WHERE *to* SKI

Edited by
Chris Gill
and
Dave Watts

B🍃XTREE

First published in Great Britain in
1994 by Boxtree Limited, Broadwall
House, 21 Broadwall, London SE1 9PL

This edition published 1995

10 9 8 7 6 5 4 3 2 1

ISBN 0 7522 1689 9

Editors Chris Gill and Dave Watts
Assistant editors Ian Porter, Ian Stratford
Editorial assistants Mandy Crook,
Dennis Shrives, Nicola Cunningham,
Seb Leber, Alice Finlay
Production editors Kate Targett,
Christopher Madigan, Tom Crawley
Production assistants Joe Fox,
Adrian Taylor
Contributors Alan Coulson, Adam Ruck,
Nicky Holford, James Hooke,
Chris Allan, Katrina Moran,
Jonathan Swinfen, Helena Wiesner,
Tim Perry
Nightlife consultant Bert Walsh

Design by Fox Design Consultants
Photo credits: see page 4
Colour reproduction by
Monarch Lithogravure
Printed and bound in Portugal by
Printer Portuguesa

A CIP catalogue entry for this book is
available from the British Library.

Contents

Photo credits

Cover	Grindelwald – Grindelwald Tourist Office
p57	Badgastein – Gasteiner Bergbahnen Ag
p73	Ischgl – Tourismusverband Ischgl
p77	Kitzbühel – Tourismusverband Kitzbühel
p81	Lech – Verkehrsamt Lech
p93	Obergurgl – Lohmann Photo/Tourismusverband Gurgl
p105	St Anton – Tourismusverband St. Anton
p113	St Johann – Fremdverkehrsverband St. Johann
p133	Zell am See – Kurverwaltung Zell am See
p140	Alpe-d'Huez – NortonWood
p144	Les Arcs – Société des Téléphériques de l'Aiguille Rouge
p152	Avoriaz – OT Avoriaz
p153	Chamonix – OT Chamonix Mont-Blanc Franc
p169	Les Contamines – Office du Tourisme, Les Contamines
p177	Les Deux-Alpes – NortonWood
p192	Megève – J C Ligcon, OT Megève
p201	Méribel – Picture A – J M Goudard, OT Méribel; NortonWood
p220	La Plagne – NortonWood
p228	La Rosière – NortonWood
p237	Tignes – NortonWood
p241	Val-d'Isère – NortonWood
p248	Val-d'Isère – NortonWood
p252	Valmorel – P. Jacques/Service Presse/Jeanne Cattini
p257	Val-Thorens – F Gros, Val Thorens
p269	Cervinia – NortonWood
p272	Cortina d'Ampezzo – Foto Stefano Zardini, Cortina d'Ampezzo
p276	Courmayeur – Associazione Operatori Turistici Monte Bianco
p288	Sauze d'Oulx – IAT Sauze d'Oulx
p293	Selva – Consorzio Turistico Val Gardena
p311	Champèry – Office du Tourisme, Champèry
p320	Crans-Montana – Photo Deprez, Crans-Montana
p324	Davos – Kur- und Verkehrsverein Davos
p340	Gstaad – NortonWood
p344	Mürren – NortonWood
p353	St Moritz – Kur- und Verkehrsverein St Moritz
p369	Wengen – NortonWood
p372	Zermatt – NortonWood
p377	Zermatt – NortonWood
p384	Aspen – Doug Child Photo, Aspen Skiing Co
p388	Aspen – NortonWood
p392	Breckenridge – Carl Scofield/Breckenridge Ski Resort
p393	Breckenridge – Bob Winsett/Breckenridge Ski Resort
p405	Jackson Hole – Bob Woodall/Wade McKoy/Jackson Hole Ski Corporation
p421	Park City – Lori Adamski-Peek/Park City Ski Corp
p428	Steamboat – Larry Pierce, Steamboat Ski and Resort Corp
p432	Taos – Robert Reck Photography/Taos Ski Valley
p436	Telluride – NortonWood
p437	Vail – Jack Affleck/Vail Photo/Vail Associates Inc
p449	Banff – Scott Rowed Photography, Ski Banff/Lake Louise
p456	Whistler – Whistler Resort Ass/Leanna Rathkelly

About this book

why Where to Ski?

"Where to Ski – ... the best ski guide ever published – will replace the Good Skiing Guide as the serious skier's first choice reference book."
Frank Barrett, Travel Editor, Mail on Sunday

"easier to find your way around ... coloured piste maps are Where to Ski's forte ..." Graham Duffill, The Times

"a worthy and comprehensive new competitor ... each resort is described with a clearly written list of pros and cons which pull few punches."
Roger Bray, London Evening Standard

"clearly laid out ... the guide I would choose is Where to Ski."
Cathy Packe, The Independent

"the most user-friendly guide ... colour lift maps and photographs ... provides an at-a-glance appraisal of which resort is good for anything from cute alpine villages to piste-side accommodation or snow-sure nursery slopes ... pulls no punches." Neil English, Mail on Sunday

"a lively new guide to resorts around the world."
Arnie Wilson, Financial Times

"This handsome, fact-packed competitor is a welcome newcomer ... Gill and Watts report at length on 250 resorts with 75 colour piste maps."
Nigel Lloyd, The Observer

"reviews 250 resorts in depth and includes a resort directory of 250 more ... a beefy book and excellent value for money at £14.99 ... Gill and Watts have gone for user-friendliness ... and been successful."
Ski Survey (magazine of the Ski Club of Great Britain)

We started the first edition of this new annual guide to ski resorts by setting out the ways in which we had improved on existing guides. In this second edition, happily, we're able to leave that job largely to the reviewers quoted above. As they've noticed, *Where to Ski* is comprehensive, detailed, hard-hitting, colourful and user-friendly; skim through it yourself, and we're confident you'll agree.

Where to Ski has another advantage, too: it's up to date. Most of the purely factual information in this book – new lifts, pass prices, package holiday programmes – is up to date for the 1995/96 ski season. And we've gone to great lengths to make sure that new resort developments for this coming season are reflected in our evaluations.

But that's only half the story. In the end, what you want from a guide book of any kind is reliable guidance; and you'll only get that if the judgements the editors have made are sound. If you're an experienced skier, you'll be able to test this aspect of *Where to Ski* by picking a resort you know well, and seeing how accurately we describe it and how fairly we assess it. If you're not, you'll have to use other ways of weighing us up.

Track records, perhaps. Chris was founding editor of the Good Skiing Guide, generally recognised at birth (in 1985) as the best ski resort guide so far; he continued to edit the guide until 1992, when his ambitions for the guide diverged from those of the publishers. Dave contributed to the Good Skiing Guide from the beginning, and became one of its mainstays. For over a decade, we have been evaluating and comparing ski resorts – not simply writing entertaining magazine and newspaper articles about them. Between the two of us, we know a bit about this game.

We also know a bit about editing magazines and books. When the Good Skiing Guide was launched, Chris was editor of Holiday Which?, while Dave was editor of Which? itself. More recently, Dave has displayed his skills in developing Daily Mail Ski magazine. When he joined the magazine three years ago it was already the biggest ski magazine in Britain; now, it's the most authoritative, too.

It won't escape your notice that *Where to Ski* carries advertisements. Does this mean that we are less impartial than we might otherwise be? No. Most of the ads come from tour operators offering catered chalet holidays. We have accepted no advertising at all from ski resorts. So we are under no pressure to compromise our views on resorts, which is what this guide is all about.

We've been careful to make sure that we take other people's views of ski resorts fully into account. *Where to Ski* has made a lot of use of reports from hundreds of holiday skiers. Last year, the 50 best earned free copies of the first edition. This year, we're giving away 100 copies – and we'll continue to offer all other reporters a hefty discount on the price of the book. Please help us to make the next edition even better than this one, by sending in a report this winter. There's more information on page 8.

In practice, anyone who goes skiing this winter can have a free copy of this edition. We're continuing our ingenious scheme which means you can reclaim the cost of *Where to Ski* when you book your holiday. It can be a package or an independent holiday, booked any time up to the end of April 1996, for any number of people. Details are given on page 9.

We'll now be starting to plan improvements for next year's *Where to Ski*. If you have any suggestions, we'd love to hear from you. Our address is on the facing page.

Where to Ski needs help

Where to Ski is produced by a small team working in two widely separated locations – Theydon Bois (Essex), and a few miles outside Bath. Now that the book is established as an annual publication, we are looking for full-time or part-time staff at both of these locations to assist in the compilation and production of future editions.

We envisage these assistants working on other projects, as well as Where to Ski. Some would be closely related, such as our contributions to Daily Mail Ski magazine. Others are publishing projects entirely unrelated to skiing. We don't have fixed ideas about the roles of these new assistants, or the levels at which they will operate. But we are looking for some particular skills and aptitudes.

You must be a keen and widely travelled skier. We are not looking for experts, either in ski technique or ski resort evaluation, but for people with a broad experience of ski resorts in a number of countries. Complete familiarity with a small number of resorts is no substitute for this breadth of experience.

You must have experience of working in some editorial capacity in book, magazine or newspaper publishing – perhaps at a relatively senior level, managing the editorial process, perhaps as an assistant. Whatever level you're operating at, you must be able to use your time efficiently, juggling competing priorities without fuss.

You must be a competent user of desktop publishing systems, and be happy to spend long periods at the screen at certain times of the production cycle. We use Quark Xpress on Macs, but we are prepared to consider people whose experience is on other systems.

You must have a fanatical eye for accuracy and detail, and the persistence to ensure that each publication you're involved in is as accurate and reliable as it can possibly be, within the constraints of time and money available.

You must have the language skills and confidence to interrogate tourist offices and other foreign sources of information in French, and preferably in German or Italian as well.

Whatever editorial and related skills you claim, you'll have to be able to demonstrate them, partly by showing us what you've done in the past and partly by undertaking a couple of short tests.

You must be capable of playing a flexible part in a small team, turning your hand to chores that seem beneath you and having a go at challenges that seem disconcertingly ambitious.

If you see yourself meeting these requirements, write to us enclosing a CV, a summary of your skiing experience, a 100-word summary of the merits of your favourite ski resort and a rough idea of the salary you are looking for.

Write to Editorial Vacancies, Where to Ski, The Old Forge, Norton St Philip, Bath BA3 6LW.

Get next year's edition free

and help make it even better

There are too many ski resorts for us to visit them all every year, and even in the resorts we do visit there are too many hotels, chalets, bars, nightspots and mountain restaurants for us to hope to see them all. So we are very keen to encourage more skiers to join our already healthy band of correspondents, who send in reports on their holiday experiences. To encourage readers, we'll be giving away 100 copies of next year's edition to the writers of the best reports.

If you reported on your holiday last year, we'll be sending you a new report form just before the season starts. If you didn't but would like a form, just drop us a line to the address below; no stamp is necessary. But we're always happy to receive reports, whether they are on the form or not. Many reporters would rather use their word processor than struggle to write legibly, and we certainly want to encourage that. But all reports should be clearly set out in a structured way that we can easily handle. (Imagine sifting through a dozen rambling letters to see what people think of a particular ski school, and you'll understand why a clear structure is important.)

The structure we favour is closely related to the structure of the resort chapters of the book – and indeed you'll find it helpful when compiling a report to have the relevant chapter to hand, to see what we've said in this edition. Here are the headings we'd like you to use:

HOW IT RATES
Give the resort marks out of five for:

The skiing
Snow
Extent
Advanced
Intermediates
Beginners
Convenience
Queues
Mountain restaurants
The rest
Scenery
Resort charm
Not skiing

OVERVIEW
Summarise the main pros and cons of the resort:

The resort
What did you like?
What did you dislike?
What surprised you?
Who does it suit?
The skiing
What did you like?
What did you dislike?
What surprised you?
Who does it suit?

DETAILED ASSESSMENT
Under each heading, summarise your view of the resort in as much detail as you can. Where appropriate (in the starred sections, probably) give your particular recommendations:

Snow reliability
For advanced skiers
For intermediate skiers
For beginners
For cross-country
Queues
Mountain restaurants*
Ski schools*
Facilities for children*
Choice of location*
Chalets*
Hotels*
Self-catering apartments*
Where to eat*
Après-ski*
For non-skiers*

Write to:
Where to Ski
FREEPOST
The Old Forge
Norton St Philip
Bath
BA3 6UB

Get your money back

Where to ski comes FREE

Where to Ski has built strong links with Ski Solutions over the last two or three years, sharing staff and involving Ski Solutions clients in reporting on resorts. So we're delighted that we have been able to put together this special offer for readers.

You can reclaim the full price of Where to Ski when you book a 1995/96-season skiing holiday. All you have to do is book the holiday through the specialist ski travel agency Ski Solutions. The price of the book will be knocked off your final payment.

Ski Solutions are Britain's longest-established and most respected ski travel agency. You can buy whatever kind of holiday you want through them, so you're not losing out on breadth of choice.

Ski Solutions sell the complete range of package holidays offered by all the bonded tour operators in Britain, ranging from the smallest one-resort chalet operators (who otherwise sell directly by mail) to the mass-market operators who mainly sell through the brochure racks of high-street travel agents.

Ski Solutions can also tailor-make holidays for independent-minded skiers who want to go their own way – whether it's a long weekend in Chamonix or an 18-day tour of the best half-dozen resorts in the Rockies.

CLAIMING YOUR REFUND

Claiming your refund is easy. Right at the back of the book is a page which comprises two vouchers. When you make your definite booking, tell Ski Solutions that you want to claim a refund. Cut out the vouchers and send one to Ski Solutions and one to Where to Ski (the addresses are on the vouchers). That's all there is to it. When your final invoice arrives, it will show a refund of the price of the book.

Introduction

the editors ramble

THE SNOW MUST GO ON

It was touch and go, but it was all right on the night, as it were. In fact it was more than all right, it was brilliant: 1995 was a vintage year for snow in the Alps, and in some other parts of the northern hemisphere. After a nightmarish November and December, during which even the highest resorts accumulated negligible amounts of snow, the New Year brought heavy falls which were repeated at frequent intervals through the season in most parts of the Alps.

As is now the norm, there were heavy falls right at the end of the conventional season, creating superb conditions for the few holiday skiers prepared to get up into the mountains in April and May. At the back end of the season, the snow depths in some French resorts, in particular, seemed ridiculous. At the top of Flaine's Grandes Platières, poles said by locals to be about 8m high were still barely visible when we were there in early April, making the officially claimed upper-slope depth of 4m seem decidedly tame.

In parts of the States, too, there was a super-abundance of snow. The storms that wreaked havoc in the coastal regions of California had less damaging effects in the Sierra Nevada, where they created the basis of snow depths in the order of 5m for much of the winter, and extended the season well into summer.

Nature seems to have shifted the skiing season back a month or two. When, we wonder, will skiers and the ski business respond?

HIGH ANXIETY

Readers of last year's edition may recall our admission that the special attention given to high-level accommodation in *Where to Ski* – you'll find a section on 'Staying up the mountain' in many resort chapters – is in part motivated by the revelation of scientists in Davos that male hormone levels increase at high altitude. Driven by this knowledge, we scoured our files to find the highest bedrooms in the skiing world, and concluded that they were to be found not in the Rockies, as we expected, but closer to home – in the Swiss Alps. Zermatt was, we concluded, the testosterone capital of the skiing world, thanks to the Kulmhotel Gornergrat at 3100m.

Well, apparently we were wrong. The February 1995 issue of the Ski Club of Great Britain's organ *Ski Survey* put us right, with the news that there are higher lodgings to be had in Italy, in a little resort called Val Senales. The Grawand Berghotel there, we were told, is located a full 112 metres higher than the Kulmhotel Gornergrat. And so it seems to be. We bow to the omniscience of the venerable Ski Club, and there stands the record – unless, of course, you know different. Or until someone builds a lodge at the base station of Colorado's Arapahoe Basin (3290m). Or they start taking lodgers at Saas Fee's Mittelallalin restaurant (3500m).

Last year, we asked readers for first-hand reports on any 'variations in sexual appetite (or indeed performance) at high altitude'. The response has been modest, in every sense. Our most explicit correspondent reported that the three couples in her group 'had never identified this side effect, and were agreed that the opposite effect seemed more likely'. What a let-down! Perhaps among this year's readers there are some who can contribute some more positive evidence on this vital question? All replies treated in confidence.

This important area of biological science is evidently not taken very seriously by our friends at Crystal Holidays, whose brochure dropped on to the office doormat just as we were finalising the book for printing. Their latest invention is 'ski weddings' – holiday, ceremony, photographer and cake in a single package deal. And where do they offer the deal? Breckenridge (2925m), Banff (about 1350m) and Kaprun (785m). Breckenridge seems the obvious choice.

HEIGHT OF DISCOMFORT

Or is it? We have had several reports this year reinforcing our own experience of staying in the very highest American resorts, approaching 3000m in altitude – which is that the risk of altitude sickness of some sort is not negligible. Our report forms don't encourage evidence about such things – there is no section headed 'Observations on maladies related to the location of the resort' – but over the years we have had a steady trickle of reports of illness in Breckenridge, in particular – and many reporters who have not been ill have found themselves short of breath. This year, for example, one family who have skied twice at Aspen (2420m) without ill effects reported that in Breckenridge 'We all suffered for three days, but Jenny, who has low blood pressure, for much longer. You should stress the difference the extra 500m altitude makes.'

Well, here we are, stressing it. The air pressure at 2900m is only about 70% of that at sea level, which means that your body is starved of oxygen to a significant degree. In an ideal world, you would not travel directly to super-high resorts, but would approach them gradually. A night or two in Denver (1600m) might help, although that still leaves a 1300m leap up to resort altitude. Idaho Springs, at 2300m on the road up to the resorts, might make a better base camp. In a less than ideal world, take precautions: don't over-exert yourself when you first arrive, especially if you are not fit; rest and drink frequently; eat a little and often, including complex carbohydrates (found in biscuits, bread, pasta).

In case you want to avoid the whole issue, here is a list of major American resorts in descending order of altitude:

Copper Mountain	2960m	Vail	2500m
Breckenridge	2925m	Snowbird	2470m
Crested Butte	2855m	Mammoth Lakes*	2430m
Keystone	2835m	Aspen	2420m
Taos	2800m	Park City	2105m
Winter Park	2745m	Steamboat	2100m
Telluride	2660m	Jackson Hole	1925m
Alta	2605m	Lake Tahoe	1890m

*The Main Lodge at Mammoth Mountain is higher, at 2715m.

THAT'S A BIT STEEP

Wouldn't it be helpful if ski runs were graded in some uniform way, so that you could confidently choose a resort to suit you by glancing at a piste map, and confidently set off down a blue run in the knowledge that it will contain no nasty surprises? Sadly, we're still a long way from this ideal state of affairs.

This came home to us with particular force last winter in Val-d'Isère, a resort that continues to show complete indifference to the anxieties of timid skier. In poor visibility we rode for the first time the new Borsat Express chair-lift, which the piste map showed as leading to two of the easiest green runs on the mountain. At the top we were amazed to find the start of the run was a short very steep pitch which deserved at least red if not black status. Imagine the reaction of a poor beginner straying up there in search of the easy runs it eventually leads to.

This winter we came across an impressive firm of mountain planners in Whistler, Canada. They specialise in assessing mountain terrain and designing lifts and runs to make the most of it – their client list is impressive, including top US resorts such as Vail, Steamboat and Sun Valley as well the local Blackcomb mountain (which has won numerous mountain design awards). One of the things they do is computer-assisted assessment and design of runs suitable for different standards of skier; they then recommend gradings to their clients (they split skiers into eight clearly defined ability categories). Mostly their clients accept their proposals for new runs and lifts. But often they don't accept their gradings: 'It's okay until the marketing guys get involved. But they want a breakdown of the terrain between green, blue and black runs that attracts the maximum number of skiers whatever the truth about the terrain.'

That explains why Val-d'Isère has green runs with moguls, why Les Deux-Alpes has reclassified its fearsome runs back to town as red rather than black and why La Thuile has red runs that are half the gradient of some Val-d'Isère greens. What is needed is a clear international standard so that blatant fiddles like this can't happen.

DRIVING SNOW
One way and another, we've done a lot of driving in the Alps; a car is our favourite mode of transport, despite loudly expressed but often ill-founded environmental objections. But we continue to learn lessons about the business of making safe and sure progress on slippery surfaces. Most recently, it dawned on us that modern tyres intended for use on dry and wet (rather than snow-covered) roads have evolved in ways that seem almost designed to make them useless on snow. On a trip last winter, in a Scandinavian front-wheel-drive car equipped with tyres made by one of Europe's leading manufacturers, we were brought to a halt by a dusting of snow on a negligible gradient. Our analysis of the reason: that the tyre tread consisted essentially of straight rings of rubber with straight channels between them. Fine for avoiding aquaplaning, no doubt, but useless on snow.

There was a time when some everyday tyres – connoisseurs may recall the Pirelli Cinturato, for example – were almost as good on snow as special winter tyres. Now, it's worth paying close attention to the tyres you're equipped with, and considering whether you're asking for trouble using them in the mountains.

REPORTERS' FAVOURITES
We have again analysed where our reporters spend their skiing time, and here are the results – last winter's top 15 resorts, with their positions in the previous year's ranking given in brackets:

1 Courchevel, France (2)
2 Val-d'Isère, France (5)
3 Tignes, France (5)
4 La Plagne, France
  Serre-Chevalier, France
6 Flaine, France (11)
  Val-Thorens, France (8)

8 Alpe-d'Huez, France (7)
  Méribel, France (1)
  Obergurgl, Austria (10)
  Zermatt, Switzerland (3)
12 Chamonix, France
  Les Deux-Alpes, France
  Obertauern, Austria
  Verbier, Switzerland (6)

Last year we treated Val and Tignes as a single destination, and it/they came in 5th place. The five resorts with no figure in brackets are new to the list; Gressoney and Sauze d'Oulx, both in Italy, almost made it into the list, too. Four resorts that were in last year's top 13 have disappeared: Les Arcs, France (number 4 last year), Cervinia, Italy (9), Morzine, France (12), Saalbach-Hinterglemm, Austria (13).

What does all this mean? Not a lot. But it is interesting that the top resort with our readers is about the most expensive in the Alps. How do they cope with Courchevel prices? First, most reporters (16 out of 24) stayed in catered chalets or chalet-hotels run by British tour operators – the classic way to keep the basic holiday cost down in a pricey French or Swiss resort; 5 self-catered, and only 3 stayed in hotels. Secondly, over half our reporters either avoided using mountain restaurants altogether, or used them only occasionally ('we treated ourselves to lunch on the first and last day').

Méribel's slide to number eight in the list is difficult to explain; we suspect it reflects the fact that readers don't bother to tell us about a resort that they guess we'll have lots of other reports on, rather than a decline in readers' interest in the place.

If you have strong views on the desirability of British companions on chair-lifts, another resort list may be of more interest – a list of the most popular resorts with British package holidaymakers, produced by Crystal. Here it is:

1 Val-d'Isère, France	6 La Plagne, France
2 Courchevel, France	7 Cervinia, Italy
3 Livigno, Italy	8 St Anton, Austria
4 Méribel, France	9 Kitzbühel, Austria
5 Sauze d'Oulx, Italy	10 Val-Thorens, France

Perhaps the big surprise here is Livigno, on which we never get more than a handful of reports, and which can't compete with the other resorts on the list in terms of extent of skiing. But having revisited the place last season we can understand its appeal: its combination of low cost, reliable snow, traditional surroundings and a fair-sized ski area is difficult to match.

COOL RECEPTION

A reader who went to Tignes at New Year suggests that we should warn others like himself – that is, skiers with little experience of high resorts in midwinter – that temperatures can be fiercely low, and that special precautions may be necessary. In particular, small children should be extravagantly well wrapped up and should not ride open chair-lifts in very low temperatures, especially if there is a wind. Our correspondent reports that in Tignes there were signs in five languages, and staff were effectively preventing children from riding the chairs on the coldest days, which is reassuring.

FLAVOURS OF THE SEASON

It didn't take a genius to predict that Italy would enjoy a resurgence of popularity last season, and it doesn't take a genius to predict that the trend will continue this season unless the lira shows a dramatic revival. But it is perhaps worth restating here, for the benefit of those who are a bit out of touch with Italian skiing, that the appeal of the place does not rely on price alone. In particular (and in contrast to the popular image of Italy), the lifts are largely modern, and resort management is efficient. Italy has something in common with America: the local visitors are in the resort for a short time (weekends, in the Italian case), and want hassle-free skiing while they're there.

Our second prediction is again tied to exchange rates: If the Canadian dollar stays at about its current level, we expect interest in skiing in Canada to grow even stronger. The flight to western Canada is not appreciably longer than that to Colorado, and the reward is spectacular scenery, impressive ski areas and – for the moment at least – bargain prices once you've arrived. At present the pound buys almost 10% more dollars than it did last season, and 20% more than the year before.

The decline of the US dollar over the last two years has been much less pronounced, and there does not seem much prospect of a return to the heady days of 1992 and 1993, when the pound bought over $1.70. But $1.60 is an acceptable rate, and there are certainly package bargains to be had. When we travelled to California last January, to research our new chapter on Heavenly and to update the one on Mammoth, Virgin were filling hotels there with British skiers travelling on packages costing £379 for a flight and a half-share in a bedroom and basic car hire. Even allowing for the inevitable extra costs, that's an impressively low price for a transatlantic holiday.

In contrast to the Italian and transatlantic exchange rates, the pound's value against the Austrian schilling and the French and Swiss Francs has continued to decline since the high-point of 1992. All three countries are now 20 to 25 per cent more expensive than they were four years ago – and in Switzerland there is the additional impact of the imposition of VAT to take into account. Small wonder that the Swiss share of the British market is dwindling.

AN IMMEDIATE SAVING

If you are keen to save on your skiing costs, you should find the chapter starting on page 23 helpful in steering towards cheaper options. But wherever you're off this winter, you can at least get the cost of this book shaved off the cost of your holiday by taking up the special offer to readers made by the specialist ski travel agency Ski Solutions. It's a simple procedure, and there's no catch. Details are on page 9.

FEEL THE QUALITY

And finally, a word about our sponsors. Well, our advertisers. We've been gratified to find that practically all the chalet holiday companies that had the confidence to take serious amounts of advertising space in the first edition are also advertising their holidays in this second edition. And to find that a number of companies that understandably took a more cautious approach have now come into the fold.

Of course, advertisers take space in a publication like this in order to promote their products. But we are well aware that many of the advertisers you will find in these pages are here partly because they think *Where to Ski* deserves to succeed, because they think it is good for skiers and skiing, and because they realise it needs support. It certainly does – even if sales were double our wildest dreams, the proceeds would not meet the cost of preparing and printing new annual editions of colour book like this. So to readers we say this: if you like *Where to Ski*, when you come to book look first at the companies who have supported it.

Skiers who think of themselves as having outgrown chalet holidays, in particular, may find the 'Selected chalet' ads (mainly to be found in French resort chapters) illuminating. If you think of the chalet holiday as a rather primitive affair, built down to a price, you are way behind the times. You will find in these ads – especially perhaps the ones in Méribel, Courchevel and Val-d'Isère – some of the most comfortable and charming accommodation in the Alps.

What's new?

lifts and snow for '96

AUSTRIA
Hintertux queue busting
People staying in the Tux valley with a lift pass for more than five days will be able to use a separate entrance at the bottom lift station of the Hintertux glacier, so avoiding the queues of day trippers who arrive when snow is bad elsewhere. There will also be some artificial snow on the lower slopes. And the off-piste run from Tuxer Joch to the valley will be improved.

Mayrhofen's Penken misery done away with
At long last, relief is in sight for Mayrhofen's long-suffering visitors. The inadequate Penken cable-car is being replaced by a big gondola for this season – 15-person cabins, 2,000 pers/hr, 10 minutes to the top. The gondola will also go that vital bit higher than the cable-car (in the process, performing the impressive trick of going round a bend at full speed), so that there will no longer be an irritating walk up to get to the Penken chairs. The only fly in this ointment is that getting up to (and back down from) the main beginners' area on the Ahorn will be as inconvenient and time-consuming as ever.

Niederau gets its first gondola
The main Markbachjoch chair out of the village is to be replaced by an 8-person gondola, which should eliminate any peak-time queues. There will also be a new 6km cross-country track on top of Markbachjoch.

Important bottlenecks removed at St Anton
The tiny cable-car up from St Christoph to Galzig is to be replaced by a high-speed quad chair-lift. This will make St Christoph an even more attractive lunch venue as you'll be able to get back into the skiing quickly in the afternoon. Two T-bars to Galzig will also be replaced by a high-speed quad. Although this will cut down queues it is likely to make the Galzig blue runs even more crowded than before.

Söll improvement
Two drags at Söll are to be replaced by quad chairs, each representing a 50% improvement in lift capacity. The bigger of the two, the 400m vertical Keat, will be a high-speed lift with wind bubble.

Stubai access improved
The older of the two gondolas up to the Stubai glacier near Neustift is to be replaced, which may reduce peak season queues.

FRANCE
Quicker way to the heights in Les Arcs
A 4-person chair-lift and new drag lift will replace the existing two Grand Col drags in the Arc 2000 sector. These serve red and black pistes starting from a height of 2850m – the resort's highest skiing except that served by the Aiguille Rouge cable-car.

Minor flaw in Courchevel's lift system proves intolerable
The only complaints about lift queues we get from Courchevel visitors concern queues to get out of Méribel-Mottaret, in the next valley. But there is no denying that it is possible to queue for the top lifts giving access to Méribel and much of Courchevel's best skiing – the Vizelle gondola and the massive and fast Saulire cable-car. So without further ado, in goes another new gondola: the 4-person Vizelle lift is being replaced by an 8-person one.

End of Signal trouble in Les Deux-Alpes
The long Signal chair lift serving a north-facing blue run which starts below the top of the Jandri Express is to be replaced by a four-seater, tripling its capacity from 900 to 2,700 people per hour.

Slight improvement at Les Menuires
The slow, old four-person Mont de la Chambre gondola out of the resort is to be renovated and the cabins changed for next season. But we understand the capacity of the lift won't change – queues may move more quickly, however, if it doesn't break down quite so often.

End of the Méribel bus rip-off
The biggest grouse most people have had about Méribel is the 15 francs a time they had to pay to use the ski bus. So it's great news that next season the bus will be free – let's hope they put on more buses, otherwise they'll be very oversubscribed. And there's a new three-person chair-lift in Mottaret, intended to relieve the pressure on the first and second stations of the Plattières gondola.

Six-seaters to the fore in La Plagne
Last season's installation of a six-seat chair-lift from Montchavin towards the main La Plagne ski area is to be followed by another monster out of Plagne Centre, replacing the Colorado chair and (we hope) relieving the queues for the Grande Rochette cable-car.

Italians get access to Val-Thorens
The long awaited gondola from Orelle in the Maurienne valley into the Val Thorens skiing is due to open for the 1995/6 season. This will make the Trois Vallées into the Quatre Vallées, though we doubt they'll change their name. And it will mean that Italians will be able to race through the Frejus tunnel to ski the area – which might lead to increased weekend crowds. Also in Val Thorens, the Cascade chair-lift out of the village is to be upgraded to a six-seater.

Vars gets a new quad chair
Vars (in the southern French Alps, linked to Risoul's skiing) is to get a new four-person chair-lift.

ITALY
Progress at Madonna di Campiglio
The Pradalago cable-car out of Madonna is to be replaced this season – by a gondola, we understand.

SWITZERLAND
Crans-Montana takes a leap forward
The great frustration of skiing in Crans-Montana – that its highest and some of its best skiing is accessed by an inadequate queue-producing cable-car – is to be ended by the opening of a jumbo-gondola with 30-person cabins and a capacity five times that of the old cable-car.

No more Flims excuses
Progress between the two main sectors of the Flims-Laax skiing will be considerably smoothed by the installation of one of Switzerland's first six-seater chair-lifts (see also St Moritz), from the valley station of Plaun up to Crap Sogn Gion above Laax. At the same time, the attractions of rustic Falera as a base will be greatly increased: the slow old chair-lift up to Curnius will be replaced by a fast quad chair.

Lenzerheide: not quite such a drag
Two drags at Alp Stätz are being replaced by a quad chair this season. Sadly, they are not among the many very long drags that make this otherwise amiable ski area rather hard work.

St Moritz continues to invest
The campaign to replace the drag-lifts in St Moritz with fast, comfortable chairs goes on. The several new quad chairs installed last year are followed this year by Switzerland's first six-seater, from

Marguns to Trais Fluors. At the same time, snowmaking is to be installed in the only major sector of the skiing in the St Moritz region that lacks it – the tough skiing sector, Lagalb.

Verbier cuts down on collisions

A tunnel is being built between Attelas and La Chaux to avoid collisions at a point where two crowded pistes cross – a notorious accident blackspot. The slopes between Gentiannes and La Chaux and between Attelas 3 and Medran are being improved. We are also told that the piste map and piste marking are being improved – not before time and we reserve judgement until we see the results.

Villars and Diablerets: properly linked at last

The link between Villars and Les Diablerets has always been a rather tenuous one, involving a tiring plod along the ridge from the top of the Diablerets skiing to get into the Villars skiing, and the descent of an unpatrolled, unprepared black run when moving in the opposite direction. This year, at last, both problems will be solved by a new chair-lift in one direction and a gentle new piste in the other.

USA AND CANADA

Aspen's jet set keep their speed up

Aspen adds two more high-speed quad chair-lifts on Snowmass mountain. One will serve a new Two Creeks base lodge area; the other will go up to Elk Camp and allow swifter access to the easy intermediate skiing available from there.

Mammoth on the move

When we visited Mammoth Mountain last January, engineers were working around the clock to complete installation of the latest toy bought by Mammoth boss Dave McCoy – an elevated monorail linking the main base area to the Chair 2 parking lot on the way up from the town of Mammoth Lakes. The idea is that the town and the base area should eventually be linked.

Taos speeds up

Taos is installing its fourth high-speed quad chair-lift. This will replace the long, slow Chair 2 to the top of the mountain. And the resort's airport will have scheduled flights from Albuquerque.

Telluride links old and new

The long-awaited gondola linking the atmospheric Old West town via the top of the mountain to the hideous new purpose-built Mountain Village is at last due to open this winter. But there are no guarantees that it will be open for the start of the season. It will open until late at night to allow Mountain Village residents to escape to the old town for civilised dinners and evening drinks. The main chair out of the Mountain Village will become a 'Chondola' – a high-speed quad where some of the chairs are replaced by gondola cabins. And at the top of the 'Chondola' there will be a 'Magic Carpet' conveyor belt to take beginners up the gentle nursery slopes.

Vail powers ahead

The slow chair from Mid-Vail to Wildwood Shelter is to be replaced by a high-speed quad. This should reduce queues for the existing high-speed quad leaving Mid-Vail for the Summit ridge. There will also be additions to the already impressive snowmaking system. In Beaver Creek a new Elkhorn chair-lift will be added providing more accommodation with ski-in, ski-out access and adding 30 acres to Beaver Creek's skiing. An eating facility at the top of the Strawberry Park Express is also planned. The link with the next door resort of Arrowhead is planned to be completed by the 1996/7 season.

New mountain opened at Banff

New lifts at Sunshine ski area at Banff will open up Goat's Eye Mountain, previously unskiable except by hiking. This will provide some excellent new, tough runs, above and below the treeline.

Resort shortlists

The ratings and lists of pros and cons at the start of each resort chapter will help you spot resorts to suit you. But for a real shortcut, here's a list of the best (and worst). Most lists embrace European and North American resorts, but some we've confined to the Alps, because America has too many qualifying resorts (eg beginners) or because America does things differently, making comparisons invalid (eg off-piste).

RELIABLE SNOW IN THE ALPS
Alpine resorts with good snow records or lots of snowmaking, and high or north-facing slopes
Argentière, France p153
Cervinia, Italy p266
Courchevel, France p169
Hintertux, Austria p68
Lech/Zürs, Austria p80
Obergurgl, Austria p91
Saas Fee, Switzerland p348
Val-d'Isère/Tignes, France p241/235
Val-Thorens, France p255
Zermatt, Switzerland p372

OFF-PISTE SKIING
Alpine resorts where, with guidance, you can have the time of your life
Alpe d'Huez, France p137
Andermatt, Switzerland p307
Argentière/Chamonix, France p153
Davos/Klosters, Switzerland p321
La Grave, France p188
Lech/Zürs, Austria p80
St Anton, Austria p103
Val d'Isère/Tignes, France p241/235
Verbier, Switzerland p359
Zermatt, Switzerland p372

BLACK RUNS
Steep skiing within the safety of the piste network
Alta/Snowbird, Utah p382/419
Andermatt, Switzerland, p307
Les Arcs, France p144
Argentière/Chamonix, France p153
Aspen, Colorado p383
Jackson Hole, Wyoming p403
Taos, New Mexico p429
Telluride, Colorado, p433
Val d'Isère/Tignes, France p241/235
Zermatt, Switzerland p372

HIGH-MILEAGE PISTE SKIING
Extensive intermediate skiing
Alpe d'Huez, France p137
Davos/Klosters, Switzerland p321
Flims/Laax, Switzerland p328
Milky Way: Sauze d'Oulx (Italy), Montgenèvre (France) p288/207
La Plagne, France p217
Portes du Soleil, France/Switz. p224
Sella Ronda/Selva, Italy p292
Trois Vallées, France p240
Val-d'Isère/Tignes, France p241/235
Whistler, Canada p455

MOTORWAY CRUISING
Long, gentle, super-smooth pistes to bolster frail confidence
Les Arcs, France p144
Aspen, Colorado p383
Breckenridge, Colorado p390
Cervinia, Italy p266
Cortina, Italy p271
Courchevel, France p169
Megève, France p190
La Plagne, France p217
La Thuile, Italy p300
Vail, Colorado p437

RESORTS FOR BEGINNERS
Alpine resorts with gentle, snowsure nursery slopes and easy runs to progress to
Alpe d'Huez, France p137
Les Arcs, France p144
Cervinia, Italy p266
Courchevel, France p169
Isola 2000, France p189
Montgenèvre, France p207
Pamporovo, Bulgaria p457
La Plagne, France p217
Saas Fee, Switzerland p348
Soldeu, Andorra p475

SKIING CONVENIENCE
Piste-side accommodation
Les Arcs, France p144
Avoriaz, France p149
Courchevel, France p169
Flaine, France p182
Isola 2000, France p189
Les Menuires, France p195
Obertauern, Austria p96
La Plagne, France p217
Valmorel, France p250
Val Thorens, France p255

WEATHERPROOF RESORTS
Alpine resorts with snowsure skiing if the sun shines, and trees in case it doesn't
Courchevel, France p169
Courmayeur, Italy p276
Flims, Switzerland p328
Montchavin/Les Coches, France p217
Schladming, Austria p114
Selva, Italy p292
Serre-Chevalier, France p230
Sestriere, Italy p299
La Thuile, Italy p300
Zermatt, Switzerland p372

BACK-DOOR RESORTS
Cute little villages linked to big, bold ski areas
Les Brevières (Tignes), France p235
Champagny (La Plagne), France p217
Falera (Flims), Switzerland p328
Leogang (Saalbach), Austria p97
Montchavin (La Plagne), France p217
St-Martin (Trois Vallées), France p240
Samoëns (Flaine), France p182
Stuben (St Anton), Austria p103
Vaujany (Alpe d'Huez), France p137
Villaroger (Les Arcs), France p144

SNOWSURE BUT SIMPATICO
Alpine resorts with high-rise skiing, but low-rise buildings
Andermatt, Switzerland p307
Arabba, Italy p292
Argentière, France p153
Ischgl, Austria p70
Lech/Zürs, Austria p80
Méribel, France p199
Obergurgl, Austria p91
Obertauern, Austria p96
Saas Fee, Switzerland p348
Zermatt, Switzerland, p372

RESORTS FOR FAMILIES
Accommodation surrounded by snow, not by traffic
Les Arcs, France p144
Avoriaz, France p149
Flaine, France p182
Isola 2000, France p189
Montchavin, France p217
Mürren, Switzerland p344
Saas Fee, Switzerland p348
Serfaus, Austria p119
Valmorel, France p250
Wengen, Switzerland p367

BUDGET SKIING
Cheap packages, cheap lifts, cheap drinks and meals
Bardonecchia, Italy p262
Arinsal, Andorra p474
Borovets, Bulgaria p478
Gressoney, Italy p281
Kranjska Gora, Slovenia (Directory)
Livigno, Italy p282
Poiana Brasov, Romania p481
Soldeu, Andorra p475
Sierra Nevada, Spain p476
Sauze d'Oulx, Italy p288

MOUNTAIN RESTAURANTS
Alpe d'Huez, France p137
La Clusaz, France p164
Courmayeur, Italy p276
Kitzbühel, Austria p75
Megève, France p190
Saalbach-Hinterglemm, Austria p97
St Johann in Tirol, Austria p110
St Moritz, Switzerland p353
Selva, Italy p292
Zermatt, Switzerland p372

DRAMATIC SCENERY
Banff, Canada, p449
Chamonix, France p153
Cortina, Italy p271
Courmayeur, Italy p276
Jungfrau resorts (Grindelwald, Mürren, Wengen), Switzerland p333/344/367
Heavenly, California p399
Saas Fee, Switzerland p348
St Moritz, Switzerland p353
Selva, Italy p292
Zermatt, Switzerland p372

VILLAGE CHARM
Alpbach, Austria p54
Champéry, Switzerland p311
Courmayeur, Italy p276
Crested Butte, Colorado p396
Lech, Austria p80
Mürren, Switzerland p344
Saas Fee, Switzerland p348
Telluride, Colorado p433
Wengen, Switzerland p367
Zermatt, Switzerland p372

LIVELY NIGHTLIFE
Chamonix, France p153
Ischgl, Austria p70
Kirchberg, Austria p75
Kitzbühel, Austria p75
Saalbach, Austria p97
St Anton, Austria p103
Sölden, Austria p120
Soldeu, Andorra p475
Val d'Isère, France p241
Verbier, Switzerland p359

 # And finally ...

Some resorts you might want to leave off your shortlist.

SHAME ABOUT THE FAME?
Resorts that remain popular despite poor snow records
Gstaad, Switzerland p337
Kitzbühel, Austria p75
Megève, France p190
Söll, Austria p124
Wengen, Switzerland p367

INSUFFERABLE QUEUES
Argentière, France p153
Avoriaz, France p149
Kitzbühel, Austria p75
Mayrhofen, Austria p85
Verbier, Switzerland p359

HIDEOUS VILLAGES
Flaine, France p182
Les Menuires, France p195
La Plagne, France p217
Sierra Nevada, Spain p476
Tignes, France p235

SNOW + ROCK

Britain's No.1
Ski, Snowboard &
Mountain Specialist

Going skiing?
Go to Snow+Rock

We offer the biggest choice with the best service. Visit one of our shops, or ring 01932 569569 to order your FREE copy of our 200 page Mail Order Ski Catalogue*, or the NEW Snowboard Book - a guide to the latest and most woofable snowboard stuff!

*Available from October 1995.

by **Katrina Moran** *and* **Jonathan Swinfen**
authors of
The Ultimate Guide to Snowboarding

Let's go boarding now

come and be a goofy * *with me*

It's not by chance that the French call snowboarding 'Le Surf' – the sport has its roots in the California of Beach Boy days. Bored with the monotony of long winter months, American surfers picked up their boards and headed for them there hills. After various gravity-defying experiments, using surf boards on the snow, these beach refugees eventually hit on a successful formula. They began to have 'fun, fun, fun' and a whole new sport was born. Over the past 20 years or so, the growth of snowboarding has been phenomenal. And it is estimated that by the year 2000, one in three people on the slopes will be a boarder.

Once you've been bitten by the boarding bug, the chances are you'll hang up your skis forever. Here's a guide to resorts to consider, either for a first go, or for a more serious snowboarding holiday.

IDEAL FOR 'L' PLATES
Top resorts for beginners:
Austria: Lech, Seefeld; France: Alpe-d'Huez, La Plagne, Isola 2000, Val-d'Isère/Tignes; Italy: Cortina d'Ampezzo, Madonna di Campiglio; Switzerland: Adelboden, Davos, Leysin, Saas Fee; USA: Copper Mountain, Vail, Winter Park.

For a learner, good tuition is essential. Teaching standards vary enormously, so choose a resort which has a specialist school or one that can provide specialist instructors.

The USA, where snowboarding is still more popular than anywhere else, offers excellent tuition. Austria, France and Switzerland lead Europe in snowboard instruction and specialist schools. Surprisingly, in the cheaper destinations – Andorra, Bulgaria and Romania – good tuition is difficult to find.

Although Italy doesn't rank among Europe's snowboarding elite, the school at Madonna di Campiglio offers some of the best tuition you'll find this side of the Atlantic. And Cortina d'Ampezzo has perfect slopes for beginners and a good school.

HOT HALFWAY HAUNTS
Top resorts for intermediates:
Austria: Hintertux, Ischgl, Sölden, Zell am See; France: Avoriaz, Courchevel, Les Arcs, Méribel, Val-d'Isère; Italy: Courmayeur, Sauze d'Oulx; Switzerland: Arosa, Crans-Montana, Gstaad, Arosa, Villars; North America: Grand Targhee, Squaw Valley, Steamboat, Whistler.

We've chosen these resorts as top destinations for intermediates for a number of reasons. They have vast areas of wide, often tree-lined runs easily accessible to an intermediate snowboarder. There's also stacks of off-piste skiing. No need to be defeatist about this – even as an intermediate, you'll find powder much easier on a board than on skis. If you do go off-piste, always hire a guide. Finally, these resorts have good lift systems with few drag-lifts to the higher areas.

Austria has a very positive attitude towards snowboarding and Ischgl is no exception. You'll have the chance to see many professional boarders in action. If they inspire you, Ischgl has excellent freeriding and advanced courses.

Avoriaz is acknowledged as the capital of European snowboarding, It has excellent runs and is exceptionally pro-snowboarding. Avoriaz has adopted a very American attitude: while giving boarders their

* 'Goofy' means you ride a snowboard with your right foot forward. 'Regular' riders lead with their left foot.

own areas such as fun parks (where you can jump off picnic tables etc should the fancy take you), they've also managed to exercise control of the sport and create a good relationship with skiers. Chalet Snowboard operate chalet holidays here specially for snowboarders.

The good lift system at Les Arcs makes the area very accessible. You'll find the best intermediate cruising pistes at Arc 2000, but head for Arc 1800 for good off-piste. If you're comfortable in powder, you can't do better than try Le Fornet in Val-d'Isère, where the wide open slopes let you carve large turns to your heart's content.

Boarders were once banned at Squaw Valley – but the resort is now organised so that skiers and boarders co-exist in perfect harmony. There are some separate runs and good fun parks. Squaw, with challenging but accessible runs, is probably one of the best places for skiers who want to be snowboarders for a few days.

UTOPIA FOR SERIOUS BOARDERS

Top resorts for experts:
Austria: Axamer Lizum, St Anton; France: Argentière, Chamonix, Les Deux-Alpes, Tignes, Val-d'Isère, Val-Thorens; North America: Breckenridge, Jackson Hole, Mt. Batchelor, Stratton, Vail, Whistler

If you're an experienced boarder, then these resorts are for you. They provide the thrill of riding some of the most challenging off-piste runs in the world. There's also plenty of scope for trying out freestyle – halfpipes and snowboard parks are par for the course.

St Anton has steep, mainly off-piste runs but there are many good qualified guides and instructors who will keep you safe.

For excellent off-piste boarding and a good halfpipe, Les Deux-Alpes is a good choice. It also gives you the chance to explore the unpisted paradise of La Grave.

Chamonix has some excellent snowboard guides for off-piste. There are plenty of powder possibilities and extreme couloirs, especially above Argentière. But Chamonix is the resort for the fully initiated boarder – a definite no-go area for learners. If you haven't mastered the sport, its jargon and dress etiquette, you could feel like a Sir Cliff Richard fan at a Guns 'n Roses concert.

Jackson Hole has done a great deal for snowboarders and has attracted a huge following. If halfpipes are your scene, then Stratton has one of the biggest. Many freestyle riders come here for the whole season purely to ride the pipe. Like Whistler, Stratton has technique clinics. But Whistler is the place for summer camps, held on the Blackcomb glacier.

SNOWBOARD-FRIENDLY RESORTS

Top Ten all-round resorts: Austria: Ischgl; France: Les Arcs, Avoriaz, Tignes, Val-d'Isère; Italy: Madonna di Campiglio; Switzerland: Saas Fee; North America: Squaw Valley, Vail, Whistler.

These resorts make our Top Ten because they've made a concerted effort to attract and welcome snowboarders. They provide facilities such as specialist schools, parks, halfpipes and a good variety of terrain.

by Chris Allan

Money talks

the cost of skiing

First the bad news. As the pound continues to fall against the currencies of the major Alpine nations, the cost of a skiing holiday has continued to rise. Whoever it was who said that 'the best things in life are free', they clearly hadn't stayed in a 3-star hotel at Courchevel 1850, bought a lift pass in Zermatt or supped a Jägertee in Lech. Now the good news. The lira is in worse straits than the pound, so Italy continues to offer amazing value. The degree to which a skiing holiday can seriously damage your wealth varies enormously depending on the country and the type of accommodation you choose. But it doesn't stop there – the costs of lift pass, ski school, equipment hire and food and drink all have their knock-on effect.

Will the reportedly hard-up Duchess of York be bidding a sad *aufwiedersehn* to private chalet holidays in glitzy Klosters? Of course, Fergie could go down-market and opt for a 4-star hotel package in Klosters at around £875 a week. If that's still too expensive, the Duchess shouldn't despair – there are plenty of ski packages around at affordable prices. She could try an apartment holiday in Bulgaria's Borovets for around just £225 in low season, provided she's prepared to share. If Fergie doesn't fancy cooking and wants rather more night life, a hotel holiday in Andorra's Soldeu wouldn't set her back much more. And, if she scours the brochures, she'll find that there are discounts or even free holidays for Beatrice and little Eugenie.

Skiing is an expensive business but you don't have to win the National Lottery to go. A holiday in one of the 'glam' resorts will be pricey. But with so many packages and resorts available, you can choose from hundreds of offers from the Vails and the Verbiers of the ski world down to bargain-basement resorts such as Poiana Brasov and Borovets.

We've checked the cost of packages to some of the most popular destinations for Brits in Europe and North America. We've also compared the cost of lift passes, ski school and ski and boot hire. And, thanks to the readers who sent us price information, we've been able to get an idea of the costs of eating and drinking on the mountain.

EUROPEAN EXPENSES

We looked at the brochures of some of the major tour operators and worked out typical costs of 3-star and 4-star hotels, chalets and studios (including flights, transfers and half-board in hotels and chalets) for two people sharing a room for a week in high season. We chose a cross-section of resorts, from the top to the bottom of the market. On the next page, we list them in price order, based on the cost of 3-star hotel packages.

Last year, Courchevel won our gold medal as Europe's most expensive resort. This year it has really excelled itself – it's become even more Franc-sapping. A week in a 3-star hotel at 1850m can set you back around £830. The price gap between Courchevel and its nearest rivals, Val-d'Isère and Zermatt (still in silver and bronze position), has widened to a margin of around £150 a week. Trailing quite some distance behind come Verbier, St Anton, Wengen, Obergurgl and Valmorel. Way behind these and around 45% cheaper than Courchevel, come the top Italian resorts of Courmayeur and

Cervinia. Eastern Europe is miles behind – a week in a 3-star hotel works at less than half the price of any of the top three resorts.

The same pattern emerges if you look at the costs of staying in a 4-star hotel. But the price of chalet holidays is much more evenly spread, making the top resorts much more affordable. In nearly all of the expensive resorts, chalets work out very much cheaper than a 3-star hotel – and that's before you start adding your wine and bar bill and other extras on to the hotel cost. Of course you can get much plusher chalets than the ones we looked at – these are likely to cost a bit more.

A studio can work out quite a lot cheaper – the way to keep costs down is to pack people in. The brochure prices normally assume four in a one-room studio but for our comparisons we added on small print supplements to get the true prices for two living in relative comfort. But remember there's no food included in our prices.

EUROPEAN PACKAGES	3★ Hotel £	4★ Hotel £	Chalet £	Studio £
Courchevel	830	1,260	550	550
Val-d'Isère	680	840	520	440
Zermatt	670	840	520	500
Verbier	620	840	600	–
St Anton	600	770	510	440
Wengen	570	710	490	430
Obergurgl	560	660	420	–
Valmorel	560	–	430	370
Serre-Chevalier	530	–	460	390
Cervinia	480	580	–	350
Courmayeur	460	640	450	–
Söll	430	520	370	–
Soldeu	390	450	–	320
Sauze d'Ouix	390	420	370	320
Borovets	330	380	–	–
Poiana Brasov	300	340	–	–

Notes: All prices are for February for two people sharing a room and include flights and transfers. Hotel and chalet prices are half-board. Not all types of accommodation were available in all resorts.

LIFT PASSES

Next, the cost of a six-day lift pass. The Swiss certainly come into their own here, with Verbier and Zermatt most expensive by far. Surprisingly, St Anton and tiny Obergurgl in Austria are more expensive than the huge French ski areas of the Trois Vallées and Val-d'Isère/Tignes. Italy is a real bargain, with resorts such as Courmayeur and Sauze d'Oulx costing not much more than half the Verbier price. Eastern Europe is cheaper by a third again.

LIFT PASS PRICES

Verbier	£165	Söll	£102
Zermatt	£162	Serre-Chevalier	£102
St Anton	£140	Cervinia	£89
Obergurgl	£137	Courmayeur	£87
Courchevel	£132	Sauze d'Oulx	£85
Wengen	£129	Soldeu	£83
Val-d'Isère	£123	Borovets	£61
Valmorel	£113	Poiana Brasov	£55

SKI AND BOOT RENTAL

Much the same pattern emerges for ski and boot hire. Charges are highest in Switzerland and Courchevel. The top Austrian and other French resorts follow. Hiring equipment in Italy is around half the price charged in Wengen and Zermatt, and costs pretty much the same as in Andorra, Bulgaria and Romania.

BOOT & SKI HIRE PRICES

Wengen	£86	Obergurgl	£51
Courchevel	£82	Cervinia	£42
Zermatt	£82	Söll	£41
Verbier	£75	Poiana Brasov	£39
St Anton	£61	Courmayeur	£38
Val-d'Isère	£61	Borovets	£37
Serre-Chevalier	£53	Sauze d'Ouix	£36
Valmorel	£52	Soldeu	£30

SKI SCHOOL

Ski school fees are more difficult to analyse simply because the number of hours and days of tuition varies from resort to resort. We've included only those which operate for six full days. Yet again the top French and Swiss resorts lead the pack. A week's ski school in Val-d'Isère will cost over 50 per cent more than in St Anton.

SKI SCHOOL FEES

Val-d'Isère	£135	Obergurgl	£99
Wengen	£133	St Anton	£88
Courchevel	£126		
Zermatt	£119		

THE TOTAL BILL

If you add on the price of all the extras to the costs of staying in a resort and buying a lift pass, the total can be quite staggering.

For example, staying in a 3-star hotel, buying a lift pass, hiring equipment and going to ski school will cost you around £1,170 in Courchevel, £890 in St Anton. Leaving out ski school allows you to make a wider comparison. The Courchevel costs then come to £1,045, compared to £800 in St Anton, £510 in Sauze d'Oulx and £430 in Borovets.

The costs don't stop there unless, of course, you lunch on tap water and digestive biscuits brought from home. How much more you'll spend will depend largely on how much you eat and drink. But again, where you go will make an enormous difference. From the information that so many of you sent us, the pattern is clear.

Top Swiss and French resorts are again by far the most expensive, with Courchevel and Méribel pretty much on a par with places like Wengen and Zermatt. The most expensive Austrian resorts (such as Lech and Obergurgl) aren't far behind, and are about as costly as Val-d'Isère and Verbier. Average price Italian resorts such as Selva and Bormio are likely to cost around half as much for lunch on the mountain as the top Swiss and French places. Again, Andorra is cheap, but Eastern Europe is rock-bottom – the cost of drinks and snack meals is literally negligible.

NORTH AMERICAN EXPENSES

At first glance, the brochure prices for North American resorts will look cheaper than those we've listed. That's because we've worked out what it would cost for two people sharing a room – brochure prices are normally based on four. When you compare prices with Europe, bear in mind that North American hotel costs exclude dinner, although you can eat out cheaply (or expensively if you like).

Surprisingly, perhaps, North America works out no more expensive than Europe – despite the trans-Atlantic flight costs. Hotel packages to Vail, Whistler and Breckenridge are on a par with half-board in the top French and Swiss resorts. Banff and Mammoth prices are on a par with medium-priced European resorts such as Obergurgl and Valmorel.

NORTH AMERICAN PACKAGES		3★ Hotel £	4★ Hotel £	Chalet £	Studio £
Vail	1 wk	770	1,100	650	720
	2 wks	1,100	1,600	910	1,100
Whistler	1 wk	720	740	620	790
	2 wks	990	1,050	860	1,120
Breckenridge	1 wk	710	750	600	750
	2 wks	1,030	1,120	820	1,030
Banff/L. Louise	1 wk	560	640	–	590
	2 wks	680	810	–	750
Mammoth	1 wk	570	610	–	600
	2 wks	770	870	–	830

Lift passes and ski school prices are generally on a par with Europe's top resorts (though Vail's ski school must rank among the world's priciest). The costs of hiring equipment are cheaper than Europe's grandest.

	Lift pass £	School fees £	Equipment hire £
Vail	150	260	50
Mammoth	142	131	57
Banff	130	109	36
Breckenridge	123	124	48
Whistler	137	157	63

Given the air fare costs and the problems of jet lag, it makes sense to go to North America for two weeks rather than one. Of the resorts we looked at, Vail is the most expensive – a lift pass and 3-star hotel, without dinner, will set you back around £1,400 for a fortnight. Mammoth works out at around £350 cheaper. And in Canada, two weeks in Banff costs around £300 less than in Whistler.

As far as the price of food and drink are concerned, North America compares quite favourably with Europe.

by **Dave Watts and Alan Coulson**

Off-piste adventure

life in the wilderness

More and more British skiers are now discovering that there's more to skiing than piste-bashing. For many, the attraction of being in the mountains is the peace, tranquility and beauty of getting away from the hordes on the piste and enjoying the scenery and solitude of the mountains. Plus, of course, the challenge of skiing steep terrain, and natural snow that hasn't been flattened by piste groomers.

You can try out off-piste at many of the Alps' top resorts. Val-d'Isère, Verbier, Zermatt, Chamonix and St Anton, for example, are all well organised to provide off-piste guiding and teaching.

Val-d'Isère would be a good place to get started and has a well established reputation for adventurous skiing as well as an amazing piste network. It has a couple of small independent schools (Alpine Experience and Top Ski) specialising in off-piste and powder skiing; you can join a group for a half-day, or sign up for longer expeditions. Many keen skiers go to Val-d'Isère and ski off-piste every day with one of these schools. We've tried them both and had splendid days each time.

Many off-piste novices are now finding they can join off-piste groups without worrying about whether they can manage, in the knowledge that the new wide Fat Boy skis that they hire will keep them safely afloat. If you haven't yet tried them, do so next season – you'll be amazed how easy they make skiing off-piste in powder and crud. They are now easy to hire in the top resorts and the off-piste schools encourage their use.

Chamonix can legitimately claim to be the off-piste capital of the world. It's a real mountain town, much more than 'just' a ski resort, and it does attract many of the best skiers and most accomplished guides in the business. Jewel in the crown for those wanting to go off-piste without climbing is the amazing Grands Montets at Argentière, where the off-piste opportunities are endless – and frequently extreme. Much less taxing is Europe's most famous off-piste run, the Vallée Blanche – 24km of stunning scenery across glaciers manageable even by an average intermediate (see page 155). Although it may well be the world's busiest off-piste route, when you're out there in amongst all that ice and thin air it still feels like a long way from home.

For many keen off-piste skiers, La Grave rivals Chamonix. It is certainly something very special – 2000 vertical metres of rough, tough mountainside that never sees a piste machine and all just a short walk away over the top from adjacent Les Deux-Alpes. It's the only resort with virtually no pistes.

WEEK LONG COURSES

If you are keen on getting started by going on a proper organised course, rather than just trying off-piste or touring for the odd day as part of a largely piste-based holiday, there are a few tour operators who specialise in this area.

Fresh Tracks is probably the main specialist off-piste operator. They have a range of courses in Chamonix, La Grave, Verbier, Alpe d'Huez and Flaine, aimed at four different standards of skier ranging from off-piste novice through to powder expert. Powder Byrne also has Introduction to Powder courses in Grindelwald, where you can use the new Fat Boy skis. And they have Adventure courses for more accomplished off-piste skiers in Klosters, Grindelwald and tiny Grimentz in Switzerland and Gressoney in Italy.

Both these operators also offer ski safaris, where you travel between resorts using their lift systems to access off-piste runs between them. 'Soft' safaris include luggage transportation between valley-based lodgings. There may be some uphill walking but not much. Fresh Tracks offer a route from Tignes to Chamonix via Champagny, Les Arcs, Sainte-Foy and Courmayeur, with a finishing flourish down the Vallée Blanche. And Powder Byrne have a safari from Grindelwald to Zermatt at the end of March.

At the other end of the scale, you can try traditional touring – carrying a hefty pack and doing a significant amount of climbing using proper touring skis. Skins – made of artificial fibres – attach to the base of your skis and the heel binding releases to allow the skis and skier to glide effortlessly uphill (or at least with less effort than it would be without them). On downhill stretches the skins are removed, the heel clicked back into place, and away you go.

Fresh Tracks organise full-scale tours, staying overnight in mountain huts, in both the Alps and Morocco's Atlas mountains. The Ski Club of Great Britain also has touring holidays. And even Inghams now feature an introductory ski touring package at Kühtai in the Austrian Tyrol – perhaps a sign of things to come. The Haute Route, the classic high-level route from Chamonix to Zermatt, is a week's hard labour needing considerable stamina, good touring equipment and luck with the weather. It's one to aspire to, but not for the novice.

SAFETY FIRST

One thing that is very different about skiing in areas other than on prepared and patrolled pistes is the degree of responsibility you assume for your own and other's safety. Skiing off-piste should never be treated casually: accidents happen even close to marked runs and within area boundaries. Avalanches are the biggest danger, and a constant threat on slopes of black-run gradient. Snow stability is influenced by many factors and only an experienced mountain guide who has done his homework can accurately judge how dangerous a particular slope is likely to be. There is only one safe rule: ski with a guide. Although mere ski instructors are allowed to take groups off-piste only fully qualified UIAGM (International Association of Mountain Guides) guides are authorised to guide groups on glaciers. They are trained to know where it's safe to ski and where there's crevasse danger – and will carry all the necessary rescue gear in case one of their party should be unlucky enough to tumble into one.

Whenever you venture off-piste your guide should give everyone in your party an avalanche transceiver and training on how to use it. This enables you to search for any of your group caught by an avalanche – it transmits and receives radio signals when the victim is within range; the resulting beeps become louder as you get nearer.

It also makes sense to wear Recco strips. These contain reflective diodes. A Recco Rescue System detector unit sends out a signal which comes back to the detector if it is reflected. Many resorts (including, for example, Verbier, Zermatt, Lech, St Anton, Ischgl, Courmayeur, Cortina, Avoriaz, Chamonix, the Trois Vallées, La Grave, Mammoth, Vail and Aspen) have Recco detectors to help find skiers buried in avalanches – and every Swiss rescue helicopter has one too. Recco strips cost around £11 and can be attached to your boots. They are also built into some clothing (all Nevica gear and some Degre 7 and Tenson). It's a small price to pay for the additional chance they give you of being found if you are caught by an avalanche.

ADVENTURE IN THE NORTH AMERICA

Many North American resorts have reasonably accessible deep-snow skiing – often bowls and chutes beyond the groomed areas but within the area boundary and cleared of avalanche danger.

Take Crested Butte, for example – a lovely little western town in with some tremendous lift-served off-piste that they call The Extreme Limits. There's masses of steep, exhilarating terrain – and there are daily guided tours for good skiers. The terrain can be as hairy as you want it to be – it hosts the US Extreme Skiing Championships. Other resorts with great, untamed, steep terrain include Snowbird and Alta in Utah, Jackson Hole in Wyoming and Whistler in Canada.

And North America has snowcat skiing, something that isn't available in Europe – see page 385 for how this cheaper version of heli-skiing works.

TAKE TO THE AIR

If it's powder that you're hungry for, and powder that hasn't previously been touched, rent yourself a helicopter.

The biggest operation in Europe is in Zermatt, but there are cheaper alternatives in Italy including the Courmayeur and La Thuile areas. The great thing here is you can buy just one ride. For about £150, for example, you can fly to near the top of Zermatt's Monte Rosa at over 4000m and ski down with a guide through the glaciers to Furi – a spectacular morning's skiing. Powder Byrne organises courses including heli-skiing in Grindelwald and Zermatt.

But the place where heli-skiing is biggest and best is the Canadian Rockies – there's a huge amount of wilderness out there just made for heli-skiing. Two outfits with a long history in the business continue to dominate the scene – CMH and Mike Wiegele – and both have links to British tour operators.

Last year I tried it for the first time – with the Mike Wiegele operation. I went along with the pre-conceived idea that it was an easy way for the filthy rich to throw money away. Now, sadly, I'm hooked – and wish I was filthy rich. Heli-skiing in Canada for a week is an entirely different concept from heli-skiing in Europe. It is not a question of having one or two lifts and runs in a day. Your helicopter drops you somewhere in the wilderness in thigh-deep powder. You ski for maybe half an hour in virgin snow to a pick-up point somewhere else in the wilderness, where your helicopter arrives to whisk you away to more wilderness. The process is repeated perhaps twelve times in a day – interrupted only by a 20-minute break for lunch (flown in to you by the helicopter, of course).

If the weather's bad you ski in the trees (easier than it sounds because they are widely spaced). If it's good you may be on the highest glaciers. Wherever you are, you'll have the skiing experience of a lifetime. And when the helicopter has gone the only sound you hear is the whoops of delight you find yourself and your companions involuntarily screaming.

At the end of the day you are flown to your lodge for a sauna, hot tub, massage or beer – followed by dinner, an early night and another day of powder. Paradise like this doesn't come cheap – the basic cost is around £2,500 for a week (or £1,250 for three days early and late season with Wiegele) which doesn't include your airfare or additional vertical feet. You have to pay extra once you've skied more than a certain number of vertical feet – our group went 30,000 feet over in three days, which cost around £200 extra.

It's a lot of money. But everyone I spoke to there had no doubt it was worth it. My advice: treat yourself to the ski holiday of a lifetime. But then start saving again – most people get hooked and 70 per cent of customers are repeat bookers.

by **Chris Allan**

Drive to the Alps

and ski where you please

The days when driving to the Alps was the preserve of the most intrepid of motorists, spurred on by a pioneering spirit, have long gone. The advent of the Channel Tunnel and the tremendous improvements made to the motorway networks in northern France and the Alps have made life much, much easier for the growing number of Brits who decide to drive down. You can now get to most resorts easily in a day. If that's not enough to tempt you away from flying, just think about the freedom that a car would give you once you're in the Alps.

If the snow's bad in your resort, or if the lift queues are horrendous, you can try somewhere else. And a car will give you a perfect means of daily escape if it turns out that you don't like the resort you've booked into or find the skiing rather limited.

Of course, if you drive, there are certain things you'll miss out on. Who can forget those long, care-free hours in the airport departure lounge, the on-board meal, the challenge of carting around skis, boots and luggage, not to mention the pleasures of the three-hour coach transfer up to the resort?

If you've never tried driving to the Alps, you don't know what you're missing. For starters, if you're taking your family or going self-catering, just think of all the extra things your can cram in that you'd otherwise have had to leave behind.

One of the most important plus-points as far as we're concerned is that we can add two extra days' skiing to a holiday while taking only one extra day off work. We cross the Channel early on a Friday morning and return nine days later on the Sunday evening. That means we get a full day's skiing both Saturdays.

Of course that involves overnight 'stop-offs' but then variety is the much-needed spice of holiday life. On the trip down, you can ski for one or two days in a resort and then move on to your final destination. It's easy to combine resorts you might think of as being very far apart. You could stop off in Chamonix for a couple of nights before driving on to Courmayeur, Cervinia or La Thuile in Italy. You could stop off in Valmorel before going on to the Trois Vallées or Val-d'Isère. If you're going to Zermatt or Saas Fee, you could stop off and ski Wengen or Mürren before putting the car on the train for the half-hour journey through the Lötschberg tunnel, which takes you to the Valais. The possibilities are endless – all it takes is a couple of hours' drive.

After a full day's skiing on the final Saturday, if you drive for a few hours in the direction of home, you won't find Sunday's journey too demanding. In France, you'll be spoiled for choice as far as comfortable and reasonably priced hotels are concerned – particularly in cities such as Mâcon or Strasbourg. You'll be able to enjoy a good, non-ski-resort meal at good non-ski-resort prices. And, what better way is there to round off the holiday than a superb French Sunday lunch?

Taking a car means you can tailor your holiday to your needs. You can simply use it for the journey and then forget about it. You can enjoy day trips to other resorts or spend the week touring. It also enables you to escape far from the madding crowd.

The Audi A6 TDI, more economica

The Audi A6 2.5 TDI returns an amazing 58.9mpg, which works out at only 3.98 pence per m
pence per mile to run. So for miniature fuel bills, drive an Audi A6 T

han many small cars.

comparison the smaller model next to it costs a colossal 4.3
a colour brochure call 0800 99 88 77.

Audi. Vorsprung durch Technik.

AS YOU LIKE IT

If you fancy skiing in several resorts, you can use one as a base and make day trips to nearby places when the fancy takes you. If you do this you can still take advantage of the favourable accommodation prices offered by tour operators – and get a discount for driving. The discount varies from operator to operator and also depends on whether you go in high or low season – but you can expect to get from around £70 to £120.

The key to turning this kind of holiday into a success is to go for a resort which offers easy road access to others. A good choice is the Tyrol. The resorts to the east of Innsbruck offer many options to would-be day-trippers. Söll is a convenient base for exploring the other resorts in the Ski Welt area, as well as such resorts as Alpbach and Kitzbühel.

Further east, in Salzburg province, you can use Zell am See as a base for excursions to Badgastein and Saalbach, while Flachau is a convenient base for visiting the resorts covered by the Top Tauern lift pass, such as Schladming and Obertauern. Although western Austria is not ideal for this sort of holiday, you could use St Anton as a base and make day-trips to Lech, Zürs, Ischgl and Serfaus.

In the southern French Alps, Serre-Chevalier and Montgenèvre are ideal bases for day-tripping. If the extensive skiing offered in Serre-Chevalier isn't enough for you, Montgenèvre is within easy reach by car. It's at one end of the Milky Way ski area which includes Sauze d'Oulx and Sestriere in Italy – you can drive on to them or reach them on skis. On the French side of the border, a few miles south, there's Puy-St-Vincent. The major resorts of Alpe d'Huez and Les Deux Alpes are also within range. An added bonus is that these resorts share lift pass arrangements.

The Chamonix valley is an ideal destination for day-trippers. It offers a terrific amount of skiing covered by the Mont-Blanc pass – Chamonix, Megève, Les Contamines, Courmayeur plus a few more. Flaine and its satellites are also fairly accessible – so is Verbier if the Col des Montets and Col de la Forclaz are open.

You could consider resorts on the Swiss side of the Portes du Soleil, such as Morgins and Champéry, as a base for trips to such resorts as Verbier, Crans-Montana and those in the Chamonix Valley as well as skiing the Portes du Soleil circuit.

Because the resorts are so remote, Italy provides more of a headache for skiing day-trippers. Courmayeur is a notable exception – with quick access to La Thuile and, through the Mont-Blanc tunnel, to the Chamonix Valley and a slow trip to Cervinia. And in some parts of the Dolomites it's useful to have a car – to get from Cortina to the Sella Ronda circuit, for example.

Although eastern Switzerland provides more of a challenge to day-trippers, you might find that it's well worth the effort. Lenzerheide is about the best choice of base-camp. Flims, Arosa, Davos and St Moritz are all within striking distance. From St Moritz you could even go over to Livigno in Italy.

AROUND THE ALPS IN SEVEN DAYS

If you've got really itchy skis and want to ski as much of the Alps as possible, then consider making a Grand Tour by car, moving every day or two to a different resort and enjoying the complete freedom of going where you want, when you want. Except in high season, there's no need to book any accommodation before you go. So you can leave your decision about which part of the Alps you want to visit to the last moment and go wherever the snow is best.

You may have the impression that if you take a touring holiday you'll be spending more time on the road than on the piste. This

Audi

isn't the case – provided you plan your route carefully. And there's no need to eat into the skiing day. An hour's drive after the lifts have shut is all it takes to travel quite a distance.

Many of the areas that are great for day-trippers are also worth considering if you're going on tour. These include Western Austria, the Tyrol and the Chamonix valley. Take western Austria, for example; you can start with Lech, Zürs and St Anton, move on to Serfaus and Ischgl, then go down to Obergurgl, perhaps stopping at Sölden on the way. You can draw up the kind of schedule, albeit fairly hectic, for France's Tarentaise that the keen, expert skier would drool over. Imagine a week in which you could ski the Trois Vallées, La Plagne, Les Arcs, and Val-d'Isère/Tignes.

Italy is far more suitable for tourers than day-trippers provided you're prepared to put up with some slow drives on winding passes. You can start in Livigno, drive to Bormio and then to the Dolomites, visiting Madonna di Campiglio and Selva, and finish your Italian expedition in Cortina.

Eastern Switzerland also offers a very attractive touring holiday. You can start in Davos/Klosters, take in Lenzerheide and Arosa and end up in Flims. You could even include St Moritz if you're prepared to put up with a little extra driving. Again in Switzerland, you can easily combine several resorts in the Bernese Oberland. You could, for example, ski in Gstaad, Adelboden, Grindelwald, Wengen and Mürren. But do remember that the last two are car-free so you'll have to leave your car in Lauterbrunnen.

There's no need to confine yourself to one country – why not sample more than one nation's skiing delights? You could imitate the famous Haute-Route by starting in Argentière in France and ending up in Switzerland's Saas Fee. On the way you could ski in Verbier and Zermatt and even Crans Montana if time permits.

The major thing that you'll have to watch out for with a touring holiday is the cost of accommodation. Checking into a resort hotel as an independent traveller for a night or two won't come cheap. You can save money by staying down the valley. Many places have excellent access to the main ski areas. For example, you can take the funicular from Bourg-St-Maurice to Les Arcs; a gondola links Brides-Les-Bains to Méribel. You can let the train take the strain in Lauterbrunnen for Wengen and Mürren; and Täsch for Zermatt.

FAR FROM THE MADDING CROWD

If you've ever been irritated in a lift-queue or restaurant by unavoidably having to listen to someone else's conversation about England's chances of regaining the Ashes, or the state of the NHS, you'll probably have wished you could have got away from it all rather more than you have done.

By travelling independently, you can boldly go where not too many Brits have gone before and explore new frontiers which British tour operators rarely or only occasionally offer. There are hundreds of resorts in the Alps to discover – and in many you'd be unlucky if you heard another British voice.

TRAVEL TIME

The French Alps are the number one destination for most motoring British skiers. The journey time is surprisingly quick. From Calais for example, you can cover the 900km (560 miles) to Chamonix in just nine hours plus stops – all but the final few miles is on motorways. Although some areas of the Alps are less straightforward to get to, the majority are within a day's driving range provided you cross the Channel early.

Neither move

The Audi A6 is fitted with one of the world's most sophisticated engine management systems.

next move, the Audi A6 takes just 0.006 secor

THE AUDI A6, £18,675. PRICE CORRECT AT TIME OF GOING TO PRESS. EVERY NEW AUDI BENEFITS FROM AN UNRIVALLED CUSTOMER CARE PACKAGE COMPRISING 3
MILES AND UP TO 6 YEARS AUDI ON CALL VEHICLE RECOVERY AND ASSISTANCE, INCLUDING 3 YEARS

The Audi A6.

without thinking.

...nile Grandmaster Daniel King takes several minutes thinking of his
...r a colour brochure call 0800 99 88 77.

Audi. Vorsprung durch Technik.

THE COST OF A TICKET TO DRIVE

The cost of driving depends, of course, on how many passengers you cram into your car. If you're booking accommodation through a tour operator who offers a generous discount to drivers, you may find driving as cheap as flying even if there are only two or three of you. You'll pay from around £130 return to take your car with one passenger on a short channel crossing. Allow £100 to £200 for petrol, depending on where you're going and in what sort of car. Don't forget French motorway tolls – the trip from Calais to Albertville and back will cost around £100. And to use Swiss motorways you need a permit costing SF40. In the Alps you can expect to pay for using many of the tunnels – for example, about £15 or £20 for a one-way trip through the Mont-Blanc tunnel (it depends on car size).

WHICH WHEELS?

A 4WD car is a great asset in the Alps. You'll have far more control when going downhill, as well as the ability to climb uphill. We've driven a lot in snow in 4WD cars with knobbly tyres and have never had to use snow-chains. Next best is a front-wheel drive car. The size and boot capacity of the car are clearly important. Four adults, plus luggage cooped up in a small family saloon for 700 miles doesn't make for a comfortable or harmonious journey. Special enclosed roof racks are available, capable of holding a lot of baggage as well as skis.

GETTING THE CAR READY

Alpine weather and roads are likely to make unusual demands on your car – it pays to make sure that:
• the tread on your tyres (including the spare) is up to scratch
• you test the battery if you suspect that it's dodgy
• the anti-freeze is strong enough to survive temperatures which could drop to -30°C overnight
• you have a similarly strong solution of winter screenwash
• you check the handbook to see if you need to do anything to adapt the car for cold weather; you may for example, have to adjust the engine air intake, or use a thinner oil
• you fit headlight beam deflectors; if they normally throw a lot of light upwards, fit special fog lights which will be a big help if you have to drive at night when it's snowing.

CAR COVER

Even if you have fully comprehensive insurance, it will often be down-graded to third party as soon as you leave the UK, unless you've made arrangements to extend it – allow at least a couple of weeks for this. Most companies don't charge for such extensions. Although it's no longer compulsory to carry a Green Card in other EU countries, it's a good idea to ask your insurance company for one.

If your car breaks down, you could face a big bill, lengthy delays and utter disruption to your holiday plans. You can buy peace of mind by taking out a breakdown insurance policy. National Breakdown's UK breakdown insurance also covers the Continent.

SAFE DRIVING

Except in severe weather, you're only likely to come across serious snow conditions on approach roads to fairly high resorts. Unless you've got a 4WD car you'll need chains on the car's driving wheels – not simply to keep you safe and mobile but also to stay on the right side of local laws. You can keep the chains on while you're driving on ordinary roads; but you'll have to drive very slowly and for a limited period only. The instructions should have information about this.

Audi

If you've never used chains before, it's well worth having a practice run at putting them on. The first time we had to fit them, we spent a very unhappy hour lying in the road-side slush as the snow came down and our fellow motorists cursed us in a variety of languages as they squeezed past us on a narrow mountain road.

Even if the road surface seems dry and free of ice, still take great care – there could be icy patches on shaded areas. You can't afford to relax in relatively warm weather – there's nothing more treacherous than ice that's melting. Be especially cautious when going downhill. If the road surface is slippery, keep your speed down and brake by using your engine – change down in good time. Brake on the straight, not on bends – otherwise the front wheels may lock and you'll slide straight on. If the back wheels slide and the car starts to spin, steer into the slide.

MOUNTAIN MOTOR MAINTENANCE

Your car will be in for quite a culture shock having, perhaps, left a nice warm garage for overnight temperatures way, way below freezing. So:
• overnight, park on flat ground and in a place where your car will be sheltered from the wind
• leave the car in gear with the hand-brake off; you could have problems if the hand-brake freezes in the 'on' position
• lift the wipers away from the windscreen
• if you're not planning any trips, it's worth taking the car out for short drives just to keep the battery ticking over.

RECOMMENDED ROUTES

From the Channel there are essentially only three 'gateways' into the Alps. For the French and some of the Swiss Alps, you go via the French motorways and **Mâcon**. For most of the Swiss and some of the Austrian Alps you aim for **Basel**. For all of the Austrian Alps you can go via **Ulm** – and for some Austrian resorts it's the only sensible route. Normally, once you've picked your destination you'll be able to see which gateway you need; our maps of Austria (page 52), France (page 136), Italy (page 261) and Switzerland (page 304) will help. Then you can concentrate on deciding how to get to that gateway from a particular port.

Where you have a choice of route, you may wish to bear in mind that German motorways are free, whereas French ones charge tolls that are not negligible (Calais to Albertville and back £100). German ones have no speed limit, making them potentially quicker but rather scary in wet weather. And their petrol stations rarely accept credit cards. To use Swiss motorways, you have to buy a sticker for your windscreen (SF40 for a calendar year). These are sold at the border, and you're expected to buy one unless you have a pretty convincing route-plan involving no motorways.

DESTINATION: FRENCH ALPS

Wherever you're starting from, the gateway is **Mâcon** and the initial target is Beaune. If you're taking the short crossing to Calais, Boulogne or Dunkirk, the route is via Reims, Troyes and Dijon. From Le Havre or Caen your route sounds even simpler: the A13 to Paris then the A6 south. But you have to get through or around Paris. The most direct way around the city is the notorious périphérique – a hectic multi-lane urban motorway close to the centre, with exits every few hundred yards. But this is not the quickest if is jammed with traffic. The more reliable alternative is to take a series of motorways and dual carriageways through the south-west fringes of Greater Paris. The route (or one of the routes – there are a couple of

Audi

This map should help you plan your route to the Alps. As we've explained in the text, all the main routes from the Channel and all the routes up into the mountains funnel through three 'gateways', picked out on the map in larger type – Mâcon, Basel and Ulm. Decide which gateway suits your destination, and pick a route to it. Occasionally, different Channel ports will lead you to use different gateways.

Audi

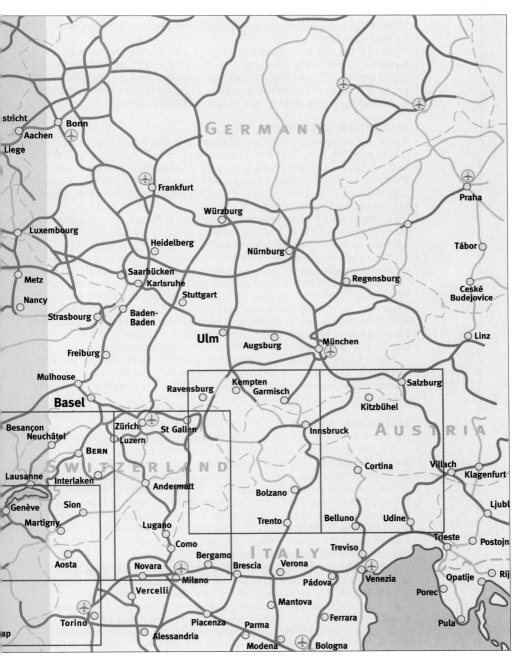

The boxes on the map correspond to the areas covered by the more
detailed maps at the start of the main country sections of the book:
Austria page 52
France page 136
Switzerland page 304.
There is also a not-so-detailed map of the Italian Alps on page 260.

Audi

variants) is signed, but not easy to follow without a detailed map and a good navigator.

At Mâcon, the routes start to diverge; you go east on the A40 for **Geneva** to get to the northern resorts – Chamonix, the Portes du Soleil and so on; take the A43 off the Lyon bypass for **Chambéry** to get to the central Tarentaise mega-resorts; and take the A48 south off that road for **Grenoble** to get to the southern resorts.

DESTINATION: SWITZERLAND

There are two gateways for Switzerland. For the Valais resorts of Champéry, Verbier, Saas Fee, Zermatt and so on, and those in Vaud such as Villars and Les Diablerets, aim for **Mâcon** and then Geneva. Don't be tempted to aim for Lausanne, two-thirds of the way along lake Geneva – the route nationale from Besançon to the Swiss border via Pontarlier is slow going.

If you're going further east, the gateway is **Basel**. This presents more alternative routes than any other gateway. From Calais the obvious route is via Reims, Metz and Strasbourg, then across the border to the autobahn up the Rhine valley. But from ports further east, other routes are viable – via the Belgian motorways to Luxembourg and into France to pick up the Calais route; or Belgian motorways towards Cologne, then all the way up the Rhine valley. From the Normandy ports, you have a choice of going via Paris to join the Calais route at Reims or heading south, as if for Geneva, and turning left at Beaune. This is the better bet – slightly quicker, more scenic, and better equipped with good places for lunch.

From Basel, the routes diverge: you go on to **Bern** for the Bernese Oberland, to get to such resorts as Wengen and Grindelwald; to **Lucerne** for resorts in central Switzerland; and to **Zürich** for resorts in the Grisons – Davos, Flims and so on.

DESTINATION: AUSTRIA

For the Vorarlberg resorts in western Austria (notably Lech and Zürs) and for St Anton just inside the Tyrol, the best gateway may be **Basel** – particularly if starting from the Normandy ports. You drive through Switzerland, and cross into Austria at **Feldkirch**.

But for most purposes the gateway is **Ulm**, between Stuttgart and Munich. From the short-crossing ports there are several ways to get to it, but the basic choice is the same as those for Basel: via France and Strasbourg; via Belgium, Luxembourg and Strasbourg; or via Belgium and the Rhine valley. Our basic advice to those thinking of starting from the Normandy ports is: Don't.

From Ulm, routes diverge. For the Vorarlberg and Arlberg resorts, head south to cross into Austria at Bregenz and join the Basel route at **Feldkirch**. For Innsbruck and neighbouring resorts, branch south-east off that route, crossing into Austria between Füssen and **Reutte**, and then negotiating the low Fern pass to get to the Inn valley. For resorts further east, carry on through Munich and cross into Austria at **Kufstein** for resorts in the eastern Tyrol (Kitzbühel and neighbours) or **Salzburg** for resorts in Salzburg province (Zell am See, Badgastein), Styria (Schladming), and Carinthia (Badkleinkirchheim).

DESTINATION: ITALY

Italian resorts are spread out over the whole length of the Alpine range. They are reached by passes or tunnels from France, Switzerland or Italy. The possibilities are set out in detail in our introduction to Italian resorts on page 261.

Audi

by **Dave Watts**

Weekend skiing

seems longer than you think

I'd always been sceptical of weekend ski trips. Surely it can't be worth the hassle – let alone the expense – of flying out, getting a transfer, arriving late, worrying about the weather and then making the return journey after a couple of days skiing.

Then I tried it for the first time in April 1994 – and was immediately converted.

I left the office at 4.30pm on Friday after having put in a full week. By 7pm I was in the air en route to Geneva. By midnight (French time) we'd arrived at our hotel in Chamonix. Snow was falling, and there was plenty of it on the ground at resort level (a mere 1035m). What must it be like at 3275m at the top of the Grands Montets, I wondered?

Dawn broke and it was still snowing. All the lifts were shut except for the Les Houches area which had been closed due to lack of snow a few days before. So we went there and had tremendous powder skiing in the trees all the way from the top (1975m) to the bottom – and the trees made seeing the ground possible. What a day!

That evening we had a superb French dinner followed by a crawl around several of Chamonix's lively bars – many of which featured live music.

Then it was Sunday – and still snowing. Someone suggested driving through the Mont Blanc tunnel to Courmayeur in Italy. As so often happens in the area, we emerged at the other end into clear skies and brilliant sunshine. Once we got to the top of the cable-car and skied our first run, it became clear that the mountain had been shut the previous day and we were in for a day of virgin powder skiing. The pistes had been well groomed and the packed powder made for wonderful intermediate cruising – which is what Courmayeur is all about. Go off the piste for a few metres and there was two or three feet of fresh, light, untracked powder. None of us were good powder skiers but we had great fun practising and falling around in the perfect snow.

The only thing we stopped for was lunch – a typical Italian lunch of pizza and pasta at the wonderfully rustic Maison Vieille mountain restaurant.

That evening, after a quick sauna and Jacuzzi, we went ten-pin bowling at the brand new bowling centre near the hotel before a meal of local Savoyarde fare and an early night in preparation for the next day's final highlight.

Monday dawned to clear skies and a 6.30am start. We paused briefly to feel sorry for our colleagues back in England confronting that familiar Monday morning feeling on their way to work. But then there was a serious choice to make. Take the first cable car up the Aiguille du Midi to the 3790m start of the 24km Vallée Blanche and make the first tracks down it for days. Or head for the Grands Montets where there was fresh powder and we'd been told the top cable car leading to awesome skiing would be open. For two of us there was no contest – a morning of fresh powder on the Grands Montets beckoned. For the other three in our group, the majesty and spectacular glacial seracs and crevasses of the Vallée Blanche were irresistible.

Both groups had a marvellous morning – and miraculously made it down for the rendezvous time of 1pm, a quick shower, pizza lunch and transfer back to Geneva airport in time for a late afternoon flight. By 6pm we were back at Heathrow. We all agreed we felt we had been away for a week, had done a tremendous amount of skiing and were fully refreshed by our break. But we'd only been gone for 72 hours.

And what did all this cost? Crystal, who we'd travelled with, had three-day breaks like this on offer last season for from £250 to £300 in 'Small & Friendly' bed and breakfast accommodation. Add on £65 for a three-day lift pass (which covers a day in Courmayeur) and £60 for food and drink, and you've got a marvellous ski break in one of the world's top resorts for around £400.

Some operators, such as White Roc, Ski Weekend and FlexiSki, specialise in organising weekend and ten-day holidays rather than the usual one or two weeks. I'm also a convert to ten-day breaks – my annual ski holiday is always of this length, with a week at one resort and visits to others on the way out and way back (yes, I drive rather than fly). Ski Solutions and other specialist ski travel agents (see Black and White Pages at the end of this book) can also arrange weekend breaks.

And if you are going to Courchevel, Méribel or Val-d'Isère a good way to organise the flight and transfer is to take the Air France Ski Elite deal. This covers scheduled return flight to Lyon, transfer by taxi or mini-bus to and from the resort, a free mountain tour with an ESF ski instructor, Carte Neige insurance and a complimentary day's trial of the latest ski equipment. Prices started at £276 last season depending on your departure airport. You can also change your flight back if you are having such a great time you want to stay longer.

Choosing your resort

get it right first time

Most British skiers, unlike those lucky enough to live closer to the Alps, get to go skiing only once or twice a year – and then only for a week at a time in most cases. So choosing the right resort is crucially important. This book is designed to help you do just that. Here is some advice on how to use it to best effect.

Lots of factors need to be taken into account. And the weight you attach to each of them depends on your own personal preferences and on the make-up of the group you are going on holiday with. On page 18, you'll find shortlists of resorts which are outstanding in various key respects. For most people cost will be an important factor. That's why we've devoted a whole chapter to it – see page 23.

WHICH RESORT?
Each resort chapter is organised in the same way, to help you choose the right resort. This short introduction explains how they work.

We start off with a How it Rates section, in the margin, where we rate each resort from 11 points of view – the more stars the better. For major resorts we then give lists of the main good and bad points about the resort and its skiing, picked out with ✔ and ✘. These lists are followed by a summary in **bold type**, in which we've aimed to encapsulate the essence of the place and to weigh up the pros and cons, giving our view of who might like it. These sections should give you a good idea of whether the resort is likely to suit *you,* and whether you should read our detailed analysis of it.

You'll know by now whether this is, for example, a high, hideous, purpose-built resort with superb, snow-sure skiing for all standards of skier but absolutely no nightlife, or whether it's a pretty, traditional village with gentle wooded skiing ideal for beginners if only there was some snow.

We then look at each aspect of the resort in more detail.

THE RESORT
Resorts vary enormously in character and charm. At the extremes of the range are the handful of really hideous modern apartment-block resorts thrown up in France in the 1960s – step forward, Les Menuires – and the captivating old traffic-free mountain villages of which Switzerland has an unfair number. But it isn't simply a question of old versus new. Some purpose-built places (such as Valmorel) can have a much friendlier feel than some traditional resorts with big blocky buildings (eg Davos). And some places can be remarkably strung out (eg Vail) whereas others are surprisingly compact (eg Wengen).

The landscape can have an important impact – whether the resort is at the bottom of a narrow valley (eg Ischgl) or on shelf with panoramic views (eg Crans-Montana). Some places are working towns as well as ski resorts (eg Bormio). Some are full of bars, discos and shops (eg St Anton). Others are peaceful backwaters (eg Arabba). Traffic may choke the streets (eg Châtel). Or the village may be traffic-free (eg Mürren).

In this first section of each chapter, we try to sort out the character of the place for you. Later, in the Staying there section, we tell you more about the hotels, restaurants, bars and so on.

THE SKIING

The ski area Some ski areas are vast and complex, while others are much smaller and lacking variation. The description here tells you how the ski area divides up into different sectors and how the links between them work. You'll need to understand this to make the most of the descriptions of the skiing that come later. Read this section together with the piste map for the resort.

Snow reliability A crucial factor for many people and one which varies enormously. In some resorts you don't have to worry at all about there being no snow to ski on, while others (including some very big names) are notorious for treating their paying guests to ice, mud and slush. Whether a resort is likely to have decent snow on its slopes normally depends on the height of the skiing, the direction most of the slopes face (north good, south bad), its snow record and how much artificial snow it has (we list this figure in Ski Facts).

For advanced/ intermediate/ beginner skiers Most (though not all) resorts have something to offer beginners. But remarkably few will keep an advanced skier happy for a holiday. As for intermediates, whether a resort will suit you really depends on your standard and temperament. Places such as Cervinia and Obergurgl are ideal for those who want easy cruising runs but have little to offer intermediates looking for more challenge. Others, such as Sölden and Val-d'Isère, may intimidate the less confident intermediate who doesn't know the ski area well. We sum up the skiing for different grades of skier and describe outstanding runs or areas.

For cross-country We don't pretend that this is a guide for avid cross-country skiers. But if you or one of your group wants to try it our summary here will help you gauge whether the resort is worth considering or a wash-out. It looks not just at the amount of cross-country available but also its scenic beauty and whether or not the tracks are likely to have decent snow (many are at low altitude).

Queues Another key factor. Not only is standing in queues tedious – it also robs you of valuable skiing time. Most resorts have improved their lift systems enormously in the last ten years, and monster queues are largely a thing of the past. But there are notable exceptions – such as Verbier and Kitzbühel.

Mountain restaurants Here's a subject that divides skiers clearly into two opposing camps. To some, having a decent lunch in civilised surroundings – either in the sun, contemplating amazing scenery, or in a cosy Alpine hut, sheltered from the elements – makes or breaks their holiday. Others regard a prolonged mid-day stop as a waste of valuable skiing time as well as valuable spending money – they prefer a sandwich on the mountain top or a quick, cheap self-service snack. We are firmly in the former camp. We get very disheartened by places with miserable restaurants and miserable food (eg many resorts in America); and there are some resorts that we go to regularly partly because of the cosy huts and excellent cuisine (eg Zermatt).

Ski school This is an area where we rely heavily on your reports of your own or your friends' experiences. The only way to judge a ski school is by trying it. Reports on ski schools are always extremely valuable and frequently disappointing.

Facilities for children If you need crèche facilities don't go to Italy. In other countries, facilities for looking after and teaching children can vary enormously between resorts. We say what is available in each resort, including what's on offer from tour operators – often the most attractive option for Brits, particularly those who like catered chalet holidays (explained later in this section). But, again, to be of real help we need reports from people who've used the facilities.

STAYING THERE

In some resorts such as St Anton and Zermatt, choosing where in the resort to stay is very important – otherwise you might end up with long treks to and from the lifts or being woken at 2am by noisy revellers. We tell you what to take into account.

How to go The basic choice is between catered chalets, hotels and self-catering accommodation. Catered chalets remain a peculiarly British phenomenon. A tour operator takes over a chalet (or a hotel in some cases), staffs it with young Brits (or antipodeans), fills it with British guests, provides half-board and free wine with dinner, lets you drink your duty-free booze without feeling guilty and often provides free ski guiding to help you get the best out of the area. And we love it! It is a very economic way of visiting the top resorts – see our chapter on costs on page 17. And it makes for a very sociable holiday. Standards of accommodation and cuisine can vary a lot.

Hotels, as ever, can vary a lot but, especially in France and Switzerland, can work out very expensive. Apartments can work out the most economical way of going skiing but French ones, in particular, tend to be very small – it's not unusual for brochure prices to be based on four people sleeping in a one-room studio, for example. To be comfortable, find out the apartment size and put fewer people in than the number it is advertised for.

In this section we have looked at the accommodation of all three types that is available through British tour operators. For hotels and self-catering we also look at what's available for independent travellers who want to fix their own accommodation. With hotels we've given each a £££ rating – the more pound signs, the pricier.

Staying up the mountain / down the valley If there are interesting options for staying on the slopes or in valley towns, we've picked them out. The former is often good for avoiding early-morning scrums for the lifts, the latter for cutting costs considerably.

Eating out The range of restaurants varies enormously between resorts. Even some big ones, such as Les Arcs, may have little choice because most of the clientele stay in their apartments and self-cater. Chalet-dominated resorts such as Méribel can also have a surprisingly limited choice. Others, such as Val-d'Isère, have a huge range available, including national and regional cuisine, pizzas, fondues and international fare. American resorts, in particular, generally have an excellent range of restaurants – everyone eats out.

Après-ski Tastes and styles vary enormously. Most resorts have pleasant places in which to have an immediate post-skiing beer or hot chocolate. Some then go dead. Others have noisy bars and discos until the early hours. And, especially in Austrian resorts, there may be a lot of events such as tobogganing and bowling that are organised by British tour operator reps. We've done our best to summarise what you'll find. But when we are touring around inspecting resorts, discos that don't get lively until midnight don't come high on our

You don't have to ski alone
...to be an individual!

SKI
SOLUTIONS

*Britain's original
and largest specialist
ski travel agency*

ABTA

SKI SOLUTIONS

The first and only place you need to call to book your ski holiday.

We are a ski travel agency as opposed to a ski tour operator. When you call us you immediately place at your disposal a choice of thousands of holidays offered by a wide variety of different reputable, fully bonded tour operators, both large and small.

By calling Ski Solutions first, rather than ringing round lots of ski tour operators, you can make *an instant short-cut to finding you ideal ski holiday*. To start the snowball rolling, simply ring us and give us a very rough idea of what kind of holiday you are seeking and when:

- **How many in your party?**
- **Are there any children? What ages?**
- **What levels of skier?**
- **Traditional or modern resort?**
- **Where, ideally, do you want to fly from?**
- **What standard of hotel, chalet or apartment?**

Our experienced staff will gently "cross-examine" you, asking what you did and didn't enjoy about past ski holidays and allowing you to reveal any personal preferences.

Acting on what you have told them, our staff will then research and compile a shortlist of appropriate holidays and will send this together with relevant brochures and other information. (If you're in a hurry, we can even fax these details to you.)

We do all the hard work for you by working out exactly what each option will cost with each operator, taking into account all the various complicated supplements and discounts. (Because they spend each day immersed in ski brochures, our staff are experts on the small print.) Without any financial obligation on your part, we can "hold" provisionally the holidays that

particularly interest you for a couple of days, giving you time to discuss things with any others involved.

After further discussions with you we will then book the holiday of your choice. The price of the holiday will be *exactly as in the brochure:* our service is absolutely *FREE*. Indeed, it actually saves you money in terms of time and phone bills.

If, by chance, we cannot find you a suitable holiday in one of the many brochures, then we are happy to tailor-make the perfect holiday for you through our A La Carte department, which works closely with many of the world's top ski resorts.

Between us the 12 staff of Ski Solutions have skied over 100 resorts on both sides of the Atlantic and we have a first-hand up-to-date knowledge of the hotels, chalets and apartments offered by most of the operators in these places.

Because we are primarily a travel agency and not a tour operator, we have the luxury of being able to sell you the holiday you want rather than the holiday we need to sell.

Discounts for *Where to Ski* readers
**Book through Ski Solutions and we'll refund the cost of this book
– see page 9.**

Call us *now!*
0171 602 9900

84 Pembroke Road, Kensington, London W8 6NX
Facsimile 0171-602-2882

agenda. So we are largely dependent for this section on hearing from those of our reporters who are keen après-skiers. And we are very grateful to the several tour operators who have helped us put together this section for certain resorts.

For non-skiers You might be surprised to hear that this is an area where we do consider ourselves experts. That's because one of us is married to a dedicated non-skier who loves the mountains and has been on no fewer than 20 Alpine holidays while setting foot on skis just once. If you'd like any more specialised advice – eg which are the easiest resorts to get the Times in; which bar terraces get the sun first in Méribel, Zermatt, Wengen, Saas-Fee and Val-d'Isère; how to save mountain restaurant tables for ten for two hours in peak season – address your enquiries to Mrs Watts.

Austria

Austria has traditionally been the favourite destination for British skiers. But last season, for the first time, France overtook it – claiming around 30 per cent of the market compared with Austria's 25 per cent. The resurgence of interest in Italy is also hitting the Austrians' business. But for a large number of Brits, Austria will remain number one. For beginners and cautious intermediates seeking reassuring surroundings rather than challenges, it's difficult to beat Austria's blend of friendly and often pretty villages and similarly captivating ski areas. Most of its ski areas, however, do lack the extent and/or the altitude that French resorts offer, and there are lots of experienced skiers who won't consider going to Austria except to visit steep, snowy St Anton or to ski one of the several excellent glaciers. The good skiers who take a different view are mainly those who like the lively nightlife that is a particular feature of Austrian resorts.

Austria is the heartland of the mainstream package ski holiday, sold over the counter by high-street travel agencies and based on hotel or guest-house accommodation. Austria has vast amounts of this reliably comfortable accommodation, and a huge number of resorts, large and small – you can buy packages to over 100 Austrian resorts this winter. Chalet and self-catering packages are less widely offered.

Most of these resorts are real villages in valley bottoms, with skiing on the wooded slopes above them. They have expanded enormously since the war, but practically all the development has been in traditional chalet style; the German demand for summer holidays is as important to Austria as skiing, and the villages of the Tyrol have to look good without the snow that is the saving grace of many French and even some Swiss resorts.

The skiing is often quite limited. There are many Austrian resorts that a keen skier could explore fully in half a day. Those who start their skiing careers in such resorts may not be worried by this – and it certainly means that there is nothing to distract you from concentrating on learning to ski properly. But those who have developed a taste for travelling around on skis find that the list of acceptable Austrian resorts is quite a short one.

Unfortunately, several of the resorts on that short list bring you up against another problem – low altitude, and therefore poor snow conditions. Kitzbühel is at 760m, Söll at 700m, Zell am See at 755m. When considering altitudes, you do have to remember that in winter Europe gets colder the further east you go – so 700m isn't as low in skiing terms as 700m would be in France. But it's still low, and the top heights of Austrian resorts are relatively low too – typically 1800m to 2000m. And snowmaking is not as widespread here as in France, Italy or Switzerland.

The resorts of the Arlberg area, at the western end of the Tyrol – St Anton, Lech and Zürs, stand apart from these concerns, with excellent snow records and extensive skiing. And there are other resorts where you can be reasonably confident of good snow, such as Obergurgl and Ischgl, not to mention the reliable year-round skiing on glaciers such as those at Hintertux, Neustift and Kaprun. But for most other resorts our advice is to book late, when you know what the snow conditions are like.

Nightlife is an important feature of Austrian skiing for many regular visitors. It ranges from lively hotel bars selling large volumes of beer, through Tyrolean evenings and activities organised by the representatives of UK tour operators, to much more sophisticated discos and nightclubs in resorts such as Lech, Ischgl and Kitzbühel.

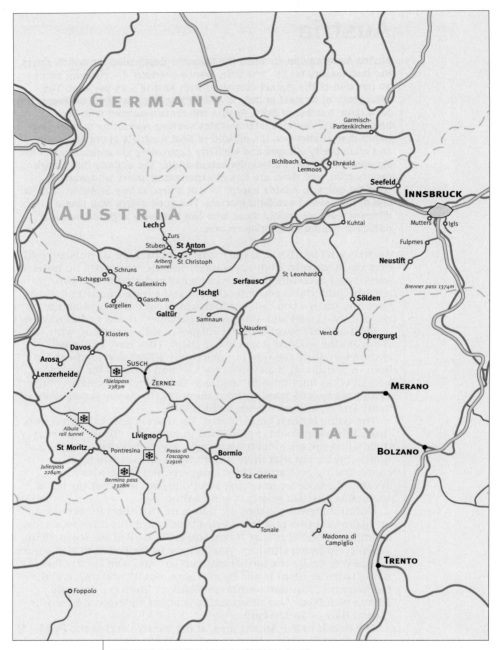

GETTING AROUND THE AUSTRIAN ALPS

The dominant feature of Austria for the ski driver is the thoroughfare of the Inn valley, which runs through the Tyrol from Landeck via Innsbruck to Kufstein. The motorway along it extends, with one or two breaks, westwards to the Arlberg pass and on to Switzerland.

The Arlberg – which divides Tyrol from Vorarlberg, but which is also the watershed between Austria and Switzerland – is one of the few areas where driving plans are likely to be seriously affected by snow. The east-west Arlberg pass itself has a long tunnel underneath it; this isn't cheap, and unless you're in a tearing hurry you may want to take the high road when it's clear, passing through Stuben,

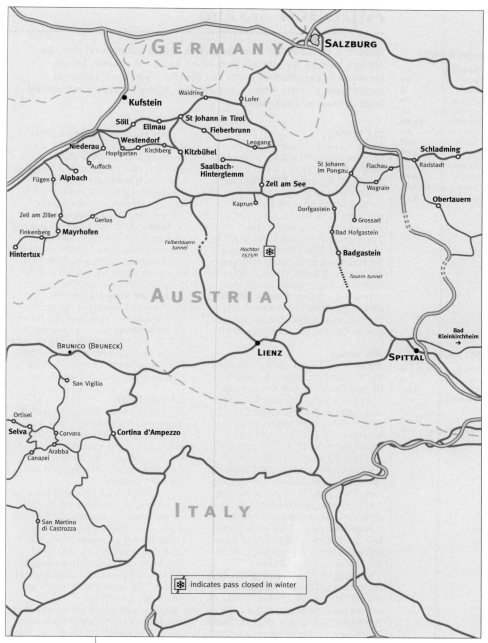

indicates pass closed in winter

St Christoph and St Anton instead of missing all three. The Flexen pass road to Zürs and Lech (which may be closed by avalanche risk even when the Arlberg is open) branches off just to the west of the Arlberg summit, and in snow it is best approached from the west.

At the eastern end of the Tyrol, the Gerlos pass road from Zell am Ziller over into Salzburg province (1628m) is occasionally closed. Resorts such as Bad Kleinkirchheim, over in Carinthia, are easily reached by motorway, thanks to the Tauern and Katschberg tunnels. There is the alternative of driving over the Radstädter Tauern pass through Obertauern (1739m), or of using the car-carrying rail service from Böckstein (just beyond Badgastein) to Mallnitz.

Alpbach 1000m

Alpbach is an old British favourite – there is even a British ski club, the Alpbach Visitors. We go there in numbers partly out of habit, but also because it is exceptionally pretty and friendly – 'you are a guest, not a tourist,' says a recent visitor – and because its tiny ski area is not without interest, even for good skiers.

THE RESORT

Alpbach is a captivating place in summer and winter alike – one of the prettiest villages in a province that is renowned for them. It lies near the head of its valley, slightly elevated and looking south across the valley towards the Wiedersbergerhorn, where most of the skiing takes place. Traditional chalets crowd around the immaculate little church, and open fields (including the nursery slopes) are just yards away. The Inn valley is only a few miles to the north, and expeditions eastward to the Kitzbühel area or westward to Innsbruck and beyond are possible. The Hintertux and Stubai glaciers are within reach.

THE SKIING

Alpbach's **ski area**, on two flanks of the Wiedersbergerhorn, is small and simple. The main gondola goes up from the isolated roadside lift-station of Achenwirt (830m), a mile from the centre; slower alternatives go up from Inneralpbach (1050m), half-way round the mountain on its east side, and they all meet at Hornboden (1890m). Two recently built drags take the skiing up to 2025m. The small ski area down at Reith is on the ski pass.

Like most lowish resorts in Tirol, Alpbach cannot claim great **snow reliability**; but at least most slopes face north. The village nursery slope and a run down the top stage of the gondola have artificial snow.

Although Alpbach can't generally be recommended for **advanced** skiers, the reds and the two (short) blacks are not without challenge, and runs of 1000m vertical are not to be sniffed at. There are a couple of off-piste routes to the valley, short ski tours are also offered, and the ski schools take the top classes off-piste a lot.

Terrain is ideal for **intermediate** skiers; the problem is that it's limited. This resort is for practicing technique on familiar slopes, not high mileage.

Beginners love the sunny nursery slopes, reassuringly close to the village centre, and higher slopes can be used when snow is poor. But this is not a resort for confidence-building: most of the longer runs are red.

There are pretty **cross-country** trails up the valleys beyond Inneralpbach (1050m); the most testing is 9km long and climbs 300m.

Serious **queues** are rare, thanks to the efficient gondola. But the resort does attract some weekend trade.

There are as many **mountain restaurants** as the small ski area can squeeze in. Hornboden now has a popular table-service restaurant as well as self-service. There is something to be said for descending to Achenwirt.

Alpbach and Alpbach Innertal are the two **ski schools**, and we have had excellent reports of the former. Both operate ski nurseries; the former takes **children** from age 4, from 9.30 to 4.15. (They bring the children back on the ski-bus at the end of the day.) The non-ski nursery operates from 9.15 to 4pm (noon on Saturday).

STAYING THERE

Alpbach is a small village, so there's no need to worry about where you stay. The very centre is undoubtedly most convenient, both for the ski-bus and for après-ski. The backwater of Inneralpbach is convenient for skiing, and suits families.

There isn't much choice of **how to go** – hotels and pensions dominate UK package programmes. Of the three smart 4-star places with pools, the Alpbacherhof gets most votes. But most simpler places also get good reports. Haus Thomas, Haus Angelika and Haus Theresia are recommended again by last season's visitors. Some self-catering is offered.

Eating out means eating in hotels, or at least in restaurants attached to hotels. The Reblaus, Jakober and Hotel Post are recommended.

The **après-ski** scene is typically Tirolean, with a great deal of noisy tea-time beer swilling in the bars of central hotels such as the Jakober. In the evening the Waschkuch'l is good for a quiet drink. There are two discos – the Schneeloch and the Weinstahdl.

There is more to amuse **non-skiers** than you might expect, including swimming and curling (400m from the centre), pretty walks, and excursions to Innsbruck and beyond.

Bad Kleinkirchheim 1080m

Having local-boy-made-good Franz Klammer as its ski ambassador has helped to put Bad Kleinkirchheim on the international map. The old spa town has developed its ski area substantially in recent years, and now offers attractive intermediate terrain.

THE RESORT

Bad Kleinkirchheim is Franz Klammer's home town and is in the far south-east of Austria's mountains, away from the usual skiing destinations. To attract custom, 'BKK' has developed from a summer spa with a limited ski area into a fair-sized ski resort. The result is modern lifts and a positive attitude towards making improvements.

The drawback to having spa origins is that the village is laid out in a sprawling manner, less than ideal for skiers. The most convenient place to stay is close to the Priedröf and Maibrunnbahn lifts.

BKK has a sophisticated, relaxed feel, with superb spa facilities.

THE SKIING

The BKK and St Oswald **ski areas** are now linked by both lift and piste – the former has two-thirds of the skiing. Both are made up of mostly flattering intermediate runs. Two lifts – a quad chair and a long drag – service the skiing immediately above BKK. Those staying near the tennis centre have a gondola to whisk them up to the far end of BKK's area. Two short chair-rides take skiers from central BKK to the St Oswald skiing, while a little drag enables a speedy return.

Being east of the Tauern Pass, BKK can have completely different weather from the rest of Austria. In recent years **snow reliability** has been noticeably better at times and much worse at others. It is sufficiently distant from most other resorts to avoid a massive invasion when its conditions are better; portable snowmaking helps matters when the situation is reversed. However, it's essentially a low, sunny ski area where late holidays in particular are risky. The top of the skiing is only a little over 2000m.

This is not a resort for **advanced skiers**. The red from the top of the Lärchegg drag is a tough run when icy. The World Cup downhill course is surprisingly easy at 'normal' speed. The Franz Klammer run is better, but finishes with a walk to a bus stop.

The area is ideal for improving **intermediates**, the majority of runs being long, wide and flattering, as well as nicely uncrowded. St Oswald's partly open skiing provides welcome variety to an area that can otherwise seem a little 'samey'.

St Oswald is best for complete **beginners**, with better nursery slopes and very easy runs at the top of the Nockalm. Near-beginners will enjoy the blue running parallel to the bottom part of the World Cup downhill course.

BKK takes **cross-country** seriously, keeping its 40km of trails well maintained. BKK has the largest loop, running around its golf course, but St Oswald has snowsure trails at the top of the Nockalm.

Queues are not a problem, though we have no reports of how the new St Oswald link works at peak periods.

Mountain restaurants are generally attractive, without any being really special. Waldratte, at the gondola mid-station, has a good ice-bar for drink-only customers.

St Oswald is good for **children**. There is a fine ski kindergarten and the Farmhouse apartments have a free nursery.

STAYING THERE

Good quality is the norm in BKK's **hotels**. Ronacher is well-placed, luxurious and has excellent spa facilities. Eschenhof is similar. Gasthof Weisses Rössl is a good-value 3-star. The Farmhouse village at St Oswald is a high-standard **self-catering** complex.

There is no need to pay a lot for quality when **eating out**. The cheap and cheerful Zirkitzerhof is popular. The Farmhouse has its own restaurant, but Gasthof Schneeweiss has perhaps the best food in St Oswald.

Apart from a good video-disco-bar, complete with chat-up phones on the tables, this is a quiet resort, with little else of the usual jolly Austrian **après-ski**.

Superb spa facilities, with indoor and outdoor thermal pools, fitness centres, whirlpools, saunas and so on, make this a great choice for a certain type of **non-skier**. However, there is little else to do than take good walks. Those with cars can visit Villach (36km away) for a shopping spree.

Badgastein 1000m

HOW IT RATES

The skiing

Snow	***
Extent	****
Advanced	***
Intermediates	****
Beginners	**
Convenience	**
Queues	***
Restaurants	****

The rest

Scenery	***
Resort charm	***
Not skiing	****

✔ Four separate, varied ski areas which together make up one of Austria's largest ski circuses covered by one pass

✔ Great skiing for confident intermediates, with lots of long, challenging red runs

✔ Relatively snowsure by the standards of most low-altitude Austrian resorts, with artificial snow and the high Sportgastein ski area as back-up

✔ Lots of good, atmospheric, traditional mountain restaurants

✔ Plenty of non-skiing facilities, especially related to its origin as a spa resort

✔ Unusual setting, architecture and ambience for a ski resort

✘ Ski area doesn't really suit beginners or timid intermediates

✘ Biggest and smallest ski areas accessed direct from Badgastein but other two a bus-ride away. Buses can be infrequent and crowded and having a car would be handy

✘ Sedate spa town atmosphere not to everyone's taste and can suffer from local traffic on the narrow streets

✘ Bus rides or steep walks to skiing or après-skiing from some accommodation

ORIENTATION

The spa resort of Badgastein sits at the head of eastern Austria's Gastein · valley. From the railway station above the resort centre, a gondola rises into the main ski area, which spreads north down the west side of the valley to Bad Hofgastein (8km by road) – a resort which gets less international attention but is about as big. The separate ski area of Dorfgastein (8km further north) is linked to Grossarl in the next valley to the east. 9km up the valley from Badgastein, beyond Böckstein (where cars bound for Italy must be loaded on to trains), is a separate area, small but high, at Sportgastein. Rail excursions to **Zell am See** and **St Johann im Pongau** are easy, while car drivers can also visit snowsure **Obertauern** and **Kaprun**.

The Gastein valley has some of Austria's best and most extensive skiing for intermediates. We have always been impressed with it on our visits, and yet it is very little known on the British market. Perhaps that is because of its unusual character. Badgastein grew up as a spa town with large, austere stone buildings. It is built in a deep gorge, with a steep road winding down from top to bottom. The atmosphere is elegant, but slightly faded rather than pristine. The après-ski matches the village – none of the Tyrolean-style lederhosen clad knees-ups here. Elegant tea rooms, sophisticated bars and a casino are more the style. The spa facilities are those you'd expect of a town born because of its hot springs and health cures rather than the skiing. It's a far cry from a standard chalet-style Austrian farming village turned ski resort.

But then so is the skiing. There are lovely long runs, above and below the treeline – mostly steepish reds. It's much more of a place for confident skiers than timid intermediates. And there's a lot of it. The biggest local ski area, reached by gondola from the top of town, is linked to that of nearby Badhofgastein to form an impressively large circuit. There's also a smaller local area on the opposite side of the valley – usually quiet and ideal for bad-weather days because of its tree-lined runs. And then there's snowsure Sportgastein further up the valley, and the big Dorfgastein-Grossarl circuit down the valley. Add together all these areas and there's more than enough to keep even the keenest skier happy for a week.

So it's really a question of whether you fancy the spa-type town rather than typical ski resort atmosphere. The main alternative places to stay are Badhofgastein (another spa town) and quiet, rustic Dorfgastein – see pages 60 and 61.

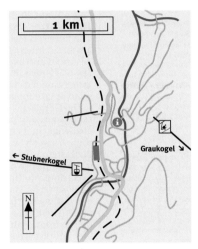

SKI FACTS

Altitude 840m-2685m
Lifts   53
Pistes   250km
Green/Blue   24%
Red   66%
Black   10%
Artificial snow   40km

SKI SCHOOL

94/95 prices in
schillings

Badgastein
Manager Werner
Pflaum
Classes 6 days
6hr: 10am-4pm, 1hr
lunch; 3hrs: 1pm-4pm
6 full days: 1,650
Children's classes
Ages: up to 14
6 full days: 1,380
Private lessons
55 mins
450 for 55 mins; each
additional person 120

Luigi
Manager Luigi
Kravanja
Classes 6 days
5hr 15min: 10am-3.15
with 1hr lunch
6 full days: 1,350
Children's classes
Ages: 4 to 14
6 full days including
lunch: 1,950
Private lessons
1hr or full-day
420 for 1hr; each
additional person 100

 # The resort

Badgastein is an old spa that had its heyday many years ago; it has spread widely, but still has a compact core. Its central buildings are a bizarre combination (smart, modern, hotel-shopping-casino complex, baroque town hall and concrete multi-storey car park) and it has a cramped horseshoe layout on a very steep hillside. It is set in what is virtually a gorge, complete with waterfall crashing beneath the main street. The thick surrounding woods lend a degree of charm, and the main road and railway bypass the centre.

Skiers will feel more at home in the area up around the railway station and main lift, where much of the recent expansion has taken place.

Badgastein is a formal resort. People tend to be smartly dressed for hotel evening meals, and the general ambience of the village is sophisticated, quiet and relaxed.

 # The skiing

On the whole, this is an area that suits confident intermediates best; most of the skiing is graded red, and rightly so. Where there is a blue option, it is not always a very attractive one – and not always as easy as a timid intermediate might hope.

THE SKI AREA
Fragmented, but adds up to a lot
The extensive main ski area is made up of two distinct sectors, above Badgastein and Bad Hofgastein, linked

mid-way between the resorts via the side-valley of Angertal.

From the upper part of Badgastein a gondola goes up to **Stubnerkogel**, from where you can ski back towards the resort or down to Angertal. This valley has lifts going up towards **Schlossalm** above Bad Hofgastein, from where a variety of pistes lead off in different directions. The runs back to Angertal are south-facing and low, but this section is well covered by artificial snowmakers.

The much smaller **Graukogel** area lies at the other side of Badgastein. This is a steep, straightforward mountain with just three lifts. With pistes set in broad swathes through the forest, the area is a great asset in bad weather and quiet at other times.

High, wild **Sportgastein** has the best snow in the area, now served by a new eight-person gondola; but there

LIFT PASSES

95/96 prices in schillings

Gastein Super Ski Pass
Covers all lifts in Gastein valley and Grossarl, and buses, trains and road tolls between the resorts.
Beginners Day- and points-tickets for baby-lifts.
Main pass
1-day pass 400
6-day pass 1,910 (low season 1,620 – 15% off)
Senior citizens
Over 65 male, 60 female: 6-day pass 1,580 (15% off)
Children
Under 15: 6-day pass 1,150 (40% off)
Under 6: free pass
Short-term passes
Single ascent on selected lifts, time card (2, 3 and 4 hours) and half-day passes available.
Alternative periods
5 or 10 days in one season.
Notes Discounts for students (under 26) and groups of over 20.
Alternative passes
Gastein Super Ski Pass only available for 3 days or more. Passes for shorter periods cover only Badgastein/Bad Hofgastein. Single ascent passes available for lifts in Dorfgastein and Sportgastein.
Credit cards: Yes

CHILDCARE

Both ski schools run ski kindergartens.

There is kindergarten at the Grüner Baum hotel, taking children aged 3 to 8, from 9.30 to 4pm. Skiing is available, with a special lift. A free shuttle bus is offered.

are only a few pistes: red and blue variants of one long run down the narrow mountainside.

Dorfgastein and, in the next valley, **Grossarl**, share another extensive area of red and blue runs.

Buses and trains between the different areas are covered by the lift pass. But they can be overcrowded and a bit of a scrum.

SNOW RELIABILITY
Good for a low-altitude resort
Although the area is essentially a typically Austrian low altitude one, there is a battery of snowmakers in crucial sections, and the higher sector of Sportgastein is an important fallback. This part of the Alps also has a good snow cover record in relation to its height, and there is a lot of skiing above mid-station height.

FOR ADVANCED SKIERS
Fast cruises rather than challenge
The terrain is really better suited to advanced intermediate than to truly advanced and expert skiers. There are few black runs but there are long, interesting reds with steepish terrain which make for great fast cruising.

The Graukogel is the World Cup skiing area, and provides some challenge on its upper slopes. The route between Stubnerkogel and Badgastein is fairly steep, and often icy, with plenty of room for off-piste excursions on the open, top section.

Sportgastein is worth the trip, especially with the efficient new lift in place. There are off-piste possibilities on the front of the mountain, and a long off-piste trail off the back drops almost 1500m from Kreuzkogel to Heilstollen in the valley (on the bus route). Dorfgastein has some of the least demanding slopes in the area, but there is a fine black run down to the village.

FOR INTERMEDIATE SKIERS
Not for the leisurely cruiser
Good intermediates will love all the areas on the ski pass – more than enough to keep you happy for a week. A particular delight is the beautiful 8km run, well away from the lifts, from Höhe Scharte down to Bad Hofgastein. The open north-facing slopes of Stubnerkogel down into Angertal are good, for both skiing interest and snow cover. The same is true of the Graukogel runs. None of the skiing is boringly easy.

But the area as a whole is uncomfortably challenging for early intermediates. The Grossarl and

Schlossalm sectors have less demanding pistes than other sectors, and the open bowl around the main cluster of restaurants at Schlossalm is reassuringly blue in gradient. Most intermediates will enjoy the network of red runs above Dorfgastein and Grossarl, as well as the whole Schlossalm sector.

FOR BEGINNERS
Unsuitable slopes
Inadequate nursery slopes are dotted around. Only the good ski school makes this resort in any way suitable.

FOR CROSS-COUNTRY
Extensive, but low and fragmented
There is an impressive 90km of trails, but all are along the valley floor, making only the small loop at Sportgastein reasonably reliable for snow. Another drawback is the scattered nature of the loops. Bad Hofgastein is by far the best base for cross-country skiing, with long trails stretching almost to Badgastein.

QUEUES
Buses are the problem
In the past, Sportgastein has experienced queues when conditions were poor elsewhere, but this has been put right by the powerful new gondola opened two years ago. Otherwise there are few problems outside the peak season in late February.

Morning queues to get out of the valley and for the Bad Hofgastein mid-station cable car are the worst. Bus queues can be a problem too. Buses between villages are infrequent, and Badgastein's in-village transport (essential for some accommodation) is unreliable and erratic.

MOUNTAIN RESTAURANTS
One of the pleasures of this area
Numerous atmospheric, traditional huts are dotted around. Good value and good food are the norm. Badgastein's places are more expensive than those in the rest of the valley, but they are still cheap compared to most of the Alps.

Bad Hofgastein's smart Schlossalm has a large terrace, plus yodelling! The Aeroplanstadl on the 8km Höhe Scharte run, Hamburger Skiheim, at Schlossalm(with 'barbecue in the snow'), and Dorfgastein's Panoramastube are all jolly places, while the Wengeralm, also above Dorf, is a cosy, upmarket refuge with a good terrace. Two new restaurants were built at Sportgastein, as part of the new gondola construction.

GETTING THERE

Air Salzburg, transfer 2hr. Linz or Munich, transfer 3½hr.

Rail Mainline station in resort.

PACKAGES

Crystal, First Choice Ski, Inghams, Made to Measure, Ski Miquel, Ski Partners, SkiBound

Bad Hofgastein Austrian Holidays, Crystal, First Choice Ski, Inghams, Made to Measure

Dorfgastein Club Europe

ACTIVITIES

Indoor Fitness centre (swimming, sauna, gym), thermal baths, squash, bridge, tennis, bowling, indoor golf, darts, casino, museum, theatre, concerts **Outdoor** Natural ice rinks (skating and curling), sleigh rides, horse-riding, ice climbing, toboggan runs, ski-bob, 35km cleared paths

TOURIST OFFICE

Postcode A-5640
Tel 00 43 (6434) 25310
Fax 253137

SKI SCHOOL
English widely spoken

The two ski schools have good reputations. Most reporters have used the main Schi & Rennschule. Instructors are enthusiastic and English standards are generally good, with some British and Swedish teachers. Optimal use of time and good division of abilities are other positive comments.

Class size seems to vary, which is not uncommon where English speakers make up a small proportion of guests. It all depends on how many of the limited number of one's fellow Brits having tuition happen to be at your ability level when you are visiting. Group lesson prices are high for short courses – it's worth booking for the week. Schischule Luigi concentrates on guiding, touring, snowboarding and children.

FACILITIES FOR CHILDREN
Reasonable

Badgastein hardly seems an ideal resort for small children, but there are facilities for all-day care, of which the kindergarten at the Grüner Baum sounds the most inviting.

 # Staying there

Getting around Badgastein is not easy, so it is worth picking your location with care. For most skiing purposes, the best place to stay is in the upper part of town, close to the Stubnerkogel gondola station.

HOW TO GO
Packages mainly to hotels

Although apartments make up nearly 15 per cent of the total beds available, British tour operators sell mainly hotel-based packages.

Chalets Ski Miquel's Tannenburg is a traditional old hotel now run as a chalet-hotel. It is a short walk from the gondola and offers good value for money – although wine is extra.

Hotels This is an upmarket spa resort, and it has lots of smart hotels with excellent spa facilities – almost as many 4-stars as 3-stars.

£££££ Elizabeth Park Luxury hotel popular with British skiers looking for excellent facilities, style, comfort and formality. Unfortunately, poorly placed for skiing, but does run a courtesy bus.

££££ Salzburger Hof 4-star with excellent spa facilities, a longish walk from the village gondola.

££££ Schillerhof Reliable 4-star in good position, opposite Graukogel lift.

££££ Wildbad 4-star within reasonable walking distance of the main lift.

££££ Grüner Baum Splendidly secluded Relais & Châteaux place, tucked away in the Kötschachtal.

£££ Mozart Well placed for buses. Good food but 'a bit like Fawlty Towers' says one reporter.

£££ Alpenblick Good value, less formal 3-star; well placed for skiing.

Self-catering Plenty of apartments available to those booking directly.

EATING OUT
Something for most tastes

There is a fair range of restaurants, including surprisingly fine Chinese and seafood places. The Bellevue Alm is one of the liveliest places to eat at, whilst the à la carte menus at the 3-star hotels Nussdorferhof and Mozart are good value.

APRES-SKI
Varied, but no oom-pah-pah

Soaking in one of the spas is a popular activity – see *For non-skiers,* overleaf.

There are elegant tea rooms, numerous bars and discos, sophisticated dances, and casinos, but the general ambience is rather subdued.

This part of Austria has not imported the informal Tyrolean-style 'oom-pah-pah'; neither are there any lively bands. The tea-dance at the Bellevue Alm is the only real concession to Kitzbühel-style fun. The best tea-rooms are the Causerie, in the Elizabeth Park, Wiener, in the Salzburger Hof, the Weismayr and the Panorama. Eden's Bar and Manfreda's Bar are pleasant for a quiet drink. The Hexen Haüsl is a more informal little wooden schnapps bar.

Haggenblooms has live music and gets full of young Swedes out to have a good time. The Bunny Bar is more sophisticated than its name suggests. The various functions in the Grüner Baum are the most informal hotel entertainment, but the elegant Ritz and Felsen bars in the Satzburger Hof and the Elizabeth Park respectively are more typical of the scene later on.

The Gatz and the Blockhaüsl are the main clubs. The casino gives you a generous amount of free chips, so those with will-power and/or luck can have a surprisingly inexpensive couple of hours there. Bowling and a casino trip are likely to be organised by tour operator reps.

FOR NON-SKIERS
Great variety of things to do
Provided you don't mind the style of the place, Badgastein has a lot to offer non-skiers, whether active or not. The spa facilities are superb. 17 thermal radon springs originate in the town and are very well used – various baths, thermal mud, massage, underwater therapy, inhalation, 'drinking cures', and all sorts of regenerative, preventative and specific illness treatments are provided.

The Gastein Healing Gallery is a highlight – a train takes you down into an old gold-digging tunnel where you have the opportunity to lie on benches inhaling radon in steam-room-like heat and humidity for a couple of hours! The Rock Pool is a large indoor pool hewn out of the rock, heated naturally by hot springs.

Meeting up the mountain is no problem, though walkers can't get to the best mountain restaurants easily.

There are organised coach trips to Kitzbühel, Salzburg and Goldegg Castle, and trains run to the resorts of Zell am See and St Johann im Pongau.

Bad Hofgastein 860m
Bad Hofgastein is a sizeable quiet, old spa village set out spaciously in a broad section of the valley. It has an impressive old Gothic church, traditional-style buildings, elegant quiet hotels, narrow alleys and a babbling brook. Everything is kept in pristine order. Although rather sprawling, the village has a pleasant pedestrianised area which acts as a central focus. Because of the spa 'cures' there's a relatively high proportion of part-time and non-skiers pottering about during the day, notably at the curling rinks in Kurpark. Several reporters have also emphasised how pretty the place looks in the evenings, under the soft glow of night lamps. The large public spa building, the Kurzentrum, is the only relative blot on the landscape, though it's not exactly an eyesore.

The best location to stay is in the pedestrian zone, which is relatively handy for most things including the slopes. However, ski convenience is not generally a strong point and a high proportion of hotels are a long walk from the single village lift station. Many people catch the inner-village ski-bus.

Buses to the other Gastein valley ski areas are infrequent (half-hourly to Badgastein, hourly to Dorfgastein, twice daily to Sportgastein), and several reporters have found the timetable in Dorfgastein particularly difficult to decipher. Note the 5pm bus home from there doesn't stop at the lift-station as all other services do – you have to trek to the main road.

Bad Hofgastein's lift is a short funicular that takes you up to a mid-station (1302m), above which most of the skiing takes place. Here, you have a choice between a cable-car and two-stage chair. Both the funicular and the much lower capacity cable-car can generate big queues (30 minutes in rush hour during peak season is not unusual). At such times, the chair is an

---

Selected chalets in Badgastein

obvious alternative to the cable-car and there's closed-circuit TV at the funicular base station which shows skiers the situation up at the cable-car.

Skiers ski the same area as those staying in Badgastein, and beginners staying in Bad Hofgastein have to catch a bus to the limited nursery area over at Angertal.

Bad Hofgastein makes a fine base for cross-country skiers when its lengthy valley floor trails have snow.

We have received complimentary reports of the two ski schools, both of which have a fair number of English-speaking instructors. One is based at Angertal, and runs the village ski kindergarten there, which can be very inconvenient for parents. Lack of many English-speaking children to play with may be another drawback.

Bad Hofgastein is essentially a hotel resort. They tend to be large, good quality and many have their own fine spa facilities. Some are within easy walking distance of the funicular, a few provide courtesy transport, and most of the rest are close to bus stops.

The Palace Gastein is a big 4-star with superb leisure facilities, including pool and thermal baths. The elegant Germania is similarly comfortable. The high quality Norica is atypically modern in design, but is well positioned in the pedestrian zone. The Alpina is another well located 4-star, five minutes from the slopes. The Astoria is well appointed but quite poorly positioned and doesn't supply courtesy transport. The old 3-star Alte Post was disliked by a reporter this year who found service at dinner too rushed and the hotel too far from the lift. The Kaiser Franz also looks charming but again, we have received negative reporter comments. The Kürpark is much more popular, for its good food, service and location in the pedestrian zone. Gasthof Reiter is poorly positioned but provides a useful inexpensive, informal B&B.

There is a good range of restaurants, and many hotels offer good formal dining. The Moserkeller is a nice, intimate restaurant. The Pyrkerhöhe, on the slopes just above town, is worth an evening excursion. Pension Maier is one of the better informal places. The Tele Pizza Bar cooks outside on an open fire at lunchtimes in fine weather. It's also good inside in the evenings, as are the Tschickeria and Da Dimo pizza and pasta places.

Après-ski is very quiet by Austrian standards. Some reporters have been disappointed; others have loved the peacefulness. There are, however, a few animated places around. The Picolo ice bar in the middle of town is lively immediately after skiing. Frankies bar is quite lively and popular with locals. Evergreen has a friendly atmosphere. Visions is a spacious modern disco, while Kuchuck and C'est la Vie had loud music and were full of teenagers when we looked in.

Most of Bad Hofgastein's clientele prefer something more sedate. Café Weitmoser is an historic little castle popular for its cakes after skiing. The outdoor bar of the Ostereicher Hof is a pleasant spot to catch the last of the sun. Another atmospheric tea-time rendezvous is the Tennishalle. Later, the West End bar is a cosy place for a quiet drink. The Glocknerkeller in Pension Zum Toni and the Rondo bar in Hotel Käruten have live music in a low-key ambience.

The Badgastein casino provides free taxis to and from town. A bowling evening is organised by tour reps. The Kurzentrum is the centrepiece of the things to do when not skiing, being arguably an even more impressive spa facility than that of Badgastein. It has an impressive thermal pool, and offers a range of therapies Other off-slope amenities include artificial and natural ice skating, indoor tennis, squash, sleigh rides. Lovely walks and riding.

Dorfgastein 830m

Those who wish to ski the Gastein valley but would prefer not to stay in large, commercialised villages should consider Dorfgastein. Prices are lower, and the atmosphere more friendly and informal – a contrast to its rather cold setting sheltered from the sun.

The extensive ski area is more suitable for inexperienced skiers than the steep slopes above Badgastein. Runs are long and varied, amid lovely scenery. Unfortunately the low-altitude nursery slopes can be cold and icy. Badhofgastein's funicular is 15 minutes away by bus (infrequent and sometimes crowded). Those not interested in venturing that far can buy a local pass costing 75 per cent of the Gastein Valley lift pass price.

There are a few shops and après-ski places, a five- or ten-minute walk or short bus-ride from the slopes. Café St Ruperb is a nice village pizzeria. The Kirchenwirt and Romerhof are comfortable hotels. Pension Schihause is cheaper, does good food, and is next to the slopes. There is an outdoor heated pool with sauna-solarium, a bowling alley and a ski kindergarten.

Ellmau 800m

HOW IT RATES

The skiing

Snow	*
Extent	****
Advanced	*
Intermediates	****
Beginners	****
Convenience	***
Queues	****
Restaurants	**

The rest

Scenery	***
Resort charm	***
Not skiing	***

✔ Large, pretty, easy ski area

✔ Cheap by Austrian standards

✔ Quiet, charming family resort – more appealing than neighbouring Söll

✔ Excellent nursery slopes (but see minus points)

✘ Very poor snow record, yet limited snowmaking set-up

✘ Poor lift and bus connections to remainder of Ski-Welt ski area

✘ Queues can be a severe problem when snow is in short supply

✘ Lack of nightlife other than rep-organised events

✘ Little difficult skiing

✘ Nursery slopes vulnerable when snow is in short supply

Like nearby Söll, Ellmau gives access to the large, unthreatening ski area now known as Ski-Welt (though we still think of it as the Grossraum). From some points of view it is attractive. Ellmau is a pleasantly quiet alternative to Söll, but offers more holiday amenities than other neighbours such as Scheffau. Its nursery slopes and its main lifts are both more convenient than most in this area. But there are snags.

We have received quite a few holidaymakers' reports on Ellmau, and we have yet to receive one that does not mention the problem of a lack of snow, at least on the lower half of the ski area. To make matters worse, the links between Ellmau and the rest of the Ski-Welt ski area are poor, particularly when the snow-cover is less than perfect. And the alternative means of access to more snowsure slopes – the ski-bus service – is also exasperatingly feeble.

Ellmau is a likeable village; whether it makes a sensible base for a ski holiday booked well in advance is another matter. Skiers looking for a quiet, pretty Austrian village with a fair amount of reliable, hassle-free skiing have safer options available.

ORIENTATION

Ellmau sits at the north-eastern corner of the Ski-Welt ski area, on the road between St Johann and Wörgl. A funicular railway goes up from a large car-park on the edge of the village into the skiing. The Ski-Welt is ringed by valleys and roads, with lifts from several other resorts. **Going** and **Scheffau** (covered by this chapter) are nearby; **Söll, Itter, Hopfgarten** and **Brixen** are spread around the high-point of Hohe Salve.

Westendorf is covered by the Ski-Welt pass, although its ski area is separate. **Kitzbühel, Waidring, Fieberbrunn** and **St Johann** are all within easy range for day-trips.

🏠 The resort

Although a sizeable resort, and becoming more commercialised each year, Ellmau remains a quiet, pretty place, complete with traditional chalet-style buildings, welcoming bars and shops, and a picturesque old church. Unfortunately its Alpine charm is spoilt a little by the main road that runs along the edge of the village, and by its frequent lack of snow on the rooftops and streets.

By Austrian standards the nightlife is rather tame, and although non-skiing diversions have recently been improved, the village doesn't really amount to much more than a pleasant dormitory for skiers.

SKI FACTS

Altitude	620m-1830m
Lifts	90
Pistes	250km
Green/Blue	37%
Red	53%
Black	10%
Artificial snow	50km

🎿 The skiing

The Ski-Welt is reputedly the largest ski circus in Austria, but most of the time it hardly compares in size, and never in quality, to St Anton, Ischgl, Saalbach and the Gastein valley. Most of its runs are short, and not difficult.

THE SKI AREA
Slow links to the rest of Ski-Welt
At least Ellmau is close to the best skiing in the area, above Scheffau. The village funicular (served by a free shuttle bus which tours the village) takes skiers up to Hartkaiser, from where a fine long run leads down to Blaiken (Scheffau's lift station). A choice of gondola or two-stage chair then goes back up to Brandstadl, the start point for three varied and long alternatives back to Blaiken.

Immediately beyond Brandstadl, the skiing becomes rather bitty; an array of short runs and lifts link Brandstadl to Zinsberg. From there, excellent, long, south-facing pistes lead down to Brixen. A short bus-ride takes skiers from Brixen to Westendorf's pleasant separate ski area. Part way down to Brixen you can head towards Söll – either by the steep Hohe Salve or by circumnavigating the latter using a series of easy runs. Hohe Salve also provides access to a long, west-facing run down to Hopfgarten. If you want to include the fine long run down to Itter in your tour, it's best to do so before getting to Hochsöll.

LIFT PASSES

95/96 prices in schillings

Ski-Welt Wilder Kaiser-Brixental
Covers all lifts in the Wilder Kaiser-Brixental area, from Going to Westendorf, and the ski-bus.
Beginners Points cards for lifts available (25 point 70). Small drags are 5 points.
Main pass
1-day pass 340
6-day pass 1610
Children
Under 15: 6-day pass 915 (43% off)
Under 5: free pass
Short-term passes
Single ascent on some lifts, half-day passes up to noon and from 11am, noon and 2pm to the end of the day.
Alternative periods
Passes available for 5 skiing days in 7, 7 days in 10 and 10 days in 14.
Notes Discounts for physically disabled skiers and children with a Kinderkarten (child's card) of 70%.
Alternative passes
Ellmau ski pass covers 13 local lifts (adult 6-day 1,375).
Credit cards Yes

CHILDCARE

The Ist Ski School has a playroom open from 9am. The Hartkaiser school opened a ski nursery last season. The Top-Ski school welcomes children and provides lunchtime care on request. There is also a village non-skiing kindergarten

Returning to Ellmau is a time-consuming business. Getting back to Blaiken via the Süd drag is quicker, but the buses to Ellmau are irregular.

Ellmau and Going share a pleasant little section of skiing on Astberg, slightly apart from the rest of the area and well suited to the unadventurous or for families. One piste leads to the funicular for access to the rest of Ski-Welt. The main Astberg chair is rather inconveniently positioned, midway between Ellmau and Going.

SNOW RELIABILITY
Very poor
Ellmau has a poor snow record. The north-facing Eiberg area above Scheffau holds its snow well, but is small and gets terribly congested when snow is in short supply. Ellmau skiers are better off getting a bus to St Johann at such times; changing at St Johann for Waidring's high Steinplatte area is even better.

FOR ADVANCED SKIERS
Not suitable
There's a steep plunge off the Hohe Salve summit, and a little mogul field between Brandstadl and Neualm, but the area isn't really suitable except for those prepared to seek out worthwhile off-piste opportunities. The Morderer ski route from Branstadl down to Scheffau is a highlight.

FOR INTERMEDIATE SKIERS
For the unadventurous or families
Unfortunately most of the best runs are among the least snowsure. Good intermediates will enjoy the runs to Brixen and those on Hohe Salve. Skiers of mixed ability will enjoy a good variety of pistes above Blaiken, while moderate skiers have fine runs down to all the valley villages, including long ones alongside the Ellmau funicular. Ellmau is particularly well placed for timid skiers, with the quiet, easy slopes of Astberg on hand.

FOR BEGINNERS
One of the best Ski-Welt villages
Ellmau has an array of good nursery slopes – snow permitting. East of the village is a vast area of gentle slopes that spreads across to Going. The area next to the funicular station, west of the village, is smaller but still very satisfactory, with the Astberg chair opening up a more snowsure plateau at altitude. The Brandstadl-Hartkaiser area has another section of short, easy runs. Near-beginners looking for a rest from drag-lifts have a nice long piste running the length of the funicular.

FOR CROSS-COUNTRY
Plenty of valley trails
When there is snow, there are long and quite challenging trails along the valley towards St Johann and Kirchdorf, and an easier one to Scheffau and via Söll to Itter. But trails at altitude are lacking.

QUEUES
Few local problems
Again, snow-cover dominates the analysis. With good snow, the worst areas are quite distant from Ellmau. Hochsöll can be a bottleneck – particularly the Hohe Salve chair. The Blaiken gondola gets oversubscribed at weekends and when snow is poor elsewhere. At such times, everyone wants to head for Eiberg's reliable snow, and the higher lifts on and around Eiberg suffer bad queues.

The poor, valley bus service and the roundabout links between Hartkaiser and the rest of the Ski-Welt are more of a problem, causing greater delays in practice than any lift queues.

MOUNTAIN RESTAURANTS
Stick to the little huts
'Little huts good, big huts bad' is a simple but fairly accurate description. The smaller places are fairly consistent in providing wholesome, good-value food in pleasant surroundings, although perhaps only the one at Neualm deserves special mention. The larger self-service restaurants are rather functional (the Jochstube at Eiberg is an exception) and suffer queues. Going is a good spot for a quiet lunch.

SKI SCHOOL
Dual language can waste time
The school has a good reputation except that classes tend to be very large. The high number of Dutch in the village means dual language tuition is not uncommon, and this can waste a great deal of class time. As well as the main ski school there is a mountaineering school that organises daily tours in the Wilder Kaiser group as well as the Kitzbühel mountains.

FACILITIES FOR CHILDREN
Fine in theory
Ellmau is an attractive resort for families, and the kindergarten facilities seem satisfactory. We have no recent reports on how they work in practice.

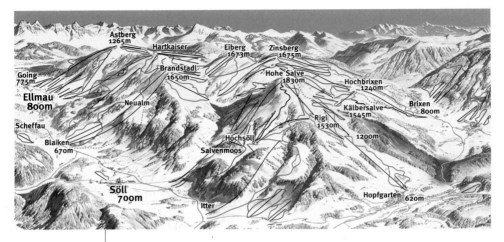

SKI SCHOOL

95/96 prices in schillings

1st Ellmau
Manager Friedl Fuchs
Classes 6 days
4hr: 10am-noon and
2pm-4pm
6 full days: 1300
Children's classes
Ages: 4 to 14
6 full days: 1250
Private lessons
Hourly or full day
(4hr)
450 for 1hr; each
additional person 200
(94/95)

Ellmau-Hartkaiser
Manager Dietmar Maier
Classes 6 days
4hr: 10am-noon and
2pm-4pm
6 full days : 1300
Children's classes
Ages: 4 to 14
6 full days: 1250
Private lessons
Hourly or full day
450 for 1hr; each
additional person 200
(94/95)

Top
Manager Hans Peter Haider
Classes 6 days
4hr: 10am-noon and
2pm-4pm

GETTING THERE

Air Salzburg, transfer 2hr.

Rail Wörgl (18km), St Johann in Tirol (14km), Kufstein (15km), bus to resort.

 # Staying there

Ellmau has a compact centre, but its accommodation is scattered. Hotel position is quite important: keen, experienced skiers will want to be close to the funicular. Après-skiers will want to be more central, close to the village facilities and up to 20 minutes' walk or a bus-ride from the railway. Near-beginners might want to be near the Astberg chair, half-way between Ellmau and Going. The main nursery slopes are also at the Going end of the village, beside the ski school, but there are some on the road to the funicular.

HOW TO GO
Lots of chalet-style hotels
Ellmau is essentially a hotel and pension resort, though there are plenty of private apartments that can be booked locally.
Chalets Crystal's converted little pension is pleasant, and convenient for intermediates but a trek from the village centre and nursery slopes.
Hotels Ellmau is typical of Austrian resorts that have expanded since World War II, with many comfortable, modern, chalet-style hotels, largely indistinguishable at first sight.
£££££ Bär Elegant but relaxed Relais & Châteaux chalet that seems almost out of place in Ellmau – twice the price of any other hotel.
£££ Hochfilzer Central, well equipped and described by a reporter as 'the best encountered in 22 years'.
£££ Christoph Large, comfortable, multi-facility place in secluded position on the outskirts – quite handy for the funicular.
£££ Sporthotel Similar in style to the Christoph, but opposite the ski school and main nursery slopes.

£££ Alte Post Pleasant and central, though not self-evidently 'alte'.
££ Pension Claudia Good bedrooms, next to the ski school.
£ Gasthof Au Cheapest place in town, five minutes from the funicular and ten from the centre.
Self-catering There is a wide variety. Basically you get what you pay for. The Bauer Annemarie is under the same management as the hotel Christoph and equally well placed for lifts. Conveniently close to the nursery slopes is Feyersinger Martin.

WHERE TO EAT
Hotel-dominated
Most people are on half-board so there are not many restaurants. The hotel Hochfilzer has a reputation for good food and is open to non-residents. The Lobewein and Buchingerstüberl are worth a visit. Café Bettina, midway between the funicular and town, is good for afternoon coffee and cakes.

APRES-SKI
Limited but varied programme
The rep-organised events include bowling, sleigh rides, Tyrolean folklore and inner-tubing, but there is little else. The Memory bar is lively, but not for those who hate passive smoking.

FOR NON-SKIERS
Excellent new sports centre
The Kaiserbad leisure centre, opened last winter, has made Ellmau much more appealing for active non-skiers. There are many excursions available, including Innsbruck, Salzburg, Rattenburg, Vitipeno or even Venice (six hours each way). St Johann in Tirol is a nice little town only a few miles away by bus. Other facilities are very limited. Valley walks are spoilt by the busy main road.

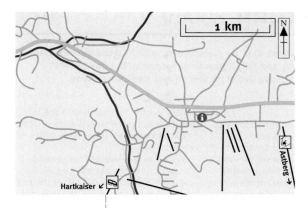

1 km

N

Hartkaiser

Astberg

ACTIVITIES

Indoor Swimming pool, sauna, solarium, tennis, squash, bowling, golf, billiards, ski museum, theatre
Outdoor Winter hiking, natural ice rink, curling, toboggan run, sleigh rides, cleared walking paths, para-gliding, hang-gliding

PACKAGES

Airtours, Crystal, Inghams, Neilson, Rank STS, SkiBound, Thomson

Scheffau Crystal, First Choice Ski, Thomson

TOURIST OFFICE

Postcode A-6352
Tel 00 43 (5358) 2301
Fax 3443

Scheffau 745m

Scheffau is one of the most attractive of the Grossraum villages: a rustic little place complete with pretty white church, it is spacious yet not sprawling, and has a definite centre. It is tucked away a kilometre off the busy main Wörgl road, which increases the charm factor at the cost of ski convenience (the Grossraum lifts are at Blaiken, on the opposite side of the main road). The nursery slopes are in the village, however, and this makes Scheffau a poor choice for mixed-ability parties. When snow conditions are very good it is possible to ski down to the main road from the village. Ski convenience freaks have the option of staying in Blaiken, where there are several hotels.

A gondola and parallel two-stage chair give rapid and generally queue-free access directly to the Grossraum's best (and most central and snowsure) section of pistes. This makes Scheffau (or more accurately Blaiken) arguably the best place to stay for skiers who want to ski every run in Austria's largest ski area.

The pistes above Blaiken are some of the longest and steepest in the Grossraum, while nearby Eiberg is the place to go when snow is poor.

Links from Ellmau and Söll are awkward (or impossible) when snow is poor, which is another attraction of being based in Scheffau or Blaiken.

The village nursery slope is adequate when snow-cover allows it to operate. Higher skiing suitable for novices is an inconvenient and expensive distance away up the main mountain, though

there are plenty of options for improving beginners.

Given full snow-cover there are few queuing problems, but delays can be long when poor conditions elsewhere force Söll, Hopfgarten and Brixen skiers into the Scheffau section. At such times the two-stage valley chair can be a useful alternative to the oversubscribed gondola.

The ski school is quite well regarded by intermediates, but beginner class sizes can be far too big (around 15).

Hotels dominate the accommodation scene. The modern Alpin Tirol is one of the best, and has the only pool in town. Gasthof Weberbauer is a lovely, olde-worlde place at the centre of the village, and the Waldrand, of a similar standard, is popular. The Wilder Kaiser is the best hotel at Blaiken. Nearby are the good value gasthofs Waldhof (right next to the gondola), Aloisia and Blaiken.

There is a distinct lack of village restaurants, and those staying in B&B places are advised to book tables well in advance.

Scheffau après-ski is unlikely to draw Blaiken residents up the hill. Pub Royal is the only bar with much animation, though the Kaiseralm disco livens up at weekends. The usual rep-organised events such as bowling and tobogganing are available.

Walking apart, there is little for non-skiers to do. Tour operators organise excursions to Innsbruck and Salzburg.

Scheffau is a good family choice: both the ski kindergarten and non-ski nursery have good reputations.

Going 775m

Going is a tiny, attractively rustic village, well placed for the limited but quiet slopes of the Astberg and for the vast area of nursery slopes between here and Ellmau. Prices are low by Austrian standards, but it's not an ideal place for skiing the whole of the Ski-Welt on the cheap: the bus service to Ellmau is poor, and the skiing link depends on resort-level snow which is not reliable.

Going is ideal for families looking for a quiet time, particularly if they have a car for transport to Scheffau or St Johann when the Astberg's low runs lack snow.

Fieberbrunn 800m

HOW IT RATES

The skiing
Snow	**
Extent	*
Advanced	*
Intermediates	**
Beginners	****
Convenience	**
Queues	****
Restaurants	**

The rest
Scenery	***
Resort charm	****
Not skiing	***

SKI FACTS

Altitude	800m-1870m
Lifts	25
Pistes	50km
Green/Blue	34%
Red	50%
Black	16%
Artificial snow	10km

PACKAGES

SkiBound

TOURIST OFFICE

Postcode A-6391
Tel 00 43 (5354)
6304
Fax 2606

Beginners could do worse than try Fieberbrunn, with its good nursery slopes, pretty tree-lined skiing and jolly Tyrolean atmosphere. But any decent intermediate skier will soon tire of its limited and unexciting skiing.

THE RESORT

Fieberbrunn is a non-commercialised, atmospheric resort that is very attractive, despite the fact that it sprawls along the valley road for 2km. It has all the classic 'Tyrolean charm' elements: wooden chalets, pretty church, cosy little bars and coffee shops, sleighs, tea dances and friendly locals. Much of the village is also pleasantly set back from the road and railway, allowing peace interrupted only by church bells! Light sleepers can escape these by staying in one of two large hotels out near the main lift-station, served by a bus (regular but sometimes overcrowded) from the village. Beginners should stay in the centre, however, near the nursery slopes. The resort is very popular with the Dutch but has relatively few British visitors these days.

THE SKIING

The **ski area**, with its 34km of piste (50km including neighbouring St Jakob), is best suited to beginners and leisurely intermediates who like very pretty skiing. The tree-lined runs are attractive but don't offer much variety. Most of the skiing is on north-facing slopes which reach 1870m.

Fieberbrunn is in a snow pocket, which means better **snow-cover** than usual at this altitude. But its above-average snowfall record has led the village to rest on its laurels: there are few snowmakers. New for 1994, however, were snow-guns on the village nursery slopes. Nearby Waidring's Steinplatte (on the same lift pass) provides particularly snow-reliable skiing. There are few lift queues normally.

Fieberbrunn holds little attraction for **advanced skiers**, or indeed for good **intermediates**. Its prettiest runs are the easy Doischberg reds, which would be blue in many resorts. The Streuböden runs to the village are pleasant cruising territory, while the Reckmoos chair accesses steeper, open skiing. Some of the most popular runs can get very crowded at weekends. Guided off-piste excursions, including some towards Kitzbühel, are popular.

Beginners have broad nursery slopes conveniently close to the village centre. Graduation to the long, gentle Streuböden runs is comfortable.

Cross-country skiers have 40km of good trails.

Weekday **queues** are rare outside the peak morning ski school rush for the Streuböden lifts. But when the rest of the Tyrol, especially Kitzbühel and Söll, is short of snow, Fieberbrunn is often invaded by large numbers of skiers. Sunny weekends are also busy, though overcrowded pistes are a greater problem than queues.

Fieberbrunn's **mountain restaurants** are a little disappointing, though there are a couple of good ones at the Streuböden mid-station and at Reiteralm.

The **ski school's** reputation is high, though classes can be large.

Children's facilities include a ski kindergarten which takes children from the age of 4. There is no longer a non-ski kindergarten, but baby-sitting is available.

STAYING THERE

Fieberbrunn is essentially a hotel resort. The 4-star Fontana (very expensive) and 3-star Lindauhof (half the price) are the only hotels near the main slopes. On the other side of town, near the railway station, is Fieberbrunn's other top-quality hotel, Schloss Rosenegg, with a swimming pool complex. More central, cheaper places include the 3-star Metzgerwirt and Grosslehen and pensions Pirker and Mariandl.

Restaurants are mainly hotel-based. The candlelit Weinstubli in the Rosenegg is good for a splurge. Hotel Alte Post has a particularly pleasant restaurant. La Pampa is an excellent specialist Mexican establishment.

Après-ski is livelier at 4pm than after dinner. The Enzianhütte, Lindauhof and Siglu snow bar at the foot of the slopes are atmospheric; the first two have good tea dances. Later, the expensive Londoner Pub is popular but overloud – conversation is impossible. Riverhouse is classier, with quieter music and live shows.

For **non-skiers**, there are cleared walks, and the train station opens up excursion possibilities to Salzburg, Innsbruck and Kitzbühel.

Galtür 1585m

Galtür stands in sharp contrast to its brash neighbour, Ischgl. It is a good base for a quiet, relaxing family holiday, with ideal and uncrowded intermediate pistes among splendid high-mountain scenery. If you want more extensive or challenging skiing, Ischgl is only a short bus-ride away.

HOW IT RATES

The skiing

Snow	****
Extent	*
Advanced	**
Intermediates	***
Beginners	****
Convenience	***
Queues	****
Restaurants	**

The rest

Scenery	***
Resort charm	***
Not skiing	**

SKI FACTS

Altitude	1635m-2465m
Lifts	12
Pistes	40km
Green/Blue	20%
Red	65%
Black	15%
Artificial snow	6km

PACKAGES

Crystal, Made to Measure, Thomson

TOURIST OFFICE

Postcode A-6563
Tel 00 43 (5443) 521
Fax 52176

THE RESORT

Galtür is a charming, peaceful, traditional village clustered around a pretty little church, amid impressive mountain scenery at the head of the Paznaun valley, beyond Ischgl. The valley is wider and sunnier here than at Ischgl. The local slopes are a short bus-ride away at Wirl, where there are also a couple of hotels. The more extensive skiing of Ischgl is a 20-minute bus-journey away and is covered by the lift pass.

THE SKIING

A high-speed quad whisks skiers into the heart of the **ski area**, opening up a spacious section of long runs towards a large lake. The scenery is impressive and all the steeper descents have easier variants. The pistes are wonderfully uncrowded, but there is a high proportion of drag-lifts.

The **snow reliability** is usually good, but there's not much snowmaking, so the lower pistes can suffer from thin cover at times.

There is nothing very challenging for **advanced skiers**: many runs are overgraded. The black descending the length of the Breitspitz chair to the lake is perhaps the most fun. There is also wonderful ski-touring from Galtür – guides can be arranged for both day and overnight tours. Otherwise a trip to Ischgl is recommended.

The black runs are ideal for good **intermediates**. Average skiers will be able to ski over most of the mountain, with the lake seeing the finish of some of the best runs. Less adventurous skiers will enjoy the overgraded runs, and the meandering blue down to the Wirl chair.

There are fine nursery slopes at Galtür itself and at Wirl, and though the piste map shows the area to be short of blue runs, there are in fact plenty of 'graduation' pistes for improving **beginners**. Galtür would be an excellent choice for a quiet family holiday with young children learning to ski and mum and dad not looking for anything too challenging.

Galtür has 60km of excellent **cross-country** trails, many of them at high altitude (ending at over 2000m).

Queues are very rare. Remarkably, few Ischgl visitors come to Galtür – no matter how bad the queues there.

The solitary **mountain restaurant** is adequate, but many prefer to ski down to the hotel Almhof at Wirl for lunch.

The **ski school** has a very high reputation, particularly for friendliness and small classes.

There is a non-ski nursery and ski kindergarten at Wirl, both taking **children** from 3 years old. Although lack of English-speaking tuition and supervision may be a problem, facilities are good and ski classes are fun. Lunchtime supervision of older children in ski school is also available.

STAYING THERE

Though small, Galtür has plenty of accommodation – around 3,500 beds. Most brochures only list top-of-the-range hotels, but there is cheaper accommodation. Position is not important within the compact village, but families may prefer Wirl.

The Almhof is a comfortable 4-star **hotel** at Wirl, with pool, sauna and jacuzzi. The Ballunspitz is a good-value 3-star on the edge of Galtür (you can pole home from Wirl). The cheapest place close to lifts is the Pension Gorfenhof. Good central hotels range from the 4-star Post to the Pension Cultura.

Self-catering accommodation is available; the Alp Aren apartments are good value and Gasthof Alpkogel has large apartments for groups.

Restaurants are mostly hotel-based. The Post, Rössle and Alpenhotel Tirol all have good food. Cheaper places for eating out are the Alpkogel and the Landle.

Nightlife is quiet and there is no evening bus service to the more energetic **après-ski** of Ischgl . The Wirlerhof (tea dancing) and Almhof are jolly between 4pm and 6pm. After dinner, the Tanz Café, Leo's Keller and the Igloo bar are the most animated nightspots (though not throbbing). The Post disco is very expensive.

Galtür has a superb sports centre with pool, tennis and squash. There is a natural ice rink, but otherwise off-slope facilities are limited. Attractive walks are in short supply, and the mountain restaurant is inaccessible to **non-skiers**.

Hintertux 1500m

HOW IT RATES

The skiing

Snow	*****
Extent	**
Advanced	***
Intermediates	***
Beginners	*
Convenience	**
Queues	***
Restaurants	**

The rest

Scenery	***
Resort charm	***
Not skiing	*

SKI FACTS

Altitude	1500m-3250m
Lifts	20
Pistes	86km
Green/Blue	35%
Red	55%
Black	10%
Artificial snow	none

PACKAGES

Juns Alpine Tours

TOURIST OFFICE

Postcode A-6293
Tel oo 43 (5287) 606
Fax 5287 624

Hintertux has one of the best glacier skiing areas in the world. It's popular with national ski teams for summer training. In winter, it provides guaranteed good snow even when the resorts of the nearby Zillertal are suffering badly.

THE RESORT

Hintertux is a tiny village set in a bleak position at the dead-end of the Tux valley. Surrounded by steep mountains on all sides except to the north, the village is in shade for much of the day in mid-winter. It consists of little other than a small collection of hotels and guest-houses. Its lifts lie a 15-minute walk away, across an enormous car park which gets filled with day-visitors' cars and coaches, especially when snow is poor in lower ski areas. There are more hotels near the lifts. The nearest bank, doctor and chemist are in Lanersbach, 5km down the valley (see Mayrhofen chapter). Between the two villages are the hamlets of Madseit and Juns.

THE SKIING

Hintertux has a fair-sized **ski area**, with surprisingly challenging skiing for a glacier. The main chain of lifts rises in four stages up the eastern side of the north-facing glacier. A choice of gondola and chair go up to Sommerbergalm (2100m), then to Tuxer-Ferner (2660m); then it's fiercely cold chairs only to 3050m and finally to Gefrorene Wand ('frozen wall') at 3250m. There are links across to another 1000m-vertical chain of lifts below Grosser Kaserer on the west side of the glacier, and behind Gefrorene Wand is the area's one sunny piste, served by a chair. Back at Sommerbergalm is a small area of skiing below Tuxer Joch (2310m), start of an excellent off-piste run down a secluded valley to Hintertux.

The glacier area is of course snowsure, and the remaining skiing is high and north-facing, making for reliable **snow-cover**.

There is more to amuse **advanced skiers** here than on any other glacier, with runs of justifiably black grading on the west side, and skiing beneath glacier level that is consistently steep.

The whole area is particularly suitable for good or aggressive **intermediates**. The long runs down from Gefrorene and Kaserer are tests, while the off-piste route from Tuxer Joch to the valley is not difficult apart from the unnerving initial traverse. Moderate skiers love the glacier, and there is a pleasant tree-lined run to the valley from Sommerbergalm.

Novices have to take the bus to the nursery slopes at Madseit or Juns. There are a couple of fine near-**beginner** runs at the top of the glacier, but you need a full lift pass.

There are **cross-country** trails between Madseit and Lanersbach.

There are few **queues** until Hintertux is invaded by skiers from other, lower resorts, when there can be long queues at the bottom station and for some lifts up the mountain.

Queues for the inadequate glacier-area **mountain restaurants** can be even worse. The one at Tuxer Joch is less crowded, but hardly a gourmet experience. Gletscherhütte, at the top of the mountain, has great views but is very expensive.

The **ski school** has a good reputation and English is surprisingly widely spoken. There's a **children's** section and Lanersbach has a nursery.

STAYING THERE

Most of the **hotels** are large and expensive and have spa facilities. But there's also a selection of pensions. For maximum ski-convenience, stay next to the lifts, not in the village. The 4-star Neuhintertux and 3-star Vierjahreszeiten are both close to lifts. Pensions Jörglerhof, Kössler and Willeiter are right in the heart of the village. There are no cheap places close to the lifts.

There are plenty of **apartments**. The 3-star Nennerhof is the highest quality and best-placed, in the centre.

Restaurants are hotel-based, so expensive. The Berghof and Alpenhof have good reputations. The Vierjahreszeiten is pleasant and informal.

Lanersbach and Mayrhofen are within easy reach by car. Otherwise there is very little **nightlife**. The hotel Rindererhof, at the foot of the slopes, has a lively tea dance.

The spa facilities are excellent, but some walks are relatively uninspiring. In general, **non-skiers** would be much better off in Mayrhofen.

Skiing Hintertux from **Lanersbach** has its advantages, particularly for ski-drivers, who can reach the glacier lift-station in 10 minutes and be better placed for ski excursions along the Ziller valley. Lanersbach has more amenities – see Mayrhofen chapter.

Innsbruck 575m

British skiers are not inclined to think of Innsbruck as a ski resort. It is a sizeable city and a major Alpine crossroads. In summer it is an attractive tourist destination, with plenty of historic and cultural (as well as scenic) interest. But a ski resort? Well, yes. It is at the heart of a little group of ski areas that share a common lift pass, and has some skiing of its own right on the edge of the city. You have to travel by car or bus to most of the ski areas, but that is a bearable hardship if you like the idea of a civilised urban base.

INNSBRUCK

The Inn valley is a broad, flat-bottomed trench hereabouts, but Innsbruck manages to fill it from side to side. It is a sizeable city, with an excellent range of winter sports facilities (it has twice hosted the Winter Olympic Games) as well as a captivating medieval core. It has smart modern shopping areas, museums, concert halls, theatres and other attractions that you might seek out on a summer holiday but don't dream of when going skiing. It has 1200m vertical of skiing on the south-facing slopes of the Hungerburg, reached by cable-car from the suburbs; but for visitors, if not for residents, skiing at Innsbruck usually means skiing on the other side of the trench, to east or west of the side-valley that reaches southwards towards the Brenner pass and Italy. The Brenner road is a major pipeline for goods and tourists between Germany and Italy, and opens up the possibility of interesting excursions (skiing and non-skiing) to the Dolomites and beyond.

The Innsbruck ski pass covers the lifts in all the resorts described here, which are served by a free ski-bus. If there is insufficient snow for skiing locally, free buses run to the Stubai glacier beyond Neustift (described in a separate chapter, page 89).

IGLS

Igls (900m) is a resort in its own right, although a small one. It is a leisurely, even sedate little place that barely seems part of the modern skiing world; frankly, we find it difficult to imagine spending a whole week here – but people do.

The skiing consists essentially of a single run with slight variations on- and off-piste. It is an excellent, long, testing red of about 1300m vertical, which formed the men's Olympic downhill course in 1976 when Franz Klammer took ski racing (and the gold medal) by storm. There is a ski school with all-day ski kindergarten (of which we've had a good report), and a non-skiing kindergarten.

AXAMER LIZUM

Axamer Lizum (1600m) could scarcely offer a sharper contrast to Igls. It offers a much higher, more varied and interesting ski area, with the most reliable snow in the area. It is the standard local venue for weekend skiers – hence the huge car park which is the most prominent feature of the 'resort'. You can stay up here (there's a 4-star hotel beside the lifts) but no one in their right mind would do so. If you're going to stay in a morgue-like skiing service station, you might as well stay in one with a lot more to ski.

The vertical drop on the main east-facing slopes back to the main lift stations is only in the order of 700m, which makes Igls look impressive. But there is much more variety here, on open red and blue runs below the peaks of Hoadl and Pleisen. From the latter, a long easy black run, well away from lifts and other intrusions, goes all the way to Axams on a shelf above the Inn valley at 880m – a great way to end the day. There is more accommodation here, and at Birgitz and Götzens nearby.

On the other side of the Axamer Lizum base station is a genuinely black slope served by a chair-lift, with a connection at the top to Mutters.

There are two ski schools, both with all-day ski kindergartens.

MUTTERS

Mutters (830m) is a charming, rustic village at the foot of a long, narrow ski area giving delightful easy cruising down from the link with Axamer Lizum to the village – a very respectable vertical of 900m.

TULFES

Tulfes (900m) gets overshadowed by Olympic Igls and Axamer Lizum, but has a very worthwhile ski area – red runs at the top, blue lower down – with the biggest local vertical of almost 1500m.

Also close to Innsbruck, but not covered by the lift pass, is Seefeld, dealt with separately on page 118.

Ischgl 1400m

HOW IT RATES

The skiing
Snow	****
Extent	****
Advanced	***
Intermediates	****
Beginners	**
Convenience	***
Queues	**
Restaurants	**

The rest
Scenery	***
Resort charm	****
Not skiing	***

✔ Old Tyrolean village which has grown quite large but retained much of its atmosphere and charm

✔ High ski area by Austrian standards, with reliable snow record

✔ Lots of good intermediate skiing, extending over the Swiss border to duty-free Samnaun

✔ Lively après-ski

✘ Lift queues can still be something of a problem, despite improvements

✘ Quite a number of long T-bars

✘ Not ideal for beginners, for various reasons

✘ Rather expensive, particularly initial package price

Ischgl seems curiously neglected by the British. It has most of the ingredients that make Austrian resorts so popular – a traditional village, lively nightlife, and a choice of smartly rustic hotels or modest B&Bs. And to this familiar recipe Ischgl adds important extras: by Austrian standards its ski area is big (linked to Samnaun in Switzerland) and high, with good, reliable snow.

So what's the problem? It appears to be limited availability of package holiday rooms, rather than any drawback to the resort itself. Continued improvements in the lift system are gradually tackling the queues. The resort is dominated by Germans and Scandinavians – whether that's a good or bad thing depends on your point of view. It isn't cheap. But neither are many Austrian resorts these days. For a group of mixed-ability intermediate skiers, it's worth putting on your short-list.

ORIENTATION

Ischgl is tucked away down the long, narrow Paznaun valley south-west of Landeck.

Like the valley, it's a long, narrow resort at the foot of steep north-facing slopes.

Three gondolas go up into the skiing, two from the eastern end of town and one from the west. The main ski area starts at the top of these lifts and spans the border into Switzerland, where there's a cable-car back from Ravaisch, below the duty-free village of **Samnaun**.

The Silvretta lift pass covers all this area plus the skiing of **Galtür** at the head of the valley and the smaller areas of **Kappl** and **See**. These areas are all linked by a rather infrequent bus service. If you have a car, visits to **St Anton** are easy.

 ## The resort

The village is set in a steep wooded valley and gets little sun in early season. We've had a report from one non-skier who went for a week in late January and found nowhere in the village to sit out in the sun.

The main street is bypassed and almost traffic-free, making it a pleasant place for a stroll in the early evening. The architecture is a mixture of old original buildings, traditional Tyrolean-style hotels and shops, and more modern-looking recent additions. It's possible to walk from one end of the village to the other in ten minutes or so. It's far from flat though – and the ups and downs can be quite treacherous when there's snow or ice on the ground; we've seen quite a few nasty falls.

There's a good selection of bars, an excellent sports centre and a fair number of shops to stroll round.

 ## The skiing

Ischgl has a fair-sized, relatively high, snowsure ski area ideally suited to intermediates. Most of the pistes are red, with very few black or easy blue runs. The opportunity of skiing over the border to duty-free Samnaun in Switzerland adds spice to the skiing.

THE SKI AREA
Cross-border cruising

Gondolas from both ends of the village go up to the sunny **Idalp** plateau at 2310m, where the ski school meets. A third goes about 300m higher to Pardatschgrat, from where it's an easy ski down to Idalp – with the alternative of testing red and black runs towards Ischgl. Lifts radiate from Idalp, leading to a wide variety of predominantly north-west- and west-facing intermediate runs.

A short ski brings you to the base of the drags serving the **Höllenkar** bowl, leading up to the area's south-western extremity at Palinkopf. There are further lifts beyond Höllenkar, on the slopes of the Fimbatal.

The mountain ridge above Idalp, ranging from around 2700m to 2900m, forms the border with Switzerland. On the Swiss side the hub of the skiing is **Alp Trida** at 2265m, surrounded by south- and east-facing runs. From here an enjoyable and scenic red run goes down to the hamlet of Compatsch, from where there is an infrequent bus to Ravaisch, for the cable-car back, and Samnaun.

From the Palinkopf area there is a very beautiful run to Samnaun itself, away from all signs of lifts, down an unspoilt valley. It is not difficult skiing, but it doesn't always have ideal snow conditions and is prone to closure by avalanche risk.

SKI FACTS

Altitude 1400m-2870m
Lifts 41
Pistes 200km
Green/Blue 25%
Red 60%
Black 15%
Artificial snow 45km

LIFT PASSES

95/96 prices in schillings
VIP Skipass
Covers all lifts in Ischgl, Samnaun and Mathon and local buses.
Main pass
1-day pass 380
6-day pass 1850
(low season 1685 – 9% off)
Senior citizens
Over 60: 6-day pass 1395 (25% off)
Children
Under 15: 6-day pass 1115 (38% off)
Under 6: free pass
Short-term passes
Single and multi ascent passes for main cablecars; half-day pass from 11.30 (345), trial ticket from 2pm (210).
Alternative periods
5 skiing days in 7, 10 days in 14 and 10 days in the season.
Notes VIP skipass is only available to those staying in Ischgl, Samnaun or Mathon on presentation of guest card. Discounts for physically disabled and groups.
Alternative passes
Silvretta ski pass covers Ischgl, Samnaun, Galtür, Kappl and See (adult 6 days 2390), 68 lifts and use of ski bus, See is 15km away.

SNOW RELIABILITY
Very good

All the skiing except the runs back to the resort is above 2000m and much of it on the Ischgl side is north-west- or north-facing. So snow conditions are often good here even when they're poor elsewhere (which can lead to crowds when bus-loads of skiers arrive from lower resorts). The run from Idalp back down to Ischgl has artificial snowmaking facilities all the way, with most of the variants from the mid-station of the gondolas benefiting from artificial snow.

FOR ADVANCED SKIERS
Some attraction

Ischgl can't compare with nearby St Anton for exciting skiing, and many of the runs marked black on the piste map barely deserve their rating. But there is plenty of challenging and beautiful off-piste skiing to be found with the help of a guide – and because there are fewer expert skiers around, it doesn't get skied as much as it would in a more 'macho' resort. The wooded lower slopes of the Fimbatal, near the Paznauner Taya restaurant, are delightful in a snowstorm – and since the glades are used as pasture in the summer, you needn't worry about damaging infant trees.

The best steep piste skiing is the Fimba Nord run from Pardatschgrat towards Ischgl. If snow conditions are poor near the bottom, you can ski the top half of this repeatedly by catching the gondola at the mid-station.

FOR INTERMEDIATE SKIERS
Something for everyone

Most of the skiing is ideal for intermediates. No matter what your standard, you should be able to find runs to suit you.

At the tough end of the spectrum our favourite runs are those from Palinkopf down to Gampenalp and on along the valley to the secluded restaurant at Bodenalp. You can now ski the top of these runs repeatedly, thanks to a recently built chair-lift up from Gampenalp to Palinkopf. Sadly this has also meant the runs no longer have the attraction of being away from civilisation.

There are also interesting and challenging runs (some marked black) down the Hollspitz chair, and from both the top and bottom of the drag-lift from Idjoch up to Greitspitz.

For easier motorway skiing, there is lots of choice, including the Swiss side, where the runs from the border down to Alp Trida should prove ideal.

So should the runs that take you back to Idalp on the return journey. But there are frequent moans from intermediates about the red runs down to Ischgl itself; neither is easy, and conditions can be tricky despite the artificial snow. One reporter recommends starting out from Pardatschgrat and switching to the Idalp piste at the mid-station.

FOR BEGINNERS
Not ideal

Beginners go up the mountain to Idalp, where there are good sunny nursery slopes and a short beginners' drag-lift – and good snow as some compensation for the inconvenience. The blue runs on the east side of the bowl offer pleasant progression. But away from this area there are few runs ideal for the near-beginner. You'd do better to learn elsewhere and come to Ischgl after getting two or three years' experience. If you want to stay in the Paznaun valley area, Galtür would be a better choice.

FOR CROSS-COUNTRY
Plenty in the valley

There is 28km of cross-country track in the Paznaun valley between Ischgl, Galtür and Wirl. This tends to be pretty sunless, especially early in the season, and is away from the main ski area, which makes meeting downhill skiers for lunch rather inconvenient. We've also seen people doing cross-country high up in the Fimbatal, towards Gampenalp, though this isn't an official trail. Galtür would be a better cross-country skier's choice, with 60km of loops.

QUEUES
Still some bottlenecks

There can be lengthy waits at key lifts at peak times. The main Silvrettabahn gondola can be a problem during the morning peak, especially when people are being bussed in from other resorts. We've managed to avoid this on our visits by taking one of the two gondolas at the other end of the village, but we're told this isn't always a foolproof method.

The other notorious waits are for the cable-car out of Samnaun in the early afternoon and then for the lifts up from Alp Trida after that. The new quad chair-lift up to Viderjoch, opened last winter, has helped, but hasn't entirely solved the problem. The real solution to all this will arrive this coming season, when an astonishing double-decker cable-car holding 180 people (by some way a

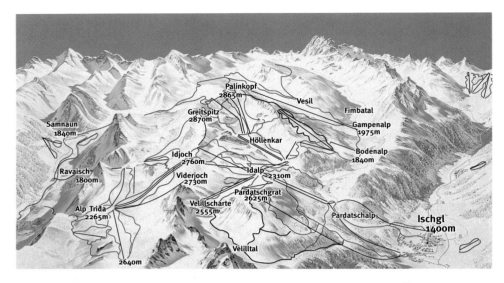

CHILDCARE

The childcare facilities are all up the mountain at Idalp. There's a ski kindergarten for children aged 3 to 5; from age 5 they go into a slightly more demanding regime in an 'adventure garden'; lunch is included in both arrangements, which are open 6 days a week. Toilet-trained children can be left at a non-ski nursery; lunch is available.

world record) will go all the way up from Ravaisch to Greitspitz, from which point Ischgl-based skiers will have a choice of routes home. Since the obvious one is down the Höllenkar bowl, we presume something will be done to improve the Höllboden chair from the bottom of the bowl up to Idalp, which is already unpleasantly inadequate in the afternoons.

MOUNTAIN RESTAURANTS
Mostly large and crowded

In general, Ischgl isn't the place to go for either culinary delights or charming small mountain restaurants. The clear exception, at least on the latter score, is the Paznauner Taya, above Bodenalp – an exceptionally rustic chalet imported from eastern Austria, and understandably very popular. There is table service upstairs and often a band playing on the large terrace. Down the mountain in the Fimbatal (most easily reached by means of the long runs from Palinkopf) is the quieter rustic restaurant (with table service) at Bodenalp, accessible to non-skiers who enjoy the walk from the mid-station of the gondola.

The main restaurant at Idalp is a big self-service cafeteria, and there's a smaller crowded alternative nearby. The restaurant at Pardatschgrat tends to be quieter.

The restaurants on the Swiss side at Alp Trida are pleasant, and La Marmotte has pricey table service as well as self service. There is a huge sunny terrace with an outdoor bar and barbecue. They take schillings, but don't forget the prices are marked in Swiss francs – and aren't cheap.

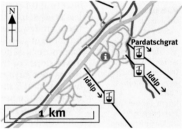

SKI SCHOOL
Language problems

The ski school meets up at Idalp and starts very late (10.30am to 12.30pm and 1.30pm to 3.30pm). We've heard from both supporters and critics of the school. There are few British skiers here, and the standard of English of the instructors is variable, so it's quite possible that you will end up in a mixed-language group. The instructor having to explain everything twice can slow things down, as can the large size of classes.

As well as normal lessons the ski school organises off-piste tours – this area is one of the best in the Alps for ski touring.

FACILITIES FOR CHILDREN
High-altitude options

Taking small children up the mountain with you rather than leaving them behind at village level is an unusual arrangement. An observer reports that the facilities 'looked good, with helpful girls', but we have no first-hand reports of the service they actually provide. The ski kindergarten is a new facility that was opened only last season.

GETTING THERE

Air Innsbruck, transfer 2hr. Zurich, transfer 5hr.

Rail Landeck (30km); frequent buses from station.

PACKAGES

Crystal, Inghams, Made to Measure

Samnaun Inghams

Staying there

On or near the main street is the best place to stay. Both the main lift-stations are an easy walk from there and the nightlife is on your doorstep. Beware of accommodation set up the steep hillside (some roads are so steep that tour operators' coaches may not make it to the door) or across the bypass road at the far side of the valley floor from the main village – though this does have the advantage of getting more sun.

HOW TO GO
Expensive packages
As is the norm in Austria, you pay for altitude. Much of the accommodation is expensive, particularly the mostly upmarket places sold through tour operators. There is, however, a big choice of cheaper little pensions.

Travelling most of the way by train is easy – the nearby town of Landeck has a main-line station.

Chalets There aren't any catered chalets run by tour operators.

Hotels Ischgl has a splendid selection of hotel and B&B accommodation, ranging from the luxurious and expensive to the plain but comfortable and good-value.

£££££ Madlein Convenient and quiet. Near the two quieter gondolas. Modern family-run chalet built in traditional style. Reportedly comfortable rooms. Facilities include swimming pool, sauna, steam room and solarium. Nightclub and disco.

£££££ Solaria Near the Madlein and just as luxurious, but with a 'friendly family atmosphere'. Splendid carved

wooden ceiling to restaurant, and wood-panelled wine bar. Swimming pool, sauna, steam room, solarium, fitness room and squash courts.

££££ Goldener Adler Traditional 250-year-old hotel right in the middle of the village. Wood-panelled and painted restaurant. Sauna, steam room, jacuzzi and solarium.

££££ Sonne One of Ischgl's oldest hotels. Well modernised, but with some very small rooms. In the centre of the village. Lively stube, with traditional squeeze-box music. Sauna, steam room, jacuzzi, solarium.

£££ Astoria Comfortable B&B hotel that faces the main Silvrettabahn gondola.

£££ Christine Probably the best B&B in town. Right opposite the end of the main run down from Idalp. One of the liveliest cafés at the end of the day.

£££ Erna Small, central B&B. Firmly recommended by a reporter who has holidayed in Ischgl 20 times.

££ Alpenrose Popular, good-value pension close to Pardatschgratbahn.

Self-catering Mainstream operators such as Inghams and Crystal have some very attractive apartments with all mod cons – a bargain compared with hotel prices in this expensive resort. Some of this accommodation books out early.

EATING OUT
Plenty of choice
Our favourite places for dinner are the traditional Austrian restaurants and stubes, of which there's a wide choice. The Goldener Adler probably serves the best food around and has a splendid traditional dining room. The Wippas stube in the Sonne is lively

and serves good food. For pizza there's the very popular and 'excellent' Nona and the Trofana-Alm, which is as much a bar as restaurant, and for fondue the Kitzloch with its galleried tables overlooking the dance floor. La Bamba is the new kid on the block, a restaurant-bar serving Mexican specialities. The Grillalm, Salner and Tirol are also popular eateries.

APRES-SKI
Very lively
Ischgl is one of the liveliest resorts in the Alps, both immediately after skiing and after dinner.

At the end of the skiing day the Café Christine gets packed and does great coffee and cakes, as well as alcohol. If you get up to dance to the disco music, make sure someone is saving your seat for you, unless you're happy to join the stand-up crush for the rest of the time.

The Kitzloch at the bottom of the run down from Pardatschgrat is just as lively and a bit more rowdy – dancing on tables and communal congas are common. Niki's Stadl across the road is worth a visit too, with comedy spots as well as music. In good weather the ice bar of the Elisabeth hotel by the Pardatschgratbahn is popular. The Post hotel also has a busy outdoor bar beneath a giant umbrella. The Wippas stube at the hotel Sonne also gets crowded and has live music but no dancing. Other places for tea dancing include the Wunderbar of the hotel Madlein and the Trofana-Alm.

Most of these places are also popular later on, and there's no shortage of other joints to choose from. The Taja Bar and Seespitz are two of the most popular haunts.

All this action is, however, rather one-dimensional. Ischgl is popular with beer-swilling Germans and 'crazy' Swedes whose idea of a good time revolves around drinking. There are, for example, few stylish discos in which to strut your stuff. The main exception is the Wunderbar, which becomes a sophisticated nightclub in the evenings with international floor shows and disco nights. For a final nightcap after other places close, you can head for the Guxa, a smart, comfortable bar.

FOR NON-SKIERS
Fair by high-village standards
Although the resort is best suited to keen skiers, there's no shortage of things for non-skiers to do. There are plenty of walks (24km of marked paths) and a splendid sports centre with an interesting pool and sauna, steam room and solarium. There's another sports centre in Galtür with swimming, tennis and squash.

It's easy to get around the valley and to Landeck by bus. But meeting skiers for lunch presents problems: the restaurants at the top stations of the gondolas are crowded and characterless. And if you stay in the valley you won't see much sun – certainly not in the early season.

STAYING DOWN THE VALLEY
Too far without a car
Ischgl is fairly isolated. We don't recommend staying down in the main valley unless you have a car and want a touring holiday. Landeck is the nearest big town. It has good shopping and is well positioned for trips to surrounding ski resorts, including Serfaus, Nauders, Sölden and St Anton.

You could consider staying up the valley instead, in Galtür. It is quieter, sunnier and considerably cheaper than Ischgl. It would be a good base for a quiet family holiday. But if you intend to ski Ischgl most of the time, bear in mind that the bus service isn't frequent. The last bus home is disappointingly early in the evening and tends to be a real crush. See report on page 67.

A more radical alternative is to stay in Pfunds – a valley village on the Swiss side of the ski area but actually just in Austria. There are several hotels, of which the major one is the Post; this has linked up with the village ski school to offer interesting 'safari' holidays, involving guided skiing in several ski areas that are easily reached by car – Ischgl-Samnaun among them.

Samnaun 1840m
The main attraction of staying in Samnaun is to ski the Ischgl-Samnaun skiing without the worst of the queues. The village itself is nothing special and consists of not much more than a handful of shops and hotels. It is very quiet. Its duty-free status makes it a useful stopover for those who want to restock on booze and tobacco. If you're touring around in a car, it's also a cheap place to fill up.

ACTIVITIES
Indoor Silvretta Centre (bowling, billiards, swimming pool, sauna, steam baths, solarium), museum, library, cinema, gallery, tennis courts
Outdoor Curling, skating, sleigh rides, hiking tours

TOURIST OFFICE
Postcode A-6561
Tel 00 43 (5444) 5266
Fax 5636

Kitzbühel 760m

The skiing

Snow	**
Extent	****
Advanced	***
Intermediates	****
Beginners	***
Convenience	**
Queues	*
Restaurants	****

The rest

Scenery	***
Resort charm	****
Not skiing	****

✔ *Vibrant nightlife*

✔ *Plenty of off-slope amenities, both for the sporty and the not-so-sporty*

✔ *Large, attractive, varied ski areas offering a sensation of travel to piste and off-piste skiers*

✔ *Beautiful medieval town centre (but see minus points)*

✔ *A surprisingly large amount of cheap and cheerful accommodation*

✔ *Jolly mountain restaurants*

✘ *Unreliable snow conditions, and a snowmaking installation that is still small relative to the ski area*

✘ *Peak-season and weekend lift and bus queues that are shockingly bad by today's standards*

✘ *Surprisingly little tough skiing*

✘ *Disjointed ski areas, with quite a lot of bussing to get around them*

✘ *Traditional charm spoilt by heavy traffic in and around the town*

✘ *Disappointing nursery area*

✘ *Crowded pistes*

'Been there, skied it, bought the t-shirt'. Kitzbühel is an impressive name to drop in the pub when discussing ski resorts. Every Ski Sunday viewer knows that the Hahnenkamm downhill race is the most challenging on the World Cup circuit. And over the years the resort has successfully cultivated an international reputation as a rather special, even glamorous resort. But the Hahnenkamm race course is irrelevant to most skiers; it is specially prepared for the famous race, and is completely untypical of Kitzbühel's skiing, which is mostly easy. And there is nothing very special about standing in long lift queues, fighting for places on crowded buses and skiing on ice and slush. We have visited Kitz countless times over the years, and rarely found decent snow on the lower slopes of the main ski area – last season was about the best. It does of course get good snow at times, and the resort has recently made serious investments in snowmaking, but the spread-out nature and low altitude of the ski area mean that the problem is unlikely to go away.

Equally surprising to visitors impressed by the PR image of Kitz is the fact that the resort is very far from exclusive. It has its expensive, elegant hotels, but it also has a huge amount of hotel and pension accommodation that is quite inexpensive – and not surprisingly attracts quite a few low-budget visitors, many of whom are young and intent on a good time.

And yet the reports we receive on Kitzbühel are almost all from fans, most of whom are regular visitors. For them, its unique combination of historic town and extensive ski area outweighs other considerations.

Kitzbühel is a sizeable town in a broad valley, with its two local ski areas on opposite sides. The main Hahnenkamm area is reached by cable-car from quite close to the centre, or from an out-of-town gondola at Klausen, on the road to **Kirchberg**, another sizeable resort which shares the skiing. The smaller Kitzbüheler Horn ski area is reached by gondola starting some way from the centre. Nearby is a small chain of lifts above the village of **Aurach.**

A fourth ski area, just about accessible on skis from the Hahnenkamm, links the valley village of **Jochberg** to the high outpost of **Pass Thurn.**

Lots of resorts in the eastern Tyrol are accessible by car or public transport.

 ## The resort

Set at a junction of pretty valleys, Kitzbühel is a large, animated town, with a beautiful walled medieval centre – complete with quaint church, cobbled streets and attractively painted buildings – which is traffic-free during the day. But the much-publicised old town represents only a relatively small part of Kitz; the resort spreads widely, and busy roads girdling the old town reduce the charm factor markedly. Visitors used to peaceful little Austrian villages are likely to be disappointed by its essential urban nature. For those who like it, the sophisticated towny ambience is what 'makes' Kitz.

 ## The skiing

Snow and lift queues permitting, the skiing suits intermediate skiers well. Although more advanced skiers can find things to do, there are many better places for experts.

THE SKI AREA
Big but bitty
Kitzbühel has four ski areas, two of them just about connected. The **Hahnenkamm** is by far the largest, and the most accessible from the town. It is reached via a cable-car or two chair-lifts, from the top of which a choice of steep and gentle runs lead down into Ehrenbachgraben; from there several chair-lifts fan out in

SKI FACTS

Altitude	800m-2000m
Lifts	64
Pistes	160km
Green/Blue	50%
Red	42%
Black	8%
Artificial snow	10km

LIFT PASSES

95/96 prices in schillings

Kitzbühel
Covers all lifts in Kitzbühel, Kirchberg, Jochberg, Pass Thurn, Bichlalm and Aschau, linking buses, and swimming pool.

Beginners Points cards valid on 15 mainly drag-lifts (adult 10 point card 150).

Main pass
1-day pass 390
6-day pass 1890
(low season 1740 – 8% off)

Senior citizens
Over 60: 6-day pass 1510 (20% off)

Children
Under 15: 6-day pass 945 (50% off)
Under 4: free pass

Short-term passes
Single ascent tickets for the major lifts; hourly refunds on day tickets; day tickets can be bought in hourly steps from 11am.

Notes 5% reduction for groups of over 15 people. The season pass is valid in Gstaad and Davos/Klosters.

different directions. One takes you to the gentle peak of Steinbergkogel, the high-point of the sector at 1975m. Beyond is the slightly lower peak of Pengelstein. On the far side of Pengelstein several long runs lead down to the valley to the west of the ski area; ski-buses link their end-points at Aschau and Skirast with Obwiesen, Kirchberg and Kitz. From Obwiesen, a slow series of lifts can take you up to Ehrenbachhöhe, the focal point of the whole Hahnenkamm sector.

Pengelstein is the start of the 'ski safari' route to Kitzbühel's most remote but most snowsure ski area, **Jochberg-Pass Thurn**. The piste finishes at Trampelpfad, a short walk from the Jochberg lifts. A parallel piste from Steinbergkogel appears on the piste map, but at Hechenmoos, where it ends, is more than a walk from Jochberg. Jochberg-Pass Thurn is a not inconsiderable area, despite the shortness of most of the runs. By local standards they are high, and have the best snow in the area – well worth the excursion even when snow is acceptably good lower down. Runs lead to Pass Thurn, the terminus of the ski-bus, where it is well worth ending the day to ensure a seat.

The very small **Bichlalm** area is of little interest except for getting away from the crowds and working on your suntan. When conditions are good, the top station (Stuckkogel) accesses an off-piste route to Fieberbrunn. A train returns you to Kitz.

The **Kitzbüheler Horn** is equally sunny, with repercussions for snow-cover, but much of its skiing is above the 1270m-high mid-station, accessed by a modern gondola close to the railway station. The second stage leads to a sunny bowl at around 1660m, but the alternative cable-car takes you up

to the summit of the Horn, from where a fine, solitary east-facing piste leads down into the Raintal on the far side, with a chair-lift returning to the ridge. There are widely spread blue, red and black runs back towards town.

The piste map could be greatly improved, especially by the addition of altitudes and mountain restaurants.

SNOW RELIABILITY
Overdue improvements
Kitzbühel's skiing has one of the lowest average heights in the Alps, and when snow disappears from its wealth of valley-bound pistes the ski area is drastically reduced in size. Long lift queues result, and many of the mountain restaurants become inaccessible. Such problems are sadly common. The introduction of snowmakers in recent years has improved matters, notably on the main Hahnenkamm piste early in the season, but most of the area remains unprotected. The best plan is to book late when snow-cover is known to be good. Otherwise, take a car for snow-searching excursions (which may take you far afield).

FOR ADVANCED SKIERS
Plan to go off-piste
Steep piste skiing is concentrated in the ring of runs down into the bowl of Ehrenbachgraben, the most direct of which are challenging mogul fields. Nearby the Streif red, which is the basis for the downhill race-course, is also good fun, particularly when ice adds to the challenge. (Bravos are prevented from throwing themselves down the famous near-vertical Mausfalle by a wicker fence.) When conditions allow there is plenty of off-piste potential, some of it safely close to pistes, some requiring guidance.

SKI SCHOOL

95/96 prices in schillings

Hahnenkamm
Manager Helmut Egger
Classes 6 days
4hr: 2hr am and pm
6 full days: 1400
Children's classes
Ages: up to 14
6 full days including lunch: 2280
Private lessons on request

Kitzbüheler Horn
Manager Wasti Zwicknagl
Classes 6 days
4hr: 2hr am and pm
5 full days: 1350
Children's classes
5 full days including lunch: 2050

Red Devils
Manager Rudi Sailer
Classes 6 days
4hr: 2hr am and pm
6 full days: 1400
Children's classes
Ages: 4 to 11
6 full days including lunch: 2230
Private lessons
on request

Total
Manager Ernst Hinterseer
Classes 6 days
4hr: 9.30-11.30 and 1pm-3pm
6 full days: 1400
Children's classes
Ages: 4 to 11
6 full days: 1480
Private lessons
on request

FOR INTERMEDIATES
Lots of alternatives

The Hahnenkamm area is prime intermediate terrain. Good intermediates will want to do the Streif run, of course, but the long 1000m-vertical red down to Klausen from Ehrenbachhöhe is equally satisfying. The long runs down to the Kirchberg-Aschau road make a fine end to the day; earlier, they are rather spoilt by the lack of return lifts.

The east-facing Raintal runs on the Horn are perhaps the best 'yo-yo' skiing in the whole area for good intermediates, though the long runs back to town from the ridge are disappointingly easy.

The runs above Jochberg are particularly good for mixed abilities, with plenty of varying routes from the top of the mountain down to Wirtsalm. Moderate skiers also have some fine runs either side of Pengelstein, including the ski safari route, and the Hieslegg piste above Aschau. The short high runs at the top of the Pass Thurn skiing are ideal for timid skiers. There are also easy routes down to both Pass Thurn and Jochberg. Much of the Horn and Bichlalm is also cruising territory, including very long glides down to town when conditions allow.

FOR BEGINNERS
Not ideal

The Hahnenkamm nursery slopes are no more than adequate and prone to poor snow conditions. The Horn has a high, sunny nursery-like section, and precocious learners will soon be skiing home from there on the long Hagstein piste. There are also plenty of easy runs to progress to.

FOR CROSS-COUNTRY
Plentiful but low

There are nearly 40km of trails dotted about, but all are at valley level and prone to lack of snow. When conditions are good, try the quiet Reith area.

QUEUES
A serious drawback

Although Kitzbühel has improved its lift system, it still lags behind other places of similar size and standing, and remains one of the worst resorts for queues at the start of the day. The Hahnenkamm cable-car has a capacity of an incredible 380 people an hour, so it's not surprising that queues are serious. There is the alternative of a slow chair (naturally, this gets busy too) or of going out to the Klausen gondola. Catching a bus can also involve long delays in peak season and at weekends. Overcrowded pistes are generally a greater problem than queues once up both the Horn and Hahnenkamm. The Silberstube drag-lift – the only way back to the Hahnenkamm from Pengelstein – has now been replaced by a quad chair.

MOUNTAIN RESTAURANTS
A highlight

'One of the reasons we keep going back,' says one of our Kitz regulars. There are many restaurants, none of them marked explicitly on the resort piste map. Avoid the large self-service places and stick to the smaller huts. Most of the Horn restaurants have their fans, the Hornköpfl particularly so thanks to good food, reasonable prices, sunny terraces and few queues. Alpenhaus is good for a lively lunch,

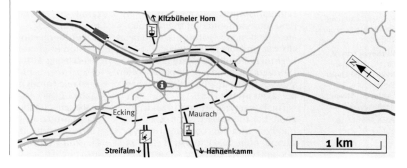

the Gipfelhaus quieter. The Bichlalm in the next-door sector is also good for a quiet lunch. In Pass Thurn-Jochberg sector the Jägerwurzhütte and Trattenbachalm are recommended, and Panoramaalm has (surprise!) great views. The Ochsalm and Brandseit are two of the best in the Hahnenkamm sector – though there are lots of others, both close to town and further away on west-facing slopes.

SKI SCHOOL
Off-piste guiding a bargain
There are now four ski schools, and at least one reporter says that the resort's increased teaching capacity – aided no doubt by the spur of competition – has put an end to the over-large classes that have long been a problem here. The original school, Rudi Sailer's famous Red Devils, runs regular off-piste guiding groups at normal class rates – an excellent way to explore outside the pistes without the usual expense of hiring a guide. In contrast to the 220-strong Red Devils, the other schools emphasise their small scale and personal nature. Ernst Hinterseer's Total school is the best-established of the newcomers – started in 1989/90 – and includes video analysis.

FACILITIES FOR CHILDREN
Not an ideal choice
Provided your children are able and willing to take ski instruction, you can deposit them at any of the four schools. The Total school has the advantage of post-skiing supervision until 5pm. But parents who have to hurry back to the resort can't make the most of the skiing day here.

 Staying there

The size of Kitz makes choice of location important. Staying in the old town has advantages other than aesthetic. It's reasonably equidistant from the two main lift stations either side of town, both being within walking distance. However, the Hahnenkamm is very much the larger (and more snowsure) of the two ski areas, and many visitors prefer to be as close as possible to its cable-car. Beginners should be aware that the Hahnenkamm nursery slopes are often short of snow, at which time novices are taken up the Horn.

The bus service around town is good, but the sheer weight of numbers, and the congested one-way system, often make journeys slow and uncomfortably crowded – one reporter

this year found it sometimes 'impossible to get on or off.' Having a car is very useful for quick access to the Pass Thurn-Jochberg and Bichlalm ski areas and the Klausen gondola, which is relatively queue-free.

HOW TO GO
Mainly hotels and pensions
Kitz is essentially a hotel resort, and UK package offerings reflect this.
Chalets A few tour operators run chalet-hotels here. Crystal have a couple of plain but pleasant and very conveniently positioned places close to the Hahnenkamm slopes and, new for this season, the up-market Chalet Melona with antique furniture, en-suite bathrooms, four course meals and sauna. Skibound run a characterful old coaching inn 8 minutes' walk from the main cable-car. Neilson have the chalet-hotel Hummer near the Kitzbüheler Horn gondola.
Hotels There is an enormous choice, with 4-star and 3-star hotels forming the core of the resort.
££££££ Tennerhof Much-extended, luxuriously converted farmhouse in big garden with renowned restaurant. Beautiful panelled rooms.
££££££ Schloss Lebenberg Modernised 'castle' with smart pool, and free shuttle bus to make up for secluded but inconvenient location. Free nursery for kids aged 3-plus.
££££ Goldener Grief Historic inn, elegantly renovated; vaulted lobby-sitting area, panelled bar, casino.
££££ Weisses Rössl Smartly traditional, with a welcoming bar-sitting room area (open fire); food can be good, but one reporter calls it 'boring and badly prepared'.
£££ Schweizerhof Comfortable chalet in unbeatable position right by Hahnenkamm cable-car.
£££ Maria Theresia Big, comfortable modern chalet.
£££ Hahnenhof Small converted farmhouse retaining rustic charm.
£££ Strasshofer A favourite with more than one of our reporters – 'central, family-run, friendly, good food, quiet rooms at back'.
£ Mühlbergerhof Small, friendly pension in good position.
Self-catering Although there are plenty of apartments in Kitz, very few are available through tour operators. Many of the best (and best-positioned) places are attached to hotels. The 4-star Garni Ludwig and 3-star Garni Christophorus, Haselberger and Pension Hillebrand all have good apartments close to the cable-car.

CHILDCARE
All four ski schools cater for small children, offering lunchtime supervision as well as tuition on baby slopes – generally from age 3. There is no non-ski nursery, but babysitters and nannies can be hired.

GETTING THERE
Air Salzburg, transfer 2hr. Munich, transfer 2½hr. Innsbruck, transfer 2hr.

Rail Mainline station in resort. Postbus every 15 mins from station.

PACKAGES
Airtours, Austrian Holidays, Crystal, First Choice Ski, Inghams, Kings Ski Club, Lagrange, Made to Measure, Neilson, PGL Ski Europe, Rank STS, Ski Europe, Ski Partners, SkiBound, Solo's, Stena Sealink, Thomson

Kirchberg Crystal, First Choice Ski, Neilson, Ski Choice, Ski Partners, SkiBound, Stena Sealink, Top Deck

Pass Thurn Club Europe

ACTIVITIES

Indoor Aquarena Centre (2 pools, sauna, solarium, mud baths, aerated baths, underwater massage – free entry with lift pass), indoor tennis hall, 2 squash courts, fitness centre, beauty centre, bridge, 2 indoor riding schools, local theatre, library, museum, chess club, casino

Outdoor Ice-rink (curling and skating), horse-riding, sleigh rides, wildlife park, toboggan run, ballooning, ski-bobs, guided excursions, flying school, hang-gliding, para-gliding, 40km of cleared walking paths

EATING OUT
Something for everyone

There is a wide range of restaurants to suit all pockets, down to good-value pizzerias and fast food outlets (even McDonald's). Some of the 4-star hotels have excellent restaurants; the Weisses Rössl and Maria Theresia are recommended. But the Unterbergen Stuben vies with the Schwedenkapelle for the 'best in town' award. Good cheaper, less formal places include the Huberbräustube, Sportstüberl and Zinnkrug. Goldene Gams does a good fondue and has live entertainment.

APRES-SKI
A main attraction

Nightlife is a great selling point of Kitz. There's something for all tastes from throbbing bars full of the young, free and single, to quiet little places popular with local workers, nice cafés full of calories and self-consciously smart spots for the fur-coat brigade to flaunt themselves.

Much of the action starts quite late; immediately after skiing the town is jolly without being much livelier than many other Tyrolean resorts – try the Mockingstube, near the cable-car, which often has live music. Cafés Praxmair and Pirchl are two of the most atmospheric tea-time places, where many a diet has been ruined by their cakes and pastries. Later the lively English-style Big Ben bar is a focal spot, while the quieter Seppi's and Glockenspiel are also popular. Das Lichtl, Royal Dancing, Grief Kellar, Drop In, and Take 5 are other lively nightspots. The Londoner Pub is the loudest, most crowded place in town, with sing-a-long and dance-a-long guitar music. It's run largely by Australians and is something of an acquired taste; one reporter described it as 'crowded, smoky, expensive but probably my favourite ski bar'.

Tour reps organise plenty of the usual events, and there's also a casino for more formal entertainment.

FOR NON-SKIERS
Plenty to do

The Aquarena leisure centre is very impressive, with two pools, sauna, solarium and various health activities. One of the many other diversions is a, surprisingly worthwhile, museum. The railway also affords plenty of scope for excursions (to Salzburg and Innsbruck, for example) and there are a number of rep-organised coach trips available. Meeting skiers for lunch can be tricky, but Jochberg is one fairly convenient possibility.

Kirchberg 850m

Anyone going to Kirchberg expecting a quiet, rustic little haven from which to ski Kitzbühel will be sadly disappointed. Kirchberg is a large, crowded, lively, commercialised village very popular with young Brits, Scandinavians and Germans. It suffers the same traffic congestion and inconvenient layout of its famous neighbour, without its compensating medieval town centre. Nor are prices much lower here.

There is a choice of ski schools: here as in Kitz there is a Total school. Meeting points are spread about. Beginners, for example, start over on the Gaisberg mountain, on the opposite side of town from the main area. There are non-ski and ski kindergartens at Obwiesen, 2.5km out of town, near the Elisabeth-Zeinlach hotel complex. Total's Snow Adventure ski kindergarten will keep children until 5pm. The village Krabbelstube crèche accepts babies.

Like Kitz, Kirchberg is essentially a hotel-pension resort, with a wide choice of modern chalet-style places available. Choice of location is important. Beginners have slopes within walking distance of the village, but experienced skiers wishing to avoid crowded bus journeys should look for a hotel a couple of kilometres out of town near the Maierl chair

The 3-star Elisabeth and Zeinlach twin-hotel complex, even further out at Obwiesen, provides the best slope-side accommodation. They are particularly good for families, with shared games and playroom amenities, and kindergartens on hand (see above). Those preferring a central village location will appreciate the 4-star multi-amenity Tiroler Adler, which has a fine leisure complex and a bus stop right outside. The 3-star Landhaus Brauns is also comfortable and has a good position next to the nursery slopes.

Nightlife is very lively, to the point of rowdiness at times. The best bars in town for good, lively fun and atmosphere without getting silly are Le Moustache, Vis a Vis and Charlie's Club. Habitat is a cheaper, more basic place full of Brits. The Londoner is a raucous spot catering for rich teenagers. All the usual Tyrolean-style entertainment is available, plus rep-organised sleigh rides etc.

Kirchberg does not have as much to offer non-skiers as Kitzbühel, but still provides plenty to do – and has the same range of excursion possibilities.

TOURIST OFFICE

Postcode A-6370
Tel 00 43 (5356) 2155
Fax 2307

Lech 1450m

HOW IT RATES

The skiing

Snow	****
Extent	***
Advanced	****
Intermediates	****
Beginners	****
Convenience	***
Queues	**
Restaurants	**

The rest

Scenery	***
Resort charm	****
Not skiing	***

✔ Picturesque Alpine village

✔ Fair sized, largely intermediate piste network

✔ Excellent off-piste skiing

✔ Easy access to tougher skiing of St Anton and other Arlberg resorts

✔ Sunny ski area with excellent snow record and extensive snowmaking

✔ Lively après-ski scene

✔ Very chic resort, good for posing and people-watching

✔ Some captivating hotels and restaurants

✘ Very expensive

✘ Surprising dearth of atmospheric mountain restaurants

✘ Very little tough piste skiing

✘ Can be bad for queues

Lech is one of the most glamorous and expensive resorts in Austria. It shares a ski area with neighbouring and equally upmarket Zürs. The skiing could fairly easily be linked with that of neighbouring St Anton. The fact that it hasn't been emphasises the difference between Zürs' and Lech's rich and royal visitors and the hoi polloi of its equally famous neighbour.

Lech is for those who don't mind fur coats, do like well groomed, snowsure, easy piste skiing and are content to enjoy a comfortable winter holiday in pampered comfort and style in a traditional Alpine village. There is challenging skiing available (mainly off-piste) and the tough skiing of St Anton is only a short bus- or car-ride away. But it is the part-time skier, who enjoys the après and the strolling as much as the skiing, who will get the most out of the resort. It helps to have a deep pocket.

ORIENTATION

Lech is set towards the end (in winter) of a high valley leading off the main Switzerland-Innsbruck motorway near to St Anton. Its own main ski area is reached by a choice of chairs or cable-car from various points in town (the cable-car goes to Oberlech, a mini-resort 300m above Lech in the middle of the ski area). Another cable-car also goes up the opposite side of the valley to link up with the skiing of **Zürs**, which you pass through on the road into Lech. Zug is a tiny hamlet 3km up another dead-end valley. The Arlberg ski pass covers not only these two resorts but also **St Anton, Stuben** and **St Christoph**, all reachable by car or local bus.

 The resort

Lech is Austria's answer to glitz-and-glamour resorts such as Courchevel and Zermatt. People come here to be seen. The village offers cosy old-world Austrian charm, complete with onion-domed church and covered wooden bridge over the river, combined with every modern convenience. It lies in a small valley with good views of the mountains on all sides.

The main street is bordered on one side by the Lech, a gurgling river, and by enticing and pricey shops on the other. In good weather it is a picture of open air cafés, dancing in the street and a fashion show of fur coats and horse-drawn carriages.

While some of the best hotels are right in the centre, they are not obtrusive. There are no towering monstrosities in Lech and the village remains picturesque despite its growth and popularity. Recently it has become associated with Princess Diana's annual pilgrimage to the Arlberg hotel. She is Lech's best-known celebrity but there are many others. Princess Caroline of Monaco

goes to neighbouring Zürs.

The clientele is largely German and Austrian, with very few Brits. The fur coat count is one of the highest in the Alps. And it helps to be able to afford a helicopter transfer out if the high Flexen Pass on the road in and out is shut – which it can be for days on end after an exceptional snowfall. The top hotels are owned by a few families and have large numbers of regular guests who come back year after year.

The first settlers in Lech came from the Valais region of Switzerland in the 11th century. The village is named after the river Lech, originally the 'Licca' which means stonewater. Skiing started in the early 1900s. The Lech ski school was founded in 1925 and the first T-bar was built in 1939. Lech's most famous son is Patrick Ortlieb, Albertville Olympic downhill champion in 1992. He was born and learned his skiing in Oberlech.

Oberlech is a small, traffic-free collection of hotels and chalets set on the piste above Lech and served by a cable-car which works until late at night, allowing access to Lech's much livelier nightlife.

Zug is a hamlet, 3km from Lech

which connects with the Lech-Oberlech ski area. The small amount of accommodation is mostly bed and breakfast with one 4-star hotel, the Rote Wand, which serves the best Kaiserschmarren (a delicious pancake and fruit desert) in the Arlberg. From Lech, Zug makes a good night out: you can take a horse-drawn sleigh for a fondue at the Rote Wand, Klosterle or Auerhahn, followed by a visit to the Rote Wand disco.

SKI FACTS

Altitude 1445m-2450m
Lifts   86
Pistes   260km
Green/Blue   30%
Red   40%
Black*   30%
Artificial snow 18km
* includes ski routes
  – see text

 # The skiing

For such an upmarket resort the lift system is surprisingly antiquated and badly planned in many ways. But perhaps that reflects the fact that its clientele are there primarily for a relaxing and social winter break, rather than wanting to clock up as much ski mileage as possible between dawn and dusk. The runs are also designed to flatter leisurely skiers, with a lot of gentle wide blue and red runs.

THE SKI AREA
One-way traffic
Lech's main ski area centres on **Oberlech**, which can be reached from the village by chair-lifts as well as the cable-car. The wide open slopes are perfect for intermediates and the area, served by 16 lifts, also accesses off-piste for experts. **Zuger Hochlicht** is the highest point of this sector, at 2380m, and the views from here and

Kriegerhorn below are stunning. As at St Anton, the toughest runs here are now classed as 'ski routes' or 'high-touring routes' rather than pistes, with all the confusion that involves (see St Anton chapter). The only official pistes back to the main skiing from Zuger Hochlicht are now gentle blues, and the only way down to Zug is a ski route.

To get to the Zürs ski area and the linked Lech-Zürs-Lech circuit, you take the **Rüfikopf** cable-car in the opposite direction from Lech's main ski area. This goes from the centre of town. From the top there are long cruisey pistes, via a couple of lifts, down to Zürs. The circuit can only be skied in a clockwise direction. This

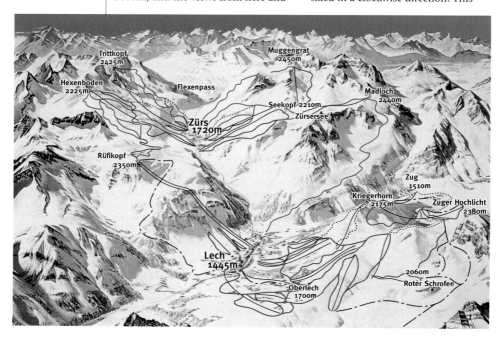

LIFT PASSES

95/96 prices in schillings

Arlberg Ski pass
Covers all St Anton, St Christoph, Lech, Zürs and Stuben lifts, but not the buses between them.
Beginners Limited day passes covering a few lifts; adventurous second-week skiers need an area pass.
Main pass
1-day pass 455
6-day pass 2030
(low season 1830 – 10% off)
Senior citizens
Over 65 male, 60 female: 6-day pass 1750 (14% off)
Over 80: 100
Children
Under 15: 6-day pass 1220 (40% off)
Under 6: 100
Short-term passes
Single ascent tickets on some lifts throughout Arlberg. Half-day tickets (adults 340) from noon, afternoon 'taster' tickets (185) from 3pm. Day tickets have by-the-hour reimbursement.
Notes Arlberg pass also covers Klösterle (10 lifts), 7km west of Stuben.
Snowman ticket (100) for children under 6 and adults over 80 covers whole season. Special reductions during wedel, firn and snow crystal weeks.

means that in school holidays and other busy periods the linking lifts and runs can get crowded.

All the skiing at Zürs is above the treeline. There are two areas on either side of the village. The more difficult runs are off the top of the **Trittkopf** (on the same side as the runs down from Lech).

On the other side of the valley, chairs go up to **Seekopf** and Zürsersee with intermediate runs down. There's a chair up to Muggengrat (at 2450m the highest point of the Zürs skiing) from below Zürsersee. This has a blue back under it and a lovely long red away from all the lifts back down to Zürs. But most people head for the Madloch-Joch chair. This accesses the long red run all the way back to Lech. You can peel off part way down and ski to Zug and the chair-lift up to the Kriegerhorn above Oberlech.

SNOW RELIABILITY
One of Austria's best

Lech and Zürs both get a lot of snow, but Austrian weather station records show a big difference between them despite their proximity. Lech gets an average of almost 8m of snow between December and March, almost twice as much as St Anton and three times as much as Kitzbühel, but Zürs gets half as much again as Lech. The altitude is high by Austrian resort standards and there is excellent snowmaking on Lech's sunny lower slopes.

This combination, together with excellent grooming, means that the Lech-Zürs ski area normally has good skiing from December until April. And the snow is frequently better here than on St Anton's predominantly south-facing slopes.

FOR ADVANCED SKIERS
Off-piste is main attraction

There are no black pistes on the piste map, only the two types of off-piste route referred to above. Skiing these with a guide is the official recommendation, though many ignore the advice. The truth is that good skiers will get a lot more out of the area if they do have a guide. There is plenty of excellent off-piste that isn't marked on the map, much of it accessed by long traverses. Especially in fresh snow, it can be wonderful.

Many of the best runs start from Zuger Hochlicht or the Steinmähder chair, which finishes just below it. Some routes involve a short climb to access bowls of untracked powder. From the Kriegerhorn there are shorter off-piste runs down towards Lech and

a very scenic long run down to Zug. There are also good runs from Salober Kopf at the northern end of the ski area. One of the problems with all these, however, is that most are south- or west-facing and can suffer from getting a lot of sun.

At the end of the season, when the snow is deep and settled, the off-piste off the shoulder of the Wöstertäli from the top of the Rüfikopf cable-car down to Lech can be superb. There are also good runs from the top of the Trittkopf cable-car in the Zürs sector, including a tricky one above the Flexen Pass down to Stuben.

Good skiers will also enjoy cruising some of the steeper red runs and will want to visit St Anton once or twice during the week, where they will find more challenging piste as well as off-piste skiing.

Heli-skiing is available from either the Kriegerhorn or the Flexen Pass.

FOR INTERMEDIATE SKIERS
Flattering variety for all

The piste skiing in the Oberlech area is nearly all immaculately groomed blue runs, the upper ones above the trees, the lower ones in wide swathes cut through them. It is ideal territory for leisurely skiers not wanting any surprises. And even early intermediates will be able to ski the circuit to Zürs and back, the only red run involved being the beautiful long (and not at all difficult) piste back to Lech from the top of the Madloch chair in Zürs.

More adventurous intermediates should take the Steinmähder chair to just below Zuger Hochlicht, or the cable-car all the way up, and from there take the scenic red run all the way to Zug (the latter part on a 'ski route' rather than a piste). If you want to record the speed of your schuss there is an electronic speed indicator at the Weibermahd chair-lift in Oberlech.

Zürs has much more interesting red run skiing, on both sides of the valley. We particularly like the west-facing reds down from the Trittkopf cable-car and the usually quiet run back to Zürs from the Muggengrat chair, which starts in a steep bowl.

FOR BEGINNERS
Easy skiing in all areas

The main nursery slopes are in Oberlech, but there is also a nice isolated area in the village dedicated purely to beginners. There are also good easy runs to progress to, both above and below Oberlech.

SKI SCHOOL

95/96 prices in schillings

Lech and Oberlech
Classes 6 days
4hr: 10am-noon and
1pm-3pm
6 full days: 1540
Children's classes
Ages: 3½ to 12
6 full days: 1420
Private lessons
Full day
2140 for full day;
each additional
person 160

CHILDCARE

There are ski
kindergartens in Lech
(2161-0) and Oberlech
(3236) taking children
from age 3, from 9am
to 4pm.

GETTING THERE

Air Zurich, transfer
3hr. Innsbruck,
transfer 2hr.

Rail Langen (15km);
12 buses daily from
station, buses
connect with
international trains.

PACKAGES

Inghams, Made to
Measure, Ski Choice,
Ski Club of GB, Ski
Les Alpes

Zürs Made to
Measure

FOR CROSS-COUNTRY
Picturesque valley trail

There are two cross-country trails in
Lech. The longer one is 15km; it
begins in the centre of town and leads
through the beautiful Zug valley,
following the Lech river and ending
up outside Zug. The other begins
behind the church and goes to
Stubenbach (another hamlet in the
Lech area). In Zürs there is a 3km track
starting at Zürs and going to the
Flexen Pass. This starts at 1600m and
climbs to 1800m.

QUEUES
Can be bad

Even early starters may well find
queues at the Rüfikopf cable-car as the
morning rush heads off towards Zürs.
Similarly the crucial Madloch chair at
the top of the Zürs area generates
queues of people going towards Lech.
The problem is that the circuit goes
only one way, so everyone is headed
in the same direction. Other
bottlenecks can include the Zuger
Hochlicht lift, Trittkopf cable-car and
getting up from Zürs to Seekopf where
new chair-lifts still can't cope with the
volume in high season and holidays.
All this is despite the proud boast that
the region limits skier numbers to
14,000 a day for more enjoyable
skiing. The Oberlech region rarely
causes problems.

However, one reporter found no
problem queues when he was there
last New Year. So you may hit lucky!

MOUNTAIN RESTAURANTS
Not enough

A lack of cosy Alpine restaurants sends
many frustrated lunchers back to Lech
and Zürs to be sure of an enjoyable
meal. One of the best mountain
restaurants is Seekopf (reached by the
Seekopf chair-lift) which has a lovely
sun terrace. Also popular is the self-
service Palmenalpe above Zug, but it
does get very crowded. There are a few
good places set prettily around the
piste at Oberlech but all get crowded;
our favourite is the Goldener Berg. For
a gourmet blow-out in Zürs, Chesa
Verde in the hotel Edelweiss and the
restaurant in the hotel Hirlanda both
feature in Gault-Millau but are not
cheap. The hotel Rote Wand in Zug
serves more casual fare. Café Schneider
in Lech serves good local dishes.

SKI SCHOOL
Excellent

The ski schools of Lech, Oberlech and
Zürs all have good reputations and we
have had no bad reports of them. But
in peak periods it might be as well to
book in advance as many of the
instructors are hired regularly every
year by an exclusive clientele. While
the instructors speak good English, as
they are used to foreigners, they may
not have picked up the typical British
sense of humour. Group lessons are
divided into no less than 12 ability
levels, which augurs well for optimum
use of time.

FACILITIES FOR CHILDREN
Oberlech's fine if you can afford it

We haven't got many reports on Lech,
and hardly any from families, who
presumably find it rather expensive.
But Oberlech, in particular, makes an
excellent choice for those who can
afford it, and at least one of the hotels
there – the Sonnenburg – has an
impressive in-house nursery.

 # Staying there

Lech is big enough for some of the
cheaper accommodation to be quite a
walk from the lifts. Unless you're
heavily into nightlife, staying up in
Oberlech is very attractive.

HOW TO GO
Luxury dominates

Chalets There are no catered chalets in
Lech so far as we know.
Hotels There are several 5-star hotels,
and dozens of 4-star and 3-star ones,
but also countless more modest places
charging one-tenth of the 5-star rates.
££££ Arlberg A favourite with
certain royal(ish) persons. Elegantly
rustic chalet, centrally placed. Pool.
££££ Krone One of the oldest
buildings in the village, in a prime
spot by the river.
££££ Tannbergerhof Splendidly
atmospheric inn on main street, with
outdoor bar and hugely popular disco
(tea-time as well as later). Pool.
££££ Sonnenburg (Oberlech) Luxury
on-piste chalet (popular for lunch).
Good children's facilities. Pool.
££ Haus Angerhof Beautiful ancient
pension, with wood panels and quaint
little windows.
££ Haus Fernsicht Pension with spa
facilities.
££ Haus Rudboden Right by the
nursery slopes.
Self-catering There are no apartments
available through tour operators.

EATING OUT
Not necessarily expensive
There are over 50 restaurants in Lech with nearly all the hotels having dining rooms. For reasonably priced meals try the Montana, which has an excellent wine cellar, the Krone, Ambrosius (above a shopping arcade), or the Post, which serves Austrian nouvelle-type food. The Madlochblick has a typically Austrian restaurant, very cosy with good solid food. For pasta and other Italian fare there is Pizza Charly. In Oberlech there is a good fondue at the Alte Goldener Berg, a tavern built in 1432. In Zug the Rote Wand is excellent for fondues and a good night out. Also try the Alphorn, the Gasthof Alpenblick and the Klosterle.

APRES-SKI
OK but pricey
The umbrella bar of the Berg hotel at Oberlech is popular immediately after skiing. Then the 'beautiful people' head down to Krones ice bar, which has a lovely setting by the river, or to the outdoor bar of the Tannbergerhof.

Inside the Tannbergerhof, there's a tea dance disco. Dancing in the streets is quite common. If you're looking for a disco there's the Arlberg hotel's Scotch Club, owned and run by former Olympic champion, Egon Zimmermann, and others in the hotels Almhof-Schneider and Krone. The latter's Side Step specialises in 60s and 70s music. The Pfefferkörnd'l is a good place for a drink, and is particularly popular for its after-skiing cocktails and gourmet snacks. You can also get a steak or pizza there until 11.30pm. For a change of scene after skiing, there's the champagne bar in Oberlech's hotel Montana, or later the Rote Wand in Zug has a disco.

Taxi James is a shared mini-bus taxi which charges a flat fare of 40 schillings for any journey in Lech/Zürs – you phone and it picks you up within half an hour.

FOR NON-SKIERS
Poseurs' paradise
Many visitors to Lech don't ski. If armed with a limitless credit card the shopping possibilities are enticing and the main street is often filled with fur-clad browsers. Strolz's plush emporium in the centre of town is a good place to up the rate at which you're spending schillings.

It's easy to get to Oberlech or Zug to meet skiers for lunch – or for them to come back to the village. The village outdoor bars make ideal posing positions – but make sure you are immaculately groomed or you'll feel out of place. An excursion to St Anton, to see how the other half live, is possible, though Lech clientele may feel more at home getting off the bus at chic St Christoph. For the more active there are 25km of walking paths and a variety of sporting activities – the walk along the river to Zug is especially beautiful.

Zürs 1720m
Ten minutes' drive towards St Anton from Lech, Zürs is almost on the Flexen Pass, with good snow virtually guaranteed. Zürs was a tiny hamlet used for farming during the summer only until (in the late 1890s) the Flexen Pass road was built and Zürs began to develop, entering the ski scene in the early 20th century.

The village is even more exclusive than Lech, with no hotels of less than 3-star standing, and a dozen 4-star and 5-star hotels around which life revolves. But the opulence is less overt here. There are few shops. Nightlife is quiet, though there are discos in the Edelweiss, Mara and Zürserhof hotels. There's also a piano bar in the Alpenhof and a good après-ski watering hole is Gerhard's Bar. Later on Matthie's Stub'l and Kaminestub'l are worth trying. Serious dining means the Zürserhof and the Lorünser – make sure you have a platinum credit card for these. For something cheaper try spaghetti in the basement of the hotel Edelweiss. Princess Caroline (who stays at the Lorünser) managed to get a plate of spaghetti here at 5am.

Zürs has its own ski school, but many of the instructors are booked for the entire season by regular clients, and more than 80% of them are hired privately. The resort has its own kindergarten.

ACTIVITIES
Indoor Tennis, squash, hotel swimming pools and saunas, cinema, museum, art gallery, hotel spas (massage and balneotherapy)
Outdoor 25km of cleared walking paths, toboggan run (from Oberlech), natural ice rink (skating, curling), sleigh rides, fun park, billiards, paragliding

TOURIST OFFICE
Postcode A-6764
Tel oo 43 (5583) 21610
Fax 3155

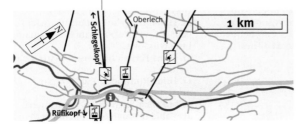

Mayrhofen 630m

HOW IT RATES

The skiing

Snow	✱✱✱
Extent	✱✱
Advanced	✱
Intermediates	✱✱✱
Beginners	✱✱
Convenience	✱
Queues	✱
Restaurants	✱✱✱

The rest

Scenery	✱✱✱
Resort charm	✱✱✱
Not skiing	✱✱✱✱

✔ *Excellent children's amenities*

✔ *Lively après ski – but it's easily avoided if you prefer peace*

✔ *Wide range of non-skiing facilities*

✔ *One of the more snowsure ski areas in the Tyrol, with the added safety of the Hintertux glacier nearby*

✔ *Various nearby areas on the same lift pass, and reached by free bus*

✔ *Easy road and rail access*

✔ *The Penken cable-car is being replaced, at last*

✘ *No skiing at village level, even for beginners*

✘ *Long queues for lifts up and down the mountain, unlikely to be cured entirely by the new Penken lift*

✘ *Inconveniently situated lifts, some out of town, can mean walks and buses*

✘ *Sprawling, commercialised village*

✘ *Little difficult skiing*

✘ *Small, crowded local ski areas*

Mayrhofen is a British favourite which wears two distinctly different hats. Many young or youngish visitors like it for its lively nightlife. But it is also an excellent family resort: its amenities include highly regarded kindergartens and a new fun pool with a special children's area. Fortunately, the liveliest of the nightlife is confined to a few very popular places, easily avoided by families in such a large resort.

But there are other considerations. Having skiing that is remote from the village is forgiveable; having remote skiing accessed by inconvenient and inadequate lifts is not. Mayrhofen visitors have put up with inadequate lifts (and promises of improvements) for years; but it really does look like there will be a new gondola up to the Penken this season. Fingers crossed.

The Zillertal pass covers all the resorts in the valley, including the excellent glacier at Hintertux (see page 68). If you're thinking of spending more than a day up there, there is something to be said for basing yourself closer to the glacier – perhaps at Lanersbach, a pretty, rustic village with a respectable local ski area, described at the end of this chapter.

ORIENTATION

Sitting in the flat-bottomed Zillertal, Mayrhofen is a cable-car ride from both its ski areas. Lifts also access the main area from **Finkenberg** and **Mühlbach**, villages either side of town. A frequent free bus serves several other resorts covered by the area pass, notably **Hintertux, Lanersbach** and **Gerlos**.

SKI FACTS

Altitude	630m–2250m
Lifts	30
Pistes	91km
Green/Blue	27%
Red	58%
Black	15%
Artificial snow	4½km

🏠 The resort

Mayrhofen is a large resort – big enough to be called a town, but not towny in character. It's essentially a traditional little village of a few bars, restaurants, hotels large and small, and sports shops – but multiplied twenty-fold. As the village has grown, architecture has been kept traditional, but the place is so sprawling and commercialised it can hardly be considered charming.

The main street is surrounded by almost every kind of tourist amenity – except ski lifts. The new Penken lift station, like the old one, will be on the edge of the village centre, while the Ahorn cable-car is out in the suburbs, about 1km from the centre.

Despite its 'lively' reputation, Mayrhofen is not dominated by lager louts. They exist, but tend to congregate in a few particular and easily avoided bars. The central hotels are mainly slightly upmarket places, and overall the resort has a pleasantly civilised atmosphere.

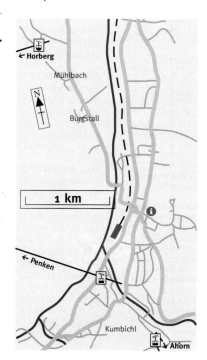

SKI SCHOOL

95/96 prices in schillings

Uli Spiess
Manager Uli Spiess
Classes 6 days
4hr: 10am-noon and
1pm-3pm
6 full days: 1450
Children's classes
Ages: 4 to 12
6 full days including
lunch: 2230
Private lessons
500 for 1hr; each
additional person 200

Manfred Gager
Manager Manfred
Gager
Classes 6 days
4hr: 10am-noon and
1.30-3.30
6 full days: 1450
Children's classes
Ages: 4 to 14
6 full days including
lunch: 2230
Private lessons
500 for 1hr; each
additional person 200

SMT Mayrhofen Total
Manager Max Rahm
Classes 6 days
4hr: 10am-noon and
1pm-3pm
6 full days: 1450
Children's classes
Ages: 4 to 14
6 full days including
lunch: 2170
Private lessons
500 for 1hr; each
additional person 200

Mount Everest
Manager Peter
Habeler
Classes 6 days
4hr: 10am-noon and
1pm-3pm
6 full days: 1440
Children's classes
Ages: 4 to 14
6 full days including
lunch: 2160
Private lessons
470 for 1hr

Ski School Special
Manager Hannes
Brandner
Classes 6 days
4hr: 10am-noon and
1pm-3pm
6 full days: 1450
Children's classes
Ages: 4 to 14
6 full days including
lunch: 2160
Private lessons
500 for 1hr

 # The skiing

Mayrhofen has two skiing mountains, one of which (Penken) is mainly suitable for intermediates, the other (Ahorn) only for beginners. Neither has much to offer advanced skiers.

THE SKI AREA
Highly inconvenient
Both skiing sectors are served by very queue-prone cable-cars, a bus-ride apart, which usually have to be ridden down as well as up. An unpisted run from **Ahorn** is the only trail from mountains to village. Needless to say, changing ski areas or meeting friends for lunch in the village is a serious waste of good skiing time. Access to the **Penken** is also provided by the gondolas a couple of kilometres either side of the resort at Hippach and Finkenberg. It is possible to ski back down to Finkenberg and Hippach when snow is good. The Finkenberg run is only a path. The unpisted Hippach trail is the best run in the area for good skiers, but rarely has good snow cover.

SNOW RELIABILITY
Good by Austrian standards
Although the highest lift goes no higher than 2280m, the area is reasonably good for snow-cover because (apart from the unreliable valley runs) all of Mayrhofen's skiing is above 1580m. Mayrhofen is also fortunate in having one of the best glaciers in the Alps within day-trip range, at Hintertux.

FOR ADVANCED SKIERS
Go elsewhere
Mayrhofen is not a sensible base for good skiers unless they aim to go touring. The long unpisted run down to Hippach is the only worthwhile local skiing, and this is rarely skiable.

FOR INTERMEDIATE SKIERS
Problematic
Mayrhofen's ski area is sufficiently small to disappoint the avid piste basher, yet just difficult enough to be unappetising for the nervous intermediate. If you come between those categories, its short, mainly open runs spread across the Penken and next-door Gerent may suit you.

On the other hand, the Ziller valley is excellent for intermediates willing to travel. Each of the main ski areas covered by the valley pass is sufficiently large and varied to make an interesting day's skiing.

FOR BEGINNERS
Overrated: big drawbacks
Despite its reputation for ski teaching, Mayrhofen is less than ideal for beginners. The Ahorn nursery slopes are excellent – high, extensive and sunny – but it's a tiresome journey to reach them. The overcrowded slopes and restaurant add to the hassle. The Penken nursery area is less satisfactory.

FOR CROSS-COUNTRY
Go to Lanersbach
In theory there is a fine 20km trail along the valley to Zell am Ziller, plus small loops conveniently in, or close to, the village. But snow at 600m is not reliable. Vorderlanersbach has a much higher, more snowsure trail running to Madseit.

QUEUES
An end in sight?
Mayrhofen has for years been one of the worst resorts in the Alps for queues at the beginning and end of the day. So it's good news that the Penken is to get a new gondola for the 1995/96 season, carrying 2,000 pers/hr and operating in winds of up to 90 km/hr. (It will also go higher than the old lift, cutting out the irritating walk up to the chair-lifts.) Although this represents a tripling of capacity, we doubt that it will eradicate delays; it certainly won't do much for the Ahorn queues. Once away from the busy area close to the Penken lift, intermediates have surprisingly queue-free skiing. The buses to and from the out-of-town gondolas are often crowded, particularly the Finkenberg one, which also serves Hintertux.

MOUNTAIN RESTAURANTS
Penken good, Ahorn bad
The Penken is very well endowed with mountain restaurants, most of which are attractive and sunny and serve good-value food. The Ahorn has only one restaurant, which is inadequate for the hordes of beginners using it.

SKI SCHOOL
You name it, they do it – well
Mayrhofen's popularity is founded on its four ski schools, which between them provide a wide range of services. We have received positive reports on many of them, including the ordinary group and private lessons. There's also ski guiding around the Zillertal, and ski tours with the Mount Everest school to the Hoher Riffler and Rastkogel summits. Snowboarders are also well catered for, with their own specialist section of the Total school.

LIFT PASSES

95/96 prices in schillings

Mayrhofen/Zillertal
Coverage depends on period – see notes.

Main pass
1-day pass 340
6-day pass 1965

Children
Under 15: 6-day pass 1180 (40% off)
Under 6: free pass

Short-term passes
Half-day pass for Mayrhofen only.

Alternative periods
Zillertal pass available for 4 days skiing in 6, 5 days in 7, 6 days in 7 and 10 days in 14.

Notes 1- to 3-day pass covers Penken/Ahorn area only; 4-day and over includes all 154 Ziller valley lifts (including Hintertux glacier), 430km of piste, ski bus and railway.

Alternative passes
Zillertal pass without Hintertux glacier (6 days 1550 for adults, 930 for children).

CHILDCARE

All five ski schools run children's classes, and ski kindergartens where lunch is provided – Spiess at Ahorn, Gager at Penken, the other two at both ski areas. All take children aged 4 to 12 or 14, and appear to operate only until the end of ski teaching at 3.30.

Wuppy's Kinderland non-skiing nursery at the fun pool complex takes children aged 3 months to 7 years, 8.30am to 5pm.

The Sporthotel Strass has a playroom.

GETTING THERE

Air Salzburg, transfer 3hr. Munich, transfer 3hr, Innsbruck, transfer 1½hr.

Rail Local line through to resort; regular buses from station.

FACILITIES FOR CHILDREN
Excellent but inconvenient

Mayrhofen has put childcare at the centre of its pitch, and the facilities both for skiing and non-skiing children are excellent. However, we prefer to take our offspring to resorts where they don't have to be bussed around and ferried up and down the mountain.

 Staying there

In such a large sprawling village, with two widely separated lifts, location is important. The original centre of the village, around the market place, church and bus/railway stations, is now on the periphery of things. The most convenient area is on the main street, as close as possible to the Penken cable-car.

HOW TO GO
Plenty of mainstream packages

There is a wide choice for package-buyers and independent travellers – except for chalet fans.

Chalets Equity Total Ski have the only catered chalet we are aware of. It's a traditional villa conversion, well located close to the Penken cable-car, high street and swimming complex.

Hotels There is an enormous choice of hotels. There are dozens of cheap pensions, but most British skiers stay in the larger, better hotels. Most of the packaged hotels are centrally located in a good position for village amenities but a fair walk from the Penken cable-car, and a bus-ride from the Ahorn lift.

£££££ Elisabeth The resort's only 5-star hotel, an opulent chalet in a fair position near the post office.

££££ Manni's Well-placed, smartly done out; pool.

£££ Sporthotel Strass Best-placed of the 4-stars, very close to the Penken cable-car. Lively bar, disco, fitness centre, solarium, pool and children's playroom.

£££ Waldheim Smallish, cosy 3-star gasthof, close to the Penken lift.

£££ St Georg Poorly positioned for amenities, but ideal for those wanting a multi-facility quality hotel in peaceful surroundings.

£££ Jägerhof Another peaceful hotel with good facilities, mid-way between the two cable-cars.

£ Claudia, Monika Cheap little twin guesthouses in a good position.

£ Kumbichl, Kumbichlhof Adjoining pensions, right next to the Ahorn cable-car.

Self-catering Although there's a wide choice of apartments for independent holidaymakers, we are not aware of any packages on the UK market.

EATING OUT
Wide choice

Most Brits come here on half-board, but there is a large choice of restaurants catering for most tastes and budgets. The Hotel Rose has a particularly good but informal restaurant.

APRES-SKI
Lively but not rowdy

Nightlife is a great selling point. Mayrhofen has all the standard Tyrolean-style entertainment such as folk dancing, bier kellers and tea-dances, along with bowling, sleigh rides, tobogganing and several lively bars and discos. The Movie bar, Scotland Yard pub and the Sporthotel's Arena video disco are particularly rocking places to go. Although après-ski is lively, it usually avoids becoming too rowdy; Mayrhofen is no 'Benidorm am Ziller'.

FOR NON-SKIERS
Good for all but shoppers

There's lots to do. The village travel agency arranges trips into Italy, while Innsbruck is easily reached by train. There are also good walks and sports amenities. Meeting skiers for lunch is not a problem; at least non-skiers can wait for the crowds to disperse before going up the mountain. Shopping is the one disappointment – just a lot of sports shops and souvenir places.

Finkenberg 840m

Finkenberg offers a welcome alternative to Mayrhofen, being a much smaller, quieter village with far better access to and from the Penken skiing. It is no more than a collection of traditional-style hotels, bars, cafés and private homes awkwardly dispersed along a steep section of the busy main road between Mayrhofen and Lanersbach. There are two distinct halves – the original village around the church, and a second cluster of buildings conveniently close to the gondola station, just over five minutes' walk away.

The gondola gives queue-free access to the Penken (Mayrhofen-based skiers tend to use the Hippach gondola rather than this one) and, importantly, a speedy ride home for beginners (and all other skiers when the Katzenmoos path is not skiable). Thus Finkenberg residents can be

PACKAGES

Airtours, Austrian
Holidays, Crystal,
Equity Total Ski, First
Choice Ski, Inghams,
Made to Measure,
Snowcoach Club
Cantabrica, Stena
Sealink, Thomson,
Timescape Holidays
Finkenberg Crystal

ACTIVITIES

Indoor Bowling, 3
hotel pools open to
the public, massage,
sauna, jacuzzi,
Turkish baths (in
hotels, but open to
non-residents),
adventure pool
(aquaslide, rapids,
whirlpool), squash,
fitness centre, chess,
indoor tennis centre
at Hotel Berghof (3
courts, coaching
available), indoor
riding-school, pool
and billiards, stamp-
swapping, cinema.
Outdoor Natural
skating-rink, curling,
horse-riding, horse
and dog sleigh rides
and racing, 45km
cleared paths, hang-
gliding, para-gliding,
tobogganing (2 runs
of 2.5km)

TOURIST OFFICE

Postcode A-6290
Tel oo 43 (5285)
2305
Fax 411633

tucking into coffee and cake in their
favourite café while Mayrhofen guests
are freezing to death, queuing in the
dark for their cable-car home.

Finkenberg has a nursery slope in
the village which, given good snow,
means that beginners do not need to
buy the full lift pass. But it's a sunless
spot, and good conditions are far from
certain at this altitude.

Cross-country skiers have to get a
bus up to Lanersbach.

There are two ski schools. The
Klauss-Kroll school has a particularly
good reputation.

Like Mayrhofen, Finkenberg prides
itself on its ability to give children a
good time. But it is not a resort for
young tots: there is no non-ski crèche
and the ski nursery doesn't take
children under the age of 4.

All hotels are within walking
distance of the gondola, and many of
the more distant ones run minibuses
to the lift station. The 4-star Margit is
particularly well positioned in the new
sector, and the equally comfortable
Stock is close to the lift station, on the
edge of the original village. The 3-star
Gasthof Panorama is well placed in
the new part. In the centre of the
original village the 4-star Eberl, the
3-star Garni Austria and 2-star Pension
Troppmair are six or seven minutes
from the gondola.

Restaurants are mostly hotel-based.
The Stock has one of the best and
most expensive. The Neuwirt is a good
mid-range place, while the
Finkenberghof has an appetising
cheaper menu.

Finkenberg is quiet in the evenings.
The main après-ski spots are Pub
Laternall and Cafe Zum Fink'n, and
there are rep-organised events such as
tobogganing and bowling. Mayrhofen
is a short taxi-ride away and offers a
far wider choice of evening action.

Swimming, curling and ice-skating
are available, and the local walks have
been recommended, but most non-
skiers find themselves spending a lot
of time down in Mayrhofen.

Lanersbach 1300m

Lanersbach is an attractive, spacious,
traditional village spoilt only a little
by the busy road up to Hintertux,
which passes the main lift station.
Happily, the area around the pretty
church is hidden away off the road,
yet within walking distance of the lift.
The village is small and
uncommercialised, but it has all you
need in a resort. And prices are low.

The Eggalm ski area, now accessed
by a cable-car, has a high point of

2300m at Beil, and a small network of
pleasantly varied, mostly wooded
pistes leading back to the village and
across to the Rastkogel sector, above
nearby Vorderlanersbach. This sector
(also accessed by its own modern
gondola) goes higher (top station
2500m) but is not so pretty or
interesting. The two sectors total
33km of piste. Snow conditions are
usually good, at least in early season;
by Austrian standards, this is high
skiing, but the Vorderlanersbach
sector, in particular, gets a lot of sun.

There are no pistes to challenge
good skiers, but there is a fine off-piste
route starting a short walk from the
Lanersbach top station and finishing
at the village. Intermediates should
enjoy the wonderfully uncrowded,
well groomed runs. Lanersbach's
nursery slope is rather small, and
finding an English-speaking instructor
can be a problem.

Lanersbach is the best base in the
area for cross-country, with 23km of
trails running up the valley to
Madseit.

Lanersbach is essentially a hotel
resort. The Lanersbachhof is a multi-
amenity olde worlde 4-star close to the
lifts but is also on the main road. The
cheaper 3-star Pinzger and Alpengruss
are similarly situated. The 3-star
Bergkristall is central, but reasonably
close to the cable-car.

Restaurants are mainly hotel-based.
The Bergfried and Central hotels have
good but expensive restaurants.
Gasthof Jäger is a cheaper place with a
charming restaurant. Zum Post does
'top-quality' pizza.

Nightlife is quiet by Austrian
standards, though the Mondschein
Keller and Sporthotel Kirchler bar have
plenty of atmosphere, and there is a
disco which livens up at weekends.
The Picolo nightclub was reported to
be the happening place last season, if
anywhere was.

Non-skiers are fairly well catered for
considering the size of the resort.
Some of the better hotels have
facilities such as pools, jacuzzis and
fitness rooms open to non-residents.
Just outside the village is a tennis
centre, also offering squash and ten-
pin bowling. Mayrhofen is a
worthwhile excursion, while Salzburg
is just within range.

The non-ski nursery takes children
from age 2, the ski school from 4.
Lanersbach is a generally child-
friendly village, though a lack of
English-speaking supervision, tuition
and other children to play with could
be a problem.

Neustift 990m

HOW IT RATES

The skiing
Snow	*****
Extent	**
Advanced	**
Intermediates	***
Beginners	**
Convenience	*
Queues	***
Restaurants	**

The rest
Scenery	***
Resort charm	****
Not skiing	***

SKI FACTS

Altitude	1000m-3210m
Lifts	36
Pistes	65km
Green/Blue	65%
Red	31%
Black	4%
Artificial snow	None

PACKAGES

Alpine Tours, Crystal, Inghams, Made to Measure, Ski Valkyrie

TOURIST OFFICE

Postcode A-6167
Tel 00 43 (5226)
2228
Fax 2529

Neustift earns its prominent place here for a curious reason – the quality of the glacier skiing 20km away at the top of the Stubai valley. It has its own little ski area where unadventurous intermediates can potter happily about – but so have dozens of other little Tyrolean villages that we have relegated to a footnote at the back of the book. However, the Stubaigletscher is one of the best skiing glaciers in Austria, and that means one of the best in the world.

THE RESORT

Neustift is a very attractive, traditional Tyrolean village about half-way along the Stubai valley, south-west of Innsbruck. It is the closest large community to the glacier, but not the only village in the valley with ski-resort status. Down the valley towards Innsbruck, Fulpmes has a more extensive local ski area, and plenty of accommodation both in Fulpmes itself and in the satellite village of Telfes. Mieders, still further down the valley, has some skiing too. The Stubai valley lift pass covers all these resorts and the glacier lifts, as well as the ski-bus.

THE SKIING

Neustift's local **ski area** is a narrow chain of slopes and lifts – mainly drags – from Elferhütte at 2080m down to the village. With the exception of one short blue run at altitude, the skiing is all graded red. This main area is on the south-east side of the valley; there is also a nursery area at village level, on the other side.

The Stubai glacier is a much more extensive area of blue and red runs (and one short black) between 3200m and the first station of the main access lifts, at 2300m. The glacier is broken up by rocky peaks, giving more sense of variety in the skiing than is normal on a glacier. But the landscape is harsh and unattractive, with lots of moraine. The bus service to the glacier is sadly inadequate – intervals are at least 30 minutes and can be much longer, and there is insufficient capacity.

On the glacier **snow reliability** is not a problem. The local slopes face roughly north, but are of typically modest Austrian altitude. The sunny village nursery slopes are unreliable.

The local skiing does not have much to offer **advanced skiers**, and the glacier is not in the same league as Hintertux for challenge, but there are long runs to be done, including a 4km ski route down the east side of the glacier, and a splendid 10km ski route down a deserted bowl back to Mutterberg in the valley at 1750m.

For **intermediate skiers**, the local skiing rather falls between two stools:

it is not easy, but it is not extensive – so its main appeal is to the confident intermediate who wants to practise technique rather than get around. The glacier is splendid intermediate territory, whatever your standard.

This is not a resort for **beginners**; the village nursery slopes are attractive, but too sunny – though they do have snowmakers.

There are 100km of **cross-country** trails in the Stubaital, including some trails at altitude reached by the lifts serving the Fulpmes and Mieders Alpine skiing. Mieders is the best base. There are trails on the glacier.

There can be serious **queues** for the access lifts to the glacier – worst, of course, when snow conditions lower down are poor.

The **mountain restaurants** in both sectors are no more than adequate – a mixture of primitive mountaineering huts and big impersonal cafeterias. There are great views to be had outside the tiny cabin at the top of the glacier, at Jochdohle.

There are **ski schools** both in Neustift itself and at the glacier. Guided ski tours are available. **Children** can be looked after all day.

STAYING THERE

If you fly into Innsbruck, you can be in the resort an hour after landing. There are lots of 4-star and 3-star **hotels**. The 3-star Tirolerhof is excellent – comfortable and relaxed, with good food. It has its own ski school and ski hire shop. The central 4-star Sonnhof and, on the way out of town to the glacier, the Fernau are also recommended.

Most of the **restaurants** are hotel-based. There is some **après-ski** activity, focused on the Romanstuben and the Hully Gully.

Neustift has quite a lot to offer **non-skiers**. There is skating, swimming, tennis, squash and bowling. The Stubaital looks like heaven for toboggan enthusiasts; all the villages have impressive runs – at Neustift, for example, there is an 8km run from the top of the main chair-lift. Innsbruck is only minutes away by bus.

Niederau 830m

HOW IT RATES

The skiing

Snow	*
Extent	*
Advanced	*
Intermediates	**
Beginners	****
Convenience	***
Queues	****
Restaurants	**

The rest

Scenery	***
Resort charm	***
Not skiing	**

SKI FACTS

Altitude	830m-1900m
Lifts	37
Pistes	42km
Green/Blue	65%
Red	30%
Black	5%
Artificial snow	none

PACKAGES

Alpine Tours, First Choice Ski, Inghams, Lagrange, Neilson, PGL Ski Europe, Thomson

Auffach Alpine Tours, PGL Ski Europe

Mühltal Alpine Tours, Winterski

Oberau First Choice Ski, Inghams, PGL Ski Europe, Thomson

TOURIST OFFICE

Postcode A-6311
Tel oo 43 (5339) 8255
Fax 2433

An attractive, though spread out, resort with a small, quite varied ski area, that has a strong British following. Good for families and beginners, so long as there is decent snow. Sadly, this is far from guaranteed.

THE RESORT

Niederau is a popular example of what Austria does so well: the unspoilt, hassle-free, family ski village. It's more convenient than Waidring and Fieberbrunn, cheaper and prettier than Obergurgl, and less commercialised than Westendorf. It has a lovely setting in a pretty valley and is made up of pleasant chalet-style buildings – even if it does lack village atmosphere.

A cluster of restaurants and shops opposite the Markbachjoch gondola is the nearest thing to a focal point, but few hotels are more than five minutes' walk from one or other of the two main lifts up into the skiing. The roads are quiet, except on Saturdays.

The resort is geared towards families looking for a friendly, unsophisticated but civilised atmosphere. Niederau has strong British connections, with a faithful following returning each year.

The Wildschonau lift pass covers the higher ski area of Auffach, a bus-ride away in the next valley, and the nursery slopes in and around the pretty village of Oberau on the col between the two.

THE SKIING

The small local **ski area** is spread over a broad, wooded mountainside which does not rise above 1600m. Mountain access is via a chair or new 8-person gondola – these are just a few minutes' walk apart, in central Niederau. The Markbachjoch gondola gives immediate access to a novices' plateau at 1500m and the area's steepest runs, back to the village. Easier runs to Niederau open up from the plateau. The other chair doesn't go so high, but is surmounted by a steep drag to the high-point of Lanerköpfl (1600m). A choice of red runs descend to the village.

A reliable half-hourly bus (free) goes to Auffach. Its sunny ski area is narrower, but taller (up to 1900m, with a vertical of 1000m). The main lift is a two-stage gondola. There are few **queues** in either area.

Snow reliability is a problem, made worse by a lack of snowmaking. When it is impossible to ski back to Niederau, its ski area is tiny. Because of its mid-station, Auffach is not as badly affected in such circumstances.

The few black runs don't have much appeal, and **advanced skiers** should go elsewhere.

Good **intermediates** may find the ungroomed gully black runs awkward rather than interesting and the whole ski area much too small to keep them interested for more than a day or two. Leisurely skiers have some interesting runs to enjoy; the long main Auffach piste is the highlight.

Niederau is suitable for **beginners** and moderate intermediates, but has surprisingly little for those in-between. Excellent nursery slopes lie at the foot and top of the mountain, but the low ones lose the sun each afternoon.

The 35km of **cross-country** trails along the valley are good when snow is abundant, and there is a new 6km trail on top of Markbachjoch.

Mountain restaurants are scarce but good, causing lunch-time queues. Many return to the village for lunch.

The **ski school** has a good reputation but classes can be large (we have one report of 17 in a class).

The ski kindergarten and non-ski nursery take **children** from age three.

STAYING THERE

The Austria, very near the centre, is reported as comfortable but shabby and near church bells which chimed 90 times at 6am. Vicky and Schneeberger are well-placed 3-stars. Staffler is a lively, central 2-star. Pensions Bergwett and Lindner are basic, good-value B&Bs. Haus Jochum has spacious and comfortable **self-catering** accommodation positioned close to the Tennladen drag.

Hotels Alpenland and Wastlhof have reputations for good-value restaurants if you're **eating out**.

Niederau has a nice balance of **après-ski**, neither too noisy for families nor too quiet for the young and lively. Hotel Staffler's Cave Bar is the liveliest place in town, except when instructors take clients into the Sport Café for a yodel. A number of places have live music: hotel Vicky, the Sonnbergstuberl, the Starchenhof and the Alm pub.

For **non-skiers**, walks are limited and there is little to do except swimming and excursions to Salzburg, Innsbruck, Vienna and Rattenburg.

Obergurgl 1930m

HOW IT RATES

The skiing

Snow	*****
Extent	**
Advanced	**
Intermediates	***
Beginners	****
Convenience	****
Queues	*****
Restaurants	**

The rest

Scenery	***
Resort charm	****
Not skiing	**

✔ One of the most reliable resorts for snow in the Alps, especially good for a late-season holiday

✔ Excellent ski area for beginners, unadventurous intermediates and families

✔ Normally queue- and crowd-free

✔ Retains village charm despite modern development

✔ Jolly tea-time après-ski

✘ Small ski area with no difficult runs

✘ Very bleak setting, with little skiing possible in bad weather

✘ Few off-slope amenities except in hotels

✘ Quiet nightlife by Austrian standards

✘ Expensive

Cruising down the Festkogl on a sunny Sunday morning, with seemingly the whole piste to yourself, sending up plumes of powdery snow, Obergurgl can seem idyllic. Few places can rival it for trouble-free, snowsure skiing. When you add high-quality hotels, a civilised atmosphere and very jolly tea-time après-ski, Obergurgl becomes the perfect resort for a certain type of skier. This is borne out by the remarkably high proportion of Obergurgl regulars who have been going there annually for years. It's best to book early to avoid disappointment.

But the Obergurgl-Hochgurgl ski area is not for everyone. Our postbag confirms this. Reporters either love it or hate it. There's no other resort where views are so sharply divided.

So what's the downside? The ski area is small and almost entirely easy. It also lacks variety, making the skiing feel even more limited. Keen piste-bashers will have explored it all in a day or two. Its slopes are high, treeless and can be cold and bleak in early season and poor weather. The village itself is made up primarily of hotels, with little in the way of shops or a vibrant nightlife. Those expecting something even remotely akin to other high Austrian resorts such as Ischgl or Lech will be sadly disappointed.

ORIENTATION

Obergurgl lies in a remote, bleak spot at the head of the Ötztal beyond Sölden. A gondola from near the entrance to the village gives access to all the local skiing and a chair-lift from above the village centre to part of it.

The Hochgurgl ski area is a bus-ride away, usually reached by chair-lift from Untergurgl. There's some accommodation at Hochgurgl.

Sölden (short bus or car journey) and **Kuhtai**, a worthwhile high ski area near Innsbruck, (long car journey) are the main ski excursion possibilities. Much closer is the tiny ski-touring launch-pad of **Vent**.

 ## The resort

Obergurgl is based on a traditional old village, set in a remote spot, the dead end of a long road up past Sölden. It is the highest parish in Austria and is usually under a blanket of snow from November until May. The surrounding mountains are bleak, with an array of avalanche barriers giving them a forbidding appearance.

Once they have arrived, most people don't use their cars. Obergurgl has no through-traffic and few day visitors, so the village is usually traffic-free.

Despite its fairly small size, Obergurgl is a village of parts. At the entrance to the resort is a cluster of hotels near the main gondola. The road then passes a second group of hotels around the ice rink, up the hillside to the left, before coming to the village proper. This starts with an attractive little square, with church, fountain, and the original village hotel (the Edelweiss und Gurgl).

Village atmosphere is jolly during the day and immediately after skiing,

but can be subdued at night when most people stay in their hotels. The resort is popular with British families and well-heeled groups of adults looking for a relaxing winter break.

Hochgurgl, a bus-ride away, is little more than a handful of hotels at the foot of its own ski area.

 ## The skiing

For a well-known and popular resort, Obergurgl's ski area is surprisingly small and lacking in interest and challenge to any who think of themselves as adventurous intermediates or better. You also don't get a sense of travelling anywhere on skis, as you do in most resorts. That's because you just ski up and down north-west facing slopes, without travelling from area to area or down into a valley and up the other side. There are, however, some good off-piste runs to explore with a guide.

The lift pass is very expensive for the amount of skiing and number of lifts. We've had several complaints about

SKI FACTS

Altitude 1800m-3080m
Lifts	22
Pistes	110km
Green/Blue	32%
Red	50%
Black	18%
Artificial snow	1km

LIFT PASSES

95/96 prices in
schillings
Obergurgl ski pass
Covers all lifts in
Obergurgl, Untergurgl
and Hochgurgl, and
local ski-bus.
Beginners Lift pass or
points card.
Main pass
1-day pass 420
6-day pass 2090
(low season 1840 –
12% off)
Senior citizens
Over 60: 6-day pass
1280 (39% off)
Children
Under 15: 6-day pass
1280 (39% off)
Under 5: free pass
Short-term passes
Half-day (from 11am,
noon or 2pm).

poor piste-marking and maintenance
making life very tricky at times. One
worrying story told how 'One of our
party went over the unmarked edge of
the piste in poor visibility and broke
her leg.' Another reported 'large stones
6" high and 12" wide not marked.'

THE SKI AREA
Fragmented cruising
The ski pass covers the two separate
ski areas of Obergurgl and Hochgurgl.
Adventurous skiers may prefer to leave
their last day free for an excursion to
Sölden – which unfortunately has no
pass-sharing arrangements with
Obergurgl.
   The **Obergurgl** ski area is the
smaller of the two. It is in two
sections, well linked by piste in one
direction, more loosely in the other.
   The Festkogl gondola from near the
village entrance takes you to the
highest skiing area, served by two
drags and two chairs, one of which
reaches 3035m. From these runs you
can ski back to the gondola base or
over to the Gaisberg area, which has a
high point of 2670m reached by a
long, slow chair-lift. There are four
other short lifts here as well as the
chair-lift up to the area from just
above the village square.
   You can ski along by this access lift
back to town and pole your way over
to the Festkogl gondola to start the
circuit again. Improving the Gaisberg-
Festkogl connection would improve
the skiing considerably.
   The regular and reliable free ski-bus
service takes you to Untergurgl, a few
minutes away. From there a chair-lift
takes you to **Hochgurgl** (also
reachable by car and the occasional
bus – two or three times a day).
Another chair-lift takes you from
Hochgurgl to the heart of the skiing,
which is served by four drags. Two
alternative chair-lifts up from here
take you to spectacular views of the
Italian Dolomites and to the 3080m
Wurmkogl summit. A single tree-

lined run leads down from Hochgurgl
to the bottom of the Untergurgl chair
and the bus home.
   Despite the small size of the ski area
we've had several complaints about
the piste map being difficult to follow.

SNOW RELIABILITY
Excellent
Obergurgl is arguably the most
snowsure of Europe's non-glacier
resorts. It has a justifiably popular
mid-December white week and regular
late-season visitors who book well in
advance. The skiing is high, and there
is virtually no tree-lined skiing. Wind
and white-outs can shut the lifts and,
especially in early season, severe cold
can curtail skiers' enthusiasm.

FOR ADVANCED SKIERS
Not generally recommendable
There is a fair amount of enjoyable
off-piste skiing to be found with a
guide – especially from the Obergurgl
ski area – and the top ski school
groups often go off-piste when there is
little avalanche danger. This is a well-
known area for ski-touring .
   The most challenging official piste is
the Hohe Mut mogul field beneath the
slow, old chair-lift at Gaisberg. But
this is often irritatingly awkward
rather than pleasurable, being icy,
worn and difficult to follow in places.

SKI SCHOOL

95/96 prices in
schillings

Obergurgl
Classes 6 days.
4hr: 10am-noon and
2pm-4pm.
6 full days: 1520
Children's classes
Ages: from 5
6 full days including
lunch: 2620
Private lessons
Half- and full day.
1400 (for half-day, for
1 to 2 people)

Hochgurgl
Classes 5 days.
4hr: 10am-noon and
2pm-4pm.
5 full days: 1490
Children's classes
Ages: from 5
5 full days: 1490
Private lessons
Half- and full day.
1350 (for half-day, for
1 to 2 people)

The other blacks are rather overgraded and there's little challenge for good skiers. Advanced skiers will soon tire of cruising the predominantly short runs, no matter how powdery the snow. Excursions by local bus to Sölden are possible.

FOR INTERMEDIATE SKIERS
Good but limited
The ski areas have some perfect intermediate terrain, made even better by the normally flattering snow conditions. The problem is there's not much of it. Keen piste-bashers will quickly tire of skiing the same runs all the time and be itching to catch the bus to Sölden, down the valley.

Hochgurgl has the bigger area of easy runs. These make good cruising. For more challenging intermediate runs head over to the Vorderer Wurmkogellift, on the right hand side as you look at the mountain.

The run down from Hochgurgl to the bus at Untergurgl is about the only tree-lined skiing in the area, and the only run served by artificial snow. Less confident intermediates can find this tricky but necessary unless they want to wait for an infrequent Hochgurgl bus or take an expensive taxi home.

The Obergurgl area has more red than blue runs but most offer no great challenge. The area served by chairs at the top of the Festkogl gondola is easy cruising. And there is a long enjoyable run down the gondola, with a scenic off-piste route in the adjoining valley.

In the Gaisberg area, there are very easy runs in front of the Nederhütte and back towards town. The bottom drags here serve very short but sometimes tricky and bumpy runs.

FOR BEGINNERS
Good for first-timers or improvers
There is an adequate nursery slope above the village, and the Gaisberg run under the chair out of town can be completed as soon as a modicum of control is achieved.

Near beginners can ski from the top of the four-person Wurmkogel chair to Hochgurgl village (600m vertical) without any problems. The quality of the snow at Obergurgl makes the area a good (but expensive) choice for beginners compared with most lower Austrian resorts.

CROSS-COUNTRY
Limited but snowsure
Four small loops: two at Obergurgl, one at Untergurgl and another at Hochgurgl give a mere 13km of trail. They are, however, relatively snowsure and all pleasantly situated, the lower ones run alongside the river. Instruction is available.

QUEUES
No problems
Lift queues are rare – even at Christmas and New Year. The resort is too remote to attract day trippers, and its authorities do not encourage 'bussing-in' when lower villages are struggling for snow.

MOUNTAIN RESTAURANTS
Little choice
Compared with most Austrian resorts, mountain huts are not very numerous and not very special. The Nederhütte at Gaisberg is one of the jolliest, often with live music. David's at the bottom of the lowest drags is friendly, cheerful and good value. The Schönwieshütte,

a 10-minute walk from the piste above here, is in a beautiful setting – as is the tiny hut at the top of the Hohe Mut chair. At Hochgurgl, the tiny hut at Wurmkogel has stunning views into Italy and basic food. Many skiers return to Obergurgl and Hochgurgl for lunch. Hotels Edelweiss and Jenewein in Obergurgl are particularly convenient, if expensive. Café Josl is a cheaper alternative. In Hochgurgl, hotel Riml has excellent reasonably priced food.

SKI SCHOOL
Good and bad
This year we've had good reports of the Obergurgl ski school, with reasonable class sizes of eight to ten and good English spoken: 'excellent tuition and organisation' and '10 out of 10 for the ski school'. But we've also had disgruntled customers: 'I had to enlist the help of an Inghams rep to escape from a class of unfit, overweight, overhung geriatrics.' No reports of the Hochgurgl ski school this year – though last year we heard of large classes and lack of interest and English among the instructors.

FACILITIES FOR CHILDREN
Check out your hotel
For a village with obvious appeal to families, Obergurgl doesn't seem to put itself out to cater for children. There is no ski kindergarten catering for tots who want to start early, and no special arrangements for lunchtime care of young children attending classes. The key factor would appear to be hotel facilities; many offer childcare of one sort or another, and the Alpina is particularly recommended. One reporter complained that adult and children's classes were arranged for different times and places, which meant dropping-off and meeting their kids was often difficult.

⬆ Staying there

The Festkogl gondola area at the village entrance is the best place for getting into the skiing and for ease of access by car. However, it's a long walk or a ski-bus from the village centre and the nursery slopes.

Accommodation around the ice rink is perched above the village, with very steep, sometimes treacherous walks to and from other amenities. It's a very short ski to the chair-lift and a pole or ski to the Festkogl gondola.

Many of Obergurgl's mainly middle-aged clientele much prefer the convenience of staying in the village centre, being close to the Gaisberg lift and well placed for the ski-bus. Ski-drivers have underground parking bang in the centre of town.

HOW TO GO
Plenty of good hotels
Virtually all package accommodation is in hotels and pensions, but there are a number of comfortable apartments available to independent travellers. Demand for rooms in Obergurgl exceeds supply, and for once it is true that you should book early to avoid disappointment. Inghams have by far the largest allocation, including much-sought-after self-catering accommodation.
Hotels Obergurgl's accommodation is of high quality: most of its 30 hotels are of 4-star rating, and none is less than 3-star. Within each rating, hotels are uniformly comfortable. In our fat file of reports we have hardly any complaints. The main ones come from couples staying in the Deutschmann who had to share tables and 'awful breakfasts' at the Haus Konigstall.
££££ Edelweiss und Gurgl
The focal hotel – biggest, oldest, among the most appealing; on the central square. Pool.
££££ Alpina Big, smart chalet with excellent children's facilities – kindergarten and playroom. Pool.
££££ Jenewein Recently refurbished, friendly staff, excellent food; good central position next to main lift.
££££ Gamper Best rooms very comfortable, good food; at far end of village, past the square.
££££ Crystal If you don't mind the ocean-liner appearance, one of the best hotels in Festkogl lift area.
£££ Fender Good all-rounder with friendly staff; central
£££ Wiesental Comfortable, well positioned, good value.
£££ Granat-Schlössl Amusing pseudo-castle, surprisingly affordable.
££ Alpenblume Good B&B hotel well-placed for Festkogl lift.
££ Haus Gurgl B&B near Festkogl lift; friendly, pizzeria, same owners as Edelweiss und Gurgl.
Hochgurgl has equally good hotels.
£££££ Hochgurgl The most luxurious in the area – the only 5-star. Pool.
£££ Laurin Well equipped, traditional rooms, excellent food.
Self-catering Inghams have an allocation in Lohmann, a high-standard large modern apartment block. It is well placed for the skiing, less so for the village centre below.

CHILDCARE
The ski schools at Obergurgl and Hochgurgl take children over the age of 5, but do not offer any special care arrangements.

The village kindergarten (305) takes children from the age of 2.

The Alpina and Austria hotels (among others) have in-house kindergartens.

PACKAGES
Crystal, First Choice Ski, Inghams, Made to Measure, Thomson
Hochgurgl Inghams

GETTING THERE
Air Innsbruck, transfer 2hr. Salzburg, transfer 3hr. Munich, transfer 4hr.

Rail Train to Ötz; regular buses from station, transfer 1½hr.

ACTIVITIES

Indoor Swimming pool (at Hotel Muhle, open to the public), saunas, whirlpools, steam baths, massage, bowling, pool and billiards, squash, table tennis, shooting range
Outdoor Natural skating rink (open in the evenings), curling, sleigh rides

TOURIST OFFICE

Postcode A-6456
Tel 00 43 (5256) 466
Fax 353

Bookable independently, the 3-star Pirchhütte Garni has apartments close to the Festkogl gondola, while the Wiesental hotel has more central ones.

EATING OUT
Wide choice, limited range
Hotel dining rooms and à la carte restaurants dominate. The commendable Pic Nic is the only independent restaurant, and hotel Madeleine has a good separate pizzeria. Hotel Alpina has a particularly good reputation for its food, while the restaurant at the Gasthof Gamper is pleasantly cosy.

APRES-SKI
Lively early, quiet later
Obergurgl is reasonably animated immediately after skiing, but things are pretty quiet later on. The Nederhütte mountain restaurant has a lively tea dance three times a week, and the Umbrella Bar outside the Edelweiss hotel is popular when the weather is good.

Later on, the crowded Krumpn's Stadl barn is the liveliest place in town with live music on alternate nights – it has also been recommended for its fondues. The Josl, Jenewein and Edelweiss hotels have atmospheric bars. Discos are uninspiring, but hotel Alpenland's bowling alley is popular.

Hochgurgl is very quiet at night except for Toni's Almhütte bar in the Olymp Sporthotel – one of three places in the resort which have live music. Hotel Hochfirst has a disco but it's difficult to believe much atmosphere is generated.

FOR NON-SKIERS
Very limited
There isn't much during the day. Innsbruck is over two hours by post-bus. Sölden (20 minutes away) has a leisure centre and shopping facilities. You can walk to the restaurants in the Gaisberg area to meet skiers for lunch. The Hochfirst hotel has a good health centre; be aware that it's mixed-sex and no clothes are allowed.

STAYING IN HOCHGURGL
Very quiet
The usual advantages of staying part way up a mountain are ski convenience, good snow and no queues. Obergurgl itself scores well in these, but Hochgurgl does have some good hotels, including the most luxurious in the area (the hotel Hochgurgl). It is even quieter than Obergurgl – great if you're looking for a quiet comfortable time with the easy skiing right on your doorstep.

Obertauern 1740m

Because of its excellent snow record, Obertauern is often chosen by skiers who are worried about conditions in lower Austrian resorts and don't mind the lack of tradition, charm and limited skiing. It has a small intermediate circuit, plenty of beginners' slopes and some challenges for better skiers. But it can get very crowded when snow in lower resorts is poor.

THE RESORT

In the land of postcard resorts grown out of rustic villages, Obertauern is something of an oddity – a mainly modern development at the summit of the Tauern pass road. Built in (high-rise) chalet-style, it's not unattractive – but it is strung out. There is no real central focus of shops and bars.

THE SKIING

The Tauern pass road divides the **ski area** into two unequal parts, well-linked to make a user-friendly well-signed circuit that can be skied clockwise or anti-clockwise. However, reporters complained about the piste map and poor piste maintenance.

Most of the pistes are on the sunny slopes north of the resort: a wide, many-faceted basin of mostly gentle skiing, with a few steepish mogulled pitches punctuated by long schusses. The vertical range is rather limited and runs are short. Skiers used to big areas will soon feel they have seen it all.

The slopes on the other side of the road have Obertauern's highest and most difficult skiing. Even here, though, the top station is less than 600m above the resort. You can ski the circuit in a couple of hours.

The resort exploits the exceptional **snowfall** record of its high bowl. In the unlikely event of a shortage, there is plenty of snowmaking lower down.

Advanced skiers would naturally incline towards the Zehnerkar and Gamsleiten sectors to the south-west. There are some genuinely steep pisted and off-piste runs from the Gamsleiten chair, but it is prone to closure by wind and avalanche danger. For a greater challenge and longer descents you can join guided ski tours to peaks above the top lifts.

For **intermediates** the biggest draw is Obertauern's circuit. Stay lower for easier pistes, or try some of the tougher runs higher up. The central point of the north area is Hochalm, from where the Seekareck and Panorama chairs take you to challenging, often mogully runs for better intermediates. The chair to Hundskogel leads to a red and a black. And over at the Plattenkar quad there are two splendid reds.

Obertauern has very good nursery slopes, with three drag-lifts for **beginners** close to the village. After the first couple of lessons it's possible to go up the mountain, because the Schaidberg chair leads to a drag-lift serving a high-altitude beginners' slope and it is an easy run back home.

There is a 15km **cross-country** loop in the heart of the resort.

When neighbouring resorts don't share Obertauern's good snow, non-residents arrive by the bus-load. The lift system is erratic and, on the circuit, high-speed quads may be followed by slow two-person chairs – so some big **queues** can build up. The runs served by high-speed quads can get crowded too.

The **mountain restaurants** are plentiful and good, but crowded. The Kringsalm is recommended.

Of the several **ski schools,** most tour operators use the Krallinger – and its kindergarten. We have enthusiastic reports of both, despite classes as large as 15. But one regular visitor rates the Willi Grillitsch school 'much the best'.

STAYING THERE

Practically all **accommodation** is in hotels (mostly 3-star and 4-star) and guest-houses. Location is not a major consideration. The 4-star Enzian is welcoming and comfortable, with good food and an outstanding wine cellar. The Edelweiss, Petersbuhel and Alpina are also recommended.

Eating out is mostly in hotels (the Enzian is recommended) and the busy après-ski bars at the foot of the north-side slopes. The Hochalm restaurant at the top of the quad chair sometimes serves early-evening meals.

Après-ski is lively and varied. The Latschnstub'n has an outside terrace, music and dancing and is the best immediate après-ski place. Later the atmospheric Lutzeralm has farmyard-style decor and a disco. The Taverne complex has various bars and includes a pizzeria and disco – it's good for mixed age groups and has special evenings including erotica and karaoke.

Non-skiers won't find much here beyond an impressive sports centre (with tennis). Salzburg is an easy trip.

Saalbach-Hinterglemm 1000m

HOW IT RATES

The skiing

Snow	***
Extent	****
Advanced	**
Intermediates	*****
Beginners	***
Convenience	****
Queues	***
Restaurants	****

The rest

Scenery	***
Resort charm	****
Not skiing	**

✔ Large, well-linked, intermediate ski circuit with a good mix of open and tree-lined runs

✔ Little walking to the lifts from central accommodation

✔ Saalbach is a big but pleasant, affluent and lively village

✔ Both villages are now traffic-free in the centre

✔ Atmospheric mountain restaurants throughout the ski area

✔ Sunny skiing

✔ Large snowmaking installation and excellent piste maintenance

✔ Lively nightlife, especially in Saalbach

✘ Large number of low, south-facing slopes that suffer from the sun

✘ Not much difficult skiing

✘ Nursery slopes in Saalbach are not ideal – sunny, and busy in parts

✘ Saalbach has now spread along the valley and some accommodation is far from central

✘ Expensive by Austrian standards – especially Saalbach

✘ Can get rowdy at night in Saalbach

ORIENTATION

Saalbach and Hinterglemm, their centres 4km apart, have spread along a narrow dead-end valley floor to the point where they almost merge, and a few years ago they adopted a single identity. The ski area spreads across north- and south-facing mountainsides, with lifts and runs connecting the villages via both. **Leogang** is a quiet village in the next valley to the north, its long, north-facing ski area forming a spur from the main area.

Right at the eastern periphery of the Tirol, the resort is rather isolated from the rest of the province; but several resorts in Salzburg province are reachable by road – **Badhofgastein, Kaprun** and **Zell am See,** the last a short bus-ride away.

Traditional Austrian ski villages are charming by day and lively by night, but have a reputation for small ski areas, long walks or bus-rides to lifts (followed by queues), too many of the dreaded T-bars, and poor snow-cover, thanks to their low altitude. Saalbach-Hinterglemm answers all such criticisms.

Its ski circus is large by all but the highest French standards, much of the accommodation has something approaching ski-to-the-door convenience, the lifts are modern and, although it is quite busy, the ski area is free of any serious bottlenecks. There are snow-cover problems, particularly on the sunny side of the valley late in the season, but Saalbach's impressive snowmaking operation and its snow-pocket location provide conditions that are much better than the Tyrolean norm.

It has some very lively nightlife but, as in most resorts popular with Scandinavians, can get rowdy when people get drunk.

 The resort

Saalbach is one of the most attractive ski villages in Austria. Wedged into a narrow valley, with skiable slopes coming right down to the village centre, its traditional-style buildings are huddled together around a classic onion-domed church.

Purists will point out that the old look is false, with practically all the buildings being modern reproductions – the main exceptions are the Post inn and the church. But the result is a close approximation to Austrian charm with French ski convenience.

Saalbach is quite upmarket. It has a number of large, expensive hotels, and few cheap and cheerful pensions. The attractive main street is lined with hotels, restaurants and ski shops, is festooned with fairy lights and comes complete with gigantic snowman. Thanks to the face-lift the resort got in readiness for the 1991 World Championships held here, the village

centre is now traffic-free; there is a completely pedestrianised zone and another area with car access only allowed for reaching hotels. A tunnel and underground car park hide the four-wheeled beasts. The valley road bypasses the village.

Hinterglemm is a more scattered and less appealing collection of hotels and holiday homes. It has a small, pleasantly traffic-free, zone in the centre. It offers a cheaper, though by no means inexpensive, alternative to Saalbach, and has far better access to the north-facing slopes.

Despite the generally high prices of Saalbach in particular, it has a youthful, not over-sophisticated atmosphere. It attracts a cosmopolitan, brash clientele, particularly from Germany and Scandinavia. When we were there last season there were drunken Swedes staggering around in their ski boots at 7.30pm, and stripping off their shoes and socks to jump into the ice cold stream at midnight.

SKI FACTS

Altitude	930m-2095m
Lifts	60
Pistes	200km
Green/Blue	54%
Red	37%
Black	18%
Artificial snow	17km

LIFT PASSES

95/96 prices in
schillings
**Saalbach-
Hinterglemm-Leogang**
Covers all the lifts in
Saalbach,
Hinterglemm and
Leogang, and the ski
bus.
Main pass
1-day pass 390
6-day pass 1895
(low season 1510 –
20% off)
Senior citizens
Over 65 male, 60
female: 6-day pass
1095 (40% off)
Children
Under 15: 6-day pass
1095 (40% off)
Under 4: free pass
Short-term passes
Day pass refundable
by the hour; day pass
price reduced hourly
from 11am; single and
return tickets on main
lifts.
Notes 6-day pass for
6-10 yrs 830. Special
rates for children over
Christmas (15% off
pass price) and Easter
(free passes for
accompanied
children).

 # The skiing

The ski area is a 'circus' of almost
exclusively intermediate skiing, much
of it on lightly-wooded slopes. Few
runs are likely either to bore the
aggressive intermediate or to worry
the timid one. And there are sufficient
open sections and changes of pitch
and direction to give pistes variety.
There is some genuinely black piste
skiing, but not much of it.

THE SKI AREA
User-friendly circuit
The complete circuit of the valley can
be skied only in an anti-clockwise
direction, there being no lift from
Vorderglemm, at the eastern
extremity, up to the north-facing
slopes. But a truncated clockwise
circuit can be undertaken, crossing to
the south side of the valley at Saalbach
itself. The valley floor is very narrow,
so there is very little walking necessary
when changing hillsides. Where you
end up at the end of the day is not
important because of the excellent bus
service which runs every 20 minutes.

The south-facing slopes have a good
deal of skiing above 1400m, albeit on
rather short runs. Five sectors can be
identified – from west to east,
**Hochalm, Reiterkogel,
Bernkogel, Kohlmaiskopf** and
Wildenkarkogel. The last connects
via Schönleitenhütte to the Leogang
skiing – a small, open area at altitude,
which leads to a long, narrow north-
facing slope down towards the village,
broadening towards the bottom. An
eight-person gondola brings you most
of the way back.

The connections across Saalbach-
Hinterglemm's south-facing slopes
work well: when traversing the whole
hillside you need to ski down to the
valley floor only once, whichever
direction you are going in. This occurs
at Saalbach itself, where a very short
walk across the main street is
necessary to get from the Bernkogel
piste to the Kohlmaiskopf lift and vice
versa. Both these runs are well
endowed with snowmakers to ensure
the link normally remains skiable, and
there is a choice of lifts going up –
chair-lifts, plus a multi-cabin cable-car
to Kohlmaiskopf .

The north-facing slopes are different
in character – two more distinct
mountains, with long runs from both
to the valley. Access from Saalbach is
by a solitary, queue-prone cable-car to
Schattberg. The high, open, sunny
slopes behind the peak are served by a

new quad chair opened last season.

From Schattberg, long runs go down
to the village, to Vorderglemm and to
Hinterglemm. From here, lifts go up
not only to Schattberg but also to the
other north-facing mountain,
Zwölferkogel, which is served by a
two-stage eight-person gondola. Drags
serve open slopes on the sunny side of
the peak, and a little-used gondola
provides a link from the south-facing
Hochalm area.

SNOW RELIABILITY
Better than most of the Tyrol
The excellent condition of Saalbach's
slopes when hosting the 1991 World
Championships, at a time when
nearby Kitzbühel was really struggling
after two weeks of sun, testified to the
importance of Saalbach's array of
snowmakers. These cover several lower
runs on both sides of the valley.

The resort also claims 'snow pocket'
status. And excellent piste
maintenance helps to keep the slopes
in the best possible condition. But an
altitude range of 900m to 2100m is
only a slight advance on Kitzbühel
and, with 60 per cent of the runs
facing south, Saalbach inevitably
suffers when the sun comes out.

FOR ADVANCED SKIERS
Little steep stuff
There is little testing skiing. Off-piste
guides are available, but snow
conditions and forest tend to limit the
potential. The long (4km) run beneath
the length of the Schattberg cable-car
is the only truly black run, but even
this is far from really challenging.

Worthwhile runs are the 5km
Schattberg West-Hinterglemm red
(and its scenic ski route variation), and
the Zwölferkogel-Hochalm link. Now
that it is served by two gondolas,
Zwölferkogel is where better skiers are
likely to spend most of their time.

FOR INTERMEDIATE SKIERS
Paradise
This area is ideal for both the great
British piste-basher, eager to clock up
the miles, and the more leisurely skier.
The south-facing pistes have mainly
been cut through the pine forest at an
angle, allowing plenty of movement
across the ski area on easy runs.

For those looking for more
challenging skiing, the most direct
routes down from Hochalm,
Reiterkogel, Kohlmaiskopf and
Hochwartalm are good fun. All the
south-facing slopes are uniformly
pleasant and, as a result, skiers tend to
be fairly evenly distributed over them.

SKI SCHOOL

95/96 prices in schillings

Hannes Fürstauer
Courses start Sun or Mon
Classes 6 days.
4hr: 10am–noon and 1pm–3pm.
6 full days: 1500
Children's classes
Ages: from 5
6 full days: 1500
Private lessons
Hourly and daily.
500 for 1hr, for
1 to 2 people. Each additional person 100
Lift priority No

Wolfgang Zink
Courses start Sun or Mon
Classes 6 days.
4hr: 10am–noon and 1pm–3pm.
6 full days: 1500
Children's classes
Ages: from 6
6 full days: 1500
Private lessons
Hourly and daily.
500 for 1hr, for
1 to 2 people. Each additional person 100
Lift priority No

Willi Fritzenwallner
Classes 6 days.
4hr per day.
6 full days: 1500
Children's classes
Ages: from 6
6 full days: 1500
Private lessons
Hourly.
500 (for 1hr, for
1 to 2 people. Each additional person 100
Lift priority No

Hinterholzer
6 days 4hr per day
6 full days 1500

Mitterlengau-Hinterglemm
6 days 4hr daily
6 full days 1500

Hinterglemm-Thomas Wolf
6 days 4hr per day
6 full days 1500

OTHER SCHOOL
Schönleiten
Hengenhauser

Only the delightful blue from Bernkogel to Saalbach gets really crowded at times. The alternative long ski route is very pleasant, taking you through forest and meadows.

The north-facing area has some more challenging runs, and a section of relatively high, open skiing around Zwölferkogel which often has good snow. None of the black runs is beyond a competent intermediate, while the long pretty cruise from Limbergalm to Vorderglemm gets you away from lifts for most of the time and is particularly quiet and pleasant first thing in the morning.

FOR BEGINNERS
Best for improvers
Saalbach's two nursery slopes are very well positioned for convenience, right next to the village centre. But they are both south-facing, and the upper one gets a lot of intermediate traffic taking a short-cut between the Kohlmaiskopf and Bernkogel areas. The lower one is very small, but the lift is free.

Alternatives are trips to the short, easy runs at Bernkogel and Schattberg. There is also a little slope at the foot of the Schattberg but the ski school seem loath to use it – so it's great for pottering about on your own at lunchtime. It's rather sunless and a little steeper than the other nursery areas but perfectly useable.

Hinterglemm's spacious nursery area is separate from the main ski area. Being north-facing, it is much more reliable for snow later on in the season, but it consequently misses out on the sun in midwinter.

There are lots of easy blue runs to move on to, in all sectors of the area.

FOR CROSS-COUNTRY
Go to Zell am See
Trails run beside the road along the valley floor from Saalbach to Vorderglemm and between Hinterglemm and the valley end at Lindlingalm. In midwinter these trails get very little sun, and they are in any case not very exciting. The countryside beyond nearby Zell am See offers more scope.

QUEUES
Busy, but only one long delay
The Schattberg cable-car is an obvious problem, with half-hour waits routinely encountered in the morning peak period. Otherwise, much depends on snow conditions. When all runs are in good shape there are few problems, other than small morning peak queues to leave

Saalbach. When snow conditions are poor, the Bernkogel chair and the following drag get very busy, as do any lifts servicing the better snow.

Saalbach-Hinterglemm does not get as overrun at weekends as other Tyrolean resorts – it's less accessible for the Munich hordes than the Grossraum area and its neighbours.

MOUNTAIN RESTAURANTS
Excellent quality and quantity
The south-facing slopes are liberally scattered with attractive little huts that serve good food. And they do not simply rely on good weather; many have pleasant rustic interiors where an animated atmosphere is generated, sometimes with the assistance of music. (There is a tax on establishments that provide music, and this is passed on to the customer through higher prices.)

The Panorama on the Kohlmaiskopf slope and the Turneralm close to Bründelkopf serve particularly good food. The little Bernkogelalm hut, overlooking Saalbach, has a great atmosphere. The large hut above the main Saalbach nursery slope gets packed at 4pm, when ski-booted customers dance to disco music.

On the north-facing slopes there are relatively few places. The Gipfelhütte at Schattberg West is adequate. We had great Tiroler Rösti, served in the pan, at the place between the chair-lifts on the way down. Ellmaualm, at the bottom of the Zwölferkogel's upper slopes, is a quiet sunny retreat with good food but suspect loos.

SKI SCHOOL
An excess of choice
We're all in favour of competition between ski schools but visitors to Saalbach-Hinterglemm may feel that they are faced with rather too much of this good thing. Two or three schools offers a choice; eight or nine begins to look like a recipe for confusion. It certainly makes life difficult for the editors of resort guides: the few reports we have are all on different schools, half of them not clearly identified. But we have a half-hearted endorsement of Wolfgang Zink (aka Ski Pro) and a whole-hearted one for private lessons with Mitterlengau-Hinterglemm.

FACILITIES FOR CHILDREN
Hinterglemm tries harder
Saalbach doesn't go out of its way to sell itself to families, although it does have a ski kindergarten. Hinterglemm, perhaps seeing itself as more of a family resort, has some good hotel-

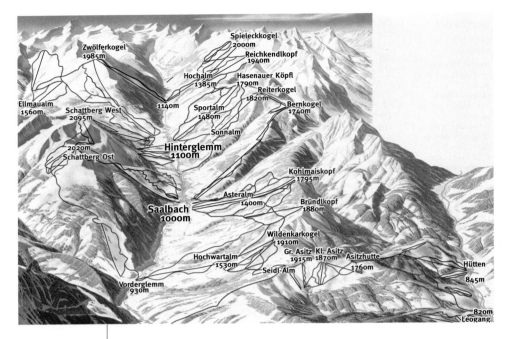

CHILDCARE

Some of the ski schools take children from age 4 or 5 and can provide lunchtime care – there are special ski areas in both villages.

Several hotels have nurseries, and some in HInterglemm are open to non-residents, including the Egger, Glemmtalerhof, Lengauerhof and Theresia. The Glemmtalerhof is part of a group of 'Partner-hotels' which operate a shared nursery.

PACKAGES

Airtours, Austrian Holidays, Club Europe, Crystal, First Choice Ski, Inghams, Kings Ski Club, Made to Measure, Mogul Ski, Neilson, PGL Ski Europe, PGL Teen Ski, Rank STS, Ski Club of GB, Ski Leogang, Ski Partners, SkiBound, Sloping Off, Thomson

Leogang Mogul Ski, Ski Leogang

based nursery facilities – the one at the Theresia is reportedly excellent. Hotels in both resorts are identified in the resort literature as 'child-friendly' if they conform to a long list of requirements ranging from electric socket covers in bedrooms to provision of ice-skates.

 Staying there

The walk to lifts from Saalbach's central hotels is minimal. Unfortunately Saalbach has seen a fair amount of expansion in recent years, and many of the cheaper hotels used by British tour operators tend to be situated in the least convenient part of the village, along the road towards Hinterglemm. In Hinterglemm itself, position isn't so important. Most of the accommodation is near a lift.

HOW TO GO

Cheerful doesn't mean cheap

Chalets Crystal has the only catered chalets that we are aware of in the main resorts – in central Hinterglemm. It offers a relatively cheap alternative to the mostly expensive hotels.
Hotels There are a large number of hotels in Saalbach, mainly 3-star and above. Most of the more expensive ones have excellent positions in the village centre, whereas the cheapest places tend to be less conveniently placed along the road to Hinterglemm – or in Hinterglemm itself, which is

rather less ritzy than Saalbach. Be aware that some central hotels are affected by disco-noise
Saalbach
££££ Alpenhotel Luxurious, with a wealth of facilities, including an open-fire lounge, disco, pub and small pool.
££££ Berger's Sporthotel Liveliest of the top hotels, with a popular daily tea dance, good bar and disco. Good pool.
££££ Kendler Position second to none, right next to the Bernkogel chair.
££££ Saalbacher Hof Retains a friendly feel despite its large size.
£££ Haider Best-positioned of the 3-stars, right next to the main lifts.
£££ König Slightly cheaper 3-star, particularly well placed for ski school and nursery slopes.
Hinterglemm
££££ Theresia Hinterglemm's top hotel, and one of the best-equipped for families. Out towards Saalbach, but nursery slopes nearby. Pool.
£££ Wolf Small but well-equipped 4-star in the the nursery-sharing scheme. 'Especially good' food, excellent position. Pool.
££ Pension Austria Half-way between the villages, and so good value by local standards for those who don't mind catching a bus every morning.
££ Pension Spatz Good value, friendly welcome, good position near centre of village.
Self-catering There's an enormous choice of apartments for independent travellers.

GETTING THERE

Air Salzburg, transfer 2hr. Munich, transfer 3½hr.

Rail Zell am See; hourly buses from station, transfer ½hr.

ACTIVITIES

Indoor Swimming pools, sauna, massage, solarium, bowling, billiards, tennis, squash (Hinterglemm)
Outdoor Floodlit tobogganing, sleigh rides, skating, ice hockey, curling, 35km of cleared paths

TOURIST OFFICE

Postcode A-5753
Tel 00 43 (6541) 7272
Fax 7900

EATING OUT
Wide choice of hotel restaurants

Saalbach-Hinterglemm is essentially a half-board resort, with relatively few non-hotel restaurants. Peter's restaurant, at the top of Saalbach's main street, is atmospheric and serves excellent meat dishes cooked on hot stones. The Wallner Pizzeria on the main street is good value. The Auwirt hotel on the outskirts of Saalbach has an à la carte restaurant that is better than the hotel's 3-star status would suggest. The simple Hochleiten hotel in Hinterglemm also has a surprisingly good restaurant. Otherwise general hotel standards and style are reflected in their restaurants.

APRES-SKI
Excellent but expensive

Après-ski is very lively, pretty much from immediately after skiing until the early hours, perhaps quietening down a bit at dinner time while most people are tucking-in back at their hotels.

In Saalbach the tiny Zum Turn (next door to the church and cemetery) is an atmospheric former medieval jail – skiers arrive at 4pm and many are still there in ski boots at 11pm. The Pub on the main road out of town is packed with young Brits and snowboarders enjoying the karaoke. The Neuhaus Taverne has live music and no admission charge. Kings Disco livens up after midnight. The Panther Bar has jungle decor, discreet music and well-heeled clientele. Zum Herrn'Karl, Hellis and Bergers are other popular places.

In Hinterglemm, there are a number of ice bars, including the Schirm in the centre of town, which are busy straight after skiing. Later on, the Londoner is the biggest attraction – live and disco music, smart, friendly, with a plastic card you collect on the way in and buy your drinks on. Bla Bla is small, modern and smart, with reasonable prices. The Alm Bar has good music and some dancing.

Tour operators reps organise events such as tobogganing, sleigh-rides and bowling.

FOR NON-SKIERS
Surprisingly little to do

Saalbach is not a very entertaining place for non-skiers. There are few shops other than supermarkets and skiing equipment places, and meeting skiers for lunch isn't going to be easy unless you can persuade them to descend to one of the resorts. Walks tend to be restricted to the paths alongside the cold cross-country trails or along the Saalbach toboggan run to Spielberghs. But there are excursions by bus and train (or car) to Kitzbühel and Salzburg.

Leogang 800m

Leogang is an attractive, although rather scattered farming community-cum-mountain resort. The lack of any central focus has repercussions for skiers: many of the hotels are a long way from the main lifts, and the bus service is disappointingly infrequent.

Leogang is, however, a much less expensive alternative to Saalbach-Hinterglemm. It is also far quieter, smaller and less commercialised than its neighbours. Situated on the St Johann-Bischofshofen road, and having a mainline railway station, Leogang is also better placed for independent travel access and for taking day excursions.

The link with Saalbach is fairly reliable: the gondola towards Asitz is followed by a couple of short pistes and lifts, with all the skiing above a lofty 1590m. These pistes are red, but not difficult. Less experienced intermediates can amuse themselves on the blue slopes served by the first stage of the gondola, or on the separate little ski area closer to the village centre.

Beginners have good nursery slopes, conveniently placed just above the village. If snow is poor, the higher slopes are not too steep, though icy conditions can be a problem for novices.

Leogang is the best of the local villages for cross-country. There are 25km of trails, with a connection to Saalfelden, plus a panoramic high-altitude trail which links through to other resorts. Given good snow, trails are kept in fine condition.

The Leogang Altenberger ski school has a high reputation – good attitude and a surprising number of English-speaking instructors. But we've had a bad report of the smaller Schischule Diesenberger, complaining of mixed abilities and languages in the same class, with no English spoken. There is a non-ski crèche, and ski school starts at 4 years old.

Ski Leogang runs a catered chalet in a converted farmhouse in Hütten, a tiny hamlet west of Leogang, which is better positioned for the skiing and the gondola than the main village.

There are convenient hotels in each price category. The luxury Krallerhof has its own nursery lift which can be used to ski across to the main lift station. The 4-star Salzburgerhof, and much simpler Gasthof Asiztstuberl, are the best-placed hotels, within a two-minute walk of the gondola. Gasthof Stockinggut is a fine 3-star, within reasonable walking distance of the main lift, and also has a good free minibus service to the slopes, driven by the hotel's 'nothing is too much trouble' manager. The informal Rupertus is better placed, right next to the gondola, and closer to the village.

Restaurants are hotel-based. The Krallerhof has the excellent food you would expect. The much cheaper Gasthof Hüttwirt has a high reputation for wholesome Austrian home cooking.

The rustic old farming chalet Kralleralm is very much the focal tea-time and evening rendezvous. Its atmosphere seems to please everyone, which is just as well, there being very little else available. The Stockinggut does, however, have an entertainment programme including a cow-milking competition!

Excursions to the pleasant nearby town of Saalfelden and the lovely city of Salzburg are the main attractions for non-skiers. Other facilities include swimming and tennis.

St Anton 1305m

✔ Extensive ski area with good skiing for adventurous intermediate and advanced skiers

✔ Heavy snowfalls, backed up by snowmakers, generally give good snow-cover despite sunny slopes

✔ Much improved lift system has greatly reduced queuing problems

✔ Easy rail access, direct from Britain

✔ The liveliest, most varied après-ski around (but see minus points)

✔ Despite resort expansion, village retains distinct Tyrolean charm

✗ Skiing doesn't suit beginners or timid intermediates

✗ Pistes can get crowded

✗ Long walks or bus-rides to lifts from much accommodation

✗ All the tough skiing is off-piste

✗ Surprisingly little to amuse non-skiers

✗ Nightlife can get rowdy, with noisy drunks in the early hours

St Anton has, along with Wengen and Mürren, a strong British tradition. From the 1920s, successive generations learned to ski here, adopting the distinctive 'feet together' style of the famous Arlberg ski school. Sir Arnold Lunn helped start the Kandahar race here in 1928. The resort has remained popular with good British skiers.

It has also become one of the world's Meccas for ski bums. That's a reflection of the wonderful, tough skiing available in the bowls below the Valluga – the best that Austria has to offer. These are now all off-piste. In good snow conditions they are superb. Sadly, conditions are often less than perfect except just after a fall, because of their south-facing aspect. But if you are lucky with the snow you'll have the time of your life.

There's a lot to offer adventurous intermediate skiers too. As well as the generally challenging St Anton pistes, there is all the skiing of Lech and Zürs to explore, a short bus-ride away.

The ski bum ethos extends to the large number of late-night discos and bars. The resort is an ideal choice for the hard-drinking, disco-loving, keen skier who can stand the pace of getting to bed late and being up for the first lift. But it's not for those who like a quiet life and gentle, uncrowded pistes.

ORIENTATION

St Anton is at the foot of the road up to the Arlberg pass, at the eastern end of a ski area that spreads across to **St Christoph** and above the pass to Rauz and **Stuben**. A cable-car from the centre of town goes up towards the famous Valluga skiing.

On the other side of the main road, a gondola goes up to the Rendl ski area.

Regular buses go to **Zürs** and **Lech**, which share another extensive ski region covered by the Arlberg lift pass.

Serfaus, Nauders, Ischgl and **Sölden** are feasible outings.

The resort

St Anton is a long, sprawling mixture of traditional and modern buildings crammed into a narrow valley, between a busy road and mainline railway. In terms of sheer size, you might call St Anton a town, but it lacks a 'lived in' feeling, being essentially just a very overgrown village full of tourism-related facilities.

It is an attractively bustling place, full of life, colour and noise, and positively teeming with a lively young international ski clientele, eager to sample the skiing and après-skiing

Although it is crowded and commercialised, St Anton is full of character, and its traffic-free main street retains Alpine charm and traditional-style buildings.

Most of the resort's ski slopes and lifts start immediately beyond the railway tracks.

⤒ The skiing

St Anton vies with Val-d'Isère for the title of 'resort with most undergraded slopes'. There are plenty of red pistes which would be black in many other resorts, and plenty of blues which would be red. Strangely, there are no black pistes. There are very popular black runs marked on the piste map but they are all given off-piste status. Some are classified as 'high-touring routes' – this means they are not marked, not groomed, not patrolled and not protected from avalanche danger. There are also some 'ski routes'. These have some markers, are groomed occasionally in part, but are not patrolled and are protected from avalanches only in 'the immediate vicinity of the markers'.

The piste map says that high-touring routes require 'extensive mountain experience and expert guidance' and

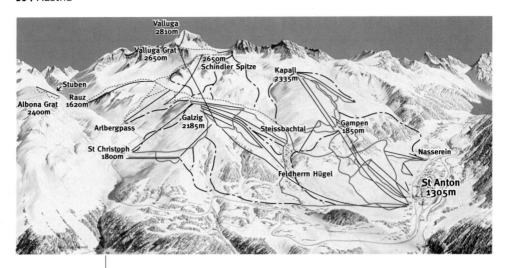

SKI FACTS

Altitude 1305m-2650m
Lifts   86
Pistes   260km
Green/Blue   30%
Red   40%
Black*   30%
Artificial snow   18km
* includes ski routes
– see text

ski routes are recommended only for people with 'good Alpine experience or with a ski instructor'. And yet between them these grades of run cover much of the best skiing for good skiers. And they are commonly skied by holiday skiers without the services of an instructor or guide – many people who visit St Anton couldn't afford one.

This has caused much confusion; one life-long St Anton fan has written to us to say, 'I started to ski as a five-year-old in St Anton in 1962 and skied there every year until 1981. Since then I have been back on four occasions. The resort has gone overboard on not marking what used to be black runs on the piste map. And now the indicators at the top and bottom stations do not show whether these runs are open or closed (or even that they exist). There are some beautiful runs, but they are steep, south-facing and prone to avalanches. It is outrageous that there is now no indication of whether I should ski them or not.'

We understand the resort is reviewing its piste grading system during the 1995-96 skiing season and may well convert some existing reds to blacks and blues to reds. Let's hope it will also do something more to help people decide whether off-piste routes are safe to ski.

THE SKI AREA
Large linked area

St Anton's ski area is made up of several sectors, all except one of which are linked, on a predominantly south-facing mountain.

Starting on the east, you have the choice of a four-person chair or ancient funicular up to **Gampen**.

From there pistes lead back to St Anton and Nasserein, or in the opposite direction across to the links with the Valluga-Galzig ski area. Or you can go up higher to **Kapall** and ski down unmarked routes – ending up at the same places.

A four-person chair is the quickest link to **Galzig**. This brings you out just above the mid-station of the cable-car up from St Anton. From here you can ski in most directions, including back to town, down to St Christoph (from where there's a new high-speed quad back up) or back to Feldherrn Hügel. The blue pistes down from here are some of the most crowded we've come across at peak periods.

You can get up to St Anton's most famous skiing, the bowls below the **Valluga**, from Galzig in one of two ways. For the second stage of the cable-car, you can take a ticket which allocates you a place on a specific cable-car (the first available) and ski around locally until it's time for your ride. Or you can ski to the Schindlergrat three-person chair, which delivers you to the same height (2650m) but on a different peak. There's a tiny third stage of the Valluga cable-car which takes you up to 2810m, but this is mainly for sightseeing. The only way to ski from there is off the back, off-piste to Zürs. You are not allowed to take skis up the lift without a guide.

From both the second-stage of the cable-car and the Schindlergrat chair, you can ski down a long, beautiful ski route to Rauz, the western end of St Anton's own skiing.

From Rauz you can ski across the road and along to Stuben, where a

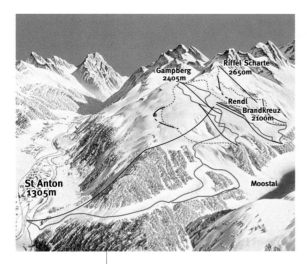

Gampberg
2405m

Riffel Scharte
2650m

Rendl

Brandkreuz
2100m

St Anton
1305m

Moostal

falls of snow. They often have much
better conditions than other ski areas
of a similar height. But many of the
slopes face south- or south-east,
causing icy or heavy conditions at
times, particularly late in the season. It
can be vital to time your runs off the
Valluga to get decent conditions.

The lower runs are now well
equipped with artificial snowmaking,
which ensures the home runs remain
open (but not necessarily enjoyable) as
long as it's cold enough at night to
make snow.

FOR ADVANCED SKIERS
One of the world's great areas
St Anton vies with Chamonix, Val-
d'Isère and a handful of others for the
affections of good skiers. It has one of
the most consistently challenging
large ski areas in the world.

The jewel in its crown is the variety
of off-piste possibilities in the bowls
accessed by the Valluga cable-car and
Schindlergrat chair. You can see tracks
going all over the mountain. No way
(except the red run) is easy. Some
descents look terrifying. In good snow
this whole area is delightful for good
skiers. There are two main high-
touring routes down – both giving
little respite during the long, steep,
often mogulled descents. The
Schindlerkar gully is the first you
come to, and the steeper. For the
wider, somewhat easier Mattun run,
you traverse over further at the top.
Both these feed down into the
Steissbachtal gully where there are lifts
back up to Galzig. The Schweinströge

LIFT PASSES
95/96 prices in
schillings
Arlberg Ski Pass
Covers all St Anton,
St Christoph, Lech,
Zürs and Stuben lifts,
but not linking buses.
Beginners Limited
pass covering
beginners' lifts.
Main pass
1-day pass 455
6-day pass 2190
(low season 1970 –
10% off)
Senior citizens
Over 65 male, 60
female: 6-day pass
1750 (20% off)
Over 80: free pass
Children
Under 15: 6-day pass
1310 (40% off)
Under 6: 100
Short-term passes
Half-day from noon,
single and return
tickets on certain lifts,
also 'taster' passes
starting 3pm.
Notes Arlberg pass
also covers Klösterle
(10 lifts), 7km west of
Stuben. Arlberg
Special pass for 6
days or longer,
reduction of about
200, available for
guests staying in St
Anton area and for
children under 15.
'Snowman' card for
under 6s, and senior
citizens over 80, 100
for season. Discounts
during wedel, firn and
snow crystal weeks.

slow two-stage chair-lift takes you to
the predominantly north-facing
Albona ski area.

The final ski area, **Rendl,** is separate
and reached by gondola from just
outside town (there are buses from the
village, but if you don't happen to
encounter one about to leave it's
quicker to walk). Six lifts serve the
west-facing runs at the top here, with
a single north-facing piste returning to
the gondola bottom-station.

SNOW RELIABILITY
Very good except late season
If the weather is coming (as it often is)
from the west or north-west, the
Arlberg gets it first, and as a result St
Anton and its neighbours get heavy

SKI SCHOOL

95/96 prices in
schillings

Arlberg
Manager Richard
Walter
Classes 6 days
4hr: 2hr am and pm,
from 9.30
6 full days with guest
card: 1490
Children's classes
Ages: 5 to 14
6 full days with guest
card and including
lunch: 2305
Private lessons
Half- or full day
2100 for full day;
each additional
person 160)

St Anton
Manager Franz
Klimmer
Classes 6 days
4hr: 10am-noon and
1pm-3pm
6 full days with guest
card: 1350
Children's classes
Ages: 5 to 14
6 full days: 1270
Private lessons
Half- or full day
1900 for full day;
each additional
person 150)

starts off in the same direction as the
red ski route, but you traverse the
shoulder of the Schindler Spitze and
down a narrow gully.

Lower down the mountain, very
difficult trails lead off in almost every
direction from the Galzig summit.
Osthang is an extremely tough, long
mogul field that leads down to
Feldherrn Hügel. Not much less
challenging are trails down to
Steissbachtal, St Christoph and past
Maiensee towards the road. These
lower runs can be doubly tricky if the
snow has been hit by the sun.

The Kandahar men's downhill
course is a long run between Gampen
and town. There are countless
opportunities for off-piste skiing in the
Kapall-Gampen area, including the
beautiful Schöngraben unmarked
route to Nasserein.

The Rendl area across the road has
plenty of open space beneath the top
lifts and, with an accompanying
guide, there is some delightful skiing
off the back of this ridge.

The Albona mountain above Stuben
has north-facing slopes that hold good
powder and some wonderful, deserted
off-piste descents including beautifully
long runs to Langen (where you can
catch the train) and back to St Anton.

On top of all this, bear in mind that
many of the red runs on the piste map
are long and challenging too.

The ultimate challenge, though, is
perhaps to go with a guide off the
back of the third stage of the Valluga.
The initial pitch is very, very steep.
But once you have negotiated that,
the run down to Zürs is very beautiful
and usually deserted.

FOR INTERMEDIATE SKIERS
Some real challenges
St Anton is suited to good rather than
simply aggressive intermediates. They
will be able to try the Mattun run
from Vallugagrat for example (see
above). The red run from Vallugagrat
to Rauz is a very long, tiring, varied
run (over 1000m vertical), which is
ideal for good (and fit) intermediates.
Alternatively, you can turn off from
this part-way down and take the
Steissbachtal to the lifts back to
Galzig.

The Kapall-Gampen section is also
full of interest, with sporty bumps
among trees on the lower half. Skiing
from Kapall to town (over 1000m
vertical), keeping to the left of the
Kandahar funicular and ending up on
a piste called Fang, is a fun run.

Less adventurous intermediates will
find St Anton less to their taste. There

are few easy cruising pistes. The most
obvious are the blues from Galzig.
These are reasonably gentle but get
very crowded, particularly at peak
times when people ski them while
waiting their turn for the advance-
ticket Valluga cable-car. The blue to St
Christoph, served by drag-lifts, is
probably the best bet. The narrowish
blues betweeen Kapall and Gampen
can have some challenging bumps.

Intermediates looking for easy
cruising will find the best by taking
the bus to Lech.

Mixed intermediate abilities are best
suited to the Rendl area. A good
variety of trails suitable for good and
moderate skiers criss-cross, including a
lovely long tree-lined run (over 1000m
vertical from the top) back to the
valley gondola station. This is the best
run in the whole ski area when
visibility is poor, though it has some
quite awkward sections.

FOR BEGINNERS
A lousy choice
St Anton has neither decent nursery
slopes nor easy runs for beginners to
progress to. Experienced skiers who
are desperate to ski the Arlberg but
are taking novices on holiday would
be better off staying in Lech or Zürs
and taking the bus to Rauz when
they want to ski St Anton. Pettneu is a
similar option. However, the bus
service from there to St Anton is
disappointing.

FOR CROSS-COUNTRY
A suitable valley
There are a couple of uninspiring trails
near town in the valley, another at St
Jakob 3km away, and a pretty trail
through trees along the Verwalltal to
the foot of the Albona ski area. There
is also an insignificant little loop at St
Christoph. Snow conditions are
usually good, but St Anton is not
really a cross-country resort. Total
trails 40km.

QUEUES
Improved, but still a problem
Queues are not the problem they
once were. But the same can be said
of virtually all resorts, and relative to
other resorts St Anton is below
average. The ticketing system for the
Valluga cable-car is intelligent, but
throws pressure on other lifts in the
area. The worst delays however are for
the Schindlergrat chair – 20 minutes is
quite common in peak season.

St Christoph's tiny cable-car is being
replaced for this season by a high-
speed quad. This will make St

Christoph an even more attractive lunch venue as you'll be able to get back into the skiing more quickly.

Two T-bars to Galzig are also being replaced with a high-speed quad. Although this will cut down on the queues, the Galzig blue runs are likely to be even more crowded than before.

MOUNTAIN RESTAURANTS
Plenty of choice
Huts are generally quite good, though there is a distinct difference between the nice little table-service ones and the characterless cafeterias. Two of the best are just above town, the Sennhütte and Rodelhütte. The Rendl Beach and Kapall Grabli are others worth a visit. The Mooserwirt serves typical Austrian food, and the Krazy Kanguruh burgers, pizzas and snacks.

Unfortunately, St Anton's best known hut, the Ulmer, on the way to Rauz from Valluga, tends to disappoint due to unfriendly service and overcrowding.

Having lunch in St Christoph or Stuben is also a useful idea. The St Christoph choices include the Maiensee Stuben and the excellent but expensive Hospiz Alm, where you can sit in a slide which delivers you to the lavatories. Stuben's Gasthof Berghaus and Hotel Post are both good.

SKI SCHOOL
Great for advanced skiers
The new St Anton ski school has brought much-needed competition to the Arlberg ski school, which had slipped, from its previously high standards, during the 1980s. Nowadays both schools come up with the goods, with classes kept at a reasonable level (8 to 10). Few schools are as well geared-up for teaching advanced skiers.

Most reporters who have hired a guide to ski off the top of the Valluga have had a great day.

FACILITIES FOR CHILDREN
Getting better
St Anton might not seem an obvious resort to choose for family holidays, but there are no good reasons to avoid it if the skiing suits you, and the resort works increasingly hard to accommodate families' needs. The youth centre attached to the Arlberg ski school is excellent, and the special slopes both for tots (at the bottom) and bigger infants (up at Gampen) are well done. Reports on these facilities would be very welcome.

Last season, Mark Warner opened a welcome chalet-hotel with a crèche.

 # Staying there

The village itself is reasonably compact, but location is worth considering with a bit of care. Staying as close to the main ski-lifts as possible has obvious advantages, though noise in the streets may disturb light sleepers. Quite a bit of the accommodation 'in' St Anton is actually in the quieter suburb of Nasserein, a short bus-ride or 10- to 15-minute walk from the centre and the nightlife. It isn't too inconvenient for skiing when there is resort-level snow. A drag-lift and short ski takes you to the main lifts, and skiing home is possible from Gampen.

St Anton itself spreads up the hill to the west of the centre, towards the Arlberg pass. Places up here in and beyond Oberdorf can be up to 20 minutes' walk from the centre – but can be quite convenient for skiing, provided there is good snow-cover at resort level.

HOW TO GO
Austria's main chalet resort
St Anton has a very wide range of accommodation, from quality hotels to cheap and cheerful pensions and apartments. What sets it apart from other Austrian resorts for British skiers is the number of chalets. Practically all our reporters stayed in catered chalets.
Chalets Chalets are fairly expensive, though few are particularly luxurious and many are well away from the centre up the hill or at Nasserein.

There are chalets bang in the centre of things but these are apartment-based. Bladon Lines have a couple. They also have the comfortable Aitken and charming old hunting lodge Arlhof, both 5 minutes' walk up the hill. Ski Val's well furnished Baren is out at Nasserein, as are Ski Total's well liked modern chalets. Crystal have a selection of places, including a pleasant small chalet out near the Rendl cable-car – particularly good for those who want to be a little removed from the noisy nightlife, but just an easy walk from the main lifts and village centre. Mark Warner have some of the nicest chalets in St Anton, close to the slopes on the hill west of the centre; the piste is close, but it's a taxi for nightlife. And last year they reopened the central Rosanna as a chalet-hotel, with en-suite bathrooms throughout. Neilson have two chalets in Nasserein and one in St Jakob.
Hotels The market is somewhat polarised: there is one 5-star hotel, lots

CHILDCARE
The kindergarten at the Jugendcenter (2526) takes toilet-trained children aged 30 months to 14 years, from 9am to 4.30. Ski tuition with the Arlberg school in a special snow-garden is available for children aged 5 (exceptionally 4).

PACKAGES
Austrian Holidays, Bladon Lines, Chalet World, Chalets 'Unlimited', Crystal, First Choice Ski, Inghams, Made to Measure, Mark Warner, Neilson, PGL Ski Europe, Ski Equipe, Ski Les Alpes, Ski Total, Ski Val, Ski Valkyrie, Thomson
Pettneu Crystal
Stuben Chalets 'Unlimited', Ski Total

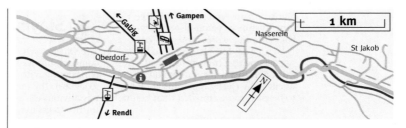

of 4-stars, rather fewer 3-stars (with and without restaurant); and then a great mass of cheaper B&B pensions spread around the valley.

£££££ St Antoner Hof Best in town, but its position on the by-pass is less than ideal except for curling (the rink is opposite) and motoring. Pool.

££££ Schwarzer Adler Centuries-old inn on main street. Widely varying bedrooms.

££££ Neue Post Comfortable if uninspiring 4-star at the centre of affairs, close to both lifts and nightlife.

££££ Grischuna Welcoming family-run place in peaceful position up the hill west of the town; close to the slopes, five minutes to the cable-car.

££££ Berghaus Maria Charmingly furnished, slightly further up the hill (hotel shuttle to lifts). Pool.

£££ Valluga About the cheapest of the 3 stars, but rather on the edge of things on the by-pass.

£££ Goldenes Kreuz A comfortable B&B hotel half-way to Nasserein, well positioned for skiing home.

Self-catering There are plenty of apartments available to independent travellers but package deals are few and far between.

STAYING DOWN THE VALLEY
Nice and quiet
Beyond Nasserein is the more complete village of St Jakob – reachable on skis, but dependent on the ski-bus in the mornings. The Brunnenhof is an attractive little hotel with a highly regarded rustic restaurant.

Pettneu is a quiet little village further down the valley, with its own ski area that is best for beginners. It's best suited to skiers with a car.

EATING OUT
Mostly informal
People ski hard and eat hard in St Anton. Plain, filling fare is the norm, with numerous places serving healthy portions of traditional Austrian home-cooking, American, Italian and fondue. Several reporters on a budget have commented on the excellent value of the Bahnhof restaurant – 'a

far cry from British Rail'. The fondue is particularly recommended. Dixies is the place for a lively meal in modern surroundings where American Western-style cuisine is enjoyed. The Reselehof is one of the best Tyrolean-style inns for Austrian cooking. The Fuhrmannstube has excellent value Austrian specialities and Amalienstüberl is good for both food and beer. The Trödlerstube is recommended for Tyrolean specialities.

APRES-SKI
Throbbing till late
Every form of informal fun is available from karaoke to late discos; from 'English' pub-style bars to brash 'drunken Scandinavian' joints. Sophisticates are less well provided for. The infamous Krazy Kangaru remains popular. But the Mooserwirt is even more so – live band, standing room only, dancing on the beams in ski boots. The Underground bar has a great atmosphere and live music, but gets terribly full. The Hazienda is equally lively and popular, and the Piccadilly pub is good for those who want a home from home. The Drop In disco throbs into the early hours. The rather inaptly named Chic Bar is the place for karoake. The Stanton is another popular place in the centre of town. If you want to concentrate on drinking rather than dancing, Pub 37 is a bit quieter. One reporter complained of 'very few single females' – a drawback of skiing such a self-consciously 'macho' resort.

FOR NON-SKIERS
Not very relaxing
St Anton is a sprawling town, not especially attractive outside the centre, and with surprisingly little to offer the non-skier. Many of the most attractive mountain restaurants are not readily accessible by lift for pedestrians. The centre is lively with a fair selection of shops. Getting by bus to the other Arlberg resorts is easy but buses tend to run only early morning and late afternoon, so make excursions a long day. Lech would arguably be a better,

GETTING THERE
Air Innsbruck, transfer 1½hr. Zurich, transfer 3hr.
Rail Mainline station in resort.

ACTIVITIES
Indoor Swimming pool (also hotel pools open to the public, with sauna and massage), tennis, squash, bowling, museum, cinema in Vallugasaal
Outdoor 15km of cleared walks, natural skating rink (skating, curling), sleigh rides, tobogganing, paragliding

TOURIST OFFICE
Postcode A-6580
Tel 00 43 (5446) 22690
Fax 2532

if pricier, base for a non-skier, though St Anton's mainline railway station does at least allow easy access to Innsbruck.

St Christoph 1780m

A small, exclusive collection of hotels, restaurants and bars right by the Arlberg Pass and with drag-lifts and a cable-car into the ski area. Good place for a nice lunch. Expensive and deadly quiet place to stay. The most expensive hotel of all – much the most expensive in this whole area – is the huge Arlberg-Hospiz.

Stuben 1410m

Stuben is an interesting alternative to St Anton, quite the opposite of the large, noisy resort. Dating back to the 13th century, it's a small unspoilt village where personal service and quiet friendliness are the order of the day. Modern developments are kept to a minimum. The only concessions to the new ski era are a few unobtrusive hotels, a ski school, two bars, a couple of banks and a few little shops. The old church and traditional buildings, usually snow-covered, make Stuben a really charming Alpine village. The north-facing local slopes retain snow well, though the queue-free village chair can be a cold ride. Lech and Zurs are nearby, accessed by infrequent but timetabled buses. Stuben has sunny nursery slopes separate from the main ski area, but lack of progression runs make it unsuitable for beginners. Evenings are quiet, but several places have a pleasant atmosphere. Willie's Stubli is the most animated rendezvous. Hotels Mondschein and Albona have bars with dance areas. The S'Murmele and Gasthof Berghaus bars are quieter. buses and taxis are extortionate). Most people stay here on half-board, but the Sport Café is a good-value pizza place for those in B&B. The charming old Post is a very comfortable 4-star renowned for its fine restaurant (available through Ski Total, who also run a catered chalet operation). Haus Erzberg is a good pension. Kolerhaus is a simple, inexpensive B&B. Stuben doesn't have much to offer non-skiers.

St Johann in Tirol 650m

✔ Most accommodation reasonably close to lifts

✔ Slopes liberally endowed with restaurants

✔ Plenty of non-skiing activities and things to do in the evening

✔ Well placed for visiting neighbouring ski resorts

✔ Highly regarded ski school

✔ Few Brits by Tyrol standards

✔ Good snow record for height

✘ Very small ski area, with little to interest good skiers

✘ Busy town makes it unsuitable for families with small children

✘ Weekend crowds from Germany

✘ Can be especially busy when nearby ski areas with less reliable snow are suffering

In some ways St Johann falls between two stools. Its ski area is small and predominantly easy. Yet it is a far from ideal choice for families and others who traditionally turn to the Tyrol for 'small and friendly' resorts – the town is too busy to suit them. But with no fewer than 18 mountain restaurants, fairly convenient ski lifts and plenty of off-slope facilities, St Johann is a fine choice for leisurely, part-time skiers who like to spend as much time pottering about having coffee and lunch as they do actually skiing.

St Johann also suits the most energetic of skiers who want to tour around visiting surrounding ski resorts and have plenty of evening entertainment awaiting their return.

ORIENTATION

St Johann is ten minutes by car or train from **Kitzbühel**. The main gondola accesses its whole mountain. Lifts also go up from the hamlet of **Eichenhof**, on one side of the ski area, and the separate little village of **Oberndorf**, on the other. Other resorts surround the place – **Fieberbrunn** and **Waidring** share an area lift pass with St Johann. **Kirchdorf** is also close. **Leogang** and **Zell am See** are within reach, as is **Kaprun**'s glacier.

SKI FACTS

Altitude	670m-1700m
Lifts	18
Pistes	60km
Green/Blue	41%
Red	47%
Black	12%
Artificial snow	7km

🏠 The resort

St Johann is a sizeable town with a life outside skiing. The compact centre is wedged between a railway track, main roads and converging rivers. It is fairly attractive, certainly atmospheric, and has retained some traditional character. The main street is full of old wooden chalet buildings housing hotels, restaurants, cafés and homely bars. The five-minute walk between centrally-placed hotels and the lift involves picking your way through town traffic and clambering over railway tracks.

St Johann has some growing and sprawling industrial and residential suburbs. Eichenhof to the east is convenient for the skiing (it has lifts starting there) but it is quite a trek along a busy road to the town centre.

🎿 The skiing

St Johann's small local skiing area is on the north-facing side of the Kitzbüheler Horn – the 'back' side of Kitzbühel's 'second' and smallest mountain. It would have been easy to link these two resorts' skiing, but up-market Kitzbühel appears to have no desire to mix with its poorer neighbour.

THE SKI AREA
Small and easy

The main access lift is a gondola which transports skiers to the top of the ski area at **Harschbichl** (1700m). From there, a choice of north-facing pistes lead back through the trees towards town.

Two chair-lifts and the mid-station of the gondola allow repeated skiing of the upper part of the mountain, and there are further chairs and drags on the lower part.

The top-station and one of the chairs also access a sunnier sector of west-facing pistes that lead down to a car park just above the hamlet of Oberndorf, served by another chair.

None of the skiing is particularly challenging and average intermediates could ski the whole area in a day.

SNOW RELIABILITY
Altitude problems

Lack of altitude is an obvious problem. But St Johann's skiing takes place on by far the snowier side of the Kitzbüheler Horn – its snow pocket location 'steals' some of Kitzbühel's snow. This, together with its largely north-facing slopes, means that St Johann often has better conditions than its famous neighbour (and the nearby Grossraum). Snowmakers also help when it is cold enough. They cover one piste from 1400m to town,

LIFT PASSES

95/96 prices schillings
St Johann lift pass
Covers all lifts and ski bus.
Beginners Points card, and half-day passes for nursery drags.
Main pass
1-day pass 330
6-day pass 1550
(low season 1420 – 8% off)
Children
Under 15: 6-day pass 795 (49% off)
Under 6: free pass
Short-term passes
Half-day (morning pass valid till 12.30, afternoon pass valid from 12.30), 'late sleeper' pass from 11am, 'try out' pass from 2pm.
Alternative periods
5 in 6 days and 11 in 13 days.
Alternative passes
Schneewinkl 6-day pass also covers Fieberbrunn, Steinplatte, Waidring and other small resorts (6 days 1650 for adults, 990 for children, 94/95 prices).

SKI SCHOOL

95/96 prices in schillings

St Johann
Manager Ulli Arpe
Classes 6 days
4hr: 10am-noon and 1.30-3.30
6 full days: 1280
Children's classes
Ages: from 4
6 full days including lunch: 1820
Private lessons
Hourly, half- or full day
450 for 1hr for 1 to 2 people; each additional person 110

Eichenhof
Classes 6 days
4hr: 10am-noon and 1.30-3.30
6 full days: 1360
Children's classes
Ages: from 4
6 full days including lunch: 1360
Private lessons
Hourly or full day
450 for 1hr for 1 to 2 people; each additional person 120

with both red off-shoots to the valley chair also endowed.

There are several nearby ski areas, such as Waidring's Steinplatte, that are also reasonably snowsure if St Johann is suffering. The glacier at Kaprun has guaranteed snow but gets very crowded when snow is scarce elsewhere. The Hintertux glacier and Obertauern are worth an hour's drive at such times.

FOR ADVANCED SKIERS
Totally unsuitable

There is nothing here to challenge a good skier. The long black run on the piste map is actually a moderate red – and it is often closed because it suffers the effects of the strong afternoon sun. Your best hope would be a solid week of snow, when you could practice your powder technique.

FOR INTERMEDIATE SKIERS
A small amount for all

The slopes are pleasantly varied, with something for everyone. Decent skiers have a fairly direct-running piste between Harschbichl and town (runs 1b and 2b), and the black mentioned above. There are some easier red runs, but the best of them (3a and 4b) are served by long drags. The Penzing piste (6a) is served by a more comfortable chair. Less adventurous skiers have plenty of options, with the long meandering run between the mid-station of the gondola and town completely covered by snowmakers.

FOR BEGINNERS
Good when snow is abundant

The main nursery slopes are excellent but have no snowmakers. The skiing served by the second stage of the chair out of town has much more reliable snow and is suitable for beginners who have a little dry slope experience. Near-beginners and fast learners have a fine easy run (2a) from the mid-station of the gondola back to the bottom.

CROSS-COUNTRY
Excellent valley trails

Given good snow St Johann is one of the best cross-country resorts in Austria. A wide variety of trails totalling 74km fan out from the cross-country centre just beyond the main road to Salzburg.

QUEUES
Good except when 'invaded'

Queues are relatively rare when St Johann is not hit by hordes from Germany and surrounding resorts.

At weekends, during 'Fasching' week (mid-February) and any time Kitzbühel is struggling for snow, the gondola can get long morning queues. The second stage of the Eichenhof drag is another bottleneck. But overcrowded pistes are a bigger worry at such times.

MOUNTAIN RESTAURANTS
Amazing array

With 18 restaurants spread over just 60km of piste, St Johann must have the densest array of huts of any sizeable ski area in Europe. Needless to say, most are pleasantly uncrowded and competitively priced. None is worthy of special mention, but many are very welcoming.

SKI SCHOOL
Good attitude

The St Johann and Eichenhof schools have a good reputation for English, tuition and friendliness, though large classes can be disappointing.

There's a specialist snowboard section, 'White Wave', which has its own half-pipe. (Three of the top performers in the world are based here.) There's a large cross-country set-up and off-piste guides are available.

FACILITIES FOR CHILDREN
Good resort and hotel amenities

St Johann is keen to attract families and provides first-class facilities for children. The village nursery, geared to the needs of workers rather than visitors, offers exceptionally long hours. We have no recent reports on how all this works in practice.

 # Staying there

Most accommodation is central, but hotels beyond the railway track close to the lifts are better placed for the skiing. There is plenty of parking in this area, ski school is on the doorstep, and traffic noise is negligible. The railway is not far away, but not a problem; St Johann isn't exactly Clapham Junction. Cross-country skiers would be better placed at the other side of town, their trails being beyond the main road and river.

HOW TO GO
Plenty of hotel packages

British tour operators concentrate on hotels plus a few pensions but there are numerous apartments available to independent travellers.

Chalets We are not aware of any British-operated chalet parties.

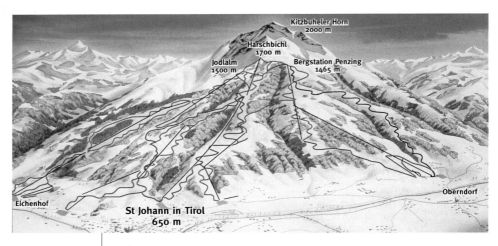

Kitzbuheler Horn 2000 m

Harschbichl 1700 m

Jodlalm 1500 m

Bergstation Penzing 1465 m

Eichenhof

Oberndorf

St Johann in Tirol 650 m

CHILDCARE

Both ski schools have special areas for children aged 4 or more to take lessons, and can provide lunch-time care. The St Johann school's kindergarten takes younger children from 9.30 to 4pm. It has a fairytale playground and a special Dwarfs' Express snowmobile lift.

The Eichenhof ski school cares for children under 4 years.

There's a free children's party at Café Rainer in the resort centre every Friday afternoon.

Hotels All the hotels are of 3-star or 4-star rating – about equally divided. Most of the best-placed hotels for skiing are 4-stars. Then there are dozens of B&B pensions.

££££ Brückenwirt Smartest in town, but wrong side for skiing.
£££ Fischer Central family-run 3-star, warmly recommended by a regular visitor.
£££ Goldener Löwe Vast, 200-bed 3-star in the centre of town. It has widely differing room standards, the simplest offering excellent value.
£££ Post House number one on the village plan: 13th century inn on the main street.
£££ Park Comfortable 4-star at the foot of the slopes.
£££ Sporthotel Austria Ditto, with more amenities including a pool.
£££ Sonne Cheaper, but comfortable place in the same area.
££ Moser Much smaller, cosier main-street hotel in the same price range as the Löwe's cheaper rooms.
££ Kaiserblick A modest B&B in a quiet spot, yet close to amenities.

Self-catering The Alpenblick (expensive), Gratterer (mid-range) and Helfereich (very cheap) are some of the best-situated apartments.

EATING OUT
Large range of options

There is a wide variety of restaurants, which stick mostly to good old-fashioned Austrian cooking. The Huber-Bräu is unusual in that it's a working brewery where you can taste the local beers before moving on to the surprisingly good food. The Bären, hotels Post and Park, plus the Rettenbachstuberl specialise in tasty Tyrolean dishes. Serving international cuisine in addition to Austrian fare, the Lemberg, Lowengrill and the Crystal and Fischer hotels have all been recommended by reporters. For a special meal, locals assure us the Ambiente is a fine establishment.

A couple of non-Austrian places recommended by locals are the Rialto for pizza, and the Hasianco for Mexican and pizza.

APRES-SKI
Plenty for all tastes

Ice bars and tea dancing greet you as the final run of the day is completed, and St Johann has plenty of evening animation without the rowdiness of some neighbouring Tyrolean resorts.

Café Max ice bar, at the bottom of the main piste, has friendly service, music and a large umbrella. Bunny's Pub is perhaps the most popular bar in town, with live music and occasional karaoke. De Klomp is rustic, popular with locals, friendly and a good place for a quiet drink. La Scala and Die Firma are disco bars. Café Rainer has live music. Platzl is a comfortable late night bar with excellent service. Pub Max is a teenage video bar.

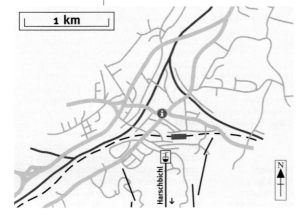

1 km

Harschbichl

N

GETTING THERE

Air Salzburg, transfer 1½hr. Munich, transfer 2hr. Innsbruck, transfer 2hr.

Rail Mainline station in resort.

PACKAGES

Club Europe, Crystal, PGL Ski Europe, Rank STS, Ski Choice, Ski Partners, SkiBound, Thomson

Kirchdorf Crystal, Snowcoach Club Cantabrica

Oberndorf Lagrange

Waidring Lagrange, Thomson

ACTIVITIES

Indoor Swimming, sauna, steam baths, solarium, 2 indoor tennis halls, fitness centre, massage, bowling

Outdoor Artificial skating rink, curling, sleigh rides, floodlit toboggan run, 40km cleared paths, ballooning, sightseeing flights

TOURIST OFFICE

Postcode A-6380
Tel 00 43 (5352) 62218
Fax 65200

Sleigh-ride, toboggan, Tyrolean and nine-pin skittles evenings are organised by tour reps.

The resort also has an entertainments programme, with something on most evenings. Some of the events you might see are: four o'clock snowboarding demonstrations followed by glühwein; floodlit ski-jumping or ski-acrobatics; after-skiing parties at the gondola base-station; and concerts at the festival hall.

FOR NON-SKIERS
A very good choice
There are plenty of things on offer, including an excellent public pool, indoor tennis, a new artificial ice-rink and 40km of cleared walks. There is also more worthwhile shopping in St Johann than is usual in a ski resort. Train excursions to Salzburg, Innsbruck, and to a lesser extent Kitzbühel, are interesting.

Waidring 780m
Anyone who wants to learn to ski in a traditional Tyrolean village, but baulks at the thought of long walks to lifts, poor snow and over-commercialised nightlife, should consider Waidring. This quiet, unspoilt, friendly place, complete with onion-domed church, has its nursery slopes right in the village, a stone's throw from most hotels, and has a good snow record for its height.

Most British visitors are couples or families on 'learn to ski' packages; it's not a place for action-seeking youngsters. Nightlife revolves around simple, organised fun – sleigh rides, bowling, tobogganing, Tyrolean folklore and a ski instructors' ball. The Keller Bar of hotel Post is good for a quiet drink, and Café Schneidermann has a civilised atmosphere.

The ski school employs English-speaking instructors from several countries who seem to go out of their way to make lessons enjoyable. Most of the week is spent on the nursery slopes before graduation to the main ski area, the Steinplatte (10 minutes away by bus). This is ideal for second-year skiers and nervous intermediates. The slopes are wonderfully uncrowded on weekdays, but Germans arrive en masse at weekends. However, the two newly-installed quad chairs ensure queueing is minimal even then, unless there's a shortage of snow in surrounding resorts. Mountain restaurants are pleasant. Try the Stellenalm on the piste back to the car park. Cafés Schneidermann and Weinstube are good for lunch in the

village. Buses run to St Johann and Fieberbrunn (both on the area lift pass) and to Ellmau and Kirchberg. Cross-country skiers have 30km of trails.

The Waidringerhof is a central 4-star hotel with all mod cons, including indoor pool, which has been praised by reporters for good food and friendliness. The good-value Tiroler Adler is virtually next to the nursery slopes. Gasthof Brücke is less well placed but popular for good food, value and friendliness. The ski kindergarten is open all day and accepts children from 3 years old (younger if they can ski morning and afternoon). There's no nursery but baby-sitting can be arranged.

Kirchdorf 640m
Kirchdorf is very similar to Waidring – quiet and traditional, with nursery slopes on the doorstep. It's five minutes by bus from St Johann, 20 from the Steinplatte. You can buy a weekly pass that includes a day in Kitzbühel. Kirchdorf also has a new day-care centre that accepts children as young as 3 months. Both this and the ski kindergarten are open all day. There's a specialist cross-country ski school and 80km of trails.

Après-ski is livelier than in Waidring, with several bars and a good disco at the Wintersteller. We have a rave review of the restaurant in Gasthof Zur Mauth. Other good places are the Zehenthof and Giovanni's. The 3-star Wintersteller is one of the best hotels. The Tasma is comfortable, with leisure facilities and a bar with open fire. Gasthof Oberhabachhof is simple but handy for the slopes. Gasthof Marienstetten is poorly positioned but has a children's playground.

Schladming 745m

✔ *The different mountains add up to a large amount of skiing by Austrian standards*

✔ *Charming town with a life independent of skiing and tourism*

✔ *Excellent nursery slopes*

✔ *Very short airport transfer*

✔ *Excellent snowmaking operation and superb piste maintenance*

✔ *Very sheltered slopes, among trees*

✔ *Close to snowsure Obertauern and Dachstein glacier*

✘ *Unconnected ski areas are individually small, and buses between them infrequent*

✘ *Nursery slopes (at Rohrmoos) are inconvenient unless you stay beside them – and beginners are expected to pay for a full lift pass*

✘ *Little difficult skiing*

✘ *The skiing lacks variety – one mountain is much like the others*

To link or not to link, that is the question. Schladming gets rave reviews from most of its customers, in most respects – not least for its uncommercialised, pretty town centre. One constant whinge concerns the as yet unconnected ski areas. But it may be this very inconvenience that keeps Schladming pleasantly unspoilt and uncrowded. If and when the projected linking lifts are put in place, Schladming will have a ski area to rival those of Kitzbühel and Söll in the Tyrol; but it may also come to suffer some of the same overcrowding and vulgarity.

Meanwhile, Schladming has another major plus-point. Its huge investment in snowmakers stands in stark contrast to the belated efforts of its Tyrolean competitors to give holiday skiers something other than grass, slush and ice.

ORIENTATION

Schladming sits at the eastern fringe of Austrian skiing (in Styria), in a broad valley running east-west. The main gondola into the Planai skiing starts close to the town centre; a drive out of town is the elevated suburb of Rohrmoos, where chair-lifts access the skiing on Hochwurzen. There are two further sizeable ski areas, reached from **Pichl** or **Gleiming** and from **Haus**.

The ski pass also covers a fifth area at Galsterbergalm, above **Pruggern**, and several other small ski areas at **Stoderzinken**, **Ramsau** and the **Dachstein** glacier. The glacier is a 45-minute bus-ride away, and has only a handful of runs, but the views are superb.

The Top Tauern area pass also covers resorts such as **St Johann im Pongau**, **Flachau** and snowsure **Obertauern**.

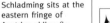 ## The resort

The old town of Schladming has developed both its skiing and mercantile interests without spoiling the charm of its attractive centre. A large woodyard, brewery and railway station are separated from town by a river, while the modern sports centre, tennis halls and Sporthotel, plus the lift stations, have also been consigned to the outskirts.

The main road also bypasses the town. The resort centre is compact, with most shops, restaurants and bars (and some of the most appealing hotels) gathered around the oblong pedestrian-only main square, which is prettily lit at night.

 ## The skiing

All four of the hills local to Schladming have been developed for skiing; most of it takes place on the wooded north-facing slopes that line the main valley, with some runs down into the side valleys at higher altitudes. The skiing throughout is as consistent in standard as it is in its nature: most runs are easy reds, ideal for the intermediate majority.

THE SKI AREA
Series of poorly connected sectors

Planai, Reiteralm and Hauser Kaibling are the main sectors; Hochwurzen has less skiing, but has the main valley-level nursery slopes at its foot – at Rohrmoos.

Planai is accessed by gondola from the east edge of town. There is a little east-facing open section at the top, but otherwise all runs are typically village-bound through forest. One run branches off towards Rohrmoos at the foot of the **Hochwurzen** sector, but you have to get a lift down (then up and through a tunnel) to complete the link. A two-stage chair rises above Rohrmoos and its nursery slopes, to a cable-car which accesses the upper slopes on the mountain proper.

Hauser Kaibling, a bus-ride away, is accessed by a gondola and a small cable-car from either side of Haus village. A small open section at the top has the only real off-piste in the whole area.

Rieteralm lies beyond Hochwurzen; it is accessed by a chair from Pichl, or the Gleiming gondola.

SKI FACTS

Altitude   745m-2015m
Lifts   78
Pistes   140km
Green/Blue   29%
Red   61%
Black   10%
Artificial snow   48km

LIFT PASSES

95/96 prices in
schillings
**Skiparadies
Dachstein-Tauern**
Covers all lifts in the
Dachstein/Tauern
region and ski bus.
Credit cards Yes
Main pass
1-day pass 365
6-day pass 1825
(low season 1695 –
7% off)
Children
Under 15: 6-day pass
915 (50% off)
Under 5: free pass
Short-term passes
Half-day from 11am,
noon and 1.30, 'trial'
ticket valid for 2½hr.
Alternative periods
1½- and 2½-day
passes.
Notes Discounts for
groups and senior
citizens on request.
Alternative passes
Day passes for
Ramsau/Dachstein
(excluding the
glacier),
Galsterbergalm and
Stoderzinken ski
areas only; Top-
Tauern Skicard covers
Dachstein/Tauern,
Obertauern, Lungau
and Sportwelt Amadè.

SKI SCHOOL

95/96 prices in
schillings

**WM Keinprecht
Schladming**
Classes 5 days
4hr: 2hr am and pm
5 full days: 1300
Children's classes
Ages: from 4
5 full days including
lunch: 1800
Private lessons
1hr, 2hr or 4hr
450 for 1hr; each
additional person 200

SNOW RELIABILITY
Excellent in cold weather
Schladming's impressive snowmaking
operation is a real boon when lack of
snowfall rather than high
temperatures is the problem.
Consequently, it is a particularly good
choice for early holidays; for late
holidays it doesn't have the required
altitude, but the northerly orientation
of the slopes and superb piste
maintenance help keep the slopes in
good shape longer here than in some
neighbouring resorts. The run to Pichl
is not fully covered by snowmakers,
but is the only valley run in the whole
area without full artificial snow cover
– an impressive achievement.

FOR ADVANCED SKIERS
Strictly intermediate stuff
Schladming's status as a World Cup
downhill venue doesn't mean macho
skiing. The skiing is almost exclusively
gentle, the steep finish to the men's
downhill course being an exception,
and the moderate mogul slopes at the
top of Planai being another. Hauser
Kaibling's off-piste skiing can be good,
but it's a rather limited area. Excellent
piste grooming and quiet slopes at off-
peak times allow fast skiing. The
women's World Cup run is
particularly pleasurable in this respect.

FOR INTERMEDIATE SKIERS
Generally flattering runs
The two World Cup pistes, and the red
that runs parallel to the Haus
downhill course, are ideal for fast
intermediates. The open sections at
the top of Planai and Hauser Kaibling
also have some challenging slopes.
Moderate skiers have the whole area at
their disposal. Many concentrate on
Planai, but Reiteralm has some of the
best runs. Hauser Kaibling is the best
mountain for timid skiers, with a
lovely meandering blue running from
top to bottom and a quiet, easy little
section with good snow at the
summit. Unfortunately, skiing this
involves a long walk back to the main
ski area. Runs are so well-bashed that
intermediates will find Schladming's
slopes generally flattering.

FOR BEGINNERS
Good, particularly for improvers
Complete beginners start on the
extensive, but inconvenient and low-
altitude Rohrmoos nursery area – and
they are expected to pay for a full lift
pass. Another novice area near the top
of Planai is more convenient for most
people, has better snow, and superior
ski school.

FOR CROSS-COUNTRY
Extensive network of trails
There is enormous scope, given
sufficient snow-cover, with 250km of
trails in the area. Schladming has
loops along the main valley floor,
beyond the furthermost reaches of
Alpine skiing, to Moosheim and
Mandling respectively. The Untertal
and Obertal valleys, between Planai
and Hochwurzen, have more trails.
Further afield there are more snowsure
trails at Stoderzinken, and the
Dachstein glacier has small loops with
spectacular views. The 1999 World
cross-country championships are
being held at Ramsau, a 20-minute
bus-ride from Schladming.

QUEUES
One or two bottlenecks
The Planai gondola can suffer 30-
minute delays on peak-season
mornings. The main Haus lift also
experiences short queues at such
times. However, there are few other
problems. Surprisingly, given its
proximity to less snowsure resorts,
Schladming does not suffer too badly
from invasions when conditions are
generally poor. Those in search of
snow tend to go higher.

MOUNTAIN RESTAURANTS
Plenty of nice places dotted around
There are attractive restaurants in all
sectors, though Planai probably has
the edge – Mitterhaus at the extremity
of the piste system is particularly
pleasant, Onkel Willy's is popular for
its live music, open fire, indoor nooks
and crannies and large terrace, and the
refurbished Schladmingerhütte at the
top of the Planai gondola has some of
the best food. The Knapphof at Hauser
Kaibling is also good, and particularly
interesting because it's owned by
Helmut Höflehner's family and has
many racing mementos on show. The
Imbisstube provides a good lunch if
you're in the Reiteralm area.

SKI SCHOOL
Satisfaction all round
There are two main schools, which
seem to impress reporters. Charly
Kahr's WM Schladming school, based
at Planai, is complimented for all
aspects of its operation, from
standards of English to friendliness
and organisation – and proudly claims
local boy Arnold Schwarzenegger as a
regular client. Beginners are
recommended to start at Rohrmoos,
where the Tritscher school has a
much-improved recent record. We
haven't heard anything recently about

**Schladming-
Rohrmoos/Tritscher
Classes** 5 days
4½hr: 10am–noon and
1.30–4pm
5 full days: 1300
Children's classes
Ages: 4 to 14
5 full days including
lunch: 1800
Private lessons
1hr (between normal
course times), half-
day or full day
450 for 1hr; each
additional person 150

CHILDCARE
Huberta's Kinder-
spiel-eck (22962)
takes children aged
1 to 10, from 9.15 to
4.15.

At Rohrmoos, the
Stocker nursery
(61188) takes children
from 18 months.
There is also a
KInderwelt nursery
(61301).

Children in ski school
can be looked after
from 9am to 5pm.

GETTING THERE
Air Salzburg, transfer
1½hr.

Rail Mainline station
in resort.

the smaller Hoppl and Onkel Willy
schools – or about the two schools
based in Haus.

Snowboarders are well catered for by
a specialist school. Ramsau is the best
place to get cross-country tuition.

FACILITIES FOR CHILDREN
Rohrmoos is the place
The extensive gentle slopes that make
up the suburb of Rohrmoos could
have been designed to build up the
confidence of young skiers. Whether
in the nursery or proper ski school
classes, this is where we would head
with children. That's the theory;
reports on the practice welcome.

Staying there

Much of the accommodation is
central, but some hotels and most
apartments are on the outskirts.
Staying on the east fringe of town is
convenient for skiers, the Planai
gondola being on that side. But the
walk from central hotels to the lift is
no great burden.

Rohrmoos has the advantage of
doorstep skiing for beginners, and
some like its peace and quiet, plus
good-value hotels. But there is little
else going for it. There is little to do
but ski in the daytime and drink in
the evenings – and Schladming is
further away than tour operators using
Rohrmoos would have you believe.

HOW TO GO
Packages means hotels
Packaged accommodation is in hotels
and pensions, but there are plenty of
apartments for independent travellers.
Chalets None that we know of.
Hotels Most of the accommodation is
in modestly priced pensions –

including some towny places in the
centre, as well as the usual suburban
chalets – but there are also a few more
upmarket hotels. Staying at the resort
entrance, near the Planai and
Rohrmoos chairs, is good value. Hotels
in this part of town are cheaper than
their centrally-placed opposition.
££££ Sporthotel Royer Big, smart,
comfortable multi-amenity place, on
the outskirts but within walking
distance of the main Planai lift.
£££ Alte Post Characterful old inn
with best position in town – on the
main square, a few minutes from
gondola. Very good food, but some
rooms are rather small by 4-star
standards.
£££ Stadttor Similarly priced,
although less charming and well
placed, but with more creature
comforts. Special deals for families.
£££ Neue Post Large rooms, good
food, in centre of town.
Recommended by recent reporter.
£££ Schladmingerhof Bright, modern
chalet in peaceful position, a bus-ride
from centre in Untere Klaus.
Self-catering The Plattner apartments
are comfortable and reasonably well
placed, eight minutes from the
gondola. Ferienhaus Girik is cheaper
and the best-positioned apartment
house in town, close to the gondola.

EATING OUT
Plenty of choice
There is a wide choice of informal
places. The Kirchenwirt hotel
restaurant has excellent home-
cooking. Giovanni's does the best
pizza. Others worth a visit are the
Vorstadtstub'n, Falbach and Lisi's. The
Jaegerstubl in the hotel Neue Post is
good, but more expensive, while the
Alte Post is the best place for a blow-
out meal.

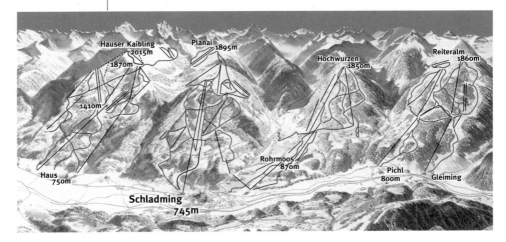

ACTIVITIES

Indoor Swimming, sauna, bowling, indoor tennis court, squash, museum
Outdoor Ice skating, curling, 6km toboggan run, sleigh rides, 50km of cleared paths in the Schladming and surrounding area, para-gliding

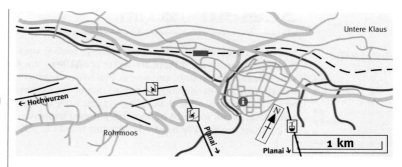

PACKAGES

Club Europe, Crystal, Equity Total Ski, Made to Measure, Neilson, Rank STS, SkiBound, Thomson

Haus in Ennstal
Equity Total Ski

APRES-SKI
Pleasantly animated

Après-ski used to be quiet by Austrian standards, but seems to get livelier every year – without yet going overboard on the lederhosen that is such a feature of some major Tyrolean resorts.

Numerous cafés and bars have a jolly atmosphere immediately after skiing. The ski-booted tea dance at the Touralm on Hochwurzen is great fun. Charley's Treff umbrella bar opposite the Planai is lively immediately after skiing, as is the Siglu (in a big plastic igloo-like bubble).

Beizel is a smart, beautiful bar attracting a varied age group. Hangl Bar mostly attracts the over 30s with its wooden decor and middle of the road music – the back room has special nights such as karaoke and evergreen. The Pub has a nautical theme, loud music and a quiet room at the rear. La Porta is more sophisticated while Raudis is a scruffy hard rock bar.

Our favourite bar was the Gondel Treff with an international football theme (lots of scarves draped around), big screen video for sports matches, a friendly tee-total host (Johann) and various gimmicks such as motorised lollipops and tequila mit worm – popular with locals and Dutch.

The Sondarbar is a central disco with a great DJ from Ghana and three bars including a quieter one at the rear.

FOR NON-SKIERS
Good for all but walkers

Lazy non-skiers should find adequate diversions. Some mountain restaurants are easily reached (though single gondola rides are very expensive). The town shops and museum are worth a look. Schladming has a railway station, making trips to beautiful Salzburg very easy. Buses run to the old walled town of Radstadt. For the more active, the public swimming pool and ice rink are supplemented by excellent sport facilities at Sporthotel Royer.

Haus 750m

Unlike Rohrmoos, Haus is a real village with a life of its own. It has a fair amount of accommodation plus its own ski schools and kindergartens.

The Hauser Kaibling lifts are a little peripheral, but the user-friendly nursery area is more handily placed between town and gondola station.

Haus is a railway stop, so excursions are easy, but non-skiers would be better off in Schladming. The same could be said of anyone looking for nightlife. It's a good choice for families looking for a quiet time, or those wishing to escape from their fellow Brits and experience a bit of the 'real' Austria – though Schladming itself isn't exactly over-commercialised or noisy.

Hotel prices are generally lower here. The Gurtl is a small, friendly, excellent-value hotel with good food. The Hauser Kaibling is a good, more upmarket place.

TOURIST OFFICE

Postcode A-8970
Tel 00 43 (3687) 22268
Fax 24138

Seefeld 1200m

In a book called Where to Ski Cross-country, Seefeld would have one of the leading entries – even if there are better places than the Alps to wear skinny skis (Norway, classically), and one or two better resorts in the Alps than Seefeld (such as Kandersteg). It is also one of the best mountain resorts in which to do things other than skiing – particularly curling, skating and swimming, for all of which its facilities are very impressive. For downhill skiing there are literally hundreds of better resorts in this book.

THE RESORT

In one competing publication that shall be nameless, we've seen Seefeld likened to Salzburg, Innsbruck and Kitzbühel. A more misleading comparison would be hard to construct: there are parts of Seefeld that are of medieval origin, but they are far from typical. The village is a classic post-war Tyrolean tourist development: modern, chalet-style, and with the warm glow of wood skillfully applied to interiors and exteriors alike. It attracts large numbers of well-heeled Germans of (or approaching) pensionable age; these people can afford to ski more or less where they like, so it is in a sense fashionable – and by Austrian standards rather expensive.

Seefeld sits on an elevated plateau to the north of the Inn valley, not far from Innsbruck, to which it is linked by railway. Ehrwald and Garmisch (over the nearby border in Germany) are also within easy reach.

THE SKIING

Seefeld's **ski area** consists of two main sectors, both on the outskirts and reached from most hotels by ski-bus. Gschwandtkopf is a rounded hill giving 300m vertical of intermediate skiing down two main slopes. Rosshütte is a more extensive but still very limited area. A funicular goes up to the main congregation area at 1800m, and a cable-car then goes up to 2100m. There is one main slope, served in addition by three drags. Runs go down from Rosshütte into the adjacent Hermannstal, with return by chair or the funicular. From Rosshütte another cable-car spans the Hermannstal to the shoulder of Härmelekopf at 2050m, whence there is an excellent red to the village.

With reasonable altitudes by Austrian standards and a serious snowmaking installation in both main sectors, **snow reliability** is not a serious problem. But most of the slopes are sunny in the morning or afternoon, affecting snow quality – particularly on Rosshütte.

The Rosshütte sector has some genuine challenges for **advanced skiers** – seriously steep off-piste routes, with and without climbing. These are great for skiers popping out from Innsbruck for the day, but no basis for a week-long holiday.

Only the most timid **intermediate skiers** should think of coming here. Gschwandtkopf is tiny, and Rosshütte is a two-run ski area.

This is an excellent resort for **beginners** – particularly those who are not dead set on becoming ace downhillers by the end of week one. The central village nursery slopes are broad and gentle; there is also a beginners' slope at Gschwandtkopf, but the slope and its lift get very busy.

The excellence of Seefeld's **cross-country** trails is one of the reasons why Innsbruck has been able to hold the Winter Olympics twice. More recently, the Nordic World Championships have been held here.

Queues are rarely a problem.

The **mountain restaurants** in both sectors are adequate, but most people eat lunch in the village.

We lack reports on the **ski school**; **children** can be looked after all day, and there is a non-ski kindergarten.

STAYING THERE

The upmarket nature of the resort is made very clear by the range of **hotels**. There are no fewer than seven 5-star places, and almost 30 4-stars. To find anything less than 3-star standard, you have to look at pensions, and there are plenty of them. The Felseneck, not far from the sports centre, is one modest B&B that has been recommended.

Most of the **restaurants** are hotel-based. The lively **après-ski** scene also revolves largely around hotel bars, many of which have live music. Four hotels have tea-dancing.

Seefeld is great for **non-skiers**. The facilities are far too numerous to list, but include eight tennis courts, two skating rinks and 40 curling lanes. The public pool is superb, with special areas for non-swimmers and children.

Serfaus 1430m

Serfaus offers the charm and nightlife of a typical Austrian village but with a decent ski area, fairly reliable snow and the huge benefit of being largely traffic-free. The resort deserves to be better known on the British market.

THE RESORT

Serfaus is an attractive and friendly village of traditional chalet-style buildings. It is largely traffic-free, with a big car park on the outskirts and a unique underground railway from there to the lifts, stopping off in the village en route. Few hotels are too far from one of the stations. This allows traditional charm to be preserved while reducing the effort of getting from one end of the long village to the slopes at the other end. A skating rink, sleighs and an old church add to the village charm.

Most visitors are well-heeled (though not particularly sophisticated) Germans and Dutch, who give the numerous bars and cafés a jolly atmosphere. Serfaus has few British visitors, but deserves more. The sunny shelf setting adds to the attraction.

THE SKIING

Though not as impressive a **ski area** as nearby Ischgl, Serfaus is far from negligible, served by lifts less prone to wind and queues. The 80km of sunny pistes spread westwards from the resort. The ski area is long and thin and reaches the respectable height of 2685m. Most of it is above the tree-line and served by drags.

The underground drops skiers at the main lift-station, from where a gondola and cable-car transport you to the mid-station. A second stage of the gondola rises to Lazid at 2350m. There are long reds from here back to the village and drags beyond lead to the highest Mindersjoch sector.

There's the skiing of neighbouring Fiss to explore too, linked in both directions. It's smaller than the Serfaus area, but is somewhat steeper.

The high average ski height, and snowmakers on four important pistes and the children's nursery area, make Serfaus reasonably **snowsure**.

There are few challenging slopes for **advanced skiers**, on- or off-piste, but it is a good area for ski-touring.

Good **intermediates** have a couple of short, steep runs between Lazid and the mid-station, while the most testing of the long runs is the pretty Alpkopf-village piste. Virtually the whole area has ideal runs for average intermediates. Less experienced skiers

have wonderful long runs from Plansegg to the village, dropping gently almost 1000m vertical.

Both the village and mid-station nursery slopes are good, and there is ample opportunity for **beginners** to progress to longer runs. The **ski school** has a good reputation but there have been complaints about standards of English in group classes.

The 60km of **cross-country** trails are excellent and include some very pretty trails at altitude.

The replacement of the Lazid chair by a second-stage of gondola has improved the mid-station **queues**. The Scheid and Plansegg drags can be bottlenecks in the early morning and late afternoon respectively.

The seven **mountain restaurants** are adequate for the size of the ski area. The Masiner, on Mindersjoch, is atmospheric, and has a good ice bar. Skiing down the cross-country trail from Alpkopf is well worth it for a quiet lunch at Rodelhütte.

Facilities for **children** are excellent. The crèche takes children aged 2 to 7 all day. Ski kindergarten is available to 4-year-olds and above, and is also open all day. Our one concern would be the lack of English-speaking children to play with.

STAYING THERE

Most accommodation is in comfortable chalet-style **hotels**. Hotel Löwen is a charming old hotel with a tasteful modern wing and lots of facilities. The Alte Schmeide is closest to the slopes. The Post is an attractive, central 3-star. There are plenty of centrally-positioned pensions, too.

Restaurants are mainly hotel-based. Many hotels have a good 'farmer's buffet' once a week. Alte Serfaus is a jolly restaurant and bar.

Après-ski is lively and traditional. There are half a dozen dance bars. The most popular is Patschi's. The four discos liven up late.

There is not a great deal for **non-skiers**, though the better hotels have pools and sauna open to the public, and there are beautiful walks to enjoy. Going up the gondola to meet skiing friends for lunch is easy. For car-drivers several interesting excursions are possible – including St Moritz.

Sölden 1380m

HOW IT RATES

The skiing

Snow	****
Extent	***
Advanced	**
Intermediates	****
Beginners	**
Convenience	***
Queues	**
Restaurants	***

The rest

Scenery	***
Resort charm	**
Not skiing	**

✔ Good snow reliability by Austrian standards, with a high proportion of skiing above 2000m

✔ Glacier skiing in spring and summer

✔ Very lively nightlife

✔ Ski convenience good from all package accommodation

✔ Short transfers from Innsbruck airport and Ötz railway station

✔ Very few T-bars for an Austrian resort

✘ Little challenging skiing

✘ Poor choice of resort for beginners and timid skiers

✘ Glacier skiing areas normally closed in winter

✘ Large village lacking much charm

✘ High-season queues can be bad

Sölden tends to disappoint. Its ski area is not as large, challenging or varied as most people expect. Many are also surprised to find the glacier lifts closed and, even when open, a bus-ride away.

This disappointment is partly the fault of tour operators. They tend to market Sölden as something akin to Ischgl or St Anton simply because, like those places, it is a big, lively, snowsure Austrian resort. However, it lacks the charm of the former, the tough runs of the latter and, most notably, the large, well-linked ski areas of both.

Sölden is, in fact, best suited to skiers who have enjoyed Mayrhofen's nightlife, intermediate runs and (usually) good snow, and who want to try an area that's more convenient, larger and slightly more challenging, with fewer queues – and enjoy a throbbing après-ski scene.

ORIENTATION

Sölden sprawls for more than 2km along the Ötz valley floor, just before the road starts rising steeply towards Obergurgl. Lifts lead into the two linked ski areas from either end of town, the northern ones accessing Hochsölden. The road to Hochsölden and the separate glacier skiing area starts from the southern edge. Nearby **Obergurgl** and **Vent** and distant **St Anton** are reachable by public transport and the resorts around **Innsbruck** are all feasible car outings.

SKI FACTS

Altitude	1380m-3060m
Lifts	33
Pistes	101km
Green/Blue	42%
Red	44%
Black	14%
Artificial snow	10km

 ## The resort

Sölden has mainly traditional Tyrolean-style buildings and it is set in a tree-filled valley. Yet, despite this, it lacks Alpine charm. It is a large, traffic-filled, rather characterless place which sprawls along both sides of a main road and river.

The geographical centre has a church and post office, but there is no real focus. There are numerous bars, cafés, hotels and typical touristy ski resort shops along its length.

The two main village lift-stations are at opposite ends of town, sufficiently distant from one another to make what is supposed to be 'central' accommodation a long walk or a bus-ride from both.

Sölden attracts a young, lively crowd – mostly made up of Germans – and is not a suitable resort for people looking for a quiet evening ambience. The bars and discos throb until the early hours.

Hochsölden, set over 700m above Sölden, is little more than a collection of fairly up-market hotels and is much quieter than its brash neighbour in the valley below. It's reachable by car, and served by day-time buses.

 ## The skiing

Sölden's immediate ski area is made up of two similar-size sectors separated by a small valley. Both suit moderate-to-good intermediates. Sölden's two glaciers don't normally enter into the winter equation – see Snow reliability.

THE SKI AREA
Lacking variety

An impressive high-capacity two-stage gondola, at the southern edge of town, whisks skiers up to the top of the 3060m **Gaislachkogl**. From here a single piste runs down to Gratl, also reachable by the Innerwald chair and a further lift. This area is served by a number of chairs which allow you to reach **Gaislachalm** at the southern extremity of the ski area and Gampealm in its centre, from where a chair goes up to the other section of the ski area above **Hochsölden**.

Hochsölden can also be reached from the northern end of the village by a chair which goes right to it, and a gondola which finishes above it at Giggijoch. There is a network of runs above Hochsölden, served by chairs and drags. This section allows less

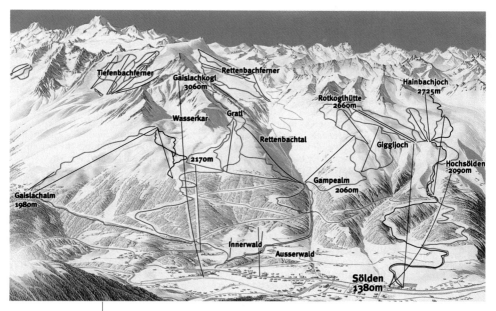

LIFT PASSES

95/96 prices in schillings

Ötztal Arena
Covers all lifts in Sölden, Hochsölden, Gaislachkogl and the Rettenbach and Tiefenbach glaciers (when open).

Beginners Points tickets, valid on lifts in Innerwald and Hochsölden areas.

Main pass
1-day pass 440
6-day pass 2020
(low season 1740 – 14% off)

Senior citizens
Over 65 male, 60 female: 6-day pass 1580 (22% off)

Children
Under 15: 6-day pass 1150 (43% off)
Under 6: free pass

Short-term passes
Half-day, 'hourly' cards refundable when you hand them in, single ascents for main cable-cars and chair-lift, only for non-skiers.

Alternative periods
Passes available for 5 days skiing in 7 and 10 days in 14.

Alternative passes
Separate passes for Vent (6 days 1,470 for adults, 1,020 for children, 94/95 prices).

horizontal movement, most pistes heading towards Hochsölden with lifts returning straight back. You can ski from near the top of this section back to Gampealm and catch a chair-lift into the Gaislachkogl-Gaislachalm sector of the skiing.

Both sectors have runs through trees to the village, and you can ski pretty much to any part of the village.

SNOW RELIABILITY
Good, but not that good
Sölden's two glaciers don't act as a snow guarantee in quite the normal way. They are generally not open in winter (the road up to the lifts is prone to avalanches) so you can't simply head for the glacier whenever you fancy skiing on perfect snow, as you can in Tignes, Hintertux or Zermatt, say. But if spring comes early, the glaciers are a very useful fall-back.

Similarly, the main area's top height of 3060m is deceptive: the lift serves only a single red piste. Most of the skiing is below 2700m. But most of it is also above 2100m – a decent height in Austrian terms – so it is reasonably snowsure. It faces east, so gets some sun, and the lower slopes depend heavily on snowmakers in late season.

FOR ADVANCED SKIERS
Don't believe the hype
Sölden has managed to gain a reputation for being suitable for good skiers but this simply isn't the case. Admittedly Sölden has little really easy skiing, but nor is there much to challenge the proficient.

None of the black runs is difficult. A steep plunge down the Gaislachkogl off-piste route is a highlight when conditions allow. Another good off-piste route is to ski from Gratl directly to the Mautstelle restaurant on the road up to the glacier. It's only a short walk to lifts.

Adventurers should note that there is a mountain guides' office in Sölden, and that at the top of the valley is one

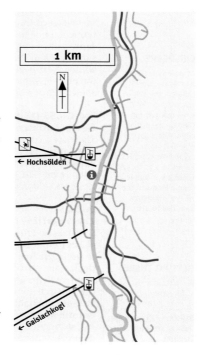

SKI SCHOOL

95/96 prices in
schillings

Sölden/Hochsölden
Classes 6 days
4hr: 10am-noon and
1.30pm-3.30pm
6 full days: 1600
Children's classes
Ages: 3 to 8
6 full days: 1600
Private lessons
2hr or daily
1200 for 2hr

Total Vacancia
Classes 6 days
2½hr: 9.30-noon or
1pm-3.30
6 half-days: 1050
Children's classes
Ages: up to 4
6 full days: 1500
Private lessons Yes

CHILDCARE

As well as ordinary
classes for older
children, the ski
schools run ski
kindergartens for
children aged 3 or
more. The main
school is open
9.30pm to 4pm, Total
Vacancia 9.30 to 3.30.
There are a couple of
child-minders in the
village – numbers
from the Tourist
Office.

GETTING THERE

Air Innsbruck, transfer
1½hr. Salzburg,
transfer 4½hr.

Rail Ötztal (35km); 12
daily buses from
station.

of the premier ski touring areas of the
Alps. Some of the tours launch off
from the remote little hamlet of Vent,
which comes under the Sölden
marketing umbrella.

FOR INTERMEDIATE SKIERS
Something for all but the nervous
Nearly all of Sölden's skiing should
really be classed as red run skiing,
ideal for the average adventurous
intermediate. Good intermediates
have several easy black runs to try, but
many may find the long, quiet piste
down to Gaislachalm the most fun.
It's ideal for fast skiing. The north-
facing run beneath the Stabele chair is
quite challenging in parts and tends to
have good snow. It can be the second
half of a fine 1000m vertical run from
the Gaislachkogl summit.
   The less experienced the skier, the
further north they should head. The
Giggijoch and Rotkogl sections above
Hochsölden are good for moderate
skiers, although the south-facing piste
to Gampealm can get very icy.
Immediately above Hochsölden is a
small section of easy runs, but timid
skiers are not really at home on
Sölden's slopes.
   Intermediates of all standards will
enjoy a day out on the slopes of
Obergurgl and Hochgurgl up the road.

FOR BEGINNERS
A poor choice
The only slopes for complete novices
are inconveniently situated just above
the village at Innerwald; they are
prone to poor snow, yet no
snowmakers are provided. These
slopes are also dark and cold in mid-
winter. Near-beginners can start at the
top of the Giggijoch gondola, but
Sölden is not a place for novices.

FOR CROSS-COUNTRY
Limited mileage
There are a couple of uninspiring
loops at the back of town by the river,
plus a small area at Zwieselstein. Total
trails 16km. The one factor in its
favour is Sölden's altitude.

QUEUES
They're getting there
Sölden is no longer one of the worst
places for queues in the Alps, thanks
to the upgrading of its lift system over
the last six years. The notable
improvements are the installation of
the Gaislach gondola and Hainback
four-person 'bubble' chair. But delays
can still be lengthy when Sölden is
full, during the morning peak at the
gondola stations, especially the

Giggijoch. New Year is a bad time to
visit, when overcrowded pistes add to
the problems. Towards the end of the
season there may be queues for the
gondolas down at the end of the day,
and for the glacier lifts (if open).

MOUNTAIN RESTAURANTS
Crowded
The restaurants tend to get very
crowded and the quality of the food is
nothing special. We like the two in
the Gaislachalm area best. They are
quieter than most, have good food,
views and jolly accordion music. The
Rauthalm at the bottom of the
Mittelstation chair is rather low down
the mountain but very welcoming,
with good omelettes and Tyroler
Gröstl (rösti). There's a big terrace and
outside bar at Gampealm.
   The Rotkoglhütte has great top-of-
the-world views. The atmospheric
little Obstlerhütte, at the foot of the
Rotkogl chair, is also worth a visit.

SKI SCHOOL
One or two problems
We haven't had many reports on
Sölden's ski schools, and in particular
we lack reports on the newish Total
Vacancia school, which offers the
distinct alternative of half-day tuition
– 'the quickest road to success,' they
say, and they may be right. Lack of
spoken English has been a problem in
the past (Sölden doesn't get huge
numbers of British visitors). Beginners
should be warned that the village
nursery slopes are pretty sunless in
midwinter.

CHILDREN'S FACILITIES
Half-hearted
Sölden doesn't go out of its way to
cater for children; there is no proper
day-care nursery, and the ski
kindergartens keep rather short hours.
The hotel Edelweiss up at Hochsölden
has its own nursery, and this upper
satellite resort has attractions for a
family holiday.

 # Staying there

The two main lifts lying out at the
edges of town make staying in the
geographic centre inconvenient. The
featureless nature of Sölden, and the
similarity of its two linked ski areas,
means there is no great advantage in
staying at one end of the village in
preference to the other. The
impressive sports centre and pool is at
the Giggijoch gondola (northern) end
of town. Those near the Gaislachkogl

ACTIVITIES

Indoor Freizeit Arena sports complex (swimming, sauna, solarium, gym, bowling, tennis, shooting, badminton, billiards, cinema) **Outdoor** Skating, curling, toboggan run, para-gliding, sledging and sleigh rides

PACKAGES

Crystal, Inghams, Made to Measure, Thomson

Hochsölden Inghams

TOURIST OFFICE

Postcode A-6450
Tel 00 43 (5254)
22120
Fax 3131

---

gondola have slightly faster access to the top of the mountain each morning. Some accommodation is located just above Sölden, at Innerwald: useful for drivers as it has a large car park and marks the start of the glacier road.

Innerwald is also useful for those wishing to stay in a quiet area, but still have the bright lights of Sölden within walking distance. Ski convenience is good there too, a chair-lift taking skiers into the main area, and a returning piste allowing skiing almost to the door.

Hochsölden is good for those wanting a quiet time in a comfortable hotel.

HOW TO GO
Plush or basic?

Pensions and apartments dominate and independent travellers have a wide choice of cheap accommodation.
Chalets There are no catered chalets.
Hotels Most tour operators use Sölden's better hotels, rated 3-star or 4-star. All the hotels at Hochsölden are 4-star.
££££ **Central** Monster chalets make up the best and one of the biggest hotels in town. Shuttle to the lifts. Swimming pool.
££££ **Tyrolerhof** Big but friendly 4-star, well placed for the slopes and Giggijoch gondola.
££££ **Regina** Very comfortable 4-star right next to the Gaislachkogl lift.
££££ **Edelweiss** Large 4-star in Hochsölden with first-class leisure amenities including swimming pool. Satellite TV in rooms.
£££ **Granat** Best B&B hotel in Sölden, well placed off the road, yet close to the Giggijoch lift.
£££ **Waldcafe** Most attractive and best-positioned of Innerwald's hotels, 80m from the chair-lift.
££ **Stefani** Opposite the Waldcafe: pleasant good-value B&B pension.
Self-catering Some hotels have apartments. The Posthausl ones are good quality and well placed, though on the main road. Much cheaper and quieter are the Gerhard apartments opposite the Innerwald chair.

EATING OUT
Good range

There is a wide selection of restaurants. The good-value Café Hubertus does everything from snacks to full meals. The Nudeltopf and Café Corso vie for the title of 'best pizzas in town'. Other informal places worth a visit are the Pension Sonnenheim, Cafés Stefan and Philip, plus Dominic's. Of the many hotel restaurants the Birkenhof's is pleasantly traditional, and one of the best in town. The Kupferpfanne in the Tirolerhof and Otztaler Stube in the Central are also good.

APRES-SKI
Throbbing nightlife

Sölden is a happening place. There are a great number of lively piano bars, umbrella bars, discos and organised evenings. Café Philip at Innerwald is the liveliest post-skiing venue. Those skiing home from Rotkogl can have a similarly lively end to the day in the Obstlerhutte beneath Hochsölden. Taking the blue, rather than black, run home in the gathering darkness is advisable after a few glühweins.

A little later, the Après-Ski Club and Berglands keller bar are two of the most popular places. The glass-fronted Dominic's and the Hinterher on the main street get extremely crowded; they frequently have live bands later on. The Stamperl and Pfiff are other 'happening' bars. Madeus in the Alpenland hotel and the Centro Club are perhaps the best discos.

The toboggan evening is not the usual tame affair. Plenty of Dutch courage is built-up with drinking and dancing before an exciting 6km run back to town from the Gaislachalm mountain restaurant. And it takes place every night!

The Sonnblick Scene is the focus of the limited nightlife in Hochsölden.

FOR NON-SKIERS
Disappointing for a large resort

Given the size of Sölden there is surprisingly little to do. Buses run to Innsbruck and there may be an organised excursion to Igls. Walks are not particularly interesting. Mountain bikes are available and there is a large sports centre and swimming pool facility. The skating rink is merely a flooded, and frozen, tennis court.

Söll 700m

HOW IT RATES

The skiing

Snow	*
Extent	****
Advanced	*
Intermediates	****
Beginners	***
Convenience	**
Queues	***
Restaurants	**

The rest

Scenery	***
Resort charm	***
Not skiing	**

✔ Large, pretty, easy-intermediate ski area

✔ Short airport transfers and easy road access

✔ Plenty of cheap and cheerful pensions for budget skiers

✔ Improved lift system has reduced queues

✔ Has the highest and steepest skiing in the Ski-Welt area

✘ Very poor recent snow record, and few snowmakers

✘ Long walks or inefficient bus to the lifts from most accommodation

✘ Little challenging skiing

✘ Local skiing is the most crowded in the Ski-Welt area

✘ Poor links to the most snowsure section of Ski-Welt area

✘ Mostly short runs in local sector

In the 1980s Söll became known as prime lager-lout territory but, for some years now, the resort's reputation for rowdy behaviour has been undeserved, sustained mainly by the efforts of British tabloid 'journalists'. Apart from anything else, the high value of the Austrian schilling has ensured that cost-conscious lager drinkers now prefer Eastern Europe and Andorra. Family skiers now make up a large portion of Söll's clientele, and young people bent on having a riotous time should not assume that they will find one.

But Söll still has a serious weakness: the Ski-Welt region is not reliable for snow. The slopes in the shadow of the Hohe Salve can have fairly decent cover (aided by snowmakers, recently introduced). But the Itter, Hopfgarten and Brixen slopes are often slushy or bare, and the best snow in the Ski-Welt, above Scheffau, is not easily accessible on skis or by bus. And only with a car can you hope to do much skiing in more remote snowsure resorts.

With good snow, Söll is great for a lively holiday spent bashing undemanding pistes in pretty scenery – at modest cost. But early bookers should beware.

ORIENTATION

Söll sits in a wide valley, a few miles off the main road through the Tyrol. From a base station 1km out of the village, a gondola goes up to the mid-mountain junction of Hochsöll, from where the skiing spreads over to **Hopfgarten**, **Brixen**, **Scheffau** and **Ellmau**. The skiing of **Westendorf** is separate, but covered by the area lift pass.

Other resorts such as **Fieberbrunn, St Johann, Waidring, Kirchberg** and **Leogang** (for Saalbach) are easily accessible by car, much less so by bus.

 ## The resort

Söll remains a small, friendly village, though development has left it feeling rather cramped. At least everything (except the skiing) is readily to hand, and new buildings have been designed to look traditional. The pretty surrounding scenery adds to its charm, and the village benefits from being some way off the busy main road.

Unfortunately it is not well placed for skiing. Its lifts are a 15-minute walk from the village centre across the main road, and much further from some accommodation. What's more, the ski-bus service is poor. There is some accommodation near the lifts.

 ## The skiing

The Ski-Welt, or Grossraum as it used to be called, is supposed to be the largest completely linked ski area in Austria, but that doesn't make it a Trois Vallées. It's a typically small, low, pastoral Austrian hill multiplied several times. One section is pretty much like any other, with almost all the skiing best suited to intermediates. Runs are short and scenery attractive rather than stunning – although the panoramic views from the Hohe Salve are impressive on a clear day.

THE SKI AREA
Short run network

A gondola takes all but complete beginners up to the shelf of Hochsöll, where there are a couple of short lifts and connections in several directions.

A two-stage chair rises to Rigi, from where you can ski to Hopfgarten or Itter, or get a further chair to the high point of Hohe Salve – also accessed directly by a long chair from Hochsöll. Hohe Salve is the start of runs down to Kälbersalve – steep at first, and south-facing – and then on down to Brixen or up by chair to Zinsberg, which in

↙ Hohe Salve

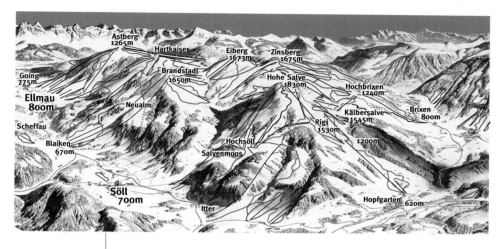

SKI FACTS

Altitude	620m-1830m
Lifts	90
Pistes	250km
Green/Blue	37%
Red	53%
Black	10%
Artificial snow	50km

turn is an access point for Eiberg, the most snowsure section of the Ski-Welt. This protracted route is tiresome and crowded when snow is in short supply; but a cable-car from Hochsöll offers an alternative route, cutting out the tricky Hohe Salve.

The excellent long runs from Brandstadl down to Blaiken are also accessed from Zinsberg.

SNOW RELIABILITY
Very poor
With a very low average ski height, and important links that get too much sun, the Ski-Welt's lack of snow is a real weakness. It is one of the least snowsure areas in the Alps, and distant from more reliable resorts. The slopes below Hohe Salve can keep artificial snow, but on top of that peak the snow tends to blow off.

FOR ADVANCED SKIERS
Not a lot
The plunge straight off Hohe Salve towards Hochsöll and the black run alongside the Brixen gondola represent the only challenging piste skiing. There are further black runs in the Scheffau and Ellmau sectors, but most good skiers will need to seek amusement off-piste – from Scheffau's Brandstadl down to Söll, for example.

FOR INTERMEDIATE SKIERS
Something for everyone
The most direct of the runs between Brandstadl and Blaiken, the Hohe Salve red, and the pistes down to Brixen suit good intermediates. Moderate skiers have an enormous choice. With good snow, the lower woodland runs down to Söll, Hopfgarten and Itter offer some of the

Selected chalets in Söll

Neilson *Ski with the leaders*   T **0113 239 4555** F **0113 239 3275**

Club Sonnenhof SLEEPS 32
Part of the Neilson Club Hotel range, the Sonnenhof is the ideal choice for a lively ski holiday. It is located in a quiet setting, just 700m from the centre of Söll, and 200m from the nearest ski bus stop. All rooms have en suite facilities and a balcony. Our own staff prepare and serve an extended Continental breakfast, afternoon tea and a three-course evening meal with wine.

LIFT PASSES

95/96 prices in schillings
Ski-Welt Wilder Kaiser-Brixental
Covers all lifts in the Wilder Kaiser-Brixental area from Going to Westendorf, and the ski-bus.
Beginners Points tickets (100 points 280). Most beginner lifts cost from 5 to 10 points.
Main pass
1-day pass 340
6-day pass 1610
Children
Under 15: 6-day pass 915 (43% off)
Under 5: free pass
Short-term passes
Single ascent on some lifts, half-day passes up to noon and from 11am, noon and 2pm to the end of the day.
Alternative periods
5 in 7 days, 7 in 10 days and 10 in 14 days.
Alternative passes
Söll only pass available (1375 6-day pass for adults, 775 for children), covers 12 local lifts.
Credit cards Yes

SKI SCHOOL

95/96 prices in schillings
Söll-Hochsöll
Manager Sepp Embacher
Classes 5 days. 2 hr or 4hr: 10am-noon and 2pm-4pm
5 full days: 1260
Children's classes
Ages: 5 to 14
5 full days: 1220
Private lessons
Hourly, or full day (4hr)
460 for 1hr; each additional person 150

Austria
Manager Hans Wohlschlager
Classes 6 days. 4hr: 10am-noon and 2pm-4pm
6 full days: 1280
Children's classes
Ages: 5 to 14
6 full days: 1220
Private lessons Hourly or daily
430 for 1hr; each extra person 170

most interesting skiing in the area. The runs down to Ellmau are enjoyable, but it's a bit of a trek to get over there. Early intermediates have plenty of cruising terrain on the higher slopes between Hochbrixen and Brandstadl. The varied long runs from Zinsberg down to Brixen are good for groups of mixed abilities.

FOR BEGINNERS
OK when snow is good
The nursery slopes are between the main road and the gondola station, and are perfectly adequate when snow is abundant – gentle, spacious and uncrowded. This year the beginner's drag has been extended by 200m. In poor snow the Hochsöll area is used, though one of the most suitable runs is served by a chair rather than drag. Near-beginners and fast learners can ski home to the bottom station when the meandering blue from Hochsöll is not too icy.

FOR CROSS-COUNTRY
Neighbouring villages are better
Söll has 35km of local trails but they are less interesting than those between Hopfgarten and Kelchsau or the ones around and beyond Ellmau. Lack of snowcover is a big problem.

QUEUES
Much improved
Continued introduction of new lifts has greatly improved this once queue-prone area. The Blaiken gondola is to be avoided on weekend mornings, and the tiresomely slow Hohe Salve chair can become over-subscribed. However, most delays are directly related to conditions: when snow is in short supply, the linking lifts to and from Zinsberg and Eiberg get busy.

MOUNTAIN RESTAURANTS
Good, but crowded
Restaurants are generally pleasant, and there are quite a few jolly little chalets dotted about, but those at Hochsöll, in particular, can get very busy. The otherwise pleasant Stockalm, Kraftalm and Grundalm are also prone to crowds. The Alpenrose, near the top of Hohe Salve, has a good sun terrace, generous portions and reasonable prices. Further afield the Neualm, half-way down to Blaiken, is one of the best huts in the Ski-Welt. The Jochstube at Eiberg is self-service but has a good atmosphere and excellent Tiroler Gröstl. The Filzalm above Brixen is a good place for a quick drink on the way back from the circuit – but don't miss last lift connection.

SKI SCHOOL
The usual reservations
The two schools have fairly good reputations, though there are occasional reports of over-large classes and poor spoken English – more of a problem with the 'red' Austria school than the bigger Söll-Hochsöll school, which is more widely used by tour operators. With the latter, groups of five to eight can book an instructor for a set price, but even for eight this works out very expensive.

FACILITIES FOR CHILDREN
Rapidly becoming a family resort
The ski kindergarten of the Söll-Hochsöll school generally gets good reports, and there is a new Mini Club, which looks after children aged 3 to 5 who don't want to spend all day skiing. Reports welcome. Although the main nursery slope is fairly child-friendly, there is also a special kids-only drag and slope on the opposite side of the village to the main lifts.

 # Staying there

Ski-convenience fans have a few options out near the lifts but most accommodation is in or around the village centre. Being on the edge of town nearest the lifts is the best bet for those who are prepared to walk to the slopes. The other side of town is better for those who prefer the bus, since you can board there before it gets too crowded. Be aware that some guest-houses are literally miles from the centre and lifts, and that the ski-bus does not serve every nook and cranny of this sprawling community.

HOW TO GO
Mostly cheap and cheerful gasthofs
There is a wide choice of simple gasthofs, pensions and B&Bs, and an adequate amount of better-quality hotel accommodation – mainly 3-star. As far as we know, none has a pool. There are apartments, too, but not through tour operators.
Chalets Crystal have a charming wood-clad chalet but it's poorly situated 7 minutes' walk from a ski-bus stop.
Hotels
£££ **Greil** The only 4-star – attractive place, but out of the centre on the wrong side for the lifts and pool.
£££ **Postwirt** Attractive and central old 3-star that is a hub of the nightlife.
£££ **Austria** Also central, and a bit quieter.
£££ **Bergland** Small 3-star, well placed mid-way between the village and lifts.

CHILDCARE

The ski schools take children from age 5, starting them off in special snow-gardens. The Söll-Hochsöll school's is next to Gasthof Eisenmann, on the nursery slopes; while based here, children can be looked after from 9.30 to 4.15. Once they progress to Hochsöll, care has to be arranged with the instructor.

Next to the main ski kindergarten, the same school now operates a Mini Club for children aged 3 to 5 – fun and games, with skiing available. It is open 6 days a week, 9.30 to 4.30.

PACKAGES

Airtours, Crystal, First Choice Ski, Inghams, Neilson, Ski Partners, SkiBound, Thomson

Hopfgarten Contiki, Ski Hillwood, Top Deck

Itter Crystal

GETTING THERE

Air Salzburg, transfer 2hr. Innsbruck, transfer 1½hr.

Rail Wörgl (13km) or Kufstein (15km); bus to resort.

ACTIVITIES

Indoor Swimming, sauna, solarium, massage, bowling, rifle-range, squash **Outdoor** Natural ice rink (skating, curling), sleigh rides, 3km floodlit toboggan run, para-gliding, hang-gliding

TOURIST OFFICE

Postcode A-6306
Tel 00 43 (5333) 5216
Fax 6180

£££ **Theresa** Comfortable, 'superb' food, but a 10-minute walk out of the centre on the wrong side.
£££ **Panorama** newish 3-star on opposite side of town to lifts but with own bus stop; wonderful views; very pleasant rooms; best cakes around.
£££ **Ingeborg** Next to the lifts.
££ **Feldwebel** Central 2-star.
££ **Schirast** Next to the lifts.
££ **Garni-Tenne** B&B gasthof between centre and main road.
Self-catering We are not aware of any packaged apartments, but there are plenty for independent travellers. The central Ferienhotel Schindlhaus has nice accommodation, though the best apartments in town are those attached to the Bergland hotel.

EATING OUT
A fair choice
Some of the best restaurants are hotel-based. Hotels Greil and Postwirt are of a high standard but the Schindlhaus is reputed to be the best. Hotel Alpenschloss, up the hill above Söll, is supposed to have a very good restaurant too. Café Einstein and the Brunhof cook excellent pizzas, while other places worth a visit include the Dorfstub'n, Venezia and Al Dente.

APRES-SKI
Seen better (or worse) days
Söll is not as raucous as it used to be and its nightlife has lost momentum. But it's by no means dead. Pub 15's floor is swimming in beer, a sleazy remnant of the yob days, but is lively. Vis A Vis is a more pleasant, urban bar. The ski bar of the Postwirt has a singalong and the bar of the Austria hotel is popular for its live guitar music and atmosphere. The Mirabell is a much quieter alternative for a convivial drink. Every kind of organised evening event is available. The Whisky Mühle is a large disco which can get a little rowdy. The Klaus is a smaller nightclub, with a friendlier atmosphere – a better place to bop. One fun evening activity is the toboggan run from Hochsöll.

FOR NON-SKIERS
Not bad for a small village
You could spend a day in the wonderfully equipped Panoramabad quite happily: sauna-ing, swimming, lounging around. The baroque church would be the pride of many tourist towns. There are numerous local excursions, including trips to Salzburg, Innsbruck and even Vipiteno over in Italy. The local bus goes to Kufstein and St Johann. Walks are quite pretty.

Hopfgarten 620m
Hopfgarten is well worth considering as a base for skiing the Ski-Welt – an unspoilt, friendly and traditional resort tucked away several kilometres from the busy Wörgl road. Most hotels are within five minutes' walk of the queue-free chair that provides access to Rigi and Hohe Salve – the high-point of the Ski-Welt circus. The resort's great weakness is that you're unlikely to be able to ski down to 620m on the south-west-facing home slope. The village is a good size – small enough to be intimate, large enough to have plenty of off-slope amenities.

For a change of scene, and perhaps less crowded pistes, Westendorf (covered by the ski pass) is a short bus-journey away – see separate chapter. There are additionally a few lifts at Kelchsau, a bus ride from Hopfgarten but on the Ski Welt lift pass.

When snow allows, the runs down to Hopfgarten and the nearby villages of Brixen and Itter offer some of the best skiing in the Ski-Welt. But the fine (and relatively snowsure) runs above Scheffau are irksomely distant.

There is a convenient nursery slope in the village, but it is sunny as well as low, so lack of snow-cover is likely to mean excursions up the mountain to the higher blue runs served by chair-lifts – at the cost of a lift pass.

Hopfgarten is one of the best cross-country bases in the area. There are fine trails to Kelschsau (11km) and Niederau (15km), and the Itter-Bocking loop (15km) starts nearby. Westendorf's trails are also close.

Although few British tour operators go to Hopfgarten, English is widely spoken in the two ski schools, thanks to the large number of Australians who take lessons via Contiki Travel.

Cheap and cheerful gasthofs, pensions and little, private B&Bs are the norm here. The exceptions are the comfortable but rather expensive hotel Hopfgarten and Sporthotel Fuchs, both of which are well placed for the main lift. Also centrally placed, and better value, are numerous little gasthofs such as the Krone and Oberbräu. The Lukas is one of the best-positioned B&Bs.

Après-ski is generally quiet, though a lively holiday can usually be ensured by booking through the Aussie-dominated Contiki Travel. Lift Stubl has a good tea-time atmosphere, while the Silver Bullet is the main rendezvous later. The ubiquitous Tyrolean evening is popular. Though most of the restaurants are hotel-based, there are exceptions, including a Chinese and a pizzeria.

The village has plenty of non-skiing amenities, including swimming, riding, bowling, ice-skating, tobogganing and parapenting. The railway provides excursion possibilities, including trips to Salzburg, Innsbruck and Kitzbühel.

Hopfgarten is a family resort, providing a fine nursery in the hotel Hopfgarten which is open to non-residents. Children are taken from 3 years. The ski kindergarten takes them from 4, and staff are friendly. The tour operator Ski Hillwood specialises in family holidays to Hopfgarten.

Itter 700m

Itter is a tiny village half-way around the mountain between Söll and Hopfgarten, with nursery slopes close to hand and a gondola just outside the village (reachable on skis) into the Ski-Welt via Hochsöll. There is one hotel, half a dozen gasthofs and a similar number of B&B pensions. There is a ski school and an associated ski hire shop, and when conditions are good it makes a good beginner's resort.

Brixen 795m

Brixen im Thale is a very scattered roadside village at the south-eastern edge of the Ski-Welt circus, close to Westendorf. Although one of the least aesthetically pleasing villages in the area, its queue-free, high-capacity gondola and the chain of snowmakers on its main piste give Brixen a more go-ahead feel than its neighbours. This is some compensation for the inconvenience of the place: its main hotels are clustered around the railway station, a bus-ride from the lifts.

When snow-cover is good, Brixen has some of the best skiing in the Ski-Welt. All three pistes leading down to the village lift station are fine runs in different ways: a black provides an interesting short cut from Hohe Salve; an unpisted route runs the length of the village gondola; and a much easier, prettier piste with artificial snow leads home from Holzalm. Another easy route home, strictly for the end of the day, is a lovely long, away-from-the-lifts run finishing close to the village centre. There is also a very small area of north-facing runs, including the nursery slopes, on the other side of the village below Kandleralm. A free bus runs to Westendorf every 45 minutes.

Brixen is a better base for good skiers than any other Ski-Welt resort. Two of the three runs to the village are challenging, and tend to be very icy. The Hohe Salve black is another test.

Intermediates will find plenty to do, staying close to home and skiing the interesting runs down to Brixen, Hopfgarten and Itter, or going over to Scheffau's skiing.

The nursery slopes are across the valley at the foot of the Kandleralm area – an inconvenient bus-ride from the village. They have the attractions of seclusion and shade, but meeting up with other skiers for lunch is a hassle. At the top of the gondola is some of the best terrain in the area for the improving novice. A special beginner's lift pass keeps costs down.

Brixen is one of the best cross-country villages in the Ski-Welt. There is a long trail to Kirchberg, and more leisurely loops that circumnavigate nearby Westendorf. Hopfgarten's trails are also nearby. A 5km loop up the mountain at Hochbrixen provides fine views, fairly reliable snow and a chance to meet up with Alpine skiers.

The surprisingly large ski school runs the usual group classes, and mini-group sessions for five to seven people, which are a third more expensive. Lack of English-speaking tuition can be a problem.

Brixen has plenty of hotels. The multi-amenity 4-star Alpenhof and Sporthotel, and the cheaper 3-star Hetzenauer are situated in the nearest thing to a village centre, some way from the lifts. The 3-star Gasthof Brixnerwirt and the less expensive Mairwirt are better placed for ski convenience, though still a lengthy walk from the gondola. Both are situated right next to the large white church, which has noise implications. Several little pensions are in an isolated position near the lifts, and are very inexpensive because they are out of town. These include Gästehaus Hofer and the Hubertus.

Restaurants are mainly in-house. The Sporthotel and Alpenhof have the best. The Loipenstub'n and Brixner Thalhof are much less expensive, cosier places. The latter has a pleasant sun terrace. Après-ski is very quiet by Tyrolean standards, but livelier Westendorf is a short taxi-ride away.

Non-skiers can play tennis, take excursions to Salzburg, Innsbruck and Kitzbühel or use the sports facilities of the Alpenhof and Sporthotel (both have a pool and fitness room).

Brixen is not as suitable for children as other Ski-Welt resorts, but it does have an all-day ski kindergarten with optional lunch-time supervision.

Westendorf 800m

Westendorf is a small but lively resort that is part of the Ski-Welt pass-sharing arrangement (along with Söll, Ellmau, Brixen and others) but not part of the main skiing circuit. Its own slopes are not without interest (except for experts), and the friendliness of the village wins many repeat visitors.

THE RESORT

The village is a compact Tyrolean charmer, complete with attractive onion-domed church and sleighs. It attracts more Germans than Brits, and more Dutch than either.

THE SKIING

The local **ski area** is a small section of leisurely skiing. A two-stage gondola takes you to Talkaser (1760m), from where you can ski various north-west-facing runs back to the resort. There are short west-facing and east-facing runs below the two low peaks of Choralpe (1820m) and Fleiding (1890m), either side of Talkaser. A couple of red runs from Fleiding go down beyond the lifts to hamlets served by buses. The main Ski-Welt area is nearby at Brixen; there's a good bus service.

The **snow reliability** of Westendorf's slopes is slightly better than that of some other Ski-Welt resorts, but there are limits to what shade and good maintenance (with some snowmaking on the lower runs) can achieve at this altitude.

Essentially Westendorf is far from suitable for **advanced skiers**, but we have reports from some who have been happy pottering about off-piste. Leisurely **intermediates** have a fair amount of pretty, uncrowded skiing. Most pistes are of blue difficulty, whatever their official grading.

Second-year skiers and confident **beginners** have nice runs both between the mid-station and village, and alongside the Choralpe chair. The extensive nursery slopes are Westendorf's pride and joy.

There are 30 km of local **cross-country** trails, less than in many neighbouring resorts. One trail links up with the Brixen route to Kirchberg. Snow-cover is a big problem.

Given good conditions, **queues** are rare except at Fasching, and far less of a problem than in the main Ski-Welt area. If poor weather closes the upper lifts, queues do become long.

Mountain restaurants are adequate. Alpenrosenhütte is small and friendly; Brechhornhaus is quiet; Gassnerhof is good if you don't mind catching a bus back to town; and Talkaiser and Choralpe are both busy.

The two **ski schools** have quite good reputations, though classes can be over-large and may cram English and Dutch together.

Westendorf sells itself as a family resort and amenities are good. Both the crèche and the ski kindergarten are open all day, but apparently close when demand tails off. Ski school takes **children** up to the age of 15.

STAYING THERE

Although the village is small, location is worth considering. Staying in the centre puts you conveniently close to the village nursery slopes, and a five-minute walk from the lifts into the main ski area, on the edge of the village. But staying on the other side of the village, further from the lifts, may be preferable to putting up with the church bells at six in the morning.

There are a couple of central 4-star **hotels** – the Jakobwirt and the 'excellent' Schermer – and a dozen 3-star ones, but most reporters have stayed in more modest guest-houses. Pension Wetti is popular, and far from the church bells. Pension Ingeborg is highly recommended, and next to the gondola. The Schermhof **apartments** are of good quality.

Most of the best **restaurants** are hotel-based – the Schermer, Mesnerwirt and Jakobwirt are good. A taxi to Berggasthaus Stimlach is well worth it, as is the sleigh ride to the Almaheuf restaurant. Something a little different is an excellent French place, Chez Yves.

The **nightlife** is quite lively, but it is a small place with a limited range of options. Kibo's Café is a pleasant tea-time place. Hausberger does the best coffee and cakes. Gerry's is about the liveliest bar, and the main Dutch meeting place. The Brit-dominated Post and the Cow Shed are also lively. Quieter, more mellow bars include the Schermer and Sporer Stuberl. The discos liven up at weekends.

For **non-skiers** Westendorf is rather limited. There are excursions by rail or bus to Innsbruck, Salzburg and Kitzbühel. Walks and sleigh rides are very pretty. The ice rink is natural, and at this altitude unreliable.

Zell am See 755m

✔ Pretty, tree-lined skiing with great views down to the lake

✔ Lively, but not rowdy, nightlife

✔ Charming old town centre with beautiful lakeside setting

✔ Lots to do off the slopes

✔ Enormous range of cross-country trails in the area

✔ Kaprun glacier skiing nearby

✔ Varied terrain including some genuinely black runs – though not many of them

✗ Sunny, low ski area often has poor conditions despite snowmakers

✗ Old-town charm spoilt somewhat by busy main road and development

✗ Trek to lifts from much accommodation

✗ Less suitable for beginners than most small Austrian resorts

✗ Kaprun glacier gets horrendous queues when it is most needed

Zell am See is an unusual resort – not a rustic village like most of its small Austrian competitors, but a lakeside town on an important through-route, with a charming old centre that seems more geared to summer visitors than to winter ones. It's a pleasant place and the skiing has more variety and challenging terrain than is normal in a small area. But there isn't enough to keep a keen intermediate or better happy for a week. And Zell's ski area is extremely sunny, making the snow there rather unreliable.

One attraction is the proximity to the Kaprun glacier and its guaranteed good snow. But Kaprun is within easy reach of many low-altitude resorts, all of which run buses to the glacier when snow is in short supply. The result can be horrendous queues (for buses as well as lifts) both to and from the glacier.

So, while Zell has its attractions – not least its charm and spectacular views – it has drawbacks from the skiing point of view. It is an attractive base for skiers who enjoy travelling around. Having a car makes it easy to visit numerous ski resorts nearby – including Saalbach-Hinterglemm, Badgastein-Bad Hofgastein, Wagrain, Schladming and Obertauern.

ORIENTATION

Zell am See sits beside a large lake that virtually fills its broad valley. The skiing is on a horseshoe-shaped mountain, one arm of which approaches the town. A gondola goes up that arm from the edge of town, but other lifts are more remote – cable-cars 2km 'inland', and another gondola 3km away at **Schüttdorf**, beyond the southern end of the lake.

Kaprun is only a few minutes by bus; **Saalbach** and **Bad Hofgastein** are easily reached by bus and train respectively; **Wagrain** and, at a push, **Obertauern** are car outings.

SKI FACTS

Altitude	760m–2000m
Lifts	55
Pistes	130km
Green/Blue	38%
Red	50%
Black	12%
Artificial snow	9.5km

 ## The resort

Zell am See is a long-established, year-round resort town in a lovely setting between a large lake and a mountain. Its charming, traffic-free medieval centre occupies a flat promontory, and it's around this attractive core – with everyday towny shops as well as ones catering for summer tourists – that the resort has developed. Unfortunately, the result is a less than convenient ski resort; much of the accommodation is a long walk from the nearest lift, and separated from it by the busy road through the town. There is also accommodation out by the cable-car station, and on the road up to it.

Quite a number of British visitors stay in the satellite resort of Schüttdorf. Some of the accommodation here is quite close to the gondola, but the place is much less appealing than Zell itself, especially for après-skiers. It also has a very sunny home piste which, unlike the Zell ones, has no snowmakers.

 ## The skiing

Despite claims to the contrary, Zell has a fairly small ski area, best suited to intermediates. The fan-shaped ski area has its easier runs along its horseshoe ridge, with steeper pistes heading down into the centre.

THE SKI AREA
Varied but limited

The town gondola goes to Mittelstation. From there you can ski to the double cable-car station at the end of the valley via two runs, one easy, the other steep. Alternatively, a chair from this mid-station goes up to Hirschkogel, where it meets the lifts up from Schüttdorf. Continuing along the ridge via a couple of short lifts brings you to the Schmittenhöhe top-station, also reached from the valley floor by cable-car. A gentle cruise and a single short drag-lift moves you to Sonnkogel. Here several routes lead down to Sonnalm mid-station, where a piste runs to the valley floor.

LIFT PASSES

95/96 prices in schillings

Europa-Sportregion Kaprun-Zell am See
Covers all lifts in Zell and Kaprun, and buses between them.
Beginners Points card or limited pass.
Main pass
1-day pass 400
6-day pass 1930
(low season 1800 – 7% off)
Senior citizens
Over 65 male, 60 female: 6-day pass 1740 (10% off)
Children
Under 15: 6-day pass 1196 (38% off)
Under 6: free pass
Short-term passes
Half-day pass from 11.30 for Zell only; reduces in price by the hour through the day.
Alternative periods
5 in 7 days and 10 in 14 days.
Notes Day pass valid on Zell am See, Schmittenhöhe only.
Alternative passes
Zell am See only; Kaprun glacier.

CHILDCARE

All three ski schools take children from age 4 and offer lunch-time care. The Areitbahn school runs a snow kindergarten and play room for children from age 3, from 9am to 4.30. This is up the mountain at Areitalm (handy for Schüttdorf residents).

There are two village nurseries. Ursula Zink (6343) takes children from age 3, from 9am to 4pm; younger children looked after on an hourly basis. Feriendorf Hagleitner (7935) takes children from age 12 months, from 10am to 4pm.

SNOW RELIABILITY
Poor, despite artificial support
Zell am See has chosen to cover its north-east-facing pistes with snowmakers, while leaving its sunnier slopes in the hands of nature. This seemingly illogical approach is presumably designed to maximise the chance of continuous snow down to Zell; not much consolation to skiers based in Schüttdorf. Also, most of the slopes covered are the steeper ones, unsuitable for the moderate majority.

The Kaprun glacier is, of course, snowsure, but the queues when the glacier is in demand are horrendous.

FOR ADVANCED SKIERS
Two tremendous blacks
There is more steep skiing in Zell than in most ski areas of this size, but not enough to entertain a good skier for a week. All except one run back to the valley are black. When we were there last February both black runs 1 and 2 were immaculately groomed each night and made for fabulous fast skiing on steep slopes – and deserted first thing. They both have substantial artificial snow facilities. Off-piste opportunities are limited.

FOR INTERMEDIATE SKIERS
Bits and pieces for most grades
Good or aggressive intermediates have a choice of fine, long runs, but this is not a place for those keen on high-mileage. All pistes graded black are within a brave intermediate's capability. Moderate skiers have a lovely run between Areit and Schüttdorf when conditions are good (not too often). Some of Sonnkogel's pistes are also suitable. Timid skiers can cruise around the ridge all day or ski past Mittelstation and cut across to the cable-car stations on an easy blue. The Hirschkogel runs are best for mixed abilities.

FOR BEGINNERS
Two low nursery areas
There are small nursery slopes at the cable-car area and at Schüttdorf, the former being covered by snowmakers. Near-beginners and fast learners have plenty of short, easy runs at Schmittenhöhe, Breiteckalm and Areitalm. Some of them are often used by complete beginners, due to poor snow conditions lower down, but it means buying a lift pass.

FOR CROSS-COUNTRY
Excellent if snow allows
The valley floor has extensive trails, including a superb area on the Kaprun

golf course. Unfortunately, there is very little at altitude except a 2km loop at the top of the Zell gondola.

QUEUES
Not normally a problem
Zell am See doesn't have too many problems except at peak times, when the Schmittenhöhe cable-car is by far the worst spot, followed by the Hirschkogel chair. When snow is poor there are few queues at Zell during the day, because many residents are away queueing at Kaprun; but getting down by lift can involve delays.

MOUNTAIN RESTAURANTS
Plenty of little refuges
As well as anonymous lift-station places there are plenty of cosier, more atmospheric huts. Among the best are Glocknerhaus (below Hirschkogel), Kettingalm, Areitalm and Brieteckalm. The Berghotel restaurant at Schmittenhöhe is good, but expensive.

SKI SCHOOL
Good attitude
The three schools (two in Zell, one in Schüttdorf) have quite good reputations. Standards of English, tuition and friendliness are all reported as high, though we lack very recent reports. Snowboarding seems to be enthusiastically supported. There are also specialist cross-country centres at Schüttdorf and at Kaprun.

FACILITIES FOR CHILDREN
Schüttdorf's the place
We have no recent reports on the workings of the childcare provisions, but staying in Schüttdorf has the advantage of direct gondola access to the Areitalm snow-kindergarten, and fairly convenient access to one of the two village nurseries (Ursula Zink is at Zeller-Moos, just outside Schüttdorf).

 # Staying there

Choice of location is tricky, and will depend on your own priorities. Our three favourite strategies would be to stay: in a beautiful lakeside setting (which gets you on the ski-bus before it's too crowded), at the upper edge of the town centre (walking distance from the Zell gondola), or near the cable-car station at Sonnenalm.

Before Zell improved its lift system it was well worth staying in Schüttdorf to avoid the queues. Perhaps it still is during peak season, but Schüttdorf is a characterless dormitory with little else going for it. Being closer to Kaprun is,

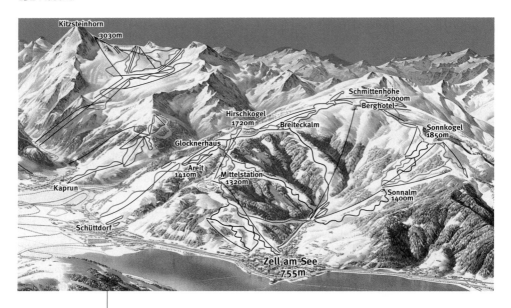

SKI SCHOOL

Schmittenhöhe
Courses start Sunday and Monday
Classes 6 days
Full day: from 9.30
6 full days: 1550
Children's classes
Ages: from 4
6 full days: 1700
Private lessons
Hourly or daily
500 for 1hr; each additional person 100

Wallner-Prenner
Courses start Sunday and Monday
Classes 6 days
Full day: from 9.30
6 full days: 1500
Children's classes
Ages: from 4
6 full days: 1650
Private lessons
Hourly or daily
500 for 1hr; each additional person 100

Areitbahn
Courses start Sunday and Monday
Classes 6 days
Full day: from 10am
6 full days: 1500
Children's classes
Ages: from 4
6 full days: 1650
Private lessons
Hourly or daily
500 for 1hr; each additional person 100

perversely, a drawback unless you have a car. Trying to get on a glacier bus is tough, as they tend to be full when they leave Zell. Families wishing to use the Areitalm nursery and cross-country skiers stand to gain most from staying in Schüttdorf.

HOW TO GO
Choose charm or convenience
There is a very wide range of hotels or pensions and apartment accommodation, but tour operators have ignored the latter.
Chalets This season there are no catered chalets so far as we are aware.
Hotels There is a broad range of hotel and guest-house accommodation, with a slight upmarket bias – 4-star hotels outnumber 3-stars.
££££ Salzburgerhof Best in town – the only 5-star. Nearer the lake than

the gondola, but with courtesy bus service. Excellent pool.
££££ Tirolerhof Excellent, friendly 4-star chalet in the old town, popular with Brits. Good pool, jacuzzi and steam room. Good food.
££££ Eichenhof Poor position on the outskirts of town. But popular and well run, with a minibus service, great food and lake views.
££££ Alpin Modern 4-star chalet next to the Zell gondola.
££££ Zum Hirschen Comfortable, central 4-star, easy walk to gondola, sauna, steam, splash pool, popular bar.
££££ Schwebebahn Attractive 4-star in secluded setting by cable-cars.
£££ Berner 3-star by the Zell gondola.
£££ Erlhof Way out of town, in a completely peaceful setting across the lake: a rustic 4-star chalet with the best food in the area.

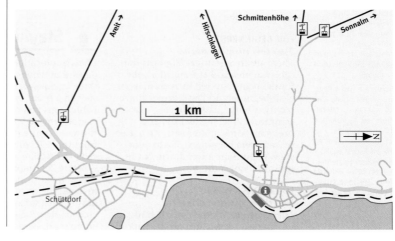

GETTING THERE

Air Salzburg, transfer 2hr. Munich, transfer 3hr.

Rail Station in resort.

PACKAGES

Airtours, Altours Travel, Crystal, First Choice Ski, Inghams, Lagrange, Made to Measure, Neilson, PGL Ski Europe, PGL Teen Ski, Rank STS, Ski Choice, Ski Leogang, SkiBound, Thomson

Kaprun Airtours, Austrian Holidays, Crystal, First Choice Ski, Inghams, Made to Measure, Neilson

Schüttdorf Airtours, Neilson

ACTIVITIES

Indoor Swimming, sauna, solarium, fitness centre, spa, tennis, squash, bowling, museum, art gallery, cinema, lessons in self-defence and judo, library, massage, ice skating
Outdoor Riding, skating, curling, floodlit toboggan runs, plane flights, sleigh rides, shooting range

TOURIST OFFICE

Postcode A-5700
Tel 00 43 (6542) 2600
Fax 2032

££ **Hubertus** B&B pension next to the Zell gondola.
££ **Margarete** B&B next to cable-car.
Self-catering The budget Karger Christine apartments are well placed for the Zell gondola. Apartment Hofer is a mid-range place close to the Ebenberg lift (which links to the gondola). More comfortable places are the 3-star Diana and Seilergasse (both in the old centre) and the Mirabell, which is close to the Zell gondola.

STAYING UP THE MOUNTAIN
Widely spread choices
As well as the big hotel at the top of the Schmittenhöhe cable-car, there are a couple of mountain restaurants with rooms. Breiteckalm is high up on the southern arm of the ski area, Sonnalm is at the northern arm mid-station.

EATING OUT
Plenty of choice
There is a good range of restaurants, with more non-hotel places than is usual in a small Austrian resort. The Ampere is a quiet, sophisticated place; Guiseppe's is a popular Italian restaurant with excellent food; and Kupferkessel and Traubenstüberl both do wholesome regional dishes. There are Chinese restaurants in both Zell and Schüttdorf. Car drivers could try the good value Finkawirt, across the lake at Prielau, or the excellent Erlhof.

APRES-SKI
Plenty for all tastes
Après-ski is lively and varied. Reps organise a full programme of the usual Austrian evening entertainments. Ice-hockey matches are lively; tea-dances and high-calorie cafés are popular at tea-time; and there are bars and discos a-plenty. On a sunny afternoon Schnapps Hans ice bar outside the Berghotel at the top of the cable-car really buzzes, with loud music, singing and dancing on the bar, all choreographed by a crazy DJ. The Diele disco bar is arguably the liveliest place in town, with a mixed age group for 4pm après and a younger crowd after dinner. Crazy Daisy on the main road has two crowded bars – downstairs with a nostalgia theme and upstairs with live guitarist, popular with Brits. Evergreen has a live band, 60s and 70s music and is popular with a more mature crowd – we loved it! Viva disco allows no under 18s and was advertising erotic shows on our visit. Other places include the smart Hirschkeller, cave-like Lebzelter Keller and, for a quieter drink, Sportstuberl with old ski photos and Insider bar.

NON-SKIERS
Spoilt for choice
There is plenty to do in this year-round resort. The train trip to Salzburg is a must, and Kitzbühel is also well worth a visit. Innsbruck is also just about in reach.

Walking across the frozen lake to Thumersbach is often possible in early or mid-season.

Sports facilities are impressive, and include swimming, sauna, a fitness centre, tennis (Schüttdorf), skating and riding (Schüttdorf). Other activities include a museum, sleigh rides and flights.

Kaprun 785m

Kaprun is a spacious village with lots of Tyrolean charm. There is a small, ski area on the outskirts of the village, and a separate nursery area – both suited to early intermediates.

The glacier skiing is a bus-ride away, and is accessed by a choice of an old underground funicular or a newer gondola, met by a quad chair. The main skiing is in a big bowl above the top of the funicular and chair. Skiing is mainly gentle blues and reds with one tougher run from the very top at 3029m. Snow is nearly always good and the area forms one of the better summer ski areas, as well as being a winter fallback. The main drawback is the queues, which can be appalling when the crowds are bussed-in.

Off-slope activities are good, and include a fine sports centre. Nightlife is quiet, but there are organised events. The Baum and Nindl bars are the liveliest. Good restaurants include the Dorfstadl, the Bella Musica and the Schlemmerstuberl. Many of the hotels are large, comfortable places. The Orgler, Mitteregger and Tauernhof are three of the best. Good cheaper hotels include Abendruh and Heidi. Haus Annelies is a pleasant B&B.

Zell am Ziller 575m

Although overshadowed by its near neighbour in the Zillertal, Mayrhofen, Zell has skiing of comparable scale and character, with similarly inconvenient lift arrangements. What it doesn't have is the vitality of the larger resort. Not long ago it used to be popular with Brits and tour operators. But as we went to press it looked like only one tour operator was going there this season.

THE RESORT

Skiing seems rather incidental to Zell – partly because it is one of the main communities of the Zillertal and partly because the ski lifts are some distance away, and the pistes even further. With an ornately decorated church and a brewery, Zell sits in the flat bottom of the Ziller valley, a few miles from Mayrhofen. It is not unpleasant, but lacks ski resort atmosphere.

THE SKIING

Zell's skiing is almost entirely for intermediates. It takes place on two mountains: Kreuzjoch and Gerlosstein. The main Kreuzjoch **ski area** is approached by gondola from Rohr, a short bus-ride across the valley to the east. It goes up to Wiesenalm (1310m); there is no piste back to the valley. The heart of the skiing, with runs above and below in every direction, is the sunny shelf of Rosenalm (1745m). One of the chairs from here goes to 2410m, the high-point of the skiing.

The Gerlosstein cable-car starts a longer bus-ride away at Hainzenberg and gives access to a much smaller area – consisting mainly of two chair-lifts meeting at the peak of Arbiskogel.

You have a choice of the local ski pass or the wide-ranging Zillertal pass, also covering valley trains and buses. The bus service to the local slopes is good, but geared towards skiing one area or the other all day. The service in the middle of the day is poor.

By Tyrolean standards the skiing is quite high, but the Kreuzjoch slopes get the afternoon sun, so **snow reliability** is better early in the season than late. Most of the Gerlosstein slopes are roughly north-facing, so snow is usually better.

Neither area has much to offer **advanced** skiers. The only black, from Arbiskogel at the top of the Gerlosstein area, is short and barely deserves its grading. There is off-piste skiing between the runs at Kreuzjoch.

Whether **intermediate** skiers will like Zell depends on how concerned they are about the inconvenient access to the skiing and the limited extent of it. There are essentially only half a dozen runs, and although the terrain is quite varied, the runs themselves are similar in character – with the exception of the secluded 3km red from Karspitz to Wiesenalm. Gerlosstein is worth visiting, especially for the red run from top to bottom (900m vertical). The best skiing in this area, however, is at Gerlos, a bus-ride beyond Hainzenberg, where 50km of varied terrain awaits.

Although Rosenalm is an excellent nursery area (and there is another at Gerlosstein), the effort and cost of getting there mean that Zell is far from ideal for **beginners**.

The valley floor provides some long, flat **cross-country** loops.

There are **queues** for the main gondola (downwards as well as up) at peak times, and for the nursery lifts below Rosenalm. The Gerlosstein cable-car copes, except when snow is poor at Kreuzjoch.

The **mountain restaurants** are adequate – mostly pleasant chalet-style self-service places.

The two **ski schools**, Lechner and Pro Zell, both have Rosenalm ski kindergartens and offer lunchtime care. Pro Zell also runs a nursery.

STAYING THERE

The centre of Zell is quite compact, but the village now spreads across the valley towards the lift station and the foot of the Gerlos road. You can stay close to the Kreuzjoch lifts, or indeed the Gerlosstein ones (at Hainzenberg), but most visitors stay centrally.

Choice of how to go is pretty well confined to **hotels** and guesthouses. The 4-star Theresa and Zapenhof have pools, the latter open to the public.

Eating out is limited to traditional Tyrolean fare, largely in hotel-based restaurants, and a couple of pizzerias. Hotel Dörflwirt is well regarded.

There's a fair amount of informal **après-ski**. Café Reiter is a friendly place with a twice-weekly tea-dance, hotel Zellerhof has Tyrolean evenings; the Piccadilly bar is dark and cramped but popular for its live music; and the Tony Keller is a late-hours disco.

This is not an ideal resort for **non-skiers** but it is not without sports facilities, and it is well placed for interesting excursions.

France

France has now overtaken Austria as the most popular destination for British skiers. It's not difficult to see why. France has the biggest linked ski areas in the world; for keen piste bashers who like to ski as many miles of piste in a day as possible, these are unrivalled. It also has some of the toughest, highest, wildest skiing in the Alps, and some of the longest, gentlest and most convenient beginner runs. French skiing takes some beating. French resort villages aren't quite so uniformly recommendable; but, equally, they don't all conform to the standard image of soulless purpose-built resorts, thrown up without any concern for appearance during the building boom of the 1960s and 70s.

Certainly France has its fair share of Alpine eyesores, such as Les Menuires, central La Plagne, Flaine, Tignes and Les Arcs. The redeeming features of places like this are the splendid quality of the skiing they serve, the reliability and quality of the snow and the amazing ski-in, ski-out convenience of most of the accommodation. But the French have learnt the lesson that new development doesn't have to be tasteless to be convenient – look at Valmorel, Belle Plagne and Les Coches, for example.

If you prefer, there are genuinely old mountain villages to stay in, linked directly to the big ski areas. These are not usually as convenient for the skiing, but they give you a feel of being in France rather than a skier-processing factory. Examples include Montchavin or Champagny for La Plagne, Vaujany for Alpe-d'Huez, St-Martin-de-Belleville for the Trois Vallées and Les Carroz or Samoëns (a short drive from the slopes) for Flaine. There are also old villages with their own ski areas, which have developed as resorts while retaining their ambience – such as Serre-Chevalier and La Clusaz.

And France has Alpine centres with a long mountaineering and skiing history. Chief among these is Chamonix, which sits in the shadow of Mont Blanc, Europe's highest peak, and is the centre of the most radical off-piste skiing there is.

France has advantages in the gastronomic stakes. While many of its mountain restaurants serve fast food, it is generally possible to find somewhere to get a half-decent lunch. And in the evening most resorts have restaurants serving good traditional French food as well as regional specialities. And the wine is decent and affordable.

In general, especially at today's exchange rate (FF7.6 when we went to press), France is not a cheap place to ski. It can even work out more expensive than Switzerland, especially if you choose a hotel-based holiday in a smart resort in high season.

One good development over the last few years has been the end of the ski school monopoly of the Ecole de Ski Français. Most resorts now have at least one competing ski school, often aimed at non-French visitors, and this has raised teaching standards (and standards of spoken English and customer care) considerably.

France also helps beginners by using four grades of piste instead of the usual three. The very easiest runs are graded green and, except in Val-d'Isère, they are reliably gentle. (Under Ski facts in our major resort chapters we've lumped green and blue runs together – but bear in mind that some blues can be quite challenging.)

The one big drawback of many French resorts (though not all) is the lack of nightlife. But nightlife isn't important to many British skiers. Of the people who filled in questionnaires for us on French resorts, 90 per cent said they couldn't help us with the nightlife section because they skied so hard all day that all they wanted to do after dinner was to fall into bed.

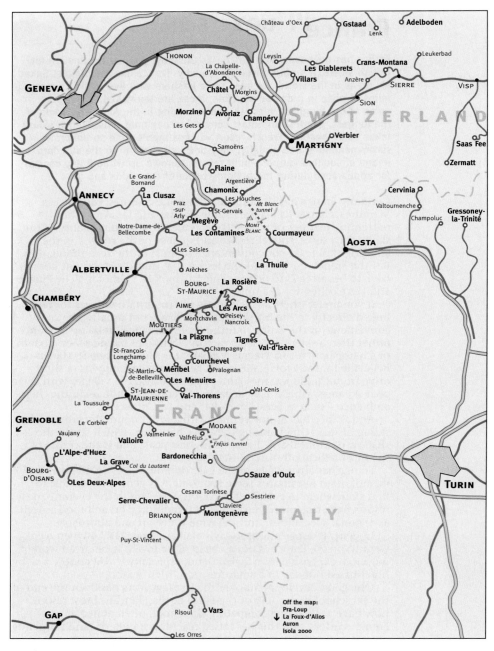

GETTING AROUND THE FRENCH ALPS

Pick the right gateway – Geneva, Chambéry or Grenoble – and you
can hardly go wrong. The only pass is on the approach to Serre-
Chevalier and Montgenèvre – the 2058m Col du Lauteret. But the
road is a major one, and generally kept clear of snow or reopened
quickly after a fall. The tunnels into Italy present no difficulties
other than expense and claustrophobia. Crossing into Switzerland
involves two passes between Chamonix and Martigny that are not
super-high but not reliably open – the Col des Montets (1461m) and
Col de la Forclaz (1527m). When necessary, one-way traffic runs
beside the tracks through the rail tunnel beneath the passes.

0 | 30

Scale in km

Alpe-d'Huez 1860m

HOW IT RATES

The skiing

Snow	★★★★
Extent	★★★★★
Advanced	★★★★
Intermediates	★★★★
Beginners	★★★★★
Convenience	★★★★
Queues	★★★
Restaurants	★★★★

The rest

Scenery	★★★★
Resort charm	★
Not skiing	★★

✔ Extensive sunny ski area, with excellent runs for all standards

✔ Efficient, modern lift system

✔ High skiing in stunning scenery

✔ Very little walking to and from most accommodation

✔ Well maintained pistes, including extensive snowmaking

✔ Some good rustic mountain restaurants

✔ Charming traditional villages in the valleys

✘ Little tree-lined skiing for bad-weather days

✘ Many of the runs can be icy early in the day in good weather

✘ Many of the tough runs rely on a high cable-car running

✘ Spread-out, charmless resort with a hotch-potch of architectural styles; seems to have developed without any real planning

✘ Some crowded runs

Alpe-d'Huez is one of France's best all-round resorts, with top-quality skiing for all and fine non-skiing facilities. It has some great tough runs (on- and off-piste) set amid spectacular, high mountain scenery – with glacier skiing from 3330m. Lower down it has extensive intermediate and beginner terrain too.

In good conditions, there are few places to rival Alpe-d'Huez for the extent and variety of the skiing – it's one of our favourites. It has a big British following too; again this year the reporters were almost unanimous in their praise. But in poor conditions it can be disappointing. The slopes get a lot of sun and can get icy. There's very little skiing in the trees – white-outs can make skiing impossible and wind can shut the top lifts.

Although Alpe-d'Huez isn't attractive, there are peaceful smaller villages which link with the skiing. Keen skiers should give the Alpe-d'Huez area a go.

The resort

Alpe-d'Huez is a large, amorphous resort. It has grown quickly in a seemingly unplanned way since being a venue for the 1968 Grenoble Winter Olympics. Its buildings come in all shapes, sizes and designs. There's even an amazingly futuristic building housing the church (which holds regular organ concerts). There's no real central focus to the resort, though its main street is in the geographic centre and forms quite a main part of the village infrastructure. The swimming

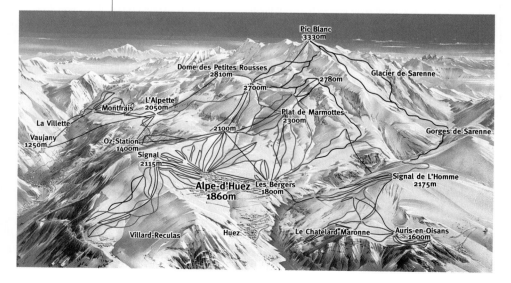

ORIENTATION

Alpe-d'Huez is a large village spread across an open mountainside, high above the Romanche valley, east of Grenoble. It lacks a definite centre – the lower end of town near the tourist office has a bucket-lift up to the main gondola station. And there's a cross-town chair-lift and a regular free bus. The main lift station at the top of the village has numerous lifts going in all directions, including the main high-capacity gondola. Another gondola heads up to the main skiing from the lower end of town (Les Bergers). One chair from here goes to one of Alpe-d'Huez's three smaller ski areas, another to the mid-station of the main gondola. The slopes spread across and down to **Auris, Villard, Oz** and **Vaujany,** hamlets which all have accommodation and lifts back up.

Outings by road are feasible to other resorts covered on the lift pass, including **Serre-Chevalier, Les Deux-Alpes** (also linked by helicopter) and **Montgenèvre.**

SKI FACTS

Altitude	1350m-3330m
Lifts	85
Pistes	227km
Green/Blue	46%
Red	30%
Black	24%
Artificial snow	32km

pool, ice skating and some of the shops, bars and restaurants are to be found there. The rest of the resort spreads out in a triangle, with lift stations close to all three apexes. There's an efficient free bus service.

Many reporters have remarked on the surprising friendliness of the place, and in terms of ambience, this once quiet 'typically French' resort gets more animated and interesting each year. It now has an extremely good Palais des Sports, with lots of activities on offer, and 32 bars, 44 restaurants and three discos to choose from.

✦ The skiing

Alpe-d'Huez isn't normally thought of as a ski area in the same class as bigger names such as Val-d'Isère, Méribel or La Plagne. But it deserves to be. It has extensive and varied skiing and as much to offer a group with mixed skiing abilities as any of those French giants. And the scenery is much more spectacular. If anything, Alpe-d'Huez's piste map understates the difficulty of its skiing. There are some red runs that would be black in other resorts and a few blues that would be red.

THE SKI AREA
Several well-linked areas

Changes in height mark fairly distinct ski areas. The tops of the mountains are rugged and steep, with black runs and steep off-piste runs only. The middle section is mainly tough reds and the lower section has the gentlest of blue and green runs.

The ski area can essentially be divided into four sectors. The biggest of these is accessed by the main gondolas out of the village. One of these (the biggest – with massive stand-up cabins) goes up in two stages to 2700m. The runs below its mid-station and below the top of the other gondola are the easy section. The big gondola delivers you to a cable-car which takes you up to the highest point of 3330m at **Pic Blanc**, from where there are endless steep options for good skiers. Above the mid-station, a couple of slow old chair-lifts serve a selection of long and difficult red runs. All the runs get a lot of sun because they face west or south.

The second sector can be accessed by skiing down black runs from the Pic Blanc or mid-mountain area, or by skiing down to the lower Bergers part of the village. From here a spectacular chair-lift-ride down into the Sarenne gorge (where you can get one to

return to the village) and up the other side brings you to more lifts up over the north-facing slopes of the **Signal de l'Homme** area. From the top you can ski back down towards the gorge, down south to Auris or west to the old hamlet of Chatelard.

The other end of town from Signal de l'Homme is the small **Signal** sector, reached by drag-lifts next to the main gondola or a chair lower down. Runs go down the other side to the old village of Villard-Reculas. The long drag-lift back is tricky in parts and sheds a fair number of its riders.

The fourth skiing sector is the **Vaujany-Oz** section of largely north-facing slopes. Oz can be reached by skiing straight down from the mid-station of the big gondola out of Alpe-d'Huez, underneath the gondola back up from Oz. Or you can go to the top-station of the Alpe-d'Huez gondola and take a beautiful run down along a shelf on the mountain towards Vaujany and the mid-station of the huge cable-car back up (at Alpette). You can ski down to Oz from here and a gondola brings you back up. Or skiing north from here leads you to the Vaujany sector of the skiing around Montfrais, where the gondola up from Vaujany arrives. Here there is a choice of five lifts, including one back to Alpette; from there you catch the second stage of the cable-car up to 2810m, and then can ski back to the top of the main Alpe-d'Huez gondola.

SNOW RELIABILITY
Good but...

The slopes get a lot of sun and the amount of skiing above 2300m is relatively limited. They can get icy in good weather (even at the top) and there have been occasions in recent seasons when nearby Serre-Chevalier, though lower lying, has had better conditions on its north-facing runs. However, under normal circumstances the runs are relatively snowsure. Moreover, the natural stuff is backed up by extensive snowmaking in the Vaujany and Oz sections as well as all the way down from the top of both of the Alpe-d'Huez gondolas. There are 385 snow cannon.

FOR ADVANCED SKIERS
Plenty of blacks and off-piste

This is an excellent resort for good skiers. Unlike so many ski areas, the black runs here are long. The run beneath the Pic Blanc cable-car is famous for its sudden plunge on exiting a tunnel through the mountain. Unfortunately this mogul

LIFT PASSES

95/96 prices in francs
Grandes Rousses
Covers all lifts in Alpe-d'Huez, Auris, Oz, Vaujany and Villard-Reculas.
Beginners Premières Traces (First Steps) daily lift pass (67) covers 16 lifts in beginners' area, Moyenne Altitude (mid-altitude) daily pass covers 39 lifts (133) in Alpe-d'Huez, Villard-Reculas and Oz.
Main pass
1-day pass 200
6-day pass 960
(low season 768 – 20% off)
Senior citizens
Over 60: 6-day pass 864 (10% off)
Children
Under 13: 6-day pass 672 (30% off)
Under 5: free pass
Notes Reduction for teenagers (14-18) 10% off (864 for 6-day pass).
Pass for 6 days or more includes one day's skiing at each of the Grande Galaxie resorts (Les Deux-Alpes, Serre-Chevalier, Puy-Saint-Vincent and the Milky Way) and free entrance to the sports centre.
Alternative passes
Passes for Auris only (15 lifts), Oz only (10 lifts), Vaujany only (10 lifts), Villard-Reculas only (8 lifts), Oz-Vaujany (19 lifts) and Moyenne Altitude (39 lifts). A pedestrian pass costs 320.

SKI SCHOOL

95/96 prices in francs
ESF
Classes 6 days
5½hr: 9.40-12.40 and 2.30-5pm;
6 full days: 890
Children's classes
Ages: 3 to 12
6 full days: 760
Private lessons
Hourly
170 for 1hr, for 1 to 2 people

field attracts a lot of macho intermediates who get in the way of good skiers as they struggle down. The run splits into three further blacks; all finish back at the cable-car station.

Another series of steep runs starts at Pic Blanc, including the longest black run in the Alps (16km with a vertical drop of almost 2000m). This starts off with a steep mogul field, but once you are off the glacier (which is open for summer skiing) it levels out and is pleasantly varied. There are stunning views on the upper part and the long lowest section (a gentle path) is beautifully set in a narrowing gorge by the side of a frozen river. There are several off-piste variants of this run, all finishing in the Sarenne gorge.

Other very long off-piste routes that take skiers well away from the pisted area (so a guide is essential) lead all the way down from Pic Blanc to Vaujany, over 2000m vertical below.

Another series of steep runs starts at the top of the Clocher de Macle chair (the second of the slow chairs up from near the mid-station of the main Alpe-d'Huez gondola). These include a beautiful long, lonely black leading back to the village, with an option to ski across to the Signal de l'Homme access chair in the Sarenne gorge.

As well as the black runs, plenty of the upper red runs are tough enough to give good skiers a challenge. These include the Canyon and Balme runs accessed by the chair from the gondola mid-station. And there's off-piste on the lower half of the mountain that is excellent in good snow conditions, including lovely runs through scattered trees and bushes at the extreme northern edge of the skiing above Vaujany.

FOR INTERMEDIATE SKIERS
Much improved
Additions to the ski area in recent years have increased the number of suitable runs between the tough and easy extremes.

Good intermediates now have a fine selection of runs all over the area. In good snow conditions the variety of the runs is difficult to beat. Every section of the skiing has some challenging red runs to test the adventurous intermediate. The most challenging are the Canyon and Balme runs mentioned above. These would be graded black in many resorts. There are lovely long runs down to Oz and to Vaujany. The off-piste among the bushes and trees above Vaujany, mentioned above, is a good place to start your off-piste

career in good snow. The Villard-Reculas and Signal de l'Homme sectors also have long challenging reds. The Chamois red from the top of the gondola down to the mid-station is beautiful but can get very crowded. Fearless intermediates should enjoy the long Sarenne black run, also mentioned above. After the first steep mogul field it's not at all difficult. But it is set in extraordinarily beautiful scenery – and you'll be able to say you've skied the world's longest black!

For less ambitious intermediates, there are usually blue alternatives, except from the top of Pic Blanc, the short top part of Signal de l'Homme and part of the run down to Villard-Reculas. The main Couloir blue from the top of the big gondola is a lovely run, well served by snowmakers, but it does get extremely crowded (and scary because of that) at times – keep to the left, where it is less crowded.

Early intermediates can get all the way over to Vaujany by taking the blue from the gondola mid-station to Oz, and then the gondola up from there to Alpette. From Alpette there's a very wide and gentle run to the Montfrais sector of great cruising runs above Vaujany. The blue down to the mid-station of the Vaujany gondola is picturesque and well-served by snowmaking. Early intermediates will also enjoy the gentle slopes leading back to Alpe-d'Huez from the main mountain, and the Signal sector.

FOR BEGINNERS
Good facilities
The large network of green runs immediately above the village is as good a nursery area as you will find anywhere. This has been especially true since the network of greens to the left of the main gondola (as you look at the mountain) became a dedicated beginners-only area, where fast skiing is banned. Add to this ski convenience, good tuition, a special lift pass covering 15 lifts, and usually reliable snow and Alpe-d'Huez is difficult to beat.

There's another good beginners' area with gentle green runs at the top of the Vaujany gondola – useful for Vaujany residents.

FOR CROSS-COUNTRY
High-level and convenient
There are 50km of trails, with two easy loops and two demanding circuits, all at around 2000m and consequently relatively snowsure. All trails are within the Alpine ski area and a cross-country user's pass costs 165 francs.

International Classes 6 days
4½hr: 2½hr am, 2hr pm
6 full days
(94/95): 1085
Children's classes
Ages: 5 to 12
6 full days
(94/95): 910
Private lessons
Hourly
175 for 1hr, for 1 to 2 people (94/95)

CHILDCARE

The main schools both run ski kindergartens. The ESF Club des Oursons, at Les Bergers and near the main gondola (76803182), takes children from age 4, ski school hours. The SEI (76804277) runs the Club des Mickeys for children aged 3½ to 4, the Club des Marmottes for those aged 5 to 12. The Eterlous kindergarten (76804327) has a private ski area and takes children aged 2½ to 14 all day; it also offers a child-minding service (until 6pm) for babies of 6 months or more.

The Club Med nursery takes children from 4, with or without tuition.

QUEUES
Generally few problems

Outside French holiday periods and busy weekends, the modern lift system ensures there are few queues. The main delays are usually for the Pic Blanc cable-car and Lièvre Blanc chair from the main gondola mid-station to the main areas of challenging skiing. These are frustrating for good skiers. Queues can also build up for the gondolas out of the village. The main gondola is usually quicker and takes you higher (the right hand side of the queue is quicker). The new chair from Les Bergers to the mid-station helped reduce the queues last season. The bottom section of the Vaujany cable-car never suffers from queues; nor do the gondolas out of Oz.

MOUNTAIN RESTAURANTS
Some excellent rustic huts

Mountain restaurants are generally good and there are plenty of rustic places you don't find in many French purpose-built resorts. At Montfrais, above Vaujany, Les Airelles is a rustic hut, built into the rock, with a roaring log fire, classical music and excellent good-value food. The Chalet du Lac Besson is a peaceful, rustic haven on the cross-country circuit between Alpette and the big gondola, with good table-service food; getting there is tricky for downhillers, easier for cross-country skiers and walkers.

The pretty Forêt de Maronne hotel at Chatelard, below Auris, is delightful and has a good choice of traditional French cuisine. The Combe Haute, at the foot of the Chalvet chair in the gorge towards the end of the Sarenne run, is welcoming but gets very busy. The Perce-Neige, just below the Oz-Poutran gondola mid-station, is so good it's permanently packed. La Plage des Neiges is one of the best huts available to beginners. The Bergerie at Villard-Reculas has good views. The Alpette and Super Signal places are also worth a visit. Even the large self-service places such as Marmottes, at the top of the gondola from Les Bergers, have above-average food. The restaurants in the Oz and Vaujany sectors tend to be cheaper.

SKI SCHOOL
Contrasting views of the schools

The sound reputation the ESF once enjoyed here has been lost of late. We've had reports of 14 or 15 people in group classes and mixed views on standards of English. In contrast, the International School limits classes to eight and standards of English are reported high. It is linked to Ski Masterclass run by a Brit, Stuart Adamson. However, other reporters have preferred the ESF, notably for superior standards of technical tuition. Ski évolutif is an option. Instruction is also available in off-piste, ski touring, mono and freestyle. The Bureau des Guides has a good reputation – very useful for good skiers who want to try the excellent off-piste.

FACILITIES FOR CHILDREN
Good reports

We've had a rave review of the International School for children: 'started the week snowploughing nervously down greens, ended up skiing parallel down reds ... only three in the class'. Children who need lunchtime care or breaks from skiing must go to Les Eterlous – though one reporter this year told us that the ESF advertised lunchtime supervision that failed to materialise.

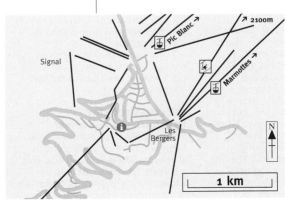

GETTING THERE

Air Lyon, transfer 3hr. Geneva, transfer 4hr. Grenoble, transfer 1½hr.

Rail Grenoble (65km); daily buses from station.

Staying there

Staying close to one of the gondolas is useful, and most accommodation used by British operators is well placed for skiing. Les Bergers, at the entrance to the resort, is convenient for skiing (it has its own nursery area) but is a trek to most of the other resort facilities. Being near the village bucket-lift is handy if you're not close to the slopes. And there is a free bus service.

HOW TO GO
Something of everything
Chalets There are quite a few chalet-hotels. Neilson have two – both near the centre of the resort and both with good value bars. The modern Bel Alpe

is now managed by Ski Miquel. It's well run and conveniently located. Crystal run a decent chalet-hotel in the centre. Skiworld have a convenient, simple old hotel annexe next to one of the Neilson chalet-hotels.
Hotels There are more hotels than is usual in a high French resort and a clear downmarket bias, with more 1-stars than 2- or 3-stars, and only one 4-star. There is a Club Med.
££££ Ours Blanc Central. Luxurious inside, with lots of warm wood. Good food. Superb fitness centre. It runs a free minibus to the lifts.
£££ Chamois d'Or Good facilities, modern rooms (some with balconies), one of the best restaurants in town and well placed for main gondola.
£££ Cimes South-facing rooms with

Selected chalets in Alpe d'Huez and Vaujany

PACKAGES

AA Ski-Driveaway, Airtours, Alpine Options Skidrive, Altours Travel, Chalets 'Unlimited', Club Med, Crystal, Driveline Europe, Equity Total Ski, First Choice Ski, French Impressions, Fresh Tracks, Inghams, Kings Ski Club, Lagrange, Le Shuttle Holidays, Made to Measure, MasterSki, Motours, Neilson, PGL Ski Europe, Ski Ardmore, Ski Club of GB, Ski France, Ski Miquel, Ski Partners, Ski Valkyrie, SkiBound, Skiworld, Stena Sealink, Thomson, Travelscene Ski-Drive

Vaujany Made to Measure, Ski Peak, Ski Valkyrie

ACTIVITIES

Indoor Sports centre (tennis, gym, squash, aerobics, body-building, climbing wall, sauna), library, cinema, swimming pool, billiards, bridge
Outdoor Artificial skating rink (skating and curling), 30km of cleared paths, outdoor swimming pool, hang-gliding, para-gliding, all-terrain carts, quad-bikes, ice climbing

TOURIST OFFICE

Postcode 38750
Tel 00 33 76803541
Fax 76806954

balconies, excellent food; close to cross-resort lift and pistes.
£££ Grandes Rousses Comfortable, excellent food, friendly staff; close to pistes and lifts.
£££ Petit Prince Pretty public rooms, sunny bedrooms; handy for the Grand Sure chair to Signal.
££ Beau Soleil The best-situated 2-star, offering good value.
££ Les Gentianes Close to the Sarenne gondola in Les Bergers; a wide range of rooms, the best of them comfortable.
Self-catering There is an enormous choice though most British operators' allocations are in the same few, mostly simple, apartment blocks.

The Rocher Soleil are in a different class from most, offering unusually comfortable, spacious accommodation with good communal facilities including access to a heated outdoor pool. Their position, opposite the Sarenne gondola in Les Bergers, is good for ski convenience and those wanting a particularly quiet time away from the main village.

The Pierre et Vacances places are much more central, but are not up to the usual standards of the chain. They remain, however, better than some apartments in this resort.

The Residence Les Horizons d'Huez apartments are short on space but superior to the usual 'French box'.

The Christiania, near the lifts in Les Bergers, and the spacious but less convenient Meteor apartments are recommended by a regular visitor.

EATING OUT
Good value

Alpe-d'Huez has 44 restaurants, many of which are good quality and good value by French purpose-built resort standards. Ancolie and Pomme de Pin are top of the range in quality and price. Cremaillere is highly recommended by a frequent visitor for its excellent food; it gives aperitifs gratis and even lays on a free taxi there and back. Au P'tit Creux gets a similarly positive review for excellent food, ambience and value. L'Aquarium is a good French restaurant, though several reporters have commented on its excellent paella. Genepi is a nice old friendly place with good cuisine. Au Vieux Guide also has admirable food, though the animal skins used for decor are an acquired taste. Saint Huron, Fromagerie and Edelweiss are others worth a try. Oregano, Tremplin and Pizzeria Pinocchio have good wholesome Italian fare. The latter, together with La Taverne, is said to do the best pizza.

APRES-SKI
Variable according to season

The evening ambience varies a great deal according to season and time of the week. It can be pretty dead mid-week in January, extremely lively on peak-season weekends.

The Lincoln pub, complete with karaoke and Newcastle Brown, attracts many Brits. The little Avalanche bar is popular with locals and is often the liveliest thanks to its resident singer. P'tit Bar takes some beating for atmosphere, and also has a fun singer. Sporting is a large but friendly French rendezvous which has a live band. Chamois, Menandiere and Charlies are other popular places with live music. Le Chalet opened last season and quickly became popular. Three discos liven up whenever the French are in town en masse. The Igloo is popular with locals, is not too big and has loud music. Most Brits prefer the Apples and Pears. English films are shown occasionally in the cinema, the ice rink is open till eleven, and the village swimming pool closes at seven.

FOR NON-SKIERS
Good by purpose-built standards

There is a wide range of facilities, including a new indoor pool, older open-air heated pools, Olympic-size ice rink and splendid sports centre. Be warned: take proper trunks – Bermuda-style shorts are reportedly banned from the pool. There's also a winter driving school. Shops are numerous, but limited in range. You can take helicopter rides to Les Deux-Alpes for the day with skiing companions. A car is useful for interesting excursions to Grenoble and Briançon. It's a shame that the better mountain restaurants aren't easily accessible to non-skiers.

Vaujany 1250m

Vaujany is a tiny rural village perched on the hillside opposite its own sector of the Alpe-d'Huez skiing. It has a giant 160-person cable-car (one of the biggest in the world) that whisks you, in two stages, to 2800m, from where you ski down a lovely red to the top of the main gondola up from Alpe-d'Huez and the bottom of the Pic Blanc cable-car. If you hate morning queues this is the place to be – no-one has ever seen the cable-car full. So time it right and you'll be right on and up the mountain in minutes.

The first stage gives you direct access to both the Oz and Vaujany sectors of the skiing. There's also a gondola from the village direct to the bottom of the Vaujany skiing and nursery slopes, with a mid-station at La Villette, an even smaller hamlet than Vaujany (just one tiny bar-restaurant). You can't normally ski back to Vaujany – only to the mid-station.

The lifts are paid for with the substantial income the community receives from a massive hydro-electric power project that it allowed to take place (but which is unobtrusive).

Vaujany has four simple hotels. The Rissiou is run by a British tour operator (Ski Peak). It has a popular bar (frequented by the lift operators and ski instructors), pleasant dining room which serves excellent French cuisine (and has a good inexpensive wine list), and fairly basic bedrooms. The staff are friendly and the maitre d'hôtel is efficient and pleasantly eccentric. Ski Peak also has catered chalets in Vaujany and La Villette and some self-catering accommodation. It runs a minibus to ferry guests around.

The Cîmes, over the road, is less rustic but useful for a change of bar scenery. The Etendard, by the lift station, and Grandes Rousses, in the village above the road, are run by a Belgian tour operator and cater for a young, lively crowd – the Etendard bar gets noisy and packed at the end of the day.

There's a disco up in the old village, usually heaving with Belgians from the Etendard, and a nightclub run by the mayor's son, which is usually very quiet. There's an open-air ice rink, well-stocked sports shop, small supermarket, a couple of restaurants and a few chickens wandering the streets. And there's a bit of (tasteful) development going on up the mountainside. But essentially Vaujany is for those who want a quiet time and easy access to a big skiing area from a tiny, unspoiled French village.

Vaujany has its own ski school – we've had a glowing report of it this year (only three in a class of beginners). And there's a big, brand-new day nursery by the lift station.

Oz-Station 1350m

Oz is a purpose-built little place up in the heart of the main ski area, above the attractive original old village of Oz-le-Oisans. Its two large apartment blocks, which are the focus of the place, have been built in a sympathetic style, with much use of wood and stone. The village also benefits from being the only resort in the area with trees on all sides.

It has the basics required of a tiny, family ski resort – good access to the slopes, ski school, sports shops, nursery slopes, a couple of bar-restaurants and a supermarket. A choice of gondolas move away in different directions, from where you can ski off to all points in double-quick time. The main run home is liberally endowed with snow cannon.

Auris 1600m

Auris is a series of wood-clad, chalet-style apartment blocks with a few shops, bars and restaurants. Beneath it is the original old village, complete with attractive, traditional buildings, a church and all but one of the resort's hotels. This is a pleasant base for those with a car. They can nip up to the upper village to start skiing locally, and also have speedy access to the valley for excursions to neighbouring resorts such as Serre-Chevalier. The upper village is pleasantly set close to the thickest woodland in the area. It's a fine family resort, with everything close to hand, including a nursery that takes children from 18 months and a ski kindergarten for 4- and 5-year-olds. There's also a ski school.

Evenings are unsurprisingly quiet, with just four bar-restaurants to choose from. The Beau Site, which looks like an apartment block, is the only hotel in the upper village. Down the hill, the attractively traditional Auberge de la Forêt, hotel Emaranches and a selection of gîtes give you a feel of 'real' rural France. Over the hill, in a secluded spot, is a fourth hotel – the cosy open-fired Forêt de Maronne. A 'down and up' chair takes skiers over to Alpe-d'Huez, but there is a fair amount of skiing to explore on the local slopes, for which there is a special lift pass. This covers 45km of piste for just over half the cost of the full area pass. Most of the skiing is intermediate, though Auris is also the best of the local hamlets for beginners.

Villard-Reculas 1500m

Villard is a secluded village, complete with an old church, set on a small shelf wedged between an expanse of open snowfields above and tree-filled hillsides below. It's a farming community, with just the bare essentials of a 'resort' – one hotel, a few apartment buildings, supermarket and a couple of bars and restaurants. Its local slopes are linked over the mountain to Alpe-d'Huez, and essentially have the skiing of the large resort in microcosm – good village nursery slopes and mostly steep, sunny intermediate runs. One surprise is the lack of snowmakers, often leaving the runs home icy and patchy.

Les Arcs 1600m–2000m

✔ *Skiing to and from the door of much of the accommodation*

✔ *Opportunity for beginners to learn by ski évolutif method*

✔ *Excellent children's facilities*

✔ *Few queues outside the 2000 area*

✔ *Plenty of tree-lined skiing as bad weather option*

✘ *Villages are purpose-built and lack charm*

✘ *Very quiet in the evenings*

✘ *Little for non-skiers to do*

✘ *Nearly all accommodation is in apartments; there's a lack of chalets and cheap hotels*

At first sight Les Arcs has a lot going against it. Its architecture can at best be described as functional, at worst downright ugly. But look again and you'll find that the resort has too much going for it to be dismissed at first sight, especially by keen skiers who don't want much other entertainment. It has an unusual mixture of attractions.

There are some beautiful, long runs through the trees down to traditional rustic French villages. There's a splendid high area of tough runs with good snow above Arc 2000. Beginners can learn quickly using the ski évolutif method of starting on short skis and gradually moving up to longer ones. Intermediates will find plenty of cruising runs to keep them happy. And the lift pass covers days out in other major Tarentaise resorts if you want to explore further afield.

It's a very good resort for families. Its children's facilities are impressive, particularly for those who have the inclination and funds to stay in one of the several hotels with children's clubs – or at Club Med.

There are remarkably few Brits around outside 1800 – Les Arcs remains an essentially French resort.

ORIENTATION

Les Arcs is made up of three resorts linked by road, high above the railway terminus town of Bourg-St-Maurice in the Isère valley. 1800 is the focal spot, though all three villages have numerous lifts into different parts of the ski area. 1600 is linked directly to Bourg by funicular as well as road. 2000 is the newest and bleakest, but most convenient for the highest, best skiing.

At the perimeter of the ski area are a couple of old villages – Peisey-Nancroix-Vallandry on the west and Le Pré-Villaroger on the east. Both have links into the Les Arcs skiing.

Day trips are possible to **La Rosière** on the other side of the valley from Bourg, **La Plagne, Val-d'Isère-Tignes,** the **Trois Vallées,** **Pralongnan-la-Vanoise** and **Les Saises**. The six-day lift pass gives unlimited access to La Plagne, plus a day per week in each of the others.

 ## The resort

Les Arcs has three villages, all fairly similar in many respects. All are purpose-built, relatively unattractive, apartment-dominated places, well positioned for doorstep skiing but lacking off-slope activities.

By far the largest of the three is 1800. It is also the central focus of the ski area, with lifts in numerous directions. It has three sections. The 'battleship' architecture of giant apartment blocks and shopping arcades synonymous with Les Arcs dominates Charvet and Villards. More pleasant on the eye is Charmettoger, at the periphery of the resort as a whole, with smaller, wood-clad buildings nestling among trees.

Charmettoger is also more consistently ski-convenient – some of the 'battleships' have been built at right angles to the slopes, falling away down the hillside on which the resort is built, and are so long that if you are unlucky enough to be staying at the far end of one, walks to lifts can be longer and more tiring than is stated in the brochures.

If 1800 has a centre, it's the Hotel du Golf. Essentially where Charvet meets Villards, it's the focus of après-ski. The slopes and a couple of main lifts are just outside the door, and the village nursery and mini-club are nearby. The two arcades that house most of the shops, bars and restaurants are either side.

2000 is just a few hotels, apartment blocks and the Club Med huddled together in a bleak spot, with little to commend it but immediate access to the highest, toughest skiing.

1600 has the advantage of being at the top of the Bourg-St-Maurice

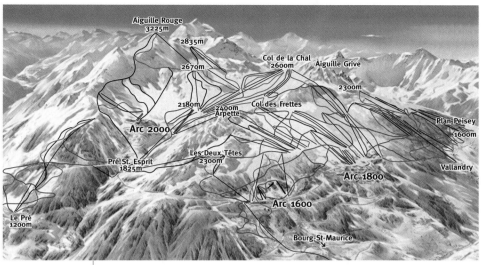

SKI FACTS

Altitude 1200m-3225m
Lifts   79
Pistes   150km
Green/Blue   54%
Red   32%
Black   14%
Artificial snow   12km

LIFT PASSES

94/95 prices in francs
**Massif Aiguille
Grive-Aiguille Rouge**
Covers all lifts in Les
Arcs and Peisey-
Nancroix, including
funicular from Bourg-
St-Maurice.
Beginners Five free
lifts; one in 1600 and
two each in 1800 and
2000.
Main pass
1-day pass 205
6-day pass 940
Children
Under 12: 6-day pass
800 (15% off)
Under 7: free pass
Short-term passes
Half-day, 145.
Notes All passes
cover La Plagne and
allow 1 day in La
Rosiere and La Thuile.
6-day pass and over
allows one day each
in Tignes-Val d'Isère,
the 3V, Pralognan-la-
Vanoise and Les
Saises; 10% reduction
on weekly pass for
families.

funicular, giving easy access to
'civilisation' for shopping, train
transfers and trips to other ski resorts.
It is set in the trees and has a friendly
feel to it; it enjoys good views along
the valley and towards Mt Blanc. It's
particularly user-friendly for families:
uncrowded, compact, set on even
ground and traffic-free. The road to
Bourg and the other villages bypasses
the resort, with the car park on the
outskirts. Things are even quieter at
night than they are during the day.
You might say 1600 combines the
functionality of Flaine with the
villagey feel of a more human place.

 # The skiing

Les Arcs' ski area is smaller than
neighbouring La Plagne's. But it has
more skiing suitable for good skiers
and a good mixture of high, snowsure
skiing and accessible low-level
woodland skiing ideal for bad weather.

THE SKI AREA
Well planned, and varied
The ski area is very well laid out and
moving around it is quick and easy.
All three villages are ski-in but not ski-
out places, having few runs
immediately beneath them. Each has a
number of lifts fanning out, none of
which are 'must-takes'. Virtually any
lift will do to gain height, after which
there is a plethora of runs criss-
crossing the mountainsides for access
to other sections.

    1600 and **1800** share a west-facing
mountainside with runs back to and
between both villages. At the southern
end of their skiing are runs down to

and lifts up from **Peisey-Nancroix**
and **Vallandry**. From the 1600 and
1800 skiing you take lifts up to a ridge
and ski down into the **2000** ski area.
On the opposite side of the bowl in
which 2000 is set, lifts take you to the
highest skiing of the area, served by
the **Aiguille Rouge** cable-car which
takes you to 3225m. As well as a
variety of steep runs back to Arc 2000
from here, you can take a lovely long
run right down to the hamlet of
Le Pré near Villaroger (over 2000m
vertical). This is arguably the longest
continuously interesting piste in the
Alps, with no boring sections as is the
case with runs claimed by other
resorts to be longer. This is at the
extreme opposite end of the ski area
from Peisey-Nancroix. You can also
reach Le Pré from below 2000, via a
short drag-lift. A chair brings you back
up.

    All three resorts have a floodlit piste,
officially open twice a week.

SNOW RELIABILITY
Good – plenty of high skiing
A high percentage of the skiing is
above 2000m and a fair amount on
north-facing slopes. While the highest
skiing from Aiguille Rouge is more
suitable for good skiers, there are easy
north-facing runs starting from
2600m. There is limited artificial snow
on some runs back to 1600, 1800 and
Peisey, but none down to Le Pré.

FOR ADVANCED SKIERS
Challenges on- and off-piste
Although it does not have the macho
reputation of Chamonix, Verbier or
neighbouring Val-d'Isère, Les Arcs is
not a bad choice for advanced skiers.

SKI SCHOOL

94/95 prices in francs

ESF
Classes 6 days
3hr: am or pm
6 half-days: 600
Children's classes
Ages: 3 to 13
6 half-days: 580
Private lessons
Hourly
180 for 1hr

International (Arc Adventure)
Classes 6 days
5hr: 2½hr am and pm
6 full days: 780
Children's classes
Ages: from 4 to 13
6 full days: 780
Private lessons
Hourly
170 for 1hr

Virages
Classes 6 days
3hr per day
6 3hr days: 670
Children's classes
Ages: from 3
6 3hr days: 680
Private lessons
Hourly
185 for 1hr

Speed skiing on the Olympic slope

The 1992 Olympic speed skiing course is open to anyone mad enough to have a go! Actually, it's not too dangerous – you go from some way below the competition start at the top, and the stopping area is very wide, flat and immaculately groomed. The only deaths that have occurred have been from elite performers skiing blind, with head down for maximum streamlining, hitting the timing mechanism. You get a mini-medal for averaging 90kph between the timing posts, a bronze medal for 110kph, silver for 130kph, and gold for 150kph.

One run, including hire of special skis and glasses and the streamlining helmet (great for photos!), is FF60, or an all-day pass is FF160. It takes a long time to prepare the course after a snowfall (it's too steep for a piste-basher to get up or down), so don't be surprised to find it closed.

There are a number of truly black runs above Arc 2000, and a couple in other areas. The Aiguille Rouge cable-car is key for accessing several of the steepest runs, and when this is shut (as it often is in bad or windy weather) the area's interest for advanced skiers is severely limited. The Aiguille Rouge-Le Pré black, with a vertical drop of over 2000m, is superb, with remarkably varying terrain. There is also a great deal of off-piste potential, with powder skiing after a fresh snowfall among trees above 1600 and down towards Peisey, very difficult steep bowl skiing beneath Aiguille Rouge, and lovely runs on the outer edge of the ski area at Grand Col (served by new lifts this season).

FOR INTERMEDIATE SKIERS
Plenty for all standards
One strength of the area is that most main routes have easy and more difficult alternatives, making it good for mixed-ability groups. There's lots to challenge, yet leisurely skiers are able to move around without getting too many nasty surprises. An exception is the solitary Comborcières black linking 1600 with Pré-St-Esprit. This long mogul field justifies its rating and can be great fun for strong intermediates, but too many near-novices attempt it, causing an overcrowded piste, which is exasperating for speedier skiers. Taking the Lac red is a more comfortable route to 2000.

The woodland runs at either end of the ski area, above Peisey and Le Pré, and the bumpy Cachette red down to 1600 are also good for better intermediates. Those wishing to 'go for it' will like Peisey: its well-groomed runs are remarkably uncrowded much of the time – ideal for fast skiing. The over-confident should avoid the Le Pré

black, due to a narrow section which demands technical proficiency rather than guts. Better skiers will enjoy it all the way down.

The lower section is good for mixed-ability groups, with a choice of routes through the trees. The red runs down from Arpette and Col des Frettes towards 1800 are quite steep but usually well groomed.

Leisurely types have plenty of cruising terrain. Many of the runs around 2000 are rather bland and prone to overcrowding. The blues above 1800 are nice, though busy, motorways, whilst the easier of the pistes down to Peisey are pleasantly quiet. The pretty Mont Blanc run is a lovely glide.

FOR BEGINNERS
1800 best for complete novices
There are nursery slopes conveniently situated just above all three villages. The ones at 1600 (used for night skiing) are rather steep for complete beginners, while those at 2000 get crowded with intermediate through-traffic at times. The sunny, spacious runs at 1800 are best. Fast learners can take the gondola up to Col de la Chal at 2600m for 'top of the world' views and usually great snow on the easy runs down towards Arc 2000.

FOR CROSS-COUNTRY
Very boring locally
Short trails, mostly on roads, close to all three villages, is the extent of it unless you travel down to the Nancroix Valley, where there are 40km of pleasant trails.

QUEUES
2000 is the only problem area
There are few queues except at Arc 2000. Even when snow is good in other sections, too many skiers seem

CHILDCARE

The ESF branches in all three stations take children from 3. The International school's Club Poussin in 1800 starts at 4.

At 1600 the Baby Club at the hotel de la Cachette (79077050) takes children from 4 months to 12 years, from 8.30 to 6pm, with ski lessons available for those aged 3 or more.

At 1800 various arrangements are offered by the Pommes de Pin nursery (79415542). The nursery itself takes childrem aged 1 to 6, from 8.45 to 5.45. Children aged 3 to 9 can join the Mini-Mini club or Mini-Maxi club, which means morning and afternoon ski classes, with lunch by arrangement.

There are children's clubs at several hotels other than the Cachette – Golf (1800) ages 3 to 6, Aiguille Rouge (2000) 3 to 6, Latitudes (1800) 4 to 12, Eldorador (2000) 4 to 12 – this is one of their 'family villages'. The Club Med (2000) has comprehensive childcare facilities.

GETTING THERE

Air Geneva, transfer 3½hr. Lyon, transfer 3½hr. Chambery, transfer 2½hr.

Rail Bourg-St-Maurice; frequent buses and direct funicular to resort.

to make a bee-line for the runs above the highest village. The cable-car is a particular bottleneck. At holiday times overcrowded pistes can be as big a problem as queues, especially on some of the blue runs.

MOUNTAIN RESTAURANTS
Very little choice
Mountain restaurants are low in both quality and quantity. The large place at Pré-St-Esprit has a good sun terrace and cheap (by local standards) pizza and pasta. The older, smaller restaurant here, Chez Béliou La Fumée, has a rustic atmosphere and good food. The two refuges in the Planay area are attractive, but their food isn't.

Chez Léa is perhaps the better of the two. The Poudreuse near the top of the Vallandry chair-lift is one of the best. La Ferme down at Le Pré has a nice terrace and good prices. The restaurant at the top of the Col de la Chal has fabulous views but lousy service.

SKI SCHOOL
Ski évolutif recommended
The ESF ski school is renowned for being the first in Europe to teach ski évolutif, where beginners learn parallel turns right from the start on short skis, cutting out snowploughs and gradually moving on to longer and longer skis. Such tuition is only available to the over 12s.

Tuition is also available in powder, mogul and racing techniques.

Again, this year we've had nothing but glowing reports of the International (also known as Arc Adventure) in Arc 1800. This seems a better bet than the ESF – which we've had mixed reports of in all three villages.

FACILITIES FOR CHILDREN
Good reports
We have an enthusiastic report on the Pommes de Pin Mini-Mini club (1800) – with the slight reservation that advance bookings appear to be a waste of time. The mini-club at the Latitudes (1800) is also recommended – 'friendly, good English' – as is the one at the Eldorador (2000). We have no reports on the ski schools, but it is worth noting that the International school at 1800 claims to operate a maximum group size of six for children aged 4 and 5 – a welcome change from the French tendency to lead infants around in huge groups.

 # Staying there

Although essentially a consistently ski-convenient resort, self-caterers staying in 1800 can be unlucky (see page 144). Charmettoger is the best bet, but it has few facilities and is quite far from the children's facilities and ski school.

HOW TO GO
Geared towards self-catering
Although all the big tour operators come here, their accommodation is limited – mostly rough-and-ready apartments. The tour operator charter train to Bourg-St-Maurice is very convenient, with one of the shortest transfers to any resort. There is a Club Med 'village' at Arc 2000.

Chalets The only catered chalet available (Skiworld) in Les Arcs itself is a cheap and cheerful place on the piste among the trees above 1600. It offers great value compared to the expensive hotels and cramped apartments. It has a pleasant open-fired lounge, but bedrooms vary enormously – the spacious top-floor rooms are much the best.

Hotels The choice of hotels in Les Arcs is gradually widening, but they still seem rather ordinary and expensive – those in 1800 particularly so. All-in packages of full board accommodation and lift pass can be attractive.

£££ **Golf** (1800) A super-pricey 3-star; the best in Les Arcs, with recently renovated rooms, sauna, gym, kindergarten and covered parking.

£££ **Trois Arcs** (1600) Central.

££ **Aiguille Rouge** (2000) Daily free ski guiding.

££ **Eldorador** (2000) Comfortable, excellent food, regular entertainment ('some nights better than others').

Self-catering Over three-quarters of the resort beds are in apartments, mostly tight on space, so paying extra for under-occupancy is a sound investment. Given the lack of nightlife, atmosphere and off-slope facilities, cable TV may be worth considering, even if you wouldn't normally watch television on holiday. The Ruitor apartments are some of the best, in one of the smaller blocks at the foot of the slopes, close to a lift. They are well equipped and nicely situated, among trees between Villards and Charmettoger. The Nova residences in Villards, which house a kindergarten and mini-club, and the Pierre et Vacances places, the Arnoise and Grand Arbois, are about the best of the rest on the British market.

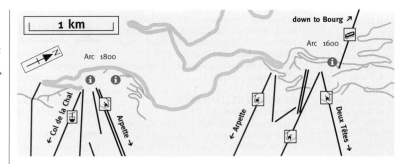

PACKAGES

AA Ski-Driveaway, Club Med, Crystal, Driveline Europe, First Choice Ski, French Impressions, Inghams, Lagrange, Le Shuttle Holidays, Made to Measure, Motours, Neilson, PGL Ski Europe, Ski Club of GB, SkiBound, Skiworld, Stena Sealink, Thomson, Travelscene Ski-Drive, UCPA

Peisey-Nancroix
Peisey Holidays

Vallandry
Equity Total Ski

ACTIVITIES

Indoor Squash (3 courts 1800), Chinese gymnastics, saunas (1600, 1800), solaria, multi-gym (1800), bridge (1800, 1600), cinemas, amusement arcades, music, concert halls, fencing (2000), bowling (1800) **Outdoor** Natural skating rinks (1800 and 2000), floodlit skiing, luge run, speed skiing (2000), ski-jump, climbing wall (1800), organised snow-shoe outings, 10km cleared paths (1800 and 1600), hang-gliding, horse-riding, sleigh rides, helicopter rides to Italy

TOURIST OFFICE

Postcode 73706
Tel 00 33 79415545
Fax 79074596

EATING OUT
Cook it yourself
Most people cook for themselves, which is pretty wise. Le Green restaurant in the Hotel du Golf has haute cuisine at sky-high prices. The Gargantus in 1800 is a welcome exception to the general mediocrity in the more informal places. L'Equipe specialises in Savoyard dishes. Casa Mia does good pizza and pasta.

APRES-SKI
Early to bed!
The Hotel du Golf in 1800 is the centre of very limited nightlife, with a jazz band and disco. The cinemas at 1800 and 1600 have English-language films once or twice a week. Otherwise it's make-your-own-atmosphere in one of the bars. Pub Russel, in 1800, is usually the most animated. The Blue Bar, an American-style cocktail joint, is the focus in 2000. It has occasional live music and stays open till late. 1600 is completely dead – there are a couple of cosy bars, one with an open fire, but they never seem to have more than a handful of punters in to give them any atmosphere.

FOR NON-SKIERS
Very poor
Les Arcs is not the place for a non-skier. There is very little to do off the slopes. It doesn't even have a swimming pool. A shopping trip to Bourg-St-Maurice, preferably on Saturday for the market, and a few walks are the main options available.

Bourg-St-Maurice 840m
Staying in Bourg-St-Maurice has its advantages. It's a real French town, without much charm, but with cheaper hotels and restaurants and easy access to other ski resorts for day trips. The funicular takes skiers straight to 1600 in seven minutes. However, those without a car will find the walk from town to the funicular a trek in ski boots.

Le Pré 1200m
A charming, rustic little hamlet with a chair-lift up to the Arc 2000 ski area. It has a few small bars and restaurants but not much more, and is a short drive from Villaroger on the road between Bourg-St-Maurice and Val-d'Isère. The Aiguille Rouge restaurant has been recommended.

Peisey-Nancroix 1350m
This small village dates back to AD1000, though its most striking feature is the fine baroque church. The other, mostly old, buildings house a small selection of shops, restaurants and bars, a short drive above the main Moutiers-Bourg road. The main tree-lined skiing of Les Arcs starts a five-minute gondola ride above the village, at Plan-Peisey-Vallandry. Skiing home off-piste is feasible.

All three reporters who stayed here last season recommended it highly for its very French atmosphere and pretty tree-lined easy red runs home.

Avoriaz 1800m

✔ Good position on the main Portes du Soleil ski circuit, giving access to a very extensive, quite varied ski area suitable for all grades of skier

✔ Avoriaz is the best base in the area for good skiers, and has the best snow

✔ Ski-from-the-door convenience

✔ Excellent family apartments

✔ Resort-level snow and ski-through, car-free village give an Alpine atmosphere

✔ Good children's facilities

✘ Bold architecture, not to the liking of traditionalists

✘ Disappointing number of lift bottlenecks, and some crowded pistes

✘ Skiing doesn't go much higher than the village

✘ Portes du Soleil circuit involves some low-altitude links that are far from snowsure

✘ Unhelpful piste map system

✘ Little to do but ski

✘ Few alternatives to self-catering

✘ Pricey by local French standards

Avoriaz is not our favourite resort in the Portes du Soleil (that would be Swiss Champéry), nor is it that of our reporters, who go to Châtel and Morzine in larger numbers. But it has clear attractions. In a low-altitude area where snow is not reliable, Avoriaz has the best there is – on relatively high, north-facing slopes of varying difficulty. The Linga sector of Châtel's skiing is also easily accessible. And the Hauts Forts sector facing the village offers much the most challenging terrain in the Portes du Soleil.

So, assuming you're set on the Portes du Soleil, why not choose Avoriaz? Several reasons. For us, the character of the village is the main problem. We don't mind sleeping in purpose-built ski stations in order to get instant access to high-altitude skiing, but there is no really high-altitude skiing here. The Portes du Soleil is mainly about pottering among attractive low-altitude villages, and we'd rather be based in one. Another factor that may clinch the decision for many is cost – Châtel and Morzine are cheap by French standards; Avoriaz is not. Queues, which can be a nuisance, are not a reason to stay away: they affect those skiing the Portes du Soleil from other bases just as much as they affect Avoriaz-based skiers – more so, in fact.

ORIENTATION

Avoriaz is perched high above the established valley resort of **Morzine**, to which it is linked by piste and lift. It is one of the main resorts on the Portes du Soleil ski circuit, and has good links to **Châtel** in one direction and **Champéry** in the other. Trips by car are possible to **Flaine** and **Chamonix**.

🏔 The resort

Avoriaz is a purpose-built resort perched impressively above a dramatic, sheer rock face. Cars and coaches have to stop at the edge of town, and a horse-drawn sleigh or snow-cat transports skiers and their luggage to the accommodation. The village is set on a considerable slope, but there are ski lifts in town and moving around on foot is straightforward except when pathways are icy (which is not uncommon).

Avoriaz usually has snow all over its byways, and being able to ski through it adds to the convenience of the place; it's also one of its great selling points. Pistes, lifts and off-slope activities are close to virtually all the accommodation. Skiing from the door is usually possible, but many of the pistes finish at the foot of town, a lift-ride away from home.

SKI FACTS

Altitude 1165m-2275m
Lifts   224
Pistes   650km
Green/Blue   54%
Red   33%
Black   13%
Artificial snow 11km

LIFT PASSES

95/96 prices in francs
Portes du Soleil
Covers all lifts in all
12 resorts, and
shuttle buses.
Beginners Reduced
price (and area) half-
day and day pass.
Main pass
1-day pass 195
6-day pass 885
Senior citizens
Over 60: 6-day pass
584 (34% off)
Children
Under 16: 6-day pass
584 (34% off)
Under 5: free pass
Short-term passes
Ascent and/or return
on the téléphérique;
half-day pass (from
noon) 136.
Alternative passes
Pass covering the 42
lifts of Avoriaz only:
147 per day (94/95
price).

SKI SCHOOL

95/96 prices in francs
ESF
Classes 6 days
5hr: 2½hr am and pm
6 full days: 790
Children's classes
Ages: 4 to 11
6 full days: 630
Private lessons
1hr, 1½hr or 2hr
165 for 1hr, for 1 to 2
people; 3 to 6 people
210 per hour

94/95 prices in francs
L'Ecole de Glisse
Classes 6 days
2½hr, am or pm
6 half-days: 850
Private lessons
Hourly
160 for 1hr

The village is composed of angular, dark, wood-clad high-rise buildings, mostly apartment blocks. Reactions to the architecture vary. But even critics must concede that the place has a distinct style, unlike the dreary cuboid blocks thrown up in the 1960s in Flaine and Les Menuires.

When snow-covered, the compact car-free village has an Alpine feel despite the architecture. It is also pleasantly cosmopolitan, with the numerous British joined by plenty of Scandinavians, Germans and Spaniards. The evenings are not ultra-lively, which is just as well since much of the accommodation is very close to the bars and nightclubs.

 # The skiing

The slopes closest to Avoriaz are mainly bleak and tree-less but relatively (note that word) snowsure. They suit all standards of skier, including advanced skiers, who also have quick access to the most challenging skiing in the Portes du Soleil, extending down into the trees below the resort.

The whole Portes du Soleil circuit can be done by moderately competent skiers. (The terrible piste maps give more cause for concern than the slopes!) The circuit breaks down at Châtel, where a bus or long walk is necessary, depending on the direction of travel (see below). The ski areas of Morzine and Les Gets are part of the Portes du Soleil network but are not actually on the core circuit. To get to them you have to get across to the far side of Morzine – most easily reached by skiing or riding the cable-car down to Les Prodains then taking the bus.

Avoriaz encourages snowboarding, and has a special area with half-pipe at the foot of the Hauts Forts sector.

THE SKI AREA
Short runs and plenty of them
The village has lifts and pistes fanning out in all directions. Staying close to Avoriaz assures the comfort of riding mostly chair-lifts – some other parts of the Portes du Soleil (particularly around Champoussin and Super-Châtel) have a lot of drags. Facing the village are the slopes of **Arare-Hauts Forts**; this is essentially short-run 'yo-yo' skiing, but when the snow conditions allow there is a long alternative down to Les Prodains. You ski down a little way to get to the lifts for this sector; you do the lifts off to the left making for the **Chavanette**

sector on the Swiss border – a broad, undulating bowl where you can ski anywhere. Beyond the border at the col is the infamous Swiss Wall – a long and impressive mogul slope with a tricky start, but not the terror it is cracked up to be unless it is icy (it gets a lot of sun). Lots of skiers doing the circuit (or returning to Champéry) ride the chair down, so don't hesitate to do the same. At the bottom of the Wall is the broad, open skiing of Planachaux, above Champéry, with links to the even broader open skiing around Les Crosets and Champoussin. There are several ways back from this sector, but much the most amusing is the chair up the Wall, with a grandstand view of skiers struggling down beneath you.

Taking a lift up from Avoriaz (or traversing from some of the highest accommodation) takes you to the ridge behind the village, where pistes go down into the **Lindarets-Brocheaux** valley, whence lifts and further runs in the excellent Linga sector lead eventually to Châtel. Getting back is basically a matter of retracing your steps, although there are several options from Lindarets.

Morgins is effectively the resort diametrically opposite Avoriaz on the circuit, and the state of the snow there may encourage you to ski anticlockwise rather than clockwise, so as to avoid the low, south-facing slopes down from Bec de Corbeau.

SNOW RELIABILITY
High resort, low skiing
Although Avoriaz is high, its skiing doesn't go much higher – and some parts of the Portes du Soleil circuit are much lower. Considering their altitude, the north-facing slopes between Hauts Forts and Avoriaz hold their snow particularly well. Chavanette also has fairly snowsure skiing. Elsewhere on the circuit, don't be surprised to find poor conditions.

FOR ADVANCED SKIERS
Several testing runs
The tough skiing tends to be rather dotted about. The challenging runs down from Hauts Forts to Prodains (including a World Cup downhill course) are excellent. There is a tough red, and several long, truly black runs, one of which cuts through trees – particularly useful in poor weather. Two chair-lifts serve for 'yo-yo' skiing on the lower runs, which snow cannon help to keep open. The famous Swiss Wall at Chavanette will naturally be on your agenda, and Châtel's Linga sector is well worth the

CHILDCARE

Les P'tits Loups (50740038) takes children aged 3 months to 5, from 9am to 6pm; indoor and outdoor games, and so on.

The Village des Enfants (50740446) takes children aged 3 to 16, from 9am to 5.30, combining ski tuition with lots of other activities.

The Club Med in Avoriaz is one of their 'family villages', with comprehensive childcare facilities.

GETTING THERE

Air Geneva, transfer 2hr.

Rail Cluses (35km); bus and cable-car to resort.

PACKAGES

AA Ski-Driveaway, Airtours, Chalet Snowboard, Club Med, Crystal, Driveline Europe, First Choice Ski, French Impressions, Inghams, Kings Ski Club, Lagrange, Le Shuttle Holidays, Made to Measure, Motours, Neilson, Ski Choice, SkiBound, Stena Sealink, Thomson, Travelscene Ski-Drive

---

trip. It's not a great area for off-piste adventures, but there is plenty of skiing just outside the pistes in all of these sectors.

FOR INTERMEDIATE SKIERS
Virtually the whole area
Although some sections lack variety, the Portes du Soleil is excellent for all grades of intermediates when snow is in good supply. Timid skiers not worried about pretty surroundings need not leave the Avoriaz sector; Arare and Chavanette are gentle, spacious, 'ski anywhere' areas. To ski the long cruise between Chavanette and Les Brocheaux, you can take a short chair down to avoid the initial steep mogul field. The pretty run to Ardent is also quite easy. Champoussin has a lot of easy skiing, reached without too much difficulty via Les Crosets and Pointe de l'Au. Better intermediates have virtually the whole area at their disposal. The runs down to Pré-la-Joux and L'Essert on the way to Châtel, and those either side of Morgins, are particularly attractive. The long, sunny runs down to Grand-Paradis near Champéry are also a must when snow conditions allow; they offer tremendous views. Good intermediates will no doubt want to take on the Wall, but the fairly new chair to Pointe de Mossette from Les Lindarets provides an easier route to Champéry.

FOR BEGINNERS
Convenient and good for snow
The nursery slopes seem small in relation to the size of the resort, but are adequate because such a high proportion of skiers are intermediates. The slopes are convenient for accommodation and restaurants; they are sunny, yet good for snow, and they link well to longer, easy runs.

FOR CROSS-COUNTRY
Varied, with some blacks
There are 45km of trails, a third graded black, mainly between Avoriaz and Super-Morzine, with other fine trails down to Lindarets and around Montriond. The only drawback is that several trails are not loops, but 'out and back' routes.

QUEUES
Long at peak times
There are a disappointing number of bottlenecks. In mid- and late-season, long queues form to get out of Avoriaz at morning and afternoon peaks, and to get to the top of the village in the early evening (although the six-person

---

chair has made things a lot better). Both the Arare and Chavanette sectors get long weekend queues. Going to Arare and skiing across to the Chavanette drags saves time in the mornings. Things are better in January and early February.

MOUNTAIN RESTAURANTS
Good choice over the hill
Avoriaz has a poor reputation for mountain restaurants because of the mediocre places close to the village, but there are plenty of good places only slightly further afield. The chalets in the hamlets of Les Lindarets – surely one of the great concentrations of mountain restaurants in the Alps – and Les Marmottes are generally charming. Particular Lindarets favourites are the simple Pomme de Pin and the Cremaillerie, just below it, which specialises in chanterelle mushrooms. Others worth a visit are at the top of the Chavanette chair, Pré-la-Joux and Super-Châtel.

SKI SCHOOL
Good, but watch the queues
The ESF ski school has quite a good reputation, although classes can be large and queues may cut down the tuition time. The Ecole de Glisse provides useful competition. Their tuition prices are double those of the ESF, but classes have a maximum of six. They also offer more options for adventurous skiers. Both schools have progressive snowboarding sections.

FACILITIES FOR CHILDREN
Looking good
The central 'children's village', run by Annie Famose, is a key part of the appeal of Avoriaz for many French families. Its facilities are excellent – a chalet full of activities and special slopes complete with Disney characters. We lack recent reports on how this goes down with British children. Children aged 7 to 16 can be looked after for a whole week without parental involvement – sounds marvellous. The car-free village must be one of the safest in the Alps for children, but there are still sleighs, skiers and snow-cats to watch out for.

 # Staying there

The main consideration when choosing where to stay in the quite steeply sloping village is your evening habits. By day you can get around with the help of ski-lifts. If you plan to be out on the town every night,

ACTIVITIES

Indoor Health centre 'Altiform' (sauna, massage, solarium, gym, aerobics, jacuzzi), squash, turkish baths, volleyball, cinema, bowling **Outdoor** Para-gliding, hang-gliding, snowshoe excursions, dogsleigh rides, walking paths, sleigh rides, skating, curling, snow-scooter excursions, helicopter and light aircraft flights

remember that what goes down must later come back up.

The resort is nominally divided into half a dozen 'villages'. The Village-de-la-Falaise is the most recent area of development; it is quite separate from the rest and is close to the entrance car parks and reception facilities.

HOW TO GO
Self-catering dominates
Alternatives to apartments are few.
Chalets There are several available, all of them comfortable and attractive but designed for small family groups. Neilson and Crystal both offer chalet accommodation. If snowboarding is why you've come to Avoriaz, Chalet Snowboard's place at Les Prodains, separated from the main resort by a cable car, is the place to stay.
Hotels There are only two 3-star hotels and a Club Med 'village', which is near the top of the resort.
£££ Dromonts The original Avoriaz construction. In the middle of the resort, reasonably well placed for skiing and après-skiing.
£££ Hauts-Forts Close to the bottom of the village, so you can walk up to it after skiing.
Self-catering We are unaware of any particularly comfortable apartments; most tend to be cramped if the full allocation is taken up. Many of the better ones are in the new Falaise area, by the resort entrance, reasonably convenient for most things. The Elinka & Malinka is better equipped than most. Other Falaise apartments are simple but slightly more spacious. Up at the top of the resort – good for views and skiing from the door but little else – the Sirius apartments are reasonable.

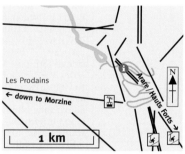

Les Prodains

← down to Morzine

Arête / Hauts Forts →

N

1 km

EATING OUT
Good; booking essential
There are numerous restaurants. The hotel Dromont's Bistro has some of the best French cuisine in town. Booking is essential. L'Igloo is also very good, but expensive. L'Ortolan, in the Elinka & Malinka complex, is friendly and good value (by local standards). There are the usual cheaper Italian places: Pizzeria Barbara is one of the best, Tex Mex and brunch in US One are also good value.

APRES-SKI
Lively, but not much choice
Nightlife lacks variety, but a few bars have good atmospheres. Le Chouca and The Place are lively and have bands, the Succa is popular, and La Taverna, Le Taraillon and Bar Fantastique are worth a visit. Happy hour in US One (also open late) is popular, as is the Midnight Express nightclub (free entry, pricey drinks).

FOR NON-SKIERS
Not much at the resort
Non-skiers are advised to go to Morzine for shops, sports facilities, riding and plenty of good walks.

TOURIST OFFICE

Postcode 74110
Tel 00 33 50740211
Fax 50741825

Chamonix 1035m

ORIENTATION
See page 156

HOW IT RATES

The skiing

Snow	★★★★
Extent	★★★
Advanced	★★★★★
Intermediates	★★
Beginners	★
Convenience	★
Queues	★★
Restaurants	★★★

The rest

Scenery	★★★★★
Resort charm	★★★★
Not skiing	★★★★

✔ A lot of very tough skiing, especially off-piste

✔ Access to arguably the most famous off-piste ski route of them all – the Vallée Blanche

✔ Amazing views of the Mont Blanc massif and surrounding glaciers

✔ Ancient mountain town, steeped in history and Alpine traditions

✔ Unforgettable cable-car ride to the Aiguille du Midi

✔ Well-organised and extensive cross-country trail system

✔ Plenty for non-skiers to do

✔ Easy access by road, rail and air

✘ Ski areas completely separate from each other – a car is most useful

✘ Virtually no ski-in, ski-out accommodation

✘ The extent of the piste skiing in most areas is quite limited

✘ Runs down to the valley floor are often closed due to lack of snow

✘ Popularity and too many old lifts mean crowds and queues

✘ Mixed-ability groups will find it difficult to stick together and keep everyone happy

✘ Bad weather can shut down the best skiing

Chamonix could not be more different from France's well-known, purpose-built ski resorts. There is no huge area of well-connected lifts and groomed pistes. Unless you are content to ski one mountain and pick your place to stay accordingly, you have to drive or take a bus each day to your chosen ski area. There is all sorts of terrain, but it offers more to interest the good skier than anyone else; to make the most of the area you need a mountain guide rather than a piste map. Chamonix is neither convenient nor conventional, but it is special and – understandably – a Mecca for advanced skiers.

Both the skiing and the scenery are dramatic – the Chamonix valley cuts deeply through Europe's highest mountains and glaciers. The views are stunning and the skiing is everything really tough skiing should be – not only steep, but high and long. If you like perfectly manicured pistes accessed by queue-free bubbles, stick to the Trois Vallées; but if you like your skiing and your scenery on the wild side, give Chamonix a try. But be warned: there are those who try it and never go home – lots of them.

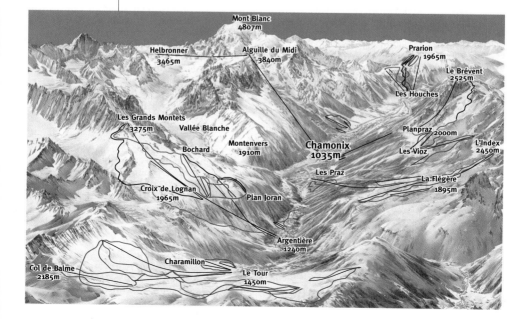

SKI FACTS

Altitude	1035m-3840m
Lifts	48
Pistes	140km
Green/Blue	35%
Red	45%
Black	20%
Artificial snow	4km

LIFT PASSES

95/96 prices in francs
Ski pass Mont Blanc
Covers lifts in 13
resorts in the Mont
Blanc region (plus
Courmayeur in Italy 4
days out of 6) and ski
buses in each resort,
except the Grand
Montets cable-car.
Beginners Points
tickets or pay by the
ride on nursery lifts.
Main pass
6-day pass 920
(low season 920 for 7
days)
Senior citizens
Over 60: 6-day pass
640 (30% off)
Children
Under 12: 6-day pass
640 (30% off)
Under 4: free pass
Short-term passes
Half-day passes for
limited areas; single
and return tickets on
most lifts.
Notes Day passes
only cover individual
areas (Les Houches,
Le Brévent, La
Flégère, etc). Grands
Montets cable-car
costs extra (30 for 1
ascent, 460 for 20,
94/95 prices).
Alternative passes
Passes available for
all the individual
areas (Le Brévent, La
Flégère, Balme, Les
Houches, Les Grands
Montets, Argentière
and Le Tour).

 # The resort

Chamonix is a busy little town with
hundreds of hotels and restaurants,
visitors year-round, a lively Saturday
market and generally lots of bustle
and business.

The centre of town is full of
atmosphere, with cobbled streets and
squares, beautiful old buildings and a
fast-running river. Sadly, unsightly
modern buildings have been built on
to its periphery (especially in the
Chamonix Sud area near the Aiguille
du Midi cable-car station) and some of
its lovely old buildings have been
allowed to fall into disrepair. Sadly,
too, traffic clogs the streets
surrounding the pedestrianised centre.
But the views of the mountains of the
Mont Blanc massif on one side and
the Aiguilles Rouge on the other more
than make up for that.

Vantage points in the town and,
even better, in some of the ski areas,
offer an overwhelming spectacle of
mountains and glaciers. The town
squares and pavement cafés are busy
most of the day, and especially on
sunny afternoons, when skiers,
shoppers and sightseers sip their
drinks and stare at the glaciers pouring
down the mountainsides. It all makes
for a very agreeable and distinctively
French atmosphere.

The shops in Chamonix cover the
range from those dealing in high-
priced, high-tech ski equipment to
some surprisingly tacky souvenir
shops completely full of rubbish. But
it remains essentially a town for
mountain men rather than poseurs.

There are regular buses to and from
all the ski areas. But having a car is
very useful to give you more flexibility
and the ability to get easily to other
resorts covered by the Mont Blanc
pass, such as Megève, Cormayeur and
Les Contamines.

 # The skiing

Once you get over the initial
impression that the place is hopelessly
disconnected and awkward to ski, you
come to realise that there is actually a
reasonable variety of skiing available,
though seldom in the same place.
There is excellent tough skiing on the
pistes at Les Grands Montets and Le
Brévent and some classic off-piste
routes, many over the glaciers that
dominate much of the higher terrain.
Some of these routes suit intermediate,
but confident and guided skiers quite

well and some are best reserved for
those with outrageous hairstyles and a
'bad' attitude. Intermediate skiers are
best served at La Flégère, Le Tour and
Les Houches. Several of the beginners'
areas need snow-cover down to the
valley floor to be operational.

THE SKI AREA
Very fragmented

For those who really like getting about
a bit, the Mont Blanc ski-pass covers
14 resorts, 25 ski areas, over 200 lifts
and 700km of piste. The resorts
covered extend far beyond the
Chamonix valley – including St-
Gervais, Megève, Les Contamines and
even Courmayeur in Italy.

The ski areas within the Chamonix
valley – and there are a dozen of them
– are either small, low, beginners'
areas or are restricted to a patch of
suitable terrain on the valley side with
cable-car or gondola access from the
valley floor. The modern 6-seater
gondola for **Le Brévent** departs a
short but steep walk from the centre of
town, and the cable-car above it takes
you to the summit at 2525m. At **La
Flégère**, like Le Brévent, the skiing is
mainly between 2000m and 2500m
and the views across to Mont Blanc
are themselves worth the price of the
lift pass. There have recently been
improvements to the system at **Les
Grands Montets** above Argentière
but the top cable-car to the 3300m
summit is still relatively low-capacity.
The area above Les Houches is served
by a cable-car to **Bellevue** and a
gondola to **Prarion**; there's no skiing
above 2000m but there are links over
to St-Gervais. The skiing at **Col de
Balme**, above Le Tour, is mostly at
opposite ends of a wide, sunny bowl
reached by the almost-parallel gondola
and chair-lift.

To get the most out of each area
you'll need the local area piste map –
the valley map is not sufficiently
detailed. We are impressed with the
Grands Montets piste map, produced
by Iain Cleaver, the Briton in charge
of marketing the Grands Montets. It
includes brief descriptions of each run,
with assessment of suitability for
different standards of skier, a history
of the ski area, advice on safety and a
feedback form to send to the lift
company – and all in French and
English versions.

SNOW RELIABILITY
Good high up; poor low down

The top runs on the north-facing
slopes above Argentière are almost
guaranteed to have good snow-cover,

SKI SCHOOL

95/96 prices in francs

ESF
In both Chamonix and
Argentière
Classes 6 days
4½hr: 9.45-noon and
2.15-4.30
6 full days: 740
Children's classes
Ages: 4 to 12
6 days (9am-5pm)
including supervised
lunch: 1100
Private lessons
1hr, 2hr, half- or full
day
190 for 1hr, for up to
4 people

and skiing normally lasts well into May. Finding the top lift shut because of the weather is more of a worry. The Col de Balme area above Le Tour doesn't have the highest skiing but has a snowy location and a good late-season record. The largely south-facing slopes of Brévent and Flégère and the low-altitude slopes of Les Houches can suffer in warm weather and runs to the resort are frequently closed. Snowmaking is restricted to two of the small, beginner areas.

FOR ADVANCED SKIERS
Head for the Grands Montets
Les Grands Montets above Argentière is justifiably renowned for the amount of tough, exciting skiing that this seemingly not very large area provides. A supplement is charged for each ride on the top cable-car. If you've got the legs and lungs, climb the 121 steep

metal steps to the observation platform at the top and take in the stunning views and stimulating air. Bear in mind that it's a long way down again – 200 more steps once you are down to the cable-car before you hit the snow.

The black pistes – Point de Vue and Pylones – start with a narrow and lumpy section and are then long and exhilarating. The Point de Vue sails right by some dramatic sections of glacier, with marvellous views of the crevasses. The off-piste routes from the top are numerous and often dangerous; the Pas de Chèvre joins with the Vallée Blanche, but only after a fairly epic journey, and there's a scenic route through the Argentière glacier. From the Bochard covered chair-lift, you can head down the Combe de la Pendant bowl for 1000m vertical of wild, unpisted

---

The Vallée Blanche

This is a trip you do for the stunning views and glacial scenery rather than the skiing, which is easy and well within the capability of the average intermediate. It is a classic tour, not to be missed by anyone who is there when conditions are right.

Go in a guided group – despite the ease of the skiing, dangerous crevasses lurk to swallow those not in the know – and prepare for extreme cold at the top. It does get extraordinarily busy at times – going early on a weekday gives you the best chance of avoiding the worst of the crowds.

The cable-car is a stunning ride that takes you to 3790m. There are snack-bars and the '3842' restaurant, if time allows. Across the bridge from the arrival station on the 'Piton Nord' is the 'Piton Central' and the highest point of the Aiguille du Midi – the view of Mont Blanc from the summit terrace should not be missed.

A tunnel through the rock and ice of the 'Piton Central' delivers skiers to the top of the infamous ridge-walk down to the start of the skiing. Many parties rope up for this walk and a fixed guide-rope provides further security. You might still feel envious about those strolling nonchalantly down in crampons – you may wish you'd stayed in bed.

After that the skiing seems a doddle; mostly effortless gliding down gentle slopes with only the occasional steeper, choppy section to deal with. So stop often and enjoy the surroundings fully – no written description or amateur photography can do it justice. The views of the ice, the crevasses and seracs, are simply mind-blowing.

There are many variants on the classic route, all of which are more difficult and more hazardous – the 'Vraie Vallée' is for experts only and the 'Envers du Plan' is a direct descent down to the Refuge du Requin – the mountain hut where everyone takes a break and admires the recently-negotiated ice fall. Snow conditions may well not allow skiing the full 24km route back down to Chamonix, in which case the station at Montenvers (1910m) is the target. A short gondola links the edge of the glacier to the station where everyone piles onto the train for Chamonix.

Book your guide the day before at the Maison de la Montagne or other ski school offices. You can join a group for FF300, or have your own guide for FF1,350 (up to five skiers – then FF160 extra per additional skier).

ORIENTATION

Strung out for 20km along the Chamonix valley are several ski areas, some with attached villages – from **Les Houches** at one end to **Argentière** and **Le Tour** at the other. Chamonix is at the centre of it all, with a cable-car soaring up from the southern fringe to the Aiguille du Midi and the famous Vallée Blanche run, and lifts from the northern fringes up to Le Brévent and La Flégère.

The ski areas around **Megève** are covered by the lift pass, as is **Courmayeur** in Italy, a short drive through the Mont Blanc tunnel. Swiss resorts such as **Verbier** are also within reach over the Col des Montets.

mountainside. The continuation down the valley side to Le Lavancher is equally testing and suffers frequently from lack of snow on the steep sections. To get the best out of the area you really need to have a local guide. Without one you either stick to the relatively small number of pistes or put your life at risk.

At Le Brévent there's more to test good skiers than it might first seem from the map – there are a number of variations on the runs down from the summit; some are steep and icy and the couloir routes are very steep and very narrow. The skiing in the Col de La Charlanon is uncrowded and includes one marked red run and lots of excellent off-piste.

At La Flégère there are several good off-piste routes flanking the main skiing area and a pretty tough run back to the village when snow-cover permits. Le Tour boasts little tough skiing on-piste but there are good off-piste routes from the high points to the village and over into Switzerland.

FOR INTERMEDIATE SKIERS
It's worth trying it all

For early or less-confident intermediates, the best areas are at the two extreme ends of the Chamonix valley skiing. The slopes of the Prarion-Bellevue system above Les Houches weave gently through the trees and are the least likely to intimidate anyone. The area is good for intermediate skiers wanting to build confidence. Likewise, the Col de Balme area above Le Tour is good for easy cruising.

A trip to Courmayeur in Italy one day makes an interesting change of atmosphere. Try it when the weather's bad in Chamonix – the sun is often shining on the other side of the Mont Blanc tunnel.

More adventurous intermediates will also want to try the other three main areas, though they may find the Grand Montets tough going. The bulk of the skiing at Le Brévent and La Flégère provides a sensible mix of blue and red runs; at Brévent the slopes

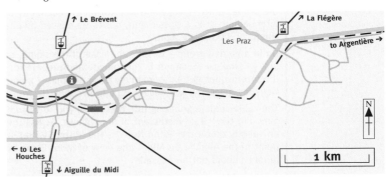

Selected chalets in Chamonix and Argentière ADVERTISEMENT

have been redesigned to achieve this. If the weather is good then you shouldn't miss a guided trip down the Vallée Blanche, perfectly within a competent intermediate's capability.

FOR BEGINNERS
Best if there's snow in the valley
If there is snow low down, the nursery lifts at La Vormaine, Les Chosalets, Les Pelerins and Le Savoy are fine for teaching first-timers; learners will not be bothered by faster skiers. The Planards and Glacier du Mont Blanc lifts both benefit from snowmaking and also provide some progression from the nursery areas. But beginner skiers would really be better advised to learn elsewhere, and come to Chamonix when they can appreciate the tough high-mountain terrain that is its hallmark.

FOR CROSS-COUNTRY
A good network of trails
Most of the 42km of prepared trails lie along the valley between Chamonix and Argentière. There are green, blue, red and black loop sections and the full tour from Chamonix to Argentière and back is 32km. All these trails are fairly low and fade fast in spring sun.

QUEUES
Some notable blackspots
The upper cable-car and the Bochard lift at Les Grands Montets access some of the best skiing and, not surprisingly, can provide some serious queues. It can also get busy at the end of the day when runs to the valley have been closed – the cable-cars at Les Houches and La Flégère suffer more from this than the gondolas at Col de Balme and Le Brévent.

The only significant amount of skiing to benefit from shelter among the trees is at Prarion-Bellevue. In poor weather, most of the rest of the skiing can close and the queues, particularly for the Bellevue cable-car, can be absolutely horrendous.

MOUNTAIN RESTAURANTS
Stunning views
The Panoramic restaurant at the top of Brévent enjoys the best views and also does a six-course 'gastronomic' menu. The food's fine but the place is dull. The Altitude 2000 is a straightforward self-service joint with a sunny terrace, as is the bar-restaurant at La Flégère.

The Grands Montets is well off. The newish restaurant at Plan Joran serves good food and has a table- as well as self-service section. And the Chavannes, just down from the Croix

de Lognan lift station, is a great place for a long lunch, whatever the weather – last season we had one of the best steak au poivres we've ever had. But it's not cheap.

At Le Tour, the Col de Balme refuge needs a bit of uphill work to get there, but it wouldn't be as nice if it didn't. The restaurants in the Prarion-Bellevue area are pleasant and good value.

Chamonix
Le Tour

SKI SCHOOL
The place to try something new
All the ski areas can provide traditional lessons with the ESF, but the schools here are particularly strong in some specialist fields – off-piste, glacier and couloir skiing, ski touring, snowboarding and cross-country. English-speaking instructors are plentiful. At the Maison de la Montagne in Chamonix, there is the main ESF office and also the HQ of the Compagnie des Guides de Chamonix Mont Blanc, which has taken visitors to the mountains for 150 years.

Competition is provided by a number of smaller, independent guiding and teaching outfits such as Stages Vallençant and Yak and Yeti Services. And there are many internationally-qualified British guides who base themselves in Chamonix.

This year we've had reports of some miserable guides from the Compagnie des Guides on the Vallée Blanche run. And we've had a very positive report on the Ski Sensation school and guides in Argentière.

FACILITIES FOR CHILDREN
Better than they were
The Panda Club is used by quite a few British visitors. This year's reports on it are enthusiastic – though there have been reservations expressed about the Argentière base being inconvenient for meeting up and skiing with your children for the afternoons.

GETTING THERE

Air Geneva, transfer 1½hr. Lyon, transfer 3½hr.

Rail Station in resort, on the St-Gervais-Le Fayet/Vallorcine line.

CHILDCARE

The ESF runs ordinary classes for children aged 6 to 12. For children aged 4 to 6 there are lessons in a snow-garden. And children in either category can be looked after all day (and amused when not skiing) from 8.45 to 5pm.

The day-care centre at the Maison pour Tous (50531224) takes children aged 18 months to 6 years from 8.15 to lunchtime.

The Panda Club takes children aged 3 months to 12 years. For those up to 18 months there is a crèche in Chamonix (50558612). Older babies are taken here or in Argentière (505404760), where the club has its own skiing area, open to children aged 3 or more.

Some of the more expensive hotels will provide child-minding – the Alpina is one. Club Med has comprehensive in-house arrangements – their place here is one of their 'family villages', with a crèche taking babies from 4 months.

ACTIVITIES

Indoor Sports complex (sports hall, weight training, table tennis), indoor skating and curling rinks, ice hockey, swimming pool with giant water slide, saunas, 2 indoor tennis courts, 2 squash courts, fitness centre, Alpine museum (open school holidays), casino, 3 cinemas, library, 10-pin bowling
Outdoor Ski-jumping, snow-shoe outings, mountain biking, hang-gliding, para-gliding, flying excursions, heli-skiing

 # Staying there

The obvious place to stay is in Chamonix itself – it's central, has all the amenities going and some of the skiing is close at hand. For those with a clear preference to do most of their skiing either at Argentière, Les Houches or Le Tour, it would be sensible to look for accommodation nearby. Whatever the choice, no location is convenient for everything so be prepared for some commuting – a car is a big advantage – especially for visiting other resorts on the Mont Blanc lift pass. The Chamonix bus runs frequently between Chamonix and the different local ski areas, but only till about 7pm. It's free to holders of the Mont Blanc ski-pass.

HOW TO GO
Pile into the car and drive
There is currently a reasonable choice of packages to both Chamonix and Argentière. Given the value of having a car in the resort and the good road links to Chamonix, a ski-drive package should be considered.
Chalets Many are run by small outfits that cater for this specialist market. Quality tends to be quite high and prices relatively low, making for great value. Bladon Lines runs a chalet in a luxury apartment block with swimming pool. The Ski Company Ltd have the one very expensive place in town (featured in Tatler's World's Top 50 Villas to Rent!). Bigfoot also have an upmarket operation. Collineige have the largest selection – all of them very comfortable. Cheaper places are offered by Huski, Neilson and several other big tour operators. Inghams has a chalet next to the Hotel Sapenière, with the food coming from the hotel's kitchen. Childcare specialists Ski Esprit also have a place.
Hotels The place is full of hotels, many of them modestly priced – several available through packages from the UK – and a few rather pricey. Practically all are small, with fewer than 30 rooms. If you have a car, location isn't crucial apart from the usual considerations about traffic. There is a Club Med 'village'.
££££ Albert 1er Smart, expensive, traditional chalet-style hotel with much the most ambitious food in town (Michelin star).
££££ Auberge du Bois Prin A small modern chalet with a big reputation; great views; bit of a hike to the centre; a shorter one to the Brévent lift.
££££ Mont Blanc Central, luxurious.

££££ Jeu de Paume (Lavancher) Alpine satellite of a chic Parisian hotel: a beautifully furnished modern chalet half-way to Argentière.
£££ Alpina Much the biggest in town: modernist-functional place just north of centre; child-minding available.
£££ Labrador (Les Praz) Scandinavian-style chalet close to the Flégère lift.
££ Sapinière Traditional hotel with good food; run by long-established Chamonix family; reasonable site on the Brévent side of town.
££ De L'Arve By the river, just off main street; smallish recently refurbished rooms.
££ Richemond Lovely old building and nice grounds, near the centre.
££ Vallée Blanche Smart low-priced 3-star B&B hotel, handy for centre and Aiguille du Midi cable-car.
££ Pointe Isabelle Not pretty, but central location; friendly staff, good plain food, well equipped bedrooms.
££ Roma Simple but satisfactory B&B hotel in hassle-free location on south side of centre; friendly patron.
£ Faucigny Cottage-style; in centre of Chamonix; cheap.
Self-catering There are hundreds of properties for renting throughout the valley – chalets, apartments and rooms (some on a B&B basis). Those that find their way into UK package brochures are typically in large purpose-built blocks, usually in Chamonix Sud – convenient but charmless. The Balcons du Savoy look much better, are well situated and have use of a swimming pool, steam room and solarium. The Splendid & Golf apartments in Les Praz have been created from the tasteful restoration of the old hotel of that name – the Flégère cable-car is nearby.

EATING OUT
Plenty of quality places
The good hotels all have good restaurants – the Eden at Les Praz and Bois Prin in Chamonix are first-rate – and there are many other good places to eat. The Sarpe is a lovely 'mountain' restaurant and The Impossible is rustic but smart and features good regional dishes. The Monchu and the Sanjon are good for Savoyarde specialities, and along the Rue des Moulins there are several more pleasant places to choose from. There are a number of ethnic restaurants – Mexican, Spanish, Japanese, Chinese etc – and lots of brasseries and cafés. The Grand Taverne is a lively grill-brasserie that stays open late, as does Poco Loco – possibly the narrowest eating-place in the Alps but good for a quick burger or

PACKAGES

AA Ski-Driveaway, APS Chalets, Airtours, Bigfoot, Bladon Lines, Chalets 'Unlimited', Chinook-It, Club Med, Collineige, Crystal, Driveline Europe, First Choice Ski, French Impressions, Fresh Tracks, HuSki, Inghams, Jean Stanford, Lagrange, Made to Measure, Motours, Neilson, Ski Addiction, Ski Club of GB, Ski Esprit, Ski Les Alpes, Ski Valkyrie, Ski Weekend, Stena Sealink, The Ski Company Ltd, Thomson, Travelscene Ski-Drive, White Roc

Argentière Chalets 'Unlimited', Collineige, Crystal, Jean Stanford, Lagrange, Peak Ski, Poles Apart, Ski Amis, Ski Club of GB, Ski Esprit, Ski France, Ski Valkyrie, Trail Alpine, White Roc

Les Houches Chalets 'Unlimited', Lagrange, Motours

TOURIST OFFICE

Postcode 74400
Tel 00 33 50530024
Fax 50535890

something in a baguette. For something completely different try the restaurant of the catering college – the students get to practise and you get good food at a knockdown price.

APRES-SKI
Lots of bars and music

There's a good sports centre and swimming pool, as well as a ten-pin bowling alley.

Many of the bars around the pedestrianised centre of Chamonix get busy for a couple of hours at sundown. La Terrasse is a good spot for a glass of wine or coffee, and the Cheval Rouge, nearby, has good draught beer and Eurosport on TV. Later on there are numerous lively venues. The Jeckyl and Hyde has live bands, a strong Irish influence and a clientele largely of chalet staff and British workers. The Cantina has live music and is open late. The Wild Wallaby is really, er, wild. It's popular with Brits and Scandinavians and the owner, Luscious Louise, encourages drinking contests and 'biggest, baddest burp' competitions. Drivers Bar has a much more French atmosphere and is small. Also recommended are Chambre 9 and the Choucas video bar. There are plenty of bars and brasseries for a quieter drink too.

Disco fun is provided by the Pele and the Refuge and there are also 'bars de nuit' which have a similarly young crowd – the Blue Night is occasionally jazz- or country-flavoured. The casino features both English and French roulette – and if you don't know the difference, you shouldn't be there.

FOR NON-SKIERS
An excellent choice

There's more for non-skiers to do here than in many resorts, and in spring it's a very pleasant place for a stroll by the river or a cable-car trip to admire the scenery at closer quarters. Scenic flights offer superb all-round views but are not for the nervous flier. Excursion possibilities are numerous – Annecy, Geneva, Courmayeur and Turin are within striking-distance and the St-Gervais-Martigny railway line runs through the valley. The Alpine Museum is an interesting diversion and there are good sports facilities.

Argentière 1240m

The old village is in a lovely setting towards the head of the valley – the Glacier d'Argentière pokes down towards it and the Aiguille du Midi and Mont Blanc still dominate the scene down the valley. There's now a

fair bit of modern development spread around the main street but it still has a certain cachet that brings people back year after year. Many of the winter residents these days are young, happy and broke, but there's also a smattering of more seasoned Alpine visitors. The small village of Le Tour, just beyond Argentière, is quiet and picturesque, and the place most likely to have snow in the streets.

Jean Stanford and Collineige both have comfortable catered chalets, and childcare specialists Ski Esprit are also represented.

A number of the hotels are simple, inexpensive and handy for the village centre – less so for the skiing. On the main street are the Couronne and the Dahu – popular with weekenders. The Grands-Montets is a large chalet-style building, right next to the skiing and Panda Club for children. The Montana is in a pleasant location but neither in the centre nor at the skiing.

Restaurants are informal and inexpensive. The Dahu Brasserie does an excellent fixed-price menu and decent wine by the jug – probably the best value in town. The Fis, attached to the hotel Couronne, is almost as good. Chez Luigi claims 'Ici nous faisons vraie pizzas'; they're certainly good and the wine list is a lot better than you'd expect. The Samoyède is a bistro with Mexican dishes and occasional cheap beer. The R'mize à Ravanel outside the village specialises in mountain dishes.

The Office is the happening place in Argentière, from breakfast till late. The Trace video bar has games, a big collection of ski-videos, some cool customers and sometimes good music. The Eschoppe is in an unpromising location but plays the best music. The Stone bar is good for late drinking.

Les Houches 1010m

Les Houches is an unremarkable village, which sprawls along a busy main road. Views of Mont Blanc are impressive, but the shadow of the massif makes it a dark, cold place. The 3-star Mont Alba is perhaps the best hotel, with good rooms, a pool and a gym. The Beausite is comfortable, the Bellevarde, Cottage and Peter Pan inexpensive. The best food is at the pricey Barberine; Peter Pan is good value. Après-ski is very quiet; the Perce Neige is the focal bar.

Ski and non-ski kindergartens are available for children.

Châtel 1190m

HOW IT RATES

The skiing

Snow	**
Extent	*****
Advanced	***
Intermediates	****
Beginners	**
Convenience	**
Queues	***
Restaurants	***

The rest

Scenery	***
Resort charm	***
Not skiing	**

✔ *Very extensive, pretty, intermediate ski area – the Portes du Soleil*

✔ *Wide range of cheap and cheerful, good-value accommodation*

✔ *Easily reached – close to Geneva, and one of the shortest drives from the Channel*

✔ *Pleasant, lively, French-dominated old village, still quite rustic in parts*

✔ *Local skiing relatively queue-free*

✔ *Good views*

✘ *Low, with no local snowmakers*

✘ *Inconvenient nursery slopes*

✘ *Time-consuming journey to Avoriaz to get to the best snow (and best tough skiing) in the area*

✘ *Queues can be a problem on the Portes du Soleil circuit*

✘ *Over-subscribed bus services*

✘ *Congested village traffic, especially at weekends*

✘ *Not much nightlife*

Like neighbouring Morzine, Châtel offers a blend of attractions that is uncommon in France – an old village with plenty of facilities, cheap accommodation by French standards, and a large ski area on the doorstep. Châtel's original rustic charm has been largely eroded in recent years, but some of it remains, and the resort has one obvious advantage over smoother Morzine: it is part of the main Portes du Soleil ski circuit.

The circuit actually breaks down at Châtel, but this works in the village's favour. Whereas skiers doing the circuit from other resorts have the inconvenience of waiting for a bus mid-circuit, Châtel residents have the advantage of being able to time their bus-rides to avoid waits and queues. Skiers mainly interested in the local slopes should also consider Châtel. For confident intermediate skiers, Châtel's Linga has few equals in the Portes du Soleil, while the nearby Torgon section has arguably the best views. The Chapelle d'Abondance slopes are pleasantly uncrowded at weekends, when many other sections are crowded. Châtel is not, however, ideal for beginners – the nursery slopes are up at Super-Châtel.

ORIENTATION

Châtel lies near the head of the wooded Dranse valley, at the north-eastern limit of the French-Swiss Portes du Soleil ski circuit (see page 224).

Directly above the village, reached by gondola, is the outpost of Super-Châtel, with skiing links to **Morgins** and **Champéry** in Switzerland, and to **Torgon**. Morgins is also reached by road over a low pass. The other main French Portes du Soleil resorts – **Avoriaz** and **Morzine** – are quite easily reached on skis, but not by road. A few kilometres down the valley is **La Chapelle-d'Abondance**.

 The resort

Châtel is a slightly tatty, overdeveloped, but nonetheless attractive old village. Although there is a definite centre, the village sprawls along the road in from lake Geneva, and the diverging roads out – up the

hillside towards Morgins and along the valley towards the Linga ski lifts at L'Essert. Lots of French and Swiss holidaymakers take cars and use them, and the centre gets clogged with traffic during the evening rush-hour. It's even worse at weekends, because the resort is easily accessible to day-trippers from Geneva.

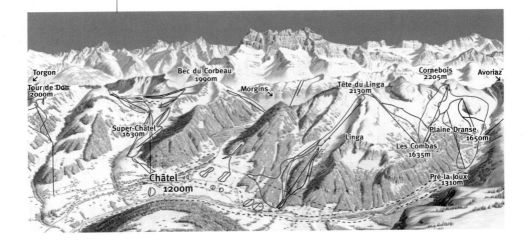

SKI FACTS

Altitude 1200m-2200m
Lifts   228
Pistes   650km
Green/Blue   51%
Red   40%
Black   9%
Artificial snow   11km

LIFT PASSES

95/96 prices in francs
Portes du Soleil
Covers all lifts in all
12 resorts, and
shuttle buses.
Main pass
1-day pass 195
6-day pass 885
Senior citizens
Over 60: 6-day pass
584 (34% off)
Children
Under 16: 6-day pass
584 (34% off)
Under 5: free pass
Short-term passes
Morning and
afternoon passes for
the Portes du Soleil
(both 136), and for
Châtel only (morning
75, afternoon 89,
94/95 prices).
Alternative periods
5 non-consecutive
days pass for Châtel
only available (adult
610).
Notes Discounts for
holders of the Carte
Neige (5%), families
(15%) and family
Carte Neige (22%).
Carte Neige gives
insurance cover and
discounts at ESF, ice
rink and some shops.

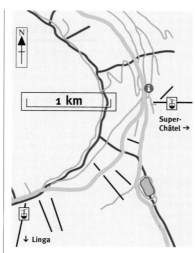

 The skiing

The Portes du Soleil as a whole is
classic intermediate skiing, and
Châtel's local slopes are very much in
character. Confident intermediates, in
particular, will find lots to enjoy in the
Linga sector.

THE SKI AREA
The PdS circuit breaks down here
Châtel sits between two sectors of the
Portes du Soleil circuit, linking the two
with a frequent but not entirely
adequate ski-bus service. **Super-
Châtel** is directly above the village –
an area of open and lightly wooded
easy skiing where beginner classes take
place, accessed by a choice of gondola
or two-stage chair from the top of the
village. From here you can ski over to
the quiet little Torgon sector or move
clockwise around the Portes du Soleil
circuit, crossing the Swiss border to
Morgins and then Champoussin and
Champéry, before crossing back into
France above Avoriaz.
    The **Linga** sector starts a bus-ride
out of the village, and leads more
directly to Avoriaz. For competent
skiers Linga has some of the most
interesting skiing in the Portes du
Soleil, though the best of it leads back
in the direction of Châtel and is
therefore not skied by those in a hurry
to reach Avoriaz or do the complete
anti-clockwise circuit. If time is of the
essence it is quicker to avoid Linga
altogether by staying on the bus to
Pré-la-Joux. From here it's a short lift
and schuss to the hamlet of Plaine
Dranse; then a single lift and run to
Les Marmottes, where there is a choice
of final lifts towards Avoriaz.

SNOW RELIABILITY
Poor – the main drawback
The main runs on Linga and down to
Pré-la-Joux are north-facing, but a lot
of the skiing around Châtel is sunny,
the altitudes hereabouts are low, and
there are virtually no snowmakers. So
snow is not entirely reliable. When it
is in short supply, the bus to and from
Pré-la-Joux is terribly oversubscribed
by people heading for Avoriaz (itself
not absolutely snowsure), and you
have to take a chair at Crête des
Rochassons because there is no
artificial snow on the crucial south-
facing piste to Les Marmottes. The
sunny Morgins-Champoussin area
struggles badly at such times, and its
Portes du Soleil link closes.

FOR ADVANCED SKIERS
Avoriaz might suit you better
It's a long way from here to Les Hauts
Forts above Avoriaz and the 'Swiss
Wall' between Avoriaz and Champéry.
There's a genuine black mogul field
between Cornebois and Plaine Dranse,
but the best local skiing is beneath the
Linga gondola and chair – a pleasant
mix of open and wooded ground
follows the fall line fairly directly. An
unpisted trail from Super-Châtel
towards the village is also fun.

FOR INTERMEDIATE SKIERS
Some of the best runs in the PdS
When conditions are right the Portes
du Soleil is an intermediate's paradise.
Good intermediates need not venture
far from Châtel; Linga has some of the
best red runs in the whole area. But
the Champéry-Avoriaz sector also
beckons. Moderately good skiers can
do the whole circuit without any
problems, and will particularly enjoy
the runs around Les Lindarets and
Morgins. Even timid skiers can do the
circuit, provided they take one or two
short-cuts and ride chairs down
trickier bits. The recently built chair
from Les Lindarets to Pointe de
Mossette provides a red run into the
Swiss skiing and also speeds up the
whole journey.
    Leaving aside attempts to complete
the whole circuit in both directions,
there are rewarding out-and-back
expeditions to be made clockwise to
the wide open snowfields above
Champoussin, beyond Morgins, and
anticlockwise to the Hauts-Forts runs
above Avoriaz.

FOR BEGINNERS
Inconvenient slopes
The nursery slopes are fine, but they
are in an inconvenient position up at

Alternative passes
Châtel pass covers 50 lifts in Châtel, Linga, Super-Châtel, Barbossine and Torgon (adult 6-day pass 660).

SKI SCHOOL

94/95 prices in francs
ESF
Classes 6 days
2hr am; 2½hr pm
6 afternoons: 495
Children's classes
Ages: 5 to 16
6 afternoons: 440
Private lessons
1hr or 1½hr
163 for 1hr, for
1 to 3 people

95/96 prices in francs
International
Classes 6 days
3hr: 9am-noon or
2pm-5pm; 2hr: noon-2pm
6 mornings: 610
Children's classes
Ages: from 8
5 mornings 510
6 afternoons 610
Private lessons
1hr or 2hr
165 for 1hr; each
additional person 15

95/96 prices in francs
Stages Henri Gonon
Courses including 6 days' accommodation and pass and 5 half-days' tuition:
adults 2950
children 2500

CHILDCARE

The ESF runs a ski kindergarten for children aged 5 or more, with lunch provided.

Le Village des Marmottons (50733379) takes children from age 14 months to 10, from 8.30 to 5.30, with ski tuition for those aged 3 or more.

Super-Châtel. Near-beginners not wanting tuition have some nice runs around Super-Châtel and nearby Tour de Don, and there's some gentle skiing above Pré-la-Joux.

FOR CROSS-COUNTRY
Pretty, if low, trails
There are plenty of pretty trails along the river and through the woods on the lower slopes of Linga (42km), but snow-cover can be a problem.

QUEUES
Lots of bottlenecks can occur
Queues vary enormously according to conditions and time of year. Given good snow in January, there are no problems apart from a couple of bottlenecks in Avoriaz. Poor conditions from February onwards can cause major delays. Beginners can face bad queues to get down from Super-Châtel, and skiers getting to and from Avoriaz face constant delays en route. Pré-la-Joux is a particular black spot.

MOUNTAIN RESTAURANTS
Variable
There are atmospheric chalets to be found, notably a couple at Plaine Dranse (Chez Crépy is recommended for cold days – there is a wood fire next to the bar) and further afield in the Marmottes-Lindarets section close to Avoriaz. The Perdix Blanche down at Pré-la-Joux scarcely counts as a mountain restaurant, but is nevertheless an attractive spot for lunch. Beginners have the very pleasant, if pricey, Chalet Neuf at Super-Châtel.

SKI SCHOOL
Diminishing complaints
Ski teaching in Châtel seems to be settling down, after a period in which the local schools seemed to be putting more effort into undermining British ski instructors working here than on the more productive business of raising their own standards.

FACILITIES FOR CHILDREN
Increasingly sympathetic
The Marmottons nursery has good facilities including toboggans, painting, music and videos. It used to have a reputation for harshness that British clients found difficult to come to terms with, but to judge by recent reports the increasing level of British business in Châtel has led to a softening of the regime – and good English is said to be spoken.

 # Staying there

Frequent free ski buses link the two valley lift stations. The Super-Châtel station is close to the village centre and can be reached on foot from much of the accommodation. The Linga gondola is a bus-ride for even the most determined of walkers. Snow conditions permitting, it is possible to ski back to town from Super-Châtel and Linga. The most convenient place to stay is close to the Super-Châtel lifts. The nursery slopes are served by these lifts, and timid intermediates are likely to prefer the skiing towards Morgins. A central position also has its advantages for skiers aiming for the more challenging skiing of Linga and Avoriaz: getting on the navette here may add a few minutes to your journey, but at least you get a seat before the bus gets overcrowded.

HOW TO GO
A wide choice, including chalets
Although this is emphatically a French resort, the days are long gone when packages from Britain were difficult to track down.
Chalets Although a fair number of operators have places here, most are one-chalet operations, often not well positioned and fairly simple. Ski Addiction's is the best-positioned chalet, five minutes from the village centre and the Super-Châtel gondola. Skibound have a similarly simple place. A more traditional and comfortable chalet is the Ski Club of GB's. A small chalet-hotel is available through Freedom, with en-suite facilities in every room.
Hotels Practically all of the hotels are 2-stars, mostly friendly chalets, wooden or at least partly wood-clad, and none of the trio of moderate 3-stars is particularly well placed.
££ Macchi Modern chalet, most central of the 3-stars.
££ Fleur de Neige Well maintained and welcoming old chalet on edge of centre; Grive Gourmande restaurant does about the best food in town.
££ Belalp Very comfortable, with excellent food.
£ Kandahar One for peace-lovers: a Logis, down by the river, a walkable distance from the centre.
Self-catering Many apartments here are privately-owned summer retreats, and standards vary even within one operator's allocation. Many of the better places are available through self-drive specialists. French Impressions have a good selection of traditional-

GETTING THERE

Air Geneva, transfer 1½hr.

Rail Thonon les Bains (42km).

PACKAGES

Chalets 'Unlimited', First Choice Ski, Freedom, French Impressions, Lagrange, Made to Measure, MasterSki, Ski Addiction, Ski Club of GB, Ski Partners, SkiBound, Sloping Off, Snowfocus, Snowise, Travelscene Ski-Dri

ACTIVITIES

Indoor Swimming pool, bowling, cinema, library **Outdoor** Skating rink, para-gliding, horse-drawn carriage rides, helicopter rides, dog-sledding, snow-shoe excursions

TOURIST OFFICE

Postcode 74390
Tel 00 33 50732244
Fax 50732287

style chalets. Two of the best are the Gelinotte – out of town but close to the Linga lifts and children's village, and Les Erines – central and close to the Super-Châtel gondola. The Flèche d'Or apartments are not so well positioned, either for lifts or shops.

EATING OUT
Fair selection

There is an adequate number and range of restaurants. The Vieux Four has good nouvelle cuisine served in a traditional atmosphere, the Bonne Ménagère is a modest, good-value place, the Fiacre does good pizza, and out-of-town the Kitchen is worth the taxi ride for superb raclette in cosy surroundings. Also worth a trip is the restaurant of the Cornettes hotel in La Chapelle-d'Abondance. The Fleur de Neige hotel has a good restaurant.

APRES-SKI
All down to bars

Châtel is fairly lively at tea-time but gets quiet at night. Busy bars supply some atmosphere; the most popular place is the Isba video bar. The unsophisticated Slalom is another Brit haunt; one reporter thought the management aggressive towards a clientele behaving like 'Brits abroad'. La Godille – close to the Super-Châtel gondola and popular at tea-time – has a more French feel. Otherwise there's a bowling alley, and one of the cinemas shows English-language films a few times a week. The Dahu disco, just out of town on the road to Morgins, livens up at weekends. Jean's is another club.

FOR NON-SKIERS
Morzine is much better

Those with a car have some entertaining excursions available: Geneva, Thonon and Evian. Otherwise there is a little to do but take some pleasant walks along the river. The Portes du Soleil as a whole is less than ideal for non-skiers who like to meet skiing companions for lunch: skiers will probably want to have theirs in a different country.

La Chapelle-d'Abondance
1010m

This unspoilt, rustic farming community, complete with old church and friendly locals, is 5km along a beautiful valley from Châtel. It's had its own quiet little north-facing ski area of easy wooded runs for some years, but has recently been put on the PdS map by a new gondola and three chair-lifts that now link it to Torgon and, from there, Super-Châtel. This new section remains essentially only a spur of the PdS circuit. But, taken together with Chapelle's own little area, it is worth exploring – good at weekends when Châtel gets crowded.

Lack of English-speaking instructors is reported to be a big drawback to using the local ESF ski school, which also runs a ski kindergarten for 4-year-olds. There is no non-ski nursery. Nightlife is virtually non-existent: just a few quiet bars, a cinema and torchlit descents. However, there are a number of good, reasonably-priced restaurants, notably the Cornettes and the Alpage.

La Chapelle makes the occasional appearance in tour operator brochures, but most accommodation has to be booked independently. The hotel Ensoleillé has been recommended. The Cornettes, Alpage and Chabi are other hotel options. The Airelles apartments have received a favourable report.

La Clusaz 1100m

ORIENTATION

La Clusaz has one of the shortest transfer times from Geneva: it is only 50km away.

The resort is rather sprawling, with accommodation along a winding road as well as in the village centre. Lifts serve the several separate skiing sectors from different points, with pistes back to most areas of the village. Les Etages is a much smaller accommodation centre where two of the sectors meet. The lift pass also covers **Le Grand-Bornand**, a ten-minute bus-ride away. If the Col des Aravis is open, a day-trip by car to **Megève** is possible.

✔ Traditional mountain village, with character retained despite development into fairly major resort

✔ Fairly large, interesting ski area, best suited to beginners and intermediates

✔ Very French atmosphere

✔ Prices low by French resort standards

✔ Very short transfer time from Geneva and easy to reach by car from UK

✔ Attractive mountain restaurants

✘ Snow conditions unreliable because of low altitude

✘ Not enough challenges to keep good skiers happy for a week

✘ Congested with traffic at times (though improvements are planned for this season)

Few other major French ski resorts are based around what is still, essentially, a genuine mountain village rather than a purpose-built resort. It exudes Gallic charm and atmosphere, despite its expansion in recent years. It is proud of its skiing heritage, the latest manifestation of which is local boy Edgar Grospiron, who won gold for bumps skiing at the Albertville Olympics.

Combine that with a fairly large, spread-out, mainly intermediate ski area with five separate interlinked sectors and you've got a good basis for an enjoyable, relaxed week, especially if you're a Francophile.

La Clusaz has one big problem – its height, or rather the lack of it. Together with a lack of substantial snowmaking facilities, this means that its lower slopes are often bare or in poor condition. Snowmaking has been installed over the last couple of seasons, but the high natural snowfall has meant that it has not been tested in really poor conditions.

The resort

Until a few years ago La Clusaz was frequented almost entirely by the French. But it has now developed into a major international resort – for both summer and winter seasons.

The village is built at the junction of a number of narrow wooded valleys, which mean that it has had to grow in a rather rambling and sprawling way. But it has retained the charm of a genuine French mountain village and the planners have successfully avoided the monstrous architecture that has been inflicted on many other French resorts. The village has been developed around the original old stone and wooden chalet buildings and, for the most part, the new buildings have been built in similar style and blend in

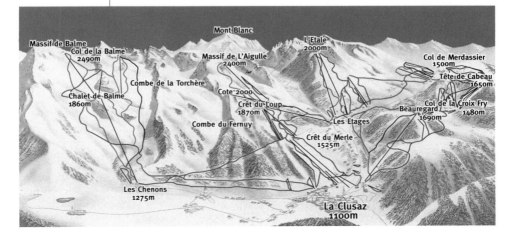

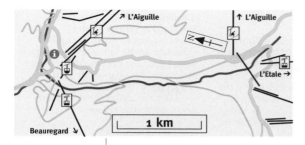

The skiing

Like the village, skiing at La Clusaz is rather spread out – which makes it all the more interesting. There are five main areas, each interconnecting with at least one of the others.

THE SKI AREA
Five interlinked areas
Several points in the village have lifts giving access to the predominantly west- and north-west facing slopes of the **Aiguille** mountain. From there you can ski to the **Balme** area on a choice of off-piste trail or easy green track. La Balme has the resort's highest skiing (normally the best snow) and a speed skiing track. From La Balme there are more woodland tracks which, perhaps with a bit of poling, take you back to the village.

Going the other way from L'Aiguille leads you to the **Étale** area via another choice of easy runs and the Transval cable-car, which has been built to shuttle skiers between the two areas in both directions. From the bottom of L'Étale, you can ski back along another path to the village and the cable-car up to the fourth skiing area of **Beauregard** which, as the name implies, has splendid views and catches a lot of sunshine.

From the top of Beauregard you can link via yet another easy piste and a two-way chair-lift with the fifth ski area of **Col de la Croix-Fry/Col de Merdassier/Manigod**. You can ski from here to L'Étale.

SKI FACTS
Altitude	1100m-2490m
Lifts	56
Pistes	130km
Green/Blue	71%
Red	25%
Black	4%
Artificial snow	1km

well. The centre comes complete with large old church, fast-flowing mountain stream and a sympathetically designed modern shopping centre. Around this, narrow roads and alleys run in a confusing mixture of directions.

La Clusaz has a very friendly feel to it. The villagers welcome visitors every Monday evening in the main square with vin chaud and the local Reblochon cheese. There's a regular weekly market, and there are several typically French bars, ranging from the type you'd expect in any rural French village to modern ones with loud rock music.

For much of the season La Clusaz is a quiet and peaceful place for a holiday. But in peak season and at weekends the place can get packed out with French and Swiss families and the singles crowd. It is one of the most accessible resorts from Geneva – good for short transfer times but bad for crowds. And when the locals arrive in force, traffic and parking can be a problem; but a new road layout is apparently to be introduced this year.

Selected chalets in La Clusaz

Aravis Alpine Retreat
T 00 33 5002 3625 F 00 33 5002 3982

La Ferme des Hirondelles
Possibly the most breathtaking place in the world. Traditional French village, charming 19th century Alpine farmhouse, flexible skiing, outstanding cuisine. Once there, you'll never want to leave.

LIFT PASSES

94/95 prices in francs
La Clusaz pass
Covers all lifts in La
Clusaz.
Beginners Points
cards cover all lifts
(60 points 97).
Main pass
1-day pass 135
6-day pass 680
Senior citizens
Over 60: 6-day pass
530 (22% off)
Children
Under 13: 6-day pass
530 (22% off)
Under 4: free pass
Short-term passes
2hr pass, half-day
passes from 9am to
1pm and from 11am or
12.30 to the end of
the day.
Notes Pass covers 40
lifts of Le Grand
Bornand (6km away).
Reductions for
families, groups and
holders of the Carte-
Neige La Clusaz,
which provides
insurance cover and
reductions in some
shops.

SKI SCHOOL

94/95 prices in francs

ESF
Classes 6 days
4hr: 9am-11am,
3pm-5pm
5 full days: 730
Children's classes
Ages: 5 to 12
5 full days: 587
Private lessons
Hourly
170 for 1 to 3 people;
220 for 4 to 5 people

SNOW RELIABILITY
Poor on lower slopes

Most of the skiing is west or north-
west facing and tends to keep its snow
fairly well. That's fortunate, because
most of it is below 2000m. The best
snow is usually at La Balme where the
north-west-facing slopes reach over
2400m. The resort itself is only just
over 1000m and the runs back can be
tricky or bare when snow is poor; but
there are now enough snowguns to
keep at least one run open to village
level, when temperatures allow. The
main lifts down from Beauregard and
Crêt du Merle will carry skiers down as
well as up.

FOR ADVANCED SKIERS
Limited

The best piste skiing for good skiers is
at La Balme, where a number of fairly
challenging runs lead from the top
lifts back down to the top of the
gondola. But the only black in the
area is the speed skiing piste which
leads right back down to the bottom.

On L'Aiguille, there are a couple of
good off-piste itineraires – the Combe
du Fernuy towards La Balme and the
Combe de Borderan towards Les
Etages. There's a black run down the
face of Beauregard that can be tricky
in poor snow conditions. And the red
run from the top of Étale is fairly steep
at the top.

Other than that, good skiers will
find La Clusaz skiing pretty tame.

FOR INTERMEDIATE SKIERS
Good if snow is good

Most intermediates will love La Clusaz
if the snow conditions are good. Early
intermediates will delight in the
gentle slopes at the top of Beauregard
and over on La Croix-Fry, where
there's a network of gentle tree-lined
runs. And they'll be able to travel all
over the area on the gentle green
linking pistes, where poling or walking
is more likely to be a problem than
any fears about steepness.

L'Étale and L'Aiguille have more
challenging but wide blue runs. The
best snow is usually on the top half of
the mountains here.

More adventurous intermediates will
prefer the steeper red slopes and good
snow of La Balme, from the top of
which there are wonderful views. This
is a fairly substantial area with good
lifts (a high-capacity gondola from the
bottom linking to a fast quad chair).

FOR BEGINNERS
Splendid beginner slopes

The best nursery slopes are up the
mountain at the top of the Beauregard
cable-car and at Crêt du Merle. The
Beauregard area has lovely gentle
green runs to progress to, including
one long run round the mountain
right back to the village.

FOR CROSS-COUNTRY
Excellent

La Clusaz has much better cross-
country facilities than many resorts,
with a total of 70km of loops of
varying difficulty. The main area is
near the lake at Les Confins, reached
by bus. There's also a lovely area at the
top of the Beauregard cable-car.

QUEUES
Not a problem

Except on peak weekends or if the
lower slopes are shut because of snow
shortage, lift queues aren't a problem.
The worst bottleneck used to be the
top half of La Balme. But the slow old
chair was replaced by a fast quad two
seasons ago.

MOUNTAIN RESTAURANTS
High standard

Mountain restaurants are one of the
resort's strong points. There are lots of
them and, for the most part, they are
rustic and charming, and serve good,
reasonably priced – often Savoyard –
food. The Vieux Ferme at Merdassier is
charming and excellent value. The
civilised Vieux Chalet, just above the
top of the gondola from the village,
has a good reputation but has just
changed hands. There are several
other good restaurants higher up in
the Aguille sector, of which the Bercail
is said to be the best. The restaurant at
Beauregard by the cross-country trail is
sunny and peaceful, with good food.

SKI SCHOOL
Mixed reports

There are tales of large classes and
poor instruction in group lessons, but
we've heard from some satisfied
customers too – especially those who
took private lessons. Locals say Croix
Fry is better organised than La Clusaz.

FACILITIES FOR CHILDREN
Excellent – in theory

The childcare arrangements seem
carefully considered, but the only first-
hand report we've had is a bad one of
the kindergarten. Generally, however,
the resort is one where families can
feel at home – provided they keep
away from the traffic.

CHILDCARE

The ESF runs a ski kindergarten for children aged 3 to 5, at normal class hours.

The two all-day kindergartens operate 8.30 to 6pm. The Club des Mouflets (50326957) offers creative activities and indoor games for non-skiing children aged 8 months to 4 years, with the babies looked after in a special section. The Champions' Club (50326500) takes children aged 3 to 6 for indoor and outdoor games, with the option of skiing in the ESF kindergarten or (if over 5) in a proper ESF class.

GETTING THERE

Air Geneva, transfer 1½hr. Lyon, transfer 2½hr.

PACKAGES

Aravis Alpine Retreat, French Impressions, Lagrange, Made to Measure, Over the Hill, Silver Ski, Ski Amis, Ski Arrangements, Ski Valkyrie, Ski Weekend, SkiBound, Stena Sealink

ACTIVITIES

Indoor Various hotels have saunas, massage, jacuzzi, weights room, aerobics, sun beds and swimming pools
Outdoor Para-gliding, hang-gliding, micro-light flights, open-air heated swimming pool, snow-shoe excursions, snowmobile rides, winter walks

TOURIST OFFICE

Postcode 74220
Tel 00 33 50326500
Fax 50326501

 # Staying there

Much of the accommodation is a fair walk from an access lift to the skiing and the bus system is somewhat erratic. It's best to stay close to the start of one of the main access lifts near the centre of town.

HOW TO GO
Decreasing choice of packages
If you're set on La Clusaz, book early: last season's good snow led to demand for packages far outstripping supply. And Enterprise and Crystal have recently dropped the resort, severely reducing the choice of packages, particularly if you're going by plane or train (drivers have a wider selection). A car is useful around the resort, and the drive from the Channel is a relatively short one.

Chalets Ski Aravis have a high-standard farmhouse conversion with all mod cons, including en-suite rooms, well located close to the village centre and lifts. A cosy open-fired, exposed-beamed old chalet is available through Martin Brodier. The Silver Ski chalet is on the slopes and offers good value; it's not well placed for the village but is ski-convenient if there is resort-level snow. Towards the bottom end of the market, SkiBound have a place that is well positioned for the nursery slopes.

Hotels Small, friendly 2-star family hotels are the mainstay of the resort.
£££ Beauregard Best in town – comfortable, big by local standards; on the fringe of the village. Pool.
£££ Croix-Fry In a peaceful spot with good views, just beyond the col of the same name, on the fringe of the ski area – a rare French example of a really cosy, rustic chalet.
£££ Alp'Hôtel Comfortable modern chalet close to the centre, with one of the better restaurants. Pool.
£££ Alpen Roc Big but stylish, central and comfortable, although one reporter called his room 'very cramped'. Pool.
££ Vieux Chalet In a splendid piste-side setting overlooking the village, this is a favourite spot for lunch and dinner and has a handful of pleasant rooms. The food is probably the best in town.
££ Christiania Traditional, simple family hotel in the centre. Quiet, small rooms, and decent food.
Self-catering Martin Brodier have a very old chalet sold as a single booking to self-caters. It's fairly simple but charming and very well

placed – just off the main square close to the village gondola. French Impressions also have little self-catering chalets; one sleeps four. The one out near the Etale cable car, 2km from town, is best: spacious, open fire, views, garage, and pine-clad.

EATING OUT
Good choice
There's a wide choice of restaurants in town, with a number of others a short drive away, including the Vieux Chalet, which probably does the best food in the resort – traditional and modern. La Caleche and St Jacques are also good. L'Ecuelle is the place to go for good seafood, or steak that you cook yourself on a little brazier on the table. The Beau Site and Val d'Or hotels and La Dent Creuse are other mid-range restaurants worth a try. Chez Georges, La Cordee and L'Outa are unpretentious places that have been recommended for their great value for money. At the other end of the price scale is the fairly formal Symphonie restaurant in the hotel Beauregard. We're told the best food in the area is out at the Ferme du Lormay.

APRES-SKI
Very quiet except at weekends
La Clusaz is a typically quiet French family resort during the week, but weekenders liven it up appreciably. Le Pressoir is a focal bar, popular for its skiing videos and draught Guinness. The Salto and Montmartre bars are other animated haunts. L'Ecluse disco has a gimmick that brings in the customers despite its very high prices: the glass dance-floor has a floodlit stream running beneath it. (There is no early evening entrance reduction.) The other two discos are cheaper but by no means inexpensive.

Other entertainments include floodlit skiing and ice-skating, and there's a cinema.

FOR NON-SKIERS
Quite good
The village is a pleasant enough place for strolling around, though the traffic can be quite annoying. It's easy to get to several different mountain restaurants for lunch. There are good walks along the valleys and a day in Annecy is a pleasant excursion.

STAYING UP THE MOUNTAIN
Cheap and panoramic
The Relais de l'Aiguille at Crêt du Loup has five adequate bedrooms that are about the cheapest in the resort.

Les Contamines 1160m

HOW IT RATES

The skiing

Snow	****
Extent	**
Advanced	**
Intermediates	***
Beginners	***
Convenience	**
Queues	**
Restaurants	****

The rest

Scenery	***
Resort charm	****
Not skiing	**

SKI FACTS

Altitude	1165m-2487m
Lifts	26
Pistes	120km
Green/Blue	42%
Red	35%
Black	23%
Artificial snow	3km

PACKAGES

Chalets 'Unlimited',
Ski Total

SKI TOTAL

helped us to compile
the eating out and
après-ski sections.
Our thanks to them.

TOURIST OFFICE

Postcode 74170
Tel 00 33 50470158
Fax 50470954

✔ *Traditional unspoilt French village*

✔ *Fair-sized intermediate ski area*

✔ *Good snow record for its height*

✔ *Lift pass covers several nearby resorts, easily reachable by road*

✘ *Limited for experts and beginners*

✘ *Not for nightlife lovers*

✘ *Ski area a bus-ride from main village*

✘ *Can be some lengthy queues*

Les Contamines is an unspoilt village with pretty wooden chalets, weekly market in the village square and prices typical of rural France rather than ski resorts. Its local ski area offers substantial, surprisingly snowsure intermediate terrain. It is included in the Mont Blanc area lift pass, which also covers the neighbouring resorts of Chamonix, Megève and Courmayeur.

THE RESORT

The village is compact but the lifts are a bus-ride or long walk from the centre. There is accommodation by the lift at Le Lay, but staying in this uninspiring spot defeats the purpose of choosing this charming resort. A car is useful but the Mont Blanc lift pass gives free access to the local ski bus and buses to other resorts.

THE SKIING

From Le Lay a two-stage gondola climbs up to the **ski area**. Another gondola leads from a little further up the valley. Above these, a sizeable network of open, largely north-facing pistes fans out. You can drop over the ridge at Col du Joly (2000m) to a series of south-facing runs – with these, the area totals a respectable 120km.

Many of the runs are above 1800m and north- or north-east-facing, and the mass of Mont Blanc is said to trigger heavy snowfalls, making for reliable **snow conditions**.

The steep western section has black runs which are enjoyable but not terribly challenging for **advanced skiers**. The main attraction is the substantial off-piste potential – do take a guide. You also have the other Mont Blanc resorts – notably Chamonix.

The black runs are manageable for good **intermediates** and the rest of the skiing is ideal for average skiers, with the best runs from the gondola's top station to its mid-station.

In good snow, the nursery area in the village is adequate for **beginners**. There are other areas at the mid-station and top of the gondola, but no long greens to progress to.

There are **cross-country** trails of varying difficulty totalling 29km.

Queues in the morning at the gondola can be a problem, especially when skiers are bussed in from other resorts. Some lifts higher up can have queues, but these are being reduced by

the introduction of more fast quads.

The lift company wickedly leaves off the piste map those lovely rustic **mountain restaurants** which it doesn't own. La Ferme du Ruelle is a jolly barn. Chalet du Col du Joly has great views. Best of all are two cosy chalets – Roselette and Buche Croisée.

We have had mixed reports on the **ski school**. Some parents thought their children's classes too strict and overcrowded. There are excursions to other resorts, including a guided group to the famous Vallée Blanche.

There is an all-day crèche for **children** up to 7, and the ski school takes children from the age of 4. The sheltered kindergarten is conveniently adjacent to the gondola mid-station.

STAYING THERE

The only operator running **chalets** is Ski Total, praised by reporters for its good-value chalets and free shuttle bus. There are a dozen modest **hotels**. Only the Chemenaz, 200m from the lifts, reaches 3-star status. The 2-star Chamois is popular, with sauna, whirlpool and a ski-bus stop outside. Cheaper places include the Christiana, Moranches and Gai Soleil (a Logis).

The Hameau du Lay **apartments** are pleasant and close to the lifts.

Recommended **restaurants** are the Bohème, the Husky and Op Traken. Ty Briez is an atmospheric little crèperie, and it becomes a drinks rendezvous later. **Après-ski** is quiet. Brasserie de Rhodos is a pleasant spot for jazz. The Tetras Pub and the Saxo at the base station are popular at tea-time. Later, the Cressoua is one of the more animated bars. The Igloo is the livelier of the two discos.

There are good walks and a natural ice-rink, but St-Gervais (10 minutes by bus), Megève and Chamonix have more to offer **non-skiers**. You can take a train ride up from St-Gervais on the Mont Blanc tramway.

Courchevel 1300m–1850m

✔ *Very extensive, varied skiing, part of the famous Trois Vallées area*

✔ *Great easy runs for near-beginners*

✔ *Much of the accommodation is very convenient for skiing*

✔ *Very impressive lift system*

✔ *Excellent piste maintenance, and widespread use of snowmakers*

✔ *Wooded setting is pretty, and gives useful skiing in bad weather*

✔ *Appealing old village at 1300*

✔ *Some great restaurants*

✔ *Surprisingly unpretentious for such an upmarket resort*

✘ *Some pistes get unpleasantly busy*

✘ *Generally characterless villages, with intrusive traffic in places*

✘ *Not much après-ski animation, except in 1850*

✘ *Expensive, particularly the ultra-pricey 1850*

✘ *Little to do but ski*

Courchevel is the favourite resort of the Paris jet set, who fly directly in to the mini airport at 1850. But it is not intimidatingly smart and, unlike many other fashionable places, it has skiing that is excellent in every respect. Its slopes are the most extensive, varied and immaculately groomed of the whole Trois Vallées. It has everything, from long gentle greens to steep, narrow couloirs, with plenty of blues, reds, black mogul fields – and tree-lined runs for bad weather. Many visitors are content to ski the Courchevel sector alone. But there is good access to the rest of the Trois Vallées for those who want it.

Courchevel 1300 is a pleasant village, and the posh bits of 1850 are stylishly woody, but overall the resort is no beauty. Well, nothing's perfect. Courchevel is much more French than Méribel, but getting more popular with the British.

ORIENTATION

Courchevel consists of four satellite villages (five if you include newly-built La Tania) widely scattered around the lower fringes of the north-eastern end of the Trois Vallées. The resorts are named after the altitudes at which they are set. A road connects 1850 with 1300 via 1650 and 1550. 1850 is the focal resort, having direct lift and piste links with 1300 and 1550, though all five centres have gondolas up into the main area. 1650 lies at the periphery, from where the skiing spreads west above the other villages to the link with **Méribel** and **Mottaret**. St-**Martin-de-Belleville, Les Menuires** and **Val-Thorens** are reached on skis via the Méribel-Mottaret valley. **Champagny** (La Plagne ski area) and **Valmorel** are easy road outings.

🏠 The resort

Courchevel is made up of four villages known by their altitudes (plus nearby La Tania). They differ widely in skiing access, character and facilities. Bus services (covered by the lift pass) link the villages – a frequent one between 1850 and 1650, hourly down to 1550 and 1300.

1850 is by far the largest village, and is very much the focal point of the area. It is certainly the place to stay if you're looking for nightlife or what few non-skiing facilities are available. 1850 is self-consciously upmarket, with some of the highest prices in the Alps. But style is radiated by the rich clientele rather than the village itself, which is a messy sprawl that has a surprising amount of traffic and associated fumes. The jet set are able to retreat to the woody suburbs.

A number of chalets and hotels are pleasantly sited among the trees that surround the village – ideal for skiing to the door but making evening trips into town a bit of a trek. The most convenient place to stay is close to the main lift station and the new Forum

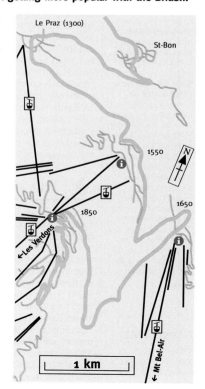

SKI FACTS

Altitude 1300m-2740m
Lifts   200
Pistes   600km
Green/Blue   49%
Red   37%
Black   14%
Artificial snow 60km

LIFT PASSES

95/96 prices in francs
Three Valleys
Covers all lifts of
Courchevel, Méribel,
Les Menuires,
Val-Thorens and
St-Martin-de-Belleville
and buses in
Courchevel only.
Beginners 13 free lifts
in the Courchevel
valley.
Main pass
1-day pass 215
6-day pass 1035
(low season 910 –
10% off)
Senior citizens
Over 60: 6-day pass
776 (25% off)
Over 80: free pass
Children
Under 16: 6-day pass
776 (25% off)
Under 5: free pass
Short-term passes
Half-day pass (from
12.30) covers 68 lifts
in Courchevel valley
only.
Notes Over 70s get a
50% discount on
main pass price.
6-day pass and over
valid for one day each
in Tignes-Val-d'Isère,
La-Plagne-Les Arcs,
Pralognan-la-Vanoise
and Les-Saises.
Alternative passes
Premières Neiges
covers Courchevel
and Méribel for first 2
weeks of the season
(6 day pass 649,
94/95 price). Vallée
de Courchevel (6 day
pass 845) covers 68
lifts in Courchevel.

sports and accommodation complex.

1650 is less pleasant on the eye, and has little in the way of facilities. It is set at the foot of a separate branch of the ski area, linked at only two points to the skiing above 1850. This makes 1650 inconvenient for skiing the Trois Vallées, but also means it is relatively quiet. Most of the accommodation is fairly close to the lifts.

1550 is a very quiet, featureless resort, a gondola-ride or short ski beneath 1850. It has the advantage of having essentially the same position in the ski area as 1850, with much cheaper accommodation and restaurants. But once skiing is finished, things change: 1550 is further by road from 1850 than 1650 is. Although small, it's a scattered place, with some accommodation a fair way from the gondola.

1300 (or Le Praz) is the most attractive of the resorts. It's a traditional village set amid woodland, although the charm factor has been undermined by recent expansion triggered by the Olympics, including the building of the Olympic ski jump. It's still a quiet place with good links into the skiing above 1850, and has the advantage of tree-lined slopes on its doorstep for bad-weather skiing. 1300 has a nursery slope with a free drag-lift but no ski school, which means that beginners need a lift pass to ride up and down to and from 1850. Near-beginners wanting access to long easy runs also face rides down as well as up: the pistes back to 1300 are red and black, and at this altitude conditions are often poor.

The new accommodation centre of **La Tania** is nearby – it's purely a quiet, small, purpose-built base with lower prices than Courchevel. Our one reporter on the place this year was very happy there.

 # The skiing

There are three sections to the local ski area, though everywhere is so well linked that it is essentially just one big network. The central 1850 section is suitable for all, the wooded 1300 area is best for good skiers, while 1650 has mainly very easy skiing. It is possible to ski back to all the villages, but the runs to 1300 can close due to lack of snow. Courchevel's skiing is a high-class operation. Piste maintenance is superb, snowmakers abundant and lifts modern, fast and comfortable. The ski area is also very well laid out. The main complaint we've had is that

many people find the piste map hard to follow because it is too small.

Many reporters recommend buying only a Courchevel pass, and buying daily extensions for the Trois Vallées.

THE SKI AREA
Highly interesting

The **1850** section is the largest, with a great network of lifts and pistes spreading out from the village, which is very much the focal point. The main axis of the area is the Verdons gondola, leading to a second gondola and a (nearly) parallel cable-car up to **La Saulire** (2740m), one of the two gateways to Méribel and all points to Val-Thorens. The Saulire sector offers a wide range of intermediate and advanced skiing, including a number of couloirs.

To the right, looking up the mountain, the Chenus gondola from 1850 goes up towards the second of the Méribel departure points, the **Col de la Loze**. Easy and intermediate runs go back to 1850, with more difficult skiing in the woods above La Tania and **1300** – splendid when snow is in good supply.

To the left of the Verdons gondola is the gentle **Biollay** sector, reached by the Jardin Alpin gondola which also serves some of the higher hotels. This is great beginner terrain, and gives access to 1650.

The **1650** area offers a good mixture of intermediate and beginner skiing, with the genuinely steep Chanrossa black at the top making one of the two links with 1850's Saulire and Biollay skiing. Neither link is easy: the drag connecting to the blue and green runs of the Biollay sector is unpleasantly steep, and apparently not open to children. Getting to and from the Méribel valley from 1650 is more of an effort than from elsewhere.

SNOW RELIABILITY
Very good

Courchevel's snow is often much better than neighbouring Méribel's because many of its slopes are north- or north-east-facing. The combination of this, its height, an abundance of snowmakers and excellent piste maintenance usually guarantees reliable skiing down to at least the 1850 and 1650 villages, and to Bouc Blanc (1680m), above La Tania.

FOR ADVANCED SKIERS
Some black gems

Tough runs make up only a small proportion of the skiing; Courchevel is certainly not in the same league as

SKI SCHOOL

95/96 prices in francs

ESF in 1850
Classes 6 days
5hr: 9.30am–noon and
2.30–5pm; 2½hr: am
or pm
6 full days: 980
Children's classes
Ages: from 4
6 full days: 760
Private lessons
2½hr morning, 2hr
lunchtime, 2½hr
afternoon, 7hr full day
1450 for full day, for
1 to 4 people

94/95 prices in francs

ESF in 1650
Classes 6 days
4½hr: 9.30am–noon
and 2.45–4.45; am
(2½hr) or pm (2hr)
6 full days: 840
Children's classes
Ages: from 3
6 full day: 670
Private lessons
2½hr morning, 2hr
lunchtime, 2hr
afternoon, 7hr full day
1400 for full day, for
1 to 6 people

94/95 prices in francs

ESF in 1550
Classes 6 days
3hr: am or pm
6 mornings: 680
Children's classes
Ages: from 3
6 mornings: 590
Private lessons
3hr morning, 3hr
afternoon, 7hr full day
1300 for full day, for
1 to 6 people

Ski Academy
Classes 5 days
2hr: am
5 mornings 650
Private lessons
1500 for full day for 1
or 2 people

Ski Masterclass
British-run ski school
Classes 5 days, 2hr
am or pm: 695
Children's classes
5 days, 3hr am or
pm: 840

Chamonix, Val-d'Isère or St Anton for
steep expert terrain. But there is plenty
to interest good skiers. The Saulire
cable-car gives access to Courchevel's
three famed couloirs which, though
not terrifyingly narrow or very long,
are certainly steep – especially the
Téléphérique. Running parallel to
these is a fine black from La Vizelle to
Les Verdons. The Vizelle gondola also
accesses the Suisses black. The quite
difficult Chanrossa run is also nearby.
For a change of scene and a real test of
stamina, a couple of long (700m
vertical), genuinely steep blacks cut
through trees from the top of the
Chenus gondola to 1300. (If they ever
cut a run down the fall-line on this
slope, it will be a run to reckon with.)

There is off-piste skiing all over the
place, with the steepest pitches, not
surprisingly, close to the black pistes.
You are never far from a piste, and
new snow gets quickly skied.

Good skiers also have the rest of the
Trois Vallées to race around.

FOR INTERMEDIATE SKIERS
Paradise for all levels

All grades of intermediate skiers love
Courchevel. Less experienced skiers
have wonderful long runs above 1650
in the Pyramide-Grand Bosses areas.
The Biollay sector also has fine easy
runs, merging with those coming
down from Verdons.

Average skiers can negotiate most of
the red runs without too much
difficulty. Our favourite is the long,
sweeping Combe de la Saulire run
from top to bottom of the cable-car.
This is especially pleasant first thing in
the morning, when it is immaculately
groomed and free of crowds. (It's a
rather different story at the end of the
day.) The Bouc Blanc runs through the
trees towards La Tania are also
particularly attractive. This section
also has fine red runs down to the
1850 area, with easier blues running
alongside. The Marmottes and Creux
area behind La Vizelle have some of
the most challenging intermediate
pistes, which can get quite bumpy –
and crowded with ski school groups.

Excursions to Méribel and the rest of
the Trois Vallées can be undertaken by
all intermediates. Less adventurous
skiers should go via Col de la Loze.

FOR BEGINNERS
Great graduation runs

There are excellent nursery slopes
above both 1650 and 1850. At the
former, lessons are likely to begin on
the short drags close to the village, but

quick learners will soon be able to ski
from close to the top of 1650 area all
the way down to the village. The
Pralong area, near the altiport above
1850, is another fine nursery area. An
easy green links this area with the
skiing above 1650, so adventurous
novices have the opportunity to move
far afield. The Bellecôte green run
down into 1850 is an excellent long,
gentle slope – though it would be
better if it were quieter. It is served by
the Jardin Alpin gondola, and by a
drag-lift which is one of a dozen free
beginner lifts in Courchevel. 1550 has
a tiny nursery area, but a gondola
swiftly transports skiers up to 1850.

FOR CROSS-COUNTRY
Long wooded trails

All the villages have some cross-
country, but 1300 is by far the most
suitable, with trails through the woods
towards 1550, 1850 and Méribel.
Given sufficient snow, there are also
several loops around the village.

QUEUES
Superb lift system copes well

Even at New Year and Easter, when
1850 in particular positively teems
with skiers, queues are minimal
thanks to the excellence of the lift
system. The Verdons gondola had its
capacity doubled a year or two ago,
alleviating this old bottleneck. Only
the Saulire cable-car generates much
of a queue, and that moves very
quickly – the cars are huge and the
cable short. What's more, the parallel
Vizelle gondola is being upgraded
from four-person to eight-person
cabin this season.

Most complaints from Courchevel-
based skiers concern lifts in the other
valleys. Remember that the lift home
from Mottaret at the end of the day
can become over-subscribed.

MOUNTAIN RESTAURANTS
Very expensive

Mountain restaurants are plentiful by
French purpose-built resort standards,
though prices are high – and a striking
proportion of 1995 reporters said they
relied on picnics or bars of chocolate.
Prices vary widely, and a little
exploration pays off. For example, the
bar of the hotel Courcheneige on the
Bellecôte piste is half the price of
places in central 1850.

The big Chalet de Pierres, on the
Verdons piste just above 1850, is one
of the highlights for those inclined to
extravagance – a comfortable and
smooth place in traditional style,

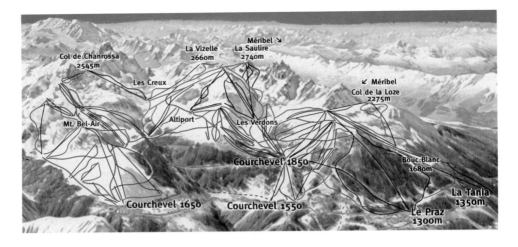

Selected chalets in Courchevel

Selected chalets in Courchevel

FlexiSki   T 0171 352 0044   F 01490 440446

The Lodge SLEEPS 20
Probably the most luxurious chalet in the Alps, boasting 10 stunning bedrooms all with ensuite facilities. Superb setting, only 5 minutes' walk up the Bellecote slope from the centre of Courchevel 1850.

Simply Ski *Chalet specialists*   T 0181 742 2541   F 0181 995 5346

Simply Ski offers a choice of seven chalets in Courchevel 1300 and 1850. Chalets range from the comfortable to the totally luxurious. Chalet L'Ancolies, one of the most luxurious chalets available in Europe, is equipped and run to the highest standards and is suitable for the most discriminating of guests. All the chalets are traditional in appearance, offer a friendly welcome and are well positioned for skiing and local amenities.
Friendly chalet staff
Cordon Bleu cuisine
Ski leader service
Creches and children's clubs
Children's ski lessons
Competitive prices and discounts
Scheduled and charter flights
Snowtrain and Snowdrive

Chalet L'Ancolies ➔

Ski Scott Dunn *Upmarket holiday specialists*   T 0181 767 0202   F 0181 767 2026

Ski Scott Dunn have the best quality chalets available in Courchevel 1850. Accommodation ranges from 6-person to 14-person chalets, and all are well located either by the Bellecôte piste or close to the centre. A full crèche is available and staffed by NNEB nannies.
Ski guiding available.

Cristal de Roche A (Sleeps 8) ➔

GETTING THERE

Air Geneva, transfer 3½hr. Lyon, transfer 3½hr. Chambery, transfer 2½hr. Direct flights to Courchevel altiport from London at weekends only (contact tourist office for details)

Rail Moûtiers (24km); transfer by bus or taxi.

PACKAGES

AA Ski-Driveaway, Airtours, Alpine Action, Bladon Lines, Chalet World, Chalets 'Unlimited', Crystal, Finlays, First Choice Ski, FlexiSki, French Impressions, Inghams, Lagrange, Le Shuttle Holidays, Le Ski, Lotus Supertravel, Made to Measure, Mark Warner, Motours, Neilson, PGL Ski Europe, Powder Byrne, Silver Ski, Simply Ski, Ski Activity, Ski Arrangements, Ski Choice, Ski Club of GB, Ski Equipe, Ski Esprit, Ski France, Ski Les Alpes, Ski Olympic, Ski Savoie, Ski Scott Dunn, Ski Val, SkiBound, Skiworld, Stena Sealink, The Ski Company, Thomson, Travelscene Ski-Drive, White Roc

La Tania Alpine Action, Crystal, French Impressions, Inghams, Lagrange, Le Shuttle Holidays, Neilson, Ski France, Stena Sealink

Le Praz Le Shuttle Holidays

CHILDCARE

There are kindergartens in 1850 (79080847) and 1650 (79083584) which take children from age 2, until 5pm. The ESF branches in all three main parts of the resort have ski kindergartens; minimum age is 3 in 1550 (79082107) and 1650 (79082608) and 4 in 1850 (79080772).

doing excellent food (including superb cakes) with about the highest prices of all. The busy self-service restaurant at the airport is good value by local standards, with good food and a fine terrace well placed for watching aircraft. The Verdons is well placed for skier-watching, and serves good value food by local standards. The Chenus is an atmospheric self-service place. Le Casserole, above 1650 at the foot of the Grandes Bosses drags, is a good self-service place. Mont Bel-Air, a bit higher up, is also recommended. A trip down to the Bistrot du Praz at 1300 is recommended for a gourmet blow-out on a bad-weather day. There are plenty of places to eat in central 1850 too; prices drop as you walk away from the lift station.

SKI SCHOOL
Masterclass rules
The Courchevel ESF is the largest ski school in Europe, with bases at 1850, 1650 and 1550, and a total of almost 500 instructors. Of course, this is a reflection of the number of people taking private lessons in this affluent resort. As elsewhere, the number of pupils in a class depends on demand. Reports this year run from six in a group in January to a Class 3 group of 25 in the February peak. That apart, people are generally content with the standards of instruction and English.

Ski Academy, an independent group of French instructors now coming up to its third season, aim to offer 'a more personal, friendly service', and claim their dozen or so instructors speak 'fluent English'. 'Adequately clear English' would be nearer the mark, in our experience, but the school has another attraction: it operates a maximum class size of seven.

Most of our reporting readers used the British-run Masterclass school – perhaps partly because of the eulogy we gave them in the last edition. This year, sadly, the picture is rather more mixed: some reports are very enthusiastic, others highly critical of the detached attitude of instructors. Lessons are short (two hours) and relatively expensive, but classes are small (maximum eight pupils).

FACILITIES FOR CHILDREN
British families don't use them?
We have one report this year from a family that used the excellent-looking ski kindergarten in 1850. The 5-year-old concerned 'loved it', despite the large number of children. There are English-speaking instructors, and the general atmosphere is 'jolly'.

An in-house chalet crèche with British nannies is an alternative that many families have found attractive. The Simply Ski operation in 1300 has been recommended, and in 1850 there is Ski Scott Dunn. Bladon Lines in 1850 offer private nannies on various terms – free in low season if you fill a chalet for eight or more. Crystal have a crèche (open to all their clients) in one of their 1550 chalets.

Family specialists Ski Esprit have several chalets and two crèches in 1300, and last year introduced their own Ski Sprites ski classes – specially contracted Ski Academy instructors, and a class size limited to eight children. Reports on the childcare are all enthusiastic – 'wonderful nannies' – those on the tuition generally so.

 # Staying there

All the resorts are convenient for the skiing. So the choice of which to go for depends on how much importance you attach to nightlife (1850 best), charm (1300 best) or the quality and price of your accommodation.

HOW TO GO
Value chalets and apartments
Huge numbers of British tour operators go to Courchevel, with a wide choice of accommodation.

Chalets There are plenty of chalets available, including some very comfortable ones and a few that you might call luxurious.

Simply Ski's exceptionally smart L'Ancolies, in 1850, is elegantly furnished, and comes with numerous mod cons and cordon bleu cooking. It's initially sold as a single booking to groups, but can be available by the room as a late booking. The same company also have a selection of much cheaper but very attractive places in 1850 and 1300.

FlexiSki have an exceptionally comfortable large chalet this year to add to their contrasting places in 1850 – a spacious luxury duplex a stone's throw from the main lift station, and a characterful little wooden place among the trees.

Ski Scott Dunn have some upmarket chalets full of creature comforts, mostly located in or near the attractive Jardin Alpin area above 1850.

Bladon Lines have a good middle-market selection in 1850; the Petit Chapiteau is 'excellent'. Lotus Supertravel have one of the biggest selections; Orsiere 3 has been recommended.

ACTIVITIES

Indoor Artificial skating rink, bridge, chess, squash, swimming and saunas (hotels), gymnasium, health and fitness centres (swimming pools, sauna, steam-room, jacuzzi, water therapy, weight-training, massage), bowling, exhibitions (galleries in 1850 and 1650), cinema, games rooms, billiards, language courses
Outdoor Hang-gliding, para-gliding, flying lessons, parachuting, floodlit skiing, ski jumping, toboggan run, snow-shoe excursions, snowmobile rides, dog-sleigh rides, 35km cleared paths, 2½km toboggan run, curling, ice-climbing, flight excursions

TOURIST OFFICE

Postcode 73122
Tel 00 33 79080029
Fax 79081563

Le Ski have a fine selection in 1650, and will carefully steer you to the right chalet for your needs. Finlays have a good reputation in 1550, and last year added a place in 1850. Crystal have places in all parts, with cheap options in 1300; their Bellevue in 1550 has an 'excellent' location. Neilson and Crystal provide very good value in La Tania – Neilson's Tangara is 'superb, in a good quiet location'. All the chalets of family specialists Ski Esprit are in 1300; we have good reports of the Merisiers ('nicely renovated, excellent food') and the YaCa ('very comfortable').

There are also plenty of chalet-hotels. Ski Val and Ski Activity share the superbly positioned, cheap and cheerful Tournier; the food gets rave reviews, the plumbing doesn't. Ski Val's Isba has also had generally good reports, especially for food.

Hotels There are nearly 50 hotels in Courchevel, mostly at 1850. Three-quarters of these are graded 3-star and above, though some would have lower ratings in other countries.

££££ Chabichou (1850) The only French ski resort hotel with two Michelin stars. Big, beautiful bedrooms to match.

££££ Grandes Alpes (1850) In pole position, on the piste right next to the main lifts.

£££ Courcheneige (1850) Pleasantly informal, large chalet on the piste above the resort.

£££ Ducs de Savoie (1850) Pleasant, wood-built; well placed in the trees for skiing to the door, but only five minutes' walk from the village.

£££ Sivoliere (1850) No beauty, but charming and comfortable inside and pleasantly set among pines.

£££ Golf (1650) Pleasant, good value 3-star, in a superb position on the piste next to the gondola station.

££ Chanrossa (1550) This attractive 2-star is a friendly, well placed hotel.

££ Peupliers (1300) Well placed and cheap by local standards.

Self-catering There's a large selection of apartments, though high-season packages can get sold out early. Neilson and Crystal have apartments in the smart and superbly positioned new Forum complex; watch out, though, for cramped windowless bedrooms. Inghams have good apartments at the foot of the slopes in 1650, perfect for families.

Crystal and Neilson have good, attractively priced places in La Tania.

EATING OUT
You pay for quality

Restaurants are, in the main, high in quality and super-high in price. Self-caterers on a budget may be forced to cook for themselves whether they want to or not! Among the best, and priciest, restaurants are the Michelin 2-stars Chabichou and Bateau Ivre in 1850. The 'friendly' Bercail also has a high reputation, notably for seafood.

Many staying in 1850 venture to the other villages in search of lower prices. The Chanrossa hotel restaurant and the Cortona pizza place in 1550 are good value by local standards. Also recommended are the Lizard and the Plouc (for eat-in or take-away pizza) at 1650. Bistrot du Praz in 1300 is pricey but excellent.

APRES-SKI
1850 has it

If you want nightlife, it's got to be 1850. There are some exclusive night clubs, such as the Dakota, New-St-Nicholas, Bergerie and Grange, with top Paris cabaret acts and sky-high prices. L'Equipe seems to be readers' favourite nightspot; opinions are divided on the Wednesday karaoke sessions. Jacques, L'Arbe, Tee-Jay's and the (relatively) cheap and cheerful Potinière are also popular bars. The Chabichou piano bar is good for a quiet drink.

The Croisette cinema has a couple of English-language films each week. Concerts take place from time to time.

The lower villages are quieter, though buses run late enough for cinema and bar excursions to 1850, and the 1650 scene has improved in recent years. Its Signal bar is friendly, full of French and renowned for its views at the back and its incredibly strong Mutzig. Le Plouc is an intimate, welcoming French bar with good music. Even the uninspiring Green Club livens up occasionally these days. In 1300 the pizzeria tucked away in the shopping mall is the social hub, with live music and modest prices.

FOR NON-SKIERS
1850 isn't bad

A pedestrian ski pass for the gondolas and buses in the Courchevel and Méribel valleys makes it easy to meet skiers for lunch and get around the area. A fair amount of strolling around and posing goes on in 1850. And the new Forum sports centre in 1850 is an asset. You can take flights from the altiport around the area.

Selected chalets in Courchevel

Le Ski *The chalet specialists*   T 01484 548996   F 01484 451909

Chalet Le Sabot de Venus
SLEEPS 22
Excellent facilities. One minute walk to village and lifts. This chalet has everything you want from skiing accommodation – it is next to the ski lifts, most rooms have en suite facilities and there is even a log fire! Apart from the main living areas (see left), the chalet is thickly carpeted throughout which helps give Le Sabot its warm and comfortable feeling.

Le Ski have the largest range of chalets in Courchevel.
 All the 11 chalets are less than 3 minutes' walk from the lifts.

Le Ski was formed 11 years ago and continues to offer delicious food and a full-time ski guiding service.

Le Ski also have four catered chalets in Val d'Isère.
Try them out. After all, they are the chalet specialists!

Le Ski *The chalet specialists*   T 01484 548996   F 01484 451909

Chalet Le Mollard SLEEPS 16
Superb position and facilities. Only 2 minute walk to the ski lifts. Le Mollard (right) lies in a wonderful location with beautiful, uninterrupted views down the Courchevel valley. This 3 year old chalet has modern facilities and is particularly popular with large parties.

Le Ski have chalets for as few as 7 guests and as many as 22. Call for a brochure.

Le Ski *The chalet specialists*   T 01484 548996   F 01484 451909

Chalet Les Carlines SLEEPS 9
Traditionally furnished with beautiful views. One of Le Ski's oldest and most popular chalets – the facilities are good and the rooms are a decent size. The lounge (see right) is very bright and has lovely views and a large old log fire.
Les Carlines has a wonderful atmosphere and, like all our chalets, you can book the whole place for your party or just take one or two rooms.

Le Ski are very flexible – give them a call!

Les Deux-Alpes 1650m

HOW IT RATES

The skiing

Snow	****
Extent	***
Advanced	***
Intermediates	**
Beginners	***
Convenience	***
Queues	**
Restaurants	*

The rest

Scenery	****
Resort charm	**
Not skiing	**

ORIENTATION

Les Deux-Alpes is a narrow village spread along a long main street, sitting on a high, remote col. Access is from the Grenoble-Briançon road to the north or by gondola from Venosc. The main ski area is on the eastern side of the street, with a small, unlinked area to the west. The main lift up to the east is the 20-person Jandri Express gondola from near the centre. The smaller Diable gondola leaves from the southern end. The newest development is Le Village, in an isolated position above the resort entrance. This has a chair-lift to the skiing.

From the top, you can get to the experts' resort, **La Grave**. The six-day pass covers a day in each of **Alpe-d'Huez**, **Serre-Chevalier**, **Puy-St-Vincent** and the Milky Way resorts from **Montgenèvre** to **Sauze d'Oulx**. All are easily reached by car, road conditions permitting.

✔ High, snowsure skiing including an extensive glacier area, with stunning views, that's normally open winter and summer

✔ Attractions both for beginners and advanced skiers

✔ Efficient, modern lift system

✔ Animated village with lively, varied nightlife

✔ Rare opportunity for those who like hotels to find good value in a modern French resort

✗ Piste network much smaller than many skiers expect

✗ Ski area even more limited when runs to resort are incomplete, and/or glacier lifts closed

✗ Very congested skiing in places

✗ No easy runs back to the resort – slopes are steep, and snow conditions often poor

✗ Virtually no woodland skiing, so little skiing possible in bad weather

✗ Long, straggling village, not especially ugly but busy with traffic

✗ Poor mountain restaurants

Les Deux-Alpes is very different from most modern French resorts. In comparison with scores of medium-sized resorts, Les Deux-Alpes has a perfectly adequate ski area. But the place tends to be sold on the British market as a member of the big boys' league – and in that company its skiing (or its piste skiing, at least) can't compete. Anyone expecting another Alpe-d'Huez, La Plagne or Val-d'Isère will be disappointed. Whatever your standard of skiing, you need to be content to ski the same runs repeatedly if you're staying for a week.

In some other respects, Les Deux-Alpes is streets ahead of most high-altitude French resorts. It may not be a pretty village, but it is much more appealing in the evening than many of its rivals, thanks to the unusually large number of lively and varied bars and discos – many of which remain busy until the early hours. It's not a particularly smart resort either, so bar and restaurant prices – as well as hotel prices – aren't prohibitively high.

 ## The resort

Les Deux-Alpes is a large, sprawling collection of hotels, apartments, bars and shops, most of which line the long, busy main street. Although there is no centre as such, and lifts are spread fairly evenly along the village, a couple of focal points are evident.

The resort has grown up haphazardly over the years – it is very far from being purpose-built – and there is a wide range of building styles, from old chalets, through monstrous 1960s blocks, to more sympathetic recent developments. Fans point out that it looks better as you drive out than as you drive in, because all the apartment buildings have their balconies facing the remote southern end of the resort.

The village is unusually lively for a French resort, which helps the general ambience. Bars, restaurants and nightclubs that originally catered for young French weekenders now

generate a suitable atmosphere for the growing lively Brit contingent. The resort is popular with Italians too, especially at weekends.

Traffic flows along a one-way system and can be heavy at times, making Les Deux-Alpes less than ideal for families.

SKI FACTS

Altitude 1300m-3570m
Lifts	63
Pistes	200km
Green/Blue	62%
Red	28%
Black	10%
Artificial snow	4km

LIFT PASSES

95/96 prices in francs
Super ski pass
Covers all lifts in Les
Deux-Alpes, entry to
swimming pool and
skating rink.
Beginners 2 free lifts;
'Première trace' pass
(covers 19 lifts).
Main pass
1-day pass 178
6-day pass 890
(low season 801 –
10% off)
Senior citizens
Over 60: 6-day pass
668 (25% off)
Children
Under 13: 6-day pass
638 (25% off)
Under 4: free pass
Short-term passes
Half-day 140
Notes Main pass of 2
days or more includes
one day's skiing in La
Grave. 6-day pass
includes one day's
skiing in Alpe-d'Huez,
Serre-Chevalier, Puy-
Saint-Vincent, and the
Milky Way.
Alternative passes
3 limited area passes:
'Ski première trace'
covers 19 lifts (82 per
day), 'Ski sympa'
covers 27 lifts (105
per day), 'Grand ski'
covers 39 lifts (136
per day).

 # The skiing

There are two ski areas, one either side
of the village. The main one has three
distinct sections, each of which has
different characteristics, making it
suitable for different types of skier.
Consequently, while the area as a
whole has skiing suitable for all
grades, there are few places good for
mixed-ability parties.

For a big resort, Les Deux-Alpes has
a disappointingly small ski area;
although extremely long and tall (it
rises almost 2000m) it is also very
narrow, with just a few runs on the
upper part of the mountain, served by
a few long, efficient lifts. Intermediate
skiers and confident beginners, in
particular, should beware. Many of the
higher blue runs are easy and crowded
– incredibly so at times – and most of
the red runs immediately above the
resort are steep and, especially in poor
snow conditions, tricky. In good
weather, at least, the skiing has
considerable attractions for advanced
skiers (largely off-piste, including
excursions to La Grave over the top of
the ski area). For novices there are very
easy green runs on guaranteed good
snow on the glacier, as well as good
village nursery slopes; but it's a long
ride up and down – and very cold,
especially in early season.

Helicopter trips to Alpe-d'Huez are
easily arranged and good value.

THE SKI AREA
Long, narrow and fragmented
The western **Pied-Moutet** side of Les
Deux-Alpes' skiing is relatively little-
used. It is served by lifts from various
parts of town but reaches only 2100m.
As well as the short runs back to town
which get the morning sun, there's an
attractive, longer north-facing run off
the back which goes down through
the trees to the small village of Bons.
This is one of only two tree-lined runs
in Les Deux-Alpes. The other drops
down to Mont-de-Lans and is the only
piste in the resort which can be skied
directly from both ski areas. These
runs are worth knowing about in poor
visibility.

On the main, **eastern side** of the
valley, the broad, steep slope
immediately above the village offers a
series of relatively short, testing runs,
with a number of nursery slopes
interspersed among them at the
bottom of the hill.

The ridge above the village has lifts
and gentle runs along it, and behind it
the deep, steep Combe de Thuit. Lifts

span the combe to the main mid-
mountain station at 2600m, passing
over the smaller lift junction of Lac du
Plan in the process. The middle
section of the skiing, above and below
2600m, is made up primarily of blue
cruising runs and is very narrow. At
one point there is essentially just a
single run down the mountain – a
broad ledge which skirts the Combe
de Thuit back to the 'home' ridge.
There are various chair-lift-served
diversions you can take from the main
channel, and it is now possible to
avoid the Thuit ledge by taking the
Gours run (previously off-piste) to the
bottom of the combe, where a new lift
takes you up to the 'home' ridge. (We
understand that the planned new lift
shown on our map, back up to 2600m,
will not now be built.)

The top **Glacier du Mont-de-Lans**
section, served by drag-lifts and the
warmer Funi Dôme Express
underground funicular, has some fine,
very easy runs which afford great
views and are ideal for beginners and
less adventurous skiers. Good skiers
can trek across to neighbouring La
Grave's challenging slopes.

SNOW RELIABILITY
Excellent on higher slopes
The snow on the higher slopes is
normally very good, even in a poor
winter – one of the main reasons for
Les Deux-Alpes' popularity. Above
2200m most of the skiing is north-
facing, and the top glacier section has
summer skiing and guaranteed good
winter snow. At Les Deux-Alpes you
should worry more about bad weather
shutting the lifts, or extremely low
temperatures high up, than about
snow shortage.

But the runs just above the village
face west, so they get a lot of
afternoon sun and can be icy at the
beginning and end of skiing. Artificial
snow on some of the lower slopes
helps keep them skiable.

FOR ADVANCED SKIERS
Off-piste is the main attraction
With good snow and weather
conditions, the area offers wonderful
off-piste skiing. A particular attraction
is La Grave, reached by a drag-lift (to
3570m) and a trek from the top of Les
Deux-Alpes' skiing at Dôme de la Loze.
From there it's a vertical drop of over
2000m to La Grave. (See separate entry
on page 188.) The downside is that in
bad weather the link is often closed.

Back on the Les Deux-Alpes side,
there are several good off-piste runs,
including a number of variations from

SKI SCHOOL

95/96 prices in francs

ESF
Classes 6 days
3hr: am; 2½hr: pm
6 mornings: 700
Children's classes
Ages: 6 to 12
6 mornings: 585
Private lessons
1hr over lunchtime or
full day Sunday
175 for 1hr, for 1 to 3
people

**International
St-Christophe
Classes** 6 days
3hr: am; 2½hr: pm
6 mornings: 620
Children's classes
Ages: 6 to 12
6 mornings: 490
Private lessons
1hr over lunchtime
185 for 1hr, for 1 to 3
people

CHILDCARE

Both ski schools run
kindergartens on
more-or-less identical
terms – taking
children aged 4 to 6
until 5pm. The ESF
(76792121) is slightly
more expensive and
does lunch only on
request, but starts at
9.15am whereas the
ESI de St Christophe
(76790421) starts at
9.30am. The Crèche
du Village offers an
excellent service for
babies from 6 months
to 2 years, from
8.30am to 5.30pm.
Garderie du
Bonhomme de Neige
for children aged 2 to
6 years.
List of babysitters
available from the
tourist office.

underneath the top stage of the Jandri
Express down to the Thuit chair-lift.
The best-known ones are now marked
on the piste map. Off-piste skiers may
regret that the run down the gunbarrel
of Les Gours is now a red piste.

The Tête Moute chair-lift, from the
top of the Diable gondola, serves the
steepest black run around. The brave
can also try off-piste variations here
between the rocks.

Most of the runs back down to the
resort are marked red on the piste
map, but they deserve a black rating.
They are usually mogulled and often
icy early on because they get the
afternoon sun. Some, in fact, used to
be black (and still had black piste
markers when we were there in 1994)
but were downgraded a few years ago –
perhaps to broaden the resort's appeal.

FOR INTERMEDIATE SKIERS
Limited cruising
Les Deux-Alpes can disappoint
intermediates. A lot of the skiing is
either fairly tough or boringly bland.
The steep runs just above the resort
put off many. As one of our reporters
(who classes himself as an 'advanced'
skier) said, 'I myself fell from top to
bottom. I was lucky. A girl in the
"Tour of the Pistes" broke her back.
You cannot afford to be complacent
getting back.' There is a green zig-zag
trail home but this is narrow in places,
often crowded and can be icy.

The runs higher up generally have
good snow, and aggressive
intermediates can enjoy great, fast
cruising, especially on the mainly
north-facing pistes served by the
chair-lifts off to the sides. You can
often pick gentle or steeper terrain in
these bowls as you wish, but avid
piste-bashers will ski all there is to
offer in a couple of days. Most of our
keen skier reporters made use of their
lift passes to take excursions to Alpe-
d'Huez and Serre-Chevalier.

Less confident intermediates will
love the quality of the snow and the
gentleness of most of the runs. Their
problem might lie in finding the pistes
too crowded, especially if snow is poor
in other resorts and people are bussed
in. At the end of the day, the worst of
the crowds and the steep lower slopes
can be avoided by taking the Jandri
Express down from the mid-station.

FOR BEGINNERS
Good slopes, shame about crowds
Les Deux-Alpes has great potential for
beginners. The nursery slopes beside
the village are spacious and gentle.
The glacier has a fine array of very

easy slopes. Unfortunately the weather
can be hostile, not just on the glacier,
but over a ravine high above which
the glacier access lifts have to travel.
Consequently glacier skiing is far from
assured. The run below chair 37 (Séa)
is the only other piste at altitude
suitable for beginners, but it does get
very crowded.

FOR CROSS-COUNTRY
Need very low altitude snow
There are three small, widely dispersed
areas. Le Petite Alpe, near the entrance
to the village, has a couple of
snowsure, if insignificant, trails but,
given good snow, Venosc (950m),
reached by a gondola down, has the
only worthwhile picturesque ones.
Total trail distance is 20km.

QUEUES
Can be a problem
Les Deux-Alpes has a great deal of
hardware to keep queues minimal,
since the village is large in relation to
its ski area. But, especially in mid- and
late-season, peak morning queues can
be long for the Jandri Express and
Diable gondolas. The Jandri queue
moves quickly and, if you are headed
for the top, it is worth joining to avoid
further queues for the second stage.

Problems can also occur when skiers
are bussed in from neighbouring
resorts when snow is in short supply.
At such times the lower slopes at Les
Deux-Alpes are likely to be out of
action too, causing even longer queues
for the Jandri Express. The top lifts are
prone to closure if it's windy, putting
pressure on the lower lifts.

MOUNTAIN RESTAURANTS
Dreary
Mountain restaurants are scarce (there
are only six) and generally pretty poor.
La Pastorale, at the top of the Diable
gondola, is the best, but it can have
huge queues for the loo. The
Panoramic at 2600m is fairly friendly
and worth a try. Reasonable
intermediates and above might
consider skiing back to the village for
lunch. Le Bimbo is well placed for the
slopes, next to the ice rink.

SKI SCHOOL
One of the better ESFs
There are two ski schools, both of
which have good reputations for
standards of tuition and English,
although class sizes can be large.
Guiding services for excursions to La
Grave are reportedly good. The School
of Adventure section will take you to
nearby resorts on the lift pass.

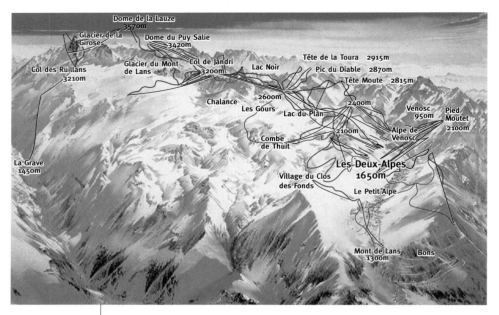

GETTING THERE

Air Lyon, transfer 3½hr. Grenoble, transfer 2hr. Chambery, transfer 3hr. Geneva, transfer 4½hr.

Rail Grenoble (70km); 4 daily buses from station.

PACKAGES

AA Ski-Driveaway, Airtours, Alpine Options Skidrive, Bladon Lines, Chalet Freestyle, Chalet Snowboard, Chalets 'Unlimited', Crystal, Equity Total Ski, First Choice Ski, French Impressions, Inghams, Lagrange, Le Shuttle Holidays, Made to Measure, Motours, PGL Ski Europe, Ski Partners, Ski Valkyrie, Ski White Knights, SkiBound, Skiworld, Thomson, Travelscene Ski-Drive, UCPA

FACILITIES FOR CHILDREN
Fine for babies

Babies can safely be entrusted to the village crèche, and there are chalet-based alternatives. Bladon Lines can provide nannies on varies – free for whole chalet bookings on certain dates – and Crystal have a crèche in one of their properties. But there are many better places for older children, whether skiers or not.

↟ Staying there

Alpe de Venosc, at the southern end of town, has many of the nightspots and hotels, the most character, the fewest cars and the best shops. It also has immediate access via the Diable gondola to the tough skiing around Tête Moute, but getting elsewhere is a roundabout business compared with going up the Jandri Express.

The geographical centre has a popular outdoor ice rink, some good restaurants and bars, and a variety of ways up the mountain, including the Jandri Express. The village straggles north from here, becoming less convenient the further you go. 'Le Village' consists of a cluster of apartments, a sports centre, a chair-lift and little else, and is an inconvenient distance from the rest of town.

There's no doubt that staying near to the Jandri Express or the Diable gondola is the best place to be, especially for early risers, who can then avoid any queues. There's a regular free bus service around town.

HOW TO GO
Wide range of packages

Les Deux-Alpes has something for most tastes, including that rarity in high-altitude French resorts, good inexpensive hotels.

Chalets There are a number of 'catered chalet' packages available, but some use cramped apartments rather than real chalets. If you don't mind this, consider Ski White Knights, personally run with great enthusiasm by proprietor Robin Dann. Thomson have some good-looking real chalets on the northern edge of town, a bus-ride from the lifts. Skiworld have some simpler places. Bladon Lines has more comfortable but expensive chalets. Tessa is the best-situated. Crystal also have a large selection, including the

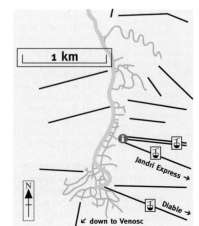

ACTIVITIES

Indoor 2 sports centres; Club Forme (squash, swimming pool, sauna, jacuzzi), Tanking Centre (floatation chambers, physiotherapy, pressotherapy, sauna, jacuzzi, turkish baths **Outdoor** Ice-skating, swimming pool, climbing wall, snow-shoe excursions

TOURIST OFFICE

Postcode 38860
Tel 00 33 76792200
Fax 76790138

comfortable, well positioned Chantal.

Hotels There are over 30 hotels, of which the majority are 2-star or below.
£££ Bérangère Smartest in town, although dreary to look at, with Michelin-starred restaurant and pool; on-piste, but at the less convenient north end of resort.
£££ Farandole Better placed for nightlife and shopping, and within comfortable walking distance of the Diable bubble and east-facing slopes.
££ Chalet Mounier Attractive modern building. Good reputation for its food, and well placed for the Diable bubble and nightlife.
££ Souleil'Or Looks like a lift station, but appearances are deceptive. Pleasant and comfortable, and well placed for the Jandri Express gondola.
££ Edelweiss Good value, and popular with British clients.
££ Brunerie Cheap and cheerful large 2-star with plenty of parking for ski drivers, and quite well positioned.
Self-catering Many of the apartments are stuck out at Le Village, at the north end of the resort, so it is well worth shopping around for more centrally situated ones.

STAYING DOWN THE VALLEY

If we were planning to spend a week skiing Les Deux-Alpes, it would be with the intention of staying in the lively resort. But staying down the valley has great attractions for anyone thinking of travelling around to Alpe-d'Huez, La Grave and Serre-Chevalier – cutting travelling time as well as costs.

Close to the foot of the final ascent to Les Deux-Alpes are two near-ideal places, both Logis de France. At Le Freney, on the N91 Grenoble-Briançon road, is the cheerful 13-room Cassini. Nearby, at Mizoën, just north of the N91, is the even more appealing 10-room Panoramique, with excellent food and friendly owners as well as the advertised views.

EATING OUT
Plenty of choice

The village restaurants are much better than those up the mountain. The Bérangère has a Michelin star and

Chalet Mounier has the reputation for some of the best food in town. Le Petit Marmite has good food and atmosphere at reasonable prices. Booking is essential. Bimbo is excellent. Brugi, Palate and Crêpes à Gogo are all worth a visit. Smokey Joe's does some good Mexican food. Visitors on a budget can get a relatively cheap Italian meal at either Vetrata or the Spaghetteria.

APRES-SKI
Unsophisticated fun

Les Deux-Alpes is one of the liveliest of French ski resorts, with plenty of bars to choose from. The Rodeo has a mechanical bucking bronco which attracts great numbers of rowdy après-skiers, many of them Brits. Mike's (which tour operators use a lot for quiz nights) and the Windsor are other noisy British enclaves. Smokey Joe's is recommended for its FF10 dice throwing – what you throw determines what drink you get! Bar Brazillienne is recommended for 'great music and tremendous atmosphere'.

There are plenty of quieter places around too. Most of the discos are expensive and take an age to warm up. La Casa, at the northern edge of town, is our favourite: it gets going at a reasonable hour and isn't too expensive – except coat checking, which is compulsory and pricey.

FOR NON-SKIERS
Not recommended

Les Deux-Alpes is not a particularly good choice for inactive non-skiers. It is quiet during the day, the shopping is uninspiring and the village is rather cut off, with little public transport for excursions. The pretty village of Venosc is well worth a visit, and you might be tempted to take the helicopter flight with skiing friends to Alpe-d'Huez for the day. For the active there are plenty of sports facilities.

Given the standard of mountain restaurants, competent skiers ought to be quite happy to return to the resort to meet non-skiers for lunch, but in practice this will depend on how icy the lower slopes are.

Flaine 1600m

HOW IT RATES

The skiing
Snow	****
Extent	****
Advanced	****
Intermediates	*****
Beginners	*****
Convenience	*****
Queues	****
Restaurants	**

The rest
Scenery	****
Resort charm	*
Not skiing	*

✔ Big, varied ski area, with off-piste challenges for experts as well as extensive intermediate terrain

✔ Reliable snow in the main bowl

✔ Compact, convenient village – skiing from the door if you're lucky

✔ Excellent facilities for children, and a car-free central area

✔ Generally scenic setting, and glorious views from top station

✔ Short transfer from Geneva airport

✘ Dreary architecture

✘ Very little nightlife

✘ Not a place for non-skiers

So long as you don't care about the uncompromising architecture or lack of lively evening ambience, Flaine has a lot going for it. Many keen skiers, especially those with children, love it.

There is some very pleasant and convenient accommodation. For families it theoretically wears the crown – if you want to spend a holiday with your kids, there is everything to help you. Whether families will be so happy in practice may depend on how well the ski schools perform – and the signs this year are that last year's problems have been resolved.

Flaine has slopes that intermediates will love, and lots of them. With its links to Samoëns, Morillon and Les Carroz, the Grand Massif is one of the big ski areas of France. Flaine caters well for beginners too, with free access to nursery slope lifts. But there is also challenging skiing for advanced skiers – particularly for those prepared to take guidance and go off-piste. We went there last season on an advanced skiing course, and came back impressed.

ORIENTATION

Flaine is set at the foot of a bleak, largely treeless bowl and reached by a long winding road up from Cluses in the valley below. It is only 70km from Geneva and has a very short airport transfer (around 90 mins). Flaine Forum is the main centre, with all the hotels and the two main gondolas into the skiing. Flaine Forêt lies above Forum and can be reached via a pair of funicular lifts. It has chair- and drag-lift access to the skiing, or you can ski down to Forum. The new development of Hameau-de-Flaine is a good 15-minute walk or short bus-ride from the skiing.

Flaine shares the Grand Massif ski area with the lower resorts of **Les Carroz, Samoëns 1600** and **Morillon**. Expeditions to **Chamonix** and neighbouring resorts are possible.

 ## The resort

In our unofficial vote for Ugliest Resort in the Alps, Flaine was narrowly beaten by Les Menuires. Like 'Les Manures', it has a nickname based on how horrid it looks: 'Phlegm'. The concrete massifs that are its buildings were conceived in the sixties as 'an example of the application of the principle of shadow and light'. Hmm. They look particularly shocking the first time you see them from the approach road way above – a mass of blocks nestling at the bottom of a beautiful snowy bowl. The one good thing about them is that from the ski slopes you can hardly see them – they do blend into the grey rocks.

In recent times, in common with other French Alpine carbuncles, efforts have been made to improve Flaine's looks. The new development of Hameau-de-Flaine is built in a much more attractive chalet style – but is inconveniently situated a good 15-minute walk or a short bus-ride from the slopes. On a smaller scale, the interiors of much of the accommodation are now looking pretty classy.

Whatever the aesthetic problems of Flaine, when it comes to having an easy holiday, the planners made no mistakes with the layout. There is supermarket and speciality food shopping close to all the Forum and Forêt accommodation; ski hire shops are a short hop away; the lifts are easy to get to, and trips to organise ski passes, school and so on are no problem.

There are two main parts to the main resort. All the hotels, and some apartments, are set down in Forum. The focus of this area is a three-sided snow-covered square, with the fourth side being the piste back from the slopes. Watch out for skiers when you're strolling from the hotels on one side to the bars and shops on the other. Flaine Forêt has its own bars and shops and most of the apartment accommodation. Neither centre is very lively at night.

There are children all over the place; they are catered for with play areas, and the resort is supposed to be traffic-free. This has become pretty lax, in fact, and there is an uncomfortable amount of traffic around; but the central Forum itself, leading to the pistes, is pretty safe.

SKI FACTS

Altitude 700m-2480m
Lifts   80
Pistes   260km
Green/Blue   39%
Red   46%
Black   15%
Artificial snow   5km

LIFT PASSES

95/96 prices in francs
Grand Massif
Covers all the lifts in
Flaine, Les Carroz,
Morillon, Samoëns
and Sixt.
Beginners Four free
lifts. Ski pass for
beginners covers 3
more lifts (80 per day
for adults, 65 for
children).
Main pass
1-day pass 175
6-day pass 820
Senior citizens
Over 60: 6-day pass
580 (29% off)
Children
Under 16: 6-day pass
580 (29% off)
Under 5: free pass
Alternative passes
Flaine area only
(1 day pass 160 for
adults, 120 for
children).

 # The skiing

THE SKI AREA
A big white playground

With its 260km of pistes, the Grand
Massif claims to be the third largest ski
area in France (behind the Trois
Vallées and Espace Killy – the Franco
Swiss Portes du Soleil doesn't count).
Whatever the truth, Flaine provides a
comfortably spacious playground.

The day begins for most skiers at the
Grandes Platières high-capacity
stand-up gondola, which speeds you
in a single long stage up the north face
of the Flaine bowl to the 2480m high-
point of the Grand Massif, and a
magnificent view of Mont Blanc.

Most of the runs are reds (though
there are some blues), curling away to
the right as you look down the
mountain and offering alternative
tracks down the barren, treeless,
rolling terrain back to Flaine or to
chairs in the middle of the wilderness
going back to the summit.

On the far right, a broad cat-walk
leads to the experts-only **Gers** bowl.
Until last season this arm of the ski
area was a dead-end, but now a long,
winding blue piste has been created to
the outskirts of Sixt (770m), which has
its own little west-facing ski area
offering red and black slopes of 700m
vertical. The creation of this piste, a
massive undertaking in itself, is to be
followed by the construction of a lift
back into the Flaine skiing.

Back at Grandes Platières, the
alternative is to head left down the
long red Méphisto (all the reds in this
area have diabolic names – Lucifer,
Belzebuth etc) to the **Aujon** area. This
opens up another sector of the bowl,
again mostly red runs but with some
blues further down. The lower slopes
here are used as slalom courses. This
sector is also reachable by gondola or
drag-lifts from below the resort.

The pistes in the Flaine bowl are
mostly punchy medium-length runs.
For a collection of longer cruises, head
out of the bowl via the Grands Vans
chair, reached from Forum by means
of a slow bucket lift (aka télébenne or
'yogurt pots'). From the top, you go
over the edge of the bowl and have a
choice of three different resorts to
head towards, each with its own lifts
and skiing. The lie of the land
hereabouts is complicated, and the
piste map does not represent it clearly.

In good snow there is a choice of
blues and reds winding down to **Les
Carroz** (1140m) or **Morillon**

(700m), the latter with a half-way
point at 1100m – Morillon Grand
Massif. There are only mogully blacks
and reds down towards **Samoëns
1600** and on down to Vercland, a
couple of miles from Samoëns itself.

Getting back to the crucial Grands
Vans drag-lift for the return to Flaine
can be complicated, so don't leave it
too late. Many reporters complain
about this bent drag-lift, and rightly;
in a premier league ski area, a key end-
of-day connection like this should not
depend on a tricky button-lift.

Arrival back in Flaine can cause a
problem: some reporters have
complained that it's difficult to ski
between the top of the resort and
Forum. The trick is to loop round
away from the buildings and approach
from under the gondola.

SNOW RELIABILITY
Usually keeps its whiteness

The main part of Flaine's skiing lies on
the wide north- and north-west-facing
flank of the Grandes Platières. Its
direction, along with a decent height,
means that it keeps the snow it
receives. And in recent seasons this
area of the Alps has enjoyed good
snowfalls. The runs towards Samoëns
1600 and Morillon are north-facing
too, but the lower parts are frequently
unpleasant or unskiable. The Les
Carroz runs are west-facing and can
suffer from strong afternoon sun, but
one of the runs has snowmaking. So
do the slopes close to Samoëns 1600
and Morillon Grand Massif, and most
of the Aujon sector, back at Flaine.

FOR ADVANCED SKIERS
Great fun with guidance

Flaine's family-friendly reputation
tends to obscure the fact that it has
some seriously testing skiing. But
much of it is off-piste. And although
some of Flaine's off-piste skiing looks
like it can safely be explored without
guidance, this impression is mistaken.
The Flaine bowl is riddled with rock
crevasses and pot-holes, and should be
treated with the same caution that
you would use on a glacier. There have
been some tragic cases of off-piste
skiers coming across nasty surprises,
including a British skier falling to his
death only yards from the piste.

All the black pistes on the map
deserve their grading. The Diamant
Noir, down the line of the main
gondola, is a testing 850m descent,
tricky because of moguls, narrowness
and other skiers rather than because of
great steepness; the first pitch down
from the summit plateau is one of the

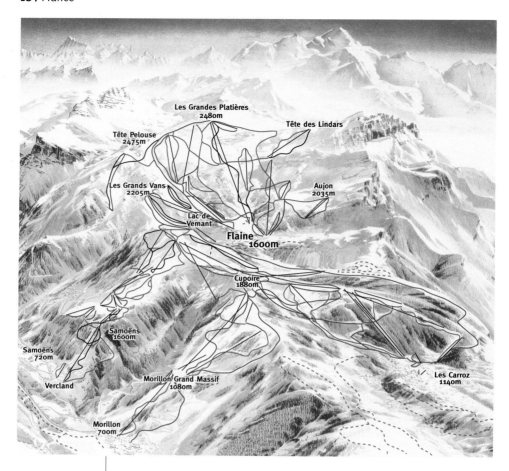

most unnerving, with spectators applauding on the overhead chair-lift.

To the left of the Diamant Noir as you look down are several short but steep off-piste routes through the crags of the Grandes Platières.

The Lindars Nord chair serves a shorter slope that often has the best snow in the area, and some seriously steep gradients if you look for them.

The Gers drag-lift, outside the main bowl beyond Tête Pelouse, serves great expert-only terrain. The piste going down the right of the drag is a proper black, but by departing from it you can find slopes of up to 45°. To the left of the drag is the impressive main Gers bowl – a great horseshoe of about 550m vertical, powder or moguls top to bottom, all off-piste. You can choose your gradient, from steep to very steep. As you look down the bowl, you can see more adventurous ways into the bowl from the Grands Vans and Tête de Veret lifts.

There is further serious piste skiing on the top lifts above Samoëns 1600.

Ski touring is a possibility in the Desert de Platé area, behind the Grandes Platières, and there are some scenic off-piste routes from which you can be retrieved by helicopter – notably the Combe des Foges, next to Gers. Make sure the pilot gives you the exciting ride home, not the tame one.

FOR INTERMEDIATES
Something for everyone

Flaine is ideal for all levels of intermediate, with a great variety of piste (and usually the bonus of good snow conditions, at least above Flaine itself). The diabolically named reds of the Flaine bowl are not really as hellish as their names imply – they

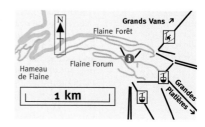

SKI SCHOOL

95/96 prices in francs

ESF

Classes 6 days
4hr: 10am-noon and
2.30-4.30
6 full days: 690
Children's classes
Ages: 3 to 12
6 full days: 580
Private lessons
1hr, 2hr or 6hr
185 for 1hr, for 1 to 2
people

International
Classes 6 days
4hr: 9.30-11.30 and
2.30-4.30
6 full days: 655
Children's classes
Ages: 4 to 12
6 full days: 525
Private lessons
1hr, 2hr or full day
170 for 1hr

Flaine Super Ski
Advanced skiers only

Independent
instructors
Hired by the day,
hour or week; contact
Guy Pezet 50937978

CHILDCARE

Both schools operate
ski kindergartens. The
ESF's Rabbit Club
(50908100) takes
children aged 3 to 12,
until 5pm. The SEI's
Club de la Souris
Verte (50908441)
takes children aged 4
to 12, until 5pm. The
hotel Les Lindars
(50908166) has a
nursery for babies
aged 3 months to 2
years, and a snow
garden for children up
to 7. Both schools
will pick up children
from Les Lindars for
lessons, and deliver
them at the end of
the class. There is
also an independent
nursery, the Petits
Loups (50908782).

tend to gain their status from steep
sections rather than overall difficulty,
and they're great for improving
technique. There are gentler cruises
from the top of the mountain –
Cristal, taking you to the Perdrix chair
which goes back up to the top, or
Serpentine, all the way home.

All intermediates will enjoy the
long, tree-lined runs down to Les
Carroz, as long as the snow is good.
You can choose between red routes or
slightly easier blues, one of which
constantly underpasses and flies over
the road out of Flaine, allowing races
between skiers and coach drivers!

A trip to Morillon Grand Massif will
yield some pleasure for those who
want to clock up the kilometres; the
journey to Samoëns 1600 is suited
more to the better intermediate who
likes the odd dose of moguls.

FOR BEGINNERS
Very good
There are excellent nursery slopes
right by the village, served by free lifts
which make a pass unnecessary until
you can go higher up the mountain.
There are no very long green runs to
progress to, but some gentle blues (see
For intermediates).

CROSS-COUNTRY
Very fragmented
The Grand Massif as a whole claims
64km of cross-country tracks but little
of it is around Flaine itself. Two 3km
loops lie just below the resort and a
600m practice loop is found off the
road to Les Carroz, near the Chalet de
Molliets mountain restaurant. There
are extensive tracks over the mountain
between Morillon and Les Carroz with
some tough uphill sections. And
Samoëns 1600 has its own tracks.

But the majority of the cross-
country is on the valley floor –
dependent on low snow. In a good
winter, Samoëns would make the best
base for cross-country enthusiasts.

QUEUES
Few real problems
There are three obvious crush points
when the resort is full. The main
apparent one is the Grandes Platières
gondola at the start of the day, but it
is an efficient lift and the queue moves
quickly. It's just that, as one reporter
complains, it feels like the Northern
Line at rush hour.

The other bottlenecks – again only
at holiday times – are the chair over to
Samoëns and the twin drags back.

MOUNTAIN RESTAURANTS
Not a lot
In the Flaine bowl, there are hardly
any restaurants above the upper
outskirts of the resort. The Desert
Blanc, at the top station, is a run-of-
the-mill, two-room self-service
snackery, with a terrace overlooking
Mont Blanc. The Blanchot, at the
bottom of the Serpentine, run is
popular and rustic but has basic food.

At Forum level, just across the piste
from the main gondola, is a pair of
chalets containing the welcoming and
comfortable Michet, with very good
Savoyard food and table service, and
the self-service Eloge – friendly but
with very limited food. In a similar
position up the mountain, at Forêt
level, Chalet Bissac has a good
atmosphere, traditional decor, a huge
warming fire, self service and excellent
plain food. The nearby Cascade is self
service, modern and stylish, with a
good terrace and amazing hi-tech loos,
but the food can be disappointing.

Outside the bowl, the Oasis, above
Morillon, and the Chalet des Molliets
beside the road up from Les Carroz,
are recommended.

SKI SCHOOLS
On the up?
Last year we had critical reports of the
International school, particularly
concerning language and class size.
This year, the only criticism we have
had concerned 'follow me' tuition,
and most reporters have been happy
both with the International and ESF
schools. There are several small
specialist schools, of which Flaine
Super Ski is one. And there is a group
of independent instructors, whose
services can be booked directly or
through the British operators Fresh
Tracks and Over the Hill. We can
testify to the excellence of at least one
of the group – Guy Pezet, who acts
informally as the leader.

FACILITIES FOR CHILDREN
Parents' paradise? Possibly
Flaine prides itself on being a family
resort. Last year we had some
disturbing reports from parents,
particularly concerning the
International school's childcare.
Happily, this year there are no
reservations. One party of five
children aged 4 to 9, for example,
were all 'well looked after and taught',
and will be going back next year.

The place to stay if you have
children is hotel Les Lindars, designed
specifically as a parents' hotel, with
nursery, all-day crèche (open to non-

GETTING THERE

Air Geneva, transfer 1½hr.

Rail Cluses (30km); regular bus service (Mont Blanc Bus).

PACKAGES

AA Ski-Driveaway, Airtours, Bladon Lines, Chalets 'Unlimited', Crystal, First Choice Ski, French Impressions, Fresh Tracks, Inghams, Kings Ski Club, Lagrange, Le Shuttle Holidays, Made to Measure, Motours, Neilson, Over the Hill, Ski Choice, Ski Club of GB, Ski Safe Travel, Stena Sealink, Thomson, Travelscene Ski-Drive

Les Carroz AA Ski-Driveaway, Lagrange, Le Shuttle Holidays, Winterski

Morillon Lagrange, Mogul Ski, Rank STS, Winterski

Samoëns Lagrange, Mogul Ski

TOURIST OFFICE

Postcode 74300
Tel 00 33 50908001
Fax 50908626

UK Representative

Erna Low Consultants
9 Reece Mews
London SW7 3HE
Tel 0171 584 2841
Fax 0171 589 9531

residents, but residents have priority), ski school pick-up and drop-off service, a children's dining-room, in-house babysitters in the evening, even an automatic nappy-dispenser! Some other accommodation units, including the Forêt, have children's clubs.

 # Staying there

As a purpose-built resort, Flaine does not spark off much discussion of location – everywhere is convenient, except Hameau-de-Flaine. That is a good 15 minutes' walk or quick bus-ride away from the skiing.

HOW TO GO
Plenty of apartments
Accommodation is overwhelmingly in self-catering apartments. These are mostly based on the Forêt level and linked by lift to Forum, where more shops are located.
Chalets There are few catered chalet options. Crystal have a couple of attractively traditional Scandinavian-style huts in Hameau, offering a good degree of comfort. Airtours have some unusual, simple accommodation packaged chalet-style with half-board and wine: an allocation of rooms in the Cascade restaurant, on the slopes just outside the village. The lounge has satellite TV.
Hotels There are just four hotels, (assuming the renovation of the Flaine is completed for this season – it was closed last winter), all around Forum.
£££ Totem The smartest hotel, with prices to match. Modern, quite stylish, great views of Aujon skiing, excellent food; but the rooms are unremarkable (some are apparently worse), and some of the staff unhelpful.
££ Les Lindars Great hassle-free holidays for families: free children's facilities, modern, smart and pleasant public rooms, functional bedrooms.
££ Flaine Renovated for this season?
£ Aujon Large and rather impersonal, but good value, and liked by most visitors. Rooms are comfortable, buffet breakfasts 'excellent', dinners acceptable (with the bonus of free house wine). Pleasant modern bar.
Self-catering Flaine seems to have realised that people choose this option on price grounds, not because they like cooking and cleaning. So they offer convenient facilities to help, such as a pizza and morning bread and croissant delivery.
Most favoured by the many Brits visiting Flaine is Forêt. Apartments are attractive, as French self-catering

blocks go – the predominance of wood is a welcome relief from the concrete outside. This is one of the most recently renovated in Flaine's ongoing face-lift. It also boasts hotel facilities such as a restaurant, bar and kindergarten. A similar set-up which is almost as popular is the Grand Massif. Both are right next door to the Forêt shopping centre. Residence L'Arche is said to be 'luxurious'.
Along with the many apartments at Forêt, Flaine-Front-de-Neige has some accommodation, down through the trees from Forum, at the resort's edge.
Out at Hameau, various tour operators have allocations in high-standard, spacious apartments. These are more comfortable than anything in the main village.

EATING OUT
Mostly fast food
Most people eat in their apartments or hotels (Totem and Lindars take outside bookings), but there are alternatives, and hotel residents are encouraged to use them – vouchers are available as part payment for your meal out. The bulk of the eateries are downmarket pizzerias and burger bars. For a more refined meal, the Perdrix Noire in Forêt is a good bet – smart, busy and friendly. The Michet (see Mountain restaurants) is open in the evening. In the mid-range, Trattoria is a good Italian, Chez la Jeanne is the best pizza restaurant. Chez Daniel offers crêpes and Savoyard specialities such as *pierrade* in a surprisingly woody environment.

APRES-SKI
Hello! Anybody there?
You see a few parents snatching a quick demi in the bar, then it's back to the child-minding. After dinner there's little happening.
Earlier, the dreary White Grouse pub is boisterous: extreme ski videos compete with rock music and British punters trying to get pints in before the end of happy hour.
Later, the more French Cîmes Rock is the only really lively joint, with live bands on towards midnight. Flaine's two nightclubs, the expensive Shelby and the 'seedy' Diamant Noir (with several pool tables) are not worth losing sleep over.

FOR NON-SKIERS
Curse of the purpose-built
As with most purpose-built resorts, there is little to recommend Flaine to non-skiers. There are few walks, and no town to explore.

ACTIVITIES

Indoor Top Form centre (swimming pool complex with sauna, solarium, gymnasium, massage), arts and crafts gallery, cinema, auditorium, indoor climbing wall
Outdoor Ice-rink, snow-shoe excursions, hang-gliding, para-gliding para-skiing, helicopter rides, snowmobiles, snow scooters, high mountain outings, ice-driving car circuit, all-terrain carts and motorbikes (in spring)

Les Carroz 1140m

This is a spacious, sunny, traditional, family resort where life revolves around the village square with its pavement cafés and array of interesting little shops. It's popular in summer as well as winter, and has a 'lived-in' feel, with much more animation than Flaine.

The gondola and chair-lift take you straight into the Grand Massif ski area – but there's a steep 300m walk from the village centre.

Apartments make up a high percentage of the beds available, but there are plenty of hotels. The main hotel, the 3-star Serrages, is opposite the lift station. The 1-star Airelles is in a good spot, half-way between the centre and the lifts. The Croix de Savoie (2-star) and Sapins (1-star) are in quiet, secluded areas on the outskirts of the village. The Belles Pistes hotel is bang in the centre. It's British-owned and popular for its good French cuisine.

The village centre has a pleasant atmosphere after skiing, and the ski school's torchlit descent is something of a highlight – it's preceded by fireworks and concludes with *vin chaud* and live jazz in the square. The Marlow and Squatt bars have regular live music, the latter becoming a disco after 11pm. The other two discos only liven up at weekends.

Other resort amenities include tobogganing, snowmobiles, floodlit skiing, ice skating, a cinema (weekly films in English), a health club, a kindergarten, banks and parapenting. There's also horse-riding if the valley is free of snow.

The kindergarten has a good reputation, though we suspect that lack of English-speaking supervision and companions could be a problem.

Les Carroz is probably best for self-drivers who want to stay in a genuine village while having the snow reliability of Flaine a short drive away.

Samoëns 720m

This is probably the most beautiful ski resort in France. It's certainly the only one to be listed as a 'Monument Historique'. Medieval fountains, rustic old buildings, an ancient church – it's all there. In the centre of the village is an impressive 8.5 acre botanical garden with thousands of plants from around the world. The traditional-style bars and restaurants give you a feel for 'real' rural France.

The ski slopes are a bus-ride away, but most people here have cars. The local skiing is generally testing, except around the mid-station of Samoëns 1600, and only confident skiers should consider basing themselves here.

We've had very positive reports of the hotels Sept Monts (3-star) and Drugères (2-star). Other possibles are the Neige et Roc and Glaciers (both 3-star) and Gai Soleil (2-star). There are numerous good restaurantss – the 19th-century Tornatta is certainly worth trying.

The centre for four o'clock cocktails is the Cheminee, while later the Café is the main rendezvous. The Louisiana disco livens up at weekends.

Samoëns has its own ski school, ski kindergarten and nursery (taking children from 6 months). But English-speaking care and tuition is unlikely in this French resort.

La Grave 1450m

La Grave is the Alps' best-kept secret. Its skiing is almost exclusively tough, off-piste stuff in spectacular scenery, with a vertical drop of 2100m. Good skiers who love off-piste, are willing to hire a guide and don't need 4-star comfort should give it serious consideration. It ranks with Val-d'Isère, St Anton and Chamonix for off-piste skiing, but comes at a fraction of the price, and includes the rustic charm of a village dating back to the 12th century.

HOW IT RATES

The skiing

Snow	***
Extent	**
Advanced	*****
Intermediates	*
Beginners	*
Convenience	***
Queues	****
Restaurants	**

The rest

Scenery	****
Resort charm	***
Not skiing	*

PACKAGES

Fresh Tracks, Neilson, Ski Club of GB, Ski Valkyrie, Ski Weekend

SKI FACTS

Altitude 1450m-3550m
Lifts   4
Pistes   5km
Green/Blue   100%
(This figure relates to pistes; practically all the skiing is off-piste)
Artificial snow   none

TOURIST OFFICE

Postcode 05320
Tel 00 33 76799005
Fax 76799165

THE RESORT

La Grave is a remarkably unspoilt old mountaineering village set on a steep hillside against impressive glacial scenery that is dominated by the majestic 4000m Meije, the last major European peak to be conquered by mountaineers. The drab local stone and busy main road which separates the village from the ski area reduce the charm somewhat, but it still has a genuinely rustic feel. Prices are more in line with rural France than with the exorbitant levels normally charged in ski resorts, but there isn't much there – a handful of small hotels, sports shops, food shops and bars. The single lift is conveniently close, but a car is useful in case poor weather closes the skiing. Les Deux-Alpes, Serre-Chevalier and Alpe-d'Huez are all around 30 minutes' drive away; Les Deux-Alpes can also be reached on skis over the top of the mountain.

THE SKIING

A three-stage gondola ascends into the **ski area** and finishes at 3200m. A few drag-lifts above here take you up to 3550m and serve the flat glacier terrain and the link over to Les Deux-Alpes. But the reason that people come here is to ski the legendary off-piste slopes back down towards La Grave. There are no marked or patrolled pistes back down at all. Various itineraries are marked on the map (the Itineraires des Vallons de la Meije and Itineraires de Chancel), but none should be attempted without a guide because of the danger from crevasses and cliffs, quite apart from the risk of losing your way or being caught by an avalanche.

Obviously this resort is best visited when **snow** is known to be good. Incomplete cover not only reduces the size of the ski area – if there's no snow above the village, you can only ski down to one of the gondola mid-stations – it also means less-than-satisfactory powder.

Advanced skiers are the only people who should contemplate a stay in La Grave. The variations in the routes you can take down are enormous: some end up in neighbouring villages or on roadsides where you can be picked up by taxi or bus; others take you right back to the village. Wherever you go, you need a guide.

Intermediates and **beginners** should go elsewhere. Don't be tempted to stay in La Grave with the intention of skiing Les Deux-Alpes most of the time – the link is often shut by poor weather.

La Grave has a couple of **cross-country** loops (total 12km); the longer one goes to the neighbouring hamlet of Les Freaux. A further 18km are available near Villar d'Arene.

There are short **queues** only at weekends – at the bottom station first thing in the morning and at the mid-station later.

The **mountain restaurants** at mid-station and Chancel are quite good. At the top station there's a basic old climbers' hut with a terrace. The **guiding** service is good, and inexpensive by French standards.

Children's baby-sitting can be arranged through the tourist office.

STAYING THERE

There are no luxurious **hotels**. The Edelweiss is a comfortable, friendly, family-run 2-star with good home cooking. The Castillian is another 2-star, 100m from the lift. The Chaumine Skiers Lodge (Freephone: 0800 893601) is run by a small British company. It provides guides and has mini-buses for trips to other resorts.

Self-catering studios are bookable through the tourist office.

Most people **eat** in their hotels. The Lou Ratel bar-restaurant does raclettes, while the Candy snack bar serves hamburgers and crèpes. The Candy has music too, but most people are too tired from hard skiing to venture out for any **après-ski**.

Non-skiers will probably find La Grave much too small and quiet. The interesting towns of Briançon (35km) and Grenoble (75km) are within reach if you have a car.

Isola 2000

HOW IT RATES

The skiing

Snow	***
Extent	**
Advanced	**
Intermediates	***
Beginners	*****
Convenience	*****
Queues	***
Restaurants	**

The rest

Scenery	***
Resort charm	*
Not skiing	*

SKI FACTS

Altitude	1840m-2610m
Lifts	24
Pistes	120km
Green/Blue	54%
Red	35%
Black	11%
Artificial snow	none

PACKAGES

Made to Measure,
Neilson, Travelscene
Ski-Drive

TOURIST OFFICE

Postcode 06420
Tel 00 33 93231515
Fax 93231425

A scheduled flight and a short (90km) transfer from Nice, with some decent from-the-door skiing, Isola is high on convenience as well as altitude. Like many purpose-built French resorts, it has been extended in a sympathetic, traditional style. But its original buildings are irredeemably block-like.

THE RESORT

Isola is one of the many small, high, purpose-built resorts in the French Alps, but differs from the rest in its extreme southern location, with access via Nice. One reporter says, 'On very clear days you can see the sea.'

Built by a British property company in the late 1960s, Isola aimed itself squarely at the family market. Front de Neige is a complex of apartments, shops, bars, restaurants and a couple of hotels that makes up the core of the resort, with nursery slopes and lifts on the doorstep.

Various owners have since worked hard to glamourise the image of the resort with new hamlets of more luxurious, wood-clad apartment blocks. But the main complex has become tatty at the same time, with shops closing down.

THE SKIING

According to the piste map, there are three **ski areas**, St Sauveur, Pélevos and Levant. Really it is one linked area in a horseshoe shape around the resort. Due to the great base height of Isola – the lowest skiable point is at 1840m – most of the skiing is above the tree-line. The main access point is the gondola from the centre of the complex to Pélevos at 2320m, and from there all three areas can be accessed more or less directly.

Isola can get different weather from other major French resorts. Sometimes it has masses of **snow** when the rest of the French Alps have none; at other times it misses out. Reporters who visit year after year say that although they never find all the lifts open, there is always snow – and plenty of strong southern sun. The north-facing slopes of St Sauveur and Pélevos tend to keep their snow well.

Advanced skiers head for St Sauveur, which has Isola's longest and most challenging runs, as well as its best off-piste skiing. There are good blacks here – and from the chair to Mont Mené. The Pélevos area is an interesting cluster of red and blue runs where **intermediate** skiers can take their pick of difficulty. The more adventurous can try the challenging St Sauveur sector, where there is a choice

of steep reds and blacks. The south-facing slopes below the Col de la Lombarde, in the Levant sector, are also intermediate.

There are excellent nursery slopes for **beginners** right in the heart of the resort, and an easy progression to greens, then blues, nearby.

There is a 4km loop just above the village, but little else to recommend Isola to **cross-country** enthusiasts.

Because it is the only central main lift, the gondola is prone to **queues** at peak times. And weekends see the arrival of day-trippers from Nice, causing further bottlenecks.

There is only a handful of **mountain restaurants.** The best is the excellent Génisserie at the foot of St Sauveur's skiing.

The ESF **ski school** has a good reputation for its English and its teaching – both in the traditional way and ski évolutif – but, as ever, class size is a gripe among reporters.

Isola has an all-day crèche, and a snow garden for **children** starting out on skis. English is widely spoken.

STAYING THERE

Accommodation is largely in **self-catering** apartments; the newer, better-appointed Bristol and Les Adrets complexes are recommended.

There is one excellent luxury hotel (at a price), the Diva, with wonderful cuisine. The other **hotels** (in the original building) are Le Druos, Pas du Loup and Le Chastillon. The last two are available through Neilson, who offer weekends as well as the usual weekly packages.

The number of British operators serving Isola 2000 has declined and, with it, the vitality of the **après-ski** scene outside high season and weekends, when skiers from the Riviera arrive. That's the time to go to L'Equateur and La Tanière.

Despite its new Aquavallée leisure centre, Isola is hardly the place for a **non-skier** to spend a week: the resort name does mean 'island', after all. However, you could top up your tan and then treat yourself to the £300 package that helicopters you to Monte Carlo for a night, with dinner at the Café de Paris and entry to the Casino.

Megève 1100m

✔ Large, very pretty, ski area, ideal for intermediates

✔ Gourmet mountain lunches in attractive surroundings

✔ Excellent area for cross-country skiing

✔ Plenty of things to do other than skiing

✔ Charming old village centre

✘ Often poor snow, especially low down; yet little snowmaking

✘ Three separate ski areas, two linked by lift but not by piste

✘ Traditional, rustic charm spoilt by bad traffic congestion around town

✘ Not much challenging piste skiing

Megève used to be France's most fashionable ski village, popular with its chic clientele for its gentle, woodland skiing, rustic charm, pretty scenery, attractive mountain restaurants, lovely walks, sophisticated nightlife and friendly locals. It has certainly lost that title now to Courchevel: it no longer boasts a single restaurant with Michelin stars; Courchevel has two.

The problem is that, for keen skiers, Megève's facilities have been overtaken by France's high, snowsure, purpose-built resorts. In good snow years, Megève's pretty tree-lined skiing is ideal for gentle intermediate cruising and gourmet lunching. But in poor years, Megève's ski area can suffer because of its shortage of high altitude skiing and paucity of snowmaking facilities. And the town's rustic charm is now marred by severe traffic problems.

Megève still attracts its fair share of Beautiful People, complete with fur coats and fat wallets. But many are there as much for the posing as the skiing.

The area lift pass covers the relatively snowsure skiing of several nearby resorts, including Chamonix, Les Contamines and Courmayeur in Italy. So if you are prepared to take a car and tour around, you are guaranteed good skiing. Alternatively book late when you know the snow is good, or find a tour operator who will transport you to neighbouring resorts in times of snow shortage.

ORIENTATION

Megève sits in a pretty, sunny setting by the main Albertville-Chamonix road that bypasses only the medieval centre of town. It's one of France's largest resorts, surrounded on three sides by a sprawl of ever-expanding suburbs.

Lifts lead up into the three different ski areas from opposite ends of town – and there's a gondola into one from near the centre. There are also access lifts further from town. **St-Gervais** and **Le Bettex** share Megève's main ski area. And the Mont Blanc lift pass covers many other resorts, including the **Chamonix** valley and **Courmayeur** in Italy.

 ## The resort

Megève is very much a tale of two cities. It is in a lovely setting and has a beautifully preserved traditional old centre, which is pedestrianised and comes complete with open-air ice rink, horse-drawn sleighs, cobbled streets and a fine church. There are lots of smart clothing, jewellery, food, antique and gift shops.

Megève has expanded enormously and is surrounded by a strangulation of modern roads and traffic. Thankfully the main road bypasses the centre, and there are expensive underground car parks. But the cars are a problem – especially at weekends when the crowds arrive and at the end of the day when people are driving back from skiing excursions.

The clientele are mainly well-heeled French couples and families, who come here as much for an all-round winter holiday and for the people-watching potential as for the skiing. The nightlife is, as you'd expect for such a resort, lively and varied.

 ## The skiing

Megève's skiing is predominantly easy intermediate cruising, much of it prettily set in the woods. But there are tough runs to be found.

THE SKI AREA
Pretty but low

There are three separate ski areas, two of them linked by cable-car – but not by pistes. The two linked areas are Rochebrune and Mont d'Arbois. A gondola within walking distance of central Megève serves both areas. From the mid-station, you can catch the cable-car, followed by a gondola, up to Mont d'Arbois (1840m), or you can carry on up the gondola to Rochebrune (1750m).

Rochebrune can also be reached directly by an ancient cable-car from the southern edge of town. From Rochebrune you can go up to Alpette (1880m), the starting point for Megève's historic downhill course. A network of gentle, wooded, east-facing slopes served by drag-lifts (and a high-

LIFT PASSES

94/95 prices in francs
Rocharbois-Mont Joly
Covers all lifts on
Rochebrune, Côte
2000, Mt d'Arbois,
Megève, St-Gervais,
Mt Joux and Mount
Joly.
Beginners Pay by the
ride.
Main pass
1-day pass 148
6-day pass 764
(low season 630 –
18% off)
Senior citizens
Over 60: 6-day pass
634 (17% off)
Children
Under 12: 6-day pass
634 (17% off)
Under 5: free pass
Short-term passes
Half-day pass
available morning or
afternoon.
Alternative passes
Mont Blanc Evasion
pass covers all lifts in
Megève, St-Gervais,
St-Nicolas and
Combloux, available
for 1 day or season,
(1-day pass 155 for
adults, 129 for
children). Mont Blanc
ski-pass covers all
lifts in the 13 resorts
of the Mont Blanc
area (700km of piste
and 190 lifts) and the
buses between them
plus Courmayeur in
Italy 4 days out of 6
(6 days 920 for adults
and 640 for children,
95/96 prices). Jaco
pass valid for Le
Jaillet, Christomet and
Combloux.

speed quad since last year) takes you across to Côte 2000 – the sector's furthest and highest point, at 2015m.

Mont d'Arbois is Megève's largest and most interesting ski area. It's also accessed by another gondola starting at Princesse, way out to the north-east of town. From the top you can ski on north-facing slopes to Le Bettex and on down to St-Gervais at around 900m. Yet another two-stage gondola returns skiers to Mont d'Arbois, with its mid-station at Le Bettex. You can work your way over to Mont Joux and Megève's highest (2350m), most snowsure skiing – a small area.

The third, and quietest, area is **Le Jaillet**, accessed by gondola from just outside the northern edge of town. Above the top of the gondola (1600m) are predominantly easy, east-facing pistes. The high-point is Christomet to the west, served by a two-stage chair. In the other directions a series of long tree-lined runs and lifts serve the area above Combloux.

SNOW RELIABILITY
The area's worst feature
Last season was a bumper year for snow in Megève – there was skiing right to the bottom until the resort closed in late April. But things aren't always so rosy.

The problem is that the slopes are low (the resort map contains hardly any height information), sunny and served by little artificial snow. There is very little skiing above 2000m. So in a poor snow year, or in a warm spell, snow cover and quality can suffer badly. And because the resort itself is so low, it often rains there when it is snowing in higher places.

The relatively snowsure Mont Joly and Le Bettex sections are very small.

FOR ADVANCED SKIERS
Off-piste is the main attraction
The Mont Joly and Mont Joux sections offer the steepest skiing. The top chair here serves slopes of a genuinely black 33°, and the slightly lower Epaule chair has some steep runs back down and also accesses some good off-piste, as well as pisted, runs down to St-Nicolas-de-Véroce. There is an off-piste route down to neighbouring Les Contamines from here too.

The steep area beneath the second stage of the Princesse gondola can be a play area of powder skiing among the trees. Côte 2000 has a small section of steep skiing, including some off-piste.

Because few 'powder hounds' go to Megève, you can often find untracked powder days after the last snowfall.

FOR INTERMEDIATE SKIERS
Superb if the snow is good
Good intermediates will enjoy the Mont d'Arbois area best. The black runs below the Princesse gondola are perfectly manageable. The runs served by the Grand Vorassel drag and the most direct route between Mont d'Arbois and Le Bettex are also interesting. Similarly testing are the steepest of the Jaillet sector pistes above Combloux. Nearby, the Christomet bowl is probably the best area for mixed abilities, with the same lift giving access to three widely differing runs.

Moderate skiers are particularly well suited to Megève. A plethora of comfortable reds lead down to Le Bettex and Princesse from Mont d'Arbois, while nearby Mont Joux accesses long, similar-standard runs to St-Nicolas. Alpette and Côte 2000 are other suitable sections.

Timid skiers can get a great deal of mileage in. All main valley-level lifts have easy routes down to them (although the Milloz piste to the Princesse mid-station is a little steep). Particularly good, long, gentle cruises are available between Mont Joux and Megève via Mont d'Arbois. But whichever sector you go to, you'll find easy, well-groomed blue runs – the main problem you are likely to encounter is the poor quality or thin snow-cover.

FOR BEGINNERS
Several nursery areas
The large amount of very easy skiing makes Megève a good choice for near-beginners. And there are plenty of nice little nursery areas dotted around at the base of most ski areas. Unfortunately all of them are prone to poor snow conditions – in which situation you're better off going up to Jaillet or Mont d'Arbois.

FOR CROSS-COUNTRY
An excellent area
There are 75km of varied trails, spread throughout the ski area, some of which are at reasonable altitude (1300m–1550m). Meeting up with Alpine skiers or walkers at one of the many mountain huts is a particular attraction of this area.

QUEUES
Much improved
Megève has improved its lift system of late, and nowadays is relatively queue-free during the week, except at peak holiday time. But school holiday and sunny Sunday delays can be long at

times, especially for the Petite Fontaine and Lanchettes lifts in the Rochebrune sector and at the mid-station of the Princesse gondola.

Overcrowded pistes at Mont Joux and Mont d'Arbois are a problem at busy periods. Queues are noticeably genteel, a far cry from the push and shove of more macho resorts.

MOUNTAIN RESTAURANTS
The long lunch lives
Megève is one of the great skiing gourmet venues. The Mont d'Arbois area is particularly well endowed with mountain restaurants.

Several of the little old chalets around St-Nicolas have both great charm and fine food, while L'Alpage at Les Communailles beneath Mont Joux is worth a visit, and is particularly recommended for good salads and the plat du jour. The Club House at Mont d'Arbois is a nice place, but popular with the Megève poseurs with dogs and fur coats.

Self-service places are cheaper and less leisurely, but still reasonably good quality. Chez Tartine is a very friendly self-service spot at the Princesse mid-station. Le Rosay on Mont Joux is also friendly and generally quite good. The Igloo has both self-service and table-service sections; the staff in both are helpful and it has wonderful views of Mont Blanc.

Further afield, Côte 2000 is popular for its atmosphere, friendly service and good quality, while La Caboche is handily placed for an end-of-day drink. Forestier and Alpette are other recommended spots.

CHILDCARE
There are four kindergartens dotted around the sprawling resort, all offering skiing. Age limits and hours vary. Alpage (50211097), next to the Mont d'Arbois gondola: ages 3 to 6, until 5.30. Caboche (50589765) at the Caboche gondola station: ages 3 to 10, until 5.30pm. Meg'Loisirs (50587784) is a comprehensive nursery: ages 1 to 6, until 6pm or even 7pm. Princesse (50930086), out at the Princess gondola: ages 3 to 6, until 5pm.

SKI SCHOOL
Adventurous
The two ski schools both have broad horizons, offering expeditions to the Vallée Blanche and heli-skiing (in Italy) as well as conventional tuition. The International school also advertises outings to the Grands Montets at Argentière.

FACILITIES FOR CHILDREN
Language problems
A comfortable low-altitude resort like Megève attracts lots of families who can afford day-care. The facilities seem impressive – all four kindergartens offer a wide range of activities as an alternative to skiing. Lack of English-speaking staff (and companions) could be the main drawback, and many parents of pre-skiing children will prefer the more predictable crèche services of Ski Esprit, who have chalets here (see following section).

SKI SCHOOL

95/96 prices in francs

ESF
Classes 6 days
4hr: 9.30-11.30 and
3pm-5pm
6 half days: 470
Children's classes
Ages: 5 to 12
6 full days: 730
Private lessons
Hourly or daily
180 for 1hr, for 1 to 2
people

International
Classes 6 days
2hr: 10am-noon, 1pm-
3pm and 3pm-5pm;
3hr: 10am-1pm
6 mornings (2hr): 585
Children's classes
Ages: 4 to 12
6 full days: 875
Private lessons
Hourly or daily
200 for 1hr, for 1 to 2
people

GETTING THERE

Air Geneva, transfer
1½hr. Lyon, transfer
3hr.

Rail Sallanches
(13km); regular buses
from station.

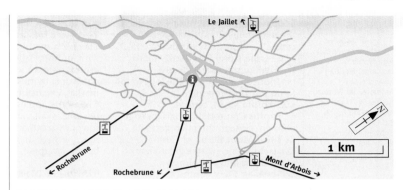

  # Staying there

Staying in the traffic-free centre of
town gives you the best atmosphere
and puts you within walking distance
of the Chamois gondola.

HOW TO GO
Few packages
Relatively few British tour operators go
to Megève. Although it's a chic resort
with five 4-star hotels, there are plenty
of simpler, charming hotels and
good-value chalets available.
Apartments tend to be expensive but
of a good standard.
Chalets Jean Stanford now offer
tuition-inclusive holidays with British
instructors at their characterful chalet-
hotel Sylvana. This former one-star
hotel is well located for the skiing,
close to the Rochebrune cable-car. For
most of the season you can ski back to
the chalet. The family specialist Ski
Esprit has a charming old villa with
lots of personal touches and an

exceptionally comfortable traditional-
style modern chalet (all bedrooms
have en-suite bathrooms). Both are
pleasantly located away from the town
congestion, 10 minutes' walk out of
the centre. Ski Barrett-Boyce has a cosy
open-fired place five minutes' walk
from the centre.
Hotels Megève may not be France's
smartest resort any longer, but it still
attracts enough affluent visitors to
sustain some exceptionally stylish and
welcoming hotels.
££££ Loges du Mont Blanc Megève's
traditional leading hotel – very elegant
and fashionable. Right in the centre,
and therefore close to the main
gondola.
££££ Chalet du Mont d'Arbois
Prettily decorated former Rothschild
family home in a secluded position
between the two gondolas.
££££ Fer à Cheval French rustic-chic
at its best, with a warmly welcoming
wood-and-stone interior. Excellent
food, and a fitness centre to redress
the balance. Close to the centre.

Selected chalets in the Megève area

PACKAGES

AA Ski-Driveaway, Chalets 'Unlimited', Jean Stanford, Lagrange, Made to Measure, Ski Ardmore, Ski Barrett-Boyce, Ski Club Megeve, Ski Esprit, Ski Les Alpes, Snowman Skiing, White Roc

St-Gervais Alpine Tours, Lagrange, PGL Ski Europe, Ski Barrett-Boyce, Snowcoach Club Cantabrica

ACTIVITIES

Indoor 'Palais des Sports' (climbing wall, swimming pool, sauna, solarium, skating, gym), judo, classical and contemporary dance classes, music lessons, bridge, tennis, yoga, archery, language classes, museum, library, cinemas, pottery, casino, concert and play hall, body-building hall, table-tennis, tennis, bowling

Outdoor 50km of cleared paths, snow-shoe excursions, skating rink, riding, sleigh rides, plane and helicopter trips, para-gliding, curling, horse-riding, rock-climbing, mountaineering

TOURIST OFFICE

Postcode 74120
Tel 00 33 50212728
Fax 50930309

££££ **Grange d'Arly** Wrong side of the road, but still quite close to the centre – a beautifully furnished chalet.
£££ **Ferme Hôtel Duvillard** Smartly restored farmhouse, perfectly positioned for skiing, at the foot of the Mont d'Arbois gondola.
£££ **Alpina** Small, central.
££ **Sapins** Comfortable logis on edge of town, close to the main gondola.
££ **Idéal-Mont Blanc** At Combloux: a Relais du Silence with a great view of Mont Blanc and a pool.
Self-catering The weekend specialist White Roc has expensive but comfortable apartments within easy walking distance of the main gondola. Chalet operator Jean Stanford will also put together a self-catering package, using local contacts for apartments.

EATING OUT
Very French

Megève is a très chic French town whose restaurants are mainly high-quality, if expensive. Michel Gaudin is probably the best in town and does very good-value set menus. The Fermes de Marie, Chalet du Mont d'Arbois and Mont Joly are not far behind in quality but much more expensive. The Tire Bouchon and Sapinière are two of the best value, Vieux Megève is a delightfully cosy grill, Le Chamois cooks the ubiquitous fondue very well and Côte 2000 is an intimate candlelit place. The Pizzeria del Mare is good value, and the Phnom-Penh serves food rather different from normal French cuisine.

APRES-SKI
Plenty to try

Nightlife is lively, and less formal than it used to be. The Chamois and Sapinière bars are animated tea-time places. The Puck is an atmospheric locals' bar, Club des Cinque Rues is a very popular jazz club-cum-cocktail bar, while Harries Bar is an informal rendezvous popular for its wide range of beers, a weekly live band, karaoke and satellite TV. Village Rock and the Enfants Terribles are other lively spots.

The bar at the chalet-hotel Sylvana is a good place for a quiet, inexpensive drink in a friendly atmosphere. Senso is the liveliest disco. The fur and poodle brigade frequent Le Rols Club. The Esquinade Club (with casino) is another jet-set spot.

The weekly broomball match, on the open-air ice rink, between the British and French is a good chance to let your hair down.

FOR NON-SKIERS
There are lots around

There is something for most tastes, with an impressive sports centre, a central outdoor ice rink, plenty of outdoor activities and a weekly market. Excursions to Annecy, Chamonix and even Courmayeur are possible. Walks are excellent outside town, with 50km of marked paths, much at high altitude. Meeting skiers up the mountain for lunch is easy.

STAYING IN OTHER RESORTS
A couple of places a car-drive away

Praz-sur-Arly (1035m) and Notre-Dame-de-Bellecombe (1130m) are much cheaper options for independent car travellers.

Praz is a small, quiet place, but has hotels, restaurants, bars, sports club, ski school and ski kindergarten. It has a fair-sized ski area of its own, with short, mainly easy north-facing runs.

Notre-Dame is a little further along the road past Praz, a pleasant enough village with mainly apartment accommodation, some simple hotels, and several bars and restaurants – L'Equipe is the most popular. Notre-Dame has its own varied, pretty ski area, with attendant ski school.

St-Gervais 850m

St-Gervais is a handsome 19th-century spa town set in a narrow river gorge, half-way between Megève and Chamonix, at the turn-off for Les Contamines. It has direct access to the Mont d'Arbois skiing via a 20-person gondola from the centre of town. At the mid-station is Le Bettex (1400m), a small collection of hotels, private chalets and new apartments, more conveniently situated for the skiing but with little evening animation.

You can go up in the opposite direction from St-Gervais, towards Mont Blanc on a rack and pinion railway, which takes you to the Les Houches skiing. The only way back to St-Gervais from here on skis is off-piste, and there's frequently not enough snow. St-Gervais and Le Bettex both have their own ski schools.

Its position makes St-Gervais a very convenient base for touring the different ski resorts of the Mont Blanc region. It also makes it fairly full of traffic much of the time.

In St-Gervais, the Val d'Este hotel is conveniently situated in the town centre (as are the spacious Alpen Rose apartments), while the chalet-style Carlina on the outskirts has swimming pool, gym and sauna. In Le Bettex, the Arbois offers stylish accommodation.

Les Menuires 1850m

HOW IT RATES

The skiing
Snow	****
Extent	*****
Advanced	****
Intermediates	*****
Beginners	***
Convenience	*****
Queues	****
Restaurants	***

The rest
Scenery	***
Resort charm	*
Not skiing	*

✔ Part of the biggest linked ski area in the world

✔ Some great local skiing for good skiers

✔ Swift access to both the Méribel and Val-Thorens ski areas

✔ You can ski directly to and from nearly all accommodation

✔ Extensive artificial snow facilities mean snow-cover rarely a problem

✔ Probably the cheapest place to stay in the Trois Vallées area

✗ Main intermediate and beginner slopes into town get a lot of sun and snow deteriorates rapidly in warm weather; artificial snow turns into artificial slush

✗ The ugliest resort in the Alps

✗ Nursery slopes are busy as well as over-exposed to the sun

Les Menuires' big problem is its looks. Frankly, it's hideous. However, you can rent an apartment here for much less than you'd pay in the more chic Trois Vallées resorts.

It has good access to the Trois Vallées skiing. With 200 lifts and 600km of pistes plus endless off-piste possibilities, no keen skier will be bored in a fortnight here. Local skiing on La Masse is some of the best in the Trois Vallées for good skiers, with usually excellent snow. Many Courchevel- and Méribel-based skiers overlook it because it is set apart from the main circuit.

If you want to stay in a quiet, traditional Savoyard village, nearby St-Martin-de-Belleville is worth considering as a base.

ORIENTATION

Les Menuires now spreads up the valley towards Val-Thorens, with the building of two new satellites – Reberty and Les Bruyères.

A slow, old, two-stage gondola (due to be renovated for 1995/96) is the main lift out of the main resort. From its top you can ski direct to **Val-Thorens** and **Méribel** (and from there, on to **Courchevel**). The chair-lift alternatives are often quicker, and the quickest lift up to the link with Val-Thorens and Méribel is the two-stage high-capacity Les Bruyères gondola. On the other side of the valley a fast two-stage gondola now takes you to the top of La Masse.

Lift passes for six days or more also give you a day in **Val-d'Isère/Tignes** and **La Plagne** or **Les Arcs, Les Saisies** and **Pralognan-la-Vanoise**. But it's quite a drive to get to these resorts – Les Menuires is a long way up its valley.

 ## The resort

Despite being 'smartened up' for the 1992 Winter Olympics (the men's slalom was held here), Les Menuires still manages to win our coveted Ugliest Resort in the Alps award, narrowly beating Tignes and Flaine. The original resort, the centre of which is known as La Croisette, is particularly horrendous.

Its newer outposts of Reberty and Les Bruyères are built in a somewhat more pleasing style. But, taken as a whole, the motley collection of mainly huge apartment blocks, varying wildly in design, make a disjointed blot on the Alpine landscape. The main advantage of most accommodation is its ski-in, ski-out convenience.

The new outposts have their own shops and bars. The main centre has an indoor shopping complex which is dark and claustrophobic. However, there are some pleasant bar and restaurant terraces facing the slopes.

 ## The skiing

Les Menuires' skiing has two main attractions: La Masse, and the swift links to the skiing of the rest of the Trois Vallée. It suits all standards except complete beginners. But local skiing for intermediates and beginners is spoilt by the orientation of the main slopes, which get the full force of the afternoon sun; despite considerable artificial snowmaking, they can be icy early in the day and heavy later.

THE SKI AREA
A good base for the Trois Vallées
Les Menuires and St-Martin-de-Belleville share a local ski area with 120km of runs and 50 lifts. The west-facing slopes have the vast bulk of the skiing. The main gondolas take you up to the **Mont de la Chambre** (2850m), from where you can ski back towards the resort or down to Val-Thorens or the Méribel skiing. Chairs and drags serve the local slopes, and you can work your way north by piste and lift, and ski down to the charming old village of St-Martin-de-Belleville.

The north-east-facing slopes of **La Masse** (2805m) usually have excellent snow on the top half and are served by a two-stage high-capacity gondola.

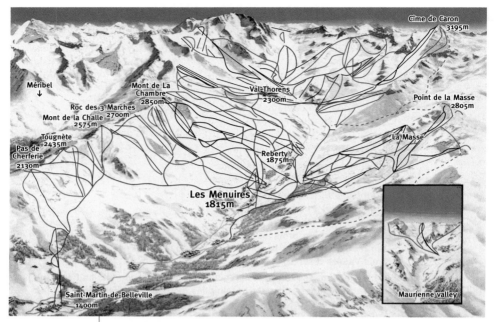

Cime de Caron 3195m
Méribel ↓
Mont de La Chambre 2850m
Val-Thorens 2300m
Point de la Masse 2805m
Roc des 3 Marches 2700m
Mont de la Challe 2575m
La Masse
Tougnète 2435m
Reberty 1875m
Pas de Cherferie 2130m
Les Menuires 1815m
Saint-Martin-de-Belleville 1400m
Maurienne valley

SKI FACTS

Altitude	1400m-2850m
Lifts	200
Pistes	600km
Green/Blue	49%
Red	37%
Black	14%
Artificial snow	60km

SKI SCHOOL

95/96 prices in francs

ESF

Classes 6 days
5½hr: 3hr am, 2½hr
pm; half-day am or
pm
6 full days: 910
Children's classes
Ages: up to 15
6 full days: 765
Private lessons
Hourly
175 for 1 or 2 people

International
Classes 6 days
2½hr am or pm
6 half-days: 620
Children's classes
Ages: up to 15
6 half-days: 545
Private lessons
Hourly
175 for 1 or 2 people

SNOW RELIABILITY
Cover guaranteed but not quality

La Masse's height and orientation
ensure good snow for a long season.

The opposite, west-facing slopes are
supplied with abundant artificial snow
(the resort boasts 277 snow cannon).
But although cover there is guaranteed
– so long as the weather is cold
enough to make snow – the quality of
the snow is often found wanting,
especially on the lower slopes.

FOR ADVANCED SKIERS
Hidden treasures

La Masse has some of the steepest and
least well-known piste skiing in the
Trois Vallées – most skiers doing the
'circuit' skip it. Long reds and blacks
come down either side of the top stage
of the gondola. Other steep blacks,
usually mogulled, are served by the
Dame Blanche and Lac Noir chairs.

From the top there are also some
marvellously scenic itineraires. The
wide, sweeping, but not too steep, Lac
du Lou takes off down towards Val-
Thorens. Others lead off in the
opposite direction to various villages
from which you need transport back,
but the Les Yvoses run takes you back
into the Les Menuires lift system.

The easy access to the rest of the
Trois Vallées skiing means that good
skiers are spoilt for choice. Within an
hour of leaving your door you can be
skiing the steepest slopes of Méribel or
Val-Thorens. Courchevel won't take
much longer.

FOR INTERMEDIATE SKIERS
600km of pistes to choose from

The Trois Vallées is an intermediate
skier's paradise. Virtually everywhere
you go you'll find a blue or red piste to
suit your tastes.

The local skiing at Les Menuires is
virtually all blue and red. But because
most slopes face west, the snow is
often better elsewhere. In good snow,
however, you may find little reason
for leaving the local area.

There are both pistes and itineraires
down into Méribel, and five different
peaks you can approach it from. Even
a second- or third-time skier should
have no problem cruising from valley
to valley. In poor snow conditions the
attractions of Val-Thorens become
evident, and there's blue-run access
via the Montaulever drag as well as red
runs from the top of the mountain.

FOR BEGINNERS
Try elsewhere

Although there are wide and gentle
slopes for beginners, we think you'd
be better off for your first ski holiday
in a resort which offers more of a real
Alpine atmosphere and is easier on the
eye. Good skiers can get away from Les
Menuires and into beautiful Alpine
scenery. Beginners are stuck with it in
view all day.

Apart from that, the snow quality is
a worry. We've seen beginners
struggling on ice first thing and in
thick slush in the afternoon. The blue
slopes immediately above the resort
can also get extremely crowded.

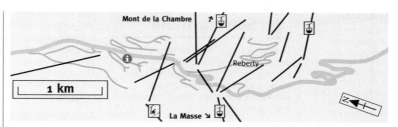

LIFT PASSES

95/96 prices in francs
Three Valleys
Covers all 3V resorts.
Beginners Points card
for some ski lifts (25
points, 74).
Main pass
1-day pass 215
6-day pass 1035
(low season 932 –
10% off)
Senior citizens
Over 60: 6-day pass
776 (25% off)
Over 80: free pass
Children
Under 16: 6-day pass
776 (25% off)
Under 5: free pass
Short-term passes
Half-day passes from
12.30: Les Menuires
and St-Martin (adult
128), La Masse area
(adult 103).
Notes 6-day pass and
over valid one day
each in Tignes-Val-
d'Isère, La Plagne-Les
Arcs, Pralognan-la-
Vanoise and Les
Saisies. Reductions
for families, students.
Alternative passes
Vallée des Belleville
pass: 78 lifts and
240km piste in Les
Menuires, St-Martin
and Val-Thorens
(adult 6-day 965). Les
Menuires and St-
Martin pass covers 48
lifts and 120km of
piste (adult 6-day
850).

FOR CROSS-COUNTRY
Valley hike
There are 28km of prepared trails
along the valley floor between
St-Martin and half-way between
Les Menuires and Val-Thorens.

QUEUES
Can be bypassed
La Masse used to be queue-prone, but
that has been solved by the new high-
capacity gondolas. The one remaining
problem is the slow, four-person Mont
de la Chambre gondola towards the
Méribel skiing – although this was
being renovated in summer 1995, we
understand the capacity will remain
the same.

MOUNTAIN RESTAURANTS
Have lunch in St-Martin
The restaurant at the top of the first
stage of the La Masse gondola is fairly
pleasant. But a lot of people prefer to
head for the restaurants of the old
village of St-Martin-de-Belleville. The
Bouite, in nearby Saint-Marcel, is
typically French and delightful for a
blow-out. It's reachable off-piste
(follow the signs) and you can get a
taxi to the lifts afterwards. The

restaurant at the foot of the second
chair up from St-Martin is also worth
visiting. Locals recommend Le Petit
Savoyard, Le Necou and Chalet 2000,
around Reberty and Bruyères.

SKI SCHOOL
Overcomes language barrier
Reporters are full of praise, despite
English not being widely spoken, and
we have reports of children enjoying
themselves in multi-national classes.
One mum states, 'My daughter, who is
quiet and shy at times, loved every
minute and preferred to ski with the
school rather than me!'
Classes are usually small, by
European standards, with a guaranteed
maximum of ten.

FACILITIES FOR CHILDREN
All-embracing
This is very much a family resort, and
the childcare arrangements seem well
organised. We have one report on the
ESF ski kindergarten which is very
enthusiastic, despite the fact that the
child was the only English-speaker in
the class – 'On departure day our
four-year-old was crying, "Daddy, I
want to go to school".'

CHILDCARE

The ESF-run Village des Schtroumpfs (79006379) takes children aged 3 months to 7 years. It has a nursery for babies, a Baby Club for toddlers and a leisure centre for older children, with indoor and outdoor activities and ski lessons for children aged 2½ or more.

At Reberty-les-Bruyères, the Marmottons offers similar facilities, and the SEI runs a ski kindergarten.

GETTING THERE

Air Geneva, transfer 3½hr. Lyon, transfer 3½hr. Chambery, transfer 2½hr.

Rail Moûtiers (27km); regular buses from station.

PACKAGES

AA Ski-Driveaway, Airtours, Club Med, Crystal, Inghams, Lagrange, Le Shuttle Holidays, Made to Measure, Motours, SkiBound, Travelscene Ski-Drive

St-Martin-de-Belleville ABT Ski, Chalets 'Unlimited', Chalets de St Martin, MasterSki, Poles Apart, Ski Total, Stena Sealink

ACTIVITIES

Indoor Sports club, body-building, table tennis, library, games room, theatre, 2 cinemas, fitness centres
Outdoor 2 outdoor heated swimming pools, plane and microlight rides, hang-gliding, guided walks, snow-scooters, artificial skating rink, snow-shoe excursions, para-gliding

TOURIST OFFICE

Postcode 73440
Tel 010 33 79007300
Fax 79007506

Staying there

Despite the fact that the resort is designed for the convenience of skiers, you may wish to think quite hard about location. The central area around La Croisette is best for shops and après-ski.

HOW TO GO
Cheap, rough-and-ready packages
Most of the big, but few of the small, tour operators go to Les Menuires. They have a fair selection of hotels and apartments. There are, perhaps surprisingly, no catered chalets. There is a Club Med above Reberty.

Hotels It comes as a slight surprise to find that there are some quite smart hotels here – although none above 3-star grading, and none with a pool.
££££ Latitudes Best in town, on the lower fringe of Les Bruyères.
££ Menuire Neat, well equipped new place on the southern fringe of the resort.
££ Ours Blanc Wood-clad chalet on the slopes above Reberty 1850.
Self-catering Apartments are cheap but not so cheerful. It's a classic 'French box' resort, so paying extra for under-occupancy is an astute move. L'Oree des Pistes and Residence Le Villaret are among the least objectionable, and the latter has a communal lounge with open fire, and a TV/video room. The Pierre et Vacances places are not up to the usual standard of the chain, but are still better than some other apartments in the resort.

EATING OUT
Good authentic French cuisine
Though some restaurants lack atmosphere at times, there's no shortage of good food. Savoyard specialities and 'real' French food are the order of the day. Reporters have recommended the Chaudron, Ruade and Bouquetin, but locals assure us that La Marmite du Geant is the best in town. Others we have liked are the Auberge de Lanau and Belle Epoque.

APRES-SKI
Improving but still very limited
The young people who are attracted here by low prices have done their best to bring a spark of life to the nightlife scene, but it's still pretty quiet. The Pub is a gathering point for Brits, and other possibles are Pop 2000, Osian and the Calgary. There's little else to do but drink, though you can have an expensive bop at the uninspiring Liberty disco.

FOR NON-SKIERS
Forget it
Les Menuires is a resort for keen skiers who want to ski the world's most extensive ski area on a budget. It's not the place for non-skiers, though there are some pretty walks and a good open-air swimming pool.

St-Martin-de-Belleville 1400m
St-Martin is a traditional Savoyard village, with old church, small square and old wooden and stone buildings. It is the administrative centre for the whole Belleville valley (which includes Les Menuires and Val-Thorens).

In 1950 it didn't even have running water or electricity. In the 1960s and 1970s the nearby purpose-built ski resorts were developed. St-Martin became a bit of a backwater. But in the late 1980s a couple of slow chair-lifts were built, linking it to the Trois Vallées skiing. It is now well worth considering as a quiet alternative to the mega-resorts.

The main disadvantages are the slow, cold 30-minute ride up into the skiing each day and the run back which doesn't survive if it's too warm for snowmaking. At least the bottom chair-lift was slightly upgraded last season. A rolling carpet was installed so the lift can now be run faster, cutting the ride by five minutes.

A new Grangeraies district has been built to extend the accommodation at the foot of the slopes. It blends in well, in contrast to its neighbours up the valley. There are a few hotels – the Alp-hôtel and the Edelweiss are traditional-style 3-stars – and a good variety of apartments. The few tour operators cover all styles of accommodation. Ski Total and Chalets de St Martin have several chalets. ABT Ski has a recently built chalet-hotel, convenient for skiing – with a sauna and jacuzzi, and plans for an outdoor bar and restaurant for lunches. We've had good reports of the rooms, food, staff and ambience – the only complaint was about the number of steps from the street to the room. Headwater package the main hotels.

There are a few restaurants and bars. The Pourquoi Pas piano bar is the most popular with tourists. There's a pizzeria, as well as more traditional restaurants.

The ski school is said to have some instructors with poor English, and was so quiet in low season there were only two classes – beginners and others, leading to very different standards in the second group. We've had a good report of the ski kindergarten.

Méribel 1400m–1700m

HOW IT RATES

The skiing

Snow	****
Extent	*****
Advanced	****
Intermediates	*****
Beginners	***
Convenience	***
Queues	****
Restaurants	****

The rest

Scenery	***
Resort charm	***
Not skiing	***

ORIENTATION

Méribel occupies the central valley of the Trois Vallées system. It consists of two main villages. Mottaret is around 200m higher and ten minutes further up the valley than the original resort of Méribel (now known as Méribel Centre), which is built along a winding road and has several 'centres' with shops and restaurants. Both resorts are served by lifts which take you quickly up to the ridges leading to **Courchevel, Val-Thorens** and **Les Menuires** as well as Méribel's own skiing.

Lift passes for six days or more also give you a day in **Val-d'Isère-Tignes** (just over an hour away), **La Plagne** or **Les Arcs** (30 and 45 mins respectively), **Les Saisies** (an hour) and **Pralognan-la-Vanoise** (45 mins).

For the Olympics, a new gondola was built from Brides-les-Bains, an old spa town way down in the valley, which served as the Olympic Village for the games, up to Méribel Centre. There's a mid-station at the old village of **Les Allues**, which has put the place back on the map as a possible place to stay.

✔ In the centre of the biggest linked ski area in the world

✔ Ideal for intermediates who love covering as many miles as possible

✔ Plenty for advanced skiers

✔ Modern, constantly improved lift system means little queueing and rapid access to all ski areas

✔ Good piste maintenance and snowmaking means reliable snow

✔ Village purpose-built in pleasing chalet-style architecture

✔ Some accommodation convenient for skiing (most at Mottaret)

✘ Not the place to go if you want to get away from fellow Brits

✘ Main village spread out, straggling along a long, winding road that is mostly well away from the slopes

✘ Expensive

✘ Satellite resort of Mottaret is rather lifeless

For keen piste-bashers, Méribel is difficult to beat. It is slap in the middle of the Trois Vallées – the biggest inter-linked ski area in the world. With 200 lifts and 600km of pistes, and endless off-piste possibilities, no keen skier will be bored in a fortnight here. Méribel's local skiing is probably the least interesting in the region. But that is still good by any standards.

If you don't like skiing with hordes of Brits, be warned: more British tour operators go here than any other resort. And it's not cheap. Indeed, the 1992 Olympics seems to have prompted the resort to move significantly upmarket. Several very comfortable and expensive hotels were built for the Games, and others were renovated, and food and drink prices have hit Swiss resort heights. But one of us learned to ski here, the other visited it on his second trip, and we both go back whenever we can.

The resort

Méribel was founded by a Brit, Peter Lindsay, in 1939. It has retained a strong British presence ever since.

The original village of Méribel-les-Allues (now known as Méribel Centre) has grown enormously over recent years and is built each side of a road which winds its way up from the village centre at about 1400m to the Altiport (an airport with snow-covered runway and little planes with skis) at around 1800m. All the buildings are wood-clad, low-rise, chalet style. It is one of the most tastefully designed of French purpose-built resorts.

Méribel-Mottaret started life in the early 1970s. It looks modern, with wood-clad apartment blocks built alongside the piste. But even Mottaret is much more attractive than many resorts built for ski convenience.

Méribel Centre rises from just above the main lifts, along the side of the main piste. Although some accommodation is right on the piste, much of it is a fair hike away.

There are a few accommodation centres on the way up to Altiport. The

main one is Belvedere, an upmarket enclave separated from the rest of the resort by the main home piste. Before that lie Altitude 1600 and Plateau de Morel, both with a fair collection of shops and restaurants. The hotels and apartments of Altiport are isolated but beautifully set in the woods. Lifts leave from here towards Courchevel.

At Mottaret, the original village is set beside the piste on the east-facing slopes. New development has since taken place on the other side of the valley. Both sides are served by lifts for pedestrian access – but the gondola up the original village stops at 7.30pm and it's a long, tiring walk after that if you're staying near the top. Mottaret has many fewer shops and bars and less après-ski than Méribel Centre.

The skiing

The main attraction of Méribel is the skiing of the immense Trois Vallées region, so read the entries for Courchevel, Les Menuires and Val-Thorens as well as this one.

It's keen piste-bashers who will get the best out of what Méribel has to

SKI FACTS

Altitude 1450m-2950m
Lifts 200
Pistes 600km
Green/Blue 49%
Red 37%
Black 14%
Artificial snow 60km

offer. The grooming of the slopes is about the best in the Alps, which means there is endless cruising to be had – as well as more challenging skiing. And the lift system is so efficient that decent skiers can travel to the far end of the ski area and still be back in time for a late lunch. The Méribel valley tends to have rather inconsistent grading of runs, with some reds trickier than some blacks and others easier than some blues.

THE SKI AREA
Highly efficient lift system
The Méribel valley runs north–south. On the eastern side gondolas leave both Méribel and Mottaret for **La Saulire** at around 2700m. From here you can ski back down towards either village or down the other side in a choice of directions to join the Courchevel skiing.

From Méribel Centre a gondola rises to **Tougnète**, on the western side of the valley, from where you can ski down to Les Menuires or St-Martin-de-Belleville. You can also ski to Mottaret from here. From there a chair then a drag take you to another entry point for the Les Menuires skiing.

The Mottaret area has seen rapid mechanisation over the last decade. The **Plattières** gondola rises up the valley to the south, ending at yet another entry point to the Les Menuires skiing. To the east of this a totally new ski area was opened up a few years ago by the building of a big stand-up gondola to the top of **Mont Vallon** at nearly 3000m. A high-speed quad from near this area goes south up to **Mont de la Chambre**, giving

direct access to the skiing of Val-Thorens, as well as Les Menuires.

All the Méribel skiing, like the skiing throughout the Trois Vallées, interconnects without having to walk.

SNOW RELIABILITY
Great piste-maintenance
The Méribel skiing isn't the highest in the Trois Vallées, and snow conditions are often better elsewhere. But the grooming of the runs is excellent and the lower runs now have a substantial amount of snowmaking. So lack of snow here is very rarely a problem, though ice or slush low down at the end of the day can be.

At the southern end of the valley, towards Les Menuires and Val-Thorens, a lot of the runs are north-facing and keep their snow well, even when snow is in generally short supply. It's the west-facing La Saulire side, which gets a lot of sun in the afternoon, where snow conditions deteriorate first – but then you can always ski over the other side in Courchevel, and the north-east-facing slopes above Altiport generally have decent snow.

FOR ADVANCED SKIERS
Exciting choices
The extent of the Trois Vallées' skiing means advanced skiers are well catered for. In the Méribel valley one of the most enjoyable runs is the long, steep, mogulled Combe de Vallon run down the right hand side of the Mont Vallon gondola. This is red on the map but deserves a black grading. There are wonderful views from the top of the gondola of the unspoilt

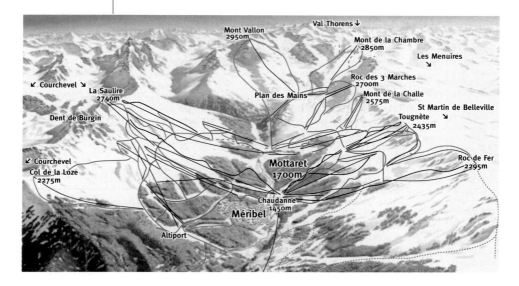

nature reserve behind, where skiing is banned. And there's a beautiful itineraire (strangely not marked on the piste map) in the next valley to the main pistes, leading to the bottom of the gondola.

The newish chair-lift up towards Val-Thorens has seen the conversion of parts of the old itineraires into official red runs, which are often crowded. Though sadly less isolated now, this remains one of our favourite valleys: there is still plenty of opportunity for skiing off-piste in the wide open bowls on the way back from Val-Thorens and Les Menuires.

A good mogul run is down the side of the double drag-lift which leads from half-way up the mountain at Mottaret to Mont de la Challe. And there is a steep black run all the way down the gondola from Tougnète back to Méribel Centre. Apart from a shallow section near the mid-station, this is unrelenting most of the way.

At the north end of the valley the La Face run was built for the women's downhill in the 1992 Olympics. Served by the two-stage Olympic Express high-speed quad, it makes a splendid cruise for a good skier when it is freshly groomed, and you can terrify yourself just by imagining what it must be like to go straight down.

On the La Saulire side, there are a couple of black runs marked on the piste map. But neither is as steep or demanding as those on the opposite side of the valley.

Throughout the area there are good off-piste opportunities. The ESF runs excellent-value guided groups.

Selected chalets in Méribel

Simply Ski *Chalet specialists*   T 0181 742 2541   F 0181 995 5346

Ski Scott Dunn *Upmarket holiday specialists*   T 0181 767 0202   F 0181 767 2026

LIFT PASSES

95/96 prices in francs
Three Valleys
Covers all lifts in Courchevel, Méribel, Les Menuires, Val-Thorens and St-Martin-de-Belleville.
Beginners One free lift in Mottaret and one in Méribel; reduced price lift pass with beginners' lessons.
Main pass
1-day pass 215
6-day pass 1035
(low season 932 – 10% off)
Senior citizens
Over 60: 6-day pass 776 (25% off)
Over 80: free pass
Children
Under 16: 6-day pass 776 (25% off)
Under 5: free pass
Short-term passes
Half-day pass (from 12.30) available for Vallée de Méribel (adult 128).
Notes 6-day pass and over valid for one day each in Tignes-Val-d'Isère, La Plagne-Les Arcs, Pralognan-la-Vanoise and Les Saisies.
Alternative passes
Vallée de Méribel pass covers 120km of runs in Méribel and Mottaret (adult 6-day 845, child 6-day 591).
Credit cards: Yes

FOR INTERMEDIATE SKIERS
Paradise found
Méribel and the rest of the Trois Vallées is a paradise for intermediate skiers. There are few other resorts where a keen piste-basher can cover as many kilometres in as short a period of time. Virtually all the pistes on both sides of the Méribel valley will suit advanced intermediates. Most of the reds are on the difficult side.

For less adventurous intermediates, the run from the second station of the Plattières gondola back to Mottaret is ideal, and used a lot by the ski school. It is a gentle, north-facing, cruising run which is well groomed and generally has good snow.

Even second-year skiers should find the runs over into Les Menuires and Courchevel well within their capabilities, opening up further vast amounts of intermediate skiing.

This section on intermediate skiing may seem short. That's because virtually every piste in the Trois Vallées region is ideal intermediate terrain. To describe them all would take a book in itself. If you're an intermediate skier, don't miss it!

FOR BEGINNERS
Not ideal
Méribel isn't ideal for beginners but has a good green run to progress to.

The resort lacks good nursery slopes set apart from the main skiing. There is a small one at Rond Point, mainly used by the children's ski school.

But the best area for beginners is at Altiport, now accessible direct from the village at Altitude 1600 by chair-lift. There is a gentle out-of-the-way area here which can be treated as a nursery slope. And, once you can take a drag-lift, there are two which lead to one of the best and most attractively situated beginner pistes we know. It is gentle, wide and tree-lined, and has little through-traffic of better skiers because it is pretty much a dead end.

FOR CROSS-COUNTRY
Scenic routes
The main area is in the woods near Altiport. There is about 17km of prepared track here, a pleasant introduction to those who want to try cross-country for the first time.

There is also a track round the frozen lake at Mottaret, and for the more experienced there is an 8km itinerary from Altiport to Courchevel.

QUEUES
Virtually non-existent
The huge investment in lifts that has been made consistently over the years has paid off in making the area virtually queue-free despite the huge numbers of skiers. If you do come across a queue, there is generally an alternative route available.

The old four-person gondola from Mottaret to La Saulire can generate queues, especially from mid-afternoon onwards, with skiers going back to Courchevel. But this can be avoided by taking the gondola from Méribel Centre or the chair from the Altiport to Col de la Loze.

The Plattières gondola at Mottaret can also get crowded at ski school time, when the school gets priority. Simply avoid the peak period.

MOUNTAIN RESTAURANTS
Places you won't want to leave
There is lots of choice by the standards of most French purpose-built resorts.

The Pierres Plates, at the top of the La Saulire gondolas, has magnificent views and you can watch hang-gliders taking off, though the food is nothing special. Chardonnet, at the mid-station of the Mottaret gondola, has table-service and excellent food but is expensive. Rhododendrons, at the top of the Altiport drag, has a modern but atmospheric wooden dining room. The Altiport hotel has a great outdoor buffet in good weather and the 'best tarts in town', but again is expensive. Les Crêtes, below the top of the Tougnète gondola, is family-run, has good service and is one of smallest mountain restaurants in the Trois Vallées. La Sittelle, above the first section of the Plattières gondola, has decent food and magnificent views towards Mont Vallon. Les Castors, at the bottom lift station, has the best-value food and excellent spaghetti served in individual copper pots.

SKI SCHOOL
No shortage of instructors
The three main schools all have plenty of English-speaking instructors and we've had good reports on them.

The ESF is by far the biggest, with over 300 instructors. It has a special International section with instructors speaking good English and run by Pat Graham (who also runs his own ski clinics in the resort). We've had good reports recently but classes can be over-large, and it's best to book in advance in high season.

Reports on Ski Cocktail were generally more encouraging; for

SKI SCHOOL

95/96 prices in francs

ESF
In Méribel and
Mottaret
Classes 6 days
5hr: 9.30-noon and
2.30-5.00
5 full days: 940
Children's classes
Ages: 5 to 12
5 full days: 740
Private lessons
1hr to 2½hr,
lunchtimes only
185 for 1hr

94/95 prices in francs
International
In Méribel and
Mottaret
Classes 6 days
4½hr: 9.30-noon and
2.45-4.45
5 full days: 840
Children's classes
Ages: 5 to 12
5 full days: 662
Private lessons
1hr to 2½hr,
lunchtimes only
185 for 1hr

95/96 prices in francs
Ski Cocktail
Classes 6 days
2hr am or 3hr pm
6 mornings: 750
Children's classes
Ages: 6 to 12
6 half days: 895
Private lessons
on request

Magic in Motion
English-speaking
school with course
maximum of 7
people.

CHILDCARE

The ESF runs P'tits
Loups kindergartens
at both Méribel and
Mottaret, with snow
gardens for children
aged 3 to 5 and
proper lessons for
older ones. Open 9.15
to 5pm.

Club Saturnin in the
tourist office building
in Méribel takes
children aged 2 to 8,
with skiing available
for those aged 3 and
ESF lessons for those
aged 4 or more.

example: 'Good tuition. Well
organised, punctual, conscientious,
friendly instructors with a good sense
of humour.' They appear to keep class
sizes down to reasonable numbers too.

As well as standard group and
private lessons, there are some
interesting alternatives. For example,
the ESF runs full-day off-piste guided
tours, and Magic in Motion will
arrange heli-skiing from Italy.

FACILITIES FOR CHILDREN
Lots of choice
Despite our fat file of reports on
Méribel, none deals first-hand with
the childcare facilities. Two observers
have remarked on instructors shouting
at tearful tots. Several chalet operators
run their own crèches, with British
nannies. Snowtime devote a floor of
one chalet (Tronchet) to theirs. Mark
Warner have a crèche in their chalet-
hotel, and the option of a nanny
service for those taking over other
chalets completely. Crystal offer a
nanny service in their chalets Martine
and Marcelle. Meriski run a crèche in
its own chalet. Ski la Vie offers a
nanny service and after-skiing care.

 # Staying there

The choice here is enormous. From
the skiing point of view, Mottaret is
hard to beat. It offers ski-in, ski-out
convenience and the quickest access
to the other valleys.

For those who prefer chalet
accommodation, a more villagey
ambience and a greater choice of
shops, bars and restaurants, the best
place would be around or just above
the village centre of Méribel. The main
thing to check is how far your
accommodation is from the piste– a
fair amount is a long hike (and the
resort is built on a hill, remember).
The local buses will be free this season
and many operators run their own
minibus services to the lifts.

HOW TO GO
Huge choice but few cheap options
Package holidays with all types of
accommodation are easy to find both
with big tour operators and smaller
Méribel specialists. There is a Club
Med, occupying the swanky new
Aspen Park hotel at Rond-Point.
Unusually, the deal here does not
include ski pass and tuition,
broadening the appeal of the Club
Med package somewhat.
Chalets Méribel has more chalets
dedicated to the British market than

any other resort. Some fair-sized chalet
companies operate only in Méribel.
The range of possibilities is vast. Here
are just a few of the options available.

Snowtime are Méribel specialists and
have the largest range of
accommodation in the resort. This
includes a well-above-average chalet-
hotel (the Parc Alpin), which benefits
from having en-suite facilities, a small
pool and an in-house crèche. Several
reporters have praised this operation,
especially the excellent food, flexible
meal times and private tables.

Simply Ski have a couple of very
luxurious chalets – including one
specially built for them which opened
last season.

Ski Scott Dunn come to the resort
for the first time this season, with two
top-of-the-range chalets.

Meriski have a good selection of
places at the top end of the market
and an old mountain refuge, isolated
after the lifts shut.

Budget-conscious Skiworld have a
selection of good-value chalets and
chalet apartments in both Méribel
and Mottaret.

Bladon Lines have a wide selection
across the price, comfort and
convenience range. The Eden is good
for those looking for a large chalet
close to the main lifts.

Crystal have a large choice, from ski-
convenient 'real' chalets, far from
town, to centrally located apartment
conversions. Ski Activity have a small
allocation of good-value, well-
positioned accommodation.

Mark Warner also have an
interesting range of comfortable
places, including a chalet hotel.

Mottaret chalets tend to be towards
the lower end of the Méribel market
but most of them are more ski-
convenient than many of the Méribel
Centre counterparts.
Hotels Méribel has some excellent
hotels with reputations for high-
quality accommodation and food. But
they don't come cheap. A lot of
renovation and repositioning went on
at the time of the Olympics, and there
are now lots of smart hotels with
health and fitness facilities.
£££££ Antares Best in town; beside
the piste at Belvedere. Ambitious
cooking. Pool, fitness room etc.
£££££ Chalet Luxurious, beautifully
furnished wooden chalet at Belvedere,
with lovely rooms and all mods cons –
outdoor pool, fitness room etc.
££££ Grand Coeur Our favourite
almost-affordable hotel in Méribel.
Just above the village centre.
Welcoming, mature building with

Selected chalets in Méribel

PACKAGES

AA Ski-Driveaway, Airtours, Alpine Action, Alpine Options Skidrive, Bladon Lines, Chalet World, Chalets 'Unlimited', Club Med, Crystal, Equity Total Ski, First Choice Ski, French Impressions, Inghams, Kings Ski Club, Lagrange, Le Shuttle Holidays, Lotus Supertravel, Made to Measure, Mark Warner, Meriski, Motours, Neilson, Over the Hill, Poles Apart, Silver Ski, Simply Ski, Ski 3000, Ski Activity, Ski Arrangements, Ski Bon, Ski Choice, Ski Experience, Ski France, Ski La Vie, Ski Les Alpes, Ski Partners, Ski Scott Dunn, Ski Valkyrie, Ski with Julia, SkiBound, Skiworld, Snowcoach Club Cantabrica, Snowtime, Stena Sealink, The Ski Company, The Ski Company Ltd, Thomson, Travelscene Ski-Drive, White Roc

Brides-les-Bains

Alpine Options Skidrive, Crystal, French Impressions, Kings Ski Club, Lagrange, Motours, Rank STS, Ski Partners, Stena Sealink, Top Deck

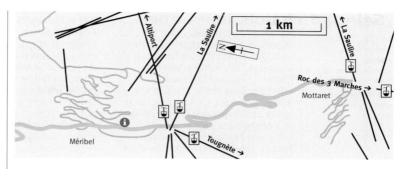

plush lounge. Magnificent food. Huge jacuzzi, sauna, etc.

££££ Altiport Modern and luxurious hotel, isolated at the foot of the Altiport lifts. Convenient for access to Courchevel, not for Val-Thorens.

££££ Mont Vallon The best hotel at Mottaret, with a reputation for good food, and excellently situated for the Trois Vallées skiing. Pool, sauna, jacuzzi, squash, fitness room, etc.

££££ Chaudanne One of the oldest Méribel hotels, but completely renovated with a new sports centre – pool, and the rest. Excellent food.

£££ Grangettes Near the lift station. Good food; friendly staff.

£££ Adray Télébar Welcoming piste-side chalet with pretty, rustic rooms, good food and popular sun terrace.

£££ Oree du Bois Just off the piste at Rond Point, convenient for skiing but not for nightlife. Old hotel offering good value for money. Sauna, steam room and jacuzzi.

££ Roc A good value B&B hotel, in the centre, with a bar-restaurant and crêperie below.

Self-catering There are a huge number of apartments and chalets to let in

both Méribel Centre and Mottaret. Take care to make sure that the place you book is conveniently situated – see above. You also need to shop around to avoid 'French boxes'.

Ski Peak act as agents for a four-bedroomed apartment, and Snowtime offer many variations, from studios to a self-catered chalet.

Inghams have apartments that are owned by 3-star hotels, and as a result benefit from having access to numerous facilities such as an open-fire lounge, swimming pool and health centre.

Bladon Lines have some good accommodation which books out very early. Their Brimbelles apartments are particularly comfortable and well positioned, close to the main lifts and the village square.

EATING OUT
Fair choice

There is a reasonable selection of restaurants, from ambitious French cuisine to fairly cheap pizza and pasta. For the best food in town, in plush surroundings, there is nothing to beat the top hotels – the Antares, Grand

GETTING THERE

Air Lyon, transfer
3½hr. Geneva,
transfer 3½hr.
Chambery, transfer
2½hr.

Rail Moûtiers (18km);
regular buses to
Méribel.

ACTIVITIES

Indoor Parc des
Sports Méribel
(skating rink,
swimming pool), Club
Forme Mottaret (spa,
sauna, solarium,
gym), library, bowling,
billiards, video club,
bridge, fitness
centres, jacuzzi,
planetarium, 2
cinemas, concert hall
Outdoor Flying
lessons and
excursions, snow-
mobiles, snow-shoe
excursions, para-
gliding, hang-gliding,
10km of cleared
paths, motor-trikes,
sleigh rides

TOURIST OFFICE

Postcode 73551
Tel 00 33 79086001
Fax 79005961

Coeur, Allodis and Chaudanne. Other
top restaurants include Chez Kiki, for
expensive but good charcoal-grilled
food. The Jardin d'Hiver has great, if
expensive, fish platters, and Les
Castors is another fine place.

But our favourite is down in Les
Allues, where the Croix Jean-Claude
serves excellent-value French cooking
in a pretty dining room.

We also like the Snowtime-run
French Connection at Altitude 1600
(where moules and ribs are
particularly good) – especially on the
nights when there's live music from
an Edith Piaf soundalike.

Back in town, try the Galette, the
Glacier and the Refuge. There's plenty
of choice for local cuisine, including
the Cave, Plantin and Cro Magnon, all
of which are particularly popular for
raclette and fondue. One reporter
recommended the Crocodile
restaurant in the Hameau at Mottaret.

APRES-SKI
Méribel has come to life

Méribel's après-ski scene used to be
dead. It has improved beyond all
recognition in the last few years. The
liveliest places are in Méribel Centre
rather than Mottaret and tend to
attract a lot of British revellers.

Immediately after skiing, the Rond
Point bar (also known as Yorkies after
the previous owner) is usually packed
and sometimes has live music. The
focal spot at 1600 is the French
Connection. Down in Centre, La
Taverne is packed with Brits straight
after skiing, as is the Pub (run by Mark
Warner). The Refuge and the
Capricorne attract more of a French
crowd. Jack's, at the Tremplin, is a
newer bar that's popular with resort
staff (possibly because they get a 50
per cent discount). Later on, live
music brings in the crowds at the Pub,
Artichaud, French Connection and
Rond Point. There is late dancing at
Les Nuits Blanche and Scott's (run by
Mark Warner). Les Saints-Pères, a cave-
style disco on the fringe of town,
attracts more of a French crowd.

In Mottaret the bars at the foot of
the pistes get packed after skiing –
especially the terraces on a sunny day.
The Rastro and DownTown are the
most popular, though reporters
inform us that Zig Zag has lower
prices. Later on, Plein Soleil sometimes
has live music, and the Rastro disco is
the main venue for late revellers.

Both villages have a cinema which
shows new films in English up to three
times a week.

FOR NON-SKIERS
Flight of fancy

Méribel is essentially a keen skier's
resort. It attracts nothing like the
number of poseurs that go to
Courchevel. But as purpose-built
French resorts go, Méribel is one of the
most attractive architecturally, and
not a bad choice for the non-skier.

Méribel Centre is the best choice to
stay for non-skiers. There is a good
public swimming pool near the lift
station. You can also take joy-rides in
the little plane which operates from
the Altiport. The cinema often shows
films in English.

The non-skier's pass covers all the
gondolas and cable-cars in the Méribel
and Courchevel valleys and makes it
very easy for non-skiers to get around
the mountain and meet skiing friends
for lunch. The buses are free.

STAYING DOWN THE VALLEY
The old village and a revived spa

If you want a quiet time, some tour
operators have places in the old village
of Les Allues down the road from the
resort and connected by the gondola
up from Brides-les-Bains. There are a
couple of bars and a good-value hotel
which serves some of the best food in
the area and has been well renovated,
La Croix Jean-Claude. Rooms are
small, however, and we've had
complaints about poor service.

Brides-les-Bains itself is an old spa
town which served as the Olympic
village at the 1992 Winter Games and
is now trying to turn itself into a
winter as well as summer resort. It's
cheap and has some simple hotels and
a casino. But reporters who've stayed
there say it's dead. And the long
gondola ride to Méribel is tedious, and
not covered by the lift pass. It also
shuts at the end of the skiing day, so
you can't enjoy Méribel's early après
ski. If you are driving, it makes a good
base for visiting other resorts as well
as the Trois Vallées, and the car would
be useful for getting to and from
Méribel or Courchevel and into the lift
system proper.

Further down the valley is the rather
dull town of Moûtiers, which has a
handful of hotels at less than half the
price of those in Méribel. It would be
fine for a couple of nights on a touring
holiday, but pretty miserable for a
whole week. The hotel Ibis is probably
the most reliable.

From Moûtiers by car you can get
reasonably quickly to not just the
Trois Vallées resorts but also to
Valmorel, La Plagne and Les Arcs.

Montgenèvre 1850m

✔ Good, convenient nursery slopes, with easy progression to longer runs

✔ Few queues on weekdays

✔ Doorstep skiing from some accommodation; a short walk from the remainder

✔ Reliable snow on local north-facing slopes

✔ Attractive old village centre tucked away off main road

✔ Great potential for car-drivers to ski large intermediate ski areas

✗ Expensive compared to neighbouring Italy

✗ Poor base for skiing the Italian Milky Way resorts

✗ Slow lifts, short runs and continual pass-checking can be irritating

✗ Main road and tatty bars reduce village charm; former also reduces convenience and family appeal

✗ Virtually nothing for non-skiers

✗ Little to challenge good skiers

Montgenèvre has a number of things going for it, but being a suitable base from which to ski the Milky Way is not one of them. The village is situated at one uninteresting end of the large ski area, a time-consuming trek from much of the best skiing, and lift pass arrangements make regular visits across the border an expensive business – you pay a daily supplement.

Unfortunately, the more central Milky Way villages have other drawbacks. Expensive Sestriere is a characterless place in a bleak setting; brash Sauze d'Oulx is not to everyone's taste; while little Sansicario and Clavière are really glorified lift base-stations with accommodation. Consequently, Montgenèvre is likely to remain a popular Milky Way base. Serious skiers should consider driving to the resort. This allows quicker access to the Milky Way's best skiing, prevents problems when the skiing links are shut because of poor snow, and simplifies day-trips to other French resorts. If you want to ski around the Milky Way a lot, pop over to Italy on day one and buy a weekly pass for the whole area.

ORIENTATION

Montgenèvre is a roadside village set in a high pass only 2km from the Italian border, relatively close to Turin. Its two facing ski areas are accessed from opposite sides of the narrow village. On each side the major lift up is a gondola. The skiing spreads east across the Italian border, via Clavière, Cesana and Sansicario to **Sauze d'Oulx** and **Sestriere** in the ski region known as the Milky Way. **Serre-Chevalier**, **Alpe-d'Huez** and **Puy-St-Vincent**, all with lift pass sharing arrangements, are easily reached by car.

 ## The resort

Perceptions of Montgenèvre as a village can vary enormously. This is understandable. At first glance it appears a dour, inhospitable place – a small, apparently purpose-built village of tatty-looking bars and restaurants set on a high, sometimes windswept and often busy, main road. The observant will also spot that the main ski lifts are inconveniently placed on the other side of the main road from the accommodation.

Appearances are, however, deceptive. Tucked away off the main road is a charming old village, complete with quaint church and friendly natives. Being covered in snow for much of the season accentuates the charm factor, as do the pleasantly wooded mountains either side of the village. Ski convenience, though far from ideal for families, is good. Other than crossing the road, there is little walking to be done in this compact village, where all accommodation is less than five minutes from a lift. Furthermore, the

underrated Chalvet area is on the same side of the road as the village. For their part, the cheap and cheerful cafés and bars add an animated atmosphere sometimes missing from French resorts. The lack of a bank is a nasty surprise. There's a limited post office exchange service and hotel rates are reported to be extortionate.

 ## The skiing

Montgenèvre's local skiing is best suited to leisurely intermediates, with lots of easy cruising on blues and greens, both above and below the tree-line. The local upper slopes are particularly bland, but the skiing gains in interest further afield. Average intermediates and better will want to ski the whole of the Milky Way (see the chapters on the Italian resorts of Sestriere and Sauze d'Oulx).

SKI FACTS

Altitude	1850m-2580m
Lifts	23
Pistes	65km
Green/Blue	48%
Red	33%
Black	19%
Artificial snow	12km

SKI SCHOOL

95/96 prices in francs

ESF
Classes 6 days
5hr: 9.15-11.45 and
14.15-16.45
6 half-days: 515
Children's classes
Ages: Up to 12
6 half-days: 485
Private lessons
Hourly or daily
165 for 1hr, for 1-2
people

THE SKI AREA
Slow going

Lifts serve north-facing slopes in the **Les Anges-Le Querelay** sector across the main road from the village and the south-facing slopes of **Le Chalvet**, which lead straight up from the village. The north-facing slopes have a high altitude link to **Cesana** and the rest of the Milky Way skiing, or you can ski a network of runs above and back down to Montgenèvre itself. The Cesana link involves a long drag-lift with a 200m walk at the top, followed by an often-unbashed mogul field – making the route a chore for less able skiers. The Chalvet area's link with the Milky Way skiing is easier but lower, via **Clavière**, just across the Italian border and down the road from Montgenèvre.

Getting to the best of the Milky Way's skiing is time-consuming. From Clavière you have to go through Cesana and up to **Sansicario** (at least six lifts) before you hit a worthwhile network of pistes; you can access either **Sestriere** (probably the best skiing of the Milky Way region) or **Sauze d'Oulx** (also good).

It's a long day out on skis to and from these areas, often made more difficult by a lack of snow in the Cesana area. Getting back to Cesana from the top of the Sansicario skiing is a single long run (actually several connecting pistes). Things slow up again after Cesana, with a three-stage chair and drag making for a long spell without skiing, before you cruise down to Clavière and get a chair-lift to the home run. You often get the

feeling you are doing a lot of travelling without much skiing. A car is helpful to speed up the journeys to and from the best skiing.

SNOW RELIABILITY
Milky Way links can be a problem

The high, north-facing local slopes have a fine snow record. The south-facing area is less reliable, particularly late-season, but like the north-facing area is supplemented by artificial snow on its main village-bound piste.

Sestriere is also snowsure, thanks to its altitude and huge snowmaking installation, but getting between the two areas on skis is difficult at times of snow shortage. The pistes either side of the connecting Cesana valley are often bereft of snow, closing the Milky Way connection.

FOR ADVANCED SKIERS
Limited, except for skiing powder

There is very little challenging piste skiing in the Montgenèvre-Clavière-Cesana sectors. Many of the runs are overgraded on the piste map, with none of the blacks being much more than tough reds in reality. There is, however, ample opportunity for off-

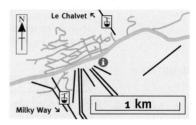

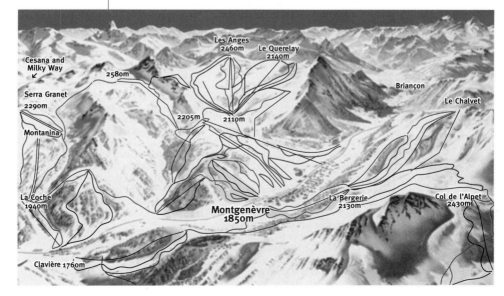

LIFT PASSES

95/96 prices in francs
Montgenèvre
Covers Montgenèvre
lifts only.
Beginners One free
drag-lift. Petit Réseau
day pass covers 7
lifts (80).
Main pass
1-day pass 120
6-day pass 630
(low season 523 –
17% off)
Senior citizens
Over 60: 6-day pass
480 (24% off)
Children
Under 12: 6-day pass
480 (24% off)
Under 5: free pass
Short-term passes
Single ascent for foot
passengers of Le
Chalvet (30). Half-day
pass from 1pm (90).
Notes 6-day pass and
over allows free days
at Alpe-d'Huez and
Les Deux-Alpes.
Extensions available
at a supplement for
Puy-St-Vincent and
Serre-Chevalier.
Reductions for
families.
Alternative passes
Montgenèvre-Mont de
la Lune (Clavière)
(adults 125 per day,
children 95, 94/95
prices). Voie Lactée
(Milky Way) covers
Montgenèvre,
Clavière, Césana,
Sansicario, Sauze
d'Oulx, Grangesises,
Borgata, Sestrières,
(adults 170 per day,
children 145, 94/95
prices).

CHILDCARE

The Halte Garderie
takes children aged
1 to 4, from 9am to
5.30. Meals are not
provided.

The ESF's
kindergarten takes
children aged 3 to 5.

piste excursions when conditions are right. There's a lonely north-east-facing bowl on the Chalvet side of Montgenèvre, served by a drag-lift from below the gondola mid-station, that is superb in good snow and has a black and red run too, with a chair to bring you back up. On the opposite side, both the runs from the top drag-lift on the Franco-Italian border can be fun. Unfortunately, there is no returning lift from the Italian side to allow repeated skiing in that direction (you get back to Montgenèvre via lower lifts, just above Clavière). The open section between Montanina and Sagna Longa on the Italian side is another good powder area. Drivers should visit Sestriere for the best challenging skiing.

FOR INTERMEDIATE SKIERS
Plenty of cruising terrain
The overgraded blacks are just right for adventurous intermediates, though none holds the interest for very long. The pleasantly narrow tree-lined runs down to Clavière from Plan del Sol, the steepest of the routes down in the Chalvet sector (including the lonely bowl mentioned for advanced skiers above), and the Montquitaine-Clavière piste (by the chair linking Clavière with Montgenèvre) are all fine in small doses. The Sagna Longa blacks are particularly uninteresting. Tours to the rest of the Milky Way are very rewarding, offering a real sensation of getting around the mountains on skis.

Average intermediates will enjoy many of the red runs, though most are rather short. The longest ones are down from the top of the Chalvet sector and from the Franco-Italian border at the top of the ski area opposite.

Skiing to Cesana via the lovely sweeping red starting at the top of the Coche drag and skiing home from La Coche via Plan del Sol is easier than the red gradings suggest, and these can be tackled by less adventurous intermediates, who also have a wealth of cruising terrain high up at the top of the north-facing Anges and Querelay slopes above Montgenèvre. These are served by several upper lifts, but you also have the option of continuing all the way down to the village. These long, gentle slopes are every bit as flattering as the famous motorways of Courchevel and Cervinia.

Further afield, skiing down to Clavière from the top of the Coche drags on the Italian border is a beautifully gentle cruise.

FOR BEGINNERS
Excellent for novices and improvers
There is a fine selection of convenient nursery slopes with reliable snow at the foot of the north-facing area. Progression to longer runs could not be easier, with a very easy green starting at Les Anges (2460m) and finishing at the roadside far below.

FOR CROSS-COUNTRY
Having a car widens horizons
Montgenèvre is the best of the Milky Way resorts for cross-country enthusiasts, but it's useful to have a car. There are just two trails locally, totalling 20km, but a further 30km of track starts 8km away in the Clarée valley. One village trail is an easy loop that takes you parallel to the road, through the golf course, to the border post just outside Clavière; the other is a steeper route that climbs through woods in the opposite direction.

QUEUES
No problems most of the time
The ski area is wonderfully uncrowded during weekdays, when surrounding resorts have snow. At weekends and when nearby Bardonecchia is snowless, some lifts become oversubscribed. However, the improved links between Sauze d'Oulx and the impressive artificial snow of Sestriere now make bussing in from the former less likely.

MOUNTAIN RESTAURANTS
Head for Italy
These are in very short supply. Most local area skiers travel back to the village for lunch. The Ca del Sol café-bar does a good pizza. Milky Way skiers have several nice spots in Italy. Tucked away in the trees at Sagna Longa is the excellent Lo Scoiattola – atmospheric, friendly, cheap, and great pasta and antipasta.

SKI SCHOOL
Very varied reports
Comments on the school vary greatly, from very good to very poor. They tend to push pupils hard, which suits some but not others. One reporter was complimentary about the instructors' enthusiasm for the mountains.

FACILITIES FOR CHILDREN
Lack of English likely to be problem
The intrusive main road apart, Montgenèvre would seem a fine family resort. The only report we've had on the ski school's children's classes was complimentary of both class size and spoken English.

GETTING THERE

Air Turin, transfer 2hr. Grenoble, transfer 3hr. Lyon, transfer 4½hr.

Rail Briançon (10km) or Oulx (17km); 3 or 4 buses per day from station.

PACKAGES

Equity Total Ski, First Choice Ski, Lagrange, Made to Measure, Rank STS, Ski Ardmore, Ski Ça Va, SkiBound, Thomson

Cesana Torinese PGL Ski Europe, SkiBound

Clavière Equity Total Ski, Neilson, PGL Ski Europe, SkiBound

ACTIVITIES

Indoor Library, cinema
Outdoor Natural skating rink, curling, hang-gliding, para-gliding, snow-scooters, sledge runs

TOURIST OFFICE

Postcode 05100
Tel 00 33 92219022
Fax 92219245

 # Staying there

There are hotels, chalets and apartments available, all of which are cheap and cheerful places. Luxury-lovers should not stay here. Location is unimportant, as Montgenèvre is such a small place.

HOW TO GO
Limited choice
Tour operators concentrate their operation on catered chalets, though a few apartments are also available and one or two operators now package hotels as well.
Chalets Ski Ça Va have arguably the best places in town, with a choice between a wooden hut and an old stone house, the latter in the attractive old village centre. The basic Bois de Sestriere and Boom chalets (Thomson) are popular for providing good value, ski-convenient accommodation, but the former is not suitable for light sleepers. Reporters state that it has been cheaply converted, and its thin walls fail to keep out early morning noise from the main road on which it is positioned. The disco attached to Boom has closed down – presumably all the complaints about inadequate sound-proofing were finally heard above the racket. First Choice Ski also have a couple of cheap and cheerful places.
Hotels There are a handful of simple places, even the priciest of them offering good value.
££ Valérie Rustic old 3-star in the village centre.
££ Napoléon 3-star on the roadside.
£ Chalet des Sport About the cheapest hotel rooms in the Alps.
£ Hotel La Grange Another cheap and cheerful place with tiny rooms and basic food.
Self-catering Résidences La Ferme d'Augustin are simple, ski-to-the-door apartments on the fringes of the main north-facing slopes, five minutes' walk (across the piste) from town.

EATING OUT
Cheap and cheerful
There are a dozen places to choose from, mostly pizzerias. Reporters have recommended the Ca del Sol and the

Tourments. A reasonable pizza can be had in the Estable, Napoli or Transalpin. Chez Pierrot and the Jamy are the classiest places in town – and arguably the only ones to have much of an authentic French feel. The 3-star Napoleon is the only hotel with a restaurant open to non-residents, but it's yet another pizzeria! A trip over the border to Clavière is well worthwhile – the cheaper prices will pay for the taxi fare – and the Pian Del Sole hotel is a pleasant place to sample 'real' Italian food.

APRES-SKI
Mainly bars, but fun
Although the range is limited, the mainly like-minded 20- to 35-year-old clientele generate quite an atmosphere in a couple of bars. Le Graal is a friendly, unsophisticated place with satellite TV and occasional live entertainment; the Ca del Sol bar is a cosy old place with an open fire and a twice-weekly guitarist who sings slightly bawdy songs. Stevie Nick's is the better of the two discos, and livens up quite well at weekends. Playboy is smaller but a lively nightclub. The Refuge and the Jamy are the focal café-bars at tea-time.

FOR NON-SKIERS
Very limited
There is very little to do. There is a weekly market and you can walk along the cross-country routes, but the main attraction is a bus-trip to the beautiful old town of Briançon.

STAYING IN OTHER RESORTS
Only for the dedicated skier
Cesana and Clavière are small, not particularly attractive villages with little in the way of resort infrastructure, and Cesana has the disadvantage of being a 15-minute walk from its lifts. Clavière has been introduced onto the 'Learn to ski' tour operator market by Neilson. Its nursery slope is small and steep but nicely uncrowded and snow-reliable, and there are plenty of longer runs suitable for progression. Both resorts are for dedicated intermediates who want to make the most of the Milky Way skiing and want a quiet time, without much après-ski.

Morzine 1000m

✔ Part of the vast Portes du Soleil lift network

✔ Larger local ski area than other Portes du Soleil resorts

✔ Good nightlife by French standards

✔ Quite attractive old village – a stark contrast to Avoriaz

✔ One of the easiest drives from the Channel (a car is very useful here)

✔ Few queues locally (but see minus points)

✘ Avoriaz queues limit access to Portes du Soleil circuit

✘ Bus-ride or long walk to lifts from much accommodation

✘ Very poor recent snow record, with few snowmakers

✘ Low altitude or very inconvenient nursery slopes

✘ Very little for good skiers if Avoriaz Prodains runs are closed

✘ Weekend crowds

Morzine is a long-established French resort, popular for its easy road access and gentle tree-filled ski area, where children do not get lost and bad weather rarely causes problems. But it seems that most British visitors are not families in search of a quiet time so much as keen skiers wanting to 'do' the Portes du Soleil. Some are graduating from Austria's smaller but similarly friendly ski areas, while others come in order to compare the Portes du Soleil with the Trois Vallées. For such skiers, the main drawback to staying in Morzine is the strong possibility of poor local snow conditions, and the frustration involved in getting to, and through, queue-prone Avoriaz.

Such problems can, however, be avoided by taking a car. A little-used gondola awaits at Ardent, a short drive from Morzine; from there you can ski the circuit clockwise via Châtel, missing out Avoriaz. There are buses, but not frequent ones. If snow is poor, Avoriaz is normally the first thought – but it's everyone else's first thought too. If you have a car, you have the alternative of visiting nearby Flaine, a resort far better than Avoriaz at coping with crowds looking for snow. Morzine is one of the easiest ski resorts to drive to from the Channel – there is a motorway from Calais to nearby Cluses.

ORIENTATION

Morzine is a large year-round resort village that sprawls on both sides of a river and on several levels. Its local skiing is shared with higher, smaller Les Gets. Lifts go up from the village into the Pléney sector, and from La Grangette, 2km from the centre, into the Nyon sector. The area is part of the Portes du Soleil lift-pass region, but is only tenuously linked to the main circuit: a gondola from the opposite side of the resort is the first in a series of lifts towards **Avoriaz**, which is on the main circuit along with **Châtel**, **Morgins** and **Champéry**. Car outings to **Flaine**, **Chamonix** and even **Courmayeur** are also feasible.

 ## The resort

Morzine is a large, traditional, towny mountain resort which sprawls amorphously on both sides of a river gorge and on several levels. Under a blanket of snow, its chalet-style buildings look charming, and in spring the village quickly takes on a spruce appearance. But at this altitude in France, the blanket of snow often gives way to slush and mud, which is less appealing. Perhaps because the French share our view that the resort suits car drivers, there are lots of them, and the resort suffers.

At the foot of this road, next to the river, is the old centre of Morzine, but most resort amenities are clustered up the hill around the Le Pléney lifts.

Accommodation is widely scattered, and a good bus service operates on six routes around the town, giving access to outlying lifts (though not linking them very cleverly).

Morzine is essentially a family resort. Consequently village ambience tends to be fairly subdued.

 ## The skiing

The local skiing, like that of the main Portes du Soleil area, suits intermediates well, with excellent slopes for beginners and near-beginners too.

THE SKI AREA
No need to go far afield

Morzine may not be an ideal base for skiing the Portes du Soleil circuit, but it has an excellent local ski area.

A cable-car and parallel gondola rise from the edge of central Morzine to **Le Pléney**, where numerous routes return to the valley, including a run down to Les Fys – a quiet junction of chairs which access **Nyon** and, in the opposite direction, the ridge separating the Morzine from the **Les Gets** skiing. Nyon is also accessed by cable-car, situated a bus-ride out of Morzine. The Nyon sector is also connected to the skiing of Les Gets higher up the valley that separates the two, with a lift up from Le Grand Pré to Le Ranfolly.

SKI FACTS

Altitude	975m-2020m
Lifts	224
Pistes	650km
Green/Blue	54%
Red	33%
Black	13%
Artificial snow	11km

SKI SCHOOL

95/96 prices in francs

ESF

Classes 6 days
5hr: 9.30-noon and
2.30-5pm; 2½hr: am
or pm
6 half-days: 520
Children's classes
Ages: Under 12
6 full days including
lunch: 1210
Private lessons
Hourly
165 for 1 to 2 people

The Nyon sector has two peaks – Pointe de Nyon and Chamossière – accessible from Nyon and Le Grand Pré respectively.

Connections between Pléney and Nyon are not easy for the uninitiated, owing to an inaccurate piste map and poor piste directions. Returning from Les Gets has to be via Le Ranfolly, from where you can ski home to Morzine without using a lift, via a path to central Morzine.

Beyond Les Gets is another small sector, chiefly of interest to Les Gets residents, on the front and back of Mont Chéry. The walk across the resort from the bottom of the Chavannes sector is a bearable one.

A third ski area starts at **Super Morzine**, accessed from town by gondola. A series of pistes and lifts transport skiers to Avoriaz. This section is very much an access route, used mainly by Morzine clientele moving to and from Avoriaz in the morning and afternoon respectively. The alternative is a bus-ride or short drive to Les Prodains, from where you can get a cable-car to Avoriaz or a chair-lift into the **Hauts Forts** skiing above it.

By bus or car you can also move swiftly to Ardent, from where a gondola accesses **Les Marmottes**. From here you can ski towards Châtel or get a lift up to Avoriaz.

SNOW RELIABILITY
Very poor

Morzine has a very low average ski height, and when snow disappears from the valley, both of the main ski areas become very small and unconnected. At such times, the queues to and from Avoriaz are long. Snowmakers have at last been introduced to the area – most noticeably on the two main runs to the valley from Nyon – but many more are needed.

FOR ADVANCED SKIERS
Limited; better than many in area

The run down from Pointe de Nyon is challenging, but it is the cable-car at Les Prodains which is the place to head for, taking you up to Avoriaz. The Hauts Forts black runs, including the World Cup downhill course, are excellent. Unfortunately, these runs are often closed due to lack of snow. The far end of the Chamossière section occasionally has some good off-piste skiing.

FOR INTERMEDIATE SKIERS
Something for everyone

Good intermediates will enjoy the challenging blacks down from the Chamossière and Pointe de Nyon high points. The former also accesses a fine long red to Blanchots. Mont Chéry – remote from Morzine on the far side

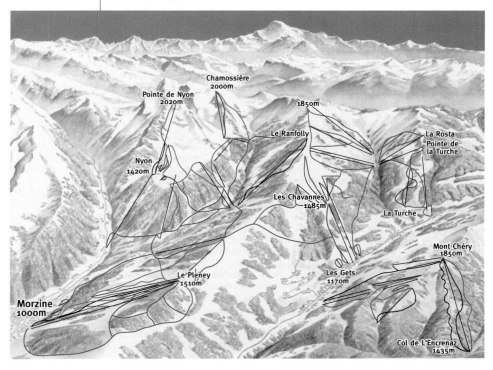

of Les Gets – has some fine steepish runs which are worth skiing over to. Moderate skiers have a great number of runs to choose from, though most are rather short.

Le Ranfolly accesses a series of moderate runs on the Les Gets side of the ridge, and a nice piste back to Le Grand Pré. Le Pléney has a compact network of pistes that are ideal for groups with mixed abilities: mainly moderate intermediate runs, but with some easier alternatives for the timid, and a single challenging route for the aggressive skier. Nyon's skiing is rather bitty for those not up to at least Chamossière runs.

Timid skiers have plenty of options on Le Pléney, including a snow-gun-covered cruise from the summit back to the main lift station. Skiing from Le Ranfolly to Le Grand Pré is another nice run. And skiing down to Les Gets from Le Pléney is particularly easy when conditions allow (the run is south-facing).

FOR BEGINNERS
Good for novices and improvers
The village nursery slopes are quite good: wide, flat and convenient, and benefiting from snow guns. Fast learners have the inconvenience that the slightly longer, steeper runs are over at Nyon. However, precocious novices also have the option of easy pistes around Le Pléney. Near-beginners can ski over to Les Gets via Le Pléney, and return via Le Ranfolly. The skiing at Les Gets suits near-beginners well.

FOR CROSS-COUNTRY
Good variety
There is a wide variety of cross-country trails, not all at valley level. The best section is in the pretty Vallée de la Manche beside the Nyon mountain. The Pléney-Chavannes loop is pleasant and relatively snow-reliable. A network of trails runs between Super-Morzine and Avoriaz, and around Montriond lake.

QUEUES
Few problems when snow is good
Queues are not a problem in the local area. The Nyon cable-car and Belvédère drag (Le Pléney) are weekend bottlenecks. Queues to and from Avoriaz are much improved in recent times, but are still bad when snow is in short supply. Bottlenecks in the Avoriaz sector make skiing the Portes du Soleil circuit a rushed affair for those without a car.

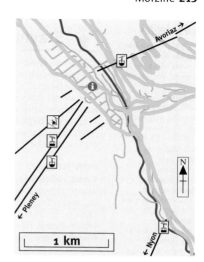

1 km

MOUNTAIN RESTAURANTS
Within reach of some good huts
The nice little place at the foot of the d'Atray chair is perhaps the best of the local huts. The Chavannes self-service is good for lunch in the Les Gets area. Les Lindarets, Les Marmottes and Plaine Dranse are not too far and have some of the best restaurants in the whole Portes du Soleil. The restaurant at the top of the Zore chair, above Super-Morzine, is good, but most skiers pass it by in their haste to get to or from Avoriaz.

SKI SCHOOL
Children's classes get good reports
Most British visitors to Morzine appear to be intent on skiing the Portes du Soleil rather then taking tuition, and consequently we lack feedback on adult schools. The ESF children's classes have a good reputation. Morzine also boasts the British Alpine Ski School, where you are guaranteed tuition in English. Reports please.

FACILITIES FOR CHILDREN
Stick to Ski Esprit
We have always been quite impressed by the facilities of the Outa crèche, but a reporter who took his two-year-old there last January tells of unfriendly staff, little spoken English and a worrying staffing ratio of one to seven children. Ski Esprit's facilities for children here are comprehensive, with three in-chalet crèches, an afternoon Snow Club for children attending morning ski school and their own Ski Sprites tuition scheme, using specially contracted instructors. But one reporter complains that sometimes less than half the morning lesson was spent on the slopes.

LIFT PASSES

95/96 prices in francs

Portes du Soleil
Covers all lifts in 12 resorts, and shuttle buses.

Beginners Limited area passes in Avoriaz, only half-day or day passes available for Morzine-Les Gets area.

Main pass
1-day pass 195
6-day pass 885

Senior citizens
Over 60: 6-day pass 584 (34% off)

Children
Under 16: 6-day pass 584 (34% off)
Under 5: free pass

Short-term passes
Half-day passes available for the Portes de Soleil (adult 136), Avoriaz only (adult 115, 94/95 price) and Pléney-Nyon-Les Gets only (adult 105).

Notes Discounts for groups of 13 or more and holders of the Carte Neige.

Alternative passes
The Pléney-Nyon-Les Gets pass covers 85 lifts in the vicinity of Morzine and Les Gets (6 days 695 for adults, 522 for children, 94/95 prices); 6-day pass including 5 days in Pléney-Nyon-Les Gets and 1 day in Portes du Soleil (730 adults, 550 children).

CHILDCARE

The Halte Garderie l'Outa (50792600) takes children aged 2 months to 4 years, from 8.30 to 6pm. From age 3 they can have one-hour introductory ski lessons. The Centre de Loisirs takes children aged 4 to 12, ferrying them to and from ESF lessons.

 # Staying there

As the extensive network of bus routes implies, Morzine is a town where getting from A to B can be tricky. It is well worth making sure that your accommodation is near the lifts that you expect to be using, which for most visitors means the gondola and cable-car to Le Pléney.

HOW TO GO
Good-value hotels and chalets
The tour operator market concentrates on cheap and cheerful hotels and chalets. Independent travellers have a wider choice, notably of apartments.

Chalets There's a wide choice, with something to suit all tastes. Position varies enormously: you can be in the centre of town or on the slopes with skiing to the door; many are on the outskirts, however, without either convenience.

The Ski Company Ltd have two chalets. One is a delightful 200-year-old farmhouse in Essert-Romand, a hamlet just outside Morzine, well placed for starting the day at Ardent, using the operator's minibus. It featured in Tatler's World's Top 50 Villas to Rent. The other, not far away on the outskirts of Morzine, is a modern Scandinavian-style affair.

Morzine specialists Ski Moose have one of the best selections, most convenient for the Pleney lifts and the town centre; one is close to the Super Morzine gondola. Trail Alpine have the ultimate place for Portes du Soleil ski convenience, at the Prodains cable-car station. A minibus provides access to Morzine.

Childcare specialists Ski Esprit have in-house crèches in three chalets. The central Gourmets – formerly a 1-star hotel – is arguably the best positioned. The Ski Chamois chalet-hotel is cheaper, but it's up the mountain at the top of the Nyon cable-car – convenient for the skiing but very isolated. However, its DIY après-ski and value for money make it popular with reporters.

Thomson have a basic, badly positioned place, but it's cheap and could suit those with a car. Crystal's Coralie is perhaps the best chalet available through a big operator.

Hotels The range of hotel accommodation is wider than it at first appears – the handful of 3-star hotels includes some quite smooth ones. But the core of the resort is its modest accommodation – dozens of 2-stars and quite a lot of 1-stars. If there

is a resort with more hotels in the Logis de France group (14 at the last count), we have yet to find it.

££££ Dahu Best in town: upmarket 3-star, complete with comfortable, elegant public areas and good restaurant and pool complex. Some distance from all lifts and public buses except the Ardent route, but with private shuttle. Pool.

££££ Airelles Central 3-star close to Pléney lifts and both Prodains and Nyon bus routes. Good pool.

££££ Champs Fleuris Comfortable 3-star right next to Pléney lifts. Pool.

£££ Tremplin Slightly simpler, but just as close to the lifts.

£££ Bergerie Rustic, old-fashioned chalet with a few rooms and many more studios, in centre.

££ Côtes Simple, upwardly mobile 2-star, with more studios than rooms. Recently installed pool compensates for poor position on the edge of town.

££ Equipe One of the better 2-stars, superbly placed next to the Pléney lift.

Self-catering The Eterlou apartments are well equipped and good value but their poor position makes them best suited to self-drivers. The Télémark apartments offer high quality accommodation, and are close to the Super-Morzine gondola.

EATING OUT
A fine choice across the price range
Morzine is a gourmet's resort. The expensive La Chamade has high-quality French cuisine, Café Chaud is an atmospheric place that does good fondue, Les Airelles has a fine restaurant known for its hot buffets and is open to non-residents, and Le Dahu also has good food. L'Etale and Le Varnay are worth visiting.

APRES-SKI
One of the livelier French resorts
Nightlife is good by French standards, though far from wild. Dixie's and Le Bowling are two of the most animated bars. The former has occasional live music, Eurosport/MTV and Murphy's on tap, for skiers who are 'not bitter' about all the snow melting. Boppers head for Opéra Rock or Laury's and teenagers of varying ages for Le Wallington, a ten-pin bowling alley-cum-disco-cum-pool hall-cum-bar. There are also two cinemas.

FOR NON-SKIERS
Quite good; excursions possible
There is a fine sports centre with a large ice rink and, although there is no public pool in Morzine, Les Gets has one and some of the hotels have their

GETTING THERE

Air Geneva, transfer
1½hr. Lyon, transfer
3½hr.

Rail Cluses or Thonon
(30km); regular bus
connections to resort.

PACKAGES

APS Chalets, Chalets
'Unlimited', Crystal,
First Choice Ski,
Lagrange, Le Shuttle
Holidays, Made to
Measure, Neilson, Ski
Chamois, Ski Choice,
Ski Esprit, Ski France,
Ski Moose Chalet Co,
Ski Valkyrie, Ski
Weekend, SkiBound,
The Ski Company Ltd,
Thomson, Trail Alpine,
White Roc

Essert-Romand Made
to Measure, The Ski
Company Ltd

Les Gets AGD Travel,
Chalets 'Unlimited',
Fantiski, Made to
Measure, Ski Famille,
Ski Hillwood, Ski
Total, Sloping Off

ACTIVITIES

Indoor Skating,
curling, bowling,
cinemas, sauna,
massage, gym, table
tennis, fitness track,
swimming pool
Outdoor Horse-riding,
sleigh rides, para-
gliding, snow-shoe
classes, artificial
climbing wall, tennis

TOURIST OFFICE

Postcode 74110
Tel 00 33 50790345
Fax 50790348

own. Buses runs to Thonon, which is a useful shopping excursion, and car owners can drive to Geneva, Annecy or Montreux. There are lots of very pretty walks, and other amenities include horse-drawn sleigh rides, horse-riding, saunas and parapenting.

Les Gets 1170m

Les Gets is not a sensible base for skiing the Portes du Soleil circuit, but its local ski area has a far larger, denser array of pistes than any of the resorts on the circuit, and is perfectly adequate for many intermediates. The good children's facilities, pleasant trees, French ambience, ski convenience, nice village restaurants, fine nursery slopes and reasonable prices make Les Gets an excellent choice for families and others looking for a civilised, atmospheric ski holiday venue. Weekend crowds are a drawback, but lack of snow is a more serious one. Snowmakers would greatly improve the appeal of Les Gets.

Les Gets is a little old village of mainly traditional chalet buildings, 6km from its much larger neighbour, Morzine. Although the village has a scattered appearance, most of the facilities are conveniently close to the main lift station. Les Gets is on a through road (Cluses-Morzine to Avoriaz), but it does not intrude too much, by-passing most of the village. There is a fair amount of nightlife but most places are quiet except at weekends. The atmosphere becomes more chic at weekends.

As well as the ski area shared with Morzine, Les Gets has skiing on Mont Chéry, on the other side of the village, accessed by gondola and parallel chair from the edge of the resort, with a further chair leading to the summit. Much of this section gets too much sun, but at least most of it is reasonably high. Beyond Mont Chéry summit is Les Gets' steepest skiing, down the back of the mountain. These are 'yo-yo' runs served by a solitary returning chair.

The quite good village nursery slopes are convenient for most accommodation, but Chavannes has better and more snow-reliable ones. Progression to pistes is simple, with a very easy run between Chavannes and the resort, and a couple of nicely meandering routes from La Rosta. Easy pistes between Le Ranfolly and Les Chavannes, and down to La Turche, mean precocious beginners can get a lot of mileage in without getting any lifts in a downward direction.

Keen cross-country skiers would be better off in Morzine, which has an excellent array of trails. But Les Gets has a good variety of loops on Mont Chéry and Les Chavannes – a total of 46km.

There are three ski schools, reports of which have been generally favourable. Group sizes can be large, though Ecole de Ski Plus guarantee classes of no more than nine. Beginners should shop around if conditions are less than perfect, looking for lessons at Chavannes.

The Ski Alpin pass covers all Les Gets, Nyon and Pleney lifts. The local ticket saves approximately £20 on the cost of a Portes du Soleil pass, and is well worth considering for moderate or timid skiers if snow conditions are good.

Many visitors stay in private chalets, quite a few of which are now on the British market in catered form. Most are pleasant, comfortable no-frills places. There are surprisingly few hotel beds and apartments available.

All the hotels are 3-star and below, mostly cheap and cheerful old 2-stars. The Crychar is one of the best hotels in town, at the foot of the slopes, 100m from central Les Gets. The Ours Blanc is also comfortable and central, and known for its good food. The Labrador, of similar standard, is closer to the edge of town, though still an easy walk from the Chavannes chair.

The Praz Du Soleil and Bouillandire are simple, but pleasant good-value apartments five minutes from the main lifts.

After skiing, the hotel Bellevue at the bottom of the slopes is the natural rendezvous point. The English-run Prings and Irish-run Irlandaise also attract some trade.

Les Gets has a surprisingly wide variety of restaurants. Most of the hotels have worthwhile restaurants, including the Alpages, which does good fondues. The Tirol is perhaps the best of the pizza places. The Schuss and the Stade are others. The Vieux Chene is a very popular rustic place doing Savoyarde specialities. The Flambeau and Tourbillon are also recommended. El Rapido is a Mexican cantina, of all things!

Nightlife is quiet, particularly on weekdays. The Irlandaise and Prings bars can get quite lively. Magnetic Theatre is a very style-conscious piano bar, sometimes with other live music. The Igloos is a small disco, popular with the locals. The Jeckyll & Hyde is a less crowded alternative. Tour ops organise evening events, including bowling at the good two-lane alley.

SKI TOTAL

helped us to compile the eating out and après-ski sections in Les Gets. Our thanks to them.

Morzine is a better choice for non skiers, although Les Gets has a good fitness centre with swimming, saunas, massage, weights and so on, and an artificial ice rink. Outings to Geneva, Lausanne and Montreux are possible.

There is a non-ski nursery for children aged 3 months to 2 years, and two ski-kindergartens. The 'Ile des Enfants', run by the Ski Espace school, is reputedly the better of the two, and is open from 8am to 6pm, taking children from 3 years old. The ESF-run Club Fantaski has been criticised for inattentive supervision and having a roadside slope used by other skiers.

Get your money back
by booking through Ski Solutions

You can reclaim the price of Where to Ski when you book a 1995/96-season skiing holiday. All you have to do is book the holiday through the specialist ski travel agency Ski Solutions. The price of the book will be knocked off your final payment.

Ski Solutions are Britain's longest-established and most respected ski travel agency. You can buy whatever kind of holiday you want through them, so you're not losing out on breadth of choice. Ski Solutions sell the complete range of package holidays offered by all the bonded tour operators in Britain, ranging from the smallest one-resort chalet operators (who otherwise sell directly by mail) to the mass-market operators who mainly sell through the brochure racks of high-street travel agents. Ski Solutions can also tailor-make holidays for independent-minded skiers who want to go their own way – whether it's a long weekend in Chamonix or an 18-day tour of the best half-dozen resorts in the Rockies.

Where to Ski has built strong links with Ski Solutions over the last two or three years, sharing staff and involving Ski Solutions clients in reporting on resorts. So we're delighted that we have been able to put together this special offer for readers.

Claiming your refund is easy. At the back of the book is a page which comprises two vouchers. When you make your definite booking, tell Ski Solutions that you want to claim a refund. Cut out the vouchers and send one to Ski Solutions and one to Where to Ski (the addresses are on the vouchers). That's all there is to it. When your final invoice arrives, it will show a refund of the price of the book.

La Plagne 1800–2100m

✔ Extensive ski area, best suited to intermediates

✔ Excellent nursery slopes

✔ High snowsure skiing, including a glacier area

✔ High, purpose-built resort units are convenient for skiing, and some are not unpleasant

✔ Attractive, traditional-style villages lower down share the skiing

✔ Wooded runs of lower resorts good for poor-weather skiing

✔ Good cross-country trails

✘ Few sustained challenging runs

✘ Lower villages often suffer from poor snow conditions

✘ Unattractive architecture in some of the higher resort units, which are now getting tatty as well

✘ Some long queues during peak season

✘ Not much green-run skiing for nervous beginners to go on to

✘ Nightlife very limited

✘ A couple of persistent lift bottlenecks in the high resorts

La Plagne has one of the biggest areas of consistently intermediate skiing around. And above the main purpose-built resorts it is high, snowsure skiing. There's mile after mile of motorway cruising, usually with some more difficult options. There are also pretty runs down through the trees to traditional and quasi-traditional connected villages. These are, in general, more attractive but less convenient for the skiing than the seven separate purpose-built centres higher up. Taken as a whole, La Plagne has considerable attractions for all skiers except those after the steepest pistes.

 ## The resort

La Plagne consists of no fewer than 11 separate 'villages'; seven are purpose-built at altitude on or above the tree-line and linked by road, lifts and pistes; the other four are widely spaced in the valleys below.

Even the resorts built up the mountain vary considerably in style and character. The first to be built, in the 1960s, was Plagne Centre, at around 2000m – still the focal point for shops and après-ski. Typical of its time, it consists of big ugly blocks and dark, depressing passageways which house the shops, bars and restaurants.

Above it, and linked by cable-car, is the even more obtrusive Aime la Plagne – a single great apartment block in the shape of a giant chalet.

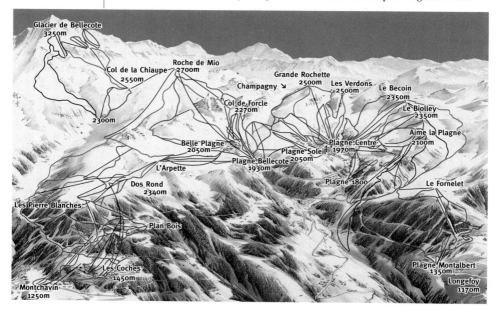

ORIENTATION

La Plagne is a big and complex ski area containing 11 identifiable resorts and seven interlinked sectors of skiing. La Plagne itself consists of seven resort units dotted around a high, fragmented bowl, above the tree-line. On lower wooded slopes outside this bowl are four satellite villages – **Champagny-en-Vanoise** to the south, Montalbert to the west, Montchavin and Les Coches to the north.

Day-trips to **Les Arcs** are easy, to **Val-d'Isère**, **Tignes** or the **Trois Vallées** more time-consuming.

SKI FACTS

Altitude	1250m-3250m
Lifts	113
Pistes	210km
Green/Blue	66%
Red	28%
Black	6%
Artificial snow	5km

Below these two, and somewhat out of the way, is Plagne 1800, a more tasteful chalet-style development.

A short walk above Plagne Centre is the newest incarnation of La Plagne, Plagne Soleil, still as yet small but with its own shops and very convenient for the slopes.

Plagne Villages is an attractive collection of small-scale apartment and chalet developments built in traditional Savoyard style and around 50m higher than Plagne Centre. Again, it is very convenient for skiing.

The large apartment buildings of Plagne Bellecôte, on the other hand, are built an inexplicably awkward walk below the local lifts. Above it is Belle Plagne – as its name suggests, built in a pleasing style, with something of the Disneyesque neo-Savoyard look of Valmorel.

Accommodation in all these developments on the mountain is largely self-catering, and popular with French families, who pack the resort during peak season weeks. In low-season it can be eerily empty. There are some hotels in Plagne Centre.

Then there are the lower resorts in the valleys – the old villages of Montchavin and Champagny, on opposite sides of the ski area, and the newly developed villages of Les Coches (near Montchavin) and Montalbert. For a description of each, see the end of this chapter.

⛷ The skiing

La Plagne is an ideal resort for intermediate skiers of all descriptions. There are wide motorways for early intermediates and long excursions for the more adventurous. Beginners are well catered for by good ski schools that operate on easy, accessible nursery slopes.

THE SKI AREA
Multi-centred; can be confusing
La Plagne boasts 210km of pistes over a wide terrain that can be broken down into seven distinct but inter-linked sectors. From Plagne Centre you can take a lift up to **Biolley,** from where you can ski back to Centre, to Aime la Plagne or down gentle runs to **Montalbert**, from which you ride several successive lifts back up. But the main lift out of Plagne Centre leads up to **Grande Rochette**. From here there are good sweeping runs back and an easier one over to Plagne Bellecôte, or you can drop over the back into the predominantly south-facing

Champagny skiing (from which a lift arrives back up at Grande Rochette and another brings you out much further east). From the Champagny sector there are great views over to Courchevel, across the valley.

From Plagne Bellecôte and Belle Plagne, the main gondola heads up to **Roche de Mio**, from where runs spread out in all directions. You can ski back down towards La Plagne proper, or down towards Champagny in one direction and **Montchavin** in the other. Montchavin can also be reached by taking a chair from Plagne Bellecôte. If you change gondolas at Roche de Mio, you go down to the mid-station at Col de la Chiaupe (there's no skiing down to it in that direction) then up again to the **Bellecôte glacier**. The easy glacier skiing here is open only in summer, but the gondola gives access to some of the steepest winter skiing in the area. You have to catch the gondola at the mid-station to get back up to Roche de Mio.

SNOW RELIABILITY
Good except in low-lying villages
In general, the bulk of La Plagne's skiing is very snowsure, with much of it being between 2000m and 2700m on the largely north-facing open slopes above the purpose-built centres. The Bellecôte glacier drags are normally shut in winter.

The runs down to the valley resorts can cause more problems, and you may have to take the lifts home at times. This is particularly true of the Champagny sector, where the two home runs are both south-facing and quickly lose their snow in warm weather. The runs down to Les Coches and Montchavin are north-facing and now have artificial snow.

FOR ADVANCED SKIERS
A few good blacks and off-piste
There are two exceptional black runs leading down from the Bellecôte glacier, both of which take you away from the lift system and are beautiful long runs with a vertical drop of over 1000m. A chair-lift takes you back to the mid-station of the glacier gondola. The other long black run is the Emile Allais down from above Aime la Plagne through the forest, finishing at 1400m, with a couple of drag-lifts taking you back up. This is surprisingly little-skied, north-facing and very enjoyable in good snow. But it's not seriously steep: the shorter Coqs and and Morbleu runs in the same sector are much more so.

LIFT PASSES

La Plagne
Covers all lifts in
La Plagne and
Champagny-en-
Vanoise.
Beginners Free baby-
lift in each centre.
Main pass
1-day pass 209
6-day pass 960
(low season 720 –
25% off)
Senior citizens
Over 60: 6-day pass
720 (25% off)
Children
Under 16: 6-day pass
720 (25% off)
Under 7: free pass
Short-term passes
Half-day pass (153).
Single ascent on
inter-area links.
Notes 6-day pass and
over covers Les Arcs
for duration of pass,
and one day each in
Tignes-Val d'Isère, the
Three Valleys,
Pralognan-la-Vanoise
and Les Saisies.
Reductions for
groups.
Alternative passes
Limited passes
available in the main
areas (La Plagne,
Champagny,
Montchavin).
'Discovery' passes in
each area.

The long, sweeping Mont de la Guerre red run, with a 1250m vertical drop down from Grande Rochette-Les Verdons to Champagny, is also a beautiful run in good snow – a rare event because of its orientation.

There are other good long reds to cruise around on. But good skiers will get the best out of La Plagne if they hire a guide and explore the vast off-piste potential. There are very popular off-piste variants from the Bellecôte glacier black run down to the restaurant at Les Bauches (a drop of over 1400m), from where you can ride chairs back to the main skiing above Les Pierres Blanches, or cruise down to Montchavin. You can also head down off-piste to Peisey-Nancroix and the lifts up to the Les Arcs skiing.

Another beautiful and out-of-the-way off-piste run from the Bellecôte glacier is over the Col du Nant glacier and down into the valley of Champagny-le-Haut.

Unfortunately, especially in the early part of the season, the glacier gondola can be closed by high winds or poor weather. This greatly reduces the area's interest for good skiers.

In fresh snow, skiers who enjoy picking their way through woods in search of fresh light powder will not be disappointed by the forests above Montchavin and Montalbert.

FOR INTERMEDIATE SKIERS
Great variety: a chance to improve
Virtually the whole of La Plagne's ski area is a paradise for intermediates, with blue and red runs wherever you look. Your main choice will be whether to settle for one area for the day and explore its skiing thoroughly, or just cruise around the pistes that form the main arteries of the network.

For early intermediates there are plenty of gentle blue motorway pistes in the main La Plagne bowl, and a long, interesting run from Roche de Mio back to Belle Plagne which includes a long, dark (and often very cold) tunnel. In poor weather the best place to be is in the trees on the gentle runs leading down to Montchavin-Les Coches or to Montalbert. The easiest way over to the Champagny skiing is from the Roche de Mio area rather than Grande Rochette.

Better intermediates have lots of delightful long red runs to try. Roche de Mio to Les Bauches is a drop of 900m. There are challenging red mogul pitches down from the glacier to the mid-station of the gondola at Col de la Chiaupe. And the main La Plagne bowl has enjoyable reds in all

sectors. The Champagny sector has a couple of tough reds – Kamikaze and Hari Kiri – leading from Grande Rochette. The long Mont de la Guerre red is a satisfying run for adventurous intermediates.

FOR BEGINNERS
Excellent facilities for the novice
La Plagne is a good place to learn to ski, with generally good snow and above-average facilities for beginners, especially children. Each of the main centres has nursery slopes on its doorstep. There are not many long green runs to progress to, but no shortage of easy blues.

CROSS-COUNTRY
Open and wooded trails
There are close to 100km of prepared and marked cross-country pistes in La Plagne and its surrounding satellites. The most beautiful of these are the 35km set out in the Champagny-le-Haut valley. Here the pistes loop and wind through wild countryside, often in good sunny conditions. The north-facing areas have more wooded trails that link the various centres. There is a 12km route around Les Coches-Montchavin and a longer, 25km route that begins low down at Longefoy (1350m) and winds up through Montalbert to Plan Bois at 1700m. Plagne Bellecôte, Belle Plagne and Plagne Villages are similarly linked by a less arduous, 24km route.

QUEUES
Bottlenecks in high season
When the resort is full there can be big queues to get out of the high-altitude centres at the start of the day. The old gondola from Plagne Bellecôte via Belle Plagne to Roche de Mio is still a bad bottleneck, despite the alternative roundabout ways available. The higher gondola can also get very oversubscribed when snow is poor lower down (and the return pistes can get very crowded). The gondola from Plagne Centre to Grande Rochette can also generate queues (after lunch as well as first thing). This season the adjacent Colorado chair-lift will be replaced by a six-seater, which should help to relieve the pressure.

MOUNTAIN RESTAURANTS
Functional; lacking in charm
Mountain restaurants are numerous, varied and seldom crowded, as many skiers prefer to descend to their resort at the end of the morning. The British-run Lincoln in Plagne Soleil and the Grange in Plagne Bellecôte get

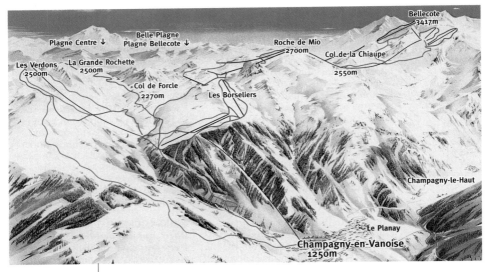

SKI SCHOOL

95/96 prices in francs

ESF
Schools in all centres.
Prices do vary; those
given here are for
Plagne Centre
Classes 6 days
2½hr, 3hr, 5hr, 6hr,
depending on centre
and time of day and
season
6 full days: 740
Children's classes
Ages: Up to 14
6 full days: 650
Private lessons
Hourly
180 for 1hr

Eric Laboureix
Ski and mountain
sports school in Belle
Plagne

Oxygène
Private school in
Plagne Centre

good reports. Many skiers based in the central resort units like skiing over to Montchavin or Champagny for lunch.

There are the usual large self-service restaurants. Particularly popular are the two on the Roche de Mio and Grande Rochette summits. There are smaller quieter alternatives for those who prefer more leisurely rest-stops. One ideal restaurant refuge in poor weather is Le Sauget, above Montchavin, which serves sensibly priced local Savoyarde dishes in a pleasant family-run setting. We also liked the restaurant at the top of the Champagny gondola – friendly staff, both table- and self-service, beautiful views from the terrace over to Courchevel, good basic cooking.

SKI SCHOOL
Adequate for all levels
Each centre has its own ESF ski school which is generally well run and offers classes for all standards. Groups can be large in peak season. Instructors speak English of varying standard, according to reporters – even in the resort units most popular with British visitors. One reporter, at least, succeeded in getting a different instructor by registering a complaint. Ski évolutif is popular. More popular still are the snowboarding and monoski lessons. Alternative and specialist schools are at last beginning to develop here, but we lack reports on them.

FACILITIES FOR CHILDREN
Good choice
Children seem to be well catered for. The nursery at Belle Plagne is 'excellent, with good English spoken'. The Club Med at Aime la Plagne is one of their 'family' villages. La Plagne and its satellites are fast becoming the chalet-crèche capital of the Alps. Crèches are provided in several of the villages by: Ski Esprit; Simply Ski and Crystal, and we have positive reports on the services of all three companies. One reporter was 'very impressed' by the tuition in Esprit's specially arranged ESF lessons in Les Coches.

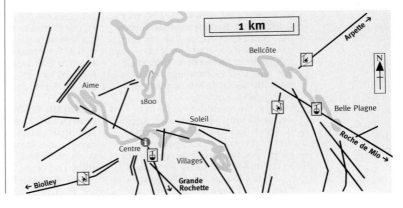

CHILDCARE

There are ESF ski kindergartens in all the high resort units, generally taking children from age 3. The ESF also runs all-day nurseries in most of the villages, mostly taking children aged 2 to 6. In Centre, the independent Marie Christine nursery does much the same.

The deal in the outlying satellite villages is similar, except that in Montchavin and Les Coches very young skiers are handled by the Nursery Club.

Staying there

Door-to-door skiing is the norm in the high altitude resorts. This means that, unless you miss a crucial linking lift, you can nearly always ski home. There is, however, an efficient bus system linking the resorts, which runs until after midnight and might tempt you to explore the après-ski in different areas. Most people, however, are happy to use the après-ski facilities most immediately accessible.

HOW TO GO
Plenty of packages
For a resort which is very apartment-dominated, there are a surprising number of attractive chalets available through British tour operators. There

are few hotels, but some attractive, simple 2-stars in the lower villages. There is a Club Med 'village' at Aime la Plagne. Accommodation in the outlying satellite resorts is described at the end of the chapter.

Chalets There's a large number available, though many are of a similar standard, type and position – fairly simple, small and in 1800. Of the big tour operators, Crystal have the biggest and best selection, with comfortable places in 1800 and Belle Plagne – and Crystal chalet-goers form the biggest group of this year's reporters. In 1800 their Bobsleigh is 'basic but adequate'; Les Circes is 'well appointed – lounge a little cramped for 14'; Nicole is 'new, with masses of storage space – a delight', but the public rooms are 'very cramped'.

Selected chalets in La Plagne

GETTING THERE

Air Geneva, transfer 3½hr. Lyon, transfer 3½hr. Chambery, transfer 2½hr.

Rail Aime (18km); frequent buses from station.

PACKAGES

AA Ski-Driveaway, Airtours, Alpine Options Skidrive, Altours Travel, Chalet World, Chalets 'Unlimited', Club Med, Crystal, First Choice Ski, French Impressions, Inghams, Lagrange, Le Shuttle Holidays, Made to Measure, Mark Warner, Neilson, PGL Ski Europe, Silver Ski, Simply Ski, Ski Beat, Ski Club of GB, Ski France, Ski Partners, SkiBound, Skiworld, Stena Sealink, Thomson, UCPA

Champagny France des Villages, French Impressions, Lagrange, Le Shuttle Holidays, Made to Measure, Ski Bon

Les Coches AA Ski-Driveaway, Chalets 'Unlimited', French Impressions, Lagrange, Made to Measure, Motours, Simply Ski, Ski Esprit, Ski Olympic, Travelscene Ski-Drive

Montalbert Ski Amis, Ski Amis

Montchavin Chalets 'Unlimited', Lagrange, Made to Measure, Simply Ski, Ski Esprit

Skiworld have simple chalets that are difficult to beat for price. Silver Ski offer a good selection of comfortable places in Centre and Plagne Villages.
Hotels There are very few, all of 2-star or 3-star grading. Probably the most comfortable place, if you're looking for a package, is Club Med, up at Aime la Plagne.
££ Graciosa Well-run 14-room hotel in Plagne Centre.
££ Eldorador 'Excellent' hotel in Belle Plagne – spacious rooms, generous buffet breakfast.
Self-catering La Plagne is the ultimate apartment resort, but many of the blocks are similar in standard. In-house communal facilities such as lounges, restaurants and the like are not as commonplace here as in most French purpose-built resorts. Fortunately, many tour operators have allocations in the above-average Pierre et Vacances apartments in Belle Plagne. The same chain also has reasonable places in Les Coches. Crystal have some mostly quite simple places in many of the main villages.

EATING OUT
Emphasis on convenience.
Throughout the resort there is a good range of restaurants, with something to suit most pockets and tastes, but the emphasis is on less expensive pizzeria-style dining which suits the self-catering family. Some satellite villages cater more for the diner interested in the regional dishes: raclette and Savoyard fondue restaurants are popular (La Ferme in

Plagne Bellecôte is recommended). Le Bec Fin in Plagne Centre is a popular choice for traditional French cuisine in a more formal setting, as is Le Matafan in Belle Plagne. Hotel Les Glières, in Champagny, serves good Savoyard food in friendly rustic surroundings.

APRES-SKI
Nothing exclusive or original
La Plagne has a wide range of après-ski amenities catering particularly for the younger crowd. Each centre produces a weekly events bulletin listing special forthcoming events, particularly those run by the hotel 'animateurs'. There is an ice rink and outdoor heated pool at Plagne Bellecôte, ten pin bowling and electronic golf at Belle Plagne, and most large hotels or apartment blocks have games rooms. Tom's Bar at Plagne 1800 is a favourite for the beery British crowd.

FOR NON-SKIERS
OK for the active
Non-skiing activities have evolved throughout La Plagne to offer the visitor a strong alternative to bashing the pistes. As well as the sports and fitness facilities, winter walks along marked trails during the March and April sunshine are particularly pleasant. It's also easy to get up the mountain on the gondolas, which both have restaurants at the top. The Olympic bobsleigh run is a popular evening activity. Excursion possibilities are limited.

Try the Olympic bobsleigh run

If the thrills and spills of the slopes aren't enough, you can try the 1992 Winter Olympic bobsleigh run. The 1.5km run drops 125m, has 19 bends and you can go in a proper four-man bob or in a special bob raft.

With the bob, you are one of two passengers wedged between the driver and brakeman. You reach a maximum speed of 100-105kph and the pressure in some turns can be as high as 2-3g. The ride lasts for 50 seconds and is not recommended for people suffering from heart, vascular or back problems, or for pregnant women. It costs FF430 a go.

The bob raft is padded and mounted on 20cm wide skids. The good news is that it goes slower – a mere 75-80kph and takes around one and a half minutes. The bad news is it has no professional driver or brakeman – just four terrified punters crammed in together. It costs FF160 a go.

For both, the price includes the ride itself, the loan of a helmet and a diploma. Additional insurance is available (yours may not be valid).

The course is generally open to tourists from Tuesday to Sunday from 5pm to 8pm (from 2pm on Tuesday and Friday) from Christmas to mid-March – though the season may be shorter if it's not cold enough.

ACTIVITIES

Indoor Swimming pool (Bellecôte), sauna and solarium in most centres, skating (Bellecôte), squash (1800), fitness centres (Belle Plagne, 1800, Centre, Bellecôte), cinemas, bowling

Outdoor Bob-sleigh (La Roche), 30km marked walks, paragliding, skidoos, rafting, climbing, skating, hang-gliding, snow-shoe excursions, helicopter rides

STAYING IN OTHER RESORTS
A good plan

Montchavin is a relatively unspoilt old farming community where rustic timber haybarns and cowsheds are much in evidence. Restaurant terraces set in orchards at the foot of the slopes add to the scene. There are adequate shops, a kindergarten and a ski school. Reaching the La Plagne skiing still involves four lifts, but the standard of them was greatly improved last season, with a six-seater chair-lift replacing the infamous bent Pierres Blanches drag-lifts. The local slopes are well-endowed with snowmakers, a cheap local lift pass covers 30km of mostly easy, pretty, sheltered skiing, with nursery slopes at village level and up at Plan Bois. Those who do venture further afield can return from Roche de Mio (2,700m) in one lovely long swoop. Après-ski is quiet, but the village doesn't lack atmosphere and has a couple of nice little bars. Simply Ski and Ski Esprit both have chalets with crèches. Ski Esprit's Mont Blanc is ideally placed beside the piste, and has 'unusually well appointed rooms'. The Bellecôte is a modest hotel with a decent restaurant, the Boule de Neige.

Les Coches is a sympathetically designed modern resort that several reporters have liked for its 'small, quiet and friendly' feel. It has its own ski school and kindergarten, and skiing arrangements are much the same as at Montchavin. Ski Esprit and Crystal have chalets with crèches. Simply Ski's Tresallet is 'a lovely, cosy chalet with basic bedrooms but comfortable, nice living/dining room'. Crystal's Nikita is 'very pleasant'.

Montalbert is a traditional village with quicker access into the main skiing – though it's a long way from here across to the Bellecôte glacier. The main village lift is being upgraded to a quad chair this season. The local slopes are easy and wooded – a useful insurance against bad visibility. The Aigle Rouge is a simple hotel.

Champagny-en-Vanoise is a charming old village in a pretty wooded setting. The south-facing local slopes mean you often have to get a gondola home at the end of the day, but Champagny is better placed than any of the other outlying villages for access into the main area. There are routes from the gondola station to summits above Centre and Bellecôte, the former being a particularly speedy affair using just one further lift. Given good snow, there are lovely runs home from above Centre (2,500m). There are several hotels, of which the two best are both Logis The Glières is a rustic old hotel with varied rooms, a friendly welcome and good food. L'Ancolie is smarter, with modern facilities.

TOURIST OFFICE

Postcode 73211
Tel 00 33 79097979
Fax 79097010

UK Representative

Erna Low Consultants
9 Reece Mews
London SW7 3HE
Tel 0171 584 2841
Fax 0171 589 9531

Portes du Soleil

The Portes du Soleil vies with the Trois Vallées for the title of World's Largest Ski Area, but its skiing is very different from that of Méribel and neighbours. It is spread out over a much larger area, most of which forms part of a central circuit straddling the French-Swiss border; smaller areas branch off from that circuit. The skiing is great for keen intermediate skiers who like to travel long distances in a leisurely fashion. There are few of the tightly packed networks of runs that encourage you to stay put in one area.

The main resorts and the skiing are described in four chapters – Avoriaz, page 149, Châtel, page 160, Morzine and Les Gets, page 211, and Champéry (and the other small Swiss resorts), page 311.

Purpose-built **Avoriaz** has the most snowsure skiing. Its main slopes face north and are the highest in the area – though still low by French standards. It also has the most densely packed section of runs, ski-in ski-out convenience and good lift links to Champéry, Châtel and Morzine. Prices are high for this normally modest area.

The other villages are generally attractive but less snowsure – and those in France are noticeably cheaper. Staying in one of them and travelling to the better snow of Avoriaz would seem a shrewd plan. But beware: many of the important links around the circuit are low, sunny and distressingly short of snowmakers.

Morzine is the closest and best-linked alternative. It's a summer as well as a winter resort – a pleasant, bustling little town with a sizeable, pretty ski area of its own. Being a town it has good shops and restaurants, traffic, lots of walking to the lifts, plenty to do. The local skiing is shared with unspoilt user-friendly **Les Gets**.

The other main French resort is **Châtel**. It's on the main circuit, and given good snow has some of the best skiing in the area. Although an old village, it's a busy, traffic-jammed place.

Champéry is the obvious choice for those looking for something more peaceful and attractive. It's a classic Swiss charmer, linked by cable-car to the main circuit. A lack of village nursery slopes may be a drawback for families and other beginners.

Morgins, in contrast, has excellent village slopes – but its local skiing is otherwise very limited. **Champoussin** and **Les Crosets** are purpose-built mini-resorts between Champéry and Morgins, with extensive slopes all around – and excellent links to Avoriaz.

Risoul 1850m

Reasonable prices, ski-convenience, good snow, few queues and a large ski area: Risoul has a lot going for it, particularly for intermediates, beginners and families. And it's one of the more attractive purpose-built resorts.

HOW IT RATES

The skiing

Snow	✱✱✱
Extent	✱✱✱
Advanced	✱✱
Intermediates	✱✱✱✱
Beginners	✱✱✱✱
Convenience	✱✱✱✱
Queues	✱✱✱✱
Restaurants	✱✱

The rest

Scenery	✱✱✱
Resort charm	✱✱
Not skiing	✱

SKI FACTS

Altitude	1850m-2750m
Lifts	58
Pistes	175km
Green/Blue	59%
Red	34%
Black	7%
Artificial snow	4km

PACKAGES

Airtours, Crystal, First Choice Ski, Inghams, Lagrange, Neilson, SkiBound, Thomson

TOURIST OFFICE

Postcode 05600
Tel 00 33 92460260
Fax 92460123

THE RESORT

Risoul, opened only in 1977, is now featured by all the big British tour operators, but remains a relatively undeveloped, quiet, apartment-based resort, popular with families. Set among the trees, with excellent views over the Ecrins National Park, Risoul is made up of wood-clad chalet-style buildings, small restaurants and open-air cafés, which give it a friendly feel. The village lacks many resort amenities – a pool, for example – and the ski area is seriously short of comfortable, fast lifts and mountain restaurants. Watch out for long transfers from Turin airport.

THE SKIING

The sunny **ski area** is shared with neighbouring Vars and is the biggest in the southern French Alps, offering 170km of pistes. The slopes leading back into Risoul are attractively wooded and good for bad-weather skiing. Above them are open slopes set in a big sunny bowl.

The top of the skiing above Vars reaches 2750m and the Vars skiing is accessed by a long drag, which has the advantage that wind is unlikely to close the link. Returning from Vars over the top is via some of Risoul's steeper skiing, though there is an easier route via Col de Valbelle. New lifts are planned, which will improve the area, particularly for better skiers.

Risoul's skiing is entirely above 1850m, so despite its southerly position (only 300km north of Nice) and sunny aspect, **snow reliability** is reasonably good. The nursery area has snow-cannon back-up.

Risoul does not yet offer much to interest **advanced skiers**. The main top stations access a couple of steepish descents, and there are six black runs in all. There are some good off-piste opportunities if you have a guide, especially in the trees. The whole area is best suited to **intermediates**, with some good long reds and blues in both the Risoul and Vars sectors. Virtually all Risoul's runs head towards the village, making it difficult to get lost in even the worst of weather. So intermediate children can be let off the leash with the minimum of worry.

Beginners have good, convenient, autonomous nursery slopes and a free lift. Graduation to longer pistes is straightforward.

There are a couple of short **cross-country** loops, including a snowsure and scenic trail along the top ridge of the Alpine ski area.

Risoul has arguably the quietest large ski area in France. **Queues** are very rare except in the French school holidays – even then delays are short.

There are more **mountain restaurants** than it appears from the piste map. But many people prefer to ski down to Vars or return to the village for lunch.

We have extremely conflicting reports of the **ski school**. Small classes are a consistently positive feature, lack of good English a similarly ever-present negative comment. Hopefully, the latter will change as more and more Brits visit, many on 'Learn to Ski' packages which guarantee instruction in English.

Risoul is very much a family resort. It provides an all-day nursery for **children** over 6 months. The ski kindergarten takes children aged 3 to 5, and children's ski school starts at 6 years old. The services are reportedly good but expensive.

STAYING THERE

Nearly all Risoul's visitors stay in apartments. **Hotels** are in short supply. The Dahu is used by some British tour operators but we have had complaints about poor food and a noisy disco. **Chalets** are becoming more widely available, and most of the operators who go there now offer them. The Mélèzes, Christiana and Belvedere **self-catering** units are good by French standards, though they can vary.

There's plenty of choice for **eating out**, from pizzerias to good French food, and it's mostly good value. More expensive are the Traderidera, Oasis and Assiette Gourmande.

Après-ski is limited to a few quiet bars. The best are the Licorne, Cimbro, Chérine, l'Eterlou, Thé 'n Thé and L'Ecureuil. The Dahu disco, for all its noise, is uninspiring. Risoul is not recommended for **non-skiers**.

La Rosière 1850m

✔ *Fairly big area of intermediate skiing, linked to La Thuile in Italy*

✔ *Quiet, pleasant resort built in traditional style*

✔ *Convenient for visiting other resorts of the Tarentaise*

✔ *Splendid view across the Tarentaise valley towards the Les Arcs ski area*

✗ *South-facing slopes can mean poor snow conditions in good weather*

✗ *Little in the way of tough piste skiing*

✗ *Not much nightlife*

La Rosière (like La Thuile in Italy, with which the skiing is linked) is not well known on the British market. For beginners and intermediates it deserves consideration. It's also a good choice for families and those wanting a quiet, relaxing week. Unlike many French purpose-built resorts, it has been built in traditional style, with chalets tucked away in the woods and no hideous high-rise buildings. And its prices are much lower than in the better-known (and nearby) Tarentaise resorts.

The south-facing aspect of most of the slopes means it is very sunny – handy in early-season cold weather but a drawback in warm weather when the snow can deteriorate. However, if that is the case, you can always ski over to Italy where the north-facing slopes usually remain good.

ORIENTATION

The resort is set along a winding road, with lifts at the top end just above the centre of town. From here a chair- and drag-lift take you up into the skiing. From the outlying district of Les Eucherts, another drag-lift goes up to mid-mountain. The skiing spreads right along the flank of the largely south-facing mountain and goes up to a high point of 2400m. It also extends below La Rosière to 1150m in Les Ecudets.

The skiing is linked to that of **La Thuile** in Italy. On the French side, **Les Arcs** is on the opposite side of the valley and easily reached by funicular from Bourg-St-Maurice. **La Plagne, Val-d'Isère-Tignes** and the **Trois Vallées** are all within easy reach by car.

SKI FACTS

Altitude	1150m-2640m
Lifts	33
Pistes	135km
Green/Blue	45%
Red	37%
Black	18%
Artificial snow	10km

 ## The resort

La Rosière has been built in traditional chalet style beside the road which zig-zags its way up to the Petit St Bernard pass to Italy from Bourg-St-Maurice and Seez in the valley. In winter the road ends in a snow bank at the top of the village, by the lifts. This is also home to some friendly St Bernard dogs, usually eager to pose for photos.

The village makes a pleasant contrast with the stark architecture of resorts such as Les Arcs and La Plagne across the valley. All the buildings are attractive and many are dotted around discretely in the woods. But there really isn't that much there other than accommodation and a few shops. Expect peace, quiet and friendly locals but not a lively nightlife.

Also expect few British, as La Rosière hasn't been discovered by many tour operators yet.

 ## The skiing

The first lift was built in 1962 and the resort has developed gradually since. The link with Italy means it has a big ski area for such a little-known resort.

THE SKI AREA
Best for intermediates and novices

The skiing is on the largely south-facing flank of the mountain above the resort. Most runs, especially those

back to the resort, are well groomed and make for easy cruising.

The chair and drag out of the village take you into the heart of the skiing, from where a series of drags and chairs spread across the mountain take you up to **Col de la Traversette** (2400m). From there you can ski over the ridge and ski to the lifts which link with **Italy** at Belvedere (2640m). You should note, though, that these top lifts are prone to being closed by wind or heavy snow.

SNOW RELIABILITY
Surprisingly good

Despite its south-facing direction, relatively low height (most of the skiing is between 1850m and 2400m) and most of the area's artificial snow being on the Italian side, La Rosière has a remarkably good snow record. But in warm weather expect the snow to be better on La Thuile's slopes.

FOR ADVANCED SKIERS
Little excitement

Advanced skiers will find little to amuse them. The steepest skiing is on the lowest slopes, down the Marcassin run to Le Vaz (1500m) and Ecudets or Eterlou to Les Ecudets (1150m). Even these aren't especially steep but probably deserve their black ratings because of the poor snow conditions you may encounter at these heights.

Other than that there are some good off-piste itineraires to be explored with a guide. And you can go heli-skiing by

LIFT PASSES

95/96 prices in francs
Domaine International
Covers all lifts in La Rosière and La Thuile.
Beginners 2 free lifts. Points card (50 points 260 (94/95 price), lifts cost from 3 to 7 points).
Main pass
1-day pass 160
6-day pass 786
Senior citizens
Over 60: 6-day pass 519 (34% off)
Over 70: free pass
Children
Under 12: 6-day pass 519 (34% off)
Under 4: free pass
Short-term passes
Half-day pass 12.30-5pm (adult 107). Half-day 9am-1pm and 12.30-5pm La Rosière only (adult 87).
Alternative periods
6-day (non-consecutive) pass available (adult 743).
Notes Passes of 6 days and over allow 1 day in Les Arcs.
Alternative passes
La Rosière-only pass covers 18 lifts (6-day: adult 661, child 430).

CHILDCARE

The Village des Enfants takes children aged 1 to 10, with ski lessons available for those aged 3 or more.

SKI SCHOOL

95/96 prices in francs
ESF
Classes 6 days 5hr: 9.15-11.45 and 2.30-5pm
6 full days: 620
Children's classes
Ages: 4 to 12
6 full days: 590
Private lessons
Hourly
145 for 1 or 2 people

skiing over into Italy for the helicopter. This is reputed to be the cheapest heli-skiing in Europe.

FOR INTERMEDIATE SKIERS
Cross-border delight
On its own La Rosière would be nothing special. But taking account of all the linked La Thuile skiing too, there's a big area to explore.

Apart from the lowest runs down to below the main village, the bottom half of La Rosière's local skiing area is mainly gentle, open blue and green runs, ideal for early intermediates to brush up their technique. The top half of the mountain, however, below Le Roc Noir and Col de la Traversette boasts somewhat steeper and more interesting red runs.

The red over the ridge from Col de la Traversette has good snow and views, but is narrow for its top section. Weaker intermediates can avoid it by taking the Chardonnet chair down.

FOR BEGINNERS
Good for families
La Rosière has good nursery slopes and short beginner lifts at the main slopes above the village and at the altiport, near the cross-country tracks. Combine that with the resort's quiet and friendly ambience and you've got a good combination for a family's first skiing holiday.

FOR CROSS-COUNTRY
Pretty setting
La Rosière has four trails totalling 12km, prettily set around the tree-line in the altiport area, with good views over the valley.

QUEUES
A good reputation
La Rosière has a reputation for being queue-free. When we were last there, in 1994, we found it much busier than on the Italian side and encountered a couple of substantial queues, especially for the Les Eucherts and Plan du Repos lifts. But reporters there in the 94/95 season only had minor waits returning from La Thuile.

MOUNTAIN RESTAURANTS
In short supply
The only real mountain restaurant is the Plan du Repos, at mid-mountain. This is a pleasant self-service place with decent food and a huge sunny terrace. But it can get very crowded, with long queues at peak times. Combine that with La Thuile's basic fare and you can see that gourmets won't find the ski area to their liking.

There are also a couple of tiny bars near the top which are fine for picnics. Many people ski down to the village for lunch. Toni's Bar in the Relais du Petit St Bernard at the foot of the pistes is convenient and has good food and service.

SKI SCHOOL
Mixed reports
Reporters were divided in their views. For example, one said, 'Instructor was very keen on jumping over rocks. Started with six people, ended with two! Also poor English.' Another thought, 'Very good and safety-conscious, worked hard; friendly.' One general good point appears to be small classes, and one couple had an excellent private lesson with a British instructor from the ESF.

FACILITIES FOR CHILDREN
Apparently good
Many reporters have observed the caring and patient supervision that children get in the snow garden of the Village des Enfants, although we lack first-hand reports. Ski Olympic can arrange a nanny service, given enough notice and enough demand.

 # Staying there

The most convenient accommodation is in the main village, near the lifts, or just below in Le Gollet or Vieux Village. There is also some by the other main lift up, in Les Eucherts, and more in rural old hamlets further down the mountain, though you need a car to make the most of staying there. The free ski-bus is efficient – and every 15 minutes at peak times. But it stops at 6pm. And one reporter complained of arduous walks from chalet to bus and bus to lifts.

HOW TO GO
Not a lot of choice
As far as we know, Ski Olympic are once again the only operators selling packages here – in two chalets.
Chalets Ski Olympic has a couple of cheap places well liked for everything except their position, a bus-ride or very long walk to the lifts.
Hotels There are half a dozen 2-star places. Prices are low.
££ Relais Petit St-Bernard The main hotel, at the top of the village on slopes. 'Warm and comfortable.'
££ Solaret Out of the village, at the satellite hamlet of Les Eucherts.
££ Belvédère Welcoming family-run place 6km down towards Bourg.

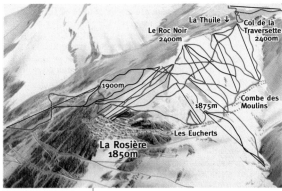

Le Roc Noir
2400m

La Thuile ↓

Col de la
Traversette
2400m

1900m

1875m

Combe des
Moulins

Les Eucherts

La Rosière
1850m

GETTING THERE

Air Geneva, transfer
3½hr. Lyon, transfer
3½hr.

Rail Bourg-St-Maurice
(23km); frequent
buses to resort.

PACKAGES

Ski Olympic

ACTIVITIES

Indoor Fitness Club
(body-building,
aerobics, sauna,
Turkish baths, jacuzzi,
Californian baths,
hammam, massage)
cinema
Outdoor Para-gliding,
cleared paths, husky
walks, floodlit skiing,
ski jump, flights over
Mont Blanc, heli-
skiing, toboggan run
for the children, 3 km
of marked walking
paths

TOURIST OFFICE

Postcode 73700
Tel 00 33 79068051
Fax 79068320

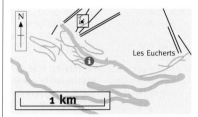

N

Les Eucherts

1 km

Self-catering Since First Choice Ski
pulled out of La Rosière last year, we
are unaware of any other tour
operators with apartments here. There
are a number of self-catering places
bookable independently, including
some ski-to-the-door ones in the upper
part of the village.

STAYING DOWN THE VALLEY
Only if skiing other resorts

There are some ancient hamlets where
you can rent gîtes, or you can stay in
the valley village of Seez or the bigger
town of Bourg-St-Maurice – both are
connected to the ski area by post bus,
though it's infrequent and expensive
(FF44 Bourg–La Rosière). If you did
this, however, it would make sense to
ski some other resorts too –
particularly Les Arcs, which is directly
connected to Bourg by funicular.

EATING OUT
Good for a small resort

There's a surprisingly wide choice of
restaurants, many of which have been
praised in reports. The Eterlou,
Pitchounette, Christophi, Plein Soleil
and Toni's Bar Pizzeria are all well
liked. The classiest place in the area,
however, is perhaps the Chaumière,
down in nearby Montvalezan – a
popular old atmospheric farmhouse
with excellent food. We are told of a
new restaurant, L'Ancolie, opening at
Les Eucherts this season – reports
would be welcome.

APRES-SKI
Limited

La Rosière is essentially a quiet family
resort, though the two main bars in
town, Toni's and the Yeti, can be
lively at tea-time. Later, the former
becomes a cosy place for a quiet
drink in front of any open fire, while
the Yeti remains fairly animated. One
reporter also recommends the Neige
et Chocolat for a friendly break
immediately after skiing. On some
nights there is floodlit skiing at the
top of the village.

FOR NON-SKIERS
Not much of interest

Non-skiers will find La Rosière very
limited. They'll soon get bored of
admiring the St Bernards (although if
you're very nice they may be allowed
to take you for a walk!). There are
scenic flights and a cinema. Walks are
good while they last, but only 3km of
them are marked.

Sainte-Foy-Tarentaise 1550m

HOW IT RATES

The skiing

Snow	***
Extent	*
Advanced	***
Intermediates	***
Beginners	**
Convenience	***
Queues	*****
Restaurants	*

The rest

Scenery	***
Resort charm	***
Not skiing	*

SKI FACTS

Altitude	1550m-2620m
Lifts	5
Pistes	25km
Green/Blue	23%
Red	54%
Black	23%
Artificial snow	½km

PACKAGES

Ski Arrangements

TOURIST OFFICE

Postcode 73640
Tel 00 33 79069170
Fax 79069509

This small ski area in the Tarentaise has been developed only since 1990. The millions who flock to the nearby mega-resorts never give it a thought. But those in the know are well rewarded. It is truly an undiscovered, uncrowded gem with some wonderful skiing for advanced and intermediate skiers.

THE RESORT

There isn't one; that's the charm of this place; it's skiing without the frills and some good skiing to boot. Ste-Foy is a tiny mountain hamlet of a few buildings – the latest addition is the largest, and houses the ticket office, ski shop and café. It's set in surroundings which are pleasant – though not outstandingly pretty – and there's a satisfying feeling of the area being undefaced by ski-lifts and skiers. It's set 8km off the main road between Val-d'Isère and Bourg-St-Maurice: turn off at the village of the same name.

THE SKIING

Rumoured to be 'where the Val d'Isère instructors ski on their days off', Ste-Foy's skiing is an undiscovered, often deserted gem. If you are staying in one of the nearby well-known Tarentaise resorts such as Val, Tignes or Les Arcs, do take a day off to give Ste-Foy a try, especially after a fresh snowfall.

The **ski area** spreads over the mountainside directly above the village and on both sides of the three chair-lifts which rise, one above the other, from 1550m to the Col de l'Aiguille (2620m). The top lift – the Aiguille – gives access to almost 600m vertical of skiing above the tree-line and to off-piste routes on the back of the mountain. The lower two chairs serve a number of pleasant green, blue and red runs through the trees and back to the base station. There are plans to cut some steeper trails alongside the lower lifts, and these should prove their worth when weather conditions on the open upper slopes are poor.

The slopes are north- or west-facing. **Snow reliability** is good on the former but can suffer on the latter. However, because of the lack of crowds, a fresh fall of powder is skied out much less quickly than in the nearby larger resorts; you can make fresh tracks days after the latest storm.

Advanced skiers can pass many a happy hour on Ste-Foy's upper slopes, and although there are currently only two marked black runs, there's lots of scope for challenging skiing all around the Aiguille chair. The off-piste and touring routes on the back of the mountain require guides – pick-up and

return to Ste-Foy can be arranged through the ESF.

Intermediate skiers should have a field-day at Ste-Foy. There's 1000m vertical of uncrowded red runs – ideal for confidence building, for sharpening technique or just for clocking up the miles. The higher slopes are the more difficult ones – the Aiguille run is a superb test for confident intermediates.

For complete **beginners** there is a small drag-lift near the base station; after which it's a case of getting on the Grand Plan chair and looping down on the Plan Bois trail – a pleasant, gentle run through the trees and the only real beginners' run.

There are no prepared **cross-country** trails, but you can lay some original tracks through the woods.

The three chair-lifts are all quads, and there are never any **queues** – it's not unusual for the highest chair to be so quiet that it's only started up when someone needs a ride.

There are two rustic **mountain restaurants** at the top of the first chair, both converted from barns and serving good food. The café adjacent to the ticket office serves pizzas, meals and snacks, and has a large terrace overlooking the valley. There is one other bar-restaurant, housed in an improbable-looking ruin nearby, which locals recommend highly for both food and ambience.

There is a **ski school** and a very good chance that any classes will not be too large. There are no special facilities for **children.**

STAYING THERE

It may be possible to rent a room in one of the few houses or farms nearby. Hotel Monal in the village of Ste-Foy, down at the turn-off in the valley, is clean and well-run, and serves wonderful food. There's a wider choice of accommodation in Bourg-St-Maurice, and there's a limited bus service from there to the skiing. But most people will want to stay in one of the major resorts and take a day trip to Ste-Foy, so having a car is handy.

On a busy day there may be a short-lived **après-ski** scene at Ste-Foy – the bar in the ruin is likely to be livelier than the main café.

Serre-Chevalier 1350m–1500m

✔ Fairly big ski area, ideally suited to intermediates, with lots of blue and red cruising runs

✔ Interesting mixture of wooded skiing (ideal for poor visibility, white-out conditions) and open bowl skiing above the tree-line

✔ One of the few big French ski areas based on old, picturesque villages

✔ Good-value and atmospheric old hotels, restaurants and chalets

✔ Buses link all the villages, so you can end the day wherever you like

✔ Lift pass covers several other major resorts easily reached by car

✔ Some good off-piste opportunities

✘ A lot of indiscriminate new building at the foot of the lifts, creating unattractive first impression

✘ Piste skiing limited for advanced and expert skiers

✘ Lots of slow, old lifts on the higher slopes

✘ Serious queues during French school holiday periods

✘ Limited nightlife

✘ Busy road runs through the resort villages

✘ Little to amuse non-skiers

ORIENTATION

Serre-Chevalier is made up of a string of villages – 13 in all – set on a valley floor running roughly east-west below the predominantly north-facing ski slopes. The three main villages are Monêtier (Serre-Chevalier 1500) at the western end, Villeneuve (Serre-Chevalier 1400) in the middle and Chantemerle (Serre-Chevalier 1350) at the eastern end, spread over a distance of 5km and linked by regular ski buses. Chair-lifts go up into the linked skiing from Monêtier, gondolas and cable-cars from the other two.

All the villages have charming old hamlets as well as modern new development areas.

The skiing connects with the lift up from the medieval walled town of **Briançon**, 5km further down the valley.

The six-day area lift pass also covers a day's skiing in each of **Les Deux-Alpes**, **Alpe-d'Huez**, the **Milky Way** ski area and **Puy-St-Vincent**.

Serre-Chevalier is one of the less well known of the major French resorts to British skiers. It deserves better. If you love old French villages with a genuinely French atmosphere and traditional restaurants, hotels and crêperies, try it. It is one of the few resorts with the sort of ambience that you might choose for a summer holiday – a sort of Provence in the snow.

And the skiing is equally likable. Although there is skiing on only one side of the long valley, it is split into different segments, so you really feel you are travelling around as you tour them on pistes and lifts. Intermediates will appreciate the skiing most, but in good snow conditions there are excellent off-piste opportunities to keep good skiers happy too. What really sets it apart from the French norm is the amount of woodland skiing, making Serre-Chevalier one of the best places to be when snow is falling (though there's plenty of open skiing too).

 ## The resort

Monêtier is the smallest, quietest and most unspoilt of the main villages, with a distinctly Provençal feel to its narrow streets, stone buildings with shutters and small square with a fountain. New building, in sympathetic style, has taken place on the other side of the main road, near the lifts into the skiing.

Villeneuve has three major gondolas out of the village. The central area of new development near the lifts is modern and fairly charmless. But the hamlet of Le Bez is peaceful and traditional, with old small stone chalets and barns. Across the main road and river the old village of La Salle is an enticing traditional village of stone houses, hotels, bars, restaurants and crêperies.

Chantemerle has more tasteless modern buildings in the centre and along the main road. But there's

another old sector a couple of minutes' walk from the lifts with a lovely old church and most of the restaurants, bars and small hotels.

As spring approaches, the charm of these old villages is diminished by the usual curse of French Alpine scenery – corrugated iron roofs.

Briançon is not strictly Serre-Chevalier. But it is now linked into the same skiing area and offers a fair amount of accommodation. It feels like a town – it is the highest in France, in fact – rather than a ski resort. The modern part of town is in the valley surrounding the lift station, with a wide selection of shops, bars, hotels and restaurants. Higher up is the fortified old town with narrow cobbled streets, well worth an excursion even if you are staying elsewhere. Many of the best restaurants are also in the old town. The profusion of barracks reflects the town's historic role as guardian of the link between France and Italy.

SKI FACTS

Altitude 1325m-2780m
Lifts   77
Pistes   250km
Green/Blue   42%
Red   46%
Black   12%
Artificial snow   13km

LIFT PASSES

94/95 prices in francs
Grand Serre-Chevalier
Covers all lifts in
Briançon, Serre-Che
and Le Monêtier.
Main pass
1-day pass 160
6-day pass 805
(low season 603 –
25% off)
Senior citizens
Over 60: 6-day pass
635 (21% off)
Over 80: free pass
Children
Under 16: 6-day pass
635 (21% off)
Under 4: free pass
Short-term passes
Morning (up to 1.15)
and afternoon pass
(from 12.30) (adult
120). Half-day passes
available for each
area.
Alternative periods
8 non-consecutive
day pass available
(adult 1,060).
Notes Further
discounts for children
aged 4 to 8 and
senior citizens aged
70 to 79. Passes of 6
days or more give
one day in each of
Les Deux Alpes, Alpe
d'Huez, Puy-St-
Vincent and Voie
Lactée (Milky Way).
Reductions for
families.
Alternative passes
Passes covering
individual areas of
Serre-Che (adult 6-day
690, Briançon (adult
6-day 525) and Le
Monêtier (adult 6-day
575).

 # The skiing

Serre-Chevalier's skiing is ideally
suited to intermediates, with miles of
easy cruising blues and reds, both
above and below the tree-line. Trees
cover almost two-thirds of the
mountainside; the runs here are very
pretty and offer some of France's best
wooded skiing if the weather is poor.

THE SKI AREA
Interestingly varied and pretty
Serre-Chevalier's 250km of pistes are
spread in four main sectors above the
Grenoble-Briançon highway.

From **Monêtier** in the west, two
chair-lifts take you to mid-mountain
and further lifts to the highest point
in the Serre-Chevalier ski area
(2780m), from which you can link
with the other sectors. Skiing from
Monêtier towards Villeneuve, the
main link is a red piste which is much
more interesting than the narrow,
flattish tracks you take when travelling
in the other direction.

Villeneuve and **Chantemerle**
both also have a choice of major lifts
into the skiing, and a network of
chairs and drags makes skiing between
these sectors easy. This area forms the
heart of the Serre-Chevalier skiing.

From the area above Chantemerle a
pair of drag-lifts takes you to the link
with the **Briançon** skiing. From there
you can ski all the way down to the
edge of town – a long run with great
views of the valley and the town of
Briançon itself.

SNOW RELIABILITY
Good – especially the upper slopes
Most of the slopes face north or north-
east and therefore hold their snow
well, especially high up (and much of
the skiing is above 2000m). Long runs
down into Briançon and Chantemerle
have artificial snow-making, as do a
shorter run down to Monêtier and a
couple of sections above Villeneuve.

FOR ADVANCED SKIERS
Head off-piste
There are long black pistes down to
Villeneuve, Chantemerle and
Monêtier, but none is fearsomely
steep. About the best is the beautiful
Tabuc run which takes you away from
the lifts, around the side of the
mountain, through woods to
Monêtier. This is generally narrow and
in places genuinely steep, but levels
out towards the bottom. When we
skied it a couple of seasons back the
snow was good and it had just been

groomed. In poor snow and with big
moguls it can be very tricky.

The top bowls above Villeneuve and
Chantemerle have a few black runs –
especially good are the two from the
top of the Eychauda drag and the wide
Balme run.

But the main interest for advanced
skiers is the off-piste, both above and
through the trees. In good snow this
can be superb. Highlights include:
Tête de Grand Pré to Villeneuve
(involving a climb from Cucumelle);
Croix de la Noire to Chantemerle
(short climb); off the back of
l'Eychauda to Puy-St-André (isolated
and beautiful, taxi ride home); l'Yret
to Monêtier via Vallon de la
Montagnolle (steep at the start, very
beautiful). And the off-piste Mecca of
La Grave is only a few miles away over
the pass towards Grenoble.

FOR INTERMEDIATE SKIERS
Ski wherever you like
Serre-Chevalier's skiing is ideally
suited to intermediates, who can buzz
around from piste to piste and area to
area without worrying about coming
across anything too surprising or
challenging. Looking at the piste map
it might appear that red runs far
outnumber blues. But most of the reds
are at the easy end of the grading
scale, and even nervous intermediates
should have no problems with most –
especially in the light of the intensive
grooming that goes on.

There's plenty to challenge the more
adventurous intermediate though.
Many of the runs are wide enough to
be able to choose a faster pace. The
Cucumelle run in the Fréjus sector is a
beautiful long red run with a
challenging initial section. In the
bowls, you can normally pick your
own route – to offer as much
challenge as you are looking for. And
many of the runs down to the valley,
including the Olympique down to
Chantemerle and the Grande
Gargouille towards Briançon, have
steep pitches.

The runs either side of the little-used
Aiguillette chair in the Chantemerle
sector are quiet, enjoyable fast cruises.

FOR BEGINNERS
Good at Villeneuve
All three main villages have nursery
areas at the bottom of the slopes
(though at Chantemerle it's small, and
you generally go up to Serre Ratier or
Grande Alpe). Villeneuve has good
slopes, and excellent green runs to
progress to above the tree-line at the
top of the Fréjus gondola. The

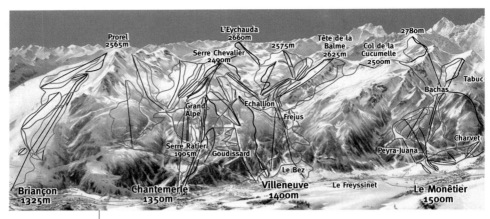

CHILDCARE

Each of the three main villages has its own non-ski nursery that takes children all day (9am to 5pm) or for a half-day. At Villeneuve, Les Schtroumpfs (92247095) caters for kids from age 6 months; meals not provided. At Chantemerle, Les Poussins (92240343) takes them from age 8 months; meals provided. At Monêtier, Garderie de Pré-Chabert (92244575) takes them from age 18 months (6 months out of school holiday times); meals not provided.

SKI SCHOOL

94/95 prices in francs

ESF
In all centres
Classes 6 days
5hr: 3hr am and 2hr pm; half-day am or pm
6 full days: 780
Children's classes
Ages: Up to 12
6 full days: 780
Private lessons
Hourly
165 for 1 to 2 people

International
Group lessons and special courses

Chantemerle sector is less suitable, but also has some easy high skiing. Both these sectors have green paths that wind down from mid-mountain; whether they are worth skiing is another question. All of Monêtier's easy skiing is at resort level, next to the excellent nursery slopes.

FOR CROSS-COUNTRY
Excellent if the snow is good
There are 45km of tracks along the valley floor, mainly following the gurgling river between Monêtier and Villeneuve and going on up towards the Col du Lautaret.

QUEUES
Avoid French school holidays
More than most resorts, Serre-Chevalier seems to be severely affected by the presence of French families during the February holidays, when there are serious queues to get up and around all sectors of the skiing. Head for the isolated Aiguillette chair, at the extreme eastern side of the Chantemerle sector, where crowds are rare. At other times, even in high season, there are few problems.

MOUNTAIN RESTAURANTS
Few, but quite good
For such a traditional French resort and large ski area, mountain restaurants are relatively thin on the ground, especially in the Briançon sector. The big Grande Alpe restaurant offers good value. The Bachas, above Monêtier, is small, rustic and self-service, and has a good sun terrace with views. There's a choice at both Serre Ratier, above Chantemerle, (where Jaques A is an excellent self-service choice) and at Echaillon, above Villeneuve. Our favourite is the Pai Mai in the hamlet of Fréjus, just off the Cucumelle run down from the col above Villeneuve: it has a welcoming

atmosphere and table service – but it is expensive, and one report says it is less good than it was.

SKI SCHOOL
Good reports
There's an International school, which is said to try harder than the ESF. Both seem to have relatively small classes and reasonable English. People in classes seem to have fun. We've had no bad reports at all on them.

FACILITIES FOR CHILDREN
Facilities at each village
We don't have many reports on child-care, and they mostly come from skiers staying in Villeneuve – but they are enthusiastic, speaking of 'endlessly patient' instructors and 'excellent staff with good English' at Les Schtroumpfs. The ski school will take children from the age of 4.

⬆ Staying there

The central resorts of Chantemerle and Villeneuve are more convenient for getting in to the main skiing than the two extremities, Monêtier and Briançon. And the link between the Monêtier and Villeneuve skiing relies on high chair-lifts that can be closed by wind. But frequent buses run along the valley, so location isn't crucial.

Perhaps more important to the feel of your holiday will be whether you stay in an 'old' or 'new' part of the resort. What makes Serre-Chevalier different from so many of the competing French resorts with similar-sized ski areas is the old-world charm and genuinely French ambience of the traditional hamlets and villages that make up the resort. If you are a Francophile, go for accommodation in one of the rustic areas, not in a modern suburb.

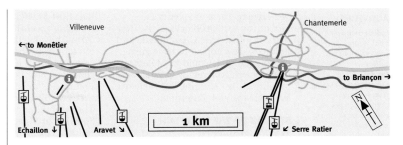

GETTING THERE

Air Turin, transfer 2½hr. Grenoble, transfer 2½hr. Lyon, transfer 4hr.

Rail Briançon (6km); regular buses from station.

PACKAGES

Airtours, Airtrack, Altours Travel, Bladon Lines, Chalets 'Unlimited', Club Europe, Crystal, Equity Total Ski, First Choice Ski, Hannibals, Inghams, Kings Ski Club, Lagrange, Made to Measure, Neilson, PGL Ski Europe, Rank STS, Ski Ardmore, Ski Club of GB, Ski Miquel, Ski Partners, SkiBound, Stena Sealink, Thomson

Briançon Airtrack, Alpine Options Skidrive, Alpine Tours, Lagrange, Motours

HOW TO GO

A good choice of packages

There's a surprisingly wide choice of package operators for a resort which is still rather off the British beaten track.

Chalets Bladon Lines have a good selection of rustic chalets in Le Bez and Villeneuve, ranging from the beautifully furnished, highly recommended Montalembert to a cheap, simply furnished old farmhouse. Ski Miquel have a chalet in Monêtier. Crystal have a range of good-value places in Villeneuve and Chantemerle. The Jerome is one of the best, with an open-fire lounge and a sunny terrace with good views, but it is a tiring uphill walk from the lifts. Neilson now run the Club Yeti – a cheap and cheerful chalet-hotel at the entrance to old Chantemerle, a stone's throw from the lifts.

Hotels One of the features of this string of little villages is that it has a range of attractive, modest hotels.

In Monêtier:

£££ Auberge du Choucas Smart wood-clad rooms, and a stone-vaulted restaurant with good food.

In Villeneuve:

££ Lièvre Blanc Former coaching inn, with a large stone-vaulted bar. Being steadily improved by British owners; popular with UK operators; has its own ski guide and ski hire shop.

££ Christiania Traditional hotel on main road, crammed with ornaments.

££ Vieille Ferme Stylish conversion – wood, tiles and white walls – on edge of village.

££ Cimotel Modern and charmless, with good-sized but simple rooms and 'excellent' food. Next to the piste and close to a main lift.

£ Le Chatelas Prettily decorated simple chalet right on the river (once a sawmill); small, cheap rooms.

InChantemerle:

££ Le Clos 200-year-old family-run chalet, with friendly service, basic rooms, a nice bar and good food.

££ Plein Sud Modern; pool and sauna.

££ Boule de Neige Comfortable 2-star in the old centre.

£ Ricelle Charming, but tucked away in Villard-Laté on the other side of the valley from the skiing. Good food at modest prices.

Selected chalets in Serre-Chevalier

Neilson *Club Yeti*   **T** 0113 239 4555 **F** 0113 239 3275

Club Hotel Yeti SLEEPS 39
The Club Hotel Yeti is located close to the centre of Chantemerle, just yards from the nearest lift. Run by Neilson staff, the property offers a comfortable standard of accommodation and a lively après-ski bar. The food is good and there is plenty of it, with an extended Continental breakfast, afternoon tea and a three-course dinner with wine.

ACTIVITIES

Indoor Swimming pool, sauna, fitness centres, cinemas, bridge

Outdoor At Chantemerle: skating rink, ice driving circuit, para-gliding, cleared paths, snow-shoe walks. At Villeneuve: horse-riding, cleared paths, para-gliding, snow-shoe walks. At Monêtier: skating rink, cleared paths. Also hang-gliding, husky dog-sleigh rides

TOURIST OFFICE

Postcode 05240
Tel 00 33 92247188
Fax 92247618

Self-catering There are plenty of modern apartment blocks in the new parts of Villeneuve, Chantemerle and Briançon. Few appear to have great charm. Our pick would be Mélezes in Chantemerle, offered by Crystal, and Moulins de la Guisanne in Villeneuve, available through Enterprise.

STAYING UP THE MOUNTAIN
Worth considering
The chalet-hotel Serre Ratier, at the mid-station of the cable-car out of Chantemerle, does full board at reasonable rates.

EATING OUT
Unpretentious and traditional
In Monêtier, the Auberge du Choucas has the best sophisticated eating. The Alliey is more of a family restaurant, and it has an excellent wine cellar.

In the old part of Villeneuve, La Pastorale has an open-fire grill and good-value menu. The Marotte is a tiny stone building with classic French cuisine. The Noctambule specialises in fondue and raclette. And there are a couple of good crèperies – the Bretonne and the Petit Duc. Over in Le Bez, Le Bidule is 'really excellent'.

In Chantemerle, Amphore has good pizzas and grills. The Couch Ou is good value for fondue and raclette and has a pizzeria upstairs. The Crystal is candlelit, and is the smartest (and most expensive) place in town. The Clos has a wide choice of food and Kandahar is a charming little pizzeria. The charmingly rustic Ricelle offers amazing value for money.

APRES-SKI
Quiet streets and few bars
Serre-Chevalier isn't the place to go for wild nightlife. The village streets are usually deathly quiet, and having a car is handy of you want to try the scattered bar scene.

In Villeneuve the Lièvre Blanc is popular with Brits, and L'Iceberg is a pub-style bar frequented mostly by teenagers. Both are preferable to the only other animated place in Villeneuve, the Frog – a cramped, uninspiring tour rep joint. In Chantemerle, the Yeti is focal for everyone, particularly its lively cellar bar, which has live music twice a week. The bar in the Clos hotel is better for a quiet drink; the Caveau disco is in the basement. The discos rarely come to life except at weekends. The Baita in Villeneuve is perhaps the pick of them. Even Chantemerle's karaoke bar fails to attract customers most evenings.

FOR NON-SKIERS
Nothing special
Serre-Chevalier doesn't hold many attractions for non-skiers, and it's certainly not the place for avid shoppers. But the old town of Briançon is well worth a visit. And there are plenty of activities on offer. The swimming pool in the hotel Sporting in Villeneuve is open to non-residents from 3pm to 9pm.

Briançon 1325m
The highest town in Europe, Briançon is linked by gondola to the Serre-Chevalier ski area. It has a lovely 17th-century upper quarter, complete with impressive fortifications, narrow cobbled streets and typically French provincial restaurants, auberges and patisseries. However, the area surrounding the lift station, at the opposite and lower end of town, is an ugly urban sprawl, full of busy roads, large car-parks and petrol stations.

The gondola, followed by a choice of short lifts, brings you to the link to the rest of the Serre-Chevalier skiing. The east-facing local slopes (all intermediate) are the sunniest in the area, but snowmakers ensure that the main pistes down to the gondola mid-station (1625m) stay open throughout the season, and the run to town remains complete for much of it.

The ski school has a high reputation, though the lack of English speakers is a drawback. The nursery and ski kindergarten care for children all day if required, the former accepting them as young as 6 months.

Packages are mostly geared towards car-driving self-caterers, but independent travellers have plenty of modestly priced hotels available. The Vauban is a very comfortable 3-star; La Chaussée de Paris a central 2-star; Mont Brison is a good B&B.

The Signal du Prorel apartments are next to the gondola, with the ski kindergarten close by. The Relais de la Guisaine apartments are also nearby. Both are fairly simple, but not as cramped as many in French resorts at higher altitude.

There are numerous restaurants; some of the best are in the old part. One reporter gave the Auberge de la Paix a rave review for quality and value. Le Passe Simple, Le Péché Gourmand and L'Entrecôte are worth a try. The old town itself is the main off-slope attraction – there are wonderful views if you climb up through the ramparts. There is ice-skating and swimming, and Grenoble is a worthwhile excursion.

Tignes 2100m

✔ *One of the best ski areas in the world for lift-served off-piste skiing*

✔ *Huge ski area, with ideal skiing for all standards of intermediate and for good skiers*

✔ *Good snow guaranteed for a long season*

✔ *Highly convenient, with skiing to the door of most accommodation*

✔ *Good lift system, with swift access to skiing of Val-d'Isère*

✘ *Ugly buildings – getting tatty, as well as being purely functional in design; traffic can be a problem, too*

✘ *Can be cold and bleak*

✘ *Little skiing below the tree-line – and it's inaccessible from Tignes if the high lifts are closed*

✘ *No green runs for beginners to progress to*

✘ *Limited après-ski*

✘ *Poor mountain restaurants*

The appeal of Tignes is simple: good snow, spread over a wide area. Tignes and Val-d'Isère together form the enormous Espace Killy – a Mecca for expert skiers, and ideal for adventurous intermediates. Whereas Val-d'Isère has a huge British presence, Tignes is much more French. It is also more reliable for snow: set at 2100m, it is one of Europe's highest resorts, with good snow right back to the resort for most of the season. The skiing goes up to 3500m, and up there lasts all year round.

Access to the highest skiing was greatly improved a couple of seasons back by the opening of a fast underground funicular and fast quad chairs almost to the top. Queues are now much less of a problem, and the amount of skiing you can get through each day is greatly increased.

If what you want from a ski holiday is Ski, Ski, Ski ... Sleep ... Ski, Ski, Ski ... Sleep, and you don't want much nightlife or care about high prices, about finding attractive places for long lunches or about the aesthetic appeal of the place where you are staying, Tignes is one of the best choices you can make. If you want pretty surroundings or lively nightlife, go elsewhere.

ORIENTATION

Tignes has two main centres: Tignes-Le-Lac and Val-Claret.

Tignes-Le-Lac has a high-capacity gondola linking it directly with the Val-d'Isère skiing on one side and a choice of chairs up the other.

Val-Claret is linked on skis and is a few minutes by bus. It has a slow chair direct to the Val-d'Isère skiing, drags, a chair up the other side and a fast quad chair and underground funicular to the Grande Motte glacier ski area.

The old villages of Tignes-Les-Brévières and Les Boisses are linked by lift and piste. And numerous other resorts are within an hour's drive. A six-day pass covers a day in several other resorts, including **Les Arcs** or **La Plagne** and the **Trois Vallées**.

 ## The resort

Tignes was created before the French discovered how to make purpose-built resorts look acceptable – as in Valmorel, Mottaret and Belle-Plagne. The main centres of accommodation – Tignes-le-Lac and Val-Claret – are just plug-ugly. They're now looking very tatty in places, too. And more than one reporter complains about the traffic, especially at Le Lac's busy central roundabout.

Large concrete blocks, some wood-clad, some not, set beside a conspicuous road, don't make for an aesthetically pleasing holiday base. But they are very convenient for the skiing. And there's a very reliable and frequent free ski-bus that links Le Lac, Val-Claret and all the accommodation which is not ski-in, ski-out. Both centres have their own shops, restaurants and bars.

Some tour operators have places in Le Lavachet, 10 minutes' walk from Le Lac. It's more villagey, with a compact horseshoe of small restaurants. It also has the best bar in Tignes, and mainly ski-in, ski-out accommodation.

Below the resort are two smaller settlements, different in style. Tignes-les-Boisses is quietly set in the trees near a military camp. Tignes-les-Brévières is a renovated old village at the lowest point of the Tignes skiing.

 ## The skiing

The skiing of the Espace Killy has few rivals for the attention of advanced and expert skiers. There is almost limitless off-piste as well as on-piste challenge. Intermediates too will have a great time here, with mile after mile of cruising runslinked by efficient lifts.

Tignes has all-year-round skiing on its 3500m Grande Motte glacier. And the resort height of 2100m generally means good snow-cover right back to base for most of the long season.

The main drawback of the area is that it can become unskiable in bad weather. There's no woodland skiing except towards Tignes-les-Boisses and Tignes-les-Brévières – a tiny fraction of the total ski area, and reachable only by road if the high lifts are closed.

SKI FACTS

Altitude	1550m-3500m
Lifts	102
Pistes	300km
Green/Blue	_%
Red	29%
Black	9%
Artificial snow	24km

THE SKI AREA
High, snowsure and varied
Tignes' biggest asset is the **Grande Motte** glacier, especially now that access to it has been speeded up hugely by the long-awaited opening of the underground funicular from Val-Claret, which whizzes you up to over 3000m in six minutes. (This was originally intended to be open for the 1992 Olympics but eventually started operating in spring 1993.) The snow up here, with a cable-car taking you up a further 500m, is always good, even on the warmest spring day. There are chairs and drags to play on, as well as beautiful long runs back to the resort and a link over to Val-d'Isère.

Lifts from both Val-Claret and Tignes-le-Lac take you up to **Tovière**, from where you can ski back to the village or down into Val-d'Isère's skiing. Going up the opposite side of the valley takes you to an area of drags and chair-lifts serving predominantly east-facing runs – splendid for early-morning sun – and leading to some delightful off-piste runs down the other side to the La Plagne and Les Arcs ski areas. The east-facing skiing splits into two main sectors, linked in both directions – **Col du Palet** and **Aiguille Percée**. From the latter, you can ski down on blue, red or black runs to the old village of Tignes-les-Brévières, from which there's now an efficient gondola back.

SNOW RELIABILITY
Difficult to beat
Few resorts can rival Tignes for reliably good snow-cover. The whole region, not just the glacier area, usually has good cover from November to May. The sunniest lower slopes now have substantial snowmaking facilities.

FOR ADVANCED SKIERS
An excellent choice
There's no lack of challenge here for good skiers. On piste, our favourite run is the Vallon de la Sache black from Aiguille Percée down to Tignes-les-Brévières. This long run takes you down a secluded valley, right away from the lifts, with beautiful views. It isn't particularly steep or narrow except for a couple of short pitches, and is manageable by adventurous intermediates. There are also off-piste variants, for which you need a guide.

The other long black run, from Tovière to Tignes-le-Lac, is steep and heavily mogulled at the top and bottom but has a long easy section in the middle. Parts of this get a lot of afternoon sun.

But it is the off-piste possibilities

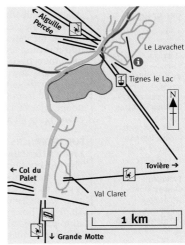

LIFT PASSES

95/96 prices in francs
L'Espace Killy
Covers all lifts and
resort buses in Tignes
and Val d'Isère.
Beginners Free lifts
on all main nursery
slopes; special
beginners' half-day
pass.
Main pass
1-day pass 209
6-day pass 960
Senior citizens
Over 60: 6-day pass
810 (16% off)
Over 80: free pass
Children
Under 13: 6-day pass
675 (30% off)
Under 5: free pass
Short-term passes
Half-day pass from
12.30 (adult 145).
Single ascents to
Palafour.
Alternative periods
14 non-consecutive
days (adult 1810).
Notes 1-day pass and
over valid for one day
in La Plagne-Les Arcs.
6-day pass and over
valid for one day each
in the Three Valleys,
Pralognan-la-Vanoise,
Les Saisies and
Valmorel. On 3- to 15-
day passes, pass
reimbursed if all lifts
are shut due to bad
weather. Discount on
new passes on
presentation of
previous season's
pass. Extra discount
for senior citizens
aged 70 to 79.

that make Tignes an excellent ski area for good skiers. Go with one of the off-piste guided groups that the ski schools organise and you'll have a wonderful time.

One of the big adventures is to ski to Champagny (linked to the La Plagne ski area) or Peisey-Nancroix (linked to the Les Arcs ski area) – very beautiful runs, and not too difficult. Your guide will organise return transport. It was on the route to Champagny two seasons ago that a group of British doctors and their guide were caught in an avalanche after a fresh snowfall, with fatal results. But thousands of other groups skied the same route during the season in perfect safety.

Another favourite descent of ours is the Tour de Pramecou, from the Grande Motte glacier. After some walking and beautiful away-from-it-all skiing, you end up on a steep, smooth north-facing slope which takes you back to Val-Claret. There are other descents across the glacier to the bottom of the two Leisse chairs, which take you back up to the arrival point of the funicular.

The off-piste served by the Col des Ves chair is often excellent. To the left (looking up) there are wonderfully secluded, scenic and challenging descents. On the right, lower down, is a less heavily skied and gentler area, ideal for off-piste initiation.

Then there's the whole of the Val-d'Isère skiing to sample, too.

FOR INTERMEDIATE SKIERS
One of the best
Only the Trois Vallées has intermediate runs in greater quantity than L'Espace Killy. But there's more than enough here to keep even the

keenest intermediate happy for a fortnight. And, in the unimaginable event that you did get bored, remember that a six-day or longer pass covers a day in the Trois Vallées and a day in La Plagne or Les Arcs too.

Tignes' local skiing is ideal intermediate terrain. The red and blue runs on the Grande Motte glacier nearly always have superb snow. The glacier run from the top of the cable-car is a very gentle blue. The Leisse red run down to the double chairs can get very mogulled but has good snow. The long red run all the way back to town is a delightful long cruise – so long as it isn't too crowded – and has a lot of snowmaking guns on the lower section to ensure good cover.

From Tovière, the Campanules red and the blue 'H' run to Val-Claret are both enjoyable cruises and generally well groomed. But again, they can get very crowded, especially at the end of the day when skiers are returning from Val-d'Isère. The direct way down from the top to Tignes-le-Lac is a steep black mogul field, but there are red and blue alternatives.

On the other side of the valley, we particularly like the Ves red run from the Col des Ves chair – the highest point of Tignes' non-glacier skiing at 2845m. After an initial mogul field the run becomes an interesting undulating and curvy cruise, usually with good snow and a few moguls. It's never crowded because of the low capacity of the double chair which serves it.

The runs down from Aiguille Percée to Tignes-les-Boisses and Tignes-les-Brévières are also scenic and enjoyable. There are red and blue options as well as the beautiful black Vallon de la Sache which is easily

SKI SCHOOL

95/96 prices in francs

ESF
Classes 5 full days
9am-12noon and 1.45-
4.45 or half-days am
or pm
5 full days: 900
Children's classes
Ages: 4 to 12
5 full days: 840
Private lessons
Hourly or daily
170 for 1hr

Evolution 2
Classes 5 days
am or pm
5 half-days: 590
Children's classes
Ages: 5 to 14
5 half-days: 390
Private lessons
Hourly or daily
180 for 1hr

OTHER SCHOOLS
International
Henri Authier
Ski Action

SPECIALIST SCHOOLS
Stages 2000
Assoc. 9 Valleys
Kebra Surfing
Ski Fun

CHILDCARE

The Petits Lutins
kindergartens in Le
Lac and Val-Claret
(79065127) take
children aged 3
months to 6 years.

The recently opened
hotel Diva in Val-
Claret (79067000) has
a nursery taking
children from age 18
months.

The Marmottons
kindergarten in Le Lac
(79065167) takes
children from 2 to 10,
with skiing with
Evolution 2
instructors for those
aged 3½ or more.

GETTING THERE

Air Geneva, transfer
4½hr. Lyon, transfer
4½hr. Chambery,
transfer 3½hr.

Rail Bourg-St-Maurice
(25km); regular buses
or taxi from station.

skiable by an adventurous
intermediate (see For advanced skiers,
above). Brévières is a good place for a
mid-morning break, especially if you
need to recover from the Sache run.

The runs down from Aiguille Percée
to Le Lac are gentle, wide blues. The
Bluets red from the top of the Aiguille
Rouge chair is a more interesting and
challenging alternative.

FOR BEGINNERS
Little attraction
The nursery slope in Le Lac is
convenient, snowsure and gentle, and
is kept nicely separate from the main
area by a man-made bank of snow.
There are, however, no green runs at
all to progress to, and the blues near
both main villages get fairly crowded
with skiers hurtling through to the lift
stations. In poor weather, because of
the height and lack of trees, beginners
could find it cold and intimidating.
We really think beginners would be
better off going elsewhere.

FOR CROSS-COUNTRY
Interesting
The Espace Killy has 44km of cross-
country trails. There are tracks on the
frozen Lac de Tignes, along the valley
between Val-Claret and Tignes-le-Lac,
at Les Boisses and Brévières and up the
mountain on the Grande Motte.

QUEUES
Very few
The new Grande Motte funicular and
parallel high-speed chairs have
removed the worst bottleneck. But
there can still be hordes of people
waiting for the funicular. If there are,
it's often quicker to take the chair. The
worst queues now are usually for the
cable-car above the funicular. Half-
hour waits here are still common,
especially when lower snow is poor.
Inevitably, the improvements to the
lifts have increased pressure on the
pistes, to the point where the run
down from the Grande Motte can be
seriously unpleasant. In late
afternoon, queues can build up for the
slow Tovière chairs to return from Val-
d'Isère. Both these problems are
avoided if you take the roundabout
blue Génépy run from the glacier and
go up the double Fresse drag to the
Col de Fresse instead. Progression
across the mountainside from the Col
du Palet sector towards the Aiguille
Percée depends on the inadequate
Grand Huit chair; the piste map shows
a projected new lift above it (the
Grapillon), but it is not clear when
this lift will be built.

MOUNTAIN RESTAURANTS
Neither cheap nor cheerful
Mountain restaurants are not a
highlight. It's easy to eat in the resort;
recommendations in central Le Lac
include the Calèche and the Troika.

The big one at the top of the
funicular has great panoramic views
and a huge terrace; the terrace is
invaded every few minutes by the next
funicular-full of skiers clumping across
to the piste, but on a wild day it's
almost cosy inside.

The Chalet du Bollin restaurant, at
the top of the short Bollin chair from
Val-Claret, is probably the best in the
main ski area, with table service and a
good plat du jour. The restaurant just
above the mid-mountain lift junction
going up to Col du Palet is pleasant,
with a big terrace.

In Les Brévières it's much cheaper to
walk round the corner into the village
than eat at one of the two places by
the piste. La Sachette is recommended.
Les Boisses has the best restaurant in
the area in La Cordée.

Reporters continue to protest at the
practice of charging even big-spending
customers FF2 for using the toilet.

SKI SCHOOL
Enormous choice
There are no fewer than nine schools,
plus various independent instructors.
The ESF and Evolution 2 are the main
ones, with sections in both resort
centres. They provide every form of
tuition, including off-piste, moguls,
racing and inter-resort off-piste
excursions. Reports of the classes are
mixed – Evolution 2 is said to be
much less good for English than
French-speakers. It may be worth
trying one of the smaller schools such
as International, Henri Authier or Ski
Action. Based in Le Lac, Stages 2000
specialises in off-piste tuition;
Association 9 Valleys does mostly
inter-resort circuits and extreme
skiing; Kebra and Ski Fun are specialist
snowboarding schools, one in each
centre. British ski guru Ali Ross runs
week-long ski clinics, bookable
through Ski Solutions, on which we
continue to get enthusiastic reports.
Fred Foxon is also said to be
'absolutely first-class'.

FACILITIES FOR CHILDREN
Apparently good
Our one reporters on the Marmottons
kindergarten judges it 'well run and
happy', confirming observations from
the side-lines. We lack reports on the
other arrangements, including the
new hotel Diva nursery.

PACKAGES

AA Ski-Driveaway, Alpine Options Skidrive, Altours Travel, Bladon Lines, Chalets 'Unlimited', Club Med, Crystal, Fantiski, First Choice Ski, French Impressions, Inghams, Kings Ski Club, Lagrange, Le Shuttle Holidays, Made to Measure, Motours, Neilson, PGL Ski Europe, Premier Ski, Rank STS, Ski Arrangements, Ski Beat, Ski Choice, Ski Club of GB, Ski France, Ski Olympic, Ski Valkyrie, SkiBound, Skiworld, The Ski Company, Thomson, Travelscene Ski-Drive, UCPA

ACTIVITIES

Indoor 'Vitatignes' in Le Lac (balneotherapy centre with spa baths, sauna etc), 'Espace Forme' in Le Lac, Fitness Club in Val-Claret (body-building, aerobics, squash, golf practice and simulation, sauna, hammam, Californian baths, jacuzzi, swimming pool, massage), cinema, covered tennis court, bowling, climbing wall, 'La Banquise M and M's' for children (ice skating, snow sliding, solarium, snow activitues, climbing activities) **Outdoor** Natural skating-rink, hang-gliding, para-gliding, helicopter rides, snow-mobiles, husky dog-sleigh rides, diving beneath ice on lake, heli-skiing

TOURIST OFFICE

Postcode 73320
Tel 00 33 79061555
Fax 79064544

 # Staying there

Location isn't crucial, but there is something to be said for staying in the cluster of buildings around the church in Le Lac: swift lift access to Val-d'Isère, and Harri's bar is not far.

HOW TO GO
Disappointing range of options
Although all three main styles of accommodation are available through tour operators, there isn't a lot of choice in any category, especially for those who like their creature comforts.
Chalets The choice is very limited in comparison to Val-d'Isère, or many other major French resorts for that matter. Many chalets are also surprisingly inconvenient for the skiing, and tend to be of a fairly similar standard to one another – reasonably comfortable but far from luxurious. We particularly like Skiworld's good-value Les Martins in Le Lac – cosy, eight minutes from the large gondola, ski-to-the-door off-piste. Their Club Tovière in Lavachet is also 'comfortable, and in a good location'. Bladon Lines have places on the outskirts of Val-Claret, a short bus-ride from the lifts. They also have the cosy Alpaka chalet-hotel in Le Lac.
Hotels The few hotels are small and simple, or (in a couple of cases) small and quite luxurious.
££££ Ski d'Or Smooth little Relais & Châteaux hotel; a modern chalet in Val-Claret, with the best food in town.
£££ Curling Tastefully renovated for the Olympics; in Val-Claret.
£££ Campanules Big modern chalet in Le Lac, with well equipped rooms.
£££ Diva Opened two years ago and enthusiastically recommended for 'spacious rooms, helpful staff and superb food'. Close to the funicular.
££ Terril Blanch Well run place next to the lake.
££ Neige et Soleil Excellent family-run place in Le Lac – central, clean, cosy, comfortable, with good food.
£ Lavachey Very friendly, plain B&B place with 'very pleasant bedrooms with balconies', next to Tovière lift in Le Lac.
Self-catering In upper Val-Claret, close to the Tovière chair, the Residence Le Boursat apartments are about the best on offer – not too cramped, are reasonably well equipped and have a communal lounge.
    The Chalet Club in Val-Claret is a collection of simple studios, but has the benefit of free indoor pool, sauna and in-house restaurant and bar.

EATING OUT
Good places dotted about
Le Lavachet has a cluster of quite nice places; we particularly liked the Tex-Mex at the Cavern, and have had good reports of the Osteria. Finding anywhere with some atmosphere is difficult in Le Lac, though some of the food is good. The Arbina has a high reputation and the Tocade has also been praised. The Bouf'Mich and Winstub (Alsatian cooking) are two of the better places in Val-Claret. Budget skiers here should try the Italian at the Stelvio or Pignatta. But the Cordée in Les Boisses is a must if you have a car – unpretentious surroundings, great traditional French food and cheap. The most ambitious food in town is found at the hotel Ski d'Or.

APRES-SKI
Early to bed
Tignes is desperately quiet at night, though Val-Claret has some early-evening atmosphere. The Wobbly Rabbit is popular with Brits – good for happy-hour jugs of margarita, and notorious for the closing-time strip routine performed by *la patronne*; it also serves Mexican and Thai food. The Corniche is more cosmopolitan, with live music.
    Le Lac is virtually dead, even immediately after skiing – though there is a cinema with bowling and video games for the kids.
    Late revellers head for Harri's in Lavachet, the most animated bar in town, though it's quite large and takes some filling before it warms up. The satellite TV here is popular

FOR NON-SKIERS
Forget it
Despite the range of alternative activities, Tignes is a resort for keen skiers, where non-skiers are liable to feel like fish out of water.

STAYING DOWN THE VALLEY
Only for visiting other resorts
See the Val-d'Isère chapter; the same considerations apply broadly here. But bear in mind that there are rooms to be had in simple hotels on the edge of the Tignes skiing. Most comfortable is the 2-star Melezes at Les Boisses, but there are even simpler alternatives in the same hamlet (the Cordée and Marais) and in Les Brévières (the Perdrix Rouge and the Génépy).

Trois Vallées

Despite competing claims, notably from the Portes du Soleil, the Trois Vallées is in a league of its own. There is nowhere like it for a serious piste basher who wants to cover as much mileage as possible while rarely skiing the same run repeatedly. And it has a lot to offer every standard of skier, from beginner to expert.

The skiing of the three valleys and their resorts are described and evaluated in four chapters – Courchevel, page 169, Méribel, page 199, Les Menuires, page 195, and Val-Thorens, page 255.

None of the resorts is cheap. **Les Menuires** is the cheapest but it is also by far the ugliest, and lacking in decent accommodation. It does, however, have some of the best steep piste skiing in the Trois Vallées on its north-facing La Masse mountain. Its near neighbour, **St-Martin-de-Belleville**, is a small, attractive, traditional village and offers good-value accommodation. The lifts into the skiing are slow, and the run home is south-facing.

Val-Thorens, set at 2300m, is Europe's highest ski resort and has the Trois Vallées' highest skiing. The snow here is pretty much guaranteed to be good, and there are two glaciers to choose from. But the setting is bleak, and skiing can be limited in bad weather; and the purpose-built resort isn't to everyone's taste.

Méribel's purpose-built satellite, **Mottaret**, is the best-placed of all the resorts for getting to any part of the system in the shortest possible time. **Méribel** itself is 200m lower, and has long been a favourite for British skiers, especially those going on chalet holidays. It is probably the most attractive of the main Trois Vallées resorts, built in chalet style beside a long winding road up the hillside, with some inconveniently situated accommodation.

Courchevel 1850 is the most expensive and fashionable of all the Trois Vallées resorts. The other satellites (1300, 1550 and 1650) are somewhat less pricey but don't have the same choice of nightlife and restaurants. The skiing around Courchevel is thought by many to be the best in the Trois Vallées, with runs to suit all standards and some of the most immaculately groomed slopes you'll find anywhere. The snow tends to be better than in neighbouring Méribel because many of the slopes are north-facing.

La Tania is a small place built for the 1992 Olympics and it still has very few facilities and very little evening animation. It is another good-value option, though.

Val-d'Isère 1850m

HOW IT RATES

The skiing

Snow	★★★★★
Extent	★★★★★
Advanced	★★★★★
Intermediates	★★★★★
Beginners	★★★
Convenience	★★★
Queues	★★★★
Restaurants	★★

The rest

Scenery	★★★
Resort charm	★★★
Not skiing	★★

✔ Huge ski area linked with Tignes, with runs for all standards

✔ Some of the best lift-served off-piste skiing in the world

✔ High altitude means snow is more-or-less guaranteed, even in a poor season

✔ Choice of six ski schools for on- and off-piste lessons and guiding

✔ Wide range of chalets, hotels and self-catering offered by dozens of UK tour operators

✔ For a high, keen skier's resort, the town is attractive, and very lively at night

✘ Piste grading understates the difficulty of many runs, and piste grooming verges on the negligent

✘ You're quite likely to need the ski-bus at the start or end of the day – perhaps both

✘ British visitors and residents can be dominant, especially in low season

✘ Not much skiing to do when the weather is bad

✘ Lifts and runs get crowded if snow is poor in lower resorts, and some key lifts at altitude need improvement

✘ Disappointing mountain restaurants

ORIENTATION

Val-d'Isère spreads along a remote valley which is a dead-end in winter. On your way in you pass the modern apartments of La Daille, from where a funicular goes to the Bellevarde skiing. The centre is 2km further on, where a road goes up a side valley, passing under the nursery slopes to Val's main lift station from which two cable-cars and parallel high-speed chairs head up in different directions into the Bellevarde and Solaise sectors. This side-valley road goes to the resort's main area of recent development. The valley road continues 3km to the old hamlet of Le Fornet, where a cable-car serves a fourth sector.

The ski area links with that of **Tignes**. A six-day lift pass gives a day's skiing in **Les Arcs** or **La Plagne**, plus the **Trois Vallées** – easily reached by car. Other resorts nearby are **Ste-Foy** and **La Rosière**.

More keen British skiers choose Val d'Isère than any other ski resort. And they aren't wrong: for adventurous skiers of any standard, there are few places to beat it. The key attractions are simple: the snow normally comes early (and stays late) even in a poor winter, and there is an enormous amount of wonderful skiing to suit all standards. The extent of lift-served off-piste skiing naturally attracts advanced skiers in particular. But you don't need to be an expert to enjoy Val – both the editors of this guide have had successful holidays there with mixed family groups. At the same time, the undergrading of pistes and relatively relaxed attitude to grooming mean that early intermediates must be steered to the right runs if their confidence is to be built up rather than demolished.

The list of drawbacks above may look long, but it's a list of mainly petty complaints. For some visitors, dependence on the ski-bus may matter, even though the free service is one of the most efficient in the Alps. The bus is necessary partly because of the rather strung-out nature of the place but ironically it has become more important recently because of lift improvements: lots of people based in central Val now start their day with a bus-ride to the super-quick funicular at La Daille.

The village is not exactly pretty, but it was improved enormously in appearance and ambience in the years leading up to the 1992 Olympics. One of our main reservations is its domination by the British – not just holiday skiers but also the hundreds imported each season to staff the chalets, shops and bars, plus of course the ski bums a resort like this pulls in. But for others this is a plus-point, and there's no denying that it results in a vibrant après-ski scene in which Brits can feel perfectly at home. And in high season, when the French arrive in numbers, the effect is much less pronounced.

SKI FACTS

Altitude	1550m-3500m
Lifts	102
Pistes	300km
Green/Blue	62%
Red	29%
Black	9%
Artificial snow	24km

LIFT PASSES

95/96 prices in francs

L'Espace Killy
Covers all lifts and resort buses in Tignes and Val d'Isère.

Beginners 11 free beginners' lifts on main nursery slopes.

Main pass
1-day pass 209
6-day pass 960

Senior citizens
Over 60: 6-day pass 810 (16% off)
Over 75: free pass

Children
Under 12: 6-day pass 675 (30% off)
Under 5: free pass

Short-term passes
Half-day pass from 12.30 (adult 145).

Alternative periods
14 non-consecutive days (adult 2,385).

Notes 1-day pass and over valid for one day in La Plagne-Les Arcs. 6-day pass and over valid for one day each in the Three Valleys, Pralognan-la-Vanoise, Les Saisies and Valmorel. On 3- to 15-day passes, pass reimbursed if all lifts are shut due to bad weather. Discount on new passes on presentation of previous season's pass.

 # The resort

Val-d'Isère is classic ribbon development. As you drive in from La Daille, the apartments and chalets lining the road increase in density, and then give way to shops, bars, restaurants and hotels. As you approach the centre the legacy of the 1992 Olympics becomes more evident: new wood- and stone-cladding, culminating in the tasteful pedestrian-only Val Village complex.

Despite the fact that the valley is a dead-end in winter, there is a lot of traffic around, making the centre feel towny rather than villagey. Still, many first-time visitors find the resort much 'prettier' than they expected.

La Daille is a complex of high-rise apartment blocks – convenient for skiing, but hideous. Locals insist that they blend in superbly with the environment in the summer.

 # The skiing

For good skiers, there are few areas to rival the skiing offered by L'Espace Killy (as the linked ski areas of Val d'Isère and Tignes are known). Its attractions are as much its splendid off-piste runs as its groomed runs. But there are significant on-piste challenges too. Intermediates of all standards will find enough to keep them interested for several visits – though there are complaints about overcrowded pistes at peak periods. Contrary to popular opinion, there are some good areas for novices too.

THE SKI AREA
Vast and varied
Val-d'Isère's skiing divides into three main sectors. **Bellevarde** (2770m) is the mountain which is home to both Val-d'Isère's famous Men's Downhill courses – the OK piste, which opens each season's World Cup programme in early December, and the Face de Bellevarde Olympic course, which made such spectacular viewing in 1992 but which costs so much to prepare that it may never be used again. You can reach Bellevarde by the funicular from La Daille or by cable-car or high-speed chairs from Val.

From the top you can ski back down to the main lifts, play on a variety of drags and chairs on the top half of the mountain or take a choice of lifts to get over to the Tignes skiing.

Solaise is the other mountain accessible directly from the centre of Val-d'Isère. The Solaise cable-car was Val's first major lift – begun illicitly during the Occupation in 1940 and finished in 1942. The parallel high-speed quad Solaise Express chair-lift takes you a few metres higher. Once up, a short drag takes you over a plateau and down to a variety of chairs which serve this very sunny area of predominantly gentle pistes.

From near the top of this area you can catch a drag or chair over to the third main skiing area, above and below the **Col de l'Iseran** (with skiing going up to 3300m on the Pissaillas glacier), which can also be reached by cable-car from Le Fornet in the valley. The chair-lift is spectacular: it climbs over a narrow ridge and then drops suddenly down the other side. You can also ride the chair-lift back if you don't want to catch the bus from Le Fornet. The drag-lift isn't the easy option, though. It's short and steep. At the top you ski through a narrow tunnel leading to an awkward black run which is often closed. The skiing you reach is predominantly easy, with spectacular views and access to the region's most beautiful off-piste runs.

SNOW RELIABILITY
Unbeatable
In years when lower resorts have suffered, Val-d'Isère has rarely been short of snow. Its height of 1850m means you can almost always ski back to the village, especially because of the snowmaking facilities on the lower slopes of all the main routes back to town. Last season it was virtually the only resort with decent snow at Christmas – and had superb cover right through until May.

Much of the skiing is north-facing (or northish) and plenty is between 2300m and 3000m, even ignoring the higher glacier skiing. The pistes would be in even better condition if the resort took piste grooming as seriously as they do in the Trois Valleés.

FOR ADVANCED SKIERS
One of the world's best
Val-d'Isère is one of the top resorts in the world for good skiers. The main attraction is the huge range of beautiful off-piste possibilities. There are lots of well-known and well-skied runs which have their starting points marked on the piste map. And there are many more which aren't marked.

Don't be tempted to launch off on these runs without a guide. We've seen horrific accidents through skiers who didn't know the terrain hitting rocks and skiing over precipices.

SKI SCHOOL

95/96 prices in francs
ESF
Classes 6 days
5½hr: 3hr am, 2½hr
pm
6 full days: 1030
Children's classes
Ages: from 4
6 full days including
lunch: 1540
Private lessons
1hr, mornings,
afternoons, or whole
day
185 for 1hr

94/95 prices in francs
Snow Fun
Classes 6 days
3hr am and 2½hr pm
6 mornings: 580
Children's classes
Ages: up to 13
6 full days: 920
Private lessons
Hourly or daily
170 for 1hr

94/95 prices in francs
Top Ski
Specialise in small
off-piste guiding
groups (max 6)
Classes 4 mornings
(9am-1pm): 920
4 full days (9am-1pm,
2pm-4pm): 1280
Other courses
On-piste tuition
including slalom and
mogul clinics
Children's classes
Ages: 7 to 16
4 mornings on-piste:
720; off-piste: 920
(tuition and safety)
Private lessons
am (8.45-1pm), pm
(2pm-4.30) or full-day
(8.45-4.30)
750 for 2½hr pm; full-
day (1,650) or am
(1,250)

Alpine Experience
Specialise in off-piste
guiding and teaching
for small groups
(max 6)

But the runs are normally quite safe with a guide. And a guide needn't cost a lot: several schools run guided groups you can join for a modest fee.

Two of our favourite off-piste runs are outstandingly beautiful and not at all difficult. The Tour de Charvet starts from the top of the Grand Pre chair-lift in the Bellevarde sector, with a long traverse into a big bowl, then wends its way though a narrow gorge before the ski out to the bottom of the Manchet chair up to Solaise.

The Col Pers starts with a traverse from the top drag or chair-lift on the Pissaillas glacier and opens up into a huge open bowl with glorious views. There are endless variants on the way down. Most bring you out just below the source of the Isère river, where you drop down into the very beautiful, narrow Gorges du Malpasset and ski on top of the frozen Isère back to the Le Fornet cable-car. This is a good area for spotting chamois grazing in the sun on the rocky outcrops above you.

There is excellent piste skiing for good skiers, too. Many of the red and blue runs – even one or two greens – are steep enough to get mogulled, so the small number of blacks is not the limitation it might seem.

On Bellevarde the famous Face run is the main attraction – mogulled from top to bottom, but not worryingly steep. Epaule is the sector's other black run – where the moguls are hit by long exposure to sun and can be slushy or rock-hard too often for our liking. On Solaise the main attractions for bump enthusiasts are the runs back down under the lifts to the village. There are several ways down: all steep, though none fearsomely so.

Apart from all this, there's Tignes' skiing to explore – as much again.

FOR INTERMEDIATE SKIERS
Quantity and quality
Val-d'Isère has as much to offer intermediates as it does good skiers. But timid skiers should be aware that many runs are under-graded.

In the Solaise sector is a network of gentle blue runs ideal for building confidence. And there are a couple of beautiful runs from here through the woods to Le Laisinant, from where you catch the bus – these are ideal for bad weather, though prone to closure in times of avalanche danger.

The runs in the Col de l'Iseran sector are flatter and easier – ideal for early and hesitant intermediates. Those marked blue at the top of the glacier could really be graded green.

Bellevarde has a huge variety of runs

ideally suited to intermediates of all standards. From Bellevarde itself there is a choice of green, blue and red runs of varying pitch. And the wide runs from Tovière normally give you the choice of groomed piste or moguls.

A snag for early intermediates is that runs back to the valley can be testing. The easiest way is to ski down to La Daille, where there is a green run – but it should be graded blue (in some resorts it would be red) and gets very crowded and mogulled at the end of the day. None of the runs from Bellevarde and Solaise back to Val itself are really easy.

The blue Santons run from Bellevarde takes you through a long, narrow gun-barrel which often has people standing around plucking up courage, making things even trickier.

On Solaise there isn't much to choose between the blue and red ways down – they're both mogulled and narrow in places. At the top, there's no option other than the red mogul run in full view of the lifts. It's just a question of choosing how big you want your moguls – the largest are on your right. Many early intermediates sensibly choose to ride the lifts down – take the chair for a spectacular view.

FOR BEGINNERS
OK if you know where to go
Val-d'Isère has a superb nursery slope right by the centre of town. What's more the lifts serving it are free – no coupons, never mind a lift pass.

Once you get off the nursery slopes, there are some easy runs, but you have to know where to find them; many of the greens would be blue, or even red, in other resorts. One experienced Val-d'Isère instructor admitted: 'We have to have plenty of green runs on the piste map, even if we haven't got many green slopes – otherwise beginners wouldn't come here.'

A good place for your first real runs off the nursery slopes is the Madeleine green run on Solaise. The Col de l'Iseran runs are also gentle and wide; they're less easily accessible but the snow is normally the best around.

There are no really easy runs back to the valley – you'll have to ride down.

FOR CROSS-COUNTRY
Limited
There are a couple of loops towards La Daille and another out past Le Laisinant. More picturesque is the one going from Le Châtelard (on the road past the main cable-car station) to the Manchet chair. But keen cross-country skiers should go elsewhere.

QUEUES

Few problems

Queues to get out of the resort have been pretty much eliminated by the building of the funicular and high-speed chair-lifts up the mountains as alternatives to the two main cable-cars. The slow Manchet chair-lift was replaced in 1993 by a high-speed quad that has alleviated the queues there.

At the end of the day, there's usually a wait for the chair back from Col de l'Iseran to Solaise. To get to Tignes, it's quicker to take the new high-speed quad to Col de Fresse than the slow Tovière chairs.

Returning from Val-Claret at the end of the day may involve a lengthy wait for the slow Tufs chair, but there are no further lifts necessary to get home.

Selected chalets in Val-d'Isère

CHILDCARE

Garderie Isabelle (79411282) at La Daille takes children from age 2½, from 8.30 to 5.30. The Petit Poucet (79061397) in the Residence les Hameaux at Val takes children aged 3 to 8, from 9am to 5.30. Both provide indoor and outdoor activities and delivery to and collection from ski school .

Snowfun's Club Nounours takes children aged 3 to 6 for lessons of 1hr30, 2hr or 3hr. Older children can be left in classes all day.

The ESF runs a ski nursery for aged 4 up, with rope tows and a heated chalet.

MOUNTAIN RESTAURANTS
Disappointing for a major resort

The mountain restaurants mainly consist of big self-service places with vast terraces at the top of major lifts. The best are in the Bellevarde sector, on the runs down to La Daille.

The Crech'Ouna just across the slope from the funicular station at La Daille, is a charming, civilised place and now has an outside terrace too. But the food is not all it used to be.

Other recommendations: Le Tufs, just below Crech'Ouna – a newer table-service restaurant, terrace, good pizzas and Savoyard fare; Trifollet, around halfway up the La Daille gondola – relatively new, table-service, terrace overlooking the men's downhill piste; La Folie Douce, at the top of the gondola – recommended by several reporters for service with a smile; Marmottes, in the middle of the Bellevarde bowl – not unpleasant, and handy for mixed groups to meet at.

An alternative is to ski to town, to one of the restaurants overlooking the nursery slopes. Our favourite is the big terrace of the Brussels. The restaurant near the cross-country course at Le Châtelard is also worth trying. When skiing at the Col de l'Iseran, much the most pleasant plan for lunch is to descend to the rustic Arolay at Le Fornet – especially on a wintry day.

SKI SCHOOL
A very wide choice

There are six ski schools plus several private instructors to choose from. ESF and Snow Fun are the two biggest, with a full range of group and private lessons. This year we've had bad reports of the ESF: 'we were the only English-speakers and were paid no attention' and 'the instructor did not stop if someone had fallen'. And we've had lots of satisfied Snow Fun pupils: 'excellent' and 'well organised' were typical comments. But there was a report of some women finding their male instructor a 'chauvinist pig'.

Top Ski, Evolution 2 and Alpine Experience all specialise in taking skiers off-piste in small groups which they put together – excellent for good skiers who want to make the most of Val-d'Isère's vast off-piste possibilities. We've had great days off-piste with both Top Ski and Alpine Experience. But we have to say – and this is an unfashionable view, which will win us no friends – that we have found Top Ski's tuition rather less impressive.

Mountain Masters has a reputation for 'inner skiing' teaching methods, has small classes and video analysis.

All the schools have teachers who speak good English – in many cases it's their native language. In peak periods it's best to book in advance, especially with some of the off-piste schools who have only a handful of teachers each. Heli-skiing can be arranged – you are taken to Italy because heli-skiing is banned in France.

FACILITIES FOR CHILDREN
Good tour op possibilities

The two resort crèches are small, get booked up early and don't cater for the under-2s. So it's not surprising that tour operator facilities are more important to British visitors. Mark Warner's Cygnaski jumbo-chalet (see below) has been the basis of an excellent family holiday for one of us; it has a spacious nursery.

We have personal experience of the incompetence and indifference of the ESF ski nursery; stay away.

 # Staying there

The location of your accommodation isn't crucial. Free shuttle buses run along the main street linking the main lift stations. It is one of the most efficient bus services we've come across; even in peak periods, you never have to wait more than a few minutes. But in the evenings frequency plummets and it may be quicker to walk. Dedicated après-skiers will want to be within walking distance of the central T-junction – most of the bars and restaurants are here, around the main street. The recent development up the side valley beyond the main lift station is mainly attractive, and no more than a pleasant stroll from the centre.

HOW TO GO
Lots of choice

More British tour operators go to Val-d'Isère than to any other resort except Méribel. The choice of chalets and chalet-hotels, in particular, is vast. There is a Club Med 'village'.

Chalets There is everything from budget chalets to the most luxurious you could demand. The resort has a fair number of chalet operators who don't go anywhere else, of which YSE is the most prominent. YSE and the very upmarket Ski Company Ltd have the best chalets in town, notably their respective luxurious mountain lodges. And Ski Scott Dunn have three luxury chalet apartments here this season, for the first time.

ACTIVITIES

Indoor Swimming pool, sports hall (basketball, volleyball, table tennis, badminton, trampoline and gymnastics), library, bridge, health centres in the hotels Christiania, Brussel's and Sofitel (sauna, hammam, jacuzzi, body building, massages, solarium etc), cinema, fitness club (body building, step, aerobics, sauna, massage, solarium)
Outdoor Walks in Le Manchet valley and Le Fornet, natural skating rink, curling, hang-gliding, quad bikes, all-terrain karts, ice driving, snow-mobiles, para-gliding, shoe-snow outings, heli-skiing, microlight trips, bungee jumping

Val-d'Isère Properties and Lotus Supertravel both have a selection of small, very comfortable places. Finlays have a good, small range, including central, beautifully appointed Squaw Valley apartments. Bladon Lines have a large range, from intimate places to chalet-hotels, including the 68-bed Fôret. Silver Ski has a good-value little chalet in central Val. Le Ski have an almost-new place in the Joseray area – handy for the cable-cars. Neilson have an attractive Savoyarde-style chalet near the cable-car. Other big operators have struggled to acquire chalets here. Their catered 'chalet' holidays are exclusively in apartment conversions.

There is quite a choice of chalet-hotels. At the bottom of the price range is Ski Val's Tarentaise. YSE's Crêtes Blanches is much the most comfortable, verging on the luxurious. Bladon Lines' recently renovated Fjord is stylishly simple, and its Grand-Nord and Forêt have bars that are among the liveliest in town. Mark Warner's absolutely central Moris is possibly even livelier; in contrast, the family-oriented Cygnaski, half-way to La Daille, is much quieter.

The best-value chalets tend to be away from the centre, at Le Fornet, Le Châtelard and Le Laisinant. Le Ski have a good choice here.

Hotels There are 40 to choose from, mostly 2- and 3-star, but for such a big international resort surprisingly few are notably attractive.
££££ Christiania Recently renovated big chalet, probably best in town. Chic, with friendly staff. Sauna.
££££ Latitudes Modern, stylish. Piano bar, nightclub. Leisure centre: sauna, steam room, whirl-pool, massage.
££££ Blizzard Renovated for Olympics. Indoor-outdoor pool behind. Convenient.
£££ Grand Paradis Excellent position. Good food.
£££ Brussels Excellent position. Large terrace, which is popular for lunch. Leisure centre.
£££ Savoyarde Rustic decor. Leisure centre. Good food. Rooms a bit small.
££ Sorbiers Modern but cosy B&B.
££ Kern Basic but good value.
££ Vieux Village Traditional old hotel. Good value.
££ Samovar In La Daille. Traditional hotel with good food.
Self-catering There are thousands of properties to choose from. UK operators offer lots of them, but they tend to get snapped up by early-booking ski-drivers. Local agency Val-d'Isère Agence has a particularly good brochure. As in all French resorts, most apartments are small, but you can find bigger places if you scour the brochures. UK operator Val-d'Isère Properties has a good selection.

The Rocher Soleil apartments are worth considering, with their satellite TVs, heated outdoor pool, leisure centre, lounge, bar and restaurant.

Finlays have a good selection, most of which are bang in the centre. Other recommendable apartments: Rond Point des Pistes, Jardins de la Balme, Châtelard, Hauts de Rogonay, Jardins de Val.

EATING OUT
Plenty of good, affordable places
Restaurants here have to satisfy the still predominantly French market, so standards are high and prices lower than in London. Although there are, among the 70-odd restaurants, some which specialise in Italian, Alsatian, Tex-Mex, even Japanese food, most offer good French dishes.

You can get a good meal for less than £15 in numerous very pleasant places, such as the very popular Perdrix Blanche (everything from Savoyard to sushi), Lodge and Taverne d'Alsace (in plush new premises). Less well known but equally good value are the Olympique, Florence, Au Bout de la Rue (English-owned, excellent

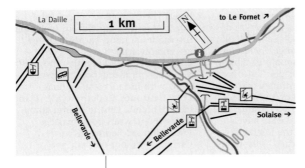

La Daille · 1 km · to Le Fornet ↗ · Bellevarde · ← Bellevarde · Solaise →

PACKAGES

AA Ski-Driveaway, Alpine Options Skidrive, Altours Travel, Bladon Lines, Chalet World, Chalets 'Unlimited', Club Med, Crystal, Finlays, First Choice Ski, French Impressions, Inghams, Kings Ski Club, Lagrange, Le Shuttle Holidays, Le Ski, Lotus Supertravel, Made to Measure, Mark Warner, Motours, Neilson, PGL Ski Europe, Silver Ski, Ski 3000, Ski Arrangements, Ski Choice, Ski Club of GB, Ski France, Ski Les Alpes, Ski Olympic, Ski Scott Dunn, Ski Val, Ski Valkyrie, Ski Weekend, SkiBound, Skiworld, Stena Sealink, The Ski Company Ltd, Thomson, Trail Alpine, Travelscene Ski-Drive, UCPA, Val d'Isère Properties, White Roc, YSE

GETTING THERE

Air Geneva, transfer 4½hr. Chambery, transfer 3½hr. Lyon, transfer 4½hr.

Rail Bourg-St-Maurice (30km); regular buses from station.

TOURIST OFFICE

Postcode 73155
Tel 00 33 79060660
Fax 79060456

French cooking) and 1789. The Crech'Ouna is also worth a visit (see Mountain restaurants) – we'd welcome more reports of the food here.

The best restaurants in town are the Solaise, Grande Ourse or the hotels Savoyard and Tsanteleina.

Those on the tightest budgets should try the pizzas in Chez Nano, next to Dick's T-bar, or the Pacific, next to the Moris pub, which serves generous portions of pasta and seafood. G-Jay's and the Pavillon are recommended for breakfast.

APRES-SKI
Very lively
Nightlife is surprisingly energetic, given that most people have spent all day skiing hard. After skiing there are lots of bars to fall into – you can save money by following the happy hour crawl from bar to bar, as prices change at different times. The famous Dick's T-Bar (under new ownership but same style) and the much smaller G-Jays are run by Brits for Brits; Bananas, Bar Jacques and the Perdrix Blanche bar attract more locals; and Brasserie des

Sports, Boubou's and the Saloon are pretty much French-only enclaves. The Pavillon is more civilised and includes a champagne bar. In La Daille the Brighton Rock (run by SkiBound) has cheap happy-hour beer.

There are lots of late bars, many with music and dancing into the early hours. For those that hate such things or have skied themselves to a standstill, there are quiet hotel bars, piano bars and cocktail lounges. Dick's becomes the busiest disco in town late evening, often with a queue outside, but it has several little alcoves where those whose age exceeds their Continental shoe size can have a civilised chat. Dick's is, however, so British you may think it lacks the cosmopolitan, slightly chic and trendy feel of French places, such as Club 21. Other good bars are the Alsace, Couleur Café and Café Face. And try the 10-drink cocktail special at Bar Jacques! Live music can often be found at the Forêt, the Aventure, Brussel's, Café Face, Pavillon, Pacific and Club 21.

Several British-run chalet hotels have bars that get very lively at times including Forêt, Grand Nord and Moris. The Forêt has karaoke nights.

FOR NON-SKIERS
Not good, except for sporty types
Val is primarily a skier's ski resort. Inactive non-skiers won't find many diversions, and may have trouble getting their skiing companions to commit themselves to a pedestrian-accessible lunchtime rendezvous.

The best walks are up the Manchet valley. The range of non-skiing activities is quite wide. But the mainstream facilities are surprisingly poor: the swimming pool building is small and showing its age. They could do with a smart new sports centre.

The range of shops is better than in most French resorts.

STAYING DOWN THE VALLEY
Not a great idea
Val-d'Isère is a long way up its dead-end valley. If you're driving out to the Alps you could consider staying half an hour away in rustic Ste-Foy (which has its own delightful and deserted ski area – see page 229) or even further away in Bourg-St-Maurice. But if you do that you'll really want to consider skiing different resorts each day rather than just Val-d'Isère.

Valloire 1430m

Little-known on the British market, Valloire offers a surprisingly extensive ski area, ideally suited to intermediates. It also has a rustic French feel to it and retains a life as a farming community, as well as a ski resort.

THE RESORT

Valloire is an unspoilt, old, working village, tucked away above the Maurienne valley. Despite having developed into a significant-sized ski resort, it has retained a feeling of 'real' France, complete with impressive old church, crêperies, fromageries, reasonable prices, villagey atmosphere and friendly locals.

THE SKIING

The 150km of piste are spread over three similar-sized, lightly wooded **ski areas** – Sétaz, Valmeinier and Crey du Quart. The skiing is almost entirely intermediate, Les Karellis (a 45-minute drive) being better for more taxing runs (and for superior snow and scenery). A gondola leads up towards Sétaz and a chair towards Crey du Quart and the link with the skiing of next-door Valmeinier. One reporter complained about poor piste marking and an unclear map, which could lead beginners into difficult areas.

Reliable **snow-cover** is not a strong point, though Valloire does have a better recent snow record than similar but lower 'real' French ski villages such as La Clusaz, Morzine, Châtel and Megève. Important links are too low, sunny and lacking artificial snow to ensure the whole area is usually skiable. The main piste to the village is fully served by snow cannon, whilst the Valmeinier area holds snow well.

There is not much to challenge **advanced skiers**, though the Cascade and Olympiques pistes are fun. The mogul field down to Valmeinier 1500 represents the greatest challenge.

Valloire is very much an **intermediate** area. Several of the pistes towards Valmeinier, and the JBM run to Valloire, are suitable for good intermediates, but average skiers have the widest choice of runs, with plenty of options in all three sections. A variety of pistes head to and from Valmeinier, making mixed-ability excursions a straightforward affair. The Crey du Quart section is particularly good for easy skiing.

The limited village nursery areas are adequate in low season when snow cover is good. Otherwise there are good nursery slopes up the mountain, at the top of the Sétaz gondola, but a full lift pass is needed to reach them. There are plenty of easy pistes suitable for improving **beginners**, and there are 40km of **cross-country** trails.

There are long delays when the Italians hit town en masse, but thankfully this is not a common occurrence. Otherwise there are few **queue** problems when snow-cover is complete. The Lac de la Veille (Crey) drag and Valmeinier 1500 chair can become oversubscribed when it is not. Understandably, the village gondola gets busy for a short period when ski school starts.

Mountain restaurants are in very short supply but are good quality. The Thimel is perhaps the best.

Reports consistently suggest the **ski school** has lapsed badly of late – large classes and poor organisation.

The nursery, which takes **children** from 6 months old, has a good reputation. The ski kindergarten is for 3- to 7-year-olds, but is open mornings only.

STAYING THERE

There's a fair choice of hotel and apartment accommodation. SkiBound have the rustic Timelets **chalet**. The Grand (3-star) and Christiania (2-star) are the best **hotels**, and both are well placed. The Centre is shabbier and noisier, but its food and position are good. Plein Sud is an adequate SkiBound club hotel which is well placed, though the cheapest rooms are extremely basic. The Rocher St Pierre **apartments** are good by French standards. The simple Val d'Aurea accommodation is well placed.

Most of the **restaurants** are pizza and fondue joints. The Crêperie and Asile des Fondues are perhaps the best of these. The Gastilleur has the best French cuisine in town.

Après-ski is quiet, though far from dead. The hotel bars of the Touring and Plein Sud, and American Dodgers, are lively. Piano Bar has live music. The Mammoth and Swell discos warm up at weekends.

There are few amenities for **non-skiers**, and Valloire feels somewhat cut off from civilisation.

Valmorel 1400m

✔ Fairly large ski area provides something for everyone

✔ Probably the most tastefully designed of all French purpose-built resorts

✔ Excellent ski convenience

✔ Beginners and children particularly well catered for

✔ One of the most accessible of the Tarentaise resorts by road and rail

✔ One of the cheapest of the French resorts widely available from UK tour operators

✘ Limited challenging skiing

✘ Fairly low ski area, so good snow not guaranteed

✘ Little variety in accommodation and in restaurants and bars

✘ Some frustrating bottlenecks mar a good lift system

This is the purpose-built resort where they got it right. Built from scratch in the mid-1970s, Valmorel was intended to look and feel like a mountain village: a traffic-free main street with hamlets grouped around it, low-rise buildings and traditional Savoie stone and wood materials throughout. The end-result is an attractive, friendly sort of place, even if it does have a 'Disney World' feel to it. There is easy access between the accommodation, the village centre and the skiing.

The ski area is large, by most standards – though it can't rival its huge neighbours, the Trois Vallées or Val-d'Isère-Tignes. But with good snow conditions and the whole system open, there's enough skiing to keep most grades of skier except experts happy. As the snow conditions deteriorate, the variety of available skiing reduces rapidly and the flaws in the lift system can start to show through.

Unashamedly aimed at the middle-ground (intermediate skiers, families and mixed-ability groups), it does have considerable appeal to those groups because it has been so well put together.

ORIENTATION

Valmorel, a short drive from Moûtiers, is the main resort in 'Le Grand Domaine' – a ski area that links the Tarentaise with the Maurienne, by way of the Col de la Madeleine. The skiing stretches over to Saint-François and Longchamp on the Maurienne side. Chair-lifts and a gondola from the compact village provide access to all the main sectors of the skiing.

All the mega-ski areas of the Tarentaise are within reasonable driving distance – the **Trois Vallées, La Plagne, Les Arcs** and even **Val-d'Isère-Tignes**. An off-piste tour through a number of these resorts starts from the Col du Gollet above Valmorel.

🏠 The resort

Happily for Valmorel and its visitors, the place was built with more than just convenience in mind – it also manages to look pretty good. Bourg-Morel is the heart of the resort – a traffic-free street where you'll find most of the shops, the restaurants, visitor information – just about everything – in a 200m stretch. It's pleasant and usually lively, with a distinctly family feel. And the skiing is right at hand, with the main pistes back and chair-lift out meeting at the end of the street. Nearby is an information board showing lift and piste status, and what's on locally.

Dotted around the hillside, but not very far from the Bourg-Morel centre, are the six 'hameaux' which contain most of the accommodation. Most of it is self-catering and of a reasonably high standard.

We've had a report of a jolly New Year's Eve in town, with lots of fireworks, a parade and torch jugglers.

The skiing

Beginners and intermediates will take to it. Those looking for more of a challenge will find it more limited. Variety is provided by a number of sectors of quite distinctive character, and the system is big enough to provide interesting, if hardly epic, exploratory trips to its farthest boundaries. Some visitors find the piste map inadequate, especially for the Longchamps sector, and there are a couple of long, awkward drag-lifts.

THE SKI AREA
A big system in miniature

The 48 lifts and 163km of piste spread out in an interesting arrangement over a number of minor valleys and ridges either side of the Col de la Madeleine, with Valmorel at the eastern extremity of the system and runs coming down into the village on three sides.

The most heavily used route out of the village is via the **Beaudin** chair which takes you over the main pistes

SKI FACTS

Altitude	1200m-2550m
Lifts	48
Pistes	163km
Green/Blue	69%
Red	19%
Black	12%
Artificial snow	8km

LIFT PASSES

95/96 prices in francs
Le Grand Domaine
Covers all lifts in
Valmorel and St-
François Longchamp.
Beginners One free
drag lift. Limited area
lift pass covers
beginner lifts and
runs.
Main pass
1-day pass 163
6-day pass 880
(low season 697 –
21% off)
Senior citizens
Over 60: 6-day pass
753 (14% off)
Children
Under 13: 6-day pass
753 (14% off)
Under 4: free pass
Short-term passes
Half-day from 11.30
(142) and 12.30 (121).
Saturday morning
until 1pm.
Alternative passes
Valmorel Domaine
covers 24 lifts in
Valmorel only (6 days
840 for adults, 708
for children).

back. From the top of the chair a
network of lifts and pistes takes you
over to the **Col de la Madeleine** and
beyond that to Lauzière (the highest
point of the ski area at 2550m) or the
slopes of **Saint-François** and
Longchamp at the far western end of
the ski area.

The Pierrafort gondola for the
Mottet sector and the Crève-Cœur
chair for the **Gollet** area take off from
Hameau-du-Mottet at the top end of
the village. Both areas have their own
runs back towards the village, or good
skiers can work their way over to the
Beaudin and Madeleine sectors (tough
runs down only) in the other direction. There's an easy link
in the other direction.

Adjacent to the village there are
nursery areas with good easy runs.

SNOW RELIABILITY
Sort of average
With a top station of 2550m and
much of the skiing below 2000m,
good snow conditions are not
guaranteed. Lower runs are frequently
closed, and even Lauzière, which has
the system's high point but faces
south, and Gollet can suffer quite
quickly during sunny spells. Mottet is
north-facing and usually has the best
snow. Artificial snowmaking covers
the almost 600m vertical from
Beaudin down to village level.

FOR ADVANCED SKIERS
Better than you might think
Although not renowned for its tough
skiing, there are challenging runs.
Gollet is usually a good place for
moguls – plenty of them but not too
big and not too hard. There are steep
black runs below the top section of
the Mottet chair and some interesting
off-piste variants. From the drag-lift up
towards the Madeleine sector, there
are a couple of fine runs (one off-piste
but indicated on the piste map).

The Lauzière chair can seem a bit of
a trek, but once there you'll probably
find it under-used and a lot of fun,
provided it hasn't suffered too much
sun. There are three marked runs and
plenty of acreage in which to pick
your own route – there are some steep
pitches and often some big bumps.

Ski-touring is a very popular activity
in the region, and trips such as the
Nine-Valley safari can be organised
from Valmorel.

FOR INTERMEDIATE SKIERS
Plenty to keep you busy
Lots of scope, though many skiers
seem to mill around Beaudin and the
Arenouillaz drag and Biollène chair –

the adjacent runs are quite friendly.
The runs down into the Celliers valley
are more testing, particularly the two
reds served by the Madeleine chair,
which are too difficult for early
intermediates to cope with
comfortably. The main thoroughfare
back to the village – from Beaudin
along the line of the snow cannons –
is graded blue then red, and the red
stretch can be quite daunting at the
end of the day. The artificial snow
tends to pile up in surprisingly large
heaps, as do tired beginners.

For a day out, the slopes around
Saint-François-Longchamp are within
easy striking distance, and form a big
area of mainly broad, flattering runs.
The Côte drag, which can be reached
on the return trip, is little used and
serves two pleasant runs with some
good terrain for practising off-piste.

The red route from the top of Mottet
is outstandingly boring on the upper
half – more push-and-walk than skiing
– but the views are some
compensation, and the lower half is
much better. The runs back to the
village, served by the Pierrafort
gondola, are graded blue but are long,
interesting and in parts tricky. The
adjacent Gollet slopes also provide
plenty of scope for good intermediates
to amuse themselves.

FOR BEGINNERS
An excellent choice
Valmorel suits beginners – there are
dedicated learning areas right by the
village for both adults (at Bois de la
Croix) and children (in the snow
garden of the children's club), and lots
of expertise among the instructors.
The terrain does not allow extensive
nursery areas in the valley, so progress
from novice to beginner usually sees
the children heading for the top of the
Pierrafort gondola and the adults for
the Beaudin sector. The lifts accessing
these areas can be used to return to
the village. If the snow-cover is
complete, there is a very pleasant
green run through the trees down to
Combelouvière.

FOR CROSS-COUNTRY
Inconvenient and not extensive
Valmorel is not the place for
aficionados; more for those giving it a
try. Trails adding up to 23km, at a
number of different locations in the
valley (and therefore likely to have a
limited season only), can be reached
by special bus from Valmorel itself.

SKI SCHOOL

94/95 prices in francs

ESF
Classes 6 days
2½hr am or pm
6 half-days: 550
Children's classes
Ages: 4 to 12
6 half-days: 510
Private lessons
Hourly
160 for 1 or 2 people

CHILDCARE

Saperlipopette
(79098445) provides
care for children aged
from 6 months to 7
years, from 8.30 to
5pm. Those aged 18
months to 3 are given
'a gentle and amusing
first experience with
the snow'. Those
aged 3 to 7 have
indoor activities as
well as ski classes
(divided into three
levels), and there is a
snow play area for
those who do not
wish to ski.

QUEUES
Occasional (avoidable) problems
Queues build up for the Beaudin chair
at ski school times. These can be
avoided by using the alternative
Lanchettes chair. Once into the skiing
area, there are only two bottlenecks to
worry about – the Madeleine chair,
which provides the only access to the
Saint-François and Lauzière side, and
the Frêne drag, almost as critical to the
return journey. Simply avoid using
them at peak times.

MOUNTAIN RESTAURANTS
Fair to middling
There are six of them: none is
appalling nor wonderful. At least a
couple of them do deserve more of a

mention: the Altipiano, below the
Mottet chair, and the Deux Mazots, at
Col de la Madeleine (and which
doubles as a roadside café in summer),
provide table-service, good food, and
some ambience, without charging silly
prices. Le Prariond, most of the way
down from Mottet, is, depending on
your point of view, either a fun place
to have a drink at the end of the day
or just plain loud.

SKI SCHOOL
Good, especially for first-timers
We've had several good reports this
year on the ski school. Instructors
generally speak good English and are
enthusiastic and imaginative. The
main criticism is the familiar one that
classes can be too large – plus the fact
that English-speaking classes are
sometimes held in the afternoons
only. Teaching for first-timers and for
children is a speciality of the resort,
and likely to produce good results.

FACILITIES FOR CHILDREN
First-rate but book early
Saperlipopette is a comprehensive
childcare facility – one of the few in
the Alps that gives the impression of
having been thought out as
thoroughly as those in America.
  One parent this year reported: 'Very
high standards of equipment, facilities
and routine. Very good English-
speaking staff always reported on what
children had done and eaten, and for
how long they slept.'
  Prices vary with the seasons.
Advance booking is essential except
for very quiet times.

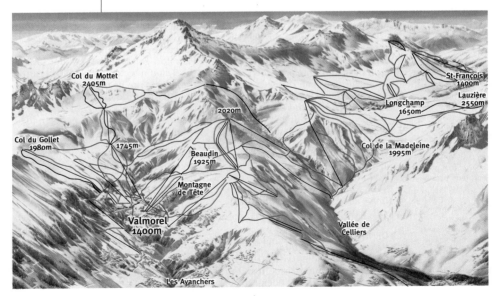

GETTING THERE

Air Geneva, transfer 3¼hr. Lyon, transfer 3½hr. Chambery, transfer 2½hr.

Rail Moûtiers (6km); regular buses from station.

Staying there

Athough it is basically a traffic-free resort, there are convenient drop-off points for all the accommodation. At the bottom end of Bourg-Morel is the base station of the Télébourg, a cross-village lift providing access to the 'Hameau-du-Mottet'. Between the other hameaux and Bourg-Morel, walking doesn't take long – but some of the pathways should be graded red. Hameau-du-Mottet probably wins the convenience contest – it is at the top of the Télébourg, and access to main lifts and from return runs is good.

A car is of no use in the resort but very handy for trips to other resorts of the Tarentaise.

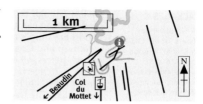

HOW TO GO

Take a package for value

Self-catering packages are the norm in Valmorel, though there seem to be more catered chalet deals available every year. There are few hotels in Valmorel, but tour operators have an allocation in most of them. If you're travelling independently and prefer more traditional surroundings, Les Avanchers is a possibility.

Selected chalets in Valmorel

Simply Ski *Chalet specialists*   T 0181 742 2541 F 0181 995 5346

Simply Ski offers a choice of three comfortable chalets, each providing a warm and friendly welcome. Chalets Beaudin and Fontaine are conveniently positioned in the centre of Valmorel, close to ski lifts, ski school, kindergarten and local amenities. Chalet Penagos is on the edge of the village, 100 metres from the Lanchette chair lift and it is possible to ski right back to the door.

Friendly chalet staff
Cordon Bleu cuisine
Competitive prices and discounts
Ski leader service
Scheduled and charter flights
Snowtrain and Snowdrive

Chalet Penagos →

Ski Crystal   T 0181 399 5144 F 0181 390 6378

Chalets Jean-Marie, Henri and Madeleine (each sleeping 11 to 14, 10 to 14, 11 to 15 respectively) are quietly located in the Hameau de la Fontaine area, with the lifts only 2 minutes walk and the village centre approximately 5 minutes away. Each comprises two apartments, directly opposite one another, with their own private access and a living/dining area in one of the apartments. An ideal choice for families or large groups.

← Nanny service is available in Valmorel

OTHER CHALET HIGHLIGHTS
Chalets Jean-Marie and Henri offer a **Nanny Service** where qualified nannies look after children aged between 6 months to 5 years, for either five full or half days between 9.30 and 4.30.
Premier Service is available in all chalets when a group books the entire chalet, and provides many extra comforts over and above the standard chalet services.
One week prices start from just £249 per person including return flights.

PACKAGES

AA Ski-Driveaway,
Altours Travel, Chalets
'Unlimited', Crystal,
Equity Total Ski,
French Impressions,
Inghams, Lagrange,
Made to Measure,
Motours, Neilson,
Simply Ski, SkiBound,
Stena Sealink,
Thomson, Travelscene
Ski-Drive

**St-François-
Longchamp** SkiBound

ACTIVITIES

Indoor Keep-fit club,
sauna, gym, cinema
Outdoor Snow-shoe
outings, 12km of
prepared walks,
tobogganing, floodlit
skiing, para-gliding

SIMPLY SKI

helped us to compile
the eating out and
après-ski sections.
Our thanks to them.

TOURIST OFFICE

Postcode 73260
Tel 00 33 79098555
Fax 79098529

Chalets Though there are more on the market each year, the range isn't wide – most are simply catered apartments.

Neilson and Crystal offer a selection of such places, all of which are fairly cheap and cheerful. For those looking for a 'proper' chalet, it's got to be Simply Ski. The traditional-style, simply furnished chalet Penagos has received plenty of complimentary remarks from reporters. On the edge of the village, it's 10 minutes' walk to the centre but you can ski back to the door. The same company also has smaller, central apartment-chalets, ideal for a family or small group looking for sole use.

Hotels There are only three hotels, and only the central hotel du Bourg expects casual callers – the others, up the hill a little way, basically cater for people staying the week on half-board.
£££ Planchamp Best in town, family run, with a good French restaurant.
££ Hotel du Bourg Simple place in the middle of Bourg-Morel – not recommended by this year's reporter.
££ La Fontaine Across the piste from the Planchamp.
Self-catering Most people do – 8,500 apartment beds are distributed throughout the six hamlets and they are generally well-equipped. While it's great having a view over the piste, the downside of certain locations in Mottet and Planchamp is the proximity of some very noisy snow guns: the sound-proofing is not quite good enough for light sleepers.

Among the most comfortable are the Creve-Coeur apartments in the Spie Loisirs sector, next to the ski kindergarten and crèche, with good connections to the centre. The Hameau Planchamp apartments are less comfortable but better than some, and well positioned for the skiing.

EATING OUT
Good enough but rarely thrilling
You can check out the menus of most of Valmorel's restaurants in 15 minutes wandering up and down the main street. The pattern soon emerges – pizzas, pasta, fondues and a smattering of Savoie fare. There's also couscous and galettes available; not a huge variety but enough, and you're likely to get decent food and fair value. Many of the places need to be booked for any chance of a seat at a reasonable time.

Grill le Creuset is a bit smarter than most, for that special meal. The restaurant of hotel Planchamp is the other relatively upmarket place with prices to match. The Vadrouille does

local dishes and has a lively atmosphere. The Pierrade and the Petit Savoyarde are mid-range places recommended by reporters. The Grenier in Mottet offers a bit of everything. Both in a slightly different location. Locals also recommend the the Galette and the Perce Neige. A pizza or shared fondue in the popular Chez Albert or the Petit Prince is the best bet if you're on a tight budget.

APRES-SKI
Unexciting
Immediate après-ski is centred on the outdoor cafés at the end of Bourg-Morel and Le Grenier. Both are lively spots. The after-dark activities are, like everything else, concentrated around that main street. The Vadrouille is a pleasant and lively bar, Café de la Gare has live music, Ski Roc and Petit Prince are popular with locals, while the Perce-Neige frequently gets packed and boisterous. Cocktails can be enjoyed in more polished surroundings at the Shaker in hotel La Fontaine. There's one disco, Jeans, which is often neglected but occasionally buzzes.

You may catch the occasional musical event at the village hall, or a street parade (there's a Mardi Gras with medieval costumes and fireworks). Once a week there's floodlit skiing and the ski instructors generally turn out to race each other. A two-screen cinema and a wine-tasting evening are other possibilities.

FOR NON-SKIERS
Pleasant but boring
It's not a great place to hang around if you're not skiing – there are some marginal activities which, together with the usual café-based pastimes, can help to pass a few days. There are some cleared walks around the village and at the top of all the main lifts; and there's a pretty baroque church and some good lunch venues in Les Avanchers. Several mid-mountain restaurants are accessible to non-skiers, and it's also quite a practical proposition for skiers to return to the village for a lunchtime meet.

Snow-shoe treks and dog-sleigh trips can be organised – you can even learn to 'mush' the dogs.

STAYING DOWN THE VALLEY
Appealing
There are three small hotels in Les Avanchers – the Cheval Noir, the Charmette, and the Crey – handy enough if you prefer the ambience of the old village, and you have a car.

Val-Thorens 2300m

HOW IT RATES

The skiing
Snow ★★★★★
Extent ★★★★★
Advanced ★★★★
Intermediates★★★★★
Beginners ★★★★
Convenience ★★★★★
Queues ★★★★
Restaurants ★★★★

The rest
Scenery ★★★
Resort charm ★
Not skiing ★★

✔ *Part of the biggest linked ski area in the world, the Trois Vallées*

✔ *The highest resort in the Alps, with north-facing slopes guaranteeing good snow for a long season*

✔ *Ski area good for all standards*

✔ *Swift access to the Méribel and Les Menuires ski areas*

✔ *Can ski directly to and from nearly all accommodation*

✘ *Purpose-built style doesn't suit all tastes, although efforts to make the village more attractive have improved the ambience*

✘ *Can be cold and bleak in bad weather – no skiing below the tree-line*

Val-Thorens' great attraction is its height and the north-facing direction of most of its slopes. It has the highest skiing in the Trois Vallées (up to 3200m) and a couple of glaciers, more or less guaranteeing good snow conditions for a long season – October to May, plus summer skiing. On top of all this you have the skiing of the rest of the Trois Vallées on your doorstep. For the keen skier looking for the best snow, it's difficult to think of anywhere better.

The resort is purpose-built and opened in the early 1970s. When we first visited it, we thought it very ugly and unfriendly. But recent efforts to smarten the place up have paid off: it's now car-free; small trees have been planted; and the compact design, with friendly squares, makes it feel rather more pleasant than some other French purpose-built resorts.

ORIENTATION

Val-Thorens is built high above the tree-line on a west-facing mountainside at the head of the Belleville valley, with pistes going past virtually all the accommodation. You can ski from your door to a variety of lifts that link to all the main ski areas.

A gondola takes you from the top of the village down and then up to the huge Caron cable-car, which goes to the area's highest point (3200m). Or you can ski down to the gondola's mid-point to join it. A number of chair-lifts lead up into the main north-facing Val-Thorens skiing. Or a 25-person gondola will whisk you east to the Péclet glacier.

From the resort centre and its western edge, chair-lifts lead up towards the skiing of the **Méribel** valley. You can also ski to **Les Menuires** from the top here.

 ## The resort

Val-Thorens is a classic purpose-built resort, with skiing from many of its doors. But it is not as hideous as some – notably Les Menuires, just down the road. The buildings are mainly medium-rise and wood-clad, and the more recent ones are distinctly stylish. The village has streets that are now largely traffic-free, which also helps. There are shopping arcades, a fair choice of bars and restaurants, and a good sports centre. Despite the northerly orientation of the slopes, the village is quite sunny.

 ## The skiing

Take account of its abundance of high slopes, the extent of its local skiing and the easy access to the other resorts of the Trois Vallées, and the attraction of Val-Thorens to keen skiers becomes clear. The main disadvantage is the lack of trees. Val-Thorens can be bleak in cold weather – and heavy snowfalls can make skiing impossible.

THE SKI AREA
High and snowsure
The resort has a wide piste going right down the front of it and leading, in turn, to a number of different lifts out. The biggest is the enormous Funitel de

Péclet gondola, each with a 25-person cabin. This takes you to one of the two glaciers, with its own lifts.

You can also ski from here to the larger **Montée du Fond** ski area, which can be reached directly from the resort too. From the top of a network of ideal intermediate runs you can also ski down into the relatively new 'Fourth Valley' of the **Maurienne**. For the coming season a new gondola is due to open from Orelle, right down in the valley – which will presumably allow access to crowds over from Italy at weekends.

The 150-person **Cîme de Caron** cable-car to the highest lift-served point in the Trois Vallées, at 3200m, can be reached from the Montée du Fond area or by taking a gondola or the fast four-person Boismint 2 chair.

Going the opposite way up from the resort leads you to the **Méribel** skiing via two chair-lifts. **Les Menuires** can be reached using these lifts too, or by skiing the easy Boulevard Cumin along the valley floor.

SNOW RELIABILITY
Difficult to beat
Few resorts can rival Val-Thorens for reliably good snow cover – accounted for by its altitude and the north-facing direction of most of its slopes. It even has two summer skiing areas on glaciers. The only place where you are likely to find poor snow is on the

LIFT PASSES

95/96 prices in francs

Three Valleys
Covers all lifts in Courchevel, Méribel, Les Menuires, Val-Thorens and St Martin-de-Belleville.
Beginners 2 free lifts in Val-Thorens.
Main pass
1-day pass 215
6-day pass 1035
(low season 932 – 10% off)
Senior citizens
Over 60: 6-day pass 776 (25% off)
Over 80: free pass
Children
Under 16: 6-day pass 776 (25% off)
Under 5: free pass
Short-term passes
Half-day pass from 12.30 for Val-Thorens lifts only (adult 125).
Notes 6-day pass and over valid for one day each in Tignes-Val d'Isère, La Plagne-Les Arcs, Pralognan-la-Vanoise and Les Saisies. Reductions for families.
Alternative passes
Val-Thorens pass covers 32 lifts (6 days 770 for adults, 540 for children); Vallée des Belleville pass covers 78 lifts and 240km piste in Les Menuires, St-Martin and Val-Thorens (adult 6-day 975, child 755).
Credit cards: Yes

south-facing runs on the way back from an excursion to the rest of the Trois Vallées, and on the south-facing runs down into the Maurienne valley.

FOR ADVANCED SKIERS
Few big challenges on-piste
Val-Thorens' local skiing is primarily intermediate terrain. But you'll certainly enjoy racing down the good snow on predominantly red runs. The runs down from the Cîme de Caron cable-car are probably the most challenging – with the red around the side narrower than, and almost as steep as, the black down the face. The Cascades run back into town from the Péclet direction is also worth trying (to be served by a new six-seater chair for the coming season). The Marielle Goitschel run down from the connection with Méribel is one of the easiest blacks we've come across – but its snow suffers from being south-facing and from the weight of traffic of skiers travelling to Val-Thorens.

There are three good itineraires. Two lead to the bottom of the chair in the Maurienne valley. And the long Lac du Lou itineraire leaves from the summit of the Cîme de Caron and joins the run from the La Masse area of Les Menuires. There is also a great deal of unmarked off-piste skiing, for which you will need a guide.

FOR INTERMEDIATE SKIERS
Unbeatable quality and quantity
Although Val-Thorens is not in the centre of the Trois Vallées, it will take a decent intermediate only 90 minutes or so to get to Courchevel at the far end, if not distracted by the endless skiing opportunities on the way. The

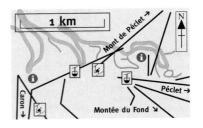

scope for intermediates throughout the Trois Vallées is enormous.

The local skiing in Val-Thorens itself is some of the best intermediate terrain in the region. The majority of the pistes are easy cruising reds and blues, made even more enjoyable by the usually excellent powdery snow.

The snow on the red Col run is always some of the best around. The blue La Moraine run below it is very gentle and popular with the ski schools. In general the runs on the top half of the mountain are steeper than those back into the resort.

The Montée du Fond 1 and 2 lifts serve a good variety of red runs. And adventurous intermediates shouldn't miss the Combe du Caron black run underneath the cable-car: it is very wide and usually has good snow.

FOR BEGINNERS
Good late-season choice
The slopes at the foot of the resort are very gentle and provide convenient, snowsure nursery slopes. There aren't ideal long green runs to progress to, but the blues back into town are very easy. Because of the resort's height and bleakness, beginners can find it cold early in the season and intimidating in bad weather.

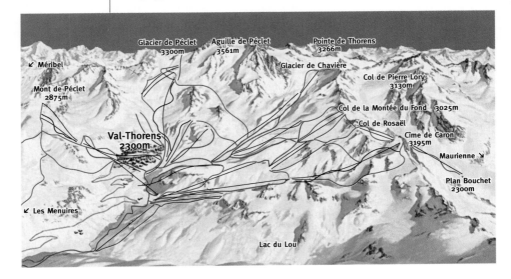

SKI SCHOOL
95/96 prices in francs
ESF
Classes 6 days
5hr 30min: 9.15-12.15
and 14.15-16.45
6 full days: 988
Children's classes
Ages: 4 to 12
6 full days: 810
Private lessons
Hourly
180 for 1 to 2 people

International
Known as Ski Cool
Classes 6 half-days
3hr, am or pm 680
(beginners only)
5 half-days: 600
Children's classes
Ages: up to 12
5 mornings: 520
Private lessons
Hourly or daily
190 for 1hr, for 1 to 2
people

FOR CROSS-COUNTRY
Try elsewhere
Val-Thorens is a poor base for cross-country, with only 4km of local trails.

QUEUES
A few bad lift bottlenecks
Val-Thorens has a very modern lift system, offering choices of routes. This means that queues are, for most of the area, not a problem most of the time. The biggest queues we've come across have been at the slow, old two-person Col chair (now fed by a high-speed quad, so it's not surprising queues build up) and for the Cîme de Caron cable-car – we've heard of 45-minute queues here, but the most we've experienced has been 20 minutes.

There can also be long queues for the 3 Vallées 1 and Plein Sud chair-lifts back towards Méribel in mid-afternoon, and for the short village lift at the end of the day.

Reporters who've been here in high season when snow has been in short supply elsewhere tell us that queues can become a significant problem, particularly if people are bussed in from lower resorts.

MOUNTAIN RESTAURANTS
Lots of choice
Moutière, just below the top of the chair of the same name, is one of the more reasonably priced of Val-Thorens' mountain huts (which are generally thought by reporters to be expensive). We liked the Chalet de Génépi, on the run down from the Moraine chair. It has an open fire, good soup and on a mid-morning stop

on the terrace, we enjoyed the medley of sixties hits.

The Plan Bouchet refuge in the Maurienne valley is very popular and welcoming, but bar service can be slow. You can stay the night there too.

On the other side of the valley the Chalet Plain Sud, below the chair of the same name, has excellent views.

SKI SCHOOL
Plenty of courses
There are two main schools, the ESF and the International school (known as Ski Cool), which between them offer a wide range of options. This year we've had good reports of private lessons with both schools. As well as the usual group lessons, the ESF have shorter duration, smaller-class sessions (two hours for five days, with a maximum of eight skiers). They also have a Trois Vallées group for those who want to cover a lot of ground while receiving tuition. This is available by the day or the week, and can include off-piste. Ski Cool also

Selected chalets in Val-Thorens

CHILDCARE

Marielle Goitschel's Children's Village (79000047) takes children aged from 3 to 16, from 9am to 5.30, 7 days a week. The ESF can provide all-day care and offers classes for children from age 2½. It also runs Mini club crèches in two locations, at the top and bottom of the resort, taking children from age 3 months.

GETTING THERE

Air Geneva, transfer 3½hr. Lyon, transfer 3½hr. Chambery, transfer 2½hr.

Rail Moûtiers (35km); regular buses from station.

PACKAGES

AA Ski-Driveaway, Airtours, Alpine Options Skidrive, Altours Travel, Bladon Lines, Crystal, Equity Total Ski, First Choice Ski, French Impressions, Inghams, Lagrange, Le Shuttle Holidays, Made to Measure, Motours, Neilson, Poles Apart, Ski Choice, Ski Club of GB, Ski France, Ski Valkyrie, SkiBound, Skiworld, Stena Sealink, Thomson, Travelscene Ski-Drive, UCPA, White Roc

ACTIVITIES

Indoor Sports centre (tennis, squash, climbing wall, roller, golf simulator, swimming pool, saunas, jacuzzi, volley ball, weight training, table tennis, fitness, badminton, football), games rooms, music recitals, cinema, beauty centre
Outdoor Walks, snow-mobiles, snow-shoe excursions, parapenting

TOURIST OFFICE

Postcode 73440
Tel 00 33 79000808
Fax 79000004

offers numerous courses, with the bonus of class sizes guaranteed not to exceed ten. They specialise in teaching beginners, who get an extra day's tuition (six instead of five), and offer an 'Evoluski' package that includes equipment hire and lift pass. Tuition is ski évolutif: you start on short skis and work your way up. Ski Cool also have off-piste courses. There are several specialist guiding outfits.

FACILITIES FOR CHILDREN

The childcare arrangements are comprehensive and well-run. The ESF crèche at the top of the village is recommended for everything except its inconvenient location. Classes for very young children may not materialise, but private lessons with an instructor called Bernard who specialises in children get rave reviews. Children who have reached third-star standard in ski school can go off in guided groups around the Trois Vallées led by Fabienne Pandier.

 Staying there

Everywhere is fairly ski-convenient, but there are two quite distinct parts of the village, with a nursery slope separating the two. There is more animation in the upper section, Péclet, than in the lower part, Caron, which is dominated by apartments. It is not a big place, so walking from one part to the other is no problem.

HOW TO GO

Surprisingly high level of comfort
Accommodation tends to be of a higher standard than in many French purpose-built villages, and there's plenty of choice too.
Chalets These are catered apartments, and many are quite comfortable. Neilson, Thomson and Crystal all have well appointed places and budget-price Skiworld moved in last season.
Hotels There are a dozen hotels, mainly 3-stars. Most of those listed are grouped around the nursery slope that almost divides the resort in two.
£££££ Fitz Roy Swanky but charming Relais & Châteaux place with lovely rooms and about the best food in town. Pool. Well placed, just in the upper part of the resort.
££££ Val Thorens Welcoming and comfortable; next door to the Fitz Roy.
£££ Sherpa Highly recommended for pleasant atmosphere and excellent, substantial food. Less-than-ideal

position at the top of the resort.
£££ Bel Horizon Small, friendly, family-run 3-star with good food and south-facing rooms. On piste near bottom of resort.
Self-catering There is a wide range of options, including apartments of a much higher standard than the norm in France. Reporters this year recommended Chalet le Val Chavière in Péclet and Residence Montana in Caron. They are comfortable with lots of mod cons and facilities.

Most of the other good places are in Caron. Les Temples du Soleil are the nicest of the Pierre et Vacances apartments in the Trois Vallées, and have plenty of amenities. The Olympiades apartments are in a good central position but have small rooms.

EATING OUT

Surprisingly wide range
Val-Thorens has something for most tastes. At the top of the range, gourmets will enjoy the Fitz Roy hotel and Chalet des Glaciers. Sherpa is another hotel with fine cuisine. Several reporters have recommended the Montana in Caron. Tavern le Scapin du Lou is a nice brasserie. Matafan, El Gringo's Café and the Temples du Soleil pizzeria are informal places worth a try. One family made special mention of how child-friendly all the restaurants were.

APRES-SKI

Limited but improving
Val-Thorens is much livelier at night than many of our reporters expected. That's because of the large Dutch and Scandinavian presence and the associated amount of drinking that goes on. It can be pretty noisy at throwing out time. Most people recommended the Ski Rock Café (with karaoke), El Gringo's (with a pub and karaoke as well as its good Mexican restaurant) and the Frog and Roast Beef (with cheap food and live music). The Lincoln, Viking and Malaysia cellar bar (live music) were also mentioned. There are three discos, of which the Agora is generally thought to be the best – though expensive.

FOR NON-SKIERS

Forget it
Val-Thorens is a resort for keen skiers. It's not the ideal place for non-skiers. But there's a good sports centre and plenty of outdoor activities, and you can get up to some of the mountain restaurants, but not the best, by lift.

Vars 1850m

Vars is a not very attractive purpose-built resort in the southern French Alps, which has the more interesting section of the fair-sized intermediate ski area that it shares with neighbouring Risoul.

THE RESORT

Vars is a sizeable resort, most of which has been purpose-built. It is bigger and has far more in the way of shops, restaurants, hotels, nightlife and other amenities such as squash, saunas and the like than Risoul, and it is equally ski-convenient and reasonably priced. Village architecture is unattractive, but Vars is not a complete eyesore thanks mainly to surrounding woodland. There are two centres: the original and geographic one, which has most of the accommodation and shopping, where the main gondola starts, and Point Show – a collection of bars, restaurants and shops, surrounding a main lift station, 10 minutes' walk from central Vars. The resort is very French, and locals are friendly to those making at least some attempt at the native tongue. Neighbouring Ste-Marie is a hamlet well linked to the skiing; being a popular summer resort, it actually has more hotels than Vars.

THE SKIING

Vars has the larger and more varied section of the **ski area**'s 170km of piste, with many more options for better skiers. There is also a good mix of open and wooded skiing on mountains either side of the village. The Peynier area is much the smaller and reaches only 2275m. The main skiing is the other side of the valley, with direct links to the skiing of Risoul. The two local areas are linked via a shortish walk across Ste-Marie, or by a two-stage gondola that rises up both mountains from just outside the village. The link to Risoul can be made in two places – near the top of the ski area, above 2500m, and lower down at the Col de Valbelle. Vars has very little skiing above 2500m and its slopes get a lot of sun, but there is virtually no skiing below village level (1850m), and the main pistes down to the village have artificial snow – so **snow reliability** is not bad.

There is little of challenge for **advanced skiers**, though the Crête de Chabrière top section accesses some off-piste, an unpisted route and a tricky couloir at Col de Crevoir.

The smaller of the two mountains, Peynier, is useful for better **intermediates**, having the only

black run of any length in the whole area, and some uncharacteristically long reds down to Ste-Marie (although these can be closed). The remainder of the skiing is mainly comfortable reds, ideal for average skiers. There is a good network of easy pistes throughout the central section, with a comfortable route to Risoul via Col de Valbelle.

Beginners have a nursery area of free lifts conveniently close to central Vars, with plenty of 'graduation' runs throughout the area. Precocious learners will be able to ski over to Risoul by the end of the week.

There are **cross-country** trails that start at the edge of town, but those above Ste-Marie are more extensive. **Queues** are rare outside the French holidays, and even then Vars is not overrun as some family resorts are.

The area is short of **mountain restaurants**. Many skiers return to base or visit Risoul for lunch. The Zizanie and Heureux Geleski are the best. Les Canettes is 'to be avoided'.

At the **ski school**, the lack of English-speaking tuition is an obvious problem. The well-equipped crèche takes **children** aged 18 months to four years. Ski school also has a nursery and a ski kindergarten.

STAYING THERE

With only a handful of hotels, Vars is dominated by **apartment** accommodation. Of the **hotels**, Le Caribou is the smartest place in town (with a swimming pool). L'Ecureuil is a modern, chalet-style 2-star. The Franou is no beauty, but its restaurant has a good reputation and it is well-positioned. Le Vallon is right next to the gondola station in Ste-Marie.

The range of **restaurants** is impressive, with numerous pizzerias, crêperies and fondue places, together with some more formal haunts. Chez Plumet has fine French cuisine; Pepito's and Chez Robert are good-value pizza joints; and Escondus is an elegant pricey establishment.

Après-ski is quite animated at tea-time, but less so after dinner, except during holidays and weekends, when the Look and the more glitzy Lem discos warm up. There is a cinema.

Non-skiers' amenities are disappointing, given the size of Vars.

TOURIST OFFICE

Postcode 05560
Tel 00 33 92465131
Fax 92465654

Italy

For a couple of years now, Italy has been on the up – and about time, too. British skiers used to go there in large numbers, attracted mainly by modest prices but also by the Italian way of doing things. Then, during the 1980s, we rather lost interest. Prices weren't low enough to compete with Andorra and Eastern Europe for the custom of low-budget beginners, while more experienced skiers were seduced by the ever-expanding lift networks of the French Alps. One or two particular British favourites, such as Sauze d'Oulx, were hit by snow shortages before the Alps in general started to suffer from erratic weather.

The tide has been turned, no doubt, mainly by exchange rates. For the last two winters, Italy has been a bargain, and lots of British skiers have taken advantage of it. Having done a fair bit of skiing in Italy recently, we predict that the revival will be sustained. Lift systems have been modernised; snowmaking – something that the Italians were early to catch on to – is now very widespread; piste grooming and resort organisation in general are improved.

The Italian approach to skiing is a relaxed one; the Italian approach to visitors is a friendly one; and the Italian approach to food and wine is an enthusiastic one. No other country offers quite the same mix. And there's a bonus: many Italian resorts enjoy splendid settings – in the Dolomites, the scenery is simply stunning.

Although there aren't huge numbers of them (on the international market, at least), Italian resorts vary as widely in characteristics as they do in location – and they are spread along the length of the Italian border, from Sauze and neighbours across the French border from Montgenèvre, all along the Swiss border to the Dolomites, an area that used to be part of Austria. There are high, snowsure ski-stations and charming valley villages, and ski areas that range from one-run wonders to some of the most extensive skiing in the world.

On our recent tours of resorts in north-east and north-west Italy, we've been struck by several things. As we've noted above, Italian resorts have pulled their socks up in recent years; most are no longer lagging in the new-lift stakes. And we'd forgotten how impressive the scenery is (something the brochures tend to overlook).

A lot of Italian skiing, particularly in the north-west, seems flatteringly easy. This is partly because the piste grooming is immaculate, and also because piste grading seems to overstate difficulty. Nowhere is this clearer than in La Thuile (located in Italy, despite its French name). Its ski area connects (just) with that of La Rosière (across the valley from Les Arcs) and, when we last visited, skiing from one to the other was like moving from the shelter of harbour to the open sea. Red runs on the La Thuile side were virtually motorways; at La Rosière, they offered challenging moguls.

We have also been struck by the way Italian skiing continues to be weekend-oriented. Except in the Dolomites, which depend largely on German custom, resorts can be quiet as the grave during the week, especially in low season, and come to life on Friday night or Saturday morning when the weekenders from Italy's affluent northern plain arrive. If, like us, you quite like having the hotel bar to yourself (not to mention the pistes), this is a real advantage. If you're looking for a social whirl, you could be disappointed.

In general, Italians don't take their skiing too seriously. Lifts may close for lunch, and mountain restaurants are generally welcoming places serving satisfying food, encouraging leisurely lunching. And at current exchange rates, prices in most resorts are noticeably low (though not in all – see our feature on the costs of skiing).

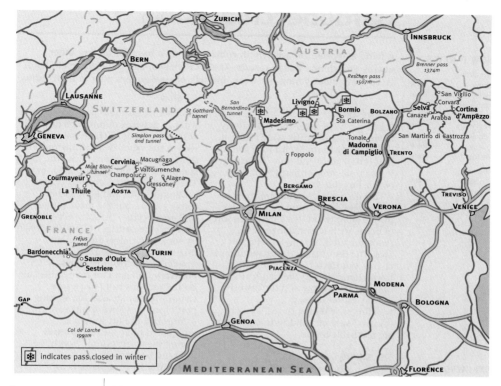

DRIVING IN THE ITALIAN ALPS

There are four main geographical groupings of Italian resorts, widely separated (our map is drawn to a much smaller scale than those of the other Alpine countries, because it has to cover much more ground). Getting to some of these resorts is tricky, and getting from one area to another can involve very long drives.

The handful of resorts to the west of Turin – Sauze d'Oulx, Bardonecchia and neighbours – are easily reached from France via the Fréjus tunnel from Modane, or via the good road over the pass that the resort of Montgenèvre sits on.

Further north, and about equidistant from Milan and Turin, are the resorts of the Aosta valley, Courmayeur and Cervinia the best-known among them. Courmayeur is the easiest resort to reach from Britain, thanks to the Mont Blanc tunnel from Chamonix in France. The road down the Aosta valley is a major thoroughfare carrying heavy goods traffic, but the roads up to some of the other resorts are quite long, winding and (at least in the case of Cervinia) high. The Aosta valley can also be reached from Switzerland via the Grand St Bernard tunnel. The approach is high, and may require chains.

To the east is a string of scattered resorts, most close to the Swiss border, many in isolated and remote valleys involving long drives up from the nearest Italian cities, or high-altitude drives from Switzerland. The links between Switzerland and Italy are more clearly shown on our Switzerland map on page 304. The major routes are the St Gotthard tunnel between Göschenen, near Andermatt, and Airolo – the main route between Basel and Milan – and the San Bernardino tunnel reached via Chur.

Finally, further east still, are the resorts of the Dolomites. Getting there is easy, over the Brenner motorway pass from Innsbruck, but getting around the intricate network of valleys linked by narrow, winding roads can be a slow business.

Bardonecchia 1310m

A fairly extensive ski area worth considering as a base for touring other nearby French and Italian resorts. The local slopes, and the town itself, tend to be fairly quiet during the week, but lots of weekenders pour in from Turin.

HOW IT RATES

The skiing

Snow	**
Extent	***
Advanced	*
Intermediates	***
Beginners	**
Convenience	**
Queues	***
Restaurants	***

The rest

Scenery	***
Resort charm	*
Not skiing	**

SKI FACTS

Altitude	1290m-2750m
Lifts	26
Pistes	140km
Green/Blue	55%
Red	41%
Black	4%
Artificial snow	13km

PACKAGES

Airtours, Chalets 'Unlimited', Crystal, Equity Total Ski, Neilson, PGL Ski Europe, Rank STS, Ski Ardmore

TOURIST OFFICE

Postcode 10052
Tel 00 39 (122) 99032
Fax 902266

THE RESORT

Bardonecchia is a sizeable old railway town, set in a beautiful wide valley, at the entrance to the Fréjus road tunnel that links France and Italy. It has two separate ski areas either side of town, both a bus-ride away.

This description could almost be of Chamonix, but Bardonecchia is a far from similar resort. It's a middling sort of place, with reasonable prices, moderate nightlife and a useful ski area. The resort lacks classic mountain charm, but has a traditional market-town character. But the frequent lack of resort-level snow and the intrusive railway rather detract.

Valfréjus, Valloire, the Milky Way resorts (Sauze etc) and Serre-Chevalier are reachable by car.

THE SKIING

The two **ski areas** are different in some ways. The larger one is a wide section of low (little above 2000m), tree-lined, north-facing pistes above three valley lift stations – Campo Smith on the edge of town, Les Arnauds and Melezet. Jafferau is a tall, thin mountain of long, partly open, west-facing runs. Chairs are generally antiquated and there are no bottom-to-top lifts. Jafferau is the less popular area, yet it has sunnier skiing, and is certainly preferable at weekends when the Torinese hit town. All runs lead back to the town chair-lift, the top-to-bottom piste descending an impressive 1460m from the high-point of 2750m.

Although the area doesn't have a particularly good record for **snow reliability**, there is plenty of relatively snowsure skiing above the middle stations, and the main pistes above Campo Smith have snowmaking on them. South-west-facing Jafferau quickly loses snow below mid-station.

In the Campo Smith-Melezet sector, the highest run, which can have moguls, and a medium-length black from Pra Magnan are the most interesting for **advanced skiers**. There is some off-piste in the trees when conditions allow. Jafferau is worth a visit for the long top-to-bottom reds.

Virtually the whole 140km is suitable for **intermediates**. Good

intermediates should head for Jafferau, where a network of fine runs finishes at the mid-station. There is a wealth of reds in the other area – skiing quickly down the tree-lined red from the top station to Campo Smith is great fun. There are plenty of leisurely cruises.

Campo Smith and Melezet have nursery areas, but the inconvenience of Bardonecchia, lack of special lift pass and the paucity of English spoken by some instructors are obvious disadvantages for **beginners**.

A varied, valley-level **cross-country** trail goes for many miles in both directions from just above Campo Smith; Melezet is a starting point for other long excursions.

Although the lift system is antiquated there are few **queues** during the week. Campo Smith is a weekend bottleneck.

Mountain restaurants are generally pleasant and uncrowded. All but one are prettily sited in trees.

The large **ski school** has a good reputation, except for over-large classes and unreliable English.

For **children**, there is a non-ski nursery and an all-day ski kindergarten at Campo Smith.

STAYING THERE

Accommodation is almost exclusively in **hotels**. The Tabor is a small, well-run 3-star. The chef and owner prides himself on the home-made cooking. The Park Hotel Rosa (4-star) is 10 minutes' walk from both the town centre and Campo Smith.

The Ronco **apartments** are inexpensive and only a couple of minutes' walk from Campo Smith.

There are numerous **restaurants** and pizzerias but some of the best places are in hotels (eg the Tabor). Loc Cá Fiore, at Campo Smith, is handy for Ronco-dwellers.

Being very much a working town, Bardonecchia lacks the usual **après-ski** atmosphere. A number of bars are good for a quiet drink among the locals, and become quite animated at weekends. Tour op reps organise some events. Only one disco.

For **non-skiers,** the town holds little interest except for its weekly market – though there are good sports facilities, including tennis and skating.

Bormio 1225m

HOW IT RATES

The skiing

Snow	✱✱✱
Extent	✱✱
Advanced	✱
Intermediates	✱✱✱
Beginners	✱✱
Convenience	✱✱✱
Queues	✱✱✱
Restaurants	✱✱✱✱

The rest

Scenery	✱✱✱
Resort charm	✱✱✱✱
Not skiing	✱✱✱✱

✔ Good mix of high, snowsure pistes and woodland runs with artificial snow, giving some excellent long runs when conditions are right

✔ Several good neighbouring ski resorts on same lift pass

✔ Interesting, attractive, old town centre – quite unlike any other ski resort

✔ Good mountain restaurants

✘ Skiing all of medium steepness – not suitable for beginners, timid intermediates or experts

✘ Rather confined main ski area, with second area some way out

✘ Many slow lifts up the mountain, despite modern access lifts

✘ Long airport transfers

✘ Crowds and queues on Sundays

✘ Central hotels are inconvenient for skiing, while those near the lifts form an ugly urban sprawl

Bormio is a highly unusual resort. If you like cobbled medieval Italian towns and don't mind a lack of Alpine resort atmosphere, you'll find the centre very appealing – though you're unlikely to be staying right in the middle. The ski area too suits a rather specific and perhaps rather uncommon breed of skier: you need to enjoy red runs and very little else, but you need to be happy with a limited range of them – unless, that is, you're prepared to take the bus out to the Val di Dentro skiing, or make longer outings, to Santa Caterina.

ORIENTATION

Bormio sits in a remote part of Lombardy, at the foot of the Stelvio pass, close to the Swiss and Austrian borders. Airport transfers are long (4 to 5 hours).

A gondola and cable-car leave from the southern edge of town to the main ski area. A second area lies well outside town to the west, served by lifts at Oga, Le Motte or Val di Dentro.

Santa Caterina (20mins) and **Livigno** (40km but 1½hr on a poor road) are accessible by bus, their lifts covered by the Valtellina lift pass, which also gives one free day a week in **St Moritz** (3hrs away). The **Passo Tonale** glacier is also within easy reach by car.

SKI FACTS

Altitude	1225m–3010m
Lifts	28
Pistes	62km
Green/Blue	36%
Red	46%
Black	18%
Artificial snow	7km

 The resort

Bormio began life as a Roman spa, and the thermal bathing facilities remain. It has a wonderfully preserved 17th-century town centre, complete with cobbled streets, markets with washing troughs, and old façades for today's shops, restaurants and cafés. Fortunately the town has escaped the dreariness and formality of many European spas. It's a colourful place where promenading is an important part of the evening scene, but not as lively as some Italian resorts, such as Courmayeur.

Between the town centre and the ski lifts, over the other side of the river, lies a characterless urban sprawl consisting largely of hotels built for the convenience of skiers – saving almost all of a 15-minute walk or a bus-ride. The ski-bus is reliable but not frequent. Most people walk.

The skiing

Bormio has good (but limited) skiing for confident intermediates who like long runs, with a nice mix of high, snowsure pistes and lower wooded slopes. Beginners, intermediates who prefer blue runs and the advanced are less well provided for.

Both the piste map and the piste marking could do with some substantial improvement.

THE SKI AREA
One-dimensional

The main ski area is tall (1800m vertical drop) and narrow, with virtually all the pistes facing north-west and heading down towards town. The two-stage **Cima Bianca** cable-car goes from bottom to top (3010m) of the skiing via the mid-station at **Bormio 2000**. The alternative gondola goes up to **Ciuk** at 1620m. Drag- and chair-lifts above these mid-stations serve all the runs, including those from the very top. The gondola means only the lowest 400m vertical is lost when runs to the resort have no snow and you have to ride down.

New lifts above **Oga** and **Val di Dentro** have made this once insignificant ski area, a short bus-ride out of Bormio, a useful addition to Cima Bianca. The area is now large enough to merit one or more day-trips. Half the runs are east-facing and not high, but some are north-facing and the mainly tree-lined skiing is very pleasant.

Day-trips further afield (see Orientation section) add greatly to the interest of a skiing trip to Bormio.

SNOW RELIABILITY
Good above mid-station

The runs above Bormio 2000 are usually snowsure, and the snowmaking facility on the lower slopes is impressive. The high, shaded, north-facing slopes of Santa Caterina (1735m to 2725m) usually have good

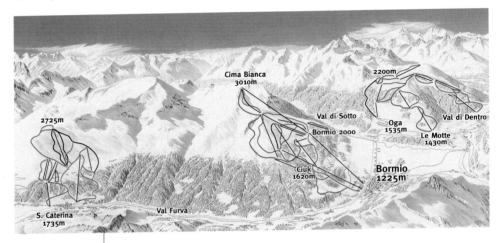

LIFT PASSES

Alta Valtellina
Covers all lifts in Bormio, Valdisotto, Valdidentro (all in local area), Santa Caterina (12km away) and Livigno (40km away) plus one free day in St Moritz.
Main pass
1-day pass 44,000 (94/95 price)
6-day pass 220,000 (low season 195,000 – 12% off)
Senior citizens
Over 65: 6-day pass 150,000 (32% off)
Children
Under 14: 6-day pass 135,000 (38% off)
Notes Day pass price covers Bormio lifts only.
Alternative passes
Up to 3-day pass for Bormio only (adult 3-day pass 120,000, 94/95 price).

CHILDCARE

Children's ski classes are offered by some of the ski schools, but there are no special arrangements for all-day care, and no non-ski kindergartens.

GETTING THERE

Air Bergamo, transfer 4hr.

Rail Tirano (40km); regular buses from station.

snow, and are not far away. However, the summer ski area at Passo Stelvio is not open in winter.

FOR ADVANCED SKIERS
Rather limited
There is little challenging skiing in Bormio's small ski area. Long, steep off-piste routes between Cima Bianca and the Ornella drag to the west are feasible when conditions allow. Otherwise there are a couple of short black runs. Bormio is said to be one of Franz Klammer's favourite ski areas; but it's the length of the runs, not their difficulty or extent, that have impressed him.

FOR INTERMEDIATE SKIERS
A few options for all grades
The men's 1985 World Championship downhill course starts with a steep plunge, but otherwise is no more than a tough red, which makes ideal skiing for strong intermediates. The Stella Alpina run down to 2000 is another fairly steep piste.

Many of the runs are less tough, ideal for average skiers. The longest is a superb top-to-bottom cruise, excellent for the less aggressive skier. The Oga area is similarly suitable for early intermediates. The runs beneath Ciuk in the main area and above Le Motte in the other can get quite icy at times. Santa Caterina has good intermediate skiing too.

FOR BEGINNERS
Many better Italian resorts
There are small nursery areas at both Ciuk and 2000, but novices would be better off at nearby Santa Caterina or Livigno. Near-beginners have a nice, quiet little area beneath 2000, using the Ornella drag, but no very flattering pistes to move on to.

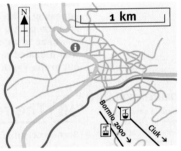

FOR CROSS-COUNTRY
Go to Santa Caterina
There are some trails either side of Bormio, towards Piatta and beneath Le Motte and Val di Dentro, but cross-country fans would be better off at snowsure Santa Caterina.

QUEUES
Much improved
Bormio has had a reputation for queues. Recent improvements to the lift system and the opening of Oga-Le Motte area have greatly improved matters. But both sections of the cable-car suffer delays in the morning peak period and on Sundays. And when the lower slopes are incomplete, queues form to ride the gondola down at the end of the day. Otherwise there are few problems except during carnival week (end of February).

MOUNTAIN RESTAURANTS
Good fare everywhere
The mountain restaurants are uniformly good for value and food. Even the efficient self-service at 2000 has a good choice of dishes. At La Rocca, above Ciuk, there is a welcoming chalet and a smart, modern place with table or self service. Cedrone, at 2000, has a good

CRYSTAL HOLIDAYS

helped us to compile the Eating out and Après-ski sections. Our thanks to them.

SKI SCHOOL

95/96 prices in lire

Bormio 2000
Classes 6 days
2hr: 9am-11am, 11am-1pm or 2pm-4pm
6 2hr days: 140,000

Nazionale
Classes 6 days
2½hr: 10am-12.30 or 2pm-4.30
6 2½hr days: 120,000
Private lessons
Daily
40,000 per hour; each additional person 5,000

Sertorelli
Italian-speaking instructors only.
Classes 6 days
2½hr
6 2½hr days: 170,000

Anzi
Small school based at Ciuk offering package of accommodation and instruction.

Capitani
Italian-speaking instructors only.

Alta Valtellina
Downhill and cross-country tuition.

PACKAGES

Airtours, Altours Travel, Crystal, First Choice Ski, Inghams, Thomson

ACTIVITIES

Indoor 2 museums, library, thermal baths, squash, swimming pool, sauna, massage, sports hall, skating rink
Outdoor Ski-bob, toboggan run, horse-riding, walks in the Stelvio National Park

TOURIST OFFICE

Postcode 23032
Tel oo 39 (342) 903300
Fax 904696

---

terrace and a play area for children. The Baita da Mario, at Ciuk, is a very welcoming table-service restaurant. The Oga area has two huts, one of them set among trees on the run to Val di Dentro.

SKI SCHOOL
Short lessons

There are six schools, some with outposts at 2000 and one based at Ciuk. Most Brits get sent to Scuola Italiano Bormio 2000 by their tour operators, but in the past we've had some negative reports of their group tuition. All the schools seem to limit their classes to half-day sessions, which some reporters considered too short. The Nazionale private lessons have received enthusiastic reports.

FACILITIES FOR CHILDREN
Typically Italian – limited

There is no crèche or ski kindergarten. But the Sertorelli and Bormio 2000 schools, at least, seem to make some effort to cater for children. The latter has a roped-off snow garden at its mid-mountain chalet.

 # Staying there

Bormio is big enough for location to be of some importance. The basic choice is between convenient locations on the ski-lift side of the river and the vitality of the town. Several major hotels are on the Via Milano, leading out of town, which is neither convenient nor atmospheric.

HOW TO GO
Probably on a hotel package

Bormio is not a chalet resort, but there are plenty of apartments available. However, hotels dominate the package holiday market.
Hotels Most of Bormio's 40-plus hotels are 2-star and 3-star places, though there are a handful of 4-stars.
££££ Palace Only luxurious place in town, on the Via Milano.
£££ Baita dei Pini Best placed of top hotels: on the river, equidistant from lifts and centre. Excellent food, good facilities, fitness room and a piano bar.
£££ Posta Right in the pedestrian heart of the town, rated a 4-star but with some 'pretty basic' rooms.
££ San Lorenzo Friendly 3-star on edge of old town.
££ Nevada Comfortable 3-star, very well placed for the cable-car.
££ Alu Ditto.
££ Ambassador Chalet Welcoming place close to the gondola.

££ Derby Large, attractive 3-star.
£ Piccolo Mondo Small, basic but friendly B&B place with good breakfasts, close to Ciuk lift.
£ Genzianella Cheap, well positioned for the gondola.
£ Dante Good-value, central 2-star.
Self-catering The plain, modern Residence Jolly is close to the centre.

EATING OUT
Plenty of choice

There is a wide selection of restaurants. The atmospheric Taulà does excellent modern food with great service. The Kuerc is popular but also pricey by local standards, due to its prime location in the main square. The Primo Piatto, in the Piccolo Mondo hotel, and the Vecchia Combo are other places worth a try. There are excellent pizzerias, including the Jap – in a vault near the main square.

APRES-SKI
Tea-time promenading

Nightlife is fairly subdued. Many people just like to do early evening promenading and visit the elegant Mozart tea-room, which has classical music. A more hectic tea-time pursuit is to stop off at the Rocca mountain café for a 'Bombardino' (hot advocat, brandy, whiskey and cream) and then ski down in the gathering darkness. Bar Cristallo is then a popular rendezvous at the bottom of the piste. Just around the corner is the relaxing terrace of the Jolly Bar. Another option is the Bar Nevada, next to the cable-car station. Clem's Pub and the Piano Bar are two of the livelier after-dinner spots. Shangri-La is a friendly bar. La Terra is the karaoke joint. The Kings Club, the only disco, gets busy at weekends – free entry for Brits.

Every Wednesday there's a floodlit ski race open to all. Tour reps organise a trip to the Roman baths, skidoo rides and a quiz evening.

FOR NON-SKIERS
Take in the thermals

Bormio offers plenty of distractions, including thermal baths, riding and walks in the Stelvio National Park. Ritzy St Moritz and duty-free Livigno are popular excursions.

STAYING UP THE MOUNTAIN
Contrasting possibilities

The modern Girasole, at Bormio 2000, is simple but well run, with a warm welcome and lots of events to counter the isolation. The Baita da Mario at Ciuk is quieter and more traditional in style. Both can be reached by road.

Cervinia 2050m

HOW IT RATES

The skiing

Snow	*****
Extent	***
Advanced	*
Intermediates	****
Beginners	*****
Convenience	***
Queues	***
Restaurants	***

The rest

Scenery	****
Resort charm	**
Not skiing	*

ORIENTATION

Cervinia is at the head of a long valley up from the Aosta valley on the Italian side of the Matterhorn. It is fairly compact with a lot of accommodation near the centre, at the foot of the nursery slopes. A series of drag-lifts from here takes you into the ski area. But the main gondola and cable-car up are an awkward uphill walk away. There is more accommodation further out at the Cielalto complex and on the road up to it.

The skiing links to **Valtournenche** further down the valley (covered by the lift pass) and **Zermatt** over in Switzerland (daily supplement payable). Day trips by car are possible to **Courmayeur, La Thuile** and the Monte Rosa resorts of **Champoluc** (you can ski there off-piste) or **Gressoney**.

✔ Extensive ski area with miles of long, gentle runs, usually with excellent snow

✔ Ideal for early intermediates and skiers who aren't looking for steep challenges or nasty surprises

✔ High, sunny and snowsure slopes amid impressive scenery

✔ Link with Zermatt in Switzerland provides more of the same type of skiing and some spectacular views

✔ Although expensive by Italian standards, still cheap in contrast to other Alpine countries

✘ Very little skiing to interest good or aggressive intermediates and above – especially since the Furggen cable-car closed

✘ Almost exclusively above-the-tree-line slopes, with little skiing possible in bad weather

✘ Lifts prone to closure by wind, particularly early in the season

✘ Village not unpleasant in the centre, but an eyesore in general

✘ Tiresome amount of walking to and between lifts

✘ Few off-slope amenities

What brings skiers to Breuil Cervinia (as the resort now styles itself) is what brought climbers to the original village of Breuil in the 19th century: altitude. For climbers it was a launch-pad for assaults on the nearby Matterhorn (Monte Cervino). For skiers, it offers an unusual combination: slopes that are gentle as well as extensive, and sunny as well as snowsure.

For skiers who like to cover the miles without worrying about the slopes being too steep, there is nowhere like it. But better skiers should steer clear. They'll find the slopes tame and the link with Zermatt disappointing because it doesn't access Zermatt's best skiing.

The resort

When the old climbing village of Breuil made the transition to international ski resort sixty years ago, it boasted smart hotels and equally impressive lifts. Unfortunately, neither the village nor (until recently) the lift system kept pace with the times.

The village was allowed to develop in a rather haphazard way with no consistent style to the architecture. The result is an uncomfortable hotch-potch, neither pleasing to the eye, nor as offensive to it as some of the worst of the French purpose-built resorts. The centre is pleasant and traffic-free. But the surrounding apartment blocks and hotels, some quite a hike up the hill above the cable-car, make the village feel less friendly and welcoming. As one visitor told us, 'The architects must have been on drugs at the design stage.'

As well as the usual ski shops there are some very smart Italian clothes shops and jewellers, with upmarket Italian prices to match. The resort fills up with day-trippers and weekenders from Milan and Turin at peak periods. As well as their money they bring cars, making the village surprisingly traffic- and fume-ridden at times.

The resort is expensive by Italian standards, but no longer for the rich and trendy. There is a lively clientele, and a high proportion of Brits.

There are surprisingly few off-slope amenities, such as kindergartens, marked walks and swimming and spa facilities. And for those staying out of the centre there are some awkward walks and no bus – though some hotels have courtesy buses.

The skiing

Cervinia's main skiing is on a high, large, open, sunny, west-facing bowl. It has Italy's highest skiing and some of its longest runs (13km from Plateau Rosa down to Valtournenche – with only a short drag-lift part-way). Nearly all the runs are accessible to all standards of intermediate skier. More of a problem for skiers than steepness is the weather. If it's bad, the top lifts often close because of high winds. And even the lower slopes may be unskiable because of poor visibility. There is little woodland skiing.

SKI FACTS

Altitude 1525m-3480m
Lifts	36
Pistes	96km
Green/Blue	40%
Red	48%
Black	12%
Artificial snow	7km

LIFT PASSES

95/96 prices in lire
Breuil-Cervinia
Covers all lifts on the Italian side of the border including Valtournenche.
Beginners Points tickets in Cretaz area only (150 points 155,000).
Main pass
1-day pass 51,000
6-day pass 240,000
Short-term passes
Half-day from noon for Cervinia. Single and return tickets on some lifts.
Notes Daily extension for Zermatt lifts around Klein Matterhorn and Schwarzsee (37,000).
Alternative passes
Limited area passes for Carosello (4 lifts) and Cretaz (8 lifts). Day pass covering Cervinia, Zermatt and Valtournenche (67,000). Valle d'Aosta ski pass covers all lifts in Courmayeur, La Thuile, Gressoney, Alagna, Champoluc, Pila, Cervinia and Valtournenche (adult 6-day 254,000).

THE SKI AREA
Very easy skiing

Cervinia has the biggest, highest, most snowsure area of easy skiing we've come across. A newish gondola and ancient cable-car leave from above the village centre, though it's a steep climb up to them. These take you to the main mid-mountain base of **Plan Maison** (2555m). From there a further gondola and cable-cars go up to **Plateau Rosa** (3480m) and the link with Zermatt.

From Plateau Rosa you can go left on a blue run to a large network of drag- and chair-lifts serving Cervinia's easiest skiing and linking back to Plan Maison again. Don't miss the sign to Italy and left turn near the top, otherwise you'll end up on the **Zermatt** lift system – paying the daily supplement. This area can also be accessed by drags from the village centre and you can ski back there or to the gondola and cable-car station.

If you go right at Plateau Rosa you ski down the splendid wide Ventina run, which you can take all the way down to Cervinia (8km). Or you can branch off left down towards **Valtournenche**. The skiing here is served by a number of lifts above the initial gondola from Valtournenche to Salette at 2245m. The top of the Ventina run can be skied repeatedly by taking the giant 140-person cable-car. And there's a chair to play on – but no other lifts serve this sector and you can't ski back to Plan Maison (though you can take the gondola down to there if you like).

There is also the small, little-used **Cieloalto** area, served by three lifts to the south of the cable-car at the bottom of the Ventina run. This can be very useful in bad weather as it has the only trees in the area.

From Plan Maison a cable-car used to go up to **Furggen** (3490m) and access Cervinia's steepest skiing. But this old lift has been closed down, and it's not known when a replacement will be built.

There is floodlit skiing some evenings, just above the village.

SNOW RELIABILITY
Superb

The ski area is one of the highest in Europe and, despite getting a lot of afternoon sun, can usually be relied upon to have good snow conditions. Lifts being closed due to wind is a bigger worry.

The village nursery slopes and bottom half of the Ventina run have snowmaking facilities.

FOR ADVANCED SKIERS
Forget it

This is not the resort for good skiers. There are several black runs dotted about but most of the these would be graded red elsewhere. The beautiful, long, lonely piste from Furggen was the only worthwhile run, and with the cable-car out of action that is no longer accessible.

Good skiers paying the expensive Zermatt supplement in search of tough runs will be disappointed. The Trockener Steg-Schwarzsee area close to Cervinia has a great deal of easy skiing and only a few challenging pistes. Getting to and from the other, more challenging ski areas on a day trip isn't practical. And the link to Zermatt is often closed because of high wind.

FOR INTERMEDIATE SKIERS
Miles of long, flattering runs

Virtually the whole area can be skied comfortably by average intermediates. And if you are the sort of skier who thrives on wide, easy, motorway pistes, you'll love Cervinia's skiing. It has more long, flattering runs than any other resort. The high proportion of red runs on the piste map is misleading: most of them would be graded blue elsewhere.

The easiest skiing is on the left hand side as you look at the mountain. From top to bottom here, there are gentle blue runs and almost equally gentle reds in the beautiful scenery at the foot of the south face of the Matterhorn.

On the right, as you look at the mountain, is the best area for more adventurous intermediates. The Ventina run is a particularly good fast cruise. The long run down to Valtournenche is easy for most of its length. Good intermediates will be able to ski the black runs.

The trip over to Zermatt will bring you first of all to even gentler motorways than on the Cervinia side, but then to some more challenging pistes around Schwarzsee.

If you want to have a look at the village of Zermatt, allow plenty of time. The run down can be tricky, the lifts back time-consuming.

There's also the bonus of even more spectacular scenery. The view of the Matterhorn is the classic one you see on all the pictures (you wouldn't recognise it from the Cervinia side), and the view of the glacier below when you ride the Klein Matterhorn cable-car to Europe's highest piste skiing is breathtaking.

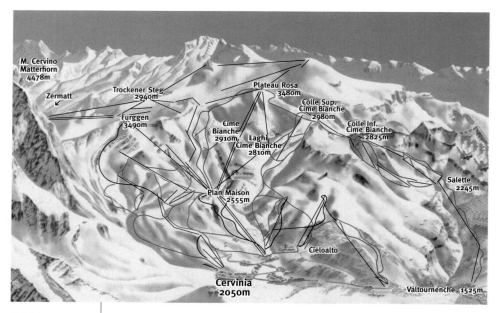

FURGGEN

The cable-car to Furggen has been taken out of commission. We understand that the resort intends to replace it, but the timing is unclear.

FOR BEGINNERS
Pretty much ideal
Complete beginners will start on the good village nursery slope, and should graduate quickly to the fine flat area around Plan Maison and its gentle green runs. Fast learners will be able to cover a great deal of ground by the end of the week, and end up skiing the blue run all the way from the top to the bottom of the mountain. The very easy runs down to Salette, on the way to Valtournenche, are a must.

FOR CROSS-COUNTRY
Hardly any
There are a couple of short trails, but this is not a cross-country resort.

QUEUES
Can still be problems
Although much improved recently, the lift system still has drawbacks. Access to the Plan Maison mid-station is crucial for most skiers, with the result that the two main access lifts get oversubscribed in peak season and at busy weekends – even though they jointly carry 2,850 skiers an hour. The alternative is a roundabout sequence of drags and chairs.

Plateau Rosa, at the top of the mountain, is another important junction that in the past has had serious access problems.

But the inadequate cable-cars from Plan Maison have had some of the pressure taken off them by a new gondola to Laghi Cime Bianche with a capacity (2,400 skiers an hour) three times that of the two cable-cars

combined. Above that is a big modern cable-car that shifts crowds quickly.

There can be queues for the lower lifts when the upper lifts are shut because of high wind.

MOUNTAIN RESTAURANTS
Good choice
The food in mountain restaurants is generally good, wholesome stuff, and helpings are liberal. But the toilet facilities are primitive.

The restaurants are also not marked on the piste map, except on the Valtournenche side, where they are cheaper and less crowded – and, in our experience, serve good food. The one at the bottom of the Roisette chair has great views and a good platter of local salami and cheeses. The Motta, at the top of the drag-lift of the same name, has an excellent local speciality (Suppa di Valdostani – bread, cheese and vegetable soup). Back on the Cervinia side, the Etoile on the Roc Nere piste has good pasta, puddings and atmosphere. Baita Cretaz, near the

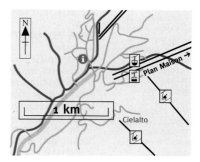

SKI SCHOOL

95/96 prices in lire

Cervino
Classes 6 days
2hr 50min: 10am-
12.50
6 days: 180,000
Children's classes
Ages: any
6 days: 180,000
Private lessons
Hourly
49,000 for 1 or 2
people; each
additional person
5,000

CHILDCARE

The ski school runs a
snow garden with
mini-lift at the foot of
the Cretaz slopes, but
there are no all-day
care arrangements.
Nor is there a non-ski
kindergarten.

GETTING THERE

Air Turin, transfer
2½hr. Geneva,
transfer 2½hr.

Rail Châtillon (27km);
regular buses from
station.

PACKAGES

Airtours, Crystal, First
Choice Ski, Inghams,
Thomson

bottom of the Cretaz pistes, is good
value and has excellent service and
presentation. The British-run Igloo, at
the top of the Bardoney chair just off
the Ventina piste, is popular and
apparently does 'amazing' chicken
sandwiches, good hot punch and has
a UK-style loo. Les Clochards, on the
edge of town, has tasty pasta. The
Bontadini da Lombard, on the blue
run back from Plateau Rosa, has good
main courses and glüwein.

SKI SCHOOL
Varied reports
Cervinia has one main ski school, the
Cervino. We continue to get mixed
reports about both the standard of
tuition and the quality of instructors'
English. One reporter said their group
asked the teacher to repeat his
instructions in French because that
was easier to understand. Classes tend
to be large. There is a separate school
up at the satellite of Cieloalto.

FACILITIES FOR CHILDREN
Do-it-yourself
The ski school children's classes is
about it. The ski area, with its long
gentle runs, should suit families.

Staying there

Most visitors to Cervinia accept that
it's not a very convenient resort and
put up with some walking (there's no
public bus service). Central hotels are
quite convenient for the Cretaz drags,
but not for the main gondola station.
There are more convenient hotels,
some of them mentioned below.

HOW TO GO
Plenty of hotel packages
Most of the big tour operators come
here, providing between them a wide
selection of hotels, though other
accommodation is thin on the
ground. A lot of the accommodation
out of the main village is private,
some of it time-sharing.
Chalets We know of no catered chalets.
Hotels There are 44 hotels, mostly 2-
star or 3-star, with half a dozen 4-stars.
£££££ Cristallo The only 4-star which
is in any way luxurious; pool, sauna,
massage. Steep walk up the hill
towards the Cielalto lift.
££££ Hermitage Small, smartly
furnished chalet just out of the village
on the road up to Cielalto. Pool.
££££ Punta Maquignaz Captivating
chalet-style 4-star, recently opened, in
centre near Cretaz lifts.

£££ Sporthotel Sotorelli Excellent
food, large buffet breakfast, sauna and
jacuzzi. Ten minutes from lifts.
£££ Neiges d'Antan Family-run chalet
in peaceful setting 4km down the road
in Perreres, with charming rustic
furnishings.
£££ Excelsior Planet Pleasant, central
3-star with a pool.
£££ Astoria Slightly down-at-heel, but
right by the main lifts, with friendly
staff and 'excellent' dinners.
£££ Furggen Modern hotel above the
resort on the Cretaz slopes, with skiing
from the door.
££ Breithorn Good food. One of a
number of good-value (by local
standards) 2-stars.
££ Marmore Clean, warm, with
'substantial' food; mid-way between
the lift stations.
Self-catering There are many
apartments in the resort but few are
available through British tour
operators. The Cristallino apartments
are fairly simple but guests have use of
the fine facilities of the Cristallo next
door. The Residence La Pineta is of a
similar standard, five minutes from
the gondola and cable-car.

CRYSTAL HOLIDAYS

helped us to compile the eating out and après-ski sections. Our thanks to them.

ACTIVITIES

Indoor Hotel with swimming pools and saunas, bowling, casino, fitness centre **Outdoor** Natural skating rink (until March), bob-sleigh run, horse-riding, para-gliding, hang-gliding, mountaineering, walks, heli-skiing

TOURIST OFFICE

Postcode 11021
Tel 00 39 (166)
949136
Fax 949731

EATING OUT
Expensive for Italy

Cervinia's 49 restaurants allow plenty of choice, though the range of food isn't vast. It helps if you like pasta, pizza or polenta-based meals. Prices are uniformly high. Some of the best hotels have good, but expensive, restaurants open to non-residents.

The Chamoix and Matterhorn are excellent, but are particularly pricey. The Grotta belies its unfortunate name with good food. Casse Croute serves probably the biggest, and best, pizzas in town. The Pania is good for local specialities. KL has traditional home cooking. The simple Dau is one of the best places for a relatively cheap meal.

APRES-SKI
Disappoints many Brits

Plenty of lively Brits come here looking for action but there isn't much to do but tour the mostly fairly ordinary bars. The Café Whymper, White Rose and Copa Pana have a 'pleasant atmosphere, good prices and generous measures' says one reporter.

The Underground Kellar Bar, with Irish music, is lively in the early-evening. The Dragon Bar is a major congregating spot for Brits. Satellite TV, videos, Fosters lager and karaoke are provided. The Pellissier Bar and Yeti Pub are other places popular with Brits. More cosmopolitan bars that can have atmosphere are Lino's, Pippo's and Café des Guides (with mementos of the owner's mountaineering trips to the Himalayas). The Scotch Club has occasional live music, but it doesn't really get going till after midnight.

There are three discos, which liven up at weekends. Brits seem to prefer the Chimera. Blow Up and the Princess are more Italian in atmosphere. There are several tour-rep-organised events such as bowling, snowmobiling, quiz nights and various meals – with fondue, pizza and local specialities.

FOR NON-SKIERS
Little attraction

There is little to do. The pleasant town of Aosta is reached easily enough, but it's a four hour round trip. Village amenities include hotel pools, fitness centre and large natural ice rink. The walks are disappointing. The mountain restaurants reachable by gondola or cable-car have little going for them.

STAYING UP THE MOUNTAIN
To beat the queues

Up at Plan Maison, the major lift junction 500m vertical above the resort, Lo Stambecco is a 50-room 3-star hotel ideally placed for early nights and early starts. Available through Inghams.

Less radically, the Cime Bianche is a rustic 3-star chalet on the upper fringes of the resort (in the area known as La Vieille).

STAYING DOWN THE VALLEY
Great home run

Valtournenche, 9km down the road, is cheaper than Cervinia, has a genuine Italian atmosphere and a fair selection of simple hotels, of which the 3-star Bijou is the best. Except at weekends (when a lot of day-trippers arrive) the gondola is a queue-free way into the Cervinia skiing, though the drag-lifts above mean it takes time. And the exceptionally long run back down is a nice way to end the day. (It involves a short drag, so you can't leave it too late.) The main street through the village is very busy with cars going to and from Cervinia.

Cortina d'Ampezzo 1220m

HOW IT RATES

The skiing

Snow	★★★
Extent	★★★
Advanced	★★
Intermediates	★★★
Beginners	★★★★★
Convenience	★
Queues	★★★
Restaurants	★★★★

The rest

Scenery	★★★★★
Resort charm	★★★★
Not skiing	★★★★★

✔ *Magnificent Dolomite scenery – perhaps the most dramatic of any ski resort*

✔ *Marvellous nursery slopes and good long cruising runs, ideal for nervous intermediates*

✔ *Access to the vast amount of skiing on the Dolomiti Superski pass*

✔ *Attractive, although rather towny, resort, with lots of upmarket shops*

✔ *Good off-slope facilities, as you might expect of an Olympic venue*

✘ *Several separate ski areas, inconveniently spread around all sides of the resort and linked by buses*

✘ *Expensive by Italian standards*

✘ *Gets very crowded during Italian holidays, but rather quiet at other times*

✘ *Very little tough skiing*

Nowhere is more picturesque than chic Cortina, the most upmarket of Italian resorts. Dramatic pink-tinged peaks rise sheerly from the top of the ski slopes, giving picture-postcard views from wherever you are. (Those amazing shots in the movie Cliffhanger were filmed here.) As many people come for the views as for the skiing.

Cortina's skiing is fine for its regular upmarket visitors from Rome and Milan, many of whom have second homes here and enjoy the strolling, shopping, people-watching and lunching as much as the odd leisurely excursion on to the slopes. For complete beginners and leisurely intermediates, the splendid nursery slopes and long easy runs are ideal. For keen piste bashers, Cortina's fragmented ski areas can be frustrating; but the fairly easy access to the Sella Ronda and other Dolomiti Superski resorts is some compensation. For good skiers the skiing is limited, with few tough runs and the best of those liable to poor snow conditions because they face south.

ORIENTATION

Cortina is a town, rather than a village, spreading across a broad valley. The main valley runs north-south, but minor roads go off to east and west and give access to some of the skiing. The two main areas are reached by cable-cars on opposite sides of the town. **San Cassiano** is not far away to the west, with skiing links from there to **Corvara** and the other Sella Ronda resorts.

 ## The resort

In high season, you'll find more non-skiers (or very part-time skiers) in Cortina as you will real skiers. It attracts the rich and wealthy from the big Italian cities, many of whom have second homes here. Fur coats and glitzy jewellery are the norm.

The resort itself is spread widely around the town centre, with exclusive chalets scattered around the woods and roads leading off into the surrounding countryside. The centre is the traffic-free Corso Italia, full of chic shops and a hive of activity in early evening, when everyone parades up and down, window-shopping and people-watching. The cobblestones and picturesque church and bell tower add to a thoroughly Italian atmosphere. Surrounding the centre is a horrendous one-way system, often clogged with traffic and stinking of exhaust fumes. This makes an unpleasant contrast with the stunning scenery on view wherever you look.

Few places can claim to match Cortina for the beauty of its setting.

We first arrived in the dark. The next morning, walking down to breakfast, we noticed a painting showing a stupendous view on the wall of the hotel staircase. By the end of breakfast we'd woken up, and when we walked back up the stairs we realised the 'painting' was in fact a window, and the view was of the Cristallo peak at the back of the hotel; no artist could have imagined anything more stunning.

Unlike the rest of the Dolomites, Cortina is pure Italy. It has none of the Germanic traditions of Selva and the Sud Tirol, and does not attract many German visitors.

 ## The skiing

Cortina first leapt to fame when it hosted the 1956 Winter Olympics, for which many of its existing facilities were built. At the time, it was one of the most modern resorts around. Now it feels distinctly behind the times. Its widely spread ski areas are as different from the classic modern French purpose-built resorts as you can get.

SKI FACTS

Altitude 1225m-2930m
Lifts   52
Pistes   140km
Green/Blue   53%
Red   42%
Black   5%
Artificial snow   25km

LIFT PASSES

94/95 prices in lire
Cortina d'Ampezzo
Covers all lifts in
Cortina, San Vito di
Cadore, Auronzo and
Misurina, and ski-
buses.
Main pass
1-day pass 47,000
6-day pass 231,000
(low season 201,000
– 13% off)
Senior citizens
Over 60: 6-day pass
185,000 (20% off)
Children
Under 15: 6-day pass
162,000 (30% off)
Short-term passes
Half-day pass from
1pm (4,200).
Notes Discount prices
for senior citizens and
children for 2-day
passes and over only.
Alternative passes
Dolomiti Superski
pass covers 464 lifts
and 1180km of piste
in the Dolomites
(adult 6-day 243,000).

THE SKI AREA
Inconveniently fragmented

Cortina has several smallish separate
ski areas, each a fair trek from the
centre of town. The largest is the
Socrepes area, accessed by chair- and
drag-lifts a bus-ride from town. This
interlinks with Cortina's highest
skiing area of **Tofana**, reached by a
two stage cable-car from just outside
the centre of town.

On the opposite side of the valley is
the tiny **Mietres** area. Another cable-
car from the east side of town leads to
the **Faloria** area, from which you can
ski down to the long slow chairs that
lead up into the limited but dramatic
skiing beneath the **Cristallo** peak.

There are several other tiny ski areas
reachable by road. The most notable
of these is a cable-car from Passo
Falzarego (2150m) up to Lagazuoi
(2750m) leading to a beautiful red run
down to Armentarola.

A car is in some ways helpful in
making the most of the skiing covered
on the Dolomiti Superski pass. But the
bus service is good, and with the aid
of a timetable you can construct very
satisfactory expeditions.

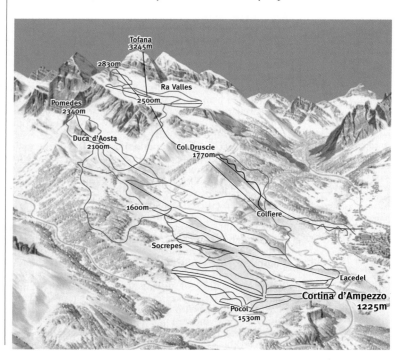

SKI SCHOOL

94/95 prices in lire

Cortina
Classes 6 days
2½hr: 9.30am-noon;
2hr: noon-2pm
6 2½hr days: 250,000
Children's classes
Ages: under 15
6 full days (9.30-3.30)
including lunch:
760,000
Private lessons
Hourly
55,000 for 1hr; each
additional person
15,000

Azzurra Cortina
Classes 6 days
3½hr: 9.15am-1pm;
3hr: 1pm-4pm;
6½hr: 9.15-4pm
6 3½hr days: 420,000
Private lessons
Hourly
56,000 for 1hr; each
additional person
14,000

SNOW RELIABILITY
Good, with plenty of artificial help

Like most other Dolomite resorts, Cortina has invested heavily in artificial snowmaking, so expect good cover on the main Socrepes slopes and on the south-facing runs of the Cristallo area. The record of natural snowfalls is an erratic one – the snow here can be good when it's poor on the north side of the Alps.

FOR ADVANCED SKIERS
Limited

There are a couple of challenging short runs but nothing like enough to keep a good skier happy for a week.

The run down from the second stage of the Tofana cable-car at Ra Valles goes through a gap in the rocks, and a steep, narrow, south-facing section gives you wonderful views of Cortina, deep down in the valley below. This isn't as precipitous as it looks from the cable-car, but is often tricky because of poor snow conditions.

The same is true of Cortina's other steep run, from the top of the Cristallo area at Forcella Staunies. The top chair-lift takes you to a steep, narrow, south-facing couloir. This is frequently shut because of either avalanche danger or poor snow.

Other than that, good skiers will have to be content with cruising the many long red runs in the area, or exploring the Superski region.

FOR INTERMEDIATE SKIERS
Fragmented and not extensive

Skiers who enjoy cruising runs among beautiful scenery and don't mind skiing the same runs repeatedly will get the most out of Cortina. But don't expect a huge interlinked ski area.

The red runs at the top of the Tofana area are short, but normally have the best snow. The skiing here goes up to over 2800m and is mainly north-facing. But be warned: the only way down is by cable-car or the often tricky black run described above.

The reds from the linked Pomedes area are longer and offer good, fast cruising, served by three chair-lifts.

The Faloria area has a whole string

CHILDCARE

Both schools offer all-day classes for children – the Cortina school from 9.30 to 3.30, the Azzurra school from 9am to 4pm.

The Mini Club, at the Socrepes lifts, (860942) takes children aged 2 to 8, from 8.30 to 8pm. Comprehensive care arrangements are offered by an outfit called Natural...Mente (5086), which takes children from age 12 months, from 8am to 6pm.

GETTING THERE

Air Venice, transfer 3hr.

Rail Calalzo (30km) or Dobbiaco (32km); frequent buses from station.

PACKAGES

Crystal, Powder Byrne

---

of fairly short north-facing reds. And the Cristallo area that you can ski to from here has just one long red run, from below the top couloir back down, served by slow old chairs.

FOR BEGINNERS
Wonderful nursery slopes
The Socrepes area has some of the biggest nursery slopes and best progression runs we have seen. Unfortunately we have had few reports on the ski school, so we can't recommend it conclusively as an ideal beginner resort.

And some of the forest paths marked blue can be icy and intimidating for a novice skier. But if you stick to the main pistes, you'll find ideal gentle terrain.

FOR CROSS-COUNTRY
One of the best
Cortina has 74km of prepared trails, mainly in the woods to the north, towards Dobbiaco. There are also trails beneath the Cristallo ski area.

QUEUES
No problem for early birds
Most Cortina holiday-makers rise late, lunch lengthily and stop skiing early – if they ski at all. That makes for few lift queues and generally uncrowded pistes. And out of the peak Christmas-New Year and February high seasons, the resort can be extraordinarily quiet. One lone skier found 'disconcertingly deserted pistes' which could be 'intimidating when descending steep slopes in total solitude'. But another reporter says that peak-season, peak-time queues can be 'chaotic'.

MOUNTAIN RESTAURANTS
Good but expensive
Lunch is a major event for many Cortina visitors. At weekends you often need to book to make sure of a table. Many of the restaurants can be reached by road, and non-skiers arrive mid-morning to sunbathe and admire the views. Prices are high, and some menus (and wine lists) tempting. We had one of the most expensive (and most enjoyable) skiing lunches ever at El Camineto, at the bottom of the main Pormedes lifts, where white-jacketed waiters minister to your needs. The Pic de Tofana, nearby, is also recommended, as is the Rifugio Pomedes, up the mountain.

The Socrepes sector has several hotels along the road going up its edge – and close to the bottom of the slopes is the best restaurant in the resort, the Michelin-starred Tivoli.

The little Cinque Torri ski area, on the way up to Passo Falzarego, has two restaurants; the Rifugio Averau offers spectacular views as well as good food.

SKI SCHOOL
Few reports
With such an upmarket Italian clientele, we'd expect tuition here to be good, but we have no reports on the standard of English spoken. We suspect it may be poor, as it generally is in this emphatically Italian area. There is a separate guiding school, the Gruppo Guide Alpine, which offers off-piste, ski-touring and special high altitude weeks. Snow-boarding also has its own section.

FACILITIES FOR CHILDREN
Better than average
By Italian standards the childcare facilities are outstanding, with a choice of all-day care arrangements for children of practically any age. Given the very small number of British visitors, you can't count on good spoken English.

 # Staying there

There's a wide range of hotels both in the centre and scattered around the outskirts. Wherever you stay, it's unlikely to be convenient. To get the most out of the town, staying in the centre and resigning yourself to being a bus-ride from the lifts is probably the best bet. If you have a car, your choice is quite a bit wider.

HOW TO GO
Now with more packages
British tour operators have no catered chalets or self-catering allocations, but hotel packages are increasingly widely available. Upmarket Powder Byrne were in the resort last year for the first time, offering a choice of five hotels.
Hotels There's a big choice, especially at the luxury end, where there are two 5-star and fifteen 4-star hotels. But the resort is not literally exclusive: there are cheaper places – down to 1-star and 2-star pensions at a fraction of the price of the top end.
£££££ Miramonti Spectacularly grand hotel in extensive grounds, 2km south of town. Pool.
££££ Poste Reliable 4-star, at the heart of the town in more ways than one.
££££ Parc Victoria Elegantly rustic 4-star, at Faloria end of town centre.
£££ Olimpia Comfortable B&B hotel in centre, close to Faloria lift.
£££ Menardi Welcoming roadside

CRYSTAL HOLIDAYS

helped us to compile the eating out and après-ski sections. Our thanks to them.

ACTIVITIES

Indoor Swimming pool, saunas, museums, art gallery, cinema, indoor tennis court, public library **Outdoor** Olympic ice-stadium (2 rinks), curling, ice hockey, sleigh rides, horse-riding school, ski-bob run, olympic ski jump, 6km walking paths, toboggan run, heli-skiing

TOURIST OFFICE

Postcode 32043
Tel 00 39 (436) 3231
Fax 3235

inn, a long walk from centre and lifts. **££ Trieste** Neat roadside chalet, not quite such a long walk from the centre and lifts.

Self-catering There's a wide choice of chalets and apartments available for independent travellers.

EATING OUT
Huge choice

There's an enormous selection of places, both in the town centre and a little way out, doing mainly Italian food. The very smart and pricey El Toulà is in a beautiful old barn, just on the edge of town. Many of the best restaurants are further out – such as the Tivoli (which gets a Michelin star), Meloncino (a charming chalet), Leone e Anna, Rio Gere and Baita Fraina. Good central restaurants include: the Passetto, Ariston, Buca Dell' Inferno, Cazzetta, Croda and Ra Stua; some of these are quite reasonably priced. Harry's Grill is one of the few good places not specialising in Italian food.

APRES-SKI
Lively in high season

Cortina is a lively social whirl in high season, with lots of well-heeled Italians staying up very late (which is why the slopes are so quiet). But in low season, it can be very quiet – one reporter found it 'difficult to find a bar open after 10.30pm'.

Don't go if the sight of fur coats upsets you: during the early evening walkabout, every other person will be wearing one.

Bar Lovat is one of the most popular tea-time spots, notably for its home-made pastries. Bar Embassy is yet another place with a high calorie

count, serving freshly made *Krapfen* – a jam and cream speciality. The new Bar Bellevue, with its large terrace overlooking the pedestrian zone, has become the 'in' place. Bar Cristallino is an elegant spot where young and old rub shoulders. The Enoteca is a welcoming wine bar, popular with locals after skiing. Later the hotel de la Poste is a 'must' for observing the rich and glamorous over an aperitif. Terrazza Viennese, attached to hotel Ancora, is another fashionable spot. The Orange American Bar has good music. In peak season, there are enough customers to give all the numerous discos a great atmosphere. Some of the best are the Metro, Hyppo, Belvedere and Limbo.

FOR NON-SKIERS
A classic resort

Along with St Moritz, Cortina rates as one of the leading resorts for non-skiers and essentially part-time skiers.

The setting is stunning, the town attractive, the shopping extensive, the mountain restaurants easily accessible by road (a car is handy) and there are plenty of other activities to keep you occupied.

There's ice skating, major ice hockey matches and even an ice disco on the Olympic ice rink. If you're there at the right time, you can watch sleds careering down the Olympic bobsleigh run. There's horse jumping and polo on the snow occasionally.

Cortina is also a cultural centre, with several museums and art galleries, including the Mario Rimoldi, which has the largest private collection in Italy of painting and sculptures by leading modernists.

Courmayeur 1225m

✔ Stunning views of Mont Blanc massif

✔ Pleasant range of intermediate runs

✔ Much of the ski area is served by artificial snowmaking

✔ Good mountain restaurants

✔ Charming, traditional village, with car-free centre and some stylish shops

✔ Lively, but not rowdy, evening atmosphere and nightlife

✔ One of the shortest, easiest drives from the Channel, and short airport transfers

✗ Lack of good nursery slopes and easy runs for beginners to progress to

✗ No tough piste skiing

✗ Relatively small ski area, with mainly short runs

✗ Slopes get very crowded at weekends

✗ Tiresome walk and cable-car journey to and from the skiing (except from Dolonne)

✗ Not much for active non-skiers to occupy themselves with

ORIENTATION

Courmayeur is just on the Italian side of the Mont Blanc tunnel, by the main route down the Aosta valley.

The skiing is separate from the village. You get up to it via a huge cable-car from the edge of town, and come back the same way. There's some accommodation on the same side of the valley as the skiing, in Dolonne, from where a gondola goes to the ski area. Those with a car can drive to another cable-car a few kilometres towards Mont Blanc at Entrèves. From La Palud, a little further away, another cable-car takes you up to the off-piste skiing of the Mont Blanc massif, including the Vallée Blanche down to **Chamonix** in France (also an easy drive through the tunnel), covered by the lift pass. **La Thuile** is an easy drive the other way and **Cervinia** is reachable.

Courmayeur is very popular, especially at weekends, with the smart Italian set from Milan and Turin. It's easy to see why: not only is it very easy to get to, thanks to the road up to the Mont Blanc tunnel, but it is certainly the most captivating of the Val d'Aosta resorts, with splendid scenery as well as abundant village charm and a relaxed but stylish après-ski scene.

The scenery, the charm and the nightlife must weigh heavily with the many British skiers who go there too. Certainly, the ski area is unlikely to be the main attraction, given its limited range of difficulty, its inconvenient location across the valley from the village and, particularly, its limited size. A keen piste-basher will ski Courmayeur's runs in a day, then be wondering what to do for the rest of the week.

Courmayeur makes a good day trip from Chamonix (the weather on the southern side of Mont Blanc can be quite different from that on the northern side) or a jolly week for those who want to party as much as ski. It also appeals to a quite different kind of skier, who wants to explore the spectacular Mont Blanc massif with the aid of a guide and local peaks with the aid of a helicopter.

The resort

Courmayeur is a traditional old mountaineering village which, despite construction of the nearby Mont Blanc tunnel road and proliferation of modern hotels, has retained much of its old-world charm. (The road passes close to the village, but generally has surprisingly little impact on it.)

The village has a charming traffic-free centre of cobbled streets, attractive shops and well-preserved old buildings, the most impressive of which is the church. An Alpine museum and a statue of a famous, long-dead mountain rescue hero add to the historical feel of the place. The potential that cobbles have for treacherous walking when icy is well appreciated – the streets are well maintained.

There is great atmosphere in the village centre, the focus of which is

Selected chalets in Courmayeur

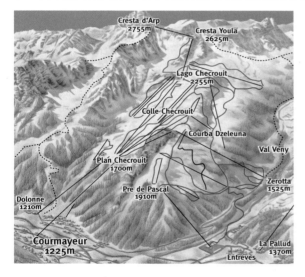

SKI FACTS

Altitude	1295m-2755m
Lifts	28
Pistes	100km
Green/Blue	50%
Red	40%
Black	10%
Artificial snow	15km

the Via Roma. Immediately after skiing, lots of skiers fill up the numerous atmospheric bars, which include some of the most civilised places we have encountered. Others wander in and out of the many varied small shops, which include a salami specialist and a good bookshop. At weekends people-watching is part of the evening scene, as ski jackets are outnumbered by the fur coats of the Milanese and Torinese.

The village extends away from the centre in several directions, including southwards to the area around the cable-car station. Dolonne, across the valley, is a quiet suburb – inconvenient for the nightlife.

⛷ The skiing

The main ski area suits intermediates, with few difficult or easy runs, but it is surprisingly small for such a well known, large resort. The pistes are varied in character if not in gradient, and pretty. Piste marking could be improved.

THE SKI AREA
Small but interestingly varied
The ski area is separate from the village: a cable-car ride is necessary at the start and end of the day. This, the only lift from Courmayeur itself, transports skiers to the bottom of the skiing at **Plan Checrouit** (where you can store your skis and boots).

The ski area has two distinct sections, both almost entirely for intermediates. The north-east-facing Checrouit area catches the morning sun, and has open, above-the-tree-line skiing. The 25-person, infrequently running Youla cable-car goes up to the top of Courmayeur's piste skiing at 2625m. There is a further cable-car to Cresta d'Arp (2755m). This serves only long off-piste runs – and apparently is now open only for skiers accompanied by guides.

Skiers tend to follow the sun over to the north-west-facing slopes down towards **Val Veny** in the afternoon. These are interesting, varied and tree-lined. Connections between the two areas are good, with numerous alternative routes.

LIFT PASSES

94/95 prices in lire

Courmayeur Mont Blanc

Covers all lifts in Val Veny and Checrouit, and the lifts on Mont Blanc up to Punta Helbronner.

Beginners Free nursery lifts at Plan Checrouit and top of Val Veny cable-car (which can be paid for by the ride).

Main pass

1-day pass 44,000
6-day pass 220,000
(low season 190,000 – 14% off)

Short-term passes

Single ascent on some lifts and half-day pass (adult 30,000) available.

Notes Passes of 6 or more days are valid for one day in the Chamonix valley.

Alternative passes

Valle d'Aosta area pass covers all lifts in Courmayeur, Gressoney, Alagna, Champoluc, La Thuile, Pila, Cervinia and Valtournenche (adult 6-day 238,000). Mont-Blanc ski region pass covers all lifts in 13 resorts around Mont Blanc.

Apart from the main ski area, you can take a cable-car up to the shoulder of **Mont Blanc**. This should only be done with a guide, as all the skiing here is off-piste and on glaciers. You can do the famous Vallée Blanche down to Chamonix from here without the horrific initial ridge walk you encounter if you take the cable-car up from Chamonix.

SNOW RELIABILITY
Good except late season

Courmayeur's skiing is not high – mostly between 1700m and 2250m. But much of it faces north or north-west, and there is virtually blanket coverage of artificial snow on the main runs.

FOR ADVANCED SKIERS
Off-piste is the only challenge

Courmayeur has little challenging piste skiing. The only black run is not difficult, and few moguls form anywhere else. However, some of the red runs are sufficiently steep to test advanced technique, especially if they're icy. And on our last two visits (both in April) we were lucky enough to have knee-deep powder and fantastic skiing among the trees.

The classic off-piste runs from Cresta d'Arp go in three different directions – a clockwise loop via Arp Vieille to Val Veny, with close-up views of the Miage glacier; eastwards down a deserted valley to Dolonne or Pré St Didier; or southwards through the Youla gorge to La Thuile.

On Mont Blanc, the Vallée Blanche is not a challenge (though there are more difficult variations and the views are stunning), but the Toula glacier route on the Italian side from Punta Helbronner to Pavillon most certainly is, often to the point of being dangerous. There's also heli-skiing available on the peaks above the Val Ferret, north-east of the resort.

FOR INTERMEDIATE SKIERS
Ideal gradient but limited extent

The whole area is suitable for most intermediates. But it is small. The avid piste-basher, who doesn't like to ski the same run twice in a day, will find it very limited.

The open east-facing Checrouit section is pretty much ski-anywhere territory, where you can choose your own route and make it as easy or difficult as you like. The blue runs here are about Courmayeur's gentlest. The red pistes running the length of the Bertolini chair are more challenging and very enjoyable, with

several off-piste excursions possible. If you ski past the bottom of the chair, you link in with the pretty, wooded slopes heading down to Zerotta. This whole north- and west-facing area has great views of Mont Blanc and the Ghiacciaio della Brenva.

The Zerotta chair dominates the area, with numerous alternatives starting at its top. It's a good area for mixed abilities, with runs of varying difficulty meeting up at several places on the way down to Zerotta.

The Vallée Blanche, reached from La Palud, has truly spectacular scenery. Although off-piste, the skiing is easy enough for an adventurous intermediate to try. But you should ski with a guide because the routes aren't marked and there are always crevasses to be wary of.

FOR BEGINNERS
Consistently too steep

Courmayeur is not well suited to beginners. There are several nursery slopes but none is ideal. The area at the top of the main cable-car from Courmayeur gets crowded with more experienced skiers and there are few easy runs for the near-beginner. The small area served by the short Tzaly drag, just above the Entrèves cable-car top station, is the most suitable beginner terrain, and it tends to have good snow.

FOR CROSS-COUNTRY
Beautiful trails

There are good trails dotted around Courmayeur. The best are the four covering 20km at Val Ferret, to which there is a bus service. Dolonne also has two short trails, and a skiable path runs from Entrèves to Zerotta, which is useful for meeting up with Alpine skiers for lunch. Total trails 35km.

QUEUES
Weekend cable-car black spots

The lift system is generally excellent. The Checrouit and Val Veny cable-cars suffer queues only at weekends, and even these can be beaten with an early start. Skiers also show remarkable patience in waiting long periods for the infrequently running Youla cable-car. Otherwise, no problems. Overcrowded slopes at the weekends, particularly those running down to Zerotta, are a greater problem.

MOUNTAIN RESTAURANTS
Lots – some of them good

The small ski area is lavishly endowed with 27 establishments ranging from rustic on-piste huts to larger self-service places at main lift stations. There is a large gap in quality between snack bars and fully fledged restaurants. Some snack bars sell little more than uninspiring hard sandwiches and cardboard pizza. They also rely on good weather, having better terraces than interiors. Most of the restaurants serve delicious pizza and pasta.

One of the better snack bars is at the top of Dzeleuna chair. Several restaurants are excellent. Château Branlant, next to the Chiecco drag at Plan Checrouit, is recommended for good food, atmospheric interior, friendly service and good views of beginners struggling up the drag and down the piste. Maison Vieille, at the top of the chair of the same name, has a rustic dining room and good food. The rather neglected restaurant, poorly positioned for trade just above and to the right of the bottom of the Pra Neyron chair, is good value, with staff eager to please.

Ristorante Zerotta is expensive, but has good food and a sunny terrace well placed for people-watching. The Petit Mont Blanc, in the same sector, is also recommended.

SKI SCHOOL
Not a strong point
Reports on the ski school vary widely, with some criticism of chaotic organisation at the start of the week. Standards of English seem erratic, which is very disappointing given Courmayeur's large number of British customers. There is a thriving guides' association ready to exploit the area's off-piste potential.

FACILITIES FOR CHILDREN
Mark Warner have a crèche
Although the resort's childcare arrangements are well ahead of the Italian norm, most parents will be more attracted by the crèche at Mark Warner's chalet-hotel in Dolonne, which takes children from 4 months.

↑ Staying there

The cable-car station is on the southern edge of town, a fair distance from much of the accommodation. There is no ski-bus alternative to walking. Once up the mountain, there is another short walk to the other lifts before you can start skiing.

Having accommodation close to the cable-car is obviously advantageous. But don't stay too close to the Mont Blanc road, which can be very noisy. However, having this major route on the doorstep does afford particularly easy access for ski-drivers. Most hotels have some parking spaces. Parking at the village cable-car is very limited, but drivers can go to Entrèves, a few kilometres away, where there is a large car-park at the Val Veny cable-car. Buses, infrequent but to a timetable, link Courmayeur with La Palud, just beyond Entrèves, for the Punta Helbronner-Vallée Blanche cable-car.

HOW TO GO
Plenty of hotels
Courmayeur's long-standing popularity ensures a wide range of packages, mainly in hotels. Interski stay out of town and bus people in (and to other resorts) each day.

SKI SCHOOL
94/95 prices in lire

Monte Bianco
Classes 6 days
3hr: 10am-1pm
6 half-days: 170,000
Children's classes
Ages: over 6
6 half-days: 170,000
Private lessons
Hourly
47,000 for 1 to 2 people; each additional person 5,000

CHILDCARE
The Kinderheim at Plan Checrouit (845073) takes children from age 6 months, from 9.30 to 4pm. They can join ski school classes from 10am to 1pm.

GETTING THERE
Air Geneva, transfer 2hr. Turin, transfer 2hr.

Rail Pré-St-Didier (5km); regular buses from station.

PACKAGES
Airtours, Bladon Lines, Crystal, First Choice Ski, Inghams, Interski, Mark Warner, Stena Sealink, Thomson, White Roc, Winterski

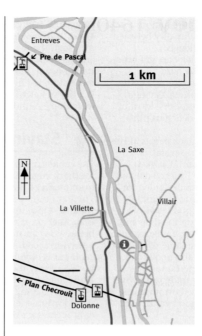

ACTIVITIES

Indoor Swimming pool and sauna in Hotel Royal and at Pré-St-Didier (5km), skating rink, Alpine museum, cinema, bridge, library
Outdoor Walking paths in Val Ferret and Dolonne, para-gliding

TOURIST OFFICE

Postcode 11013
Tel 00 39 (165) 842060
Fax 842072

Chalets Courmayeur isn't a major chalet resort, but Bladon Lines have three simple, cheap units here. Lamastra is a complete house, above the town at Villair, 15 minutes from the cable-car. Donzelli and Marconi are in one larger chalet, with their good central location reflected in slightly higher prices. Mark Warner have a comfortable chalet-hotel in Dolonne – the Telecabine, sharing a building with the gondola base station. It has an in-house crèche (see Facilities for children).
Hotels There are nearly 50 hotels in Courmayeur, evenly distributed between the star ratings.
££££ Pavillon Comfortable 4-star near cable-car, with one of the two pools in town. Friendly staff.
££££ Royal Large well positioned hotel, with the other swimming pool.
££££ Palace Bron Small but tall, elegantly furnished chalet above the town at Plan Gorret.
£££ Berthod Friendly, family run hotel near centre. Recommended by two reporters this year.
£££ Cristallo Well placed 3-star, just off via Roma; attractively furnished, well equipped rooms, 'excellent' food.
£££ Grange Rustic, stone-and-wood farmhouse at Entrèves.
££ Edelweiss Friendly, cosy, good-value place close to the centre.
££ Lo Scoiattolo Good rooms, good food, shame about the position – at opposite end of town from cable-car.

Self-catering There is quite a lot of self-catering accommodation available. Bladon Lines has some and the tourist office staff speak good English.

EATING OUT
Jolly Italian evenings
There is a great choice of restaurants. Many of them make up for what they lack in quality by serving enormous portions. The touristy but very jolly Maison de Filippo in Entrèves is for gluttons – its speciality is a fixed-price, 36-dish menu. Further out, at Val Ferret, Chalet Proment (Floriano's) is attractively rustic, with a warm welcome and wonderful local cooking. For a serious meal out in the centre try Pierre Alexis, which has good food, service and value. The Pizzeria Tunnel serves enormous pizzas, and is very popular, so book well in advance. The Turistica is one of the cheapest, good-value places in town. La Petite Bouffe, at Dolonne, has a good set meal which includes Clochard disco entrance.

APRES-SKI
Stylish bar-hopping
Courmayeur has a lot of evening atmosphere. Après-ski is centred on lively bars and a couple of discos that do not liven up till late. Ziggy's and Steve's are popular bars. The American 49 is another, although this gets so crowded that only a one-drink visit is advisable. The Red Lion is worth a visit if you're missing English pubs. Our favourites are the Roma and the back room of the Posta, both with comfy armchairs to collapse in. The Abat Jour disco plays 70s pop, whilst Dolonne's excellent Clochard night club has the latest sounds.

FOR NON-SKIERS
Very limited for sporty types
Inactive non-skiers will find the village pleasant and may find the shops diverting. There are some interesting excursions – by cable-car up to Punta Helbronner and by bus to Aosta or Chamonix. It's easy to go up the main cable-car to Plan Checrouit to meet skiers for lunch up the mountain. But, considering the size of the resort, there is little for sporty non-skiers.

STAYING UP THE MOUNTAIN
Why would you want to?
The idea of visiting Courmayeur and not making the most of the charming village seems perverse – if you're that keen on getting onto the slopes in the morning, this is probably the wrong resort. But there are simple rooms in the Christiania at Plan Checrouit.

Gressoney 1640m

Gressoney is at the heart of the Monterosa ski area – Italy's answer to the Trois Vallées. Not surprisingly, the skiing of this little-known area is less extensive; it is also mostly easy. But it offers the same sensation of travel on skis, amid impressive scenery and a relaxed atmosphere. For piste skiers it is actually a two-valley system; for off-piste skiers this region has more to offer.

HOW IT RATES

The skiing

Snow	★★★
Extent	★★★
Advanced	★★
Intermediates	★★★★
Beginners	★★
Convenience	★★★★
Queues	★★★★
Restaurants	★★

The rest

Scenery	★★★★
Resort charm	★★★
Not skiing	★

SKI FACTS

Altitude	1640m-2970m
Lifts	30
Pistes	70km
Green/Blue	31%
Red	63%
Black	6%
Artificial snow	12km

PACKAGES

Crystal

Champoluc Crystal

TOURIST OFFICE

Postcode 11020
Tel 00 39 (125)
366143
(125) 307876

THE RESORT

Gressoney la Trinité is a quiet, neat little village in a rather enclosed setting at the heart of the three-valley Monterosa ski area, east of Cervinia. It sits a couple of miles from the head of the narrow central valley, which runs roughly north-south. Gressoney St Jean, a more substantial and appealing village 5km (and 250m vertical) down the valley, has its own ski area, separate from the main system.

The main resort in the eastern valley is Champoluc; in the western valley it is Alagna. Expeditions by road to Cervinia, La Thuile and Courmayeur are possible.

THE SKIING

The Monterosa **ski area** is relatively extensive, and very scenic. The piste skiing is almost all easy (and very well groomed). The terrain is undulating and fragmented; runs are attractively varied, but many of the lifts serve only one or two defined pistes. The lift system is impressively modern, with several high-speed chair-lifts. There are lifts out of the village, but the main linking lifts are at the head of the valley, at Stafal.

La Trinité's local ski area is centred on the sunny shelf of Gabiet (2300m). Chairs and drags serve the area below it, and above it a long 12-person gondola goes up to Passo dei Salati (3000m). From here, a serious off-piste run makes the link with the pistes of the Alagna valley. You can descend to Orsia or Stafal (both in the Gressoney valley), where chair-lifts go up towards the Colle Bettaforca (2705m), the link with the Champoluc valley.

The area's **snow reliability** is good, thanks to altitude and extensive snowmaking on west-facing runs.

There is not much to interest **advanced skiers**, apart from one black of 700m vertical (most blacks on the badly printed piste map turn out to be blues). At Alagna there is a long black run (roughly 7km for only 850m vertical) from the top of the cable-car at Punta Indren (3260m). But there are great off-piste possibilities from the high points of the lift system in all three valleys, and some excellent heli-

drops. Powder Byrne are running an adventure skiing course here this year.

For **intermediate** skiers who like to cover a bit of ground, the area is fine, with long runs from the ridges down into the valleys.

Beginners are adequately catered for on the lower slopes at La Trinité, but Champoluc's sunny area at Crest (1950m) is better.

There are long **cross-country** trails around St Jean, and shorter ones up the valley; but Brusson, in the Champoluc valley, has the best trails.

Only at weekends, when the Italians arrive, are there **queues**.

The **mountain restaurants** are adequate, no more; the Lys mountain refuge at Gabiet (with very simple food) is the most captivating.

The **ski school** doesn't get much chance to practise its English. As far as we know, there are no special facilities for **children**.

STAYING THERE

For keen skiers who don't mind isolation, **accommodation** at Stafal, at the head of the valley, is the best choice. The best hotel is the 4-star Monboso – a big modern chalet. At La Trinité, the main accommodation for skiers is half a mile outside the village, at the foot of the slopes.

Eating out possibilities are limited. **Après-ski** is very quiet; some discos may open up at weekends.

Non-skiers should go elsewhere.

STAYING IN THE OTHER VALLEYS

Champoluc is another attractive, quiet chalet-style village with a handful of hotels and only a couple of sports shops. Access to the Gressoney valley involves taking a series of lifts and runs across the mountainside to Colle Bettaforca – and much the same in reverse at the end of the day. The hotel Villa Anna Maria is a captivatingly creaky wooden chalet, tucked away amid trees a short walk from the lifts.

Only good skiers with plans to go off-piste should base themselves in **Alagna**. The piste skiing is very limited, and it does not include the connection to Gressoney.

Livigno 1815m

✔ High altitude plus snowmaking ensures a long season and a good chance of snow to resort level

✔ Large choice of beginners' slopes

✔ Modern and improving lift system, with few queues

✔ Cheap by Alpine standards, with the bonus of duty-free shopping – a great place to treat yourself to the new skis you've been wanting

✔ Cosmopolitan, friendly village with some Alpine atmosphere

✔ Long, snowsure cross-country trails

✘ No difficult piste skiing

✘ Long airport transfers

✘ Skiing links across the valley depend on buses, overcrowded at peak times

✘ Village is very long and straggling, and a bit prone to tattiness

✘ Very few non-skiing amenities

✘ Bleak, windy setting – not a good place in bad weather

✘ Lack of really comfortable hotels bookable through tour operators

✘ Nightlife can disappoint – it's not as lively as many expect

Livigno is not an outstanding resort in any respect, and it has some important drawbacks – in particular, it is not an easy place to get to or to get around. But it offers the unusual combination of a fair-sized intermediate ski area, high altitude and low prices – thanks to its duty-free status, lower even than most other Italian resorts. It cannot compete with eastern Europe on cost, but as a relatively snowsure alternative to the Pyrenees or to the smallest, cheapest resorts in Austria, Livigno seems very attractive.

The scale of the duty-free shopping in the resort may come as a surprise – there are countless camera and clothes shops. But the bars are not particularly cheap, and the resort succeeds in attracting a wide range of visitors, so lager louts are not a problem. It's a pleasant enough place in which to spend time, although it looks a bit of a mess, taken as a whole.

ORIENTATION

Livigno is an amalgam of three villages; the centres of the northernmost, Santa Maria, and the central focus, San Antonio, are about 1km apart. San Rocco is about 3km further south. The resort sits in a wide, remote valley close to the Swiss border. The ski area spreads evenly over mountains either side, with lifts into both sections from the northern end of the resort, and just into the westerly half from the southern extremity.

The area lift pass covers **Bormio** and **Santa Caterina**, an easy drive away to the south-east if the high pass is open, and a 6-day pass covers a day in **St Moritz** to the south-west, which is more reliably accessible via a road tunnel to the north (alternating one-way traffic – expect queues at peak times).

SKI FACTS
Altitude	1815m-2795m
Lifts	29
Pistes	100km
Green/Blue	42%
Red	46%
Black	12%
Artificial snow	4km

The resort

Livigno mainly consists of a continuous string of hotels, bars and supermarkets lining a single street running along a flat, wide valley floor. The buildings are small in scale and mainly traditional in style, giving the village quite a pleasant atmosphere.

The original hamlet of San Antonio is the nearest thing Livigno has to a centre. Here, the main street and those at right angles linking it to the busy by-pass road are nominally traffic-free; but this is Italy, so the traffic ban is not entirely effective. (There is a petrol station right in the middle, rather spoiling the surroundings of the central and historic Alpina hotel.)

The road that skirts the 'traffic-free' area is constantly busy, and becomes intrusive in Santa Maria. Germans arriving in Livigno for duty-free shopping as well as skiing add to traffic nuisance. The local bus services, running on three colour-coded routes, are free and frequent, but get overcrowded at peak times, morning and afternoon, and stop in the early evening.

The skiing

The skiing appeals mainly to beginners and intermediates. There is quite a lot of it, at least in comparison with the other cheap and cheerful destinations that Livigno competes with.

THE SKI AREA
Improved links
There are three ski areas, all suitable for moderate and leisurely skiers. Thanks to a new lift built a couple of seasons ago, two of them are now reasonably well linked.

The ridge of **Mottolino** is reached by a smart and efficient gondola (replacing a famously cold drag-lift) from Teola, a tiresome walk or a short bus-ride from San Antonio. As well as north-west-facing runs back towards Livigno from Monte della Neva, the high point at 2660m (reached by an antique chair that can be fiercely cold), there are north-east-facing pistes and lifts on the other side of the ridge, above Trepalle, on the road to Bormio. On the other side of the valley, closer to town, chairs in the middle of a row

LIFT PASSES

95/96 prices in lire
Alta Valtellina
Covers all lifts in
Livigno, Bormio
(40km away, but 1hr
30min by a very poor
road), Valdidentro
(30km away) and
Santa Caterina (50km
away) plus one free
day in St Moritz (6-
day pass+).
Main pass
1-day pass 45,000
6-day pass 220,000
(low season 195,000
– 12% off)
Senior citizens
Over 65: 6-day pass
150,000 (32% off)
Children
Under 13: 6-day pass
150,000 (32% off)
Short-term passes
Afternoon pass for
Livigno only 33,000.
Notes Day pass price
is for Livigno lifts
only.
Alternative passes
Livigno only pass for
up to 2 days (adult 2-
day 85,000).

SKI SCHOOL

94/95 prices in lire
Livigno
Classes 6 days
2hr: 9am-11am or
11am-1pm
6 2hr days: 105,000
Children's classes
Ages: from 5
6 2hr days: 95,000
Private lessons
Hourly
42,000 for 1hr; each
additional person
6,000

Livigno Inverno-Estate
Classes 6 days
2hr: 9am-11am or
11am-1pm
6 2hr days: 105,000
Children's classes
Ages: from 5
6 2hr days: 95,000
Private lessons
Hourly 42,000 for 1hr;
each additional
person 6,000

OTHER SCHOOLS

Livigno Italy

Azzura Livigno

of nursery slopes take you up to **Costaccia** (2370m), where a long high-speed quad chair-lift now goes along the ridge towards the **Carosello** sector. The linking run beyond this lift – to the mid-station of the Carosello gondola – and (more especially) the linking run back from Carosello are not runs you would ski for pleasure; depending on the snow conditions and the wind, energetic poling may be needed. The Carosello skiing is usually accessed by the optimistically named Carosello 3000 gondola at San Rocco, which goes up to 2750m. Most of the runs return towards the valley, but there are a couple of runs on the back of the mountain, on the west-facing slopes of Val Federia.

Direction-finding is tricky, thanks to very patchy signposting and a very approximate piste map, and information about which lifts are running is hard to come by.

SNOW RELIABILITY
Very good, despite no glacier
Livigno's ski area is high (you can spend most of your time skiing around the 2500m mark), and with snowmakers backing up nature on the lower slopes of Mottolino and Costaccia, the valley has one of the longest of ski seasons.

FOR ADVANCED SKIERS
Not recommended
The piste map shows a few black runs but these are not steep – though they may be difficult when (as on the occasion of our most recent visit) they are left open despite appallingly bad snow conditions low-down. There is off-piste skiing to be done, but not many people do it.

FOR INTERMEDIATE SKIERS
Flattering slopes
Few pistes follow the fall line directly, so good intermediates looking for a challenge are liable to be disappointed. Learning to ski off-piste may be their best option. The runs on the back of Carosello down to Federia are more challenging than most, and bumpy at times. Moderate skiers have virtually the whole area at their disposal. The long run beneath the Mottolino gondola is one of the best. Leisurely types have several long cruises. Passo d'Eira-Teola, Monte della Neve-Sponda drag, and Costaccia's easy skiing are all enjoyable. The run underneath the new Vetta chair, at the top of the Costaccia sector, is a splendid slope for confidence-building – 1.5km long, dropping only 260m.

FOR BEGINNERS
Excellent but scattered slopes
A vast array of nursery slopes along the sunny lower flanks of Costaccia, and other slopes dotted around the valley, make Livigno an excellent novices' resort – although some of the slopes at the northern end are on the steep side. There are lots of longer runs suitable for fast learners and near-beginners.

CROSS-COUNTRY
Good snow, bleak setting
Long snowsure trails (50km in total) follow the valley floor, making Livigno a good choice, except that the scenery is bleak and the road not usually far away from the trail. Staying in Santa Maria is best, being close to a nicer trail along the Val Federia. There is a specialist cross-country school, and the resort organises major cross-country races.

QUEUES
Few problems these days
Lift queues are not usually a problem; the Mottolino gondola relieved the major bottleneck. There may be a short delay for the Carosello gondola on holiday mornings. There has been quite a lot of recent investment in fast new chair-lifts, both at Carosello and Mottolino, so queues up the mountain are not a worry. Overcrowded pistes at Mottolino, particularly at weekends, are a greater problem, as are queues for buses and mountain restaurants.

MOUNTAIN RESTAURANTS
More than adequate
While there are few great culinary delights by the standards of some Italian resorts, many reporters have commented on the consistent adequacy of huts. The modern self-service places at the top of Mottolino and Carosello are perfectly acceptable (the latter's bar has impressive woody decor and painted ceilings), and there are some more charming places lower down. One of the best is not marked on the piste map – Mama's at Passo d'Eira, at the low point of the Mottolino ridge. The welcoming Tea del Vidal is at the base of the same sector, making Mottolino the best bet for serious lunchers, though Costaccia's Tea del Plan is also pleasantly rustic and sunny, with good food, and Tea Bork, in the trees near the bottom of Carosello, offers 'Tyrolean-style atmosphere, complete with music'. When skiing Carosello, lunch in the valley at the hotel Sporting (close to the gondola station)

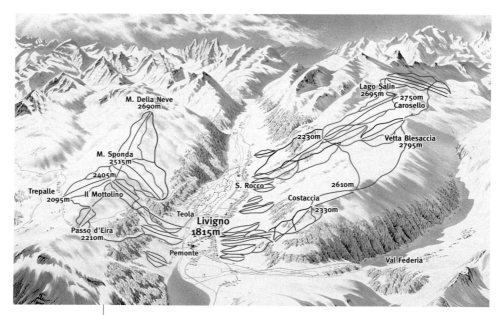

GETTING THERE

Air Bergamo, transfer 5hr.

Rail Tirano (48km); regular buses from station.

PACKAGES

Airtours, Crystal, First Choice Ski, Inghams, Panorama, Thomson

CHILDCARE

There are no all-day care facilities.

is a popular alternative – excellent cheap pizza. The Bellavista is another resort-level recommendation.

SKI SCHOOL
Short lessons a drawback
There are several schools. English is widely and well spoken, and recent reports are generally favourable. But one reporter notes a reluctance to get beginners off the nursery slopes and up the mountain, and another is highly critical of a 'pathetic' standard of tuition, which achieved 'absolutely nothing'. Many visitors consider the lessons too short at two hours a day ('an hour and a half some days').

FACILITIES FOR CHILDREN
Bring your own
The schools run children's classes, but (as so often in Italy) there are no special arrangements for all-day care, with or without ski tuition.

 Staying there

In such a long village, with fragmented skiing, location of accommodation can be important. And tour operators tend to be a little vague at times, stating that a particular hotel is 'close to the lifts'. Which lifts?

Beginners should avoid San Rocco (the Carosello end of town), because your ski school is likely to meet a bus-ride away in San Antonio. The latter is the best all-round location now that there is lift access via Costaccia to

Carosello – though it will still be quicker to take a bus out to the Carosello gondola. Much of the nightlife is in San Antonio.

HOW TO GO
Lots of hotels, some apartments
Livigno has an enormous range of hotels and a number of apartments.
Chalets Crystal have a handful of attractively priced catered chalets here – some apartment conversions, others in pleasantly rustic individual chalets.
Hotels Most of the hotels are small 2- and 3-star places, with a couple of 4-stars out of the centre.
£££ Intermonti Huge, modern 4-star with all mod cons (including a pool); some way from the village, on the slopes of Mottolino – reachable on skis by going off-piste.
££ Europa One of the better 3-stars, within walking distance of the Mottolino gondola and village centre.
££ Bivio Bang in the centre of things, close to ski school and lifts; the only hotel in central Livigno with a pool.
££ Steinbock Nice little place, far from major lifts but only five minutes' walk from some nursery slopes.
££ Teola Quiet place, a little way up Mottolino slopes; recommended (despite small bedrooms) for 'good food and friendly staff'.
££ Larice Stylish little 3-star well placed for Costaccia lifts and slopes.
££ Montanina Good central 2-star
££ Sporting Basic but satisfactory B&B hotel, next to Carosello gondola.
££ Gimea Quiet B&B hotel, 300m from Carosello gondola, with

CRYSTAL HOLIDAYS

helped us to compile the Eating out and Après-ski sections. Our thanks to them.

ACTIVITIES

Indoor Sauna, gym, body-building, games room, indoor golf and tennis club, cinema
Outdoor Cleared paths, skating rink, snow-mobiles, sleigh rides, para-gliding

TOURIST OFFICE

Postcode 23030
Tel 00 39 (342) 996379
Fax 996881

'excellent rooms'.
££ Camana Veglia Charming old wooden chalet with popular restaurant, well placed in Santa Maria.
£ Silvestri Well liked by several reporters, reasonably handy for lifts, ski school and nightlife.
Self-catering All the big tour operators that come here have apartment options. Most are cheap and cheerful; position is perhaps the most important thing to consider. The Primavera apartments are more comfortable than their rustic exterior suggests, and well placed for Costaccia. Bait da Bark are reasonably well appointed, and convenient for the Carosello gondola. Airtours have simple places well located for nightlife and the Mottolino gondola.

EATING OUT
Value for money
Livigno has an appetising range of good (though mainly simple) restaurants, many hotel-based. Hotel Concordia has some of the best cooking in town, and the Camana Veglia restaurant is superior to the hotel's 2-star rating. Mario's has one of the largest menus in town, serving seafood, fondue and steaks in addition to the ubiquitous pizza and pasta. The Bellavista is a charming little restaurant. Bait dal Ghet has excellent pizzas, the Rusticana wholesome, cheap food. The Vecchia Lanterna, Ambassador and Mirage are others worthy of mention.

APRES-SKI
Lively, but disappoints some
Many reporters have expressed disappointment in the nightlife. It's not that there isn't action, but simply that the scene is quieter than some people expect in a duty-free resort – that is, quieter than in Andorra. Also, the best places are rather dotted about, leaving the village as a whole rather lacking evening atmosphere. The San Rocco end of town is particularly quiet, and ideal for those looking for peaceful surroundings.

At tea-time the Tea del Vidal, at the bottom of Mottolino, gets quite lively. But most skiers seem to return to their hotels for a quiet drink. Galli's pub, in San Antonio (not to be confused with the Galli in San Rocco), is popular

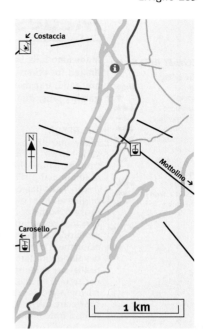

with lively Brits at such times. Most after-dinner nightlife doesn't really get going until after 10pm. Galli's is again popular, notably for its music, games and karaoke. Foxi's cellar video bar is more Italian and stylish. Mario's is another good video bar, with an organist (livelier than it sounds!). The Underground pub is a cheap and cheerful, noisy place. The Cielo is a chic and expensive nightclub with live music, popular with Italians. Brits tend to prefer the less sophisticated Koleodis disco. Other après-ski is limited to a few tour-rep-organised events such as early-evening snowmobiling and a party night with games.

FOR NON-SKIERS
Disappointing but improving
Livigno is not a good place for non-skiers. Walks are uninspiring and there is no sports centre or public swimming pool. The few hotel pools are kept for the exclusive use of guests. Excursions to Bormio and St Moritz are the most popular things to do, although snowmobiling, ice skating and a new indoor golf and tennis centre may keep a few people happy.

Madesimo 1545m

HOW IT RATES

The skiing

Snow	***
Extent	*
Advanced	***
Intermediates	**
Beginners	***
Convenience	***
Queues	***
Restaurants	**

The rest

Scenery	***
Resort charm	**
Not skiing	*

SKI FACTS

Altitude	1550m-2950m
Lifts	23
Pistes	43km
Green/Blue	35%
Red	45%
Black	20%
Artificial snow	9½km

PACKAGES

Airtours, Crystal, Inghams, Ski Partners, SkiBound, Thomson

TOURIST OFFICE

Postcode 23024
Tel 00 39 (343) 53015
Fax 53782

Madesimo falls between stools – its steep skiing is too tough for some, too limited for others. The village is old but lacks real charm. The nursery slopes are good, but there are few easy runs to progress to. But Madesimo is gaining fans, due primarily to low prices.

THE RESORT

Madesimo sits in a remote, pretty side valley a two- to three-hour drive north from Bergamo which ends in a dramatic hairpin bend ascent to the resort. The village claims 17th-century origins and has old farm buildings to prove it, some of them converted into bars and restaurants. But the remainder of the village is a random assortment of piecemeal modern development. Pitched roofs and timber are evident, but so too is concrete. The delightful old church, narrow streets and little shops in its centre are overlooked by what appears to be a hideous airport control tower (the hotel Torre).

THE SKIING

A two-stage cable-car is the primary lift into the **ski area**, with chair and drag alternatives to the first section. Most runs return straight to the village, but the top station accesses pistes on the far side of the mountain. The altitude is respectable, but most of the slopes get too much sun for the **snow** to be particularly reliable.

Advanced skiers need the upper section to be open so that they can take on the famous Canalone run – a long, consistently steep black gunbarrel which keeps its snow well and is therefore not usually as terrifying as its reputation suggests.

The best **intermediate** runs also start from the top station, dropping down into the beautiful Valle di Lei area, separate from the rest of the skiing. The reds descending from the cable-car mid-station are also very pleasant, passing through pretty woodland. Some of the easier runs have steeper sections that could prove awkward for nervous or inexperienced skiers. The nursery slopes are fine, but improving **beginners** have few really easy pistes to graduate to.

There's plenty of **cross-country** skiing dotted around the area, but you need a car to reach most of it.

There are weekend **queues** for the cable-car, but otherwise there are few lift delays.

The **mountain restaurants** are not particularly appealing.

Having been popular with British school groups, Madesimo has plenty of **ski school** instructors who speak some English. Tuition is reportedly good and classes not too large.

There are no public **children's facilities**, but the Cascata e Cristallo 4-star hotel has a Mini club for children aged 4 or more. Madesimo is, however, better suited to families with older children who can ski quite well.

STAYING THERE

The village centre is a tight cluster of buildings with both main lift stations a short walk away. A 500m strip of ribbon development finishes at the nursery slopes.

A fair choice of **hotels** is available through tour operators. The Emet is the more traditional of the two 4-stars. The Cascata e Cristallo is a large, modern, multi-amenity place. The Ferrè is highly recommended: a small modern 3-star hotel in the centre with 'first-class service, good-sized rooms and excellent food'; it has a popular après-ski bar. The Liro and the Soldanella are small, simple 2-stars in a central position. Inghams offer well-equipped but poorly positioned **self-catering** apartments.

Eating out is one of Madesimo's delights. Taverna Verosa is atmospheric, good value and popular for pizzas cooked over an open fire. Osteria Vecchia is a charming, traditional place with some of the best and most expensive food in town. Dogana Vegia is one of the original 17th-century village buildings, and serves tasty local specialities. Go to La Clessidra for good fondue. Tec de L'Urs is also good-value.

Après-ski is fairly quiet. There are several pleasant cafés for a tea-time cappucino and cakes. Later the log-cabin-style Cantinone bar in the hotel Andossi has a good atmosphere. The piano cellar bar in the Meridiana and the Ferrè are other focal spots. The Facsimile Videoteque and Queen's are discos that liven up at weekends. Tour reps organise several events.

It's not a place for **non-skiers**, unless they just like walks and excursions. The nearby medieval town of Chiavenna, and a trip to St Moritz, are highlights.

Madonna di Campiglio 1520m

Madonna is a sort of poor person's Cortina – a pleasant village amid splendid Dolomite scenery, with an affluent and almost exclusively Italian clientele, despite qualities that should make it attractive to many intermediates. In contrast, Folgarida and Marilleva, with which Madonna shares quite an extensive ski area, have a history of British group and school business.

HOW IT RATES

The skiing

Snow	***
Extent	***
Advanced	**
Intermediates	****
Beginners	****
Convenience	**
Queues	***
Restaurants	****

The rest

Scenery	****
Resort charm	***
Not skiing	***

SKI FACTS

Altitude	1520m-2505m
Lifts	49
Pistes	150km
Green/Blue	43%
Red	41%
Black	16%
Artificial snow	40km

PACKAGES

Airtours, Altours Travel, Crystal, Inghams, Winterski

Folgarida Altours Travel, Equity Total Ski, Winterski

Marilleva Equity Total Ski, Winterski

TOURIST OFFICE

Postcode 38084
Tel 00 39 (465)
442000
Fax 440404

THE RESORT

Madonna is a largely modern, but pleasant, traditional-style village that has spread widely across its prettily wooded valley beneath the impressive Brenta Dolomites. It is on a through-road, but most of the traffic is local and the road bypasses the focal piazza. There is another area of development about 1km to the south, and between the two a frozen lake that is used for skating and other diversions.

The resort attracts an affluent Italian clientele, with almost as many 4-star hotels as 3-stars, and the kind of smart clothes shops that you find in Courmayeur and Cortina. A high proportion of Madonna's customers potter about the village during the day, and promenading is an important ritual in the early evening.

THE SKIING

The terrain, as in other Dolomite areas, provides a lot of intermediate skiing, both above and below the treeline. There are three **ski areas** around Madonna itself, each with a handful of lifts and runs. Cable-cars from the edges of the village serve Cinque Laghi to the west and Pradalago to the north, and a rather less convenient gondola accesses Monte Spinale to the east. Just outside the village and 130m vertical above it, another gondola serves Passo Groste – the highest area, reaching 2505m, and also accessible via Spinale. Pradalago is linked by lift and piste to Monte Vigo (2180m), where the ski areas of Folgarida and Marilleva also meet.

Although many of the slopes are sunny, they are at a fair altitude, and all three resorts have invested heavily in snowmakers. As a result, **snow reliability** is reasonable.

Madonna's status as a World Cup racing resort should not lead **advanced skiers** to expect a lot. Even the 3-Tre race-course is no more than a steep red. Pista Nera is a good mogul field in the Folgarida section, and the Spinale and Groste sections can provide good off-piste skiing.

Cinque Laghi, Madonna's racing mountain, is ideal for good **intermediates**. Moderate skiers will love the area, and will have no difficulty exploring virtually the whole network. The tree-lined runs above Folgarida are particularly lovely pistes. Groste and Pradalago have long easy runs for the less experienced, although the former can get crowded.

It's a good resort for **beginners**, provided they don't mind taking a bus out to the excellent main nursery slopes at Campo Carlo Magno (run by a separate lift company). There are fine long runs to progress to.

Madonna is big on **cross-country** quality if not quantity. The 30km of trails are very pretty, running through the woods over the pass towards Folgarida. There is a specialist school.

Except at Christmas and New Year, there are few **queues**; but the cable-cars out of the village can get busy. The 500 pers/hr Pradalago cable-car is to be replaced by a gondola for the 1995-96 season.

The **mountain restaurants** are a highlight, serving good food in civilised settings, with lovely views.

With several **ski schools** in operation, classes tend to be multi-standard and multi-lingual. They are also frustratingly short – two hours.

STAYING THERE

There is a ski-bus, but it is not free and it doesn't run in the evening – so in this widely spread resort it's worth thinking about location. There is a wide choice of **hotels**. The 4-star Miramonti takes some beating for all-round convenience. The Spinale Clubhotel (with pool) is close to the Spinale gondola. Hotel Bellavista is a friendly, excellent 2-star right by the Pradalago lift. Some self-catering accommodation is sold by tour ops.

There are 20 **restaurants** to choose from, limited mainly to Italian dishes. Belvedere da Lele, Le Roi and Stube Diana are recommended.

The **après-ski** scene is reported to be quite muted, although there are bars and discos, and tour reps and the ski school organise evening events.

For **non-skiers**, Madonna is a fair resort. Window-shopping and walking are the most popular diversions, but there is also skating and swimming.

Sauze d'Oulx 1510m

✔ *Large and uncrowded ski area suitable for most abilities*

✔ *Linked into Milky Way*

✔ *Mix of open and tree-lined runs provides skiing in all conditions*

✔ *Entertaining nightlife*

✔ *Some scope for off-piste adventures*

✔ *One of the cheapest major resorts there is – and more attractive than its reputation suggests*

✗ *Brashness and Britishness of resort will not suit everyone*

✗ *Lots of slow, old lifts, making progress around the ski area slow*

✗ *Crowds at weekends*

✗ *Very little challenging piste skiing for good skiers*

✗ *Poor snow reliability in late season*

✗ *Steep walks around the village, and an inadequate ski-bus service*

Sauze d'Oulx is still living down the reputation that it had in the early 1980s of being prime lager-lout territory. Its nickname – 'Suzy does it' – only served to increase the expectations of those who went there. Then it faded from the British package holiday scene – partly because it had serious snow problems before the rest of the Alps. Now it's back, but in slightly reconstructed form. The village still has something of the feel of a Spanish summer resort relocated to the Alps, with bars and shops conspicuously aimed at the British. But it's no longer fair to liken the place to Benidorm; the resort's nightlife is lively, but the extreme behaviour of earlier years has been curbed and the resort attracts many respectable customers. There always were two sides to the resort – the downmarket package hotels and brash bars alongside the comfortable second homes and one or two smart restaurants catering for affluent Italians. The two now seem much more in balance.

The ski area offers little to challenge the more advanced skier, but it is attractively varied and prettily wooded, and its size and good ski school make it a good choice for improving skiers who wish to get some kilometres under their belts with the minimum expense. Short school hours and the need to ride lifts to the main nursery slopes make it less attractive to beginners.

People looking for an affordable combination of serious skiing and animated nightlife, not just wild nights, could do a lot worse than Sauze. And those for whom nightlife matters little – families, for example – need not stay away. Most reporters seem to like the resort more than they expected to.

ORIENTATION

Sauze d'Oulx sits on a gentle mountain shelf facing north-west across the Valle di Susa. Chair-lifts go up from the top of the village and from two points on its fringes. There is also a chair-lift into the skiing from the nearby, lower hamlet of **Jouvenceaux**.

The area is part of the extensive 'Milky Way' region, with easy access to the slopes of **Sestriere** and **Sansicario**. **Claviere** and **Montgenèvre** (just over the French border) are part of the same network, but a longer trek, and more quickly reached by car than on skis.

Excursions by road are possible beyond Montgenèvre to **Briançon** and **Serre-Chevalier**, and to **Bardonecchia**.

SKI FACTS

Figures relate to the whole Milky Way area

Altitude	1390m-2825m
Lifts	97
Pistes	400km
Green/Blue	12%
Red	67%
Black	21%
Artificial snow	65km

 The resort

Although it's not immediately obvious, Sauze has an attractive old core, with narrow, twisting streets and the occasional carved stone drinking fountain; houses have huge stone slabs serving as roof slates.

Most of the resort, however, is modern and undistinguished, made up of block-like hotels, relieved by the occasional chalet, spreading down the steep hillside, from the foot of the ski slopes to the village centre and beyond. Despite the shift in clientele, the centre is still quite lively at night, with late-closing bars that are usually quite full, as well as a handful of discos that do most of their business at the weekend.

Out of the bustle of the centre, where most of the bars and nightclubs are located, there are quiet wooded residential areas full of secluded apartment blocks, and a number of good restaurants are also tucked out of the way of the front line.

Traffic roams freely through the village, which can become congested both in the mornings and in the evenings as cars vie for the most convenient parking spaces and the

LIFT PASSES

94/95 prices in lire
La Via Lattea
Covers all lifts in
Sauze d'Oulx,
Sestriere, Sansicario,
Cesana and Clavière.
Beginners Points
book (85 points
95,000), with lifts
costing from 1 to 12
points.
Main pass
1-day pass 39,000
6-day pass 215,000
(low season 195,000
– 9% off)
Children
Under 13: 6-day pass
193,000 (10% off)
Under 8: free pass
Short-term passes
Some single ascent
passes and afternoon
pass (27,000).
Notes Includes one
free day in each of:
Alpe d'Huez, Les Deux
Alpes, Serre-Chevalier
or Puy-St-Vincent.
One day extension for
Montgenèvre 17,000.
One day extension for
Pragelato 10,000.
Alternative passes
La Via Lattea VIP card
also covers
Montgenèvre and
Pragelato.

quickest ways out of town respectively. This can also lead to the roads becoming slushy and dirty during the day and icy and treacherous at night – a hazard in a resort with few pavements. As the snow withdraws up the mountain later in the season, the dirt stays behind, and one reporter complained of the streets being particularly dusty.

The area is surrounded by trees, and on a good day the views across the Valle di Susa, to the towering mountains forming the border with France, can be quite spectacular.

⛷ The skiing

Sauze's skiing is excellent intermediate terrain. The piste grading fluctuates from year to year if you believe the resort's map – and we're not sure we've caught up with the latest changes from blue to red and red to blue. But most reporters agree that many of the runs graded red should in any case be blue; challenges are few, and far between. (The same might be said of the whole extensive Milky Way area, of which Sauze is one extreme.)

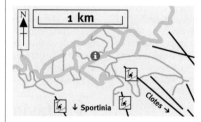

THE SKI AREA
Big and varied enough for most
Sauze's local skiing is spread across a broad wooded bowl above the resort, ranging from west- to north-facing. The main lifts are chairs, from the top of the village up to **Clotes** and from the western fringes to **Sportinia** – a sunny mid-mountain clearing in the woods, with a ring of restaurants and hotels (see Staying up the mountain, page 291) and a small nursery area.

The high-point of the system is **Monte Fraiteve**. From here you can ski westwards on splendid broad, long runs down to Sansicario – and on to chair-lifts near Cesana Torinese which link with the skiing of Claviere and then Montgenèvre, in France – the far end of the Milky Way. You can ski back towards Sauze, on some of the steepest terrain in the area. But there is no longer a piste southwards to Sestriere – you get to that resort from the lower point of Col Basset.

As in so many Italian resorts, piste marking, direction signing and piste map design are not taken seriously, and finding your way can be tricky.

The linked skiing of Sestriere and Montgenèvre is dealt with separately.

SNOW RELIABILITY
Poor in late season
Sauze's very poor snow record in the mid-1980s was mainly to do with a lack of snowfall. In normal winters, a bigger worry is that many of the slopes get a lot of afternoon sun. At these modest altitudes, late-season conditions are far from reliable. There is snowmaking on a couple of slopes, notably the key home run from Clotes to the village.

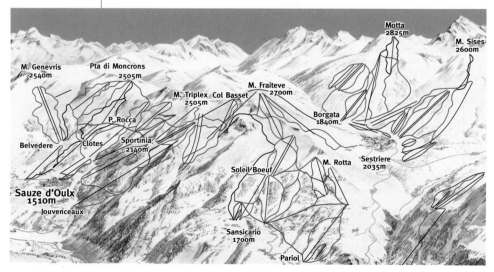

SKI SCHOOL

94/95 prices in lire

Sauze Sportinia
Classes 6 days
3hr: 10am-1pm
6 3hr days: 160,000
Children's classes
Ages: from 6
6 3hr days: 160,000
Private lessons
Hourly
41,000 for 1hr

Sauze d'Oulx
Classes 6 days
3hr: 10am-1pm
6 3hr days: 170,000
Children's classes
Ages: from 4
6 3hr days: 170,000
Private lessons
Hourly
42,000 for 1hr

Sauze Project
Italian-speaking
school only

CHILDCARE

The village
kindergarten (858396)
has English and
Italian staff and takes
children aged from 6
months to 6 years,
from 9am to 5pm.
You have to provide
lunch, but it can be
heated up.

PACKAGES

Airtours, Crystal, First
Choice Ski, Inghams,
Neilson, Panorama,
Ski Club of GB, Ski
Partners, SkiBound,
Thomson, Winterski

Jouvenceaux Neilson

GETTING THERE

Air Turin, transfer 2hr.

Rail Oulx (5km);
frequent buses.

FOR ADVANCED SKIERS
Head off-piste

Very little of the piste skiing is
challenging. Virtually at opposite ends
of Sauze's local area are the best slopes
– a high, north-facing run from the
shoulder of M Fraiteve, and the sunny
slopes below M Montcrons. The main
interest is in going off-piste. There are
plenty of minor opportunities within
the piste network, but the highlights
are long, top-to-bottom descents of up
to 1300m vertical from M Fraiteve,
ending (snow permitting) at villages
dotted along the valleys. The best-
known of these runs (which were until
recently marked on the piste map) is
the Rio Nero, down to the road near
Oulx. When snow low down is poor,
some of these runs can be cut short at
Jouvenceaux or Sansicario.

FOR INTERMEDIATE SKIERS
Splendid when there's snow

Practically the whole area is skiable by
confident intermediates. For less
confident skiers there is plenty of
scope, though the piste grading
doesn't help; it picks out only the very
easiest runs in blue.

At the higher levels, where the
slopes are open, the terrain is
interestingly lumpy, allowing a choice
of route. Lower down are pretty runs
through the woods, where the main
complication can be route-finding.
The mountainside is broken up by
gullies, and pistes that appear to be
quite close together may have no easy
connections between them.

The long slopes above Sansicario
form a splendid intermediate area.

FOR BEGINNERS
The are better choices

Sauze is not ideal for beginners: its
village-level slopes are a bit on the
steep side and the main nursery area is
up the mountain, at Sportinia. Equally
importantly, the mornings-only
classes don't suit everyone.

FOR CROSS-COUNTRY
Severely limited, even with snow

There is very little cross-country
skiing, and it can't be considered
reliable for snow.

QUEUES
No real problems

There may be 10-minute waits at
Sportinia when ski school classes are
setting off or immediately after lunch,
but otherwise the system has few
bottlenecks. Many lifts are ancient
(the recently installed high-speed
quad up to Sportinia is a conspicuous

exception), and breakdowns on drag-
lifts may be a bigger nuisance than
queues.

MOUNTAIN RESTAURANTS
Some pleasant possibilities

Restaurants are numerous, and
generally pleasant. The hotel
Capricorno, at Clotes, is one of the
most civilised and appealing lunch-
spots in the Alps. It is not cheap,
though. There are more modest mid-
mountain restaurants across the
mountainside, with the main
concentration at Sportinia, where
service is friendly and deck chairs
come free with a drink or meal. The
Capanna Kind is deservedly popular.

SKI SCHOOL
Good reports

This is one Italian resort where a lack
of English in the ski schools is not
likely to be a problem. Equally
importantly, reports suggest that
tuition is enthusiastic and effective –
though there are niggles (about
reluctance to move pupils between
classes, for example). Classes are only
half-day, but at least they give three
hours' tuition.

FACILITIES FOR CHILDREN
Consider Neilson

As well as the resort kindergarten,
there is the possibility of plugging into
the arrangements Neilson offer at the
hotel des Amis, down in Jouvenceaux:
a crèche for children aged 6 months to
2 years and a children's club for those
aged 3 to 8.

Staying there

Most of the hotels are reasonably
central, but the Clotes lift is at the top
of the village, up a short but steep hill,
and the Sportinia chair is an
irritatingly long walk beyond that.
There is a ski-bus, but it is infrequent
and unreliable, and gets very crowded
in the morning peak.

HOW TO GO
Packaged hotels dominate

All the major mainstream operators
offer hotel packages here, but there are
also one or two chalets.
Chalets As well as the Crystal chalets
(see Staying up the mountain),
Neilson have a simple chalet, with log
fire, 1km outside the village.
Hotels Simple 2-star and 3-star hotels
form the core of the holiday
accommodation, with a couple of
4-stars and some more basic places.

CRYSTAL HOLIDAYS

helped us to compile the eating out and après-ski sections. Our thanks to them.

ACTIVITIES

Indoor Bowling, cinema, sauna, massage
Outdoor Artificial skating rink, floodlit tobogganing, torchlit descents, heli-skiing from Sestriere

TOURIST OFFICE

Postcode 10050
Tel 00 39 (122) 85009
Fax 85497

£££ **Capricorno** Small, charming; at Clotes (see Staying up the mountain).
£££ **La Torre** Cylindrical landmark 200m below centre, very popular with reporters – 'excellent' rooms and buffet-style food; free wine; inadequate mini-buses to lifts.
££ **Hermitage** Neat chalet-style hotel in about the best position for skiing – beside the home piste from Clotes.
££ **Gran Baita** Comfortable place in quiet, central back-street, with 'excellent' food and good rooms, some with spectacular sunset views from their balconies.
££ **Biancaneve** Recommended despite 'smallish' rooms; close to centre.
££ **Des Amis** Down in Jouvenceaux, but close to bus-stop; small, simple hotel run by Anglo-Italian couple, with childcare facilities offered through Neilson.
Self-catering There are apartments and chalets available locally, but none as far as we know through UK tour operators.

EATING OUT
Caters for all tastes and pockets
Typical Italian banquets of five or six courses can be had in the upmarket Don Vincenzo and U Cantun restaurants. The Italian chef at the Del Falco cooks a particularly good three-course 'skier's menu'. In the old town, Del Borgo serves perhaps the best pizza in town, and has a very friendly atmosphere. Nearby is La Griglia, which is full of character and does a good steak. U Lampione's is the place to go for 'pub grub' – good-value Chinese, Mexican and Indian food.

APRES-SKI
Suzy does it with more dignity
Once favoured almost solely by large groups of youngsters, some of whom were very rowdy, Sauze now attracts middle-aged skiers, families, couples and more sober young people.

Recent reporters young and old have been impressed by the number and atmosphere of Sauze's bars. The Assietta terrace is popular for catching the last rays of the sun after skiing. The more discerning then move on to the pleasant Scotch Bar, while nearby, the once-famous Andy Capp's Pub still attracts punters looking for a 'home from home'. Other early-evening places include the Max Bar, popular for its satellite TV, the small cocktail bar Moncrons, and the U Lampione Pub, in the old town, recommended for its crêpes. After dinner, more places warm up. Those who like to rub shoulders with the locals should try the small Cotton Club bar for a chic aperitif. Gossips has a popular band which plays six nights a week, covering everything from Frank Sinatra to Bon Jovi. Torinese weekenders pack it out on Saturday nights. The Derby Bar has fun games such as nail bashing. Gran Trun is a downmarket relic of the 'old Sauze', popular for its pool table. The two discos are quite different: Newlife is a large club which has special promotions, theme nights and so on; Schuss is an intimate little place, very popular with reporters.

Tour reps organise various activities, including torchlit descents, bowling and 'broomball' on the ice rink. There's also a karaoke bar, mostly frequented by locals; once a week it's taken over by Brits for a quiz and party night.

FOR NON-SKIERS
Go elsewhere
Sauze is not a particularly pleasant place in which to while away the days: the shopping is limited, all the lifts are chairs, and there are few non-skiing activities.

STAYING UP THE MOUNTAIN
You pays your money . . .
In most resorts, staying up the mountain is an amusing thing to do and is often economical – but usually you pay the price of accepting simple accommodation. Here, the reverse applies. The 4-star Capricorno, up at Clotes, is one of the most comfortable hotels in Sauze, certainly the most attractive and by a wide margin the most expensive. It's a charming little chalet beside the piste, with a smart restaurant and terrace (a very popular spot for a good lunch on the mountain) and only eight bedrooms.

Not quite in the same league are the places up at Sportinia, of which the best is the 3-star Monte Triplex. This season, Crystal are running the hotel's annex, the Turistico, as a jumbo chalet. They also have a smaller chalet here. Both give access to the facilities of the Monte Triplex.

Sansicario 1700m
If any resort is ideally placed for exploration of the whole Milky Way, it is Sansicario. It is a smart, purpose-built, self-contained resort mainly consisting of apartments linked by monorail to the little shopping precinct. The 40-room Rio Envers is a comfortable, quite expensive hotel.

Selva/Sella Ronda 1565m

HOW IT RATES

The skiing

Snow	****
Extent	*****
Advanced	***
Intermediates	*****
Beginners	****
Convenience	***
Queues	***
Restaurants	****

The rest

Scenery	*****
Resort charm	***
Not skiing	***

✔ Enormous, beautiful ski area, particularly well suited to intermediate skiers

✔ Very impressive snowmaking set-up – the most extensive in Europe

✔ Attractive, panoramic mountain huts with good food

✔ Much improved lift system with few bad bottlenecks

✔ Good nursery slopes

✔ Best nightlife in the Sella Ronda

✔ Excellent value

✘ Small proportion of tough runs

✘ High proportion of short runs, few long ones

✘ English not universal in ski school

✘ Not the most attractive of the Dolomite ski villages

✘ Erratic snow record; and heavy dependence on artificial snow and modest top heights make skiing vulnerable to warm weather

✘ Main language is German, which detracts from jolly Italian feel

The skiing of the Sella Ronda has been revolutionised over recent years by heavy investment in both the lift system and artificial snowmaking. Both are now among the best and most extensive in Europe. Combine that with extraordinarily picturesque Dolomite scenery, a lift pass which covers over 460 lifts and 1100km of runs, cheap Italian prices and jolly mountain refuges, and you have a compelling case for going on a skiing holiday there. One drawback for some people is that German, rather than Italian, is the main language – and there's a strong German influence.

Only expert skiers who find the lack of challenging skiing frustrating will be disappointed with the skiing. If what you want is a feeling of travelling around on skis, there's little to beat the Sella Ronda – a trip around the Gruppo Sella massif that is easily skiable in a day by an average intermediate. On the way round you will hit many separate local ski areas worth exploring.

If you don't want to stay in Selva there are plenty of smaller, quiet, attractive places on the circuit to base yourself in.

ORIENTATION

Selva is the biggest of the linked resorts that encircle the enormous Gruppo Sella massif, making up the Sella Ronda ski circus. It straggles along a road which follows the Val Gardena, and is now virtually merged with the next village of Santa Cristina. Gondolas rise in two directions. One heads east from the top of the nursery slopes towards Colfosco and Corvara and the clockwise route round the Sella Ronda. The other heads south from the village itself to Ciampinoi and the anti-clockwise route. Spreading far afield, the skiing takes in numerous villages, including **Colfosco, Corvara, Arabba, Canazei, Ortisei** and **San Cassiano. Cortina** is an easy excursion if the roads are open. Its ski area, like many others reachable by car, is covered by the Dolomiti Superski pass.

 ## The resort

Selva is a long roadside village which suffers from traffic but retains a fair level of charm. It has traditional-style architecture, with an attractive central church. And it enjoys a lovely setting among trees beneath the impressive pink-tinged walls of the Gruppo Sella massif and Sassolungo.

Despite its World Cup fame (it's known as Val Gardena, the name of the valley) and animated atmosphere, Selva is neither upmarket nor brash. It is essentially a good-value, lively but civilised family resort with none of the fur coats, poseurs, trendies or ski bums of some large, well-known places. The quite newly available short transfer from hassle-free Verona airport is another plus point.

The area is famous for its wood carvings and you'll find them everywhere – on lamp-posts, doorways, interiors and for sale in shops.

The locals have their own Ladino dialect, which has resisted being absorbed into either German or Italian. The main language, however, is German – as are most of the visitors. Place names are normally given in both German and Italian. Selva is also known as Wolkenstein and the Gardena valley as Gröden. For many years the area was under Austrian rule and the influence is still strong.

 ## The skiing

There really is a vast amount of skiing here, all amid stunning scenery and practically all of it ideally suited to intermediate skiers who don't mind shortish runs. You can set off for the day, pick an area that takes your fancy and explore the local skiing. Or you can set off on the trip round the Sella Ronda circuit. And many separate ski areas – including Cortina – are covered on the lift pass. Buying a cartographic map (3000 lira) from the tourist office is much better than relying on the free piste maps.

SKI FACTS

Altitude 1230m-2520m
Lifts 86
Pistes 175km
Green/Blue 29%
Red 57%
Black 14%
Artificial snow 78km

THE SKI AREA

High mileage piste excursions

A gondola and parallel-running chair go up from Selva to **Ciampinoi**, from where several pistes spread out across the mountain and lead back down to Selva, **Santa Cristina** and **Plan de Gralba**. These include the famous World Cup downhill run which takes place in mid-December each year. From Plan de Gralba, you can head off towards **Passo Sella**, **Canazei** and the rest of the Sella Ronda.

Across the valley from the Ciampinoi gondola is a short chair which links with the Dantercëpies gondola. This accesses the Sella Ronda in the opposite direction or you can ski back down the Ladies downhill to Selva. From the top you ski straight down to **Colfosco**, then lifts link with **Corvara** and from there to **Arabba** and the rest of the Sella Ronda.

Throughout the Sella Ronda there are diversions you can take to ski areas not directly on the circuit. The biggest is the **Alta Badia** area to the west of Corvara, from which you can ski down to **San Cassiano** and **La Villa**.

Local to Selva is the **Seceda** area, accessed by a gondola a bus-ride from town. You can ski back down to the bottom of here or to **Ortisei**. And from Ortisei a cable-car goes up the

other side of the valley to **Alpe di Siusi** and its virtually flat plateau of easy skiing, cross-country and walks.

SNOW RELIABILITY

Excellent when the weather is cold

The skiing in the area is not high. There's very little above 2200m. Most is between 2000m and 1500m. And the Dolomites miss out on many of the snowstorms which affect the Alps to the north. That was why the area invested so heavily in snowmaking machinery after a series of lean snow years. It now has the biggest snowmaking capacity in Europe, covering 78km of runs. Only the high Arabba, Passo Sella and Pordoi sections lack cannons. All other areas

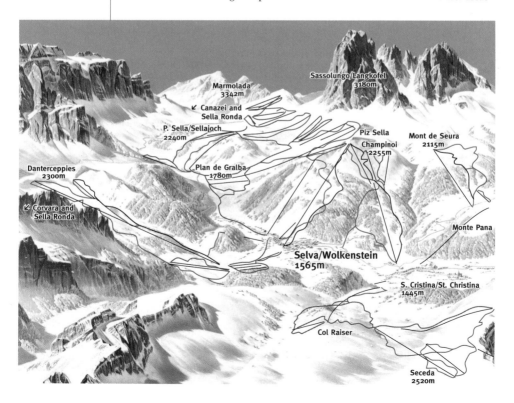

LIFT PASSES

95/96 prices in lire
Dolomiti Superski
Covers 464 lifts and 1180km of piste in the Dolomites, including all Sella Ronda resorts
Main pass
1-day pass 54,000
6-day pass 266,000
(low season 233,000
– 13% off)
Senior citizens
Over 60: 6-day pass 213,000 (20% off)
Children
Under 14: 6-day pass 187,000 (30% off)
Under 6: free pass
Alternative passes
Val Gardena pass covers all lifts in Selva, S Cristina, Ortisei and Castelrotto, and ski-bus between Selva and Ortisei.

have snowmakers on at least the main runs to resorts, and almost all Selva's local pistes are liberally endowed.

The only problem therefore arises in poor snow years when temperatures are too low to make snow. Late season is more of a risk than early season, as night-time temperatures are more likely to be above freezing.

FOR ADVANCED SKIERS
Staying in Arabba is better
Arabba has the best steep skiing, though it's rather distant from Selva with a lot of bland skiing en route. The north-facing black and red runs from Porta Vescovo back to Arabba are served by an efficient high-capacity gondola and are great fun. The Val Gardena World Cup piste, the 'Saslonch', is one of several steepish runs between Ciampinoi and both Selva and Santa Cristina. Unlike many World Cup pistes it is kept in racing condition, for Italian team practices, but is open to the public much of the time. It's especially good in January, when it's not too crowded. The unpisted trail from the top of the Saltaria chair on Alpe Di Siusi down to Santa Cristina is not difficult, but pleasantly lonely.

There is also some exciting off-piste to be explored with a guide. The run from Sass Pordoi (the highest point in the region at 2950m) to Colfosco finishes in the spectacular narrow descent through the Val Mezdi. The ski schools arrange group trips here. But overall, off-piste is limited because of the sheer-drop nature of the tops of the mountains in the Dolomites.

In general, advanced skiers might find the region as a whole too tame, especially if they are looking for a lot of steep challenges or moguls.

FOR INTERMEDIATES
A huge network of ideal runs
The Sella Ronda region is renowned for its easy skiing. The runs down from Dantercëpies to Colfosco and Corvara, and across the valley from there in the Alta Badia are superb for early or unadventurous intermediates – it is a big area of confidence-boosting runs. These are easily reached from Selva, though returning home from Dantercëpies may be a little daunting. Riding the gondola down is an option. Nearer to Selva itself, the runs at the top of Ciampinoi and those of the Plan de Gralba area are nice and gentle. The Alpe di Siusi runs above Ortisei are likely to prove too flat, with too much poling involved for even the most nervous skier.

Average intermediate skiers have an extraordinarily large network of suitable pistes, though there are few long runs. The beautiful swoop down the far side of the Seceda massif from Cuca to Ortisei is perhaps the best long run. The Mont de Seura above Santa Cristina is very pleasant, but skiing both to and from it involves tackling unpisted trails. The Plan de Gralba area, the runs either side of the Saltaria chair, and the main pistes down to La Villa and San Cassiano are other particularly nice spots.

The runs back down to the valley direct from Ciampinoi are a bit more challenging, as are the descents from Dantercëpies to Selva.

As long as the better skiers in a party can resist schussing off into the distance every time one of the many very easy runs is negotiated, the Sella Ronda circuit is ideal for mixed abilities wishing to do day-long excursions together. There are no awkward sections that have to be taken, and when there are no queues most intermediates can complete a circuit in five hours (and any stops).

FOR BEGINNERS
Great slopes, but...
Near-beginners have numerous runs, and the village nursery slopes are excellent – spacious, convenient, and kept in good condition by snow cannons. But we have reservations about the ski school – see opposite.

FOR CROSS-COUNTRY
Beautiful trails
There are over 70km of trails all enjoying wonderful scenery. The 12km trail up the Vallunga-Langental valley is particularly attractive, with neck-craning views all around. The largest section of trails (40km) has the advantage of being at altitude, running between Monte Pana and Seiseralm, and across Alpe di Siusi.

QUEUES
Much improved: few problems
New lifts have vastly improved this once badly queue-prone area. Bottlenecks are no longer common and, except for peak periods, most areas are now fairly queue-free.

But in busy periods some of the Sella Ronda lifts can have delays. The chairlifts from Arabba in both directions can be a problem. The drags from Colfosco to Selva are another bottleneck. The Plan de Gralba cable-car on the Selva to Passo Sella road can also have a queue, but there is a chair alternative.

GETTING THERE

Air Verona, transfer 3hr. Innsbruck, transfer 3hr.

Rail Chiusa (27km); frequent buses from station.

SKI SCHOOL

94/95 prices in lire
Selva Gardena
Classes 6 days
4hr: 9am-1pm or 1pm-5pm; 2hr: 11am-1pm
6 4hr days: 200,000
Children's classes
Ages: 4 to 12
6 6hr days: 360,000
Private lessons
Hourly
47,000 for 1hr for 1 person; each additional person 10,000

Other schools:
S. Christina

CHILDCARE

The ski school runs a kindergarten for children aged 1 to 4, with skiing available for the older children. Those attending proper ski school classes can be looked after all day.

MOUNTAIN RESTAURANTS
One of the area's highlights

Our reporters are unanimous in their praise for the mountain huts – there are lots of them and virtually all offer good food, atmosphere and value for money. As well as restaurants, there are lots of snow bars to stop off at for a quick grappa.

The little place at Piz Sorega above San Cassiano is called a 'ski bar' but it is also a fine restaurant. The Panorama is a small, cosy, rustic sun-trap at the foot of the Dantercëpies drag. The Scoiattolo, at the bottom of the Dantercëpies gondola, alongside the nursery area, is very atmospheric.

On the way down to Plan de Gralba from Ciampinoi, the Vallongia Rolandhütte is renowned for its apple strudel, but is actually a fine all-round restaurant – watch out for the huge St Bernard dog. Nearby the Gran Paradis is good for watching racers but gets rather busy. The Clerchütte at Ciampinoi is a very lively place. The triumvirate of little huts above Colfosco – Forcelles, Edelweiss and Pradat – are all very pleasant.

Way over at Lagazuoi, beyond San Cassiano, the Scotoni restaurant is worth the excursion, serving some of the best food in the area, including spit-barbecued pig. Capana Alpina is another one to try in this area.

Those skiing the Alta Badia should try the excellent Cherz above Passo di Campolongo. The Gamsbluthütte above Santa Cristina is a major sunbathing spot. Lupo Bianco, at the bottom of Val Zalei between Passo Sella and Canazei, is a notable rendezvous point and sun-trap. Capanna Bill, on the far side of Arabba beyond Passo Padon, has stunning views of the Marmolada glacier.

SKI SCHOOL
Don't count on English

Lack of English-speaking instruction is a problem. This year one reporter tells us 'all English speakers put together regardless of competence.' If you are lucky enough to be in a suitable group and to get a good English-speaker or understand German or Italian, the lesson is likely to be useful. Selva has a good reputation for standards of tuition and private lessons are reported to be very good.

FACILITIES FOR CHILDREN
Good by Italian standards

There are comprehensive childcare arrangements, but given the lack of British visitors it would be surprising if English were routinely spoken.

 # Staying there

Selva is the biggest and liveliest of the places actually on the Sella Ronda circuit at which to stay. Ortisei is the administrative centre of the Val Gardena – pretty, and more of a complete community – but it is not so conveniently situated for the skiing. For a brief description of the other villages on or near the circuit, see the end of this chapter.

In Selva itself, the most convenient position to stay is near one of, or between, the two main gondolas. But there is a very good, free, regular bus service throughout the valley until early evening, so position isn't crucial.

HOW TO GO
Surprisingly few packages

Selva and the Sella Ronda area has made a comeback in a few British tour operators' programmes after being dropped for several years.

Chalets There is now quite a wide choice of catered chalets, with three operators in the resort; and some of the properties are of good quality, with en-suite bathrooms.

First Choice have the attractive, modern Splendid, on the edge of the village, 500m from the Ciampinoi lifts. Their Elise is a smaller apartment-based chalet in a superb position opposite the Ciampinoi gondola. Crystal have several chalets, most close to the centre and lifts. The Salvan is particularly comfortable. Bladon Lines and Crystal both have floors of the Vanadis, and Bladon Lines also have the simpler and less convenient Wiesenheim.

Hotels There are 10 4-stars, over 30 3-stars and numerous lesser hotels. Few of the best hotels are well positioned.
£££ **Gran Baita** Large, luxurious sporthotel, with lots of mod cons including indoor pool. A few minutes' walk from centre and lifts. Highly recommended by recent reporters.
£££ **Aaritz** Best-placed of the 4-stars, opposite the gondola.
££ **Astor** Family-run chalet in centre, below nursery slopes. Good value.
££ **Olympia** Well positioned, central 3-star, recommended by reporters.
££ **Solaia** 3-star chalet, superbly positioned for lifts and slopes, recommended by reporters.
Self-catering There are plenty of apartments to choose from – some more convenient than others. The 3-star Rondula apartments are in a pretty chalet building just out of town near the Ciampinoi chair.

PACKAGES

Bladon Lines, Crystal, First Choice Ski, Inghams, Ski Club of GB

Arabba Ski Beach Villas

Campitello First Choice Ski, Inghams

Canazei Crystal, First Choice Ski, Inghams, Simply Ski

La Villa Ski Beach Villas

San Cassiano First Choice Ski

ACTIVITIES

Indoor Swimming, sauna, solaria (in hotels), bowling alley, squash, artificial skating rink, ice hockey, curling, museum, indoor golf, concerts, cinema, billiards, tennis
Outdoor Sleigh rides, torch-light descents, horse-riding, extensive cleared paths around Selva and above S Cristina and Ortisei, ski-bob

TOURIST OFFICE

Postcode 39048
Tel 00 39 (471) 795122
Fax 794245

EATING OUT
Plenty of good-value choices

Selva offers the best of both Austrian and Italian food at prices to suit all pockets. The higher-quality restaurants are mainly hotel-based. The Antares and Laurin have particularly good menus while the Olympia is renowned for its fondues. The Freina specialises in traditional Austrian food and large meals suitable for two or three people to share (good value). Da Rino has some of the best pizzas in town, whilst the Ciampinoi pizzeria serves excellent pasta and Austrian dishes in a lively atmosphere.

APRES-SKI
Above average for a family resort

Nightlife is lively and informal, though the scattered nature of the village means there is little on-street atmosphere. The Luisl, Speck and Laurin kellers are the liveliest bars in town. The Sun Valley and Savoy nightclubs have live bands. Hotel Stella has an atmospheric bar but its disco can lack atmosphere except at weekends. The Médel disco is just out of town, but worth the taxi-ride. Tour operators organise a lively bowling evening. The Friday tea dance at the Scoiattolo mountain hut is a must – oompah, yodelling etc.

FOR NON-SKIERS
Good variety

Excursions are difficult without a car, but otherwise there is a fair amount to do. The lovely walks are the highlight. The charming town of Ortisei is close by and well worth a visit for its large hot-spring swimming pool, shops, restaurants and lovely old buildings. Numerous good mountain restaurants, nicely scattered around the different sections of ski area, can be reached by gondola or cable-car from the village or nearby. Car-drivers have Bolzano and Innsbruck within reach.

Ortisei 1235m

Ortisei is a charming market town that has a life outside skiing. It's full of lovely old buildings, pretty churches

and pleasant shops. The lift station that accesses the south-facing side of the skiing is conveniently central, but skiers wishing to start on the north-facing Alpe di Siusi slopes have to negotiate the busy main road that skirts town. The nursery area, ski school and ski kindergarten are at the foot of these slopes, but families have a fair range of accommodation available to them on the piste-side of the road. The fine public indoor pool and ice rink are also here. A central hotel is equidistant from both lift stations. The south-facing Seceda slopes give the fastest access to Selva.

There is hotel and self-catering accommodation to suit all tastes and pockets, but we are not aware of any available through tour operators. Many of the more expensive hotels have good pool and health facilities. The 4-star Adler is very central. The unfortunately named hotel Hell is close to the Alpe di Siusi lifts. If you have a car, the out-of-town Perla and Rodes, both 3-stars, take some beating for value. Inexpensive, central places include the 2-star Beleval, Garni Dr. Senoner and the Pra Palmer B&B. The best apartments – such as the Stella Rondula – are clustered around the Seceda chair. The simpler Aquila-Kirchmayr and Oswald apartments are close to the centre and north-facing slopes respectively.

There are many good restaurants, mainly specialising in local dishes. The Grien is expensive but very good. Villa Emilia and Dolimiten Madonna are both worth a try. The immediate après-ski atmosphere is quite jolly, but things are fairly subdued later. The Cosmea bar is the place to go if returning from the north-facing slopes at the end of the day; the Albergo Sureghes taverna has live music; the Posta has a Tyrolean-style stube.

Non-skiing facilities are plentiful. Apart from exploring the town, there are good indoor swimming, tennis and ice skating centres, squash, bowling, sauna and tobogganing. There are lovely walks, and some mountain restaurants are within reach by cable-car.

Corvara 1570m

Corvara is the most animated Sella Ronda village east of Selva, with plenty of hotels, restaurants, bars and sports facilities. It's well positioned within the ski area, with village lifts heading off in different directions towards the reasonably equidistant Selva, Arabba and San Cassiano. The main shops and some hotels are

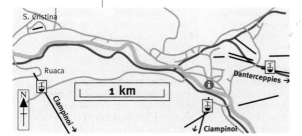

clustered around a small central piazza, but the rest of the place sprawls along the valley floor.

Hotel Sassongher is perhaps the best hotel in town, but it's not particularly well placed for the skiing. The Posta is a more central, quality hotel. The Eden is a good, cheaper option. The Pradat is an attractive pension, well placed for the lifts, which has the only babysitting service in town. Ardent après-skiers should visit the Posta Zirm, which has great tea dances. It becomes a nightclub later, when its main rival is the Sassongher keller bar. The Arabesque bar is best for a quiet drink. There are a number of good-value restaurants: the Adler, Perla and Panorama are examples.

There's a ski kindergarten but English is not widely spoken, and there's no nursery. Non-skiers have an indoor pool, bowling, squash, indoor tennis and an ice rink.

Colfosco 1645m

Colfosco is a smaller, quieter version of Corvara, 2km away. It has a fairly compact centre with a sprawl of large hotels along the road towards Selva. It's connected to Corvara by a horizontal-running chair-lift. In the opposite direction, a series of irritatingly short lifts head off to the Passo Gardena and on to Selva.

There are several large hotels that between them provide plenty of services. The top-class Cappella and Kolfuschgerhof hotels both have indoor pools and provide most of what little nightlife there is. The Centrale is a cheaper place to stay. The rustic, cramped Garni Peter bar is the one lively après-ski haunt; it often has live music and a tea dance. Restaurants worth a try include the Stria, Tabladel and Matthiaskeller.

San Cassiano 1530m

San Cassiano is a pretty little village, set in an attractive, tree-filled valley. It's a very quiet, slightly upmarket resort, full of well-heeled Italian families and comfortable hotels, but little else. The local skiing, the Alta Badia, though sizeable and fully linked, is something of a spur of the main Sella Ronda circuit. Moving further afield is a tiresome business for adventurous skiers who want to do the circuit.

First Choice has a couple of quite different catered chalets. One is a large, comfortable pension-conversion. The other is a smaller, more basic, rustic place. Among the best hotels in each category are the Rosa Alpina (4-star), Tyrol (3-star),

Alexander (2-star), Plang (1-star) and Jasmin (B&B). The Ciasa La Ro and Ciasa Ulli are good apartments.

The Pitscheiderhof is perhaps the best restaurant in town, and others worth a try are the Diamant, La Stüa, Frohsinn and Antersies. The Ski Bar at the base of the village chair is the main après-ski spot.

The tea dance in Corvara's Posta Zirm is a must for those wanting something lively. Ski there at the end of the day, taxi home afterwards. Later nightlife is very limited. The Rosa Alpina hotel has dancing and there's a bowling alley in the Diamant hotel. Walking in the pretty scenery is the main non-skiing activity. Swimming is the other. There is no nursery or ski kindergarten.

La Villa 1435m

La Villa is similar to neighbouring San Cassiano in most respects – small, quiet, pretty, unspoilt – but is slightly closer to Corvara, making it rather better placed for the main Sella Ronda circuit. Beach Villas has a large, good-value catered chalet here. La Bercia Pizzeria is recommended for chalet girls' nights off. Village amenities include pool, bowling, ski kindergarten (no nursery), and ice skating on a frozen lake.

Canazei 1440m

Canazei is a sizeable, bustling, pretty, roadside village of narrow streets, rustic old buildings, traditional style hotels and nice little shops, set in the Sella Ronda's most heavily wooded section of mountains. It has reasonably animated nightlife and plenty going on generally. It is not, perhaps, an ideal choice for some British families due to the busy road and lack of English spoken in the ski school and nursery facilities.

A 12-person gondola is the only mountain access point, but it shifts the queues (which can be long) quickly. A single piste back to the village is linked to runs returning from both Selva and Arabba. The village nursery slope is inconveniently located, but it's unlikely to be used after day one. The local Belvedere slopes are uniformly easy and particularly well endowed with mountain restaurants.

Crystal have an apartment-based catered chalet in Canazei, ten minutes from the lift. There are no luxury hotels, but the 3-star Croce Bianca offers elegant comfort and old-world charm. It's also central and close to the lift. The much cheaper Diana is a charming place, five minutes from the village centre. The friendly, comfortable Azola is a long walk from the gondola – and the bus service is reputedly erratic. The Palace Dolomiti is another hotel with a touch of class, and particularly popular for its cuisine and central position. The Astoria is another good choice available on the British market.

There are numerous restaurants. The Stala, Principe, Rosticceria Melester and Te Cevana are all worth a try. Nightlife is fairly jolly, if limited in scope. Two happening places dominate – the Montanara bar and Gatto Nero bar disco.

There's a fair amount to do for non-skiers. Walks are beautiful, clothes shopping worthwhile. There's a good pool, sauna, Turkish baths, and ice skating in neighbouring Alba. There is an all-day nursery and ski kindergarten available.

Campitello 1445m

This is a smaller, quieter village than neighbouring Canazei but, with the exception of Selva, is the most prominent of the Sella Ronda resorts on the British package market. It remains, however, very unspoilt, with little English spoken.

By the high standards of the Sella Ronda, the village is nothing special to look at, particularly when there's little snow – which is much of the time – but it's still pleasant. It's remarkably quiet during the day, having no slopes to the village.

A cable-car takes skiers up into the Sella Ronda circuit. If you don't wish to return by lift at the end of the day, skiing down to Canazei and catching a bus back is an option. We had a good report of the beginners' class in the ski school this year – though English was a problem.

The Rubino is an elegant 4-star hotel well placed close to the cable-car. The good 3-star Sella Ronda is also very convenient for everything. The 3-star Enrosadira is less well positioned, a tiring uphill walk from the cable-car. Pension Festil is similarly placed but offers a useful cheap and cheerful B&B option. Campitello is much livelier and the neighbouring village of Pozza has ice skating and night-skiing. There are no children's facilities.

Arabba 1600m

Arabba is a small traditional village, uncommercialised to the point where basic resort infrastructure is in short supply. But the lifts into the Sella Ronda in both directions make it very convenient. It is much more of a serious skiers' resort than its sunny, family-oriented neighbours. The high north-facing slopes have the best natural snow in the Dolomites, and the nearby Marmolada glacier opens in February (for a supplement).

Apartment-conversion chalets and self-catering accommodation are available through Beach Villas. The chalets are cheap, comfortable and close to the lifts. The self-catering apartments are in the same building as some chalet accommodation.

Hotels are available to independent travellers. The 4-star Sport is the best. The Porta Vescovo is a large, comfortable, multi-amenity 3-star with the only pool in town. The Evaldo is a simpler 3-star. Albergo Pordoi is a 2-star with character, and Garni Erika is a pleasant 1-star.

Venues for eating out are limited. Al Forte, 3km out of town, is best. Al Tablé, 7 Sass and Ru De Mont are cheap and cheerful pizzerias.

The après-ski is also very limited. The Al Fegole bar is the smartest place in town. Bar Peter, and the bars of Pension Erika and Albergo Pordoi, are others worth a try. The Delmonego family's bar-caravan, at the bottom of the piste, is the tea-time rendezvous.

Non-skiers are marooned and children's facilities are non-existent.

Sestriere 2000m

Sestriere was built for snow – high, with north-west-facing slopes – and it now has very extensive snowmaking facilities. It attracts lots of smart Italians but not many British – perhaps because the village is not what we generally look for in an Italian resort. Sestriere's international profile will doubtless be raised next season, when it hosts the 1997 World Championships.

HOW IT RATES

The skiing

Snow	****
Extent	****
Advanced	***
Intermediates	****
Beginners	***
Convenience	****
Queues	***
Restaurants	**

The rest

Scenery	***
Resort charm	*
Not skiing	*

SKI FACTS

Figures relate to the whole Milky Way area

Altitude	1390m-2825m
Lifts	97
Pistes	400km
Green/Blue	12%
Red	67%
Black	21%
Artificial snow	65km

PACKAGES

Club Med, Crystal, Equity Total Ski, Neilson, Stena Sealink

Sansicario Equity Total Ski, Stena Sealink

TOURIST OFFICE

Postcode 10058
Tel 00 39 (122)
755444
Fax 755171

THE RESORT

Sestriere was the Alps' first purpose-built resort. It sits on a broad, sunny and windy col at 2000m. Neither the site nor the village looks very hospitable, though the buildings have benefited from recent investment.

THE SKIING

Sestriere is at one extreme of the big Franco-Italian Milky Way **ski area**. The local skiing has two main sectors: Sises, directly in front of the village (which has a brightly floodlit piste), and Motta, above Borgata – a satellite village 2km away to the north-east and 150m lower.

Drag- and chair-lifts predominate on the local north-west-facing slopes. The chair-lift link to Monte Fraiteve, on the other side of the resort, has been removed, because the south-facing run it served was often bare of snow. As a result, access to Sansicario and the rest of the Milky Way is via the gondola from Borgata to Col Basset, at the top of the Sauze d'Oulx skiing, and a drag-lift back up to Monte Fraiteve.

With most of the local slopes facing north-west and ranging from 1840m to 2820m, it is fair to expect them to have **snow-cover** for most of the season, even without the snowmaking that covers practically all of the Sises sector and about half of Motta.

There is a fair amount to amuse **advanced skiers** – steep pistes served by the drags at the top of both sectors, and off-piste opportunities in several directions from here and from the lifts on Monte Fraiteve.

Both sectors also offer plenty for **intermediate skiers**, who can also expect to explore practically all of the Milky Way areas, time permitting. The terrain is excellent for **beginners**, with several nursery areas and the gentlest of easy runs down to Borgata.

There are two **cross-country** loops covering a total of 15km.

Although the lifts are mainly modern, with several quad chairs, **queues** for the main lifts occur at the weekends and holidays. The lifts from Borgata to Sestriere inevitably become crowded at the end of the day, as everyone skiing Motta or returning

from Sauze has to use this link.

The local **mountain restaurants** are fair – the one at Sises is best – but there are better ones further afield.

Lack of English-speaking tuition can be a problem in the **ski school**.

An all-day crèche takes **children** between 3 and 6 years.

STAYING THERE

Sestriere is not the most convenient of purpose-built resorts, but choice of location is not crucial. If you want to make use of Sestriere's nightlife or shops, don't be tempted to stay in Borgata. Most **accommodation** is in apartments, but there are a dozen hotels, mostly of 3-star or 4-star status.

The central 4-star Grand Hotel Sestriere is an ugly low building, but is comfortable and well placed. Just out of the village (but not far from a lift, and with courtesy transport) is the luxurious Principi di Piemonte. The Savoy Edelweiss is a central, attractive 3-star. The distinctive round towers of the Torre and Duchi d'Aosta are occupied by Club Med.

The comfortable Residence Bellavista apartments, at the entrance to the resort, are equidistant (10 to 12 minutes' walk) from the main lifts, though skiing from nearby is possible.

The numerous 3- and 4-star hotels offer plenty of options for **eating out**. For example, the Grand has good local specialities. The Gargotte, I Tre Rubinetti and the Last Tango grill have good Italian and French food across the price range.

Après-ski is lively at weekends, quiet at other times. The Prestige and Palace are just two of the many little bars that liven up. The Rendezvous is a cosy piano bar. The Black Sun piano-bar-cum-disco and the Tabata club are great fun at weekends. The Pinky is perhaps the best of the relaxed bars that double as pizzerias or snack joints, with lots of low sofas in the classic Italian style.

There is a fair amount for active **non-skiers** to do, but it is not a very attractive place in which to while away the days, despite some smart shopping. Strangely, there is no indoor swimming pool.

La Thuile 1450m

HOW IT RATES

The skiing
Snow	****
Extent	***
Advanced	**
Intermediates	****
Beginners	****
Convenience	***
Queues	****
Restaurants	*

The rest
Scenery	***
Resort charm	***
Not skiing	**

✔ Fair-sized, very quiet ski area linked to La Rosière in France

✔ Excellent beginner and easy intermediate skiing

✔ Unusual mix of modern purpose-built accommodation at foot of slopes and more villagey atmosphere of the old town, a ten-minute walk away

✘ All the seriously tough piste skiing is low down, and most of the low tree-lined skiing is tough

✘ Mountain restaurants very disappointing

✘ Not the place for lively après-ski

La Thuile is surprisingly little known on the British market. It deserves better. It has a fair-sized ski area of its own as well as being linked with La Rosière in France (they have a shared lift pass). The skiing best suits beginners and intermediates in search of little challenge, but it is not devoid of interest for good skiers, particularly if the snow conditions are good, when there is the choice of venturing off-piste above the Petit St Bernard pass between France and Italy (closed in winter) or skiing the short but serious blacks through the trees above the village. It has an excellent lift system and uncrowded runs.

The resort itself is an unusual mixture of old and new, with both a modern, purpose-built complex at the foot of the slopes and an old, partly restored mining village over the river.

ORIENTATION

La Thuile consists of two quite distinct parts. An old mining village sits across a river from a new purpose-built resort at the foot of the lifts. A fast chair and a gondola speed you up the mountain with further high-speed chairs to the top.

The skiing links with **La Rosière**, over the border in France. **Courmayeur** is within easy reach by road, **Chamonix** is just through the Mont Blanc tunnel and **Cervinia** is about an hour's drive away.

The resort

At the foot of the lifts is a modern purpose-built complex, with accommodation, splendid leisure centre, bars, restaurants and shops. It looks and feels much like a typical French purpose-built resort such as La Plagne or Tignes, but with a distinctly Italian atmosphere.

Cross the river and things are completely different. La Thuile started life as a mining town but became depopulated, and large parts of it fell into disrepair until the skiing area was developed and boom times returned.

Much of the old village has been restored and new buildings tastefully added around it. But parts remain in ruins, with a slight 'ghost town' feel to them. There's a reasonable selection of restaurants and bars, but not much in the way of shopping other than food and ski gear.

The skiing

For a little-known resort, La Thuile offers a surprisingly large amount of skiing. And it is normally very uncrowded, with quiet pistes and no lift queues. Beginners and early intermediates will get the most out of it, although most of the lower runs in the woods are seriously steep. Although many of La Thuile's runs are

marked red, they often deserve no more than a blue rating. The ski area has a reputation for being very cold, especially early in the season – many of the runs are north-facing.

THE SKI AREA
Big and gentle
The lifts out of the village take you to **Les Suches** (2200m), with black runs going back down directly to the village through the trees, and reds taking a more roundabout route. From here chairs and drags take you to the top of the mountain and a number of different gentle bowls accessed from **Chaz Dura** (2580m). You can also drop down over the back from here to the Petit St Bernard road.

The link with **La Rosière** in France is via Belvedere (2640m) and the Col de Traversette (2400m) and is quite a tiresome journey. In contrast with La Thuile's mainly north- and east-facing runs, La Rosière's skiing is largely south-facing and, although the runs in France tend to be steeper, the snow in Italy tends to be better.

SNOW RELIABILITY
Good
Most of La Thuile's skiing is north- or east-facing and above 2000m. So the snow generally keeps in good condition. There's also a reasonable amount of snowmaking both above the tree-line and on a couple of the runs home.

SKI FACTS

Altitude	1150m-2640m
Lifts	33
Pistes	135km
Green/Blue	45%
Red	37%
Black	18%
Artificial snow	10km

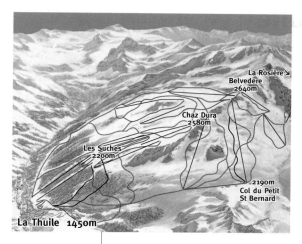

La Thuile 1450m

LIFT PASSES

95/96 prices in lire
Dominio Internazionale
Covers all lifts in La Rosière and La Thuile.
Beginners One baby-lift in village. Points tickets (50 points 60,000).
Main pass
1-day pass 43,000 (94/95 price)
6-day pass 215,000 (low season 190,000 – 12% off)
Children
Under 4: free pass
Short-term passes
Half-day from 1pm.
Notes Discount of 10% for groups of 25 or more.
Alternative passes
Valle d'Aosta pass covers La Thuile, Courmayeur, Gressoney, Champoluc, Alagna, Cervinia, Valtournenche and Pila (adult 6-day 238,000, 94/95 price).
Credit cards: Yes

SKI SCHOOL

95/96 prices in lire
Rutor
Classes 6 days
2½hr: 10am-12.30; 2hr: 1pm-3pm
6 2½hr days: 155,000
Children's classes
Ages: from 6
6 2½hr days: 155,000
Private lessons
Hourly
49,000 for 1 or 2 people; each additional person 5,000

FOR ADVANCED SKIERS
Rather limited

The only steep pistes are those down through the trees from Les Suches back to the resort. The steepest of these, the Diretta, is serious stuff. What's more, because they are low (below 2000m) these runs can suffer from poor conditions and become very tricky indeed.

The rest of the skiing is tame by comparison. The best of it, for good skiers, is the area above the Petit St Bernard road, served by the San Bernardo and Fourclaz chairs, where there is some genuinely black terrain and plenty of opportunity to venture off-piste. You'll find many of the other red runs seem overgraded.

An added attraction of La Thuile, for those who can afford it, is its heli-skiing. This includes drops on the Ruitor glacier, with a 20km run into France, ending at La Rosière.

FOR INTERMEDIATE SKIERS
Something different

La Thuile has some good intermediate skiing, and its link with La Rosière in France adds a sense of adventure as well as doubling the extent of the skiing. Together, the two resorts offer a large and varied ski area, with over 130km of runs. However, timid intermediates are better off staying on home ground: the route back from La Rosière involves a short but tricky red right at the start, and most of the terrain at La Rosière – particularly on the top half of the mountain – is fairly challenging.

On the Italian side, the bowls above Les Suches have numerous gentle, groomed blue and red runs, ideal for easy cruising and practising your technique. There are also long roundabout red runs down through

the trees back to the resort.

The red runs on the other side of the top ridge, down towards the Petit St Bernard road, offer a greater challenge for more adventurous intermediates. But La Thuile's skiing really suits less ambitious intermediates best.

FOR BEGINNERS
Good, but not much English

There are nursery slopes both at village level and at Les Suches. There's a good gentle green run above Les Suches to progress to, and some shallow blues too. But none of these are segregated from the main ski area. The main problem for beginners is likely to be the lack of English in the ski school (see next page).

FOR CROSS-COUNTRY
Varied choice

La Thuile has 16km of tracks of varying difficulty on the valley floor.

QUEUES
Very rare

The resort has a very effective lift system for the number of skiers it attracts, starting with an exceptionally powerful gondola and parallel high-speed chair up to Les Suches. You can usually walk straight on to any of the lifts; it's only at peak weekends that you might find queues.

MOUNTAIN RESTAURANTS
Very disappointing

La Thuile was the only resort last season in which we failed to have a decent lunch up the mountain. And the locals recommend skiing back to town for lunch.

Although there are several ristorantes marked on the piste map, most serve little more than sandwiches and snacks. If you are coming to Italy for the pasta, you'd be better off going elsewhere. The biggest facility is the self-service cafeteria at Les Suches which lacks atmosphere but serves good home-made Italian

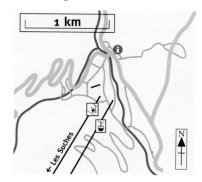

food. Just below there's a pleasant hut.

Many of the on-slope places operate the typical Italian system of paying before you collect your food.

SKI SCHOOL
Good but foreign
Several of the reporters we've heard from praise the ski school for reasonably-sized classes and fair instruction. Repeatedly, the biggest reservation is the lack of instructors who speak good English.

FACILITIES FOR CHILDREN
Very poor
La Thuile doesn't seem to cater much for children (or, perhaps more accurately, their parents). There is no kindergarten or crèche. Ski school starts at six years.

⬆ Staying there

Undoubtedly the most convenient place to stay for the skiing is in the modern purpose-built Planibel complex at the foot of the slopes. But many people find this rather soulless and prefer to stay in the old town over the river (served by a free bus service) or in one of the more traditional buildings nearer the slopes.

HOW TO GO
Some choice of packages
The number of tour operators going to La Thuile is gradually increasing.
Chalets Bladon Lines have the only catered chalet in town, an apartment conversion in a ramshackle old block, but it is reasonably comfortable by the standards of such places. It offers good value and books out very early.
Hotels The choice is between the swanky but characterless 4-star Planibel, three 3-stars and 10 simpler places.
££££ Planibel American-style 'resort hotel' with all mod cons, including covered driveway for unloading your trunk, and underground parking. Right at the base of the lifts. Pool and other facilities.

£££ Eden Comfortable modern hotel in traditional wood and stone style, conveniently close to the lifts and Planibel centre.
££ Chalet Alpina Simple place with the atmosphere of a catered chalet, on outskirts of the resort.
Self-catering The Planibel apartments have received nothing but praise from a number of our reporters. They're spacious, well-equipped, ski-convenient and offer great value for money. Not surprisingly, they usually book out early.

EATING OUT
Limited range, consistently good
There are only eleven restaurants in La Thuile but we've received positive reports on most of them. The Bricole and Marmottes both serve excellent traditional Italian food. Lisse also has authentic Italian fare at cheaper prices. The always-busy Lo Creton, Relais and Grotta vie for the title of Best Cheap and Cheerful Pizzeria. The Maison de Laurent and Tufeja are also popular.

Booking at all the above is advisable if you want to eat at popular times.

APRES-SKI
Early to bed
A few of the bars fill up after skiing, notably the Buvette and Bon Chon in the Planibel complex, but most of the evenings tend to be taken up by a leisurely meal, after which people retire for the evening. The Rendezvous bar has karaoke but the Bricolette and Bricole have more atmospheric bars. The Bricole and Paradiso discos warm up at the weekend.

FOR NON-SKIERS
Not the best choice
La Thuile has little to attract non-skiers. The Planibel complex has an excellent range of leisure facilities including a huge swimming pool and indoor ice rink. But there's little in the way of attractive walks or shopping. Excursions to Courmayeur and Chamonix can be organised. Meeting at the top of the gondola for lunch is easy, but not terribly enticing.

CHILDCARE
There are no all-day childcare arrangements

GETTING THERE
Air Geneva, transfer 2¹⁄₂hr. Turin, transfer 2¹⁄₂hr.

Rail Pré-St-Didier (10km); regular buses to resort.

PACKAGES
Bladon Lines, Crystal, First Choice Ski, Interski, Neilson, Ski Valkyrie

ACTIVITIES
Indoor Skating rink, 2 swimming pools, gymnasium, 10 pin bowling, solarium, sauna, jacuzzi, massage, amusement arcade, billiards, squash
Outdoor Winter walks, heli-skiing

TOURIST OFFICE
Postcode 11016
Tel 00 39 (165) 884179
Fax 885196

Switzerland

Switzerland is home to some of our favourite ski resorts. For sheer charm and spectacular scenery, the 'traffic-free' villages of Wengen, Mürren, Saas Fee and Zermatt take some beating. Many resorts have impressive ski areas too – including some of the biggest, highest and toughest skiing in the Alps. For fast, efficient, queue-free lift networks, Swiss resorts rarely come up to French standards – and the worst are positively abysmal. But there are compensations: the world's best mountain restaurants, for example. Prices in resorts and up the mountain are high; but what you get for your money is first-class.

Downhill skiing in its modern form was invented in Wengen and Mürren, which were persuaded to open their summer railways in winter to take their British guests up the mountain to ski. They remain firm favourites with their regular British visitors, who return every year to savour the special atmosphere of these tiny villages and their awesome views of the Eiger, Mönch and Jungfrau.

While France is the home of the purpose-built ski resort, Switzerland is the home of the traditional mountain village which has transformed itself from farming community into year-round holiday resort. Many of Switzerland's most famous ski resorts are as popular in the summer as in the winter, or more so. This creates resorts with a much more lived-in feel to them and a much more stable local community. Many of the resorts are still run and dominated by a handful of families who were lucky or shrewd enough to get involved in the early development of the resorts.

This has its downside as well as advantages. The ruling families are able to stifle competition and prevent newcomers from taking a slice of their action. New ski schools, competing with the traditional school and pushing up standards, are much less common than in other countries, for example. And in many resorts, British tour operators are severely restricted in the amount of ski guiding they can offer their guests – a popular service which the ski schools see as taking business away from them.

Swiss resorts have a reputation for efficiently relieving you of your money. And the reputation is well earned: it is undoubtedly true that Switzerland is an expensive place in which to ski. Nothing is cheap; but the quality of the service you get for your money is generally high. Swiss hotels are some of the best in the world. The trains run like clockwork to the advertised timetable (and often they run to the top of the mountain, doubling up as a ski-lift). The food is almost universally of good quality, and much less stodgy than in neighbouring Austria. Although it is expensive, there are fashionable resorts in France that can cost you even more. And in Switzerland it is generally true that you get what you pay for. Even the cheapest wine, for example, is not cheap; but it is reliable – duff bottles are very rare.

Although reliable standards are among the key features of Switzerland, there are notable exceptions. Verbier has Europe's most expensive lift pass; for £165 (at summer 1995 exchange rates) you get the right to stand for hours in queues for inadequate and badly planned lifts – see page 359. Wengen and Grindelwald share an excellent intermediate ski area which has suffered a series of very poor years for snow-cover. And yet they have been painfully slow to invest in artificial snowmaking facilities, which means that they are falling way behind the standards of service that keen skiers now expect – and the service provided by many less prestigious resorts such as those in the Italian Dolomites.

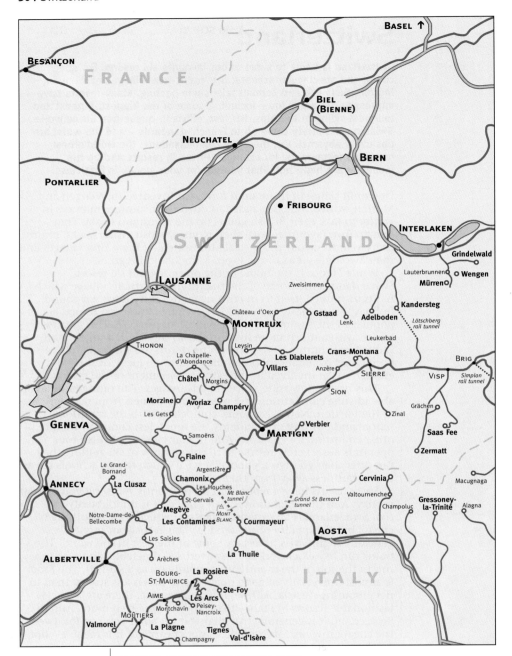

GETTING AROUND THE SWISS ALPS

Access to practically all Swiss resorts is fairly straightforward when approaching from the north. Many of the high passes that are perfectly sensible ways to get around the country in summer are closed in winter, which can be inconvenient if you are moving around from one area to another. There are car-carrying rail tunnels beneath the passes either side of Andermatt (Furka leading westwards to Brig, and Oberalp leading eastwards to Sedrun, Flims and Chur).

St Moritz is more awkward to get to. The main road route is over the Julier pass. This is normally kept open, but at 2284m it is naturally prone to heavy snowfalls that can shut it for a time. The

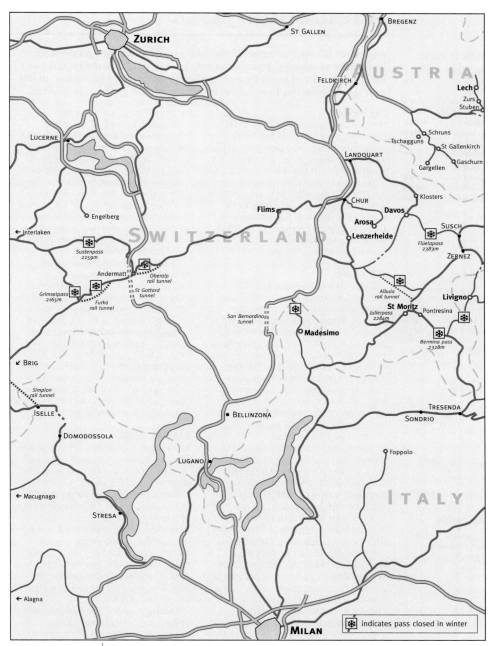

Scale in km
0 — 30

fall-back is the car-carrying rail tunnel under the Albula pass.

These car-carrying rail services are painless unless you travel at peak times, when there may be long queues – particularly for the Furka tunnel from Andermatt, which offers residents of Zürich the shortest route to the Valais resorts (Zermatt etc). Another rail tunnel service that's very handy for skiers is the Lötschberg tunnel, linking Kandersteg in the Bernese Oberland with Brig in the Valais. There's no quicker way from Wengen to Zermatt.

There is a car-carrying rail tunnel linking Switzerland with Italy – the Simplon. But most of the routes to Italy are kept open by means of road tunnels. See the Italy introduction for more information.

Adelboden 1355m

HOW IT RATES

The skiing

Snow	**
Extent	***
Advanced	**
Intermediates	***
Beginners	****
Convenience	***
Queues	***
Restaurants	**

The rest

Scenery	***
Resort charm	****
Not skiing	****

SKI FACTS

Altitude	1400m-2355m
Lifts	50
Pistes	130km
Green/Blue	48%
Red	44%
Black	8%
Artificial snow	2km

PACKAGES

Inghams, Kuoni, Made to Measure, Plus Travel, Swiss Travel Service

TOURIST OFFICE

Postcode CH-3715
Tel 00 41 (33) 738080
Fax 734252

Adelboden is unjustly neglected; for intermediate skiers who attach more importance to relaxing, pretty surroundings than to ski convenience, it has a lot of appeal. It will never be a convenience resort, but its investment in lifts over recent years has been heavy, and has produced great improvements.

THE RESORT

Adelboden comes quite close to the chocolate-box image of the Swiss mountain village: old wooden chalets with overhanging roofs line the quiet main street (cars are discouraged), and 3000m peaks provide an impressive backdrop. Adelboden is in the Bernese Oberland, a couple of valleys to the west of the much better-known Jungfrau resorts (Wengen etc). These resorts are within day-trip range, as is the Gstaad area to the west.

THE SKIING

Adelboden's **ski area** is split into six sectors. Lifts from close to the main street take you to three of them. Schwandfeldspitz, directly above the village, is now reached by a cable-car-gondola hybrid. The main gondola to nearby Hochsthorn and more remote Geils-Sillerenbuhl starts below the village at Oey (where there is a car park), but a connecting mini-gondola starts from close to the main street. This is much the biggest sector, with long, gentle runs (and some short, sharp ones) from around 2200m down to around 1450m, back towards the village and over the ridge towards Lenk in the next valley. The single drag up Fleckli (1860m) remains unlinked; so does Engstligenalp, a flat-bottomed high-altitude bowl reached by cable-car, 4km south of the resort; and the even more remote, but slightly more extensive, Elsigenalp.

The skiing doesn't go very high – most of it is below 2000m – so **snow reliability** is not a strong point. But it could be worse: much of the skiing is above 1500m and north-facing. There is very little snowmaking.

For **advanced skiers** there are some genuine blacks beside the chairs at Geils, where there are also off-piste possibilities down towards both Adelboden and Lenk (though there are protected forest areas). Engstligenalp has off-piste potential too – and is a launching point for ski tours on and around the Wildstrubel.

All six areas deserve exploration by **intermediate skiers**. At Geils, there is quite a lot of ground to be covered – and expeditions across the valley to Lenk's gentle Betelberg area (covered by the lift pass) are possible.

Beginners are well catered for. There are good nursery slopes in the village and at the bottom of nearby sectors. At Geils there are gloriously long, easy blue runs to progress to.

The **cross-country** trails along the valleys towards Engstligenalp and Geils are extensive, varied and scenic.

The main access gondola is not entirely free of **queues**. When snow low down is poor, the Engstligenalp cable-car cannot cope.

There are pleasant **mountain restaurants** with terraces and immaculate loos in the Geils sector. Aebi is particularly charming. The snack bar at Hahnenmoos is 'absolute rubbish', according to one reporter.

The Swiss **ski school** gets mixed reports – 'caring, good English', but 'mix of abilities within group'. For **children** aged 4 to 6 there is a 'very good' ski nursery (9.15 to 4pm); for those aged 2 to 6, a day nursery (9am-5pm). Some hotels have nurseries: the free one at the Nevada Palace is good.

STAYING THERE

The village is compact, and there are efficient buses to the outlying areas; the ideal location for most people is close to the main street.

The choice of **how to go** is now quite wide: several UK operators, lots of locally bookable chalets and apartments, 30 pensions and hotels (mainly 3-star and 4-star, generally recommendable). The central 3-star Adler Sporthotel is one of the prettiest chalets, and is recommended. The little Bären is a classic wooden chalet – simple but captivating.

Eating out possibilities are quite varied, and include one or two mountain restaurants, including Aebi.

The **après-ski** is traditional, based on bars and tea-rooms (tea dancing at the Viktoria Eden hotel, 'great cakes' at Schmidt's). The Alte Taverne is a lovely, but pricey, old chalet with live music. Alpenrose is the cheapest bar.

There is a fair amount for **non-skiers**, and easy access to a couple of mountain restaurants. The Nevada-Palace hotel has a pool open to the public. There are indoor and outdoor curling and skating rinks.

Andermatt 1445m

HOW IT RATES

The skiing

Snow	★★★★
Extent	★
Advanced	★★★★
Intermediates	★★
Beginners	★
Convenience	★★★
Queues	★★
Restaurants	★★

The rest

Scenery	★★★
Resort charm	★★★★
Not skiing	★★

SKI FACTS

Altitude	1445m-2965m
Lifts	13
Pistes	56km
Green/Blue	29%
Red	42%
Black	29%
Artificial snow	none

Andermatt used to be a firm favourite with the Brits, but as other ski areas developed it got left behind. It's now an atmospheric old village with a small and outdated lift system giving access to some great, steep off-piste skiing.

THE RESORT

A familiar name among pre- and immediately post-war British skiers, Andermatt is now terra incognita to all but a few of the old brigade and a sporty minority of committed off-piste skiers. Historically an important Alpine thoroughfare, it has been sidelined since the opening of the Gotthard tunnel. Its primary livelihood now is not tourism but the army, whose barracks are the first buildings you see on your arrival and whose national servicemen are out in force in the bars and on the slopes.

But Andermatt is an attractive, if somewhat run-down village, with wooden houses lining the dog-leg main street, which runs from railway to cable-car stations via a hump-backed bridge that many an unchained car fails to conquer.

THE SKIING

For off-piste skiers Andermatt is one of the most inviting resorts in the world, thanks to a combination of suitable terrain, abundant snowfalls and retarded lift and piste development.

The main cable-car serves magnificent, varied skiing on the open, usually empty, slopes of the Gemsstock, and there are three more ski areas along the valley: Nätschen, Winterhorn (above Hospental) and Realp. The valley railway provides the only link between Andermatt and the latter two sectors, and offers tempting connections with resorts to the east (Davos, St Moritz) and west (Zermatt and other Valais resorts). You can put your car on some trains.

Andermatt is most definitely a resort for **advanced skiers**, with the Gemsstock boasting two superb long blacks in the north-facing bowl beneath the top cable-car, and another from mid-mountain back to the village. Much of the rest is 1500m vertical of challenging off-piste. Andermatt has plenty of guides for off-piste adventure and safaris, and heli-skiing.

Unfortunately the Gemsstock cable-car can take a while to get going after a heavy snowfall, but Winterhorn and Nätschen both provide black runs and off-piste opportunities while you wait.

Intermediates needn't be put off approaching the Gemsstock: a fine long red run, the Sonnenpiste, can be tackled, and there are two short lifts mid-mountain serving intermediate runs. Winterhorn's deceptively modest lift system offers ways down the 900m vertical of all standards, while Nätschen's south- and west-facing slopes are mostly open pistes perfect for finding your ski legs again.

There is an isolated nursery slope at Realp, along the valley towards the Furka pass, and the lower half of Nätschen has a good, long easy run back to the village. But essentially this is not a resort for **beginners**.

There is a 20km **cross-country** loop between Andermatt and Realp.

The antiquated lift system means weekend **queues** in optimum conditions. And if there are few skiers, the Gemsstock cable-car will wait ages for a decent load before ascending.

The few **mountain restaurants** are dull. Lunch is for wimps, of course, but it's best taken in restaurants in the village (see below). There is a good place at the foot of the off-piste run from Gemsstock down into Hospental.

The **ski school** has good English-speaking instructors. Mountain Reality offers excellent guiding around the breathtaking off-piste – it's great fun but hard work.

There are no special facilities for **children**; but there is skiing they can handle at Nätschen.

STAYING THERE

Accommodation is free if you're a 20-year-old Swiss male – the drawback is that you can't go home after a week. Otherwise Andermatt's beds are in small, cosy hotels and chalets.

The central Gasthaus Zum Sternen is an attractive old wooden chalet with a popular and lively restaurant and bar. The 3-star Sonne, between the centre and the cable-car, is welcoming and comfortable. The Aurora is the closest to the cable-car, and the Monopol, on the station side of the centre, has a pool. The 2-star Bergidyll, next door, is a British favourite.

Après-ski revolves around a few cosy local bars (the Ochsen is the most atmospheric) and restaurants (including the Tell and the Adler) and there are a couple of places that have dancing – the Downhill is the liveliest.

Andermatt has little for **non-skiers**.

Arosa 1800m

ORIENTATION

Arosa is in a high, remote setting at the end of a very long winding approach road from Chur. Rail access is easier. It is made up of two main centres, which are almost separate villages, Obersee and Innerarosa. Obersee, the first you come to, is the main centre and has a cable-car, chair and drag into the skiing. Innerarosa is about 1km further along and has a chair, a drag and (some way below the main focus) a gondola. Some accommodation is a long walk from the lifts, but there's a frequent, free ski-bus.

Outings by public transport or car are possible, notably to **Davos-Klosters, Flims** or **Lenzerheide**, the latter also reachable off-piste.

SKI FACTS

Altitude	1800m-2655m
Lifts	16
Pistes	70km
Green/Blue	38%
Red	57%
Black	5%
Artificial snow	1km

GETTING THERE

Air Zürich, transfer 3hr.

Rail Station in resort (Obersee); regular bus service.

✔ *Peaceful, quiet, sunny ski area*

✔ *Classic all-round winter holiday destination, with excellent non-skiing and cross-country facilities*

✔ *Very good children's facilities*

✔ *Good village transport compensates for scattered nature of the place*

✔ *Easy access by train, including packaged airport transfers*

✘ *Very limited skiing by large-resort standards*

✘ *Virtually no tree-lined runs, so little skiing feasible in bad weather*

✘ *Slopes face mainly south and east, and can get icy*

✘ *Some ugly, square, grey buildings in Obersee*

✘ *Lack of evening atmosphere*

The classic image of a winter sports resort is perhaps an isolated, snow-covered Swiss village, surrounded by big, beautiful mountains, with skating on a frozen lake, horse-drawn sleighs jingling through the streets, and people in fur coats strolling on mountain paths. Arosa is just that.

Skiing is just one of its attractions – and not an important one for many of its visitors. It's not keen skiers that Arosa aims to attract. It's people who want a relaxing time in the mountains and, maybe, want to ski a little too.

Accommodation is mainly in quiet hotels. Most people who come here don't want lively nightlife. But they do want comfort, and they don't mind paying for it. It's a pity that many of the hotels that are so comfortable within are eyesores, dating from times when pitched roofs were out of fashion.

 ## The resort

Arosa is set in a sheltered basin at the head of a beautiful wooded valley, in contrast to the open mountainside on which the skiing takes place. The approach, whether by road or rail is dramatic. The centre of the resort, Obersee, is a drab collection of Edwardian buildings – though its lakeside setting adds some charm. The remainder of Arosa is scattered over a wide area, with a substantial hill separating Obersee from the older, prettier Innerarosa.

Arosa is quiet; its relaxed ambience attracts an unpretentiously wealthy clientele of families and older people.

 ## The skiing

For such a well known and long-established resort, Arosa's ski area is tiny and lacking in any real challenge. Don't be surprised by the number of pedestrians and tobogganists you'll find around the ski area.

THE SKI AREA
Small and friendly
The slopes are spread widely over two main sectors. The **Weisshorn** skiing faces mainly south and south-east. Tschuggen, half-way to the Weisshorn peak, is the major lift junction,

reachable from both Obersee and Innerarosa. An inconveniently sited gondola below Innerarosa is the main access to the east- and north-east-facing slopes of the **Hörnli** sector.

Drags and chair-lifts allow skiing either way between the two sectors. Skiing around is straightforward, with easy routes possible between all main points. There are no potential dead-ends and it is possible to take the ski-bus home from wherever you end up.

Arosa has a US-style free ski host service every Sunday to help new arrivals get to know the slopes. It also has remarkably flexible lift passes: 4 days out of 7, 1½ days, half-day (after 12pm) and afternoon (after 2pm).

SNOW RELIABILITY
Quite good, despite sunny aspect
Although there is no very high skiing, and the slopes get a lot of sun, Arosa has relatively good cover. All the best south-facing pistes are above 2000m and the shadier Hörnli slopes usually hold their snow well. Temperatures can be very high in March though. A cannon to cover worn patches is the only artificial back-up. Arosa has little tree skiing for poor visibility days.

FOR ADVANCED SKIERS
A few off-piste options
Arosa isn't the resort for a keen advanced skier. There is a small section of steep skiing, both on- and

SKI SCHOOL

95/96 prices in Swiss francs

Swiss
Classes 5 days
4hr: 9.45-11.45 and 2.15-4.15
5 half-days: 125
Children's classes
Ages: 4 to 12
5 half-days: 115
Private lessons
Hourly or daily
120 for 2hr

CHILDCARE

The ski school runs ski kindergartens for children from age 4 to 6, from 9.45 to 4.15, at Innerarosa and behind the hotel Eden at Obersee.

The two 5-star hotels have their own kindergartens, as do some others – the 4-star Hof Maran, Seehof and Valsana, and the more modest Eden.

off-piste, at the top of the Weisshorn. But the most interesting opportunity is to ski off-piste to and from Lenzerheide via Hörnli. It's a scenic but not difficult run.

FOR INTERMEDIATE SKIERS
Best for leisurely types
This is a good area for those who want to take it easy and aren't looking for high mileage or much challenge. Keen piste-bashers will ski it all in the first day. Even the one black, the interesting Weisshorn-Carmenna run, is within the scope of good intermediates. Average skiers will particularly enjoy the long Hörnli-Innerarosa pistes. Less ambitious skiers have some lovely long cruises, the highlight of which is the Bruggerhorn-Pratschi motorway, well away from the lifts. The only woodland run of any note is one of the steeper blues.

FOR BEGINNERS
Very good beginner slopes
The Tschuggen nursery slopes are excellent and usually have good snow, but get other skiers passing through.

Innerarosa has a quieter but more limited area usually reserved for children. Quick learners will soon be able to ski all the way to Innerarosa, where there's a chair-lift straight back to Tschuggen. There are other easy runs for beginners to try too.

FOR CROSS-COUNTRY
High-quality trails
Although it lacks the sheer length of trails of many resorts, Arosa (with 29km) has some of the best, varied loops in the Alps. Guided excursions and instruction are widely available, and buses serve the scattered areas.

QUEUES
Few problems
With so many part-timers and non-skiers, and a well laid out lift system, Arosa does not suffer many queues. There can still be waits for the recently improved Weisshorn cable-car. The Hörnli drag was the worst bottleneck but was replaced last season by a quad chair, drastically cutting the wait.

MOUNTAIN RESTAURANTS
Excellent but crowded
Some of the mountain restaurants are very good, but there are too few of them, particularly considering the number of non-skiers walking around the slopes. Consequently they get crowded. Most have table-service and are expensive. Carmennahütte is the best: the barbie outside does great homemade hamburgers and there is a guy serving up pasta with meat sauce, cooked over a military field stove and served in mess tins. Tschuggenhütte is a rustic little refuge with a nice sun terrace, but gets crowded from 11am according to one regular. The Weisshornsattelhütte is rarely crowded. Hörnlihütte has a view worth the skate from the top of the

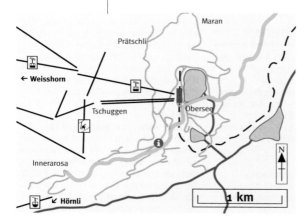

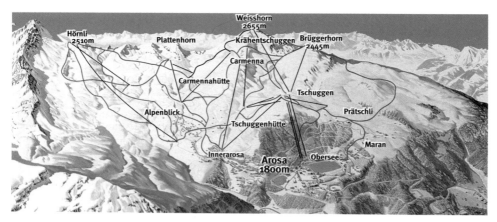

LIFT PASSES

95/96 prices in
Swiss francs

Arosa area
All lifts in Arosa ski
region.
Beginners Free baby-
lifts at Innerarosa and
Obersee. Tschuggen
area ski-pass (am, pm
or full-day) covers 7
beginner area lifts
(adult 1-day 30).
Main pass
1-day pass 52; 6-day
pass 219 (low season
186 – 15% off)
Senior citizens
Over 65 male, 62
female: 6-day pass
186 (15% off)
Children
Under 16: 6-day pass
110 (50% off)
Under 6: free pass
Short-term passes
Single ascent tickets
for pedestrians on
some lifts. Day-pass
with refund when
handed in early (58).
Afternoon pass
reduces by the hour,
from 39 at noon to
27 at 3pm.
Alternative periods
4 days in 7: 187
7 days in 14: 309
Notes Discounts for
students and groups.
Credit cards: Yes

ACTIVITIES

Indoor Hotel facilities
open to non-residents
(swimming, sauna,
massage, tennis,
squash), golf, bridge,
chess, bowling,
fitness centre, cinema,
concerts, museum
Outdoor 3 skating
rinks (2 artificial), 1
covered artificial rink,
ice-hockey, curling,
sleigh rides, 40km
cleared paths, hot-air
ballooning, ski-bob,
toboggan runs, snow-
shoe walks, para-
gliding, hang-gliding

PACKAGES

Inghams, Kuoni, Made
to Measure, Plus
Travel, Ski Choice,
SkiGower, Swiss
Travel Service

TOURIST OFFICE

Postcode CH-7050
Tel 00 41 (81) 315151
Fax 313135

gondola. Alpenblick serves huge
portions of good food but is hard to
reach from the piste. There is a little
shack at the foot of the Carmenna
drag that has the cheapest food and
drink anywhere on the mountain.

SKI SCHOOL
Plenty of English speakers
There's a big ski school and a lot of
demand for private lessons from the
affluent Arosa guests. Practically all
instructors speak at least some English,
and we have had good reports which
confirm the school's high reputation.
However, one reporter 'had a great
time for two days in a high-level off-
piste group' but thought the teaching
'fairly non-existent'.

FACILITIES FOR CHILDREN
Accommodating hotels
Arosa seems a good choice for a family
holiday, with its low-pressure
approach to skiing and lots of
alternative things to do. Observers
have been impressed by the ski
kindergartens, but we lack first-hand
reports. Bear in mind that several
hotels have kindergartens.

 # Staying there

It's a spread-out place, but location of
accommodation is not unduly
important as the resort has an
excellent ski-bus service supplemented
by hotel courtesy transport. But for
skiers (as opposed to skaters),
Innerarosa is preferable, with lifts into
both sectors of the skiing.

HOW TO GO
Plenty of hotels, few packages
Part of Arosa's charm is that it is not
big on the British market; but a few
operators go there.
Hotels Arosa is essentially a hotel
resort, with a high proportion of them
3- and 4-stars. Most reporters stayed in
4-stars. They are mainly block-like
buildings, unpleasant to behold but
enjoying excellent views.
£££££ Kulm Smart, luxurious; in
splendid position at Innerarosa. Pool.
££££ Waldhotel National Idyllic
setting in woods by piste; new but
built in traditional style; pool, sauna.
££££ Eden Refurbished last year, this
place is wild, with pop art on the
walls; designer rooms, including the
Garden of Eden suite; and fitness
centre. The hub of Arosa's nightlife.
££££ Sporthotel Valsana Well
equipped place on eastern side of
Obersee. Pool, kindergarten.

££££ Hof Maran Comfortable retreat,
up at Maran. Children's facilities,
natural ice rink; particularly well
placed for cross-country skiers.
££££ Bellevue Just below Innerarosa.
Refurbished rooms and excellent food.
££££ Hohenfels Non-ideal position
above the road between Obersee and
Innerarosa, but runs a courtesy bus
and is recommended for excellent
food and attentive staff.
£££ Seehof Quiet family hotel, ten
minutes' walk below Obersee; supplies
courtesy bus. Good, varied food.
££ Hold Good-value chalet across the
road from the Kulm at Innerarosa.
Self-catering Holiday flats are widely
available in the resort, but few are
bookable through British operators.
The Promenade studios are simple and
modern, reasonably well placed on the
main street just outside Obersee.

EATING OUT
Good, if formal
Most are hotel-based, and there is a
disappointing shortage of little rustic
stublis. For a true gourmet experience,
the tiny wood-panelled Zum Wohl
dining room in the unprepossessing
Hotel Anita is an expensive treat that
has to be booked well in advance. The
new Restaurant Roggenmoser in Hotel
Eden offers a strange but delicious
combination of Oriental and Swiss
food. The Bellevue, Cristallo, Post and
Hohenfels hotels are worth a try. The
Waldbeck serves good local dishes.

APRES-SKI
Livelier than you might think
Arosa's nightlife is wilder than its
reputation suggests. We even hear of a
transvestite show at the Hohenstube!
Early on the Rondo is a lively bar with
music, while the trendy congregate at
Barosa. The Carmenna hotel by the ice
rink has well priced drinks. Later the
popular bar of the Eden hotel has live
music, then the crowd goes downstairs
to the rather hip Kitchen, where the
sounds are up-to-date and you park
your drink on an oven, while dancing
round pots and pans.

FOR NON-SKIERS
A Swiss classic
Non-skiers have their own lift pass,
with many mountain restaurants
reachable via 35km of cleared, marked
walks. The boutiques and jewellers are
worth a look, though prices are likely
to dull the interest. Sleigh rides (some
into the ski area) are beautiful. Curling
and indoor golf are great fun, or you
can watch an ice hockey match.

Champéry 1050m

HOW IT RATES

The skiing

Snow	**
Extent	*****
Advanced	***
Intermediates	****
Beginners	**
Convenience	*
Queues	****
Restaurants	***

The rest

Scenery	****
Resort charm	****
Not skiing	***

✔ Charming rustic village with impressive mountain views

✔ Very extensive ski area, linking with Avoriaz and Châtel in France

✔ Quiet, relaxed place – yet plenty to do off the slopes

✔ Easy access for independent travellers – car, train, plane/train

✘ Local slopes suffer from the sun – facing south-east, with no snowmakers

✘ No skiing back to the village – and often none back to the valley

✘ Beginners face the hassle and expense of getting up to Planachaux, which is not as gentle as it could be

✘ Not much difficult skiing nearby

Champéry is one the prettiest of ski villages, with narrow streets, pleasantly rustic wooden buildings, informal cafés, nice little shops, and a friendly atmosphere – certainly the most appealing place from which to ski the main Franco-Swiss Portes du Soleil circuit. However, it is also one of the least reliable of Switzerland's ski resorts for snow, with sunny slopes mainly lying between 1600m and 2200m, and no local snowmakers to compensate.

With good transport links and sports facilities, Champéry is great for part-timers and non-skiers, or for families looking for a quiet time in a lovely place, especially if they have a car. But it also deserves consideration by skiers who simply put character before convenience. The north-facing slopes of Avoriaz, just across the French border, are only four lift-rides away – and we have skied fresh powder there when Champéry's lower slopes were bare and its upper ones slushy.

ORIENTATION

Champéry sits on the side of a valley separated from its ski area by a steep, fragmented mountainside. A cable-car goes up into the skiing from the railway station at the bottom of the village, and Grand Paradis, 2km further up the valley, has ski slopes down to it. The skiing is part of the main Portes du Soleil circuit, spreading north (anti-clockwise) and west (clockwise) into France and taking in **Avoriaz, Les Crosets, Champoussin, Morgins** and **Châtel**, the last four also easily reached by car.

Possible outings further afield are **Verbier, Chamonix** and **Les Diablerets**.

SKI FACTS

Altitude	1050m-2280m
Lifts	228
Pistes	650km
Green/Blue	54%
Red	33%
Black	13%
Artificial snow	11km

 ## The resort

Set beneath the dramatic Dents du Midi, Champéry is the stuff of picture-postcards. The main street that runs the length of the village is lined with old wooden chalets housing most of the hotels, bars and restaurants, liberally adorned with Swiss flags.

An attempt has been made to provide the facilities demanded by today's holiday-makers without spoiling the old-world charm. Down a steepish hill, somewhat removed from the main street, is the modern development of sports centre and large cable-car station – and a convenient new terminus for the narrow-gauge railway that comes up from the mainline town of Aigle.

The village has a friendly, relaxed atmosphere; it would be ideal for families if there was more convenient skiing available.

The skiing

Champéry's local skiing is as friendly and relaxing as the village, at least for intermediate skiers. It is far from ideal for absolute beginners, and experts have a choice of covering vast amounts of ground on the Portes du

Soleil piste circuit, or exploring the considerable off-piste possibilities reachable from the resort.

THE SKI AREA
Extensive and sunny

The village of Champéry is not quite part of the main Portes du Soleil circuit (see overall summary on page 224) but its skiing is – the sunny bowl of **Planachaux**, way above the village, with a couple of runs leading down to the valley at **Grand Paradis**, a short bus-ride from Champéry. There is no piste skiing to Champéry itself, though on rare occasions local conditions allow off-piste trips. Planachaux is rather featureless, and most skiers quickly move on – at least as far as next-door Les Crosets. You can explore the Portes du Soleil by travelling west towards Avoriaz or north-east to Champoussin, Morgins and Châtel.

There are three ways to ski to Avoriaz – via a chair-lift from the eastern side of the Planachaux bowl to Chavanette (check out the infamous 'Swiss Wall' mogul field as you ride up) or via one of two lifts from Les Crosets (the antiquated gondola to Pointe de Mossette has recently been revamped). Care should be taken to allow plenty of time to return from Avoriaz. Queues can form at some

LIFT PASSES

95/96 prices in
Swiss francs
Portes du Soleil
Covers all the lifts in
12 resorts.
Beginners Points card
(adult 50-point card
30, 94/95 price)
Main pass
1-day pass 46
6-day pass 210
Senior citizens
Over 60: 6-day pass
139 (34% off)
Children
Under 16: 6-day pass
139 (34% off)
Under 7: free pass
Short-term passes
Half-day pass to and
from noon (adult 33).
Notes Reductions for
families.
Alternative passes
Half-, 1- and 2-day
passes available for
35 lifts and 100km of
piste in Champéry,
Les Crosets,
Champoussin and La
Foilleuse (Morgins);
(adult 1-day 35, 94/95
price).

lifts, and getting up to the top of the Champéry cable-car to ride down (when it's not possible to ski to Grand Paradis) is a roundabout business. The run home is usually either closed or made awkward by poor snow.

The easy runs of Champoussin are most directly reached by taking the chair-lift (a walk across the Les Crosets car park) to Pointe de l'Au. From here there is a network of short runs and lifts to Champoussin and Morgins.

For more on skiing Avoriaz see page 149; for Châtel see page 160.

SNOW RELIABILITY
Very poor
Champéry gets a big thumbs down for lack of snowmakers. Even the little ski kindergarten relies on helicopter deliveries of white stuff when it's in short supply. The Champoussin and Morgins runs are also low and sunny, and getting to Avoriaz's north-facing slopes when conditions are poor can be unpleasant for moderate skiers.

FOR ADVANCED SKIERS
Few local challenges
Champéry is not well placed for reaching the Portes du Soleil tough runs. The Swiss Wall, on the Champéry side of Chavanette, is an intimidatingly long, steep slope, but not nearly as terrifying as its various names suggest; the main difficulty is at the very top, which can be icy when snow is in short supply or may have moguls the size of small cars when it is in abundance. There's a limit to how many times you will want to ski the Wall, and it's quite a trek to the Hauts Forts above Avoriaz – the main black-run sector in the Portes du Soleil. There's lots of scope for off-piste at Chavanette and on the broad slopes of Les Crosets and Champoussin.

FOR INTERMEDIATE SKIERS
Wonderful if snow is good
Confident intermediates have the whole of the Portes du Soleil at their disposal. Without straying across the border there is a huge amount of intermediate skiing to be enjoyed.

The runs home to Grand Paradis are as good as any when conditions allow, and enjoyable by all grades of intermediate. It's not worth dwelling too long around the bland Planachaux area, but Les Crosets is a junction of several fine runs. The pistes down from Pointe de Mossete and Grand Conche are good direct runs ideal for competent, or simply confident, skiers. The runs back from Pointe de l'Au also hold the interest. The Champoussin section is a network of short, easy pistes ideal for leisurely cruising. Skiers 'doing the circuit' tend to find these runs uninteresting and time consuming, and as such circumnavigate them, leaving this section nicely uncrowded and perfect for nervous performers. Beyond, the runs down to Morgins are delightful

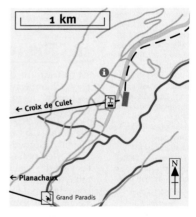

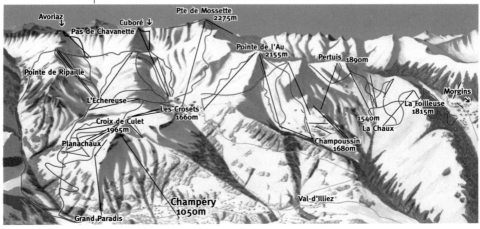

SKI SCHOOL

95/96 prices in
Swiss francs

Swiss
Classes 5 days
3hr: 9.15-12.15
5 days (15hr): 120
Children's classes
Ages: from 6
5 days (15hr): 110
Private lessons
Hourly or daily
45 for 1hr

CHILDCARE

The ski school runs a
ski kindergarten for
children aged 4 to 7,
from 9.15 to 4.30.

The non-ski
kindergarten takes
children aged 6
months to 5 years,
from 9am to 5pm –
Maison des
Schtroumpfs
(741066).

tree-lined meanders for average skiers,
and certainly the place to head for in
poor visibility. If need be, you can ski
from Planachaux to Morgins by use of
just two lifts.

FOR BEGINNERS
Go elsewhere if you have a choice
Despite its good ski school, Champéry
is far from ideal for beginners. An
expensive cable-car ride takes novices
to the steepish Planachaux runs, on
the shortest of which they receive
tuition. Beginners with a car can reach
the far more suitable Champoussin
slopes reasonably quickly.

FOR CROSS-COUNTRY
Very poor
A 7km loop is advertised, but it's
very unreliable for snow and not well
maintained.

QUEUES
Few local problems
The cable-car comfortably copes with
the village's quite small ski
population. When snow is good,
weekend crowds can be a problem –
the car park opposite the cable-car
station is not there by accident – but
Avoriaz's queues are a greater concern.

MOUNTAIN RESTAURANTS
Wide choice, some highlights
The local area is very good in terms of
numbers of mountain restaurants,
though few are particularly
memorable. Chez Coquoz at
Planachaux is recommended for its
traditional atmosphere and good

cheesy specialities. Chez Marius (or
Clavets) is a pleasant halt on the way
down to Grand Paradis. Chez Gaby,
above Champoussin, is a 'table service
delight'. Further afield, the refuges at
Marmottes-Les Lindarets are worth
heading for (see Avoriaz, page 149).

SKI SCHOOL
No worries
The few reports on the ski school that
we've had are free of criticisms and tell
of a surprising number of instructors
who speak good English.

FACILITIES FOR CHILDREN
Plenty of options
As well as the ski kindergartens and
two non-ski ones, there is the
alternative of half-day or all-day care
with the upmarket chalet operator Ski

Selected chalets in Champéry

GETTING THERE

Air Geneva, transfer 2hr.

PACKAGES

Chalets 'Unlimited', Kuoni, Made to Measure, Piste Artiste, Ski La Vie, Ski Les Alpes, Ski Scott Dunn, Swiss Travel Service, White Roc

Champoussin APS Chalets

Les Crosets Swiss Travel Service

Morgins Chalets 'Unlimited', Ski Morgins

ACTIVITIES

Indoor Swimming pool, ice skating and curling rink, Sunfit fitness centre (sauna, solarium, body building, physiotherapy) **Outdoor** Para-gliding

PISTE ARTISTE

helped us to compile the eating out and après-ski sections. Our thanks to them.

TOURIST OFFICE

Postcode CH-1874
Tel 00 41 (25) 791141
Fax 791847

La Vie, who have a crèche staffed by their own trained nannies for children aged up to 6. Piste Artiste offers a ski kindergarten and nanny services. Older children wanting to go to ski school for a half-day can spend the rest of the day in the Snowflake club.

 # Staying there

Although only a small village, much of the accommodation is not particularly well located for skiers. The new cable-car station has been consigned to the outer fringes, some way from many hotels; one or two chalets are stuck on hillsides at the periphery of things. The result, surprisingly for a small resort, is that the ski-bus is quite important – fortunately it is fairly efficient – and that having your own transport can be an advantage.

HOW TO GO
Limited packages available

There's a limited range of hotels and catered chalets available through tour operators. Champéry is one of the easiest resorts to get to – by car, train or plane.

Chalets There are a number of chalets available, mostly very small – ideal for families. Piste Artiste have a couple of well equipped chalets that, unusually, are available by the part-week. Ski la Vie have a traditional chalet and a couple of smart modern chalet-apartments. Ski Scott Dunn have a selection of traditional, creaky old places with lots of nice touches.

Hotels Champéry is essentially a hotel resort, with a good spread of accommodation from 4-star to B&B. Prices are low by comparison with many smarter Swiss resorts.

£££ Champéry Biggest and best in town, but hardly in the luxury bracket despite 4-star rating – a pleasantly comfortable chalet on the main street.

£££ Suisse Rival adjacent 4-star.

£££ Beau Séjour Comfortable, traditional 3-star at the southern end of the main street.

££ National Classic Swiss villa-style hotel on the main street, with neatly renovated bedrooms.

££ Paix Creaky old chalet near the Beau Séjour.

££ Alpes Ditto, but in a slightly inconvenient position.

£ Souvenir Central 1-star which does the cheapest half board you'll find.

Self-catering There are some apartments but none are packaged on the British market.

EATING OUT
A fair choice

Two of the best places are just outside the village. Cantines des Rives, on the other side of the valley, is a taxi-ride away. It's a beautiful traditional chalet specialising in fondue and raclette. Similarly distant is the Grand Paradis. It serves excellent, if expensive, local specialities. The use of stuffed animals to decorate the place may be off-putting for some.

Victor Hugo and 4 Saisons are impressive gourmet restaurants in the hotel Suisse. Good, less expensive places are the Vieux Chalet and the restaurants of the hotel des Alpes and hotel National. For a less formal ambience it's best to try the local specialities of the Farinet, Café du Centre or hotel du Nord, and the pizza at Cime de l'Est.

Once a week the restaurant at the top of the cable-car is open in the evening with special departures from and to the base-station. Piste Artiste organise post-skiing meals at the mountain hut Chez Marius, followed by a torchlit descent.

APRES-SKI
Something for everyone

Champéry has a convivial atmosphere at tea-time, but things are fairly sedate later in the evening. The Pub is the liveliest place in town, with noisy jukebox music earlier before a disco starts in the basic little downstairs bar around midnight. It's frequented mostly by resort workers and locals.

Far cosier places are the pleasantly informal bars in the hotel Suisse. The Bar des Guides is a pre-dinner watering hole with interesting relics and photographs of pre-war skiing. The Mines d'Or is a cellar bar, mainly frequented by ski instructors, that's good for a mellow late drink.

The Farinet is a spacious cellar night-club with upstairs restaurant which is good fun when there are enough people to give it atmosphere – mostly at weekends. Most Brits prefer it to the simpler Levant disco, which is more of a locals' haunt.

FOR NON-SKIERS
Excellent for the energetic

The Portes du Soleil has a general drawback for non-skiers, which is that skiers other than beginners are very unlikely to want to hang around (or return to) the local skiing for lunch. That aside, Champéry is very attractive for the non-skier who does not insist on a lot of animation in the village. Walks, particularly along to

Val d'Illiez, are very pleasant, and the narrow-gauge railway allows excursions to Montreux, Lausanne and Sion. There is a good range of things to do in this small village, thanks to the excellent sports centre.

Les Crosets 1660m

Les Crosets has a prime position within the Portes du Soleil, but to stay there you would have to be very keen. It's little more than a multi-lift station and car-park, with a couple of hotels and restaurants supposedly making it a mini-resort. It could be recommended only to car-driving hermits who might find it a useful base with the option to visit Champéry if they get bored. Hotel Télécabine is a homely British-run place, which reputedly provides good evening meals.

Champoussin 1580m

Champoussin is, theoretically at least, a good choice for a family looking for a quiet, user-friendly base – no traffic, ski-in, ski-out convenience, enough altitude to have snow in the village often, no noisy late-night revellers, rustic-style buildings and the comfortable Ambassador hotel with all mod cons. Last year, though, we had a report from a very bitter visitor who certainly felt her choice of resort had been a mistake. Her family's holiday was spoilt by problems with a poorly-run, impersonal ski school and a children's Miniclub where apparently kids spent much of their time standing around, no English was spoken and the unpleasant supervisor was seen shaking a small child. They fared little better at their swish hotel; it had variable food and a shortage of staff, making for almost non-existent service, and the accommodation they'd booked was not available. And all this was supervised by an unrepentant Basil Fawlty figure. Perhaps it was just a bad week, we speculated; but we wondered whether it was worth the risk of finding out.

Well, one reader felt it was, and returned a report praising the friendliness of the natives, the lively atmosphere created by the many Dutch visitors, 'stupendous views of the Dents du Midi', the proximity to the slopes, the child-friendly attitude of the comfortable Alpage hotel (two restaurants, pool, gym, disco) and the progress his daughter made in the multi-lingual Miniclub.

Morgins 1350m

Morgins can disappoint. Attracted there by visions of a quiet little Swiss village with a great ski area on its doorstep, visitors are surprised to find a scattered resort where some accommodation is a fair walk from one or both of the Portes du Soleil lifts. Although reasonably attractive, the village is not in the same league as Champéry for charm, and even those looking for peace and quiet may find too much of a good thing here. The bland local slopes lead skiers to look further afield; but with poor snow conditions affecting links, an irritating series of short lifts, and lack of public transport to Châtel, this is often easier said than done. Those expecting typical Swiss efficiency are also surprised to find poor local piste grooming and marking.

Morgins is best suited to those with a car. They can drive to Les Crosets for the highest and best of the Swiss Portes du Soleil skiing, or to the Linga gondola at Châtel.

Skiers not interested in 'doing the circuit' have the option to buy the cheaper Evasion lift pass which covers a still substantial area – Morgins, Champoussin, Super-Châtel, Torgon and La Chapelle-d'Abondance. Cross-country enthusiasts have 20km of pleasant trails.

The large 3-star Bellevue is a modern hotel, but built in traditional style, and has been praised by reporters for its friendliness and comfort. There are a couple of worthwhile restaurants – Café du Valais has good grill specialities and the Bergerie serves interesting French cuisine. The Bazot is the place for a four o'clock coffee. The Crystal bar is the only place with any atmosphere later. Off-slope amenities are indoor tennis, horse riding and a natural ice-rink.

Crans-Montana 1500m

HOW IT RATES

The skiing

Snow	**
Extent	***
Advanced	**
Intermediates	****
Beginners	***
Convenience	**
Queues	***
Restaurants	**

The rest

Scenery	****
Resort charm	**
Not skiing	****

✔ *Large ski area suitable for all but black-run skiers*

✔ *Fair amount of woodland skiing – good for bad weather*

✔ *Modern, well designed lift system, with few queues except for top lifts*

✔ *Splendid wooded setting with magnificent panoramic views*

✔ *Golf course provides excellent, gentle nursery slopes*

✔ *Very sunny skiing (see right)*

✔ *Excellent cross-country trails*

✘ *Snow badly affected by sun except in early season*

✘ *Towny resort centres composed partly of big chalet-style blocks but mainly of dreary cubic blocks – and therefore entirely without Alpine atmosphere*

✘ *Long, uphill walks to lifts from much of the accommodation*

✘ *Not much challenging skiing*

ORIENTATION

Crans-Montana is an amalgam of two villages, their centres a mile apart and their fringes now merging. They sit on a broad shelf facing south across the Rhône valley, reached by good roads as well as a funicular railway from Sierre. Gondolas go up into the main ski area from both villages. The skiing spreads east across the mountainside, with further lift base-stations (and accommodation) at Les Barzettes and Aminona.

Anzere is to the west, but the skiing is not linked. Outings by road or rail are possible, notably to **Zermatt** and **Verbier**. The smaller resorts of **Grimentz** and **Ovronnaz** are also worth bearing in mind.

When conditions are right – clear skies above fresh, deep snow – Crans-Montana takes some beating. The mountains you bounce down with the midday sun full on your face are charmingly scenic, the slopes broken up by rock outcrops and forest. The mountains you gaze at – Zermatt's Matterhorn prominent among them – are mind-blowing. When conditions are right, mountain-loving skiers may forgive Crans-Montana anything – in particular, its inconvenient, linear layout and the ugly, towny style of its twin resort centres.

Sadly, conditions are more often wrong than right. Except in the depths of midwinter, that strong midday sun quickly bakes the pistes. For the typical British skier booking six months ahead, this is enough to keep Crans-Montana off the short-list. For intermediate skiers who can time a visit according to the weather – and who are content to avert their eyes from the architecture – the resort is worth serious consideration.

The appeal of the resort to keen skiers is increased considerably this winter with the opening of a major new lift serving the top half of the mountain, where snow conditions are at their best.

 ## The resort

Crans-Montana celebrated its centenary as a resort in 1993, but is far from being a picturesque Swiss chocolate-box village. It is strung along a busy road, and its many hotels, villas, apartments and smart shops are mainly ugly blocks with few concessions to Alpine traditions.

Fortunately, the resort's many trees help to hide some of the architectural excesses, and give some areas a positively attractive appearance. And its wonderful south-facing balcony setting means you get a lot of sun as well as superb views to the great mountains beyond the Rhône. The balcony accommodates several small lakes and two golf courses, one of them home to the Swiss Open tournament.

The resort depends heavily on summer conference business and this rather sets the tone even in winter. Hotels tend to be formal, quiet and comfortable, village facilities wide-ranging but daytime-oriented, and the visitors middle-aged and dignified. In the evenings, the place lacks the Alpine-village atmosphere that many of us look for.

Crans is the more up-market village, with expensive jewellery shops, a casino, and a correspondingly high fur-coat count. It is well situated for the pretty golf course area, which has baby lifts for complete beginners, a cross-country trail and lovely walks. Montana has cheaper restaurants and bars, the main ice rink, and the station for the funicular from Sierre.

The skiing

Although it has achieved some prominence in ski-racing – hosting the world championships in 1987 and the climax of the World Cup series in 1992 – Crans-Montana is not a bravo's resort. Its skiing suits intermediates well, containing few challenges and no nasty surprises. Beginners are well catered for.

SKI FACTS

Altitude	1500m-3000m
Lifts	43
Pistes	160km
Green/Blue	37%
Red	50%
Black	13%
Artificial snow	3km

LIFT PASSES

95/96 prices in Swiss francs

Crans-Montana-Aminona
Covers all lifts in Crans-Montana and Aminona and the ski-bus.
Beginners
Points card
Main pass
1-day pass 45
6-day pass 204
Senior citizens
Over 65: 6-day pass 123 (40% off)
Children
Under 16: 6-day pass 123 (40% off)
Under 6: free pass
Short-term passes
Half-day from 11.15 (adult 35) or 12.30 (adult 30); 2hr afternoon pass from 2pm (adult 26).
Alternative periods
8 non-consecutive days (adult 295)
Credit cards: Yes

THE SKI AREA
Interestingly fragmented

Crans-Montana's 160km of piste are spread over three well-linked areas, all equally suitable for intermediates of varying abilities and persuasions.

Cry d'Err is the largest sector – an open bowl descending into patchy forest, directly above Montana. Cry d'Err itself is the meeting point of many lifts and the starting point of the cable-car up to the sector high-point of Bella Lui (2545m). Cry d'Err is served directly by two gondolas – one carrying 2,200 people per hour from just above central Montana, the other carrying less than half that number from just above Crans. Both have mid-stations; the one above Montana delivers beginners to the high-altitude nursery slopes served by the twin

Verdets drags. A third gondola goes up from the west side of Crans to Chetzeron, with a drag above going on to Cry d'Err.

The next sector, reached directly from Les Barzettes by another 2,200p/h gondola, is focused on Les Violettes, starting point of the new gondola up to the Plaine Morte glacier. There are three linking routes from Cry d'Err to the **Violettes-Plaine Morte** sector. One, starting at Bella Lui (or, strictly, from Col du Pochet, a short run and drag beyond) is officially 'for experienced skiers only' because it is off-piste; but it is largely a traverse, made awkward only by wave-like bumps and narrowness in places. Bella Lui is also the start of the Men's Downhill race course (Piste Nationale), which passes Cry d'Err and

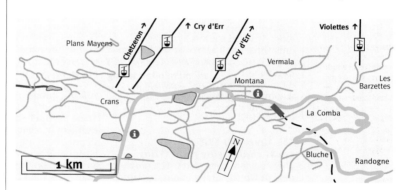

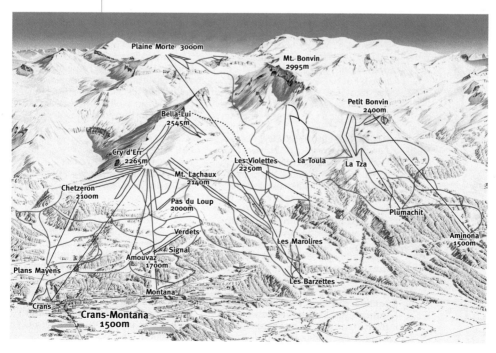

finishes at Les Barzettes. The third option is to take an easy path across from the Verdets drags, near the bottom of the Cry d'Err sector. It's high enough to reach the low mid-station of the Violettes gondola.

The third sector is above **Aminona** at the eastern-end of the skiing. This is linked in both directions to Les Violettes and there's a gondola up from the valley.

SNOW RELIABILITY
The resort's main drawback
Crans-Montana's skiing goes up to glacier level at 3000m, but this impressive fact is misleading. The solitary run down from the Plaine Morte glacier at 3000m does not make this a snowsure ski area.

Little of the other skiing is above 2250m; on a south-facing mountain, this makes for icy, patchy conditions whenever the sun hits the pistes for long. Artificial snow is available in only three small areas – at the bottom of the Piste Nationale, and on short runs beneath Les Violettes and Cry d'Err. One reporter recommends a day-trip outing to Grimentz, across the Rhône valley, when the slush at Crans is no longer bearable.

FOR ADVANCED SKIERS
Lacks challenging piste skiing
There are few steep pistes. The only moguls worthy of the name are found on the short but usually quiet run served by the Toula lifts. Plenty of off-piste is available in all sectors, but particularly beneath Chetzeron and La Tza; guides are usually easy to book.

The Piste Nationale course is far from daunting taken at 'normal' speed, but has some enormous jumps just above Les Marolies. The direct run from La Tza to Plumachit is fairly testing in places, especially when icy.

FOR INTERMEDIATE SKIERS
Lots of attractive, flattering runs
Crans-Montana is particularly well suited to intermediates. Pistes are mostly wide and, although red dominates the map, many of the red runs don't justify the grading. They also tend to be uniform in difficulty from top to bottom, with few nasty surprises for the nervous. Avid piste bashers enjoy the length of many runs, plus the fast lifts and good links that allow a lot of varied mileage to be clocked up.

The 11km run from Plaine Morte down to Les Barzettes is a fine, varied piste, starting with superb top-of-the-world views and powder snow, and finishing among pretty woods. There are several truly contrasting variants of the bottom half from Les Violettes. But many skiers love the top half so much they 'yo-yo' ski it – an even more attractive option with the new gondola expected to cut waiting times.

The short runs from Bella Lui to just below Cry d'Err have some of the best snow and quietest skiing in the area, and provide fine views of awesome Montagne de Raul. The Piste Nationale is a good test of intermediate technique, with plenty of bumps but also lots of room. The quietest area, and a good one for groups of varying intermediate standards, is the Petit Bonvin sector above Aminona. Three long runs of varying difficulty take skiers from La Tza down to Aminona, while there are also drags up at Petit Bonvin which serve short, easy runs over good snow.

A surprising number of skiers are very unadventurous, tending to linger in the unremarkable area beneath Cry d'Err, content with short runs down to Merbé and Pas du Loup.

FOR BEGINNERS
Plenty to offer the first-timer
There are three nursery areas, all excellent in their own way, with slopes of varying difficulty. Complete beginners have very gentle slopes as an option, on the golf course next to Crans. Cry d'Err has an area of relatively long, easy runs, which have the advantage of up-the-mountain views and atmosphere as well as better snow. But the runs are also used by other skiers, and do require investment in a full lift pass. The Verdets-Grand Signal run is steeper, and lazy liftmen can let the drag-lift get terribly icy. For the near-beginner, the little run served by a drag at Plaine Morte is worth trying – powder snow and great views.

FOR CROSS-COUNTRY
Excellent high-level trails
There are 17km of pretty, easy trails (skating-style as well as classic) on and around the golf course. But what makes Crans-Montana a particularly good cross-country resort is the high-level route, in and out of woods, across the whole mountainside from Plans Mayens to beyond Aminona – a 15km round-trip. Plaine Morte has a further 12km available in the summer.

You must purchase a vignette, costing SF6 a day or SF40 for the season (valid in all other Swiss resorts too). It gets you a 50% discount on the lifts up to Plaine Morte.

CHILDCARE

The Montana ski school runs a kindergarten with skiing available up at Signal (411480) for children aged 3 to 6, from 9am to 4.45.

There are several other kindergartens. In Crans, Bibiland (418142) takes children from age 2. In Montana, Fleurs des Champs (412367) takes children aged 2 months to 12 years; and Les Coccinelles (412423) takes children aged 3 to 16.

GETTING THERE

Air Geneva, transfer 3hr.

Rail Sierre (15km), Sion (22km); regular buses to resort.

PACKAGES

Inghams, Kuoni, Lagrange, Made to Measure, PGL Ski Europe, Plus Travel, Ski Club of GB, Travelscene Ski-Drive

Aminona Lagrange

SKI SCHOOL

95/96 prices in Swiss francs

Swiss
Classes
5 days
3hr: 9.30-12.30
5 days (15hr): 155
Children's classes
Ages: from 3
5 days (15hr): 155
Private lessons
Hourly
50 for 1hr

QUEUES
Imminent transformation

Access to the glacier – and, more importantly, the excellent red run of over 1000m vertical back down – did involve long waits. Even in January, if snow low down was poor, hour-long queues were not unknown. But December 1995 sees the opening of the impressive Funitel stand-up gondola with five times the capacity of the old cable-car. There is also a quad chair replacing the parallel lifts at La Tza. Minor irritations include short queues for the Barmaz chair-lifts up to Les Violettes from La Toula, and sometimes at Cabane des Bois. Delays become longer when snow lower down is in poor condition. On the other hand, the low-capacity gondola to Merbé becomes over-subscribed when wind closes the other major lifts. Crans-Montana does not get overrun at weekends.

MOUNTAIN RESTAURANTS
Disappointing for a smart resort

Mountain restaurants are generally undistinguished, but at least they tend to provide table-service. They are expensive, with main meals better value than snacks. Only the Cry d'Err sector offers much choice. The Merbé restaurant, at the Crans-Cry d'Err gondola mid-station, is the most attractive, with table-service of good food in a pleasant setting just above the tree-line. Bella Lui's terrace (with service) offers good views. The Chetzeron eatery allows 'picnics' provided a drink is purchased.

Petit Bonvin has perhaps the best of the self-service places, with superb views. The Plumachit restaurant, towards the bottom of the sector, has a large sun terrace in a pretty setting. In the Violettes sector there is not much choice; but there is a small hut 50m from the main cafeteria at Violettes itself, and a welcoming little hotel opposite the bottom station.

SKI SCHOOL
Not much to report

Both local branches of the Swiss ski school generally attract favourable comment, although class sizes can be excessive. Meeting places vary according to the standard of the class, but Cry d'Err is a common rendezvous spot. Note the unusual hours (see margin); no weekend tuition means no lessons are missed regardless of when you arrive, but also means that beginners arriving on Saturday waste the Sunday. Private lessons are easily booked, both for on- and off-piste.

FACILITIES FOR CHILDREN
Ski Esprit have moved out

The resort facilities for children are adequate, particularly in Montana. Sadly, childcare specialists Ski Esprit no longer operate their chalet with in-house crèche at Les Barzettes, 500m from the Violettes lift.

↑ Staying there

Crans-Montana is quite a sprawling place. The free ski-bus service links the villages and satellite lift-stations during the day, but there is no evening service. Buses run (on several overlapping routes) to a timetable and are fairly frequent during peak periods, less so at other times. They can get very crowded at the end of the day, but are generally an effective way of travelling between sectors. They do not cut out walks. The gondola-stations are perched above the main road, a sufficiently tiring, and often icy, walk from many hotels to warrant paying for ski and boot storage at the lift station.

The best choice of location for most people would be within a short walk of the powerful Montana gondola. But if you want to beat the queues up to Plaine Morte, you'll want to be out at Les Barzettes, at the base station of the Violettes gondola.

HOW TO GO
Much more choice on your own

The independent traveller to Crans-Montana has a wide choice of hotels and apartments. Package holidays are not widely sold in Britain.

Chalets Crans-Montana is not a major chalet resort. Ski Esprit used to be the only operator in town and even they have decided not to offer a chalet here this season.

Hotels Not surprisingly, this conference resort has a great number of mainly large, comfortable, expensive hotels. 42 of the 52 hotels are of 3-star or higher standard.

£££££ Crans-Ambassador Huge luxury place with distinctive 'chalet' roof-line, well placed for the Montana gondola. Pool.

££££ Hauts de Crans Smart modern hotel in excellent position up above Montana. Pool.

££££ Aïda Castel Beautifully furnished in chic rustic style, with hand-painted furniture and pine panelling. Between the two resort centres. Outdoor pool.

££££ Le Green Well placed near the Crans lifts; small, modern and chic.

ACTIVITIES

Indoor Hotel swimming pools, tennis, fitness centre, bowling, bridge, squash, concerts, cinema, casino
Outdoor Skating, curling, toboggan run, ski-bob, horse-riding, golf on snow

£££ La Foret Highly recommended hotel almost, but not quite, at Les Barzettes, with minibus to lifts. Pool in adjacent self-catering block.
£££ National Perfectly placed for the Crans-Cry d'Err gondola; 'quiet, comfortable, good food'.
£££ Au Robinson B&B only; well placed near the National, in Crans, with friendly service.
£ Petit Paradis Five minutes from Montana in Bluche, a family-run auberge with a welcoming restaurant.
Self-catering The number of visitor beds available in apartments outnumbers hotels five to one. Of course, not all those beds are available to rent, and very few find their way on to the British package market. Supermarkets in Montana are surprisingly cheap by resort standards.

EATING OUT
Plenty of alternatives
There is a good variety of restaurants from French to Chinese and Lebanese, although prices tend to push British self-caterers into pizzerias or supermarkets. Almost all the less expensive restaurants are in Montana. Most places do good rösti, which is relatively cheap and filling. The Carnozet has been recommended for excellent fondue. The Au Robinson hotel restaurant is good, reasonably priced by local standards, and open to non-residents. The Gréni is a welcoming restaurant on the western fringe of Montana. The Cervin up at Vermala is unusually rustic.

APRES-SKI
Can be ritzy, but otherwise quiet
The resort boasts plenty of après-ski amenities, but its clientele seems loath to use them; the several nightspots and the impressive ice rinks often lack animation. The Pub Georges & Dragon is by far the liveliest, most crowded bar; surprisingly, given its location in Crans, it has the cheapest beer in town. For peace and quiet, there are quite a few piano bars. The two cinemas change films every couple of days, and some play in English. Ten-pin bowling (not Austrian-style skittles) is about the only reorganised nightlife. Swimming is available in about a dozen hotels, at about SF10; those wanting a sauna will find the Hauts de Crans hotel good value. Bridge is played from 3pm in the Aïda-Castel.

FOR NON-SKIERS
Excellent, but little charm
There is plenty to keep non-skiers busy. There are lovely walks through and around the golf course, in and among novice downhill and cross-country skiers. Restaurants have sun terraces. Lots of activities are available.

Sierre is only a funicular ride away for serious shopping, while the larger town of Sion is only a few minutes further by rail. Montreux is also within reach. The mountain restaurants are mainly situated at the gondola and cable-car stations, which allows beginners and non-skiers to meet others for lunch at altitude.

TOURIST OFFICE

Postcode CH-3962
Tel 00 41 (27) 413041
Fax 417460

Davos 1550m

✔ *Huge amount of skiing*

✔ *Some superb long and mostly easy runs away from the lifts*

✔ *Lots of off-piste skiing, with a wide choice of marked itineraries and some well known short ski-tours*

✔ *Good cross-country trails*

✔ *Lots to do other than ski – excellent sports facilities, pretty walks, good range of shopping*

✔ *Free of hooligan skiers*

✔ *Some captivating mountain restaurants above Klosters*

✔ *Klosters is attractively villagey*

✘ *Dreary block-style buildings of Davos spoil the views*

✘ *Davos is a towny resort, rather plagued by traffic and lacking Alpine atmosphere*

✘ *Skiing is spread over six or seven essentially separate ski areas*

✘ *Some access lifts are inefficient, leading to queues, and antique T-bars are common*

Once popular with British skiers, Davos is a rather specialised taste these days (and British visitors are hugely outnumbered by Germans). Few resorts in the world have a ski area more extensive, or that offers more for all grades of skier. But the skiing has its drawbacks: it is split into five or six unlinked sectors, and relatively ancient lifts serve many of them. Skiers who are prepared to accept such drawbacks normally do so as the price of staying in a captivating Alpine village. But Davos is far from that.

Whether you forgive the flaws and fall for the resort as a whole depends on how highly you value three plus-points: the distinctive, long intermediate runs of the Parsenn area; the ability to ski a different sector every day; and the considerable off-piste potential. We like all three, and this is one of the ski areas in the Alps we always look forward to visiting.

But you don't have to stay in Davos to enjoy its skiing: Klosters offers a much more captivating alternative. Despite its royal connections, it is not an exclusive village – on the contrary, it has some exceptionally welcoming places to stay. It is less well placed than Davos for exploration of all the ski areas, but slightly better-placed for the all-important Parsenn.

ORIENTATION

Davos shares its skiing with **Klosters**, its smaller and 350m lower neighbour. Set in a broad, gently sloping valley running north-east to south-west, with skiing mountains either side. Davos has two main centres roughly 2km apart; the road and railway from Klosters come first to Dorf, where a funicular railway goes up into the main Parsenn ski area, and then to Platz, where lifts go up in opposite directions to the Strela and Jakobshorn ski areas. The Rinerhorn area starts about 6km further down the valley, at Glaris, the Pischa area 5km up a side valley. North of Klosters is the Madrisa area, start of easy tours to Gargellen in Austria.

Excursions by road or rail to **St Moritz** and **Arosa**, or by road to **Flims** and **Lenzerheide**, are possible.

🏠 The resort

Davos was one of the places in the Alps where skiing first blossomed as a leisure activity (a process in which Brits, including Conan Doyle, were much involved). And arguably it was the very first to develop skiing as a business. The railway up the Parsenn was one of the first to be built for skiers (in 1931), and the first drag-lift was built on the Bolgen nursery slopes in 1934. But by then Davos was already well developed as a health resort; many of its present-day luxury hotels are converted sanatoriums.

Sadly, converted sanatoriums are just what they look like. No-one goes to Davos because they like the look of the town – and it emphatically is a town, not a village. It is often said to be the highest town in Europe, and probably is. It is sometimes said to be Switzerland's biggest ski resort but

isn't: in terms of beds at least, Crans-Montana is much bigger, and Verbier is slightly so.

Conferences are big business – from the annual World Economic Forum at one extreme, to the Zurich Master Plumbers' convention at the other – and the place certainly has the air of a conference resort rather than a ski resort. The health business lives on, in the shape of several specialist clinics.

SKI FACTS

Altitude 810m-2845m
Lifts 55
Pistes 315km
Green/Blue 30%
Red 40%
Black 30%
Artificial snow 1km

LIFT PASSES

95/96 prices in
Swiss francs
Rega area
Covers all Davos and
Klosters, the railway
in the whole region
and buses between
the resorts.
Beginners Single and
return tickets on main
lifts in each area.
Main pass
1-day pass 52
6-day pass 259
(low season 207 –
20% off)
Senior citizens
Over 65 male, 62
female: 6-day pass
207 (20% off)
Children
Under 16: 6-day pass
155 (40% off)
Under 6: free pass
Short-term passes
Half-day passes, up
to and from 12.30,
for each area
(Jakobshorn, adult
35).
Alternative periods
Passes for 8 days
(Rinerhorn, adult 230)
and 15 days
(Rinerhorn, adult 377)
in the season, but
only for limited areas.
Notes Day pass price
is for Parsenn, Pischa,
Schatzalp, Strela and
Gotschna only.
Alternative passes
A confusing array of
passes covering
limited areas
(Jakobshorn,
Rinerhorn, Pischa,
Schatzalp and Strela,
and other
combinations).

 # The skiing

The skiing here has something for everybody, although experts and nervous intermediates need to choose their territory with care.

THE SKI AREA
Vast and varied
It's a common trick, when describing a ski area, to say how long you could stay in the resort without skiing the same run twice. But in Davos you can spend a week without skiing the same mountain twice – that is, you can ski a different mountain every day. In practice, you don't: the minor areas tend to be neglected by most visitors – but they are worth checking out, and are all the better for their neglect.

The Parsennbahn funicular from Davos Dorf takes you to the major lift junction of Weissfluhjoch (2660m), at one end of the **Parsenn** skiing. At the other is Gotschnagrat, reached by cable-car from Klosters. Between the two is the wide, open bowl of the Parsenn. From Davos Platz, another funicular takes you up to Schatzalp, at the base of the **Strela** skiing. A cable-car from the top of this sector offers a back-door way to Weissfluhjoch.

Across the valley, **Jakobshorn** is reached by cable-car from Davos Platz; this is the main snowboarders' hill. **Rinerhorn** and **Pischa** are outlying areas reached by bus or (in the case of Rinerhorn) train.

Beyond the main part of Klosters, a cable-car goes up from Klosters Dorf to the sunny **Madrisa** area.

Lift passes are monitored electronically, without the need to take them out of your pocket.

SNOW RELIABILITY
Good, but not the best
Davos is quite high by Swiss standards. Its ski areas go respectably high too – though not to glacial heights. Not much of it faces directly south, but not much of it faces directly north either – mainly the long runs on the back of the Parsenn. So snow reliability is no more than fair. The south-east-facing pistes down to Dorf from Weissfluhjoch are the ones most at risk. There is some artificial snow in each main sector, but not much.

FOR ADVANCED SKIERS
Plenty to do, on- and off-piste
A glance at the piste map may give the misleading impression that this is an intermediate's resort. Blacks are confined largely to the wooded lower

slopes of several sectors, which means excellent skiing when snow is falling – the Meierhofer Tälli run to Wolfgang is excellent – but rough skiing when snow is needed. But there are two exceptions: the trio of runs at the southern extremity of the Strela area and the runs from Gotschnagrat directly towards Klosters, on and around the infamous Gotschnawang slope. The Wang run, starting south of the peak, is formally a piste, but it is not marked (and rarely open, in our experience); there are various routes, all seriously steep. Drostobel, starting to the north, is less scary, though the overall gradient is little different.

The main appeal of the area, however, is that it is excellent for off-piste adventures and short ski-tours.

Practically all the sectors of the skiing now have at least one marked off-piste itinerary to the valley – an excellent arrangement which allows good skiers to escape the crowds without paying for guidance. The exception is Rinerhorn – but that has an excellent black piste of 1000m vertical that amounts to much the same thing.

Arosa can be reached much more quickly on skis than by road or rail, but requires a return by rail via Chur. From the Madrisa sector, you can make tours to Gargellen in Austria's Montafontal. This involves an exhausting one-hour uphill walk on seal skins on the way back.

FOR INTERMEDIATE SKIERS
A splendid variety of runs
For intermediate skiers of any temperament or tendency, this is a great ski area. But its greatest appeal is to the skier who likes to get around, with long runs to the valleys and the stimulating prospect of skiing several different areas.

The epic runs to Klosters and other places (described in the box opposite) pose few difficulties for a confident intermediate or even an ambitious near-beginner (one of the editors did the run to Klosters on his third day on skis). And there are one or two other notable away-from-the-lifts runs to the valley that are more than just woodland paths. In particular, you can ski from the top of Madrisa back to Klosters Dorf via the beautiful Schlappin valley.

FOR BEGINNERS
Platz is the more convenient
The Bolgen nursery slope is adequately spacious and gentle, and a bearable walk from the centre of Platz. But

SKI SCHOOL

95/96 prices in
Swiss francs

Swiss
Classes 5 days
4hr: 2hr am and pm
5 full days: 190
Children's classes
Ages: 4 to 16
5 full days: 154
Private lessons
Half-day or full-day
145 for half-day

CHILDCARE

The ski school runs
the Pinocchio nursery
at Bünda, on the
outskirts of Davos
Dorf, taking children
from age 3, from 8.30
to 4.30. Children can
stay in the nursery,
play about on skis or
take proper ski school
classes.

The Berghotel
Schatzalp has its own
ski nursery – see
Staying up the
mountain. The hotel
Derby in Dorf has an
indoor kindergarten.

Dorf-based beginners face more of a
trek out to Bünda.

There is no shortage of easy runs to
progress to, and they are spread
around all the sectors. The Parsenn
sector probably has the edge, with
long, easy runs in the main Parsenn
bowl, as well as in the valleys running
down from Weissfluhjoch.

FOR CROSS-COUNTRY
Long, scenic valley trails
Davos may not be in the first division
for langlaufers, but it can't be far
outside, with a total of 75km of trails
running in both directions along the
main valley and reaching well up into
Sertigtal and Dischmatal. There is a
cross-country ski centre and special ski
school on the outskirts of the town.

QUEUES
Still a problem in places
The Parsennbahn was generating
queues when we first visited Davos 20
years ago, and it is still generating
queues today. The Schatzalpbahn –
the alternative, roundabout way into
Davos' main ski area – suffers too.
Other access lifts present fewer
problems. In Klosters, queues for the
Gotschna cable-car have been much
reduced by a doubling of its capacity,
but can still be a problem at weekends.

MOUNTAIN RESTAURANTS
Stay low down
The main high-altitude restaurants are
dreary self-service affairs, but the

Strelapass hut is recommended for
good views and 'excellent' food. There
are more compelling places at or
approaching valley level – notably the
Conterser Schwendi and Serneuser
Schwendi in the woods on the way
down to the Klosters valley from the
Parsenn. These are great places to end
up as darkness falls – the Klosters
Schwendi, at least, sells wax torches to
illuminate your final descent to the
village. The hotel Kulm at Wolfgang,
midway between Davos and Klosters,
is enthusiastically recommended.

There are peaceful restaurants at or
near the bottom of the Pischa,
Jakobshorn and Rinerhorn sectors.
And the station restaurants at Saas and
Kublis are pleasant places to wait for
the train home.

SKI SCHOOL
Don't count on English
Reports suggest that better skiers, at
least, are likely to find themselves in a
German-dominated group – scarcely
surprising, given the small number of
British visitors that Davos attracts. A
Davos regular says that the school is
well organised, but that the instructors
vary widely; a familiar story.

The 'deep snow' classes guarantee a
maximum of six skiers, with half a day
per week given over to avalanche
rescue techniques and understanding
the behaviour of deep snow. Seniors
and teenagers can both enroll in
classes aimed at them. Snowboarders
have a keen specialist school.

The Parsenn's super-runs

The runs from Weissfluhjoch that head north, on the back of the mountain,
make this area special for many skiers. The pistes that continue northward to
Schifer and then to Kublis, Saas and Serneus, and the one that curls around
the mountain to Klosters, are graded red but are not difficult. What marks them
out is their sheer length (10–12km) and the sensation of travel they offer.

Until 1987, only the very top 2.5km and 400m vertical of this enormous ski
field could be skied repeatedly; once below Kreuzweg, you skied on down to
the valley and caught the train home. Usually, you did it towards the end of
the day, dawdling in the rustic restaurants in the woods on the lower reaches.
The long Schiferbahn gondola changed all that – you can now ski 1100m
vertical as often as you like. Some long-standing visitors regret the change, but
there is the added advantage that the lower runs, below the Schifer gondola
station, are quieter.

The longest runs are the marked but unpatrolled routes to Fideris and Jenaz,
the latter being 18km from Weissfluhjoch, according to official figures. Start at
the Weissfluh summit and you can add another kilometre, as well as another
200m vertical. But these are not continuous runs: they require skins for a
couple of short ascents, and payment for the use of the lifts at Fideriser
Heuberge on the way.

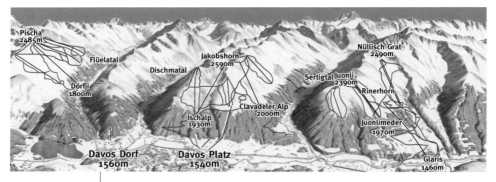

GETTING THERE

Air Zürich, transfer 3hr.

Rail Station in Davos Platz.

PACKAGES

Inghams, Kuoni, Made to Measure, Plus Travel, Ski Choice, Ski Les Alpes, SkiGower, Swiss Travel Service, White Roc

Klosters Kuoni, Made to Measure, Plus Travel, Powder Byrne, Ski Club of GB, Ski Les Alpes, Ski with Julia, SkiGower, The Ski Company Ltd, White Roc

FACILITIES FOR CHILDREN
Not ideal

Davos is a rather spread-out place in which to handle a family – and indeed the ski school nursery is in a slightly isolated spot, at Dorf's Bünda nursery slope, inconvenient for dropping off and picking up. A reporter with long experience of Davos describes the facilities as 'excellent', staff quality as highly variable. Our instinct, if the budget will stand it, would be to stay at the Berghotel Schatzalp (see Staying up the mountain).

 ## Staying there

Davos is a big, spread-out resort and although transport is good, with buses around the town as well as the railway linking Dorf and Platz to Klosters and other villages, choice of location is important. Dorf has direct but queue-prone access to the Parsenn; Platz has lifts up to the Jakobshorn and Strela sectors, the big sports facilities, the smarter shopping and more evening action.

HOW TO GO
Hotels dominate the package scene

Although the bulk of the bed spaces in Davos is in apartments, hotels dominate the UK package holiday market. As far as we know, there are no catered chalet packages in Davos, but The Ski Company Ltd operates in Klosters.

Hotels A dozen 4-star and about 30 3-star places form the core of the Davos hotel trade, though there are a couple of 5-stars and quite a few cheaper places, including B&Bs.

£££££ Fluela The more atmospheric of the two 5-star hotels, in central Dorf, and quite well placed to beat the Parsenn queues. Pool.

££££ Golfhotel Waldhuus As convenient for winter langlaufers as for summer golfers. Quiet, modern, tasteful, with 'first-rate cuisine' and 'unusually attentive' staff. Pool.

£££ Parsenn What Davos needs is more hotels that look like this attractive chalet, directly opposite the Parsenn railway in Dorf.

£££ Davoserhof Our favourite: small, old, beautifully furnished, with excellent food; well placed in Platz.

££ Alte Post Traditional, cosy; central in Platz.

££ Hubli's Landhaus 5km out at Laret, towards Klosters. Quiet country inn with sophisticated food.

Self-catering The Allod Park apartments are in a dreary block, but are reasonably comfortable, and in a happy medium position, mid-way between the Parsenn and Strela lifts.

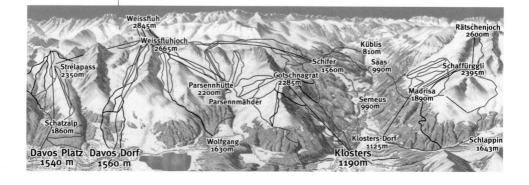

ACTIVITIES

Indoor Artificial skating rink, fitness centre, tennis, squash, swimming, sauna, cinema, museums, galleries, libraries
Outdoor Over 80km of cleared paths (mostly at valley level), natural skating rink, curling, toboggan run, horse-riding, hang-gliding, sleigh rides, para-gliding

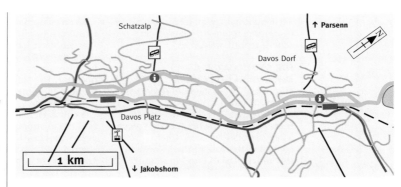

STAYING UP THE MOUNTAIN
Especially appealing for families
The Berghotel Schatzalp, on the tree-line about 300m above Davos Platz and reached by funicular (free to guests), is a 4-star hotel to rival any in the resort, complete with pool and sauna. The Strela skiing immediately above has something for everyone, but what makes the Berghotel especially interesting is that there is a nursery slope right next to it – and the hotel runs its own crèche (evenings as well as daytime) with ski tuition available. Schatzalp is also the start of the local toboggan run, a mini-Cresta.

EATING OUT
Wide choice, mostly in hotels
Most of the better restaurants are in hotels. Don't commit yourself until you've seen inside, advises a regular – 'you can find yourself in a graveyard even on New Year's Eve'. The Davoserhof's restaurant is one of the best in town, both for food and ambience. Chinese food is trendy here – the lavish Zauberberg restaurant in the Central and the Golden Dragon in the Terminus are two of the best in this category. The Fluela has a highly regarded grill room. The Derby is good for an intimate dinner dance. Sharing a fondue in the Gentiana is rather pleasant. Pizzeria Padrino and the National are two good informal places.

The Mona Lisa and Da Elio, both Italian joints, are other possibles for those not wanting to spend too much.

An evening excursion for dinner out of town is popular. Prices are lower and restaurants less formal. Teufi, Schatzalp (reached by funicular), Laret, Islen, Wolfgang and Frauenkirch all have good places. Our favourite would have to be the wholesome local fare in the basic old Landhaus in Frauenkirch.

APRES-SKI
Lots on offer, but quiet clientele
There are plenty of bars, discos and nightclubs, but we're not sure how some of them make a living. Davos guests tend to want the quiet life. The non-ski activities and numerous cafés and bars give Davos a pleasant tea-time atmosphere, but things are subdued after dinner. High calories are consumed with enthusiasm after skiing at cafés Weber and Schneider. A civilised drink can be had at several hotels – the Derby's attractive Paluda bar; the Corner bar of the Post Morosani; the piano bars in the Central and Europe.

The liveliest place in town is the rustic little Chämi bar. Its taped pop music and strange decor is popular with the young crowd. It's one of the few spots to retain a spark of life late in the evening. La Bohème, which also has music, is another. Nightclubs tend to be sophisticated, expensive and lacking atmosphere during the week. The most popular are the Cabanna, Pöstli and Europe. The intimate little Jakobshorn disco is more informal and less expensive.

FOR NON-SKIERS
Great apart from the buildings
Provided you're not fussy about building style, Davos can be unreservedly recommended for non-skiers. The towny resort has shops and other diversions, and transport along the valley (covered by the tourist tax) and up into the skiing is good – though the best of the mountain restaurants are well out of range. For the energetic, the sports facilities are excellent; the natural ice rink is said to be Europe's biggest, and is supplemented by artificial rinks both indoor and outdoor.

Spectator sports include speed skating as well as hockey. And there are lots of marked walks up in the ski areas as well as around the lake and along the valleys.

TOURIST OFFICE

Postcode CH-7270
Tel 00 41 (81) 4152121
Fax 4152100

The new winter sports museum may be of more interest to skiers than others; reports welcome.

FOR SNOWBOARDERS
Better than you'd think
Surprisingly, this staid old resort seems to have decided to cultivate snowboarders' custom. Not only is there a dedicated school, there is even a dedicated Snowboard Hotel, conveniently close to the Jakobshorn (the official Davos Fun Mountain)

Klosters 1190m
In a word association game, Klosters would normally trigger 'Prince of Wales'. The world's TV screens have shown him skiing there countless times. In 1988 he was almost killed there in an off-piste avalanche that did kill one of his companions, and now the enlarged cable-car to Gotschna – a quick way into the Parsenn skiing shared with Davos – is named after him.

Don't be put off. We don't know why HRH likes to ski in Klosters particularly, but it is certainly not because the place is the exclusive territory of royalty and aristocracy. It's a comfortable, quiet village with a much more appealing Alpine flavour than Davos, despite its lower altitude. Klosters Platz is the main focus – a collection of upmarket, traditional-style hotels around the railway station, at the foot of the steep, wooded slopes of Gotschna. The road to Davos passes through, and traffic can be a bit of a nuisance.

The village spreads along the valley road for quite a way before fading into the countryside; there's then a second concentration of building in the even quieter village of Klosters Dorf, from where a gondola goes up to the Madrisa ski area.

Although there are some nursery lifts at valley level, the sunny slopes of Madrisa are more appealing. There is a ski kindergarten up there. The hotel Vereina has a non-ski kindergarten, taking very young children on request.

Klosters' upmarket image is reinforced by UK tour operators. Powder Byrne have been here for some years, and last year they were joined by the even more exclusive chalet operator, The Ski Company Ltd.

There are some particularly attractive hotels. The central Chesa Grischuna is irresistible, combining traditional atmosphere (carved wood everywhere) with modern comfort – and a lively après-ski bar. The less central Wynegg is a favourite with British visitors, with a warmly welcoming panelled dining room and good-value bedrooms. The Vereina is a 'slightly faded' grand hotel, with 'friendly, helpful staff and very good food'. In Dorf, the Albeina is recommended ('one third of the prices I was quoted in Platz').

The evenings are quiet, but not entirely lifeless. The huts in the woods above the village attract lots of skiers on their last run of the day, particularly the Serneuser Schwendi. In the village, the Chesa Grischuna is a focus of activity from tea-time onwards, with its piano bar, bowling and expensive but popular restaurant. The Wynegg is also popular immediately after skiing, and for more affordable dinners. An alternative for eating out is the Walserhof (a rival to the Chesa Grischuna) and there are other more modest places. There is a Mexican place at the hotel Kaiser, and a pizzeria under the hotel Vereina with a famously vociferous tenor for a chef. A short taxi or sleigh ride out to Monbiel takes you to the Höhwald, a cosy stubli with good fresh fish.

In the late evening the bars of the hotels Kaiser and Vereina are popular. The Casa Antica is a small but popular disco. The Kir Royale, under the hotel Silvretta Park, is bigger and more brash. The Funny Place, under the Piz Buin, is more grown-up and expensive.

Klosters is an attractive base for walking and cross-country skiing, but has little else to offer non-skiers. The hotels Pardenn and Sport have pools, and there is curling.

Engelberg 1050m

HOW IT RATES

The skiing

Snow	***
Extent	**
Advanced	***
Intermediates	***
Beginners	**
Convenience	*
Queues	***
Restaurants	***

The rest

Scenery	***
Resort charm	***
Not skiing	***

SKI FACTS

Altitude	1050m-3020m
Lifts	25
Pistes	50km
Green/Blue	40%
Red	58%
Black	2%
Artificial snow	5km

PACKAGES

Kuoni, Made to Measure, Plus Travel, SkiGower, Swiss Travel Service

Engelberg makes a great retreat for the residents of Lucerne, less than an hour away. It attracts few British visitors, despite impressive mountains offering one of the biggest verticals in the Alps. The ski area is rather unusual, with its main mountain slopes broken up by balconies.

THE RESORT

Engelberg is one of Switzerland's longest-established year-round resorts – a bustling, rather towny village, home to an impressive 12th-century monastery, surrounded by spectacular mountains. Much of the old-world charm of the original village has been diluted by modern development. But it remains a pleasant enough place, and away from the town the valley is very scenic. Engelberg is rather isolated from other resorts, but it is possible to get to Andermatt and to the Jungfrau region.

THE SKIING

There are two contrasting **ski areas** either side of the village, their widely separated lift stations served by a regular ski-bus.

Very much the main area is Titlis, which rises an impressive 2000m from the valley floor. A two-stage gondola goes up to the shelf of Trübsee (1800m). Above this a two-stage cable-car rises to over 3000m, the second stage having the novelty of the world's first revolving cabin, allowing superb views of glacial scenery. Below the summit are some short drags; descent to Trübsee is via a single steep piste, with easier slopes lower down. Across the frozen Trübsee, a separate set of lifts serve good red runs below Jochstock (2565m). There is a roundabout run back to the valley.

The Brunni area, accessed by a gondola from the edge of town, has a small network of sunny pistes between Schonegg (2040m) and Ristis (1600m), and occasionally a run back to town.

The high, north-facing Titlis has good **snow reliability** high drags stay open into June); but the resort as a whole is not particularly reliable. However, piste grooming is excellent.

For **advanced skiers**, the big attraction is off-piste – the famous Laub. This is a steep wall dropping 1000m from the shoulder of Titlis, which is superb when conditions are right, dangerous when they are not.

There is quite a lot of skiing for confident **intermediates**, in particular some great barrelling runs off Jochstock. But there is not much very easy skiing.

There is an adequate **beginners'** slope at the Titlis mid-station and another at Trübsee. You can progress to the uncrowded, easy Brunni slopes.

Engelberg is well regarded by **cross-country** skiers, with five trails totalling 30 km amidst lovely scenery up at Trübsee and along the valley.

There are no **queue** or overcrowded piste problems except at weekends and, particularly, holiday times – New Year crowds from Lucerne can create queues measured in hours.

There is plenty of choice of **mountain restaurants**, and most are friendly and inexpensive by Swiss standards. The Titlis restaurant is good but the overcrowded, poor-value snack bar is best avoided. The cosy Sporthotel Trübsee has a vast sun terrace overlooking the frozen lake.

Unusually, the Swiss **ski school** faces competition in the form of the Neue Schischule. Both have all-day care for **children**. Hotels Regina Titlis and Edelweiss have supervised crèches.

STAYING THERE

Most package **accommodation** is in hotels, although there are lots of chalets and apartments to rent locally. The 4-star Sporthotel (less packed with amenities than its claimed 'mini-resort' status would suggest) lies up the mountain at Trübsee. The elegant 4-star Hess has nice rooms and good food. Among the 3-stars, Edelweiss is poorly placed but has good children's facilities, and the Crystal and Engelberg are central.

Eating out is mostly in hotels. The excellent Tudor-Stübli in the Hess does particularly good lamb. Bänklialp, Europe and Spannort are worth trying. The Engel's Stübli is cheaper.

Après-ski is good, particularly at weekends. The hotel Alpenclub's Spindle cellar disco draws the crowds. The Caribbean Dream Life and Peter's Pub are quieter places. The Casino Carmena in fact only has fruit machines while legal wrangles to install tables continue.

Engelberg provides plenty for **non-skiers**, with good sports facilities as well as excursions to nearby Lucerne and Zurich. For vicarious thrills, you can watch ski jumpers in training.

TOURIST OFFICE

Postcode CH-6390
Tel 00 41 (41) 941161
Fax 944156

Flims 1100m

HOW IT RATES

The skiing

Snow	***
Extent	****
Advanced	***
Intermediates	*****
Beginners	****
Convenience	***
Queues	***
Restaurants	***

The rest

Scenery	***
Resort charm	***
Not skiing	***

✔ Extensive, varied, beautiful ski area suitable for all but experts

✔ Fair amount of skiing above 2000m offsets effects of sunny south-east-facing slopes

✔ Large amount of wooded skiing for bad-weather days

✔ Virtually queue-free on weekdays

✔ Plenty to do off the slopes

✘ Sunny orientation can cause icy pistes and shut runs to the resort; most lack snowmaking

✘ Buses or long walks to lifts necessary from much of the accommodation

✘ Very subdued in the evenings

✘ Village very spread-out, which detracts from its charm

✘ Weekend crowds

Flims remains a Swiss gem undiscovered by the British. With a large, sunny ski area set above a wooded shelf, it's reminiscent of Crans-Montana – but is superior in some ways, notably in the amount of high skiing available. It also has important advantages, in skiing terms, over other Swiss resorts more widely marketed on the British scene, such as Villars, Arosa and Lenzerheide. While the likes of Kitzbühel and Wengen remain popular despite their poor snow records, Flims stays well outside the list of top resorts.

The village was for many years a summer beauty spot that had only a moderate amount of skiing available in the winter. After winning a war with local conservationists in the 1970s, Flims and nearby Laax opened up a vast new network of lifts serving an impressive 220km of pistes. Yet it remains essentially a quiet place in winter, given the spark of life only by Zürich and Chur weekenders.

Flims has some excellent, very beautiful, high skiing ideally suited to intermediates. It deserves to be better known. If the village had a bit more character we'd be recommending it even more highly.

ORIENTATION

Flims is made up of two villages, Waldhaus and Dorf, over a kilometre apart. They sit on a sunny, wooded mountain terrace. A gondola and chair-lift leave from Dorf. Most hotels run courtesy buses to and from the slopes and there's a punctual, but not frequent, post bus. The skiing spreads across the mainly south-east-facing mountainside to a second lift base-station at Murschetg (1.5km from Waldhaus), an outpost of **Laax**. There is a further lift into the skiing at **Falera** (5km from Waldhaus).

Excursions are possible by public transport or car to **Lenzerheide, Davos-Klosters** and **Arosa**, all reached via the nearby town of Chur.

 ## The resort

Flims is made up of two villages, over a kilometre apart. Dorf is by far the larger and more animated, sprawling along a busy main road which houses most of the shops, hotels, restaurants and bars. Waldhaus is a sedate, sophisticated huddle of hotels – some of them quite grand – attractively set among trees. Both resorts have stuck to the traditional look, with almost all hotels of the wooden chalet variety.

Dorf is better placed than Waldhaus for skiers, having the village lifts on its western outskirts. Given the spread-out nature of the resort, it's surprising there is no ski-bus. However a combination of hotel courtesy buses, post buses and regional buses serve guests well. There are hotels in Dorf close to the lifts, but the majority are a long walk away.

Although it's quiet, Flims has a pleasant cosmopolitan atmosphere – Germans, Dutch, Swedes, Belgians and Americans come here. Dorf is popular with fashionable families, while Waldhaus has an older, even more affluent clientele.

 ## The skiing

Flims has a big, underrated ski area, with varied skiing: some long runs and some high skiing, including a small glacier area. Because of its sunny aspect, the lower runs deteriorate quickly and it's not uncommon to be unable to ski back to the villages. And in poor visibility there is little in the way of wooded skiing.

THE SKI AREA
Impressive and well planned
The beautiful ski area has essentially four sections, each suitable for all grades but expert. The skiing has been well planned, and moving in either direction across it is straightforward, although one or two links do have inherent weaknesses.

The **Cassons** sector above Flims Dorf is the smallest sector, particularly so when runs to the village are incomplete. This is reached by the chair from the village, then a further chair or drag to the cable-car to the peak (2675m).

You can ski from here to Startgels, which is also the top of the gondola

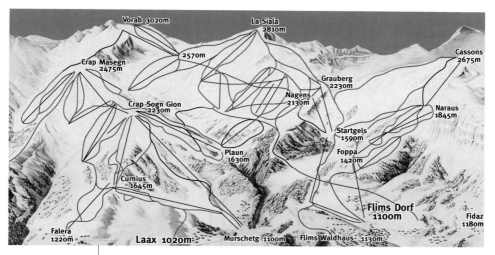

from the village. Lifts from here link in with the middle sector, **La Siala**, which is served by chairs and drags and reaches 2810m. The linking lifts cross an exposed ravine that can be rather windy.

Skiing across to the **Vorab** glacier (where the top lift reaches 3020m) from the top of La Siala is a simple matter except when La Siala's high chair is inoperative. In that case, all three routes via Plaun involve skiing short black sections of piste.

From Vorab you can ski to the biggest section of the skiing, served by eleven lifts, around **Crap Mesegn** and **Crap Sogn Gion**. You can also get from La Siala to Crap Sogn Gion by skiing down to the low-point of Plaun, where a new six-seater chair-lift (one of the first in Switzerland) provides uplift. From Crap Sogn Gion you can ski down to Murschetg, Laax or Falera.

SNOW RELIABILITY
Poor lower down, good higher up
Due to its sunny aspect, Flims is far from snowsure top to bottom, with snowmaking confined to two runs from Crap Sogn Gion – the black race-course down to Murschetg and a red to Plaun. But even if you have to ride the lifts down the lower sections, there is a lot of skiing above 2000m which usually enjoys decent snow except in late season.

FOR ADVANCED SKIERS
Bits and pieces
There is a fair amount of challenging skiing but it's rather dotted about, with the added frustration that some of it is on short sections of otherwise easy pistes. The toughest run is the steep, unpisted Cassons black, reached by making a steep climb from the top of the cable-car near the village. An off-piste excursion from the Cassons summit looks tempting but don't even think about it without a guide. You could go over a cliff.

One of the great pleasures of the whole area is the men's World Cup downhill course from Crap Sogn Gion to Murschetg. It's so long (1000m vertical) and pretty that skiing it repeatedly using the Murschetg cable-car doesn't get boring – and it is not so vulnerable to the sun now that it is equipped with snowmakers. The Nagens-Startgels run is short but steep.

Off-piste skiing is generally between pistes, but in such an extensive area there is plenty of such terrain. Ruschein, at the western extremity of the ski area, is the best sector. And the long Sattel piste from Vorab – see below – is a good and beautiful starting point. Note that many of the black runs are really 'dark red'.

FOR INTERMEDIATE SKIERS
Paradise for all
A superb area, though less confident skiers have to watch out for some easy runs that have short steep sections (normally marked black on the map). The two lower links between Siala and Dorf (Platt 'Alta and Stretg) and the run from the bottom of the Grisch drag down to Plaun (Sogn Martin) are examples.

When conditions allow, the area immediately above Flims is splendid for easy cruising. But the real highlight for early intermediates is skiing to the Vorab glacier and back on blue runs. On the way back you can take the cable-car down from Grauberg to Startgels to avoid the awkward runs in this area.

More adventurous intermediates have most of the area to choose from, though the narrow little Scansinas runs to Plaun are best avoided. The easier of the two descents from Cassons is a lovely run along the shoulder of the mountain into a valley and on to Startgels, a 1000m vertical trip. Skiing from Crap Sogn Gion to Larnags via Curnius is also great fun.

Good intermediates will enjoy the superb Sattel black run from the glacier to Ruschein on the extreme western edge of the ski area. It starts with a challenging mogul field but develops into a fast cruise and is one of the longest and most beautiful runs in the whole area.

The Crap Sogn Gion to Plaun routes along a valley are interesting, being quite steep, sheltered, and some of the few runs not to be almost directly facing the sun.

FOR BEGINNERS
Plenty of options
There is a good nursery area in Dorf, with an alternative at Startgels when snow is in short supply. Moving further afield is not a problem for quick learners. Getting the bus to the lovely easy runs above Falera is a good option. Although not a 'British' resort, there is plenty of tuition in English.

FOR CROSS-COUNTRY
One of the best
An excellent choice. There are 60km of beautiful well marked, mainly forest trails. Loops range from 3km to 20km The specialist cross-country ski school, centred at Waldhaus, has a good reputation, and gets sufficient numbers of customers to organise group classes. 3km of trail are floodlit. The only drawback is the possibility of poor snow.

QUEUES
Some delays
There is generally little queuing during the week, but we have had reports of a 20-minute midweek wait for the Cassons cable-car and of it waiting for a full load when custom was short. The resort is busier at weekends, but delays out of Flims in the morning are rarely more than ten minutes and you can choose between the gondola and chair. The chair towards La Siala can become a problem as people try to avoid some of the tough, long T-bars. Treis Palas (below Masegn) is an obvious bottleneck, but there's no need to ski there at busy periods.

MOUNTAIN RESTAURANTS
Good, wide selection
Mountain restaurants are numerous and generally good, if expensive. The large cafeterias at Cirnius, Sogn Gion and Vorab are clean, efficient and serve good wholesome food. Nagens has another good high-altitude place, but the nicest refuges are lower down. The Spaligna below Foppa, the Tegia at Larnags, and the Runcahöhe where the Stretg piste flattens out as it crosses the path down from Startgels, are among the best.

SKI SCHOOL
Plenty of English tuition
The ski school has a good reputation. Being a cosmopolitan resort, it makes wide use of English as the international language.

FACILITIES FOR CHILDREN
Expensive option
Not surprisingly, given the small number of British visitors, we lack reports on the resort childcare arrangements. If you want pre-skiing children to be looked after, you have to stay at the very expensive Park Hotel Waldhaus.

 Staying there

Although it might seem best to stay near the lifts in Dorf, in practice most of the better hotels in Waldhaus (and the remote bits of Dorf) run efficient courtesy buses to and from the slopes. These satisfy most of their guests, especially as most visitors don't often venture out on the town after dinner. Don't overlook the possibility of staying in Laax, Murschetg or rustic Falera – the last being a much more attractive option (if you like a quiet time) now that the access lift is being replaced by a fast quad chair.

HOW TO GO
Few tour operators
Only a handful of tour operators feature Flims.
Hotels Flims has over 30 hotels, the majority of which are either 3-star or simple B&B places, the latter tending to be booked out long in advance. Of the six top-notch hotels, five are in Waldhaus. Grading of hotels is accurate – you get what you pay for.
£££££ Park Enormous and very comfortable, but rather institutional, 5-star in wooded grounds at Waldhaus; the courtesy bus is essential in the mornings, but you can ski home. Pool.

CHILDCARE

The ski school runs ski kindergartens taking children from age 4 – in Flims from 9am to 4.30, in Laax from 8.30 to 4.30. Childcare in Falera is 'on request'.

Several hotels claim special facilities for children. The Park Hotel Waldhaus has its own crèche, and an independent crèche may be operating in the Adula.

GETTING THERE

Air Zürich, transfer 3hr.

Rail Chur (17km); regular buses to resort.

PACKAGES

Made to Measure, Plus Travel, Powder Byrne, Ski Choice, Swiss Travel Service

Falera

Laax Made to Measure, Plus Travel

ACTIVITIES

Indoor 4 hotel swimming pools open to public, saunas, 2 indoor tennis courts, covered hall with 4 skating rinks, bowling, fitness centres (including Prau La Selva), table tennis, whirlpool, solarium
Outdoor 60km of cleared paths, riding, natural skating rinks, curling, sleigh rides, toboggan runs, ski-bob, para-gliding, hot-air ballooning, hang-gliding, dogsleigh rides

TOURIST OFFICE

Postcode CH-7018
Tel 00 41 (81) 820 9200
Fax 820 9201

££££ Crap Ner The only 4-star in Dorf, but well away from the lifts and just as inconvenient for skiers as Waldhaus. But it's a friendly hotel with spacious, well decorated rooms and superb food. The hotel's courtesy bus is very efficient. Good pool.
££££ Adula Big, highly recommended 4-star in Waldhaus. Good pool.
£££ Grischuna Pretty little 3-star just outside Dorf, and close to the lifts.
£££ Curtgin Attractive place in quiet position on edge of town, quite well placed for the lifts.
£££ Albana Sporthotel Modern 3-star beside lifts, with focal après-ski bar.
£££ Waldeck Neat 3-star place in Waldhaus, with pleasant restaurant.
Self-catering The Minerva in Waldhaus is by far the nicest of the limited apartments available.

EATING OUT
Varied options
Flims offers a wide variety of restaurants for different tastes and budgets – Italian, Chinese, local specialities and nouvelle cuisine are some of the main choices on offer. Most restaurants are in hotels. The good value (by local standards) Chesa does a nice fondue, and has a lovely open fire. The National, by the bus station, has good fish dishes. The Meiler hotel restaurant also has a good reputation. Something a bit different is going up to the Spaligna mountain restaurant for a meal, with a toboggan run home. Little China is a good new Chinese restaurant. The Alpina Garni (Waldhaus) has some of the cheapest food in town – good pizzas.

APRES-SKI
Not a strong point
Flims is very quiet après-ski. The Spaligna trip mentioned under Eating out is the highlight of the week. The Stenna-Bar, opposite the Dorf base-station, has a tea dance, while just across the road the Albana Pub is popular with a young crowd. Later on, the focal spot is also in Dorf, at the hotel Bellevue's Caverna, an atmospheric old wine vault. Locals assure us the Iglou bar is also popular. The Park hotel is the centre of limited action in Waldhaus, having an old cellar with entertainer, plus the Chadafo bar which has dancing to live music. The Segnes and Bellavista bars are quiet. The sophisticated Viva Club comes to life at weekends.

FOR NON-SKIERS
Lots to do
There are plenty of things to do. The enormous sports centre has a huge range of activities, including shooting. And Flims has some of the best and most extensive (60km) marked walks of any ski resort. Chur is an historic old town a short bus-ride away. Other good excursions are to the impressive church at Zillis, and to Rhine Canyon, which is nature at its best. Catching the Glacier Express train from Chur to Andermatt takes you through some wonderful scenery.

STAYING UP THE MOUNTAIN
Space station St John
Even though there are entire resorts that are higher, the prospect of staying 1100m above Murschetg, in the ultra-modern 3-star Crap Sogn Gion, is an exciting one. It has all mod cons, including a pool. You can also stay above Flims in the more traditional Berghaus Nagens – it has dormitories as well as comfortable double rooms.

Laax 1020m
Laax is a quiet, spacious old farming community which has retained a lot of its original character; much of its modern development has taken place a short bus-ride away at Murschetg. This soulless complex has been built around the ski lifts and has its own hotels, shops and restaurants for those who want ski convenience above all else. Though the oldest house in Laax dates from 1615, and the setting is pleasant enough, the village is no more than routinely charming. Those looking for a traditional little gem would prefer Falera (see below).

The Murschetg cable-car (which generates peak-time queues) gives speedy access to Crap Sogn Gion, the main mid-station of the whole area. A gondola, followed by a chair, is an alternative route up the mountain. Runs lead back to Murschetg from Sogn Gion and Curnius; the routes converge at Larnags, where the village gondola has a joining station – useful for rides down when snow is becoming patchy.

Cross-country skiers visiting the area should stay in Laax. A fine trail network of 60km starts nearby.

Laax has its own ski school and ski kindergarten, run by the well known downhill racer Conradin Cathomen.

Most of the hotels are in the 3-star and 4-star categories. Although a few of those are large and modern, some semblance of traditional style has usually been attempted, and the thick pine forest which surrounds Murschetg also helps to hide the worst architectural excesses.

The Vallarosa and Signina are Murschetg 4-stars – very user-friendly and comfortable. The 4-star Arena Alva is a more attractive building in the old village, with its own transport to the lifts. The Bellaval is a pretty, traditional 3-star in the village centre. We've enjoyed staying at the charming, central old Posta Veglia, with its lively stubli and piano bar. A good central B&B is the Cathomen.

Restaurants are mostly hotel-based. The Laaxer Bündnerstuben in the Posta Veglia is the best bet for a meal in traditional surroundings. The limited nightlife scene is centred around the Bistro Bar in the Capricorn hotel, live music in the Vallarosa bar, and the ubiquitous Posta Veglia.

As at Flims, there's a fair amount to do for non-skiers. The 60km of cleared walks are one highlight. Other facilities include a riding academy, curling and skating on a nearby lake or artificial rink, sleigh rides, indoor pool, squash and a little museum.

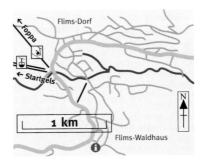

Falera 1220m

Along the road from Flims, beyond Laax, lies the attractively rustic village of Falera. It's a traditional, quiet little place, complete with two lovely old churches, and benefits from being traffic-free (parking is free at the entrance to the village). Sitting on a sunny plateau, it has good views over three valleys. Everything is close to hand, including the single village lift, ski slopes, ski school and ski kindergarten (by arrangement). In the past, the old village chair-lift has been a real drawback, taking an age (15 minutes) to rise the 400m vertical to Curnius; but this season a fast quad chair should be in place. The onward connections from Curnius are fairly rapid, so Falera must now be considered quite an attractive base, even for keen skiers.

Accommodation is mostly in apartments, but the two hotels have plenty of beds between them. La Siala is a large 4-star with pool and sauna. It also has apartments. The Encarna is a much simpler, atmospheric place.

La Siala's Spielkeller is the only real nightspot.

Café La Punt is good for tea-time cakes. The Alpenblick is an appealing restaurant, and the Aurora and Casa Seeli are other possibles for a meal.

Grindelwald 1035m

HOW IT RATES

The skiing

Snow	**
Extent	***
Advanced	***
Intermediates	*****
Beginners	***
Convenience	**
Queues	**
Restaurants	***

The rest

Scenery	*****
Resort charm	****
Not skiing	****

✔ *Dramatically set in magnificent scenery beneath the towering north face of the Eiger*

✔ *Large ski area, ideal for intermediates*

✔ *Traditional mountain village with long mountaineering history*

✘ *Village gets very little sunshine in early season*

✘ *Little challenging piste skiing for good skiers*

✘ *Long journey to top of skiing and inconvenient for visiting Mürren*

✘ *Not ideal for beginners – village nursery slopes often short of snow*

✘ *Snow cover unreliable, with little artificial help*

✘ *Queues for railway and gondola can be bad, especially when weekend visitors flock in*

Grindelwald is a much expanded, traditioal mountain village, set at the bottom of some of Europe's best climbing terrain, with the north face of the Eiger towering dramatically above. The main ski area is shared with Wengen and has stunning views – unmatched except perhaps by those from Mürren.

When conditions are good, the skiing matches the scenery – at least for intermediates. Experts will find the piste skiing unexciting, and beginners may find the snow on the lower slopes poor or non-existent. That's one of Grindelwald's main drawbacks. The ski area is low, there's virtually no artificial snow on the Grindelwald side of the ski area, and the region has suffered a series of poor years for snowfall – even the 94/95 season, a bumper year for most resorts, saw a relative shortage, though last year this region shared in the Alps' generally heavy falls throughout the winter.

But it has a loyal following of people for whom skiing is only one part of a winter holiday. It is best suited to leisurely skiers who aren't too fussed if conditions are less than ideal. Most reporters rated it highly for an all-round mountain holiday for the middle-aged and for visitors with young children. Many emphasised that it wasn't really ideal for teenagers or child-free people in their 20s and 30s.

Then there's the question of whether to stay here or in Wengen. On balance, we'd go for Wengen. Its 'traffic-free' village is prettier and more relaxing. And it has much quicker access to Mürren and its more exciting skiing.

ORIENTATION

Grindelwald is spread out along a narrow valley with mountains rising sheerly above it. The main Kleine Scheidegg-Männlichen ski area is shared with **Wengen**. Kleine Scheidegg is reached by cog railway from Grund, near the western end of town; the station for this railway is itself served by railway from the village. Männlichen is reached by gondola, also from Grund. The other ski area is First, on the opposite side of the valley, reached by a three-stage gondola from just to the east of the village centre.

Outings to other resorts are not very attractive, but you can get to **Gstaad** by rail and road, and **Adelboden** by road.

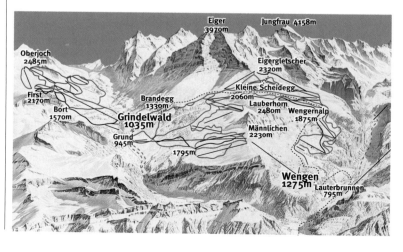

SKI FACTS

Jungfrau region –
including Wengen and
Mürren

Altitude	945m-2970m
Lifts	49
Pistes	183km
Green/Blue	30%
Red	50%
Black	20%
Artificial snow	15km

LIFT PASSES

95/96 prices in
Swiss francs
**Jungfrau Top Ski
Region**
Covers all lifts in
Wengen, Mürren and
Grindelwald, trains
between them and
Grindelwald ski-bus.
Beginners Points card
(adult 100 points 46,
lifts cost 4 to 10
points).
Main pass
1-day pass 52
6-day pass 232
Children
Under 16: 6-day pass
116 (50% off)
Under 6: free pass
Short-term passes
Single ascent tickets
for most lifts. Half-day
pass for First (adult
38), Kleine Scheidegg-
Männlichen (adult 40)
and Mürren-Schilthorn
(adult 38).
Notes Day pass price
for Kleine Scheidegg-
Männlichen area only
(98km of piste, 21
lifts), as Jungfrau Top
Ski Region pass is
only available for
2 days or over.
Discounts for
teenagers 16 to 21 (6-
day 186) and groups.
Alternative passes
1- and 2-day passes
available for First
(adult 2-day 90),
Mürren-Schilthorn
(adult 2-day 90) and
Kleine Scheidegg-
Männlichen (adult 2-
day 95, child 48).
Credit cards: Yes

The resort

Grindelwald is a traditional
mountaineering resort set either side
of the road along the foot of a narrow
valley. The buildings are primarily
traditional Swiss chalet style, with a
few grander buildings such as the
stone-built Grand Hotel Regina.

It can feel claustrophobic because of
the towering mountains rising sheerly
from the valley floor, and can be dark
in early season, when it gets no, or
very little, sun.

There is a splendid sports centre to
which entrance is now free with a
Visitor's Card. And it can feel very
jolly at times, such as during the ice-
carving festival in January, when large
and beautiful tableaux are on display.

At weekends, though, it can get very
crowded – or at least the train and the
gondola can – with coachloads of
people, especially from Germany, who
may well be staying cheaply in
Interlaken and Wilderswil.

The village tends to be more
animated at night than the other
Jungfrau resorts of Wengen and
Mürren. There's live music in several
bars and hotels, though it certainly
isn't the place for those who want to
bop every night until dawn.

The skiing

See Wengen (page 367) for a general
description of the main ski area. As
well as that, there is the separate First
ski area, now served by a three-stage
gondola which has replaced what used
to be the oldest chair-lift in the world
– you rode it sideways. The First area's
skiing is almost entirely south-facing.
So while it can be marvellous after a
fresh snowfall, the snow here
deteriorates rapidly in warm weather.
It's primarily intermediate terrain.

A three-days-out-of-seven pass is
new this year and the Jungfrau region
pass, formerly available for three days
plus, can now be had for two.

SNOW RELIABILITY
Poor
Grindelwald has had a succession of
relatively poor snow years. Its low
altitude – the skiing goes down to
below 1000m and little of it is above
2000m – and the lack of significant
amounts of artificial snow mean
Grindelwald is not a resort for which
we'd make a firm booking months in
advance. And it's not the place for a
late season holiday.

FOR ADVANCED SKIERS
Very limited
See the chapter on Wengen. The main
interest for good skiers is off-piste, and
Powder Byrne runs holidays to
Grindelwald which include off-piste
courses with mountain guide Ueli Frei.
On-piste, there's little of interest,
especially on the Grindelwald side of
the ski area shared with Wengen. The
black run marked on the piste map
from Männlichen back to Grindelwald
must qualify as one of the most overgraded runs in the world. The black
run on First which runs beneath the
gondola back to town is tougher,
especially when the snow has suffered
from too much sun. Getting to the
tougher, higher skiing of Mürren is a
lengthy business unless you've got a
car – Wengen is a much better base in
that respect.

FOR INTERMEDIATE SKIERS
Ideal intermediate terrain
Again, see the chapter on Wengen for
a description of the ideal intermediate
slopes which the two resorts share. In
good snow conditions the whole area
is perfect for intermediate skiers,
especially those who don't like
unexpected surprises.

First has some very gentle slopes
right at the top, served by a couple of
drag-lifts. This is the highest part of
Grindelwald's ski area, reaching
2485m – a few metres higher than the
Lauberhorn lift takes you. There's a
lovely long red run all the way back to
Grindelwald on the extreme eastern
side of the First ski area. In good snow,
First is a splendid intermediate
playground, and worth spending a day
or two on, although many skiers
ignore it and head straight for the
main ski area.

FOR BEGINNERS
In good snow, wonderful
Grindelwald's gentle slopes make ideal
beginner territory, with a splendid
gentle blue run through the trees to
progress to once you are off the
nursery slopes. It goes right from the
top of the train at Kleine Scheidegg
down to Grund. But you can just do
parts of it by getting off or catching
the train up at the intermediate stops
such as Brandegg and Alpiglen.

If the snow is poor, it's not good to
be a beginner in Grindelwald. The
main nursery slopes are at low altitude
at the foot of the sunny First ski area.

SKI SCHOOL

95/96 prices in
Swiss francs

Swiss

Classes 5 days
4hr: 10am-noon and
2pm-4pm
5 full days: 192
Children's classes
Ages: 3 to 14
5 full days: 192
Private lessons
2½hr or 5hr
170 for 2½hr

GETTING THERE

Air Zürich, transfer
3hr. Bern, transfer
1½hr.

Rail Station in resort.

CHILDCARE

The ski school takes
children aged 3 to 14,
and they can be
looked after at
lunchtime in the
Children's Club
kindergarten at the
Bodmi nursery slopes.
This takes children
from age 3, from 9.30
to 4pm. It apparently
ceases to function if
snow shortage closes
the nursery slopes.

In February there is
an organised
programme of
activities for
children of secondary
school age.

FOR CROSS-COUNTRY
The best in the Jungfrau region

The tourist office says that there are
between 25km and 32km of prepared
tracks, depending on snow conditions.
Almost all of this is in the valley floor
at around 1000m, so in good snow it's
delightful. In poor snow there may be
little more cross-country here than in
the rest of the Jungfrau region (where
there is hardly any).

QUEUES
Can be dreadful at weekends

The queues at Grund, for both the
gondola and the train, can be
substantial, especially at busy
weekends when all the day visitors
tend to enter the skiing via
Grindelwald rather than taking the
slower Lauterbrunnen-Wengen route.
The queue for the train, in particular,
was found by one reporter to be 'just
like being in a cattle pen; very
disconcerting, with orders being
barked at you over loudspeakers in
German. And even once you're on it,
there may be standing-room only, and
it takes 50 minutes to get to the top'.

Another reporter tells of 'waits of up
to one and a half hours to get on the
gondola after 8.45am'.

If the whole ski area is open, lift
queues higher up are not a problem.
But if snow is short on the lower
slopes, queues build up higher up.

MOUNTAIN RESTAURANTS
More choice on the Wengen side

See the Wengen chapter for restaurants
in the main ski area. On the First side,
the restaurant at Bort does extremely
good rösti. One of our reporters was
lucky enough to see chamois grazing
just below here. The First restaurant,
by contrast, is large and ugly.

SKI SCHOOL
One of the better Swiss schools

Reports consistently suggest standards
are high, with small classes and good
English spoken. One reporter says the
instructors have become charming in
recent seasons. There are special
courses such as powder and seniors'
weeks, and there's a section for people
with impaired vision.

FACILITIES FOR CHILDREN
Good reports

One reporter who has put four
children through the Grindelwald mill
has nothing but good words for the ski
school – not only caring instructors
and effective instruction but
'peppermint tea at 11am that our
5-year-old always remembers'.

 # Staying there

The most convenient place to stay for
the skiing is at Grund. But this is out
of the centre and rather charmless.

There's a wide range of hotels in the
heart of the village, which is handy
enough for everything else, including
the First ski area, at the foot of which
are the nursery slopes, ski school and
kindergarten.

HOW TO GO
Limited range of packages

Although tour operators offer a
reasonable selection of hotels, they
tend to concentrate on the upper end
of the market. Traditional little B&B
pensions and self-catering apartments
are, however, widely available to
independent bookers.

Chalets We are not aware of any
catered chalets run by tour operators.

Hotels There is one 5-star hotel, a
dozen 4-stars, and a good range of
more modest places.

£££££ Regina The one 5-star. Big and
imposing; right next to the railway
station. Nightly music in the bar. Pool.

££££ Schweizerhof Beautifully
decorated 4-star chalet at west end of
centre, close to station. Pool.

££££ Bodmi New little chalet right on
the village nursery slopes.

£££ Hirschen Excellent family-run
3-star in central position at foot of
nursery slopes, mid-way between First
gondola and railway station.

£££ Fiescherblick Hospitable chalet
on eastern fringe of village, five
minutes from the First gondola.

£££ Derby Popular, modern 3-star
right on the station.

££ Tschuggen Modest chalet in
central position below nursery slopes.

£ Wetterhorn Cosy, simple chalet way
beyond the village, with great views of
the glacier.

Self-catering There are some
comfortable apartments in a pleasant
wooden chalet in the main street. One
independent reporter recommends the
apartments of the hotel Hirschen for
comfort and spaciousness.

EATING OUT
Hotel based

There's a wide choice of good hotel
restaurants, but pizzeria-style places
are in short supply. The only one we
know is the Latino, which specialises
in home-made Italian cooking. Among
the more attractively traditional places
are: the Gepsi in the Eiger; Schmitte in
the Schweizerhof; Challi-Stubli in the
Kreuz; and the Alte Post.

PACKAGES

Inghams, Kuoni, Made to Measure, Plus Travel, Powder Byrne, Swiss Travel Service, Thomson

ACTIVITIES

Indoor Sports centre (swimming pool, sauna, solarium, massage), indoor skating rink, curling, bowling, cinema
Outdoor 80km of cleared paths, train rides to Jungfraujoch, tobogganing, snow-shoe excursions, sleigh rides, para-gliding, snowrafting, glacier tours

TOURIST OFFICE

Postcode CH-3818
Tel 00 41 (36) 531212
Fax 533088

The Kirchbuhl is good for vegetarians, the Bahnhof in the Derby for fondue and raclette. Hotel Spinne has a good restaurant for almost all tastes – the Mercato for Italian, Mescalero for Mexican, a Chinese place; and one of the best places in town for a special romantic meal, the candlelit Rôtisserie. Hotel Belvedere has a gourmet French restaurant.

APRES-SKI
Relaxed
It's a fairly subdued scene, though there's no shortage of live music. The Regina has a sophisticated dance band every evening, and the Derby has live entertainment, including rather incongruous country and western. The Spinne has reputedly the best of the two village discos. There is also a cinema, and there are ice hockey and curling matches to watch.

FOR NON-SKIERS
Plenty to do, easy to get around
There are 50km of cleared paths with magnificent views and a splendid sports centre.

It's easy to get around the mountain and meet skiing friends for lunch using both the train and gondola, and there's a special (though expensive at SF150 for five days) non-skier's lift pass. A trip to Jungfraujoch is spectacular. And an excursion by train to Interlaken is easy, and Bern possible. Day trips to Mürren are surprisingly long-winded because you have to change three times, with a lengthy wait at the first change. Helicopter flights are available.

STAYING UP THE MOUNTAIN
Several possibilities
Grindelwald, like Wengen, gives easy rail access to Kleine Scheidegg, where there are quite pricey rooms at the Kleine Scheidegg hotel and cheap dormitory space above the station buffets. There are also dormitories at the nearby Grindelwaldblick. The Bort, at the gondola station in the middle of the First area (1570m), is perhaps the most attractive of all.

Gstaad 1050m

HOW IT RATES

The skiing

Snow	*
Extent	****
Advanced	**
Intermediates	***
Beginners	***
Convenience	*
Queues	***
Restaurants	***

The rest

Scenery	***
Resort charm	****
Not skiing	****

ORIENTATION

Gstaad sits at a broad junction of valleys, with skiing on three mountains reached by lifts from the fringes of the village. One of these sectors spreads west to **Rougemont**. A separate fourth sector of skiing is accessed from **Schönried**, **Saanenmöser** and **St Stephan**. The skiing of **Zweisimmen** comes between the last two but is not linked.

Château d'Oex, a few km to the west (reached by train, bus or car) is covered by the area lift pass. So is the skiing on and down from the **Diablerets** glacier, 15km to the south. And so is **Lenk**, up valley from St Stephan, and the linked resort of **Adelboden**.

✔ Surprisingly unspoilt, unpretentious, traditional village

✔ A wide variety of après-ski in January and February

✔ Plenty of off-slope amenities

✔ Large, pretty ski area, mainly of intermediate difficulty but with off-piste possibilities

✔ Few queues, given snow-cover

✔ Excellent descents from Diablerets glacier, a few miles away

✘ Very poor recent snow record, yet no snowmakers

✘ Several widely separated ski areas, none of which is convenient to the village (though most are served by good public transport)

✘ Little steep piste skiing to challenge good skiers – token black runs on the piste map don't mean much

✘ Nursery slopes less than ideal – though some smaller resorts nearby are better equipped

✘ No inexpensive hotels in the main resort village

✘ Diablerets glacier itself is of rather limited appeal, and certainly doesn't compensate for Gstaad's local snow record

Gstaad is renowned as a jet-set resort – one of the places that's always trotted out when soppy magazines want to do a piece on where celebs ski. And it is one of the few resorts in the Alps where there is no cheap and cheerful accommodation at all – you have to go to outlying villages to find a hotel of less than 3-star standard.

But if you think this makes Gstaad another St Moritz – that is, another glitzy, self-consciously 'international' resort, you're wrong. The grandest of the hotels are tucked away in secluded grounds, and at first glance the resort still has the air of a country village, even if it is an obviously affluent one. Look again, and you see that the winding high street is lined with famous-name jewellers and designer boutiques.

For 'ordinary' holiday skiers Gstaad offers a civilised, crowd-free atmosphere, unspoilt rustic charm, beautiful scenery, high quality hotels and excellent non-skiing facilities. Those who attach a high priority to convenience, reliable snow or value for money should stay away – although there are smaller villages in Gstaad's inappropriately named White Highlands ski area that improve on the main resort in all three respects.

Rougemont, over the line into French-speaking Switzerland, is a particularly captivating and modestly priced village with a lift into the biggest of the three ski sectors that surround Gstaad. Schönried and Saanenmöser have lifts into another extensive area, away from Gstaad, that links with St Stephan.

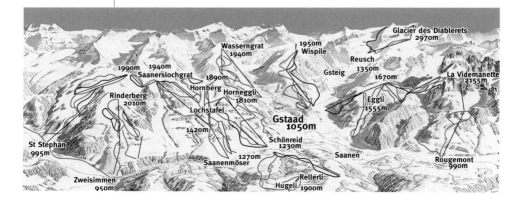

SKI FACTS

Altitude 950m-3000m
Lifts	69
Pistes	250km
Green/Blue	60%
Red	30%
Black	10%
Artificial snow	2km

LIFT PASSES

95/96 prices in Swiss francs
Gstaad Super Ski Region
Covers all lifts in Gstaad, Schönried, Saanenmöser, Zweisimmen, St Stephan, Lauenen, Gsteig, Reusch, the Glacier des Diablerets, Rougemont, Château d'Oex and Les Moulins, and the train, local buses and swimming pool.
Beginners Coupon booklet covers all lifts.
Main pass
1-day pass 46
6-day pass 233
Children
Under 16: 6-day pass 140 (40% off)
Under 6: free pass
Short-term passes
2hr (adult 32), 4hr (adult 38) passes available.
Alternative periods
Any 6 days in the season.
Notes Passes of 4 days or more are also valid in Adelboden-Lenk and Les Diablerets-Villars. Discounts for teenagers 16 to 20 and for families.

The resort

Gstaad is an attractive, traditional, long-established, year-round resort in a spacious, sunny setting surrounded by a horseshoe of wooded mountains where several valleys converge.

Life revolves around the bustling main street, which is lined by chalet-style buildings housing hotels, shops and cafés. This is also a through-route, with a fair amount of local traffic, which detracts from what is otherwise a pleasant and relaxing village. The Montreux-Oberland-Bernois (MOB) railway, which accesses numerous surrounding ski villages, loops in and out of the village on its way from Montreux to Berne; the station is conveniently positioned, close to much of the accommodation.

The skiing

The skiing is mostly pretty, intermediate stuff, with steeper slopes available to those who venture off-piste. A Ski-Data electronic lift pass system has been introduced, as in Courmayeur and other Italian resorts – you can have a programmable wrist watch instead of a conventional pass.

THE SKI AREA
Fragmented and scattered
The local topography has implications for skiers. On each of the hills separating the surrounding valleys, unconnected ski areas have evolved. They would be awkward to link in any circumstances; in such a strong conservation area, the prospect can be discounted altogether.

The three local lift stations are disposed around the southern end of the village, just too far out to be reached on foot. A ski-bus links them and the village every 15 minutes; another line, running every 30 minutes, takes in Saanen as well.

To the east is **Wasserngrat**, a small 'yo-yo' skiing area, accessed by a gondola from the eastern side of Gstaad. To the south, **Wispile** is very similar. To the west is a more complex and extensive area, **Eggli**. There is another lift into this sector from north-east of Gstaad, at Rübeldorf. And you can ski via the Chalberhöni valley to lifts up to **Videmanette**, also reached by gondola from Rougemont. From here a steep, narrow off-piste route goes down beneath the second stage of the gondola, with pistes leading down to Rougemont

from the mid-station. There is also a much easier pisted route between Videmanette and Rougemont. Finishing the day here is not a bad plan. The train is nearby and an après-ski drink while waiting for it is very pleasant in this lovely village.

The closest access point to the fourth and largest sector, spreading east from the nearby peak of **Hornberg**, is a short train trip away from Gstaad – an enclosed chair-lift at Schönried. Slightly further east, at Saanenmöser, is the major access lift – a gondola up to the higher point of Saanerslochgrat. From Saanerslochgrat a couple of short lifts and pistes lead to Parwengesattel, the top station above St Stephan, the furthermost village in the local area. Although further from Gstaad, these departure points at Schönried and Saanenmöser are not appreciably less convenient than Gstaad's local lift stations; you just need to study the timetables of the MOB and the ski-bus Line 3, and time your day accordingly. Schönried also has a lift on the sunny side of its valley, up to **Rellerli**.

The Zweisimmen ski area on **Rinderberg** is strangely bypassed by the lifts and runs linking Saanenmöser and St Stephan. Off-piste routes linking the areas are possible, though rarely skiable.

There are snowboard fun-parks at Saanersloch and Rinderberg.

SNOW RELIABILITY
Poor, despite the nearby glacier
A lack of both altitude and snowmakers has obvious repercussions for snow-cover, but at least all the ski sectors have a fair amount of north-facing skiing above the lift mid-stations, which are at altitudes ranging from around 1350m to around 1600m. The Diablerets glacier is snowsure, but is a limited area (not in the Hintertux-Stubai-Kaprun league); nevertheless, when snow is scarce it can suffer horrendous queues.

FOR ADVANCED SKIERS
Few options
Most of the piste skiing is easy; the blacks rarely exceed red difficulty, and some should be blue. There are off-piste possibilities in all the sectors, and sometimes steep ones – particularly on the wooded flanks of Wispile and on Eggli. When skiable, the run under the top gondola above Rougemont must be a challenge. The Diablerets glacier itself lacks challenge, but the black runs on the flanks of the mountain, above the Col

SKI SCHOOL

95/96 prices in
Swiss francs

Swiss
Classes 6 days
3³/₄hr: 10am-2.45, 1hr
for lunch
6 full days: 200
Children's classes
Ages: Any
6 full days: 195
Private lessons
Hourly or daily
55 for 1hr for 1 to 4
people

CHILDCARE

The ski kindergarten
takes children from
age 3, from 10am to
3pm.

GETTING THERE

Air Geneva, transfer
2¹/₂hr.

Rail Station in resort.

---

du Pillon certainly do not. The run described below, from the glacier to Reusch, is worth an hour of anyone's time. Not surprisingly in this very affluent resort, heli-skiing is available.

FOR INTERMEDIATE SKIERS
Plenty for everyone dotted about
Good intermediates will find the Wispile and Wasserngrat reds and blacks entertaining for a while, but 'yo-yo' skiing has its drawbacks. A better series of options lies in the Hornberg sector above Schönried. The moguls either side of Saanerslochgrat and at Hornberg itself, plus the steepest of the runs above St Stephan, are all good fun.

Moderate skiers will like the long runs down to Rougemont, the Wispile and Wasserngrat reds, and the fine pistes down to St Stephan. Leisurely types have plenty of choice above Saanenmöser, including long cruises to the village from Saanerslochgrat and Hornfluh. The Chalberhöni valley area is good for mixed abilities, with parallel-running pistes of varying difficulty.

Adventurous intermediates should not fail to make an outing to the Diablerets glacier, not for the flat glacier skiing but for the splendid run down from it. After a slightly tricky start, this develops into a glorious swooping run of no great difficulty, down a deserted valley which keeps its snow very well. At the 'end' of the valley, lifts take you up to Oldenegg (the mid-station of the cable-car up to the glacier) and you then resume your descent, through pretty woods to Reusch and the bus home.

FOR BEGINNERS
Château d'Oex is better
Nursery slopes at the bottom of Wispileare are no more than adequate and are prone to poor snow conditions. A small area at the top of the Wispile is fairly snowsure, but La Braye, above Château d'Oex, has the best nursery area in the region. Unfortunately, it's rather a trek from Gstaad. Saanenmöser has plenty of suitable runs for precocious learners.

FOR CROSS-COUNTRY
Good when snow allows
The 60km of trails are very pretty, and the trains and buses mean you don't have to retrace your steps. But virtually all of the trails are at valley level, and prone to loss of snow. There are slightly higher trails at Schönried, and 25km much higher at Sparenmoos near Zweisimmen.

QUEUES
Few delays
There are few queues in the main ski area except at weekends and the peak February weeks, and even then they are easily avoided when there is resort-level snow. Time lost on buses or trains is a greater problem.

MOUNTAIN RESTAURANTS
Excellent, leisurely lunches
There is no shortage of restaurants and most are attractive, if expensive. Many have table-service, which can make for longish waits at peak times. The Chemi-Stube, with great views towards Lenk, is a particularly nice place above St Stephan. The hut at the top of the Eggli gondola is another excellent spot for lunch. But Berghaus Wasserngrat – a small chalet with a big terrace – is the most captivating of all.

SKI SCHOOL
English-speaking tuition
Although few Brits frequent it, Gstaad is an international resort, with plenty of Americans among its clientele. So English is more widely spoken in this ski school than in many others in Brit-free zones. It has a good reputation too, though we lack recent reports.

FACILITIES FOR CHILDREN
Surprisingly poor
The limited hours offered by the ski kindergarten mean that parents can forget any ideas of escaping their responsibilities for a whole day's skiing. The only nursery appears to be in the Palace hotel. We shall see if the new children's play area on Eggli improves matters.

↑ Staying there

For skiing, hotel position is relatively unimportant; you're unlikely to be close to a lift, and unlikely to be far from a bus stop. Some hotels are close to the Wispile lifts, but poorly placed for everything else – including the other lifts. Best to put aside thoughts of skiing convenience and stay in the heart of the charming village.

HOW TO GO
Easy to reach independently
Gstaad is certainly exclusive, with over three quarters of its accommodation in private chalets and apartments, and the remainder of its beds in 3-star hotels and above. It is one of the easiest of ski drives from the Channel and has good train links to Geneva airport via Montreux. But you'll

PACKAGES

Made to Measure,
SkiGower

Château d'Oex
Airtours, Kuoni, Ski
Valkyrie

probably prefer to fly directly to Gstaad-Saanen airport, which now has immigration and customs facilities. About time, too.

Chalets We don't know of any catered chalets in Gstaad itself.

Hotels There aren't many hotels by usual ski resort standards – half a dozen 4-star, half a dozen 3-star and two 5-star.

£££££ Palace Extravagantly swish place overlooking the village from secluded grounds.

££££ Bernerhof Large, centrally placed 4-star with all conceivable facilities. Pool and playroom.

££££ Christiania Small, cosy 4-star, centrally placed.

££££ Gstaaderhof Large 3-star, centrally positioned but peaceful.

££££ Olden Exceptionally charming, small, family-run, prettily painted chalet, right in the centre of things, with locals' bar as well as upmarket restaurant.

£££ Posthotel Rössli Wooden chalet, close to the Olden in every way.

£££ Victoria Comfortable place, well placed for station.

£££ Rütti Cheapest hotel in Gstaad, close to Wispile gondola, 10 minutes from village centre.

Self-catering There is a wide choice of apartments for independent travellers. The Utoring has been recommended to us as a high-quality establishment , but it's not for budget skiers seeking to stay in Gstaad 'on the cheap'. The Christiania has luxury serviced apartments within the hotel building and Ludi-Haus, Selini and Bel Horizon are well positioned places in the upper price range. Less expensive, but equally central, are Sunbeam, Blum, Burn and Hänsel.

EATING OUT
You pays your money …
Restaurants are mainly hotel-based, and expensive. Hotel Bellevue's Chez Fritz is famed for its high-quality cuisine, although the elegant Chesery is perhaps the best in town. The Rialto restaurant bar is known for pasta and fish. The rustic (but big – 350-seat) Chlösterli, a seven-minute car journey out of town, is a popular place to eat and dance. Hotel Rössli's restaurant is reasonably priced. Cheap and sustaining food can be had in the locals' bar of the Olden, but don't stray into La Cave by mistake.

APRES-SKI
Sophistication and informality
During 'the season', nightlife is lively, less so off-peak. Café Pernet, the Apple Pie and Charly's are popular at tea-time, while later Henry's Bar, Richi's

ACTIVITIES

Indoor Sports centre (swimming, tennis, sauna), squash, fitness centre, cinema **Outdoor** Skating, curling, 50km cleared paths, hot-air balloons, horse-riding, sleigh rides, paragliding, helicopter flights, excursions, night skiing, saltwater swimming pools, sledging

TOURIST OFFICE

Postcode CH-3780
Tel 00 41 (30) 88181
Fax 88133

Pub and the bars of the Olden and Rialto come alive. People-watching in the Palace Hotel's GreenGo nightclub is an expensive 'must', but the Olden's La Cave, the Rütti's Keller, and the Viktoria's Taburi are arguably better places to have a bop. The Chlösterli has a live band, and Gstaad's cinema has a change of programme every two days. Nearby Saanen has floodlit skiing three nights a week.

FOR NON-SKIERS
Superb facilities
Gstaad suits non-skiers better than it suits many skiers. The tennis centre and swimming pool complex are particularly impressive, and there is a very wide range of other non-skiing things to do. There are also 50km of pretty, cleared walks, and the buses and MOB train make getting around easy, both within the White Highlands and further afield. Montreux and Interlaken are within reach. Several attractive mountain restaurants are served by gondolas.

STAYING IN OTHER VILLAGES
Worth considering
Schönried and Saanenmöser are better placed for skiing, and offer slightly cheaper accommodation, but neither has much further appeal. Schönried is a roadside straggle with four hotels, a couple of nightclubs, several restaurants and tea rooms, and one good bar (Sammy's). The 3-star Bahnhof is the third cheapest hotel in the whole area, and the good value it offers is essentially the main reason for staying in Schönried. It is situated next to the railway station, within

walking distance of the lifts.

Saanenmöser has very little infrastructure, and two of its three hotels are sufficiently luxurious to be just as expensive as many Gstaad establishments. The 2-star Bahnhof is inexpensive by local standards but is slightly pricier than its 3-star namesake in Schönried.

Saanen is very poorly situated for skiing, a bus-ride from its nearest lifts and pistes at Rübeldorf. It does, however, have plenty of restaurants and tea rooms, and (as well as slick hotels to match all but the very dearest in Gstaad) has the two cheapest hotels in the whole area. Hotel Boo is an atmospheric, rustic 3-star chalet in the village centre, while the slightly cheaper Landhaus is attractive and well placed for the railway station. Ten minutes out of the village is a youth hostel.

Rougemont is the most attractive village in the whole area – a pretty collection of rustic old chalets. Hotel Valrose is a good-value establishment close to both gondola and railway station. The hotel de Commune is a beautiful old chalet in the centre. The Viva, out of the village, is recommended for its rooms and welcome, but not food. Après-ski centres around the bars of the Valrose and Commune, and the charming, woody Cerf restaurant.

Chateau d'Oex gets more British visitors and is unspoilt, but some of its hotels are very poorly positioned for skiing the White Highlands. The good-value 3-star Beau Séjour is by far the best placed hotel, both for the local skiing and railway station.

Lenzerheide-Valbella 1470m

Lenzerheide and Valbella are separate villages that share a big intermediate ski area in a pretty wooded setting. They don't attract many British skiers, perhaps because there is nothing very distinctive about them. The skiing is rather monotonous, the villages not outstanding for charm, convenience, seclusion or animation. Langlaufers and non-skiers tend to like it best.

THE RESORTS

Lenzerheide and Valbella are set on a wide, sunny, wooded pass with skiable mountains on either side. The two villages are separated by a lake, which contributes to the classic Alpine scene. But the villages are an undisciplined sprawl of traditional and modern buildings, lacking character, with a busy road slicing through the middle of Lenzerheide and part of Valbella. They are scarcely the 'picture book villages' sometimes marketed by tour operators. The area is now patronised mainly by Swiss and German families.

THE SKIING

155km of piste are spread evenly over two facing mountains, with a circuit possible (with a little walking). The east-facing Danis **ski area** has the greater number of runs, and reaches 2430m. Reporters complain of too many long T-bars – so it's good news that two drags at Alp Stätz are being replaced by a quad chair this season. Ten minutes out of town, towards Valbella, a cable-car and gondola access the west-facing Rothorn area – more varied, taller (1400m vertical) but less extensive.

Sunny slopes and limited snowguns make the area less snowsure than the altitude would suggest, especially in the trees lower down. However, skiing is usually assured above the mid-stations at about 1900m, and plenty of two-stage lifts means lack of resort-level **snow** is not a disaster.

The slopes get steeper with altitude, so the few **advanced skiers'** runs have the best snow. The long, beautiful off-piste trail from Rothorn's summit to town is a must. Off-piste excursions to nearby resorts, including Arosa, are possible with a guide.

The area suits **intermediates** well, except that it lacks variety. The top-to-bottom run of over 1000m vertical, from the shoulder of the Weisshorn (on the Rothorn side) to Parpan, is a highlight for confident skiers. There are long cruises on Danis, and even early intermediates will enjoy the pretty run home from the middle of the Rothorn cable-car. In general the runs in the trees are very easy.

There are adequate **beginner** areas close to the villages, and easy runs to progress to. If snow is in short supply, you go up to one of the mid-stations.

With 50km of attractive trails, some on the lake, good tuition and night skiing, Lenzerheide is a leading **cross-country** resort.

There are few **queues** except at weekends, when the cable-car and Parpan lift are jammed. Delays also occur if the lower runs are snowless.

There are plenty of **mountain restaurants**, but few of distinction. Berghaus Tagntieni is recommended.

The **ski school** has a reputation for small classes, but a lack of English-speaking instructors is a problem.

The hotel Schweizerhof and the Soleval apartments have supervised **children's** facilities, open all day on weekdays. There is no public crèche or ski kindergarten.

STAYING THERE

The 4-star Schweizerhof **hotel** is central, with good food, pool, tennis and squash. The Sunstar is of similar standard, next to the nursery slopes, and with a pool. Kurhaus Alpina is cheaper, handy for Danis skiing, and has a pool. The Dieschen is a family-run 3-star, near the cable-car, with good health and fitness facilities. The 3-star Collina is recommended for its good position, good food and friendly staff. The Guarda Val is splendidly rustic, well renovated but out of town.

Soleval **apartments** are high-quality, with fitness facilities and free covered parking, 10 minutes from the village but right on the slopes.

Restaurants are mostly hotel-based. Da Elio is a good pizzeria. Hotel Lenzerhorn has dinner dances in a rustic setting.

Après-ski is quiet on weekdays but lively at the weekend. Nino's pub is the liveliest place in town. Café Aurora and the bar of the Sunstar are good for a cosy drink. There are two discos.

Facilities for **non-skiers** are good. Apart from sports (including skating – on a new indoor rink this year), there is a cinema, 35km of cleared walks around the lake and along the valley and a bus-link to nearby Chur.

Les Diablerets 1160m

Les Diablerets is a pleasant, unspoilt but rather diffuse village in a grand setting. Its amiable intermediate skiing is linked to that of Villars, and the big news this year is that the link will at last become one that intermediate skiers will enjoy. The Diablerets glacier is nearby, but you have to buy a regional pass to use it, and it doesn't add up to much.

THE RESORT

The village of Les Diablerets lies in a broad valley beside the Diablerets massif, towering a neck-craning 2000 metres above the resort. It is a diffuse village – a scattered collection of traditional-style holiday homes and modern hotels, with a cluster of shops along the main street leading away from the railway station. The road up to the village goes on over the Col du Pillon to Gstaad; Leysin is easily reached by road or railway, and Villars is linked by lifts and runs.

THE SKIING

Les Diablerets gives access to three separate **ski areas**. Two start from the village, but their base stations are widely separated. Stupidly, the piste map gives no indication of difficulty.

Meilleret is a thickly wooded north-facing intermediate area, served by drags starting a long walk from the village centre. This sector is linked to Villars (covered by the lift pass), and the link will be much improved this winter, with a new lift and piste connecting Villars to the bottom of Diablerets' Laouissalet drag-lift.

Isenau is a small open section of easy runs reached by gondola from the top of the village, with long, easy runs back down to the village.

The piste map shows a run down from Isenau to the base station of the third area, at the Col du Pillon (1545m), but it is usually reached by bus. A gondola goes up to Pierres Pointes (2215m) with a black run down. This is the limit of the skiing covered by the Diablerets pass; you need the Alpes Vaudoise pass if you want to go on up by cable-car to ski the Diablerets glacier and the runs from it (see Gstaad, page 337).

The short runs on the glacier would hardly make Les Diablerets a **snow-reliable** resort even if they were covered by the usual lift pass. The skiing is low, and half of it is south-facing, with no snowmakers.

The long black run down to Col du Pillon is dark and forbidding, but not as super-tough as it looks. There is little else for **advanced skiers**.

The Combe d'Audon piste, from the glacier to Olden, is one of the great away-from-the-lifts runs of the Alps, and can be tackled by adventurous **intermediate** skiers. Moderate skiers will enjoy the Meilleret and Isenau skiing, and can now enjoy Villars.

There is an adequate nursery slope, served by an awkward rope tow, at the foot of Meilleret, but the best **beginners'** area is at sunny Isenau. Near-beginners will find Isenau ideal, apart from using drags all day.

There is 27km of **cross-country** skiing, including a pretty trail to Vers l'Eglise and a loop up at Isenau.

During peak season and when snow is in short supply elsewhere, **queues** for the glacier lifts can be serious.

It is not a great area for **mountain restaurants**. The best lunch-spots are at valley level. Vers l'Eglise is popular. The Vioz, close to the bottom of the Meilleret slopes, is a charming chalet.

A regular user of the Swiss **ski school** reports a slight slackening of standards, but our latest report is enthusiastic. The **kindergarten** by the nursery slopes provides lunch at the hotel les Sources, where all-day care is also available.

STAYING THERE

None of the **accommodation** is close to the more important Meilleret lifts. The Ermitage and Eurohotel are incongruously modern but comfortable 4-star hotels with pools. The 2-star Mon Abri is appealingly rustic, with a good restaurant and a warm welcome, although not ideally placed. The central, simple but jolly Auberge de la Poste is good value.

The 'excellent' Locanda Livia pizzeria and jolly Poste restaurant are relatively cheap places for **eating out**. The Vioz, a cosy wood-panelled chalet on the edge of the village, is more expensive.

Après-ski is very quiet during the week, when the Poste bar is the only place with any animation. Things get livelier at weekends, but the discos remain pretty dead. Car drivers can visit the nearby Gstaad.

There is pretty walking for **non-skiers**, and excursions to Montreux and Gstaad by public transport.

Mürren 1650m

HOW IT RATES

The skiing

Snow	★★★
Extent	★
Advanced	★★★
Intermediates	★★★
Beginners	★★
Convenience	★★★
Queues	★★★
Restaurants	★★

The rest

Scenery	★★★★★
Resort charm	★★★★★
Not skiing	★★★

✔ Tiny, charming, traditional 'traffic-free' village (reached only by funicular or cable-car) with narrow paths and chocolate-box chalets

✔ Stupendous scenery

✔ Good sports centre

✔ Beautiful, challenging run from the panoramic Schilthorn, with staggering views on the way down

✔ Good snow high up even when the rest of the region is suffering – and new lifts make more of the high skiing easily accessible

✔ Nearby Wengen offers a big ski area ideal for intermediates

✗ Extent of local piste skiing very limited for all grades of skier

✗ Little nightlife for club and disco lovers

✗ Like all other Swiss 'traffic-free' villages, Mürren is gradually admitting more service vehicles – though it is still about the nearest to truly traffic-free

ORIENTATION

Mürren is set on a shelf 800m above the Lauterbrunnen valley, opposite Wengen, and is reached by two-stage cable-car from Stechelberg or two-stage railway from Lauterbrunnen. The cable-car arrives at the south end of the tiny village, the railway at the north end, no more than ten minutes' walk away. Two further stages of the cable-car go up to the high skiing of Birg and the Schilthorn. Drag-lifts nearby serve the resort's main lower ski area; an ancient, short funicular halfway along the village gives access to the rest of the skiing.

Wengen can be reached by train from Lauterbrunnen. The skiing (connected with **Grindelwald**) is covered by the Jungfrau lift pass.

Mürren is one of our favourite resorts. There may be other Swiss mountain villages that are equally pretty, but none of them enjoys views like the ones that Mürren gives across the deep valley to the Eiger, Mönch and Jungfrau massifs: simply breathtaking.

But it isn't just the views that keep us going back to Mürren. The Schilthorn run draws us back like a magnet whenever we're driving through the Oberland. The limited ski area doesn't worry us because our visits are normally one-day affairs; holidaymakers, we concede, are likely to want to explore the large intermediate ski area of Wengen and Grindelwald on the opposite side of the valley. Getting there takes time. But who cares, when you've got the most spectacular scenery in the Alps to gaze at?

Others keep going back to Mürren because it's their second home, and that of many other British families. It was here that modern skiing was more-or-less invented by Sir Arnold Lunn, who organised the first-ever slalom race here in 1922. Twelve years earlier his father, Sir Henry, had persuaded the locals to open the railway in winter so he could bring the first winter package tour here (of public school chaps, of course). British families have been coming to Mürren year after year ever since – many of them members of the Kandahar Ski Club which Sir Arnold founded.

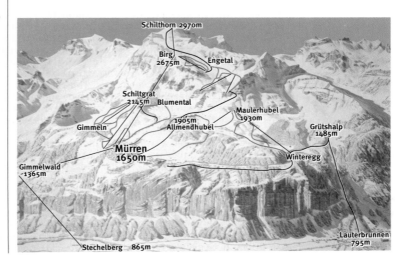

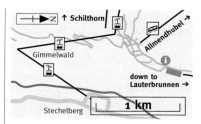

SKI FACTS

Jungfrau region –
including Wengen and
Grindelwald

Altitude	945m-2970m
Lifts	49
Pistes	183km
Green/Blue	30%
Red	50%
Black	20%
Artificial snow	15km

LIFT PASSES

95/96 prices in
Swiss francs
**Jungfrau Top Ski
Region**
Covers all lifts in
Wengen, Mürren and
Grindelwald, trains
between them and
Grindelwald ski-bus.
Beginners Points card
(adult 100 points 46,
lifts cost 4 to 10
points).
Main pass
1-day pass 52
6-day pass 232
Children
Under 16: 6-day pass
116 (50% off)
Under 6: free pass
Short-term passes
Single ascent tickets
for most lifts. Half-day
pass for First (adult
38), Kleine Scheidegg-
Männlichen (adult 40)
and Mürren-Schilthorn
(adult 38).
Notes Day pass price
for Mürren-Schilthorn
area only (35km of
piste, 16 lifts), as
Jungfrau Top Ski
Region pass is only
available for 2 days
or over. Discounts for
teenagers 16 to 21 (6-
day 186) and groups.
Alternative passes
1- and 2-day passes
available for First
(adult 2-day 90),
Mürren-Schilthorn
(adult 2-day 90) and
Kleine Scheidegg-
Männlichen (adult 2-
day 95, child 48).

The resort

Once you get there you can't fail to be
struck by Mürren's tranquillity and
beauty. It really is remarkable how
little development has taken place
over the years. The tiny village is
made up of paths and narrow lanes
weaving between tiny wooden chalets
and a handful of bigger hotel
buildings. The roofs and paths are
normally snow-covered for a long
season, giving the village a really
traditional Alpine feel.

Even in peak season, Mürren feels
peaceful and quiet. And although in
our summary above we've registered a
protest against the gradual increase in
'traffic', Mürren still isn't plagued by
electric carts and taxis as most of the
other traditional 'traffic-free' resorts
now are.

It's not the place to go for lively
nightlife, shopping or showing off
your latest gear to admiring hordes. It
is the place to go if you want
tranquillity and stunning views.

The skiing

For an internationally known resort,
Mürren has remarkably little skiing –
and much of it is tricky unless you are
a good skier. If you are used to the big
ski areas of most large French resorts
you'll soon be bored here.

But it has one of our favourite runs
in the world. And if intermediates are
happy to travel to the Wengen-
Grindelwald ski area they'll find more
than enough skiing to keep them
happy. This is covered on the area lift
pass, and is easily (though not
quickly) reached.

THE SKI AREA
Small but interesting
There are three interconnected ski
areas on the bottom part of the
mountain. The biggest of these is at
Schiltgrat, served by three drag-lifts
taking you up from behind the cable-
car station. You can also reach these
from the top of an ancient funicular

leaving from near the village centre
and serving the nursery slope area at
Allmendhubel. From there you can
also ski to the third **Maulerhubel**
area, served by a chair-lift up from the
Winteregg stop on the railway. This
lower skiing takes you from the
village's 1650m up to around 2000m.

Much more interesting is the higher
skiing reached by cable-car. The first
stage takes you to Birg at 2675m, from
where you can ski the **Engetal** area.
The final stage takes you up to the
2970m summit of the **Schilthorn**
and the Piz Gloria revolving
restaurant, made famous by the James
Bond film On Her Majesty's Secret
Service. In good snow conditions it's
possible to ski all the way down from
here (via the Engetal skiing and one
drag-lift) to Lauterbrunnen at 795m –
a distance of almost 16km and vertical
drop of 2175m. The annual Inferno
race – open to all comers, but with
roughly 5,000 applicants for the 1,400
available places – takes place in
January over this course. But the
skiing below Winteregg is all pretty
boring paths.

Mürren's high-altitude skiing has
been greatly improved by the
installation two seasons ago of two
new lifts below the Engetal. Good
skiers can now enjoy a long, testing
run from the Schilthorn without

SKI SCHOOL

94/95 prices in
Swiss francs

Swiss
Classes 6 days
2hr: 10am-noon
6 days (12hr): 123
Children's classes
Ages: from 4
6 days (12hr): 123
Private lessons
Half-day (2hr) or full-day (5hr)
100 for 2hr afternoon

descending all the way to the village, while not-so-good skiers have much more snowsure skiing available than they used to. Plans for a third new chair-lift, up to Birg, have been scrapped in favour of a more ambitious project, scheduled for next year at the earliest.

SNOW RELIABILITY
Good on the upper slopes
The Jungfrau ski region has struggled for good snow in quite a few recent winters. But when Wengen and Grindelwald (and the lower slopes here) have had problems, the Schilthorn and Engetal have often had packed powder snow because of their height and the north-facing direction of the Engetal skiing. Piste grooming is haphazard, except at Winteregg.

FOR ADVANCED SKIERS
One wonderful piste
The run from the top of the Schilthorn starts off with a steep, but not terrifying, mogul-field for the first few hundred metres. But it soon flattens out into some gentle skiing followed by a schuss to the Engetal skiing below Birg. After this, there's a wonderful wide run with stunning views to the Eiger, Mönch and Jungfrau over the valley. Now that new lifts have been built here you don't feel so far from civilisation, but the views remain staggeringly beautiful and the skiing possibilities have been expanded.

If you ignore the lifts and carry on down, you next hit the Kanonenrohr (or gunbarrel). This is a very narrow shelf with solid rock on one side, and a steep drop on the other (which is, thankfully, protected by nets). After an open slope and a scrappy zig-zag path, you then have a choice of routes back through the trees into the village or to the lower skiing.

There is a short but serious mogul run from Schiltgrat to the village (the Kandahar), but good skiers are more likely to be interested in the off-piste runs into the Blumental, both in this sector (the north-facing Blumenlucke run) and from Birg (the south-east-facing Tschingelchrachen), or the more adventurous runs from the Schilthorn.

FOR INTERMEDIATE SKIERS
Limited, but Wengen nearby
Keen piste bashers won't find enough skiing in Mürren to keep them happy for a week. You'd have to make a few expeditions to the ideal intermediate terrain of Wengen-Grindelwald.

The best easy cruising run in Mürren is the blue down to Winteregg. The reds in the other lower ski areas can get tough and mogulled, and the snow conditions can be poor. The area below Birg is much more attractive now that there are new lifts – and the snow in this high and fairly shady area is normally good.

Timid skiers should not attempt the top cable-car or the run down through the Kanonenrohr.

FOR BEGINNERS
Go elsewhere
The nursery slopes, at Allmendhubel at the top of the funicular, are fine. But once you get off those, there are no good, easy runs to graduate to. The Winteregg run and the area around Birg are about the easiest.

FOR CROSS-COUNTRY
Forget it
There is one small cross-country loop above the village in the Blumental. And there are extensive loops along the valley floor from Lauterbrunnen or Stechelberg. But snow is unreliable at valley height.

QUEUES
Generally not a problem
Mürren gets much less crowded than Wengen and Grindelwald. There are rarely queues except, occasionally, for the cable-cars. These usually arise when snow shortages bring skiers from less fortunate resorts.

MOUNTAIN RESTAURANTS
Disappointing at altitude
Piz Gloria, at the summit of the Schilthorn, has a revolving restaurant with a fabulous 360° panorama of peaks and lakes. But the service, food and welcome are disappointing and it has a functional atmosphere.

The self-service restaurant at the Birg mid-station is ordinary; there's a big sun terrace but it can get windy.

Lower down, we like the Suppenalp restaurant in the Blumental – rustic and away from the lifts, with good views and a large sun terrace.

It's easy to ski back to Mürren for lunch, where our favourite is the sun terrace at the back of the Bellevue hotel, near the foot of the funicular. The views are stunning and the alcoholic cakes well worth trying.

SKI SCHOOL
Now reliable?
The ski school has had a patchy reputation over the years, and several recent changes of management.

GETTING THERE

Air Zürich, transfer 3½hr. Bern, transfer 1½hr.

Rail Lauterbrunnen; transfer by mountain railway and tram.

CHILDCARE

The ski school takes children from age 4.

The nursery in the sports centre no longer cares for babies. It now takes children aged 3 or more all day, but those aged 2 to 3 for mornings only. There are few places, so it's advisable to book in advance through the tourist office.

PACKAGES

Chalets 'Unlimited', Inghams, Kuoni, Made to Measure, Plus Travel, Ski Club of GB, Swiss Travel Service

Lauterbrunnen Ski Miquel, Top Deck

ACTIVITIES

Indoor 'Alpine Sports Centre Mürren' swimming pool, whirlpool and children's pool, library, children's playroom, gymnasium, squash, sauna, solarium, judo, massage
Outdoor Artificial skating rink (curling, skating) free with Visitor's card, toboggan run to Gimmelwald, 15km cleared paths

TOURIST OFFICE

Postcode CH-3825
Tel 00 41 (36) 551616
Fax 553769

According to our most recent reports, the regime of Angelique Feuz, who took over in 1992, is delivering the goods: 'very high standards, very good English'.

FACILITIES FOR CHILDREN
Half-hearted
Mürren doesn't have ideal terrain for infants to find their skiing feet, and the facilities seem to echo this. The ski nursery is open only in the afternoons, and the day-care nursery at the sports centre (now limiting all-day care to children aged 3 or more) has not always met with parental approval, though we lack recent reports.

 # Staying there

Mürren is so small that location is not a concern. Nothing will be more than a few minutes' walk away. But there is something to be said for being based close to one or other of the arrival stations.

HOW TO GO
Mainly hotels, packaged or not
A handful of operators offer packages, but the range of accommodation is not wide.
Chalets As far as we know, there is now only one company offering one chalet – Chalets & Hotels Unlimited.
Hotels There are fewer than a dozen hotels, but they range widely in style.
££££ Mürren Palace Victorian pile close to the railway station – biggest and 'best' in town.
££££ Eiger Plain-looking 'chalet' blocks right next to railway station; good blend of efficiency and charm; swimming pool.
£££ Alpenruh Attractively renovated chalet next to the cable-car station.
££ Alpenblick Simple, small, modern chalet near railway station.
Self-catering There are plenty of chalets and apartments to rent in the village, but they are not packaged on the UK market. There are adequate shops, including a butcher's.

STAYING DOWN THE VALLEY
A cheaper option
See the Wengen chapter for options in Lauterbrunnen and Interlaken. If you want to ski both the Wengen and Mürren areas, Lauterbrunnen in particular is a good budget place to stay. It has a ski resort (rather than town) atmosphere and access to and from both main resorts until late (covered by your ski pass).

STAYING UP THE MOUNTAIN
Two possibilities
Two of the attractive restaurants in the Blumental – the Sonnenberg and Flora-Suppenalp – have cheap dormitory-style accommodation.

EATING OUT
Mainly in hotels
There's not a lot of choice except for hotel restaurants. The rustic Stägerstübli is the main alternative – a popular bar as well as restaurant. The hotels Bellevue, Eiger and Palace have good reputations.

APRES-SKI
Quiet
Mürren isn't a place for party animals. The main haunts are hotel based. The Tachi in the Eiger is the liveliest bar, although the Balloon bar in the Palace and the Belmont are good for a civilised après-ski drink. The Stägerstübli is the place to meet locals. Teenagers fill up the little Blienilichäller disco until it closes at a mere 2am.

FOR NON-SKIERS
Tranquillity but not much else
Other than admiring the peace and beauty, there isn't a lot to amuse inactive non-skiers. It's not the place to go for people-watching. But there is a remarkably good sports centre, with a splendidly set outdoor ice rink.
Meeting up with skiers for lunch is easy – it's no problem for them to ski down to the village and the only problem for non-skiers meeting at the top of the cable-car is the expense – SF52, around £25.

Saas-Fee 1800m

✔ *Good percentage of high-altitude, snowsure skiing*

✔ *Two crucial new lifts last season improved access to highest skiing*

✔ *Spectacular setting amid high peaks and glaciers*

✔ *Attractive, traditional, 'traffic-free' village*

✔ *Good amenities including a hillside dedicated to non-skiers*

✗ *Disappointingly small ski area*

✗ *Glacier stifles off-piste potential*

✗ *Much of the area is in shadow in mid-winter – cold and dark*

✗ *Bad weather can shut down the skiing completely*

✗ *Parts of the village are inconvenient for the skiing*

✗ *Rocky home runs need good snow-cover*

Saas-Fee is the kind of place people fall for in a big way. It's got lots of Swiss charm and the setting is just stunning – impressive glaciers and 4000m peaks surround the place.

Unfortunately, the dramatic surroundings are also the reason for Saas-Fee's skiing being rather less spectacular than its scenery – the steep terrain and extensive areas of glacier severely restrict the area's development. The tight ring of high peaks can also make the village seem dark and cold for long periods in mid-winter; which is good for the snow, not good for those seeking blue skies and sunshine. It's a place not without its faults and its critics – but it's too good to be ignored, especially if you're taking a late-season holiday. Snow conditions here are often among the best in the Alps when many other resorts are struggling to provide any skiing. That consideration, together with its Alpine charm and wonderful scenery, is enough to continue attracting skiers of all abilities.

ORIENTATION

Saas-Fee is a long, narrow, traffic-free village, around 2km from end to end. Visitors arrive at a large car-parking area at the entrance to the resort – close to the village centre and the start of the giant Alpin Express gondola. The other major lifts – two gondolas and a cable-car – start from the far, southern end of the village, at the foot of the slopes. Saas-Fee is the main resort of the Saastal – **Saas-Almagell, Saas-Balen** and **Saas-Grund** are a short bus-ride away, down in the valley. The ski areas are not linked but are covered by a single lift pass. Day trips to **Zermatt, Grächen** and **Crans-Montana** are realistic options.

SKI FACTS

Altitude	1800m-3620m
Lifts	27
Pistes	100km
Green/Blue	25%
Red	50%
Black	25%
Artificial snow	2km

 ## The resort

Like nearby Zermatt, Saas-Fee is car-free but somewhat plagued by electric vehicles. On most other counts, Saas-Fee and its more exalted neighbour are a long way apart in style. Saas-Fee still manages to feel like a village rather than a 'destination resort' – the nearly-9,000 visitor beds are well spread out and have not yet overwhelmed the attractive old chalets, cow sheds and narrow streets. And there's little of the glamour and greed that, for many, spoil Zermatt.

The spread-out nature of the village is a disadvantage – it's a long walk (or expensive taxi-ride) from one end to the other – though for skiing purposes this is less important than it was, because the new Alpin express starts below the centre.

The centre of the village is perhaps a little disappointing – there is the ski school office, the church and a few more shops than elsewhere – but it lacks a feeling of being at the heart of things. The restaurant terraces at the foot of the slopes, however, are anything but disappointing. The views up to the horseshoe of 4000m peaks is breath-taking – you can see exactly why the village is known as 'The Pearl of The Alps'.

There are some very smart hotels (plus many others that are more reasonably priced) and plenty of good eating and drinking places. During days when the spring sun is beating down, Saas-Fee is a quite beautiful place just to stroll around and relax. It's also a major centre for ski-touring – several nearby peaks can be climbed and the extended Haute Route from Chamonix ends at Saas-Fee.

 ## The skiing

The main Felskinn-Längfluh area has been improved by recent additions to the lift system. And the skiing is set in classic Alpine surroundings, providing something for everyone but, for some skiers, simply not enough kilometres of piste. It seems to have been a question of fitting in what the mountain allows, rather than designing what might be preferred. For ski-mountaineering and ski-touring, this is one of the top places.

LIFT PASSES

95/96 prices in
Swiss francs
Saas Fee area
Covers all lifts in Saas
Fee only.
Beginners Village area
pass covers 3
beginners' lifts.
Main pass
1-day pass 56
6-day pass 260
Senior citizens
Over 62: 6-day pass
240 (8% off)
Children
Under 16: 6-day pass
150 (41% off)
Under 6: free pass
Short-term passes
Single and return
tickets on most main
lifts. Half-day pass
from noon (adult 45).
Notes Discount for
groups of 20 or more.
Alternative passes
Separate passes for
each of the other ski
areas in the Saastal
(Saas Grund, Saas
Almagell, Saas Balen).
Pass for all four
villages in the Saastal
also available, and
includes free ski-bus
between them.

THE SKI AREA

A glacier runs through it

Saas-Fee's smallest ski area, **Plattjen**, is reached by gondola from the southern end of the village at the foot of the slopes. This is a small intermediates' hill – frequently used by the ski school 'middle classes' – and has only one chair-lift in addition to the gondola.

The main **Felskinn-Längfluh** area, where most of the skiing is to be found, can be reached in a variety of ways. The Felskinn cable-car, which starts a short drag-lift away from the foot of the pistes, takes you directly to Felskinn at 3000m and the entrance to the Metro Alpin (an underground funicular which hurtles through the rock beneath the glacier and emerges at 3500m. From the top of the Metro, two drag-lifts access the high point of the system – 3620m.

The new Alpin Express 30-person gondola now provides an alternative route to Felskinn. It starts on the fringe of the village, mid-way between the slopes and parking area, and gets bodies out of the village very efficiently. It has a mid-station at Maste 4.

From the same station as the Plattjen lift, another gondola leaves for Spielboden. This is met by a cable-car which takes you up to Längfluh.

Felskinn and Längfluh are themselves almost separate sectors, squeezed out onto opposite fringes of an off-limits glacier area. Connections

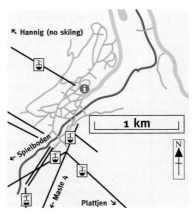

between the two were vastly improved last season by a new drag-lift which takes you up from Längfluh to a point where you can ski down into the Felskinn area. It has replaced the old snowcat service and saved you the extra SF6 that each ride used to cost. The Längfluh and Felskinn sectors are served mainly by drag-lifts, and you can ski from both all the way down to the village.

The nursery slopes are at the edge of the village and are quite extensive.

SNOW RELIABILITY

One of the best

If Saas-Fee is suffering from lack of snow, it's likely that almost everywhere else has problems too. The village is at 1800m, enough for village-level snow during much of the season.

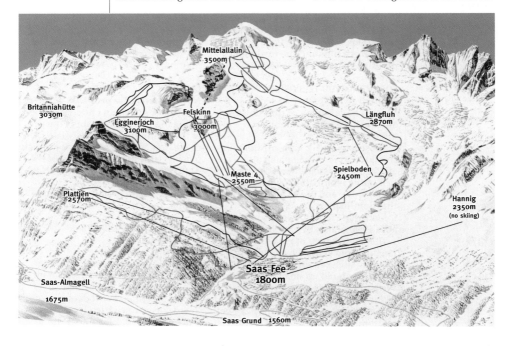

SKI SCHOOL

95/96 prices in
Swiss francs

Swiss
Classes 5 days
4hr: 9.45-11.45 and
1.30-3.30
5 full days: 178
Children's classes
Ages: from 5
5 full days: 178
Private lessons
Hourly or daily
54 for 1hr for 1 to 2
people

Most of the skiing is north-facing and much of it above 2500m, which makes Saas Fee one of the most reliable resorts in the Alps for snow. On the glacier there is skiing all year round. Even so, rocks and stones can be a bit of a nuisance on the lower slopes. A short stretch of snow cannons on the nursery slopes normally ensures that they stay in working order.

FOR ADVANCED SKIERS
A few good challenges on-piste
One of the disadvantages of Saas-Fee's glacier is the limitations it imposes on off-piste skiing – crevasse danger is extreme, and good skiers have to content themselves with the pisted areas or take a guide for limited off-piste or extensive ski-touring. Late-season ski-tours are a big feature in this region.

There is not a vast amount of steep skiing, but there's sufficient technical challenge to keep good skiers busy for a while. The highest drag-lift, on the left above Felskinn, serves two short, steep blacks and one easy one. The lift itself is a bit of a challenge – we've been lifted off the ground here several times. The extremely short Spielboden drag delivers skiers to the top of an equally short, steep and lumpy slope in full view of the terrace below – usually with an audience expecting some entertainment. The slopes around the top of Längfluh often provide good powder skiing. The long return runs to the village from both Längfluh and Felskinn are not easy, with some genuinely black sections which can be especially tricky in icy conditions.

The black runs and the tree-skiing on Plattjen are worth exploring.

FOR INTERMEDIATE SKIERS
Enough to do; plenty to see
Plattjen has a variety of runs down it, all of them skiable by ambitious intermediates.

Those looking for long cruising runs should head for Mittelallalin and try all the options from there. The top half of the mountain, down as far as Maste 4 (the end of the first stage of the Alpin Express), is ideal intermediate terrain, with the added advantage of usually excellent snow.

There is a variety of gradient, ranging from gentle blue confidence-building slopes to some steeper reds which can build up smallish bumps. We particularly like the runs at the top of the Metro first-thing on a late-season morning – though they can be mind-numbingly cold in early season.

The descent from the top right down to the village is a great challenge for those wishing to prove their stamina. Either way, via Felskinn or via Längfluh, it's a superb descent of 1800m vertical. The runs on the bottom half of the mountain all have some tricky sections, and nervous or tired intermediates would be well advised to take a lift down.

FOR BEGINNERS
A nice place to start
There's a good, large nursery area right at the edge of the village. Three lifts serve an out-of-the-way area without through-traffic of experienced skiers going back to the village. Graduates of the nursery slopes will probably want to head for the gentle blue area on Felskinn just above Maste 4 – the return trip is best completed by Alpin Express. And there are further gentle blues at the very top of the mountain, from where it's possible to ski down the glacier to the Längfluh side – again the lifts would need to be used to return to the village.

There's a useful pass for beginners who aren't ready to go up the mountain, allowing access to all the short lifts at the edge of the village.

FOR CROSS-COUNTRY
A good local trail and lots nearby
There is one short (8km) pleasant, prepared trail at the edge of the village, away from all those noisy downhillers. It snakes up through the woods, providing about 150m of climb and nice views. In the valley there are far more options, including 25km of track and plenty of suitable terrain beyond Saas-Almagell, towards Mattmark.

QUEUES
Not so much of a problem
In the past, the main criticism of the skiing has been the appalling queues at the main lifts, particularly late in the season. This problem is now much relieved with the construction of the Alpin Express, which now goes all the way up to Felskinn. This year's reporters experienced no problems – even in high season.

MOUNTAIN RESTAURANTS
A couple of gems
The main claim to fame belongs to the one at Mittelallalin – at 3500m the world's highest revolving restaurant. It doesn't actually have the best views on the mountain but it does provide 360-degrees-worth each hour. There's a perfectly good café underneath it

which doesn't rotate but is cheaper. All the major lift stations have a restaurant – generally functional rather than charming. At Spielboden there's a large terrace with good views of some tricky slopes. At Längfluh the terrace has splendid views of the huge crevasses in the glacier.

The best of the huts are slightly off the beaten track: the Berghaus Plattjen (not to be confused with the place at the top of the Plattjen lifts) and the Gletscher-Grotte, half-way down from Spielboden. Both provide excellent food and a lovely old, smoky hut kind of ambience – especially good when the weather's foul. The Britanniahütte is a real mountain refuge, awkward to get to but, if you're up to the trek, best for mountain atmosphere and views.

SKI SCHOOL
Attitude problems

It's the Swiss ski school or nothing in Saas-Fee. Unfortunately the lack of competition creates problems – too often classes are overlarge, with a wide range of abilities in a class, and some instructors have limited English.

FACILITIES FOR CHILDREN
Half-hearted

Neither the ski school nor the non-ski kindergarten takes children younger than age 5. One solution for people with younger children is to use one of the hotels that have an in-house kindergarten. Although it has no kindergarten, the hotel Beau-Site has an 'excellent' play-room.

 Staying there

Staying near one of the main lifts makes most sense. If you do end up at the wrong (north) end of the village – and most of the budget accommodation is there – using the facilities for depositing skis and boots near the lifts will ease the pain. It's worth getting a guest card for miscellaneous discounts.

HOW TO GO
Check the location

Quite a few tour operators include Saas-Fee, providing an excellent range of hotel accommodation, but chalets and apartments are few.

Chalets For a village that looks to be composed almost entirely of chalets, there are surprisingly few offered by UK tour operators – Crystal have the only ones that we know of. Their Feeblick and Schönegg chalets are simple, friendly old places. Viktoria is

more modern, and has en suite bathrooms. None is very conveniently placed for skiing.

Hotels 50-plus hotels (the number continues to increase) means lots of choice. The great majority are 3-star, with half a dozen 4-star places and a similar number of 2-star. There are also many lesser-graded but comfortable places.

££££££ Fletschhorn Elegant chalet, a long way out of the village in the wrong direction, but in a lovely tranquil setting – and with fabulous nouvelle food (Michelin star).

££££ Walliserhof Lively, ritzy 4-star, smart but rather brash. Pool.

££££ Schweizerhof Stylish new place in quiet, but not convenient, position just above centre (can leave kit at Saaserhof). 'Excellent' food. Pool.

£££ Beau-Site 'First-rate' but quiet 4-star in central, but not convenient, position. Good food. Pool.

£££ Saaserhof Modern chalet in good position, just over the river from the nursery slopes.

£££ Ambassador Modern chalet, well placed close to the nursery slopes.

£££ Alphubel At the wrong end of town, but one of the best bets for families, with its own kindergarten.

£££ Hohnegg A more rustic alternative to the Fletschhorn, in a similarly remote spot; only eight rooms.

££ Belmont The most appealing of the hotels looking directly on to the nursery slopes.

££ Zur Mühle Rustic restaurant with three bedrooms, well placed by the river bridge.

Self-catering A number of the least attractive looking buildings, at the north end of the village, house apartments which are featured by UK tour operators. Fortunately, the apartments themselves tend to be spacious, clean and well-equipped. Ski convenience is poor, but independent travellers have apartments available in better situated parts of the village. The Residence Hotel Atlantic has unusually comfortable studios, ideal for couples. They come complete with in-house hotel amenities. Families or groups could consider the Tobias and Allalin apartments.

EATING OUT
No shortage – some high class

There are 60 restaurants to choose from. Gastronomes will probably want to head for the Michelin-starred Fletschhorn (see Hotels) or the Hohnegg – their high reputations and high prices are widely judged to be

CHILDCARE

The ski school takes children from age 5, and can provide lunchtime care. The kindergarten at the Hotel Berghof (572484) takes children from age 2½ to 6, from 9am to 5pm.

A couple of 3-star hotels – the Alphubel and the Europa Minotel – have their own kindergartens.

GETTING THERE

Air Geneva, transfer 3½hr.

Rail Brig (34km); regular buses from station.

PACKAGES
Crystal, Inghams, Kuoni, Lagrange, Made to Measure, Plus Travel, Ski Choice, SkiGower, Swiss Travel Service, Thomson

Saas-Grund PGL Ski Europe

ACTIVITIES
Indoor Bielen Leisure centre (swimming, jacuzzi, steam bath, solarium, sauna, massage, tennis, gym, whirlpool), cinema, museum, concerts, badminton
Outdoor 20km cleared paths, natural skating rink (skating, curling, ice-hockey), ski-bob runs, toboggan run

TOURIST OFFICE
Postcode CH-3906
Tel 00 41 (28) 571457
Fax 571860

justified. Others will no doubt make do with the large selection of hotel restaurants and other eateries in town. Most hotel restaurants welcome non-residents and they usually offer set meals at a good price. The food tends to be traditional – the Belmont and the Tenne are typical; the latter also does charcoal grill specialities. Boccalino is cheap and does pizzas – book or get there early. Alp-Hitta specialises in rustic surroundings and food. The Skihütte is a good bet for both lunch and dinner. The hotel Dom has a splendid restaurant specialising in endless different varieties of rösti.

Locals assure us that the following are all good: Arvu-Stuba, Zur Mühle, the Gorge, the Feeloch and the Ferme.

APRES-SKI
Excellent and varied
For that tea-time drink the best places are down near the lifts, where it's usually pretty lively for at least a couple of hours. Nesti's ski-bar, Zur Mühle and the little snowbars are all popular. Later on Nesti's and the Go-Inn get busy and keep going till 1am. The Arts Club is smarter and more sophisticated, with live music. The Metro Bar is like being in a 19th century mineshaft and is popular with locals; the Happy Bar has huge wood carvings, heavy music and lots of Brits; Pop Corn is popular early and after 9pm with the younger crowd – it opens onto a snowboard shop. The Metropole has a disco and three other bars. For a quieter drink, try the Roadhouse, the tiny Sissy Bar or the traditional Christiana Stubl.

FOR NON-SKIERS
A whole 'mountain' just for you
Non-skiers are likely to enjoy Saas-Fee much better than a lot of places, except perhaps in the middle of winter, when it can seem permanently cold and dark. It's easy to travel around the mountain on the gondolas and cable-car. There is now a whole mountainside, the Hannig, dedicated to the art of non-skiing. Skiers are banned – eating, drinking, sunning, walking, tobogganing and parapenting take priority. In the village, the splendid Bielen leisure centre has the usual facilities, but also boasts a 25m pool, indoor tennis courts and an unusual lounging area with sunlamps which turn on and off at intervals.

Skating and curling are further possibilities. A close look at the glacier is a must – the views from the terrace at Längfluh are the best; at Mittelallalin there are the added attractions of the rotating restaurant and the ice-cave.

Saas-Grund 1570m
Saas-Grund stretches for 2km along the valley road and the river Vispe below Saas-Fee. The Saas-Fee road turns off from here. It is an ancient farming community which has expanded enormously in recent years, yet has managed to retain some rustic charm. It is Saas-Fee's poor relation, with correspondingly lower prices. The regular bus service means it is an acceptable alternative to staying in Saas-Fee. But don't expect the same charm, beauty or atmosphere.

There are around 15 hotels – mostly 2- or 3-star with 30 or 40 beds each and rooms at between SF50 and SF70 per person per night. The Café Sporting is good value and the hotel Rodania does fine fondues at a good price and puts on a disco.

Saas-Grund has its own pleasant, quiet, small (20km of piste) ski area. A gondola takes you up to the Kreuzboden mid-station at 2400m. A group of short lifts around here do nicely for beginners – particularly later in the season, when many lower nursery slopes have already faded away. The second stage goes to 3100m, with glorious views of the Saas-Fee ski area, a couple of nice runs down and a restaurant serving good Swiss food at reasonable prices. The bars near the base station get pretty lively when the skiing stops.

The resort has its own ski school and ski kindergarten, though we suspect a lack of English-speakers in both could be a problem. There is no non-skiing crèche.

Saas-Almagell 1670m
Ten minutes along the valley by bus from Grund lies Saas-Almagell, a compact, traditional old village. Its small, wooded ski area comes into its own in bad weather. Walkers are well catered for and the village offers 26km of fine, wooded cross-country trails in both directions through its high snow-reliable valley. Its fair range of accommodation includes 12 hotels and a pleasant, informal pension, the Edelweiss.

St Moritz 1800m

HOW IT RATES

The skiing

Snow	★★★★
Extent	★★★★★
Advanced	★★★★
Intermediates	★★★★
Beginners	★★
Convenience	★★
Queues	★★
Restaurants	★★★★

The rest

Scenery	★★★★★
Resort charm	★★
Not skiing	★★★★★

ORIENTATION

St Moritz sits in a high valley, reached from the rest of Switzerland by high passes or tunnels.

It spreads around the western end of a lake. Dorf is the main town, built on a steep hillside to the north of the lake, beneath the ski slopes of Corviglia (reached by funicular). Other lifts go up into the Corviglia skiing from **Celerina**, 2km down the valley, and from St Moritz Bad, which spreads up the valley from the the lakeside.

There are several other ski areas. The main one is Corvatsch – up the valley, on the opposite side from Corviglia, with lifts at Surlej, on the fringe of **Silvaplana**, and **Sils Maria**. There are hotels and cross-country skiing down the valley, in and around the nearby villages of **Samedan** and **Pontresina**, and 5km from St Moritz up the Bernina valley, towards the Lagalb and Diavolezza ski areas. Trips further afield to other resorts such as **Lenzerheide** and **Davos** are possible, but not easy.

✔ *Beautiful scenery – St Moritz is set next to a picturesque lake in a spectacular high valley*

✔ *Non-skiing amenities second to none – including the Cresta run*

✔ *A lot of skiing – half a dozen distinct ski areas*

✔ *Fairly snowsure skiing, thanks to altitude and extensive snowmaking*

✔ *Attracts a 'nice' class of clientele – no hooligan skiers*

✔ *Good après-ski, catering for all ages from 18 to 80, not just the jet set*

✔ *Numerous good (but expensive) mountain restaurants*

✔ *Celerina is an attractive villagey alternative to staying in St Moritz*

✔ *Painless rail access via Zürich*

✗ *Views from St Moritz Dorf (and elsewhere) are blighted by the hideous blocks of St Moritz Bad*

✗ *Dorf has an ordinary, towny feel, with little Alpine character*

✗ *No proper nursery slopes at resort level – except at Celerina*

✗ *Road access involves high mountain passes or car-carrying rail tunnels*

✗ *Long overland airport transfers – over four hours*

✗ *Lift queues can be a problem*

✗ *Not much woodland skiing*

✗ *Expensive; even the Swiss complain that St Moritz is pricey*

St Moritz is Switzerland's most famous 'exclusive' ski resort: glitzy, pricey, fashionable and, above all, the place to be seen. But, rather like Aspen in the US, St Moritz is not as snooty as its popular image might lead you to expect. In fact – heaven forbid – they have even opened a half-pipe track for snowboarders on Corviglia. What's more, the skiing – again, rather like Aspen – is superb, with something for everybody. We don't rate it highly for complete beginners, but there are worse places to learn to ski, and there is some compensation in the non-skiing diversions, which are unrivalled.

The town of St Moritz itself is surprisingly unattractive. It seems far removed from the chocolate box image of the Swiss mountain resort, all wooden huts and cows with bells round their necks. Here, many of the buildings resemble council flats (extremely neat and clean ones – this is Switzerland, after all).

St Moritz itself may be unattractive to look at, but its setting, beside the lowest in a long chain of lakes at the foot of the 4000m Piz Bernina, is spectacular. This is one of those areas where our progress on skis is regularly interrupted by the need to stand and gaze. It may not have quite the drama of the Jungfrau massif, or the Matterhorn, or the Dolomites, but its wide and glorious mountain landscapes make skiing here a special experience.

🏠 The resort

St Moritz has two distinct parts. Dorf is the main part, built on a steep hillside above the lake. This is the fashionable St Moritz – a busy, compact town with two main streets lined with expensive boutiques selling Rolex watches, Cartier jewellery and Hermes scarves, a few side lanes and a single small main square. Great big expensive hotels on the fringe of this central area stand guard over the lake, including the famous names – the Palace, the Kulm and the Carlton.

St Moritz Bad is less smart – a spa resort, spread around one end of the lake on the valley floor. There are less prestigious hotels, restaurants and shops, and it is well placed for cross-country skiing as well as walks around the lake. In winter, the lake is used for all sorts of eccentric activities, including equestrian activities (such as polo), 'ice golf' and even cricket.

Many of the modern buildings, especially down at lake level, are uncompromisingly rectangular and obtrusive. The damage done to the otherwise superb views across the lake from Dorf – not least from the posh hotels – has to be seen to be believed.

🎿 The skiing

Like the resort, most of the slopes are made for posing. There is the occasional black run, but few of them are seriously steep, and most pistes are so well groomed that you can easily swoop down with little chance that you'll make a fool of yourself on a rogue mogul. There are lots of long and generally wide runs, with varied terrain. There is tough skiing off-piste, and it does not get skied out as it does in more macho resorts. Beginners' slopes are few and far between.

THE SKI AREA
Big but broken up
There is a lot of skiing. With a claimed 350km, the Upper Engadine may not be quite in the Trois Vallées league, but it is definitely in the next division.

The skiing is in several distinct ski areas. The main ones, shown on our piste maps, are Corviglia-Marguns, close to the resort, and Corvatsch-Furtschellas, which starts a bus-ride away (although you can ski back to Bad). Diavolezza, Piz Lagalb, Alp Languard and a few other bits and pieces more remote from St Moritz make up the rest. If you want to ski

these areas (and some are well worth an outing), it helps to have a car, although the bus service is adequate.

From St Moritz Dorf a two-stage monorail train goes up to **Corviglia**, in itself a fair-sized area, with slopes facing east and south. The peak of Piz Nair, reached from here by cable-car, splits the area in two – the sunny runs towards the main valley, and the less sunny ones in the bowls to the north. From Corviglia you can ski down (conditions permitting) to Dorf and Bad, and via the lower lift junction of Marguns to Celerina – a pleasant run in good snow conditions, mostly well away from the gondola.

From Surlej, a few miles up the valley from St Moritz, a two-stage cable-car takes you to up to the north-facing slopes of **Corvatsch**. From there you have a choice of red runs down to Murtel and Alp Margun. From the latter you can work your way across the mountain to **Furtschellas**, also reached directly by cable-car from Sils Maria. Runs go down to Sils Maria and Surlej, and to the fringes of Bad.

Diavolezza (2978m) and Lagalb (2959m) are the main additional ski areas, on opposite sides of the road to the Bernina pass to Italy, less than half an hour away by bus. **Diavolezza** has excellent north-facing pistes of 900m vertical, down under its big (125-person) main cable-car, and a very popular off-piste route, off the back of the mountain, across a glacier and down a valley beneath Piz Bernina to Morteratsch. **Lagalb** is a smaller area of quite challenging skiing, with an 80-person cable-car serving the west-facing front slope of 850m vertical and a couple of drags on the south side.

SNOW RELIABILITY
Reasonable
This corner of the Alps has a rather dry climate, but the altitude means that any available precipitation is likely to be snowy. The snowmaking is quite widespread, with guns in every sector of the skiing: several easy slopes around Corviglia are covered, as is an excellent 800m vertical red run on Corvatsch (Murtel to Surlej) and much of the 900m vertical face of Diavolezza; Lagalb gets a new installation this winter.

FOR ADVANCED SKIERS
Dispersed challenges
Good skiers looking for challenges are liable to find the St Moritz skiing disappointing unless they are prepared to venture off-piste. Red runs far outnumber the black, and mogul fields

SKI FACTS
Altitude 1720m-3300m
Lifts	55
Pistes	350km
Green/Blue	16%
Red	71%
Black	13%
Artificial snow	15km

LIFT PASSES

95/96 prices in Swiss francs
Upper Engadine
Covers all lifts in St Moritz, Celerina, Surlej, Sils Maria, Maloja, Lagalb, Diavolezza, Pontresina, Punt Muragl, Samedan, Müsella and Zuoz, and the swimming pools in St Moritz and Pontresina.
Main pass
1-day pass 54
6-day pass 258
Children
Under 16: 6-day pass 129 (50% off)
Under 6: free pass
Short-term passes
Half-day pass from 11.45 (adult 45).
Alternative periods
5 (adult 248) or 10 (adult 418) days skiing in the season.
Notes Discount for groups of 15 or more. Ski pass also valid in Gstaad Superski region, and gives one days skiing in Livigno.
Alternative passes
Half-day and day passes for individual areas within the Upper Engadine.

are few and far between. There are some serious black runs, but they are dotted about the area in different sectors. (On the positive side, this means that if you want to ski the same area as less adventurous friends, there will always be something challenging to do, not far away.)

The black runs at Lagalb and Diavolezza are the most testing pistes. The direct Minor run down the Lagalb cable-car offers 850m vertical of continuous moguls.

There are plenty of opportunities to venture a little way off-piste in search of challenges – there is an excellent north-facing slope immediately above the Marguns lift junction, for example. Experts head for tough off-piste runs on Piz Nair, such as Guinness (down into the Val Suvretta) and Niarchos (named after the Greek who is a major shareholder in the lift company), or on the Corvatsch summit. More serious expeditions can be undertaken – such as down the splendid Roseg valley from Corvatsch. The off-piste potential, particularly from Corviglia and Corvatsch, is all the better for being relatively little exploited. Instructors are allowed to guide only on certain slopes; for the Roseg valley run, for example, you have to take a proper mountain guide.

FOR INTERMEDIATE SKIERS
Good but flattering
St Moritz is great for intermediates. Most of the pistes are easyish reds that could well have been graded blue.

One of the finest runs is the Hahnensee, from the northern limit of the Corvatsch lift system down to St Moritz Bad – a black-graded run that is of red difficulty for most of its 6km length and 900m vertical drop. (Start from the top of Corvatsch and you can double both these figures, but you have to ride a chair-lift in the middle.) It's a five-minute walk from the end of the Hahnensee run to the Signal cable-car up to Corviglia.

The skiing at Diavolezza is mostly intermediate. There is an easy open slope at the top, now served by a fast quad chair, and a splendid long intermediate run back down under the lift, with mogulled variants. The popular off-piste run to Morteratsch requires only a bit of energy for the gentle 15-minute climb once you've crossed the initial stretch of glacier, and a bit of nerve for the narrow ledge that follows. And the views along the way are splendid.

Lagalb is definitely the place to go for the most challenging piste skiing.

FOR BEGINNERS
Not much to offer
St Moritz is not an ideal place for beginners. It sits in a deep, steep-sided valley, with very little space for nursery slopes at the lower levels. Beginners start up the mountain, at Salastrains or Corviglia, or slightly out of town, at Suvretta. Celerina has good, broad nursery slopes at village level. Progression from the nursery slopes to intermediate runs is rather awkward, as these invariably include the odd difficult section.

FOR CROSS COUNTRY
Excellent; go to Pontresina
The Engadine is one of the premier regions in the Alps for cross-country, with 150km of trails of all levels of difficulty, amid splendid scenery and with pretty reliable snow. Pontresina is one of the best locations in the region, and also has good skating and curling rinks and swimming pools. There are floodlit loops at Bad, Pontresina and Samedan.

QUEUES
Crowds can be a problem
St Moritz has invested heavily in new lifts designed to meet international and indeed intercontinental expectations. High-speed quad chairs with bubble covers are now common – three new ones were installed last year

---

The Cresta Run

No trip to St Moritz is really complete without a visit to the Cresta Run. It's the last bastion of Britishness (until recently, payment had to be made in sterling) and male chauvinism (women have been banned since 1929 – for their own good, of course).

Any adult male can pay around £200 for five rides on the famous run (helmet and lunch at the Kulm hotel included). Watch out for the Shuttlecock corner – that's where most people come off, and the ambulances ply for trade. You lie on a toboggan (aptly called a 'skeleton') and hurtle head-first down a sheet ice gully from St Moritz to Celerina. David Gower, Sandy Gall and many others are addicts. Fancy giving it a go?

SKI SCHOOL

95/96 prices in Swiss francs

St Moritz
Classes 6 days
4hr: 10am–noon and 1.30–3.30
6 full days: 230
Children's classes
Ages: from 5
6 full days: 230
Private lessons
Half-day (2hr) or full-day (5hr)
140 for half-day

Suvretta
Small groups of 4 to 6 people
Classes 6 days
2hr, 3hr, 4hr or full-day (5hr)
1 full day: 365
Children's classes
Ages: up to 15
3 days (4hr): 170
Private lessons
Hourly or daily
80 for 1hr between noon and 1pm

CHILDCARE

The St Moritz ski school operates a pick-up service for children. Both schools provide all-day care.

Children aged 3 or more can be looked after in hotels – there are nurseries in the Carlton, the Parkhotel Kurhaus and the Schweizerhof, open from 9am to 4.30 or 5pm.

on Corviglia alone – and one reporter reckons that piste crowding is now more of a problem that lift queues. This winter, one of Switzerland's first six-seat chair-lifts will open on Trais Fluors above Marguns (at present served by a pair of drags). But it's also true that the area as a whole is over-dependent on cable-cars – most not of enormous capacity – both for getting up the mountain from resort level and for access to the peaks from mid-mountain; queues are the inevitable result. Some of the cable-cars have a system of pre-allocation of space, like the Valluga at St Anton.

MOUNTAIN RESTAURANTS
Some special places
Mountain restaurants are plentiful, and include some of the most glamorous in Europe. Prices can be high, and reservations are often necessary, especially if you want to sit in particular spots.

On Corviglia, the highlight (for those who can afford it) is the Marmite; but at £35 for a plate of pasta, the place is literally exclusive, and irrelevant to most of us. Don't expect much Alpine charm for your money: the Marmite is housed in the brand-new Corviglia lift station, known locally as the highest post office in Switzerland because of its bright yellow paintwork. At the far western end of the lift network, behind Piz Nair, is a recently built but attractive chalet, Lej de la Pesch.

On the Corvatsch side, Fuorcla Surlej is a delightfully secluded spot, as is Hahnensee, on the lift-free run of the same name down to St Moritz Bad – a splendid place to pause in the afternoon sun on the way home. On stormy days, the most captivating

place is the extremely rustic Alpetta, at Alp Margun (table service inside).

The hotel-restaurant up at Muottas Muragl, between Celerina and Pontresina, is well worth a visit. It has truly spectacular views overlooking the valley, as well as good food. But the best time to go is at sunset; the funicular runs half-hourly.

SKI SCHOOL
Internal competition
The St Moritz and Suvretta schools are apparently both branches of the national Swiss school. We lack recent reports on them. Some of the posh hotels have their own instructors, for private lessons only.

FACILITIES FOR CHILDREN
Hotel-based nurseries
Children wanting ski lessons have a choice of the two schools, but others must be deposited at one of the three hotels with nurseries: the Parkhotel Kurhaus close to the cable-car in Bad, and two others up in Dorf. Club Med has its usual good facilities.

 # Staying there

For high society you will want to stay in Dorf. If economy matters, you will probably have to stay in Bad – or stay at home. You can find convenient accommodation in either part of the resort, but not easily. Bad has the advantage that you can ski back to it from Corvatsch and Corviglia. But Celerina is our preferred base.

HOW TO GO
More packages than you expect
Considering how rarely we hear from anyone who has visited St Moritz, it's quite surprising to find that more than a handful of tour operators package the resort. But there is much more choice of accommodation open to the independent traveller. As well as the many conventional hotels, there are two branches of Club Med – and going with an operator like this, who does all-inclusive deals, is one way to cut down the impact of the high prices. The Roi Soleil Club Med hotel is the one to go for. It has a good-size pool, and is conveniently situated in St Moritz Bad, near the Signal lift.
Hotels Over half the hotels are of 4-star and 5-star quality – the highest concentration of high-quality hotels in Switzerland. We don't actually like any of the famous 5-star places, but if forced to choose would prefer the glossy, secluded Carlton or the even

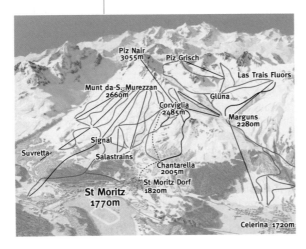

Piz Nair 3055m
Piz Grisch
Las Trais Fluors
Munt da S. Murezzan 2660m
Glüna
Corviglia 2485m
Marguns 2280m
Signal
Suvretta
Salastrains
Chantarella 2005m
St Moritz Dorf 1820m
St Moritz 1770m
Celerina 1720m

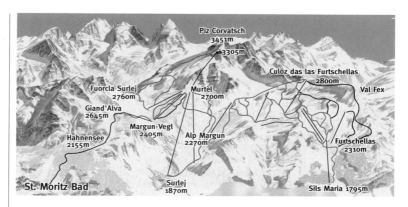

GETTING THERE

Air Zürich, transfer 4½hr.

Rail Mainline station in resort.

PACKAGES

Club Med, Inghams, Kuoni, Made to Measure, Plus Travel, Ski Club of GB, Ski with Julia, SkiGower, Swiss Travel Service

Celerina Made to Measure

Champfér Made to Measure

Pontresina Club Med, Made to Measure, SkiGower

Sils Maria Made to Measure

Silvaplana Made to Measure

ACTIVITIES

Indoor Curling, swimming, sauna, solarium, tennis, squash, museum, health spa, cinema (with English films), aerobics, beauty farm, health centre, Rotary International club **Outdoor** Ice skating, sleigh rides, ski jumping, toboggan run, hang-gliding, golf on frozen lake, Cresta run, 120km cleared paths, greyhound racing, horse-riding and racing, polo tournaments, cricket tournaments, ski-bob run, para-gliding

TOURIST OFFICE

Postcode CH-7500
Tel 00 41 (82) 33147
Fax 32952

more secluded Suvretta House to the rather staid Kulm or the Gothic Badrutt's Palace.

££££ Crystal Big 4-star in Dorf, as close to the Corviglia lift as any.

££££ Schweizerhof 'Relaxed' 4-star in central Dorf, 5 min from the Corviglia lift, with 'excellent food and very helpful staff'.

£££ Nolda One of the few chalet-style buildings, close to the cable-car in St Moritz Bad.

EATING OUT
Mostly chic and expensive

It's easy to spend £50 a head on dinner in St Moritz, not counting the wine. Even the Swiss complain about the prices.

But there are reasonable places. The Soldanella hotel has a set menu for SF35 (£17.50,) which must be the best value for money in town; the Steffani is also inexpensive by St Moritz standards; and the cosy restaurant of the Belvedere is good value and has great views of the lake. The Chesa Veglia is a swanky little restaurant in Dorf. But the best food is supposed to be out at Champfer, at Jöhri's Talvo.

On a clear day late in the season, an evening up the funicular at Muottas Muragl is recommended for a splendid sunset followed by a good dinner in the hotel's unpretentious restaurant.

APRES-SKI
Caters for all ages

There is an enormous variety of après-skiing age groups in St Moritz. Kids escape from their parents to Billy's pub, where grunge replaces fur, and the music is loud. At the sedate piano bar, on the other hand, there appears to be no-one below bus-pass age.

The fur coat count is high – people come to St Moritz to be seen. The Cresta men have no truck with fashion and all that sissy stuff, so you could adopt their baggy cords and Viyella check shirts. But forget those salopettes from Walthamstow market.

At tea-time, if you can tear yourself away from the the bars up the mountain, the obvious venue is the famous Hanselmann's, for cakes.

At midnight, the streets are full of visitors sampling the nightlife. The most famous is the Kings Disco at the Palace, where SF30 gets you in (men need a tie) and buys one drink. The other favourite is the Absolute, near the tourist office.

Others worth trying are the wood-panelled Stubli, in the lower level of the Schweizerhof, and the Cave Bar at the Steffani. The Cresta Bar, at the same hotel, is also a popular place – particularly with the British.

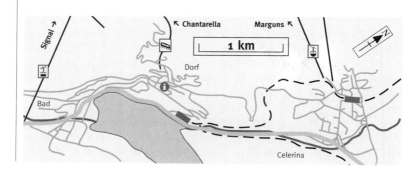

STAYING UP THE MOUNTAIN
Excellent possibilities
Next door to one another at Salastrains, just across the mountainside from Chantarella, are two chalet-style hotels, the 3-star hotel Salastrains, with 60 comfortable beds, and the slightly simpler and much smaller Zuberhütte. Great views, and no queues.

Celerina 1730m

Celerina is a much smaller, more villagey resort, with equally good access to the Corviglia skiing, and well worth considering as a cheaper and less posh base than St Moritz. The 12-room Stüvetta Veglia is a particularly appealing place to stay.

Pontresina 1780m

Pontresina is a small sedate base, in marked contrast to nearby St Moritz. It's a sheltered, sunny village with essentially a single narrow street of traditional old buildings spoilt somewhat by the sanitorium-style of architecture that blights this whole area. Position of accommodation is relatively unimportant – all the skiing involves a bus- or car-ride.

Five minutes away towards Celerina is the Muottas Muragl area, where a mountain railway serves a tiny mountain-top area with marvellous views and a single long run returning to the bottom station. Pontresina's village hill, Languard, has a single long piste.

The sheltered Engadine does not get the amount of snow one might assume from its impressive altitude.

Much is made of Pontresina being a cheaper place to stay than St Moritz, but cheaper doesn't mean cheap – hotels are still very expensive, with little in the way of self-catering options. There is another Club Med here, in addition to the two in St Moritz.

The Collina is one of the better-value luxury hotels, but some of the many 3-star places are more likely to be within the average British pocket. The Steinbock is the most attractive hotel in town, an old inn with an informal atmosphere by local standards and one of only two hotels in the category with a pool. The Rosatch Stummhaus is the other. The ugly Atlas is the best for families, as it houses the village nursery and has some cheaper basic rooms.

Dining is mostly hotel-based, but the Sarazena is an attractive old place with expensive dining on a wooden minstrel's gallery. Hotel Muller has a good stubli, and the Engadinerhof and Bernina restaurants have good reputations.

Nightlife is very quiet. The Sarazena and Engadinerhof have dance floors.

Non-skiers have the numerous facilities of St Moritz close by, while Pontresina has a free skating rink, swimming pool (covered by the lift pass), sauna and massage facilities, sleigh rides, horse-drawn buses and a cinema. Walking is, however, the main pursuit, with 140km of cleared paths throughout the Engadine.

Hotel Atlas has an all-day nursery open to non-residents. There is no ski kindergarten, but ski school starts at 3.

Verbier 1500m

HOW IT RATES

The skiing

Snow	★★★
Extent	★★★★★
Advanced	★★★★★
Intermediates	★★★
Beginners	★★
Convenience	★★
Queues	★
Restaurants	★★★

The rest

Scenery	★★★★
Resort charm	★★★
Not skiing	★★★

✔ Large, challenging ski area with a lot of off-piste potential

✔ Very lively nightlife

✔ Wide range of chalet holidays available

✔ Hardly any drag-lifts

✔ Good off-piste and other advanced-level tuition

✘ Still dreadful queues despite new lift

✘ Overcrowded pistes

✘ Very poor piste maintenance – lack of grooming, marking, safety measures

✘ Very little artificial snowmaking

✘ Long walk or a bus needed to lift from much accommodation

✘ Poorly positioned base from which to ski Four Valleys

✘ Little skiing for novices or early intermediates except paths

✘ Surprisingly little for non-skiers or cross-country enthusiasts

✘ The full lift pass is Europe's most expensive

Verbier has some of Europe's steepest and best off-piste skiing and some of its liveliest nightlife. For these two things its devotees are willing to forgive the resort its many drawbacks. But a lot of first-time visitors are sorely disappointed. They go expecting another Trois Vallées, Val d'Isère or Zermatt – a massive ski area, with varied skiing suiting most skiers from intermediate up, combined with a decent lift system. They come back disillusioned with the resort's expense, the antiquated lifts, the limited and crowded piste skiing and the often poor snow on the lower slopes. A major new lift last season eliminated one mid-mountain bottleneck. But notorious queues elsewhere are as bad as ever – hour-long waits are not uncommon at one blackspot. And the new lift has made some of the pistes even more crowded.

To get the most out of Verbier, you really need to party till late and not ski much, or to get up early, beat the lift queues and enjoy the wonderful top-to-bottom of the mountain off-piste adventures with a guide.

ORIENTATION

Verbier sits on a wide sunny balcony, gazing across a junction of valleys below. The resort is an amorphous sprawl, with its main focus 500m (40m vertical) from its main lift station. A notable secondary area, Savoleyres, is accessed from another extremity of town, a bus-ride from the centre. The skiing is part of the so-called Four Valleys area, which also includes **Nendaz, Thyon, La Tzoumaz, Siviez** and **Veysonnaz. Bruson** is also on the lift pass and reached by bus or by riding a gondola down to **Le Châble** and taking a bus from there. **Argentière** and **Champéry** (which is part of the Portes du Soleil circuit) are other possible road outings.

Verbier grouses

This year our postbag contained another fat pile of grouses from dissatisfied Verbier visitors. Here is a selection. Bear in mind that pressure was taken off Verbier last season because snow was so good elsewhere that fewer people came here for its guaranteed glacier snow. Imagine what it's like in a poor snow season:

'The queues at Tortin are still just as gruesome.'

'On our first day the queue was horrendous – one hour.'

'Annoying walks between lifts.'

'Piste map not good – difficult to see which way pistes go.'

'Lift passes are enormously expensive compared with similar areas in France … what do they do with the money?'

'It would make life easier if the runs were either named or numbered … you have no reference to where you are.'

'Several black runs have been reclassified as ski tours, which eases insurance problems and saves them having to groom them, but spoils the experience for those who have to choose other routes or go down by lift. Very disappointing.'

'Grooming conspicuous by its absence.'

'Too many cars, not enough parking.'

'Pistes from Attelas to Ruinettes become very crowded.'

But not all the feedback was bad:

'New Funispace gondola removes all queues at Ruinettes.'

'Great views, good bars.'

'Steep runs, big moguls, deep powder.'

'Ski bus service excellent.'

The resort

Verbier is an amorphous, still-expanding sprawl of chalet-style buildings, which retains a certain level of charm by not having too much concrete in evidence, and being impressively set on a wide, sunny, tree-filled balcony beneath spectacular peaks. It's a fashionable, yet informal, very lively place which teems with a young (20s rather than teens) cosmopolitan clientele. But it's no longer exclusive. Sloanes rub shoulders with Essex girls, and the mad Scandinavians often out-party British Hoorays.

The centre of town, where most of the typical touristy ski resort shops and hotels (but not chalets) are, is set around the Place Centrale. A fair proportion of the nightlife is here too, though bars are rather scattered – so there's not much evening street life.

More chalets and apartments are built each year, with much of the recent development inconveniently situated along the bus route to the Savoleyres lifts at the edge of town. There's a good sports centre and an efficient free bus service.

SKI FACTS

Altitude	1300m-3330m
Lifts	100
Pistes	400km
Green/Blue	39%
Red	42%
Black	19%
Artificial snow	25km

The skiing

Verbier is at one end of a long, strung out, interconnected ski area. Its local skiing suits good skiers best because of its steepness and the quality of the off-piste available. Further small ski areas covered by the lift pass are scattered around nearby valleys, reached by bus.

THE SKI AREA
Very spread out
Verbier has two local ski areas. **Savoleyres** is the smaller one, mainly suited to beginners and intermediates and reached by a gondola from the northern end of town. This area is underrated and under-used. It has a pleasant mix of open and tree-lined skiing (and has some of the better mountain restaurants). From the top (2355m) you can ski down to La Tzoumaz. When conditions are good you can also ski back to Verbier on south-facing slopes, but these deteriorate quickly.

Verbier's main ski area is reached by lifts from the opposite end of town, where a double gondola and chair rise to **Ruinettes** and one of the gondolas carries on to **Attelas**. Last season the ancient, small cable-car from Ruinettes to Attelas was replaced by an efficient new 30-person jumbo gondola (see 'Queues' for further details).

From Attelas you can ski back down to town or Ruinettes, over to La Chaux or down to Lac des Vaux. The La Chaux area is served by a number of chair-lifts and is the departure point of a huge cable-car up to Col de Gentianes and the glacier skiing area of **Mont-Fort**.

A second, much smaller cable-car then goes up to the high point of the Four Valleys skiing at 3330m. All the lifts to and around Col des Gentianes are accessible only if you buy the 'Général' pass. If the weather is doubtful, it may be best to get the basic Four Valleys pass and pay the daily Mont-Fort supplement whenever you need it.

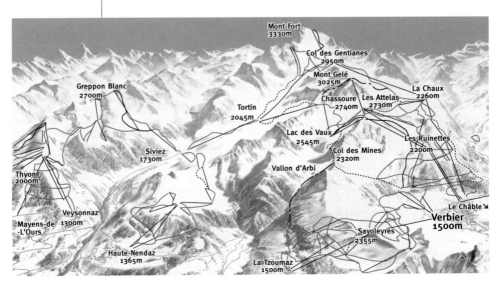

From Mont-Fort you can ski all the way down to **Tortin**, a run of almost 1300m vertical, which is now defined as off-piste. From here a cable-car returns to Col des Gentianes. An ancient gondola also leaves from Tortin for Chassoure, from where you can ski down to Lac des Vaux. A chair-lift from Lac des Vaux returns to Chassoure and the off-piste mogul run down to Tortin. Other chairs return you to Attelas. From Attelas a cable-car takes you to Mont-Gelé, from where there are only steep off-piste runs.

Tortin is the gateway to the rest of the Four Valleys' skiing. From there you ski down to **Siviez** (previously Super Nendaz). Take the chair up to the left there and you are entering the long, thin **Nendaz** sector.

Take the chair to the right and you are starting the journey to the **Thyon** and **Veysonnaz** sectors, reached by a couple of lifts and a long, easy ski along the mountain. Both these sectors suit intermediate skiers best. The way back from both sectors involves retracing your footsteps to Siviez and then Tortin.

Allow plenty of time for the queues – you don't want to be stranded in the wrong valley because, although it's not far from Verbier to Siviez on skis, it is by road. There is no bus back – and it's a very expensive taxi-ride.

The nearest and most extensive of the small unlinked ski areas is **Bruson**, reached by hourly bus from Verbier or by taking the gondola down to Le Châble and a bus from there.

SNOW RELIABILITY
Limited glacier skiing

The skiing on the Mont-Fort glacier is always on good snow. The runs to Tortin are normally snowsure too. But nearly all this is steep skiing, and much of it is now off-piste. Lesser skiers might well find themselves with a problem because most of Verbier's local skiing is west-facing and gets the hot afternoon sun. Most of it is also below 2500m and the runs to the resort can get very bare indeed. There is hardly any artificial snow.

The north-facing slopes of Savoleyres and Lac des Vaux are normally better than the rest. Veysonnaz's substantial artificial snow facilities can be reached from Verbier when conditions are poor, but the lack of snowmakers around Siviez, and the fact that there are only tough off-piste runs to Tortin, mean that many skiers have to take lifts down as well as up – and you don't get much skiing done in the course of a day.

FOR ADVANCED SKIERS
The main attraction

Verbier has some superb tough skiing, much of it off-piste and to be skied with a guide. The very extreme, almost unskiable, couloirs between Mont-Gelé and Attelas and below the Attelas gondola are some of the toughest of all. There are safer, more satisfying off-piste routes from Mont-Gelé to Tortin and La Chaux.

The front face of Mont-Fort is a wonderful, tough mogul field. It is all of black steepness, although the piste map shows a red variant. But there is some choice of gradient – from seriously steep to intimidatingly steep. Occasionally you can ski from Mont-Fort all the way to Le Châble off-piste. You can also ski off-piste via one of two spectacular couloirs off the back of Mont-Fort to Siviez. The North Face of Mont-Fort is one of the hottest runs of all for expert skiers.

Both ski routes to Tortin (one from the bottom of the drags below Col des Gentianes and the other under the Tortin gondola) are rewarding and heavily mogulled. But these runs are often spoilt by crowds of intermediates out of their depth yet refusing to take the lift down.

There is often plenty of skiable off-piste powder around the north-facing slope from Gentianes to Tortin. Attelas is also the start of shorter off-piste runs towards the village.

A couple of long, but easy, off-piste routes go from Lac des Vaux via Col des Mines. One is a popular short-cut back to town, but the other is more beautiful, passing through Vallon d'Arbi and the woods before finishing at La Tzoumaz.

The Savoleyres speed-skiing course is open to all, and is a must for all bravos. The World Cup run at Veysonnaz is a steepish, often icy, red, ideal for really fast skiing.

There is also an entertaining off-piste run from Greppon Blanc at the top of the Siviez-Thyon sector down to Leteygeon. An hourly bus service (covered by the lift pass) brings you back to Thyon. Allow a full day for this excursion.

FOR INTERMEDIATE SKIERS
Best for the adventurous

It's for keen piste-bashing intermediates that Verbier is most disappointing. The skiing available to them in the main ski area is concentrated between Attelas and the village, above and below Ruinettes, plus the little bowl at Lac des Vaux beyond Attelas and the skiing served

LIFT PASSES

95/96 prices in Swiss francs
General Four Valleys
Covers all lifts and ski-buses in Verbier, Mont-Fort, Bruson, Champex-Lac, La Tzoumaz, Nendaz, Veysonnaz and Thyon.
Beginners Station pass covers 6 beginner lifts.
Main pass
1-day pass 59
6-day pass 297
Senior citizens
Over 65: 6-day pass 178 (40% off)
Children
Under 16: 6-day pass 178 (40% off)
Short-term passes
Half-day pass from 11am (adult 51) or 12.30 (adult 44).
Alternative periods
10 non-consecutive day pass (excluding Mont-Fort, adult 468).
Notes Reductions for students, families and groups. Children under 6 years 70% off.
Alternative passes
Limited passes for Savoleyres-La Tzoumaz, Bruson-Champex, Thyon-Veysonnaz-Nendez and Four Valleys without Mont-Fort.

by the chairs at La Chaux. This is all excellent and varied intermediate territory. But there isn't much of it – this whole area is no bigger than the ski area of Alpbach, for example – and it has to accommodate half the skiers staying in what is one of Switzerland's largest resorts.

As a result, it is often crowded to a miserable degree – and this was made worse last season by the opening of the new jumbo gondola to Attelas.

Savoleyres is a more satisfying and much less crowded section. It is also a good hill for mixed abilities, with variations of many runs to suit most standards of intermediate except the very inexperienced.

The best snow for intermediates is normally on the summer skiing area served by two drag-lifts on the Mont-Fort sector. Early intermediates will probably want to take lifts down as well as to it, though the red run down to La Chaux is not too steep.

A trip across to the Bruson ski area, reached by a bus, is also worthy of a day's excursion.

FOR BEGINNERS
A poor choice
Verbier's nursery slopes are inconveniently positioned (between Savoleyres and town) and tend to suffer from too much sun. Near-beginners and fast improvers have few options, especially if they do not want to pay vast sums for their lift pass. A couple of runs down to La Chaux are easy enough, but get too crowded.

FOR CROSS-COUNTRY
Surprisingly little on offer
Verbier has surprisingly limited cross-country facilities. There is a 4km circuit in Verbier, 4km at Ruinettes-La Chaux and 30km down at Le Châble/Val de Bagnes.

QUEUES
Perhaps the worst in Europe
Verbier has improved its lift system, but so have most other resorts, and by today's standards it is one of the worst places in the Alps for queues. The new jumbo gondola from Ruinettes to Attelas has virtually eliminated queues there. But it has increased the overcrowding on the pistes back down. And it has done nothing to cut the queues at Tortin – where half-hour waits for both the ancient bubble and the cable-car are normal and over an hour for the bubble is not unusual.

The queues for the Mont-Fort cable-cars can be substantial too. The Greppon Blanc drag and

Combatzeline chair out of Siviez are also prone to delays, as is the chair back to Tortin at the end of the day. This can make skiing to and from Thyon-Veysonnaz impractical at times. The main Nendaz lift also gets half-hour queues in high season.

At the main bottom lift station at Medran, the queue problem seemed to be improving with more people deciding to take the six-person gondola to Ruinettes to meet the new lift to Attelas rather than wait for the slower four-person gondola which starts down in Le Châble and carries on all the way up to Attelas. But we hear the lift company took to blocking off the way to the four-person gondola, forcing everyone to wait for the six-person, even though empty four-person cabins were in full view – and giving no sensible explanation. The nearby chair-lift is usually a quicker alternative – but is often shut.

MOUNTAIN RESTAURANTS
Very disappointing in main area
There are not enough huts, which creates queues, overcrowding and high prices. Savoleyres is the best area. The hotel by the Tzoumaz chair takes some beating for value and lack of crowds. Chez Simon and Les Marmottes are also worth trying.

In the main ski area, the rustic Chez Dany at Clambin, on the off-piste run down from the La Chaux area, is about the best, but is a bit tricky to get to at times. It is open at night too. Carrefour is popular and well situated at the top of the nursery slopes.

The Tortin has good pasta, and a visit puts off standing in the queue for a while. The Cabane de Mont-Fort, between La Chaux and Les Gentianes, is cheerful, with good food and views, but gets very busy. Violon d'Ingres, at Ruinettes, is a large table-service place popular with several reporters.

SKI SCHOOL
Mixed reports, best for experts
Verbier is an excellent place for advanced skiers, in particular, to get tuition. Several reporters are complimentary about the off-piste lessons. These can be part of a Ski Adventure course (adults only) that takes in local powder and heli-skiing, with video analysis. More than 20 guides are available for heli-skiing, which includes trips to Zermatt and the Aosta valley. The Vallée Blanche at Chamonix, Monte Rosa tours and a trip to Zinal are cheaper excursions. If you prefer fast piste skiing, there are plenty of race competitions organised.

SKI SCHOOL

Swiss
Classes 6 days
4hr 45min: 9.15-11.45
and 2.10-4.30
6 half-days: 112
Children's classes
Ages: 3 to 12
6 half-days: 112
Private lessons
Hourly, half- or full-
day
55 for 1hr for 1 to 2
people

Fantastique
Small school
specialising in private
lessons, and
adventure skiing.

GETTING THERE

Air Geneva, transfer
2½hr.

Rail Le Châble (7km);
regular buses to
resort or gondola.

CHILDCARE

The ski school's Mini
Champion-Klub
kindergarten, near the
sports centre, has its
own drag-lift and
takes children aged 3
to 10 from 8.45 to
5pm. There is also a
ski playground up at
La Chaux, reached by
infrequent special
bus.

The Schtroumpfs non-
ski kindergarten
(316585), close to the
middle of the resort,
takes children of any
age up to 4 years
(older ones by
arrangement), from
8.30 to 5.30.

Verbier is also quite big on Telemark tuition for those looking for a completely new challenge.

One or two regular visitors reckon the ski school's standards have improved generally in recent years, and we have good reports on beginners' classes. But we've also had reports criticising the children's classes. A 6-year-old was put in a class where no English was spoken, and a 7-year-old had an instructor who was impatient and kept losing her temper.

FACILITIES FOR CHILDREN
Wide range of options
The ski school's facilities in the resort are good, and the resort attracts quite a lot of families. The ski playground up at La Chaux has also received favourable reports. Although it is not used exclusively by the ski school, space on the bus back is limited, and priority is given to ski school groups.

The possibility of leaving very young babies at the Schtroumpfs nursery is valuable. British families have the option of travelling with two family-oriented chalet operators – Ski Esprit, who have two chalets with crèches, and Mark Warner, whose Rosablanche chalet-hotel has an 'excellent' crèche.

There are considerable reductions on the lift pass price for families.

⬆ Staying there

Staying at the top of the resort, close to the Medran lift station, is convenient for the skiing and sufficiently distant from nightlife to avoid late evening noise. One reporter mentions New Year's Eve revellers dancing in the main square outside his hotel until 3am to music being blasted out by loudspeakers on hotel balconies – his hotel had to have a bouncer on the door to keep non-residents out. For self-caterers, however, the supermarkets are a tiresome walk from the lift area.

The ski-bus service is mostly good and reduces the inconvenience factor, but there are several routes running around the network of busy (congested at weekends) streets, so it is imperative to study the timetables carefully. Some accommodation has quite an infrequent service.

HOW TO GO
Plenty of options
Verbier is the chalet-party capital of the Alps. It has a higher proportion of chalets than any other resort. Given

the size of the place there are surprisingly few apartments and pensions available, though budget skiers have inexpensive B&B options in Le Châble. Hotels are expensive in relation to their grading.

Chalets There are chalets available for most types of holiday-maker. Small ones, ideal for a family or small group of friends to have exclusive use of, are particularly common. There are also large chalets good for groups, ski-to-the-door places, and others slap bang in the centre of Verbier's lively nightlife. Prices are generally surprisingly low.

There are not, however, many options for luxury lovers. Flexiski's Bouvreuil is the main exception. Owned by a Belgian Count, it's tastefully furnished with antiques and plush sofas. It's also well positioned, mid-way between Place Centrale and the lifts.

Bladon Lines has the largest selection, including two of the best in the resort, the Norma and Mondzeu. Both of these are comfortable catered apartments ideal for a small group or family. The block has a 'very good' pool. The simple Rendez Vous is one of the best located chalets available, with skiing to the door and the main lifts close by.

Silver Ski has a selection of good-value, mostly small places, generally better positioned for the nursery slopes than the main area.

Family specialists Ski Esprit have in-house crèches with British nannies in two of their chalets. The little Tai Pan is perfect for a family wanting exclusive use, and also has the benefit of ski-to-the-door convenience. The Filaos is well placed for the underrated Savoleyres ski area.

Neilson have two small, central chalets and one right by the Medran lifts. The best of Crystal's places are the comfortable chalet Djabo, close to Medran, and the Siboget catered apartments, well positioned between the lifts and centre.

The Itroz, close to the nursery slopes, offers perhaps the best value of Thomson's range.

Mark Warner leads the chalet hotel scene. The Mont Fort is close to the main lifts, whilst the old 2-star Roseblanche has the benefit of an in-house crèche, and is well positioned in a quiet spot close to both centre and lifts; it's quite simple, with some small rooms and thin walls.

Hotels There are half a dozen 4-star places, a dozen 3-star and a handful of simpler places.

FLEXISKI

helped us to compile the Eating out and Après-ski sections. Our thanks to them.

PACKAGES

Bladon Lines, Chalet World, Chalets 'Unlimited', Crystal, First Choice Ski, FlexiSki, Fresh Tracks, Inghams, Made to Measure, Mark Warner, Neilson, Peak Ski, Plus Travel, Silver Ski, Simply Ski, Ski Activity, Ski Choice, Ski Club of GB, Ski Equipe, Ski Esprit, Ski Les Alpes, Ski with Julia, Skiworld, Solo's, Swiss Travel Service, Thomson, White Roc

Nendaz Travelscene Ski-Drive

££££ Rosalp The place to stay if you can afford it, not least for the food in Roland Pierroz's restaurant, which is the best you'll find in a Swiss ski resort. Good position mid-way between centre and lifts.

££££ Montpelier Very comfortable 4-star, but out of town (a courtesy bus is provided).

££££ Rois Mages Smart little B&B hotel in secluded setting, up near the Savoleyres lift.

£££ Rotonde Much cheaper, well positioned 3-star between centre and lifts; some budget rooms.

£££ Chamois 3-star close to lifts.

£££ Poste Well placed 3-star mid-way between centre and lifts; the only hotel pool. Some rooms rather small; food and decor 'dreary' according to one reporter.

£££ Verbier Central 3-star, popular with tour operators and their clientele; renowned for good food; atmospheric, but 'olde worlde' decor is a little in need of refurbishment.

££ Auberge Well placed 2-star, mid-way between centre and lifts.

££ Farinet Central 2-star B&B hotel.

Self-catering Apartments available through tour operators are extremely thin on the ground. Self-caterers usually book direct. The comfortable Richemont and Troika apartments are close to the nursery slopes, a trek from the main lifts. The similar standard Blizzard is better placed, mid-way between Place Centrale and lifts.

The Vieux Verbier apartments have a position second to none for the skiing, next to the main lift station. Close to the town centre are the simple Carina places.

EATING OUT
Very big choice

There is a very wide range of restaurants. Hotel Rosalp is clearly the best in town, and among the best in Switzerland, with an awesome wine cellar to match its excellent Michelin-starred food.

Two-star hotel Chalet Phénix has a surprisingly good Chinese restaurant. Au Fer à Cheval is a very popular pizza/salad/breakfast place that's full of life, and Borsalino's is just as good and easier to book. Arguably the best-value Italian food in town, however, is at Al Capone's out near the Savoleyres gondola. The Spaghetti House is another inexpensive place.

The Farinet restaurant is atmospheric and has good food at affordable prices. The Vieux Verbier apartments have a surprisingly good restaurant that serves huge portions of

Swiss specialities. The Luge is a good-value, atmospheric place specialising in steaks. The Crêperie does everything from snacks to full meals.

L'Ecurie has good but expensive Swiss specialities. Robinsons and Le Caveau are others worth trying. Relais de Neige is one of the cheaper places in town. Harold's is Verbier's 'fast-food' outlet – it's less clinical and more fun than McDonalds.

APRES-SKI
Throbbing but expensive

It starts with a 4pm visit to Offshore, for people-watching and coffee (no alcohol sold). Then it's on to the Mont Fort or Nelson pubs, if you're young, loud and British. La Luge is good for a more relaxed drink in a friendly atmosphere. The Farinet is particularly good in spring, its live band playing to the audience on a huge, sunny terrace. Au Fer à Cheval is a fun place full of locals and regular Verbier-ites.

After dinner the two pubs become very lively pick-up joints, popular with Brits and locals alike. Crock No Name often has live music, and is entertaining for its cosmopolitan crowd. La Luge remains a more relaxed option. Jacky's, under the Grand-Combin hotel, is a classy haunt frequented by big spenders on their way to the Farm Club. This is an outrageously expensive nightclub which nonetheless is very popular – tables are difficult to reserve.

More within the pocket of most Brits is the noisy, glitzy Marshalls Club, which sometimes has live music. Tara Club is less smart but the noise level is more conducive to conversation, and it has a friendly atmosphere. Scotch is a bit of a dive, but it's the cheapest disco in town. It's particularly handy towards the end of your stay, when over-indulgence in the above attractions may have exhausted your flexible friend. Big Ben is another cheaper haunt, popular with teenagers. Harry's Bar is good for a midnight burger.

Something a bit different is to snowmobile up to Chez Dany or Les Marmottes for a good evening meal in the mountains, followed by a torchlit descent. It's great fun.

FOR NON-SKIERS
No great attraction

Verbier has an excellent sports centre and some nice walks, but otherwise has little for non-skiers. Montreux is an enjoyable train excursion from Le Châble. It's easy for non-skiers to walk to some of the lower mountain

ACTIVITIES

Indoor Sports centre
(swimming, skating,
curling, squash,
sauna, solarium,
jacuzzi), fitness
centre, cinema, ice
hockey, artificial
skating rink, indoor
golf
Outdoor Ski-bob,
15km cleared paths,
para-gliding, hang-
gliding, mountain-
eering, jogging tracks,
winter walking

TOURIST OFFICE

Postcode CH-1936
Tel 00 41 (26) 316222
Fax 313272

restaurants to meet up with skiers for
lunch, and there are reachable
restaurants at most of the gondola
top stations.

STAYING IN OTHER RESORTS
A lot going for them

There are advantages to staying in the
other resorts of the Four Valleys. For a
start, you can avoid the worst of the
queues if you are not travelling
around in the same direction as
everyone else (though you're still
likely to be clobbered by the waits for
the Tortin and Mont-Fort lifts if you
want to ski these sections).

Secondly, they are substantially
cheaper for both accommodation and
incidentals. What you lose is the
Verbier ambience and its range of
restaurants, bars and nightlife. If you
don't really care about those elements,
staying elsewhere is well worth
considering. Unfortunately only one
British tour operator (Travelscene Ski-
Drive to Nendaz) offers packages to
any of them.

Veysonnaz or Thyon are both small
resorts, with mainly apartment
accommodation. Veysonnaz is by far
the more attractive – an old village
complete with church. It has adequate
bars, cafés and restaurants, a disco,
sports centre with swimming pool,
and a ski school. The only hotel is the
inexpensive Magrappe, which is
situated next to the gondola. Thyon is
little more than a functional, ugly,
purpose-built place.

Nendaz is a far larger resort, with an
enormous number of beds available,
mainly in apartments. There are

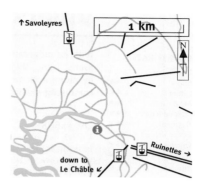

plenty of amenities, including a
skating rink, sports centre with
swimming, fitness centre and squash,
cafés, restaurants, discos, crèche and
ski school.

The Déserteur is the best-placed of
its hotels, all of which are inexpensive,
relatively simple 3-stars. Auberge les
Etagnes is a very cheap B&B situated
next to the gondola. A couple of
simple standard chalet parties are
also available.

Le Châble is a village just a gondola-
ride from Verbier. As changing
gondola cars is not necessary for
moving on to Ruinettes and Attelas,
access to the ski area can be just as
quick (or even quicker) from the
queue-free valley. Le Châble is
particularly convenient for those
travelling by train or ski-drivers who
want to visit other resorts too. The
Giétroz, Poste and Ruinette are all
simple, adequate hotels.

Selected chalets in Verbier

Simply Ski *Chalet specialists*   T 0181 742 2541 F 0181 995 5346

Simply Ski offers four comfortable
catered chalets, each offering a warm
welcome in traditional surroundings.
Chalet staff provide breakfast, tea and
dinner with a choice of wine. Chalet
Norjeanne, a superior chalet, offers an
enhanced level of cuisine and service
and is designated a 'Chalet of
Distinction'.
Cordon Bleu cuisine
Ski leader service
Scheduled and charter flights
Snowdrive
Competitive prices and discounts

Chalet Norjeanne →

Villars 1300m

HOW IT RATES

The skiing

Snow	**
Extent	**
Advanced	**
Intermediates	***
Beginners	****
Convenience	***
Queues	***
Restaurants	***

The rest

Scenery	***
Resort charm	****
Not skiing	****

SKI FACTS

Altitude	1130m-2970m
Lifts	45
Pistes	120km
Green/Blue	51%
Red	41%
Black	8%
Artificial snow	2km

PACKAGES

Chalets 'Unlimited', Club Med, Kuoni, Made to Measure, Stena Sealink, Swiss Travel Service, Travelscene Ski-Drive

Alpe des Chaux Stena Sealink

TOURIST OFFICE

Postcode CH-1884
Tel 00 41 (25) 353232
Fax 352794

With its mountain railway, gentle low-altitude ski slopes and year-round tourist trade, Villars is the kind of place that has been rather overshadowed by modern mega-resorts. But for a relaxing family holiday – perhaps combining skiing with other activities – this formula has clear attractions.

THE RESORT

Villars sits on a sunny shelf at 1300m, looking south-west across the Rhône valley towards the mountains of the Portes du Soleil. Roads go up from Ollon and Bex, a rack railway only from Bex. A busy high street lined with shops unconnected with skiing gives Villars more the air of a small town than of a ski resort; but a pleasant, reassuring town, with all but two or three of the largest hotels built in chalet style, and fields and woods close at hand. There is further accommodation well outside the main village at Barboleusaz, where a gondola serves the slopes of Les Chaux, and further up those slopes.

This season will see an improved link with Les Diablerets, to the north; and outings to Leysin and Champéry are possible by rail or road. Many other resorts (such as Verbier) are within driving distance.

THE SKIING

The railway goes on up into the **ski area**, terminating at Bretaye (1800m); a gondola from the other end of the village goes higher into the skiing.

The col of Bretaye has intermediate slopes on either side, with a maximum vertical of 300m back to the col and a couple of much longer runs back to the village. To the east, easier open slopes (very susceptible to sun) go down to La Rasse (1350m), the meeting point with the otherwise separate Les Chaux sector.

Low altitude and southerly orientation mean that Villars' **snow reliability** is not good.

This is not a resort for **advanced skiers**, although there are occasional steep pitches to be found – and small but worthwhile off-piste areas.

For **intermediates** not worried about mileage or snow reliability, there is an interesting range of pistes. Until now, reaching the similarly appealing skiing of Les Diablerets involved an intimidating, unpatrolled black stretch. Getting back required a tiring walk at the top. But from this season a chair-lift will provide a link straight to the Laouissalet drag in the Diablerets sector, and there will be a gentle piste back from the same point.

Beginners will feel comfortable on the village nursery slopes, and riding the train up to Bretaye. There is gentle skiing here, too, but also lots of people charging about in a crowded area.

The **cross-country** trails up the valley past La Rasse are long and pretty, and there are further loops in the depression beyond Bretaye.

It is mainly at weekends that **queues** appear for the lifts at Bretaye.

The **mountain restaurants** are a mixed bag. The main one at Bretaye is characterless and very busy; the small Grizzly bar at La Rasse is popular for its barbecue; Lac des Chavonnes is worth the walk from the piste (and snowmobile ride back).

Villars' Ecole Moderne, started in 1974 and still using the ski évolutif method, was one of the first of the rare alternatives to the Swiss **ski school**. There is also a Bureau des Guides offering heliskiing excursions. The Swiss school nursery takes **children** aged 3 to 12, Monday to Saturday; the Moderne school runs a nursery too. There is also a non-ski nursery in next-door Chesières.

STAYING THERE

Although the centre of Villars is quite compact, the gondola is quite a walk from the railway station. But there is a free ski-bus (reliable but busy at times) and many of the **hotels** are between the two lifts. There are three big 4-star hotels, and several mid-sized and smaller 3-star ones; the Alpe Fleurie and Renardière are our favourites. The huge Palace is now occupied by Club Med. Some UK operators offer self-catering; the Panorama apartments were recommended this year.

For many visitors, **eating out** means regional specialities in the neo-rustic Vieux Villars – though there are numerous alternatives, including a recommended pizzeria in the centre.

There is **après-ski** activity to be found. Charlie's is a very welcoming, pleasantly busy upstairs bar. Le Sporting has great olives. El Gringo is a proper disco.

There is plenty to amuse active **non-skiers**; as well as six tennis courts and lots of marked walks there is swimming, skating, curling etc.

Wengen 1275m

HOW IT RATES

The skiing

Snow	**
Extent	***
Advanced	***
Intermediates	*****
Beginners	***
Convenience	***
Queues	***
Restaurants	****

The rest

Scenery	*****
Resort charm	*****
Not skiing	****

✔ Some of the most beautiful scenery in the Alps

✔ Pretty, traditional, 'traffic-free' Alpine village which can be reached only by cog railway

✔ Large ski area, ideal for intermediates

✔ Good for non-skiers or part-time skiers who want a relaxing break

✘ Limited terrain for experts

✘ Not ideal for beginners – village nursery slopes often short of snow

✘ Snow conditions unreliable, despite some artificial help

✘ Little nightlife for club- and disco-lovers

Wengen, like Mürren across the valley, is one of our favourite resorts. As an early intermediate, one of us went to Wengen on holiday for four successive years. It has ideal terrain for someone at that stage. Combine that with the charm of the village, the friendliness of the locals and the beauty of the scenery and you can see why the place entrances many people so completely that they never go anywhere else, whatever their skiing standard.

So it is sad that these days it's a risky bet booking a holiday in Wengen months in advance. It has had a series of very disappointing years for snow (last season being a happy exception). The skiing is not high – there's little above 2000m. And the present investment in snowmaking is insufficient to transform the prospects.

But the old-world charm of the place is difficult to beat. You have to be willing to accept an old-world pace too. Taking the train up the mountain in the morning may be quaint. But quick it ain't. Wengen is a place for relaxing and enjoying winter among Europe's most glorious scenery. It's not a place for skiers who want to maximise mileage, catch the most efficient lifts or find the most challenging skiing. Relax and you'll love it. Stay tense – in working mode – and you'll find it very frustrating.

ORIENTATION

Wengen is set on a shelf high above the Lauterbrunnen valley, opposite Mürren, and can be reached only by cog railway from Lauterbrunnen. The railway arrives at the station at the southern end of Wengen's main street and carries on up, doubling up as the main ski lift out of the village as well as the only access to it. There's also a cable-car up from above the nursery slopes in the centre of the village. The skiing at the top of both lifts is shared with **Grindelwald** in the next valley. **Mürren** can be reached by taking the train down to Lauterbrunnen and a funicular and connecting train up the other side of the valley. The Wengen, Grindelwald and Mürren skiing is all covered by the Jungfrau lift pass.

 ## The resort

Wengen was a farming community long before skiing became a sport or the first train chugged its way up the mountain. Today it's a charming 'traffic-free' village, much smaller and more unspoilt than you'd expect, given its fame as host to one of the most famous downhill races on the World Cup circuit.

There's really only one main street, which is lined with chalet-style shops and hotels. The focal point of the village is at the southern end where the station and ski school meeting-area are located.

The only traffic you'll see in Wengen are the little electric hotel trucks, which gather at the station to pick up guests, and a couple of Range Rover taxis. But these can be very annoying as they tear past you while you're strolling through the streets.

The views across the Lauterbrunnen valley from the shelf upon which Wengen sits are stunning. They get even better as you travel up the mountain and the Eiger, Jungfrau and

Mönch come into view. The Mönch (Monk) is set between the other two and, mythology says, is there to protect the Jungfrau (Maiden) from the Eiger (Ogre).

There's a very strong British presence at Wengen. Many Brits have been returning to the same rooms in the same hotels in the same week, year after year. Wengen is home to the Downhill Only Club – so named when the first Brits persuaded the locals to keep the summer railway running up the mountain in winter so they would no longer have to climb up in order to ski down again.

The main street is the hub of the village. Lined with hotels and shops, it also has the ice rink, curling club and village nursery slopes giving it a pleasant open aspect. The nursery slopes double as the venue for floodlit ski-jumping and parallel slalom races on several nights a season.

The main form of transport up the mountain is the regular, incredibly punctual train to Kleine Scheidegg. There's also a cable-car from above the nursery slopes up to the Männlichen ski area.

SKI FACTS

Jungfrau region – including Grindelwald and Mürren

Altitude	945m-2970m
Lifts	49
Pistes	183km
Green/Blue	30%
Red	50%
Black	20%
Artificial snow	15km

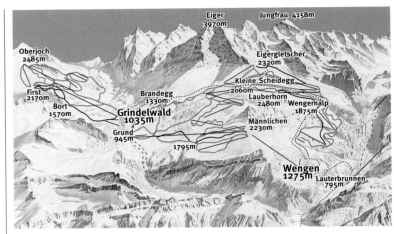

LIFT PASSES

95/96 prices in Swiss francs

Jungfrau Top Ski Region

Covers all lifts in Wengen, Mürren and Grindelwald, trains between them and Grindelwald ski-bus.

Beginners Points card (adult 100 points 46, lifts cost 4 to 10 points).

Main pass

1-day pass 52

6-day pass 232

Children

Under 16: 6-day pass 116 (50% off)

Under 6: free pass

Short-term passes

Single ascent tickets for most lifts. Half-day pass for First (adult 38), Kleine Scheidegg-Männlichen (adult 40) and Mürren-Schilthorn (adult 38).

Notes Day pass price for Kleine Scheidegg-Männlichen area only (98km of piste, 21 lifts), as Jungfrau Top Ski Region pass is only available for 3 days or over. Discounts for teenagers 16 to 21 (6-day 186) and groups.

Alternative passes

1- and 2-day passes aviable for First (adult 2-day 90), Mürren-Schilthorn (adult 2-day 90) and Kleine Scheidegg-Männlichen (adult 2-day 95, child 48).

Credit cards: Yes

The skiing

Although it is famous for the fearsome Lauberhorn World Cup Downhill course – the longest and one of the toughest on the circuit – Wengen's skiing is best suited to intermediates; early intermediates at that. There are no seriously steep pistes and the scariest part of the Downhill course, the Hundschopf jump, is shut to holiday skiers. Most runs are gentle blues and reds, ideal for cruising. On the Grindelwald side there are some long and beautiful runs down to the village. But the lower parts of these often suffer from snow shortage or poor snow conditions – and there is hardly any snowmaking on the Grindelwald side of the area.

THE SKI AREA

Picturesque playground

Most of the skiing is on the other side of the mountain from Wengen. From the top of the train at **Kleine Scheidegg** (2060m) you can ski straight down to Grindelwald or work your way across the mountain with the help of a couple of lifts to the top of the **Männlichen** (2230m). This area has a lot of skiing, served by drag-and chair-lifts. It can also be reached directly by catching the little-used cable-car up from Wengen.

On the Wengen side there are a few runs back down towards Wengen from the top of the **Lauberhorn** (2470m), but below Kleine Scheidegg there's really only one run back to Wengen.

As well as the Wengen skiing, it's easy (although a slow process) to get to Mürren and to the **First** area on the far side of Grindelwald.

SNOW RELIABILITY

Poor

Most of the skiing is below 2000m, and at Grindelwald it goes down to less than 1000m. Very few of the slopes are north-facing, and Wengen's snowmaking facilities – 20 mobile guns – can't deal with more than a fraction of the shared area. All this can mean severe problems in times of snow famine or warm weather. We've experienced wonderful skiing in late March, but we've also struggled to find skiable pistes in January.

FOR ADVANCED SKIERS

Few challenges

Wengen's skiing is quite limited for good skiers. The one genuine black run in the area takes you from Eigergletscher to Wixi. The steepest parts of the famous Lauberhorn Downhill race course are normally shut to holiday skiers. The main challenges are off-piste runs such as the Oh God from near Eigergletscher to Wixi and the White Hare from under the north face of the Eiger. There are a number of off-piste runs from the Jungfraujoch late in the season, but you must ski with a guide. For more challenging skiing it's well worth going to nearby Mürren, an hour away by train and funicular. The Wengen ski school organises heli-skiing if there are enough takers.

FOR INTERMEDIATE SKIERS

Wonderful if the snow is good

Wengen has superb intermediate slopes. Nearly all the skiing is on long blue or gentle red runs. From Kleine Scheidegg there's an easy scenic blue run all the way down through the trees to Grindelwald – or you can stop at Brandegg and catch the train back up. The run back to Wengen is gentle all the way and is a relaxing end to the day, as long as it's not too crowded.

On the Männlichen there's a choice of several gentle runs down to the mid-station of the gondola up from Grindelwald Grund. If conditions permit, you can ski right down to the bottom. There's a piste from Männlichen to Grindelwald that is marked as black on the map but is perfectly skiable by any competent intermediate skier.

For tougher skiing, head for the runs from the top of the Lauberhorn lift down to Kleine Scheidegg or to Wixi (this piste follows the start of the Downhill course). You could also try the north-facing run from Eigergletscher to Salzegg, which often has the best snow late in the season.

FOR BEGINNERS
Not ideal
There's a nursery slope in the centre of the village – although it's convenient, the snow can be unreliable. There is a beginners ski area at Wengernalp but, to get back to Wengen, you either have to climb up to the train or tackle the run down, which can be tricky in places for novice skiers. There are good, long gentle slopes to progress to – especially the run down by the railway on the Grindelwald side.

FOR CROSS-COUNTRY
There is none
There's no cross-country skiing in Wengen itself. There are tracks down in the Lauterbrunnen valley, but the snow there is unreliable.

QUEUES
Can be bad – but improving
There can be some horrific bottle-necks in peak periods, and daily scrums to board the trains that the ski school generally uses. The weekend invasion of locals and coach parties from Germany can increase the crowds enormously. Particular black spots at these times are the train and gondola from Grindelwald.

However, queues up the mountain have been alleviated a lot in the last few years. Some of the old drag- and chair-lifts have been replaced by new, fast four-person chairs, and the capacity of the Männlichen cable-car has been increased.

MOUNTAIN RESTAURANTS
Plenty of variety
A popular but expensive place for lunch is Wengernalp, where the rösti is excellent and the views of the Jungfrau are superb. The highest

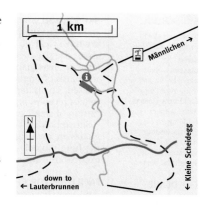

restaurant is at Eigergletscher. If you get there early on a sunny day, you can nab one of the tables on the narrow outside balcony and enjoy some magnificent views of the glacier. The station buffet at Kleine Scheidegg is good value. The Café Oberland, just below Almend, is popular at lunch-time and at the end of the day for those who want to soak up the last of the sun before returning to Wengen. Non-skiers can easily reach all of these places by train.

On the Grindelwald side of the mountain, the restaurants by the Brandegg station and the top of the Aspen drag are recommended.

SKI SCHOOL

95/96 prices in
Swiss francs

Swiss

Classes 6 days
4hr: 2hr am and pm
6 full days: 240
Children's classes
Ages: 4 to 12
6 full days: 240
Private lessons
Half- or full-day
160 for half-day; each
additional person 15

CHILDCARE

The kindergarten on
the first floor of the
Sport Pavilion takes
children aged 3 to 7,
from 8.45 to 4.30.
Children can be taken
to and from lessons
with the ski school,
which starts at age 4.

A couple of 4-star
hotels have their own
kindergartens.

GETTING THERE

Air Zürich, transfer
3½hr. Bern, transfer
1½hr.
Rail Station in resort.

PACKAGES

Club Med, Crystal,
Inghams, Kuoni, Made
to Measure, PGL Ski
Europe, Plus Travel,
Ski Club of GB, Swiss
Travel Service,
Thomson

SKI SCHOOL
Healthy competition

We have received contrasting reports
about the size of classes, from 'too
large' to 'reasonable', but tuition and
standards of English are usually
praised. The independent Privat
school receives praise for good-value
tuition of small groups.

Snowboarders are well served, and
guides are available for heli-skiing on
the Jungfraujoch and powder
excursions off the Lauberhorn.

FACILITIES FOR CHILDREN
Apparently satisfactory

Our recent reports on children's
facilities are from observers rather
than participants, but they are all
favourable. It is an attractive village
for families, with the baby slope right
in the centre, and the train giving
warm, easy access to higher slopes.

 # Staying there

Wengen is small, so location isn't as
crucial as in many other resorts. The
main street is ideally placed for the
station and the commuter trains up in
the morning. The hotels on the home
piste offer ski-in ski-out convenience.
Those who don't fancy a steepish
morning climb should avoid places set
well below the station.

HOW TO GO
Wide range of hotels

Most accommodation is in hotels.
Plenty of tour operators organise hotel
packages here. But there is only a
handful of catered chalets, and self-
catering apartments are thin on the
ground. There is a Club Med.
Chalets Surprisingly, perhaps, Wengen
has no particularly luxurious catered
chalets. Inghams' Liane is about the
best; a cosy old place eight minutes
from the centre. The Boss is a well-
located apartment conversion, whilst
the Helene is a spacious first-floor
apartment-chalet near the Liane.
Crystal has a similar selection,
including the comfortable Iris, and
attractive Spycher.
Hotels There are about two dozen
hotels, mostly 4-star and 3-star, with a
handful of simpler places.
££££ Parkhotel Beausite Unattractive
block at top of the village, near cable-
car; generally regarded as the top
hotel. Good pool; kindergarten.
££££ Sunstar Modern hotel on main
street. Comfortable rooms; the lounge
has a welcoming log fire. Live music
some nights. Large pool with views.

Food very good. Friendly staff.
££££ Regina Central position. Smart,
traditional atmosphere. Large,
chandeliered lounge. 'Best food in
Wengen.' Carousel nightclub.
££££ Silberhorn Comfortable modern
4-star in excellent central position,
with choice of restaurants. Popular
with several reporters.
££££ Caprice Small, new, smartly
furnished chalet-style hotel across the
tracks from the Regina. Kindergarten.
£££ Alpenrose Long-standing British
favourite; eight minutes' climb to the
station. Good views; 'first-class' food;
friendly staff.
£££ Eiger Very conveniently sited,
overlooking the station. Focal après-
ski bar. Renovated a few years ago –
comfortable modern rooms.
£££ Falken Further up the hill.
Another British favourite, known
affectionately (and justifiably,
apparently) as 'Fawlty Towers'.
££ Bernerhof Wooden chalet on main
street; jolly bar.
Self-catering The hotel Bernerhof's
decent Residence apartments are well
positioned just off the main street,
with the facilities of the hotel
available to guests.

EATING OUT
Lots of choice

Most of the restaurants in the village
are in the hotels. They offer a good
standard of food and service, and are
open to non-residents. It's worth
trying the Eiger which has a
traditional restaurant and a stube
which has Swiss and French cuisine.
There's no shortage of fondues in the
village. If all you want is a snack, then
try the Pizzeria at the Victoria
Lauberhorn, the Silberhorn or the
Tanne Bar. You could book a table at
Wengernalp's excellent restaurant –
the last train back to Wengen leaves at
11.45pm. If you feel a little daring,
you could ski or toboggan back.

APRES-SKI
Quietly lively

Wengen has a reputation for quiet
nightlife which is rather misleading.
Most British guests here want a
relaxing time, hence reports tend to
minimise what's on offer. But there
are a number of places where a lively
atmosphere is generated, largely by
locals and visiting Germans. A number
of reporters have been pleasantly
surprised by the action available if you
look around. The stube at the Eiger
and the tiny Eiger Bar, just round the
corner, are popular haunts for skiers at
the end of the day. If you've still got

ACTIVITIES

Indoor Swimming pool (in Park Hotel), sauna, solarium, whirlpool, massage (in hotels), cinema (with English films), bowling, billiards **Outdoor** Skating, curling, 20km cleared paths, toboggan runs, sleigh rides, paragliding, glacier flights, sledging excursions, hang-gliding

TOURIST OFFICE

Postcode CH-3823
Tel 00 41 (36) 551414
Fax 553060

energy, you could try the tea dancing at the Silberhorn or Belvedere.

The Tanne and Sinaa's are very popular bars, the latter with live music some nights and karaoke the rest. The bowling alley has the cheapest beer in town (SF4 for 0.5l). There are a couple of discos, a nightclub, dancing and live music in some of the hotels.

The cinema often shows English-language films. Sports fans can enjoy floodlit ski-jumping and slalom competitions for the locals on the slopes in the centre of the village. There are also ice hockey matches.

FOR NON-SKIERS
A good choice
Wengen is a superb resort for non-skiers who want a completely relaxing holiday. The unbeatable scenery makes just sitting around and soaking up the sun thoroughly enjoyable. And the train is ideal for non-skiers who want to get up the mountain to meet friends for lunch (there's a special, though expensive, five-day pass for non-skiers). For those who feel the need to take a little exercise there are some lovely mountain walks, ice skating, a curling club and bowling. Excursions to Interlaken and Berne are possible by train, as is the trip to the Jungfraujoch at 3455m for stunning views and a trip to the Ice Palace carved out of the glacier.

STAYING UP THE MOUNTAIN
Great views
You can stay at two points up the mountain, reached by the railway: the pricey Jungfrau at Wengernalp – a favourite lunch spot with great views – and at Kleine Scheidegg, where there's a choice of rooms in the Kleine Scheidegg hotel or dormitory space above the station buffet.

STAYING DOWN THE VALLEY
The budget option
Staying in a 3-star hotel like the Schützen or Oberland in Lauterbrunnen will cost about half as much as similar accommodation in Wengen. Lauterbrunnen isn't exactly throbbing with nightlife, but the train from Wengen runs until 11.30pm and is included in your lift pass. Staying in Lauterbrunnen has the bonus of improving your chances of getting a seat on the train to Kleine Scheidegg rather than joining the scrum at Wengen. Lauterbrunnen is also much better placed for skiing in Mürren.

You can save even more money by staying further away in the beautiful summer resort of Interlaken. Choose a hotel near Interlaken Ost station, from which you can catch a train to Lauterbrunnen (22mins) or Grindelwald (36mins). Driving takes about as long as the train on weekdays in good weather.

Zermatt 1620m

HOW IT RATES

The skiing

Snow	****
Extent	****
Advanced	*****
Intermediates	****
Beginners	*
Convenience	*
Queues	***
Restaurants	*****

The rest

Scenery	*****
Resort charm	*****
Not skiing	****

✔ Wonderful high and extensive skiing for advanced and intermediate skiers

✔ Spectacular high-mountain scenery, dominated by the Matterhorn

✔ Charming, although rather sprawling, old mountain village, largely traffic-free

✔ Reliable snow at altitude

✔ Best resort in the world for mountain restaurants

✔ Extensive heli-skiing operation for those who can afford it

✔ Nightlife to suit most tastes

✔ Smart shops

✔ Day-trips on skis to Cervinia in Italy are possible, for a different atmosphere and cheap shopping

✗ Getting to main lift stations may involve a long walk, crowded bus- or expensive taxi-ride

✗ Beginners should go elsewhere

✗ The three separate ski areas are not well linked

✗ Getting up the mountain can be a slow business

✗ Electric taxis detract somewhat from the otherwise relaxed, car-free village ambience

ORIENTATION

Zermatt is reached by mountain railway from Täsch, 6km down the valley, where visitors must leave their cars. The village sprawls along a narrow valley either side of a river, with mountains rising steeply on each side.

From near the main station a separate cog railway takes you up to the Gornergrat ski area. A five-minute walk from here is a fast underground funicular up to Sunnegga. The other main lift is at the far end of town – a brisk 15-minute walk away. From there, gondolas take you the first part of the journey up to the Klein Matterhorn and Zermatt's highest skiing.

From this area you can also ski down to **Cervinia** in Italy. The resorts of **Saas-Fee** and **Grächen** are an easy drive from Täsch.

If you are a keen skier you must try Zermatt before you die. There are few places to match it for its combination of excellent advanced and intermediate skiing, reliable snow, magnificent scenery, Alpine-village charm and (not least) mountain restaurants with an unbeatable combination of superb food and stunning views.

Some people complain that the car-free village is spoiled by the intrusive electric carts and taxis, and that the atmosphere is one of Swiss efficiency and international (or intercontinental) tourism rather than mountain-village friendliness. But the place still has a magical feel to it, particularly when you get away from the busy, modern-seeming main street into the winding snowy paths, with their old wooden buildings.

Most of Zermatt's flaws are minor when put alongside its attractions, which come close to matching perfectly our notion of the ideal ski resort. It is certainly one of our favourite resorts, and we are not alone.

 ## The resort

Zermatt started life as a traditional mountain village, then developed as a mountaineering centre in the 19th century before becoming a winter ski resort too. Summer is still as important to the resort as winter.

Be warned – Zermatt is big business. Prices are high and courteous service can be lacking. Most of the restaurants and hotels are owned by a handful of families, and their employees don't always seem happy in their work.

The village is a mixture of chocolate-box chalets and more modern buildings – most of them are built in traditional style. The main street runs past the station and is lined with large luxurious hotels and smart shops.

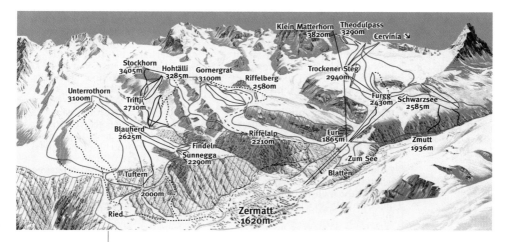

Zermatt doesn't have the relaxed, quaint feel of some other car-free resorts, such as Wengen and Saas-Fee. That's partly because the electric vehicles buzzing around the place are more intrusive and aggressive than elsewhere; partly because of the chance of unfriendly service mentioned earlier; and partly because the clientele is more overtly upmarket and jet-set, with large contingents from Japan and the US.

For a resort with such good and extensive skiing, the place has a remarkably high age profile. Most visitors seem to be over 40, and there are very few of the youthful ski bums you get in rival resorts with comparable skiing, such as Val-d'Isère, St Anton and Chamonix.

The main street, with the station square near one end, is the focal point of village life. The cog railway to the Gornergrat ski area leaves from opposite the main station, and the underground funicular to the Sunnegga area is just a few minutes' walk away. The gondola to the Klein Matterhorn (and the link to Cervinia) is a 15-minute trek from here.

The ski school office, tourist office and most of the resort's hotels, restaurants, shops, bars and nightspots are on, or a short stroll from, the main street. There's another main thoroughfare a few yards away, along the side of the river. To each side of these main arteries are narrow streets and paths, many of which are hilly and treacherous when icy.

⛷ The skiing

There is skiing to suit all standards except absolute beginners, for whom we don't recommend the resort. For intermediate and advanced skiers Zermatt has few rivals worldwide. There are marvellously groomed cruising trails, some of the best mogul skiing available, long, beautiful scenic runs out of view of the lift system, exciting heli-skiing and off-piste possibilities if you hire a guide, as well as the opportunity to ski down into Italy for the day and lunch on pasta and chianti.

THE SKI AREA
Beautiful and varied
Zermatt has three separate ski areas, at best awkwardly linked. The **Sunnegga-Blauherd-Unterrothorn** area is reached by an underground funicular starting about five minutes' walk from the station. This shifts large numbers rapidly but can lead to queues for the subsequent gondola and top cable-car (due to be replaced for the 1996/97 season). From this area you can ski – via south-facing slopes that lose their snow and two gruelling steep drag-lifts – to the second main area, **Gornergrat-Stockhorn**, which can also be reached by the cog railway from opposite the main station. New 'high-speed' trains are supposed to cut the 45-minute ride to 25 minutes – but because old trains still operate on the single-track railway, the new ones have to wait long periods to pass and end up taking just as long. A gondola makes the link back to Sunnegga.

From Gornergrat, if snow-cover permits, you can ski to below Furi to link up with the third and highest ski area, **Klein Matterhorn-Trockener Steg-Schwarzsee**. But you can't do the journey in the opposite direction: once on the Klein Matterhorn, moving to a different mountain means skiing down and getting from

SKI FACTS

Altitude	1620m-3820m
Lifts	36
Pistes	230km
Green/Blue	27%
Red	43%
Black	30%
Artificial snow	19.5km

LIFT PASSES

95/96 prices in
Swiss francs
Area Pass
Covers all lifts on the
Swiss side of the
border.
Beginners Coupon
book (100 coupons
136). Pass for
Riffelberg-Gornergrat
beginner area (adult
6-day 218).
Main pass
1-day pass 60
6-day pass 292
Senior citizens
Over 65 male, 62
female: 6-day pass
219 (25% off)
Children
Under 16: 6-day pass
146 (50% off)
Under 6: free pass
Short-term passes
Single ascent tickets
for most lifts.
Notes Daily
supplement available
to cover all lifts in
Cervinia and
Valtournenche (31).
Alternative passes
Passes for any period
available for each
area of Zermatt
(Gornergrat-
Stockhorn, Sunnegga-
Rothorn, Trockener
Steg-Klein
Matterhorn-
Schwarzsee), and
combinations of
areas. 1-day pass
available for Zermatt,
Cervinia and
Valtournenche (62).
Credit cards: Yes

one end of the village to the other to
catch a lift up. The Klein Matterhorn
gives access to Cervinia – you need to
buy a daily supplement to your lift
pass and the high lifts are frequently
shut because of high winds.

In theory you can ski back to the
village from all three areas. But in
practice the lower runs have often
been shut or unpleasant on our visits.

SNOW RELIABILITY
Good higher up, poor lower down
Zermatt has rocky terrain and a
relatively dry climate. But it also has
some of the highest skiing in Europe,
and quite a bit of snowmaking
machinery.

All three ski areas go up to over
3000m, and the Klein Matterhorn
cable-car is the highest in Europe,
ending at over 3800m and serving a
summer skiing area on the glacier.
There is a huge amount of skiing
above 2500m, much of which is
north-facing, so guaranteeing decent
snow except in freak years.

Artificial snowmaking machines
serve some of the pistes on both the
Sunnegga and Trockener Steg areas,
from around 3000m to under 2000m.
But the runs back to the resort are
often closed or tricky, despite the
artificial help.

FOR ADVANCED SKIERS
Good – with superb heli-skiing
If you've never been, Zermatt has to
be on your short-list. If you have been,
we're pretty sure you'll want to return.

For skiers who love long, fluffy
mogul pitches the skiing at Triftji,
below Stockhorn, is what dreams are
made of. From the top of the
Stockhorn cable-car there's a run
down to the T-bar that serves another
two steep 2km runs – one each side of
the lift. The whole mountainside here
is skied into one vast mogul field –
steep, but not extremely so. Being
north-facing and lying between
3400m and 2700m, the snow here is
usually the best around, which makes
the huge moguls so forgiving that
even we can enjoy them. The snag for
early-season skiers is that this whole
area is unlikely to open until well into
January, and possibly later.

You can continue down from here
to Gant and catch the gondola up to
Blauherd. On that mountain there are
a couple of wonderful off-piste
'downhill routes' from Unterrothorn,
which used to be official black pistes
and have spectacular views down
towards the village and over to the
Matterhorn.

On the Klein Matterhorn, the best
area for good skiers is Schwarzsee,
from where there are several steep
north-facing gullies through the
woods. Unfortunately, you can't ski
these repeatedly without taking the
beautiful, but slightly boring, track
they end up on down to Furi and
catching the cable-car up again.

There are marvellous off-piste
possibilities from the top lifts in each
sector, but they aren't immediately
obvious to those without local
knowledge. They are also dangerous
because of the rocky terrain.

We don't recommend anyone skiing
off-piste without a guide. But in
Zermatt we've found that more of a
problem than elsewhere. The ski
school doesn't run off-piste groups in
the same way they do in resorts such
as Val-d'Isère and Méribel. You have
to hire a guide privately for a full day,
and that's expensive unless you have a
fair-sized group. Much better value for
individuals and couples is a half-day
heli-skiing trip – provided you know
what you're in for.

Zermatt is the Alps' biggest heli-
skiing centre; the helipad resembles a
bus station at times, with choppers
taking off every few minutes. There
are only three main drop-off points, so
this can mean encountering one or
two other groups on the mountain,
even though there are multiple ways
down. From all three points there are
routes that don't require great
expertise. The epic is from the Monte
Rosa, at over 4000m, down through
wonderful glacier scenery to Furi.

FOR INTERMEDIATE SKIERS
Mile after mile of beautiful runs
Zermatt is ideal for adventurous
intermediates. Both the blue and the
red runs tend to be at the difficult end
of their grading. There are some very
beautiful reds down lift-free valleys
from both Gornergrat and Hohtälli –
we like these first thing in the
morning, before anyone else is on
them. The variant which goes to
Riffelalp ends up on a very narrow
wooded path with a sheer cliff and
magnificent views to the right.

On Sunnegga, the 5km Kumme run,
from Unterrothorn to the bottom of
the Patrullarve chair, also gets away
from the lift system and has an
interesting mix of straight-running
and mogul pitches. On Klein
Matterhorn, the reds served by the
Hörnli and Garten drags and the fast
four-person chair from Furgg are all
long and gloriously set at the foot of
the Matterhorn.

SKI SCHOOL

95/96 prices in Swiss francs

Swiss
Classes 6 days
4hr: 2hr am and pm
6 full days: 215
Children's classes
Ages: 6 to 12
6 full days including lunch: 255
Private lessons
Half- or full-day
145 for half-day for
1 to 2 people; each
additional person 5

For the less adventurous intermediate, the best areas are the blues above Riffelberg (on Gornergrat), above Sunnegga, and the runs between Klein Matterhorn and Trockener Steg. Of these, the Riffelberg area often has the best combination of good snow and easy cruising, and is popular with the ski school. Sunnegga gets a lot of sun, but the artificial snow here means that the problem is more often a foot or more of heavy snow near the bottom rather than bare patches.

On the Klein Matterhorn, most of the runs, though marked red on the piste map, are very flat and represent the easiest skiing Zermatt has to offer, as well as the best snow. The problem here is the possibility of bad weather because of the height – high winds, extreme cold and poor visibility can make life very unpleasant. To get to Cervinia, you set off from Testa Grigia with a choice of blue or red routes – even an early intermediate should find the 10km blue route right down to the village manageable.

FOR BEGINNERS
Save your money: learn elsewhere
Zermatt is to be avoided by beginners. The easiest skiing is described above. And there's no decent nursery slope area. Unless you have a compelling reason to start in Zermatt, don't.

FOR EVERYONE
A spectacular cable-car ride
The Klein Matterhorn cable-car is an experience you shouldn't miss if the weather is good. The views down to the glacier and its crevasses, as the car swings steeply into its hole blasted out of the mountain at the top, are stupendous. When you arrive, you walk through a long tunnel, to emerge on top of the world for the highest piste skiing in Europe. The top drag-lifts here are for summer skiing and are normally shut in winter.

FOR CROSS-COUNTRY
Fairly limited
There's a 4km loop at Furi, 3km near the bottom of the gondola to Furi, and 12 to 15km down at Täsch (but don't count on there being snow). There are also some 'ski walking trails' up the mountain – best tackled as part of an organised group.

QUEUES
Still some bottlenecks
Zermatt used to have one of the worst reputations for queues in the Alps. The major problems have now been pretty well eliminated. But there can still be a lengthy scrum for the gondola out of town towards the Klein Matterhorn area at the start of the day. And the lifts above the Sunnegga train can generate queues,

---

The world's best mountain restaurants

We once met a man who had been coming here for 20 years simply because of the mountain restaurants. The choice is enormous (the tourist information says 30 but it seems like more). Most of those we've tried have excellent food and many are in spectacular settings. It is impossible to list here all those worth a visit – so don't limit yourself to those we mention.

At Furi, the Restaurant Furi itself, Aroleid above it and Simi's on the road below all have large sun terraces and good reputations. The hotel at Schwarzsee is set right at the foot of the Matterhorn, at over 2500m, with staggering views of the mountain and the Trockener Steg skiing. On the way back to the village in this area, a couple of cosy, popular stopping-off points are Zum See and Blatten.

The Kulmhotel, at 3100m at Gornergrat, has both self-service and table-service restaurants with amazing views of lift-free mountains and glaciers. Further down, the Riffelalp hotel has excellent pot-au-feu and pasta; the chef came from the 5-star Mont Cervin down in Zermatt.

The large terrace of the restaurant at Sunnegga offers decent food and a great view of children's ski school classes falling down the steep ending of the blue piste nearby. Down at Findeln are several attractive rustic restaurants, including Franz & Heidy's and Chez Vrony ('unbeatable on a snowy day').

Wherever you go, don't miss trying the local alcoholic coffee known as *Schlümli Pflümli* – but only if you don't fancy skiing in the afternoon!

CHILDCARE

There are nurseries in two upmarket hotels. The Kinderparadies in the Nicoletta (661151) takes children aged 2 to 8, from 9am to 5pm. The Kinderclub Pumuckel at the Ginabelle (674535) takes children from 30 months to 6, from 9am to 5pm, and ski tuition is available on the spot.

Ski school lessons start at age 4.

especially at peak ski school periods.

To avoid the queues, start out early – really early. If you catch the Gornergrat train before 8.30am or so, you shouldn't encounter queues until late morning at the earliest.

SKI SCHOOL
Bad experiences

The ski school has a poor reputation with a lot of people we've heard from over the last few years. We're told it's improving under new management; we lack recent reports to confirm this.

Last time we were in Zermatt the school was advertising powder skiing classes, but when we enquired, they weren't happening. We also asked what would happen if we booked a half-day private lesson for powder skiing the following day and the

weather continued to be as appalling as it was then. The surly reply was that if we booked we had to have the lesson as 'you have to learn to ski in bad weather and we have to work to earn'. Great customer relations.

Things are made slightly worse by Zermatt's policy of placing strict limits on tour operator ski guiding.

FACILITIES FOR CHILDREN
Good hotel nurseries

The Nicoletta and Ginabelle hotels have obvious attractions for families who can afford them (though their nurseries are open to others). Despite an exceptionally fat file of skiers' reports on Zermatt, we have no first-hand reports on these facilities. For children of ski-school age, the resort is difficult to recommend.

Selected chalets in Zermatt

GETTING THERE
Air Geneva, transfer
4hr. Zürich, transfer
5hr.

Rail Station in resort.

PACKAGES

Bladon Lines, Chalets
'Unlimited', Crystal,
Inghams, Kuoni,
Lotus Supertravel,
Made to Measure,
Plus Travel, Powder
Byrne, Ski Choice, Ski
Club of GB, Ski La
Vie, Ski Les Alpes,
Ski Scott Dunn, Ski
Total, Ski with Julia,
SkiGower, Swiss
Travel Service,
Thomson

 # Staying there

Choosing where to stay is very important in Zermatt. The solar-powered ski-buses are crowded, and cost SF2 a go; if you can fill a taxi with your group, that can work out as cheap. Walking from one end of the village to the furthest ski lifts can take 15 to 20 minutes and can be unpleasant because of icy paths.

The best spot for most people is near the centre and the Gornergrat and Sunnegga railways. Some of the accommodation is inconveniently situated, up the steep hill across the river from the centre. The Winkelmatten area can be particularly tedious unless you intend to ski the Klein Matterhorn area most days.

Getting up to the village from Täsch is no problem. The trains run on time and have automatically descending ramps which allow you to wheel luggage trolleys on and off. You are met at the other end by electric and horse-drawn taxis and hotel shuttles.

HOW TO GO
A wide choice, packaged or not
Chalets Several operators do have places here, many of the most comfortable contained in sizeable blocks of apartments. Ski Scott Dunn's places are of this kind, including the 'excellent', 'well appointed' Bolero units, in a quiet spot close to the Klein Matterhorn lifts. The Mazot, above the restaurant of the same name, gets good reports and is quite well placed, near the river. It is now part of Bladon Lines' quite wide selection, which also includes the secluded Bambi – a good-value 'real' wooden chalet – and the dear old Diana. Crystal have several chalets, including the 'excellent, central' Aeschhorn.
Hotels There are over 100 hotels, mostly comfortable and traditional-style 3- and 4-stars, but including some luxurious and pricey and some more affordable places.
£££££ Mont Cervin Biggest and perhaps best in town. Elegantly traditional inside, despite blocky looks. Central. Good pool.
££££ Alex An established favourite, close to the station. Welcoming; charmingly decorated. Good facilities, including a pool.
££££ Ambassador Peaceful position on northern fringe, near Gornergrat station. Large pool; fitness room.
££££ Monte Rosa The original Zermatt hotel, towards southern end of village – full of climbing pictures

and mementos, but well modernised. The basement Whymperstube is named after the British conqueror of the Matterhorn, who stayed here.
££££ Ginabelle Smart pair of chalets, over the river, not far from Sunnegga lift; great for families – on-the-spot ski nursery as well as day-care.
££££ Nicoletta Bright modern chalet quite close to centre, with nursery.
£££ Julen Charming, modern-rustic chalet over the river, with Matterhorn views from some rooms.
££ Atlanta No frills, but good food; close to centre, with Matterhorn views from some rooms.
££ Alpina Modest but very friendly, and close to centre.

SKI SCOTT DUNN

helped us to compile the Après-ski section. Our thanks to them.

ACTIVITIES

Indoor Sauna, tennis, hotel swimming pools (some open to public) and a salt water pool, keep-fit centre, squash, billiards, curling, bowling, gallery and excellent Alpine museum, cinemas, indoor golf **Outdoor** Skating, sleigh rides, 30km cleared paths, helicopter flights, para-gliding, cycling

TOURIST OFFICE

Postcode CH-3920
Tel 00 41 (28) 661181
Fax 661185

Self-catering There is a lot of apartment accommodation in the village, but not much of it finds its way to the UK package market – so it sells out early. The hotel Ambassador apartments have excellent facilities. The large, comfortable Armina apartments are ideal for large families. The Malteserhaus apartments are comfortable, but sell early.

STAYING UP THE MOUNTAIN
Comfortable ski-in ski-out seclusion
There are several hotels at altitude, of which the pick is probably the Riffelalp, rebuilt from a ruin in 1988 and recommended for good food and a quiet time. It's at the first stop on the Gornergrat railway. The last train up from Zermatt is at 6pm, but if you fancy a night in town and there's room, you can stay at the Seilers' other hotels – the Schweizerhof for no extra charge, or the Mont Cervin or Monte Rosa for a supplement. At the top of the railway, at 3100m, is the Kulmhotel Gornergrat.

STAYING DOWN THE VALLEY
Attractive for drivers
In Täsch, where visitors must leave their cars, there are five 3-star hotels, costing less than half the price of the equivalent in Zermatt. The Täscherhof is next to the station; the City and Bellevue close by. It's a 13-minute ride from Zermatt, with trains every 20 minutes for most of the day; the last train down is 11.10pm.

EATING OUT
Huge choice at all price levels
There are 100 restaurants to choose from, ranging from top-quality haute cuisine to egg and chips. Among the most highly rated restaurants is the Mazot, which has prices to match the food. At the other end of the scale, Café du Pont has good-value pasta and rösti, and the Bahnhof Buffet offers good food at some of the lowest prices. For its rustic atmosphere and dried meats, try the Whymperstube.

The Chi-Ba-Bou, in the hotel Ambassador, specialises in fondue and has a good reputation. For pizza, Tony's Grotta is hard to beat – we had excellent food but surly service there. Taking the last lift up and strolling down to an early dinner in a mountain hut is worth considering – check their serving times first.

APRES-SKI
Lively and varied
There's something for almost every taste, with a good mix of sophisticated and informal fun, though it certainly helps if you have deep pockets.

When you ski back to the village from the Klein Matterhorn, there are lots of restaurants below Furi for a last drink and sunbathe. In town, there are fewer places than you might expect to have a post-skiing *glühwein* or hot chocolate. The Papperla is one of the most popular (it's busy after dinner, too). Elsie's bar, renowned for its snails and oysters, gets packed early and late. Promenading along the main street is popular, and gives the village a great atmosphere.

Later on, the hotel de la Poste complex is popular for eating, drinking, dancing and jazz. There is something for everyone in this remarkable establishment, from a quiet, comfortable bar (David's Boathouse) to a lively disco-bar (Le Broken); Pink Elephant is a jazz/piano bar; the Brown Cow is a friendly but otherwise uninspiring bar that's usually full of Brits, as it has some of the cheapest beer in town.

The dreary North Face is another cheap place, which is popular with tour reps. Two bars with dancing and a bit more atmosphere are the 'excellent, comfortable' Grampi's and the Tschuggi – a smart cellar with karaoke. Z'Alt Hischi is an atmospheric bar for a quiet drink. The Hexenbar is a similarly cosy place. The hotel Alex appeals to over-30s for eating, drinking and dancing, with 'middle-of-the-road music, quality decor and candlelit tables'.

The Vernissage is an unusually stylish, modern place – a very civilised little cinema with the projection room built into the upstairs bar.

FOR NON-SKIERS
Considerable attractions
Zermatt is an easy place for non-skiers to spend time (and money). And if lunch up the mountain appeals, this is nearly as good a resort for non-skiers as it is for skiers – it's easy to get around and meet skiing friends. The lack of a public swimming pool is no real problem, with 15 hotel pools, and there is a decent range of other activities for the energetic. The Alpine museum is recommended.

United States

As you can see from the costs chapter (page 23) skiing in the US is no longer much more expensive than skiing in many top French, Swiss or Austrian resorts. The dollar has been as weak as the pound in recent years, transatlantic fares have remained low and US accommodation offers good value for money.

Most people who try US skiing are captivated by it. Wherever you go you'll be struck by the high standards of service and courtesy you receive and by the immaculate piste grooming that happens every night. Depending on the resort you choose you may also be struck by the superb quality of the snow, the cute wild-west ambience and how easy it is to visit other nearby ski areas too. But don't fall into the trap of lumping all US resorts together – they differ enormously. And there are distinct disadvantages to American skiing too.

It was snow that first took British skiers to America in large numbers, during the Alpine snow droughts of the late 1980s. The super-high Rockies had the reputation of getting limitless quantities of super-light snow, and in those crucial years they certainly did better than the Alps. The reputation went slightly beyond the reality, but in practice it doesn't matter – most American resorts have serious snowmaking facilities anyway. What's more, they use them – they lay down a base of artificial snow early in the season, rather than using snow-guns to make up for a lack of the real thing.

This is partly a reaction to the pattern of natural snowfall. A lot of the Rockies' snow arrives relatively late in the season – something that seems to be increasingly true in the Alps, but not traditionally what we expect. When skiing in January or even February, you may encounter signs saying: 'Caution: Early Season Conditions Apply'. What they mean is that you may occasionally encounter a rock.

The state of Utah has staked a claim to the best snow conditions of all by adopting the slogan 'Greatest Snow on Earth'. The Utah resorts – particularly Snowbird and Alta – get very large amounts of snow, and it is by our standards superbly powdery stuff. But measurements of water content have shown that Colorado gets even lighter snow, justifying its 'Champagne powder' label. California, on the other hand, tends to have much heavier snow, often referred to as 'Sierra Cement'. And New England has a reputation for hard and icy conditions.

Piste grooming is taken very seriously – most American resorts set standards that few resorts in the Alps can match. But this doesn't mean that there aren't moguls – far from it. It's just that you get moguls where the resort says you can expect moguls, and not where you're expecting an easy cruise. Val d'Isère please copy. American resorts are well organised in lots of other respects, too.

Many offer free guided tours of the ski area. Lift queues are short, partly because they are highly disciplined, and spare seats on chair-lifts are religiously filled, with the aid of cheerful, conscientious attendants. Piste maps and boxes of tissues are freely available at the bottom of most lifts. Mountain 'hosts' are on hand to advise you about the best possible routes to take. Ski school standards are uniformly high – with the added advantage of English being the native language. And facilities for children are impressive too.

US resorts have the reputation of not providing opportunities for off-piste skiing, but this seriously misrepresents the position. It's true that ski areas practically always have a boundary, and that skiing outside it is discouraged or forbidden. But within the ski area there is often challenging skiing that is very much like off-piste terrain in an

Alpine resort – with the important advantage that it is much safer because it's patrolled and checked for avalanche risk.

There are drawbacks to US skiing as well, though. One is that many resorts (including big names) have ski areas that are very modest in extent compared with major Alpine areas. But many US resorts are very close to each other – so if you are prepared to travel a bit, you won't get bored. A more serious problem, as far as we are concerned, is that the skiing day is short. The lifts often shut at 3pm or 3.30pm, even late in the season. That may explain another major drawback for skiers who like a good lunch on the mountain – the dearth of decent mountain restaurants. Monster self-service cafeterias doing pizza, burgers and other fast foods are the norm – so that people can spend as much time skiing and as little time eating as possible. Small, atmospheric restaurants with table service are rare.

It's also true that much of the terrain and many of the runs are monotonous. You don't get the spectacular mountain scenery and the distinctive high-mountain runs of the Alps – most of the skiing is below the tree-line (the upside of this is that the skiing is very unlikely to be interrupted by bad weather). And because most areas have been developed specifically for the skiing with no old village or farming communities at the base, they can feel rather artificial.

The grading of pistes (or trails, to use the local term) is different from Europe. Red runs don't exist. The colours used are combined with shapes: green circles, blue squares, black diamonds. Greens correspond fairly closely to greens in Europe (that is, in France, where they are mainly found). American blues largely correspond to blues here, but also include tougher intermediate runs that would be red here; these are sometimes labelled as double blue squares, although in some resorts a hybrid blue-black grading is used instead. American blacks correspond to steeper European reds and easier European blacks. Many US resorts have double black diamonds, which are seriously steep – often steeper than the steepest pistes in the Alps and including high, open bowls.

US resorts vary as widely in style and convenience as Alpine resorts. There are old restored wild west towns such as Telluride, Crested Butte and Aspen, genuine cowboy towns such as Jackson Hole, purpose-built monstrosities such as Copper Mountain and Snowbird, and even neon-lit, skycraping gambling dens such as Heavenly. But two things they all have in common are good-value, spacious accommodation and good, reasonably priced restaurants.

Be prepared, though, for altitude problems – most resorts are higher than the 2300m of Europe's highest (Val Thorens) and some are built at almost 3000m with skiing going up to 4000m.

In the end, your reaction to American skiing may depend mainly on your reaction to America. If repeated cheerful exhortations to have a nice day wind you up, perhaps you'd better stick to the Alps. If you like the idea that the customer is king, give America a try. We love it and look forward to our annual visit.

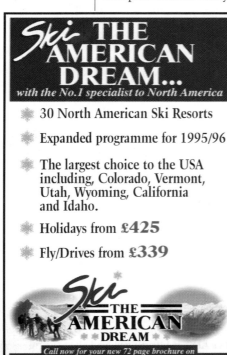

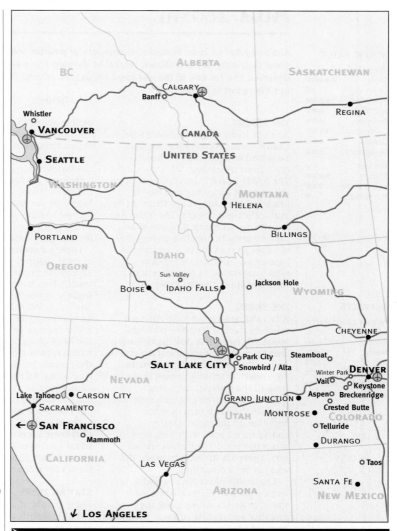

Alta 2605m

Alta's reputation is for remarkable amounts of powder snow to arrive with great regularity, for a stubborn refusal to develop the area as some say it deserves and for one of the cheapest lift passes around. The skiing is classy but the resort is limited.

HOW IT RATES

The skiing

Snow	*****
Extent	*
Advanced	*****
Intermediates	***
Beginners	***
Convenience	****
Queues	***
Restaurants	***

The rest

Scenery	****
Resort charm	***
Not skiing	*

SKI FACTS

Altitude	2605m-3215m
Lifts	12
Pistes	2200 acres
Green	25%
Blue	40%
Black	35%
Art. snow	25 acres

TOURIST OFFICE

Postcode UT 84092
Tel 00 1 (801)
7423333
Fax 7423333

THE RESORT

Alta sits at the craggy head of Little Cottonwood Canyon, 2km beyond Snowbird and less than an hour's drive from downtown Salt Lake City. The lovely peaceful location was once the scene of a bustling and bawdy mining town – long since flattened by avalanches and neglect. The 'new' Alta is a strung-out handful of lodges and parking areas that lacks a centre; life revolves around the two separate lift base areas – Albion and Wildcat – which are linked by a bi-directional rope tow along the flat valley floor.

THE SKIING

Alta's **ski area** can't have changed much in the last 20 years; no high-speed lifts here. The dominant feature seen from the resort is the steep end of a ridge that separates the two basins. To the left, from Albion base at the head of the canyon, the skiing stretches away over easy green terrain towards the black runs of Point Supreme; to the right, a more concentrated bowl with blue runs down the middle and blacks either side. There are lift links between the areas in both directions.

A base altitude of 2600m and a vertical drop of 600m are modest statistics for US resorts – but the quantity and quality of snow that falls here, and the northerly orientation of the slopes, put Alta right in the top drawer for **snow reliability**.

Small though it is, Alta is great for **advanced skiers**, who flock to the high ridges after a fresh snowfall. There are dozens of steep chutes through the trees on the front faces leading back to the Wildcat base area, and wide steep slopes around the rim of the Albion basin.

Intermediate skiers with a sense of adventure do pretty well at Alta, too – there's good variety in the standard of runs and the easier blacks offer a gradual progression. But high-mileage piste-bashers will find it very limited.

Timid intermediates and **beginners** need to stick to the Albion side, where most of the lower runs are broad, gentle and well groomed.

There's little provision for **cross-country** skiing but it does go on –

mainly across the road from the downhill slopes – and those experienced enough or willing to hire a guide could certainly venture into the surrounding back-country.

Queues are not unknown at Alta – the snow record, easy access from Salt Lake City and the rather slow chair-lifts see to that – especially in spring and on sunny weekends. At least the lift company limits the tickets sold.

There's a **mountain restaurant** in each sector of the skiing – the Alpenglow on the Albion side has a small, often busy, terrace and a slightly Alpine feel to it and Watson's Shelter on Wildcat has both cafeteria and table-service sections.

The famous Alf Engen **ski school** has been going for over 50 years, which is plenty of time to sharpen up the powder lessons in which it specialises. All the regular classes and clinics are also available and the small classes, enthusiastic teachers and low prices provide good value.

The ski school does organise **children's** lessons, and day-care for those aged over 3 months is available at the Albion ticket building – but there's little else for kids to do.

STAYING THERE

There are about a dozen places to stay – simple **hotels and apartments**. None of the locations is bad, but for the best ski-in ski-out convenience the smart Alta Lodge and the comfortable modern Goldminer's Daughter take the honours. The latter has a busy après-ski bar. Snowpine Lodge is small and welcoming, between the lift bases. We don't know of any packages.

Eating out in Alta means the Shallow Shaft steakhouse and it's worth a visit if you haven't already paid for your dinner; for most people eating in is the routine. The lodges expect to provide dinner for their guests but not for others.

Après-ski is self-contained in the lodges and rarely goes beyond a few drinks and possibly a ski movie.

Nor is there much to keep **non-skiers** occupied – it's a pleasant location but any distractions other than mountains, snow and skiers will require a trip to Salt Lake City.

Aspen 2420m

✔ *A lot of skiing, with terrain to suit all standards*

✔ *Gets better every season, with new lifts making more good skiing more accessible*

✔ *Attractive, characterful town, with lots of tempting shops*

✔ *Good for celebrity-spotting*

✔ *Lively nightlife*

✔ *Ski-in, ski-out accommodation at Snowmass*

✘ *Skiing spread over four separate mountains*

✘ *Rather sprawling town, so choice of accommodation important*

✘ *Can be very expensive (although Aspen can also be done on the cheap – see page 388)*

Aspen is well-known for its rich and famous guests, lots of whom have holiday homes here and private jets parked at the local airport. Jack Nicholson, Martina Navratilova, Jane Fonda and countless more are regulars. But don't let that put you off. Most celebs are keen to keep a low profile and disappear into the crowd, rather than be mobbed by adoring fans.

Aspen has a lot going for it. Its four mountains between them offer a lot of skiing, with enough to keep every standard of skier interested. It has the biggest vertical drop in Colorado. The town is a beautifully restored Victorian silver-mining town, with wide streets built in typical American grid fashion and a huge variety of restaurants, bars and plush shops. And the resort doesn't rest on its laurels – it is always devising new attractions and building new high-speed quads.

The main drawback of the place is that you can spend a fortune. But you don't have to: Aspen need not cost more than any other major US resort.

ORIENTATION

Aspen is a compact town with a typical American grid of streets. The skiing is on four separate mountains. Aspen Mountain starts right next to the town. There is more accommodation (and more skiing, in terms of area) at Snowmass, 12 miles to the west. The other two ski mountains – Tiehack and Aspen Highlands – are between these extremes. All the mountains are served by an efficient, free ski-bus.

Day-trips to other resorts are unlikely, but a two-centre holiday is easily arranged, and there's a special lift pass to encourage you to combine Aspen with Vail, including a free transfer between the resorts.

 ## The resort

Just over a century ago Aspen was a booming silver-mining town of 12,000 inhabitants, boasting six newspapers, an opera house and a red light district. But Aspen's fortunes took a nose-dive when the silver price plummeted in 1893, and by the 1930s the population had shrunk to 400 or so. Elegant Victorian buildings – such as the Wheeler Opera House and the Hotel Jerome – had fallen into disrepair.

The historic centre has been beautifully renovated to form the core of what is now the most fashionable ski town in the Rockies. There's a huge variety of shops, bars, restaurants and galleries – though you may find some of the prices a deterrent. Spreading out from this centre, you'll find a mixture of developments, ranging from the homes of the super-rich, on the outskirts, to the mobile homes for the workers who now find it too expensive to buy or rent in Aspen.

Twelve miles away is Snowmass, with its own mountain and modern ski-in, ski-out accommodation.

 ## The skiing

Aspen has lots of skiing for every standard; you just have to pick the right mountain.

THE SKI AREA
Widely dispersed

There are four mountains, only one accessible from Aspen town. Skiing development started in Aspen on a small scale in the late 1930s. The first ski-lift (then the world's longest chair-lift) was opened shortly after the Second World War, and Aspen hasn't looked back since. By 1958, development of Buttermilk (now Tiehack) and Aspen Highlands had started. Snowmass opened in 1967.

Getting around between the areas by free ski-bus is easy. Each area is big enough to keep you amused for a full day. And all of them have regular free guided tours.

The Silver Queen gondola takes you from right in the heart of town to the top of **Aspen Mountain** in 15 minutes. The alternative – to take three chair-lifts – is only worth considering if the queues are horrific

SKI FACTS

Altitude 2400m-3600m
Lifts 42
Pistes 4160 acres
Green 13%
Blue 44%
Black 43%
Art. snow 483 acres

for the gondola. A series of chairs including, surprisingly, only one high-speed quad, serve the different ridges – Gentleman's Ridge along the eastern edge, the Ridge of Bell in the centre, and Ruthie's to the west – with valleys or gulches in between. There are no green runs at all. In general, there are long cruising blue runs along the valley floors and short steep blacks down from the ridges. The mountain is ideal for skiers of good intermediate standard or better.

Snowmass is an entirely separate ski resort some 12 miles west of Aspen. It's the largest of Aspen's ski areas – some 2,500 acres in all – fanning out from the purpose-built village at the

base. Chair-lifts head off towards four separate peaks, the skiing of which is all interlinked. From left to right looking at the mountain, these are Elk Camp, High Alpine, Big Burn (named after the fire started by Ute Indians protesting against the mining that was ruining their terrain) and Sam's Knob. Many of the runs are wide, sweeping, perfectly groomed highways, providing relaxing and scenic skiing. But it also has some of the toughest skiing in the whole area.

Tiehack – said to be the closest ski area to an airport in the world – is famous as a learning mountain, although a fair proportion of the skiing would suit intermediates too.

The runs fan out from the top in three directions. West Buttermilk, with long, gentle runs through the woods, is ideal for beginners, as is the Main Buttermilk area (though this also has some good intermediate skiing); Tiehack, to the east, is a bit more demanding, but ideal for an intermediate skier to learn or perfect mogul, powder or tree skiing.

Aspen Highlands boasts the greatest vertical drop in Colorado – 1155m. Until 1993, it was separately owned and run, and famous for its antiquated lifts. It is now run by the Aspen Skiing Company, and last season saw two new high-speed quads that now whisk you to the top in under 20 minutes – half the time it used to take. And another 45 acres of new tough tree skiing was opened up. The skiing is a strange mixture of tough blacks and easy greens and blues. And the views from the top are the best that Aspen has to offer – the famous Maroon Bells that appear on all the scenic postcards.

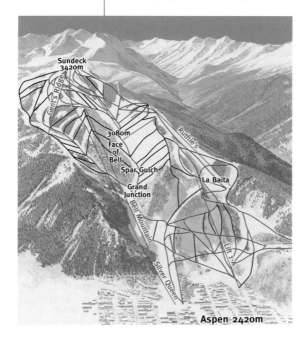

Sundeck
3420m

Gent's Ridge

3080m
Face
of
Bell

Ruthie's

Spar Gulch

Grand
Junction

La Baita

Bell Mountain

Lift 1A

Silver Queen

Aspen 2420m

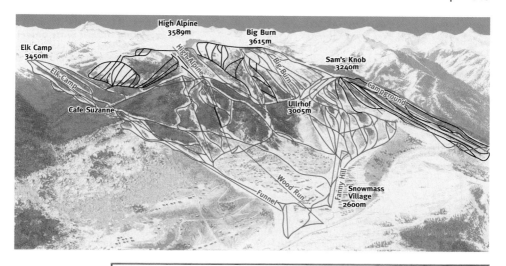

Powder tours

If you can stump up the $200 for the day's tour, this is an experience not to miss – particularly if you hire the revolutionary 'Fat Sticks' to ski on. These are skis about twice as wide as normal ones. The $35 a day ski hire is well worth it for the transformation of your powder skiing ability. If your normal experience of powder is one of continually searching for your skis that have been buried under feet of apparently pristine snow, these are for you.

Your day starts with you signing a form which relieves the Aspen Skiing Company of all responsibility for your safety and welfare, before you climb into the Silver Queen gondola just after 8am (while it is still shut to other skiers). At the top you are armed with an avalanche transceiver and instructed on how to search out your lost colleagues should they be buried under an avalanche (so far there has been no need to use these). You then pile into a heated snow-cat and are driven off onto the 'backside' of Aspen Mountain. Away from the lifts and other skiers, your two guides search out untracked snow.

The cat rejoins you at the end of each run and takes you off for the next. You're likely to squeeze in about 10 runs in all. At midday, you stop for a better-than-average buffet lunch at an old mountain cabin.

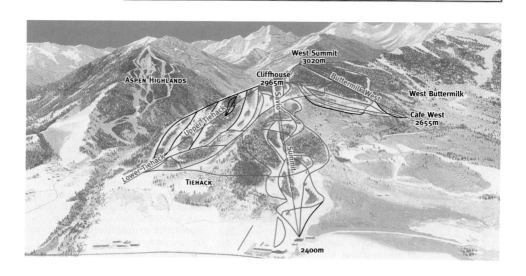

LIFT PASSES

94/95 prices in dollars
Four Mountain Pass
Covers Aspen
Mountain, Aspen
Highlands, Tiehack
and Snowmass, and
shuttle bus between
the areas.
Beginners Included in
price of beginners'
lessons; 129 for 3-day
learn-to-ski or
snowboard lessons.
Main pass
1-day pass 49
6-day pass 254
(low season 222 –
13% off)
Senior citizens
Over 65: 6-day pass
186 (27% off)
Over 70: free pass
Children
Under 13: 6-day pass
162 (36% off)
Under 7: free pass
Notes Single day
passes cover one area
only. All passes over
3 days allow one day
off, eg 6-day pass
valid for 7 days, with
one non-skiing day.
Alternative passes
Premier Passport is
designed for two-
centre holiday. Covers
all Aspen and Vail
skiing and one-way
transfer between the
resorts. Allows from
10 days skiing out of
12 up to 18 out of 21
(38 per day).

SNOW RELIABILITY
Never a problem

Aspen has a good natural snow record. In addition, all areas except Snowmass have substantial snowmaking capabilities. Immaculate grooming adds to the quality of the piste skiing.

FOR ADVANCED SKIERS
Tiehack is the only soft stuff

There's plenty of skiing to choose from – all the mountains except for Tiehack offer lots of challenges.

Aspen Mountain has a formidable array of double black diamond skiing. From the top of the Silver Queen gondola, try Walsh's, Hyrup's or Kristi, linking up with Gentleman's Ridge and Jackpot for a combination of steep slopes, moguls and trees – the longest black run on the mountain. Or head for the Ridge of Bell – and a chance to show off your mogul skills to those going up in the chair or gondola. Don't miss the expert tree and bump slopes running off the International into Spar Gulch – these are collectively called the Dumps, because they were formed out of slag and rubble dumped by the miners back in the silver-mining days. There are numerous other black challenges too – 65 per cent of the trails are black.

At Snowmass, expert skiers face a hike to get to the Hanging Valley Wall and Glades and to most of the Cirque area runs. But what a reward! Beautiful scenery, wonderful tree skiing at Hanging Valley and steep enough everywhere to satisfy the keenest. The Cirque area is mainly above the tree-line, with steep, narrow, often rocky, chutes – Gowdy's is one of the steepest in the whole area, AMF ('Adios My Friend') speaks for itself.

The runs back down under the High Alpine lift offer cruising, bumps and tree skiing within a small area. And, lower down, there's a network of long black trails down from Sam's Knob.

At Aspen Highlands, there are challenging runs from top to bottom of the mountain. At the top the Steeplechase area consists of a number of parallel natural avalanche chutes, and their elevation means the snow stays light and dry. The Olympic Bowl area, served by Chair 5, has great views of the Maroon Bells peaks and some serious moguls. Chair 8 takes you to more moguls. Chair 6 serves a nice varied area – you can cream down Thunderbowl, practice bumps on Powderbowl and enjoy good snow on the little-used Limelight.

On top of this there's the 45 acres of tough skiing opened last season.

FOR INTERMEDIATE SKIERS
More grooming than a male model

Snowmass is the best mountain for intermediate skiers and the Big Burn is definitely the first place to head for. The huge open area is a cruising paradise. The runs merge into each other, though there's a satisfying variety of terrain and some trees to add interest. Free snowcat rides take you from the top of the Big Burn chair to less accessible parts of the skiing.

The easiest intermediate skiing is reached from the Elk Camp lift – up-graded to a high-speed quad for the 1995/96 season. There's a choice of runs from the top, through spruce trees. Naked Lady lift gives you access to yet more intermediate slopes – a little trickier and more varied including some moguls. The Sam's Knob sector offers slightly more advanced intermediate skiing. Finally, Green Cabin, accessed from the top of the High Alpine lift, is a magical intermediate run cruising from top to bottom of the mountain, with spectacular views on the way.

Most intermediate skiing in Aspen Highlands is above the mid-mountain Merry-Go-Round restaurant. The most popular slope, Scarlet's Run, is directly above it. Grand Prix is a wide cruiser between trees – but watch out for the path to the right taking you back to mid-mountain, otherwise you hit a double black diamond run. Beyond Grand Prix, you can reach Picnic Point via Upper Robinson's – a table and views make it a good place to pause.

Aspen Mountain has its fair share of intermediate slopes, but they tend to be tougher than on the other mountains. Copper Bowl and Spar Gulch running between the ridges making up Aspen Mountain are great cruises early in the morning but can get crowded later. Upper Aspen Mountain, at the top of the Silver Queen gondola, has a dense network of well-groomed blues. Ruthie's has more cruising runs and less in the way of crowds. Ruthie's Run leads into the popular Snow Bowl, a wide open area with moguls on the left but groomed on the right and centre.

Tiehack may not be the obvious choice for intermediate skiers – yet it has quite a lot going for it. The Main Buttermilk runs offer good, easy slopes to practise your technique on. And good intermediates should be able to handle the relatively easy black runs in the Tiehack area and gain the confidence to progress to the somewhat tougher black pistes on other mountains.

SKI SCHOOL

94/95 prices in dollars

**Aspen Skiing
Company**
Snowmass and
Tiehack for all
abilities; Aspen
Mountain for
intermediate and
advanced only
Classes 5 days
5hr: 10.30-3.30;
3hr: 12.30-3.30
3 full days: 129
Children's classes
Ages: 7 to 12
5 5hr 45min days:
240
Private lessons
1½hr, 3hr (am or pm)
or 6hr
140 for 1½hr, for
1 to 5 people

CHILDCARE

The childcare
possibilities are too
numerous to list in
detail.

A new children's
'learning center' was
opened at Tiehack a
couple of years ago –
Fort Frog – with a
special children's
shuttle bus from
Aspen. The Powder
Pandas classes there
take children aged 3
to 6. At Snowmass,
the Big Burn Bears ski
kindergarten takes
children from age 4,
and children aged 18
months to 3 have the
Snow Cubs
playschool.

There are several all-
day non-skiing
crèches, taking
children from as
young as 12 months.

FOR BEGINNERS
Can be a great place to learn

Tiehack is a great mountain for
beginners, whether tackling skiing or
snowboarding (banned on Aspen
Mountain). West Buttermilk has
beautifully groomed, gentle and tree-
lined runs – ideal for building up
confidence. The easiest slope of all,
though, is found in the central Main
Buttermilk sector – Panda Peak.

The easiest beginner slope at
Snowmass is the wide Assay Hill, at
the bottom of the Elk Camp area.
Right next to Snowmass Village Mall is
the Fanny Hill high-speed lift and
beginners' run of the same name.
Further up, from Sam's Knob, a series
of runs offer a long, gentle cruise.

Despite its mighty vertical rise,
Aspen Highlands boasts the highest
concentration of beginners' runs in
Aspen, located below the Merry-Go-
Round restaurant. Right by the base
area, Chair 9 serves Half Inch – the
easiest beginners' slope. The biggest
problem is meeting up with more
experienced friends for lunch – they
may be on a different mountain.

FOR CROSS-COUNTRY
Back-country bonanza

There are 80km of groomed trails
between Aspen and Snowmass in the
Roaring Fork Valley – the most
extensive maintained cross-country
system in the US. And the Ashcroft Ski
Touring Centre maintains around
30km of trails around Ashcroft, a
mining ghost-town. Take the
opportunity of eating at the Pine
Creek Cookhouse, some 2.5km from
the Ashcroft trailhead: excellent food
and accessible by ski or sledge only. In
addition, there are limitless miles of
ungroomed trails. Aspen is at one end
of the famous 230-mile Tenth
Mountain Division Trail, heading
north-east and almost linking up to
Vail, with 13 huts for overnight stops.

QUEUES
Few problems

There are rarely major queues on any
of the mountains. At Aspen Mountain,
the Silver Queen gondola can have
delays at peak times, but you have
alternative lifts to the top.

Snowmass has so many alternative
lifts and runs that you can normally
avoid any problems. But the long,
slow chairs can be cold in mid-winter,
and the home slope gets very busy.

Aspen Highlands is almost always
queue-free, even at peak times.

The two lifts out of Main Buttermilk
sometimes get congested.

MOUNTAIN RESTAURANTS
Good by American standards

Even this smartest of US skiing resorts
can't compare with, say, Switzerland
for mountain restaurants. But there
are some good places.

On Aspen Mountain, try La Baita
(an Italian-style restaurant), with good
views down onto Aspen. Sundeck, at
the top, has been taken over by the
Little Nell hotel and boasts, 'You can't
find a better meal on a mountain west
of the Alps.' Fabulous views, and non-
skiers can reach it on the gondola.

At Snowmass, Gwyn's is an elegant
restaurant serving excellent food. The
best views of the mountains
surrounding this area are from Sam's
Knob restaurant and cafeteria.

Merry-Go-Round at mid-mountain
at Aspen Highlands is worth a visit,
not just for its good, if fairly basic,
cooking (the strudel is famous), but
also for the great view of skiers
approaching it (including the
freestylers on Fridays at noon). At 1pm
you could head for the Cloud Nine
picnic deck with a snack in the hope
that the ski patrollers will do their
legendary dramatic ski jump over the
54-foot sun deck.

SKI SCHOOL
Special programmes

There's a wide variety of specialised ski
instruction available – bumps, powder,
mountain racing and so on – and a
four-day Mountain Masters program
on Aspen and Snowmass, where small
groups of intermediate and advanced
skiers ski with the same instructor for
five hours a day. Video analysis,
NASTAR races, on-mountain picnics
and a farewell party are all included.

FACILITIES FOR CHILDREN
Choice of crèches?

There is no shortage of advertised
childcare arrangements, but one
reporter found care for pre-skiing
children at Snowmass was actually in
short supply (and very expensive).
We've had a rave review this year from
a mother whose 7- and 8-year-olds
loved the ski school and 'were
reluctant to ski with mummy and
daddy for the first time ever'. Each
morning they were taken by the Max
the Moose bus to Tiehack's very
impressive Fort Frog – a wooden
frontier-style fort, with lookout
towers, flags, old wagons, a jail, saloon
and native American teepee village.
They were taught by 'very impressive
instructors with great personalities –
and delivered back to Aspen to be met
at 3.30pm'.

PACKAGES

American Dream, American Skiworld, Bladon Lines, Crystal, Enterprise, Inghams, Lotus Supertravel, Made to Measure, Ski Activity, Ski Independence, USAirtours

Snowmass American Dream, Crystal, Inghams, Lotus Supertravel, USAirtours

GETTING THERE

Air Aspen, transfer ½hr. Eagle, transfer 1½hr. Denver, transfer 3½hr.

Rail Glenwood Springs (70km).

 # Staying there

In Aspen, by far the most convenient place to stay is near the Silver Queen gondola. Buses for the other ski areas also leave from nearby. For ski-in, ski-out convenience, choose Snowmass. The buses from Aspen run until 1am.

HOW TO GO
Accommodation for all pockets
Aspen Mountain and Snowmass between them have beds for some 16,000 guests in a mixture of hotels, inns, B&Bs, lodges and condos – and now there are one or two catered chalets as well.
Chalets American Skiworld have a very comfortable homestead complete with marble fireplace, just out of town. Crystal have the attractive chalet, Meadowood, near Aspen Highlands.
Hotels Aspen isn't short of luxury hotels. For cheaper places see Aspen on the cheap, below.
£££££ Ritz-Carlton Opulent city-type hotel, near the gondola. Fitness centre, outdoor pool, whirlpool spas, sauna.
£££££ Little Nell Stylish modern hotel right by the gondola, with ski-in, ski-out access. Pampers you in a

slightly more Colorado style – fireplaces in every room, outdoor pool, hot tub, sauna and more.
£££££ Jerome Step back a century in history in one of Aspen's most famous hotels. Victorian authenticity combined with modern-day luxury; swimming pool, hot tub.
££££ Sardy House Elegantly furnished, intimate little hotel on edge of centre, 10 minutes from the gondola, with comfortable, though less captivating, modern extension. Small outdoor pool, hot tub.
££££ Lenado Neat modern B&B place with open-fire lounge and cosy rooms, within walking distance of gondola.
££££ Silvertree. Large ski-in, ski-out hotel at Snowmass. Pools, hot tubs.
£££ Innsbruck Inn 'Excellent' Tyrolean-style hotel, a fair walk from centre and lifts.
Self-catering The standards here are high, even in US terms. Many of the smarter developments have their own free shuttle-buses. The luxurious Gant, with impressive communal facilities, is close to the gondola and the centre. The smart Aspen Club complex enjoys a prime position next to the gondola, with free entry to the excellent health and sports facilities. Chateau Roaring

---

Aspen on the cheap?

So, your bank balance doesn't match that of Aspen's celebrity clients, but you still want to have a good time in America's trendiest resort? Well, all it takes is a bit of planning.

Accommodation is the major expenditure. If you're prepared to risk slightly inferior snow conditions, you can save up to a third by going either early (mid-Nov to mid-Dec) or late (mid-March to mid-April).

Two favourites among Aspen's lower-cost motels are the Christmas Inn ($100 a double room per night), on the edge of town, and Aspen Manor Lodge, very close to the gondola ($120). Both throw in a big buffet breakfast. The least expensive motel rooms are at the Alpine Lodge ($70 for double with shared bath), but it's a bit of a hike out. Budget options closer to town are the Tyrolean Lodge and the Swiss Chalet, which has kitchenettes (both charge around $80). Finding a two-bed condo for under $200 is increasingly difficult; of the various management companies, Aspen Classic Properties tend to offer the most reasonable prices. There are several decent motels at under $50 in the likeable-enough town of Glenwood Springs, 45 miles north.

Eating and drinking need not cost more than in any other major US resort. Be sure to scan Aspen's two free daily papers for news of dinner specials and happy hours. The town's visitor centre stocks menus and money-saving coupons. The excellent Wienerstube serves delicious Austrian breakfasts for little more than $5. Sno' Beach Cafe in Snowmass does breakfasts from $4. There are plenty of informal dining spots, where a meal can cost less than $10. The Red Onion serves up half-price appetisers in the afternoons and good burritos and burgers. Little Annie's has big platters of trout, chicken or ribs for around $12. Mexican restaurants do good-value meals: try Su Casa or the less expensive La Cocina. Stewpot at Snowmass serves filling meals.

At night, neither the country and western Shooters, nor the rock and dance club, Double Diamond, imposes big cover charges.

Fork and Eau Claire, four blocks from the gondola, are spacious, well-furnished and with the largest outdoor pool in Aspen. There are also some luxurious individual houses on offer.

Lots of restaurants take part in the 'A la Car' scheme: you order from a book of menus, and the meal is delivered.

EATING OUT
Dining dilemma
There is an exceptionally wide choice of styles of eating, including Japanese, Thai and Swiss, as well as the more usual options. The most sophisticated and expensive food is in the top hotels, but there are some excellent upmarket restaurants around the town too. Piñons serves innovative American food in toned-down South-Western surroundings. Syzygy is a suave upstairs place with live jazz. There are some excellent Italian places, including Abetone and Farfalla (where queueing is part of the dining experience). Cache Cache does good-value French with Italian options.

Cheaper places include: Ute City Banque, serving grills and seafood in a lively atmosphere; Hard Rock Cafe – part of the famous chain, with one of Madonna's cast-off basques on display; Planet Hollywood – opened here two years ago, taking over the premises with the famous opening roof – so you can see the stars above you as well as those next to you; Poppie's Bistro Cafe – famous for its breads and puddings; and Su Casa – probably the best Mexican.

Boogies and Mezza Luna were highly recommended by one reporter this year.

Krabloonik, outside Snowmass, reachable by car or cross-country skis, has a rustic log cabin atmosphere.

ACTIVITIES

Indoor Aspen Athletic Club (racquetball, swimming, free weights, aerobics classes, sauna, steam, jacuzzi), skating
Outdoor Ballooning, para-gliding, snowcat tours, snow-shoe tours, sleigh rides, dog-sledding, snow-mobiles, tours of mines

TOURIST OFFICE

Postcode CO 81612
Tel 00 1 (303) 9251220
Fax 9253785

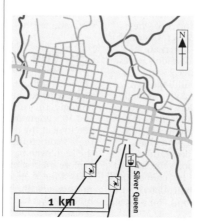

APRES-SKI
Party time
Immediately after skiing, Ajax Tavern next to the Little Nell (formerly Shlomo's) is the place to be in Aspen.

There are lots of other bars to move on to, early or late in the evening. The J-bar of the Jerome hotel and the Red Onion still have a local feel to them, attracting a changing crowd throughout the evening. There is the statutory micro-brewery, with the Flying Dog basement bar attached. Shooters Saloon is a splendid country and western dive, with pool tables and (if you're lucky) line-dancing. Legends is a livelier bar, with table football and pool. La Cantina serves the best margaritas in town. The Double Diamond is a big, brash, busy place that has video, good bands and dancing. Tippler is a quite spacious disco-bar, good for meeting people. For exclusive peace and quiet, wangle an invitation to the Caribou club.

FOR NON-SKIERS
Silver service
Aspen has lots to offer the non-skier, especially if you've got a high credit card limit and like shopping. Just wandering around town is pleasant. Getting up the mountains to meet skiers for lunch is easy. Most hotels have excellent spa facilities.

Breckenridge 2925m

HOW IT RATES

Ratings for extent, advanced and intermediates relate to the whole Ski the Summit area, including Copper Mountain, Keystone and Arapahoe Basin.

The skiing

Snow	*****
Extent	****
Advanced	****
Intermediates	****
Beginners	****
Convenience	***
Queues	****
Restaurants	*

The rest

Scenery	***
Resort charm	***
Not skiing	***

ORIENTATION

Breckenridge is based around the long Main Street, with a lot of accommodation towards the top-end where two high-speed quad chairs head up into the skiing. They lead to Peak 9, one of four mountains all linked by lifts and pistes. A regular free shuttle runs around the resort to the Peak 9 and Peak 8 lifts.

Breckenridge was bought in 1993 by the owners of nearby **Keystone** and **Arapahoe Basin**; all three are now covered on the same lift ticket. A Ski the Summit lift pass also covers **Copper Mountain**. These four ski areas are linked by free buses. Those with a car can also try the resorts of **Vail**, **Beaver Creek** and **Steamboat**, all less than two hours' drive.

SKI FACTS

Breckenridge only

Altitude	2925m-3960m
Lifts	17
Pistes	1915 acres
Green	15%
Blue	27%
Black	58%
Art. snow	362 acres

✔ Varied local ski area with something for all standards

✔ Together with Keystone, Arapahoe Basin and Copper Mountain, forms the enormous Ski the Summit ski area, linked by free buses

✔ Efficient lift system means few queues

✔ Lively bars, restaurants and nightlife by US standards

✔ Based on restored Victorian mining town, with many new buildings in attractive 19th-century style

✘ The local ski area is rather small, with few long runs

✘ At this extreme altitude there is an appreciable risk of sickness for visitors coming straight from lower altitudes

✘ The pseudo-Victorian style gets a bit overblown in places, giving the town the air of a theme park

Breckenridge was the first US resort to market itself aggressively on the British market, and at the end of the 1980s attracted large numbers of British visitors. Many were on their first American skiing trip, and came back impressed. Apparently, Breckenridge still gets more Brits than any other American resort, but we've noticed a rapid decline in the number of skiers reporting on the place – as if many of those first-timers had come back with a taste for skiing in the US, but not particularly for skiing in Breckenridge.

You can't blame them. By European standards, the local ski area is not huge – though it does have some good skiing for advanced skiers. But both they and intermediates will want to explore the rest of the Ski the Summit area on a week or 10-day trip. And if you're looking for the atmosphere of the old West, there are better – rather less Disneyesque – resorts.

Breckenridge is, however, probably the best base for exploration of the whole Ski the Summit area; it's certainly more lively and attractive than the other resorts in the conglomerate (Keystone and Copper Mountain). Between them the resorts offer an enormous amount of skiing – more than enough to keep even the keenest intermediate piste basher happy for a couple of weeks.

 ## The resort

Breckenridge was founded in 1859 and became a booming gold-mining town in the latter part of the century. The biggest ever gold nugget, weighing nearly 14 pounds and named Tom's Baby, was unearthed here. The old wooden and clapboard buildings have been well renovated and form the bottom part of Main Street. Over 250 restored Victorian buildings are included in what is Colorado's largest national historic district. New shopping malls and buildings have been added in similar style – though they are obvious modern additions.

The town centre is attractively lively in the evening, with plenty of shops and over 100 restaurants and bars. Christmas lights and decorations remain on the lamp-posts throughout the season, giving the town an air of non-stop winter festivity. This is enhanced by a number of real winter festivals such as Ullr Fest – a carnival honouring the Norse God of Winter – and Ice Sculpture championships which leave wonderful sculptures for weeks afterwards.

Hotels and condominiums built in more modern style are spread over a wide, wooded area and are linked by a regular Town Trolley. Breckenridge also boasts more ski-in, ski-out accommodation than any other Colorado resort.

 ## The skiing

The local skiing takes place on four separate peaks, linked by lift and piste. Boringly, they are named Peaks 7, 8, 9 and 10 – going from right to left as you look at the mountain. Though there's something for all standards, the keen piste-basher will want to explore the rest of Summit County too – Keystone, Copper Mountain and Arapahoe Basin. If anything, Breckenridge has the least interesting skiing of the Summit County resorts.

LIFT PASSES

94/95 prices in dollars

Breckenridge-Keystone

Covers all lifts in Breckenridge, Keystone and Arapahoe Basin.

Beginners

2 beginners' lifts. Beginners and novices have a reduced area pass in ski school.

Main pass

1-day pass 40

6-day pass 192

Senior citizens

Over 65: 6-day pass 150 (22% off)

Children

Under 13: 6-day pass 102 (47% off)

Under 6: free pass

Notes Breckenridge, Keystone and Arapahoe are all a ski-bus ride apart. Discounts for groups of over 20. Over 70s have a further discounted pass price. All passes (except day-pass) allow one non-skiing day; 6-day pass valid for 7 days with one non-skiing day.

Alternative passes

Ski the Summit coupon booklets interchangeable for lift pass at Breckenridge, Copper Mountain, Keystone and Arapahoe Basin (6 days skiing out of 7 adult 210).

SKI SCHOOL

94/95 prices in dollars

Breckenridge

Classes 6 days

4½hr: 10am-12.15 and 1.45-4pm; 2hr 15min: am or pm

6 full days: 198

Children's classes

Ages: 4 to 12

6 full days including lunch and ski-pass: 318

Private lessons

Hourly, up to 6hr

70 for 1hr; each additional person 25

THE SKI AREA
Small but fragmented

Two high-speed quad chair-lifts go from the top end of town up to **Peak 9**, one accessing mainly green runs on the lower half of the hill, the other mainly blues higher up. From there you can ski down to **Peak 10**, which has a large number of blue and black runs served by a single high-speed quad lift.

Skiing down the other flank of Peak 9 takes you to a lift up into the **Peak 8** skiing – tough stuff at the top, easier lower down. The base lifts of Peak 8 at the Bergenhof can also be reached by the town shuttle bus. From the top T-bar of Peak 8, you can traverse to the all-black **Peak 7** skiing which has no lifts of its own – you ski out back to the base of Peak 8.

At the end of the day two trails lead back down to town from Peak 8 – Sawmill to the main Peak 9 lifts and Four O'Clock down towards the centre of town. Or you can catch a bus.

SNOW RELIABILITY
Excellent

With the village at almost 3000m (the highest of the main North American resorts) and the skiing going up to almost 4000m, it's no surprise that Breckenridge boasts an excellent snow record. That is supplemented by substantial artificial snowmaking that is mainly intended for pre-Christmas use.

FOR ADVANCED SKIERS
Quite a few short but tough runs

A remarkable 58% of Breckenridge's runs are classified as 'Most Difficult' (single black diamond) or 'Expert' (double black diamond) terrain. That's a higher proportion than even in the famous 'macho' resorts such as Jackson Hole, Taos and Snowbird. But remember Breckenridge is not a big ski area by European standards, so most good skiers will want to spend a good proportion of their time exploring the other Ski the Summit resorts.

Peak 7 is an entirely off-piste skiing area. It reputedly has some good steep runs both above and through the trees. But it opened last season for the first time, and when we were there in January there wasn't enough snow.

Peak 8 has some good open skiing in Horseshoe and Contest bowls, where the snow normally remains good. But the runs are short by European standards and they aren't remarkably steep despite their double black diamond rating.

We particularly liked the skiing in the back bowls of Peak 8. This is basically ski-anywhere terrain among a thin covering of trees and bushes. Lots of runs, such as Lobo, Hombre, Amen and Adios, are marked on the trail map. But in practice you can easily skip between them and invent your own way down. It's picturesque and not too steep. Double diamond black mogul fields lead down under Chair 4 to the junction with Peak 9.

Peak 9 itself has nothing to offer advanced skiers except very steep blacks from the top down under Chair E on the North Face. These had very patchy snow covering on each of our visits, conditions which probably account for their fearsome names such as Devil's Crotch and Satan's Inferno.

Peak 10 offers much more interest. Off to the right of the chair, at the edge of the ski area, is a network of interlinking black mogul runs by the side of the downhill course – consistently steep and bumpy. To the left of the chair is a lightly wooded off-piste area, The Burn.

FOR INTERMEDIATE SKIERS
Nice cruising – but not much of it

Breckenridge has some good blue cruising runs for all standards of intermediate. But dedicated piste bashers will find it very limited and will want to visit the other Summit County resorts.

Peak 9 has the easiest skiing. It is nearly all gentle, wide blues at the top and greens at the bottom. Timid intermediates will find it delightful.

Peak 10 has a couple of more challenging runs graded blue-black, such as Crystal and Centennial, which make for good fast cruising.

Peak 8 has a choice of blues down through trails cut close together in the trees. We particularly liked the quiet Claimjumper, which is skied less than the others because of its position at the far northern end of the ski area, next to the boundary.

More adventurous intermediates will also like to try some of the high bowl skiing (see above). And Keystone and Copper Mountain both offer miles of excellent intermediate terrain.

FOR BEGINNERS
Excellent

The bottom of Peak 9 has a big, virtually flat area and some good gentle nursery slopes. There's then a good choice of green runs to move on to. Beginners can try Peak 8 too, with another selection of green runs and a choice of trails which take you right back to town.

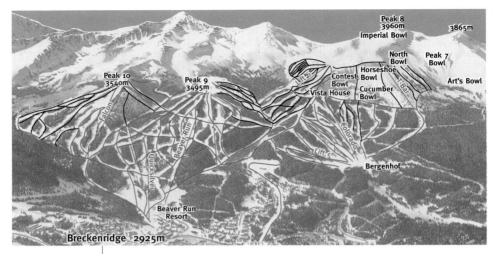

Peak 8
3960m
Imperial Bowl

3865m

North
Bowl
Peak 7
Bowl

Horseshoe
Bowl

Contest
Bowl
Art's Bowl

Vista House
Cucumber
Bowl

Peak 10
3540m

Peak 9
3495m

Falcon

Beaver Run

Quicksilver

Colorado

Lift 6

Lift 5

Bergenhof

Beaver Run
Resort

Breckenridge 2925m

FOR CROSS-COUNTRY
Specialist centre in woods
Breckenridge's Nordic Centre is
prettily set in the woods between the
town and Peak 8 (and is served by the
shuttle bus). It has 38km of trails.

QUEUES
Not normally a problem
Breckenridge's four high-speed quads
(two on Peak 9 and one each on Peaks
8 and 10) make light work of peak-
time crowds. We've never come across
serious queues and neither have our
reporters except in exceptional
circumstances, such as after watching
a competition.

MOUNTAIN RESTAURANTS
Unexciting
Mountain eating is fairly typical of US
resorts: large, efficient self-service
cafeterias which serve standard fare of
burgers, pasta, chillis in a rather
utilitarian atmosphere – and very
crowded at peak time.

Vistahaus, at the top of Peak 8, is
the best of a poor bunch and known
for its soups and pizzas.

SKI SCHOOL
Usual American efficiency
Our reporters are unanimous in their
praise for the workings of the ski
school: classes of five to eight, doing
what the class, not the instructor,
wants, special clinics on how to ski
bumps or powder or make a quantum
leap in your skiing.

A typical comments: 'Standards of
tuition were excellent, with instructors
showing genuine interest and pleasure
in your progress' and 'I went to three
special clinics on improving turns,
style and skiing bumps. They were all
excellent and my skiing leapt ahead as
a result'.

CHILDCARE

At each major lift base there is a Children's Center (453 3250), with 'fun facilities' and a complex array of options for all-day care from 8.30 to 4.30. Peak 8 takes children from 2 months, and runs a Snow Play programme for those aged 2 years; both Centers offer this for non-skiers aged 3 to 5. Special ski school classes are held for those aged 3, mornings only. Those aged 4 or 5 have their own junior ski school. Children aged 6 to 12 go into ordinary children's ski school, but all-day care is available at Kid's Castle meeting areas at each lift base.

There is also a separate Kinderhut children's ski school (453 0379) at Beaver Run Resort, with 'magic carpet' ski-lift, offering all-day care.

GETTING THERE

Air Denver, transfer 2¼hr.

PACKAGES

Airtours, American Connections, American Dream, American Skiworld, Bladon Lines, Chalet World, Crystal, Equity Total Ski, First Choice Ski, Inghams, Jean Stanford, Made to Measure, Neilson, Ski Activity, Ski Club of GB, Ski Independence, Ski Val, SkiGower, Snowed in America, Solo's, Summit Chalet Company, Thomson, USAirtours

Frisco Equity Total Ski, USAirtours

FACILITIES FOR CHILDREN
Excellent facilities

We have few reports, but the facilities for infants seem splendid, with the usual American emphasis on having fun. Teenagers have special ski school classes aimed at achieving maximum mileage and fun.

 # Staying there

Breckenridge is quite a spread-out resort. Although there is probably as much ski-in ski-out accommodation here as anywhere in the US, there is also a fair amount away from Main Street and the lift base-stations. Free shuttle buses serve most of the accommodation efficiently, but less reliably in the evening than the day.

The area between the base of Peak 9 and Main Street is the best location if you plan to go out in the evening.

HOW TO GO
Lots of choice

Over a dozen tour operators feature Breckenridge in their programme and it's easy to arrange your own holiday there too – Resort Express runs regular transfers from Denver airport to Breckenridge.

Chalets Crystal have various mock-Victorian houses – all as well equipped as you would expect in the US, and all but one close to the lifts. The other tour operators here all have similarly attractive places, though many of them are out of town. American Skiworld and Ski Independence have some well located places. Crystal and Ski Val have some particularly good out-of-town properties.

Hotels There's a good choice of style and price range, including several 'resorts' – large complexes which may include self-catering units and shops as well as hotel facilities.

££££ Breckenridge Hilton Prime location, vast rooms (it was built as condos) and good facilities make this recently renovated hotel very popular with Brits. Pool, tubs. One niggle this year: 'Dining room unstaffed and unmanaged at breakfast.'

££££ Lodge at Breckenridge Stylish new luxury spa resort set out of town among 32 acres, with great views. Private shuttle bus. Pool, tubs.

££££ Allaire Timbers Inn Exclusive new B&B (eight rooms, two suites) a little way from lifts and downtown. Good views. Tub.

£££ Beaver Run Huge resort complex with 520 spacious rooms, very convenient for the skiing.

£££ Williams House Beautifully restored, charmingly furnished four-room B&B on Main St.

££ Fireside Inn Cosy New England-style B&B. Historic part of town. Tub.

££ Breckenridge Mountain Lodge Straightforward, good-value accommodation. Tubs.

£ Breckenridge Wayside Inn Friendly budget place out of town by golf course. Tub.

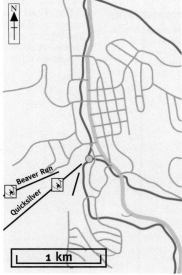

ACTIVITIES

Indoor Sports clubs, swimming, sauna, massage, jacuzzi, cinema, theatre, art gallery, library, indoor miniature golf course **Outdoor** Heli-skiing, horse- and dog-sleigh rides, rafting, fishing, snow-mobiles, snow coach rides, toboggans, scooters, mountain biking

TOURIST OFFICE

Postcode CO 80424
Tel oo 1 (303)
4535000
Fax 4533202

Self-catering There is a huge choice of condominiums, many set along the aptly named Four O'Clock run for ski-in (but not ski-out) convenience and many available through UK tour operators. Comfortable, well-equipped and conveniently located condos include Liftside Inn, Tannhaüser, Pine Ridge, River Mountain Lodge, Sundowner, Wedgewood, Tyra Summit and Wildwood. The above-mentioned Beaver Run resort has self-catering as well as hotel accommodation which is probably the most luxurious available on a package.

STAYING DOWN THE VALLEY
Good for exploring Summit County
Staying in Frisco, which is on the route of the Summit Stage shuttle between all the Summit County resorts, is a real possibility for those touring around or on a tight budget. It's a small town based on a Victorian settlement, where the stage-coach used to stop.

There are several cheap motels (including the old stagecoach stop, now the Frisco Inn), some B&B places and a Best Western hotel.

EATING OUT
Over 100 restaurants
There's a very wide range of eating places, with pretty much everything you'd expect, from typical American food to 'fine-dining', and almost every ethnic cuisine you could wish for.

The Brewery is famous for its enormous portions of appetisers such as Buffalo Wings which will fill you up cheaply – as well as its splendid brewed-on-the-spot beers. We particularly liked the Avalanche beer.

The Whale's Tail has been highly recommended for its seafood, lively atmosphere and good, half-price children's portions.

Poirier's Cajun Café has been recommended by several reporters for its spicy Creole food. The Village Pasta Co serves good fresh pasta and El Perdido 'giant quantities of fantastic Mexican food'. The Red Orchid Chinese is praised. Windy City is 'a simple pizza place but the food is great'. Café Alpine is good for Spanish tapas. Blue River Bistro offers 'a wonderful selection, cooked to perfection'. Other recommendations include Tillie's and Heartstone.

APRES-SKI
The best in Summit County
There's a good, lively after-skiing atmosphere, but things quieten down considerably later. The Breckenridge Brewery, a real working brewery with vats visible from the bar, is the 'in' place at tea-time, though it's not for those who dislike crowds and noise. Its main rival is Jake T Pounders at the Peak 9 base-station, which has live music. Jake is an unusual owner – he's a dog! The Gold Pan dates from Goldrush days, and is reputedly the oldest bar west of the Mississippi. Behind its saloon doors is a good atmosphere, with live music most nights. Shamus O'Toole's roadhouse is good if you want to meet 'redneck' locals straight out of a Burt Reynolds movie. Downstairs at Eric's is a trendy disco bar. Colts Down Under is one of the few lively late bars. Tiffany's is the livelier of the two main discos, especially on the weekly cheap night.

FOR NON-SKIERS
Far from ideal
Breckenridge is a pleasant place to wander around, and not without distractions. But a non-skier staying for a week or 10 days would find it pretty limiting, and the excursion possibilities are few. Skiers should be quite happy to return to one of the base-stations for lunchtime meetings.

Copper Mountain 2960m

SKI FACTS

Altitude	2930m-3770m
Lifts	19
Pistes	1330 acres
Green	22%
Blue	37%
Black	41%
Art. snow	270 acres

PACKAGES
Airtours, American Connections, Club Med

TOURIST OFFICE
Postcode CO 80443
Tel 00 1 (970) 9682882
Fax 9682711

Copper Mountain has little charm but great skiing. It is part of the Ski the Summit region and is well worth a day or two's skiing if you are staying in the more atmospheric resorts of Breckenridge or Keystone.

THE RESORT
Copper Mountain is a functional, purpose-built resort, high on convenience, low on charm – rather like some French purpose-built resorts. The apartment blocks are surprisingly spread out, making the free shuttle-bus pretty essential. There is little in the way of shops or ambience away from the area at the base of the skiing. The resort has a big conference market and the only Club Med ski village in North America. It's good for families, with superb children's facilities, spacious self-catering accommodation and quiet evenings. There's a fine sports club (free entrance to resort guests), with a huge pool and indoor tennis.

Copper is a Ski the Summit resort, and has half-hourly buses to the others: Keystone, Breckenridge and Arapahoe Basin.

THE SKIING
The **ski area** is quite sizeable by American standards, and it is very easy to work out where you want to ski. As you look up at the mountain, the easiest runs are on the right hand side and the terrain gradually gets steeper the further left you go. Two high-speed quads whizz you up to the tree-line, from where numerous runs head back towards the base. Further lifts serve the resort's open bowls.

Height and an extensive snowmaking operation give Copper very good **snow reliability.**

Snowcat skiing was introduced for **advanced skiers** last season in Copper Bowl, on the backside of Copper's mountain. This will continue in 1995/96 before lifts are installed to make this steep terrain more accessible. Good skiers will also enjoy the double diamond terrain of Spaulding Bowl, and there are great bump runs through the trees to the bottom of the two lifts on the left as you look at the mountain.

Good **intermediates** have the benefit of the steepest runs also being the longest. These are in the Copper Peak section. The slightly less proficient can enjoy shorter, gentler runs on the middle section of mountain, while early intermediates have gentle cruising terrain in the Union Peak section.

The nursery slopes are excellent for **beginners**, and there are plenty of very easy green runs in 'slow skiing zones' to graduate to.

Copper is one of the least impressive American areas for **cross-country**, though the 25km of trails through the woods at the base of Union mountain are quite pleasant.

Copper has a lot of skiing served by few lifts, and **queues** are a problem in peak season. However, the uncrowded pistes compensate for delays.

The one **mountain restaurant** is mediocre, and many people prefer to ski back to the base for lunch.

The **ski school** has a fine reputation, especially for teaching children.

The all-day ski kindergarten takes **children** from 3 years, and has its slopes right outside the nursery. The nursery takes children from 2 months old and, as well as the usual facilities, provides cooking and crafts. Evening babysitters are also available.

STAYING THERE
Copper Mountain is essentially a **condominium** resort. All 12 condo complexes are in excellent condition and have all mod cons. The resort has been awarded four diamonds by the American AA for accommodation standards. We have heard rave reports of West Lodge, but other places are also very good.

Copper's only **hotel** is Foxpine Inn. It has well appointed rooms and a swimming pool. There are hotels nearby, in Dillon and Frisco on the Ski the Summit bus route.

There are only half-a-dozen **restaurants**, but all are quite good. O'Shea's is an Old West-style barbecue place; Steak Out is good; Pesce Fresco's has an international menu that includes fine fish; and the sports club's restaurant does excellent salads.

Nightlife is very quiet. The 'pub' in Copper Commons is a wine bar. A multi-screen cinema is nearby. Evening sleigh rides take people out to a dinner. Other activities for **non-skiers** centre around the The Racquet & Athletic Club and West Lake.

Crested Butte 2855m

✔ Known for its 'extreme' skiing

✔ Enough non-extreme steep runs to amuse advanced skiers for a while

✔ Excellent for beginners and for near-beginners, with long easy runs

✔ Charming, tiny, restored Victorian mining town with good restaurants

✔ Alternative of convenient ski-village

✔ Excellent ski school, with a special courses for skiers with disabilities

✔ Better-than-average scenery for Colorado

✘ Skiing limited for confident intermediate piste-bashers

✘ Old town is ten minutes from ski village by shuttle bus

✘ Out on a limb, away from mainstream Colorado resorts

✘ Only one satisfactory mountain restaurant

Crested Butte is not yet well-known in Britain, but they're working on it. Among expert skiers who are at home on very steep unprepared runs – and 'extreme' skiers who like their mountains as steep as possible – it enjoys cult status, thanks to the extent and gradient of the slopes on the outer fringes of the ski area. Meanwhile, the commercial success of the place depends on beginners and timid intermediates, for whom the long groomed slopes of the main ski area are ideal. Skiers in these two groups can safely include Crested Butte on their short-lists. Mileage-hungry piste-bashers should stay away.

The resort

The skiing

Crested Butte takes its name from its mountain – an isolated peak (a butte, pronounced 'beaut') with a distinctive shape. Crested Butte started life as a coal-mining town in the late 1800s; it is now one of the most attractive resorts in the Rockies – just a few narrow streets with beautifully restored wooden buildings and sidewalks, and the tiniest imaginable town jail, straight out of a Western. Elk Avenue, the main street, is a five-minute stroll from top to bottom, and is lined with bars, restaurants and shops. There's even a classic general store, run by an old-timer.

The bars and restaurants are varied in price and character. But wherever you go you'll find genuinely friendly and hospitable locals. And mingled with them you'll find a fair share of down-to-earth celebrities.

The ski village of Mount Crested Butte is a huge contrast to the town of Crested Butte. Nearly all the buildings are modern and characterless, and you can judge the appeal of the place from the fact that its central focus is a bus station and car park – recently reduced in size by the construction of the new Mountain Lair hotel. There is a cluster of bars and restaurants at the foot of the slopes, around the large Grande Butte hotel.

It's a small area, but it packs in an astonishing mixture of perfect beginner slopes, easy cruising runs and the steepest cliff-jumping extreme skiing in North America. The only groups of people who might not be suited by this mixture are piste-bashing adventurous intermediates who like to ski different runs all the time and good skiers who don't fancy extreme terrain.

THE SKI AREA
A Jekyll and Hyde mountain
Two main lifts leave the base area. The Silver Queen high-speed chair-lift takes advanced skiers to black runs and lifts which access the steepest runs. Those just off the nursery slopes will take the Keystone lift to the easiest runs, and intermediates can access cruising blue runs from either.

SNOW RELIABILITY
Excellent – usually
Crested Butte claims to benefit from snowstorms approaching from several directions, and it has a substantial snowmaking installation which covers runs from most of the lifts. We've usually had superb snow here. But in 1994, cover in the early part of the season was thin, keeping the North Face closed until well into the season.

SKI FACTS

Altitude 2775m-3620m
Lifts	13
Pistes	1160 acres
Green	13%
Blue	29%
Black	58%
Art. snow	238 acres

LIFT PASSES

94/95 prices in dollars
Crested Butte Mountain Resort
Covers all lifts in Crested Butte only.
Beginners Beginners' lessons in ski school includes lift pass.
Main pass
1-day pass 42
6-day pass 222
(low season 153 – 31% off)
Short-term passes
Half-day pass available (adult 30).
Notes Free lift passes for first weeks of season (28/11/94 to 16/12/94), with reductions on ski hire and lodgings. All lift passes over 4 days allow for one day off, 4 days skiing in 5, 6 out of 7 days. Children under 13 pay their age for each day's skiing.

FOR ADVANCED SKIERS
Some cult terrain

For those up to leaping off cliffs and skiing steep slopes through the trees, Crested Butte has an abundance of double black diamond runs accessed by two high drag-lifts. The older North Face lift leads to a series of runs down the east flank of the mountain, where there are numerous cliffs, steep couloirs, rocks and trees to negotiate. The sign as you enter the North Face area reads 'This terrain is the steepest lift-served terrain in North America. Experts only'.

The High Lift, added a few years ago, opened up a whole new range of extreme skiing possibilities previously reached only by long climbs, including Paradise Cliffs, Paradise Headwall and a whole series of runs on the western side of the ski area.

Not all of the North Face skiing is extreme; but for the typical black-piste mogul skier Crested Butte is much more limited.

FOR INTERMEDIATE SKIERS
Not a lot

Similarly, good intermediate skiers are likely to find the area limited unless they enjoy perfecting their technique on the same few runs each day.

For early, unsure intermediates, Crested Butte has attractions. The east-facing runs down the Paradise, Teocalli and East River lifts are all wide, fairly gentle, well groomed and normally uncrowded cruising runs which can be taken fast or slow. There are usually several variations to choose from, ending up back at the same lifts.

A particularly gentle and uncrowded area is that served by the Gold Link lift, isolated from the rest of the skiing and good for near-beginners too.

FOR BEGINNERS
Excellent

There are excellent nursery slopes near the village. After that you'll be taking the Keystone chair-lift up to a choice of several long, easy green runs leading back down again. Or you can stop off part-way down to catch the Painter Boy lift. This has green runs down again or you can try the easy blues down the Gold Link lift.

FOR CROSS-COUNTRY
Looks good

There are 30km of cross-country trails near the Nordic Ski Centre in the old town of Crested Butte.

QUEUES
No problem

Queues are virtually non-existent except at peak periods. The trails are quiet and uncrowded too. Moving peak-period crowds up the mountain was speeded up a couple of years ago by replacing the main Silver Queen lift with a new high-speed quad chair.

MOUNTAIN RESTAURANTS
Only one worth visiting

Most people ski back to the base-station for lunch – not a hardship. The main restaurant at the base of the Paradise lift is fairly civilised, with a wooden interior and good choice of food. There's even a table-service restaurant inside as well as the large

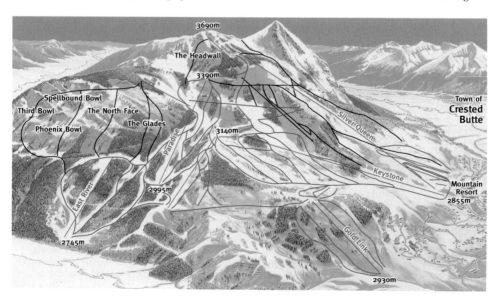

SKI SCHOOL

95/96 prices in dollars

Crested Butte
Classes 5 days
4hr: 10.30-12.30 and
1.30-3.30; 2hr: am or
pm; 3hr: from 12.45
5 2hr days: 120
Children's classes
Ages: 2 to 12
6 8hr days including
lunch: 330
Private lessons
1½hr to 6hr
76 for 1½hr; each
additional person 35

CHILDCARE

The Children's Centre
in the Whetstone
building, at the foot
of the slopes, offers a
comprehensive range
of care for children
aged 6 months to 7
years, from 8.30 to
4.30. There are
separate ski classes
for children aged 2 to
3, 4 to 7, and 8 to 12,
split into beginners
and non-beginners.

GETTING THERE

Air Gunnison, transfer
½hr. Denver, transfer
4½hr.

PACKAGES

American
Connections,
American Dream,
Made to Measure,
Mogul Ski, Ski
Activity, Ski
Independence

ACTIVITIES

Indoor Racquetball,
swimming, hot tubs,
weight-training,
aerobic classes,
saunas
Outdoor Snow-
mobiling, sleigh rides,
ballooning, winter
horse riding,
mountain barbecues

TOURIST OFFICE

Postcode CO 81225
Tel 00 1 (970)
3492221
Fax 3492250

---

self-service and outdoor barbecue
areas. The other restaurant, at the base
of the Twister lift, is accurately
described as a warming house. The
food is primitive, and many callers
bring their own.

SKI SCHOOL
A major asset
Run by French-Swiss Jean Pavaillard,
the ski school has won the Best Ski
School in Colorado vote several times
in recent years. It offers the usual
flexible options you find in US ski
schools of specialised clinics (eg
bumps, powder, racing) as well as
normal group and private lessons.
   There are free daily mountain tours
for intermediate or better skiers, and
the ski school has a high reputation
for teaching people with disabilities.

FACILITIES FOR CHILDREN
Comprehensive
Crested Butte takes childcare seriously,
and the facilities look excellent.

 # Staying there

Most of the accommodation is at the
ski village. From some places you can
stroll to the lifts; but many condos, in
particular, are much further away and
dependent on the ski-bus. There is
some accommodation in the town.

HOW TO GO
Plenty of choice
Practically all the tour operators with
serious US programmes offer packages
to Crested Butte, mainly in hotels.
Chalets We don't know of any.
Hotels You have a broad range of
options, from international-style
comfort to homely character.
£££ Grand Butte Big, anonymous,
comfortable, convenient (right at the
foot of the slopes) and used by most of
the British tour operators. Small
swimming pool; sauna and hot tub.
££ Nordic Inn B&B The oldest hotel
in the mountain village, only a short
walk from the lifts. It has an outdoor
hot tub, friendly service from Alan
Cox and his staff, and large rooms.
££ Manor Lodge Comfortable modern
hotel close to the lifts, with live
entertainment most evenings.
££ Crested Butte Lodge More
modern, nearer the centre, with an
indoor pool, sauna and outdoor hot
tub – and much more personal than
the Grand Butte.
££ The Inn at Crested Butte Brand-
new non-smoking hotel on the edge
of the old town. Outdoor hot tub.

££ Elk Mountain Lodge Renovated
miners' hotel in old town with good
rooms. B&B only.
££ Gothic Inn Five-room Alpine-style
B&B in the town.
Self-catering There are literally
thousands of apartments available to
rent, mainly in the ski village. Crested
Mountain Village apartments are
perhaps the most convenient and
have pool, hot tubs, saunas and
friendly and efficient reception
facilities. The Buttes, the Gateway
and the Plaza are also recommended.
The Three Seasons condos have plenty
of mod cons but are some way from
the lifts.

EATING OUT
Better than you'd expect
For such a small place Crested Butte
has a surprisingly high number of
decent restaurants – nearly all of them
in the old town. Top of the pile is
undoubtedly Soupcon, a tiny place in
an old log cabin just off the main
street, serving refined French food. Le
Bosquet and Timberline run it close.
The Idle Spur is the statutory micro-
brewery, doing satisfying food as well
as a range of beers.

APRES-SKI
Lively bars
The old town of Crested Butte has
plenty of diversions for a short stay,
provided you're not looking for great
sophistication or variety. Kochevar's is
an amusing Wild-West saloon,
complete with shuffleboard (the
American-size version of shove-
ha'penny). Out at the ski village,
Rafters usually has a lot going on.

FOR NON-SKIERS
Limited
Charming though it is, Crested Butte
won't keep most non-skiers amused
for very long.

STAYING UP THE MOUNTAIN
A wilderness retreat
For good skiers, cross-country skiers,
snowmobile fans and those who
simply like to get away from it all,
Crested Butte has something special.
   Irwin Lodge is a great wooden barn
of a place in a remote back-country
area, reached in winter only by snowcat or snow-mobile. It has an outdoor
hot tub, great views and fairly simple
rooms above a huge communal sitting
room with open fire. Most people go
there for the guided powder skiing,
with uplift by snow-cat. Heli-skiing is
envisaged, but not yet available.

Heavenly 1995m

HOW IT RATES

The skiing
Snow	✦✦✦
Extent	✦✦✦
Advanced	✦✦✦✦
Intermediates	✦✦✦✦
Beginners	✦✦✦✦
Convenience	✦
Queues	✦✦✦
Restaurants	✦

The rest
Scenery	✦✦✦✦
Resort charm	✦
Not skiing	✦✦

SKI FACTS

Altitude	1995m-3060m
Lifts	24
Pistes	4800 acres
Green	20%
Blue	45%
Black	35%
Art. snow	500 acres

ORIENTATION

Heavenly is at the south end of Lake Tahoe, on the borders of California and Nevada, east of San Francisco. The Heavenly skiing straddles the state line, as does the popular year-round resort of South Lake Tahoe at its foot. Access to the skiing is via any of three base stations which can easily be reached by road. The major one is California Lodge, on the outskirts of South Lake Tahoe; Boulder and Stagecoach Base lodges lie around the mountain in Nevada. There are a dozen other ski areas within an hour's drive – see page 412.

✔ Amazing views across Lake Tahoe and arid Nevada

✔ Fair-sized ski area which (unusually for America) offers a sensation of travelling around

✔ Huge amounts of easy off-piste skiing among trees

✔ Some serious challenges for advanced and expert skiers

✔ Numerous other worthwhile ski areas within driving distance

✔ Amazingly cheap package holidays

✔ A unique après-ski scene

✔ Impressive snowmaking facilities

✘ The base-town of South Lake Tahoe is quite unlike a traditional ski resort, and not attractive

✘ Very little traditional après-ski activity

✘ If natural snow is in short supply, there is very little challenging skiing

A resort called Heavenly invites an obvious first question: just how close to Heaven does it take you? Physically, close enough: with a top height of 3060m and vertical drop of 1065m, it's the highest and biggest of the dozen or more resorts clustered around scenic Lake Tahoe (see page 412 for the others). Metaphorically, it's not quite so close. The ski area has something for everyone (not least the expert), and having another dozen resorts within easy reach by car means that an interestingly varied holiday is assured. The problem we have with the place is aesthetic. One of the key features of the skiing is the amazing views, particularly north across the lake; but those skiers (like us) who value that feature are likely to be dismayed by the appearance and atmosphere of the town of South Lake Tahoe, at the foot of the slopes. If you can live with this drawback and you go with a car, you can have a great holiday here. And you can have one at an amazingly low cost, if last season is any guide – you could get a flight, room and car for £379.

 ## The resort

Heavenly's base-town of South Lake Tahoe is unlike any other ski resort we know. The Stateline area at its centre is dominated by four monstrous hotel-casinos (located just inches on the Nevada side of the line). These brash but comfortable hotels offer good-value accommodation and big-name entertainment as well as gambling. They are a conspicuous part of the amazing lake views from the ski area. More importantly, the area around the casinos is strangely devoid of 'downtown' atmosphere (never mind mountain resort atmosphere); there are few bars or shops, and the centre is bisected by US Highway 50. The rest of the town consists of low-rise motels, stores, wedding chapels and so on, spreading for miles along this busy, pedestrian-hostile highway; many are rather shabby, though this is partly camouflaged by the tall trees that surround most of them.

More than any other US resort, South Lake Tahoe is a place for the car-borne. Your base may be within walking distance of a bar, a restaurant or a shop, but don't count on it. The casinos run free shuttle-buses to pull people in to the Stateline area at night, but many of the best bars and restaurants are tucked out of the way.

The place as a whole is surprisingly downmarket. The casinos have some swanky restaurants, but are basically places where Californians and other gambling-starved Americans flock to feed their quarters into slot machines. The accommodation away from the centre includes chalet-style 'Alpine lodges', spacious condominium developments and run-of-the-mill motels. None of this accommodation is particularly smart. But most of it conforms to American norms, and (except at weekends) all of it is under-used in winter, which is why UK tour operators can offer cheap deals.

The base of Heavenly's skiing is California Lodge, beside a huge car park, a mile out of town, up a heavily wooded slope. There are medium-term plans to build a gondola into the skiing, starting close to the casinos.

LIFT PASSES

95/96 prices in dollars

Heavenly
Covers all lifts on Heavenly mountain.
Beginners Package of lesson, pass and equipment for 3hr (adult 45).
Main pass
1-day pass 44
6-day pass 234
Senior citizens
Over 65: 6-day pass 102 (56% off)
Children
Under 13: 6-day pass 102 (56% off)
Under 5: free pass
Short-term passes
Half-day passes available from 12.30 to 4pm (adult 30)
Notes
Passes of three days or more allow one non-skiing day; 6-day pass valid for 7 days, with one non-skiing day.
Credit cards Yes

⛷ The skiing

Most of Heavenly's skiing suits intermediates down to the ground. But there are also good beginner slopes at the California base area, and some splendid easy runs to progress to, while experts can find some genuine challenges at the two extremes of the area – as well as lots of fun in acre upon acre of easy off-piste tree skiing. Keep in mind that there are many other worthwhile ski areas within easy reach by car or bus (or paddle steamer!). You'll want to try at least a couple during your stay, as well as Heavenly – see page 412.

THE SKI AREA
Interestingly complex

Heavenly's mountain is quite complicated, and getting from A to B requires more careful navigation (and more skiing on tedious linking runs) than is usual in the US.

There is a clear division into the California side (the lifts and runs directly above South Lake Tahoe) and the Nevada side (above Stagecoach Lodge and Boulder Lodge). There is only one way from California to Nevada, and the three trails leading the other way soon join into one. On both sides, the terrain is complicated by ridges, which may mean that your route down the mountain involves catching a lift at some point. There are

no really easy runs on the Nevada side, apart from limited nursery slopes at the bottom.

Directly above California Lodge is a steep slope of around 520m vertical, with broad black pistes down the fall line and the narrower Roundabout blue trail snaking down. A mid-sized cable-car and two chairs go up to the first ridge, and all these lifts can be ridden down again by novices. Short easy runs go from this ridge down into a narrow wooded valley which is the starting point of the blue Roundabout run as well as the base of two further chair-lifts. These serve a variety of runs, and give access to the main skiing bowl on the California side, above the Sky Deck restaurant. The blue and black runs here are served by three chair-lifts, including the Sky Express high-speed quad.

The Sky Express chair makes the link with the Nevada side of the ski area, via the Skyline Trail catwalk. On this side there are three main bowls. The central one, above East Peak Lodge, is an excellent intermediate area served by two fast quad chairs, with a downhill extension of the bowl served by the Galaxy chair. On one side of this central bowl is the steeper, open terrain of Milky Way Bowl, leading to the seriously steep Mott and Killebrew canyons, served by the Mott Canyon chair. On the other side of the central bowl is the North Bowl, leading down to Nevada's two base lodges.

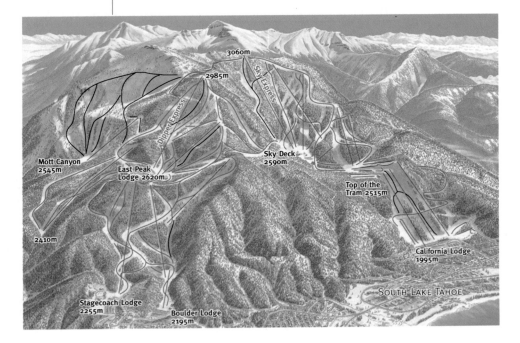

SKI SCHOOL

95/96 prices in dollars

Heavenly

Classes 5 days
2hr: from 9.45 or
12.45
5 half days: 125
Children's classes
Ages: 4 to 12
5 5hr 45min days
including pass, rental
and lunch: 270
Private lessons
1hr, 2hr, 3hr and 6hr
62 (94/95) for 1hr

GETTING THERE

Air San Francisco,
transfer 3-4hrs. Reno,
transfer 75 mins.
South Lake Tahoe,
transfer 15mins.

PACKAGES

American Dream,
American Skiworld,
Crystal, Inghams,
Ski Activity,
Ski Independence,
Virgin Snow

SNOW RELIABILITY
Impressive artificial backup

Despite spectacularly heavy snowfalls last season and a ten-year average snowfall of 250 inches (matching that of many Colorado resorts), Heavenly's recent snow record is not reassuring: California has suffered badly from drought in the early 90s, and it has not been unusual for Heavenly to go for many weeks without a heavy snowfall. Happily, the resort has very impressive snowmaking that covers 65% of the skiable area and ensures that most sections remain open most of the time. The resort often operates an irritating policy of closing off areas on Thursdays and Fridays to keep them fresh for the weekenders.

FOR ADVANCED SKIERS
Some specific challenges

Although the area as a whole is better suited to intermediates, there are some genuine challenges for the better skier. The runs under the California base lifts – The Face and Gunbarrel (often used for moguls competition skiing) – are of proper black steepness, and very testing when the snow is hard. Ellie's Run, at the top of the mountain, may offer continuous moguls too. But the really steep stuff is on the Nevada side. Milky Way Bowl offers a fairly gentle introduction to this terrain, which in most respects resembles European off-piste skiing. At the extremity of the bowl, the seriously steep Mott and Killebrew canyons are roped off, with defined gateways to steer less expert skiers to the lower gates and less steep slopes, and to keep skiers out when the crucial Mott Canyon chair-lift (installed to serve this expert skiing in 1991) is closed.

All over the mountain, there is excellent off-piste skiing among widely spaced trees, which offers tremendous fun when the conditions are right. Many of last year's visitors got the opportunity to ski these areas in near-perfect conditions, but don't count on it every year.

FOR INTERMEDIATE SKIERS
Lots to do

Heavenly is excellent for intermediates, who are made to feel welcome and secure by excellent piste grooming and signposting. The California side offers a progression from the relaxed cruising of the long Ridge Run, starting right at the top of the mountain, to more testing blues dropping off the ridge towards the Sky Deck restaurant. The confident intermediate may want to spend more time on the Nevada side, where there is more variety of terrain and some long, quite testing runs down to the base stations and to the Galaxy chair.

FOR BEGINNERS
An excellent place to learn

The California side is more suited to beginners, with gentle green runs served by the Pioneer and Powder Bowl lifts at the top of the cable-car, and good nursery slopes at base lodge level. The snow is well groomed and therefore easy to learn on.

FOR CROSS COUNTRY
A separate world

The Spooner Lake Cross Country Ski Area located close to Tahoe is an extensive meadow area of over 100km in 21 prepared trails. There are ample facilities for both instruction and ski rental. Organised moonlit tours are a popular alternative to the noise and bright lights of the casinos.

QUEUES
Some at weekends

Lift lines are generally not a problem at Heavenly, except during some weekends and public holidays when the entire Tahoe area is swamped with weekenders and day trippers. The key lifts moving skiers out from the base lodges are fast, reliable and comfortable.

MOUNTAIN RESTAURANTS
Not many options

The limited choice for lunch includes two that can be recommended on the California side. At The Top of the Tram is a table-service restaurant (Monument Peak) which makes up for its simple food with a calm atmosphere and the famous lake view (reservations necessary). And the outdoor Sky Deck has an excellent barbecue (cook your own comestibles), where Californian rock music blasts out and the cool dudes hang out. On the Nevada side, East Peak Lodge has a fair-sized terrace with interesting views over arid Nevada, but it gets hideously overcrowded when the weather drives people indoors. There's an Italian-themed place at Stagecoach Lodge, and a Tex-Mex at Boulder.

SKI SCHOOL
Good attitude

The ski school offers a full range of services, and boldly guarantees improvement; otherwise you get a second lesson free. Midweek classes can be small, and therefore very good value. They offer Quick Tips lessons,

CHILDCARE

Children between 4 and 12 can enrol in the Ski Explorers ski school programme which offers an all-inclusive day of supervision, lunch, lift access, equipment, snacks and snowplay. The programme is based at the extensive Children's Ski Centre at California Lodge, which includes an indoor play area. If children can't cope with a full day's skiing, or if the weather prevents it, the children do other activities.

ACTIVITIES

Indoor 6 casinos, 6 cinemas, cheap factory shops, ice skating, bowling, gyms, spas, Western museum
Outdoor Boat cruises, snowmobiling, horse-drawn sleigh rides, horse riding, ice fishing, hot springs, ghost town tours

TOURIST OFFICE

Postcode NV 89449
Tel 00 1 (702) 5867000
Fax 5885517

which are 20-minute, one-run lessons, starting at the top of the mountain, designed to pinpoint one or two key ways you can improve your skiing. Snowboarding lessons are popular.

FACILITIES FOR CHILDREN

We lack first-hand reports on the childcare arrangements, but they seem to be up to the usual high American standard.

 # Staying there

When deciding where to stay, you need to give careful consideration to your plans for evening as well as daytime activity. If you have a car, your options are numerous; location with a car is relatively unimportant, but you could consider basing yourself out at one of the Nevada lift stations, and driving when you want entertainment. Night owls could scarcely do better than to stay in one of the casinos. Otherwise, stay away from the centre and try to tuck yourself away in the woods.

HOW TO GO
Hotel or motel?
Accommodation in the South Lake Tahoe area is both abundant and varied, ranging from the glossy casinos to small, rather ramshackle motels. Hotel and motel rooms are easy to find midweek, but can be sold out at busy weekends. As far as we are aware, the British chalet holiday has yet to appear in this area.
Hotels Caesars, Harrah's, Horizon and Harveys are the main casino hotels, in descending order of price. Rooms booked on the spot can be quite expensive; packages are good value.
££££ Embassy Suites Luxury one-bedroom suites in a new, traditional-style building next to the casinos.
££ Tahoe Chalet Inn Clean and friendly, close to casinos. Back rooms (away from busy highway) preferable.
££ Best Western Timber Cove Lodge Bland but well run, with lovely lake views from some rooms.
Self-catering There are lots of condominiums and chalets, with units ranging in size from one bedroom to four bedrooms or more. Some are available from tour operators.

EATING OUT
Good value
For those whose appetites are not diminished by the deafening ringing of hundreds of fruit machines, the

casino hotels offer fantastic value in their buffet-style all-you-can-eat dining. They have some more ambitious 'gourmet' restaurants too – some high enough up their tower blocks to give superb lake views. Llewellyn's, on the 19th floor of Harvey's casino, has a good reputation. Among the seven or more restaurants at Harrah's is an all-you-can-eat buffet in the Forest restaurant on the 18th floor, and the more civilised Friday's Station. Caesars casino has an in-house branch of Planet Hollywood. The sprawling resort area offers a great choice of international dining, from cosy little pizza houses to large, traditional American diners, Mexican tequila-and-tacos joints and Irish pubs. As usual in the US, there is a brew-pub.

APRES-SKI
Extraordinary
America's Snow Country magazine rates this area best in the US for nightlife, and it's easy to see why. There are the usual bars and so on, but what makes the area unique is the casinos on the Nevada side of the Stateline. These aren't simply opportunities to throw money away on roulette or slot machines: top-name entertainers, pop and jazz stars, cabarets and Broadway revues are also to be found in them – designed to give gamblers another reason to stay.

Other entertainments are also on offer – for example, Caesars has a 'hot buns' night and 'tight jeans' competitions; Turtles, at the Embassy Suites, is the place for a bop to the latest hits; the Wild West Country Club has appropriate dancing.

A more unusual way to spend the evening is to dance and dine your way across the lake aboard an authentic paddle steamer.

FOR NON-SKIERS
Luck be a lady
There is little for the non-skier to enjoy apart from the casinos. Snowmobiling is available a short drive from South Lake Tahoe, and there are hot-air balloon rides. Non-skiers can use the cable-car to meet skiers at the Top of the Tram, to walk in the surrounding area and view the lake and mountains below. When the sun is shining, it is a pleasant place to while away an afternoon.

Jackson Hole 1925m

HOW IT RATES

The skiing

Snow	★★★
Extent	★★
Advanced	★★★★★
Intermediates	★★★
Beginners	★★★
Convenience	★★★
Queues	★★
Restaurants	★

The rest

Scenery	★★★
Resort charm	★★★
Not skiing	★★

✔ One of the toughest ski areas in the US, with some truly radical terrain

✔ Jackson town has more genuine Wild West character than any other US ski resort

✔ People are friendly and hospitable – they want you to have fun

✔ Good variety of cross-country skiing

✔ Beautiful, unspoilt location in a remote part of the US, with several other attractions in the region

✘ There are too few lifts and they're mainly old and slow

✘ Queues, especially for the aerial tram (cable-car), can be bad

✘ It's a long journey from the UK

✘ Primitive mountain restaurants

✘ Snow can be poor on the lower slopes

✘ Limited scope for improving beginners and timid skiers

If you're an adventurous skier and want a real American Wild West atmosphere, Jackson Hole is the place to go. Cowboys – genuine and 'dude' – roam the wooden sidewalks, fall out of saloons, play pool, and dance to country music. The tiny town is the only place for miles around for the ranchers to go. In summer there are staged gunfights every evening in the town square, underneath the elk antler archways.

But in winter you're more likely to be killed by your own foolishness in the ski area 12 miles away. Jackson Hole has serious skiing for serious skiers – steeps, jumps, narrow couloirs, bumps. Fifty per cent of the skiing is classed as 'expert' terrain – black, double-black and even blacker. It takes a very good skier to get the most out of the area. It takes good snow too – so you've got to be lucky with the weather. Anyone below adventurous and competent intermediate standard may soon get bored with the skiing – the ski area is not huge, and much of it will be beyond their capability. But there's plenty else to see, including the beautiful winter wildernesses of the nearby National Parks of Yellowstone and Grand Teton.

ORIENTATION

The town of Jackson, in the north-west corner of Wyoming, sits at the south-eastern edge of Jackson Hole – the 'hole' being the high, flat valley floor surrounded by mountain ranges. The skiing, 20km north-east, stretches up the eastern flanks of the mountains above Teton Village – a small, modern collection of lodgings, shops and restaurants. The quickest way up is the Tram (cable-car) but there is an alternative chair-lift route which doesn't take you quite to the top. On the fringe of Jackson town is the small Snow King ski area, where night skiing is possible. Within a one-hour drive is Grand Targhee resort, famous for its powder snow – buses run daily.

 The resort

The town of Jackson, a 15-minute drive away from the slopes, is a real 'cowboy' town, where skiers and ranchers meet in seemingly perfect harmony. It is small and compact, with characterful western saloons, wooden side-walks and good restaurants. Everywhere there are station-wagons and snow-mobiles, skis and stetsons, saloons and ski-bums – it's a strange mix and the effect is great. In among the cowboys and the log cabins there's now a sprinkling of upmarket galleries and downmarket souvenir shops. But, in winter at least, it retains a genuine Western feel.

 The skiing

The ownership of the ski area area changed a few seasons ago, when the founder, Paul McCollister, finally sold out after a lengthy and costly legal battle. The new owners have plans for upgrading some of the lifts. They are also working at changing Jackson

Hole's image from that of a big, tough ski mountain to one that suits intermediate skiers and family groups as well, but it is still a big, tough ski mountain. Experts and good, adventurous intermediates will love the challenges on Rendezvous Mountain but, as yet, there's not enough skiing for the less bold.

THE SKI AREA
One big mountain, one small one
What makes Jackson Hole famous is the one big mountain – **Rendezvous.** The cable-car ('Tram') to its peak provides a 1260m vertical drop – the biggest in the US – and serves terrain that's just riddled with chutes, cliffs, bumps and jumps. Signs saying 'experts only' tend to mean it.

Apres Vous mountain is adjacent to Rendezvous. Its peak is 600m lower and it has mainly blue and a few green trails, as well as a handful of blacks. There's a half-pipe for snowboarders.

Two double chairs are needed to get from the base area to the summit of Apres Vous – Teewinot and then Apres Vous. Between the line of these chairs and the Tram there's another couple

SKI FACTS

Altitude 1925m-3185m
Lifts 9
Pistes 2500 acres
Green 10%
Blue 40%
Black 50%
Art. snow 80 acres

of chairs serving Casper Bowl and the Amphitheatre. Linking runs connect the Apres Vous and Casper areas. And from there you can work your way over to the two chairs on Rendezvous.

Ski Hosts provide hourly guided tours from the top of Rendezvous. And at 1.30pm on weekdays you can usually ski with Pepi Stiegler, head of the ski school and Olympic gold medal winner.

There's also a small ski area – **Snow King** – on the outskirts of Jackson town, floodlit in the evening.

SNOW RELIABILITY
Steep lower slopes can suffer

The claimed average of between 32ft and 38ft of 'mostly dry powder' snow sounds impressive, and for a core three-month season conditions are likely to be reasonable. But the base elevation here is relatively low for the Rockies, and unlucky skiers may well find insufficient cover for the steepish lower slopes like the Hobacks to be open. Snowmaking is limited to the runs on the lower part of Apres Vous mountain.

FOR ADVANCED SKIERS
Best for the brave

After a few runs on Apres Vous to warm up, most capable skiers will want to head for the Tram and take on the best that Rendezvous mountain has to offer. There's no gentle introduction here. So it is worth pausing at the top to take in the views and pluck up your courage.

You should take the East Ridge Traverse at least once to stare over the edge of the awesome Corbet's couloir – it flattens out to 50° after the vertical entry. Corbet's is the best-known of many thrilling and potentially damaging features on a mountain that needs to be treated with great respect. It's the most famous because the Tram passes right above it and provides a great viewing platform for watching people throw themselves off its lip.

From Corbet's – top or bottom – it's possible to track over to Tensleep Bowl and the tricky Expert Chutes. Tower Three Chute is one of several accessed via the Thunder chair and is a typical example of the many steep, narrow chutes on Rendezvous.

Laramie Bowl, which can be reached from the Upper Sublette quad as well as the Tram, has its own series of chutes – the Alta Chutes – and lower down some good bump and tree skiing. Cheyenne Bowl has open bowl skiing and, below it, some lovely runs through the trees.

The lower runs, including the Hobacks, at the edge of the ski area, are generally bumpy and frequently have less-than-ideal snow because of their orientation and altitude.

There are some heli-skiing operations to nearby ranges and some serious back-country routes down from Teton Pass – use a guide. A day's skiing in the powder of Grand Targhee, just over 40 miles away, is worth the excursion – all the reporters we've heard from rave about it.

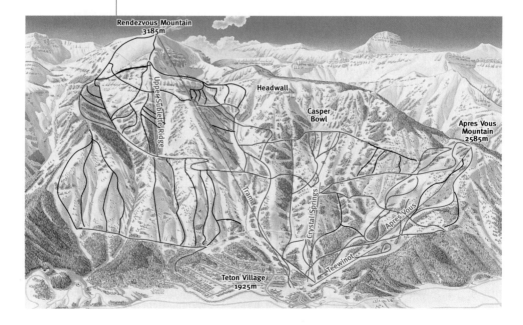

FOR INTERMEDIATE SKIERS
Exciting for some
Less adventurous intermediates will be mostly restricted to Apres Vous, with only the bolder skiers graduating to Rendezvous. There are great cruising runs all over Apres Vous. And Casper Bowl offers some quite gentle bowl skiing. There are several black runs on Apres Vous, and many suit improving intermediates testing their limits.

After that it's a case of checking out the main mountain by traversing to the Thunder chair and seeking out the few tough blues among the blacks and double-blacks. Adventurous intermediates will want to try their luck from the top – Rendezvous Trail is a good starting run and allows you to take a look at the area.

FOR BEGINNERS
A small number of suitable slopes
There's a choice of two lifts – Eagle's Rest and Teewinot double chairs – and four or five runs. These runs are broad and gentle – fine for getting started. The problem comes thereafter and the leap to tackling the runs off either the Apres Vous or Crystal Springs chairs. Beginners would really be best served going to another resort.

LIFT PASSES

95/96 prices in dollars

Jackson Hole
Covers all lifts and includes free 'Tram' tickets.
Main pass
1-day pass 45
6-day pass 246
Senior citizens
Over 65: 6-day pass 132 (48% off)
Children
Under 14: 6-day pass 132 (48% off)
Short-term passes
Afternoon pass from 12.30 (adult 34).
Notes 5 year-olds and under have free use on some lifts.
Alternative passes
Chair-lift only pass excludes Tram (adult 6-day 228). Jackson Hole Ski Three 5-day voucher book covers Jackson Hole, Grand Targhee and Snow King resorts (205, 94/95 price).

SKI SCHOOL

94/95 prices in dollars

Jackson Hole
Classes 6 days
4hr: 9.30-11.30 and 1.45-3.45; 2hr: am or pm
6 full days: 160
Children's classes
Ages: 3 to 14
6 6hr days including supervised lunch: 274
Private lessons
1hr, 2hr, half- or full-day
115 for 2hr; 130 for 2 to 3 people

CHILDCARE

The Kids Ranch (739 2691) near the Crystal Springs lift takes children aged 2 months to 5 years, from 8am to 5pm, with indoor and outdoor games and one-to-one ski lessons from age 3.

FOR CROSS-COUNTRY
Lots of possibilities

There are six centres in the valley, offering trails of various length and difficulty. The Spring Creek Nordic Centre has mainly beginner terrain and offers moonlight tours. There's a Nordic Centre at Teton Village, with 22km of trails and organised trips into the National Parks.

QUEUES
Can be awful at the Tram

The lengthy legal battle, before the ski area's change of ownership, held up much-needed modernisation of the lift system. There are frequently long queues for the 30-year-old Tram, despite the supplement payable on top of the basic lift pass. But the bad bottleneck in the key link from Apres Vous to Rendezvous was alleviated last season when the Thunder chair was upgraded to a quad.

MOUNTAIN RESTAURANTS
Ski to the base area

There's only one restaurant on the mountain – at the base of the Casper chair-lift – and it's very ordinary. The only other facilities are the snack-bars and toilets at the base of the Thunder chair-lift and Corbet's Cabin, at the top-station of the Tram. For a decent lunch, head to the base area. Nick Wilson's in the Clocktower building, the Alpenhof restaurant and the Mangy Moose are favourites.

SKI SCHOOL
Ski the Big One with confidence

Well that's what the school claims anyway. And it is the Pepi Stiegler ski school, so maybe some of that Olympic magic will rub off. Classes are typically small, with only four to six in the group, and the instructors do generate lots of enthusiasm and work hard at the 'inner game' of confidence building. At the higher teaching levels they give an introduction to the wide terrain variations that the area provides, and there are clinics for powder and mogul skiing.

All the reports we have are positive, with stress laid on fact that classes operate at all 11 levels regardless of how few people there are – two or three in a class is not at all unusual, more than eight exceptional.

FACILITIES FOR CHILDREN
Just fine

The ski area may not seem to be one ideally suited to children, but in fact there is enough easy skiing and the care facilities are good.

 # Staying there

If you want to be able to ski from the door, choose one of the hotels or condominiums in Teton Village. If you're happy with the idea of a 12-mile drive morning and evening, there's a far better choice of lodgings in the town of Jackson – and lots of other attractions. There is a regular and efficient bus service, and any lodging in town is likely to be within a five-minute walk of the town square.

HOW TO GO
Check out the package deals

There's a good variety of lodging styles on offer through UK tour operators – pretty well everything but the guest ranches are covered – and unless you're planning to visit other ski areas, it's likely there'll be a package to suit at a reasonable price.

Chalets Crystal have a comfortable catered condo five minutes' walk from Jackson town and close to a bus stop to the main ski area.

Hotels From economy motels to expensive hotels and lodges there should be a style and price to suit most tastes. There are quite a few small B&Bs in and around Jackson – they tend not to be cheap, but do give a bit of an insight to the local lifestyle (for details phone 001 307 733 1719).

££££ **Wort Hotel** The ritziest place to stay: brick-built hotel right in the centre of town and proud owner of the Silver Dollar Bar. Hot tub.

££££ **Inn at Jackson Hole** Comfortable, functional Best Western in Teton Village. Pool, sauna, hot tub.

££££ **Alpenhof** Our favourite in Teton Village. Tyrolean-style, with lots of wood and atmosphere. Good food. Pool, sauna, hot tub.

££££ **Rusty Parrot Lodge** Another stylish place in Jackson town, with a more rustic feel and handcrafted furniture. Hot tub.

£££ **Sojourner Inn** At Teton Village. It is comfortable and convenient with pool, sauna and hot tub.

£££ **Lodge at Jackson Hole** Newish western-style lodge in Jackson town, with comfortable rooms. Pool, sauna, hot tub. Report this year of 'not very friendly staff.'

£££ **Parkway Inn** Friendly, family-run place in Jackson town; nice pool.

££ **Forty-Niner Inn** Regular motel; hot tub and sauna.

Self-catering There is lots of choice at Teton Village, within and around Jackson and at more isolated locations between the two and elsewhere. The

GETTING THERE

Air Jackson, transfer ½hr.

PACKAGES

American Connections, American Dream, American Skiworld, Bladon Lines, Chalets 'Unlimited', Crystal, Lotus Supertravel, Made to Measure, Ski Activity, Ski Independence, Ski Scott Dunn

Grand Targhee American Dream

ACTIVITIES

Indoor Art galleries, ice skating, swimming, theatre, concerts and live music
Outdoor Snow-mobiles, mountaineering, horse riding, snow-shoe hikes, snowcat tours, floodlit skiing, heli-skiing, sleigh rides, dog-sledding, walks, wildlife safaris and tours of Yellowstone National Park

TOURIST OFFICE

Postcode WY 83001
Tel 00 1 (307) 7334005
Fax 7331286

Cowboy Village Resort has neat little log cabins on the edge of town. The Jackson Hole Racquet Club has good condos and facilities between town and skiing. Teton Village Property Management control many of the condos at Teton Village. The Snow King Resort Condominiums have full hotel service facilities, next to the town skiing. The Mad Dog Ranch has a country location, with great views.

There's only one large supermarket in Jackson and a number of smaller stores and delis. Teton Village has good small stores but no supermarket.

EATING OUT
It's a pleasure in Jackson

Teton Village can list about ten or so restaurants – there's a pizza place, a Mexican, a Steakhouse and a number of hotel restaurants. They're all OK but most people's favourite is the Mangy Moose and the Rocky Mountain Oyster, downstairs – good value, good fun. In Jackson it's a case of trying as many places as you can in the time available. The Cadillac Grille, with its art-deco interior, is the coolest place – and there is a burger bar attached. The Blue Lion is small, cosy and casually stylish. Louie's Steak and Seafood does just that in smart, log cabin surroundings. The Cowboy Steakhouse is attached to the Cowboy Bar and can come in very handy after a hard night on the saddle stools. Italian, Cajun, Chinese and several fast food chains are also represented. The Bunnery is a sound choice for breakfast and fresh-baked things; for bagels head for Pearl Street Bagels.

APRES-SKI
Check out the saloons

There are bars and occasional live entertainment, rather than clubs and discos; this is Wyoming, not Val d'Isère. In Teton Village, Beaver Dick's and the Pub have their fans, but the biggest draw is usually the Mangy Moose – it's a big happy, noisy place and often has good live music. The famous bars in Jackson are JJ's Silver Dollar Bar at the Wort hotel and the Million Dollar Cowboy Bar on the town square. You have to see them both. The Silver Dollar is the classier venue and has over 2,000 silver dollars inlaid into the counter. The Cowboy Bar features saddles as bar stools, a

stuffed grizzly bear and is usually the rowdiest place in town. There's quality live music every night (both kinds – country and western). The Rancher and the Shady Lady Saloon might also have live music; the Rancher is the place to play pool. The Virginian Saloon is a quieter watering hole. It's a good idea for those under 30 to carry their passports – the drinking age is 21 and is zealously enforced.

For a night out, try driving to Wilson, where the Stagecoach Inn has cowgirl waitresses, big portions of western food and live music on Sundays. Or you can go night-skiing on the local floodlit Snow King hill, on the outskirts of Jackson.

FOR NON-SKIERS
Some great outdoor diversions

There are some big outdoor attractions nearby and plenty of possibilities for trips. Yellowstone National Park is 100km to the north, and although most of the roads are closed to traffic in winter, snow-mobile and 'snow-coach' trips are permitted. The park is famous for its geysers, the wildlife and the general beauty of the surroundings. The National Elk Refuge, just outside Jackson, has the largest remaining elk herd in the US – around 8,000 strong. Visits to the Granite Hot Springs and to parts of the Grand Teton National Park are also possible. In town there are some 40 galleries and museums and a number of outlets for Indian and Western arts and crafts. Most of the larger hotels have swimming pools.

Grand Targhee 2440m

This 'resort' 42 miles north-west of Jackson has only 444 beds but is a great place to visit for a day-trip. It has a wonderful reputation for powder snow and has adopted the slogan 'Snow from Heaven not Hoses'. There are only three chair-lifts, but they give you access to unusually deserted pistes which often have splendid untracked powder nearby – all our reporters this season have praised the skiing highly. There is also a good snowcat skiing operation – you ride up in a snow grooming machine converted into a people carrier (10 people plus a couple of guides) and ski virgin slopes. Book in advance.

Keystone 2835m

✔ *Splendid intermediate ski area with immaculately groomed runs*

✔ *Huge floodlit skiing area with runs open until 10pm*

✔ *Good tough skiing at Arapahoe Basin – Colorado's highest lifts*

✔ *Part of Ski the Summit ski lift pass area*

✔ *Efficient lift system means few queues*

✔ *Luxurious condominiums in woods make for relaxed family holidays*

✗ *Very quiet in the evenings*

✗ *Resort lacks a real centre, so very little ski-village feel*

Keystone has the biggest and best intermediate skiing area of all the Ski the Summit resorts, with miles and miles of immaculately groomed tree-lined runs. It also has Colorado's biggest night skiing operation, with 13 runs operating until 10pm, a huge computerised snowmaking system to supplement the natural stuff, and the best mountain restaurant in the US. Good skiers might find it a bit limited, but with the rest of the Ski the Summit area to explore too, they should find enough to interest them for their stay – especially if nearby Arapahoe Basin is fully open.

The resort best suits keen skiers who aren't seeking lively nightlife. There are some excellent restaurants, but not much in the way of lively bars and dancing. Those who want nightlife would be better off staying in Breckenridge, and making excursions to Keystone.

The resort

Keystone was the dream of Max Dercum. He gave up his professorship at Pennsylvania State University to drop out with his wife, Edna, to Colorado in the 1940s. Max converted the old stage-coach stop into the Ski Tip Lodge, now the most atmospheric place to stay in the district.

While Max and his wife ran the ski school in Arapahoe Basin, he worked on his plans to convert the wooded mountains in front of his door into one of the best ski areas in the US. He saw his dream open for business in 1969, and it has been growing rapidly ever since. Max sold out long ago, but still lives locally.

Keystone is a sprawling resort of luxurious condominiums spread over

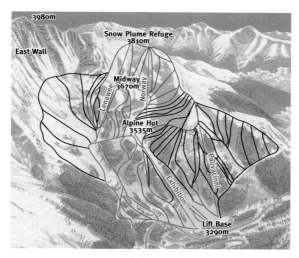

ORIENTATION

Keystone consists mainly of luxurious condominiums spread over a large area at the foot of Keystone Mountain. A high-speed quad chair goes up into the skiing from the Mountain House base, and a gondola goes up from the day-skiers' parking lot out of town.

Nearby **Arapahoe Basin** adds to the skiing of Keystone. In 1993, **Breckenridge** came under the same ownership. All three are now covered on the same lift ticket. A Ski the Summit lift pass also covers **Copper Mountain**. These four ski areas are linked by free buses. With a hire car you can also try **Vail, Beaver Creek** and **Steamboat**, all less than two hours' drive.

wooded countryside. Regular buses transport you between your accommodation and the two main centres, which both have shops, restaurants and bars. The Mountain House area lies at the foot of the main lift, and staying near here is best for ski convenience.

A couple of miles away is the picturesque lake area – a huge natural ice rink in winter. This is the other main resort centre, and includes the large and luxurious Keystone Lodge.

 # The skiing

Keystone has expanded rapidly in the last few years, most notably opening up a new $28 million mountain in 1991. It now offers the most extensive intermediate skiing in the Ski the Summit area. Nearby Arapahoe Basin (or A-Basin as it's called by the locals) is a complete contrast. Its relatively slow and ancient lift system gives access to steep, high, above-the-tree-line runs.

THE SKI AREA
A keen intermediate's dream
Three tree-lined, interlinked mountains form Keystone's local skiing – Keystone Mountain, North

Peak and The Outback. The only one directly accessible from the resort is **Keystone Mountain**. The quickest way up is by the Peru Express quad chair from the Mountain House centre or by the gondola from the car park.

From the top you can ski down on a choice of 53 runs, or drop over the back and ski down to the foot of **North Peak** and take a chair-lift up. Or you can ride the Outpost gondola which links the top of Keystone Mountain to the top of North Peak (and stays open late into the night to ferry diners to and from the mountain-top restaurants up there).

From North Peak you can ski back to the bases of both Keystone Mountain and the third peak, known as **The Outback**, served by another high-speed quad chair-lift.

Arapahoe Basin is a short shuttle-bus ride away and was developed long before Keystone. In contrast to Keystone's superb modern lifts, A-Basin is still served by a series of slow old chairs. These give it an old-fashioned feel which contrasts remarkably with the large number of young snowboarders you find here. Snowboarders are banned from Keystone's mountains.

SNOW RELIABILITY
Excellent
Keystone rarely suffers from a shortage of natural snow. But in case it does, it has one of the world's biggest snowmaking systems as back-up.

One of the main reasons for the snowmaking is to help form an early season base. Keystone traditionally vies with Killington to be the first US ski resort to open its runs for the season – normally in October.

A-Basin has no need for artificial snow. It has the highest lift-served skiing in the US, at almost 4000m, and the base-station is at an impressive 3285m. The skiing here is normally open well into June.

FOR ADVANCED SKIERS
You'll have to travel
Keystone's own skiing area isn't particularly challenging. There are some good mogul runs, such as Ambush and Geronimo on North Peak. The steepest parts of Keystone's skiing are off-piste, among the trees below the open bowls at the top of The Outback. But most of Keystone's skiing is intermediate cruising.

Arapahoe Basin, down the road, is the best place locally for those looking for a challenge. The East Wall here has some splendid steep chutes. And the

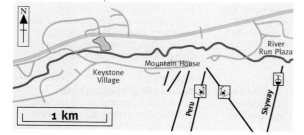

LIFT PASSES

94/95 prices in dollars

Breckenridge-Keystone

Covers all lifts in Breckenridge, Keystone and Arapahoe Basin.

Beginners Beginners and novices have a reduced area pass in ski school.

Main pass

1-day pass 40
6-day pass 192

Senior citizens

Over 65: 6-day pass 150 (22% off)

Children

Under 13: 6-day pass 102 (47% off)
Under 6: free pass

Notes Breckenridge, Keystone and Arapahoe are all a ski-bus ride apart. Discounts for groups of over 20. Over 70s have a further discounted pass price. All passes (except day-pass) allow one non-skiing day; 6-day pass valid for 7 days with one non-skiing day.

Alternative passes

Ski the Summit coupon booklets interchangeable for lift pass at Breckenridge, Copper Mountain, Keystone and Arapahoe Basin (6 days skiing out of 7 adult 210).

SKI SCHOOL

95/96 prices in dollars

Keystone

Classes 6 days 2½hr: 10.30-1pm or 1.30-5pm; 2hr 30min am or pm; evening 4.30-6.30, 2hr 6 half days: 204

Children's classes

Ages: 3 to 12 6 full days including lunch and ski-pass: 408

Private lessons

Hourly, up to 6hr 75 for 1hr

opposite side of the bowl is riddled with steep bump runs – although none of the runs is particularly long.

Copper Mountain and Breckenridge have some good challenging skiing too – Breckenridge opened a new area last season. To get the most out of the region you'll have to be prepared to travel around quite a lot – no real hassle with the free half-hourly shuttles between resorts.

FOR INTERMEDIATE SKIERS
A cruiser's paradise

Keystone's skiing is ideal for intermediates. The front face of Keystone Mountain itself is a network of beautifully groomed blue and green runs through the trees. Keen skiers who want to bash the pistes for as long as possible won't find anywhere better. Over 42% of the mountain's runs are floodlit, and open until 10pm, and the whole mountain is served by snowmaking.

The Outback and North Peak also have easy cruising blues, with The Outback having some of the steepest blue skiing, including a couple of blue-black bump runs through the trees which are pretty much off-piste and unmarked.

On top of that there's the rest of Summit County's skiing to explore. Copper Mountain, in particular, has some great intermediate terrain, and is easily reached.

FOR BEGINNERS
Nice gentle greens

The front face of Keystone Mountain has some excellent easy green runs for beginners to try once they are off the nursery slopes. Schoolmarm goes right from top to bottom of the mountain.

FOR CROSS-COUNTRY
Extensive facilities

There's a special Cross-Country and Touring Center between Keystone and A-Basin which is served by the shuttle bus. There are 29km of groomed trails. And 57km of unprepared trails take you through spectacular scenery in the Montezuma area, with great views of the Continental Divide. Some trails lead to old mining ghost-towns. The Cross-County and Touring Center runs guided tours, including a Full Moon evening tour.

QUEUES
Not a problem

Keystone has an efficient, modern lift system, and except at the morning peak there are usually few queuing problems.

MOUNTAIN RESTAURANTS
Includes the best in the US

There are only two mountain-top restaurant complexes – Summit House at the top of Keystone Mountain and The Outpost at the top of North Peak.

The Outpost, in particular, is streets ahead of most US mountain eating places. Opened three seasons ago, the whole place is beautifully designed in wood, with high ceilings, large picture windows and a big sun terrace. The self-service restaurant is well designed and sells good fresh pizza, pasta, salads and grills. But the real jewel is the table-service Alpenglow Stube, which serves haute cuisine with a Bavarian flavour. It has a luxury atmosphere rarely found in European, let alone American, mountain restaurants – they even swap your ski boots for slippers at the cloakroom.

SKI SCHOOL
Typical American excellence

As well as the normal lessons, there are skiing workshops which specialise in moguls, powder and steep terrain, and five-day courses run by Olympic medallists Phil and Steve Mahre. One reporter was very impressed by the tuition his 9-year-old had – lessons blended fun and technique well, and at the end of each day the instructor gave the child a personal debrief with written report! 'French ski schools could learn a bit here,' he said.

FACILITIES FOR CHILDREN
Excellent

Childcare facilities are excellent, with programmes carefully tailored to specific age groups, and nursery care going on into the evening. We're not surprised to learn that Keystone has twice been voted Family Resort of the Year by the magazine Family Circle.

 # Staying there

Keystone is a comfortable place to stay if you're looking for a quiet time with good restaurants but not much other evening atmosphere. The most convenient place to stay is near the Mountain House lift base-station.

But all the accommodation is well served by the shuttle buses. All the condominiums we've seen or heard about are large and luxurious.

HOW TO GO
Independent booking easy

A few tour operators offer packages and booking independently is easy. Resort Express run regular transport

CHILDCARE

The Children's Center at the base of the mountain caters for children aged 2 months to 12 years and is open from 8am to 9pm. They can also provide evening baby-sitting in your own room. From age 3, children can join in the Snowplay programmes.

The ski school's Mini Minor's Camp takes children aged 3 to 4, the Minor's Camp those from 5 to 12.

GETTING THERE

Air Denver, transfer 2hr.

PACKAGES

Airtours, American Connections, American Dream, Crystal, Made to Measure, Ski Independence, USAirtours

ACTIVITIES

Indoor Swimming, hot tubs, tennis
Outdoor Floodlit ice skating, sleigh and stagecoach rides, snowmobiling, horse-riding, dog-sledding, evening gondola trips

TOURIST OFFICE

Postcode CO 80435
Tel 00 1 (303)
4535000
Fax 4533202

from Denver airport to Keystone. There are a few hotels but most accommodation is in condominiums.
Chalets No tour operators run catered chalets here, as far as we know.
Hotels There isn't a great choice but they're all of a high standard.
££££ Chateaux d'Mont Small luxurious hotel near the lifts; only 15 suites, with private hot tubs and lots of other extravagances.
££££ Keystone Lodge Large, luxurious modern hotel in Keystone Village – a shopping and restaurant complex by the frozen lake. Pool and fitness centre.
£££ Inn at Keystone Modern, comfortable hotel a short walk from the lifts. Outdoor hot tubs. Liked by reporters who stayed there.
£££ Ski Tip Lodge Former stage-coach halt and home of Keystone's founder, Max Dercum, who restored and extended it and used broken ski tips found on the slopes as door handles – hence the name. Atmospheric old rooms, bar and lounge with log fires. Well out of town by the cross-country centre. Good restaurant.
Self-catering There are hundreds of well-appointed condominiums, most with use of a pool and hot tub. The Liftside condos are in the heart of the resort, close to the lifts, and come complete with all mod cons and good communal facilities. The equally comfortable and well positioned Frostfire condos have fewer in-house amenities but each unit has en suite whirlpool bath. The Resort condos enjoy a pretty location in the woods, a bus-ride from the lifts. The Cinnamon Ridge and Slopeside condos are other comfortable places.

STAYING DOWN THE VALLEY
Possible, good for exploring
A couple of reporters stayed in **Silverthorne**. The Days Inn was thought comfortable but basic. The Alpen Hutte was friendly and had its own private bus transfer. **Frisco** was thought a better centre for skiing the whole of the Summit region.

EATING OUT
Generally very high standard
Whether you want to eat up the mountain or in the valley, there's a good choice.
   The Summit House, at the top of the gondola on Keystone Mountain, remains busy at the end of normal skiing because of the night skiing. There's live country and western entertainment and simple food –

hamburgers, ribs and so on.
   The Outpost, on North Peak, is a hive of dining activity with the Alpenglow Stube (see Mountain restaurants) open every night for 'fine dining' as well as fondue, raclette and Tyrolean music at Der Fondue Chessel.
   In the valley, the Ski Tip Lodge by the cross-country track has good food in a charming restored building that was formerly the stage-coach halt.
   The Keystone Ranch has an award-winning restaurant that serves six-course dinners in a building based on a 19th-century homestead built in an area which the Ute and Arapahoe Indians used as their summer campground for buffalo hunting.
   There are simpler places in both the lakeside and lift station areas, such as Gassy Thomson's and Ida Belle's for typical American-style burgers, ribs and grills, the Commodore for steak, seafood and pasta, and the Bighorn Steakhouse and Pizza on the Plaza for pizza, soup, salad and sandwiches.
   You can take a dinner sleigh ride to Soda Creek Homestead, or a more unusual 'progressive dinner' – a stage-coach ride where you have each course in a different restaurant, with dessert at the Ski Tip Lodge.
   Less grandly, you can get takeaways delivered to your condominium.

APRES-SKI
Pretty quiet in the evenings
Immediately after skiing can be quite lively. The Summit House at the top of the gondola has live music and caters for night skiers as well as après-skiers. Keysters at the bottom of the gondola has karaoke and Montezuma has rock 'n roll. Some of the eateries double as bars with live music: Snake River Saloon has happy hour, 5–7pm; Ida Belle has ragtime music and a miners' tavern decor; and Dillon Inn has Country and Western.
   But places empty out quite early and Keystone isn't really the place for late-night revellers.

FOR NON-SKIERS
OK if you want a peaceful time
Keystone is one of the best places in Colorado for getting around on the mountain. The gondolas make both mountain restaurant complexes easily accessible, and the Summit Stage shuttle makes getting to Breckenridge and Copper Mountain easy.
   There are plenty of other activities, including skating on the frozen lake (the largest outdoor maintained rink in the US).

Lake Tahoe 1890m

Set high in the mountains 200 miles east of San Francisco, on the borders of California and Nevada, Lake Tahoe has the highest concentration of ski resorts in the US, with 14 downhill and seven cross-country centres. It is a very beautiful region, ideal for driving around on a tour, visiting a different ski area each day – as well as having two or three areas well worth spending several days exploring. The two areas that are best-known in Britain are Heavenly (see page 399) and Squaw Valley.

THE RESORTS

The ski areas of the Lake Tahoe region are mostly just that – ski areas, rather than fully fledged resorts with their own villages and vibrant nightlife. Some have no accommodation, others a little. But most of the areas earn their money from weekend or day-trip skiers from the local area, or from people who drive or fly up for a couple of days from the big cities on the west coast.

Don't expect a 'resort' in the European sense of the word. And you may be surprised by the influence that gambling has in the area. The California-Nevada border cuts through the region and through Lake Tahoe itself. At the border you'll find a clutch of amazingly popular, bright, brash casinos. The biggest accommodation centre (and the biggest centre for gambling and casinos) is South Lake Tahoe – for a description of that, see the Heavenly chapter on page 399. The Heavenly ski area is a short drive or bus-ride from there.

The other main resort on the British market is Squaw Valley – which has a limited amount of accommodation but little nightlife outside that. It is about a 90-minute drive from South Lake Tahoe, or a pleasant cruise across the lake on the Tahoe Queen (with live music and a jolly après-ski atmosphere on the way back). If you drive, be sure to check whether the quickest route along the west bank of the lake is open – it's often shut by Emerald Bay due to avalanche danger.

Apart from those two, you'll find lots of B&Bs and motels dotted around the lake, and a couple of quite pleasant small towns.

THE SKIING

The choice of **ski areas** is enormous, with more than enough to keep even the keenest skier happy for a couple of weeks. You just need to be prepared to drive around to the different resorts. Because US lift tickets are priced by the day, with little or no discount for a week's pass, this doesn't add much to the cost of the holiday.

When we were in the region last January, we stayed at Squaw Valley for three days and were unable to ski Squaw at all in that time because of the amount of snow falling. But we were able to ski other nearby areas instead – the beauty of the region's varied skiing. And we had a great day at Squaw a few days later by driving from our next lodgings at Heavenly.

The record for **snow reliability** isn't as good around here as in many other US resorts. But the area does have huge amounts of artificial snowmaking capacity, so lack of snow shouldn't be a problem.

Heavenly, at the southern end of the lake, has the greatest vertical drop of the region, with skiing to suit all standards and splendid lake views. See page 399 for more details.

Nearby **Sierra-at-Tahoe** is a smaller, tree-lined area – more sheltered, so useful in bad-weather.

Kirkwood, also at the south end of the lake, is renowned for its steep runs. It has fine intermediate groomed trails too (which in total account for 50 per cent of its skiing).

The major resort at the north end of the lake is **Squaw Valley**. It still makes quite a play on having hosted the Winter Olympics, even though that was way back in 1960. Squaw is unusual in having no named runs at all – and no trails marked on the piste map, just blue squares and black diamonds. The skiing is in 4,000 acres of open, above-the-treeline bowls on six linked mountains.

The skiing for expert skiers is phenomenal, with lots of steep slopes, chutes and big mogul fields – many extreme skiing movies are made here. Perhaps surprisingly, it is good for intermediates too, with lovely long groomed blue runs including a top-to-bottom three-mile cruise – 45 per cent of the terrain is rated as suitable for intermediates. Squaw is a big snowboarding centre.

Alpine Meadows has the longest season and some of the most varied terrain in the Tahoe region – skiing can last until July some years. There is

PACKAGES

Lake Tahoe American Connections, Crystal, Ski Activity, Ski Independence, USAirtours, Virgin Snow

Squaw Valley
Ski Activity, Ski Independence, Virgin Snow

TOURIST OFFICE

Squaw Valley

Postcode CA 96146
Tel 00 1 (916) 5836985
Fax 5835970

some excellent skiing for all standards, with green runs and nursery slopes at the bottom, top-to-bottom blues and some varied blacks, including high bowls and tree skiing. The mountain has slopes facing in all directions, giving good skiing whatever the weather. The major drawback is its limited vertical drop – around 550m. Still it's well worth a day of anyone's skiing trip. Snowboards are banned.

Northstar-at-Tahoe is a fairly small, almost entirely beginner and intermediate mountain close to Squaw. Although there are black runs marked on the trail map, none are seriously steep and the nine or so blacks on the back (served by a single high-speed quad) vary little in character and are really good long advanced intermediate cruises. Again, the area is very sheltered and good for bad weather days. There's a pleasant shopping, restaurant and bar area at the bottom of the mountain, with

very convenient hotel rooms and condominiums. It would be a good family choice of a quiet place to stay.

Those are the six areas we'd most recommend visiting. But there are eight other areas in the Tahoe region in case you get bored, most of which are marked on our map. There is also a substantial amount of **cross-country** skiing, which is available at most of the downhill areas as well as in dedicated cross-country areas.

Queues are rare in all the ski areas, except at peak weekends when people pour in from San Francisco and Los Angeles. Squaw Valley is even confident enough to offer a lift pass refund for any day on which you have to wait more than ten minutes. We have few reports of the **ski schools** or facilities for **children**, but have no reason to believe that they fall short of the generally excellent standards of other US resorts.

STAYING THERE

We'd recommend spending a few days at each end of the lake.

At the southern end there's little alternative to staying in the brash and rather tacky town of South Lake Tahoe – for more detail see our Heavenly chapter on page 399.

At the northern end there's more choice. Squaw Valley has three hotels, of which the Lodge at Squaw Creek is the biggest and most luxurious. It is huge, and often full of guests at conferences and seminars that allow them time off to ski. It is out of town, with its own lift into the ski area and a piste back. It has all the facilities you'd expect – pools, hot tubs, condos, a few shops and a couple of bars – all centred around the bottom of the cable-car. The cable-car itself runs in the evenings to serve the night skiing and the dining facilities at the High Camp Bath and Tennis Club at the top. This is an incredible mid-mountain base, with several restaurants and bars, outdoor pool, ice skiing, tennis and bungy jumping – though little of this was working when we were there last January.

Or you could stay in the small town of Tahoe City, right on the lake, a short drive from both the Squaw Valley and Alpine Meadows areas. It has a fair number of hotels and bars, and some good restaurants – we liked Jake's, popular with locals, airy wooden decor, lake views and excellent modern American cooking.

There are also plenty of motels and condominiums dotted around the lakeside road.

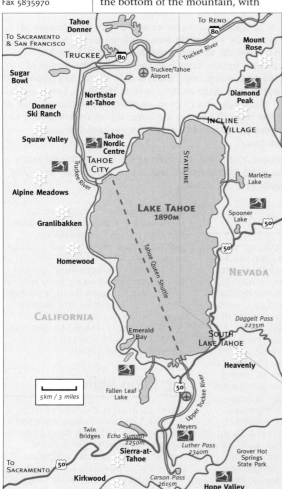

Mammoth Mountain 2430m

✔ One of North America's biggest and best ski areas

✔ Can get a lot of snow – and there's extensive snowmaking

✔ Very extensive steep bowls at the top of the lift system

✔ Plenty of easy/intermediate cruising runs lower down, in the trees

✔ Good children's facilities

✔ Extensive, well kept, snowsure cross-country trails

✔ Amazingly cheap package holidays

✗ Most of the accommodation, in the 'village' of Mammoth Lakes, is miles from the slopes

✗ Mammoth Lakes is a rather diffuse place, lacking ski resort atmosphere and a pain if you don't have a car

✗ Weekend crowds from Los Angeles

✗ No mountain restaurants worth mentioning

✗ Eccentric trail map marks runs very approximately

California doesn't conjure up skiing in most British people's imagination. They're more likely to think of surfing, beaches, wine, Hollywood and the big cities of Los Angeles and San Francisco. But since Richard Branson decided that Mammoth was his favourite resort and started offering extremely good-value packages there via his Virgin Atlantic flights to LA and San Francisco, more and more Brits have been trying Mammoth.

And they all love it – or at least the ones we've heard from do. It's easy to see why. Mammoth may not be a giant ski area in Alpine terms, but it is much bigger than most in the US, and big enough to provide a week's amusement for most skiers – except those wedded to the mega-resorts of France. It has everything from steep, high, experts-only chutes and bowls (with magnificent views) to long, easy cruising runs in the trees. Los Angeles residents discovered it years ago, and in good weather they swarm up here at weekends. But during the week the slopes are often almost deserted. And on busy days you can always try Mammoth's smaller sister resort of June Mountain, a short drive away.

The lack of an atmospheric traditional ski resort at the base of the mountain is something we guess most British visitors will put up with if they're paying the kind of prices people paid last season.

ORIENTATION

Most people stay in Mammoth Lakes, four miles (7km) from the base of the ski area and linked by efficient shuttle-buses. Lifts go up to the ski area from a few places on the road. The main base area, at the far end, has the biggest choice of lifts, including a gondola and a high-speed chair. These both connect with other lifts taking you straight to Mammoth's highest skiing.

A separate ski area called **June Mountain** is 30 minutes' drive away and is covered by the lift pass.

 ## The resort

Mammoth Lakes, a small year-round resort town four miles from the ski slopes, is the main accommodation centre. It sprawls widely – mainly along the extraordinarily wide road (called Main Street) leading towards the ski slopes, and along one or two major side-roads. Hotels, bars, restaurants and little shopping centres with well-stocked ski shops line the roadside. Mammoth may be short on ski-resort ambience, but its setting among trees and its not unattractive buildings give a pleasant enough appearance. Even the ubiquitous MacDonald's has been tastefully designed. The 'village' is usually under a blanket of snow, which also helps.

There is accommodation at the main base area of the skiing – the Mammoth Mountain Inn complex. And along the road up to the slopes lie several hotels and condos. Shuttle-buses serve four colour-coded routes, but a car is useful, especially for getting to June Mountain for a change of skiing scenery.

The five- or six-hour drive up from Los Angeles, along a very good road, is spectacular. You pass through the San Bernardino mountains and Mojave Desert before reaching the Sierra Nevada range, of which Mammoth is part. Alternatively you can fly into Mammoth's own airport.

 ## The skiing

Although Mammoth is one of America's largest ski areas, the resort's claim to have 150 trails should not be taken too seriously. The slightest variant of a run is given a separate name and number. Go to the right of a few trees and you're on trail 34, go to the left and it's trail 35.

SKI FACTS

Altitude 2430m-3370m
Lifts 31
Pistes 3500 acres
Green 30%
Blue 40%
Black 30%
Art. snow 200 acres

LIFT PASSES

95/96 prices in dollars
Mammoth Mountain
Covers all lifts at
Mammoth.
Beginners 1- (54), 2-
(126) and 3-day (206)
learn-to-ski packages
include pass, lessons
and rental.
Main pass
1-day pass 43
6-day pass 224
Senior citizens
Over 65: 6-day pass
116 (50% off)
Children
Under 13: 6-day pass
116 (50% off)
Under 7: free pass
Short-term passes
Scenic ride on
Mammoth Gondola
(adult 10); afternoon
pass available (adult
30).

SKI SCHOOL

95/96 prices in dollars
Mammoth Mountain
Classes 7 days
4hr: 10am-noon and
1.30-3.30; 2hr: am or
pm
5 full days: 175
Children's classes
Ages: 4 to 12
5 full days including
lunch: 190
Private lessons
1hr, 3hr or 6hr
60 for 1hr

Nevertheless, the 30 lifts access an impressive single ski area suitable for all standards of skier. The highest runs are almost exclusively steep powder bowls and chutes, most of which are for experts only. In general, the lower down you go the easier the skiing becomes.

Finding your way around is something else. The lifts are known by numbers allocated as they were built, so the system has no geographic logic. Chair 26 is between chairs 1 and 19, and so on. And the trail map shows trails by means of occasional symbols, not continuous lines, which makes it difficult to see where a particular run takes you. But in the end it doesn't matter a lot: head downhill, and you'll eventually come to a lift. And if you get lost, there's a fair chance you'll come across a member of the helpful mountain host service to point the way home.

Mammoth's ski area is still owned and run by its founder, Dave McCoy, who built the first lift here in the 1940s. Many people told him at the outset that it was too high, too remote and too stormy here to make it as a ski resort, so he is naturally proud that his dream of developing the inhospitable mountains of the area into one of America's top ski resorts has been turned into reality. Dave is still actively involved in running the mountain, and pursues his ideas with an amazing vigour. When we met him last winter, he had just commissioned a Disney-style monorail to link the slopes to Mammoth Lakes; it was scheduled to be built in a matter of weeks, and we don't doubt that it was.

THE SKI AREA
It's all here
There are three major lift-stations at regular intervals along the foot of the slopes, which mainly face north-east. An isolated fourth is also reachable by shuttle-bus.

At the centre of the ski area is Mid Chalet, a huge restaurant (the only one on the mountain, not counting those at the bottom of lifts). This is the mid-station of the gondola from **Main Lodge** (the main base area, furthest from town), the second stage of which goes on up to the highest point of the skiing, at 3370m. The views from the top are splendid, with Nevada to the north-east and the jagged Minarets to the west.

From the top, there are essentially three ways down. The first, on which there are countless variations (including 15 shown on the trail

map), is down the front of the mountain, which ranges from steep to very steep – or vertical if the wind has created a cornice, as it often does. The second is off the back, down to **Chair 14 Outpost**, whence chair 14 or 13 bring you back to a lower point on the ridge. The third is to follow the ridge down to the Main Lodge area – a route that can hardly be detected on the idiotic trail map. This route brings you past an area of easy skiing served by chair 12, and very easy skiing served by chairs 11 and 27.

Main Lodge has an array of other lifts fanning out over the mountain. One of them links to a triple chair for speedy access to the summit ridge.

Mid Chalet can also be reached from **Chair 2 Outpost**, on the road up from town. Other lifts from here take you into the more heavily forested eastern half of the ski area – long, gentle runs served by lifts up from **Hut 2** and **Chair 15 Outpost**, both on the fringe of town, and seriously steep stuff on the subsidiary peak, served by lifts 25 and 22.

SNOW RELIABILITY
A long season
California had poor years in 1992 and 1994 and is not generally as snowsure as Colorado or Utah. But when it snows, it snows. 1993 saw a record snowfall of 617 inches (almost 16m), and 1995 was pretty impressive: even early in the season there was a 4m base. Mammoth has, over the years, had an impressive snow record, and thanks to its height and its snowmakers, it enjoys a long season.

FOR ADVANCED SKIERS
Some very challenging skiing
The steep bowls that run the width of the mountain top provide wonderful skiing for experts. The steep chutes either side of Chair 22 also provide very challenging skiing, and being relatively sheltered are often open in bad weather when the top is firmly shut. Above Main Lodge is another steep area ideal for the advanced skier. A quiet little bowl behind the main mountain plunges down to Chair 14 Outpost. Many of the lower trails are short, by European standards, but can easily be skied repeatedly. And you can ski virtually from top to bottom all day entirely on black runs. There are plenty of opportunities for couloir-lovers, and some only for the very brave, such as Star Chute and Felipe's.

June Mountain has some steep tree-lined skiing too, and is certainly worth trying for a day.

CHILDCARE

Children's classes are handled by the Woollywood Ski Academy at the Main Lodge, which 'interfaces' with the Small World Day Care Center (934 0646) based at the nearby Mammoth Mountain Inn. This takes children from newborn to age 12, from 8am to 5pm.

GETTING THERE

Air Los Angeles, transfer 5hr. Reno, transfer 3hr. Mammoth Lakes, transfer 20 minutes.

PACKAGES

American Connections, American Dream, American Skiworld, Crystal, Inghams, Ski Activity, Ski Independence, Virgin Snow

FOR INTERMEDIATE SKIERS
Lots of great cruising

Mammoth's piste maintenance is such that intermediates can ski runs they might consider too steep in European resorts where bumps are allowed to build up on even moderately steep pistes. And there is plenty of skiing for all standards of intermediate.

Some of the mountain's longest runs, served by Chairs 9 and 25, are ideal for good intermediates. There are also a couple of lovely, fairly steep, tree-lined pistes running the length of Chair 10 down to Chair 2 Outpost.

Many of the tree-lined runs above Chair 15 Outpost and Hut 2 are flattering, while the piste between Mid Chalet and Chair 2 Outpost is the one real motorway on the mountain.

Less adventurous skiers have some good, wide runs through trees in the triangle between Main Lodge, Chair 2 Outpost and Mid-Chalet, and need not fear out-of-control skiers hurtling around the 'slow skiing' areas.

FOR BEGINNERS
Good tuition

Nursery slopes are adequate, and the excellence of tuition, piste grooming and snow quality usually makes progress very speedy. Hansel and Gretel are a couple of very easy pistes through the trees above Hut 2.

FOR CROSS-COUNTRY
Very popular

There is a fine choice of trails. Two specialist centres, Tamarack and Sierra Meadows, provide tuition and tours, and there are no fewer than eleven cross-country ski-hire shops. There are 70km of well maintained trails, including some winding through the beautiful Lakes Basin area, and miles of very pretty ungroomed tracks through forests.

QUEUES
Weekend invasions

During the week the lifts and slopes are usually very quiet, with no queues. But even the efficient lift system can struggle to cope with 15,000 skiers arriving from LA on fine weekends. That's the time to try June Mountain.

MOUNTAIN RESTAURANTS
Singular and inadequate

Although there are restaurants at the Main Lodge base area (including the cute Yodler chalet) and refreshments at other lift bases, there is only one restaurant actually on the slopes, at Mid Chalet. It is emphatically not a chalet, but a monster motorway cafe, lacking charm, atmosphere and interesting food. Even when the resort is quiet, there may be queues.

SKI SCHOOL
Excellent reports – mostly

Mammoth has a high reputation for tuition, though one recent report speaks of very large beginner classes, even mid-week. We've had very good reports of the June Mountain school, where classes as small as three don't seem unusual. For advanced skiers there are excellent classes in powder style and 'efficiency' (technique). Heli-skiing is also available.

FACILITIES FOR CHILDREN
Family favourite

Mammoth is keen to attract families. Children have a very caring ski school which works closely with the nearby nursery. There is also a special ski club for teenagers. We've had one particularly glowing report of a 3-year-old who had 'a great time' in the Small World nursery and had a private lesson one day which was an unqualified success – she 'came back with a huge smile'.

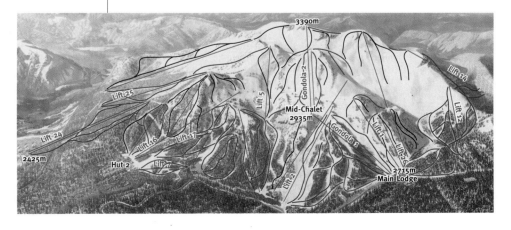

ACTIVITIES

Indoor Mammoth museum, art galleries, theatre
Outdoor Snow-mobiling, ski touring, bobsleigh, dog-sledding, tobogganing, sleigh rides, hot-air balloon rides

 # Staying there

Staying at Main Lodge, at the bottom of the slopes, is clearly most convenient for the skiing. But there's a much greater choice of bars and restaurants in Mammoth Lakes, and the efficient, free shuttle-bus service means getting to and from the slopes is easy.

HOW TO GO
Some packages, more independent
There's a catered chalet available and a few condo options, but hotels dominate the scene. Condos tend to be either out near the lifts or along the road to them, rather than in town.
Chalets American Skiworld have a place in a complex of traditional-style townhouses. It's comfortable and has the added benefit of an indoor pool and other leisure facilities on-site.
Hotels Tour operators all use the same few places. Independent travellers have a much wider choice.
££££ Mammoth Mountain Inn Motel/hotel/condo complex at the foot of the slopes. Comfortable and spacious bedrooms, but rather gloomy public rooms.
£££ Quality Inn Good, main street hotel with the biggest hot tub in town. Shuttle-bus outside. Underground car park.
£££ Alpenhof Lodge Comfortable and friendly, in central location. Well liked by reporters. Shuttle and plenty of restaurants nearby.
£££ Jagerhof Lodge British-run, friendly; much praised by reporters. At the edge of town on bus route. Restaurants close by.
£££ Alpine Lodge Refurbished town motel. Bus stop outside.
Self-catering The 1849 condos are spacious, very well equipped and nicely fitted out in pine. The Hut 2 base-station is only a couple of minutes' walk. Other top quality places well positioned for the lifts are Snowbird and Mountainback. The Summit condos are similarly convenient; though less luxurious than the above they are still comfortable, with plenty of mod cons. The same can be said of the Sierra Manor and Timberline condos. The Aspen Creek condos are other good mid-range places close to the slopes.

EATING OUT
Outstanding choice
There are no fewer than 55 restaurants in town, though you wouldn't guess it – they are dotted around over a wide area. They cater for most tastes and pockets – Japanese, Chinese, Mexican, Italian, Cajun, steak, seafood. Nevado's does excellent 'modern European' food, while the Lakefront, out of town at Tamarack Lodge, aims high with its Continental cuisine. Cheaper good places are the atmospheric Josh Slocum's and Mogul. The Stove and the Mountainside Grill are good places for a hearty meal. Roberto's does Mexican food; the Shogun Japanese. Angel's is recommended for its 'pleasant atmosphere and open fire'.

APRES-SKI
Lively at weekends
The liveliest immediate après-ski spot is the Yodler, at the Main Lodge base area – apparently an authentic Swiss chalet, transported across the Atlantic complete with authentic Swiss après-ski atmosphere. There is a pleasant evening sleigh-ride and dinner trip, but nightlife is essentially bars which come to life at weekends. Whiskey Creek is an informal eating and meeting place with rock 'n roll and country and western bands, packed with people in the late evening, even when the resort is quiet. Josh Slocum's has a lively piano bar with jazz; Rafters has live entertainment; and Gringo's does the best margaritas in town. The Cellar has an especially good selection of beers, including draught Newcastle Brown.

FOR NON-SKIERS
Mainly sightseeing
There are lots of areas of interest within reach of those with a car. These include the pretty Mono Lake, the beautiful Yosemite National Park, and the Sequoia and Kings Canyon National Parks (including Mt Whitney). Bear in mind that some of these trips will not be possible in midwinter. There's also a gold-mining ghost-town to visit. There are some diverting clothes shops, but Mammoth is essentially a place for keen skiers. Meeting for lunch up the mountain is possible, but not an attractive prospect.

TOURIST OFFICE

Postcode CA 93546
Tel 00 1 (619) 9340743
Fax 9340603

Park City 2105m

✔ Atmospheric Wild West-style main street, complete with jail and museum; convenient for the slopes

✔ Good choice of lively bars and restaurants makes nonsense of Utah's image as a puritanical Mormon state

✔ Famous for its light powder snow

✔ Well maintained slopes, and lots of snowmaking

✔ Easy road access to other major Utah ski areas

✗ Rest of town doesn't have same charm as main street – essentially an enormous sprawl of anonymous condos

✗ No long runs

✗ Little variation in skiing terrain

✗ Lack of spectacular scenery

On its own, Park City isn't worth travelling 5,000 miles for. Its ski area is small by European standards, and it has little to offer that hundreds of other resorts don't have too. But there are two compelling reasons to pay it a visit.

First, Utah has some great, tough skiing in what it likes to claim is 'The Greatest Snow on Earth'. Colorado resorts dispute that, but it's Utah that has the phrase on its car number plates. And there is usually no shortage of deep powder snow. Park City and its immediate neighbours don't get the best of it – that's reserved for Snowbird and Alta, in nearby Little Cottonwood Canyon, which have phenomenal snow records and some super-tough skiing. They and other resorts are around half an hour's drive away.

But they have little accommodation, and certainly nothing to match the second reason to visit – Park City's beautifully restored and developed main street, which grew up in the silver-mining boom years of the 1880s and makes it a much more interesting place to stay. It makes a good base for skiing many of Utah's resorts – and here, as elsewhere in the US, buying lift passes by the day rather than the week doesn't add much to the cost.

ORIENTATION

Park City is in Utah's Wasatch Mountains, 45 minutes by road from Salt Lake City. The resort is spread over a wide area, with chair-lifts and a gondola going into the skiing from the modern purpose-built 'Resort Center' near a big parking lot. This is some distance from Main Street, which is the centre of town. There's a chair-lift from one end of Main Street directly into the ski area. **Wolf Mountain** and **Deer Valley** ski areas are only a few minutes away, and linked by the free ski-buses. Road connections to other Utah ski areas – including **Snowbird, Alta, Brighton, Solitude** and **Sundance** – are good.

 ## The resort

Park City was born with the discovery of silver in 1872. By the turn of the century, it boasted a population of 10,000 (largely of Irish origin), a red-light district, Chinese quarter and 27 saloons. All this faded with the crash in the silver price. But careful restoration has left Park City with a splendid historic centre-piece.

The old wooden sidewalks and clapboard buildings of Main Street are now filled with a colourful selection of Park City's 15 art galleries, 100 smart shops and boutiques, a dozen bars and 80 restaurants. New buildings have been tastefully designed to blend in smoothly, but away from the centre the resort lacks the same charm.

The US National Ski Team headquarters is in Park City, and the resort features strongly in Utah's bid for the 2002 Winter Olympics.

The 'Resort Center' is the main base area of the skiing, with its modern buildings and its own bars, restaurants and accommodation.

Deer Valley and Wolf Mountain are almost suburbs of Park City, but all three retain quite separate identities. Deer Valley is upmarket, ready to pamper its clientele with swish hotels, ski-in, ski-out convenience and some of the most upmarket lunch spots of any US ski resort. Wolf Mountain is bold and breezy – day passes are cheaper here and snowboarders are welcome (they're banned from the Park City and Deer Valley slopes).

 ## The skiing

Although good enough to host World Cup events, the terrain is generally quite tame – smooth trails cut through the trees on rounded, low mountains. The bite in the system is in the bowls at the top of the resort's skiing.

THE SKI AREA
Nothing spectacular
From the base area, a long 23-minute gondola ride, or a slightly shorter journey on a couple of chairs, takes you up to **Summit House**. Most of

SKI FACTS

Altitude 2100m-3050m
Lifts   14
Pistes   2200 acres
Green   16%
Blue   45%
Black   39%
Art. snow   400 acres

LIFT PASSES

95/96 prices in dollars
Park City
Covers all lifts in Park
City ski area, with free
ski-bus.
Beginners Beginners'
courses (1, 3 or 5
day) includes 1 day
free ski pass on First
Time Lift.
Main pass
1-day pass 44
6-day pass 246
(low season 147 –
40% off)
Senior citizens
Over 65: 6-day pass
123 (50% off)
Over 70: free pass
Children
Under 12: 6-day pass
114 (53% off)
Short-term passes
Ascent and return on
gondola. Half-day
passes from 1pm
(adult 32). Night
skiing pass 4pm-9pm
available.
Notes All passes of
over 2 days allow 1
non-skiing day; 6 day
pass valid for 7 days,
with 1 non-skiing day.
Reductions for groups
and student groups.
Alternative passes
Multi-area books
contain vouchers that
can be swapped for
day passes in Alta,
Brighton, Deer Valley,
Park City, Snowbird,
Solitude, and Wolf
Mountain (adult 6-day
276).
Credit cards Yes

the skiing lies between here and the
base area, and spreads along the sides
of a series of interconnecting ridges.
Virtually all the terrain above Summit
House is unprepared, and accessed
only by the **Jupiter** chair which takes
you to a high point of 3050m.

The Town triple-chair, from the end
of Main Street, connects well with the
rest of the skiing.

There are a few old, wooden mine
buildings left dotted around the
slopes, which add extra atmosphere.

Night skiing on the Rockies' longest
floodlit run is available until 10pm,
but you have to pay extra.

SNOW RELIABILITY
'The Greatest Snow on Earth'

That's what Utah claims on every car
number-plate. All the main Utah
resorts benefit from their unique
position where the Pacific storms hit
the Wasatch mountains after crossing
over the arid Nevada desert and then
picking up moisture from the famous
Salt Lake. A season from late
November to early April is normally
scheduled but, with a bit of luck and
use of the extensive snowmaking, the
season is frequently extended. Thirty
per cent of runs are covered by
snowmaking. Snowbird and Alta, a
half-hour drive away, have an even
better snow record than Park City.

FOR ADVANCED SKIERS
Head for the top bowls

Jupiter Bowl is directly accessible by
chair-lift and gets skied-out first after a
snowfall. After that it's a case of hiking
along the ridge to reach the likes of
Puma and McConkey's bowls. All the
bowls include some serious terrain –
with narrow couloirs, cliffs and
cornices as well as easier ways down.

The side of Summit House ridge,
serviced by the Thaynes and
Motherlode chairs, has some little-
used black runs with occasional steep
pitches, plus a few satisfying trails in,
rather than cut through, the trees.
There's a zone of steep runs down into
town from further round the ridge,
including Willy's Run, which has seen
duty as a World Cup men's GS course.
And don't miss Blueslip Bowl near
Summit House – so called because
locals used to ski it although it was out
of bounds. If caught, they got a blue
slip which meant they were fired.

The Utah Interconnect will interest
skiers keen to see a little more of the
Wasatch Mountains back-country – it
can be completed in a day and links
Park City with four other Utah resorts.
Advanced skiers will also want to

spend days at the other nearby resorts,
notably Snowbird and Alta.

They may even want to try the Utah
Winter Sports Park down the road.
This is one of the few places where
you can learn to ski-jump – starting on
a baby jump and gradually working
your way up. They have full-scale hills
and freestyle jumps here too.

FOR INTERMEDIATE SKIERS
Limited choice

There are blue runs everywhere, apart
from Jupiter. The areas around the
King Con and the Prospector high-
speed quads have a dense network of
great (but short) cruising runs. There
are also more difficult trails close by,
for those looking for a challenge. But
there is little in between, and there are
few opportunities for long cruising
runs – most trails are in the 1km to
2km region. The Pioneer chair-lift is
slightly off the beaten track and it
serves some very pleasant, quiet runs –
ideal for warming-up and for those
not seeking too many thrills.

Intermediates will certainly want to
visit Wolf Mountain and Deer Valley
for a day each. Deer Valley has the
best-groomed runs around and offers
flattering intermediate cruising.

FOR BEGINNERS
A good chance for fast progress

Novices get started on the short lifts
near the base area. The beginners'
classes graduate up the hill quite
quickly, and there's an 'easiest way
down' clearly marked all the way from
Summit House. It's easy enough for
most beginners to manage after only a
few lessons, but it is quite long – both
the gondola and the Town chair can
be used to descend.

FOR CROSS-COUNTRY
Some trails; lots of back-country

The scope for 'back-country' skiing is
enormous – several companies in
town arrange trips to some of the
nearby National Forests, including
overnight stays in log cabins or, for
the hardy, snow caves.

There are prepared trails on both the
Park City golf course, next to the
downhill area, and the Homestead
Resort course, just out of town. Both
centres can provide lessons and
equipment hire – they charge around
$5 a day for use of their trails.

QUEUES
Peak period problems only

Lift queues aren't normally a problem.
But the slow, old gondola takes an age
to get up the mountain and there can

SKI SCHOOL

95/96 prices in dollars

Park City
Classes 5 days
4hr: 9.45-11.45 and
2.15-4.15; 2hr: noon-
2pm or 2pm-4pm
5 4hr days: 197
Children's classes
Ages: 7 to 13
5 6hr days including
lunch: 322
Private lessons
1hr, 2hr, half- or full-
day
78 for 1hr; each
additional person 15

be queues for it at the start of the day. Take the chair-lift alternatives. The Prospector chair can generate queues too, but shifts them very quickly.

MOUNTAIN RESTAURANTS
Nothing exciting
There are three restaurants, all of reasonable quality. The Mid-Mountain restaurant is an old mine building which was heaved up the mountain to its present location near the bottom of Pioneer chair; you may wonder whether it was worth the effort. The food is standard self-service fare. The Summit House is café-style – good for chilli, pizza, soup etc. The Snow Hut is a smaller log building and usually has an outdoor grill sending the smell of burgers half-way up nearby runs.

There's quite a choice of restaurants back at the base area, and that's where many skiers head at lunchtime.

If it's a gourmet lunch you are after, you'd be better-off in Deer Valley.

SKI SCHOOL
Thorough and full of enthusiasm
The official ski school offers all sorts of specialist programmes, and the usual group and private lessons. Group lessons can be excellent value: many skiers choose private lessons, with the happy result that four to six is the normal size for groups.

We've had several glowing reports on the school, but one negative one from a repeat visitor who felt that standards had slipped since 1992.

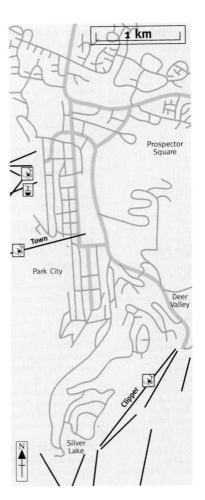

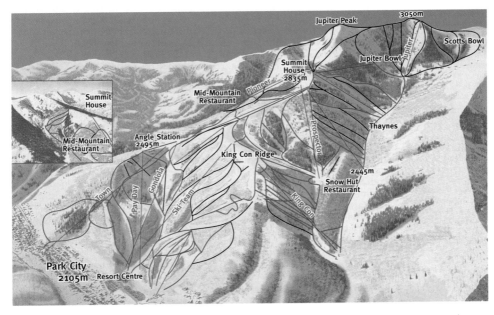

CHILDCARE

The ski school's Kinderschule takes children aged from 3 to 6, from 8.30 to 4.30, mixing tuition with other activities.

There are a dozen different nurseries in the town.

GETTING THERE

Air Salt Lake City, transfer 35 minutes.

PACKAGES

American Connections, American Dream, American Skiworld, Crystal, Made to Measure, Ski Activity, Ski Independence, Virgin Snow

Deer Valley Made to Measure, Virgin Snow

FACILITIES FOR CHILDREN
Well organised; ideal terrain

For very young children, even babies, there are a number of licensed carers who operate either at their own premises or at visitors' lodgings. The ski school deals with children under the umbrella of a separate Kinderschule. Book in advance to guarantee a place.

Staying there

It's quite practical to stay in Park City and not bother with a car – choose a location that's handy for Main Street and either the Town chair or the free shuttle bus. The bus goes from various locations in town to the base area of the skiing, it's frequent and runs till late. There's also a trolley-bus along Main Street. Regular buses serve Deer Valley and Wolf Mountain. If you plan to visit resorts such as Snowbird and Alta a few times a car would be useful, though there are buses.

HOW TO GO
Packaged independence

Park City is the busiest and most atmospheric of all the Utah resorts, and a good base from which to visit the others.

Chalets We know of no tour operators offering traditional catered chalets.

Hotels The mass of chain motels on the fringes of most American towns is missing in Park City; and rooms at typical motel prices are a little scarce.

££££ Silver King Deluxe hotel/condo complex at base of ski area, with indoor-outdoor pool.

££££ Washington School Inn Another historic building – there are quite a few around – which doubles as an hotel. Big breakfasts and après-ski snacks. Good location.

£££ Old Miners' Lodge A 100-year-old building next to the Town lift, restored and furnished with antiques.

£££ Radisson Inn Excellent rooms and indoor-outdoor pool but poorly placed for nightlife, out of town.

££ Chateau Apres Close to the ski area: comfortable but slightly faded budget place.

££ Star Hotel On Main Street, cheap, friendly and comfortable.

££ Imperial Inn Quaint B&B at top of Main Street.

££££ Homestead Relaxing country resort hotel, with accommodation in houses spread around the grounds. Miles from the downhill skiing, but well placed for cross-country and snowmobiling. Pool.

Self-catering There's a big range of self-catering units available though only a small selection – typically from the larger condo-complexes – finds its way into the brochures of tour operators. The Shadow Ridge and Park Station apartments and Park Avenue condos are typical. What they lack in character they make up for with their comfort and comprehensive facilities. Silver Cliff Village is adjacent to the skiing and provides spacious, serviced units. It also provides access to the facilities of the Silver King Hotel. Skiers travelling independently have a wider range of smaller places to choose from.

Food shopping in town is good and cheap, especially at Albertson's hypermarket; there are five liquor stores. There are also several take-away outlets – the Park City pizza company is recommended for fresh-made pasta, pizza and sandwiches, and Nacho Mamas for either take-out or stay-in Mexican food.

EATING OUT
Book in advance

Ethnic variation in the cuisine is much greater than might be expected – Szechuan, Cantonese, Japanese, Mexican, Vietnamese and Italian are all represented. Less surprisingly, there are more good steak places than the average digestive system can handle in a fortnight. The Carpetbagger at the

ACTIVITIES

Indoor Park City Racquet Club (4 indoor tennis courts, 2 racquetball courts, heated pool, jacuzzi, sauna, gym, aerobics, basketball), Prospector Athletic Club (racquetball courts, weights room, swimming pool, aerobics, spa, massage and physical therapy, whirlpool, sauna), art galleries, concerts, theatre, martial arts studio, bowling
Outdoor
Snowmobiles, ballooning, sleigh rides, ski jumping, ice skating, bobsleigh and luge track, sports and recreation opportunities for disabled children and adults

Claimjumper is worth getting hungry for. Texas Red's does Tex-Mex grub and the Depot Restaurant does steaks and lots of other things – it's also in a fine old renovated railroad building. The Barking Frog is a trendy place with an open, spacious feel. Cisero's has the best Italian food and gets packed. At the base of the skiing the Baja Cantina does great margaritas and Mexican food. There is a huge number of places to choose from but they all get busy, so book in advance. Just to clarify, Irish Camel Ltd actually serves Mexican food and El Cheapo Grill is not that cheap.

APRES-SKI
Plenty of bars
Although there are still some arcane liquor laws in Utah, Park City seems to have adopted a fairly sensible attitude to their application, and – provided you're over-21 and have your ID handy – the laws are never a serious barrier to getting a drink. The Wasatch Brew Pub makes its own excellent ale on the premises and has a good supper menu.

At the bars and clubs which are more dedicated to drinking (ie don't feature food) membership of some kind is required. This may involve handing over $5 to cover a fortnight's membership – one member can then introduce numerous 'guests' – or else there'll be some old guy at the bar already organised to sign a bunch of people in for the price of a beer. The Claimjumper, the splendidly scruffy Alamo and Pop Jenks are the most lively places and there's usually live music and dancing, at the very least at weekends. Adolph's is a bit smarter.

Steeps Café, in the gondola bottom-station, is the regular happening place straight after skiing – there's a disco and it tends to go on long after your ski clothes ought to have left.

FOR NON-SKIERS
Should be interesting
Salt Lake City has a few points of interest, many connected with its Mormon heritage, and some good shopping – Trolley Square is worth a look, as much for the buildings as the shops. Scenic balloon flights and excursions to Nevada for gambling are both popular. And there are lots of snow-based non-skiing activities – sleigh rides, snow-shoeing, ice-skating; there's even an ice-sculpture festival. Snowmobiling is big – there are 150 miles of prepared trails in lovely countryside. In January there's Robert Redford's Sundance Film Festival.

There are a couple of clubs in town with a pool, gym etc and a fairly up-market range of shops and galleries selling antiques, Western goods, expensive paintings, stuffed animals, Indian artefacts etc. The museum and old jail house are worth a visit.

Wolf Mountain 2075m
This separate ski area, formerly known as Park West, is only four miles down the road, and an easy 15-minute transfer from Park City. It's a little lower, a little less than half the size and less than half the price to ski. Snowboarding is allowed here, unlike Park City and Deer Valley. The layout of the skiing is much like that of Park City, but the bowls are reached only by hiking – no soft-option Jupiter chair here. Ironhorse peak should be avoided by beginners – one side of the ridge has good intermediate runs, the other side has only 'expert' runs. The area is almost always pleasantly uncrowded and there is a collection of lodgings, restaurants and shops at the base area.

But it wouldn't be a particularly exciting place to stay. Buffalo Bob's Paradise Café, at the bottom of Ironhorse lift, is renowned for its après-ski atmosphere – good music, grilled burgers and drinks.

Deer Valley 2075m
Just a mile from the end of Main Street, this is the 'dude' skiing capital of Utah – famed for the care and attention lavished on both slopes and guests. Valets unload your equipment in the car park, the chair-lifts are padded and it looks as if stones are hand-picked off the slopes – it's very obviously aimed at people who are used to being pampered and can pay for it. The eating places are particularly upmarket: the Huggery's seafood buffet is spectacular.

Some of the lodgings are similarly top-dollar, including the Stein Eriksen Lodge and Goldener Hirsch at Silver Lake Village at mid-mountain (but reachable by road). The terrace of Stein Eriksen and the Stag, lower down, offer excellent lunchtime cuisine unheard of in most US resorts.

The slopes are immaculate, though not all are easy – there are mogul runs and 'double black diamond' skiing in the top bowls. And some runs are left ungroomed after a snowfall, creating the conditions that incompetent but ambitious intermediates dream about: a foot of powder on a completely smooth base. Deer Valley is a recommended cultural experience.

TOURIST OFFICE
Postcode UT 84060
Tel 00 1 (801) 6498111
Fax 6475374

Snowbird 2470m

HOW IT RATES

The skiing

Snow	*****
Extent	*
Advanced	*****
Intermediates	***
Beginners	**
Convenience	*****
Queues	**
Restaurants	*

The rest

Scenery	***
Resort charm	*
Not skiing	*

✔ Quantity and quality of snow unrivalled except by next-door Alta

✔ A lot of skiing crammed into a small area

✔ Some seriously steep stuff

✔ Ski-from-the-door convenience

✔ The nightlife and airport of Salt Lake City are only a short drive away

✘ Ski area is limited, particularly for energetic piste-bashers

✘ Tiny, claustrophobic resort

✘ Uncompromising modern architecture

✘ Main cable-car generates queues, despite its impressive size

There can be few places where nature has combined the steep with the deep better than at Snowbird, and even fewer places where there are also lifts to give you access. So despite the notably charmless appearance of the purpose-built village and the limited extent of the skiing – particularly for keen intermediates – it remains one of the top US locations for hot-shot skiers. For visitors from Britain it is the main destination in Little Cottonwood Canyon, although Alta is, if anything, more compelling (see separate chapter, page 382) and anyone staying in Snowbird will certainly want to explore it. There is no shared lift pass, but buying passes by the day does not add much to the cost.

ORIENTATION

Snowbird lies 40km south-east of Salt Lake City in the Wasatch mountains, some 10km up Little Cottonwood Canyon – just beyond is **Alta** and the end of the road. The resort area and the slopes are by the road on its south side. Snowbird Centre and the base-station of the main cable-car are towards the up-canyon end of the resort; much of the rest is given over to car-parking areas. From the mouth of the canyon, good road links head for downtown Salt Lake City, the ski areas around **Park City**, and those in Big Cottonwood Canyon – **Solitude** and **Brighton**.

SKI FACTS

Altitude	2410m-3355m
Lifts	8
Pistes	1572 acres
Green	20%
Blue	30%
Black	50%
Artificial snow	none

 ## The resort

The canyon setting is rugged and grand, and it needs to be: the resort buildings are mainly large and dull – but they do provide decent lodgings and convenient skiing. If function is more important than form, Snowbird Resort, tucked right under some of Utah's most exciting slopes, will do you just fine.

The skiing

The **ski area** covers the north-facing side of the canyon up to Hidden Peak at 3355m. The famed cable-car ('Aerial Tram', with a capacity of 125 persons) takes eight minutes to reach Hidden Peak from Snowbird Centre. The toughest skiing is around the line of the Tram and in Peruvian Gulch, to the east. To the west of the Tram, in Gad Valley, there are five of the seven double chairs and skiing from very tough to very easy.

With Little Cottonwood Canyon apparently acting as the local snowfall magnet, and with north-facing slopes and all the skiing above 2400m, **snow reliability** is very good. Snowbird and Alta typically average about twice the snowfall of the Park City area or of most Colorado resorts.

Snowbird was created for and still appeals mainly to **advanced skiers**. For such a relatively compact area there is a lot of tough skiing. The trail

map is liberally sprinkled with double black diamonds, and some of the gulleys off the Cirque ridge are at least that – Silver Fox and Great Scott are very narrow, very steep and frequently neck-deep in powder. Great Scott is considered to be one of the US's steepest trails. At the edge of the ski area High Baldy is an expert trail that leads to an off-piste route to Alta. Lower down the mountain lurk the bump runs, including Mach Schnell – a great run straight down the fall line through trees. There is some wonderful off-piste skiing in the bowl beneath the Little Cloud chair, and Carbonate opens up some attractive off-piste tree skiing.

Chip's Run provides the only comfortable run down from the top of Hidden Peak for **intermediate skiers** – at 5km it's Snowbird's longest run and is now a designated Family Skiing area. It's a good place from which to enjoy the views, winding down on the east side of the Cirque ridge. Gad Valley is the best area for intermediates to ski – there are some testing runs through the trees off the Gad 2 lift.

Beginners have the Chickadee lift right down in the resort – ideal for getting started – and then there's a small network of suitable trails on the lower slopes of Gad Valley. Big Emma is a lovely smooth trail, broad enough to accommodate the widest of turns.

There are no **cross-country** trails at Snowbird. It's not that far to travel to the likes of Solitude, where there

PACKAGES

American Dream,
Crystal,
Made to Measure,
Ski Club of GB,
Virgin Snow

are 20km of trails, but keen cross-country skiers shouldn't really be here.

At Snowbird nearly everyone wants to use the Aerial Tram – for which privilege there's a supplement to pay and usually a queue to endure. The lift system is far too reliant on the Tram, and for much of the season **queues** of up to 40 minutes are the result. Some of the chair-lifts can also struggle to meet demand.

Choosing a **mountain restaurant** for lunch doesn't take long – there's the Mid Gad self-service cafeteria or else it's back to base. As fast-food chains go, the Tex-Mex Taco Bell at the bottom of the Mid Gad lift, is an off-beat alternative to the usual pizza and burger places in the Snowbird Centre. General Gritts has a good take-out deli counter, and lounging over lunch in the plaza is perfectly pleasant when the sun shines.

The **ski school** offers a quite progressive range of lessons and speciality clinics – including disabled skier programmes, women-only clinics and powder lessons using Atomic Powder Plus skis. The school also works to a maximum class size of eight, for all but Christmas and President's Weekend.

Children from age 3 can be handed over to the ski school, and the Cliff Lodge will arrange childcare for those as young as 6 weeks. Camp Snowbird provides non-skiing activities for 3- to 12-year-olds and there are occasional evening distractions like parties, games and movies to keep the kids happy. Seniors also get a good deal at Snowbird – the over-70s ski free – but it's probably not the place to introduce your granny to skiing.

 ## Staying there

Within Snowbird Resort all the lodgings and restaurants are within walking distance of each other. The Tram station is central and the Gad lifts can be reached mainly on skis. There are shuttle bus services linking the lodgings, the lifts and the car-parks, and a regular service up to Alta.

Choosing how to go depends mainly on which of the other Utah resorts are to be visited. If several are to be tackled, Salt Lake City is

TOURIST OFFICE

Postcode UT 84092-6019
Tel 00 1 (801) 7422222
Fax 7423344

probably the most practical base – driving is easy and there are good bus services too. Park City is a more inviting proposition if the extra distance to most resorts isn't a problem to you.

A few operators feature **accommodation** in Snowbird – typically rooms in Cliff Lodge, a huge hotel and restaurant complex just up the nursery slopes from the Center. The alternative is one of the three smaller condominium properties in the resort or the newer View condominiums on the ridge above Cliff Lodge.

Eating out revolves around Cliff Lodge and Snowbird Center – both house a number of restaurants. It's advisable for at least one member of a party to join the Club at Snowbird ($5) as most of the better restaurants are classed as private clubs. The Aerie and the Wildflower are quite upmarket venues, the Mexican Keyhole and the Forklift are easier on the pocket and better for families. For those not worried about budgets, La Caille, at the mouth of the canyon, provides French food and style right here in the middle of Utah.

Après-ski in Snowbird tends to be a bit muted, though the comedy club may liven things up if you're lucky with the choice of acts. A sunset swim and a few cocktails at the rooftop pool in Cliff Lodge is reputed to be the best way to meet the in-crowd. It's quite feasible to head into downtown Salt Lake City for the occasional big night out – the Rio Grande is a stylish cafe in the Amtrak station, and Squatters Brew Pub is probably the liveliest bar in town. The Zephyr club has live bands, dancing and a distinctly non-Utah feel to it.

Non-skiers will be bored at Snowbird once they've tried the Cliff Spa and it's massages, herbal treatments and the like. Best bet is to head towards the city – the Racquet Club is owned by Snowbird and has superb tennis facilities, and there are some attractions downtown, particularly around Temple Square. And there is, of course, the Great Salt Lake itself. Further afield there are the Utah National Parks – including Bryce Canyon and Arches – and some of the nation's finest scenery.

Steamboat 2100m

HOW IT RATES

The skiing

Snow	****
Extent	**
Advanced	***
Intermediates	****
Beginners	*****
Convenience	***
Queues	****
Restaurants	***

The rest

Scenery	***
Resort charm	**
Not skiing	**

✔ Medium-sized ski area with good skiing for all standards of skier

✔ Good restaurants by US standards

✔ Excellent snow record

✔ Ski-in, ski-out convenience if you stay out at the slopes

✔ Famed for its tree-skiing in fresh powder

✘ Western cowboy hype rather overdone

✘ Resort separated from old cattle town, and much less characterful

✘ Ski area rather bland

✘ Although there is some tough skiing, there isn't much

Steamboat markets itself as a real cowboy town. Its brochures usually have horse-riding, stetson-wearing, lassoo-wielding cowboys on the cover. Even Billy Kidd, the head of the ski school (who skis every day with anyone who turns up to meet him at the top of the mountain at 1pm), is decked out in cowboy gear for the brochures. The area does still have genuine working cowboys but the old 'wagon train' atmosphere doesn't permeate the ski resort or old town much. Don't go there just for the Western atmosphere.

A better reason for going is its compact area of largely easy-to-intermediate skiing. And in good snow conditions Steamboat is also one of the best resorts around for skiing off-piste among the trees. But the skiing has neither the extent of resorts such as Vail, Aspen or the Ski the Summit areas nor the distinctive character of smaller areas such as Telluride. If you are going to travel 5,000 miles across the Atlantic and you're a keen skier, you'd be well advised to combine a visit to Steamboat with a stay at another resort.

ORIENTATION

Steamboat ski resort is a 20-minute bus-ride from the cattle town of Steamboat Springs, a long drive, or short flight, from Denver.

The main lift into the skiing is a gondola from near the centre of the resort. The accommodation is spread over a fairly wide area – some on the slopes, some a bus-ride away.

If you have a hire car, **Vail-Beaver Creek, Copper Mountain, Keystone, Arapahoe Basin, Breckenridge** and **Winter Park** are all less than a two-hour drive.

 ## The resort

The ski resort is a 20-minute bus-ride from the old town of Steamboat Springs, and is much the most convenient place to stay. Near the gondola station there are a couple of shop- and restaurant-lined multi-level squares leading to the one main street. The buildings are all modern, but built with some taste and plenty of wooden façades. Much of the accommodation is built up the side of the piste, so the village does have a slightly sprawling feel to it. You couldn't call it ugly but neither is it charming.

The old town is a bit of a disappointment after the hype of the brochures. Its plus-point is that it's a genuine working cattle town. And you're likely to end up chatting to friendly locals if you try some of the bars – we drank with the local on-duty taxi driver. If you go in mid-January you'll catch the Cowboy Downhill, when cowboys pour into town to compete in a fun slalom, lassooing and saddling competition. The rest of the season, there's much less of a real cowboy presence.

The main (and almost only) street is very wide, with multiple lanes of traffic each way – it was built that way to allow cattle to be driven through town. It is lined with bars, hotels and shops, built at various times over the last 120 years, in a wide mixture of architectural styles, from old wooden buildings to modern concrete shopping plazas.

The town got its name in the mid-1800s, when trappers going along by the Yampa river heard a chugging they thought was a steamboat. It turned out to be the sound of a hot spring bubbling through the rocks.

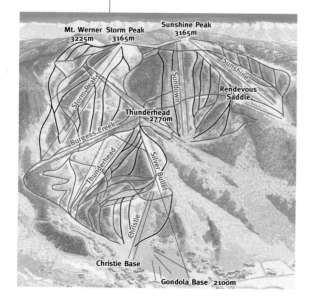

Mt. Werner 3225m — Storm Peak 3165m — Sunshine Peak 3165m — Sunshine — Sundown — Rendevous Saddle — Storm Peak — Thunderhead 2770m — Burgess Creek — Thunderhead — Silver Bullet — Christie — Christie Base — Gondola Base 2100m

SKI FACTS

Altitude 2100m-3225m
Lifts	20
Pistes	2500 acres
Green	15%
Blue	54%
Black	31%
Art. snow	390 acres

LIFT PASSES

95/96 prices in dollars
Steamboat
Covers all lifts at
Steamboat only.
Beginners Day pass
for beginners covers
two lifts at base
(adult 25).
Main pass
1-day pass 44
6-day pass 252
(low season 222 –
12% off)
Senior citizens
Over 65: 6-day pass
150 (40% off)
Over 70: free pass
Children
Under 13: 6-day pass
150 (40% off)
Short-term passes
Single ascent on
Silver Bullet Gondola
for non skiers only
(adult 12); afternoon
pass from 12.15
(adult 38).
Notes Passes of 4
days and over allow
one day non-skiing,
so 4 days skiing in 5,
6 in 7. Children up to
12 ski free when
parents buy full lift
pass and stay for 5
days or more (one
child per parent).
Discounts for groups.
Credit cards Yes

SKI SCHOOL

95/96 prices in dollars
Steamboat
Classes 6 days
4hr 45min: 10.15-
3pm; 2hr 15min: 9am-
11.15 or 11.30-1.45
6 full days: 270
Children's classes
Ages: 6 to 15
5 5hr days including
lunch: 225
Private lessons
1hr, 2hr, 3hr or full-
day
75 for 1hr

⛷ The skiing

Steamboat's ski area is prettily set
among the trees, with splendid views
down to the rolling hills below.
Although it claims to be Colorado's
second biggest ski area (after Vail), a
keen intermediate piste-basher could
cover all the marked runs in a day.

THE SKI AREA
Three flanks on a mountain
The skiing divides naturally into three
areas and all have runs to suit all
abilities. The Silver Bullet gondola
from the village rises to
Thunderhead. One ski area lies on
the face of this mountain, with runs
back to the village and a variety of
chairs to carry you back from various
points. From Thunderhead you can ski
down to the left to catch a chair up to
Storm Peak or to the right to go up
to **Sunshine Peak**. Each of these has
its own runs and lifts and you can ski
from one to the other.

SNOW RELIABILITY
Good despite low altitude
Steamboat is relatively low by
Colorado standards; it goes from
2100m to 3225m. So its highest skiing
is below the height of the base of
Arapahoe Basin. Despite this it has an
excellent snow record, getting as
much in a year as most of the higher
resorts. And over 25 per cent of the
pistes have snowmaking facilities. We
skied there after snow hadn't fallen for
a month and, though there were more
rocks and icy patches than the other
resorts we visited, there was still good
skiing to be had.

FOR ADVANCED SKIERS
Tree skiing is the highlight
The main attraction of Steamboat for
good skiers is the challenging off-piste
skiing in the trees – something which
is increasingly banned in Europe for
ecological reasons. This is particularly
wonderful after a fall of fresh powder.
But there isn't much other than that.
    The best area for tree skiing is on
Sunshine Peak below the Sundown
Express and Priest Creek lifts. There's a
huge amount of choice here. You
simply take off through the aspens
and choose a route where the trees are
spaced as you like them – wide or
narrow. There are also black pistes
marked on the map in this area. The
two to the left of the lifts as you go up
– Closet and Shadows – are only
loosely pistes; basically it's still tree
skiing but the trees have been thinned

out a bit. On the right of the lift as
you go up the blacks marked are more
genuine cleared routes.
    On Storm Peak, experts climb up
from the top of the lift to the Chutes –
where there's another wide choice of
route and the steepest slopes on the
mountain. We were told this climb
was designed to put less expert skiers
off from tackling skiing beyond their
abilities – very sensible, having seen
the 50-degree slope of Chute 1.
    Elsewhere on the mountain, you'll
find other blacks marked. But most are
easily skied by good intermediates and
make great fast runs if they've been
groomed.

FOR INTERMEDIATE SKIERS
Some long cruises
Much of the mountain is ideal
intermediate territory, with long
cruising blue runs such as Buddy's
Run, Rainbow and Ego on Storm Peak
and High Noon, One O'Clock and
Two O'Clock on Sunshine Peak. Don't
ignore the skiing on Thunderhead
either – there are a lot of good runs
which it's easy to miss out on if you
insist on being drawn up to the top of
the mountain. At the end of the day,
Vagabond is usually less crowded than
Heavenly Daze right under the
gondola.
    Some of the black runs such as West
Side and Lower Valley View also make
good challenging intermediate runs
when the bumps have been groomed
out of them.
    The runs at the far right hand side
of the ski area are very gentle –
Tomahawk and Quickdraw are marked
blue but perfectly skiable by those
who normally stick to green. This area
is known to locals as 'Wally World'
because of the ease of the terrain.
    The main problem for keen
intermediates will be the limited
extent of the skiing – not really
enough to keep you interested for a
week unless you enjoy skiing the same
runs repeatedly.

FOR BEGINNERS
Excellent learning terrain
There's a big gentle nursery area at the
base of the mountain served by four
lifts. You progress from this to take the
Christie chair-lifts to a variety of
gentle green runs such as Yoo Hoo,
Giggle Gulch and Right of Way.

FOR CROSS-COUNTRY
Plenty out of town
There's no cross-country in Steamboat
itself but a free shuttle service takes
you to the Touring Center, where

there are 30km of groomed tracks and lessons available. There are also Forest Service trails on Rabbit Ears Pass.

QUEUES
Not a serious problem
There may be queues for the gondola at the start of the day, but at least they are superbly organised. Two fast quad chairs have cut out the worst bottlenecks up the mountain, though that for the Sundown lift is reportedly long enough to merit Trivial Pursuit contests organised by the lifties. We hear that the Thunderhead lift is to become a quad this winter, too. There can be queues for the Sunshine lift serving the easiest top-of-the-mountain runs.

MOUNTAIN RESTAURANTS
Good by US standards
There are two main restaurant complexes on the mountain, both of which include unusually good table-service restaurants by US standards. The biggest is at Thunderhead. You can catch the gondola up from 8am and breakfast while waiting for the skiing to start at 9am. At lunchtime there's a choice of a big self-service restaurant, a barbecue on the sundeck, the Stoker bar and restaurant and Hazie's table-service restaurant.

At Rendezvous Saddle there's a slightly smaller alternative which has a two-floor self-service section including a pizza bar, another sundeck and barbecue and Ragnar's table-service Scandinavian restaurant. You can book for Ragnar's and Hazie's.

There's also a new snack bar and sundeck at Four Points.

SKI SCHOOL
Mixed views
We've had mixed reports of the ski school, some very positive, others rating private better than group lessons. There's plenty of choice in the programme, including a Challenge course aimed at advanced skiers, a Come Smell The Roses course aimed at 'mature' skiers and a Women's Ski Seminar programme.

FACILITIES FOR CHILDREN
Kids Ski Free
Steamboat has a better-than-usual Kids Ski Free scheme – free lift pass and free equipment hire for one child of up to age 12 per parent buying a pass and renting their own gear. Childcare arrangements are comprehensive, including communal evening babysitting in the Vacation Center – an excellent idea that ought to be

widely copied. The one weak spot seems to be that ski school ends at 3pm, and there seem to be no facilities for looking after pupils after that time.

 Staying there

Staying in the old town of Steamboat Springs is cheaper but much less convenient than staying at the resort itself. And the bus costs 50c each way. Our preference would be to stay on the slopes and make occasional excursions to the town in the evening. In case you're gripped by indecision, there is accommodation between the two – the worst of both worlds.

HOW TO GO
Plenty of packages
More tour operators go here than to many comparable mid-size US resorts. There's accommodation for all tastes, including some more downmarket places than is the US norm.
Chalets Crystal's one chalet is very comfortable, and has an outdoor hot tub; ten minutes' walk from lifts.
Hotels The smarter hotels out at the resort have less character than some of the in-town options.
££££ Ptarmigan Inn Ideally situated just above the gondola station and right on the piste, with an outdoor pool and hot tub, a sauna and good après-ski bar with a happy hour.
££££ Sheraton Big, anonymous, concrete hotel right on the main square at the foot of the slopes, with a pool and hot tub – just the sort of place we like to avoid in ski resorts.
£££ Harbor The oldest hotel in the old town. All its rooms vary in size and character and there's a sauna, steam room and two hot tubs.
££ Alpiner Lodge Bavarian style economy option in old town.
Self-catering The apartments we have seen have been universally high in quality. The best we saw were the Bear Claw condos – wonderfully spacious and individually furnished, and right on the piste at the top of the Headwall chair. The complex has a sauna, outdoor pool and hot tub, and an efficient shuttle bus system. Other recommendations include Timber Run, a short shuttle-bus ride from the centre with a number of hot tubs kept at different temperatures; the Lodge at Steamboat, close to the gondola station, also with good facilities; Thunderhead Lodge; and the aptly named Ski Inn.

CHILDCARE
The Kids' Vacation Center is run by the resort in the gondola station. The Kiddie Coral nursery takes children aged 6 months to 6 years, all day. Those aged 2 can opt for the Buckaroos programme with a one-hour private ski lesson (ski rental not included). Older children go on to the Sundance Kids group classes.

The ski school has a Rough Rider programme for children up to 15, with their own skiing skills playground area and lunchtime supervision.

The Adventure Club at Night offers evening childcare in the Vacation Center for ages 2½ to 12, from 6pm to 10.30.

GETTING THERE

Air Steamboat Springs, transfer ½hr. Yampa Valley regional airport, transfer 1hr. Denver, transfer 4hr.

PACKAGES

American Dream, American Skiworld, Crystal, First Choice Ski, Lotus Supertravel, Made to Measure, Ski Activity, Ski Independence, USAirtours

ACTIVITIES

Indoor hot springs, swimming pools, tennis, weights room **Outdoor** Bob-sledding at Howelsen Park, ice driving school, dog-sledding, snow-mobiling, ballooning, bungee jumping, hot springs, dinner sleigh rides, horse-riding, skating, Elk feeding tours

TOURIST OFFICE

Postcode CO 80487
Tel 00 1 (970)
8796111
Fax 8797844

EATING OUT
Huge variety

There's a huge choice of places to suit all pockets. Steamboat specialises in mountain-top eating – there are three places to choose from. You start by going up the Silver Queen gondola (with complimentary blankets). If you're going to Ragnar's, you then take a sleigh hauled by a snowcat for a Scandinavian meal. Or you stay put at Thunderhead. There you can go to BK's (the lunchtime self-service restaurant) for an as-much-as-you-can-eat buffet, accompanied by country and western music and dancing. Or you can try haute cuisine at Hazie's, where the menu goes somewhat upmarket from the lunchtime fare.

Down in the valley you can take horse-drawn sleigh rides to other dinner options, such as down Walton Creek canyon, to eat in heated tents with Western music.

In downtown Steamboat try L'Apogee, for French-style food, or the cheaper Harwig's Grill on the same premises. The Steamboat Yacht Club on the riverbank is recommended for seafood and views of ski-jumping. The Chart House and Coral Grill, on the outskirts of town, are recommended for seafood. For more traditional American fare try the popular Old West Steakhouse or the atmospheric ranch-style Ore House. Gorky Park has good Russian food and live gypsy music. Other options include Japanese, Russian, Chinese and Cajun.

In the resort, La Montana, El Rancho and Cantina are recommended for Tex-Mex, Mattie Silles for seafood, Cipriani's and Cugnino's for Italian and The Butcher Shop for steaks and the like.

APRES-SKI
Fairly lively

The base lodge area has a few noisy bars, but things are much quieter and less brash in the old town. The liveliest place immediately after skiing is usually the Inferno, in the square. This has live music and a happy hour. Buddy's Run, near the gondola entrance, can also be fun, with live music or comedy. Dos Amigos is the place for jugs of margarita. Or try the Tugboat Tavern in the main street. The Conservatory in the Thunderhead Lodge and the Ptarmigan Inn are for those who want a somewhat more sophisticated atmosphere.

The Old Town Pub in Steamboat Springs dates from 1904, often has live music and does Tex-Mex food. Gorky Park has live music and 27 varieties of vodka. The Loft has live country or rock bands.

There are popular micro-brewery bars in both the resort and the old town – the Heavenly Daze and Steamboat Brewery are worth trying. The nearest thing to a disco is Hershey's Bar, but the best place for a bop is the Steamboat Saloon.

There are plenty of evening activities too, including hurtling down a mile-long track in a four-person padded bobsleigh and watching floodlit ski jumping in the old town.

FOR NON-SKIERS
Lots to do

Getting up the gondola to the restaurant complex is easy. Visiting town is too. And you can go and relax in outdoor hot springs seven miles from town or learn to drive on the special ice circuit. There are plenty of other activities too.

Taos 2800m

HOW IT RATES

The skiing

Snow	****
Extent	**
Advanced	*****
Intermediates	***
Beginners	**
Convenience	***
Queues	****
Restaurants	*

The rest

Scenery	***
Resort charm	***
Not skiing	**

✔ *Some very steep and challenging skiing*

✔ *Intermediates and beginners surprisingly well catered for, given the apparent general steepness*

✔ *Small, intimate resort nestled in splendour of New Mexico Rockies*

✔ *Fascinating contrast between ski resort and Taos town*

✔ *Has perhaps the best ski school in the US*

✘ *Taos town a long drive from the resort*

✘ *Some of the best skiing is a long hike from the top lifts*

✘ *Relatively small ski area*

✘ *Very little accommodation in the resort itself*

ORIENTATION

Taos Ski Valley is the most southerly mainstream ski resort in North America, not far from Santa Fe in New Mexico. The resort itself is tiny, with little accommodation. Two chair-lifts lead from the centre into the skiing.

Taos town is 18 miles away in the valley. Much of the accommodation is there or on the road between the town and the ski resort. Although there are bus links, having a hire car is convenient.

The Taos experience is unlike any other in the US. For a start it is in New Mexico, with the ski resort set high above the arid valley and the traditional adobe town of Taos, home to many famous artists and writers over the years – including DH Lawrence. The culture is southern and very different from neighbouring Colorado. You'll see many more native American Indians around. You'll be eating spicy southern food as well as burgers and steaks.

The skiing is something different too. If you are after the steep and deep, Taos has it. It has some of the steepest skiing, both above and below the tree-line, of any resort in North America. Much of it is awkward to reach – and made deliberately so in order to keep the numbers skiing it low and the quality of the snow high.

Our main reservation about Taos is that it's such a long drive from other mainstream ski resorts. And because the ski area is not huge and the culture is so different, it would be good to combine it with a stay in a Colorado resort. If you are willing to make the five- or six-hour drive to, say, Telluride or Breckenridge, splitting your holiday between the two would be a very entertaining thing to do.

🏠 The resort

Taos Ski Valley and the town of Taos itself could be on two different planets. The resort is deep in the Sangre de Cristo mountains, some 18 miles from Taos town. Starting on the road from Taos, you travel through the flat, arid desert scenery, with its muted red-brown tones and low-built, adobe buildings, then climb into the wooded splendour of the Rockies, finally reaching the tiny resort. There are regular buses.

The resort is little more than a handful of lodges, built in chalet style at the head of a narrow valley. Space is too restricted to allow the development of a 'fashionable' resort. But there is a huge car park.

It was founded in 1955 by Ernie Blake, who was born in Germany, reared in Switzerland, married an American and fulfilled his vision of building a European-style ski resort in the southern Rockies. The ski resort is still family-run, though Ernie sadly died in 1989.

Taos town, in contrast, is sizeable, spread-out and rich in the many cultural influences – native American, Spanish and classic South-Western – which have shaped it over the centuries. It's full of art galleries, museums, restaurants and bars, as well as hotels and B&Bs.

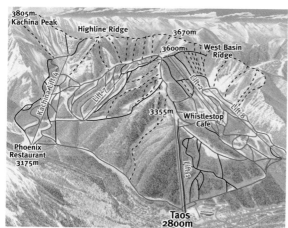

SKI FACTS

Altitude	2800m-3600m
Lifts	11
Pistes	1100 acres
Green	24%
Blue	25%
Black	51%
Art. snow	496 acres

LIFT PASSES

95/96 prices in dollars
Taos area
Covers all lifts of
Taos.
Beginners Yellowbird
Program offers 2hr
am and pm lessons
and 'free' lift pass
(adult 46 per day).
Main pass
1-day pass 38
6-day pass 210
(low season 150 –
28% off)
Senior citizens
Over 65: 6-day pass
108 (48% off)
Over 70: free pass
Children
Under 13: 6-day pass
120 (43% off)
Short-term passes
Half-day pass from
12.30 (adult 34,
94/95).
Notes Discounts for
groups of over 25
and tickets bought
over 14 days in
advance.
Credit cards Yes

 # The skiing

When you hit Taos Ski Valley, the first thing that will strike you is Al's Run, rising sheer out of the resort. Named after a local GP, it's a mogul pitch of formidable length and steepness. As it's virtually the only run you can see from the base, it's no surprise that Ernie Blake felt moved to put up a sign saying 'Don't panic! You're looking at 1/30 of Taos Ski Valley. We have many easy runs too'. They do. The ski area has runs to suit all abilities, but it is best suited to experts nevertheless.

Another of Ernie's ideas was the Martini Trees – burying hand-blown glass bottles of spirits in the snow under blue spruce trees at strategic points. Sadly, when our instructor led us to one, it had already been drained! Watch out too for Slim, an extremely life-like dummy, spread-eagled, face-down on the snow, boots down the mountain, near the top of lift 6. The sign next to him reads, 'Slim says, know how to stop sliding'. Useful advice on Taos' steep terrain, but unnerving the first time you see it.

THE SKI AREA
Small but expandable
From the top of one of the two chair-lifts out (one of which is a high-speed quad), you can ski back down to the resort or down to two further chair-lifts to take you higher. There is skiing on three separate flanks of the mountain, served by a total of eight lifts. From each of the lifts there are green, blue and black options. A unique feature of the skiing here is that many of the toughest runs (15 of those marked on the trail map) can be reached only by a lengthy climb from the top of the lifts.

SNOW RELIABILITY
Good
Taos has a good snow record (it gets around 300 inches each year). Because of its southerly position, it often gets a weather pattern different from that of the Colorado resorts further north – benefiting from storms which they miss and vice versa. In addition, almost half of the terrain is covered by snowmaking, including 85 per cent of the beginner and intermediate runs.

FOR ADVANCED SKIERS
Hike to the heights
Al's Run is the most obvious challenge for any good skier. In fact, quite often the bottom section is shut – because it's the first thing visitors see, the

resort closes it so the snow doesn't look worn.

The best terrain for expert skiers is an energetic hike from the top of the mountain. Highline Ridge and West Basin Ridge both have a collection of steep, steep chutes through the trees and rocks. They're also very narrow so, not surprisingly, they're not always open and are best skied in fresh snow, provided there's no avalanche danger.

The other major challenge is to make the 75-minute-plus hike (not easy at almost 4000m) to Kachina Peak to ski the magical, wide, off-piste bowls and powder after you've stopped to recover and admire the spectacular views.

If you're disinclined to hike, you can still get in some challenging expert skiing – nearly all big bump runs through the trees. Chairs 2 and 6 take you to the best. Walkyries Chute lives up to its name, Castor isn't much easier and Sir Arnold Lunn is long and unrelenting. Our favourite was Lorelei, where the trees are a little thinner and the views superb.

At the eastern end of the mountain, the Kachina lift gives you access to the above-the-tree-line Hunziker Bowl, High Noon and El Funko.

There's yet another area of black runs immediately above the village.

FOR INTERMEDIATE SKIERS
Good but limited cruising
Wherever you go there are easy-cruising, blue-run alternatives to the challenging steeps. But they are limited in extent compared with the variety a bigger resort such as Vail or Aspen has to offer.

At the western end of the skiing, there are lovely long blues such as Lower Stauffenberg, Bambi and Powderhorn, served by three lifts.

To the east, the Kachina lift has more cruising, blue terrain. And adventurous intermediates will enjoy the open skiing of the Hunziker Bowl.

They could also try their luck with some of the tree-lined blacks of Taos. But stick to the single black diamonds until you feel confident!

FOR BEGINNERS
Good facilities
Strawberry Hill at the base is devoted to those who've never been on skis before. This has a nursery area at the bottom, steeper pitches higher up and no through-traffic of better skiers. But the aim of Taos ski instructors is to get their students skiing from the top by the third day. There are easy green tracks all over the mountain.

CHILDCARE

The Kinderkäfig Center houses all the ski school's children's facilities under one roof. Kinderkare takes babies from as young as 6 weeks up to toddlers not quite ready to ski. Junior Elite takes pre-school children from 3 years, introducing them to skiing through games, and also does proper classes for children up to the age of 12, with lunchtime care and indoor supervised play after skiing.

SKI SCHOOL

95/96 prices in dollars
Ernie Blake
Classes 6 days
4hr: 9.45-11.45 and 1.45-3.45; 2hr am or pm
6 2hr days: 150
Children's classes
Ages: 3 to 12
6 full days including lunch, rental and lift pass: 384
Private lessons
1hr, half- of full-day 70 for 1hr; each additional person 30

FOR CROSS-COUNTRY
Not one of the best

There's no formal, groomed cross-country, but skiers with a guide can head off into the Wheeler Wilderness Area and other parts of the Carson National Forest.

QUEUES
Self-imposed limits

The resort restricts sales of ski passes to 4,800 on any one day. This is so that neither the lifts nor the slopes get too crowded. In practice this means queues are rare except for the bottom lifts at peak times.

MOUNTAIN RESTAURANTS
Take a picnic

This is not the place to go to for haute cuisine on the mountain. There are just two restaurants, neither selling the world's greatest food. At the Phoenix, you'll find you get an alcoholic drink only with food, and you're then restricted in the amount you can have. The Whistlestop doesn't sell alcohol at all. You can picnic at both places.

If you want a decent lunch, it's best to ski back to the resort – no great hardship. The large terrace of the hotel St Bernard is a favourite spot.

SKI SCHOOL
Simply the best?

Taos ski school is considered by many the best there is. Their aim is to push all the skiers they teach as far and as fast as possible – but also to have fun. To get the most out of the school, you need to enrol for a whole week, as is normal in Europe but not the US – another result of Ernie Blake wanting to bring European ways to US skiing. As testimony to the school's success, 70 per cent of guests staying in the ski resort for a week take courses.

In addition to straight group classes and private lessons, there are packages designed to encourage skiers to go to school for the whole week. Super Ski Weeks for intermediate and expert skiers provide six days' lift pass and morning and afternoon lessons, video analysis and seminar for $428 ('94/'95 prices); Ski-Better-Weeks offer six days' lift pass and six morning lessons, video analysis and race, for all levels, at $348. The Yellowbird Program for beginners includes morning and afternoon lessons for $44 per day, with a free lift ticket thrown in, and cheap ski and boot rental.

Mogul Mastery and special Women's Weekends are among the other special workshops available.

FACILITIES FOR CHILDREN
Childcare from 6 weeks old

The resort takes childcare just as seriously as it takes ski tuition, with programmes tailored precisely to different age groups, and the new Kinderkäfig building brings the various options together. The ability to deposit babies at the age of 6 weeks is more or less unrivalled.

⬆ Staying there

The first decision is whether to stay in Taos Ski Valley, in Taos town or in one of the many lodges on the drive between the two. If you stay at the resort, there's a high risk that you won't drag yourself to experience the different culture of Taos town and the surrounding area, which would be a pity. On the other hand, it's a fair old drive up and down a winding road each day to the ski resort.

HOW TO GO
Little choice

Few British skiers have discovered Taos and only a couple of tour operators put it in their brochures – and then not in a big way. But any of the US specialists will be able to put a package together for you.
Hotels There are no particularly luxurious or smart hotels – indeed that's part of the charm of the resort. There are quite a few small B&Bs. At Taos Ski Valley:
££££ Inn at Snakedance The original Taos ski hotel, this was completely rebuilt in 1993 and now boasts a panoramic, glass-walled bar, large sun terrace and new spa facilities.
£££ Edelweiss Ski-in, ski-out hotel famous for its breakfasts, fine food and live music. No TVs or phones in rooms. Sauna, hot tub.
£££ St Bernard Ski-in, ski-out hotel at the base of Al's Run; fine food, après-ski scene. Also has condos in a separate building.
£££ Innsbruck Lodge and Condos Across from the lifts, combines lodge with self-catering condos. American or Continental cooking, relaxed family atmosphere.
In Taos town itself:
££££ Historic Taos Inn Historic building just off the central plaza, with dramatic two-storey lobby, called 'the town's living room'. Adobe fireplaces, hand-loomed Indian bedspreads and local furniture. Excellent restaurant and stylish Adobe Bar, popular with locals, artists and visitors. Outdoor pool, hot tub.

GETTING THERE

Air Albuquerque, transfer 3hr.

PACKAGES

American Dream, Chalets 'Unlimited', Crystal, Made to Measure, Ski Independence

ACTIVITIES

Indoor Six local museums, galleries, film theatre and theatre, swimming pools, sauna, hot tubs, tennis, squash, raquetball and basketball courts, weights room, climbing wall, aerobics
Outdoor Day-trips (National Forest, Wild Rivers area, ancient Pueblos-Indian sites, Santa Fe and many others), horse-riding, ice skating, hiking

TOURIST OFFICE

Postcode NM 87525
Tel 00 1 (505)
7762291
Fax 7768596

££££ Casa de las Chimeneas
Charming, romantic B&B with only three rooms.
£££ Sagebrush Inn Built in 1929 in Pueblo-Mission-style adobe. Handmade Mexican furniture and local pottery and antiques. Excellent food, nightly entertainment. Tennis, outdoor pool, hot tubs.
Self-catering There's a wide selection of self-catering condos in the resort.

Kandahar has the highest location on the ski slopes, overlooking the resort and the slopes; hot tub and a steam bath.

Sierra del Sol is in the heart of Taos Ski Valley; each condo has a fireplace; hot tubs and sauna.

Rio Hondo is on the Hondo river and next to the ski slopes; hot tub and sauna; each condo has its own balcony, fireplace, living room.

Between Taos town and the ski valley is Quail Ridge Inn Resort, a large adobe-style complex, with comfortable well-appointed rooms and suites, each with a fireplace. Huge outdoor heated pool, hot tub, sauna, tennis, and fitness centre.

Haçienda del Valdez nestles in the foothills of the Valdez valley, eight miles from resort; South-Western design, wonderful views; hot tub.

EATING OUT
Spoilt for choice if you drive
At the resort, be sure to try Tim's Stray Dog. It specialises in northern New Mexico food – enchiladas, green chilli, tortilla soup – as well as burgers and other US fare, all served in a lively atmosphere, whatever the time of day. At Rhoda's Restaurant, specialities include elk, buffalo and New Mexican dishes – the menu changes daily. The Dolomite has great pizzas and fresh pasta dishes.

Between the town and resort, the locals recommend Chile Connection for the best New Mexican and Spanish food. Brett House is a charming restaurant, serving American and international food.

Another must of a different nature on the road between the resort and Taos, is Casa Fresen Bakery at Arroyo Seco. It sells fantastic bread – wholewheat, cinnamon, nut, rye – as well as mouth-watering cakes, and has a decent deli as well. Useful for those who are self-catering, but worth a visit for those who aren't.

In Taos itself, you practically fall over restaurants. Doc Martin's is so historic that you'd kick yourself if you missed it – and it serves great contemporary South-Western food too. Lambert's has a dinner menu that changes each night, specialising in lamb, fresh seafood and steaks. The Historic Taos Inn has good food in beautiful surroundings.

APRES-SKI
Ski hard, sleep early
It's generally quiet, with people skiing hard, then enjoying a meal and a quiet drink, trying to restore their energy for the next day with an early night. Some of the hotels do have live music some nights, and there's a jazz festival in the Ski Valley every January.

FOR NON-SKIERS
Plenty of sightseeing
The Taos area is good for sightseeing and a popular summer holiday spot.

The Ski Valley is too tightly packed to feature any activities other than skiing. And non-skiers are likely to prefer skiers to come back to the resort to meet for lunch than walk to the unappealing places on the mountain.

In Taos itself you'll find ice skating and swimming, and you can go on a historic walking tour. The town is rich with art galleries and museums covering the different influences on it. For example, you can visit Kit Carson's home – a 12-room adobe building bought by the famous mountain man and scout in 1843 for his bride.

Taos Pueblo, four miles outside Taos, has been the home of the Tiwa Indians for nearly 800 years and has the largest multi-storied adobe structure in the US.

Excursions to the historic and pretty city of Santa Fe are possible – and, indeed, recommended.

Telluride 2660m

HOW IT RATES

The skiing
Snow ★★★★
Extent ★★
Advanced ★★★★
Intermediates ★★★
Beginners ★★★★★
Convenience ★★★★
Queues ★★★★★
Restaurants ★★

The rest
Scenery ★★★
Resort charm ★★★★
Not skiing ★★

✔ *Charming restored Victorian silver-mining town with a real Wild West atmosphere*

✔ *Skiing for all standards, from beginners to experts, with some of the steepest mogul fields we've seen and some of the longest easy runs in the Rockies*

✔ *Dramatic, craggy mountain scenery*

✔ *Some ski-in, ski-out accommodation in newly built Mountain Village – due to be linked to the old town by gondola during 1995/6 season*

✗ *Limited amount of skiing for the keen intermediate piste-basher*

✗ *Mountain Village is something of an eyesore when seen from parts of the ski area (but it is well away from the old town)*

✗ *Limited mountain restaurants*

ORIENTATION

Telluride is an isolated resort in a dead-end valley (a 'box canyon') in south-west Colorado, with its own precarious little airport five miles out of town (and a more serious airport at Montrose, 67 miles away). The skiing starts right on the edge of the small town, with chair-lifts close to the centre of town (Oak Street base – where the new gondola is due to leave from too) and at the west end (Coonskin).

Beyond the ski area, a separate Mountain Village has been created specially for skiers and summer golfers. An eight-person gondola linking the town to the Mountain Village via the top of the mountain is due to open during the 1995/6 season.

Like so many American ski areas, Telluride is rather small; we're in no doubt high-mileage British piste-bashers used to French mega-resorts will get bored with the skiing, if there for a week. But that is our only serious reservation about a resort, we blushingly confess, we fell for on first acquaintance.

Repeat visits have only confirmed our affection for the place. The scenery is an important factor, as the resort's marketing people are well aware: the San Juan mountains are not remarkable by Alpine standards, but they are impressive enough to set Telluride apart from other resorts in the Rocky Mountains. The town may not be quite as captivating as the more rustic Crested Butte, but it has plenty of character and is pleasantly compact, and has some of the best skiing looming directly above it, so staying in the town rather than the Mountain Village is an attractive option even for keen skiers.

The company that runs the mountain has ambitious plans to extend the lift network, almost doubling the skiable area. When they find the money, Telluride will be difficult to beat.

🏠 The resort

Telluride started life in the 1870s as a silver-mining camp; when gold was found, the town boomed. It had a rough reputation for its drinking and whoring; some say its name is a shortened version of 'To hell you ride'. The town slumped in the early 1900s and became virtually depopulated

until the skiing was developed in the early 1970s. Since then it has been restored to its former glory, with painted clapboard buildings now turned into friendly, interesting shops and restaurants. It looks like a typical small Wild West town from the movies – except that the main street is busy with pickup trucks, not horse-drawn wagons. The inhabitants are a unique blend of ageing hippies, lively

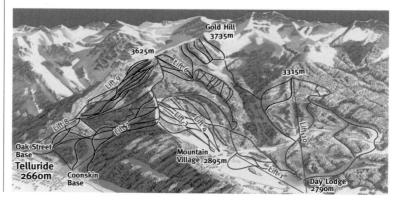

Gold Hill 3735m
3625m
3315m
Lift 9
Lift 6
Lift 8
Lift 7
Lift 3
Lift 4
Lift 10
Oak Street Base
Telluride 2660m
Coonskin Base
Mountain Village 2895m
Lift 5
Day Lodge 2790m

young people, old timers who've stuck it out through the bad times, ski bums and a smattering of celebrities who shun the glitter of Aspen.

The new Mountain Village is as different as you could imagine. It is very much the modern American leisure resort, with security guards to keep out the riff-raff, and entirely modern buildings. Most of these have been designed in a sort of post-modern Alpine style, but there is a conspicuous exception – The Peaks, a monster hotel that looks as if it came from a housing estate in Poitiers.

⛷ The skiing

The skiing has a macho reputation. It features in many of the extreme skiing videos, and it deserves to – there's some fearsomely steep terrain. But there's ideal beginner and intermediate skiing too. The trouble is that there's not much of it – this is definitely a resort for those who put quality before quantity.

THE SKI AREA
Small but quite complex
The new gondola (when it opens) and two chair-lifts climb the steep, wooded northern flank of the skiing from two points on the edge of town. The gondola will carry on down to the Mountain Village, from which chair-lifts also rise. Lifts from both sides meet at two points, which ought to have names but don't; the higher of the two is the top point of the lift system, at 3625m. Beyond this point is Gold Hill, a lightly wooded area of steep runs reached by hiking up as far as 3735m. The terrain gets flatter down towards Mountain Village; below it is the long, gentle nursery slope, and branching off from the bottom of that the world's longest high-speed quad chair-lift, serving a separate mountain (anonymous, again) with a choice of long, easy runs of 525m vertical.

SNOW RELIABILITY
Good
The height of the isolated San Juan range makes Telluride something of a snow-hole, with an average of 25 feet of snow a year. On top of that (or, in practice, underneath it) there is a considerable amount of snowmaking on the lower half of the mountain. The steep slopes above the town face roughly north, while those in the bowl above Mountain Village range from west- to north-facing.

FOR ADVANCED SKIERS
Extremely steep mogul slopes
Telluride's reputation among the US skiing cogniscenti was made by the double black bump runs directly above the town – a slope of 960m vertical. Aptly named runs such as The Plunge, Spiral Stairs and Kant-Mak-M look terrifying from Lift 9, and only a little less terrifying on the ground. Some of them are now normally half-groomed to make them accessible to less-than-expert skiers – you have the choice of a steep groomed trail or fearsome-sized bumps. There's also some great steep glade skiing on the opposite side of the lift-system high-point. The new Gold Hill area was opened a couple of years ago, and there are plans to build a lift to serve it. It offers tough glade skiing; but Telluride doesn't have the sort of high bowl skiing to set it up as a competitor to Whistler or Vail.

FOR INTERMEDIATE SKIERS
Quality not quantity
Telluride's intermediate skiing is mainly confined to the runs served by the lifts immediately above Mountain Village – runs such as Peek A Boo, Boomerang and Misty Maiden. From the top of the mountain, See Forever is a glorious cruise down the main ridge, with splendid long-range views of mountain ranges in Utah. The other blues from here towards the old town are mainly more difficult double blue squares. But there is one easy way back to town – the winding Telluride Trail.

FOR BEGINNERS
Superb – one of the best
The Mountain Village area has for years had ideal first runs in the Meadows area (served by Lift 1). This will be even better this year as the lift will be replaced by a 'chondola' – a high-speed quad chair-lift with some gondola cabins interspersed among the chairs. There will also be a 'magic carpet' conveyor belt at the top, to take beginners further up the gentle slope. The opening of the super-long Lift 10 has also opened up another three or four excellent beginners' runs – which have the big advantage of being isolated from the rest of the skiing, so beginners aren't worried by better skiers flashing past them.

FOR CROSS-COUNTRY
Very attractive
The scenic beauty of this area makes it splendid for cross-country. The Telluride Nordic Center runs over 40km of groomed trails, and there is plenty of scope for skiing ungroomed

SKI FACTS

Altitude 2660m-3625m
Lifts	10
Pistes	1050 acres
Green	21%
Blue	47%
Black	32%
Art. snow	155 acres

LIFT PASSES

95/96 prices in dollars
Telluride area
Covers all lifts in Telluride.
Beginners Learn-to-ski/shred day course includes lift pass and equipment rental (adult 70, 75 for snowboarding).
Main pass
1-day pass 45
6-day pass 234
(low season 180 – 23% off)
Senior citizens
Over 65: 6-day pass 150 (36% off)
Over 70: free pass
Children
Under 12: 6-day pass 150 (36% off)
Under 6: free pass
Short-term passes
Half-day pass available (adult 36).
Notes Passes of over 2 days allow one day non-skiing, eg 6-day pass covers 6 days in 7. Discounts for groups, and tickets bought over 14 days in advance.
Credit cards Yes

SKI SCHOOL

95/96 prices in dollars

Telluride
Classes 6 days
2hr: 10.50-1pm; 2½hr: 1.20-4pm
6 half-days: 150
Children's classes
Ages: 3 to 12
5 5½hr days including lunch: 260
Private lessons
1hr, half- or full-day 70 for 1hr; each additional person 20

CHILDCARE

The ski school runs special classes for children aged 3 or more, provides lunchtime care and runs a free Adventure Club to keep children occupied before and after lessons.

The Mountain Village Nursery takes younger children from age 2 months to 3 years, from 8am to 5pm.

GETTING THERE

Air Telluride, transfer ½hr.

trails with a guide. There are even overnight excursions where you stay in back-country huts, and heli-drops are available.

QUEUES
Rarely a problem
Despite many of the lifts being antiquated by US standards, queues are rarely a problem because of the small numbers of skiers using the resort. Lift 6 can be a bottleneck at peak weekends because of the large number of the classic tough runs it serves and the fact that it's a slow two-person chair. But the ride is long and scenic, and it makes you feel good when you see others below you struggling just as much as you did on the way down.

MOUNTAIN RESTAURANTS
Could be worse
As in many US resorts, eating on the mountain is a fairly primitive and entirely self-service affair – though both of the two options do have some merit. The main mountain cafeteria – Gorrono – is only a few hundred metres above the Mountain Village. This is a large, two-storey wooden barn offering fairly standard American fare; but it has a big outside terrace with a barbecue, and a separate bar in an old cabin. There's also a tiny hut at the top of Lift 6 – Giuseppe's – which has tables outside on the snow and serves sandwiches, chilli, soup and the like (potato and bean sauté is the speciality, and it sells out early). There are good views from up here, with the chance of the additional spectacle of Glider Bob's performance (see For non-skiers). There are alternatives worth exploring at both the Mountain Village and the town.

SKI SCHOOL
Seems impressive
The school offers the usual American range of options, including special tuition on the resort's amazing mogul slopes and some very attractive early-morning starts to get you on the snow (on- or off-piste) before anyone else. There are free mountain orientation tours daily at 10am.

FACILITIES FOR CHILDREN
At the Mountain Village
There is the thorough provision for children that is usual in the US. The ski school's Adventure Club provides indoor and outdoor play before and after lessons, and for those based in the town includes transportation to the slopes at the Mountain Village.

↑ Staying there

The key decision is whether to stay down in the town or up in Mountain Village. For us, and we guess for most British visitors, there is no choice: in the Mountain Village, you could be anywhere, whereas in the town you're in no doubt that you're in Miningville, Colorado. But the Mountain Village will be made a more attractive base when the gondola link to the old town opens – it will work till late, allowing you to spend evenings there.

HOW TO GO
Fair choice of hotels and condos
Telluride is not among the best-known American resorts in the UK, and is offered by few of the main US tour operators.
Chalets We know of no catered chalets on the British package market.
Hotels With the exception of The Peaks and one or two others, all the hotels are in and around the town.
££££ The Peaks The biggest, plushest and priciest hotel – and the biggest eyesore in Mountain Village; although built only a couple of years ago, it appears to be modelled on the concrete monstrosities thrown up by the French in the 1960s. It has already changed ownership and name (it was formerly the Doral); and it may by now have changed colour – it was painted in drab shades to minimise the visual impact in summer and autumn, thus cleverly maximising the impact in winter. Once you're inside, of course, all this is forgiven. The new owners have given the spacious public areas a warm and inviting ambience, the bedrooms are big and plush, and it has a large and very smart health spa with saunas, steam rooms, pool, squash courts, a vast range of exercise machinery and whatever else you could want. The hotel is conveniently placed for skiing, on a loop off the main beginner run (and there is a ski hire shop in the basement).
£££ New Sheridan One of the town's oldest and most atmospheric hotels, which should by now be irresistible after a $1 million renovation programme. At the heart of things on the main street.
£££ Viking Suite New place that offers luxury suites and couldn't be more convenient for the Coonskin lift out of the village.
£££ Columbia New ski-in, ski-out luxury hotel in the heart of the old town.

PACKAGES

American Dream, Made to Measure, Ski Independence

ACTIVITIES

Indoor Swimming, galleries, Athletics Club (racquetball, aerobics, weights, steam room, massage), health spa, theatre, roller skating, cinema

Outdoor Dinner sleigh rides, ice skating, hot springs, snow-mobiling, glider rides, heli-skiing, climbing instruction, sledding, skating, horse-riding, ballooning, snow-shoe tours

TOURIST OFFICE

Postcode CO 81435
Tel 00 1 (303) 7287404
Fax 7286364

£££ Pennington's Inn Luxy B&B place in inconvenient but secluded setting (with great views) outside the Mountain Village.

££ San Sophia Smart, traditional B&B close to Oak Street lift.

££ Alpine Inn Dinky B&B on main street, just west of centre.

££ Skyline Guest Ranch Genuine turn-of-the-century ranch about 15 minutes out of town, with lovely mountain views. Charming rustic rooms, excellent food and a warm welcome from owners Dave and Sherry Farny (it's known to its friends as The Farny Farm – geddit?). There's a minibus service to and from town, but only at the start and end of the day and once in the early evening. Cross-country skiing (and snow-mobile) trails start nearby.

Self-catering There are plenty of condos and houses to rent both in town and up at Mountain Village, but few offered by British tour operators.

WHERE TO EAT
A wide choice
There's pretty much anything you want. La Marmotte is the place for French cuisine, the Athenian Suite for Greek-Italian, Leimgruber's for German-Austrian, Eddie's for pizzas, One World for Chinese and a choice of venues for Tex-Mex and typical American, including the atmospheric Legends Tavern & Grille and T-Ride Country Club, where you can cook your own steaks. About the best food in town is at 221 South Oak – innovative, ambitious food in stylish surroundings. Powderhouse also takes its food seriously. Out of town, the Peaks hotel, at Mountain Village, has two restaurants for formal dining, and the Skyline guest ranch has excellent food and wine in a country setting (where you can combine dinner with snow-mobiling).

APRES-SKI
Plenty going on
Telluride has a lively bar-based après-ski scene. Leimgruber's is popular for immediate post-skiing drinking, replicating an Alpine stube – right down to a Stammtisch reserved for ski instructors and their guests, and Paulaner on draught. The San Juan Brewing Company and Baked and Brewed in Telluride both have good brewed-on-the-premises beers – the former in the spectacularly restored old railway station known as the

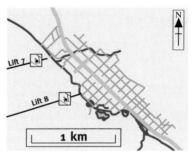

1 km

Depot (live music on Fridays). Swede-Finn Hall is a relaxed and popular bar and restaurant, with four pool tables downstairs. The Last Dollar Saloon and the bar at the New Sheraton Hotel are traditional drinking venues with lots of old-time atmosphere. Fly Me To The Moon Saloon sometimes has live music, and dancing in its basement may go on into the early hours. The Opera House is a movie theatre, but a thriving amateur rep company performs at the Nugget theatre.

FOR NON-SKIERS
Quite amusing, for a while
For a small resort there's a surprising number of non-skiing activities. A glider flight over the ski area is spectacular (ask for Glider Bob – if he has enough altitude left on the home run he'll offer to loop the loop; go for it). The local token cowboy, Roudy, can take you riding. On the whole, though, Telluride is difficult to recommend to non-skiers.

Vail 2500m

✔ *The biggest ski area in the US*

✔ *Superb piste grooming*

✔ *Ideal beginner and intermediate skiing in trails cut through trees*

✔ *Back Bowls offer the biggest area of treeless, go-anywhere skiing for intermediate and good skiers in US*

✔ *Despite its size, Vail is friendly and tastefully-built, largely in Tyrolean-style*

✔ *Excellent reputation for ski school and children's facilities*

✔ *Both Vail and Beaver Creek are largely traffic-free*

✗ *The famous Back Bowls face south, and the snow can suffer in warm weather*

✗ *Tyrolean-style architecture of Vail and modern luxury of Beaver Creek are far from the Wild West atmosphere you might look for on a trip to the US*

✗ *Expensive, especially Beaver Creek*

✗ *Some long lift queues in Vail*

Vail, Beaver Creek and now Arrowhead are all run by the same company. Vail cultivates an exclusive image – but the other two are even more upmarket.

The prices reflect the image. But many are prepared to pay them for the luxurious accommodation, relaxed atmosphere and wonderfully groomed trails you get. They make ideal beginner and intermediate terrain – the biggest in the US. Better skiers will also find runs to interest them in Vail's Back Bowls, if the snow is good, and on the steepest runs of Beaver Creek.

But these aren't the resorts to visit if you're looking for somewhere with a real feel of the Wild West. Vail was developed from scratch in the 1960s, and Beaver Creek opened in 1980. They have no buildings or traditions dating from the gold- and silver-mining days of the movies.

ORIENTATION

Vail is the biggest US ski resort. It stretches for seven miles at the foot of its mountain, beside the freeway. The skiing can be accessed from four main places: by chair from Golden Peak in the east or Cascade Village in the west by high-speed quad from Vail Village centre; and by high-speed quad or gondola from Lionshead. These are easily accessed from all accommodation by frequent free buses.

Sister resort **Beaver Creek** is ten miles to the west, and covered by the same lift pass. It is much smaller and built at the foot of its own skiing, accessed by a high-speed quad. **Arrowhead** is smaller still, and will eventually be linked-in to the Beaver Creek skiing by its own fast quad.

Other resorts within a two-hour drive include **Aspen, Breckenridge, Copper Mountain, Keystone** and **Steamboat.**

🏠 The resort

Standing in the centre of traffic-free Vail, surrounded by chalet-style wooden buildings and bierkellers, you could be forgiven for thinking you were in a top Austrian resort. And that's just how founder Pete Seibert intended it to be when he envisaged it in the 1950s. Vail is now enormous, stretching for seven miles at the foot of the biggest ski mountain in the US. There are hotels, condos, bars, restaurants and night-spots to suit every taste and pocket.

Beaver Creek, a resort developed by the owners of Vail in the 1980s, is ten miles to the west of Vail itself. It is unashamedly upmarket and luxurious, with a choice of top-quality hotels and condominiums right by the slopes. It is pedestrian-only and built around a huge square featuring exquisite bronze statues and even an open-air fire to warm you up on evening promenades.

Arrowhead is the newest addition to Vail's portfolio. A collection of luxury, secluded chalets, it was a tiny exclusive resort until bought by Vail. Arrowhead will be linked to Beaver Creek's skiing for the 1996/7 season.

Between them, Vail and Beaver Creek already have so many 'firsts' it's unbelievable: biggest ski area in the US; most high-speed quad chair-lifts in the world, most snow-grooming machines, and most ski instructors (over 1,100 of them).

SKI FACTS

Vail

Altitude	2475m-3490m
Lifts	25
Pistes	4014 acres
Green	32%
Blue	36%
Black	32%
Art. snow	332 acres

Beaver Creek

Altitude	2470m-3490m
Lifts	11
Pistes	1125 acres
Green	18%
Blue	39%
Black	43%
Art. snow	375 acres

LIFT PASSES

94/95 prices in dollars
Vail and Beaver Creek
Covers all Vail and
Beaver Creek lifts,
and ski-bus around
resort.
Beginners Half- (60),
1- (75) and 3-day
(225) Learn-to-ski
courses include lift
pass.
Main pass
1-day pass 46
6-day pass 230
Senior citizens
Over 65: 6-day pass
222 (3% off)
Over 70: free pass
Children
Under 13: 6-day pass
162 (30% off)
Short-term passes
Return trips on some
lifts for foot
passengers only. Half-
day pass from noon
available (adult 39).
Alternative passes
Premier Passport is
designed for a two-
centre holiday. It
covers all Aspen and
Vail-Beaver Creek
skiing, and one-way
transport between the
resorts. Allows from
10 days skiing out of
12 up to 18 out of 21
(38 per day).
Credit cards Yes

⛷ The skiing

Vail and Beaver Creek together have
the biggest ski area in the US. It leapt
to fame in the UK by hosting the 1989
World Championships (it is holding
them again in 1999). It is now the
number two US destination for UK
skiers (behind Breckenridge). But
although big by US standards, it's not
by European ones. It can't compare
with the likes of Val-d'Isère-Tignes and
the Trois Vallées. Its area is more like
Wengen, Kitzbühel or St Anton.

The resort's skiing stands out for
our reporters' enthusiasm for it. We've
had many reports on it, nearly all
glowing with praise. 'Brilliant',
'Excellent', 'Grooming exemplary',
'Hazard marking superb' are typical.
The main criticism – made by several
correspondents – is that some of the
runs (especially single black
diamonds) are over-graded.

THE SKI AREA
Something for everyone
The Vail and Beaver Creek ski areas are
completely separate but linked by bus
and covered on the same lift pass.
They also feel very different.

Vail gets much more crowded. Its
skiing divides neatly into two. The
front face is largely north-facing, with
well-groomed trails cut through the
trees. Efficient chair-lifts and a
gondola take you from various points
along the long valley floor to mid-
mountain, where **Mid-Vail** (3080m)
is the main focal point. From here
chairs take you to various points along
the ridge, which reaches 3430m.

From the top ridge you drop over
into the **Back Bowls**; these are
largely south-facing and rejoice in
names such as Sun Up, Sun Down,
China, Teacup and Siberia Bowls. The
bowls are mainly open, free of trees,
and for the most part unpisted. The
story goes that the bowls were
denuded of trees by the peace-loving
Ute Indians, who were driven from
their land by the white men in the
1880s and took revenge by setting fire
to their forests before they left.

Beaver Creek is overlooked by
many Vail-based skiers. That makes it
delightfully uncrowded. There's a
high-speed quad from the resort up to
Spruce Saddle, the mid-mountain
focus. From there you can carry on up
or ski down to more lifts left and
right. Going right takes you to lifts up
two separate mountains – **Grouse**
(with the best steep skiing) and
Larkspur Bowl. It also leads to what

will be the connection to the
Arrowhead ski area and the newly
developed Bachelor Gulch, from
where a new lift will bring you back to
Beaver Creek's own skiing. These
connections have much of their
infrastructure already in place.

We love Beaver Creek's skiing and
think it is vastly underrated by most
visitors who stick to Vail.

SNOW RELIABILITY
Excellent, except in the Bowls
Apart from the exceptional natural
snow record, Vail and Beaver Creek
both have extensive snowmaking
facilities, normally needed only in
early season. But one of the biggest
disappointments about Vail is that its
famous Back Bowls are largely south-
facing. That means a fresh snowfall
can often get ruined quickly if it's
sunny. In three visits we've never hit
the champagne powder conditions for
which the Back Bowls are ideal.

The steep Grouse Mountain skiing
in Beaver Creek can also suffer from
thin snow cover.

FOR ADVANCED SKIERS
Enough to keep most people happy
Vail's Back Bowls are vast areas, served
by three chair-lifts and a drag-lift. You
can ski virtually anywhere you like in
their 2,734 acres, trying the gradient
and terrain of your choice. There are
areas of interesting tree-skiing as well
as the more common tree-free
mogulled slopes. Some runs are
groomed, making it easy for groups of
mixed ability to take different routes
and ride the lifts together.

The steepest runs are probably Wow
and Forever on Sun Down Bowl,
which funnel in to the High Noon lift.

On the front face there are some
steep, often mogulled, slopes which
frequently have better snow than the
Back Bowls because of their
orientation. The Highline lift on the
extreme east of the ski area serves
three double black diamond runs –
Blue Ox, Highline and Roger's Run.
Prima, which comes down from the
ridge Summit, is also steep.

The rest of the mountain has a few
short black runs and the long Minnies
Mile which is a wonderful fast cruise
when it has been groomed.

In Beaver Creek, Grouse Mountain is
the place for experts to head for. This
is almost entirely black run territory.
We've twice found this area wonderful
but rather bare in parts. Other good
steep blacks lead down to the bottom
of Grouse from the main mountain
summit. This is called the Birds of Prey

area because of the runs named after them – Goshawk, Peregrine and Golden Eagle.

The Larkspur Bowl area has three short steep mogul runs worth trying.

The other thing good skiers will love about Beaver Creek is the lack of crowds. Even by American standards, Beaver Creek's runs are often deserted. That means it's normally safe to bomb around the immaculately groomed blue runs at speeds that you couldn't contemplate on Europe's crowded slopes. We've gone flat out with the most responsible of guides every time we've visited.

But the more macho advanced skiers may find too little to challenge them in Vail-Beaver Creek. The Back Bowls, in particular, have disappointed some of our more dare-devil correspondents, because they judge them too tame.

FOR INTERMEDIATE SKIERS
Ideal territory
The majority of Vail's front face is easy cruising, tree-lined blue runs. Particularly on the western side of the area there are excellent long blues such as the easy Born Free and the faster Simba, which both go from top to bottom of the mountain. If you drop over into Game Creek Bowl, you can try Showboat, under the lift, or other blues down from the ridge.

As well, as tackling some of the easier front-face blacks, intermediates will find plenty of interest in the Back Bowls. There are a couple of usually pisted blue runs, Poppyfields and Sleepytime, which both lead down to the Orient Express chair.

And the Silk Road blue leads from the top of the Mongolia drag-lift at the extreme eastern side of the skiing. There are wonderful views from here towards Copper Mountain (much nearer and easier to build a lift-link to than Beaver Creek). The run goes right around the ski area boundary back to the Orient Express lift, with splendid views of the virgin mountain across the river (which Vail has earmarked for expansion into to provide some much-needed north-facing bowl skiing).

All these blues are easily tackled even by early intermediates. More adventurous ones can branch out to try some of the unpisted bowl skiing, much of which is reasonably gentle. In fresh snow this can make the ideal introduction to powder skiing.

Beaver Creek is an intermediate skier's dream. There are marvellous long cruising blue runs almost everywhere you look. Centennial runs from top to bottom of the main mountain – a vertical drop of just over 1000m. It starts off green and has a black section in the centre (which can be avoided) but is genuine blue for most of its length. Harrier and Red Tail down to the foot of Grouse Mountain and Larkspur Bowl were another two of our favourite long cruises. Larkspur Bowl itself is a huge wide blue run with several variations possible on the lower part of it.

The Arrowhead area is another ideal intermediate area. Served by only one lift, there is a fair variety of runs – our favourites were Golden Bear, Cresta and the black Real McCoy.

FOR BEGINNERS
Difficult to beat
In 1993 Vail opened a new mountain-top teaching area of five runs, served by six lifts – the Eagle's Nest Beginner Park. It also has separate adult and children areas, a special area to teach safe skiing procedures, an environmental education trail and a native American village.

Combine this dedicated teaching area with Vail ski school's high reputation and you have a very appealing combination. The area is suited to both complete beginners and those trying to make a breakthrough later on in their skiing career.

Once you are off the beginners' slopes, there are plenty of easy greens to progress to – on both the top and bottom parts of the mountain. Cub's Way, Gitalong Road and the lower part of Born Free on the eastern side of the ski area are ideal. Overeasy, Ramshorn and Flapjack on the top part of the mountain are also excellent gentle runs for first-week skiers.

Beaver Creek has good village-level nursery slopes and its fair share of easy greens to progress to. Cinch runs virtually from top to bottom of the main mountain, with Dally the main alternative on the bottom half. There is a good choice of greens on the top half too.

The little-used Strawberry Park Express lift serves a lot of easy blue run skiing as well as the mountain-top cross-country area.

FOR CROSS-COUNTRY
Some of the best
Vail's cross-country areas are at the foot of Golden Peak and at the Nordic Centre on the golf course. At Beaver Creek, there's a splendid mountain-top network of 32km of tracks at McCoy Park, at the top of the Strawberry Park lift out of the resort.

QUEUES
Can be bad in Vail
Vail has some of the longest lift queues we've come across in the US. Although they move quickly and are well disciplined (as they are everywhere in the US), they come as a shock in comparison with the queue-free environment of most US resorts.

The worst queues (perhaps 20 minutes) build up for the Vista Bahn Express from the middle of town in the morning rush, the Mountaintop Express from Mid-Vail to the top and for the Back Bowl chair-lifts when the snow there is good. Weekends are the worst times because Vail is near enough to Denver to attract weekenders in significant numbers. Reporters thought the traffic-light system at the main lift notice boards was useful for identifying and allowing them to avoid the worst queues.

Beaver Creek, on the other hand, is virtually queue-free – it is amazing that more people don't go there to get away from the Vail crowds.

And the Mid-Vail queues should be alleviated for the 1995/6 season, with the upgrade of the Wildwood Shelter slow chair to a high-speed quad.

MOUNTAIN RESTAURANTS
Trying hard
While still far from a gourmet's delight, Vail is trying hard to bring its mountain dining facilities up to European standards.

The Two Elk restaurant was opened

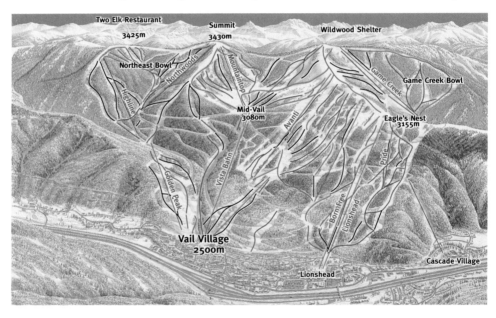

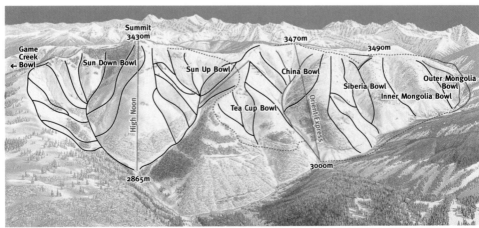

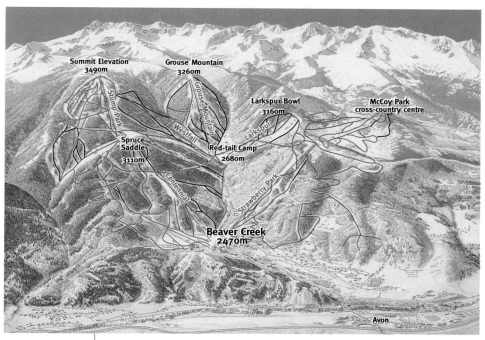

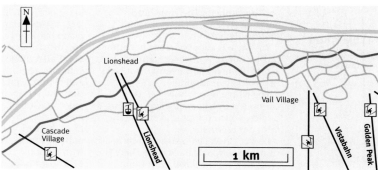

SKI SCHOOL

94/95 prices in dollars

Vail and Beaver Creek
At four locations –
Vail Village,
Lionshead, Golden
Peak and Beaver
Creek
Classes 6 days
5hr: 9.45-3.45 with
1hr lunch; 3hr 15mins:
12.30-3.45
3 full days: 210
Children's classes
Ages: 3 to 13
5 6½hr days including
rental, lift pass and
lunch: 332
Private lessons
1hr, 2hr, half- and
full-day
95 for 1hr, for 1 to 6
people

for the 1991/92 season. It is huge, and beautifully designed, featuring massive wooden pillars, a high roof and a number of different seating areas. There's a good choice of food, with salad and pasta bars, and a big selection of grills.

At Mid-Vail there are a couple of large self-service cafeterias and the best table-service restaurant on the mountain in Cook Shack (it's best to reserve a table). The Wine Stube at the top of the Lionshead gondola is also table-service, and there's a self-service restaurant there too.

At Beaver Creek, Spruce Saddle (built along the same lines as Two Elk) at mid-mountain is the main place for lunch. The exclusive Beano's Cabin is a private members' club at lunchtime, but it's worth trying to wangle your way in as a guest. It serves superb food in a beautifully-built wooden cabin

situated in the woods off the piste near Larkspur Bowl. At night it's open to all via sleigh-rides – see Eating Out, page 443.

In both Vail and Beaver Creek there are smaller places you can ski into for a swift snack.

SKI SCHOOL
One of the best in the world

The Vail-Beaver Creek ski school has an excellent reputation. All the reports we've had of it have again been glowing. It's also one of the biggest, with over 1,100 instructors in high season. This number helps keep class sizes down – as few as four is not uncommon.

We can vouch for the high standard of instruction. We've tried three different instructors, and all have been excellent. Instructors get bonuses for repeat customers, so there's a financial

CHILDCARE

Ski school tuition is based at Children's Ski Centers located at Golden Peak and Lionshead in Vail, and at Beaver Creek resort. There are separate programmes to suit children of different ages and skiing competence – Mini-Mice for children aged 3, Mogul Mice and Superstars for those aged 4 to 6.

Small World Play Schools, at Golden Peak in Vail and at Beaver Creek, take children aged 2 months to 6 years, from 8am to 4.30

GETTING THERE

Air Eagle, transfer 30 minutes. Denver, transfer 2½hr.

PACKAGES

American Connections, American Dream, American Skiworld, Bladon Lines, Crystal, First Choice Ski, Inghams, Lotus Supertravel, Made to Measure, Ski Activity, Ski Independence, Ski Val, Snow Cocktail, The Ski Company Ltd, Thomson, USAirtours

Beaver Creek
American Connections, American Dream, American Skiworld, Crystal, Inghams, Lotus Supertravel, Made to Measure, Ski Independence, USAirtours

incentive for them to give their clients what they want. In addition to normal classes and private lessons, there are specialist half-day workshops in, for example, bumps and powder. You can sign up the same day at a choice of mountain-top offices.

FACILITIES FOR CHILDREN
Excellent

The comprehensive arrangements for young children look excellent, and a report on the children's ski school this year says it is 'outstanding' with 'staff and tuition excellent.' At both Vail and Beaver Creek there are splendid children's areas with adventure skiing trails and themed play areas.

Staying there

Vail is vast in ski resort terms. The most convenient – and expensive – places to stay are in Vail Village centre near the Vista Bahn lift or in Lionshead, near the gondola. Of these we prefer Vail Village, which has the best of the mock-Tyrolean architecture and atmosphere. The Lionshead building style – which came later – is more dully modern.

But there is a lot of accommodation further out – the cheapest tends to be across the main I-70 freeway, but lacks the real Vail atmosphere.

The whole resort, however, is connected by a very efficient free bus-service, which brings universal praise from our reporters.

Beaver Creek can be reached by a shuttle bus from Vail. Staying there is an option for the wealthy. It is an unashamedly upmarket resort with a fair choice of luxurious, expensive hotels, all within an easy walk of the slopes. Nightlife and choice of bars and restaurants is much more limited than in Vail; it's not for those who want a wild time.

HOW TO GO
Package or independent

There's a big choice of packages to Vail and a smaller one to Beaver Creek. It's also very easy to organise your own visit, with regular shuttles from Denver airport by Vans to Vail. Hiring a car would be worthwhile if you wanted to visit other resorts such as Breckenridge, but is superfluous in traffic-free Vail and Beaver Creek.
Chalets The widest choice of any US resort. Supertravel have very comfortable places, with all mod cons, in East Vail. In the same area, Crystal have a selection of places, several of

which have been praised by our reporters. If you prefer West Vail, the luxurious private homes featured by Ski Activity are difficult to beat. Ski Val have an impressive, luxurious family home in a secluded spot, best for those with a car. Good apartments out at Gore Creek are also run as catered chalets by Ski Independence and American Skiworld. Top-of-the-market operator The Ski Company opened its first US chalet in Vail last season.
Hotels Vail has a fair choice of hotels, ranging from luxurious to budget. In the more upmarket Beaver Creek you can go completely overboard.
At Vail:
£££££ Lodge at Vail The best hotel in Vail, owned by Orient Express Hotels. It is right by the Vista Bahn Express, in the centre of Vail Village. Its amazing buffet breakfast features smoked salmon and cold meats as well as hot food, and keeps most people going all day, and its Wildflower restaurant is one of the best in town.
££££ Sonnenalp There are various Sonnenalp hotels in town. The most luxurious is the Bavaria House with a large sports complex and splendid piano bar-lounge. Also recommended are Austria House and Swiss House.
£££ Vail Village Inn Condo and hotel complex, recently partly renovated and rebuilt. Complaints of unfriendly staff and scruffy decor from one recent reporter. Good position. Outdoor pool.
£££ Chateau Vail (Holiday Inn) Not quite as central. Adequate comfort, with a pool.
££ Roost Lodge A popular budget option in West Vail, with comfortable rooms and friendly, helpful staff. Pool, sauna, hot tub, constant free coffee and regular cheese and wine parties.
At Beaver Creek:
£££££ Beaver Creek Lodge All-suite hotel. Luxurious. Health club with pool, sauna and so on.
£££££ Hyatt Regency Standard Hyatt luxury. Lively bar in basement.
Self-catering There are numerous options. For those who want lots of in-house amenities, the Racquet Club at East Vail is superb – high-standard apartments and town houses with use of pool, health centre and, of course, racket sports. There are plenty of cheaper options throughout the town – and several tour operators have allocations conveniently close to the Lionshead gondola.

ACTIVITIES

Indoor Athletic clubs and spas, massage, museum, cinema, tennis courts, artificial skating rink, library, galleries

Outdoor Hot-air ballooning, skating, ice hockey, heli-skiing, sleigh rides, fishing, mountaineering, snowmobiles, snow-shoe excursions, snowcat tours, bobsleighing, dog-sledding, para-gliding

STAYING UP THE MOUNTAIN
Great if you can afford it

Trappers Cabin is a luxurious private cabin up the mountain, which a group can rent by the night ($500 each for a minimum of four people). You ski in at end of the day to a champagne welcome, make a snow-shoe excursion to see the sunset, soak in an outdoor hot tub and enjoy a gourmet dinner. The cabin-keeper then leaves until morning. Splendid isolation.

STAYING DOWN THE VALLEY
Cheaper but quiet

Staying out of central Vail is certainly cheaper but not so lively. **East** and **West Vail** both have reasonably priced accommodation.

Another budget option is to stay in **Avon** at the foot of the approach road up to Beaver Creek. Day-trippers have to leave their cars here and take the shuttle bus up to the resort.

It's not a very atmospheric town but it does have a number of reasonably priced hotels and motels. The Comfort Inn is used by a fair number of tour operators.

If you rent a car, staying out of town and visiting nearby resorts makes for an interesting holiday.

EATING OUT
Endless choice

Whichever kind of food you want, Vail has it. Pizza, Burger, Tex Mex, Chinese, Japanese, Moroccan, Italian, Thai and a big choice of European-style fine dining. But expect to pay for it. Vail is not a cheap place for eating and drinking.

The Wildflower, in the Lodge, and Ludwig's, in the Sonnenalp Bavaria House, are two of the best fine-dining places in Vail. The Saddleridge, in Beaver Creek, offers a marvellous night out. It is a luxurious wooden building packed with photos and Wild West artefacts, including old six-shooters and General Custer's hat.

The sleigh-ride to Beano's Cabin in Beaver Creek also makes a fine evening out. The food and setting are several cuts above the average 'dinner sleigh-ride'.

For a budget option we liked the Hubcap Brewery in Vail Village, which as well as a choice of local ales has a filling menu of typical American food.

Recommendations from readers this year include Lancelot (for steaks), Montauk (for fish), Vendetta (Italian), Blu's (varied menu), Amigos (Mexican) and Szechuan Lion (Chinese).

APRES-SKI
Lively after skiing, but early to bed

A combination of staying at high altitude and the early opening and closing times of lifts, makes Vail's nightlife a short pre-dinner affair. Things are fairly buzzing from three till five, then it's an early evening meal before tiredness sets in for the night.

Many of our reporters have fallen into the convenient, though rather dire, Red Lion after skiing, but there are plenty of better places: the Hong Kong Café is popular for its cocktails; the Swiss Chalet attempts to recreate European 'gemütlichkeit'; King's Club is the place to go for high-calorie cake intake, and becomes a piano bar later; Louie's has live jazz; and Los Amigos and the Hubcap Brewery are other atmospheric places at around four o'clock. Sarah's Bar in the Christiana condos sometimes has tea-time live music and sing-a-long.

Cyrano's is one of the few places to stay lively throughout the evening, serving good food and becoming a disco later. Garston's also stays open late and has live bands some nights.

Cassidy's Hole In The Wall is an Old West saloon reconstruction, with live entertainment including country and western bands. A more authentic Old West scene can be experienced in the 4 Eagle Ranch, a homestead dating from the 1860s, 6km out of town. It has Western-style entertainment such as country and western barn dancing with instructions for the uninitiated.

Nick's and the Club are the main discos in town, but usually only come to life at weekends.

FOR NON-SKIERS
A lot to do

Getting around on the free bus is easy and there are lots of activities to try and walks available. Excursions to other resorts and to Denver are feasible.

TOURIST OFFICE

Postcode 81658
Tel 00 1 (303)
8455745
Fax 8455729

Winter Park 2745m

✔ *The best snowfall record of all Colorado's major resorts*

✔ *Skiing for all standards, with one of the best beginner areas and some of the steepest chutes we've seen, as well as intermediate cruising*

✔ *Town feels like a real American place rather than a ski resort*

✔ *Spectacular views*

✔ *World's leading centre for teaching disabled people to ski*

✔ *Cheap by US ski resort standards*

✘ *Not much ski resort ambience. There's no resort village at the bottom of the ski area and the town is a bus ride away, strung out along a road, with no real focus*

✘ *The nearest big ski resort to Denver, so can get crowded at weekends*

Winter Park has been a favourite ski area with locals for over 50 years. It is only a ninety-minute drive from Denver and a regular ski train still works at weekends. This local trade means the area has developed excellent skiing, with runs to suit everyone and an efficient lift system including six high-speed quads. We have to admit to being surprised by the extent and quality of the skiing and on-mountain facilities when we first visited two years ago.

The downside of Winter Park for a skiing holiday is that, because it is primarily still a locals' place, there is not much in the way of normal ski resort atmosphere or buildings. The town, where most accommodation is, is typically American – strung out along the main US40 highway. It has no real focus and certainly none of the glitz and glamour you associate with Aspen or Vail. But it does have good, quiet condo accommodation set in the woods, bars and restaurants with a local feel and some lively nightspots.

ORIENTATION

Winter Park is around 70 miles from Denver, over the Berthoud Pass and right on the Continental Divide. The town straddles the US40 highway and the main Winter Park ski area base is just above that (a bus ride from most accommodation). The skiing can be accessed from her where there is a huge car park, or from the Mary Jane base area at the foot of the adjoining, linked mountain – where there is more car parking. High speed quads and other chair lifts depart from both these areas. Other resorts within a two hour drive include **Steamboat, Breckenridge, Copper Mountain, Keystone** and **Vail.**

 ## The resort

Winter Park started life around the turn of the century as a railway town, when Rio Grande railway workers started climbing up the slopes and skiing down. One of the resort's mountains, Mary Jane, is named after a legendary 'lady of pleasure' who is said to have received the land as payment for her favours.

The railway still plays an important part in Winter Park's existence, with a station right at the foot of the ski area and regular ski trains bringing day trippers from Denver every Saturday and Sunday. The area around there is now known as Old Town Winter Park.

Most accommodation, however, is a shuttle bus ride away in downtown Winter Park which straddles the main highway. Here condos are dotted around by the roadside and in the trees either side. There are also motels and restaurants lining the road, which continues northwards to the neighbouring town of Fraser. A car would be handy but is by no means essential.

The locals are very friendly and helpful – typical small town America.

The skiing

Winter Park is one of the least-known ski areas to British skiers because until this year no mass market British tour operator has offered it. This year Crystal and Thomson both feature it for the first time – as well as specialist US operators.

And it is well worth a visit. It has a fair-sized ski area (big by US standards) and a wonderful mixture of terrain that will suit skiers of all standards.

THE SKI AREA
Interestingly divided
There are four very distinct, but well-linked, ski areas – each with its own special character. From the main base, a high-speed quad takes you up the original **Winter Park** mountain to the Sunspot restaurant area at 10,700ft. From there, you can ski in virtually all directions. Runs lead down towards the main base and link to chairs back up, or you can ski over to the **Vasquez Ridge** area on the far right. This is served by a high-speed quad which allows you to ski that area continuously or get back to the Winter Park mountain. Both these

LIFT PASSES

95/96 prices in dollars
Winter Park Resort
Covers all lifts in
Winter Park, Mary
Jane, Vasquez Ridge
and Parsenn Bowl
areas.
Beginners Pass for
Galloping Goose
beginner lift only on
Mary Jane mountain
(5 per day).
Main Pass
1-day pass 35
6-day pass 210
(Low season 150 –
28% off)
Senior Citizens
Over 61: 6-day pass
108 (48% off)
Over 70: free pass
Children
Under 14: 6-day pass
108 (48% off)
Under 6: free pass
Short-term passes
Half-day passes up to
or from 12.15pm
(adult 26, 94/95)
Alternative passes
Mini Mountain pass
covers 6 lifts on
Winter Park mountain
(adult 18, 94/95).
Notes
Passes of more than
one day allow one
non-skiing day; 6-day
pass valid for 7 days,
with one non-skiing
day. Special rates for
disabled skiers.
Credit Cards Yes

SKI SCHOOL

95/96 prices in dollars

Winter Park
Classes 6 days
4¼hr: from 9.30 or
11am; 3hr: from 11am
6 4¼hr days: 210
Children's classes
Ages: 3 to 12
6 8hr days including
pass and lunch: 360
Private lessons
1½hr, 3hr or 6hr
80 for 1½hr, for 1 or 2
people; each extra
person 20

NSCD
Special programme
for disabled skiers
Private lessons
Half-day (3hr) with
pass and special
equipment: 40
Full-day (6hr) with
pass and special
equipment: 75

areas are primarily beginner and
intermediate terrain.

From the top of Winter Park
mountain you can ski to **Mary Jane**
mountain, which has the resort's
toughest skiing. Mary Jane itself is
served by six lifts including two high
speed quads to the summit (11,200ft).
From there you can ski over to Winter
Park's newest ski area of **Parsenn
Bowl** much of which, unlike the rest
of Winter Park's skiing, is above the
treeline. This area has 99% of its runs
classified as intermediate terrain.

SNOW RELIABILITY
Among Colorado's best
Winter Park is situated right on the
Continental Divide in the highest part
of the Rockies. Its position means that
its average yearly snowfall of almost
30ft is the highest of any major
Colorado resort. As a back up, artificial
snowmaking covers a high proportion
of the runs on Winter Park mountain.

FOR ADVANCED SKIERS
Some hair-raising challenges
Expert skiers generally head for Mary
Jane, which has some of the steepest
mogul fields and hair-raising
challenges in the US. The steepest
chutes are on Mary Jane's Backside
accessed by a control gate off a long
black run called Derailer. Hole in the
Wall, Awe Chute, Baldy's Chute and
Jeff's Chute are all fearsomely steep,
narrow couloirs, bordered by rocks.
Peer down Awe Chute before backing
off, as we did, and you'll understand
why the locals have a slightly different
name for it! More manageable, wider

black mogul fields for most good skiers
are Derailer, Long Haul, Brakeman,
Railbender and Phantom Bridge.
Coming down a notch of difficulty
good skiers will enjoy cruising down
the blue/black runs on Mary Jane's
front side. There are good challenges
on Winter Park Mountain too.

FOR INTERMEDIATE SKIERS
Choose your challenge
From pretty much wherever you are
on Winter Park mountain and
Vasquez Ridge you can choose a run
to suit your ability and mood – green,
blue or blue/black. Most are well
groomed every night giving you
perfect early morning cruising on the
famous Colorado 'corduroy' pistes. If
you are more into trying powder
skiing during one of Winter Park's
frequent snow storms, we picked up a
great tip from a local. Because of the
prevailing winds, you'll normally find
the best and deepest powder by
keeping to the left hand side of the
pistes – the winds come from that
direction and dump the snow where
the trees give some shelter. Some of
our favourute blues were the aptly
named Cheshire Cat, Jaberwocky and
Bradley's Bash.

For bumps try Mary Jane's front
side, where long and perfectly formed
mogul fields normally develop.

Parsenn Bowl has stunning views
and some gentle, cruising pistes as
well as more challenging unpisted
bowl skiing. It's an intermediate
paradise and an ideal place to try your
first steps off the marked pistes.

National Sports Centre for the Disabled

If you are able-bodied, the most striking and humbling thing you'll notice
as you ride your first chair-lift up the mountain is the number of skiers with
disabilities of all sorts hurtling down the mountain faster than many of us
could ever hope to. There are blind skiers, skiers with one leg, no legs,
paralysis – whatever their problem, they've cracked it.

That's because Winter Park is home to the US National Sports Centre for
the Disabled (NSCD) – the world's leading centre for teaching skiing to
people with disabilities. There are 12 full-time instructors and 1,000 trained
volunteers who help in the programme, using techniques and adapted ski
equipment which the centre has pioneered the development of. Skiers are
placed with instructors trained to teach people with their particular
disability – more than 40 disabilities are specially catered for.

If you are disabled and want to learn to ski (or to ski again) there's no
better place to go. Lesson, lift pass and special equipment cost just $40
for a half day, $75 for a full day. It's important to book ahead so that a
suitable instructor is available. The centre can help with travel and
accommodation arrangements: NSCD, PO Box 36, Winter Park, CO 80482,
USA. Tel: 00 1 303 726 5514 ext 179. Fax: 00 1 303 726 4112.

CHILDCARE

The ski school runs special classes for children aged 3 or more and provides lunch.
The Children's centre has a non-skiing programme for children aged 2 months to 5 years. The Chlidren's Centre is open 8am to 4pm. Lessons are 10am to 3pm.

GETTING THERE

Air Denver, transfer 2 hours.

Rail Leaves Denver Sat and Sun at 7.15am and returns at 4.15pm. Journey time 2 hours.

PACKAGES

American Dream, American Skiworld, Crystal, Made to Measure, Ski Independence, Thomson

ACTIVITIES

Indoor Cinema, swimming pool, roller skating, mini-golf, lazer maze, casino trips
Outdoor Dog sledding, sight-seeing flights, snow shoe excursions, sleigh rides, 'tubing', ice skating, snow-mobiling, snowcat tours

TOURIST OFFICE

Postcode CO80482
Tel 00 1 (970)
7265993
Fax 7265514

FOR BEGINNERS
The best we've seen

A couple of seasons ago, Winter Park built Discovery Park – a 25 acre mid-mountain area specifically for beginners served by a high-speed quad. The area is roped off so that experienced skiers don't go in. It has another two of its own lifts, a nursery area, gentle beginner runs, an adventure trail through the trees and a special terrain park.

It is used for beginners and by the programme for disabled people (see Box). Once you are out of the Park, there are easy runs all the way down to the base.

FOR CROSS-COUNTRY
Lots of it

There are several different areas, all with generally excellent snow, adding up to well over 200km of groomed trails, as well as back-country tours.

QUEUES
Rarely a problem

During the week the mountain is generally quiet. At weekends the Denver crowds arrive. But even then the network of over twenty lifts includes six high-speed quads which make light work of the crowds.

MOUNTAIN RESTAURANTS
Some good facilities

For a resort which caters mainly for locals Winter Park has surprisingly good restaurant facilities. The highlight is the Lodge at Sunspot, at the top of Winter Park mountain. This beautifully built wood and glass building houses a welcoming bar, with easy chairs and a roaring log fire, a table-service restaurant and a very good self-service section. It is open on certain nights too – accessed by gondolas that are put on the main chair lift specially for night-time transport.

SKI SCHOOL
A good reputation

We've had no reader reports on the ski school. However, it consistently comes out well in US ski magazine surveys.

FACILITIES FOR CHILDREN
Some of the best

There is a Children's Centre at the Winter Park base area which houses day care facilities for non-skiing children and is the meeting point for children's ski classes. Classes are available in four age groups.

 # Staying there

Nearly all the accommodation is down in town, served by a free shuttle bus.

HOW TO GO
More packages

This season sees a massive increase in the number of tour operators going to Winter Park. We suggest you try combining Winter Park with another resort in a two-centre holiday. That way you'd see the contrast between Winter Park's 'locals' atmosphere and a normal US 'destination' resort – try Steamboat, Breckenridge or Vail.
Hotels There are a couple of hotel/condo complexes which stand out above the others.
££££ Iron Horse Resort The only ski-in/ski-out accommodation. Comfortable, with outdoor pool and hot tub. Complementary local shuttle.
££££ Vintage Quarter mile from ski area. Same facilities as Iron Horse.
Self-catering There are a lot of comfortable condo complexes dotted around town and in the woods. Snowblaze and Beaver Village both have good pool and spa facilities.

EATING OUT
A fair choice

There are lots of restaurants, with both ethnic and typical American food. You can also ride the lift up to eat at the Lodge at Sunspot on some evenings.

Our favourite local restaurant is the Crooked Creek Saloon at Fraser – as much for the atmosphere as the food. It is popular with locals, has great Old West decor and photos and serves typical American food – try the Awesome Fat Boy burger.

APRES-SKI
Surprisingly lively

Immediately after skiing, the hot spots are the Derailer Bar at the foot of Winter Park mountain and the Club Car at the bottom of Mary Jane.

Then try the Tubing Hill at Fraser Valley. You slide down on an inner tube spinning out of control if you go solo. Much more fun to join a big group, link arms and legs and hurtle down en masse.

Later on, try The Slope (in Old Town) which has live music and dancing or Adolph's, just across the road. Deno's, downtown, has nine big screen TVs usually showing sport. The Stampede has a disco and occasional live bands. The Crooked Creek Saloon (see Eating Out) is also worth trying as is the bar of the Lord Gore Arms.

Canada

Western Canada combines the best of US skiing with the best of European skiing. That combination, together with the great value offered by the weak Canadian dollar, makes it an attractive destination which increasing numbers of British skiers are discovering.

Canada offers the service and courtesy that is so striking when you first visit the US – mountain hosts to show you around the slopes, immaculately groomed runs, civilised lift queues, lots of high-speed quad chair-lifts, piste maps available at the bottom of most lifts, and lift operators who seem happy in their job and appear to want you to have a good time. But what distinguishes Canadian from American skiing is that the mountains resemble those of the Alps. You get spectacular scenery of the kind that is very rare in the US. And at the two resorts featured in most tour operators' brochures – Whistler-Blackcomb and Banff-Lake Louise – there is very extensive skiing. In fact, Whistler-Blackcomb has the biggest vertical drop and highest piste mileage in North America, and a lot of exciting skiing above the tree-line as well as woodland runs.

Banff-Lake Louise has another big plus-point. It is surrounded by Canadian National Park land and an amazing variety of wildlife that you'd never come across in Europe. Herds of elk and big-horn sheep roam the streets and roadsides. You might even see a moose or bear. Winter is Banff's low season – hotel prices are half their summer levels and the resort offers excellent value for money.

There are downsides to both these resorts though. Whistler suffers from a lot of bad weather coming in from the Pacific Ocean – it is practically on the coast. While this normally means a lot of snow up top, it can also mean a lot of rain at resort level, and days on end without sight of the sun. Banff and nearby Lake Louise have a different problem – especially in early season, temperatures can be bitterly cold (-20°C is not uncommon; -30°C not unknown). Riding a high-speed chair in very low temperatures isn't much fun. Banff also suffers from the fact that there are no villages at the bases of the ski areas – you have to stay a bus- or car-ride away.

Canada is also home to the world's most famous heli-skiing operations, where you can stay for a week in a luxurious lodge and be whirled up to virgin powder for several runs a day. We tried it for the first time last season and are addicted. Or you can try heli-skiing for a day from most resorts – a much more affordable option.

There are numerous smaller resorts in Canada's Rockies that are now appearing on the British market, mainly through specialist Canadian and North American operators. Jasper in Alberta has its own small ski area 30 minutes' drive away in the National Park, abundant wildlife, stunning scenery and a charming luxury hotel (see page 454). Panorama is a small, ski-in ski-out resort two hours south-west of Banff with the second biggest vertical

drop in North America (1310m) and a well-known heli-skiing operation as well as its own eight lifts. Kananaskis near Calgary was home to the 1988 Winter Olympics with many events being held at Nakiska five minutes away – a small, mainly intermediate ski area with artificial snow covering 80% of the terrain.

Big White is British Columbia's highest ski area and has a reputation for having plentiful snow and Canada's best powder skiing; it has convenient ski-in, ski-out accommodation. Silver Star is a newly developed ski area, with its Gaslight Era base village built in 1890s style – we have had good reports of the new White Crystal hotel there. The old town of Vernon is nearby. Sun Peaks, near the town of Kamloops, is a name for the future. Former Olympic gold medallist Nancy Greene and her husband Al Raine did much to help develop Whistler (including building the Nancy Greene Lodge). They have now sold up and moved to Sun Peaks, where they are building a slope-side hotel and Nancy is Director of Skiing. There won't be much of a village there for a few years yet but the skiing offers interesting variety and when we were there last April it was deserted and delightfully groomed. It's a convenient place to warm up for a couple of days before a heli-skiing week at one of the nearby bases.

One or two of our reporters last season had a holiday touring around Canada's less well-known resorts and trying a few days' heli- or snowcat skiing. They recommend it highly.

As well as downhill skiing, other activities such as snowmobiling, cross-country skiing and dog-sledding are widely available. The main resorts of Eastern Canada, such as Mont Tremblant and Mont Ste Anne are covered in the Resort Directory at the back of this book.

With the Canadian dollar hitting hard times, now would be a good time to give Canada's skiing a go – you'll find prices low compared with the Alps.

Banff-Lake Louise 1340–1660m

✔ *Three ski areas between them have a large amount of skiing*

✔ *Excellent snow record over long season (November to May)*

✔ *Really spectacular high mountain scenery – the best in North America*

✘ *Can be extremely cold, especially in early season*

✘ *Separate ski areas are a long drive from each other and there is no accommodation at their bases*

There are few ski areas we have such mixed feelings about as Banff-Lake Louise. They are set in the spectacular and unspoilt Banff National Park. The landscape is one of glaciers, jagged peaks and magnificent views. The valleys are full of wildlife that you'll never see in Europe.

The accommodation is tremendous value because winter is their low season. The skiing has something for everyone, from steep couloirs to gentle cruising. The snow is some of the coldest, driest and most reliable you'll find anywhere in the world. And there's a lot of it.

And yet we have mixed feelings? Only because of the 'resorts'. They don't feel like ski resorts as we know them in Europe and the US, because they are miles away from their ski slopes. Banff, in particular, feels like what it is – a summer tourist trap trying to earn some extra money from the much quieter winter season.

ORIENTATION

Banff is a summer resort with three separate ski areas nearby, 10 to 45 minutes away by efficient bus – Lake Louise, Sunshine Village and Norquay-Mystic Ridge. **Lake Louise** 'village' is a five-minute drive from the ski area of the same name.

 The resort

Most people (including the people who work on the mountains) stay in Banff – which is a 45-minute drive from the largest ski area (Lake Louise), 20 minutes from the Sunshine area and 10 minutes from Mount Norquay-Mystic Ridge.

Banff is spectacularly set, with several towering peaks rising up around its outskirts. There is lots of wildlife around. Don't be surprised to find a herd of elk or long-horned sheep outside your hotel. And watch out for black (and even grizzly) bears on the drives to and from the skiing.

Banff gained its independence from the National Park authority in 1990.

Since then it has seen substantial growth and development. But it still consists largely of one long main street and a small network of side roads built in the usual North American grid fashion.

Banff is primarily a summer, rather than winter, resort – hotel prices double for the summer season. The main street is lined with hotels, condominiums, restaurants and tacky souvenir shops – many obviously catering for the Japanese market.

The buildings themselves have been successfully confined to low-rise developments. But despite many wooden clapboard buildings, it lacks genuine charm. It's not another Aspen or Telluride for atmosphere.

The only other place to stay is Lake Louise village, a five-minute drive from the ski area of the same name. But the village is not on the lake; that's another five-minute drive. And 'village' is rather too grand an expression for the tiny collection of hotels, condominiums, petrol station, supermarket, liquor store and few shops. If Banff lacks charm, Lake Louise village lacks it even more. But it does have one excellent hotel.

In marked contrast is Lake Louise itself, site of the Chateau Lake Louise hotel. In terms of scenery, you'd be hard-pressed to find anywhere more beautiful in your skiing travels.

In 1882, Tom Watson, a surveyor for the Canadian Pacific Railroad, was the first white man to set eyes on this lake and the 3564m Victoria Glacier towering above it. On seeing the view, Watson exclaimed, 'As God is my judge, I never in all my exploration have seen such a matchless scene.' Neither have we.

SKI FACTS

Altitude	1635m-2730m
Lifts	30
Pistes	6300 acres
Green	29%
Blue	49%
Black	22%
Art. snow	870 acres

 The skiing

In sharp contrast to our lack of enthusiasm for the villages, we find the skiing hard to beat. Taking account of all three mountains, the ski area is big, and the views are the most spectacular that the Rockies have to offer, rivalling the best in the Alps.

THE SKI AREA
A lot of moving around to do
The biggest of the three ski areas (claimed to be the biggest in North America in terms of skiable acreage, but it certainly isn't in terms of marked pistes) is **Lake Louise**.

Two successive high-speed quads take you to the top of the main mountain. From here, as elsewhere,

there's a choice of green, blue or black runs to other lifts. So skiers of varying standards can ski the same lifts together. Almost all the mountain is wooded, good for when it's snowing.

From the top there's a stunning view of some of the high peaks of the Continental Divide (which runs from Canada to New Mexico), including Canada's uncanny Matterhorn lookalike, Mount Assiniboine.

Go over the back of this top ridge and you're into Lake Louise's treeless back bowl skiing, which is predominantly north-facing and so keeps its snow in good condition.

From the bottom of the bowl runs you can take a lift back to the top again or up to the **Larch** area. This is the area's other mountain and was the original Lake Louise ski area. Served by one double chair, it has a number of pretty, wooded, relatively short runs. From the bottom you can return to the top of the main mountain or ski back to the main base area along a lengthy green path.

There are plans to build a lift up Richardson's Ridge, on the far side of the back bowls, and open up a whole new area of lift-served skiing.

The Lake Louise ski area is owned by Charles Locke, who amassed his fortune in oil and on the stock market. He bought the ski area in 1981 through his appropriately named company, Locke, Stock and Barrel. His wife is also appropriately named – yes, she's called Louise!

The second largest ski area is **Sunshine Village**, 20 minutes' drive from Banff, 40 from Lake Louise village. It has the highest skiing and best snow record in the area. It prides itself on not needing any artificial snow – we skied right to the bottom in late April without seeing a bare spot.

Most of the skiing is above the tree-line, up to 2730m. If the weather is bad, it is best to ski elsewhere. But in good weather, this is a great area.

You reach the ski area by taking a long (25-minute) gondola to the main on-mountain base.

For the 1995/6 season a whole new mountain is due to be opened up by new lifts, increasing the skiable area by over 60 per cent. It's Goat's Eye Mountain – the obvious white face above Wheeler Lift on our map over the page.

Even without the new area, Sunshine has enough skiing to keep the keenest skier happy for a couple of days, with lifts fanning out in all directions and good snow throughout a long season.

LIFT PASSES

95/96 prices in Canadian dollars
Tri-area lift pass
Covers all lifts and transport between Banff, Lake Louise and Sunshine Village.
Main pass
6-day pass 279
Children
Under 13: 6-day pass 102 (63% off)
Short-term passes
Half-day pass for individual areas of Lake Louise, Sunshine Village or Mystic Ridge/Norquay.
Notes Tri-area only available for 3 days or more, and includes a coupon worth 7 dollars towards other services at Mystic Ridge/Norquay.
Alternative passes
Day passes for individual areas of Lake Louise, Sunshine Village or Mystic Ridge/Norquay, with reductions for senior citizens.
Credit cards Yes

Mystic Ridge-Norquay was Banff's first – and remains its smallest – ski area, 10 minutes' drive from town and served by just five lifts. Until a few years ago, this area was known simply as Mount Norquay. It consisted of a tiny area of easy slopes at the bottom, and one lift higher up serving a choice of some of the toughest runs in the area. Then two new lifts were added which serve tree-lined, predominantly intermediate slopes. This area opens for floodlit night-skiing once a week.

SNOW RELIABILITY
Excellent
When we were last there, we found plenty of snow everywhere on both Lake Louise and Sunshine in late April. And that was at the end of what the locals claim was the worst winter for snow in many years. Mystic Ridge-Norquay was shut due to lack of customers rather than snow. Wherever it's needed, there's artificial snowmaking.

FOR ADVANCED SKIERS
Widespread pleasure
Good skiers will want to spend most of their time at the Lake Louise area. The back bowls offer endless variations of black mogul and powder runs. Many people's favourite is Paradise Bowl – one run is marked on the map but there are at least three commonly skied routes here, and scores of other variants. Others prefer the runs on the far left, which take you right away from all signs of lifts. The two steepest are Ridge Run and Whitehorn One. Again, there are endless variations.

Because this is National Park, you can ski anywhere. But the areas outside the boundaries aren't patrolled

and there's no avalanche control. A guide is essential.

On the front of the mountain there are more tough runs, including Outer Limits, Sunset and the Men's and Women's Downhills.

Sunshine has plenty of open bumps skiing above the tree-line. One particular novelty is a short, steep pitch, near the mid-station, known as the Waterfall run – because you do actually ski down over a snow-covered frozen fall. The new ski area also promises a lot of good advanced skiing – it is mainly steep terrain.

Until that opens, Norquay has the only double black diamond runs in the region, one a 35-degree bump run, the other a steep gunbarrel. There's a decent selection of other blacks to keep you happy.

FOR INTERMEDIATE SKIERS
Ideal runs wherever you go
In all three areas, at least 45 per cent of the runs are classified as intermediate. One thing which characterises both Lake Louise and Sunshine is that there is a wide choice of runs from the top of virtually all lifts. Wherever you look there are blue and green ways down – some of the greens as enjoyable (and pretty much as steep) cruises as the blues.

On Louise, Meadowlark is a beautiful tree-lined run from the top of the Eagle chair to the base area. Juniper and Juniper Jungle are wonderful cruising runs on the western side. The Larch area has some short but enjoyable intermediate terrain. And the adventurous should try the blue-graded Boomerang which starts with a hike from the top of the highest lift, the Summit Platter drag. On many runs one side is groomed, the other left to develop moguls.

Free ski-guiding

All three areas pride themselves on their free ski-guiding services. Just turn up at one of the two or three meeting times a day and meet your 'Ski Friend' – a volunteer who will show you around the area. You are divided into groups, according to ability and the type of runs you want to ski, and off you go.

You can use the service as many times as you want in order to get the chance to ski with people of similar ability to yourself.

This sort of service is common in the US now – but there it's normally seen as a mountain orientation tour and run once a day for a group of mixed ability. The Banff-Lake Louise service is another step forward – and they claim to have invented the idea which the Americans have copied. Lake Louise alone now has eight volunteer 'Ski Friends' available each day. All the reports we've had of the guiding have been very positive.

SKI SCHOOL

95/96 prices in
Canadian dollars

Club Ski
Guided tuition of the
three areas
Classes 5 days
4hr per day
5 full days: 195
Children's classes
Ages: 7 to 12
5 5hr days including
lunch: 190

On Sunshine, we particularly liked the World Cup Downhill run, which goes right from the top of the ski area down to the mid-mountain base. And don't ignore the Wa-wa T-Bar, which gives access to the often quiet Wa-Wa Bowl and Tincan Alley.

The Mystic Ridge area linked to Norquay was developed especially to attract intermediates and has 11 tree-lined blues and a couple of sometimes-groomed blacks served by two high-speed quads. It's worth trying.

FOR BEGINNERS
Excellent terrain
Louise has a good nursery area near the base, served by a short T-bar; Sunshine a good area by the mid-mountain base and served by an even shorter hand-tow. And Norquay has a small nursery area but no real runs for progressing beginners.

Recommended graduation runs for improvers on Louise are the gentle, wide Wixwaxy (designated a slow skiing zone, so there are no lunatics bombing past you) and the slightly more difficult Deer Run or Eagle Meadows.

There are even greens round the back bowls and in the Larch area – worth taking for the views.

Sunshine has the beginners-only Meadow Park among other user-friendly greens.

If you're a complete beginner with a party of friends who are experienced skiers and you want to meet up with them regularly, we don't recommend this area as ideal. Each mountain has its own ski school and you'll want to stick to one, whereas experienced skiers will probably want to split their days between the three areas.

FOR CROSS-COUNTRY
High in quality and quantity
It's a good area for cross-country. There are trails near Banff, around the Bow River, and on the Banff Springs golf course. But the best area is around Lake Louise, which has around 100km of groomed trails of all standards – watch out for the wolf packs!

QUEUES
Deserted during the week
Never a problem except on the busiest weekends. Half of the area's skiers are up from cities like Calgary on day passes, rather than holidaying for a week or more. So it's normally quiet during the week. We're told the worst weekend queues can be for the gondola up Sunshine in the morning.

The Lake Louise area is so confident it can handle skier numbers that it offers a full refund of your ski pass on any day you have to queue for more than ten minutes at the base area.

More of a problem than queues is the cold. Temperatures can fall to as low as -30°C. The high-speed chairs can then be extremely unpleasant.

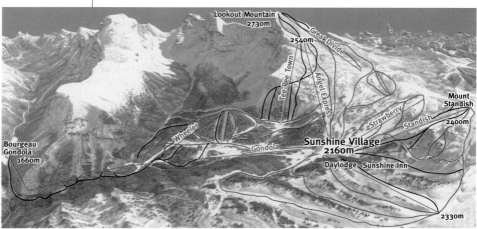

Labels on map: 2640m To Back Bowls and Larch; Top of the World 2530m; To Back Bowls and Larch; Summit; Top of the World; Eagle; 2090m; Whitehorn Lodge; Olympic; Friendly Giant; Olympic Chair; Friendly Giant Chairs; Whiskyjack Lodge 1660m

SKI SCHOOL
Caught on film
The Club Ski Program takes adults (16 and over) to all three mountains and offers a mixture of guiding and instruction, including free video analysis. We'd recommend it to anyone who wants to see the whole area while improving their technique too – reporters who've tried say it is superb. All standards are catered for. To ensure continuity, a reporter strongly recommends booking into a four- or five-day ski school course rather than taking odd lessons.

FACILITIES FOR CHILDREN
Each area has them
We have no first-hand reports of childcare facilities. But as in the US, arrangements for children seem thoroughly worked out.

 # Staying there

Wherever you stay (except at mid-mountain on Sunshine) it will be a drive or bus-ride to the slopes. Lake Louise village is the nearest place to a major ski area. But don't expect any resort ambience or much nightlife.

HOW TO GO
Superb-value hotels
There are no catered chalets available on the British market, but a wealth of hotels give plenty of options.
Hotels Summer is the peak season here. Hotel prices halve for the winter – so you can stay in luxury hotels at bargain rates.
In or near Banff:
£££ Banff Springs The luxury option in Banff, a turn-of-the-century, castle-style Canadian Pacific property. It's virtually a town within a town. It can sleep 2,000 people and has over 40 shops, 12 restaurants and bars, an Olympic-sized indoor pool and a separate outdoor pool.
£££ Caribou Lodge Opened in April 1993, on the main street, slightly out of town. It has a variety of wood-clad, interestingly and individually designed rooms, and a sauna and hot tub complex. It received a glowing report from one reporter this year.
£££ Rimrock Also opened in Spring 1993, spectacularly set, out of town on Sulphur Mountain, with outstanding views and a fully equipped health club.
££ Inns of Banff On the way into town; it has been recommended for its large rooms and health club facilities.
££ Banff Park Lodge In the town

CHILDCARE
Last year the nursery at Lake Louise took children aged 18 days to 6 years, from 8am to 4.30. The one at Sunshine Village takes children aged 19 months to 6 years, from 8.30 to 4.30. The one at Norquay's Cascade Lodge takes children aged 19 months, from 9am to 4pm. In all three, children aged 3 or more can take short ski lessons.

GETTING THERE
Air Calgary, transfer 2hr.

MOUNTAIN RESTAURANTS
Not bad for North America
All three mountains have eating facilities both at the base area and up the mountain. But most are cafeteria-style and serve the usual basics: burgers, hot dogs, sandwiches, soups.

On Louise, Temple Lodge, near the bottom of the Larch lift, is probably the most attractive, built in rustic style with a big terrace and choice of eating venues, including a table-service restaurant. Whitehorn Lodge, near the bottom of the Eagle chair, has excellent views from its balcony. At Whiskey Jack, at the base, the table-service restaurant is much better than the dire self-service cafeteria.

Sunshine Village has a choice of eating places at its mid-mountain base. The Daylodge and Old Sunshine Lodge serve fairly standard food and snacks. The Sunshine Inn (an on-mountain hotel) has the best food – table-service snacks in the Chimney Corner Lounge or a full lunch in the Eagle's Nest Dining Room.

On Mystic Ridge-Norquay, there's a new restaurant-cum-cafeteria at the main base. And the smaller, older Norquay Lodge, at the foot of the North American chair, serves snacks and has good views of skiing – but is only open at weekends and peak holiday periods.

PACKAGES

Accessible Isolation, Airtours, All Canada, American Connections, American Dream, American Skiworld, Chinook-It, Crystal, Frontier Ski, Inghams, Lotus Supertravel, Made to Measure, Neilson, Powder Byrne, Ski Activity, Ski Canada, Ski Independence, SkiBound, SkiGower, Thomson, USAirtours

Lake Louise
Accessible Isolation, All Canada, American Connections, American Dream, American Skiworld, Chinook-It, Crystal, Frontier Ski, Inghams, Lotus Supertravel, Made to Measure, Neilson, Ski Activity, Ski Canada, Ski Club of GB, Ski Independence, SkiGower, Solo's, USAirtours, Waymark Holidays

ACTIVITIES

Indoor Film theatre, museums, galleries, swimming pools (one with water slides), gym, squash, raquetball, weight training, bowling, jacuzzi, sauna, mini-golf, climbing wall
Outdoor Swimming in hot springs, ice skating, heli-skiing, horse-drawn carriage rides, sleigh rides, dog-sled rides, snowmobiles, curling, ice hockey, ice fishing, helicopter tours

TOURIST OFFICE

Ski Banff/Lake Louise
225 Banff Avenue
Box 1085
Banff, Alberta
TOL OCO
Tel 00 1 (403)
7624561
Fax 7628185

itself. Used by several British tour operators, large and central, with hot tub, steam room and indoor pool.
At Lake Louise village:
££££ Post A member of the Relais & Châteaux chain, with the best cuisine in the area, wood-panelled rooms and even a few log cabins in the grounds. Indoor pool, hot tub and steam room. Go for a room facing away from the railway to avoid the worst of the hooting trains during the night.
££ Lake Louise Inn The cheaper option in the village, still with pool, hot tub and sauna.
At Lake Louise itself:
£££ Chateau Lake Louise With stunning views over frozen Lake Louise, this 515-room Canadian Pacific-owned hotel has undergone multi-million dollar restoration over the last few years and has a choice of restaurants and a health club with indoor pool, steam room and hot tub.
££ Deer Lodge A simpler, cheaper option with a rooftop hot tub.
Self-catering Condominiums aren't as numerous as hotels but are available. The biggest complex is the Banff Rocky Mountain Resort, set in the woods on the edge of town, which has a wealth of in-house facilities including indoor pool, squash and hot tubs.

EATING OUT
International choice

The best cuisine in the region is in the Post Hotel restaurant at Lake Louise. The Chateau Lake Louise has two Alpine-style restaurants – the Walliser Stube, serving fondue and cured meats, and the Edelweiss, for more formal dining. It also has the Poppy Room, for family-style food. And there are other options in the village, such as the Station Restaurant and Frankie's Pizza and Pasta Café.

Banff has over 100 different restaurants, from McDonald's to fine dining in the Banff Springs Hotel. In between you'll find Italian, Greek, Chinese, Japanese, French and Mexican restaurants, steak houses, delis and pub snacks. The Beaujolais and Giorgio's are recommended at the top end of the price range. If you fancy fondued lizard or rattlesnake, try the Grizzly Bear.

APRES-SKI
Liveliest in Banff

One of the drawbacks of the area is that tea-time après-ski is limited because the villages are a drive from the ski areas.

But things liven up later, especially in Banff. Wild Bill's has live country and western music. The Rose & Crown has music and gets crowded. Barbary Coast often has live music and The Works nightclub and Whiskey Creek Saloon (both in the Banff Springs hotel) are popular.

Lake Louise is quieter. The Glacier Saloon, in Chateau Lake Louise, with traditional Wild West decor, often has live music until late. Charly Two's pub, in the Lake Louise Inn, has dancing until 2am. The Outpost Pub, in the Post Hotel, is worth trying, as is the Saddleback lounge, in the Lake Louise Inn.

FOR NON-SKIERS
Beautiful scenery

If you enjoy walking, the area has a lot of attractions. There are museums to visit such as The Whyte Museum of the Canadian Rockies, The Natural History Museum and The Luxton Museum of the Plains Indians. And, of course, there's the wildlife and the natural hot springs. Meeting up with skiers at lunchtime can be a drag.

There are sleigh rides, dog sledding, skating and tobogganing around the Banff Springs hotel area. Lake Louise has ice skating and broomball games.

STAYING UP THE MOUNTAIN
Worth considering

At Sunshine Village, the Sunshine Village Inn is the only ski-in, ski-out hotel. It is well run and has a good atmosphere, a big outdoor hot tub overlooking the slopes, good food and small but attractive rooms with excellent views. Unlike every other hotel in the area, it closes in summer, and its winter rates are as high as any.

STAYING IN OTHER RESORTS
The road to Jasper is stunning

An attractive option is to spend a couple of days in Jasper, with its own small ski area at Marmot Basin. The three-hour trip on the Columbia Icefields Parkway, through the Banff and Jasper National Parks, is one of the most beautiful drives in the world. The best place to spend the night here is the Jasper Park Lodge, log cabins set around a frozen lake. On the walk to breakfast, you may well encounter a herd of elk grazing outside your cabin.

Whistler 675m

HOW IT RATES

The skiing

Snow	★★★★
Extent	★★★★
Advanced	★★★★★
Intermediates	★★★★★
Beginners	★★★★
Convenience	★★★★
Queues	★★★★★
Restaurants	★

The rest

Scenery	★★★
Resort charm	★★★
Not skiing	★★

✔ *The biggest ski area in North America, with the largest vertical drop of over 1600m*

✔ *Spectacular 'Alpine' scenery with lots of 'ski-anywhere' above-the-tree-line skiing*

✔ *Good skiing for all standards*

✔ *Sea to Sky coast road from Vancouver is one of the most beautiful approaches to any ski resort in the world*

✔ *Modern pedestrianised resort built in pleasant 'West Coast' style with varied architecture*

✘ *Proximity to coast and low altitude means it can rain a lot at resort level*

✘ *Two separate ski areas are linked only at resort level*

✘ *Mediocre (but improving) mountain restaurants*

Whistler-Blackcomb has come from virtually nowhere in the 1970s to being voted the Number One resort in North America for the last three seasons by Snow Country – the US' best ski magazine.

Billions of Canadian dollars have been invested in developing two separate mountains (linked at their bases), each with considerable attractions, and two separate pedestrianised villages ten minutes' walk apart.

Both mountains have miles of skiing for all standards, the greatest vertical drops in North America, good snow guaranteed on the highest glacier runs, modern lift systems which whisk you rapidly back up the mountain and spectacular 'Alpine'-type scenery so often missing in US resorts. Between them they offer more piste skiing than any other North American resort.

So what's the catch? Only one main one as far as we're concerned. The weather. It's unpredictable in the extreme. It can be mind-numbingly cold. And because it's very near the coast, it can also be damp and dismal as the storms roll in from the Pacific. The rain normally turns to snow as you go up the lifts, but rain low down can dampen your spirits.

ORIENTATION

Whistler village and its smaller neighbour, **Blackcomb**, a 10-minute walk away, are set at the foot of their separate ski areas, a scenic 75-mile drive inland from Vancouver on Canada's west coast.

The main way up Whistler Mountain is by gondola which takes you from Whistler Village, up 1157m vertical, to the hub of the skiing. A high-speed chair-lift from **Whistler Creek**, 10 minutes by bus from the main village, also accesses the Whistler skiing. From Whistler village, a second gondola takes you part-way up Blackcomb Mountain, linking with Blackcomb's own lift system which starts with a high-speed quad from the base area. There are pistes linking both villages near the bottom of the ski area.

 ## The resort

Whistler started as a ski area in 1965 with the 'village' consisting of a few ramshackle buildings in what is now called Whistler Creek, a few miles from Whistler proper. It catered largely for day skiers from Vancouver.

Whistler village was built in the late 1970s on the site of what used to be the area's rubbish tip. Blackcomb village was developed in the 1980s. Both are traffic-free.

The architecture is varied and, for purpose-built resorts, quite tasteful. There are lots of chalet-style apartments built on the hillsides. The centres have individually designed wooden and concrete buildings, blended together in a master plan and built around a series of squares. There are no monstrous high-rise blocks. But there are a lot of large five- or six-storey hotel and apartment buildings.

The Japanese like the resort so much that they've bought up a substantial proportion of it and commissioned a replica to be built back home.

Whistler is the main resort, with nearly all the bars, restaurants and shops. It is built around two main squares – one at the base of the gondola and the other, the Village Square, a two-minute stroll away. Whistler North is being developed on the edge of the central area.

Blackcomb is much smaller and quieter with a limited range of shops and restaurants. Its 343-room Chateau Whistler hotel, built in true chateau style, dominates the views down into the village from the mountain.

Whistler Creek, a ten-minute bus-ride from the main Whistler village, is rather out on a limb with limited nightlife and eating and drinking places, though there are plans to develop it further.

There is a free bus service between Whistler and Blackcomb, with fares charged for going further out. But if you're staying centrally it's just as quick to walk between the two.

SKI FACTS

Altitude	650m-2285m
Lifts	28
Pistes	6997 acres
Green	20%
Blue	55%
Black	25%
Art. snow	70 acres

LIFT PASSES

95/96 prices in Canadian dollars

Dual Mountain Lift Ticket
Covers all lifts on both Whistler and Blackcomb mountains.

Beginners Daily program for beginners includes 2hr lesson, ski rental and pass (adult 60 per day).

Main pass
1-day pass 50
6-day pass 294

Senior citizens
Over 65: 6-day pass 210 (28% off)

Children
Under 13: 6-day pass 160 (46% off)
Under 7: free pass

Short-term passes
Half-day pass for each area separately.

Notes Dual mountain pass of 5 days or over gives one non-skiing day; 6-day pass valid for 7 days with one day non-skiing. Further discounts for 13- to 18- year-olds, (6-day pass 258).

Credit cards Yes

The skiing

The skiing has acquired a formidable reputation among good skiers. And that reputation is well deserved. There are some fearsomely steep chutes and lots of off-piste bowls.

But both mountains also have enormous amounts of well-groomed intermediate cruising terrain. Together they have over 200 marked pistes, and they form the biggest ski area, with the longest runs, in North America. But because of the low altitude of the base villages (less than 700m) it is often impossible to ski all the way back, especially in late season.

THE SKI AREA
The best in North America
Both Whistler and Blackcomb mountains have their own devotees who choose to ski just one non-stop. That practice is encouraged by the mountains being owned and run entirely separately, though two-mountain lift passes are now on sale.

The main way up **Whistler Mountain** is from Whistler Village by a long two-stage, 10-person gondola which rises over 1100m from the village at 650m to Pika's and The Roundhouse, the main mid-mountain base at 1810m.

From there runs fan out in all directions back down through the trees to a series of chairs which carry you back up again. There's no need to ski back to Whistler until the end of the day.

But the jewel in Whistler's crown only reveals itself when you reach the top of the gondola. There, high above you, lie Whistler's five magnificent above-the-tree-line bowls which reach 2178m – from left to right, Symphony, Harmony, Glacier, Whistler and West. You can ski more or less anywhere in these, and a few of the ways are pisted to make areas accessible for intermediates as well as good skiers. Last season a new high-speed quad made this skiing much more accessible.

Access to **Blackcomb Mountain** was also greatly improved by the new Excalibur 8-person sit-down gondola which opened last season. This starts in Whistler Village with a mid-station just above the Blackcomb base area. It finishes part-way up Blackcomb Mountain and is met by another new high-speed quad chair. There is also a route up Blackcomb by a series of high-speed chairs starting from the Blackcomb base area. The 1610m vertical rise from Blackcomb village at 675m to the top of the 7th Heaven Express at 2285m is the largest in North America (and impressive even by European standards).

One of the second-stage chairs, the Solar Coaster Express, takes you to the main mid-mountain base and the Rendezvous restaurant at 1860m. From here there's a wide variety of runs through the trees in all directions and for all standards. Two different peaks can be reached from a chair down to the right or a chair and a T-bar to the left. Both access the summer skiing area on the Horstman Glacier. And the T-bar also brings you (with a short climb) to the Blackcomb Glacier in the next valley – a beautiful run which takes you right away from all lifts and signs of civilisation.

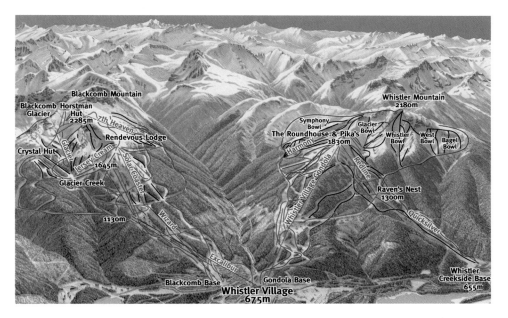

Blackcomb Mountain · Blackcomb Glacier · Horstman Hut 2285m · 7th Heaven · Rendevous Lodge · Crystal Hut · Jersey Cream 1645m · Glacier Creek · Solar Coaster · 1130m · Wizard · Excalibur · Blackcomb Base · Gondola Base · Whistler Village 675m · Whistler Mountain 2180m · Symphony Bowl · Glacier Bowl · The Roundhouse & Pika's 1830m · Harmony · Whistler Bowl · West Bowl · Bagel Bowl · Whistler Village Gondola · Redline · Raven's Nest 1300m · Quicksilver · Whistler Creekside Base 655m

SNOW RELIABILITY
Good high up, poor low down
Snow conditions at the top are usually excellent. But because the resort is low and close to the Pacific, the bottom part of the mountains can be wet or unskiable. Blackcomb has more snowmaking than Whistler Mountain – one of the reasons it shuts later (at the end of May).

FOR ADVANCED SKIERS
Few can rival it
Whistler-Blackcomb has acquired a cult reputation with professional ski bums in the last few years. Whistler Mountain's bowls alone are enough to keep experts happy for weeks. Each of the five has endless possible variations, with chutes and gullies of varied steepness and width. The biggest challenges are around Glacier, Whistler and West Bowls, with runs such as The Cirque and Doom & Gloom – though you can literally ski anywhere in this high and wide area. Access to the bowls was greatly improved last season by the new high-speed quad Harmony chair-lift.

Blackcomb has its challenging bowl skiing too. But it's not as extensive or set as dramatically as Whistler's. From the top of the Seventh Heaven lift you can traverse across to the right to Xhiggy's Meadow, where there's good sunny bowl skiing. Or if you're feeling brave you can drop over the ridge behind you down the infamous 41° Couloir Extreme (used to be called Saudan Couloir). Amazingly, there's a public race down here each year, late in the season, which attracts entrants from all over the world. Alternatively, you can walk up a little from the run down from the Glacier Express lift and ski down Ruby Bowl, Helterskelter or Spanky's to join the Blackcomb glacier run.

On both mountains there are challenging black mogul runs on the lower part below the tree-line.

If all this isn't enough, there's also local heli-skiing available – something that British Columbia is famous for.

FOR INTERMEDIATE SKIERS
Ideal and extensive terrain
Both mountains are paradise. Good intermediates will enjoy the less extreme variations in the bowls on both mountains in good weather.

One of our favourite intermediate runs is the Blackcomb Glacier from the top of the mountain at almost 2300m down to the bottom of the new high-speed quad at 1130m. This 5km run starts with a short two-minute climb up from the top of the Showcase T-bar over the ridge and into the valley hidden behind. You drop into a wide, wide bowl – the further you traverse, the shallower the slope becomes. A large part of the attraction of the run for us is being away from sight of all lifts.

You are guaranteed good snow on the Horstman Glacier runs too. This is Blackcomb's summer ski area, with typically gentle top-of-the-mountain glacier runs. Lower down there are large numbers of perfectly groomed cruising runs through the trees – perfect when the weather is bad.

On Whistler Mountain, there are easy blue pistes in Symphony, Harmony and Glacier bowls, which allow even early intermediates to try the bowls for themselves, always knowing there's an easy way down. The new Harmony Express lift and the construction of an easier way into Glacier Bowl has greatly improved the bowl skiing for intermediates. The blue path round the back from the top of the Peak chair, which skirts West Bowl, has beautiful views over a steep valley and across to Black Tusk (an apt name for the phallic-shaped top of this famous mountain).

Lower down the mountain there is a vast choice of groomed blue runs with a series of efficient fast chairs to bring you back up to the top of the gondola. It's a cruiser's paradise – especially the aptly named Ego Bowl. A great run to take at the end of the day is the Dave Murray Downhill all the way from mid-mountain to the finish in town. Although marked black on the map, it's a wonderful fast and varied cruise when it has been groomed.

FOR BEGINNERS
A great place to learn
Whistler has excellent nursery slopes by the mid-station of the gondola – and Blackcomb's slopes are down at the base area. Both also have facilities higher up if the snow lower down isn't too good.

On Whistler, Upper Whiskey Jack is a gentle first run from the top of the gondola after progressing beyond the nursery slopes. You can return to its start by various chair-lifts or continue right down to the base area on simple greens. There is a variety of other green runs, and many of the blue runs are only a little steeper or narrower.

On Blackcomb, Green Line goes right from the top of the mountain to the bottom. The top part is a particularly gentle run, with a couple of steeper pitches below the Rendezvous Restaurant and mid-mountain base.

FOR CROSS-COUNTRY
Picturesque but low
There are over 15km of cross-country tracks starting in the valley by the frozen river, on the path between Whistler and Blackcomb, and heading off towards the Lost Lake. And there is more cross-country around the golf courses. But all this is at low altitude, so conditions can be unreliable. Keen cross-country merchants can catch the train to better areas.

QUEUES
Weekend invasions
During the week there's rarely a problem with queues. At weekends, crowds pour in from Vancouver and can create a wait to get up Whistler Mountain. But the new Excalibur gondola has speeded up access to Blackcomb a lot. And once up the mountain, people are moved very quickly by the high-speed quads.

On Whistler, the new Harmony chair-lift has taken the pressure off the slow old Peak chair – which used to be the only way up.

MOUNTAIN RESTAURANTS
Blackcomb better than Whistler
Whistler's main eating venue is Pika's, at the top of the gondola. It is a fairly charmless self-service refuelling stop. It gets incredibly crowded, has a separate bar and an upstairs Sushi Bar.

The Roundhouse, a few yards up the hill, is not much better. It's a circular building with seats round the outside and the serving areas in the centre. There's a salad bar as well as the standard burgers and chilli.

Raven's Nest Café, at the top of the chair up from Whistler Creek, serves the best food on the mountain. It is tiny, with a small terrace with good views down to the creek. Its specialities are pasta and Japanese food, but we've also had great peppery paté and Caesar Salad with Cajun Chicken there.

Rendezvous is Blackcomb's mid-mountain base. It is a massive self-service restaurant, with paper plates and plastic cutlery, which also houses the ski school office. Christine's, at the same location, is the only table-service restaurant around, serving an up-market selection of food (snails, smoked salmon, steaks) and offering an award-winning wine list.

A splendid, large, attractive new restaurant, Glacier Creek Lodge, has been built at the bottom of the Glacier Express lift. This is the best place on either mountain – with good food and a wide choice including stir-fry, pasta

SKI SCHOOL
94/95 prices in Canadian dollars
Whistler and Blackcomb
Guided instruction with Ski Esprit course
Classes 6 days full-day from 8.45
6 full days: 336
Children's classes
Ages: 3 to 12
5 6hr days including lunch: 185
Private lessons
1hr or full-day
70 for 1hr

CHILDCARE

The Kids' Kamp, at the base of Blackcomb, has a huge dining area and nursery area inside, snow garden and special lifts outside. It takes non-skiing children aged 18 months to 3 years, as well as acting as the base for ski tuition.

Both ski schools have special programmes for young children. Wee Scamps on Whistler and Wee Wizards on Blackcomb take children aged 2 to 3, from 8.30 to 3.30. Super Kids and Ski Scamps take older children, with different schemes for different levels of skiing competence.

GETTING THERE

Air Vancouver, transfer 2hr.

PACKAGES

Accessible Isolation, All Canada, American Connections, American Dream, American Skiworld, Chinook-It, Crystal, Frontier Ski, Inghams, Lotus Supertravel, Made to Measure, Neilson, Powder Byrne, Ski Activity, Ski Canada, Ski Independence, Ski Miquel, SkiBound, Thomson, Trail Alpine, USAirtours

Blackcomb Frontier Ski, Ski Independence

and salad bars.

The two alternatives are tiny mountain huts built to resemble Alpine refuges. Crystal Hut, at the top of the Crystal Ridge chair, has Buffalo Burgers and Buffalo Stew. Horstman Hut, at the top of the mountain, attempts to create a Bavarian feel and does excellent strudels.

SKI SCHOOL
Very high standards

Whistler and Blackcomb have separate ski schools. The joint programme, Ski Esprit, is as much a guiding service as it is ski instruction. It runs for three or four full days and includes a welcome reception, prizes and après-ski – we've had excellent reports of it.

As well as standard group and private lessons, both mountains offer specialist courses and clinics. There is also snowboard instruction.

Children are well catered for with a variety of different programmes for different ages.

There are also highly-praised, free, twice-daily guided tours of each mountain. These are grouped by skiing standard and one reporter had two splendid sessions on Whistler with a fast-moving 'Steep and Deep' group, skiing runs he'd otherwise never have found.

FACILITIES FOR CHILDREN
Comprehensive

The facilities are as impressive as usual in North America. Blackcomb's base area has a special, slow-moving Magic Chair to get children part-way up the mountain. Whistler's gondola mid-station has a splendid dedicated kids-only area. Our main reservation about taking young children here would be the weather. Playing in a snow garden in falling snow is one thing; in falling rain, something else.

⬆ Staying there

The most convenient places to stay are the two main villages. A lot of chalets and apartments are an inconvenient bus-ride from the villages and ski areas. And Whistler Creek, though convenient for Whistler's skiing, is less so for getting to Blackcomb and has much less life than the main villages.

HOW TO GO
High quality packages

A lot of British tour operators have recently 'discovered' Whistler. Between them they offer a wide range of very comfortable accommodation,

though catered chalets are thin on the ground.

Chalets We know of no catered chalets but Frontier Ski will provide evening meals in their condos on request.

Hotels There is a very wide range. **£££££ Chateau Whistler** The top hotel, huge and impressive, modern but in traditional Canadian Pacific château-hotel style. Ideally placed at the foot of Blackcomb Mountain. It has an indoor-outdoor pool, exercise machines, saunas etc.

££££ Delta Mountain Inn Big, modern, stylish, in the heart of Whistler village; health club, covered tennis courts, pool.

££££ Crystal Lodge Formerly the Nancy Greene Lodge, now Japanese-owned; good reputation, centrally placed in Whistler, 140 rooms, friendly staff, recommended by reporters. Pool.

£££ Timberline Lodge Fairly central Whistler. Pool, hot tub and sauna.

£££ Glacier Lodge In Blackcomb. Pool, hot tub and sauna.

Self-catering There are plenty of spacious, comfortable condominiums in both chalet- and hotel-style blocks available through British tour operators.

EATING OUT
High quality and plenty of choice

There is no shortage of good places to eat. Whistler is thought expensive by Canadian standards. As a rough guide, expect pasta dishes to be between C$6 and C$10, main course meat dishes C$12 to C$20.

In Whistler Village, Umberto's is highly regarded for Italian cuisine, Val d'Isère for French, Chez Joel for fondue. Another favourite is the Keg, renowned for great steaks, seafood and its huge salad bar. Brandy's bar is a popular pre-dinner rendezvous. There are numerous Japanese restaurants catering for the substantial number of Japanese visitors. Sushi Village is good and reasonably priced.

In Blackcomb, the Wildflower restaurant in the Chateau Whistler serves excellent innovative dishes and there's a good tapas bar in the hotel too. Rua has a good reputation for Mediterranean cooking, and Monk's Grill for prime rib and steaks.

But locals reckon the best place to eat is the Rim Rock Café and Oyster Bar at Whistler Creek, especially for its seafood and salmon dishes. Highly regarded French cuisine is served at Deux Gros, a beautiful restaurant which is a five- to ten-minute walk from the village.

PISTE ARTISTE

helped us to compile the Eating out and Après-ski sections. Our thanks to them.

ACTIVITIES

Indoor Ice skating, museum, tennis, hot tubs
Outdoor Flightseeing, heli-skiing, para-gliding, snowmobiling, snow-shoe excursions, fishing, horse-riding, sleigh rides, guided tours

TOURIST OFFICE

Postcode VON 1BO
Tel oo 1 (604)
9324222
Fax 9327231

Other good value recommendations in Whistler Village include the Old Spaghetti Factory, Peter's Underground, Boston Pizza, Citta's and a burger joint called A and W.

APRES-SKI
Something for most tastes
With over 50 bars, night-clubs and restaurants, Whistler is very lively by North American standards. The two favourite bars immediately after skiing are the Longhorn at Whistler and Merlin's at Blackcomb, both at the foot of the slopes. The former has a huge terrace that is particularly popular in spring; inside, the place rocks till after midnight. Dusty's is the place to go at Whistler Creek – good beer and nachos. Citta 2000 is another popular early evening bar. Black's Pub in Whistler is favoured for its supposedly English decor, but Tapply's is arguably more interesting – a bit of a dive frequented by local workers.

The Mallard bar in Chateau Whistler and the Crystal Lodge Piano Bar are popular for a more relaxed and sophisticated time.

Later on, Garfinkel's has occasional live rock 'n roll and attracts local college students as well as tourists. Tommy Africa's is good for a thumpin', pumpin' bop and comes complete with Go-Go dancers. The Savage Beagle Club is a trendy night club and very popular with Vancouver yuppies. Waitresses sport hip-holstered tequila bottles and crossed shoulder-belts of glasses.

To experience 'redneck' Canada try the Boot – live music, pool and seemingly the cast from Thelma and Louise. Strippers are even brought in to attract punters in the off-season! It's a five-minute drive north of the village.

FOR NON-SKIERS
Not ideal
Whistler is a long way to go if you aren't going to sample the superb skiing. The villages are quiet during the day. Non-skiers can get tickets for the gondola and main chair-lifts. The health club in the Delta is open to non-residents, and there are some other activities available. Excursions to Vancouver and to Squamish (famous for its wild eagles) are easy.

STAYING DOWN THE VALLEY
We wouldn't
Staying out of town basically means staying at Whistler Creek or along the road between there and the main village. There's a regular bus service until just after midnight.

Accommodation is cheaper but the ambience is not as nice and the nightlife not nearly as lively or varied.

Scotland

✔ It's easy to get to, at least from northern Britain; short-breaks are a realistic proposition

✔ It is possible to experience perfect snow and stirring skiing

✔ Decent, cheap accommodation and good value packages are on offer

✔ Mid-week is rarely crowded

✔ There are extensive ski-touring and ski-mountaineering possibilities

✔ Minimal or no travel, language, currency and insurance hassles

✔ Lots for non-skiers to do

✘ Weather is frequently changeable and sometimes vicious

✘ Snowfall is erratic, and has been poor in several recent seasons

✘ Ski areas are small; runs tend to be short

✘ Queueing can be a problem - though usually only at peak times and if lifts are closed

✘ Little ski village ambience and few memorable mountain restaurants

So what's the point in flogging up there to find roads closed, wind strength in double figures and small ski areas with limited facilities, runs of rutted ice and lift company staff that seem less than delighted to see you? It might be fiction based on just a few old facts but it is still how some skiers, and not only those from the deep south, view the prospect of skiing in Scotland. And there's no doubt that as the masses discovered skiing in the Alps in the 1970s and early 1980s any attempt to replicate the experience in Scotland was doomed to disappointment. It seemed like whenever the snow was good either the roads were impassable or the lift-queues were unbelievable. Happily, much has changed – and if Scotland was relegated to the "probably never again" list more than a decade ago, then it's time to give it another go. The weather might still be unpredictable but skiing is a winter sport after all and there's nowhere better than Scotland to learn some respect for the mountains in winter. If you must have blue skies, perfect pistes and charming mountain restaurants, forget it. Otherwise chuck the boards in the car and get up there – you'll have a great time; or you'll hate it – but at least you'll know.

Obviously it's unfair to compare Scotland with the Alps or the Rockies – that's why we all do it. Likewise it would be sloppy to think of the five ski areas just as parts of the same thing – they're surprisingly different from one another. They do though share some characteristics, and in some ways are similar to small Norwegian downhill areas – but then there aren't many of us bother going to Norway to ski these days, so that comparison isn't very useful either. If it wasn't on our doorstep – relatively speaking – then Scotland's skiing would be of little interest. As it is, it's probably cheaper to fly to Geneva from London than it is to Inverness – just to use another unfair comparison. But it's a lot handier to nip up to Aviemore for the weekend from Newcastle than it is to nip out to Avoriaz, say.

Some up-to-date and accurate information on conditions and the weather forecast is particularly important for those contemplating a trip at short notice. Snow conditions and the weather can vary dramatically from one area to the next – especially from west to east. In general terms, snow cover has been poor in a number of recent seasons – the spectre of global warming has been hovering since the late 80s, and the desperately poor 91/92 season when the Alps also had a very lean time of it. Confidence is now returning with good snow in the last two seasons.

As the ski areas and their regional tourist boards strive to maintain or improve visitor numbers, they do appear to recognise the reality that there's a limited number of skiers who are going to book their main one- or two-week holiday at a Scottish resort. A bit more positive promotion might well help. There's long been a tradition of season-ticket holders and club skiers from all parts of Scotland and the north of England providing a hard-core at each area – but future growth is most likely to arrive via more attractive beginners' packages and the long weekend or short week break. There are plenty of skiers gasping for the chance of a cheap break to warm up for the main holiday or just to get in a few more days than usual in a season.

For novices who are really keen to learn – and who are prepared for the possibility of less than ideal conditions – Scotland should prove an excellent choice. One option is to book instruction via one of the outdoor centres, many of which also provide accommodation. They are likely to provide quality instruction, value for money and access to some alternative activities if skiing is impossible. There's no escaping the fact that conditions can be testing. Gales, icy slopes, rain, slush, fog, rocks and heather are not unheard of – for the instructors it can be like working in victim support. The 'up' side is that those who survive the learning experience and go on to ski regularly in Scotland tend to finish up as strong, versatile skiers capable of extracting maximum pleasure from the most marginal of skiing conditions.

For skiers into at least the intermediate phase of their careers, a tour (by car not ski) that takes in all five ski areas is a great way to spend a week. At a push this is feasible from the one base – in the Spey Valley somewhere – but it is far more interesting to move between the resorts, staying close to the ski area in each case. Compare and contrast the likes of Aviemore and Fort William with Tomintoul or the Kings House in Glencoe. For non-skiers in your group or for you on non-skiing days there are quite a number of reasonably amusing diversions – like distilleries, castles, ospreys, clay-pigeons and monsters (only one). Not recommended for every day of your principal ski vacation but not too bad as a fallback.

As a sweeping generalisation and for skiers who have been to a few Alpine resorts but who don't know Scottish skiing, it's fair to say that most of the slopes in most of the areas fall somewhere around the intermediate level. But it should also be stated that all areas, apart from the Lecht, do offer the occasional piece of tough or very tough skiing. Much of the terrain is suitable for ski touring and ski mountaineering; Cairngorm especially is something of a centre of expertise for these and many other mountain activities.

Scotland's failing in the eyes of many is in the softer issues – like style, ambience, attitude. All these elements are better than they were – Nevis Range has probably had a lot to do with that – but Aviemore is still ugly, Fort William is hard to like and cosy, charming cafe-bars and restaurants are still too few in number. Licensed restaurants have appeared at the slopes in the last few years, bringing not just alcohol but also much better catering. The snack-hut has not yet disappeared completely – one or two may survive as a testimony to our past.

The limited facilities at the base areas (none has accommodation) mean that après-ski – of the kind that starts at 4pm on the spectacular and sunny terrace of a magnificent chalet and goes on until it's too late for dinner – is seldom available. By 5pm almost everybody has gone. The trick is to find out if they've all gone to the same place and get there too. There is night-life, there are reasonable pubs and bars – but it's like Scotland not Switzerland.

If you do decide to go, call the relevant tourist offices for information and advice; get the latest Ski Scotland brochure and regional accommodation guides and get on up there. A car, sadly, is almost a necessity – though if Aviemore or Fort William is your only destination then the train would be an appropriate way to travel.

Cairngorm 555m

Still Scotland's main ski centre, but perhaps feeling the pressure more than ever before, Cairngorm does offer more variety in its skiing than any of the other centres and, whatever you might think of Aviemore, also has the nearest thing in Scotland to a ski village. There are plenty of places to eat and drink and at times the town is fairly lively – bordering on the boisterous. There are now ambitious plans on the table to install a bottom-to-top funicular, replacing the ageing two-stage chair system of Coire Cas.

THE RESORT

Aviemore is the main centre but a significant amount of Cairngorm business also comes in from other villages in the Spey Valley – Newtonmore, Kingussie, Nethy Bridge, Grantown and others accommodate many skiers in a variety of hotels and guest houses, B&Bs, chalets and outdoor activity centres. In general, these are more traditional Highland villages – albeit tourism-oriented – whilst Aviemore is a real one-off.

Aviemore first discovered the joys of tourism when the Victorians discovered the Highlands; but it was the developments of the 1960s that put the town on the map for skiers. The Aviemore Centre epitomises the period in which it was built; it was cheap, functional and ugly. Age has not been kind to this place – it's more ugly than ever – yet it remains the key to the success of the ski area; providing much of the accommodation and other visitor facilities. Along with the plan to build a funicular for the ski area, there are other redevelopments on their way, among them new hotels and an indoor sports centre.

Aviemore is approached by car via the much-improved A9. The London-Inverness rail line runs through the town and regular bus services link the ski area with Aviemore (about 9 miles) and other Speyside villages.

THE SKIING

The **ski area**, which lies between 555m and 1145m, is accessed from car parks about a mile apart at the base of two corries – Coire Cas (the main area) and Coire na Ciste (a narrow gulley with the toughest skiing in it). The two sectors come together at the Ptarmigan beginners' area just below the summit of Cairn Gorm. The Ciste car park is used only when the Cas is full and a shuttle bus then operates between them. There are chair lifts operating from both base areas and, as the snowline recedes up the hill, they provide access to the skiing. If you've never been on a sideways chair, this is your big chance.

There is no snowmaking but snowfences are used to trap and hold snow for as long as possible. They aren't sufficient to give high **snow reliability** over the whole area but they do help to keep the snow in place for skiing (around some of the lifts) until late May or even into June.

Advanced skiers will find the West Wall and some routes on the opposite side of the Ciste gulley very challenging – the West Wall is always closed in icy conditions; it's very dangerous. The bumps between the West Wall chair and tow and various routes down the centre of the Ciste gulley are fun. In the Cas area the White Lady, the most famous run, is frequently heavily mogulled. Some interesting off-piste excursions into adjacent corries or onto the slopes above the lift-served area are worth the trouble for those that don't object to a little walking or skinning. Be warned that there is sometimes a high risk of avalanches in these corries.

Intermediates should be able to cope with any run save the West Wall and any big moguls left lying around. The best long cruising run is M2 down from the Ptarmigan which loops round to the West Wall tow or down through the wide Aonach bowl. The run is often deserted and the snow lovely. It's a shame the alternative route alongside the Day Lodge tow and back to the Cas car park usually loses its snow early – this also means the loss of the key low-level link between the Cas and Ciste areas. The tows under the Fiacaill Ridge provide the rest of the intermediate skiing.

Beginners generally head for the Cas car park lifts – best to avoid the Ciste area at this stage – and get weaving in the somewhat congested zone below the Shieling. The runs are too narrow for those of a nervous disposition, especially with the associated hazards of snowfences, uplift lines and faster skiers. The Ptarmigan area is a much better bet if the weather is being kind – runs are smooth and wide. Unfortunately, strong winds are a feature of the Cairngorms and the Ptarmigan frequently bears the brunt of them – it can be windy even inside the cafe.

For **cross-country** skiers there are trails in the Glenmore Forest and the Highland Guides Nordic centre at Inverdruie just outside Aviemore offer courses from basic techniques to fast downhill telemarking.

The chairs are old, slow and slated for replacement so **queues** can build up at peak times, when the weather forces closures or simply on nice weekends when everyone decides to go skiing at the same time. There's congestion on the slopes at the bottom of the Cas area and at the top of White Lady where several lifts arrive near to one another and T-bars have to be allowed to retract gently – no problem if you, and everybody else, are awake and in control. Weekdays are usually fairly quiet.

There are **mountain restaurants** at each of the base areas, at the Shieling (midway up Coire Cas) and at the very top. The Ptarmigan restaurant is still the highest eating place in the land. Whilst it's an interesting building and a renowned Cairngorm landmark, it's a pretty grim restaurant. And if you wish to eat a packed lunch there you have to sit in the lobby outside the toilets. Only the cafe-bar in the Day-lodge at the Cas car park can really be recommended as a pleasant venue for food or drink, and real coffee and decent beer are available.

The lift company does not operate a **ski school** but there are a total of ten schools (including one snowboard school) from Aviemore and the surrounding area that regularly use the facilities. Some, such as Newtonmore and Insh Hall schools, will put together full packages including accommodation. The National Outdoor Centre at Glenmore Lodge offers good-value board and lodging and ski tuition at various levels – its instructors are among the best in the business. The Uphill Ski Club is based at Nethy Bridge is one of the organisations now helping disabled skiers onto the slopes. Ski Sporthaus seem well organised and good value for children – but only down to seven years old. Other schools deal with children as young as four.

TOURIST OFFICES

Cairngorm Chairlift Company
(pass prices and ski information)
01479 861261

Aviemore Tourist Office
(accommodation and ski school information)
01479 810363

STAYING THERE

There's no accommodation at the ski area. The Stakis Coylumbridge, the nearest hotel, offers good-value packages, a wooded location and the famous Cyril the Squirrel's funhouse where even the under-5's are welcome. The Red Mcgregor Hotel is centrally located in Aviemore and has a leisure centre with swimming pool. A good bet for pleasant surroundings and excellent value is a DB&B arrangement at one of the many private **hotels** or guest houses in the area. They vary from simple B&B's to upmarket hotels with serious kitchens. On the list of quality accommodation are The Ossian Hotel (Kingraig), The Scotts Hotel (Kingussie), Corrour House Hotel (Inverdruie), Morrfield House Hotel (Boat of Garten), Feith Mhor Country House (Carrbridge) and Auchendean Lodge Hotel (Dulnain Bridge).

There are chalets, cottages, houses and caravans – and even the occasional castle – to rent on a **self-catering** basis.

The bigger hotels all have **restaurants** open to outsiders – the Ossian Hotel's can't be matched. There's a strip of activity down Aviemore's main street providing fish & chips (Smithy's Chip Shop has been voted best in Scotland) and pizzas. The Boathouse Restaurant at Kincraig and the Craggan Mill at Grantown are amongst those places worth travelling for. The Old Bridge Inn offers the best bar food in the valley. And if clootie dumpling is important to you there's a place at Dulnain Bridge that's waiting for you.

For the **après-ski** late in the evening Crofter's Show Bar is the best dance haunt. Chevvy's features alternative music and is a focal point for snowboarders of the grungier variety. The Winking Owl tends to be preferred by skiers, although it does house a snowboard school. Various hotels have live entertainment from time to time and karaoke evenings still feature in many of the bars. The Old Bridge Inn is a lively, traditional pub tucked away off the main street.

Non-skiers should be able to find plenty to do in Aviemore and Speyside; in springtime the area is ideal as a base for touring the Highlands – to view Loch Ness and Ben Nevis or to visit castles and whisky distilleries, for example. Lots of alternative activities are also available, including off-road driving courses.

Glencoe 305m

The enigma remains and is going strong almost 40 years after the first lift went in. Despite recent improvements and modernisations the Glencoe skiing experience is still a rough diamond that, on a good day, won't be bettered in Scotland. The views over the moor and down the glen are superb and there's just enough skiing to keep all levels of skier fully occupied. On a bad day, the snow cover is broken, the lifts are either buried or taking frequent rests and the views are a myth. It can be a bleak and frustrating place.

THE SKIING

The **ski area**, which lies between 305m and 1108m, is on the slopes of Meall A Bhuiridh at the edge of Rannoch Moor and just east of Glen Coe – a moody and magnificent setting if ever there was one. The base area is a car park and a few buildings housing the cafe, ticket office and a museum of skiing and mountaineering. The Access lift is now a double chair and this rises to the Plateau tow, which opens up the main nursery area and provides access to the other tows and the bulk of the skiing.

The upper slopes around the top tows (one button and one T-bar) enjoy good **snow cover**, often for a season that lasts from December to May. Too much snow – burying the pylons – has been a problem in the past; the pylons are now being heightened. Snow reliability lower down is not as good and more often than not it's necessary to take the chair lift back down to the car park. If there is sufficient snow to ski this then advanced skiers will enjoy it; beginners should not attempt it and others should give it careful thought.

The tops of the mountain runs – especially Flypaper – are steep enough to be challenging to **advanced skiers** and there's scope for lots of variants around here.

Intermediate skiers can take various routes below the summit of Meall A Bhuiridh and will probably find even the 'blues' a good challenge. Etive Glades is a good place to start but expect grooming to be minimal.

Beyond the nursery slopes on the Plateau, **beginners** can take a ride up the Cliffhanger chair and loop down along Mugs Alley – after that it can be tricky to make the next move.

Queues form at the ticket windows if the car park is nearly full – as it often is on good weekends – and although the Access chair is no longer the bottleneck it was, the Plateau tow has become the problem. Beginners use it routinely for the nursery slopes

and everybody else wants to use it to access the other lifts. The solution is to walk across the plateau – five minutes or so – or get there earlier.

The Plateau cafe would be embarrassed to be called a **mountain restaurant**, as it's still a pretty basic hut, but it's warm and moist and a lot of people like that. It also serves damn fine bacon rolls. The log cabin restaurant at the car park is licensed and quite pleasant.

There is only the one **ski school** operating. It also organises the on-site ski hire and can put it all together with an acommodation deal, if required. **Children** are a problem.

STAYING THERE

The only **hotel** nearby is the splendidly isolated Kings House Hotel – about a mile away – and just the job if all that's needed is skiing, food, a decent bar and a bed. They also have a bunkhouse and an area for tents, if you're hard-up, hard or both. And whatever the weather, there is always someone camping there. Down the road a few miles are the villages of Glencoe, Ballachulish and Onich and some more options for accommodation. The Isles of Glencoe at Ballachulish is a striking new hotel with decent rooms and a good leisure centre – including whirlpool, sauna and steam room. Onich, across the bridge over the entrance to Loch Leven, has several medium-sized, good-quality hotels which are generally much less busy in winter than during the coach party season. The Outdoor Centre in Glencoe village is a good choice for families or groups looking for a ski package.

For **restaurants** it's the hotels; and for **après-ski** it is hard to beat the famous Clachaig Inn which often has live music, sometimes a beer festival and is never dull.

Non-skiers or skiers on a day off can head south to Loch Lomond and Glasgow, north to Fort William or west to Oban and the coast.

TOURIST OFFICES

Glencoe Ski Centre
(pass prices, local accommodation)
01855 811303

Fort William Tourist Office
(accommodation, general information)
01397 703781

Glenshee 640m

The striking thing about Glenshee is the way it has expanded – mainly during the 1980s – into a system that now boasts 26 lifts and has comfortably the biggest area and uplift capacity of the Scottish ski areas. It remains, however, primarily a venue for day trippers because of the lack of a major accommodation centre at hand. Most of the skiing is suitable for intermediates and beginners.

THE SKIING

The **ski area**, which lies between 640m and 1068m, does allow for more of a feeling of travelling around than any of the other areas – particularly in the Sunnyside sector where the lifts go over two ridges and then down into Coire Fionn for the most distant and highest lift, up Glas Maol. On the other side of the A93, above the Ski Centre, the runs are ranged across the slopes below and between Cairn Aosda and the Cairnwell – two more Munros which can be 'bagged' very cheaply indeed.

Glenshee suffered more than most during the recent lean winters and has now invested in snowmaking equipment – which allowed the area to open at the end of November for the 93/94 season. At present the equipment is used primarily to cover the Claybokie run but other runs are being considered and this should certainly improve **snow reliability** The season usually ends at, or shortly after, Easter.

Advanced skiers can pick out the more difficult routes around Meall Odhar and down from Glas Maol but the most challenging skiing is on the other side around the Tiger run – sometimes with big bumps – or on the front face of Cairn Aosda, for which good coverage is needed. The single chair up Cairnwell is one of those interesting, old (well thirty-something anyway) pieces of early '60s ski engineering that remains in operation. Slalom and GS courses are frequently set above the Cairnwell restaurant and the timed course may be available for those feeling competetive. The mountains visible from the ski area do look attractive for touring and off-piste exploring but little of that seems to happen – although there are apparently some moves to introduce heliskiing to the area.

Intermediates can scope out the whole place and should cope happily with just about everything. Butcharts Coire normally holds good snow and is a good warm-up area. There are several gulleys – like lower Butcharts and Coire Fionn – that are fun for practising U-turns in and, although the snow on the Sunnyside side can be quite variable, there are a lot of lifts and piste miles just waiting to be clocked up.

The nursery slopes are by the roadside – built for and dedicated to **beginners**. Progression onto the hill is then nice and gentle with a number of suitable alternatives. Most will probably stay on the same side of the road and head up the adjacent drag lifts – the east-facing slopes of Sunnyside then offer a number of good learner runs. It's also worth making the effort to get up Cairn Aosda – the views of the rest of the ski area will impress most beginners and there are some friendly runs back down to the base area.

Cross-country trails are laid in the forests at Glenisla – 12 miles away – and instruction and accommodation can be provided. Braemar Nordic Ski Centre also provides rentals and tuition.

Glenshee now has enough uplift – 18,500 per hour in total – to deal pretty well with the maximum number of skiers – around 6,000 – that the car parks can deliver. So **queues** are rarely a problem. What can happen though is that everyone arrives together and then buys tickets, rents skis and travels over to Glas Maol together; but what can you do about that? One step taken by the management is to open the ticket office early on busy days, which eases the pressure there. They also seem quite relaxed about running the lifts fairly late – weather and light permitting – which allows skiers to spread out their active hours over a longer day. Pre-booking hire equipment will save queueing with those that didn't bother.

The area does now have a decent **mountain restaurant** – on the Cairnwell side – and both the Sunnyside and base area cafes are more convivial refuelling stops since refurbishment. The Cairnwell restaurant is licensed.

The Cairnwell **ski school** is operated by the lift company from the base area and the competition is provided by Cairdsport, who have a base at Spittal of Glenshee, a few miles down the road. Prices are similar for most arrangements; the Cairnwell school is geared up for snowboard hire and lessons.

Children from the 'local' schools get lessons on the slopes here and both ski schools are well used to dealing with younger clients. There is a crèche facility for over twos but its availability is limited – talk to the ski centre if you really need it.

STAYING THERE

Convenient accommodation is scarce in Glenshee. There are a couple of **hotels** at the Spittal of Glenshee – five miles south on the A93. The one that's close to the road and imaginatively called 'The Spittal of Glenshee' is casual and inexpensive – B&B at around £20. The Dalmunzie House Hotel is a much more traditional and imposing looking place and they offer DB&B at around £40 a night.

Braemar, nine miles in the other direction, has a clutch of hotels and guest houses offering B&B from about £15 and up. The larger places – The Fife Arms and Invercauld Arms – also offer ski holiday packages. Callater Lodge Hotel is a hospitable place

serving good food and they also have two **self-catering** properties for rent. There are chalets to rent at the Spittal and a little further down the road is Dainaglar Castle – much of which is given over to rooms or self-catering units for rent.

Kirkmichael, which is 15 miles from the slopes, has a good collection of accommodation aimed at skiers and isn't far from the A9 should a trip to Cairngorm be called for.

Skiers do stay beyond the immediate area – Blairgowrie, Pitlochry and Alyth all have their fans – but commuting can become tiresome. The A93 and the infamous Devil's Elbow are not the problem they were – and the elbow's been straightened out anyway – but why drive if you don't have to?

Ballater is another possibility for a base and if both the Lecht and Glenshee are on the agenda, it's a good choice. There's the luxurious Craigendarroch hotel where B&B rates start at about £50 but you get quite a bit of pampering for your money.

Restaurants are scarce – except in hotels – but finding decent food at a reasonable price isn't hard.

Après-ski is low key and based around log fires and malt whiskies.

Non-skiers may wish to explore Deeside and grab a glimpse of the castle at Balmoral; there's also a distillery nearby. There are a selection of waymarked walks in and around Braemar.

TOURIST OFFICES

Glenshee Ski area
(lift prices, ski school information)
01339 741320

Braemar Tourist Information
(accommodation)
01339 741600

Blairgowrie Tourist Information
(accommodation)
01250 872960

The Lecht 610m

This is a beginners' area near the summit of the infamous A939 Cockbridge – Tomintoul road and only 32 miles from Aviemore. The development was started as long ago as 1977 and it says much for the persistence of management and staff that the centre continues to operate successfully despite several poor winters and the proximity of major competition.

THE SKIING

The **ski area** (610m-823m) covers the gentle east-facing slopes of a high pass with a series of parallel drag lifts and runs just above the car parks. First impressions are that it all looks a tad tedious. On the opposite side of the road is a single lift and three runs. The main area includes five beginner tows and five others, each with a run or two back down towards the road. With a maximum vertical of only around 200m, runs are short but it is more

interesting than it looks from the road. Some of the links across the hill are poorly defined and may lead no further than a clump of heather or heap of peat – the heather is often skiable but the peat never is.

The 93/94 season was exceptionally long – 135 operating days – and less affected by strong winds than Aviemore and the west coast areas. **Snow reliability** has been a problem though, and snow fence placement and grooming – or snow shuffling – has had to be developed into an art form. There is a floodlit dry ski slope – hopefully buried under mounds of snow – but it ensures some evening skiing and a bit of summer business.

The steepest slopes are off the Harrier and Buzzard tows and **advanced skiers** have to make do with cruising down these or racing themselves down the timed course. Unfortunately the base of the Harrier is actually the lowest part of the area and the Buzzard runs face west so they suffer first as the snow melts. It's not a great place for good skiers but it is worth a try if you're with a mixed ability group.

Intermediates will find the Lecht a comfortable environment in which to make progress. The terrain is not at all intimidating and the ambitious will soon be looking for challenges beyond avoiding the snow fences.

It's in the **beginners**, near-beginners and families-with-young-children markets that the Lecht has made its mark. There are good nursery zones and tows next to the car parks and it's pretty well impossible – even for kids – to get lost here. It shouldn't take many lessons to make a novice ready for the higher lifts. Some schools and other groups regularly travel to the area – often staying in village halls and the like – and take advantage of the relatively low prices and the good beginners' facilities.

There are forest and hill trails for **cross-country** skiers at the Glenmullach Ski Centre between the Lecht and Tomintoul. Equipment hire, instruction and package deals are on offer and the skiing can be very good in the picturesque Ladder hills.

Queues are not a major problem but, like all the Scottish resorts, they can arise at peak times or when the road has just been opened or other areas are shut down. Total uplift of around 8,500 per hour seems reasonable for this size of a resort.

It's not exactly a **mountain restaurant**, but the base area cafe is self-service, does decent plain food and is licensed. The collection of buildings that make up the base area and include the ticket office, shop and first aid facility all conform to a pleasing, blue-wood style and the recent planting of several thousand native species trees should, one day, further enhance appearances.

The **ski school** office is in the building nearest the slopes and provides the usual range of training options. **Children** who are too young or not interested in the skiing can be booked into the crèche for £20 a day.

STAYING THERE

Tomintoul is about six miles from the ski area and is a typical highland village with a couple of **hotels**, some B&Bs and cottages for **self-catering**. The principal hotel is The Gordon – a smartish, quiet place with a posh restaurant and an excellent selection of whiskies; they also own a four-mile stretch of fishing rights. Tomintoul and Glenlivet Highland Holidays have a range of cottages to rent and a selection of farmhouse B&Bs. Beyond Tomintoul are the Speyside villages which are still within striking distance of the Lecht and are equally well placed for the skiing at Cairngorm. Nethy Bridge, Grantown and Glenlivet are all within about 30 minutes of the Lecht and the alternative attractions at places like Glenlivet may appeal to non-skiers in the party.

Travelling east from the ski area there's the Allargue Arms at Corgarff for B&B and various other village hotels and guest houses along the roads that weave vaguely in the direction of Aberdeen.

Anyone expecting lively **après-ski** has made a mistake but for whisky afficionados this is the place. There's also a sort of whisky grocer's shop in Tomintoul with an amazing selection of the stuff on offer – some at pretty amazing prices too.

So **non-skiers** can pass the time bathed in a malty glow; they can follow the castle trail or get out and about on the Glenlivet Estate where there are paths and cycle routes.

TOURIST OFFICE

The Lecht Ski Area
01975 651440

Nevis Range 630m

It's the newest and the highest Scottish resort and it occupies the north-facing slopes of Aonach Mor – a 4000-foot peak, Britain's eighth highest and in close proximity to the Ben itself. A long gondola ride in comfortable six-seater cabins is something of a novelty in Scotland and a fair indicator of the relative sophistication of the facilities here. The extent of the lift-served skiing is slightly disappointing and only when current plans to extend into the eastern corries are put into effect will there really be enough variety for good skiers to get excited about.

THE RESORT

Fort William is only a 15-minute drive from the skiing and is one of the 'gateways to the Highlands' – familiar to generations of summer coach parties, campers, walkers, climbers and the like. The town benefits from a lovely setting at the end of Loch Linnhe, almost at the foot of Ben Nevis, and it provides everything that the visitor, skier or otherwise, needs; but it steadfastly refuses to become the kind of charming place that people fall in love with. Some hotels arrange transport to the slopes and the main west coast rail link from London does get this far – but for how long is the subject of much contemporary debate.

THE SKIING

After feasibility studies that go back to the 70's, followed by a typically protracted period of planning, consultation and contemplation, the construction was completed in 12 months and the facilities opened to the public in December 1989 – undoubtedly the biggest event to hit Scottish skiing since the early 60s and the arrival of Cairngorm and Glenshee alongside Glencoe as 'major' ski areas. The concept at Nevis Range was to establish an all-season tourist facility with the prime objective of providing high-quality uplift and runs for skiers of all levels of ability. At present the number of summer visitors almost matches the number of skiers and the skiing on offer is well suited for beginners up to strong intermediates.

The **ski area**, which lies between 630m and 1200m, occupies the Snowgoose Bowl above the gondola top station. Only when there is exceptionally good snow cover can skiing to the car park be considered – and even then it's a fairly challenging piece of 'cross-country'. In general terms the easier slopes are lower down, nearer to the gondola top station and the tougher runs are just below the summit area.

The upper part of the bowl holds snow well but rather poorer **snow reliability** at the nursery slopes has led to plans for an additional beginners' area on a part of the mountain with better snow-holding properties. The chair lift – a few minutes' walk from the gondola station – arrives at an altitude of 900 metres and is crucial to keeping skiing going late season – the upper runs are expected to last until late May.

For **advanced skiers** there are several satisfying variations on the run from summit to base, approximately 2km long. Towards the eastern limit of the area are some short black runs served by Warren's T-bar, which provide some steep pitches and quite possibly a bit of a slog back up to the lifts if you don't know exactly where to start turning left. Regulars to the area do ski into Coire Dubh at the back of the mountain via some steep and often corniced routes from the Summit ridge – the skiing is said to be excellent but until it's incorporated into the patrolled area it should be viewed as potentially hazardous to health.

When the sun shines and the views of Ben Nevis and Carn Mor Dearg are at their most spectacular, **intermediates** should head for the summit and take it all in – it's superb. The runs around the summit tow don't present a problem, and although the red runs below the summit and around the Goose T-bar are a little steeper there is usually enough width to the slopes to tackle them indirectly, if needs be. There are some easier intermediate runs around the alpha tow and a bigger choice over by the quad chair.

Beginners have a not-quite-dedicated nursery area with two friendly button tows, adjacent to the restaurant. Other skiers generally only use these lifts for access on arrival from the gondola station or on emerging from the restaurant. Having mastered these lower slopes, the Alpha tow can then be tackled and there is a pleasant green route either back towards the nursery area or across to the restaurant for a reward.

To date there have been few reported **queuing** problems but the uplift capacity is relatively low – around 5,500 per hour, excluding the gondola – and would be sorely tested on the busiest days – 2,500 skiers is the busiest day so far.

The main **mountain restaurant**, the self-service Snowgoose Restaurant and Bar, shares a building with the gondola top station and is frequently the most popular location on the mountain. Gondola trippers as well as skiers hang out here looking for warmth, food and one of the 200 seats. It's quite an attractive building and usually a pretty lively place – not least in the bar area. There's also terrace seating when the weather allows. A snack hut by the Goose T-bar may be able to rustle up a burger and the cafe by the car park does some rather nice home-baked items and that skiers' favourite – the all-day cooked breakfast. For those with a packed lunch there's the interesting and rather unexpected invitation to consume it while taking a round trip in a gondola.

The Nevis Range **ski school** is the only one on offer and provides two-hour morning and afternoon sessions as well as a range of more specialist options including telemark and snowboard instruction.

Children need to be over seven, or big for their age, to be accepted into group lessons. The under-sevens are relegated to private lessons. A crèche in the base station will look after three- to seven-year-olds.

STAYING THERE

Just for a change, why not stay on a ship? The Ski Ship Vertrouwen offers a £40 a night deal including breakfast, dinner and transportation to either Nevis Range or Glencoe. And there are many more normal B&Bs and **hotels** in and around Fort William that offer accommodation in this sort of price range – even for as little as £12 a night at some of the smaller places. The Old Pines Hotel at Spean Bridge is a much decorated establishment, noted for its restaurant and facilities for the disabled.

The two Milton hotels – the Milton and the Alexandra – both offer good-value ski packages for three- and five-day breaks.

The Moorings Hotel at Banavie is a cosy sort of place and has a decent wine bar. Nevis Bank Hotel, a little out from the centre of town, has good rooms and a lively bar with real ale. The Mercury Hotel is one of those with a resident ski school rep, who may invite you to consider signing up for a learning experience; there's also a bus to the slopes.

Self-catering units are plentiful and a cottage or chalet sleeping up to six people would be around £250 for a week. Snowgoose Activities, one of the centres providing winter skills courses, also have a 12-person bunkhouse and some self-catering units.

The Crannog, at the pier in Fort William, is one of the best seafood **restaurants** in the area – they serve fish caught by their own boat – and there's a curry house on the high street that's okay. Otherwise it's the usual array of fish & chip places, pizzerias, hotel restaurants and bars that serve food.

There's no shortage of bars in Fort William. The Nevisport bar can be a good **après-ski** venue, and there's often live music. It represents an interesting concept in total service, since it shares the purpose-built premises with Nevisport's other ventures: ski-hire, mountaineering equipment, books and maps, a cafe and a bureau de change. The Grog & Gruel sports a large selection of real ales and Crofter's is a good local bar; both are on the High Street.

Non-skiers should spend only a limited amount of time in the souvenir and wool shops in Fort William. More stimulating would be a trip to see the interesting bits of the Caledonian Canal and the Great Glen through which it passes. Neptune's Staircase consists of eight locks in quick succession; it was built by Thomas Telford and has been operating since 1822. A gondola ride and lunch with skiing friends in the Snowgoose Restaurant is also to be recommended and, depending on the weather and the snowline, a couple of short scenic walks may be possible. The two leisure centres between them offer aerobics, bowling, climbing wall, sauna, whirlpool and swimming pool.

TOURIST OFFICES

Nevis Range Tourist Office
01397 705825

Fort William Tourist Office
(accommodation)
01397 703781

Norway

HOW IT RATES

The skiing

Snow	****
Extent	*
Advanced	*
Intermediates	*
Beginners	**
Convenience	**
Queues	****
Restaurants	*

The rest

Scenery	**
Resort charm	**
Not skiing	**

✔ Probably the best terrain and facilities in Europe for serious cross-country skiing

✔ Complete freedom from the glitziness often associated with downhill skiing, and from the ill-mannered lift queues of the Alps

✔ Quiet atmosphere that suits families and older skiers

✔ Usually reliable snow conditions throughout a long season, at least in the higher resorts

✔ Some appealing hotels

✗ Very limited downhill ski areas – small, with few challenges

✗ Unremarkable scenery – nothing like the drama of the coastal fjords (or the Alps) except in Hemsedal

✗ Mountain restaurants are little more than pit-stops

✗ Prohibitively high prices (because of high taxes) for alcoholic drinks

✗ Very little apres-ski animation

✗ Short daylight hours in midwinter

✗ Highly changeable weather

✗ Limited non-skiing activities

Norway and its ski resorts are very different from the Alps, or for that matter the Rockies. Our list of ✔ and ✗ points makes the Norwegian recipe clear. Some skiers find it very much to their taste. For cross-country skiing there is nowhere like it. And for downhillers who dislike the usual trappings of skiing, and long for a simpler approach to winter holidays, it could be just the place.

But it is quite difficult to imagine the kind of dedicated downhiller who would happily spend a week in a Norwegian resort. And speaking for ourselves – well, any one of the first four ✗ points we've listed would probably be enough to put us off; when these are combined in a single destination, along with four other non-trivial drawbacks, you can count us out.

From the 1960s to the 1980s, Norway's popularity with British skiers declined steadily, until it was attracting only 1,500 or so – about one-tenth of the peak number. So in 1988 the tourist agencies launched an initiative to reverse the trend. Aided by the Alpine snow shortages at the turn of the decade and the award of the 1994 Olympic Winter Games to Lillehammer, the campaign has been a success. By 1993, numbers were up to 5,000. In 1996, that may be doubled.

There is a traditional friendship between Norway and Britain, and we think of Norwegians as welcoming people, well disposed towards British visitors. Some reporters find the reality bears this out; 'a warm welcome awaits,' says one. Sadly, our visit a few years ago left us underwhelmed by the warmth of welcome, and we're not alone. One report, for example, speaks of a 'lack of enthusiasm by townspeople – a take it or leave it approach.' But at least English is widely spoken; you'll find British TV programmes on local channels.

Cross-country skiing comes as naturally to Norwegians as walking; they are both ways of getting about the valleys, and exploring the hills. Although you can plod around short valley circuits as you might in an Alpine resort, what distinguishes

Norway for the keen cross-country skier is the network of long trails across the gentle uplands, with refuges along the way where backpackers can pause for refreshment or stay overnight before carrying on their way. Even if you're not that keen, the fact that cross-country is normal, and not a wimp's alternative to 'real' skiing, gives Norway a special appeal.

For Alpine skiing, the country is not nearly so attractive. Despite the fact that it is able to hold downhill races, and despite the recent successes of its own Alpine racers, Norway's Alpine ski areas are of limited appeal. (Although there is, of course, nowhere better to learn the tricky but eventually elegant Telemark technique, invented here.)

The site of the 1994 Olympics, the little lakeside town of **Lillehammer** (200m) is not actually a downhill ski resort at all. There is plenty of cross-country terrain around, but the nearest downhill skiing is 15km north at Hafjell. This is a worthwhile little ski area, with a vertical of 850m, eight lifts, and pistes totalling 20km with a longest run of 5km. The Olympic slalom events were held here; but the planned women's downhill and super-G races were moved elsewhere after the racers judged the course too easy. They went to Kvitfjell, about 35km further north, developed specially for the men's downhill and super-G. It's steeper but smaller – 12km of pistes.

Norway's other internationally known ski resort is **Geilo** (770m) – a small, quiet, unspoilt community on the railway line that links Bergen on the coast to Oslo. It provides all the basics of a ski resort – a handful of cafes and shops clustered around the railway station, ten hotels more widely spread around the wide valley, children's facilities and a sports centre.

Geilo is a superb cross-country resort, but very limited for downhillers. The 24km of piste are spread over two small hills – one, Vestlia, a bus-ride away, with a good informal hotel and restaurant at its foot – offering a maximum vertical of 265m and a longest run of 1.5km. None of the skiing is difficult.

Clearly the best hotel, and one of the attractions of staying in Geilo, is the Dr Holms Hotel – smartly white-painted outside, beautifully furnished and spacious inside. The luxurious Bardola is also recommended. The resort is quiet after skiing but the main hotels often provide live entertainment.

The most rewarding resort for keen downhill skiers is **Hemsedal** (650m), about 30km north of Geilo. The runs here, totalling about 35km, are more varied and longer – up to 6km, and almost 800m vertical – and the rather more craggy terrain provides testing off-piste skiing (accessible from the lifts) as well as better-than-usual scenery. As usual, there are extensive cross-country trails in the valleys and up at altitude. The slopes are some distance from the town, and the bus service is infrequent and sometimes crowded, although reliable. Reporters are impressed by the main hotel, the Skogstad.

A long way north of the other resorts is **Oppdal** (550m), which claims more downhill skiing than any of its rivals (about 80km – as much as a small Alpine resort). The total vertical is also impressive (about 900m) but most of the runs are short.

There is almost as much skiing at **Trysil** (600m), off to the east on the border with Sweden, and the runs are longer (up to 4km and 650m vertical). The skiing here takes place all around the conical Trysilfjellet, some way from Trysil itself – though there is some accommodation at the hill.

In complete contrast to all of these resorts is **Voss** (50m), a sizeable lakeside town quite close to Bergen and the sea. A cable-car links the town to the skiing on Hangur and Slettafjell, with a total of 40km of pistes.

Andorra

More than most skiing countries, Andorra invites generalisations. Perhaps it's because all the resorts are so close to one another that they are so remarkably similar, having almost all the same pluses and minuses. Low prices (including duty-free goods), simple hotels, ugly villages, lively nightlife, good ski schools, fairly reliable snow, young clientele, a lot of Anglophones, small easy ski areas and awful mountain restaurants are all fairly typical of Andorran resorts across the board.

There's an immediate temptation to compare Andorra to Eastern Europe. Many of the above pluses and minuses would be appropriate to Borovets and company, too. Perhaps the main difference is that Andorra is more expensive and attracts a mostly young and lively clientele with more money to spend.

Andorra has also proved a tough competitor, on the British market at least, for Austria. Many of the little Austrian resorts where so many of us learned to ski in the 1970s and 1980s are slowly but surely losing British custom, and this is partly because they can't compete with Andorra for providing first-time ski holidays that are not only cheap and cheerful, but also relatively snowsure. Andorra's snow reliability should not be underestimated. A combination of height and heavy investment in snowmakers puts it well ahead of much of Austria. You can book Andorra months in advance with some confidence. And an early reservation is necessary, too: late bookers can have difficulty finding an Andorra package.

However, two of the apparently crucial elements of Andorra's success – good value and nightlife – do not stand up too well under the microscope. Prices are low once you arrive, notably for drinks and ski extras such as tuition and equipment hire. But the cost of package holidays has crept up over the last few years as demand has exceeded supply. It's difficult to find a half-board package for less than £300 these days, which is not the case in many Italian resorts, never mind Bulgarian ones. And although lift passes are cheap, you have to remember they access pretty limited ski areas of the kind that come quite cheap in supposedly more expensive countries. For example, the French purpose-built resort of Valfréjus has skiing that compares favourably with anything in Andorra, yet it costs only a few pounds more. Many reporters have also been disappointed to find duty-free luxury goods not the super-bargain they had expected. As for nightlife, it certainly is very lively, with lots of throbbing bars; but if you get bored with bar-hopping there's little else.

It would seem the real secret of Andorra's success may be that it offers a sort of gathering of a particular clan – skiers (mainly young ones and many of them native English-speakers) who don't insist on a really cheap holiday but do insist on a very cheerful one.

Arinsal 1550m

Young people come here for the nightlife, and Arinsal does not disappoint. The numerous lively bars and discos are not as rowdy as in nearby Soldeu. However, some will find the nightlife very one-dimensional. There is little to do outside of bar-hopping and clubbing, and the spread-out nature of Arinsal means there is little village atmosphere but lots of cold walks between 'happening' places. The skiing is very limited, and the resort is difficult to recommend to anyone except beginners.

THE RESORT

Arinsal is a little village of Catalan slate and grey stone, near the head of a narrow valley north of Andorra-la-Vella. It has seen rapid development in recent years, giving the place a building-site appearance. Yet little new accommodation is available near the single resort-level lift, inconveniently situated a kilometre out of town. Most skiers face a long walk or a bus-ride to this chair. Fortunately the village bus service is good. Arinsal is dominated by British holidaymakers.

THE SKIING

The very small **ski area** is a narrow east-facing coomb of mainly open slopes, suitable for beginners, children and unadventurous intermediates. All runs lead straight back towards the mid-station area, ideal for parents to keep a watchful eye on children. Proposed development of the Coll d'Ature mountainside will add not only size, but much needed variety, including some relatively snowsure tree-lined runs. A rarely skied black run or a blue road down to the Arinsal chair are the only options in bad weather.

With almost all skiing above 1950m and a fair number of guns, snow is relatively assured. The **snow reliability** of the nursery slopes is a boon. Most lifts above the mid-station are drags, keeping the mountain open when it's windy.

Advanced skiers and progressive intermediates shouldn't even think about Arinsal. But some of the slopes are not entirely easy and are suitable for **intermediates** who do not mind skiing a very limited area. Piste maintenance is good.

Essentially, Arinsal is a ski area suitable for near-**beginners** or early intermediates. The nursery slopes are gentle, away from the main ski area, and well covered by snow cannons. They do not cover a particularly large area, and as a result can get very crowded in peak season.

Although everyone has to ascend the mountain by a single lift, **queues** are not a problem on weekdays. Spanish weekenders and local children can hit the slopes en masse at times.

If you rate a resort by its **mountain restaurants**, Zermatt this isn't. They're expensive, by local standards, and crowded. And they serve mediocre snacks – hamburgers and so on.

Arinsal's **ski school** is its pride and joy. It offers good technical tuition; patient instruction; English widely spoken; low prices; and lessons that are fun. Class sizes can however be very large in peak season.

There is a ski kindergarten but no non-skiing crèche for young **children**.

STAYING THERE

Arinsal is essentially a cheap and cheerful small hotel resort.

The Crest is perhaps the best **hotel** in Arinsal, and has the advantage of being next to the chair-lift; it offers half-board or B&B terms. The studio-style rooms are geared towards families, sleeping up to five. The Solana has good food but simple rooms. It is much nearer the lifts than the peripheral St Gotthard. Apartments are generally of a higher standard that the hotels. The Velvet, Poblado and Rosa Blanca apartments are all quite comfortable.

There is a fair range of **restaurants** for a small resort. Cisco's is a lively restaurant/bar serving Mexican food, Borda specialises in Catalan dishes and La Calisa has Spanish cooking. Arguably the best in town is Il Neu.

For **après ski**, Arinsal has very animated bars and discos, but if you get fed up with these, there isn't much else to do – a fondue evening is the best bet. Prices are low, but not as low as many expect of Andorra. Red Rock is a focal spot, popular for its large measures, videos and good burgers.

Arinsal has few facilities for **non-skiers**. The main thing to do is shopping in La Vella, half an hour away by infrequent bus.

Soldeu 1800m

Soldeu has a lot in common with other resorts in Andorra – limited skiing, low prices, great ski school, grim-looking village, lively bar-based nightlife. But its ski area is one of the better ones in the region, and is fairly convenient – the walk to the lifts, although irritating, is relatively short.

HOW IT RATES

The skiing

Snow	***
Extent	**
Advanced	*
Intermediates	***
Beginners	****
Convenience	***
Queues	***
Restaurants	*

The rest

Scenery	***
Resort charm	*
Not skiing	*

SKI FACTS

Altitude	1680m-2560m
Lifts	22
Pistes	50km
Green/Blue	59%
Red	32%
Black	9%
Artificial snow	9½km

PACKAGES

Airtours, Crystal, First Choice Ski, Neilson, Panorama, Ski Club of GB, Skiworld, Thomson, Top Deck

TOURIST OFFICE

Tel 00 376 851151
Fax 838738

THE RESORT

The village is a small, though ever-growing, ribbon of ugly modern buildings along a busy road, most of them hotels and bars. Other than sleeping, skiing, eating and drinking, there is nothing to do, and the poor transport facilities make excursions difficult. The ski area lies beyond a long new metal bridge, which is a simple enough walk when there is no ice about, especially if you desposit skis and boots at the chair-lift.

THE SKIING

The **ski area** is shared with El Tarter. There are a few challenges, but the skiing is most suited to timid/early intermediates.

A chair-lift rises over wooded north-facing slopes to Espiolets, a broad, extensive nursery area. From here, a short gentle run to the east takes you to a lift up to Solana (2440m). A longer gentle run in the opposite direction takes you to the foot of the open bowl of Riba Escorxada and the arrival point of the lift up from El Tarter. From here lifts ascend to both Solana and the high-point of Llosada (2560m), with blue and red runs back down. All main routes have very easy skiing options, so all but complete beginners can get around the area.

Soldeu enjoys fairly **reliable snow**. Most of the skiing is north-facing, with artificial snow available on the descents to Soldeu. Should runs to the village be incomplete, the area as whole is not unduly affected.

It's a limited area for **advanced skiers**. There are short off-piste trails down the bowl beneath Llosada, and you can sometimes play in powder among the trees above El Tarter.

The most direct of the wooded runs down to El Tarter and Soldeu are suitable for good **intermediates**, while moderate skiers will enjoy the relatively long pistes from Llosada. Timid skiers have gentle cruises throughout the area. Riba Escorxada is a fine section for mixed abilities

This is a good resort for **beginners**. The Espiolets nursery area is adequate and relatively snowsure, and there are numerous easy pistes to move on to.

The lift system is antiquated and inefficient, and free of **queues** on weekdays only because of the high proportion of beginners. When there is an influx at weekends, morning queues of 30–45 minutes develop for the village chair. There are plans to build a large gondola from the centre of town to Pla Dels Espiolets but it is unclear when that will happen.

The **mountain restaurants** are poor. The one at the top of El Tarter chair is the best of a bad bunch.

The **ski school** has a high reputation for standards of English, quality of tuition and friendliness. **Children** aged three to eight can attend a non-ski nursery. Children's ski school starts at six, but lunchtime supervision is not available.

STAYING THERE

The central 3-star Sporthotel is by far the best **hotel** in Soldeu – tastefully designed in local stone and stained pine, with good bedrooms and a pleasant and well equipped sauna/gym. Buffet breakfast is good. The popular Naudi offers good value provided you stay in the main hotel, not the more basis annexe.

The Edelweiss apartments are spacious and generally pleasant, and well placed opposite the Sporthotel, the facilities of which are available.

Though standards are not particularly high, there is plenty of choice of places for **eating out**. The Pussycat is an atmospheric restaurant with reasonable food and good service. The Duc hotel restaurant has arguably the best food in town.

Although **après-ski** is lively, it is very one-dimensional, consisting of bars and rep-organised outings. The Sol Y Nieve bar at the foot of the slopes starts things off after skiing, while later on the Edelweiss, Bruxelles and Bonnel bars are the most popular. Aspen is the main snowboard hang-out. The Naudi has a quieter locals' bar. The El Duc is the best disco.

There is little to amuse **non-skiers**. There is a very smart sports centre in Canillo (erratic bus service) with pool, ice rink, squash and gym. It is closed in the afternoons. The Sporthotel has sauna and gym, and the only all-day bar (the 'excellent' Piccadilly).

Spain

The Spanish Pyrenees were a popular British budget destination a decade ago, but then Andorra and Eastern Europe succeeded in capturing much of the Spanish trade. It's easy to see why. The mass-market resorts often struggled for snow and, even when conditions were good, skiing was far from guaranteed in many places because of the tendency for high winds to close the lifts. Although prices were low, they were lower elsewhere, and Spain also gained a reputation for low standards – poor hotels, ancient hire equipment, old lifts and so on.

But it's dangerous to generalise about Spanish skiing. There is more to the country than its downmarket image suggests. There is a well equipped Pyrenean resort with fine, snowsure skiing that compares very favourably with the best mid-size places in the Alps. And down in the south, near Granada, lies a resort which is about to host the World Alpine Ski Championships. The two resorts are certainly not downmarket (the King of Spain frequents them both), yet the exchange rate makes them relatively inexpensive. Skiing is also becoming more popular with the increasingly prosperous Spanish themselves, and as a result many of the smaller resorts are now improving their facilities.

Furthermore, the general ambience of Spanish skiing is attractive – not unlike that of Italy. There's plenty of animation, with eating, posing and partying taken seriously. Large families often lunch together, creating much merriment while huge amounts of food are consumed. Dinner starts late after such a blow out, so in turn nightlife doesn't get going before many a British punter has retired disgruntled at the lack of action.

The 1995 World Championships were due to take place in **Sierra Nevada** (2100m) in the extreme south of Spain; but at the eleventh hour they had to be postponed to 1996, due to lack of snow – with high temperatures rendering the resort's state-of-the-art snowmaking installation useless. The resort's natural snow arrives via completely different weather patterns from those supplying the Alps and Pyrenees; in 1990, when the Alps were disastrously snowless, Sierra Nevada had the best conditions in Europe. The mostly intermediate ski area is very exposed to the elements. When the wind blows, as it does, the skiing stops, and the strong sun makes the pistes either icy or soft in late season. The resort is very ugly but user-friendly, and its restaurants, bars and shops are nicely gathered around a central square. Granada's proximity means good outings, but overcrowding at weekends and holidays. Hotels are comfortable and good value.

Baqueira-Beret (1500m) is atypical of the Pyrenees – a user-friendly resort with high-standard accommodation, modern lifts and a sizeable, fairly snowsure ski area. Spanish prices make it a real bargain. The mountain seems bigger than its claim of 90km of piste would suggest, thanks to its variety. The skiing is mostly above 1800m, much of it northish-facing, backed by snowmakers. Queues are rare because most of the lifts are high-capacity chairs. There's skiing for all grades including some steep challenges. Ski Miquel have a good chalet and hotels available.

The smaller Pyrenean resorts are best toured by car: spend a day in each and drive to more sheltered places if the wind blows. The best-known, **Formigal**, and has a good ski school but is windswept. Our favourite is nearby **Panticosa**, a charming old village with sheltered, if limited skiing. **La Molina** has a sizeable ski area. It's an old place, preferable to its dreary purpose-built satellite, **Supermolina**.

Bulgaria

Bulgaria attracts skiers on a tight budget: the basic package, ski hire, school and lift pass are all very cheap. Drawbacks include limited ski areas, old lifts, and mountain food that has you reaching for the Mars bars. But there are compensations other than simply low prices. All of our reporters have been struck by the friendliness of the local people, the ski schools are excellent, the tour op-organised nightlife is good fun, and from Borovets an excursion to Sofia is recommended. The resorts also try hard to provide the sort of amenities 'Westerners' require from a holiday resort. Many of the hotels have the potential to be perfectly adequate places to stay, and Bulgaria, like the rest of Eastern Europe is struggling to raise standards. Unfortunately the shortages the country is suffering at present have so far limited what can be achieved. Progress is slow, but recognisable. Several old Bulgaria hands have commented on the improvement in food in recent years. Reports of the resorts get more positive each year, and many visitors are return bookings.

The low prices have not attracted huge numbers of young drinkers away from Andorra. Bulgaria receives young and old, families and singles alike. Consequently the atmosphere is nicely cosmopolitan, with people of different ages and walks of life mixing in together.

Bulgaria's two main ski resorts are some way apart, served by different airports, with similarly short transfer times (less than two hours). They are fairly similar places in some ways; both have good tuition ('individuals needs accounted for'), low prices (though not as low as in the days of Communism) and poor mountain restaurants ('mostly caravans with outside seating'). But the two ski areas suit different levels of skier.

Borovets (see page 478 for a full report) has intermediate skiing that a combination of steepness and poor piste grooming makes awkward for improving beginners and leisurely cruisers.

Pamporovo (1450m) is far better for beginners and early intermediates, with mostly easy skiing. Others may find 25km of short runs too limited. But the skiing is pretty and sheltered, with pistes cut through pine forest. Skiing around is easy, with no bottlenecks or hazards, and getting lost is difficult even in the worst weather. Beginners should book a 'learn to ski' package through their tour operator. It's a good deal, saving up to 80% of the cost of booking ski extras locally. (You can also get Bulgarian ski passes at half the local price by booking them from the UK.) Despite having to bus to the slopes, families praise Pamporovo. Not only is the skiing suitable but the English-speaking crèche is well regarded, and the purpose-built village has 'everything to hand'. The ski school's instructors are patient, enthusiastic and speak good English, and class sizes are usually quite small. At the heart of the village are the two hotels, Perelik and Mourgaret, both of which are good by Bulgarian standards. The food is monotonous ('it helps if you like pork'), though the buffet offers a fair choice. The Perelik has a large pool. The organised evening events are popular, and there are some bars, but Pamporovo is generally quieter and less commercialised than Borovets. Late season snowcover is unreliable.

Vitosha (1810m) is no more than a few widely scattered hotels with limited, bland skiing, and on our visit we were unable to find any nursery slopes, which was a surprise given the resort's five-star rating for beginners in one brochure. The hotels are mostly dour, and all but one are a bus-ride from the lifts. Sofia is close by, allowing short transfers and easy excursions, but the slopes get overrun at weekends. Vitosha's main saving grace is its good snow record.

Borovets 1300m

✔ Still very cheap, despite growth of economy

✔ A completely different ski holiday, with the chance to experience a fascinating although depressed culture

✔ Very good ski school

✔ Compact village – little walking to lifts

✔ Beautiful setting among thick pine forest

✗ Low standards of comfort, particularly food and other things affected by present shortages

✗ Archaic airports, airline, coaches can cause long travel delays (We strongly recommend a Sofia flight – Plovdiv airport is a disaster)

✗ Not particularly snowsure, yet no artificial back-up

✗ Small, yet steep ski area relatively unsuitable for many grades of skier

✗ Poor piste and lift maintenance

✗ Limited off-slope facilities

✗ Ugly hotels

ORIENTATION

Despite recent development, Borovets remains essentially a compact gathering of hotels. There are two focal points to the resort. The first is a central cluster of large hotels. The main village lift (a gondola) goes from here to two of the three ski sectors. Most of the slopes face north with east-facing runs beneath the top station. A couple of minutes' walk takes you to the top of the resort, where an enormous hotel overlooks the remaining village lifts, all conveniently close to one and other. There are no resorts near enough to justify a ski excursion.

For visitors who have done some research into what to expect from a Bulgarian ski holiday Borovets has few nasty surprises and some pleasant ones. It is typically Balkan, with all that implies – keen piste-bashers, gourmets, posers and those wanting creature comforts should look elsewhere. However, it is one of the few resorts to meet the needs of budget skiers seeking a reasonable ski area, pretty scenery, and convenient village lifts. Borovets is also developing, with much-needed infrastructure being provided in response to market demands. These assets put it ahead of Bulgarian and Romanian rivals, making it the best all-round ski resort in Eastern Europe.

Since the fall of Communism it is no longer true to say, 'You can't spend your money', but prices are still at least half those of the Alps. One worrying report this year told of a high number of thefts, including one couple having the contents of their hotel room loaded into their suicases and stolen. Perhaps capitalism is bringing some nasty side-effects with it.

The resort

Borovets is little more than a collection of large, ugly, modern hotels, with most of the essentials of a ski resort – bars, restaurants, shops etc – housed within them. This said, there has been new development every year since the fall of the Communist regime; some regulars believe the place is becoming too commercial and is now not as ultra-friendly or cheap as its Bulgarian rival Pamporovo. This is relative of course. It's still inexpensive by the standards of most resorts.

The beautiful wooded setting of the place provides a degree of Alpine-style charm, and trees do hide some of the worst architectural excesses.

Despite the very low prices, including cheap beer, Borovets is not dominated by young people looking to whoop it up. Many of the visitors are families on low budgets. Evening animation is centred mainly within the Rila hotel, leaving the rest of Borovets to have a muted atmosphere.

The skiing

THE SKI AREA
Biggest in Eastern Europe
The 40km of piste are spread over three sectors, two of which are loosely connected. The two largest have fairly steep skiing made more awkward by poor piste maintenance. A gondola rises over 1000m from the edge of town to service both the small, high, easy slopes of the Markoudjika sector, and the mainly long steepish Yastrebets pistes that lead back to the same lift station. A little drag lift and path connect the two. The Baraki sector is within easy walking distance of the gondola bottom station, even in ski boots, starting conveniently in front of the biggest of the village hotels, with several base lifts to choose from. Runs are short, with a ski range of just 550m upto a top station at 1850m.

LIFT PASSES

94/95 prices in pounds sterling
Borovets area
Covers all lifts in the resort.
Main pass
1-day pass 11
6-day pass 61
Children
Under 12: 6-day pass 50 (18% off)

SKI SCHOOL

94/95 prices in pounds sterling
Borovets Ski School
Classes 6 days
4hr: 10am-noon and 2pm-4pm
6 full days: 65
Children's classes
Ages: up to 12
6 full days: 46

CHILDCARE

The kindergarten in the hotel Rila takes children aged 2 to 5, from 9am to 4.30 and in the evening from 7pm.

GETTING THERE

Air Sofia, transfer 1½hr.

SNOW RELIABILITY
Not particularly good
The small Markoudjika section is relatively snowsure, but the ski area as a whole is markedly reduced when runs to the village are incomplete – there is little skiing between the top and middle stations of the gondola, and Baraki's section is drastically reduced. Despite advertisements to the contrary, there is little snowmaking.

FOR ADVANCED SKIERS
One run doesn't make a holiday
The long fairly challenging piste, and its variants, beneath the gondola is where you'll be practising those turns.

FOR INTERMEDIATE SKIERS
Some variety
Good intermediates will enjoy the red runs, most of which are fairly tough. Average performers have a lovely long blue run, dropping 1000m, from Yastrebets. Nervous skiers are not well provided for, although the short runs at Markoudjika have good snow. The lack of grooming tends to mean there are few leisurely cruises available.

FOR BEGINNERS
Not ideal
The nursery slopes are conveniently positioned at the foot of the Baraki section, but are inadequate. The excellence of the ski school is some compensation. Markoudjika is good for near beginners, though again we have to emphasise poor grooming does not make for easy progression.

FOR CROSS-COUNTRY
Not appealing
Officially there are 20 trails but the area covered is small. Few people come here to do the sport, so trails are either pleasantly or unpleasantly lonely, depending on your point of view. Trails are poorly maintained.

QUEUES
Can be dreadful
There are weeks when queues form only at ski school start and finish times, but when the resort is full and/or lacking complete snow cover lines can be long in places. The gondola and a single-person chair are the main bottlenecks. When the attractions of skiing high are particularly apparent, delays to reach Yastrebets can be serious (up to two hours). At such times skiers bussed in from Pamporovo have added to the chaos. Lifts also have a tendency to shut regularly 'for maintenance', putting strain on the others.

MOUNTAIN RESTAURANTS
Basic and inadequate
These are mostly basic little snack bars with limited seating serving good-sized portions of very simple fare. It helps if you like chips. Lunchtime queues can be more time-consuming than lift delays. Fortunately, it is not inconvenient to return to Borovets for lunch. The Ela hotel is close to the Yastrebets slopes and has bearable food. If staying on the mountain, it's probably safest to stick to pizza.

SKI SCHOOL
A justly high reputation
The Borovets ski school gives caring, patient, fun tuition four hours per day. Standards of English are surprisingly high, and classes not too large. There is also a new co-operative school, which offers similar prices and services.

FACILITIES FOR CHILDREN
Generally approved of
Reports of ski kindergarten have been highly complimentary, with a couple of exceptions castigating it for poor supervision. This was over New Year, so perhaps the normally caring staff were overworked or simply not on duty. The non-ski nursery is situated in hotel Rila.

 # Staying there

The compact nature of the resort, with everything (including lifts) within easy walking distance of everything else, makes location of hotel relatively unimportant. This said, there is some accommodation out in the countryside which relies on quite a poor ski-bus service and/or taxis (very cheap). Horse-drawn sleighs also provide a taxi service around the village; it is cheap enough to use frequently, but scarcely needed.

HOW TO GO
On a hotel package, probably
Borovets is essentially a hotel resort. Apartments are available, but cooking is difficult: there is no supermarket and nothing like the range of food you'd be used to available in shops. There are no catered chalets.
Hotels The big, modern monstrosities are conveniently close to the lifts, and there is also an attractive Scandanavian-style development out in the forest.
£ Rila Low marks for virtually everything, especially food; not recommended.

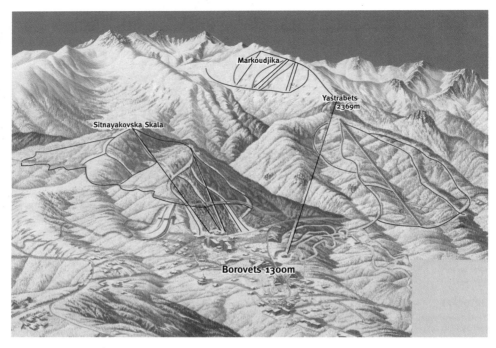

PACKAGES

Balkan Holidays, Crystal, First Choice Ski, Inghams, Neilson, Ski Ardmore, Ski Balkantours, Sunquest Ski

ACTIVITIES

Indoor Sauna, fitness centre, swimming pools, gym
Outdoor Sleigh rides, helicopter trips, mountain walks, excursions to Samokov, Sofia, Rila monastery and Plovdiv

TOURIST OFFICE

Tel 00 359 (2) 835210
Fax 800134

£ Samokov Much the better of the two big conference hotels, though its four-star rating should not be taken too seriously. Plenty of amenities but little atmosphere or character. The 25m pool is a major asset in a resort with few off-slope facilities.

£ Ela and **Moura** Friendly sister hotels, both with plenty of hot water (an important consideration here) and (at the Moura) particularly good food by local standards.

£ Edelweiss Comfortable in recently refurbished rooms (not all rooms); 10 minute walk from lifts.

£ Breza Rather spartan, but small and friendly, with lots of hot water; more rustic character than anywhere else.

£ Bor One of the less well positioned places, and rather basic – but popular for its friendliness.

£ Yagoda Chalets Studio apartments sold on a half-board basis. Part of an attractive Finnish-designed development of log cabins in the forest 3km out of town. Buses every 20 minutes during the morning rush, then hourly. Taxis about £2 each way.
Self-catering The Rila studios are clean and comfortable, but hot water can be erratic.

EATING OUT
Organised events best
Food is generally poor. The Maritsa restaurant in the hotel Samokov attempts French cuisine at the bargain price of £5 per head, but the best food

of the week is likely to be on the folklore and local village dinner evenings arranged by tour reps. Hotel Moura is the best bet at other times.

APRES SKI
Limited, but a varied range
Events organised by tour operator reps include trips to sample Bulgarian folklore and a visit to a local village for dinner. Sleigh rides and togogganing are available. Many consider the entertaining ski school show the highlight of the week. Others prefer the sumo wrestling! There are three discos – the Rila is the noisiest, the Samokov perhaps the best. The Piano Bar is the best place for a quiet drink, being one of the few bars not to have loud music or MTV. Hotel bars are also generally large and impersonal, with the notable exception of the cosy one in the Breza.

FOR NON SKIERS
Not a lot
There isn't sufficient to keep complete non-skiers happy for long, but part-time skiers have a few intriguing options open to them. Excursions to the Rila monastery by coach and to Sofia, by either coach or helicopter, are very interesting. There may also be an opportunity to see ballet in Sofia. Borovets has little to offer, but the Samokov pool is open to the public. The Piano Bar art gallery has some good works at bargain prices.

Romania

LIke Bulgaria, Romania sells mainly on cost. On-the-spot prices, in particular, are very, very low. Provided you have correspondingly low expectations – and provided you go to Poiana Brasov and not Sinaia – you'll probably come back content. If you have any interest in good living, and particularly good lunching, stay away. It's a place for beginners and near-beginners – the skiing is limited in extent and challenge, but the ski tuition is good (and cheap, of course).

There is another dimension to a holiday in Romania, which is the experience of visiting (and you could say supporting) an interesting and attractive country with an exceptionally traumatic recent history. All of our recent reporters commented on the friendliness of the local people, and most recommended exploring beyond the confines of the ski resorts. Bucharest is 'not to be missed'.

Romania's two ski resorts are in the Carpathian mountains, about 120km north-west of the capital and arrival airport, Bucharest. They are very different places, but do have one or two things in common apart from low prices ('difficult to spend £50 in a week, even if you like to drink a lot,' said one reporter). One is good tuition, with excellent spoken English, small classes of 6 to 10 pupils and a patient, friendly approach. Another is very basic mountain restaurants, with primitive sanitary arrangements that would 'shock the toughest of characters'.

The main resort is **Poiana Brasov** (1020m), near the city of Brasov. It is purpose-built, but not for the convenience of skiers: the hotels are dotted about a spacious, pretty wooded plateau, served by regular ski-buses. There is no village as such.

The main skiing consists of decent intermediate tree-lined runs of about 750m vertical, roughly following the line of the main cable-car and gondola, plus an open nursery area at the top. There are also some nursery lifts at village level. There is a black run that takes a less direct route down the mountain, which means that on average it is gentler than the red run under the lifts; it has one moderately steep pitch towards the end. Adventurous skiers would need to seek opportunities to go off-piste. The resorts gets weekend business from Brasov and Bucharest, and the main lifts can suffer serious queues.

The Bradul and Sport hotels are handy for the lower nursery slopes and for one of the cable-cars, but you can't be certain that it will be operating. None of the hotels is special, but the Alpin gets the best reports and the Ciucas is a 'good, basic' place with satellite TV. Après-ski revolves around hotels; they have bars and discos which can be quite lively at times. The two nightclubs put on cheap cabarets including 'Russian ballet dancers attempting to be erotic – quite good fun'. Non-skiing facilities are limited; there is a good-sized pool, and bowling. Excursions are 'surprisingly expensive'.

One or two companies offer holidays in **Sinaia** – a small town on the busy road from Bucharest to Brasov. When we visited it some years ago we were quite taken by the modest intermediate ski area, on largely treeless hills next to the town. In those pre-revolutionary days the town was a rather depressing place, and to judge by reports it is even more so now – one reporter was shocked and saddened by the evident poverty, and upset by the number of stray dogs around.

The abiding impression we brought back from Romania was one of resources stretched to their limits. To judge by the reports we have received, post-revolutionary Romania has not made much progress. One report tells of the loos at Bucharest airport, where three sheets of toilet paper were issued to each person on entry.

Black-and-White pages

A classified listing of the names, numbers and addresses you are likely to need when fixing a ski holiday.

Tour operators *485*

The rest *493*

Tour operators

Arranging your own accommodation in a ski resort is not difficult, whether you do it in advance by letter or phone, or do it on the spot. But most people still prefer the convenience of a package holiday, which is what most of the companies listed below are set up to provide. We've also included a few that offer accommodation without travel arrangements.

AA SKI-DRIVEAWAY
Ski drive specialist
PO Box 128, Fanum House, Basingstoke, Hampshire RG21 2EA
Tel 01256 20123 Fax 01256 493875

ABT SKI
Chalet in St-Martin-de-Belleville
Shepperton Marina, Felix Lane, Shepperton, Middlesex TW17 8NJ
Tel 01932 252025 Fax 01932 246140

ACCESSIBLE ISOLATION
Holidays in Canada
Midhurst Walk, West Street, Midhurst, West Sussex GU29 9NF
Tel 01730 812535 Fax 01730 812926

AGD TRAVEL
Catered apartments in Les Gets
Rails Farmhouse, East Hanningfield, Chelmsford, Essex CM3 8AU
Tel 01245 400684

AIRTOURS
Fast-growing mainstream operator
Wavell House, Holcombe Road, Helmshore, Rossendale, Lancashire BB4 4NB
Tel 01706 260000 Fax 01706 229032

AIRTRACK
Snow-boarding in Serre-Chevalier
16-17 Windsor Street, Uxbridge, Middlesex UB8 1AB
Tel 01895 810810 Fax 01895 254088

ALL CANADA
Holidays in Canada, with some USA
90 High Street, Lowestoft, Suffolk NR32 1XN
Tel 01502 565176 Fax 01502 500681

ALPINE ACTION
Catered chalets in the Trois Vallées
10 Kings Road, Lancing, West Sussex BN15 8EA
Tel 01903 761986 Fax 01903 761986

ALPINE OPTIONS SKIDRIVE
Self-drive and fly-drive to France
70 Glenwood Way, West Moors, Ferndown, Dorset BH22 0ET
Tel 01202 877148 Fax 01202 877148

ALPINE TOURS
Mostly Austria, with Italy, France and Slovenia
54 Northgate, Canterbury, Kent CT1 1BE
Tel 01227 454777 Fax 01227 451177

ALTOURS TRAVEL
Wide-ranging programme
41A Church Street, Staveley, Chesterfield S43 3TL
Tel 01246 471234 Fax 01246 471999

AMERICAN CONNECTIONS
US and Canadian operator
7 York Way, Lancaster Road, High Wycombe, Bucks HP12 3PY
Tel 01494 473173 Fax 01494 473588

AMERICAN DREAM
Major operator to North America
1-7 Station Chambers, High Street North, London E6 1JE
Tel 0181-552 1201 Fax 0181-552 7726

AMERICAN SKIWORLD
Specialist American part of Skiworld
41 North End Road, West Kensington, London W14 8SZ
Tel 0171-602 4826 Fax 0171-371 4904

APS CHALETS
Chalets in Haute Savoie
Spencer Court, 140-142 High Street, Wandsworth, London SW18 4JJ
Tel 0181-875 9235 Fax 0181-875 9236

ARAVIS ALPINE RETREAT
Chalet in La Clusaz
Les Hirondelles, 74450, Saint-Jean-de-Sixt, France
Tel 00 33 50 02 36 25 Fax 00 33 50 02 39 82

AUSTRIAN HOLIDAYS
Hotel holidays in Austria
5th Floor, 10 Wardour Street, London W1V 4BQ
Tel 0171-434 7399 Fax 0171-434 7393

BALKAN HOLIDAYS
Holidays in Bulgaria, Yugoslavia and Romania
Sofia House, 19 Conduit Street, London W1R 9TD
Tel 0171-491 4499 Fax 0171-491 7068

BIGFOOT
Variety of holidays in Chamonix
186 Greys Road, Henley on Thames, Oxon
RG9 1QU
Tel 01491 579601 **Fax** 01491 576568

BLADON LINES
Major operator, emphasis on chalets
56/58 Putney High Street, London SW15 1SF
Tel 0181-780 8800 **Fax** 0181-789 8358

BORDERLINE
Specialist in Barèges
Les Sorbiers, Rue Ramond, 65120 Barèges, France
Tel 01963 250117 **Fax** 00 33 62 92 66 93

CHALET FREESTYLE
Chalet specialist in Les Deux Alpes
7 Burlington Road, Leicester LE2 3DD
Tel 0116-270 3063

CHALET SNOWBOARD
Snowboard holidays in France
31 Aldworth Avenue, Wantage, Oxon OX12 7EJ
Tel 01235 767182 **Fax** 01235 767182

CHALETS DE ST MARTIN
A number of chalets in St-Martin
1-3 Vine Lane, High Street, Christchurch, Dorset
BH23 1AB
Tel 01202 473255 **Fax** 01202 480042

Les Chalets de St. Martin
The village specialists, we own and run –
- The most picturesque and well appointed catered chalets
- Superb self-catering chalets and apartments (in converted farmhouse)
- We are also agents for the hotels and French apartments in St. Martin
- Transfers arranged
Ski from 'The Village' of the 3 valleys
For a brochure: Tel **01202 473255** or **01425 276891** Fax **01202 480042**

CHALETS 'UNLIMITED'
Mainly France and Switzerland
50A Friern Barnet Lane, London N11 3NA
Tel 0181-368 4001 **Fax** 0181-368 1212

CHALETS 'UNLIMITED'
Top of the range chalets, 35 resorts
0181 343 7339

CHALET WORLD
Chalets in big name resorts
PO Box 260, Shrewsbury SY1 1WX
Tel 01952 840462

CHINOOK-IT
Adventure in Canada and USA
30 Sansom Street, Camberwell, London SE5 7RE
Tel 0171-252 5438 **Fax** 0171-252 5438

CLUB EUROPE
Schools and groups, mainly Austria
Fairway House, 53 Dartmouth Road, London
SE23 3HN
Tel 0181-699 7788 **Fax** 0181-699 7770

CLUB MED
All-inclusive holidays in 'ski villages'
106-110 Brompton Road, London SW3 1JJ
Tel 0171-581 1161 **Fax** 0171-581 4769

COLLINEIGE
Chamonix valley specialist
32 High Street, Frimley, Surrey GU16 5JD
Tel 01276 24262 **Fax** 01276 27282

COLOR LINE
Holidays in Norway
International Ferry Terminal, Royal Quay, North
Shields, Tyne and Wear NE29 6EE
Tel 0191-296 1313 **Fax** 0191-296 1540

CONTIKI
Coach-travel holidays for 18-35s
Wells House, 15 Elmfield Road, Bromley, Kent
BR1 1LS
Tel 0181-290 6422 **Fax** 0181-290 6569

CRYSTAL
Major mainstream operator
The Courtyard, Arlington Rd, Surbiton, Surrey
KT6 6BW
Tel 0181-399 5144 **Fax** 0181-390 6378

DAWSON AND SANDERSON
Holidays in Norway
60 Middle Street, Consett, County Durham
DH8 5QE
Tel 01207 591261 **Fax** 01207 591262

DRIVELINE EUROPE
Self-drive to France
Greenleaf House, Darkes Lane, Potters Bar,
Hertfordshire EN6 1AE
Tel 01707 660011 **Fax** 01707 649126

EQUITY TOTAL SKI
All-inclusive holidays
Dukes Lane House, 47 Middle Street, Brighton,
East Sussex BN1 1AL
Tel 01273 203202 **Fax** 01273 203212

FANTISKI
Holidays in France
c/o First Choice Travel Services, Warmlake Estate,
Maidstone Road, Sutton Valence, Kent ME17 3LR
Tel 01622 842555 **Fax** 01622 842458

FINLAYS
Mainly chalets in France
The Green, Ancrum, Borders TD8 6UY
Tel 01835 830562 **Fax** 01835 830550

FIRST CHOICE SKI
Major mainstream operator
Groundstar House, London Road, Crawley
RH10 2TB
Tel 0161-745 7000 **Fax** 01293 525225

FLEXISKI
Specialists in flexible breaks
Crogen Stables, Corwen, Clwyd LL21 0SY
Tel 0171-352 0044 **Fax** 01490 84446

FRANCE DES VILLAGES
Ski-drive holidays to Champagny
Model Farm, Rattlesden, Nr. Bury St Edmunds,
Suffolk IP30 0SY
Tel 01449 737664 **Fax** 01449 737850

FREEDOM
Holidays in Châtel
30 Brackenbury Road, Hammersmith, London
W6 0BA
Tel 0181-741 4471 Fax 0181-741 9332

FRENCH IMPRESSIONS
Mainly self-catering in France
The Broadway, 3-5 Crouch End Hill, London
N8 8DH
Tel 0181-342 8870 Fax 0181-342 8860

FRESH TRACKS
Off-piste specialists, mainly France
Argyll House, 1A All Saints Passage, London
SW18 1EP
Tel 0181-875 9818 Fax 0181-874 8827

FRONTIER SKI
Holidays in Canada
3rd Floor, Broadmead House, 21 Panton Street,
London SW1Y 4DR
Tel 0171-839 5341 Fax 0171-839 5761

HANNIBALS
Holidays in Serre-Chevalier
Farriers, Little Olantigh Road, Wye, Ashford,
Kent TN25 5DQ
Tel 01233 813105 Fax 01233 813432

HUSKI
Holidays in Chamonix
63a Kensington Church Street, London W8 4BA
Tel 0171-938 4844 Fax 0171-938 2312

ICELANDAIR
Holidays in ... Iceland
172 Tottenham Court Rd, London W1P 9LG
Tel 0171-388 5599 Fax 0171-387 5711

INGHAMS
Major mainstream operator
10-18 Putney Hill, London SW15 6AX
Tel 0181-780 4444 OR 0181-780 6600
Fax 0181-785 2045

INNTRAVEL
Cross-country skiing holidays
Hovingham, York YO6 4JZ
Tel 01653 628811 Fax 01653 628741

INTERSKI
Holidays with tuition
95 Outram Street, Sutton-in-Ashfield, Notts
NG17 4BG
Tel 01623 551024 Fax 01623 558941

JEAN STANFORD
Holidays in France
213 Sandcross Lane, Reigate, Surrey RH2 8LL
Tel 01737 242074 Fax 01737 242003

KINGS SKI CLUB
Lively group specialists
1st Floor, Castle Mill, Lower Kings Road,
Berkhamsted, Herts HP4 2AP
Tel 01442 876642 Fax 01442 879968

KUONI
Holidays in Switzerland
Kuoni House, Dorking, Surrey RH5 4AZ
Tel 01306 742500 Fax 01306 744222

LAGRANGE
Self-catering holidays in France
168 Shepherds Bush Road, Hammersmith,
London W6 7PB
Tel 0171-371 6111 Fax 0171-371 2990

LE SHUTTLE HOLIDAYS
Self-drive to France by tunnel
Eurotunnel, PO Box 301, Folkestone, Kent
CT19 4QY
Tel 01303 272303 Fax 01303 850355

LE SKI
Chalets in Courchevel and Val d'Isère
25 Holly Terrace, Huddersfield HD1 6JW
Tel 01484 548996 Fax 01484 451909

LOTUS SUPERTRAVEL
North America, France, Switzerland
Hobbs Court, 2 Jacob Street, London SE1 2BT
Tel 0171-962 9933 Fax 0171-962 9965

MADE TO MEASURE
Wide variety of tailor-made holidays
43 East Street, Chichester, West Sussex
PO19 1HX
Tel 01243 533333 Fax 01243 778431

MARK WARNER
Chalet holidays in big name resorts
20 Kensington Church Street, London W8 4EP
Tel 0171-393 3131 Fax 0171-393 0093

MASTERSKI
Christian holidays
Thames House, 63-67 Kingston Road, New
Malden, Surrey KT3 3PB
Tel 0181-942 9442 Fax 0181-949 4396

MERISKI
Chalet specialist in Méribel
The Old School, Great Barrington, Oxon
OX18 4UR
Tel 01451 844788 Fax 01451 844799

MOGUL SKI
School and group holidays
Royal Chambers, Station Parade, Harrogate,
Yorks HG1 1EP
Tel 01423 569512 Fax 01423 509145

MOSWIN TOURS
Small German programme
Moswin House, 21 Church Street, Oadby,
Leicester LE2 5DB
Tel 0116-271 9922 Fax 0116-271 6016

MOTOURS
French ski-drive operation
Motours House, Old Government Buildings,
Forest Road, Royal Tunbridge Wells, Kent
TN2 5JE
Tel 01892 518555 Fax 01892 518666

NSR TRAVEL
Holidays in Norway
Norwegian State Railways Travel Bureau, Norway
House, Trafalgar Square, 21-24 Cockspur Street,
London SW1Y 5DA
Tel 0171-930 6666 **Fax** 0171-321 0624

NEILSON
Major mainstream operator
Iberotravel Ltd, 29-31 Elmfield Road, Bromley,
Kent BR1 1LT
Tel 0113-239 4555 **Fax** 0113-239 3275

OVER THE HILL
Holidays for the older skier
35-37 Moulsham Street, Chelmsford, Essex
CM2 0HY
Tel 01245 346022 **Fax** 01245 354764

PANORAMA
Budget-oriented holidays
29 Queens Road, Brighton, East Sussex BN1 3YN
Tel 01273 206531 **Fax** 01273 205338

PASSAGE TO SOUTH AMERICA
Tailor-made holidays to South America
113 Shepherds Bush Road, London W6 7LP
Tel 0171-602 9889 **Fax** 0171-602 4251

PEAK SKI
Holidays in Verbier and Argentière
White Lilacs House, Water Lane, Bovingdon,
Herts HP3 0NA
Tel 01442 832629 **Fax** 01442 834303

PEISEY HOLIDAYS
One chalet in Peisey-Nancroix
Chalet Les Sapins, Peisey-Nancroix, Aime 73210,
France
Tel 01252 836186 PM OR 01344 489571
Fax 01344 489572

PGL SKI EUROPE
Specialist in school holidays
Alton Court, Penyard Lane, Ross-on-Wye,
Herefordshire HR9 5NR
Tel 01989 768168 **Fax** 01989 563162

PGL TEEN SKI
School trip specialist
Alton Court, Penyard Lane, Ross on Wye,
Herefordshire HR9 5NR
Tel 01989 764211 **Fax** 01989 765451

PISTE ARTISTE
Holidays in Champéry
Chalet Mon Travail, 1874 Champéry,
Switzerland
Tel 0800 898604 **Fax** 00 41 25 74 13 44

PLUS TRAVEL
Goes to satellites of major resorts
9 Eccleston Street, London SW1W 9LX
Tel 0171-259 0199 **Fax** 0171-259 0190

POLES APART
Holidays in France
75 Compton Avenue, Plymouth, Devon PL3 5DD
Tel 01752 257752 **Fax** 01752 229190

POWDER BYRNE
Small programme of luxury holidays
4 Alice Court, 116 Putney Bridge Road, London
SW15 2NQ
Tel 0181-871 3300 **Fax** 0181-871 3322

POWDER SKIING IN NORTH AMERICA LIMITED
Heli-skiing holidays in Canada
61 Doneraile Street, London SW6 6EW
Tel 0171-736 8191 **Fax** 0171-384 2592

PREMIER SKI
Mainly chalet holidays in Tignes
108 Grange Drive, Swindon SN3 4LD
Tel 01793 823667 **Fax** 01793 823667

RAMBLERS
Cross-country holidays
Box 43, Welwyn Garden City, Herts AL8 6PQ
Tel 01707 331133 **Fax** 01707 333276

RANK STS
School group holidays
Castle Mill, Lower Kings Road, Berkhamsted,
Herts HP4 2AP
Tel 01442 876646 **Fax** 01442 876558

SILVER SKI
Chalet holidays, mainly in France
Conifers House, Grove Green Lane, Maidstone
ME14 5JW
Tel 01622 735544 **Fax** 01622 738550

SIMPLY SKI
Holidays in France and Italy
Chiswick Gate, 598-608 Chiswick High Rd,
London W4 5RT
Tel 0181-742 2541 **Fax** 0181-995 5346

SKI 3000
Chalets in top French resorts
154-156 Victoria Road, Cambridge CB4 3DZ
Tel 01223 302747 **Fax** 01223 314423

SKI ACTIVITY
Holidays in big-name resorts
23 Blair Street, Edinburgh EH1 1QR
Tel 0131-225 9457 Fax 0131-220 4185

SKI ADDICTION
Chalets in Châtel and Chamonix
The Cottage, Fontridge Lane, Etchingham,
East Sussex TN19 7DD
Tel 01580 819354 Fax 01580 819354

SKI AMIS
Chalet holidays in the La Plagne area
Alanda, Hornash Lane, Shadoxhurst, Ashford,
Kent TN26 1HT
Tel 01233 732187 Fax 01233 732769

SKI ARDMORE
School group specialists
11-15 High Street, Marlow, Bucks SL7 1AU
Tel 01628 890060 Fax 01628 898141

SKI ARRANGEMENTS
Chalets in Val d'Isère area
Scotland Nurseries, Tansley, Derbyshire DE4 5GF
Tel 01773 602194 OR 01246 590444
Fax 01246 590654

SKI BALKANTOURS
Holidays in E Europe for schools and groups
37 Ann Street, Belfast BT1 4EB
Tel 01232 246795 Fax 01232 234581

SKI BARRETT-BOYCE
Megève and St-Gervais with tuition
14 Hawthorn Road, Wallington, Surrey SM6 0SX
Tel 0181-647 6934 Fax 0181-647 8620

SKI BEACH VILLAS
Small Italian programme
55 Sidney Street, Cambridge CB2 3QR
Tel 01223 371371 Fax 01223 68626

SKI BEAT
Chalets in La Plagne and Tignes
57 York Road, Montpelier, Bristol BS6 5QD
Tel 0117-955 7361 Fax 0117-941 2099

SKI BON
Catered chalets in Champagny and Méribel
Hilldale, Radnor Cliff Crescent, Folkestone, Kent
CT20 2JQ
Tel 01303 241560

SKI CANADA
Holidays in Canada
Cambridge House, 8 Cambridge Street, Glasgow
G2 3DZ
Tel 0141-332 1511 Fax 0141-353 0135

SKI ÇA VA
Chalet holidays in Montgenèvre
56 Fourth Avenue, Havant, Hampshire PO9 2QX
Tel 01705 484189

SKI CHAMOIS
Holidays in Morzine
18 Lawn Road, Doncaster DN1 2JF
Tel 01302 369006 Fax 01302 326640

SKI CHOICE
Mainly hotel and self-catering
27 High Street, Benson, Oxon OX10 6RP
Tel 01491 837607 Fax 01491 833836

SKI CLUB MEGEVE
Holidays in Mègeve
213 Sandcross Lane, Reigate, Surrey RH2 8LL
Tel 01737 242074 Fax 01737 242003

SKI CLUB OF GB
Holidays for club members
118 Eaton Square, London SW1W 9AF
Tel 0171-245 1033 Fax 0171-245 1258

SKI EQUIPE
Upmarket chalet operator
27 Bramhall Lane South, Bramhall, Stockport,
Cheshire SK7 2DN
Tel 0161-440 0010 Fax 0161-440 0080

SKI ESPRIT
Chalet holidays for families
Oaklands, Reading Road North, Fleet, Hampshire
GU13 8AA
Tel 01252 616789 Fax 01252 811243

SKI EXPERIENCE
Chalets in Méribel
24 College Road, Clifton, Bristol BS8 3HZ
Tel 0117-974 5351 Fax 0117-973 1179

SKI FAMILLE
Family holidays in Les Gets
Unit 9, Chesterton Mill, French's Road,
Cambridge CB4 3NP
Tel 01223 63777 Fax 01223 61508

SKI FRANCE
Chalets and catered apartments
Acorn House, 60 Bromley Common, Bromley,
Kent BR2 9PF
Tel 0181-313 0690 **Fax** 0181-466 0653

SKI HILLWOOD
Austrian and French family holidays
2 Field End Road, Pinner, Middlesex HA5 2QL
Tel 0181-866 9993 **Fax** 0181-868 0258

SKI INDEPENDENCE
Holidays in America and Canada
Osprey Travel, Broughton Market, Edinburgh
EH3 6NU
Tel 0131-557 8555 **Fax** 0131-557 1676

SKI LA VIE
Upmarket holidays in France
28 Linver Road, London SW6 3RB
Tel 0171-736 5611 **Fax** 0171-371 8059

SKI LEOGANG
Leogang specialist
6 Palace Street, London SW1E 5HY
Tel 0171-730 7234 **Fax** 0171-730 1180

SKI LES ALPES
Holidays in Switzerland and France
20 Lansdowne Gardens, London SW8 2EG
Tel 0171-720 7127 **Fax** 0171-720 7134

SKI MIQUEL
Small but eclectic programme
33 High Street, Uppermill, Nr Oldham OL3 6HS
Tel 01457 820200 **Fax** 01457 872715

SKI MOOSE CHALET CO
Chalet in Morzine
23A High Street, Wealdstone, Harrow, Middlesex
HA3 5BY
Tel 0181-427 4475 **Fax** 0181-861 4459

SKI MORGINS
Chalet holidays in Morgins
Raughton Head, Carlisle, Cumbria CA5 7DD
Tel 01697 476258 **Fax** 01697 476258

SKI NEW ENGLAND
Eastern USA holidays
Northwest House, Tinsley Lane North, Crawley,
West Sussex RH10 2TP
Tel 01293 561000 **Fax** 01293 574546

SKI OLYMPIC
Chalet holidays in France
Pine Lodge, Barnsley Rd, Doncaster, South Yorks
DN5 8RB
Tel 01302 390120 **Fax** 01302 390787

SKI PARTNERS
Hotel holidays in Austria, Italy and France
Friary House, Colston Street, Bristol BS1 5AP
Tel 0117-925 3545 **Fax** 0117-929 3697

SKI PEAK
Vaujany specialist operator
The Old Bakery, Dockenfield, Farnham, Surrey
GU10 4HX
Tel 01252 794941 **Fax** 01252 794942

SKI SAFE TRAVEL
Mainly coach holidays to Flaine
Unit 4, Braehead Estate, Old Govan Road,
Renfrew, Scotland PA4 0BJ
Tel 0141-885 1423 **Fax** 0141-812 1544

SKI SAVOIE
Holidays in Courchevel
362-364 Sutton Common Road, Sutton, Surrey
SM3 9PL
Tel 0181-715 1122 **Fax** 0181-644 3068

SKI SCOTT DUNN
Upmarket holidays
Fovant Mews, 12 Noyna Rd, London SW17 7PH
Tel 0181-767 0202 **Fax** 0181-767 2026

SKI TOTAL
European chalet holidays
10 Hill Street, Richmond, Surrey TW9 1TN
Tel 0181-948 6922 **Fax** 0181-332 1268

SKI VAL
Mainly France and America
39A-41 North End Road, West Kensington,
London W14 8SZ
Tel 0171-371 4900 **Fax** 0171-371 4904

SKI VALKYRIE
Travel agent/tour operator hybrid
56 Bower Street, Maidstone, Kent ME16 8SD
Tel 01622 763745 **Fax** 01622 690964

SKI WEEKEND
Weekend and ten-day holidays
2 The Old Barn, Wicklesham Lodge Farm,
Faringdon, Oxon SN7 7PN
Tel 01367 241636 **Fax** 01367 243833

SKI WHITE KNIGHTS
Chalet in Les Deux-Alpes
10 Woolwich Road, Greenwich, London
SE10 0JU
Tel 0181-853 5701

SKI WITH JULIA
Holidays in Switzerland
East Lodge Farm, Stanton, Broadway, Worcs
WR12 7NE
Tel 01386 584478 **Fax** 01386 584629

SKIBOUND
Group holidays specialist
Olivier House, 18 Marine Parade, Brighton,
East Sussex BN2 1TL
Tel 01273 677777 **Fax** 01273 600999

SKIGOWER
School trips, mainly Switzerland
2 High Street, Studley, Warwickshire B80 7HJ
Tel 01527 854822 **Fax** 01527 857236

SKIWORLD
Snowsure European programme
Skiworld House, 41 North End Road, West
Kensington, London W14 8SZ
Tel 0171-602 4826 **Fax** 0171-371 1463

SLOPING OFF
Schools and tailor-made, by coach
31 High Street, Handley, Salisbury, Wiltshire
SP5 5NR
Tel 01725 552247 **Fax** 01725 552489

SNOW COCKTAIL
Vail specialist
Brunel Road, Hinckley, Leicestershire LE10 0AB
Tel 01455 631022 **Fax** 01455 632774

SNOWBIZZ VACANCES
Holidays in Puy-St-Vincent
69 High Street, Maxey, Peterborough PE6 9EE
Tel 01778 341455 **Fax** 01778 347422

SNOWCOACH CLUB CANTABRICA
Coach-based holidays
Holiday House, 146-148 London Rd, St Albans,
Herts AL1 1PQ
Tel 01727 866177 **Fax** 01727 843766

SNOWED IN AMERICA
Chalets in Breckenridge
PO Box 140, Manchester M60 1GB
Tel 0161-839 8079

SNOWFOCUS
Chalet in Châtel with nannies
Cambray House, 48 Montholme Road, London
SW11 6HY
Tel 0171-924 6171 **Fax** 0171-924 4232

SNOWISE
Holidays in Châtel
The Farmhouse, Nix Hill, Manea Road,
Wimblington, March, Cambs
Tel 01354 741403 **Fax** 01354 740493

SNOWMAN SKIING
Own one hotel near Mègeve (Le Bettex)
Llangarron, Ross-on-Wye, Herefordshire
HR9 6PG
Tel 01989 770766 **Fax** 01989 770752

SNOWTIME
Holidays in Méribel
96 Belsize Lane, London NW3 5BE
Tel 0171-433 3336 **Fax** 0171-433 1883

SOLO'S
Singles' holidays, ages 30-49 or 50-69
41 Watford Way, Hendon, London NW4 3JH
Tel 0181-202 0855 **Fax** 0181-202 4749

STENA SEALINK
Ski-drive to France, Austria and Italy
Charter House, Park Street, Ashford, Kent
TN24 8EX
Tel 01233 647033 **Fax** 01233 612016

SUMMIT CHALET COMPANY
Holidays in Breckenridge
72 Whitney Court, Coram St, London WC1
Tel 0171-837 4166 **Fax** 0171-837 4166

SUNQUEST SKI
Holidays in Eastern Europe
9 Grand Parade, Green Lanes, London N4 1JX
Tel 0171-499 9991 **Fax** 0171-499 9995

SWISS TRAVEL SERVICE
Mainly hotels in Switzerland
Bridge House, 55-59 High Road, Broxbourne,
Herts EN10 7DT
Tel 01992 456123 **Fax** 01992 448855

THE SKI COMPANY
Holidays in France, with tuition
13 Squires Close, Bishop's Park, Bishop's
Stortford, Herts CM23 4DB
Tel 01279 653746 **Fax** 01279 654705

THE SKI COMPANY LTD
Luxury chalets mainly in France
c/o Abercrombie & Kent, Sloane Square House,
Holbein Place, London SW1W 8NS
Tel 0171-730 9600 **Fax** 0171-730 9376

THOMSON
Major mainstream operator
Greater London House, Hampstead Rd, London
NW1 7SD
Tel 0121-632 6282 **Fax** 0171-387 8451

TIMESCAPE HOLIDAYS
Budget holidays by coach to Austria
581 Roman Road, London E3 5EL
Tel 0181-980 7244 **Fax** 0181-980 7157

TOP DECK
Lively, informal holidays
131-133 Earls Court Rd, London SW5 9RH
Tel 0171-370 4555 **Fax** 0171-373 6201

TRAIL ALPINE
Small but varied programme
Papertree House, 68 Mostyn Street, Llandudno,
Gwynedd LL30 2SB
Tel 01492-871770 **Fax** 01492-872437

TRAVELSCENE SKI-DRIVE
Self-drive holidays, mainly in France
11-15 St Ann's Road, Harrow, Middlesex
HA1 1AS
Tel 0181-863 2787 **Fax** 0181-861 4154

UCPA
All-inclusive budget trips
c/o Action Vacances, 30 Brackley Road,
Stockport, Cheshire SK4 2RE
Tel 0161-442 6130 **Fax** 0161-442 6130

USAIRTOURS
Holidays in America
1 Raven Road, London E18 1HD
Tel 0181-559 7700 **Fax** 0181-559 7722

VAL D'ISÈRE PROPERTIES
Specialist in Val d'Isère
Hyde Park House, Manfred Road, London
SW15 2RS
Tel 0181-875 1957 **Fax** 0181-875 9236

VIRGIN SNOW
Holidays to America
Virgin Holidays Limited, Galleria, Station Road,
Crawley, West Sussex RH10 1WW
Tel 01293 617181 **Fax** 01293 536957

WAYMARK HOLIDAYS
Cross-country skiing holidays
44 Windsor Rd, Slough SL1 2EJ
Tel 01753 516477 **Fax** 01753 517016

WHITE ROC
Weekends and short breaks
69 Westbourne Grove, London W2 4UJ
Tel 0171-792 1188 **Fax** 0171-792 1956

WINTERSKI
Holidays mainly in Italy
31 Old Steine, Brighton BN1 1EL
Tel 01273 626242 **Fax** 01273 620222

YSE
Variety of holidays in Val d'Isère
The Business Village, Broomhill Rd, London
SW18 4JQ
Tel 0181-871 5117 **Fax** 0181-871 5229

AIRLINES

AIR CANADA
7/8 Conduit Street, London W1R 9TG
Tel 0181-759 2636 Fax 0181-564 7644
Linkline number from outside London 0345 181313

AIR FRANCE
Colet Court, 100 Hammersmith Road, London W6 7JP
Tel 0181-742 6600 Fax 0181-750 4488

AIR UK LTD
Liberator Rd, Norwich Airport Industrial Estate, Norwich, Norfolk NR6 6ER
Tel 0345 666777 Fax 01603 418217

ALITALIA
205 Holland Park Avenue, London W11 4XB
Tel 0171-602 7111 Fax 0171-603 5584
Linkline from outside London 0345 212121

AMERICAN AIRLINES
23/59 Staines Road, Hounslow TW3 3HE
Tel 0181-572 5555 Fax 0181-572 8646
Linkline from outside London 0345 789789

AUSTRIAN AIRLINES
5th Floor, 10 Wardour Street, London W1V 4BJ
Tel 0171-434 7300 Fax 0171-434 7363

BRITISH AIRWAYS
PO Box 10, London Heathrow Airport, Hounslow, Middlesex TW6 2JA
Tel 0345 222111

CANADIAN AIRLINES
23-59 Staines Rd, Hounslow, Middlesex TW3 3HE
Tel 0345 616767

CONTINENTAL AIRLINES
Beulah Court, Albert Road, Horley RH6 7HP
Tel 0800 776464 Fax 01293 773726

DELTA AIRLINES
Ground Floor, Oakfield Court, Consort Way, Horley, Surrey RH6 7AF
Tel 0800 414767 Fax 01293 821374

LAUDA AIR
Units 1 and 2, Colonnade Walk, 123 Buckingham Palace Road, London SW1W 9SH
Tel 0171-630 5924 Fax 0171-828 9611
Freephone number 0800 767737

LUFTHANSA GERMAN AIRLINES
Lufthansa House, 10 Old Bond Street, London W1X 4EN
Tel 0181-750 3500 Fax 0181-750 3460

NORTHWEST AIRLINES
Northwest House, Tinsley Lane North, Crawley RH10 2TP
Tel 01293 561000 Fax 01293 574537

SWISSAIR
Swiss Centre, 1 Swiss Court, London W1V 4BJ
Tel 0171-439 4144 Fax 0171-439 7375

UNITED AIRLINES
United House, Building 451, Southern Perimeter Road, London Heathrow Airport, Middlesex TW6 3LP
Tel 0181-990 9900 Fax 0181-759 7019
Freephone number 0800 888555

VIRGIN ATLANTIC AIRWAYS
Ashdown House, High Street, Crawley RH10 1BZ
Tel 01293 747747 Fax 01293 561721

AIRPORTS

ABERDEEN AIRPORT LTD
Dyce, Aberdeenshire AB2 0DU
Tel 01224 722331 Fax 01224 725724

BELFAST INTERNATIONAL AIRPORT
Belfast BT29 4AB
Tel 01849 422888 Fax 01849 452096

BIRMINGHAM INTERNATIONAL AIRPORT
Birmingham B26 3QJ
Tel 0121-767 5511 Fax 0121-782 8802

BOURNEMOUTH INTERNATIONAL AIRPORT
Christchurch BH23 6SE
Tel 01202 593939 Fax 01202 570266

BRISTOL AIRPORT
Bristol BS19 3DY
Tel 01275 474444 Fax 01275 474099

CARDIFF-WALES AIRPORT
Rhoose, South Glamorgan CF62 3BD
Tel 01446 711111 Fax 01446 711675

DUBLIN AIRPORT
Dublin, Eire
Tel 00 353 1 8444900 Fax 00 353 1 7044643

EAST MIDLANDS AIRPORT
Castle Donington, Derby DE74 2SA
Tel 01332 852852 Fax 01332 850393

EDINBURGH AIRPORT
Edinburgh EH12 9DN
Tel 0131-333 1000 Fax 0131-335 3181

EXETER AND DEVON AIRPORT
Exeter, Devon EX5 2BD
Tel 01392 367433 Fax 01392 364593

GLASGOW AIRPORT
Paisley PA3 2ST
Tel 0141-887 1111 Fax 0141-842 1412

LEEDS-BRADFORD INTERNATIONAL AIRPORT
Leeds LS19 7TZ
Tel 0113 2509696 Fax 0113 2505426

LONDON GATWICK AIRPORT
Gatwick, West Sussex RH6 0NP
Tel 01293 535353 Fax 01293 504153

LONDON HEATHROW AIRPORT
Hounslow, Middlesex TW6 1JH
Tel 0181-759 4321 Fax 0181-745 5323

LONDON LUTON AIRPORT
Luton, Bedfordshire LU2 9LY
Tel 01582 405100 Fax 01582 395313

LONDON STANSTED AIRPORT
Enterprise House, Stansted, Essex CM24 1QW
Tel 01279 680500 Fax 01279 662461

MANCHESTER AIRPORT
Wythenshawe, Manchester M90 1QX
Tel 0161-489 3000 Fax 0161-489 3813

NEWCASTLE INTERNATIONAL AIRPORT LTD
Woolsington, Newcastle-upon-Tyne NE13 8BZ
Tel 0191-286 0966 Fax 0191-271 6080

TEESSIDE INTERNATIONAL AIRPORT
Darlington, Co. Durham DL2 1LU
Tel 01325 332811 Fax 01325 332810

BREAKDOWN INSURANCE

AA FIVE STAR SERVICE
AA Five Star Postlink, Freepost, PO Box 128, Basingstoke, Hants RG21 1BR
Tel 0345 555577 Fax 01256 460750

AUTOHOME
202-204 Kettering Road, Northampton NN1 4HE
Tel 01604 232334 Fax 01604 231304

BRITANNIA CONTINENTAL
St Georges Square, Huddersfield, West Yorkshire HD1 1JF
Tel 01484 514848 Fax 01484 518961

EUROP ASSISTANCE
Sussex House, Perrymount Rd, Haywards Heath, West Sussex RH16 1DN
Tel 01444 442211 Fax 0181-680 8992

INTERNATIONAL ASSISTANCE SERVICES
32 High Street, Purley, Surrey CR8 2PP
Tel 0181-763 1550 Fax 0181-668 1262

LEISURECARE INSURANCE SERVICES
Shaftesbury Centre, Percy Street, Swindon, Wilts SN2 2AZ
Tel 01793 514199 Fax 01793 481333

MONDIAL ASSISTANCE UK
Mondial House, 1 Scarbrook Rd, Croydon, Surrey CR0 1SQ
Tel 0181-681 2525 Fax 0181-680 2769

NATIONAL BREAKDOWN
PO Box 300, Leeds LS99 2LZ
Tel 0800 800600

RAC TRAVEL SERVICES
RAC Enterprises Ltd, P.O. Box 499, Croydon CR2 6ZH
Tel 0800 550055 Fax 0181-681 8710

CAR HIRE

ALAMO
Alamo House, Stockley Close, Stockley Rd, West Drayton, Middlesex UB7 9BA
Tel 01895 443355 Fax 01895 441133

AVIS
Trident House, Station Road, Hayes, Middlesex UB3 4DJ
Tel 0181-848 8765 Fax 0181-561 2604

BUDGET
41 Marlowes, Hemel Hempstead HP1 1XJ
Tel 0800 181181 Fax 01442 276041

EURODOLLAR
Beasley Court, Warwick Place, Uxbridge UB8 1PE
Tel 01895 256565 Fax 01895 256050

EUROPCAR INTERRENT
Europcar Interrent House, Aldenham Road, Watford, Herts WD2 2LX
Tel 01923 811000 Fax 01923 811010

HERTZ
Radnor House, 1272 London Road, Norbury, London SW16 4XW
Tel 0181-679 1777 Fax 0181-679 9931

HOLIDAY AUTOS
25 Saville Row, Mayfair, London W1X 1AA
Tel 0171-491 1111 Fax 0171-355 4352

SUNCARS
Sandrocks, Rocky Lane, Haywards Heath, West Sussex RH16 4RH
Tel 01444 456446 Fax 01444 441234

Car Winter Equipment

Brindley Chains Ltd
1 Tatton Court, Kingsland Grange, Warrington
WA1 4RR
Tel 01925 825555 Fax 01925 825338
Pewag snow-chains

Discount Autoparts
122 Newmarket Road, Cambridge CB5 8HE
Tel 01223 323488 Fax 01223 324952
Thule roof systems, Kar Rite boxes, Skandibox

GT Towing Ltd
6 Hatfield Rd, Potters Bar, Herts EN6 1HP
Tel 01707 652118 Fax 01707 644638
Ski boxes and snow-chains

Kar Rite Europe Ltd
One and Two Falconer Road, Haverhill, Suffolk
CB9 7XU
Tel 01440 712829 Fax 01440 712843
Luggage boxes

Latchmere Motor Spares
93-97 Latchmere Road, London SW11 2DR
Tel 0171-223 5491 Fax 0171-228 3907
Snow-chains, roof bars, ski clamps, boxes

Motor Traveller
225 St Leonards Road, Windsor SL4 3DR
Tel 01753 833442 Fax 01753 832495
Thule racks and boxes; Milz snowchains

Snowchains Ltd
Wrotham Road, Borough Green, Kent TN15 8DG
Tel 01732 884408 Fax 01732 884564
Thule roofbars and ski-racks; Weissenfels snow-chains

Thule Ltd
Units 4 & 5 Concorde Drive, 5c Business Centre,
Clevedon, BS21 6UH
Tel 01275 340404 Fax 01275 340686

Clothing Retailers

Ski Occasions
The Priors Shopping Centre, 704 High Rd,
North Finchley, London N12
Tel 0181-445 4233 Fax 0181-445 2790
Buy and sell nearly-new ski clothing

Cross-Channel Travel

Brittany Ferries
Millbay Docks, Plymouth PL1 3EW
Tel 01705 827701 **Fax** 01752 661308
Route: Portsmouth - Caen

Hoverspeed
International Hoverport, Marine Parade, Dover,
Kent CT17 9TG
Tel 01304 240241 **Fax** 01304 240099
Routes: Dover - Calais, Folkestone - Boulogne

Le Shuttle
Cheriton Parc, Cheriton High Street, Cheriton,
Folkestone, Kent CT19 4QS
Tel 01303 271100 **Fax** 01303 850360
Channel Tunnel service, reservations not required

North Sea Ferries
King George Dock, Hedon Road, Hull HU9 5QA
Tel 01482 377177 **Fax** 01482 706438
Routes: Hull - Zeebrugge, Hull - Rotterdam

P & O European Ferries
Channel House, Channel View Road, Dover,
Kent CT17 9TJ
Tel 01304 212121 **Fax** 01304 223223
*Routes: Dover - Calais, Portsmouth - Le Havre,
Portsmouth - Cherbourg, Felixstowe - Zeebrugge*

Sally Lines
Argyle Centre, York Street, Ramsgate, Kent
CT11 9DS
Tel 01843 595522 **Fax** 01843 589329
Routes: Ramsgate - Dunkerque, Ramsgate - Ostend

Stena Sealink Line
Charter House, Park Street, Ashford, Kent
TN24 8EX
Tel 01233 647047 **Fax** 01233 646024
*Routes: Dover - Calais, Harwich - Hook, Newhaven -
Dieppe, Southampton - Cherbourg*

Equipment Distributors

Ardblair Sports Ltd
James Street, Blairgowrie, Perthshire, PH10 6EZ
Tel 01250 873863 **Fax** 01250-875289
Volkl skis and poles, Leki ski poles

Blue Ridge
The Gate Studio, Station Road, Borehamwood,
Herts WD6 1DE
Tel 0181-207 6775 **Fax** 0181-207 5650
Pre skis, Tecnica, Geze

Europa Sport
Ann Street, Kendal, Cumbria LA9 6AA
Tel 01539 724740 **Fax** 01539 726314
*Nordica boots, Kastle skis, Marker bindings, Gipron
poles*

Euroski
66/67 North Road, Brighton BN1 1YD
Tel 01273 688258 **Fax** 01273 701004
Alpina

Glacier Imports
74 Prospect Road, Southborough, Tunbridge
Wells, Kent TN4 0EH
Tel 01892 543952 **Fax** 01892 535464
*Atomic, Koflach, Ess, Oxygen (snowboarding
equipment)*

Headwall Ltd
26 Durlston Park Drive, Bookham, Surrey
KT23 4AJ
Tel 01372 456685

Mast Co
24 Albert Road, Caversham, Reading RG4 7PE
Tel 01734 471735 **Fax** 01734 461213
Fischer, Dynafit, Tyrolia, Raichle

Outdoor Leisure
Moac House, Demmings Road, Industrial Estate,
Cheadle, Cheshire SK8 2PE
Tel 0161-428 1178 **Fax** 0161-428 1243
K2

Salomon
Annecy House, Gastons Wood, Reading Road,
Basingstoke, Hants RG24 OTW
Tel 01256 479555 **Fax** 01256 465562

Sportline Ltd
Dominion House, Kennet Side, Bone Lane,
Newbury, Berks RG14 5PX
Tel 01635 48387 **Fax** 01635 38682
Head

Ultra Sport
Acton Grove, Acton Road Industrial Estate, Long
Eaton, Nottingham NG10 1FY
Tel 0115-973 1001 **Fax** 0115-946 1067
Rossignol, Look bindings

Vango (Scotland) Ltd
70 East Hamilton Street, Ladywood, Greenock,
PA15 2UB
Tel 01475 744122 **Fax** 01475 742333
Rossignol skis and boots

Ventura
Hall House, New Hutton, Kendal, Cumbria
LA8 OAH
Tel 01539 728386 **Fax** 01539 741165
Lange, Dynastar, Kerma ski poles

INSURANCE COMPANIES

ACCIDENT AND GENERAL
ISIS Building, Thames Quay, 193 Marsh Wall,
London E14 9SG
Tel 0171-512 0022 Fax 0171-512 0602
APPLE BOOKING COMPANY
Apple Barn, Smeeth, Ashford, Kent TN25 6SR
Tel 0800 414141 Fax 01303 812893
BUPA TRAVEL COVER
Sussex House (Ground floor), 58-62 Perrymount
Road, Haywards Heath, West Sussex RH16 1BR
Tel 01444 442400 Fax 01444 455204
Cover provided by Europ Assistance
BISHOPSGATE INSURANCE
Bishopsgate House, Tollgate, Eastleigh, Hants
SO53 3YA
Tel 01703 313030 Fax 01703 644614
BRITISH ACTIVITY HOLIDAY INSURANCE SERVICES
Security House, Frog Lane, Tunbridge Wells, Kent
TN1 1YT
Tel 01892 534411 Fax 01892 511980
For groups of 10 or more only
COLUMBUS TRAVEL INSURANCE
17, Devonshire Square, London EC2M 4SQ
Tel 0171-375 0011 Fax 0171-375 0022
COMMERCIAL UNION
PO Box 420, St Helens, 1 Undershaft, London
EC3P 3DQ
Tel 0171-283 7500 Fax 0171-662 8140
CORK, BAYS & FISHER
66 Prescot Street, London E1 8HG
Tel 0171-481 0707 Fax 0171-488 9786
DEREK KETTERIDGE & ASSOCIATES
Ketteridge Vaughan, New Loom House Suite 8,
101 Back Church Lane, London E1 1LU
Tel 0171-702 1912 Fax 0171-702 1909

DOUGLAS COX TYRIE
Central House, 32/66 High Street, Stratford,
London E15 2PF
Tel 0181-534 9595 Fax 0181-519 8780
EUROP ASSISTANCE
Sussex House, Perrymount Rd, Haywards Heath,
West Sussex RH16 1DN
Tel 01444 442211 Fax 01444 459292
GENERAL ACCIDENT
Pitheavlis, Perth PH2 0NH
Tel 01738 621202 Fax 01738 621843
HAMILTON BARR INSURANCE BROKERS
Bridge Mews, Bridge Street, Godalming, Surrey
GU7 1HZ
Tel 01483 426600 Fax 01483 426382
JS INSURANCE
196-197 High Street, Egham, Middlesex
TW20 9ED
Tel 01784 430043 Fax 01784 472601

JARDINE INSURANCE BROKERS
23rd Floor, Sunley Tower, Piccadilly Plaza,
Manchester M1 4BT
Tel 0161-228 3742 Fax 0161-228 6475
MATTHEW GERARD TRAVEL INSURANCE SERVICES
MG House, 7 Westminster Court, Hipley Street,
Old Woking, Surrey GU22 9LQ
Tel 01483 730900 Fax 01483 730969
McKLEAN, KENT AND COOMBER (MKC)
Nevendon Hall, Nevendon Road, Basildon, Essex
SS13 1BX
Tel 01268 590658 Fax 01268 590860
P J HAYMAN & CO
Forestry House, New Barn Road, Buriton,
Nr Petersfield, Hants GU31 5 SL
Tel 01730 260222 Fax 01730 266655
PERRY, GAMBLE & CO
Tuition House, 27/37 St George's Road, London
SW19 4XE
Tel 0181-879 1255 Fax 0181-879 1767
SNOWCARD
Lower Boddington, Daventry, Northants N11 6BR
Tel 01327 62805 Fax 01327 62805

SURETRAVEL
The Pavilions, Kiln Park Business Centre,
Kiln Lane, Epsom, Surrey KT17 1JG
Tel 01372 749191 Fax 01372 749701
TRAVEL INSURANCE SERVICE
Rowlandson House, 289/293 Ballards Lane,
London N12 8NP
Tel 0181-446 8431 Fax 0181-445 9085
VISASPORTS U.K.
62 Prince Street, Bristol, Avon BS1 4QD
Tel 0117-922 6222 Fax 0117-930 8601

WHITELEY INSURANCE CONSULTANTS
Kingfisher House, Portland Place, Halifax
HX1 2JH
Tel 01422 348411 **Fax** 01422 330345

NATIONAL TOURIST OFFICES

ANDORRAN DELEGATION
63 Westover Road, London SW18 2RF
Tel 0181-874 4806

ARGENTINIAN TOURIST BOARD
Trevor House, 5th Floor, 100 Brompton Road,
London SW3 1ER
Tel 0171-589 3104 **Fax** 0171-584 7863

AUSTRALIAN TOURIST COMMISSION
Gemini House, 10/18 Putney Hill, Putney,
London SW15 6AA
Tel 0181-780 2227 **Fax** 0181-780 1496

AUSTRIAN NATIONAL TOURIST OFFICE
30 St George Street, London W1R 0AL
Tel 0171-629 0461 **Fax** 0171-499 6038

CANADIAN TOURIST OFFICE
62-65 Trafalgar Square, London WC2N 5DY
Tel 0171-839 2299 **Fax** 0171-839 1149

CHILE - CONSULATE GENERAL
12 Devonshire Street, London W1N 2DS
Tel 0171-580 1023 **Fax** 0171-436 5204

FRENCH GOVERNMENT TOURIST OFFICE
178 Piccadilly, London W1V 0AL
Tel 0891 244123 **Fax** 0171-493 6594

GERMAN NATIONAL TOURIST OFFICE
65 Curzon Street, London W1Y 8NE
Tel 0891 600100 **Fax** 0171-495 6129

ITALIAN STATE TOURIST OFFICE
1 Princes Street, London W1R 8AY
Tel 0171-408 1254 **Fax** 0171-493 6695

NEW ZEALAND TOURISM BOARD
New Zealand House, Haymarket, London SW1Y
4TQ
Tel 0839 300900 **Fax** 0171-839 8929

NORWEGIAN TOURIST BOARD
Charles House, 5/11 Lower Regent Street,
London SW1Y 4LR
Tel 0171-839 6255 **Fax** 0171-839 6014

ROMANIAN NATIONAL TOURIST OFFICE
83A Marylebone High Street, London W1M 3DE
Tel 0171-224 3692 **Fax** 0171-224 3692

SCOTTISH TOURIST BOARD
23 Ravelston Terrace, Edinburgh EH4 3EU
Tel 0131-332 2433 **Fax** 0131-343 1513

SLOVENIAN TOURIST OFFICE
2 Canfield Place, London NW6 3BT
Tel 0171-372 3844 **Fax** 0171-372 3763

SPANISH TOURIST OFFICE
57/58 St James's Street, London SW1A 1LD
Tel 0171-499 1169 **Fax** 0171-629 4257

SWEDISH TRAVEL AND TOURISM COUNCIL
73 Welbeck Street, London W1M 8AN
Tel 0171-935 9784 **Fax** 0171-935 5853

SWISS NATIONAL TOURIST OFFICE
Swiss Centre, Swiss Court, London W1V 8EE
Tel 0171-734 1921 **Fax** 0171-437 4577

**UNITED STATES TRAVEL AND TOURISM
ADMINISTRATION**
PO Box 170, Ashford, Kent TN24 0ZX
Tel 0171-495 4466

Railways

British Rail International
Victoria Station, London SW1V 1JY
Tel 0171-834 2345 Fax 0171-922 9874

French Railways
179 Piccadilly, London W1V 9DB
Tel 0345 300003 Fax 0171-409 2408
Timetable - 0891 515477; Motorail - 0171-409 3518

German Rail
Suite 4, 23 Oakhill Grove, Surbiton KT6 6DU
Tel 0891 887755 Fax 0181-399 4700

Swiss Federal Railways
Swiss Centre, Swiss Court, London W1V 8EE
Tel 0171-734 1921 Fax 0171-437 4577

Ski Organisations

Artificial Ski Slope Instructors (ASSI)
The English Ski Council, Area Library Building,
Queensway Mall, The Cornbow, Halesowen,
West Midlands B63 4AJ
Tel 0121-501 2314 Fax 0121-585 6448

British Association of Ski Instructors (BASI)
Grampian Road, Aviemore, Inverness PH22 1RL
Tel 01479 810407 Fax 01479 811222

British Ski Association
19 Market Street, Carnforth, Lancashire LA5 9JR
Tel 01524 720322 Fax 01524 720087

British Ski Club for the Disabled
Springmount, Berwick St John, Shaftesbury SP7 0HQ
Tel 01747 828515

British Ski Federation
258 Main Street, East Calder, West Lothian,
Scotland EH53 0EE
Tel 01506 884343 Fax 01506 882952

British Snowboarding Association
5 Cressex Rd, High Wycombe, Bucks HP12 4PG
Tel 01494 462225 Fax 01494 462225

English Ski Council
Area Library Building, Queensway Mall, The
Cornbow, Halesowen, West Midlands B63 4AJ
Tel 0121-501 2314 Fax 0121-585 6448

Scottish National Ski Council
Caledonia House, South Gyle, Edinburgh EH12 9DQ
Tel 0131-317 7280 Fax 0131-339 8602

Ski Club of Great Britain
118 Eaton Square, London SW1W 9AF
Tel 0171-245 1033 Fax 0171-245 1258

Ski Council of Wales
240 Whitchurch Road, Cardiff, CF4 3ND
Tel 01222 619637 Fax 01222 619637

The Uphill Ski Club
12 Park Crescent, London W1N 4EQ
Tel 0171-636 1989 Fax 0171-436 2601
Ski organisation for the disabled

Ulster Ski Council
8 Abercorn Park, Hillsborough, County Down,
Northern Ireland
Tel 01846 683243
Ring in evenings only

SPECIALIST SKI TRAVEL AGENTS

ALPINE ANSWERS
The Business Village, 3-9 Broomhill Road,
London SW18 4JQ
Tel 0181-871 5100 **Fax** 0181-871 9676

Talk to skiers who have skied
where you want to **ski**...
Talk to skiers who have stayed
where you want to **stay**...

EXPERT ADVICE ON EUROPE, CANADA & USA

0181 871 5100
ABTA D4050

CHALET CONNECTIONS
1st Floor, 79 Street Lane, Roundhay, Leeds
LS8 1AP
Tel 0113-237 0371 **Fax** 0113-269 3305
Deals only with smaller operators

SKI ÇA VA
56 Fourth Avenue, Havant, Hampshire PO 2QX
Tel 01705-484189

♦ Tailor-made ski holidays to France,
Switzerland and USA. Independent
accommodation, flights and
insurance arranged.
♦ Chalets, Inns, Apartments,
Condos, Log cabins
♦ Brochures available on each resort
and accommodation

Ski Holiday Consultants

Phone Paul or Toni on 01705 484189

SKI LES ALPES
20 Lansdowne Gardens, London SW8 2EG
Tel 0171-720 7127 **Fax** 0171-720 7134

Ski Les Alpes
Don't have a good holiday -
—— **Have a brilliant one!** ——
With our indepth experience and excellent service, all
you have to worry about is when you can go again.
0171 720 7127
ATOL 2987

SKI OPTIONS
Hobbs Court, Jacob Street, London SE1 2BT
Tel 0171-962 9940 **Fax** 0171-962 9932

SKI SOLUTIONS
84 Pembroke Road, Kensington, London
W8 6NX
Tel 0171-602 9900 **Fax** 0171-602 2882

Ski Solutions
Britain's leading ski travel agency

*Book your 94/95 ski holiday
through us, and you can get the
price of this book refunded.*

*See our main ad on pages 48 and
49, and details of the refund
scheme on page 9.*

SKI TRAVEL CENTRE
1100 Pollokshaws Road, Glasgow G41 3NJ
Tel 0141-649 9696 **Fax** 0141-649 2273

SKIERS TRAVEL BUREAU
79 Street Lane, Roundhay, Leeds LS8 1AP
Tel 0113-266 6876 **Fax** 0113-269 3305

SNOW LINE
1 Angel Court, High Street, Market Harborough,
Leics LE16 7NL
Tel 01858 433633 **Fax** 01858 433266

Snow Line *The* Skiers
Travel Agent
EXPERT SERVICE & THE BEST DEALS
ALL SKI RESORTS IN EUROPE & USA
COMPUTER LINKED TO SKI OPERATORS **CALL TODAY**
EUROPE **01858 433633** **BEST DEALS**
Free USA **01858 434500** **for Chalets**
Service FLIGHTS **01858 434363** **Flights, USA.**
VISA MASTERCARD ABTA CO4OX DELTA SWITCH

SUSIE WARD
Hurling Burrow, Sevenmilestone, St Agnes,
Cornwall TR5 0PG
Tel 01872 553055 **Fax** 01872 553050

THE
Susie Ward.
COMPANY

**CHALETS AND HOTELS
IN TOP SKI RESORTS**
Rely on years of experience

**SUSIE WARD
01872 553055**
ABTA
D 7909

snowboarding
published by refuge publications

The Universal Snowboard Guide, the worlds first comprehensive guide on where to snowboard. Written and compiled by a snowboarder.

UNIVERSAL SNOWBOARD GUIDE
Carving Snowboard friendly resorts around the world

Info On The Best:
- Half Pipes
- Fun Parks
- Freestyle resorts
- Euro Carving Resorts
- Snowboard Hangouts
- Snowboard Life Style
- Snowboard Camps
- Summer Snowboarding

£9.99

The Scottish Snowboard Passport is the simply to use · no nonsense must, for those wanting to get the best out of Scotland .Each passport contains £7.50's worth of lift pass vouchers, a guide on all of the Scottish mountain resorts, a Scottish dry slope and snowboard shop directory, facts and tips about Scottish Snowboarding and a lot more in an 80 page pocket booklet.

Scottish
SNOWBOARD
Passport

£4.99

To order either book please-send Cheques or Postal orders payable to:

RP
Refuge Publications

Refuge Publications
45 Corrour road
Dalfaber, Aviemore
Inverness-shire.
PH22 1SS

☎

Telephone & Credit Card order line 01479 810 362

Resort directory / Index

As well as the resorts we've covered in detail there are literally hundreds more in the Alps and North America, most of them much smaller than those we've given full coverage to. Here we give brief details on another 250-plus; many of these are well worth exploring, especially if you're in the area already or touring around. We also list the pages on which you'll find the in-depth coverage of the main resorts.

Key

⌁ *Lifts*
⅄ *Pistes*
⊠ *Tour operators*

Abetone Italy
Resort in the exposed (and as such fairly reliable for snow) Appenines, less than two hours from both Florence and Pisa. Good for a ski/culture trip.
1390m; skiing 1390m–2160m
⌁ *27* ⅄ *50km*

Achenkirch Austria
Unspoilt, low-altitude Tyrolean village close to Niederau and Alpbach, in a beautiful setting overlooking a lake.
930m; skiing 950m–1780m
⌁ *14* ⅄ *25km*
⊠ *Ramblers, Winterski*

Adelboden Switzerland **306**

Akakura Japan
Old spa of some oriental charm, 150km from Tokyo, with a modern lift system serving mostly easy skiing.
770m; skiing 770m–1500m
⌁ *41* ⅄ *85km*

Alagna Italy **281**

Alba Italy
Picturesque Dolomite village with a small, quiet ski area, and well placed for access to the Sella Ronda at nearby Canazei.
1515m; skiing 1515m–2430m
⌁ *5* ⅄ *10km*
⊠ *Chalets 'Unlimited', Crystal, Simply Ski*

Alleghe Italy
Dolomite village in a pretty lakeside setting close to numerous ski areas. Cheap base from which to ski nearby Cortina.
980m ⌁ *24* ⅄ *80km*
⊠ *Altours Travel*

Alpbach Austria **54**

Alpe-d'Huez France **137**

Alpendorf Austria
Hamlet-cum-base-station 4km from St Johann im Pongau, with immediate access to the Salzburger Sportwelt ski area.
800m; skiing 800m–2185m
⌁ *59* ⅄ *200km*

Alpine Meadows USA **412**

Alta USA **382**

Altenmarkt Austria
Unspoilt village well placed just off the Salzburg-Villach autobahn for skiing numerous resorts including snowsure Obertauern and pretty Wagrain.
855m; skiing 855m–1675m
⌁ *9* ⅄ *30km*
⊠ *Alpine Tours, Made to Measure, Mogul Ski*

Aminona Switzerland **316**

Andalo Italy
Atmospheric Dolomite village near Madonna with low wooded skiing well supported by snowmakers, best for novices and leisurely intermediates.
1050m; skiing 1040m–2125m
⌁ *17* ⅄ *40km*
⊠ *Equity Total Ski, Sloping Off, Winterski*

Andermatt Switzerland **307**

Les Angles France
Characterless Pyrenean resort with a good sports centre and varied skiing worth a day trip from nearby Font-Romeu.
1600m; skiing 1650m–2375m
⌁ *19* ⅄ *40km*
⊠ *Lagrange*

Annaberg-Lungötz Austria
Peaceful village in a pretty setting, sharing a sizeable ski area with Gosau, in the Dachstein region close to Filzmoos.
780m; skiing 780m–1700m
⌁ *34* ⅄ *50km*

Anzère Switzerland
Sympathetically designed modern resort set on a lovely sunny balcony near Crans-Montana, with slopes suited to leisurely skiers but not beginners.
1500m; skiing 1500m–2460m
⌁ *12* ⅄ *40km*
⊠ *Lagrange, Made to Measure*

Aprica Italy
Ugly, straggling, characterless village between Lake Como and the Brenta Dolomites, with bland skiing, limited facilities, and no real atmosphere.
1175m; skiing 1175m–2575m
⌁ *30* ⅄ *60km*
⊠ *Equity Total Ski, Kings Ski Club, Rank STS, SkiBound, Winterski*

Arabba Italy **292**

Aragnouet-Piau France
Purpose-built mid-mountain satellite of St Lary best suited to families, beginners and early intermediates.
1850m; skiing 1420m–2500m
⌁ *32* ⅄ *80km*

Arapahoe Basin USA **408**

Arcalis Andorra
Andorra's most interesting ski area (there's no resort), 15km from La Massana, with varied, scenic and, in places, steep skiing uncharacteristic of the region.
skiing 1940m–2600m
⌁ *12* ⅄ *20km*

Les Arcs France **144**

Ardent France **149**

Åre Sweden
Traditional village 650km by
train (driving not
recommended) from
Stockholm, with by far the best
Alpine skiing in Scandanavia.
550m; skiing 550m–1240m
⛇ *29* ⛷ *100km*

Arêches France
One of the prettiest of French
resorts, with low wooded
skiing, tucked away off the
Bourg-Albertville 'B' road, a
nice change of scene from Les
Arcs.
1080m; skiing 1080m–2100m
⛇ *13* ⛷ *35km*

Argentière France **153**

Arinsal Andorra **474**

Arosa Switzerland **308**

Artesina Italy
Limited south Piedmont resort,
a short car-trip from Nice or
Monte Carlo, though
neighbouring Limone is a more
attractive day-trip.
1500m ⛇ *25* ⛷ *90km*
✉ *Equity Total Ski, Rank STS*

Aspen USA **383**

Auffach Austria **90**

Auris-en-Oisans France **137**

Auron France
Pleasant village with varied,
sheltered skiing; a stark
contrast to nearby Isola 2000.
1600m; skiing 1600m–2450m
⛇ *27* ⛷ *130km*

Avoriaz France **149**

Axamer Lizum Austria **69**

Badgastein Austria **56**

Bad Hofgastein Austria **56**

Bad Kleinkirchheim Austria **55**

Banff Canada **449**

Baqueira-Beret Spain **476**
Smart, convenient resort. Fine
skiing and lift system, and
more snowsure than the rest of
the Spanish Pyrenees. Plenty of
good accommodation.
1500m; skiing 1500m–2510m
⛇ *22* ⛷ *90km*
✉ *Ski Miquel*

Barboleusaz Switzerland **366**

Bardonecchia Italy **262**

Barèges France
Cheerful old Pyrenean spa
village that shares an
intermediate ski area with La
Mongie. Good ski school.
Unreliable snow.
1220m; skiing 1220m–2350m
⛇ *56* ⛷ *100km*
✉ *Borderline, Thomson*

Les Barzettes Switzerland **316**

Bear Mountain USA
Southern California's main ski
area, in the beautiful San
Bernadino National Forest
region, with snowmaking on
all 25 runs.
skiing 2170m–2675m
⛇ *11* ⛷ *174 acres*

Beaver Creek USA **437**

Berchtesgaden Germany
Pleasant old town close to
Salzburg, known for its Nordic
skiing but with several little
Alpine areas nearby; the Jenner
is the best.
560m; skiing 1105m–1640m
⛇ *33* ⛷ *65km*
✉ *Moswin Tours*

Bergun Switzerland
Traditional, quiet, unspoilt,
virtually traffic-free little family
resort on the rail route between
Davos and St Moritz.
1455m; skiing 1455m–2490m
⛇ *5* ⛷ *21km*

Berwang Austria
Unspoilt village nestling in a
spacious valley, close to
Lermoos. Best visited in snowy
years due to unreliable cover.
1340m; skiing 1270m–1640m
⛇ *11* ⛷ *40km*

Le Bettex France **190**

Bettmeralp Switzerland
Central village of the sizeable
Aletsch ski area near Brig,
perched high above the Rhône
valley, surrounded by
spectacular glacial scenery.
1940m; skiing 1925m–2710m
⛇ *26* ⛷ *90km*

Biberwier Austria
Limited little village with a
small ski area, best as a quiet
Brit-free base from which to ski
the Zugspitz area resorts such
as Lermoos.
990m; skiing 1000m–1840m
⛇ *7* ⛷ *25km*

Bichlbach Austria
Smallest of the Zugspitz villages
with very limited skiing of its
own, suitable as an unspoilt
base from which to tour the
area.
1070m; skiing 1070m–1260m
⛇ *4* ⛷ *5km*

Big Mountain USA
Family ski area close to
Montana's Glacier National
Park, with lots of skiing
accessed by few lifts.
1400m; skiing 1400m–2055m
⛇ *8* ⛷ *3000 acres*

Big Sky USA
Great skiing near Yellowstone
and Little Big Horn, with
plenty for all grades accessed by
few lifts, including renowned
powder.
2055m; skiing 2055m–3310m
⛇ *10* ⛷ *2400 acres*
✉ *American Dream*

Big White Canada
Convenient purpose built
family resort six hours east of
Vancouver, renowned for huge
dumps of fluffy powder.
1660m; skiing 1660m–2320m
⛇ *8* ⛷ *1000 acres*
✉ *Frontier Ski, Ski Canada*

Bivio Switzerland
Quiet village near St Moritz
with a fair amount of easy
skiing opened up by a few drag-
lifts.
1780m; skiing 1780m–2600m
⛇ *4* ⛷ *30km*

Blackcomb Canada **455**

Blatten-Naters Switzerland
Ski area amidst stunning glacial
scenery, immediately above
Brig, with the larger Aletsch
skiing nearby.
675m; skiing 1325m–2880m
⛷ *9* 🚡 *60km*

Bled Slovenia
Beautiful lakeside base from
which to drive to several
nearby ski areas. Its own skiing
is very limited but OK for a ski-
cum-sightseeing day-trip from
Austria.
500m; skiing 880m–1265m
⛷ *5* 🚡 *16km*
✉ *Alpine Tours*

Blue River Canada
Town 200km north of
Kamploops, from where you
can heli-ski the famous
Monashees and Cariboos
without being incarcerated in a
remote mountain lodge.
✉ *Chinook-It, Fresh Tracks, Ski
Scott Dunn*

Bohinj Slovenia
Lakeside village near Bled set in
a beautiful valley, with lovely
views from its plateau ski area
of short runs high above.
540m; skiing 1535m–1880m
⛷ *6* 🚡 *20km*
✉ *Alpine Tours*

Bonneval France
Unspoilt old village near
Modane with much of its
skiing above 2500m. There are
future plans to link to Val-
d'Isère over the Col de l'Isèran.
2000m; skiing 1800m–3000m
⛷ *10* 🚡 *40km*

Bormio Italy **263**

Borovets Bulgaria **478**

Bourg-St-Maurice France **144**

Brand Austria
Old family favourite,
unpopular these days, perhaps
because it lacks the charm to
compensate for its small, low
ski area. A nice outing from
Lech or St Anton.
1035m; skiing 1035m–1920m
⛷ *13* 🚡 *50km*
✉ *Made to Measure*

Breckenridge USA **390**

Briançon France **230**

Brides-les-Bains France **199**

Brixen Austria **124**

Bromont Canada
Purpose-built resort an hour
east of Montreal, with one of
the best small ski areas in the
East, popular for its night
skiing.
⛷ *6* 🚡 *140 acres*

Bruck Austria
Low, one lift 'learn to ski'
resort, but might suit
intermediates looking for a
small, quiet base from which to
ski nearby Zell am See.
560m; skiing 560m–600m
⛷ *1* 🚡 *1km*

Bruson Switzerland
Relaxing respite from Verbier's
crowds, on the other side of Le
Châble. Well placed for car
trips to Chamonix and
Champéry.
1080m; skiing 820m–2200m
⛷ *7* 🚡 *15km*

Cairngorm Scotland **463**

Campitello Italy **292**

Canazei Italy **292**

Les Carroz France **182**

Caspoggio Italy
Attractive, unspoilt village
north-east of Lake Como, with
novice/leisurely skiing and
similar slopes at neighbouring
Chiesa.
1100m; skiing 1100m–2155m
⛷ *9* 🚡 *22km*

Cauterets France
Historic Pyrenean spa town
with easy/intermediate open
bowl skiing high above it.
Particularly suitable for
families.
935m; skiing 1400m–2500m
⛷ *15* 🚡 *29km*
✉ *Lagrange, Thomson*

Cavalese Italy
Unspoilt medieval town with
its own pretty skiing and
proximity to the Sella Ronda.
You need a car to make the
most of the scattered ski areas.
1000m; skiing 1000m–2260m
⛷ *11* 🚡 *70km*
✉ *First Choice Ski*

Celerina Switzerland **353**

Cerler Spain
Very limited purpose-built
resort with a compact
amphitheatre ski area similar to
that of nearby Andorra's
Arinsal.
1500m; skiing 1500m–2355m
⛷ *11* 🚡 *35km*

Cervinia Italy **266**

Cesana Torinese Italy **207**

Le Châble Switzerland **359**

Chamonix France **153**

Champagny France **217**

Champéry Switzerland **311**

Champex Switzerland
Lakeside hamlet tucked away in
the trees above Orsieres. A nice
quiet, unspoilt base from which
to ski Verbier's Four Valleys
area if you have a car.
1470m; skiing 1470m–2190m
⛷ *4* 🚡 *8km*

Champfér Switzerland **353**

Champoluc Italy **281**

Champoussin Switzerland **311**

Chamrousse France
Functional two-centre family
resort near Grenoble, with
good, sheltered ski to the door
slopes suitable for all grades.
*1650–1750m;
skiing 1650m–2255m*
⛷ *26* 🚡 *70km*
✉ *Lagrange*

Chantemerle France **230**

La Chapelle-d'Abondance France
160

Château d'Oex Switzerland **337**

Châtel France **160**

Chiesa Italy
Attractive 'learn to ski' venue with a fairly high plateau of easy runs way above the resort. Neighbouring Caspoggio adds to the skiing available.
1000m; skiing 1700m–2335m
↟ *8* ↟ *25km*
✉ *First Choice Ski*

Le Chinaillon France
Modern, chalet-style village at the heart of the pretty, intermediate Le Grand Bornand ski area, close to La Clusaz.
1300m; skiing 1000m–2100m
↟ *40* ↟ *60km*

Churwalden Switzerland **342**

Clavière Italy **207**

La Clusaz France **164**

Les Coches France **217**

Colfosco Italy **292**

Colle di Tenda Italy
Dour modern resort that shares a good, though far from snowsure, ski area with much nicer Limone, not far from Nice or Monte Carlo.
1400m; skiing 1005m–2060m
↟ *33* ↟ *100km*
✉ *Altours Travel, Winterski*

Combelouvière France
Quiet hamlet tucked away in the trees at the foot of Valmorel's skiing, well placed for day-trips to the Trois Vallées, La Plagne and Les Arcs.
1250m; skiing 1250m–2550m
↟ *48* ↟ *163km*

Combloux France
Quiet, unspoilt alternative to Megève, with which it shares a ski area. Best for car drivers, who can easily reach the rest of the local skiing.
900m; skiing 1100m–2350m
↟ *82* ↟ *300km*

Les Contamines France **168**

Copper Mountain USA **395**

Le Corbier France
Relatively inexpensive purpose-built resort that shares an extensive, underused intermediate ski area with La Toussuire, east of Grenoble.
1550m; skiing 1500m–2265m
↟ *41* ↟ *200km*
✉ *Lagrange, Made to Measure, Motours*

Cortina d'Ampezzo Italy **271**

Corvara Italy **292**

Courchevel France **169**

Courmayeur Italy **276**

Crans-Montana Switzerland **316**

Crested Butte USA **396**

Les Crosets Switzerland **311**

La Daille France **241**

Damüls Austria
Scattered but attractive village in the snowsure Bregenzerwald area close to the German and Swiss borders. Quiet ambience and leisurely skiing.
1430m; skiing 1430m–2005m
↟ *7* ↟ *40km*

Davos Switzerland **321**

Deer Valley USA **418**

Les Deux-Alpes France **177**

Les Diablerets Switzerland **343**

Dienten Austria
Quiet village at the heart of one of Austria's largest low-altitude ski areas, close to Zell am See. A high proportion of drag-lifts is a drawback.
790m; skiing 790m–1900m
↟ *42* ↟ *160km*

Disentis Switzerland
Unspoilt old village in a pretty setting on the Glacier Express rail route near Andermatt. Scenic ski area with lovely long runs.
1150m; skiing 1215m–2905m
↟ *9* ↟ *60km*
✉ *Plus Travel*

Dolonne Italy **276**

Dorfgastein Austria **56**

Ehrwald Austria
Friendly, relaxed, pretty village with several nicely varied ski areas, notably the Zugspitz glacier, nearby. Poor bus services make having a car desirable.
1000m; skiing 1000m–2950m
↟ *9* ↟ *13km*
✉ *Crystal, First Choice Ski*

Ellmau Austria **62**

Encamp Andorra
Unattractive town, 20 minutes by bus from the Soldeu slopes, popular for its nightlife and particularly low prices.
skiing 1680m–2560m
↟ *22* ↟ *50km*
✉ *First Choice Ski, Top Deck*

Engelberg Switzerland **327**

Entrèves Italy **276**

Essert-Romand France **211**

Etna Italy
Scenic, uncrowded, short-season ski area on the volcano's flank, 20 minutes from Nickolossi, with a couple of fair runs and some easy off piste.
1800m; skiing 1800m–2350m
↟ *5km*

Falera Switzerland **328**

Falls Creek Australia
Euro-style modern on-mountain family resort, five hours from Melbourne, with a fair network of short intermediate runs.
1600m; skiing 1180m–1780m
↟ *20* ↟ *20km*

Fernie Canada
Pleasant old lumber town three hours south of Banff, renowned for huge dumps of fluffy snow and superb deep powder bowl skiing.
1065m; skiing 1065m–1800m
↟ *7* ↟ *800 acres*
✉ *Chinook-It*

Fieberbrunn Austria **66**

Fiesch Switzerland
Traditional Rhône valley resort
close to Brig, with special
facilities for school trips, and a
lift up into the beautiful
Aletsch ski area.
1050m; skiing 1925m–2710m
⛄ *26* 🏂 *90km*
✉ *SkiGower*

Filzmoos Austria
Charming, unspoilt, friendly
atmospheric village with pretty
skiing ideal for novices and
leisurely skiers. Good snow
record for its height.
1060m; skiing 1060m–1645m
⛄ *16* 🏂 *32km*
✉ *Inghams, Made to Measure*

Finkenberg Austria **85**

Fiss Austria
Nicely compact, quiet
traditional village with a sun-
kissed ski area well protected by
snowmakers that's linked to
Serfaus.
1435m; skiing 1200m–2685m
⛄ *38* 🏂 *150km*

Flachau Austria
Quiet village in a pretty setting,
well situated at the heart of the
large Salzburger Sportwelt ski
area.
925m; skiing 800m–2185m
⛄ *59* 🏂 *200km*
✉ *Club Europe, Made to Measure*

Flachauwinkl Austria
Well placed within the
Salzburger Sportwelt ski area,
but no more than a ski station
with the Salzburg-Villach
autobahn carving through it.
930m; skiing 800m–2185m
⛄ *59* 🏂 *200km*

Flaine France **182**

Flims Switzerland **328**

Flumserberg Switzerland
Collective name for
Tannenheim and
Tannenbodenalp, villages
sharing a varied ski area an
hour south-east of Zurich.
1220–1400m;
skiing 1220m–2220m
⛄ *16* 🏂 *40km*

Folgarida Italy **287**

Font-Romeu France
Family resort set in woodland,
with the biggest snowmaking
set-up in the Pyrenees
protecting its easy pistes from
the mild climate.
1800m; skiing 1750m–2250m
⛄ *31* 🏂 *30km*
✉ *Lagrange*

Foppolo Italy
Relatively unattractive but user-
friendly village, a short transfer
from Bergamo, best for families
on a budget seeking fairly
reliable snow.
1510m; skiing 1105m–2300m
⛄ *15* 🏂 *47km*
✉ *Crystal, Equity Total Ski, Ski
Partners, SkiBound, Winterski*

Formigal Spain **476**
Cheap Pyrenean resort with a
reputation for good tuition,
and lift closures due to high
winds. Sheltered Panticosa is a
nearby failsafe.
1520m; skiing 1510m–2250m
⛄ *20* 🏂 *50km*
✉ *Thomson*

Le Fornet France **241**

La Foux d'Allos France
Purpose-built resort that shares
a good, large intermediate ski
area with Pra-Loup in southern
French Alps.
1800m; skiing 1500m–2600m
⛄ *63* 🏂 *230km*
✉ *Lagrange*

Frisco USA **390**

Fügen Austria
Unspoilt village with limited
skiing best suited to beginners,
poorly placed for skiing other
Zillertal resorts.
560m; skiing 560m–2050m
⛄ *9* 🏂 *21km*
✉ *Ski Partners*

Fulpmes Austria
Sizeable village in a beautiful
valley, with a small ski area of
its own, close to Neustift and
the Stubai glacier.
960m; skiing 960m–2260m
⛄ *8* 🏂 *30km*
✉ *Alpine Tours, Crystal*

Fuschl Austria
Attractive, unspoilt lakeside
village close to St Wolfgang
and Salzburg, 30 minutes from
its ski slopes. Best suited to
part-time skiers-cum-sightseers.
670m; skiing 750m–1570m
⛄ *8* 🏂 *10km*
✉ *Crystal*

Galtür Austria **67**

Gargellen Austria
Charming, secluded village
over the hill from Klosters,
highly regarded by families and
older guests. Its Madrisa hotel
is well-liked by reporters.
1425m; skiing 1425m–2150m
⛄ *9* 🏂 *25km*
✉ *Made to Measure*

Garmisch-Partenkirchen
Germany
Large twin resort; unspoilt
traditional Partenkirchen much
the prettier. Disjointed skiing,
with superb main area of
wooded runs when the
unreliable snowcover allows;
great glacier views from
another section when it
doesn't.
720m; skiing 750m–2965m
⛄ *43* 🏂 *109km*
✉ *Moswin Tours*

Gaschurn Austria
Attractive, unspoilt, Brit-free
village with the largest of the
pretty Montafon ski areas south
of Lech, well suited to
intermediates.
1000m; skiing 900m–2370m
⛄ *26* 🏂 *100km*

Geilo Norway
Pleasant but limited resort,
with mainly Nordic skiing, and
some short Alpine pistes.
770m; skiing 800m–1170m
⛄ *18* 🏂 *25km*
✉ *Crystal, Dawson and
Sanderson, Inntravel, NSR
Travel, Waymark Holidays*

Gerlos Austria
One of Austria's few
inexpensive but fairly snowsure
resorts, tucked away near Zell
am Ziller. Queue-free, varied
intermediate ski area with old
lifts.
1245m; skiing 1245m–2300m
⛄ *18* 🏂 *52km*

Les Gets France **211**

Glaris Switzerland
Hamlet base station for the
uncrowded Rinerhorn section
of the Davos skiing. Well
placed for an excursion to St
Moritz.
1455m; skiing 1455m–2490m
⌷ *5* ⌷ *30km*

Glencoe Scotland **465**

Glenshee Scotland **466**

Going Austria **62**

Gosau Austria
Straggling village with plenty
of pretty, if low, skiing.
Snowsure Obertauern and
Schladming are within reach by
car if local conditions are poor.
750m; skiing 750m–1600m
⌷ *35* ⌷ *50km*
⌷ *Neilson*

Gostling Austria
One of Austria's easternmost
resorts, midway between
Salzburg and Vienna. A
traditional village in a pretty,
wooded setting.
550m; skiing 550m–1900m
⌷ *12* ⌷ *50km*

Gotzens Austri *59*

Gourette France
Most snowsure resort in the
French Pyrenees. Very popular
with local families, best
avoided at weekends.
1400m; skiing 1400m–2550m
⌷ *21* ⌷ *30km*
⌷ *Lagrange*

Grächen Switzerland
Uncommercialised, quiet little
family village, a contrast to its
bigger, higher near-neighbours
Zermatt and Saas Fee, but with
similarly beautiful, if less
extensive, skiing.
1615m; skiing 1615m–2865m
⌷ *14* ⌷ *50km*

Le Grand-Bornand France
Pleasant, atmospheric 'real'
provincial village with a pretty,
varied intermediate ski area,
close to Annecy and La Clusaz.
1000m; skiing 1000m–2100m
⌷ *38* ⌷ *60km*
⌷ *Lagrange, Stena Sealink*

Grand Targhee USA **403**

Grau Roig Andorra
Car park with one hotel, a few
shops and a Pizza Hut, giving
direct access to Pas de la Casa's
only tree-lined runs.
2100m; skiing 2050m–2600m
⌷ *29* ⌷ *75km*

La Grave France **188**

Gray Rocks Canada
Very popular family resort,
120km north of Montreal,
renowned for its ski school and
fun-filled all-inclusive (Club
Med style) 'ski weeks'.
⌷ *4*

Gressoney-St-Jean Italy **281**

Gressoney-la-Trinité Italy **281**

Grimentz Switzerland
Captivating, unspoilt rustic
village with high, varied skiing
served by modern lifts; near the
Rhône valley town of Sierre,
with Crans-Montana quite
close by.
1570m; skiing 1570m–2900m
⌷ *10* ⌷ *50km*

Grindelwald Switzerland **333**

Grossarl Austria
Secluded village tucked away
over the mountain from the
Gastein valley. It shares a good
sizeable intermediate ski area
with Dorfgastein.
920m; skiing 850m–2010m
⌷ *23* ⌷ *70km*

Grünau Austria
Attractive, spacious riverside
village in a lovely lake-filled
part of eastern Austria. Nicely
varied, but very low, ski area.
530m; skiing 600m–1600m
⌷ *13* ⌷ *45km*

Gstaad Switzerland **337**

Gudauri Georgia
Austro-Soviet Glasnost attempt
at a good ski hotel complex
near Tbilisi; its potential,
notably for cheap heli-skiing,
inhibited at present by
Georgia's problems.
2005m; skiing 2005m–3010m
⌷ *5* ⌷ *5km*

Hainzenberg Austria **134**

Haus in Ennstal Austria **114**

Heavenly USA **399**

Heiligenblut Austria
Picturesque village in beautiful
surroundings with mostly high
skiing. Its remote position west
of Badgastein ensures crowds
don't invade when snow is
scarce.
1300m; skiing 1300m–2900m
⌷ *14* ⌷ *52km*

Hemsedal Norway
Pleasant, friendly little family
resort, midway between Oslo
and Bergen, with limited but
varied intermediate skiing.
Reliable snowcover.
650m; skiing 650m–1450m
⌷ *17* ⌷ *35km*
⌷ *Crystal, NSR Travel,
Waymark Holidays*

Hermagor Austria
Carinthian village below the
Sonnenalpe ski area. Franz
Klammer rates this one of the
best mid-size ski areas in
Austria.
590m; skiing 1210m–2005m
⌷ *24* ⌷ *80km*

Hinterstoder Austria
Quiet, unspoilt traditional
village, 80km east of Salzburg,
with a good snow record for its
height. A fair proportion of its
skiing is above 1400m on short
easy runs.
600m; skiing 600m–1860m
⌷ *17* ⌷ *38km*

Hintertux Austria **68**

Hippach Austria
Hamlet near a queue-free lift
into Mayrhofen's main skiing.
An astute choice if Mayrhofen's
on-slope merits are more
important than its off-slope
ones.
625m; skiing 625m–2250m
⌷ *23* ⌷ *65km*

Hochgurgl Austria **91**

Hochsölden Austria **120**

Hochybrig Switzerland
No village as such, but a
purpose built complex only
64km south of Zurich, with
skiing and facilities for families.
1050m; skiing 1050m–2200m
⚲ *16* ⚲ *50km*

Hopfgarten Austria **124**

Hospental Switzerland **307**

Les Houches France **153**

Igls Austria **69**

Inneralpbach Austria **54**

Innerarosa Switzerland **308**

Innsbruck Austria **69**

Ischgl Austria **70**

Isola 2000 France **189**

Itter Austria **124**

Jackson Hole USA **403**

Jasper Canada
Friendly railroad town, 30
minutes from its small ski area,
best suited to intermediates.
Best as a two-centre holiday
with Lake Louise, Banff or
Whistler.
skiing 1720m–2415m
⚲ *7* ⚲ *2400 acres*
✉ *All Canada, American
Connections, American Dream,
Crystal, Frontier Ski, Inghams,
Made to Measure, Ski Canada,
Ski Independence, Thomson*

Jochberg Austria **75**

Jouvenceaux Italy **288**

June USA
Recipient of rave reports from
all that have visited from
nearby, lift pass-sharing
Mammoth. Quiet slopes and
superb ski school.
2295m; skiing 2295m–3080m
⚲ *8* ⚲ *500 acres*

Juns Austria **68**

Kaltenbach Austria
Village with one of the larger,
quieter Zillertal ski areas. With
plenty of skiing above 1800m
it's a good outing from lower
Tyrol resorts when snow is
scarce.
560m; skiing 560m–2265m
⚲ *15* ⚲ *32km*

Kandersteg Switzerland
Good cross-country base amidst
beautiful scenery near
Interlaken. Limited Alpine
skiing but Adelbolen and the
Jungfrau resorts are nearby.
1175m; skiing 1175m–2000m
⚲ *6* ⚲ *10km*
✉ *Inntravel, Kuoni, Made to
Measure, Waymark Holidays*

Kaprun Austria **130**

Les Karellis France
Resort with a ski area that
offers more scenic, challenging
and snowsure skiing than
nearby Valloire, which has a
weekly lift pass that allows one
free day there.
1650m; skiing 1600m–2520m
⚲ *17* ⚲ *40km*

Keystone USA **408**

Killington USA
Eastern America's biggest and
best ski area, with skiing for all
standards and an impressive
snowmaking facility. Lack of
any real village and intense
cold are drawbacks.
320m; skiing 320m–1295m
⚲ *19* ⚲ *829 acres*
✉ *American Dream, Crystal,
Inghams, Ski Activity, Ski
Independence, Ski New England,
Virgin Snow*

Kimberley Canada
Mining town turned twee mock
Austro-Bavarian-English Tudor
ski resort. It's not as tacky as it
sounds, and being in a
beautiful setting is well worth
the two-hour drive from Banff.
1280m; skiing 1280m–1980m
⚲ *7* ⚲ *450 acres*

Kirchberg Austria **75**

Kirchdorf Austria **110**

Kirkwood USA **412**

Kitzbühel Austria **75**

Kleinarl Austria
Secluded traditional village up
a pretty side valley from
Wagrain, with lifts into the
Flachau section of the
Salzburger Sportwelt.
1015m; skiing 800m–2185m
⚲ *59* ⚲ *200km*
✉ *Club Europe, Made to Measure*

Klosters Switzerland **321**

Kolsass-Weer Austria
Dated resort; low,
inconvenient, limited skiing
which used to suit those more
concerned with partying than
skiing, but now loses out to
cheaper, more snowsure
Andorra.
555m; skiing 555m–1850m
⚲ *8* ⚲ *9km*
✉ *Airtours*

Königsleiten Austria
Quiet resort that has the more
interesting half of the
pleasantly varied, fairly
snowsure ski area shared with
Gerlos.
1600m; skiing 1245m–2315m
⚲ *26* ⚲ *52km*

Kopaonik Bosnia
Modern, sympathetically
designed family resort in a
pretty setting, with the best ski
area of the regions that used to
make up Yugoslavia. Off limits
at present.
1650m; skiing 1270m–2005m
⚲ *20* ⚲ *45km*

Kössen Austria
British schools destination near
St Johann in Tirol with little to
attract others; very low,
scattered, limited skiing.
600m; skiing 600m–1700m
⚲ *8* ⚲ *20km*
✉ *Rank STS*

Kranjska Gora Slovenia
Slovenia's leading resort, close to Austria/Italy, good for cheap, fun, convenient holidays for beginners but limited (despite its World Cup status) for others.
805m; skiing 805m–1500m
⛷ *19* 🚡 *20km*
✉ *Alpine Tours, Inghams*

Kühtai Austria
Huddle of good hotels (and little else) with a small, snowsure ski area suited to intermediate skiers. Few Brits, and only 35km from Innsbruck.
2020m; skiing 2010m–2655m
⛷ *10* 🚡 *50km*
✉ *Alpine Tours, Inghams*

Laax Switzerland **328**

Le Laisinant France **241**

Lake Louise Canada **449**

Lake Placid USA
Attractive lakeside winter sports resort 15km from the small but varied Whiteface ski area. 93% snowmaking and low temperatures ensure good snowcover. Plenty of things to do off the slopes.
975m; skiing 975m–1340m
⛷ *9* 🚡 *150 acres*

Lake Tahoe USA **412**

Lanersbach Austria **85**

Lauterbrunnen Switzerland **344**

Le Lavancher France **153**

Lech Austria **80**

The Lecht Scotland **467**

Las Leñas Argentina
Up-market, Euro-style modern resort, three hours south of Mendoza, with varied, beautiful skiing. Peak season crowds and queues.
2240m; skiing 2255m–3400m
⛷ *11* 🚡 *65km*
✉ *Passage to South America*

Lenk Switzerland
Traditional, though relatively unexceptional village by local standards, that shares a sizeable area of easy, pretty skiing with Adelbolen.
1070m; skiing 1070m–2200m
⛷ *47* 🚡 *130km*
✉ *Made to Measure, Plus Travel, Swiss Travel Service*

Lenzerheide Switzerland **342**

Leogang Austria **97**

Lermoos Austria
Focal resort of the Zugspitz area, a delightful base for cross-country enthusiasts and novice alpine skiers.
1005m; skiing 1005m–2200m
⛷ *10* 🚡 *18km*
✉ *Crystal, First Choice Ski, Made to Measure, Thomson*

Leukerbad Switzerland
Major spa resort of Roman origins, with spectacular cable-car rides to mostly high skiing including a World Cup downhill course.
1410m; skiing 1410m–2700m
⛷ *17* 🚡 *60km*

Leutasch Austria
Traditional cross-country village with limited Alpine skiing but a pleasant day trip from nearby Seefeld or Innsbruck.
1130m; skiing 1130m–1600m
⛷ *9* 🚡 *7km*
✉ *Inntravel*

Leysin Switzerland
Large winter sports resort near Aigle, with a good range of facilities, but its low sunny skiing is often very limited due to lack of snow.
1255m; skiing 1255m–2200m
⛷ *19* 🚡 *50km*
✉ *Lagrange*

Lienz Austria
Pleasant town-cum-ski-resort in pretty surroundings, ideal for a skier/non-skier couple. Cortina and Badgastein are very good excursions for both parties.
730m; skiing 730m–2280m
⛷ *13* 🚡 *45km*

Lillehammer Norway
Cultural fjordside town, two to three hours north of Oslo by train/car, with its two Olympic ski areas 15 & 35km away, poorly served by bus.
180m; skiing 180m–1500m
⛷ *11* 🚡 *35km*
✉ *NSR Travel, Ramblers*

Limone Italy
Pleasant old railway town not far from Turin, with a pretty, if far from snowsure, ski area. Good for independent skiers seeking the 'real' Italy.
1010m; skiing 1010m–2150m
⛷ *33* 🚡 *100km*

Livigno Italy **282**

Lofer Austria
Quiet, traditional Brit-free village close to Salzburg with a small ski area of its own, and Waidring's relatively snowsure Steinplatte nearby.
900m; skiing 900m–1745m
⛷ *14* 🚡 *35km*

Longchamp France **250**

Loon Mountain USA
New Hampshire's premier ski area (there's no resort as such), set amidst scenic wilderness, renowned for immaculately groomed intermediate slopes.
290m; skiing 290m–910m
⛷ *9* 🚡 *234 acres*
✉ *Ski New England, Virgin Snow*

Macugnaga Italy
Two pretty villages, 1km apart, set amidst stunning scenery. Staffa has high intermediate skiing and an off-piste route to Saas Fee, Pecetto has sheltered novice runs.
1330–1390m;
skiing 1390m–2900m
⛷ *12* 🚡 *40km*
✉ *Crystal, Neilson, Solo's, Thomson*

Madesimo Italy **286**

Madonna di Campiglio Italy **287**

Malbun Liechtenstein
Quaint, civilised, user-friendly
little family resort, 16km from
the capital, Vaduz. Many guests
are regulars. Limited skiing,
with short easy runs.
1595m; skiing 1595m–2100m
⬩*6* ⬩*16km*

Malga Ciapela Italy
Well positioned resort sitting at
the foot of the Marmolada
glacier massif, with a link into
the Sella Ronda, and Cortina
nearby.
1445m; skiing 1445m–3340m
⬩*8* ⬩*18km*

Mallnitz Austria
Village in a pretty valley close
to Slovenia, with two varied ski
areas providing a fine mix of
wooded and open intermediate
skiing and good off-piste.
1200m; skiing 1300m–2650m
⬩*8* ⬩*30km*

Mammoth Mountain USA **414**

Maria Alm Austria
Charming unspoilt village east
of Zell am See with a varied ski
area that stretches impressively
over five linked mountains.
Highly recommended by
several reporters.
805m; skiing 790m–1900m
⬩*42* ⬩*160km*
✉ *Mogul Ski, Ski Partners,*
SkiBound

Mariazell Austria
Traditional Styria village with
an impressive basilica, that has
a real antiquated feel to it.
Limited ski area.
870m; skiing 870m–1625m
⬩*19* ⬩*15km*

Marilleva Italy **287**

La Massana Andorra
Lively village with no slopes of
its own, but the best base if you
want to ski several areas,
notably Pal, Arinsal and Arcalis.
skiing 1545m–2590m
⬩*44* ⬩*60km*
✉ *Snowcoach Club Cantabrica*

Mayens de Riddes Switzerland
359

Mayrhofen Austria **85**

Megève France **190**

Meiringen Switzerland
Conan Doyle's deathplace for
Sherlock Holmes. A sightseeing
centre with varied skiing, a
good outing from the nearby
Jungfrau resorts or Interlaken.
595m; skiing 1050m–2245m
⬩*15* ⬩*60km*
✉ *Made to Measure, PGL Ski*
Europe

Les Menuires France **195**

Méribel France **199**

La Molina Spain **476**
Cheap, limited resort near
Andorra with a fair amount of
quite varied skiing served by a
poorly conceived lift system.
1700m; skiing 1600m–2535m
⬩*29* ⬩*85km*

Le Monêtier France **230**

La Mongie France
By linking to Barèges, this area
(Bagneres) claims to be the
largest in the Pyrenees. La
Mongie sits in a large, treeless
bowl.
1800m; skiing 1250m–2340m
⬩*56* ⬩*100km*
✉ *Lagrange*

Montalbert France **217**

Montchavin France **217**

Mont-de-Lans France **177**

Monte Bondone Italy
Essentially a Trento
weekenders' ski area (there's no
resort and some of the lifts are
closed weekdays). A possible
outing from Andalo or
Cavalese.
skiing 1300m–2100m
⬩*9* ⬩*10km*
✉ *Rank STS, Solo's*

Montgenèvre France **207**

Mont Orford Canada
Cold, windswept lone peak
(there's no resort) with skiing
worth a trip from nearby
Montreal on a fine day.
⬩*8*

Mont Ste Anne Canada
Largest ski mountain in Eastern
Canada (there's no resort) with
an impressive night skiing
facility. Being only 40km from
Quebec city, it gets very
crowded at weekends and some
evenings.
⬩*12* ⬩*390 acres*
✉ *All Canada, SkiBound*

Mont St Sauveur Canada
Perhaps the prettiest ski village
in Canada, popular with
Montreal (60km) day-trippers
and luxury condo owners.
⬩*9*
✉ *All Canada*

Mont Sutton Canada
Varied area with perhaps the
best glade skiing in the East,
including some negotiable by
novices. Quaint Sutton village
nearby. Highly rated by a
reporter.
⬩*9*

Mont Tremblant Canada
Eastern flagship due to huge
recent investment, with a
charming new pedestrian
village and upgraded
mountain. Good but exposed,
cold skiing.
265m; skiing 265m–910m
⬩*10* ⬩*425 acres*
✉ *All Canada, Inghams,*
SkiBound

Morgins Switzerland **311**

Morillon France **182**

Morzine France **211**

Les Mosses Switzerland
Uninteresting resort and ski
area, best for a day trip if
staying in nearby Leysin, Les
Diablerets or Villars.
1450m; skiing 1450m–2350m
⬩*12* ⬩*60km*

Mottaret France **199**

Mount Bachelor USA
Interesting 360 degree ski area
(there's no resort) on an extinct
volcano in central Oregon.
Pacific sends a lot of rain.
1825m; skiing 1825m–2755m
⬩*10* ⬩*6000 acres*

Mount Buller Australia
Largest resort in Oz, built on
the mountain, 3 hours from
Melbourne, with a 360 degree
network of short runs on its
isolated massif.
1600m; skiing 1375m–1790m
⛟ 26 ⛷ 80km

Mount Cook New Zealand
Superb heli-skiing in the
Mount Cook National
Park/Tasman Glacier area
(South Island), with
intermediate as well as expert
descents.

Mount Hutt New Zealand
Steepest, most snowsure ski
area in NZ, with ocean views,
but prone to bad weather;
100km from Christchurch, a
tricky drive up from Methven.
skiing 1420m–2075m
⛟ 10 ⛷ 902 acres

Mount Lyford New Zealand
Limited but developing ski area
close to the superb whale- and
seal-watching centre, Kaikoura,
140km north of Christchurch.
⛟ 6 ⛷ 803 acres

Mount Snow USA
Twin Vermont ski areas (there's
no village as such), only 340km
from New York City, that total
the second highest mileage in
the US East.
575m; skiing 575m–1095m
⛟ 24 ⛷ 643 acres
✉ Ski New England

Mühlbach Austria
Village near Bischofshofen, a
short bus hop from one end of
an impressive five-mountain
ski area that stretches for miles
towards Maria Alm.
855m; skiing 790m–1900m
⛟ 42 ⛷ 160km

Mühltal Austria **90**

Mürren Switzerland **344**

Mutters Austria **69**

Nasserein Austria **103**

Nauders Austria
Attractive village near Samnaun
and Serfaus with a high, sunny
intermediate ski area supported
by a good artificial snow set-up.
1400m; skiing 1400m–2750m
⛟ 15 ⛷ 55km

Nendaz Switzerland **359**

Neukirchen Austria
Quiet, pretty beginners resort
with a fairly snowsure plateau
at the top of its mountain.
Intermediates have the Ziller
valley nearby.
855m; skiing 855m–2130m
⛟ 13 ⛷ 25km
✉ SkiBound, Waymark Holidays

Neustift Austria **89**

Nevis Range Scotland **469**

Niederau Austria **90**

La Norma France
Traffic-free purpose-built resort
near Modane and Val-Cenis,
with mostly easy skiing,
popular for cheap British
school trips.
1350m; skiing 1350m–2750m
⛟ 18 ⛷ 70km
✉ Lagrange, Motours

Northstar-at-Tahoe USA **412**

Nôtre-Dame-de-Bellecombe
France
Pleasant village spoilt by the
busy Albertville-Megève road.
Inexpensive base from which
to ski Megève, though it has
fair skiing of its own.
1135m; skiing 1035m–2070m
⛟ 40 ⛷ 120km
✉ SkiBound

Oberau Austria **90**

Obergurgl Austria **91**

Oberlech Austria **80**

Oberndorf Austria **110**

Oberstdorf Germany
Attractive winter sports town
with famous ski jumping hill,
near the Austrian border, with
three small ski areas. The
Fellhorn is the most
noteworthy.
2235m; skiing 805m–835m
⛟ 26 ⛷ 30km

Obertauern Austria **96**

Okemo USA
Worthwhile intermediate ski
area (there's no resort) above
the old Vermont town of
Ludlow, close to Killington.
395m; skiing 395m–1010m
⛟ 14 ⛷ 310 acres

Orcières-Merlette France
Good family resort; convenient
snowsure nursery slopes, longer
runs mostly funnel safely back
to town, useful village facilities
– eg large pool and
kindergartens.
1850m; skiing 1850m–2655m
⛟ 29 ⛷ 100km
✉ Lagrange

Les Orres France
Friendly modern resort that
enjoys great views and varied
intermediate skiing, but snow
is unreliable in this area, a very
long transfer south of Lyon.
1600m; skiing 1550m–2770m
⛟ 23 ⛷ 50km
*✉ Lagrange, Ski Ardmore,
SkiBound*

Ortisei Italy **292**

Oukaimeden Morocco
Ski area 75km from Marrakesh
that can have a surprisingly
long season. A few simple
hotels and ski hire are
available. Pistes are marked but
grooming is perfunctory.
2630m; skiing 2630m–3310m
⛟ 6 ⛷ 15km

Ovronnaz Switzerland
Pretty village set on a sunny
shelf above the Rhône valley,
with a good pool complex.
Limited ski area but Crans-
Montana and Anzère are close
by.
1350m; skiing 1350m–2425m
⛟ 8 ⛷ 25km
✉ Lagrange, Ski Ardmore

Owl's Head Canada
Steep ski mountain rising out
of a lake that affords superb
views, in a remote spot
bordering Vermont, away from
weekend crowds.
⚡ 7

Oz-Station France **137**

Pal Andorra
Andorra's prettiest ski area
(there's no resort), near La
Massana, laid out amidst pine
trees, best suited to
beginners/early intermediates.
skiing 1780m–2360m
⚡ 15 ⚡ 30km
✉ *Panorama*

Pamporovo Bulgaria **477**
Great value, family/fun resort
in a pretty setting, with skiing
for beginners and early
intermediates, good tuition and
a few decent hotels (unusual
for Bulgaria).
1620m; skiing 1600m–1935m
⚡ 13 ⚡ 25km
✉ *Balkan Holidays, Crystal,
First Choice Ski, Ski Balkantours,
Sunquest Ski*

Panorama Canada
Pretty, convenient family
resort, two hours west of Banff,
renowned for its big vertical
drop, top tuition, and superb
heli-skiing.
975m; skiing 975m–2135m
⚡ 8 ⚡ 300 acres
✉ *All Canada, Frontier Ski*

Panticosa Spain **476**
Charming old Pyrenees village
in a sheltered spot good for
calm weather, bad for
snowcover. Limited ski area
best for novices.
1165m; skiing 1165m–1885m
⚡ 7 ⚡ 25km

Park City USA **418**

Park West USA **418**

Parpan Switzerland **342**

Pas de la Casa Andorra
Sprawling mess popular with
French duty-free shoppers, in a
bleak setting with Andorra's
largest, highest skiing.
2095m; skiing 2050m–2600m
⚡ 29 ⚡ 75km
✉ *Airtours, First Choice Ski,
Lagrange, Neilson, Panorama,
Thomson, Top Deck*

Pass Thurn Austria **75**

Peisey-Nancroix France **144**

Pejo Italy
Unspoilt traditional village in a
pretty setting, with a limited
ski area. A cheap base from
which to ski nearby Madonna
di Campiglio.
1340m; skiing 1340m–2800m
⚡ 5 ⚡ 15km
✉ *Winterski*

Perisher/Smiggin Holes
Australia
Twin ski areas 30km from their
dormitory town, Jindabyne, 6
hours from Sydney, which
between them offer plenty of
short, intermediate runs.
skiing 1675m–2055m
⚡ 30 ⚡ 75km

Pettneu Austria **103**

Piancavallo Italy
Uninspiring yet curiously
trendy purpose-built village
with a mediocre ski area of
short runs, an easy car outing
from Venice.
1830m; skiing 1300m–2000m
⚡ 17 ⚡ 45km
✉ *PGL Ski Europe, Rank STS*

Piau-Engaly France
User-friendly St-Lary satellite
similar in appearance to Les
Arcs 1600, in one of the best ski
areas in the Pyrenees.
1850m; skiing 1420m–2500m
⚡ 32 ⚡ 70km

Pico USA
Low-key little family ski area
(there's no resort) with fine
views, close to Killington, in
central Vermont.
605m; skiing 605m–1215m
⚡ 9 ⚡ 160 acres

Pila Italy
Old village with a modern
section that has varied, fairly
snowsure skiing that shares an
area lift pass with nearby La
Thuile, Cervinia and
Gressoney.
1790m; skiing 1370m–2650m
⚡ 13 ⚡ 60km
✉ *Interski*

Pinzolo Italy
Atmospheric village with a life
outside skiing, that has its ski
area well supported by
snowmakers, and is a cheap
base from which to ski nearby
Madonna.
900m; skiing 900m–2100m
⚡ 9 ⚡ 30km

La Plagne France **217**

Poiana Brasov Romania **481**
Cheap, informal user-friendly
resort amidst lovely Carpathian
scenery. Fine ski school and
limited skiing make it best for
novices.
1165m; skiing 1165m–1885m
⚡ 10 ⚡ 15km
✉ *Airtours, Balkan Holidays,
Crystal, First Choice Ski,
Inghams, Neilson, Ski
Balkantours, Sunquest Ski*

Pontresina Switzerland **353**

Portillo Chile
Little more than a luxury hotel
150km north-east of Santiago,
with more snowsure, less
crowded skiing than Las Leñas
in Argentina.
2850m; skiing 2850m–3685m
⚡ 7 ⚡ 25km
✉ *Passage to South America*

Pozza di Fassa Italy
Pretty Dolomites village with
its own skiing, three other
small ski areas on its doorstep,
and access to the Sella Ronda at
nearby Campitello.
1320m; skiing 1320m–2215m
⚡ 13 ⚡ 20km
✉ *Crystal, Winterski*

Pra-Loup France
Convenient, purpose-built family resort with an extensive, varied intermediate ski area in a rather isolated position south of Gap.
1600m; skiing 1500m–2600m
⛷ *63* 🚠 *230km*
✉ *Kings Ski Club, Lagrange, PGL Ski Europe, Rank STS, Snowcoach Club Cantabrica, Thomson*

Pralognan-la-Vanoise France
Unspoilt traditional Savoie village with skiing overlooked by spectacular peaks. Champagny (La Plagne) and Courchevel are close by.
1410m; skiing 1410m–2355m
⛷ *14* 🚠 *25km*
✉ *Lagrange*

Les Praz France **153**

Le Praz France **169**

Praz-de-Lys France
Little known snow-pocket ski area near Lac Leman, that can have good snow when nearby resorts (eg La Clusaz) do not.
1500m; skiing 1200m–1740m
⛷ *21* 🚠 *50km*
✉ *Lagrange*

Praz-sur-Arly France
Traditional Haute Savoie village in a pretty wooded setting just down the road from Megève, with its own varied ski area.
1035m; skiing 1035m–2030m
⛷ *33* 🚠 *100km*

Purgatory USA
Limited Colorado resort with enough good skiing to make it a useful day out from nearby Telluride.
2670m; skiing 2670m–3290m
⛷ *9* 🚠 *692 acres*

Puy-St-Vincent France
Modern apartment complex above an old village south of Briançon; convenient access to a modest but quite varied ski area. Relatively inexpensive and popular with families.
1400–1600m;
skiing 1400m–2750m
⛷ *15* 🚠 *50km*
✉ *Alpine Tours, Rank STS, Ski Ardmore, Snowbizz Vacances*

Queenstown New Zealand
NZ's only large resort, in a stunning lakeside setting overlooked by one of its two ski mountains, the aptly named Remarkables.
skiing 1215m–1955m
⛷ *11* 🚠 *1235 acres*

Radstadt Austria
Interesting unspoilt medieval town near Schladming that has its own small ski area, with the Salzburger Sportwelt accessed from nearby Zauchensee or Flachau.
855m; skiing 855m–1675m
⛷ *9* 🚠 *30km*
✉ *Club Europe, Made to Measure*

Ramsau Austria
Charming village overlooked by the Dachstein glacier. Renowned for cross-country, it also has Alpine skiing locally, on the glacier and at nearby Schladming.
1200m; skiing 1100m–2700m
⛷ *22* 🚠 *40km*
✉ *Waymark Holidays*

Rauris Austria
Old roadside village close to Kaprun and Zell am See, with a long narrow ski area that has snowmakers on its lower slopes.
950m; skiing 950m–2210m
⛷ *11* 🚠 *25km*

Ravascletto Italy
Resort close to Carinthian Austria in a pretty tree-filled setting, with most of its skiing high above on an open plateau.
920m; skiing 920m–1735m
⛷ *12* 🚠 *40km*
✉ *PGL Ski Europe*

Red Mountain Canada
Ski area renowned for its steep and deep powder, eight hours east of Vancouver, 3km from Rossland, a charming old mining town.
1185m; skiing 1185m–2040m
⛷ *4* 🚠 *2500 acres*

Reutte Austria
500-year-old market town with many suitably traditional hotels, and rail links to nearby Lermoos, Garmisch and Innsbruck.
855m; skiing 855m–1900m
⛷ *11* 🚠 *10km*

Revelstoke Canada
Town from which you can heli-ski the Monashees without staying in a remote mountain lodge, with local skiing on Mount McKenzie for bad weather days.
460m
✉ *Powder Skiing in North America Limited*

Rhêmes-Notre-Dame Italy
Unspoilt village in the beautiful Rhêmes valley, south of Aosta, with skiing of its own and that of Courmayeur and La Thuile nearby. Hotel Granta Parey is recommended by one reporter.
⛷ *2* 🚠 *5km*

Riederalp Switzerland
Pretty car-free village perched high above the Rhône valley amidst the glorious scenery of the Aletsch ski area. Access by cable-car from Mörel, near Brig.
1925m; skiing 1925m–2710m
⛷ *26* 🚠 *90km*

Rigi-Kaltbad Switzerland
Resort on a mountain rising straight out of Lake Lucerne, with superb 360 degree views, accessed by the world's first mountain railway.
1440m; skiing 1195m–1795m
⛷ *9* 🚠 *30km*

Riksgränsen Sweden
Unique Arctic Circle Alpine ski area not open until late February. Skiing under the midnight sun (lift-served) from mid-May to June 30. 20 hours by train from Stockholm.
600m; skiing 600m–910m
⛷ *7* 🚠 *10km*

Risoul France **225**

Rohrmoos Austria **114**

La Rosière France **226**

Rougemont Switzerland **337**

Saalbach-Hinterglemm Austria **97**

Saanen Switzerland **337**

Saanenmöser Switzerland **337**

Saas-Almagell Switzerland **348**

Saas-Fee Switzerland **348**

Saas-Grund Switzerland **348**

Sahoro Japan
Ugly purpose-built Hokkaido Island complex with a limited ski area, but one of the most exotic destinations available on a package.
400m; skiing 400m–1100m
⛷ *10* 🚡 *15km*
✉ *Club Med*

St Anton Austria **103**

St Cergue Switzerland
Limited resort less than an hour from Geneva, good for families with young children.
1185m; skiing 1185m–1700m
⛷ *9* 🚡 *20km*

St Christoph Austria **103**

Sainte-Foy France **229**

St-François-Longchamp France **250**

St Gallenkirch Austria
Smaller, less attractive village than Gaschurn, with which it shares a sizeable intermediate ski area near Schruns.
900m; skiing 900m–2370m
⛷ *26* 🚡 *100km*

St-Gervais France **190**

St Jakob in Defereggen Austria
Unspoilt traditional village in a pretty, sunny valley close to Lienz and Heiligenblut, with a good proportion of its skiing above 2000m.
1390m; skiing 1390m–2520m
⛷ *14* 🚡 *25km*

St Jakob in Haus Austria
Snowpocket village with its own skiing, and a shared lift pass with charming nearby Fieberbrunn, Waidring and St Johann. Good for leisure skiers with a car.
855m; skiing 855m–1442m
⛷ *7* 🚡 *25km*

St Johann im Pongau Austria
Bustling, lively town with a small ski area of its own, but the impressive Salzburger Sportwelt skiing starts only 4km away at Alpendorf.
650m; skiing 800m–2185m
⛷ *59* 🚡 *200km*
✉ *PGL Ski Europe*

St Johann in Tirol Austria **110**

St-Lary France
Well preserved old stone Pyrenean village, a lift-ride below its fine intermediate ski area. Not unlike a downmarket, Brit-free Courmayeur.
890m; skiing 1420m–2500m
⛷ *32* 🚡 *70km*
✉ *Lagrange*

St Leonhard in Pitztal Austria
Village beneath a fine area of glacier skiing in the Oetz area, accessed by a fast new mountain railway.
1250m; skiing 1735m–3440m
⛷ *12* 🚡 *40km*

St Luc Switzerland
Quiet unspoilt rustic village on the south side of the Rhône valley, with plenty of high easy skiing.
1650m; skiing 1650m–3025m
⛷ *16* 🚡 *75km*

St-Martin-de-Belleville France **195**

St Michael im Lungau Austria
Quiet unspoilt village in the Tauern pass snowpocket with an uncrowded but disjointed intermediate ski area. Close to Obertauern and Wagrain.
1075m; skiing 1075m–2360m
⛷ *29* 🚡 *60km*
✉ *Alpine Tours, Club Europe, Ski Partners*

St Moritz Switzerland **353**

St-Nicolas-de-Véroce France **190**

St Oswald Austria **55**

St Stephan Switzerland
Unspoilt, relatively inexpensive old farming village at the foot of the largest ski area in the Gstaad Super Ski region.
995m; skiing 950m–2155m
⛷ *69* 🚡 *250km*

St Wolfgang Austria
Charming lakeside resort near Salzburg, some way from any ski slopes, best for a relaxing winter holiday with perhaps one or two days' skiing included.
540m; skiing 665m–1350m
⛷ *9* 🚡 *6km*
✉ *Airtours, Austrian Holidays, Crystal, Inghams, Neilson, Thomson*

Les Saisies France
Traditional-style Albertville Olympics cross-country venue in a pretty setting, surrounded by a wonderfully varied four-mountain Alpine ski area.
1650m; skiing 1150m–1950m
⛷ *24* 🚡 *100km*
✉ *Over the Hill*

Samnaun Switzerland **70**

Samoëns France **182**

San Bernadino Switzerland
Pretty resort south of the road tunnel of the same name, close to Madesimo, with a fair amount of skiing opened up by its few lifts.
1595m; skiing 1595m–2515m
⛷ *7* 🚡 *50km*

San Carlos de Bariloche Argentina
South America's only year-round community-cum-ski-resort, with five ski areas nearby. Cerro Catedrel is the best but gets crowded in August.
790m; skiing 1045m–2045m
⛷ *7* 🚡 *26km*
✉ *Passage to South America*

San Cassiano Italy **292**

San Martino di Castrozza Italy
Plain village in the southern
Dolomites with varied skiing in
four disjointed areas, none of
them very extensive.
1465m; skiing 1450m–2385m
🚠 *25* 🎿 *50km*

Sansicario Italy **299**

Santa Caterina Italy
Pretty, user-friendly village near
Bormio, with which, along
with Livigno, it shares an area
lift pass. It has a particularly
snowsure novice and
intermediate ski area but the
slopes are dark and cold in
early season.
1740m; skiing 1740m–2725m
🚠 *7* 🎿 *25km*
✉ *Airtours, First Choice Ski,
Rank STS, Thomson*

Santa Cristina Italy **292**

San Vigilio Italy
Charming, atmospheric
Dolomite village with a
delightful, sizeable ski area well
covered by snow cannon.
1200m; skiing 1200m–2275m
🚠 *35* 🎿 *40km*

Sappada Italy
Isolated resort close to the
Austrian border below Lienz.
1215m 🚠 *22* 🎿 *50km*
✉ *PGL Ski Europe, Rank STS*

Sauze d'Oulx Italy **288**

Savognin Switzerland
Pretty village with one of
Switzerland's best mid-size ski
areas, and a good base for
skiing top nearby resorts - St
Moritz, Davos/Klosters, Flims.
1200m; skiing 1200m–2715m
🚠 *17* 🎿 *80km*

Scheffau Austria **62**

Schladming Austria **114**

Schönried Switzerland **337**

Schröcken Austria
Bregenzerwald area village
close to the German border
with an amazingly good snow
record. Good day trip from
Lech, St Anton or Brand.
1260m; skiing 1260m–2050m
🚠 *14* 🎿 *40km*

Schruns Austria
Pleasant little town at the heart
of the Montafon ski region; a
collection of charming unspoilt
Brit-free villages and ski areas
south-west of Lech.
700m; skiing 700m–2250m
🚠 *16* 🎿 *50km*
✉ *Alpine Tours*

Schüttdorf Austria **130**

Scuol Switzerland
Year-round spa resort midway
between Davos and Samnaun,
with an impressive ski range.
1245m; skiing 1245m–2800m
🚠 *16* 🎿 *80km*

Sedrun Switzerland
Charming unspoilt old village
on the Glacier Express rail
route close to Andermatt, with
fine on- and off-piste skiing
amidst glorious scenery.
1400m; skiing 1215m–2905m
🚠 *13* 🎿 *60km*
✉ *Plus Travel*

Seefeld Austria **118**

Sella Nevea Italy
Limited but developing resort
in a beautiful setting on the
Slovenian border, with skiing
amidst dramatic scenery.
Summer glacier skiing nearby.
1140m; skiing 1190m–1800m
🚠 *11* 🎿 *8km*
✉ *Winterski*

Selva Italy **292**

Semmering Austria
Long established, civilised
wintersports resort amidst
pretty scenery, 100km from
Vienna, towards Graz. Mostly
intermediate skiing.
985m; skiing 985m–1340m
🚠 *13* 🎿 *33km*

Les Sept-Laux France
Ugly, user-friendly family resort
near Grenoble, reminiscent in
some ways of a small Avoriaz.
Pretty skiing for all grades.
1350m; skiing 1350m–2400m
🚠 *35* 🎿 *60km*
✉ *Altours Travel, Lagrange*

Serfaus Austria **119**

Serre-Chevalier France **230**

Sesto Italy
Dolomite village on the road to
Cortina surrounded by nice
pretty little ski areas.
1310m 🚠 *31* 🎿 *50km*

Sestola Italy
Appenine village a short drive
from Pisa and Florence with its
skiing, starting some way
above, almost completely
supported by snow makers.
900m; skiing 1280m–1975m
🚠 *23* 🎿 *50km*
✉ *Winterski*

Sestriere Italy **299**

Shiga Heights Japan
Largest ski area in Japan, site of
Nagano's 1998 Olympic skiing
events, 150km from Tokyo.
Happo One is a pretty pseudo-
European resort in the area.
930m; skiing 1220m–2305m
🚠 *74* 🎿 *130km*

Sierra-at-Tahoe USA **412**

Sierra Nevada Spain **476**
Very ugly but user-friendly
resort near Granada, with
superb snowmaking facilities
and great-value hotels. Suitable
for beginners and
intermediates, but strong late
season sun causes icy/soft
pistes.
2100m; skiing 2100m–3470m
🚠 *19* 🎿 *55km*
✉ *First Choice Ski, Thomson*

Sils Maria Switzerland **353**

Silvaplana Switzerland **353**

Silver Star Canada
Newly developed resort built
on an 1890's theme, with
snowsure skiing above the
town of Vernon, midway
between Banff and Whistler.
1150m; skiing 1150m–1915m
🚠 *8* 🎿 *850 acres*
✉ *All Canada, American Dream,
Frontier Ski, Made to Measure,
Ski Canada*

Sinaia Romania **481**
Depressed and depressing main-road town with a modest, open ski area.
795m; skiing 795m–1995m
⛷ *9* 🚡 *15km*
✉ *Crystal*

Siviez Switzerland **359**

Smokovec Slovakia
Spa town near Poprad, with three small ski areas on its doorstep, known collectively as North Tatras.
1020m; skiing 850m–2005m
⛷ *21* 🚡 *10km*

Smugglers Notch USA
Pretty, quiet purpose-built Vermont resort near Stowe, with award-winning children's services, voted best US family ski resort by Family Circle magazine.
315m; skiing 315m–1110m
⛷ *7* 🚡 *246 acres*
✉ *American Dream, Ski New England*

Snowbird USA **423**

Snowmass USA **383**

Sölden Austria **120**

Soldeu Andorra **475**

Solitude USA
On the Utah Interconnect route from Park City and Snowbird. More suited to intermediates than neighbouring Alta and Snowbird.
2430m; skiing 2430m–3190m
⛷ *14* 🚡 *1950 acres*

Söll Austria **124**

Sorenberg Switzerland
Popular weekend retreat between Berne and Lucerne, with a high proportion of steep, low skiing.
1165m; skiing 1165m–2350m
⛷ *18* 🚡 *50km*

South Tatras Slovakia
A ski area (there's no resort) covering both sides of Mount Chopok near Poprad.
skiing 1240m–2005m
⛷ *19* 🚡 *20km*

Spital am Pyhrn Austria
Limited village east of Schladming, 4km from its easy intermediate skiing. Nearby Hinterstoder is more interesting.
650m; skiing 810m–1870m
⛷ *10* 🚡 *18km*

Spittal/Drau Austria
Historic Carinthian town with a limited ski area starting a cable-car ride above it. A good day-trip from Bad Kleinkirchheim or Slovenia.
555m; skiing 1650m–2100m
⛷ *10* 🚡 *20km*

Sportgastein Austria **56**

Squaw Valley USA **412**

Srinagar India
Himalayan resort in trouble-torn Kashmir, best ignored at present, with a small pisted area but excellent heli-skiing.
2720m; skiing 2645m–3645m
⛷ *7* 🚡 *5km*

Stafal Italy **281**

Steamboat USA **425**

Steinach Austria
Pleasant village in picturesque surroundings, an easy outing from Innsbruck, just off the autobahn near the Brenner Pass.
1045m; skiing 1045m–2005m
⛷ *9* 🚡 *18km*
✉ *Alpine Tours*

Stoneham Canada
Leading Quebec resort, better equipped and more sheltered then most neighbours, with skiing across four mountains, including the largest night operation in Canada. 92% snowmaking.
⛷ *10*
✉ *SkiBound*

Stowe USA
Probably North America's prettiest resort; a beautifully preserved and restored old Vermont village, 10km from a mostly intermediate ski area which also has some very challenging slopes.
395m; skiing 395m–1115m
⛷ *11* 🚡 *487 acres*
✉ *American Connections, American Dream, Crystal, Ski Independence, Ski New England, Virgin Snow*

Stratton/Bromley USA
New York City weekend retreat that has two ski areas, with Bromley reputedly the warmest place to ski in chilly Vermont.
515m; skiing 515m–1175m
⛷ *18* 🚡 *458 acres*
✉ *Ski New England*

Stuben Austria **103**

Sugar Loaf USA
Developing Maine resort, five hours from Boston, with US East's best open skiing.
405m; skiing 405m–1260m
⛷ *15* 🚡 *433 acres*
✉ *Ski New England*

Sugarbush USA
Resort in upper Vermont near Montpelier, trendy in the 1960's, now a more low-key place with a well designed ski area.
455m; skiing 455m–1235m
⛷ *16* 🚡 *497 acres*

Sundance USA
Robert Redford-owned, tastefully designed family resort set amidst trees in snowsure Utah, with a fair amount of mostly intermediate skiing opened up by few lifts.
2505m; skiing 2505m–3160m
⛷ *4*

Sunday River USA
One of the more attractive resorts in the East, four hours from Boston, best for intermediate cruisers.
245m; skiing 245m–840m
⛷ *12* 🚡 *411 acres*
✉ *Ski New England*

Sunshine Village Canada **449**

Sun Valley USA
America's original glamour resort, spread over disjointed developments, most a bus-ride from the slopes. Skiing suitable for all.
1755m; skiing 1755m–2790m
⛽ *12* ⛷ *2000 acres*
✉ *American Dream, Ski Activity, Ski Independence*

Superbagnères France
Little more than a particularly French-dominated Club Med, best for a low-cost, low-effort family trip to the Pyrenees.
1880m; skiing 1450m–2260m
⛽ *15* ⛷ *15km*
✉ *Club Med*

Superdévoluy France
Ugly, purpose-built, user-friendly family resort, an hour south-east of Grenoble, with a sizeable intermediate ski area.
1500m; skiing 1470m–2470m
⛽ *32* ⛷ *105km*
✉ *Lagrange, Motours, Rank STS*

La Tania France **169**

Taos USA **429**

El Tarter Andorra
Relatively quiet, convenient alternative to Soldeu, with which it shares a ski area. Having a chalet package is a boon given the poor hotels.
1680m; skiing 1680m–2560m
⛽ *22* ⛷ *50km*
✉ *Panorama*

Tarvisio Italy
Interesting, animated old town bordering Austria and Slovenia. A major cross-country centre with fairly limited Alpine skiing.
750m; skiing 750m–1860m
⛽ *12* ⛷ *15km*
✉ *PGL Ski Europe, Rank STS*

Täsch Switzerland **372**

Tauplitz Austria
Traditional village at the foot of an interestingly varied ski area north of Schladming, close to Salzburg.
895m; skiing 895m–1965m
⛽ *18* ⛷ *25km*
✉ *Club Europe*

Telluride USA **433**

Terminillo Italy
Purpose-built resort 100km from Rome with a worthwhile ski area when its lower runs have snowcover, but not surprisingly this isn't assured.
1500m; skiing 1500m–2700m
⛽ *13* ⛷ *40km*

Thredbo Australia
Oz's best, six hours from Sydney; with uncharacteristically long (and, in places, testing) runs, snowmaking, lots of accommodation and active nightlife.
1365m; skiing 1365m–2035m
⛽ *15* ⛷ *70km*

La Thuile Italy **300**

Thyon 2000 Switzerland **359**

Tignes France **235**

Tonale Italy
Ugly resort in a bleak setting with little to offer except the not inconsiderable guarantee of snow at a bargain price. Pretty Madonna is nearby.
1885m; skiing 1885m–3015m
⛽ *28* ⛷ *80km*
✉ *Airtours, Altours Travel, Crystal, Equity Total Ski, First Choice Ski, PGL Ski Europe, SkiBound*

Torgon Switzerland
Old village in a pretty tree-filled setting, with a nearby lift connection to the Portes du Soleil.
1095m; skiing 975m–2275m
⛽ *224* ⛷ *650km*

Le Tour France
Charming unspoilt hamlet at the head of the Chamonix valley with much easier skiing than its near neighbours.
1465m; skiing 1465m–2185m
⛽ *9* ⛷ *40km*
✉ *Poles Apart*

La Toussuire France
User-friendly modern resort east of Grenoble, with a large uncrowded intermediate ski area that deserves to be better known.
1800m; skiing 1450m–2265m
⛽ *41* ⛷ *180km*
✉ *First Choice Ski, Motours*

Trafoi Italy
Quiet, traditional (Austrian-style) South Tyrol village near Bormio, worth a day trip if you can ski down to the resort; not if you can't.
1570m; skiing 1570m–2550m
⛽ *6* ⛷ *10km*
✉ *Rank STS*

Troodos Cyprus
A good outing from Greek sector coastal resorts, with interesting old villages en-route. Pretty, wooded pistes and fine views.
⛽ *4* ⛷ *5km*

Tschagguns Austria
Village with a varied little ski area of its own and the skiing and town life of Schruns a stone's throw away.
700m; skiing 655m–2085m
⛽ *12* ⛷ *50km*

Tulfes Austria **69**

Turoa New Zealand
Arguably North Island's best ski area, on a volcano's flank with superb views of its classic cone. 350km south of Auckland, near Ohakune.
⛽ *10* ⛷ *914 acres*

Turracher Höhe Austria
Tiny, unspoilt lakeside resort on a mountain shelf with varied intermediate skiing above and below it. A good outing from Bad Kleinkirchheim.
1765m; skiing 1400m–2205m
⛽ *12* ⛷ *40km*
✉ *Alpine Tours*

Uludag Turkey
Surprisingly suave, laid-back, well equipped, purpose-built resort near Bursa, south of Istanbul, popular with poseurs.
1800m; skiing 1800m–2225m
⛽ *12* ⛷ *15km*
✉ *Sunquest Ski*

Untergurgl Austria **91**

Vail USA **437**

Valbella Switzerland **342**

Val-Cenis France
Ramshackle old twin villages over the Isèran pass (closed in winter) from Val-d'Isère that have varied skiing, with the best runs above 2000 meters.
1400m; skiing 1400m–2800m
⛷ *23* 🚡 *60km*
✉ *Lagrange, Ski Valkyrie, SkiBound*

Val-d'Isère France **241**

Valfréjus France
Underrated, pleasant modern family resort near Bardonecchia, with a cheap lift pass and varied, interesting, snowsure skiing.
1500m; skiing 1500m–2730m
⛷ *13* 🚡 *52km*
✉ *Lagrange, Made to Measure, Motours, Neilson*

Vallandry France **144**

Valloire France **249**

Valmeinier France **249**

Valmorel France **250**

Val Senales Italy
In the Dolomites near Merano, this isn't so much a resort as a top-of-the-mountain hotel that's the ultimate in snowsure skiing from the door.
3250m; skiing 2005m–3250m
⛷ *10* 🚡 *24km*

Val-Thorens France **255**

Valtournenche Italy **266**

Vars France **259**

Vaujany France **137**

Vent Austria
High, remote Oztal village with just enough skiing to warrant a day-trip from nearby Obergurgl.
1900m; skiing 1900m–2680m
⛷ *4* 🚡 *15km*
✉ *Sloping Off*

Verbier Switzerland **359**

Veysonnaz Switzerland **359**

Vigo di Fassa Italy
Best base from which to ski the Fassa valley, with the Sella Ronda also close via neighbouring Campitello.
1390m; skiing 1320m–2215m
⛷ *13* 🚡 *20km*
✉ *Crystal*

La Villa Italy **292**

Villard-Reculas France **137**

Villard-de-Lans France
Unspoilt traditional village west of Grenoble, full of life and character with animated canopied cafes etc. It's also snowsure thanks to very extensive snowmaking.
1050m; skiing 1110m–2170m
⛷ *36* 🚡 *130km*
✉ *Alpine Options Skidrive, Inntravel, Lagrange*

Villaroger France **144**

Villars Switzerland **366**

Vitosha Bulgaria **477**
A few widely scattered dour hotels (there's no resort) with very limited skiing. Low budget skiers have far better options – eg Borovets, Pamporovo or Poiana Brasov.
1810m; skiing 1515m–2200m
⛷ *8* 🚡 *20km*
✉ *Balkan Holidays, Sunquest Ski*

Vorderlanersbach Austria **85**

Voss Norway
Well equipped winter sports resort attractively set on a lake, with relatively limited Alpine skiing.
60m; skiing 150m–945m
⛷ *10* 🚡 *40km*
✉ *Color Line, Dawson and Sanderson, NSR Travel*

Wagrain Austria
Traditional village at the heart of the extensive Salzburger Sportwelt intermediate ski area linking Flachau and St Johann im Pongau.
900m; skiing 800m–2185m
⛷ *59* 🚡 *200km*
✉ *Club Europe, Made to Measure, Mogul Ski*

Waidring Austria **110**

Wanaka New Zealand
Village in what must be one of the most beautiful lakeside mountain settings in the world, with two ski areas each half an hour away.
skiing 1200m–1860m
⛷ *9* 🚡 *2223 acres*

Wengen Switzerland **367**

Westendorf Austria **129**

Whakapapa New Zealand
NZ's largest ski area, on a volcano close to Turoa with similarly superb views. The Grand Chateau is a lovely old hotel in the tiny village 6km away.
skiing 1625m–2300m
⛷ *22* 🚡 *988 acres*

Whistler Canada **455**

Wildhaus Switzerland
Undeveloped farming community in stunning scenery, near Liechtenstein, popular with families and good for serious snowboarders.
1050m; skiing 900m–2260m
⛷ *21* 🚡 *50km*

Winter Park USA **444**

Yong Pyeong Korea
Largest resort in Korea, 200km east of Seoul, with snowmakers on all 19 of its exclusively short runs. Much less crowded than Japanese resorts.
750m; skiing 750m–1460m
⛷ *15* 🚡 *20km*

Zakopane Poland
An interesting old town near charming medieval Cracow and moving Auschwitz. Mostly intermediate skiing.
685m; skiing 685m–1990m
⛷ *7* 🚡 *10km*

Zauchensee Austria
Purpose-built resort with lifts
fanning out into the
surrounding Salzburger
Sportwelt area.
855m; skiing 800m–2185m
⛟ *59* ⛷ *200km*
✉ *Alpine Tours, Made to
Measure, Mogul Ski*

Zell am See Austria **130**

Zell am Ziller Austria **134**

Zermatt Switzerland **372**

Zinal Switzerland
Rustic village, pretty but for
some incongruous modern
building, with plenty of high
skiing and a striking, unusual
Matterhorn view.
1700m; skiing 1660m–2895m
⛟ *9* ⛷ *70km*
✉ *Club Med*

Zug Austria **80**

Zürs Austria **80**

Zweisimmen Switzerland
Limited but inexpensive base
from which to ski nearby
Gstaad, with its own delightful
little easy skiing area too.
950m; skiing 950m–2005m
⛟ *6* ⛷ *25km*

Ordering more copies of Where to Ski

Where to Ski is available by post at the bookshop price of £14.99, post and packing included. You don't have to use this form, but it helps us and it may help you.

Where to Ski order

TO
WHERE TO SKI, THE OLD FORGE, NORTON ST PHILIP, BATH BA3 6LW

Please supply   copies of Where to Ski at £14.99 per copy including post and packing. I enclose a cheque for   made out to Where to Ski.

Name _____

Address _____

_____

_____

_____

Ordering more copies of Where to Ski

Where to Ski is available by post at the bookshop price of £14.99, post and packing included. You don't have to use this form, but it helps us and it may help you.

Where to Ski order

TO
WHERE TO SKI, THE OLD FORGE, NORTON ST PHILIP, BATH BA3 6LW

Please supply   copies of Where to Ski at £14.99 per copy including post and packing. I enclose a cheque for   made out to Where to Ski.

Name _____

Address _____

_____

_____

_____

Pre-publication offers on the next edition

The third edition of Where to Ski will be published in early September 1996. If you would like the opportunity to buy a copy in advance of publication at a special discount price, send in this form to reach us before 31 July 1996.

Where to Ski pre-publication offers

TO
WHERE TO SKI, THE OLD FORGE, NORTON ST PHILIP, BATH BA3 6LW

Please send me details of special pre-publication discounts available on the next edition of Where to Ski. I understand that I am under no obligation to buy.

Name

Address

Get your money back

it couldn't be easier

Book your 1995/96-season skiing holiday through the specialist travel agency Ski Solutions, and the price of this book will be knocked off the cost of your holiday.

Ski Solutions are Britain's longest-established and most respected ski travel agency. You can book more-or-less any ski holiday through them, whether you want to go independently or on a tour operator's package.

To book your holiday, ask their advice, or just get hold of some brochures, phone them on 0171-602 9900. When you make your booking, tell Ski Solutions you're claiming a refund and send Part 1 of the voucher opposite to them with your booking form. Send Part 2 to us at Where To Ski. The price of this book will then be deducted from your final invoice.

MONEY BACK VOUCHER – PART 1

TO BE SENT TO
SKI SOLUTIONS, 84 PEMBROKE ROAD, LONDON W8 6NX
ALONG WITH YOUR BOOKING FORM

Name

Address

I have bought a copy of Where to Ski and
claim a refund of the £14.99 cover price.
I understand this amount will be
deducted from the cost of the holiday I
am booking through Ski Solutions. Offer
valid for bookings for 1995/96 season
holidays made before 30 April 1996.

Departure Date

Tour Operator (if applicable)

MONEY BACK VOUCHER – PART 2

TO BE SENT TO
WHERE TO SKI, THE OLD FORGE, NORTON ST PHILIP, BATH BA3 6LW

Name

Address

I have booked a 1995/96 ski holiday
through Ski Solutions and claimed a
refund of the price of Where to Ski.

Departure Date

Ski Resort(s) to be visited

Have you booked any other
holiday through Ski Solutions
in the last two seasons?   Yes ☐   No ☐

Where did you hear about Where to Ski
(please tick all that apply)?

Daily Mail Ski magazine ☐

The Independent newspaper ☐

The Independent on Sunday ☐

Other magazine or newspaper ☐

Saw in book shop ☐

Where to Ski mailing ☐

Reports on resorts help us
make Where to Ski as useful
and up-to-date as possible.
Please tick here if you would
be willing to fill in a
questionnaire about your
holiday and about how
Where to Ski could be made
even more useful to you.
We will then send you one
shortly before your
departure date.

Yes, please send me a questionnaire ☐

CUT ALONG DOTTED LINE

WHERE *to* SKI

WHERE *to* SKI

WHERE *to* SKI

WHERE *to* SKI

WHERE *to* SKI

WHERE *to* SKI

WHERE *to* SKI

WHERE *to* SKI